LAND LAW:

Text and Materials

AUSTRALIA
LBC Information Services
Sydney

CANADA and USA
Carswell
Toronto, Ontario

NEW ZEALAND
Brooker's
Auckland

SINGAPORE and MALAYSIA
Sweet & Maxwell Asia
Singapore and Kuala Lumpur

LAND LAW:

Text and Materials

Second Edition

Nigel P. Gravells, M.A. (Oxon)
Of the Middle Temple, Barrister
Professor of English Law, University of Nottingham

London
Sweet & Maxwell
1999

Published by
Sweet & Maxwell Limited of
100 Avenue Road
London NW3 3PF

Typeset by Tradespools Ltd,
Frome, Somerset
Printed in England by Clays Ltd,
St Ives plc

A CIP catalogue record
for this book is available
from The British Library.

ISBN 0 421 620102

No natural forests were destroyed to make this product, only farmed timber
was used and re-planted.

PREFACE

Four years on from the publication of the first edition of this book, the aims and objectives of this second edition remain essentially unchanged. The feedback that I have received on the first edition suggests that the structure of the book has proved to be conducive to the realisation of those aims and objectives. In that respect too the book remains essentially unchanged.

However, contrary to the apparent belief of some of my colleagues, there have been many important developments in land law in the past four years. In many instances, legislative developments have not simply added a qualification to an established principle: they have involved wholesale restructuring of the relevant law. Examples of such developments include the Trusts of Land and Appointment of Trustees Act 1996, which introduced new statutory machinery (the trust of land) to accommodate concurrent and successive interests in land, and the Landlord and Tenant (Covenants) Act 1995, which introduced new rules relating to the enforcement of leasehold covenants. These two statutes also exemplify the "evolutionary" and/or "incremental" nature of many developments: the new regime preserves expressly or by implication some of the concepts and principles underlying the old regime that has been replaced; and/or the new regime applies prospectively only so that the old regime continues to operate alongside the new regime. As a result the explanation of the law has inevitably been made more complex because such developments require the treatment of both the old and the new regimes, whether or not the treatment of the old regime is strictly necessary to an understanding of the new regime. In order fully to integrate these and other developments, the text has been substantially revised throughout the book.

While some of these developments reflect the implementation of earlier Law Commission recommendations, there has been a further series of Law Commission reports in the field of land law. Undoubtedly, the most significant of these is Law Commission Report No. 254 on Land Registration for the Twenty-First Century, published in September 1998. This consultative document includes provisional recommendations that would produce many fundamental changes in the system of registration of title and registered title conveyancing, including the introduction of electronic conveyancing. The Law Commission has indicated an intention to publish a draft Bill in 1999, following the consultation process, with a view to the introduction of legislation in 2000. It remains to be seen whether this timetable is maintained. In any event, consideration of the recommendations, some of which have implications beyond the system of registration of title, has been integrated throughout the book.

Apart from these fundamental legislative developments and proposals, other issues have generated a very significant volume of litigation, in which new doctrines have been clarified and judicial approaches have been reconsidered.

Examples include the limitation of actions in the context of registered land, the undue influence doctrine expounded in *Barclays Bank v. O'Brien* and a mortgagee's right to possession and related topics. These judicial developments have prompted expanded treatment of the relevant issues.

I have endeavoured to state the law as at March 1, 1999, but I have been able to incorporate some later developments at proof stage.

I am extremely grateful to those people who have provided practical assistance and/or less tangible (but no less valuable) support during the preparation of this second edition. In particular, Linda has again demonstrated that she has considerable reserves of patience and understanding, not least when I have appeared to be less concerned with The Brambles than with any other parcel of land (real or hypothetical); but then she doubtless hopes to benefit again from any royalties!

The Brambles   Nigel P. Gravells
Wymeswold
July 1, 1999

PREFACE TO THE FIRST EDITION

Land law has a reputation as one of the more difficult subjects in the undergraduate curriculum; it is sometimes regarded as daunting to students, not least because the relevant legislation and case law, indeed the very terminology of the subject, appear to be less than user-friendly. The aim of this book is to examine the main rules and principles of land law in a manner which makes them accessible to students while it requires but facilitates the important process of reading the primary sources of the subject.

In the scope of the subject-matter and the selection of the materials the book is designed to cover the principal substantive topics of land law which form the basis of undergraduate courses taught in most law schools. Thus, after a consideration of certain introductory matters, the book concentrates on eight main topics, each forming the subject-matter of a separate chapter. (I have excluded (or considered in outline only) certain topics which (even in these days of modularisation and semesterisation) are sometimes included in land law courses: for example, strict settlements, the rule(s) against perpetuities, profits à prendre and limitation of actions; but I do not believe that the omission of these topics means that the book presents a distorted view of land law.) The intention is that, by limiting the range of topics covered, those topics can be examined in greater depth, thereby providing a clearer understanding of the subject and its principal components.

Although the treatment of the topics necessarily varies in its detail, largely in accordance with whether they are based essentially in statute or case law, there is a general pattern in the approach. Each chapter begins with an indication of the context of its subject-matter and of the major theme(s) of the chapter. Within each chapter most sections begin with an introductory text to provide some structure and guidance. This is followed by the selected materials. The selection of materials is necessarily in part a matter of personal preference, but I hope that overall the selection is a not unreasonable reflection of the subject-matter. I have preferred extended extracts from fewer cases in the belief that this provides a better appreciation of the reasoning in the individual cases and, consequently, a clearer and more coherent understanding of their subject-matter: indeed, that belief has become stronger, with the result that at proof stage I restored passages that I had previously edited out. As originally envisaged, the book would not have included extracts from the 1925 property legislation and other statutory material, on the basis that most students acquire their own copies of the property legislation. However, I subsequently came to the view that it was essential to include certain fundamental provisions, so as to avoid creating a misleading view of the statutory basis of many of the topics under consideration. The materials in turn are followed by notes which are intended to provide, where appropriate, commentary on the extracts, indications of the views of commentators on the subject-matter and references to further primary and secondary materials. No less important for a critical study of the subject is an awareness of the defects in the current law and the proposals for reform. I have therefore included extracts (or summaries) of the reports of the Law Commission and other law reform bodies on many of the topics covered in the book.

It is hoped that overall this approach may encourage and facilitate a closer and critical study of land law; and that this in turn may persuade students that land law offers intellectual entertainment and even enjoyment.

I would like to express my sincere thanks to many people who have provided practical assistance and/or less tangible (but no less valuable) support during the writing of this book. First to Sweet & Maxwell: they suggested the project some time ago and, since then, they have continued to encourage and indulge me beyond any reasonable expectation. Secondly to my colleagues in the Department of Law at the University of Nottingham: not only do they continue to provide a friendly and stimulating environment in which to work but they also sustain the system within the Department which permits regular periods of study leave. Thirdly to my intermittent colleagues in the Law School at the University of Canterbury, New Zealand: the Canterbury Law School has become my second academic home over the past seven years; the facilities and the hospitality of friends there have made it an excellent "research haven"; and it was there that the first words of this book were committed to the word processor and it was from there that the final pages of the proofs were dispatched to the publishers. Finally to Linda: she has shown immense patience and understanding and she has provided all manner of support, all of which have made the writing of the book rather easier than it would otherwise have been; and so it will be with her that I shall spend any royalties!

University of Nottingham
May 26, 1995

Nigel P. Gravells

ACKNOWLEDGMENTS

Grateful acknowledgment is made for permission to reproduce from the undermentioned works:

ESTATES GAZETTE LTD. Extracts from the following reports:
Hussein v. Mehlman [1992] 2 E.G.L.R. 87
Griffiths v. Williams (1977) 248 E.G. 947
Dodsworth v. Dodsworth (1973) 228 E.G. 1115

HER MAJESTY'S STATIONERY OFFICE. Various extracts

THE INCORPORATED COUNCIL OF LAW REPORTING FOR ENGLAND AND WALES. Extracts from The Law Reports.

THE LAW BOOK COMPANY LTD, Australia. Extracts from the following case: *Latec Investments Ltd v. Hotel Terrigal Pty Ltd* [1965] 113 C.L.R. 265

TIMES NEWSPAPERS LTD, The Times Law Reports. Extracts from the following reports:
Appleby v. Cowley, The Times, April 14, 1982
Facchini v. Bryson [1952] 1 T.L.R. 1386

While every care has been taken to establish and acknowledge copyright, and contact the copyright owners, the publishers tender their apologies for any accidental infringement. They would be pleased to come to a suitable arrangement with the rightful owners in each case.

CONTENTS

TABLE OF CASES

*[Page references in **bold** type indicate extracts of the case]*

TABLE OF STATUTES

[Page references in bold type indicate extracts of the statute]

1

INTRODUCTORY TOPICS

A. THE SUBJECT-MATTER OF LAND LAW

1. Land law as an element of the law of property

Land law is one of the constituent elements of the law of property. Although the term "property" is commonly used to describe those things which belong to a person, in the strict sense the term denotes the condition of being owned by or belonging to some person. In this sense, therefore, "property" is a relationship. In its simplest form the law of property deals with the legal relationship between a thing and the owner of that thing; and land law deals with the legal relationship between land and the owner of that land. However, for a number of reasons land law is arguably one of the more complex elements of the law of property. First, as with other areas of property law that deal with things other than land, it is not uncommon for different persons to make competing claims to interests in respect of the same land. Secondly, the unique immovable and indestructible nature of land means that land is capable of sustaining a range of interests and relationships which do not necessarily compete with each other. Thirdly, because land does not exist in isolation but is normally physically joined to other land, it is frequently impossible to consider the relationships affecting land without considering also relationships affecting other adjoining land. For these reasons land law is commonly concerned not with a single property relationship but with a potentially complex network of relationships affecting land.

2. The subject-matter of land law in practice

These theoretical relationships may be considered from a more practical viewpoint.

2.1 *Multiplicity of interests*
The assertion that land is capable of sustaining a multiplicity of interests or relationships may be illustrated as follows. First, although a landowner may claim that he owns the land in question (the "principal land"), it will frequently be the case that other members of his family contributed part of the

purchase price. Such a contribution may confer on the contributor a share in the ownership of the land. Secondly, it is also possible that the land was purchased with the assistance of a loan from a bank or building society. In such circumstances the loan does not confer on the lender a share in the ownership of the land; but the lender will almost invariably have required the borrower to provide some security that the loan will be repaid. To that end the borrower will have granted to the lender an interest over the principal land (a "mortgage" or "charge"), which, in the event of the borrower failing to make repayment, entitles the lender to sell the principal land in order to recover the amount of the loan. Thirdly, the principal land may be located in a residential area and, with a view to maintaining that residential character, the principal landowner and his neighbours may agree that they will not use their respective land for business purposes. Subject to certain conditions, each landowner who is a party to the agreement will be under an obligation to comply with the terms of the agreement (or "restrictive covenant") and will have a right to enforce the agreement against any neighbours who fail to comply. Fourthly, the physical geography of the neighbourhood may be such that the principal landowner agrees that his neighbour may have a right to walk across part of the principal land; and the precise circumstances will determine the nature of any interest ("easement" or "licence") of the neighbour over the principal land. This represents a not uncommon scenario; and further interests and relationships can be added. For example, the principal landowner may agree that another person may occupy part of the principal land; and, again, the precise circumstances will determine the nature of any interest ("lease" or "licence") of that person in the principal land.

Land law is concerned with the nature and creation of these various interests; and, in some circumstances, it may also be concerned with the relationship between such interests.

2.2 *Ownership interests and third party interests*

The above scenario reveals two different categories of interest or right in land. The first category comprises the interest of the principal landowner in the principal land (and the interests of other contributors to the purchase price of the land), which confer what are generally termed ownership rights. (It will be seen that as a matter of theory English law does not recognise direct ownership of the land itself but rather ownership of an interest in the land which confers those rights normally associated with ownership: see *infra*, p. 21.) In practice today there are two types of ownership interest: *freehold* interests, which confer ownership rights that are potentially unlimited in duration and which in effect therefore confer absolute ownership of the principal land; and *leasehold* interests, which confer ownership rights that are limited to a fixed maximum duration. The second category of interests revealed by the above scenario comprises those interests which confer rights over the land of another person. Such rights include the rights of a bank or building society over the principal land pursuant to a mortgage; the right of a neighbour to restrain the principal landowner from using the principal land for certain purposes; and the right of a neighbour to walk across the principal land. Interests in this second category are commonly referred to as "third party interests". It may be noted that leasehold interests fall into both categories: from the point of view of the leasehold owner, the interest confers (limited) ownership rights over the principal land; but, from the point of view of the freehold owner of the principal land, the leasehold interest is a third party interest affecting his (unlimited) ownership rights.

2.3 *Land law and conveyancing*

It is important to appreciate that land law is inextricably linked with the practical process of conveyancing, whereby the ownership rights in land are transferred from one person to another. The above scenario ignored this aspect of land law but represented a snapshot view of the interests in the principal land. If, however, that scenario is extended backwards and forwards in time, the further dimension of land law is revealed. When the principal landowner first acquired his ownership interest in the land, he would have been concerned to ensure that the vendor was entitled to sell that interest; but he would also have been concerned to know whether there were any existing third party rights affecting the principal land which would be enforceable by or against him as purchaser of the principal land. Similarly, if the principal land were subsequently to be sold to a new purchaser, it would be important for both the purchaser and third parties to know whether those rights and obligations and any new rights and obligations created during the ownership of the principal landowner would be enforceable by and against the purchaser. For example, if a neighbouring landowner acquires the right to prevent the use of the principal land for business purposes or acquires a right to walk across the principal land, he will wish to ensure that those rights will continue to be enforceable irrespective of whether the principal land continues to be owned by the principal landowner or is transferred to a purchaser.

This further dimension highlights one of the central concerns of land law, the question of the enforceability of interests in land through changes in ownership of that land. Moreover, it will be seen that enforceability depends in part upon the method of creation of the interests and the machinery for their transfer and protection, which in turn depend upon whether the title to the land is registered or unregistered: see *infra*, p. 56; and see *post*, Chapters 2,3.

B. THE MEANING OF LAND

1. Statutory definition

Law of Property Act 1925, s.205(1)

General Definitions

(ix) "Land" includes land of any tenure, and mines and minerals, whether or not held apart from the surface, buildings or parts of buildings (whether the division is horizontal, vertical or made in any other way) and other corporeal hereditaments; also a manor, an advowson, and a rent and other incorporeal hereditaments, and an easement, right, privilege, or benefit in, over, or derived from land; but not an undivided share in land; and "mines and minerals" include any strata or seam of minerals or substances in or under any land, and powers of working and getting the same but not an individed share thereof; and "manor" includes a lordship, and reputed manor or lordship; and "hereditament" means any real property which on an intestacy occurring before the commencement of this Act might have devolved upon an heir.

1.1 *Real and personal property*

Provided that "land" is given its extended meaning discussed in this section, that term is preferred to "real property", which is sometimes used, albeit inaccurately, as a synonym. Historically, the term "real property" was used to denote any property which the dispossessed owner was entitled specifically to recover from the dispossessor in a "real action". By contrast, the term "personal property" was used to denote property in respect of which the dispossessed owner could bring only a "personal action" against the dispossessor, who could elect either to restore the property or to pay its value to the owner. Freehold ownership interests were classified as real property. However, leasehold ownership interests were classified as personal property since they were regarded as essentially contractual arrangements between the parties and different in kind from the feudal arrangements for land holding. Consequently, the leaseholder could recover the land itself if he were dispossessed by the person who had granted the leasehold interest; but, if the leaseholder were dispossessed by any other person, he had no entitlement to recover the land itself: he might have to be content with its monetary value. Although the leaseholder eventually became entitled to recover the land from *any* dispossessor, the classification of leasehold interests as personal property remained. On the other hand, leasehold interests are not pure personalty or simple chattels; and they are therefore classified as "chattels real". Against that background it is suggested that the term "land", which naturally includes leasehold interests, is more accurate and more readily understandable.

1.2 *Corporeal and incorporeal hereditaments*

Before leaving the terminology of real property, reference should be made to a further sub-classification. Real property comprises both corporeal and incorporeal hereditaments. The term "hereditaments" denotes property which at common law descended to the heir on intestacy. Corporeal hereditaments are (real) property rights which involve physical possession of the land and everything physically attached to the land. Incorporeal hereditaments are (real) property rights which do not involve physical possession of the land. They include rights to physical possession *in the future*: see *infra*, p. 22; and they also include certain proprietary rights over the land of another person such as rights of way and other easements: see *post*, Chapter 7.

2. Extended meaning of land

At common law the concept of land was said to be extended by the maxim "cuius est solum, eius est usque ad coelum et ad inferos" (the owner of the soil owns also everything up to the sky and down to the centre of the earth): see, *e.g. Mitchell v. Mosley* [1914] 1 Ch. 438, 450 *per* Cozens-Hardy M.R. More recently the maxim has been described as "sweeping, unscientific and impractical ... unlikely to appeal to the common law mind" and "mainly serviceable as dispensing with analysis": *Commissioner for Railways v. Valuer-General* [1974] A.C. 328, 351–352 *per* Lord Wilberforce. However, the maxim does make clear that ownership rights in land are not simply confined to the surface of that land.

2.1 *Airspace*
The first part of the maxim has never been applied literally; and the rights of the landowner in respect of the column of airspace above his land have been restricted "to such height as is necessary for the ordinary use and enjoyment of his land and the structures upon it": *Bernstein v. Skyviews and General Ltd* [1978] Q.B. 479, 488 *per* Griffiths J. Invasion of the airspace within that limit without the consent of the landowner may constitute a trespass, which is actionable irrespective of whether any damage has been caused: see, *e.g. Kelsen v. Imperial Tobacco Co. (of Great Britain and Ireland) Ltd* [1957] 2 Q.B. 334; *John Trenberth Ltd v. National Westminster Bank Ltd* (1979) 39 P. & C.R. 104.

2.2 *Underground space*
The cases support the principle that the owner of land owns any natural or man-made spaces below the surface of the land: *Metropolitan Railway Co. v. Fowler* [1892] 1 Q.B. 165 (railway tunnel); *Grigsby v. Melville* [1974] 1 W.L.R. 80 (cellar). However, the principle is probably confined to space within a reasonable distance of the surface.

2.3 *Buildings*
Buildings and structures erected on land almost invariably become part of the land, provided that they are constructed on foundations set in the ground: see *Elwes v. Brigg Gas Co.* (1886) 33 Ch D. 562, where Chitty J. stated (at 567):

This principle is an absolute rule of law, not depending on intention; for instance, if a man digs in the land of another, and permanently fixes in the soil stones or bricks, or the like, as the foundation of a house, the stones or bricks become the property of the owner of the soil, whatever may have been the intention of the person who so placed them there, and even against his declared intention that they should remain his property.

Where a structure does not have foundations set in the ground, the question whether it forms part of the land seems to depend on the principles relating to fixtures: see *infra*, p. 7.

2.4 *Fixtures*
See *infra*, p. 7.

2.5 *Strata titles*
It is clear from section 205(1)(ix) of the Law of Property Act 1925 that land
(in the extended sense under discussion) can be divided vertically or
horizontally. It is therefore possible for a person to have ownership rights over
"land" that comprises only a single floor (above or below ground level) in a
multi-storey building. In the current state of English law on the enforceability
of covenants relating to the support and repair of land and buildings, there
are very real practical difficulties which effectively restrict the way in which
such divisions of land may be made. However, the Law Commission has
proposed a new scheme of land ownership known as "commonhold" as a
response to those difficulties: see *post*, p. 805.

2.6 *Water*
Inland areas of water are regarded as areas of land covered with water: see
Attorney-General for British Columbia v. Attorney-General for Canada [1914]
A.C. 153, 167 *per* Viscount Haldane L.C. However, ownership rights over the
land covered with water do not extend to the water covering the land; and
there is no right to abstract water, other than in small quantities for domestic
or agricultural purposes, without a licence granted by the National Rivers
Authority: Water Resources Act 1991, ss.24, 27. For the rights and obligations
in relation to the flow of water over land, see *Home Brewery Co. Ltd v.
William Davis & Co. (Leicester) Ltd* [1987] 1 Q.B. 339, 345–349 *per* Piers
Ashworth Q.C.

2.7 *Flora and fauna*
Land includes all trees and plants, whether cultivated or wild, growing on the
land: see *Stukeley v. Butler* (1615) Hob. 168, 170. Ownership rights over land
include "qualified property" in wild animals and fish which are alive and on
the land at any particular time. The landowner becomes absolutely entitled to
them, but as *personal* property, only when they have been caught and killed:
see *Blades v. Higgs* (1865) 11 H.L.C. 621 (wild animals); *Nicholls v. Ely Beet
Sugar Factory Ltd* [1936] Ch. 343 (fish).

2.8 *Minerals*
Although the rights of the landowner extend to the centre of the earth, and
section 205(1)(ix) of the Law of Property Act 1925 includes mines and
minerals in the definition of land, there are exceptions to the logical
conclusion that a landowner also owns minerals found under his land.
Unmined gold and silver belong to the Crown: *Case of Mines* (1567) 1 Plowd.
310; *Attorney-General v. Morgan* [1891] 1 Ch. 432, 455 *per* Lindley L.J.; oil,
natural gas and coal belong to the Crown: see Petroleum (Production) Act
1934, s.1; Coal Industry Act 1994, s.9

2.9 *Finds*

The common law draws a distinction between articles found *in or attached to* land and articles found *on* land. As a general principle, articles in the former category belong to the owner of the land: *Elwes v. Brigg Gas Co.* (1886) 33 Ch D. 562; *Waverley BC v. Fletcher* [1996] Q.B. 334, noted at [1996] Conv. 216. The position is less clear in relation to articles found on the land but it seems that if the owner of the land is to claim such articles, he must exercise sufficient control amounting to factual possession of any article that might be on the land and must manifest an intention to exercise such control: *Parker v. British Airways Board* [1982] Q.B. 1004. Special rules apply where the articles constitute "treasure" within the meaning of the Treasure Act 1996: see Marston and Ross [1997] Conv. 273, [1998] Conv. 252.

3. Fixtures

According to the maxim "quicquid plantatur solo, solo cedit" (whatever is attached to the soil becomes part of it), personal property or chattels which become attached to land in certain circumstances lose their legal identity as chattels. According to the traditional twofold classification, they assume the status of "fixtures" and, as such, they are regarded in law as part of the land. That fundamental principle has not changed. However, in *Elitestone Ltd v. Morris* [1997] 1 W.L.R. 687 the House of Lords adopted a threefold classification, effectively sub-dividing the traditional category of fixtures into (i) chattels that have become part and parcel of the land and (ii) other fixtures. Although it is suggested that this reclassification should facilitate the resolution of disputes in relation to buildings and other large structures, both sub-categories retain the status of traditional fixtures: they become part of the land and pass with the land on any subsequent disposition; and they cannot be recovered by the former owner unless he has a right to remove them.

There are therefore two distinct issues involved: first, whether the chattel has become a fixture and/or part of the land; and, secondly, where it has, whether in the circumstances there is a right of removal.

3.1 *Nature of fixtures*

The question whether a chattel has become a fixture and/or part of the land depends upon the intention of the original owner of the chattel as ascertained from the degree of annexation and the purpose of annexation.

Holland v. Hodgson (1872) L.R. 7 C.P. 328

(Court of Exchequer Chamber, Blackburn J.)

The defendant, the owner of a mill, conveyed the property to the plaintiffs by way of mortgage to secure the repayment of a loan. The conveyance expressly included the buildings, a steam engine and "all other fixtures whatever which now or at any time hereafter during the continuance of this security shall be set up and affixed to the said hereditaments". The question arose as to whether the conveyance included over 400 looms installed in the mill. The mill had been specially adapted for the steam-powered looms; and, in order to keep the looms steady and in their proper position for working, they were fastened to the floors by nails driven through holes in their feet into (wooden plugs in) the floors. However, the looms could easily be removed without serious damage to the floors.

BLACKBURN J.:

There is no doubt that the general maxim of the law is, that what is annexed to the land becomes part of the land; but it is very difficult, if not impossible, to say with precision what constitutes an annexation sufficient for this purpose. It is a question which must depend on the circumstances of each case, and mainly on two circumstances, as indicating the intention, viz., the degree of annexation and the object of the annexation. When the article in question is no further attached to the land than by its own weight it is generally to be considered a mere chattel; see *Wiltshear v. Cottrell* (1853) 1 E. & B. 674, and the cases there cited. But even in such a case, if the intention is apparent to make the articles part of the land, they do become part of the land: see *D'Eyncourt v. Gregory* (1866) Law Rep. 3 Eq. 382. Thus blocks of stone placed one on the top of another without any mortar or cement for the purpose of forming a dry stone wall would become part of the land, though the same stones, if deposited in a builder's yard and for convenience sake stacked on the top of each other in the form of a wall, would remain chattels. On the other hand, an article may be very firmly fixed to the land, and yet the circumstances may be such as to shew that it was never intended to be part of the land, and then it does not become part of the land. The anchor of a large ship must be very firmly fixed in the ground in order to bear the strain of the cable, yet no one could suppose that it became part of the land, even though it should chance that the shipowner was also the owner of the fee of the spot where the anchor was dropped. An anchor similarly fixed in the soil for the purpose of bearing the strain of the chain of a suspension bridge would be part of the land. Perhaps the true rule is, that articles not otherwise attached to the land than by their own weight are not to be considered as part of the land, unless the circumstances are such as to shew that they were intended to be part of the land, the onus of shewing that they were so intended lying on those who assert that they have ceased to be chattels, and that, on the contrary, an article which is affixed to the land even slightly is to be considered as part of the land, unless the circumstances are such as to shew that it was intended all along to continue a chattel, the onus lying on those who contend that it is a chattel. This last proposition seems to be in effect the basis of the judgment of the Court of Common Pleas delivered by Maule J. in *Wilde v. Waters* (1855) 16 C.B. 637. This, however, only removes the difficulty one step, for it still remains a question in each case whether the circumstances are sufficient to satisfy the onus. In some cases, such as the anchor of the ship or the ordinary instance given of a carpet nailed to the floor of a room, the nature of the thing sufficiently shews it is only fastened as a chattel temporarily, and not affixed permanently as part of the land. But ordinary trade or tenant fixtures which are put up with the intention that they should be removed by the tenant (and so are put up for a purpose in one sense only temporary, and certainly not for the purpose of improving the reversionary interest of the landlord) have always been considered as part of the land, though severable by the tenant. In most, if not all, of such cases the reason why the articles are considered fixtures is probably that indicated by Wood V.-C. in *Boyd v. Shorrock* (1867) Law Rep. 5 Eq. 72, 78, that the tenant indicates by the mode in which he puts them up that he regards them as attached to the property during his interest in the property. What we have now to decide is as to the application of these rules to looms put up by the owner of the fee in the manner described in the case. In *Hellawell v. Eastwood* (1851) 6 Ex. 295 the facts as stated in the report are, that the plaintiff held the premises in question as tenant of the defendants, and that a distress for rent had been put in by the defendants under which a seizure was made of cotton-spinning machinery called "mules", some of which were fixed by screws to the wooden floor, and some by screws which had been sunk in the stone floor, and secured by molten lead poured into them. It may be inferred that the plaintiff being the tenant only had put up those mules; and from the large sum for which the distress appears to have been levied (£2000) it seems probable that he was the tenant of the whole mill. It does not appear what admissions, if any, were made at the trial, nor whether the Court had or had not by the reservation power to draw inferences of fact, though it seems assumed in the judgment that they had such a power. Parke B., in delivering the judgment of the Court, says, "This is a question of fact depending on the circumstances of each case, and principally on two considerations; first, the mode of annexation to the soil or fabric of the house, and the extent to which it is united to them, whether it can easily be removed integrè salve et commode or not without injury to itself or the fabric of the building; secondly, on the object and purpose of the annexation, whether it was for the permanent and substantial improvement of the dwelling, in the language of the civil law, perpetui usûs causâ, or in that of the year book, pour un profit del inheritance, or merely for a temporary purpose and the more complete enjoyment and use of it as a chattel". It was contended by [counsel for the defendant] that the decision in *Hellawell v. Eastwood* had been approved in the Queen's Bench in the case of *Turner v. Cameron* (1870) Law Rep. 5 Q.B. 306. It is quite true that the Court in that case said that it afforded a true exposition of the law as applicable to the particular facts upon which the judgment proceeded; but the Court expressly guarded their approval by citing from the judgment delivered by Parke B. the facts upon which they considered it to have proceeded: "They were attached slightly so as to be capable of removal without the least injury to the fabric of the building or to themselves, and the object of the annexation was not to improve the inheritance, but merely to render the machines steadier and more capable of convenient use as chattels". As we have already observed, trade or tenant fixtures might in one sense be said to be fixed "merely for a temporary purpose;" but we cannot suppose that the Court of Exchequer meant to decide that they were not part of the land, though liable to be severed by the tenant.

The words "merely for a temporary purpose" must be understood as applying to such a case as we have supposed, of the anchor dropped for the temporary purpose of mooring the ship, or the instance immediately afterwards given by Parke B. of the carpet tacked to the floor for the purpose of keeping it stretched whilst it was there used, and not to a case such as that of a tenant who, for example, affixes a shop counter for the purpose (in one sense temporary) of more effectually enjoying the shop whilst he continues to sell his wares there. Subject to this observation, we think that the passage in the judgment in *Hellawell v. Eastwood* does state the true principles, though it may be questioned if they were in that case correctly applied to the facts. The Court in their judgment determine what they have just declared to be a question of fact thus: "The object and purpose of the connection was not to improve the inheritance, but merely to render the machines steadier and more capable of convenient use as chattels". [Counsel for the defendant] was justified in saying, as he did in his argument, that as far as the facts are stated in the report they are very like those in the present case, except that the tenant who put the mules up cannot have been supposed to intend to improve the inheritance (if by that is meant his landlord's reversion), but only at most to improve the property whilst he continued tenant thereof; and he argued with great force that we ought not to act on a surmise that there were any special facts or findings not stated in the report, but to meet the case, as shewing that the judges who decided *Hellawell v. Eastwood* thought that articles fixed in a manner very like those in the case before us remained chattels; and this is felt by some of us at least to be a weighty argument. But that case was decided in 1851. In 1853 the Court of Queen's Bench had, in *Wiltshear v. Cottrell*, to consider what articles passed by the conveyance in fee of a farm. Among the articles in dispute was a threshing machine, which is described in the report thus: "The threshing machine was placed inside one of the barns (the machinery for the horse being on the outside), and there fixed by screws and bolts to four posts which were let into the earth". *Hellawell v. Eastwood* was cited in the argument. The Court (without, however, noticing that case) decided that the threshing machine, being so annexed to the land, passed by the conveyance. It seems difficult to point out how the threshing machine was more for the improvement of the inheritance of the farm than the present looms were for the improvement of the manufactory; and in *Mather v. Fraser* (1856) 2 K. & J. 536 Wood V.-C., who was there judge both of the fact and the law, came to the conclusion that machinery affixed not more firmly than the articles in question by the owner of the fee to land, for the purpose of carrying on a trade there, became part of the land. This was decided in 1856. And in *Walmsley v. Milne* (1859) 7 C.B. (N.S.) 115 the Court of Common Pleas, after having their attention called to a slight misapprehension by Wood V.-C. of the effect of *Hellawell v. Eastwood*, came to the conclusion, as is stated by them, at p. 131, "that we are of opinion, as a matter of fact, that they were all firmly annexed to the freehold for the purpose of improving the inheritance, and not for any temporary purpose. The bankrupt was the real owner of the premises, subject only to a mortgage which vested the legal title in the mortgage until the repayment of the money borrowed. The mortgagor first erected baths, stables and a coach-house, and other buildings, and then supplied them with the fixtures in question for their permanent improvement. As to the steam-engine and boiler, they were necessary for the use of the baths. The hay-cutter was fixed into a building adjoining the stable as an important adjunct to it, and to improve its usefulness as a stable. The malt-mill and grinding-stones were also permanent erections, intended by the owner to add to the value of the premises. They therefore resemble in no particular (except being fixed to the building by screws) the mules put up by the tenant in *Hellawell v. Eastwood*". It is stated in a note to the report of the case that, on a subsequent day, it was intimated by the Court that Mr Justice Willes entertained serious doubts as to whether the articles in question were not chattels. The reason of his doubt is not stated, but probably it was from a doubt whether the Exchequer had not, in *Hellawell v. Eastwood*, shewn that they would have thought that the articles were not put up for the purpose of improving the inheritance, and from deference to that authority. The doubt of this learned judge in one view weakens the authority of *Walmsley v. Milne*, but in another view it strengthens it, as it shews that the opinion of the majority, that as a matter of fact the hay-cutter, which was not more firmly fixed than the mules in *Hellawell v. Eastwood*, must be taken to form part of the land, because it was "put up as an adjunct to the stable, and to improve its usefulness as a stable", was deliberately adopted as the basis of the judgment; and it is to be observed that Willes J., though doubting, did not dissent. *Walmsley v. Milne* was decided in 1859. This case and that of *Wiltshear v. Cottrell* seem authorities for this principle, that where an article is affixed by the owner of the fee, though only affixed by bolts and screws, it is to be considered as part of the land, at all events where the object of setting up the articles is to enhance the value of the premises to which it is annexed for the purposes to which those premises are applied. The threshing machine in *Wiltshear v. Cottrell* was affixed by the owner of the fee to the barn as an adjunct to the barn, and to improve its usefulness as a barn, in much the same sense as the hay-cutter in *Walmsley v. Milne* was affixed to the stable as an adjunct to it, and to improve its usefulness as a stable. And it seems difficult to say that the machinery in *Mather v. Fraser* was not as much affixed to the mill as an adjunct to it and to improve the usefulness of the mill as such, as either the threshing machine or the hay-cutter. If, therefore, the matter were to be decided on principle, without reference to what has since been done on the faith of the decision, we should be much inclined, notwithstanding the profound respect we feel for everything that was decided by Parke B., to hold that the looms now in question were, as a matter of fact, part of the land. But there is another view of the matter which weighs strongly with us. *Hellawell v. Eastwood* was a decision between landlord and tenant, not so likely to influence those who advance money on morrgage as *Mather v. Fraser* which was a decision directly between mortgagor and mortgagee. We find that *Mather v. Fraser*, which was decided in 1856, has been acted upon in *Boyd v. Shorrock*, by the Court of Queen's Bench in *Longbottom v. Berry* (1869) Law Rep. 5 Q.B. 123, and in Ireland in *Re Dawson*, Ir. Law Rep. 2 Eq. 222. These cases are too recent to have been themselves much acted upon, but they shew that *Mather v. Fraser* has been generally adopted as the ruling case. We cannot, therefore, doubt that much money has, during the last sixteen years, been advanced on the faith of the decision in *Mather v. Fraser*. It is of great importance that the law as to what is the security of a mortgagee should be settled; and without going so far as to say that a decision only sixteen years old should be upheld, right or wrong, on the principle that communis error facitjus, we feel that it should not be reversed unless we clearly see that it is wrong. As already said, we are rather inclined to think that, if it were res integra we should find the same way.

NOTES:

1. In the context of chattel/fixture disputes, the purpose of annexation now seems to be the decisive consideration while the degree of annexation simply provides evidence of that purpose: *Berkley v. Poulett* (1976) 241 E.G. 911, 913 *per* Scarman L.J. and *Elitestone Ltd v. Morris* [1997] 1 W.L.R. 687, 692 *per* Lord Lloyd, both citing *Leigh v. Taylor* [1902] A.C. 157. The most important question seems to be whether the chattel was attached to the land simply for the more complete use and enjoyment of it as a chattel, in which case it will probably be held to have remained a chattel; or whether the chattel was attached to the land for the purposes of the permanent improvement of the land, or for the purposes of the trade or business carried on there, in which case it will probably be regarded as having become a fixture.

2. In *Botham v. TSB Bank plc* (1996) 73 P. & C.R. D1, noted at [1998] Conv. 137, the Court of Appeal adopted the same test when considering the chattel/fixture distinction in relation to a range of household items: the purpose of annexation is the decisive test but the degree of annexation may give rise to evidential presumptions. Roch L.J. then identified four guidelines. The first two are uncontroversial: ornamental items attached to the building simply for their display and enjoyment are prima facie chattels; and items that can be removed without damage to the fabric of the building are prima facie chattels. Rather more controversial are the remaining guidelines: items not owned by the landowner should not be held to be fixtures unless "the intent to effect a permanent improvement is incontrovertible" (but see notes 3 and 4, *infra*); and "items installed by a builder will probably be fixtures, whereas items installed by ... the occupier of the building may well not be" (but it is suggested that the emphasis should be on the nature of the items and the purpose of their attachment). Applying the test and guidelines, Roch L.J. concluded that the following items were fixtures: bathroom fittings and fitted kitchen units; and that the following items remained chattels: fitted carpets and curtains, light fittings, gas fires and white goods. It is arguable that many of the items in the second group would become fixtures if there were a high degree of annexation/integration.

3. The *subjective* intention of the parties (that the chattel should or should not become a fixture) does not affect the question whether the chattel has, as a matter of law, become a fixture or part of the land. In *Hobson v. Gorringe* [1897] 1 Ch. 182 the claimants to the chattel/fixture were respectively (i) the

supplier of the chattel let on a hire-purchase agreement, under which the supplier (a) retained title to the chattel until payment in full and (b) reserved the right to repossess the chattel in the event of default; and (ii) a transferee of the land by way of mortgage. The Court of Appeal held that the terms of the hire-purchase agreement were irrelevant as evidence of intention as to whether the chattel became a fixture. Smith L.J. stated (at 193):

[I]n *Holland v. Hodgson* (1872) L.R. 7 C.P. 328, Lord Blackburn, when dealing with the "circumstances to show intention", was contemplating and referring to circumstances which showed the degree of annexation and the object of such annexation which were patent for all to see, and not the circumstances of a chance agreement that might or might not exist between an owner of a chattel and a hirer thereof.

In *Melluish v. B.M.I. (No.3) Ltd* [1996] A.C. 454 Lord Wilberforce stated (at 473):

The terms expressly or implicitly agreed between the fixer of the chattel and the owner of the land cannot affect the determination of the question whether, in law, the chattel has become a fixture and therefore in law belongs to the owner of the soil: ... The terms of such agreement will regulate the contractual rights to sever the chattel from the land as between the parties to that contract and, where an equitable right is conferred by the contract, as against certain third parties. But such agreement cannot prevent the chattel, once fixed, becoming in law part of the land and as such owned by the owner of the land so long as it remains fixed.

See also *Deen v. Andrews* (1985) 52 P. & C.R. 17, 22 *per* Hirst J.; *Elitestone Ltd v. Morris* [1997] 1 W.L.R. 687, *infra*.

4. The agreement in *Hobson v. Gorringe* also raised the issue of the status and enforceability of the interest of the supplier. On the facts the court held that the right of the supplier, reserved in the agreement, to remove the chattel/fixture was no more than an equitable interest, which was unenforceable against the purchaser/mortgagee of the land who did not have notice of the right. For discussion of this issue and potential developments, see Guest and Lever (1963) 27 Conv. 30; McCormack [1990] Conv. 275; Bennett and Davis (1994) 110 L.Q.R. 448.

5. As indicated above, the chattel/fixture distinction was reconsidered in relation to buildings in *Elitestone Ltd v. Morris* [1997] 1 W.L.R. 687.

Elitestone Ltd v. Morris [1997] 1 W.L.R. 687

(HL, Lord Browne-Wilkinson, Lord Lloyd, Lord Nolan, Lord Nicholls, Lord Clyde)

The plaintiff, Elitestone Ltd, was the freehold owner of a parcel of land divided into a number of lots, one of which ("Unit 6") was occupied by the defendant, Morris. A bungalow had been erected on each lot. The main structure of the bungalow rested by its own weight on concrete pillars that were attached to the ground; and the bungalow could only be removed by being demolished. The chattel/fixture status of the bungalow arose in the context of a claim by the defendant that the bungalow formed part of the land and that he was therefore the tenant of a dwelling-house under a Rent Act protected tenancy. At first instance, the court held that the bungalow was part of the land; but the Court of Appeal reversed that decision on the ground that the bungalow was never annexed to the land and therefore remained a chattel. The defendant appealed to the House of Lords.

LORD LLOYD:

The ... issue for your Lordships is whether Mr Morris's bungalow did indeed become part of the land, or whether it has remained a chattel ever since it was first constructed before 1945.

It will be noticed that in framing the issue for decision I have avoided the use of the word "fixture". There are two reasons for this. The first is that "fixture", though a hallowed term in this branch of the law, does not always bear the same meaning in law as it does in everyday life. In ordinary language one thinks of a fixture as being something fixed to a building. One would not ordinarily think of the building itself as a fixture. Thus in *Boswell v. Crucible Steel Co.* [1925] 1 K.B. 119 the question was whether plate glass windows which formed part of the wall of a warehouse were landlord's fixtures within the meaning of a repairing covenant. Atkin L.J. said, at p. 123:

> "... I am quite satisfied that they are not landlord's fixtures, and for the simple reason that they are not fixtures at all in the sense in which that term is generally understood. A fixture, as that term is used in connection with the house, means something which has been affixed to the freehold as accessory to the house. It does not include things which were made part of the house itself in the course of its construction."

Yet in *Billing v. Pill* [1954] 1 Q.B. 70, 75 Lord Goddard C.J. said:

> "What is a fixture? The commonest fixture is a house which is built into the land, so that in law it is regarded as part of the land. The house and the land are one thing."

There is another reason. The term fixture is apt to be a source of misunderstanding owing to the existence of the category of so called "tenants' fixtures" (a term used to cover both trade fixtures and ornamental fixtures), which are fixtures in the full sense of the word (and therefore part of the realty) but which may nevertheless be removed by the tenant in the course of or at the end of his tenancy. Such fixtures are sometimes confused with chattels which have never become fixtures at all. Indeed the confusion arose in this very case. In the course of his judgment Aldous L.J. quoted at length from the judgment of Scott L.J. in *Webb v. Frank Bevis Ltd* [1940] 1 All E.R. 247. The case concerned a shed which was 135 feet long and 50 feet wide. The shed was built on a concrete floor to which it was attached by iron straps. Having referred to *Webb v. Frank Bevis Ltd* and a decision of Hirst J. in *Deen v. Andrews* [1986] 1 E.G.L.R. 262 Aldous L.J. continued:

> "In the present case we are concerned with a chalet which rests on concrete pillars and I believe falls to be considered as a unit which is not annexed to the land. It was no more annexed to the land than the greenhouse in *Deen v. Andrews* or the large shed in *Webb v. Frank Bevis Ltd* Prima facie, the chalet is a chattel and not a fixture."

A little later he said: "Unit 6 was just as much a chattel as the very large shed was in the *Webb* case and the greenhouse in *Deen v. Andrews*".

But when one looks at Scott L.J.'s. judgment in *Webb v. Frank Bevis Ltd* it is clear

that the shed in question was not a chattel. It was annexed to the land, and was held
to form part of the realty. But it could be severed from the land and removed by the
tenant at the end of his tenancy because it was in the nature of a tenant's fixture,
having been erected by the tenant for use in his trade. It follows that *Webb v. Frank
Bevis Ltd* affords no parallel to the present case, as indeed Mr Thom conceded.

For my part I find it better in the present case to avoid the traditional twofold
distinction between chattels and fixtures, and to adopt the threefold classification set
out in *Woodfall, Landlord and Tenant* (looseleaf ed.), vol. 1, para. 13.131:

> "An object which is brought onto land may be classified under one of three broad
> heads. It may be (a) a chattel; (b) a fixture; or (c) part and parcel of the land itself.
> Objects in categories (b) and (c) are treated as being part of the land."

So the question in the present appeal is whether, when the bungalow was built, it
became part and parcel of the land itself. The materials out of which the bungalow
was constructed, that is to say, the timber frame walls, the feather boarding, the
suspended timber floors, the chipboard ceilings, and so on, were all, of course, chattels
when they were brought onto the site. Did they cease to be chattels when they were
built into the composite structure? The answer to the question, as Blackburn J. pointed
out in *Holland v. Hodgson* (1872) L.R. 7 C.P. 328, depends on the circumstances of
each case, but mainly on two factors, the degree of annexation to the land, and the
object of the annexation.

Degree of annexation

The importance of the degree of annexation will vary from object to object. In the
case of a large object, such as a house, the question does not often arise. Annexation
goes without saying. So there is little recent authority on the point, and I do not get
much help from the early cases in which wooden structures have been held not to form
part of the realty, such as the wooden mill in *Rex v. Otley* (1830) 1 B. & Ad. 161, the
wooden barn in *Wansbrough v. Maton* (1836) 4 A. & E. 884 and the granary in
Wiltshear v. Cottrell (1853) 1 E. & B. 674. But there is a more recent decision of the
High Court of Australia which is of greater assistance. In *Reid v. Smith* (1905) 3
C.L.R. 656, 659 Griffith C.J. stated the question as follows:

> "The short point raised in this case is whether an ordinary dwelling-house, erected
> upon an ordinary town allotment in a large town, but not fastened to the soil,
> remains a chattel or becomes part of the freehold."

The Supreme Court of Queensland had held that the house remained a chattel. But the
High Court reversed this decision, treating the answer as being almost a matter of
common sense. The house in that case was made of wood, and rested by its own
weight on brick piers. The house was not attached to the brick piers in any way. It was
separated by iron plates placed on top of the piers, in order to prevent an invasion of
white ants. There was an extensive citation of English and American authorities. It was
held that the absence of any attachment did not prevent the house forming part of the
realty. Two quotations, at p. 667, from the American authorities may suffice. In
Snedeker v. Warring (1854) 12 N.Y. 170, 175 Parker J. said: "A thing may be as firmly
affixed to the land by gravitation as by clamps or cement. Its character may depend
upon the object of its erection". In *Goff v. O'Conner* (1855) 16 Ill. 421, 423, the court
said:

> "Houses, in common intendment of the law, are not fixtures to, but part of, the
> land. . . . This does not depend, in the case of houses, so much upon the particular
> mode of attaching, or fixing and connecting them with the land upon which they
> stand or rest, as it does upon the uses and purposes for which they were erected and
> designed."

Purpose of annexation

Many different tests have been suggested, such as whether the object which has been fixed to the property has been so fixed for the better enjoyment of the object as a chattel, or whether it has been fixed with a view to effecting a permanent improvement of the freehold. This and similar tests are useful when one is considering an object such as a tapestry, which may or may not be fixed to a house so as to become part of the freehold: see *Leigh v. Taylor* [1902] A.C. 157. These tests are less useful when one is considering the house itself. In the case of the house the answer is as much a matter of common sense as precise analysis. A house which is constructed in such a way so as to be removable, whether as a unit, or in sections, may well remain a chattel, even though it is connected temporarily to mains services such as water and electricity. But a house which is constructed in such a way that it cannot be removed at all, save by destruction, cannot have been intended to remain as a chattel. It must have been intended to form part of the realty. I know of no better analogy than the example given by Blackburn J. in *Holland v. Hodgson* (1872) L.R. 7 C.P. 328, 335:

> "Thus blocks of stone placed one on the top of another without any mortar or cement for the purpose of forming a dry stone wall would become part of the land, though the same stones, if deposited in a builder's yard and for convenience sake stacked on the top of each other in the form of a wall, would remain chattels."

Applying that analogy to the present case, I do not doubt that when Mr Morris's bungalow was built, and as each of the timber frame walls were placed in position, they all became part of the structure, which was itself part and parcel of the land. The object of bringing the individual bits of wood onto the site seems to be so clear that the absence of any attachment to the soil (save by gravity) becomes an irrelevance.

Finally I return to the judgment of the Court of Appeal. I need say no more about the absence of attachment, which was the first of the reasons given by the Court of Appeal for reversing the assistant recorder. The second reason was the intention which the court inferred from the previous course of dealing between the parties, and in particular the uncertainty of Mr Morris's tenure. The third reason was the analogy with the shed in *Webb v. Frank Bevis Ltd* [1940] 1 All E.R. 247, and the greenhouse in *Deen v. Andrews* [1986] 1 E.G.L.R. 262.

As to the second reason the Court of Appeal may have been misled by Blackburn J.'s use of the word "intention" in *Holland v. Hodgson* (1872) L.R. 7 C.P. 328. But as the subsequent decision of the Court of Appeal in *Hobson v. Gorringe* [1897] 1 Ch. 182 made clear, and as the decision of the House in *Melluish v. B.M.I. (No. 3) Ltd* [1996] A.C. 454 put beyond question, the intention of the parties is only relevant to the extent that it can be derived from the degree and object of the annexation. The subjective intention of the parties cannot affect the question whether the chattel has, in law, become part of the freehold, any more than the subjective intention of the parties can prevent what they have called a licence from taking effect as a tenancy, if that is what in law it is: see *Street v. Mountford* [1985] A.C. 809.

As for the third of the reasons, I have already pointed out that *Webb v. Frank Bevis Ltd* does not support the Court of Appeal's conclusion, because the shed in that case was held to be a fixture, albeit a fixture which the tenant was entitled to remove.

In *Deen v. Andrews* the question was whether a greenhouse was a building so as to pass to the purchaser under a contract for the sale of land "together with the farmhouses and other buildings." Hirst J. held that it was not. He followed an earlier decision in *H. E. Dibble Ltd v. Moore* [1970] 2 Q.B. 181 in which the Court of Appeal, reversing the trial judge, held that a greenhouse was not an "erection" within section 62(1) of the Law of Property Act 1925. I note that in the latter case Megaw L.J., at p. 187G, drew attention to some evidence "that it was customary to move such greenhouses every few years to a fresh site." It is obvious that a greenhouse which can be moved from site to site is a long way removed from a two bedroom bungalow which cannot be moved at all without being demolished.

For the above reasons I would allow this appeal and restore the order of the assistant recorder.

LORD CLYDE:
. . .

As the law has developed it has become easy to neglect the original principle from which the consequences of attachment of a chattel to realty derive. That is the principle of accession.
. . .

In the generality there are a number of considerations to which resort may be had to solve the problem. But each case in this matter has to turn on its own facts. Comparable cases are useful for guidance in respect of the considerations employed but can only rarely provide conclusive answers. It has not been suggested that if the bungalow is real property it can be regarded as distinct from the site so as to be excluded from the property let to Mr Morris. The question then can be simply asked whether the bungalow is a chattel or realty. On that wider approach a useful starting point can be found in the words of the old commentator Heineccius (Elementa Iuris Civilis secundum ordinem Pandectarum, Lib.I, Tit. VIII, Sec.199) where, in classifying things as moveable or immoveable he describes the latter as being things "quae vel salvae moveri nequeunt, ut fundus, aedes, ager ... vel usus perpetui causa iunguntur immobilibus, aut horum usui destinantur."

The first of these factors may serve both to identify an item as being real property in its own right and to indicate a case of accession. But account has also to be taken of the degree of physical attachment and the possibility or impossibility of restoring the article from its constituent parts after dissolution. In one early Scottish case large leaden vessels which were not fastened to the building in any way but simply rested by their own weight were held to be heritable since they had had to be taken to pieces in order to be removed and had then been sold as old lead: *Niven v. Pitcairn* (1823) 2 S. 239. In *Hellawell v. Eastwood* (1851) 6 Exch. 295, 312, Parke B., in considering the mode and extent of annexation of the articles in that case, referred to the consideration whether the object in question "can easily be removed, integré, salvé, et commodé, or not, without injury to itself or the fabric of the building." It is agreed in the present case that as matter of fact "the bungalow is not removable in one piece; nor is it demountable for re-erection elsewhere." That agreed finding is in my view one powerful indication that it is not of the nature of a chattel.

In many cases the problem of accession arises in relation to some article or articles which have been placed in or affixed to a building. An unusual, although by no means unique, feature of the present case is that the alleged chattel is the building itself. This invites the approach of simply asking whether it is real property in its own right. Apart from the considerations which I already mentioned it seems to me that it is proper to have regard to the genus of the alleged chattel. That approach was adopted in the Australian case, *Reid v. Smith* (1905) 3 C.L.R. 656.
. . .

In several cases before the Lands Valuation Appeal Court in Scotland where the issue has arisen whether particular subjects are heritable or moveable for the purposes of valuation for local taxation the test has been applied by asking the question whether the particular subjects belong to a genus which is prima facie of a heritable character and, if they are, whether there are any special facts to deprive them of that character. ... Beyond question Mr Morris's bungalow is of the genus "dwelling-house" and dwelling houses are generally of the nature of real property. While it is situated in a rural setting it evidently forms part of a development of a number of other houses whose positions are even noted on the ordnance survey map. I find no factors which would justify taking it out of the category of dwelling houses. On the contrary there are powerful indications that it and its constituent parts do not possess the character of a chattel. It seems to me to be real property.

If the problem is approached as one of accession it has to be noted that in the present case the bungalow is not attached or secured to any realty. It is not joined by any physical link which would require to be severed for it to be detached. But accession can operate even where there is only a juxtaposition without any physical bond between the article and the freehold. Thus the sculptures in *D'Eyncourt v. Gregory* (1866) L.R. 3 Eq. 382 which simply rested by their own weight were held to form part of the architectural design for the hall in which they were placed and so fell to be treated as part of the freehold. The reasoning in such a case where there is no physical attachment was identified by Blackburn J. in *Holland v. Hodgson* (1872) L.R. 7 C.P. 328, 335: "But even in such a case, if the intention is apparent to make the articles part of the land, they do become part of the land".

... Accession also involves a degree of permanence, as opposed to some merely temporary provision. This is not simply a matter of counting the years for which the structure has stood where it is, but again of appraising the whole circumstances. The bungalow has been standing on its site for about half a century and has been used for many years as the residence of Mr Morris and his family. That the bungalow was constructed where it is for the purpose of a residence and that it cannot be removed and re-erected elsewhere point in my view to the conclusion that it is intended to serve a permanent purpose. If it was designed and constructed in a way that would enable it to be taken down and rebuilt elsewhere, that might well point to the possibility that it still retained its character of a chattel. That the integrity of this chalet depends upon it remaining where it is provides that element of permanence which points to its having acceded to the ground. The Court of Appeal took the view that the bungalow was no more annexed to the land and just as much a chattel as the greenhouse in *Deen v. Andrews* [1986] 1 E.G.L.R. 262 (or, as I have already mentioned, the large shed in *Webb v. Frank Bevis Ltd* [1940] 1 All E.R. 247). But there is a critical distinction between *Deen v. Andrews* and the present case in the fact that the greenhouse was demountable while the bungalow is not. I prefer the conclusion reached by the assistant recorder.

...

NOTES:

1. For comment, see [1997] C.L.J. 498; [1998] Conv. 418.

2. Both Lord Lloyd and Lord Clyde stressed the importance of distinguishing clearly between the two issues identified above, namely whether the chattel has become a fixture and/or part of the land; and, where it has, whether there is a right of removal. The second issue is discussed below.

3.2 *Right of removal*

Where a chattel retains its status as such, it may be removed by its owner. Where a chattel loses its status and becomes a fixture and/or part of the land, there is in principle no right of removal once the owner has contracted to sell the land. Thus a purchaser of the land will also acquire all fixtures attached to the land at the time of the contract of sale, unless those fixtures are expressly excluded from the sale. Similarly, a mortgage of the land will include all fixtures in the security, so that if the mortgagee exercises his power of sale in order to recover his loan, he may include any fixtures in the sale, including any fixtures *subsequently* attached to the land: *Reynolds v. Ashby & Son* [1904] A.C. 466.

However, a right to remove fixtures has been recognised in the case of tenants under a lease or life tenants under a trust of land. Such a right is intended to encourage the improvement of the property by such limited owners, whether for the purposes of trade or personal enjoyment, without conferring an undeserved windfall on those persons who subsequently become entitled to the enjoyment of the land.

Mancetter Developments Ltd v. Garmanson Ltd [1986] Q.B. 1212

(CA, Dillon and Kerr L.JJ., Sir George Waller)

DILLON L.J.:
The law of fixtures is of very ancient origin. Originally the position was simply that anything affixed to the land became part of the land and passed with the land; quicquid plantatur solo, solo cedit. The development of a tenant's right to remove tenant's or trade fixtures was a mitigation of that rule; it came about not by any change in the concept of what is a fixture, but by a qualification of the tenant's obligation not to remove fixtures once they have been affixed to the land: see *per* Kindersley V.-C. in *Gibson v. Hammersmith & City Railway Co.* (1863) 2 Drew. & Sm. 603, 608. It is possible that, when a tenant's right to remove trade fixtures was first recognised by the courts, that right was upheld irrespective of any damage caused to the premises by the removal; thus in *Poole's Case* (1703) 1 Salk. 368 it seems to have been held that the sheriff levying execution to enforce a judgment against a sub-tenant was entitled to remove trade fixtures installed by the sub-tenant in premises notwithstanding that the premises were thereby rendered ruinous and the liability to make good the damage was left to fall on the sub-lessor under his own covenants in his head lease. Whatever the initial view of the courts, however, the position that developed was, as put in *Amos & Ferard on Fixtures*, 3rd ed. (1883), pp. 123–124:

"it appears to have been generally understood in practice, that as well where trading as where ornamental fixtures are taken down, the tenant is liable to repair the injury the premises may sustain by the act of removal..."

The extent of the liability is expressed in *Foley v. Addenbrooke* (1844) 13 M. & W. 174, 196 and 199, as being that the tenant must leave the premises in such a state as would be most useful and beneficial to the lessors or those who might next take the premises and must not leave the premises in such a state as not to be conveniently applicable to the same purpose. I would interpret this as a requirement of the law that if tenant's fixtures are removed, the premises must be made good to the extent of being left in a reasonable condition.

The right of a tenant to remove tenant's or trade fixtures arose by the common law independently of contract, though the right might be confirmed or excluded by contract. So equally, in my judgment, the obligation on the tenant to make good the damage, if tenant's fixtures were removed, arose at common law irrespective of contract, although there might also in a particular case be a relevant contract. This is demonstrated by the fact that, as between tenant for life of land and the remaindermen, the tenant for life had a similar right to remove tenant's fixtures and a similar obligation to make good damage, even though there would not have been any contract between the tenant for life and the remaindermen: see *Re De Falbe* [1901] 1 Ch. 523, 542.

The liability to make good the damage, or to repair the injury the premises may sustain by the act of removal of tenant's fixtures, must, in so far as it is a liability at common law and not under a contract, be the liability of the person who removes the fixtures, and not of the person, if different, who originally installed the fixtures and left them there. The analysis of the liability at common law is, in my judgment, that the liability to make good the damage is a condition of the tenant's right to remove tenant's fixtures; therefore removal of the fixtures without making good the damage, being in excess of the tenant's right of removal, is waste, actionable in tort, just as much as removal by the tenant of a landlord's fixture which the tenant has no right to remove is waste.

NOTES:

1. The common law right of a tenant to remove "tenant's fixtures" extends to trade fixtures: see, *e.g. Smith v. City Petroleum Co. Ltd* [1940] 1 All E.R. 260 (petrol pumps); *New Zealand Government Property Corp. v. H.M. & S. Ltd* [1982] Q.B. 1145 (theatre seating and other fittings); *Mancetter Developments Ltd v. Garmanson Ltd* [1986] Q.B. 1212 (extractor fans); and ornamental and domestic fixtures, provided that they are complete in themselves and can be removed without causing irreparable damage to the land/buildings: see, *e.g. Spyer v. Phillipson* [1931] 2 Ch. 183 (decorative wooden panelling and fireplaces); but not general agricultural fixtures: *Elwes v. Maw* (1802) 3 East 38. However, tenants under agricultural holdings and farm business tenancies are given statutory rights to remove fixtures and buildings: see, respectively, Agricultural Holdings Act 1986, s.10; Agricultural Tenancies Act 1995, s.8. A life tenant under a trust of land has a similar right to remove trade, ornamental and domestic fixtures: *Re Hulse* [1905] 1 Ch. 406, 410 *per* Buckley J.

2. The approach of the courts in some cases seems to have undermined the orthodoxy that the right of removal conferred on limited owners is a qualification of the general rule that tenants are not permitted to remove fixtures and that the right does not represent a change in the concept of fixtures. For the courts seem not always to have kept separate, or even addressed, the issues, first, whether the chattel has become a fixture and, secondly, whether it can be removed as a tenant's fixture: see, *e.g. Webb v. Frank Bevis Ltd* [1940] 1 All E.R. 247, 251 *per* Scott L.J. In *Leigh v. Taylor* [1902] A.C. 157 a majority of the House of Lords seems to have approached the case on the basis that the chattels (tapestries) either retained their status as chattels or became *irremovable* fixtures (and held them to be chattels); contrast the decision of the Court of Appeal (*sub nom. Re De Falbe* [1901] Ch. 532) that the tapestries were (removable) tenant's fixtures. This failure on the part of the courts to distinguish the issues (and the consequent blurring of the distinction between chattels and (removable) fixtures) was the subject of critical comment in *Elitestone Ltd v. Morris* [1997] 1 W.L.R. 687, *supra*.

3. As a general rule, if the tenant fails to remove his fixtures before the termination of the tenancy, consistently with their status as fixtures they remain a permanent part of the land: *Re Roberts, ex parte Brook* (1878) 10 Ch D. 100, 109 *per* Thesiger L.J.; *Smith v. City Petroleum Co. Ltd* [1940] 1 All E.R. 260, 261–262 *per* Stable J. However, the rule has been qualified. The right of removal continues to be exercisable "during such further period of possession by [the tenant] as he holds the premises under a right still to consider himself a tenant": *Weeton v. Woodcock* (1840) 7 M. & W. 14, 19 *per* Alderson B.; and the qualification seems to include holding over as a tenant at will: *Re Roberts, ex parte Brook* (1878) 10 Ch D. 100, 109 *per*

Thesiger L.J.; and continuing in possession pursuant to a statutory right under the landlord and tenant legislation or under a new lease (irrespective of whether there is a surrender of the old lease): *New Zealand Government Property Corp. v. H.M. & S. Ltd* [1982] Q.B. 1145. Moreover, even in the absence of any continuing landlord and tenant relationship, if the tenancy is terminated in circumstances which do not afford the tenant sufficient time to remove his fixtures, he must be allowed a reasonable time after the expiry of the tenancy for removal: *Re Roberts, ex parte Brook* (1878) 10 Ch D. 100, 109 *per* Thesiger L.J.; *Smith v. City Petroleum Co. Ltd* [1940] 1 All E.R. 260, 261–262 *per* Stable J. See, generally, Kodilinye [1987] Conv. 253.

C. LAND OWNERSHIP

In order to understand the theory and structure of modern land ownership, it is necessary briefly to examine its historical roots and the central doctrines of tenures and estates.

1. The doctrine of tenures

Following the Norman invasion of England in 1066, the King, who considered himself to be the owner of all land, created a system of land holding under which the right to hold land was granted to tenants in return for the performance of services. In this context the term "tenant" simply means a holder of land: it does not denote the modern landlord and tenant relationship. The different services that were required of the tenant, in effect the terms on which the land was held, were known as "tenures". Such services usually took the form of the provision of horsemen to serve in the army ("knight's service"); but the right to hold land was also granted in return for the performance of some personal service for the king ("grand sergeanty") or, where land was held by religious institutions, the performance of some religious service ("frankalmoign" or "divine service"). These tenants who received a grant of land immediately from the king ("tenants in chief") in turn granted parts of the land to other tenants ("mesne lords"), again in return for the performance of services, which, in addition to those mentioned, included the provision of agricultural services ("socage"). The process was repeated until all land was held by tenants who actually occupied it. This system of land holding, which embraced only "free" tenures such as those referred to above, resulted in the creation of the "feudal pyramid" with the King at its apex. In addition, around the lower levels of the feudal pyramid there was a system of land holding based on "unfree" tenure or "villeinage" (later "copyhold" tenure), according to which the "unfree" tenants merely occupied land on behalf of the "free" tenants. The practical difference between the two systems was gradually eroded; but "unfree" tenure was not formally abolished until 1925.

The theoretical importance of the doctrine of tenures was that there was no transfer of the ownership of the land itself; ownership remained in the King.

Initially, the doctrine of tenures also had great practical significance. First, the tenant was required to perform the specified services for his immediate overlord. Secondly, and perhaps more important, some forms of tenure involved other obligations known as "incidents" of tenure, which entitled the immediate overlord to demand various financial and other benefits from the tenant and even to recover the right to hold the land itself where a tenant died without heirs or was convicted of a capital crime. The latter incident was known as "escheat". The demise of the practical significance of the doctrine began in 1290. The Statute Quia Emptores prohibited "subinfeudation", the creation of additional levels on the feudal pyramid; instead it required the transfer of any right to hold land to take the form of "substitution" whereby the transferee simply took the place of the transferor. The effect of the Statute, combined with the operation of escheat, was the progressive reduction in the number of levels on the feudal pyramid: no new levels could be created and levels lost through escheat could not be replaced. The demise of the practical significance of the doctrine of tenures was accelerated by the absence of any real incentive to preserve socage tenure, the most common form of tenure. Socage tenure had never attracted the more valuable incidents of tenure; and the required services were generally commuted for money payments, which, as a result of inflation, ceased to be worth collecting. The process was more or less completed when the Tenures Abolition Act 1660 converted almost all free tenures into socage tenure and abolished the onerous incidents of tenure with the exception of escheat (although it was not until 1925 that all free (and unfree) tenures were converted into socage tenure). The practical result was that all land was (or was presumed to be) held directly from the Crown; no services or commuted payments were exacted (save in very exceptional circumstances); and the only remaining incident of tenure was escheat.

That remains the position today. As a matter of practical significance, the doctrine of tenures is now effectively obsolete. However, the doctrine of *bona vacantia* (replacing the former doctrine of escheat), according to which land passes to the Crown where the tenant dies intestate and without leaving any relevant relatives, serves as a reminder that the doctrine of tenures continues to form an element of the theoretical structure of modern land ownership: see *Re Lowe's Will Trusts* [1973] 1 W.L.R. 882.

2. The doctrine of estates

The above summary of the doctrine of tenures, according to which ownership of land remains in the Crown, leaves unanswered the question whether the tenant can be said to own anything. The answer provided by English law is unique. The tenant owns an abstract entity, known as an "estate", the substance of which is the entitlement to exercise what amount to ownership rights over the land for a particular period of time. Thus, while the tenure denotes the terms on which a grant of ownership rights over land was made, the estate denotes the duration of the ownership rights granted on those terms.

The modern dichotomy of freehold and leasehold estates (or ownership interests) referred to above did not exist when the doctrine of estates was first developed. The only estates recognised by the common law were the estates granted to tenants on the feudal pyramid holding land by free tenure; and those estates were accordingly all freehold estates. The modern leasehold estate had its origins outside the feudal pyramid and it was regarded as an essentially contractual arrangement between the parties. Only later was the leasehold interest afforded the protection originally confined to freehold estates and recognised as an estate, albeit different in kind from the freehold estates.

2.1 *Freehold estates*

There were three freehold estates known to the common law, all characterised by the uncertainty of the duration of the ownership rights conferred. In (theoretical) descending order of duration, they were the fee simple, the fee tail and the life estate. The fee simple was potentially the largest estate since it would continue until the owner of the estate for the time being died intestate without leaving heirs (so that the land passed to the Crown by virtue of the doctrine of escheat); the term "fee" denoted that the estate was capable of being inherited; and the term "simple" denoted the absence of restriction as to which heirs (descendants, ascendants or collaterals) could inherit and thus keep the estate in existence. The second freehold estate was the fee tail. It was theoretically of shorter duration than the fee simple because it could be inherited only by specified categories of descendants of the original grantee and the potential for its extinction was therefore greater. The third freehold estate was the life estate, which entitled the grantee to the ownership rights for the duration of his life or the life of another person (in which case the estate was known as an "estate pur autre vie").

2.1.1 *Successive freehold estates*   In separating ownership from the land itself, the doctrine of estates provided a convenient and efficient means of setting up a scheme of successive entitlement to the ownership rights over land. Suppose that the person owning the fee simple of land (F) wished to confer the ownership rights over the land on a succession of persons for their lives: first A, then (on A's death) B, then (on B's death) C; and then (on C's death) he wished the ownership rights to revert to himself (F) and his heirs. The intended substance of the arrangement is clear; but every legal system that permits the setting up of such arrangements must analyse the rights of the successive "owners". If a legal system provides for the ownership of the land itself, B, C and F can own nothing until the preceding ownership has ended. However, with the doctrine of estates English law was not so constrained. From the outset each of A, B, C and F is the present owner of an estate in the land; and, notwithstanding that for B, C and F the substance of their respective estates is the entitlement to exercise ownership rights over the land *in the future*, the estate itself is a present asset which is potentially marketable. To draw an analogy: the purchaser of a theatre ticket for a performance next week owns something now which he can sell (the ticket), notwithstanding that the ticket does not entitle him (or any purchaser from him) to view the theatrical performance until next week.

As a matter of terminology, the person whose estate entitles him to the *present* exercise of ownership rights (A) is said to have an estate *in possession*. The person whose estate entitles him to the *future* exercise of ownership rights (B, C and F) is said to have an estate *in expectancy*; but such estates are usually further classified. If the person entitled to ownership rights in the future is someone other than the grantor (B and C), his estate is referred to as an estate *in remainder*; but, if the person entitled to ownership rights in the future is the grantor (F (and his heirs)), his estate is referred to as an estate *in reversion*. However, this particular classification only applies at the outset. When the first life estate (in possession) comes to an end on the death of the estate owner, the immediately following life estate (in remainder) "falls into possession" and that life estate becomes an estate in possession; and the reclassification is repeated on each successive death.

2.1.2 *Modern significance of the doctrine of freehold estates*   In practice, arrangements of successive freehold estates are rarely encountered today, except as the remnants of land transactions from earlier times: see *post*, p. 268. Moreover, since 1997 the creation of fee tail estates (entailed interests) has been prohibited: Trusts of Land and Appointment of Trustees Act 1996, s.2(6), Sched. 1, para. 5. The fee simple in possession is therefore the only freehold estate which in practice constitutes the subject-matter of modern dealings in land; and, when someone claims to "own" land or even to "own the freehold" of land, he almost invariably means that he owns the fee simple estate in possession in that land. Nonetheless, although the fee simple is for virtually all practical purposes tantamount to absolute ownership and it can be transferred by lifetime transfer or by will, its conceptual origin as an estate in the land continues to be reflected in the possibility that, if the owner of the fee simple for the time being dies intestate without leaving relevant relatives, the right to the land reverts to the Crown under the doctrine of *bona vacantia* (formerly the doctrine of escheat): see *Re Lowe's Will Trusts* [1973] 1 W.L.R. 882.

2.2 *Leasehold estates*

The grant of a leasehold estate was characterised (and distinguished from freehold estates) by the certainty of the duration of the ownership rights conferred; thus in the case of a leasehold estate ownership rights were conferred for a fixed (maximum) period of time. This characteristic remains an essential requirement of modern leasehold estates: see *post*, p. 349.

Moreover, leasehold estates were further distinguished from freehold estates, in that, at least by the time that they were recognised as estates, they did not confer seisin on the leasehold owner. Originally seisin denoted simply the factual possession of land; but the term acquired a technical meaning of the possession conferred by the grant of a freehold estate: hence the person who would claim to own Blackacre (and who as a matter of law owns the fee simple estate in Blackacre) is formally and technically described as being "seised of Blackacre (by the tenure of socage) for an estate in fee simple (absolute) in possession". This distinction was, and continues to be, reflected in the structure of leasehold ownership as compared with the structure of successive freehold ownership. The grant of a (freehold) life estate by the fee simple owner in fact necessarily involved the creation of a succession of freehold estates; for, in the absence of an express grant of ownership rights when the life estate came to an end, the law implied the grant of a fee simple in reversion in favour of the original grantor and his heirs. However, since the grant of the life estate involved the conferring of seisin on its owner, the grantor, notwithstanding his fee simple in reversion, had no rights over the land itself during the currency of the life estate. By contrast, the grant of a leasehold estate did not involve the conferring of seisin on the leaseholder; seisin remained in the grantor, who thus continued to have the benefit of a fee simple in possession. Although the fee simple owner had deprived himself of the right to *physical possession* of the land during the currency of the leasehold estate, the fee simple continued as a fee simple in possession because the fee simple owner was entitled to receive rent from the leaseholder.

3. Ownership, possession and title

Despite the terminology of "ownership rights", it must be stressed that the current owner of an estate in possession does not own the land. Subject to certain restrictions, he is entitled to exercise those rights of use, enjoyment and disposition which are normally associated with ownership; but ownership is a concept which English law has never applied directly to land. English law, led by the available legal procedures for the recovery of land, concentrated either on ownership of the estate in the land or on possession (or seisin) of the land itself; but practical considerations of convenience and cost led to an overwhelming preference for, and ultimate predominance of, claims to land based on (the better right to) possession. The practical result was that entitlement to the ownership rights over land (or title to land) depended upon the better right to possession.

This emphasis on possession as the basis of entitlement to ownership rights and on the better right to possession rather than absolute ownership is illustrated by the case of *Asher v. Whitlock* (1865) L.R. 1 Q.B. 1.

Asher v. Whitlock (1865) L.R. 1. Q.B. 1

(Court of Exchequer Chamber, Cockburn C.J., Mellor J., Lush J.)

In 1850 Williamson took possession of and enclosed some manorial land on which he built a cottage. He lived there until he died in 1860. By his will he devised the land to his widow as long as she remained unmarried, with the remainder to his daughter in fee simple. The widow and the daughter continued to live in the cottage; and in 1861 they were joined by the defendant, who had married the widow. In 1863 both the widow and the daughter died; and the defendant continued to live in the cottage. In 1865 the plaintiffs, the heirs of the daughter, sought to remove the defendant; and they relied on the better right to possession of Williamson which they had inherited from his daughter.

COCKBURN C.J.:

The defendant, on the facts, is in this dilemma; either his possession was adverse, or it was not. If it was not adverse to the devisee of the person who inclosed the land, and it may be treated as a continuance of the possession which the widow had and ought to have given up, on her marriage with the defendant, then, as she and the defendant came in under the will, both would be estopped from denying the title of the devisee and her heir-at-law. But assuming the defendant's possession to have been adverse, we have then to consider how far it operated to destroy the right of the devisee and her heir-at-law. [Counsel for the defendant] was obliged to contend that possession acquired, as this was, against a rightful owner, would not be sufficient to keep out every other person but the rightful owner. But I take it as clearly established, that possession is good against all the world except the person who can show a good title; and it would be mischievous to change this established doctrine. In *Doe v. Dyeball* (1829) Mood. & M. 346 one year's possession by the plaintiff was held good against a person who came and turned him out; and there are other authorities to the same effect. Suppose the person who originally inclosed the land had been expelled by the defendant, or the defendant had obtained possession without force, by simply walking in at the open door in the absence of the then possessor, and were to say to him, "You have no more title than I have, my possession is as good as yours," surely ejectment could have been maintained by the original possessor against the defendant. All the old law on the doctrine of disseisin was founded on the principle that the disseisor's title was good against all but the disseisee. It is too clear to admit of doubt, that if the devisor had been turned out of possession he could have maintained ejectment. What is the position of the devisee? There can be no doubt that a man has a right to devise that estate, which the law gives him against all the world but the true owner. Here the widow was a prior devisee, but *durante viduitate* only, and as soon as the testator died, the estate became vested in the widow; and immediately on the widow's marriage the daughter had a right to possession; the defendant however anticipates her, and with the widow takes possession. But just as he had no right to interfere with the testator, so he had no right against the daughter, and had she lived she could have brought ejectment; although she died without asserting her right, the same right belongs to her heir. Therefore I think the action can be maintained, inasmuch as the defendant had not acquired any title by length of possession. The devisor might have brought ejectment, his right of possession being passed by will to his daughter, she could have maintained ejectment, and so therefore can her heir, the female plaintiff. We know to what extent encroachments on waste lands have taken place; and if the lord has acquiesced and does not interfere, can it be at the mere will of any stranger to disturb the person in possession? I do not know what equity may say to the rights of different claimants who have come in at different times without title; but at law, I think the right of the original possessor is clear. On the simple ground that possession is good title against all but the true owner, I think the plaintiffs entitled to succeed.

NOTES:

1. On the assumption that the defendant was in adverse possession, in 1865 there were three (potential) titles to the land: (i) the (documentary) title of the Lord of the Manor, (ii) the possessory title of Williamson commencing in 1850 and currently owned by the plaintiffs and (iii) the possessory title of the defendant commencing in 1861. The title of the Lord of the Manor was the

superior title of the three and he could have recovered the land in an action against either the plaintiffs or the defendant. However, he was not a party to the action and the court was concerned only with the relative merits of the two possessory titles. It followed that, since the Williamson title had commenced first, it was a better title than that of the defendant Whitlock.

2. An earlier title to land can be extinguished by a period of adverse possession if the earlier title is not asserted within the statutory limitation period. At the time of *Asher v. Whitlock* the limitation period was 20 years, so that the title of the Lord of the Manor, if not asserted, would have been extinguished in 1870 (and it would have made no difference that the 20 years' adverse possession was by two successive adverse possessors, Williamson and the defendant). Similarly, if the plaintiffs had not asserted the Williamson title before 1881, that title could have been extinguished by virtue of 20 years' adverse possession by the defendant.

3. The modern law relating to the extinction of documentary title and the acquisition of possessory title by adverse possession is considered further below: see *infra*, p. 79.

D. EQUITY

1. Common law and equity

In parallel with the development of the common rules relating to estates and other interests in land, a distinct set of rules and principles relating to land were devised by the Court of Chancery. The reason for the emergence of these rules and principles, known as "equity", is to be found in the inflexibility of the common law. The common law courts developed a system of remedies based on form. Actions could only be commenced in the courts by the issue of a writ by the King's Chancellor, and success depended upon the availability of a writ that fitted the particular case. Although at first new writs were formulated reasonably readily and their validity was recognised by the courts, the Provisions of Oxford 1258 prohibited the formulation of new writs except with the authority of the King's Council. Despite the restoration of a limited power to adapt existing writs, it was sometimes the case that no remedy was available in the common law courts to redress a novel grievance. In such circumstances, since the King was regarded as holding the residue of judicial power, the only remaining course of action was a petition to the King's Council, usually in the guise of the Chancellor. Eventually this judicial function was taken over by the Chancery, the office of the Chancellor, which was recognised as a court independent of the King's Council and distinct from the common law courts.

Originally the Chancellor exercised this jurisdiction on a case by case basis but systematisation inevitably occurred and there emerged a recognised set of equitable principles. However, equity never abandoned its fundamental rationale that its remedies were discretionary and would evolve to mitigate the injustice created by the sometimes uncompromising attitude of the common law. Equity recognised rights not recognised by the common law and granted remedies not available at common law. For present purposes, it should be noted that, although in many respects equity supplemented the common law, equity and the common law also diverged significantly in their respective approaches to certain aspects of property law.

Although the Supreme Court of Judicature Acts of 1873–1875 merged the courts of law and equity and provided that the rules of law and equity should be administered by all courts, those rules remain distinct; but in cases of conflict it is provided that the rules of equity prevail.

2. Trusts

2.1 *Development of the use/trust*
According to Maitland "of all the exploits of equity the largest and most important is the invention and development of the trust": Maitland, *Equity* (2nd ed. 1936), p. 23. As the creation of equity, the trust (and its predecessor, the use) was *ex hypothesi* a modification of the common law principles of (land) ownership. In due course the trust became a recognised mechanism of land ownership which could be expressly created in preference to the common law mechanism. However, it should be appreciated that at the outset the recognition of the trust was simply the response of equity to the injustice created by the application of the common law to unconventional arrangements in relation to land.

The common feature of these arrangements was that while the land was formally transferred to one person (the "feoffee to use", later the "trustee"), that person was not intended to receive any benefit from the land; rather he had undertaken to hold the land for the benefit of another person (the "cestui que use/trust" or "beneficiary"). Originally, such arrangements were seen as temporary: for example, a knight setting off on a crusade would transfer his land to a friend on the understanding that, during his absence, the friend would look after the land and the family of the knight. Later such arrangements were employed by the Franciscan friars who arrived in England in the early thirteenth century. Since they were prohibited by their vows of poverty from owning land themselves, they would arrange for land to be transferred to a local community "to the use of the friars". However, the most common reason for the creation of such arrangements was that they (potentially) enabled landowners to deal with their property in a more flexible manner than the common law would permit; and, in particular, they provided a means of avoiding some of the more onerous incidents of tenure which were exacted on the death of the freehold estate owner when there was a transfer of seisin to his heir. A transfer of the land during the lifetime of the fee simple estate owner to feoffees to use, to the use of the former estate owner and, on his death, to the use of his heir, ensured that when the former estate owner died there was no transfer of seisin, which remained in the feoffees to use. Moreover, since the feoffees to use could remain a continuing body of persons who owned the fee simple estate jointly, with the result that it (and seisin) never passed to any of their heirs, the effect of the arrangement was the avoidance of many of the incidents of tenure.

Provided that the feoffees to use were carefully selected and that they dealt with the land in accordance with their undertaking, these arrangements required no formal recognition. However, if the feoffees to use failed to comply with their undertaking, the intended beneficiaries of the arrangement could obtain no assistance from the common law courts. The common law was concerned only with the formal arrangement, which conferred the fee simple estate on the feoffees to use, and refused to recognise any claim of the intended beneficiaries. In these circumstances, the assistance of equity was sought; and at some time in the early fifteenth century equitable relief was first granted. Equity did not question the common law ownership of the feoffees to use; but, because equity took the view that the land would not have been transferred to the feoffees to use except on the basis that they would comply with their undertaking, the feoffees to use were compelled *as a matter of personal obligation enforced by equity* to comply with that undertaking.

The enforcement of uses and the consequential widespread avoidance of the incidents of tenure adversely affected the revenue of the King: for, as has been seen, after the Statute Quia Emptores of 1290 the feudal pyramid had begun to compress and land had increasingly been held (or presumed to be held) directly from the King. The response, "forced upon an extremely unwilling Parliament by an extremely strong-willed King", was the Statute of Uses of 1535. The Statute provided for the "execution" of all uses, with the effect that the feoffees to use dropped out of the picture and the intended beneficiaries became the common law owners of the land. However, with the abolition of the onerous incidents of tenure by the Tenures Abolition Act 1660, the motivation behind the prohibition of uses disappeared; and by the end of the seventeenth century equity was again enforcing the device in the form of the trust. Since the Statute of Uses remained in force, this was achieved by transferring land "to A and his heirs to the use of B and his heirs to the use of (on trust for) C and his heirs". The Statutes of Uses executed the first use so that the grant took effect as a transfer to B and his heirs; and, although the use/trust in favour of C and his heirs was not recognised by the common law, it was enforced in equity with the result that B held the land on trust for C. Although an abbreviated formula was later adopted ("unto and to the use of B and his heirs in trust for C and his heirs"), the use upon a use remained the theoretical basis of the trust until the Statute of Uses was repealed in 1925.

2.2 Analysis of the trust: legal and equitable ownership

The effect of the recognition of the trust was the recognition by equity of both common law (or legal) ownership and equitable ownership in land. The formal transferees acquired legal ownership of the land as trustees while the beneficiaries acquired equitable ownership. However, once the division into legal and equitable ownership was made, equity applied to equitable ownership many of the same principles that the common law had developed in relation to legal ownership. In particular, equity adopted the doctrine of estates and permitted the equitable ownership rights over land to be granted for a succession of time periods or estates. Thus a grant to trustees on trust for A and his heirs conferred the legal fee simple in possession on the trustees and the equitable fee simple in possession on A; and a grant to trustees on trust for A for life and then for B and his heirs conferred the legal fee simple in possession on the trustees, an equitable life estate in possession on A and the equitable fee simple in remainder on B. However, it must be emphasised that, where a trust is created, the legal ownership of the trustees is *formal* ownership: it involves duties of management of the trust property for the benefit of the beneficiaries but confers no substantive benefit on the trustees themselves. The real benefits of ownership are conferred on the beneficiaries of the trust, who acquire the equitable (or beneficial) ownership of the land.

2.3 *Legal and equitable estates compared*
Given the general application of the doctrine of estates to equitable ownership, it should be apparent that, following the development of the trust, there were two methods by which the fee simple owner of land could grant the ownership rights over that land to A for the duration of his life: he could grant a *legal* life estate; or he could transfer the land to trustees on trust for A for life, thereby conferring on A an *equitable* life estate. Since the owner of the life estate in each case acquired the real benefits of ownership, it may be questioned whether there was any difference between the legal life estate and the equitable life estate.

The fundamental difference was to be found in the enforceability of the respective estates against successors in title to the legal fee simple. Suppose that during A's lifetime, the owner of the legal fee simple (the grantor where A has a legal life estate; the trustees where A has an equitable life estate) transferred that legal fee simple to a third party. The question arose whether A could continue to claim the benefit of the life estate as against the transferee of the legal fee simple. A legal life estate would be enforceable since, as a general rule, legal estates were universally enforceable against the land in question, whoever acquired that land and irrespective of whether or not he knew about the legal estate at the time he acquired the land. This rule is sometimes expressed by saying that legal rights are "rights *in rem*". By contrast, the enforceability of equitable estates against transferees was initially less comprehensive. When trusts were first enforced, equity based that enforcement on the personal obligation undertaken by the trustee and remedies were directed at the trustee personally rather than at the trust property: for that reason the equitable rights of the beneficiary were referred to as "rights *in personam*". However, the enforceability of these equitable rights was progressively extended. They became enforceable against any person who succeeded to the property of the trustee on his death; against any person who acquired the trust property from the trustee by way of gift; and against any person to whom the trustee sold the trust property, if the purchaser knew about the trust. A further and final extension of enforceability was intended to include the dishonest or imprudent purchaser: equitable estates were therefore held to be enforceable against a purchaser of the trust property who had *constructive* notice of the trust, that is a purchaser who *would have known* about the trust if he had made all the inquiries that an honest and prudent purchaser would have made in the circumstances. It will be apparent that these extensions of enforceability significantly undermined the classification of equitable estates as "rights *in personam*", although it could not be claimed that they constituted "rights *in rem*". For, in contrast with legal estates, equitable estates were not enforceable against *all* persons who acquired the land. The distinction could be formulated in terms of the doctrine of notice, one of the central doctrines of equity: that an equitable estate was enforceable against all persons *except* a bona fide (good faith) purchaser of the legal estate for valuable consideration without actual or constructive notice of the trust at the time of the purchase.

Before the doctrine of notice is examined in more detail, it is necessary to refer to the wider range of equitable interests to which it applied.

3. Equitable interests

In addition to the recognition of trusts, and therefore equitable estates corresponding to the common law estates, equity recognised and enforced other interests in relation to land.

3.1 *Equitable versions of legal interests*

Equity recognised equitable versions of legal rights other than the freehold estates. Thus recognition extended to equitable leasehold interests, equitable mortgages and equitable easements, either where equity was prepared to overlook one of the substantive constituents required for the legal version of the interest or where there had been no compliance with the formal requirements for the creation of the relevant interest at common law. For example, an easement could only be a legal easement if it was granted for a period equivalent to a fee simple or leasehold estate and if the grant complied with certain formalities. However, whereas it followed that an easement purportedly granted for life and/or granted without the necessary formalities could not be recognised at law, it could be recognised as an equitable easement.

3.2 *Equitable interests having no legal equivalent*

Equity also developed a number of interests which had no legal equivalent. For the purposes of the following discussion of the doctrine of notice, it may be helpful briefly to outline three of these interests, although they will be considered in greater detail in subsequent chapters.

3.2.1 *Estate contracts*   Where a person contracts to purchase a legal estate in land, the availability of the equitable remedy of specific performance to compel the vendor to perform the contract and to transfer the legal estate means that, prior to the execution of the contract and the transfer of the legal estate, the purchaser acquires an immediate equitable interest in the land.

3.2.2 *Restrictive covenants*   Although a contract is normally enforceable only between the parties to the contract, a covenant (or undertaking) by a landowner, whereby he (the "covenantor") agrees to restrict his use of the land, is recognised as potentially enforceable against subsequent owners of the land and as conferring on the other party to the covenant (the "covenantee") an equitable interest over the land of the covenantor.

3.2.3 *Equity of redemption*   Where a landowner transferred his land to another person by way of mortgage as security for the repayment of a loan, common law took the view that if repayment were not made on the specified date, the landowner would lose forever the right to recover the land. Equity intervened to give the landowner the right to recover the land after the specified date, provided that he made full repayment. This right constituted the principal element in the landowner's equity of redemption, an equitable interest in the mortgaged land.

4. Doctrine of notice

Prior to 1926 the doctrine of notice determined the enforceability of equitable interests through changes in ownership of the land affected. Since 1926 the significance of the doctrine has diminished significantly: see Howell [1997] Conv. 431; but, as some of the cases discussed in this section illustrate, it continues to operate in certain circumstances. It must therefore be examined in more detail. The classic statement of the doctrine is to be found in *Pilcher v. Rawlins* (1872) L.R. 7 Ch.App. 259, where James L.J. stated (at 268–269):

I propose simply to apply myself to the case of a purchaser for valuable consideration, without notice, obtaining, upon the occasion of his purchase, and by means of his purchase deed, some legal right, some legal advantage; and, according to my view of the established law of this Court, such a purchaser's plea of a purchase for valuable consideration without notice is an absolute, unqualified, unanswerable defence, and an unanswerable plea to the jurisdiction of this Court. Such a purchaser, when he has once put in that plea, may be interrogated and tested to any extent as to the valuable consideration which he has given in order to shew the *bona fides* or *mala fides* of his purchase, and also the presence or the absence of notice; but when once he has gone through that ordeal, and has satisfied the terms of the plea of purchase for valuable consideration without notice, then, according to my judgment, this Court has no jurisdiction whatever to do anything more than to let him depart in possession of that legal estate, that legal right, that legal advantage which he has obtained, whatever it may be. In such a case a purchaser is entitled to hold that which, without breach of duty, he has had conveyed to him.

If a person acquiring land is to qualify as a "bona fide purchaser" or "equity's darling" and thus take free of any equitable interest affecting the land, it is for that person to establish that he satisfies each of the constituent elements of the doctrine: *Re Nisbet and Potts' Contract* [1906] 1 Ch. 386, 403 *per* Collins M.R.

4.1 *Bona fides (good faith)*

In *Midland Bank Trust Co. Ltd v. Green* [1981] A.C. 513 Lord Wilberforce
stated (at 528):

My Lords, the character in the law known as the bona fide (good faith) purchaser for
value without notice was the creation of equity. In order to affect a purchaser for value
of a legal estate with some equity or equitable interest, equity fastened upon his
conscience and the composite expression was used to epitomise the circumstances in
which equity would or rather would not do so. I think that it would generally be true
to say that the words "in good faith" related to the existence of notice. Equity, in other
words, required not only absence of notice, but genuine and honest absence of notice.
As the law developed, this requirement became crystallised in the doctrine of
constructive notice which assumed a statutory form in the Conveyancing Act 1882,
section 3. But, and so far I would be willing to accompany the respondents, it would
be a mistake to suppose that the requirement of good faith extended only to the matter
of notice, or that when notice came to be regulated by statute, the requirement of good
faith became obsolete. Equity still retained its interest in and power over the
purchaser's conscience. The classic judgment of James L.J. in *Pilcher v. Rawlins* (1872)
L.R. 7 Ch.App. 259, 269 is clear authority that it did: good faith there is stated as a
separate test which may have to be passed even though absence of notice is proved.
And there are references in cases subsequent to 1882 which confirm the proposition
that honesty or bona fides remained something which might be inquired into (see
Berwick & Co. v. Price [1905] 1 Ch. 632, 639; *Taylor v. London and County Banking
Co.* [1901] 2 Ch. 231, 256; *Oliver v. Hinton* [1899] 2 Ch. 264, 273).

For the statutory formulation of constructive notice, see now Law of Property
Act 1925, s.199(1)(ii)(a), *infra*, p. 33.

4.2 *Purchaser for valuable consideration*

The composite expression "purchaser for valuable consideration" is used
because at common law "purchaser" denotes any person who acquires land by
the voluntary act of the parties as opposed to by operation of law: see *Inland
Revenue Commissioners v. Gribble* [1913] 3 K.B. 212, 218 *per* Buckley L.J.
"Purchaser" thus includes a purchaser in the normal sense of that term, but
also a person acquiring land by way of gift or under the will of the former
owner; but the term excludes a person acquiring land on the death of the
former owner under the intestacy rules and a squatter, who acquires title to
land through adverse possession and the extinction of the previous title: *Re
Nisbet and Potts' Contract* [1906] 1 Ch. 386, *infra*, p. 35. However, for the
purposes of the bona fide purchaser rule the purchaser must provide
consideration in the form of money or money's worth (including the payment
of an existing debt: *Thorndike v. Hunt* (1859) 3 De G. & J. 563) or future
marriage; and the consideration must have been paid in full before the
purchaser discovers the equitable interest: *Tourville v. Naish* (1734) 3 P. Wms.
307.

4.3 *Purchaser of the legal estate*

Although the classic formulation of the doctrine of notice states that the
purchaser must have acquired a legal estate in the land affected by the
equitable interest, it is not necessary that he should have acquired the legal fee

simple. In appropriate circumstances, the bona fide purchaser rule extends to a person who acquires a legal lease of the land and also to a person who acquires a legal mortgage over the land. On the other hand, where a purchaser acquires an *equitable* interest only, prima facie he is bound by all existing equitable interests affecting the land, irrespective of notice: *Phillips v. Phillips* (1862) 4 De G.F. & J. 208, 215 *per* Lord Westbury; *London and South Western Railway Co. v. Gomm* (1882) 20 Ch D. 562, 583 *per* Jessel M.R. That proposition is, however, subject to qualification. First, the principle that "first in time prevails" applies only where the equities "are in *all other respects* equal": *Rice v. Rice* (1853) 2 Drew 73, 78 *per* Kindersley V.-C.; and the principle may therefore be displaced where the owner of the earlier equitable interest has been fraudulent or negligent: see *post*, p. 955. Secondly, pursuant to the "tabula in naufragio" doctrine, the purchaser of an equitable interest may not be bound by an earlier equitable interest where he later acquires a legal estate: *Bailey v. Barnes* [1894] 1 Ch. 25; and see *post*, p. 960. Thirdly, the purchaser of an equitable interest will not be bound by "mere equities" of which he has no notice: see *Latec Investments Ltd v. Hotel Terrigal Pty Ltd* (1965) 113 C.L.R. 265, *infra*.

4.4 *Notice*
The requirement that the bona fide purchaser must not have notice of the equitable interest at the time of the purchase extends to actual, constructive and imputed notice: see, *e.g. Kemmis v. Kemmis* [1988] 1 W.L.R. 1307, 1333 *per* Nourse L.J.

4.4.1 *Actual notice*   A purchaser has actual notice of all those matters within his own knowledge. However, it is not necessary that the purchaser should have acquired the knowledge directly from the owner of the equitable interest. According to Lord Cairns L.C. in *Lloyd v. Banks* (1868) 3 Ch.App. 488, 490–491, what is required is proof

that the mind of the [purchaser] has in some way been brought to an intelligent apprehension of the nature of the [equitable interest] which has come upon the property, so that a reasonable man, or an ordinary man of business, would act upon the information and would regulate his conduct by it...

On the basis that notice involves knowledge that operates upon the mind of the purchaser, it has been suggested that a purchaser will not have knowledge of a fact that he once knew if at the time of the purchase he has genuinely forgotten all about it: *Re Montagu's Settlement* [1987] Ch. 264, 284 *per* Megarry V.-C.

4.4.2 *Constructive notice*   According to section 199(1)(ii)(a) of the Law of Property Act 1925, a purchaser will be held to have constructive notice of those matters that would have come to his notice if he had made those inquiries and inspections that a reasonable and prudent purchaser would have made in the circumstances. Thus, despite the assertion that the section "really

does no more than state the law as it was before" (see *Bailey v. Barnes* [1894] 1 Ch. 25, 35 *per* Lindley L.J.; *Caunce v. Caunce* [1969] 1 W.L.R. 286, 293 *per* Stamp J.), constructive notice probably extends beyond earlier statements that referred only to "knowing something which ought to have put [the purchaser] on further inquiry" and "wilfully abstaining from inquiry to avoid notice": see *Jones v. Smith* (1841) 1 Hare 43, 55 *per* Wigram V.-C.; *Hunt v. Luck* [1901] 1 Ch. 45, 52 *per* Farwell J.; and see *Kemmis v. Kemmis* [1988] 1 W.L.R. 1307, 1317 *per* Purchas L.J.

However, provided that the purchaser can establish that he has done what a prudent purchaser would have done, it seems that the purchaser will not be bound by equitable interests that he has not discovered. On the other hand, if the purchaser has failed to act as a prudent purchaser, he will nonetheless be deemed to have notice of, and will be bound by, all those equitable interests that he would have discovered if he had acted as a prudent purchaser. The doctrine is reasonably simple to state; but it is not always so simple for the purchaser to anticipate the necessarily *ex post facto* decision of a court as to what a prudent purchaser would have done in the circumstances of the particular case. Equally, the owner of an equitable interest may be uncertain as to what he can do in order to ensure that a potential purchaser has or is deemed to have notice of that interest.

It is traditionally asserted that a prudent purchaser would investigate the documents of title and would inspect the land. However, such investigation/inspection may not exhaust the scope of constructive notice. For example, in *Kingsnorth Finance Co. Ltd v. Tizard* [1986] 1 W.L.R. 786, *infra*, p. 42, the mortgagee learned that the prospective mortgagor had children, although he had (falsely) stated on the application form that he was single. It was held that the mortgagee should have made further inquiries, which would almost certainly have disclosed that the mortgagor's wife claimed an equitable interest in the mortgaged property (based on her contributions to the purchase price); and that the mortgagee therefore had constructive notice of that interest.

4.4.2.1 *Investigation of the documents of title*   Under the title deeds system of conveyancing that applies to unregistered land, the vendor is required to provide an "abstract of title", detailing documentary evidence of his entitlement to the legal fee simple that he is purporting to sell to the purchaser. This evidence will comprise the document by which he acquired the fee simple and the documents by which each preceding owner acquired the fee simple; the evidence will also include documents relating to mortgages and certain other dealings in the land. The intention is that the documents should, first, demonstrate the entitlement of the vendor to the fee simple in the land and, secondly, reveal the (means of discovering the) existence of any third party interests over the land. It would, of course, have been increasingly impracticable and unrealistic to require the vendor to provide documentary evidence of *all* previous dealings in the land. Consequently, in the absence of any contrary agreement between the vendor and purchaser, statute specifies the period to be covered by the abstract of title. This period was first fixed at 60 years; but, as titles to land became less complicated and concerns over potential problems failed to materialise, the period was gradually reduced and the current period is 15 years: Law of Property Act 1925, s.44(1), as amended by the Law of Property Act 1969, s.23. In practice this means that the vendor must identify the person who owned the fee simple 15 years ago; and he must provide documentary evidence of the conveyance to that person (the so-called "root of title") together with documentary evidence of all subsequent conveyances of, and dealings affecting, the fee simple.

The importance of the specified period is that, since the purchaser is entitled by statute to see all the documents of title covering that period, it is assumed that a prudent purchaser would investigate all those documents. Consequently, even where the parties agree that the abstract of title should cover a shorter period, a purchaser who fails to investigate the documents of title covering the entire period specified by statute will be held to have constructive notice of those equitable interests that he would have discovered if he had investigated the documents covering the entire period: *Re Cox and Neve's Contract* [1891] 2 Ch. 109, *infra*, p. 37; *Re Nisbet and Potts' Contract* [1906] 1 Ch. 386, *infra*; and the principle applies *a fortiori* to a purchaser who fails to investigate at all: *Worthington v. Morgan* (1849) 16 Sim. 547.

Re Nisbet and Potts' Contract [1906] 1 Ch. 386

(CA, Collins M.R., Romer and Cozens-Hardy L.JJ.)

In 1903 Potts contracted to purchase certain land from Nisbet. Potts subsequently discovered that two restrictive covenants, restricting the use of the land but not mentioned in the contract with Nisbet, had been entered into in 1867 and 1872. If the covenants were still enforceable, Potts would have been prevented from using the land as he had intended and he would have been entitled to withdraw from the contract on the ground that Nisbet could not "show good title". The question of enforceability in fact depended on whether Nisbet had notice of the convenants when he purchased the land in 1901. If he did, he would have been bound by them; and Potts would also have been bound if he had proceeded with his purchase, since he clearly had notice of the covenants. On the other hand, if Nisbet did not have notice of the covenants when he purchased the land in 1901, neither he nor any subsequent purchaser would be bound by them (see *Wilkes v. Spooner* [1911] 2 K.B. 473, *infra*, p. 47). When Nisbet purchased the land in 1901, it was agreed that the abstract of title should commence in 1878 (although the current specified period was 40 years); and the abstract revealed that Nisbet's predecessor in title had acquired title by adverse possession between 1878 and 1890.

COLLINS M.R.:
It seems to me, therefore, that the principal question before us is whether or not Sir George Jessel was right in the view that he took in *London and South Western Ry. Co. v. Gomm* (1882) 20 Ch.D. 562, that an obligation created by a restrictive covenant is in the nature of a negative easement, creating a paramount right in the person entitled

to it over the land to which it relates. If that is so, then, in the present case, the squatter, by his squatting, simply acquired a right to land subject to this incident. Of course, the burden of that incident must pass to all persons who subsequently become assignees of the land, and the squatter is not entitled to hand it over freed from the obligation that was imposed on the person whose title he has ousted by his possession.

Now, is that the law or not? In the first place, I do not think there was anything inconsistent in the view taken by Sir George Jessel with the law as laid down in the leading case of *Tulk v. Moxhay* (1848) 2 Ph. 774, though, no doubt, words are used there pointing to the equity arising out of the injustice which would accrue if a person who had acquired land at a reduced price by reason of its user being subject to a restriction were afterwards enabled to pass on that land to other persons freed from that restriction receiving in return, on that ground, an increased price. That element, no doubt, does enter into consideration, when one comes to inquire what is the position of a person who acquires for value the legal estate in land subject to a right that has previously been created in another person to restrict the user of that land. The right so created is an equitable right, and, therefore, it is one capable of being defeated in certain circumstances by a person who acquires the legal estate for value. The question thus arises whether, in the circumstances of the particular case, there is anything which would make it inequitable for that person to avail himself of his legal estate to defeat that equitable right. That, as [counsel for Potts] pointed out, is an inquiry which is inevitable in cases where you are dealing with equitable rights and legal estates. But that does not in the least prevent the right in question being what Sir George Jessel considered it to be, namely, a burden imposed upon the land, and passing with the land, subject, of course, to this, that it may be defeated by a purchaser for value without notice; but the burden is upon the person who takes the land to shew that he has acquired it under such conditions as to defeat the right as against him, namely, that he has acquired it for value and without notice.

Now, that being Sir George Jessel's view in *Gomm's Case*, it seems to me that the view has been adopted more than once in this Court: *Rogers v. Hosegood* [1900] 2 Ch. 388, *Hall v. Ewin* (1888) 37 Ch.D. 74, and in *Haywood's Case* (1881) 8 Q.B.D. 403.

Therefore, it seems to me that the law is clearly established in accordance with Sir George Jessel's view of the subject, and consequently that in this case the burden of the restrictive covenant did remain imposed on the land so as to be binding upon any person who could not shew that he had bought for value and without notice. Consequently it appears to me that the squatter's title does not in any way assist the appellant in this case.

Then that brings me to the second point. Has the appellant, the present vendor, shewn—as the burden is upon him to shew—that, having bought this land for value, he bought without notice of this incumbrance? There, again, it seems to me quite clear that he has not discharged that burden. He admits that he accepted, possibly he bound himself to accept, a title commencing in 1878. He was entitled to demand a title of forty years, and it seems perfectly clear now that if he had insisted upon a title of forty years he must have had before him the existence of a covenant entered into as late as 1872 by the person whose title was displaced or "extinguished"—to use the expression in the statute—by the possession for the statutory period of the person through whom the present vendor, Nisbet, now claims. That is equivalent to notice. In point of fact, by exercising reasonable care in demanding the title to which he was entitled, Nisbet must have discovered the fact that there was this burden; and, if so, that is proof that he must be taken as having had constructive notice of it. It is not even necessary to go as far as that, because I agree with Farwell J. in this, as in all other points of the case, that, the burden being upon Nisbet to shew that he had himself bought for value without notice, he has not discharged that burden by simply saying, "I did not push my inquiries beyond that". It is said to be doubtful whether he could have actually discovered the existence of the covenant: but that does not seem to me to discharge the burden of proof that lies upon the appellant; and therefore I am of opinion, on all grounds, that he is not in a position to enforce the contract against the purchaser.

NOTES:

1. For detailed discussion of restrictive covenants, see *post*, Chapter 8.

2. In *Re Cox and Neve's Contract* [1891] 2 Ch. 109 the contract of sale dated 1890 provided that title should commence with a mortgage deed relating to the land dated 1852. When the purchasers discovered a conveyance dated 1847 (which was referred to in the mortgage deed) containing restrictive covenants, they sought to withdraw from the contract because, if they proceeded, they would be bound by the covenants. North J. held that the vendors had failed to show good title; he said (at 117–118):

Under these circumstances the vendor's advisers did not choose to commence the abstract of title with the deed of 1847, which would have shewn a title going back forty-three years, but they choose to commence with the mortgage deed of July, 1852—not a very convenient document with which to commence a title—a mortgage only thirty-eight years old. And then it is said—I never heard such a contention before—"The purchaser has been too vigilant. If he had only refrained from making the inquiries which he thought fit to make, and had not thus acquired notice of the deed of 1847, but had taken a conveyance of the property, he would have obtained a good title as a purchaser for value without notice, and could not have been affected by the restrictive covenant." Therefore, it is said, that as it is only the purchaser's own inquisitiveness which has brought this upon him, the vendor ought not to be prejudiced by the inquiry which he thus made. I think it was the vendor's duty to tell the purchaser that this deed existed, and it is the vendor's fault, and not the purchaser's inquisitiveness, which has led to the disclosure. But I must say that I dissent entirely from the proposition that the purchaser would have taken the property free from the restrictive covenant, if he had made no inquiry. On the contrary, I think he would have been bound by it, and for this reason. He had agreed by the bargain contained in the conditions of sale to accept a title of less than forty years. That cannot relieve him from all knowledge of the prior title, or, it would come to this—that, if a man was content to purchase property on the condition that he should not inquire into the title, he would acquire a title free from any existing restrictions, and would not have constructive notice of any incumbrance. Of course the law does not allow of anything so absurd as that. If a purchaser chooses to take property with a thirty-eight years' title, without going any further back, he has, in my opinion, constructive notice of that which he would actually have known if he had required a forty years' title to be shewn, and had investigated the title during that period. And, when I say a forty years' title, I mean a title deduced for forty years, and for so much longer as it is necessary to go back in order to arrive at a point at which the title can properly commence. The title cannot commence *in nubibus* at the exact point of time which is represented by 365 days multiplied by 40. It must commence at or before the forty years with something which is in itself, or, which it is agreed shall be, a proper root of title.

Under these circumstances, I think the purchaser was fortunate in discovering that which it was the vendor's duty to tell him, but which the vendor abstained from telling him.

3. The limit of this aspect of constructive notice is illustrated by *Pilcher v. Rawlins* (1872) L.R. 7 Ch.App. 259. Rawlins acquired the fee simple of certain land. He conveyed it by way of mortgage to the trustees of the Pilcher trust as security for the repayment of a loan. The surviving trustee subsequently reconveyed part of the land to Rawlins, although the loan had not been repaid, with the result that the land remained subject to the equitable interests under the trust. Rawlins then conveyed that part of the

land to other mortgagees, relying on an abstract of title which ended with the original conveyance to him and without disclosing the dealings with the Pilcher trustees. The mortgagees were held not to have constructive notice of the equitable interests since they had made all reasonable inquiries. Although the equitable interests would have been disclosed by investigation of the *complete* title, the relevant documents had been concealed in circumstances that made their discovery effectively impossible.

4. Prior to 1926 a prospective purchaser of a leasehold estate was entitled to investigate the title to the freehold estate from which it was derived. Thus, even if he agreed not to investigate it, he was deemed to have notice of those equitable interests affecting the freehold title that he would have discovered if he had investigated it: *Patman v. Harland* (1881) 17 ChD. 353, 359 *per* Jessel M.R. After 1925 a prospective purchaser of a leasehold estate is no longer entitled to investigate the relevant freehold title: Law of Property Act 1925, s.44(2); and, accordingly, he is not deemed to have notice of those equitable interests affecting the freehold title that he would have discovered if he had investigated it: *ibid.* s.44(5), although the owner of the interest may seek to establish that the purchaser had *actual* notice: *Shears v. Wells* [1936] 1 All E.R. 832, 834 *per* Luxmoore J. It follows that an equitable interest affecting land that depends upon notice for its enforceability may effectively be lost by the grant of a lease of that land.

4.4.2.2 *Inspection of the land*   In addition to investigating the documents of title, it is assumed that the prudent purchaser would also inspect the land in order to discover whether there are any adverse interests affecting the land or whether there are any persons other than the vendor in occupation of the land.

The operation of this aspect of the doctrine of constructive notice where the vendor is not in occupation of the land is governed by the rule in *Hunt v. Luck*.

Hunt v. Luck [1902] 1 Ch. 428

(CA, Vaughan Williams, Stirling and Cozens-Hardy L.JJ.)

The plaintiff's husband owned a number of freehold properties, which he leased. The rent was collected by Woodrow and at first paid directly to the plaintiff's husband. Subsequently the rent was remitted by Woodrow to Gilbert, who paid it over to the plaintiff's husband and, after his death, to the plaintiff. When Gilbert died, the plaintiff discovered that two years earlier her husband had conveyed the properties to Gilbert and that Gilbert had conveyed the properties by way of mortgage to secure the repayment of a loan. The plaintiff sought to challenge the conveyances, *inter alia*, on the ground of fraud; the defendants were the beneficiary under Gilbert's will and the mortgagees. Farwell J. rejected the challenge to the conveyances; and he further held that, even on the assumption that fraud had been established, the mortgagees did not have notice of the fraud or of the title of the plaintiff's husband. The plaintiff appealed.

VAUGHAN WILLIAMS L.J.:

I think that the conclusion of Farwell J. was right. In his judgment he, after quoting the older authorities, said [1901] 1 Ch. 45, 51: "The rule established by these two cases may be stated thus: (1) A tenant's occupation is notice of all that tenant's rights, but not of his lessor's title or rights; (2) actual knowledge that the rents are paid by the tenants to some person whose receipt is inconsistent with the title of the vendor is notice of that person's rights." In the present case I do not understand that any one suggests, and, if it is suggested, in my opinion the suggestion is ill-founded, that there was actual knowledge that the rents were paid by the tenants to some person whose receipt would be inconsistent with the title of the mortgagor, Gilbert. We have, therefore, to apply the first of the rules stated by the learned judge. Now, what does that mean? It means that, if a purchaser or a mortgagee has notice that the vendor or mortgagor is not in possession of the property, he must make inquiries of the person in possession—of the tenant who is in possession—and find out from him what his rights are, and, if he does not choose to do that, then whatever title he acquires as purchaser or mortgagee will be subject to the title or right of the tenant in possession.

That, I believe, is a true statement of the law; and the only other matter to which I need allude is the case of *Mumford v. Stohwasser* (1874) L.R. 18 Eq. 556, to which the attention of Farwell J. was called by the reporter after he had delivered his judgment in Court. Farwell J. gave an explanation of that case, namely, that in his view the passage in the judgment of Jessel M.R. (at p. 562) which appears to favour the idea that notice of a tenancy is notice of the title of the lessor, was, if the learned judge really said so, a slip of memory on his part. He did not profess to be laying down any new law; he only professed to be stating the old-established and unquestioned law. It is impossible for us to affirm the proposition so stated by him in the passage to which I have referred, unless we are prepared to disregard the other authorities, including the decision of the Privy Council in *Barnhart v. Greenshields* (1853) 9 Moo. P.C. 32, which shew that notice of a tenancy has no operation whatever as giving notice of the title of the lessor of the tenant who is in possession. Of course, if you make inquiries and get information, then you are affected by notice, but not otherwise.

Where the vendor is in occupation, the question is whether the purchaser has constructive notice of the interests of other persons in occupation; but the approach of the court in answering that question has changed significantly.

Caunce v. Caunce [1969] 1 W.L.R. 286

(Ch D., Stamp J.)

A husband and wife agreed that the wife would contribute a capital sum to the purchase price of a house, that the husband would pay the instalments on the mortgage loan and that the property would be conveyed to them in their joint names. In fact the property was conveyed to the husband alone, with the result that he held the property, subject to the mortgage, on trust for himself and the wife. He later obtained three further loans and secured repayment by mortgaging the property to the bank. On his bankruptcy, the question arose as to whether, at the time of the later mortgages, the bank had constructive notice of the equitable interest of the wife under the trust.

STAMP J.:

It is contended that an inquiry ought to have been made on the property and that if such an inquiry had been made the plaintiff would have asserted her equitable interest, ergo—so the argument runs—the bank had constructive notice of that interest. Before going on to consider this contention it is, perhaps, convenient that I should remark by way of warning that section 199 is a section designed not to extend but to limit the doctrine of constructive notice. The section does not operate so as to fix a purchaser with constructive notice of a matter of which he would not have had constructive notice prior to the coming into force of the Law of Property Act. The law, as I understand it, is this: if there be in possession or occupation of the property, contracted to be sold or mortgaged, a person other than the vendor, or, as in this case, other than the mortgagor, and the purchaser makes no inquiry of that person, he takes the property fixed with notice of that person's rights and interests, however that may be. (See the judgment in the Court of Appeal of Vaughan Williams L.J. in *Hunt v. Luck* [1902] 1 Ch. 428, 432.) Here it is said that the plaintiff was in possession or occupation. No inquiry was made of her and therefore the bank is fixed with notice of her equitable interest. In my judgment, it is here that the fallacy arises, for the plaintiff, unlike the deserted wife, was not in apparent occupation or possession. She was there, ostensibly, because she was the wife, and her presence there was wholly consistent with the title offered by the husband to the bank.

A similar point was touched upon by Lord Wilberforce in *National Provincial Bank Ltd v. Hastings Car Mart Ltd* [1965] A.C. 1175, 1248, when he said:

"For to hold that the wife acquires on marriage a right valid against third parties to remain in the house where she lives with her husband would not only fly in the face of the reality of the marriage relationship which requires the spouses to live together, as they can agree, wherever circumstances may prescribe, but would create impossible difficulties for those dealing with the property of a married man. It would mean that the concurrence of the wife would be necessary for all dealings."

In my judgment, where the vendor or mortgagor is himself in possession and occupation of the property, the purchaser or the mortgagee is not affected with notice of the equitable interests of any other person who may be resident there, and whose presence is wholly consistent with the title offered. If you buy with vacant possession on completion and you know, or find out, that the vendor is himself in possession and occupation of the property, you are, in my judgment, by reason of your failure to make further inquiries on the premises, no more fixed with notice of the equitable interest of the vendor's wife who is living there with him than you would be affected with notice of the equitable interest of any other person who might also be resident on the premises, *e.g.*, the vendor's father, his "Uncle Harry" or his "Aunt Matilda", any of whom, be it observed, might have contributed towards the purchase of the property. The reason is that the vendor being in possession, the presence of his wife or guest or lodger implies nothing to negative the title offered. It is otherwise if the vendor is not in occupation and you find another party whose presence demands an explanation and whose presence you ignore at your peril.

I would add this: Mr Nourse [counsel for the bank], in his very clear argument, has called attention to the fact that this is a conveyancing question, and I accept the point he makes that in such a matter the practice of conveyancers carries great weight. I have never heard it suggested, and no textbook or judicial utterance has been cited which suggests, that where one finds a vendor and his wife living together on the property a prudent solicitor acting for the purchaser ought to inquire of the wife whether she claims an interest in the house. Mr Nourse also points out, by reference to remarks made by Russell L.J. in the Court of Appeal, in the case to which I have already referred in the House of Lords, *National Provincial Bank Ltd v. Hastings Car Mart Ltd* [1964] Ch. 665, 700 and to the speeches of Lord Upjohn ([1965] A.C. 1229) and Lord Wilberforce ([1965] A.C. 1241) in that case, how unworkable and undesirable it would be if the law required such an inquiry—an inquiry, let me add, which would be as embarrassing to the inquirer as it would, in my view, be intolerable to the wife and the husband. Mr Nourse, I think, put it well when, in commenting on the whole of the plaintiff's case, he said it is not in the public interest that bank mortgagees should be snoopers and busybodies in relation to wholly normal transactions of mortgage. I must make it clear—because much reliance was placed, on behalf of the plaintiff, on what was said by the majority of the Court of Appeal in the *Ainsworth* case, *The National Provincial Bank Ltd v. Hastings Car Mart Ltd* [1964] Ch. 665, regarding the duty of a purchaser to make inquiries on the premises where the wife is living alone in the matrimonial home after her husband has left her—that about such a situation I say nothing whatsoever. Here the wife was living with her husband.

NOTES:

1. Stamp J. also rejected an argument that the bank had constructive notice of the interest of the wife by reason of the fact that she was herself a customer of the bank and that the bank should have inquired into the details of her account with a view to ascertaining whether she had an interest in the house. He stated that such an inquiry was not one which ought reasonably to have been made within the meaning of the Law of Property Act 1925, s.199(1)(ii)(a).

2. The approach of Stamp J., which was reinforced by, and which for a while reinforced, the "easy-going practice of dispensing with enquiries as to occupation beyond that of the vendor" (*Williams & Glyn's Bank Ltd v. Boland* [1981] A.C. 487, 508 *per* Lord Wilberforce), was subsequently the subject of considerable judicial criticism: see *Hodgson v. Marks* [1971] Ch. 892, 934–935 *per* Russell L.J.; *Williams & Glyn's Bank Ltd v. Boland, supra,* 505–506 *per* Lord Wilberforce. Although those cases concerned land with registered title (in which context the doctrine of notice is strictly speaking irrelevant), the criticism of *Caunce v. Caunce* was significant. In *Williams & Glyn's Bank Ltd v. Boland* the technical question was whether a wife was "in actual occupation" for the purposes of the Land Registration Act 1925, s.70(1)(g), (see *post*, p. 205); but the case involved similar facts and raised the same underlying issue as *Caunce v. Caunce*. Lord Wilberforce stated (at 505–506):

Then, were the wives in actual occupation? I ask: why not? There was physical presence, with all the rights that occupiers have, including the right to exclude all others except those having similar rights. The house was a matrimonial home, intended to be occupied, and in fact occupied by both spouses, both of whom have an interest in it: it would require some special doctrine of law to avoid the result that each is in occupation. Three arguments were used for a contrary conclusion. First, it was said that if the vendor (I use this word to include a mortgagor) is in occupation, that is enough to prevent the application of the paragraph. This seems to be a proposition of general application, not limited to the case of husbands, and no doubt, if correct, would be very convenient for purchasers and intending mortgagees. But the presence of the vendor, with occupation, does not exclude the possibility of occupation of others. There are observations which suggest the contrary in the unregistered land case of *Caunce v. Caunce* [1969] 1 W.L.R. 286, but I agree with the disapproval of these, and with the assertion of the proposition I have just stated by Russell L.J. in *Hodgson v. Marks* [1971] Ch. 892, 934. Then it was suggested that the wife's occupation was nothing but the shadow of the husband's—a version I suppose of the doctrine of unity of husband and wife. This expression and the argument flowing from it was used by Templeman J. in *Bird v. Syme-Thomson* [1979] 1 W.L.R. 440, 444, a decision preceding and which he followed in the present case. The argument was also inherent in the judgment in *Caunce v. Caunce* [1969] 1 W.L.R. 286 which influenced the decisions of Templeman J. It somewhat faded from the arguments in the present case and appears to me to be heavily obsolete. The appellant's main and final position became in the end this: that, to come within the paragraph, the occupation in question must be apparently inconsistent with the title of the vendor. This, it was suggested, would exclude the wife of a husband-vendor because her apparent occupation would be satisfactorily accounted for by his. But, apart from the rewriting of the paragraph which this would involve, the suggestion is unacceptable. Consistency, or inconsistency, involves the absence, or presence, of an independent right to occupy, though I must observe that "inconsistency" in this context is an inappropriate word. But how can either quality be predicated of a wife, simply qua wife? A wife may, and everyone knows this, have rights of her own; particularly, many wives have a share in a matrimonial home. How can it be said that the presence of a wife in the house, as occupier, is consistent or inconsistent with the husband's rights until one knows what rights she has? And if she has rights, why, just because she is a wife (or in the converse case, just because an occupier is the husband), should these rights be denied protection under the paragraph? If one looks beyond the case of husband and wife, the difficulty of all these arguments stands out if one considers the case of a man living with a mistress, or of a man and a woman—or for that matter two persons of the same sex—living in a house in separate or partially shared rooms. Are these cases of apparently consistent occupation, so that the rights of the other person (other than the vendor) can be disregarded? The only solution which is consistent with the Act (section 70(1)(g)) and with common sense is to read the paragraph for what it says. Occupation, existing as a fact, may protect rights if the person in occupation has rights. On this part of the case I have no difficulty in concluding that a spouse, living in a house, has an actual occupation capable of conferring protection, as an overriding interest, upon rights of that spouse.

3. In the light of these criticisms, it was rather surprising that *Caunce v. Caunce* subsequently received approval as a "workmanlike solution": see *Lloyds Bank plc v. Rosset* [1989] Ch. 350, 397 *per* Mustill L.J.

4. A rather different approach from that in *Caunce v. Caunce* was adopted in *Kingsnorth Finance Co. Ltd v. Tizard* [1986] 1 W.L.R. 783.

Kingsnorth Finance Co. Ltd v. Tizard [1986] 1 W.L.R. 783

(Ch D., Judge John Finlay Q.C.)

The matrimonial home (Willowdown) was held by the husband on trust for himself and the wife. Following the breakdown of the marriage in 1982 the wife only slept at the house when the husband was away, although she always returned to the house in the morning and the evening in order to care for the children of the marriage. Moreover, most of her clothes and other belongings remained at the house. In 1983 the husband obtained from the plaintiffs a loan of £66,000, repayment of which was secured by a mortgage over the matrimonial home. The loan was negotiated through a broker (Bradshaws). On the initial application form the husband left blank the space for the spouse's signature; and on another form he described himself as single. When the surveyor (Marshall) inspected the property (at a time arranged by the husband), the husband told him that he and his wife were separated and that the wife was living elsewhere. Although the surveyor was looking for evidence of other occupiers, he refrained from opening cupboards; and he concluded that the husband was living alone with the children. The husband later disappeared with the loan money and the plaintiffs sought possession of the house; the question arose as to whether the plaintiffs had notice of the equitable interest of the wife under the trust.

JUDGE JOHN FINLAY Q.C.:
[His Lordship quoted the above passage from *Williams & Glyn's Bank Ltd v. Boland* and concluded that the wife was in occupation. He continued:]
Willowdown, however, is not registered land. If it were, my findings that Mrs Tizard had equitable rights in the house and was at the material time in occupation would protect those rights against the mortgagee by reason of section 70(1)(g) of the Land Registration Act 1925. Do these two matters bring about the like result where the land is not registered?

[Counsel for the plaintiffs] submits that although in the case of registered land the fact of occupation confers protection, in the case of unregistered land it is not enough that the claimant is in occupation; she must be found to be in occupation by the purchaser or mortgagee, or, at any rate, the circumstances must be such that she would have been found had proper inspections, inquiries and searches been made. [His Lordship detailed the facts summarised above and continued:]
It is common ground that Mr Marshall was acting as agent of the plaintiffs. He was not instructed by the plaintiffs. He was instructed by Bradshaws. Before Mr Marshall inspected the property, Bradshaws had the document dated 12 March 1983 which Mr Tizard signed. What Mr Tizard told Bradshaws about his martial status at that stage can be inferred from what he told them later when he signed the plaintiffs' form, namely, that he was "single." In a document which gives only one alternative to "single," namely, "married," "single" must signify either bachelor or spinster as the case may be, or a widow or widower, or a person whose marriage has been dissolved. It cannot mean "married but separated." As Bradshaws were instructing Mr Marshall to make an inspection on behalf of the plaintiffs, they were acting as the plaintiffs' agents for that purpose. The fact that Mr Marshall was looking for evidence of the occupation of a female cohabitee coupled with what I infer from the two documents signed by Mr Tizard was Bradshaws' understanding of Mr Tizard's marital status, implies that Mr Marshall approached his inspection on the footing that Mr Tizard was not married; when it appeared that he was, I consider that he had a duty to communicate this new information to his principals. It follows in my judgment that the knowledge of the agent, Mr Marshall, that Mr Tizard had a wife is to be taken to be the knowledge of the principal, the plaintiffs.

The plaintiffs received Mr Tizard's application in which he described himself as single; and received Mr Marshall's report in which there was mention of a son and daughter.... Had Mr Marshall's report indicated that Mr Tizard was married, it seems to me to be clear that bearing in mind that the application stated over Mr Tizard's signature that he was single, the plaintiffs would have been put on notice that further investigation was required. Indeed, even if I am wrong in my view that Mr Marshall should have reported what Mr Tizard said about his wife, the reference to "son and daughter" in the report should have alerted the plaintiffs to the need to make further inquiries. Primarily, the plaintiffs are to be taken to have been aware that Mr Tizard was married and had described himself as single; and in these circumstances their further inquiries should have led them to Mrs Tizard.

Section 199(1) of the Law of Property Act 1925 provides:

"A purchaser shall not be prejudicially affected by notice of—(i) any instrument or matter capable of registration under the provisions of the Land Charges Act 1925, or any enactment which it replaces, which is void or not enforceable as against him under that Act or enactment, by reason of the non-registration thereof; (ii) any other instrument or matter or any fact or thing unless—(a) it is within his own knowledge, or would have come to his knowledge if such inquiries and inspections had been made as ought reasonably to have been made by him; or (b) in the same transaction with respect to which a question of notice to the purchaser arises, it has come to the knowledge of his counsel, as such, or of his solicitor or other agent, as such, or would have come to the knowledge of his solicitor or other agent, as such, if such inquiries and inspections had been made as ought reasonably to have been made by the solicitor or other agent."

"Purchaser" in that provision, includes a mortgagee: see section 205(1) of the Act.

Although a spouse's statutory rights of occupation under section 1 of the Matrimonial Homes Act 1983, and the statutory provisions replaced by that Act are capable of protection by registration as a Class F land charge, by virtue of the Land Charges Act 1972, the equitable interest of such a spouse in the matrimonial home is not capable of being so protected. The plaintiffs were prejudicially affected by the knowledge of their agent, Mr Marshall, that Mr Tizard, contrary to what he had said in his application, was married: see section 199(1)(ii)(b). That put them on notice that further inquiries were necessary; the inquiries which in these circumstances ought reasonably to have been made by the plaintiffs would, in my judgment, have been such as to have apprised them of the fact that Mrs Tizard claimed a beneficial interest in the property; and accordingly, they would have had notice of such equitable rights as she had and the mortgage in these circumstances takes effect subject to these rights: see section 199(1)(ii)(a).

I arrive at that conclusion without having considered the question: does the occupation of Mrs Tizard affect the mortgagees with notice of her rights, or are they only so affected if, as [counsel for the plaintiffs] submits, they are aware of her occupation, that is, if they find her in occupation?

On the balance of probabilities, I find that the reason Mr Marshall did not find Mrs Tizard in the house was that Mr Tizard had arranged matters to achieve that result. He told Mrs Tizard that on a particular Sunday, and I find in fact that it was the Sunday that Mr Marshall did inspect, he was going to entertain friends to lunch and would she take the children out for the day. She did; and having regard to the manner in which I find that the signs of her occupation were temporarily eliminated by Mr Tizard, the reasonable inference is that he made this request so that Mr Marshall could inspect and find no evidence of Mrs Tizard's occupation.

In *Caunce v. Caunce* [1969] 1 W.L.R. 286 Stamp J. held that where a wife who had an equitable interest in a property being mortgaged to the bank by her husband was resident with him in the property, that circumstance did not result in the bank taking the property fixed with notice of her rights because, finding her in occupation, the bank made no inquiry of her. Stamp J. said, at 293:

"Here it is said that the plaintiff was in possession or occupation. No inquiry was made of her and therefore the bank is fixed with notice of her equitable interest. In my judgment, it is here that the fallacy arises, for the plaintiff, unlike the deserted wife, was not in apparent occupation or possession. She was there, ostensibly, because she was the wife, and her presence was wholly consistent with the title offered by the husband to the bank."

In *Williams & Glyn's Bank Ltd v. Boland* [1981] A.C. 487, 505, Lord Wilberforce said in the passage I have already read: "But the presence of the vendor, with occupation, does not exclude the possibility of occupation of others." He went on to say there were observations suggesting the contrary in *Caunce v. Caunce* [1969] 1 W.L.R. 286 but he agreed with the disapproval of those and with the assertion expressed by Russell L.J. in *Hodgson v. Marks* [1971] Ch. 892, 934. Russell L.J. there stated:

"I would only add that I do not consider it necessary to this decision to pronounce on the decision in *Caunce v. Caunce* [1969] 1 W.L.R. 286. In that case the occupation of the wife may have been rightly taken to be not her occupation but that of her husband. In so far, however, as some phrases in the judgment might appear to lay down a general proposition that inquiry need not be made of any person on the premises if the proposed vendor himself appears to be in occupation, I would not accept them."

I have already stated my finding that the wife was in occupation. In the circumstances in which she was, I find that her occupation was not that of her husband. Guided by the high authority of the two passages I have just cited, Lord Wilberforce in *Williams & Glyn's Bank Ltd v. Boland* [1981] A.C. 487, 505, and Russell L.J. in *Hodgson v. Marks* [1971] Ch. 892, 934, I conclude that had Mrs Tizard been found to be in occupation by the plaintiffs or their agent and so found in the context of what had been said by Mr Tizard to Mr Marshall and stated or implied in the forms he had signed, they, the plaintiffs, would clearly either have learned of her rights by inquiry of her or been fixed with notice of those rights had not inquiry of her been made.

In the light of my finding that Mr Marshall's information about Mr Tizard's wife is to be imputed to the plaintiffs and my conclusion that further inquiries should have been made by the plaintiffs because of that imputed knowledge, do I ask myself whether such an inspection as would have disclosed that Mrs Tizard was in the premises is one which ought reasonably to have been made by them, or is the proper question: can the plaintiffs show that no such inspection was reasonably necessary? The latter appears to me to be the proper way to put it. The plaintiffs did not make any further inquiries or inspections; had they done so it would have been open to them to contend that they had done all that was reasonably required and if they still had no knowledge of Mrs Tizard's rights or claims, that they were not fixed with notice of them. But in the absence of further inquiries or inspections, I do not think that it is open to the plaintiffs to say that if they had made a further inspection they would still not have found Mrs Tizard in occupation.

I would put it briefly thus, Mr Tizard appears to have been minded to conceal the true facts; he did not do so completely; the plaintiffs had, or are to be taken to have had, information which should have alerted them to the fact that the full facts were not in their possession and that they should make further inspections or inquiries; they did not do so; and in these circumstances I find that they are fixed with notice of the equitable interest of Mrs Tizard.

I return to the submissions made by [counsel]. [Counsel for Mrs Tizard's] submission is that as Mrs Tizard was in fact in occupation, that circumstance itself fixed the plaintiffs with notice of such rights as she had; to the contrary is the submission made by [counsel for the plaintiffs] that, in the case of unregistered land, it is only where the purchaser or mortgagee finds the claimant to an equitable interest in occupation that he has notice.

I accept [counsel for the plaintiffs'] submission but subject to a significant qualification: if the purchaser or mortgagee carries out such inspections "as ought reasonably to be made" and does not either find the claimant in occupation or find evidence of that occupation reasonably sufficient to give notice of the occupation, then I am not persuaded that the purchaser or mortgagee is in such circumstances (and in the absence, which is not the case here, of other circumstances) fixed with notice of the claimant's rights. One of the circumstances, however, is that such inspection is made "as ought reasonably to be made."

Here Mr Marshall carried out his inspection on a Sunday afternoon at a time arranged with Mr Tizard. If the only purpose of such an inspection were to ascertain the physical state of the property, the time at which the inspection is made and whether or not that time is one agreed in advance with the vendor or mortgagor appears to me to be immaterial. Where, however, the object of the inspection (or one of the objects) is to ascertain who is in occupation, I cannot see that an inspection at a time pre-arranged with the vendor will necessarily attain that object. Such a pre-arranged inspection may achieve no more than an inquiry of the vendor or mortgagor and his answer to it. In the case of residential property an appointment for inspection will, in most cases, be essential so far as inspection of the interior is concerned. How then is a purchaser or mortgagee to carry out such inspection "as ought reasonably to have been made" for the purpose of determining whether the possession and occupation of the property accords with the title offered? What is such an inspection "as ought reasonably to be made" must, I think, depend on all the circumstances. In the circumstances of the present case I am not satisfied that the pre-arranged inspection on a Sunday afternoon fell within the category of "such inspections which ought reasonably to have been made," the words in section 199 of the Law of Property Act 1925 which I have already read. The plaintiffs not having established that they made such an inspection, the conclusion that I have reached by another route is, in my view, fortified. It follows that the plaintiffs' claim for possession fails.

NOTES:

1. The reasoning was criticised on the grounds (i) that it seemed to concentrate more on the bank's constructive notice of the wife's *occupation of the property* rather than on its constructive notice of her *interest in the property*; and (ii) that it imposed an excessive burden on the purchaser/ mortgagee: see [1986] All E.R. Rev. 181; [1986] Conv. 283; [1987] C.L.J. 28.

2. For the proposition that a purchaser is deemed to have notice of the interests of any person in occupation, see *City of London Building Society v. Flegg* [1988] A.C. 54, 81 *per* Lord Oliver; *Lloyds Bank plc v. Semmakie* [1993] 1 F.L.R. 34, 42 *per* Scott L.J.; and the proposition applies irrespective of the unlikely existence of the interests or their unusual nature: *Midland Bank Ltd v. Farmpride Hatcheries Ltd* (1980) 260 E.G. 493, 497 *per* Shaw L.J., 498 *per* Oliver L.J.

3. In *Midland Bank Ltd v. Farmpride Hatcheries Ltd* (1980) 260 E.G. 493 it was held that, even where the doctrine of constructive notice would prima facie operate to render an equitable interest enforceable against a purchaser, the owner of the interest was estopped from asserting such enforceability where he "set up a smoke screen designed to hide even the possible existence of some interest.... He deliberately put [the mortgagee] off the scent and [the mortgagee] accepted the mortgage as a consequence. They would not have done so but for [the interest owner's] subtle but positive indication that he had communicated all that had to be told....": *ibid.* at 497 *per* Shaw L.J.

4.4.3 *Imputed notice*   Where a purchaser employs an agent for the purposes of the transaction, any actual or constructive notice which is received by the agent is imputed to the principal: see, *e.g. Kingsnorth Finance Co. Ltd v. Tizard, supra.* The inclusion of imputed notice in the doctrine of notice is essential since purchasers and mortgages almost invariably act through agents; and it would clearly be unacceptable for their principals to be able to claim absence of notice on the basis that they did not personally receive notice of equitable interests. However, it would be no less unfair to impute to a purchaser notice of a relevant equitable interest which the agent happened to have received in the context of another transaction; and the rule is now restricted to notice acquired in the same transaction: Law of Property Act 1925, s.199(1)(ii)(b); and see *Re Cousins* (1886) 31 ChD. 671.

4.5 *Purchasers from the bona fide purchaser*

Where a bona fide purchaser has acquired land free of an equitable interest, the interest cannot normally be revived so as to bind a subsequent purchaser, even where the subsequent purchaser has notice of the interest. This proposition, which was implicit in *Re Nisbet and Potts' Contract* [1906] 1 Ch. 386, *supra*, p. 35, was expressly decided in *Wilkes v. Spooner* [1911] 2 K.B. 473.

Wilkes v. Spooner [1911] 2 K.B. 473

(CA, Jessel M.R., Vaughan Williams and Farwell L.JJ.)

Spooner was the lessee of two shops, No. 137, where he carried on the business of pork butcher, and No. 170, where he carried on the business of general butcher. He sold the lease of No. 170 to Wilkes and covenanted, in effect, that he would not carry on the business of general butcher at No. 137. Spooner subsequently surrendered the lease of No. 137 to the landlord, who knew nothing of the covenant. The landlord then granted a new lease of No. 137 to Spooner's son, who did know about the covenant. When the son started to carry on business as a general butcher at No. 137, the question arose as to whether he was bound by the covenant. Reversing the decision of Scrutton J., the Court of Appeal held that the son was not bound.

VAUGHAN WILLIAMS L.J.:
I think that this appeal must be allowed. This case has been very well argued, but really when certain conclusions of fact are arrived at, there is very little left to argue. It cannot seriously be disputed that the proposition which I quoted from Ashburner's Principles of Equity, p. 75, is good law. It is as follows: "A purchaser for valuable consideration without notice can give a good title to a purchaser from him with notice. The only exception is that a trustee who has sold property in breach of trust, or a person who has acquired property by fraud, cannot protect himself by purchasing it from a bona fide purchaser for value without notice." The learned author cites as authorities for that proposition the cases of *Sweet v. Southcote* (1786) 2 Bro. C.C. 66 and *Barrow's Case* (1880) 14 Ch.D. 432. Those cases seem to me to be conclusive authorities for the proposition stated by the author in the text, the terms of which show that he had in his mind the words used by Jessel M.R. in giving judgment in the latter case.... Under these circumstances there is really to my mind only one question that we have to decide. So far as the landlord was concerned, if he had no notice, either actual or constructive, of the covenant entered into by the father in respect of No. 137, he became upon the surrender free to deal with the property unincumbered by any equity arising therefrom, and, that being so, the only question really left to be decided is whether the landlord had notice, either actual or constructive. So far as actual notice is concerned, it cannot be suggested that there was any evidence of such notice to the landlord. All that counsel for the plaintiff were able to say was that it was not proved as a fact that he had no notice, but to my mind the only possible inference which could be drawn from the facts in this case is that there was no such notice.

But then it is said that he had constructive notice. In my judgment there were no facts proved upon which a suggestion that there was constructive notice to him can properly be based. Upon that question the case of *In re Ford and Hill* (1879) 10 Ch.D. 365 is really conclusive to show that there is nothing in the present case to justify the conclusion that there was constructive notice to the landlord. The covenant relied upon was a covenant in respect of a different estate granted by a different landlord. It is suggested that, either on the surrender or on the grant of the new lease by the landlord of No. 137, there ought to have been inquiries or requisitions made by him, which, if they had been made, would have disclosed the existence of the covenant not to carry on a general butcher's business on the premises, but to my mind there was no obligation of any kind on the landlord to make any such inquiries or requisitions. Under these circumstances I think, with all respect to Scrutton J., that he arrived at a wrong conclusion when he said, in substance, that there was constructive notice to the landlord because those inquiries were not made by him which reasonably ought to have been made. It appears to me that he must have forgotten for a moment that these were two distinct properties owned by different landlords, and that the landlord who accepted a surrender of the premises on which the pork butcher's business was carried on, and granted a new lease of them, had nothing to do with the other premises. There was, in my opinion, no failure on the part of the landlord to make any inquiry that ought reasonably to have been made by him, and from the omission to make which constructive notice to him could be inferred.

It must not be inferred from anything which I have said that I do not think that any wrong was done to the plaintiff, who took the assignment of the general butcher's shop, being induced thereto by the covenant not to carry on anything beyond the business of a pork butcher on the other side of the street. I think that a wrong was plainly done to him by what occurred, but one cannot, because a wrong was done to him, and one might be glad to throw the loss occasioned to him upon those by whom the wrong was done, derogate from the plain rights of the landlord, who, when the surrender was made and the new lease granted, had no notice of the restrictive covenant.

NOTE:

1. For a case within the exception to the principle, see *Gordon v. Holland* (1913) 82 L.J.P.C. 81.

5. Equities

Equity has intervened in the context of land law otherwise than by the recognition and development of equitable estates and interests. Equity has also recognised as potentially enforceable against third parties certain lesser rights, referred to as "equities" or "mere equities", which are of a procedural nature but ancillary to some substantive property right. For example, where by reason of a mistake a conveyance of land fails to reflect the agreement of the parties, there may be a right to have the conveyance rectified so as to effect the intended allocation of property rights; or where a conveyance is vitiated by fraud, there may be a right to have the conveyance set aside so as to restore the property rights of the person defrauded. Although the enforcement of such a procedural right depends upon the discretion of the court, it is capable of binding a third party because it is ancillary to or dependent upon some existing proprietary interest of the claimant: see *National Provincial Bank Ltd v. Ainsworth* [1965] A.C. 1175, 1238 *per* Lord Upjohn; or because the recognition and enforcement of the procedural right generates the creation or (re-) transfer of a proprietary interest: see *Latec Investments Ltd v. Hotel Terrigal Pty Ltd* (1965) 113 C.L.R. 265, *infra*. However, because mere equities are lesser rights, they will normally not bind a purchaser of a legal estate *or equitable interest* in the land unless the purchaser has notice: *Smith v. Jones* [1954] 1 W.L.R. 1089 (purchaser of legal estate); *Latec Investments Ltd v. Hotel Terrigal Pty Ltd* (purchaser of an equitable interest).

Latec Investments Ltd v. Hotel Terrigal Pty Ltd (1965) 113 C.L.R. 265

(High Court of Australia)

The mortgagees of certain land became entitled to sell the mortgaged property but the actual sale to a subsidiary company was fraudulent. The mortgagees therefore had a right to have the sale set aside (a mere equity), which would have resulted in the restoration of their equity of redemption (an equitable interest); but they took no action for five years. In the meantime, the subsidiary company had granted an equitable charge (mortgage) over the land in favour of a trustee. The question was whether the mortgagors could enforce their mere equity (the right to have the sale set aside) against the equitable charge (an equitable interest) of the trustee.

KITTO J.:

If the mortgagor had sought the intervention of the court without delay, the findings of fact with which so far I have dealt would necessarily have led to a decree setting aside the sale as against the mortgagee and the purchaser and granting consequential relief. But nearly five years went by before proceedings were commenced, and it is necessary to consider whether the mortgagor's right to relief is affected by what occurred in that time....

In my opinion the equitable charge of the trustee stands in the way of the mortgagor's success because it was acquired for value and without any notice either of the existence of the mortgagor's right to set aside the sale or of any facts from which such a right might be inferred. The trustee, of course, has not the legal estate; its rights are purely equitable; but the case falls within one of the categories described in the judgment of Lord Westbury in *Phillips v. Phillips* (1861) 4 De G.F. & J. 208 in which the legal estate is not required in order that a defence of purchase for value without notice may succeed. It is the case of a suit "where there are circumstances that give rise to an equity as distinguished from an equitable estate—as, for example, an equity to set aside a deed for fraud, or to correct it for mistake". In such a case, his Lordship said, if the purchaser under the instrument maintains the plea of purchase for value without notice "the Court will not interfere". It is true that if the mortgagor in the present case was entitled to have the mortgagee's sale set aside it had more than a mere equity: it had, as I have pointed out, an equity of redemption, and such an interest, being in respect of an estate in fee simple, has been considered an equitable estate ever since Lord Hardwicke decided *Casborne v. Scarfe* (1737) 1 Atk. 603. But each of the illustrations Lord Westbury chose was also a case where the equity was accompanied by an equitable interest which might constitute an equitable estate. So much had been shown by decisions of most eminent judges, at least twice in the ten years before his Lordship spoke: see *Stump v. Gaby* (1852) 2 De G. M. & G. 623; *Gresley v. Mousley* (1859) 4 De G. & J. 78, and Lord Westbury's judgment gives every indication of an intention to state systematically the effect of previous decisions, and not to depart from them in any degree. The illustrations therefore make it clear, it seems to me, that the cases to which his Lordship was referring were not only those in which there is an assertion of an equity unaccompanied by an equitable interest (as was held to be the case in *Westminster Bank Ltd v. Lee* [1956] Ch. 7 and *National Provincial Bank Ltd v. Hastings Car Mart Ltd* [1964] Ch. 9)—indeed he may not have had them in mind at all—but those in which an equity is asserted which must be made good before an equitable interest can be held to exist. In the latter class of cases the equity is distinct from, because logically antecedent to, the equitable interest, and it is against the equity and not the consequential equitable interest that the defence must be set up. That the defence of purchase for value without notice (in the absence of the legal estate) is a good defence against the assertion of the equity in such a case had been established long before Lord Westbury's time. In *Malden v. Menill* (1737) 2 Atk. 8, at p. 13, for example, Lord Hardwicke had refused rectification of an instrument for mistake, as against a purchaser of an equitable interest without notice, on the ground that the mistake should not "turn to the prejudice of a fair purchaser". Such cases as *Garrard v. Frankel* (1862) 30 Beav. 445 and *Bainbrigge v. Browne* (1881) 18 Ch.D. 188 were soon to be decided on the same principle. See generally *Halsbury's Laws of England*, 3rd ed. vol. 14, p. 537, para. 1008. The reason of the matter, as I understand it, is that the purchaser who has relied upon the instrument as taking effect according to its terms and the party whose rights depend upon the instrument being denied that effect have equal merits, and the court, finding no reason for binding the conscience of either in favour of the other, declines to interfere between them. Consequently the party complaining of the fraud or mistake finds himself unable to set up as against the other the equitable interest he asserts; but the fact remains that it is against the preliminary equity, and not against the equitable interest itself, that the defence of purchase for value without notice has succeeded. The maxim *qui prior est tempore* is not applicable, for it applies only as between equitable interests, the logical basis of it being that in a competition between equitable interests the conveyance in virtue of which the later interest is claimed is considered, as Lord Westbury pointed out, to be innocent, in the sense of being intended to pass that which the conveyor is justly entitled to and no more: (1861) 4 De G.F. & J. 208, at p. 215. Where a claim to an earlier equitable interest is dependent for its success upon the setting aside or rectification of an instrument, and the court, notwithstanding that the fraud or mistake (or other cause) is established, leaves the instrument to take effect according to its terms in favour of a third party whose rights have intervened, the alleged earlier equitable interest is unprovable against the third party, and consequently, so far as the case against him discloses, there is no prior equitable interest to which his conveyance can be held to be subject.

On the principle to which Lord Westbury referred it seems to me inevitable that the mortgagor's claim in the present case to have the mortgagee's sale and the transfer to the purchaser "set aside", i.e. treated as if they were only a sale and transfer of the mortgage, should fail as against the trustee.

NOTE:

1. The distinction between equitable interests and mere equities is considered further: see *post*, pp. 190, 602.

E. THE 1925 PROPERTY LEGISLATION

1. Policy of the 1925 legislation: simplification of conveyancing

The legislative basis of modern land law remains the property legislation of 1925. That legislation, comprising the Settled Land Act, the Trustee Act, the

Law of Property Act, the Land Registration Act, the Land Charges Act and the Administration of Estates Act, represented the consolidation of about 40 years of legislative reform between 1882 and 1922; and, as a general principle, references to the 1925 legislation should be construed accordingly.

The policy behind the legislation was the simplification of the conveyancing process and the facilitation of the alienability of land. The legislation sought to address three concerns relating to the conveyancing process, which were not necessarily compatible. First, the purchaser of land wished to ensure that when he purchased the land in question, he actually acquired title to that land and the full range of ownership rights over that land. This concern required the facilitation of the investigation and acquisition of title. Secondly, the purchaser wished to ensure that he was aware (before he decided to purchase) of all third party interests which might be enforceable against the land and which might affect his use and enjoyment of the land. This concern required the facilitation of the investigation of such third party interests. As will be seen, these first two concerns were addressed in part by the reclassification of interests in land, involving a reduction in the range of *legal* estates and interests affecting land and a corresponding increase in the range of *equitable* interests. However, it has already been seen that equitable interests are potentially more precarious than legal interests, to the extent that they are subject to extinction by the bona fide purchaser. Thus, while the *purchaser* stood to benefit from the reclassification of interests, the owners of third party interests, and in particular owners of those legal interests that were reclassified as equitable interests, were understandably concerned that their interests might be subordinated to the convenience of purchasers. This third concern relating to the conveyancing process required the provision of machinery for the protection of third party (equitable) interests.

The 1925 legislation therefore sought to effect a simplification of the conveyancing process by the reclassification of interests in land and by the provision of machinery for the protection of interests in land. Reclassification addressed the first and second concerns outlined above; the provision of machinery addressed the second and third concerns.

1.1 *Investigation and acquisition of title*

1.1.1 *Legal fee simple as the basis of conveyancing*   The first concern was the investigation and acquisition of title. As noted above, in most circumstances the purchaser of land wishes to acquire the legal fee simple in possession. Prior to 1926, the problem was that the legal fee simple could have been fragmented into a series of life estates, estates in fee tail and finally the fee simple (and, as will be seen, each such estate could have been the subject of co-ownership by an unlimited number of persons). Consequently, if the purchaser wished to acquire the legal fee simple in possession, because he wished to acquire immediate and continuing ownership rights, he had to identify all the various owners, investigate their various fragmented ownership rights and obtain their combined agreement to the acquisition.

It is true that trusts were frequently set up to achieve similar fragmentation of the ownership rights in equity; and in such cases the *legal* fee simple would normally have remained unfragmented in the trustees. However, since the purchaser of land subject to a trust would probably have notice of at least some of the equitable interests under the trust, he would have acquired the legal fee simple in the land subject to those interests. This "second generation" problem is discussed below.

It was necessary to deal first with the legal fee simple. The intention of the 1925 legislation was that the legal fee simple in possession should become the basis of conveyancing. This was to be achieved by providing, first, that the fee simple in possession was the only freehold estate capable of existing as a *legal* estate and, secondly, that the legal fee simple in possession was indivisible so that a purchaser would be required to investigate one title only. It followed that all other freehold estates (life estates, fee tail estates; and also fee simple estates in remainder or in reversion), which before 1926 could exist either as legal estates or as equitable estates under a trust, after 1925 could only exist as equitable interests under a trust. Thus, leasehold estates apart (see *infra*), the only available method of fragmentation of ownership rights would be under the trust machinery. For example, the grant of the ownership rights over land for the life of the grantee necessarily involved the trust machinery. The legal fee simple in possession might be owned jointly by a maximum of four trustees: Trustee Act 1925, s.34(2); and see *post*, p. 295; but that did not affect the indivisibility of the estate. The fragmentation of ownership rights operated in equity.

1.1.2 *Overreaching of other freehold estates*　　　The singling out of the fee simple in possession as the only estate capable of existing as a legal estate, and the relegation of all other freehold estates to equitable status raised the "second generation" problem referred to above. The purchaser of land could now readily investigate and purchase the legal fee simple in possession; but the land would remain subject to any trust and equitable ownership interests affecting the property of which the purchaser had notice. In practice, if the purchaser was seeking to acquire immediate and continuing ownership rights over the land, he would be unlikely to proceed with the purchase. The response of the 1925 legislation (completing the reform introduced in 1882) was that on a sale of land which was held on trust (which after 1925 meant all cases of fragmentation of ownership rights) all equitable interests under the trust would be detached from the land; and the purchaser would acquire immediate and continuing ownership rights free from those interests. In the language of land law, the equitable interests under the trust would be "overreached". However, those equitable interests would not thereby be extinguished entirely; instead they would be attached to the proceeds of sale in the hands of the trustees/vendors. Overreaching was not a new concept in the 1925 legislation. However, as a *mandatory* part of the post-1925 conveyancing process wherever ownership rights in land had been fragmented, overreaching was questionable since an equitable interest under a trust, which at the outset entitled the owner of that interest to part of the ownership rights in land, would be converted into a corresponding entitlement in a fund of money representing the proceeds of sale. On the other hand, the doctrine of overreaching was a necessary compromise for the achievement of the policy of the 1925 legislation and the objective of freely alienable land. Moreover equitable interests under trusts of land had increasingly come to be regarded as interests in property generally, although there were different considerations where the law imposed the trust machinery in cases of concurrent (rather than successive) interests in land: see *post*, p. 300.

1.1.3 *Classification of the leasehold estate*   The apparent exception to the above reclassification of estates in land was the leasehold estate. Like the freehold estates, a leasehold estate conferred ownership rights on the estate owner (albeit for a fixed maximum duration); and, since it was not the fee simple in possession, it is arguable that it should have been included in the general relegation of the other estates to equitable status. However, a leasehold estate was different in kind from the lesser freehold estates. While freehold estates tended to be created in the context of arrangements for the inheritance of family property from generation to generation (see *post*, p. 268), the leasehold estate became a more commercial transaction for which the mechanism of the trust and the doctrine of overreaching was inappropriate. The owner of a leasehold estate generally wished to occupy the property: he was not interested in an equivalent interest in a fund of money. The 1925 legislation therefore provided for leasehold estates also to take effect as legal estates. However, this concession to the role of the legal fee simple in possession as the basis of conveyancing did not compromise the theoretical integrity of the legal fee simple in possession. As has been seen, the leasehold estate differed from the freehold estates in that it did not involve seisin. Consequently, a leasehold estate existed concurrently with the legal fee simple in possession of the grantor. Furthermore, as a matter of practice, the continuance of leasehold estates as legal estates posed no serious threat to potential purchasers of the legal fee simple since the occupation of the leaseholder would normally be quite apparent on inspection of the documents of title or the land itself.

1.2 *Investigation and protection of third party interests*
Third party interests over land owned by another person posed different problems. Such interests, which include rights of way and other easements, estate contracts and restrictive covenants, are, like leasehold estates, of a commercial nature and not suited to the doctrine of overreaching. It was therefore necessary for the 1925 legislation to adopt different means of balancing the convenience of the purchaser and the protection of the third party interest. First, the legislation reduced the number of third party interests which could exist as legal interests and which would therefore be enforceable against a purchaser irrespective of notice, in accordance with the principle of universal enforceability. The content of the list of those interests which could still exist as legal interests was largely determined by the traditional definition of real property. Secondly, in respect of the wider range of third party interests which could only exist as equitable interests (whether or not as a

consequence of the reclassification of interests), the legislation introduced machinery which was designed to protect both purchasers and third parties. In essence the doctrine of notice, which had previously determined the enforceability of such interests was replaced by the principle of registration. By registering the equitable interest, the owner of the interest gave "statutory notice" to a potential purchaser, who would therefore be bound by the interest if he proceeded with the purchase; and at the same time the register provided the potential purchaser with a convenient means of discovering that interest and deciding whether to purchase the land at all.

2. Reclassification of estates and interests in land

Law of Property Act 1925, s.1

Legal estates and equitable interests

1.—(1) The only estates in land which are capable of subsisting or of being conveyed or created at law are—

(a) An estate in fee simple absolute in possession;

(b) A term of years absolute.

(2) The only interests or charges in or over land which are capable of subsisting or of being conveyed or created at law are—

(a) An easement, right, or privilege in or over land for an interest equivalent to an estate in fee simple absolute in possession or a term of years absolute;

(b) A rentcharge in possession issuing out of or charged on land being either perpetual or for a term of years absolute;

(c) A charge by way of legal mortgage;

(d) [...] and any other similar charge on land which is not created by an instrument;

(e) Rights of entry exercisable over or in respect of a legal term of years absolute, or annexed, for any purpose, to a legal rentcharge.

(3) All other estates, interests, and charges in or over land take effect as equitable interests.

(4) The estates, interests, and charges which under this section are authorised to subsist or to be conveyed or created at law are (when subsisting or conveyed or created at law) in this Act referred to as "legal estates", and have the same incidents as legal estates subsisting at the commencement of this Act; and the owner of a legal estate is referred to as "an estate owner" and his legal estate is referred to as his estate.

(5) A legal estate may subsist concurrently with or subject to any other legal estate in the same land in like manner as it could have done before the commencement of this Act.

...

(8) Estates, interests, and charges in or over land which are not legal estates are in this Act referred to as "equitable interests". . . .

2.1 *Legal estates*

2.1.1 *Fee simple absolute in possession*   The constituent parts of the term "fee simple absolute in possession" (s.1(1)(a)) have been considered (*supra*, p. 22), except for the word "absolute". The term is used to distinguish the most complete version of the fee simple from modified versions such as the determinable or conditional fee simple, which are limited, expressly or by implication, to continue until, or to commence/terminate upon, some specified event. The limitations imposed are subject to invalidation on grounds of public policy; and, although the determinable fee simple and the conditional fee simple are not always easily distinguishable, a rather stricter approach is taken to such limitations in the case of the conditional fee simple. Moreover, whereas an invalidated determinable fee simple is void, an invalidated conditional fee simple takes effect as a fee simple absolute. Any modified fee simple that survives such scrutiny should, in accordance with the policy of the 1925 legislation discussed above, take effect as an *equitable* fee simple under a trust. However, the operation of the trust machinery would have been inappropriate and inconvenient in some cases: a fee simple in land owned by a public authority for certain public purposes may be determinable when the land is no longer required for those purposes; a fee simple owned by a corporate body is determinable on the dissolution of the corporation; a fee simple acquired, in accordance with normal practice in certain parts of the country, in return for the payment of a perpetual rentcharge is conditional on continuing payments and is subject to a right to re-enter the land in the event of non-payment. In order to deal with these cases, the Law of Property Act 1925 declares that, notwithstanding that the fee simple remains in substance a determinable or conditional fee simple, it is for the purposes of the Act a fee simple absolute: *ibid.* s.7; and see the Reverter of Sites Act 1987.

2.1.2 *Term of years absolute* The term of years absolute (s.1(1)(b)), or leasehold estate, is considered in detail in Chapter 5. The word "absolute" has no discernible meaning in this context. It certainly does not have the significance that it has in the case of the fee simple absolute. As will be seen, leases almost invariably provide for early termination in the event of non-payment of rent or breach of some other term of the lease but such a provision does not prevent the creation of a term of years *absolute*. Since the legal fee simple absolute in possession fulfils the function as the basis of conveyancing, and any leasehold estate subsists concurrently with the fee simple (Law of Property Act 1925, s.1(5)), there is no requirement that the term of years absolute must be *in possession* if it is to qualify as a legal estate.

2.1.3 *Fee simple absolute in possession and term of years absolute not necessarily legal* Although the fee simple absolute in possession and the term of years absolute are the only estates capable of existing as legal estates, it does not inevitably follow that such estates will always be legal estates; they may also exist as equitable interests. For example, where land is conveyed to trustees on trust for X in fee simple (because X is a minor and not legally competent to own a legal estate in land: Law of Property Act 1925, s.1(6)), the trustees will own the *legal* fee simple absolute in possession and X will own the *equitable* fee simple absolute in possession. However, while the fee simple absolute in possession and the term of years absolute may thus exist either at law or in equity, all other estates necessarily exist as equitable *interests*: *ibid.* s.1(3). It should be noted that the terminology of "estates" is reserved for the legal fee simple absolute in possession and the term of years absolute: all other former estates, which now take effect in equity under the trust machinery are referred to as equitable *interests*: *ibid.* s.1(4), (8).

2.2 *Legal interests*

In parallel with section 1(1), the interests listed in section 1(2) are the only third party interests capable of existing as legal interests; but they may also exist as equitable interests. However, third party interests in land not listed in section 1(2) necessarily exist as equitable interests only: see section 1(3).

2.2.1 *Easements*

Easements (s.1(2)(a)) are exemplified by the right of way over land granted to the owner of neighbouring land in his capacity as landowner: see *post*, Chapter 7. Easements qualify as *legal* interests in land only where they are granted for a period of time equivalent to the fee simple absolute in possession or the term of years absolute. Moreover, the grant of a legal easement requires a deed.

2.2.2 *Rentcharges*

A rentcharge (s.1(2)(b)) is a right to periodical payments charged on land but independent of any lease or mortgage. Rentcharges qualify as *legal* interests in land only where they are created for a period of time equivalent to the fee simple absolute in possession or the term of years absolute; and only where the right to payments is a right "in possession". With certain exceptions, the creation of new rentcharges has been prohibited since 1977; and existing rentcharges are being gradually extinguished: see Rentcharges Act 1977.

2.2.3 *Charges by way of legal mortgage*

A charge by way of legal mortgage (s.1(2)(c)) is the grant of certain rights over land as a means of securing repayment of a loan advanced by the grantee to the landowner: see *post*, Chapter 9.

2.2.4 *Miscellaneous charges*

The category of charges within section 1(2)(d) has been significantly reduced in scope and is now of little practical consequence.

2.2.5 *Rights of entry*

A right of entry (s.1(2)(e)) is a means of forfeiting (or terminating) a lease where the leaseholder is in breach of its terms, or any other estate in land where the owner has failed to comply with the terms of a rentcharge charged on that land. Rights of entry qualify as legal interests only where they are attached to a legal term of years or to a legal rentcharge.

3. Machinery for the investigation and protection of third party interests

The machinery for the investigation and protection of third party interests in land differs according to whether the land has an unregistered title and is therefore subject to the title deeds conveyancing system; or whether the land has a registered title and is therefore subject to the registered title conveyancing system.

Prior to 1926 the conveyancing process in England and Wales was a private system in which the state was not involved. With a few exceptions, title to land was established by reference to title deeds and other documents; and there was no official record of dealings in land because the documents which both created and recorded rights in relation to the land were prepared and retained by the parties. Although the system of title deeds conveyancing was retained (albeit with certain modifications) by the 1925 legislation, the Land Registration Act 1925 introduced a new system of conveyancing which was based on the establishment of title by reference to a central register of title. Moreover, this system of registered title conveyancing was not limited simply to proof of title in the strict sense. The availability of the register also provided a new system of protection for third party interests which benefited or adversely affected the land.

Registration of title in fact spread rather more slowly that had originally been envisaged: compulsory registration was introduced area by area and it did not extend to the whole country until 1990; and even then registration of title was only compulsory following a conveyance on sale of the fee simple or the grant or assignment of a lease. The Land Registration Act 1997 extended the list of dispositions triggering compulsory registration to include most principal dealings in land: see *post*, p. 162. However, for a not insignificant number of properties in England and Wales title remains unregistered and there is no requirement to register until there has been a relevant disposition. Moreover, such titles will only be registered following the completion of the title deeds conveyancing procedures. It follows that an understanding of the principles of title deeds conveyancing will remain significant for some years.

It may be useful to summarise how the two systems of conveyancing deal with the various interests in land as reclassified by the Law of Property Act 1925.

3.1 *Unregistered land*

3.1.1 *Title*   It has been seen that the intending purchaser of the legal fee simple absolute in possession must obtain from the vendor documentary evidence of his entitlement to the estate that he is purporting to sell. Such evidence must normally commence with a good "root of title" at least 15 years old and must cover all subsequent dealings with or affecting the fee simple. The title to a legal term of years must also be established by relevant documentary evidence. Assuming that the purchaser acquires the legal fee simple absolute in possession (or the legal term of years absolute), the question is the extent to which the purchaser is bound by third party interests.

3.1.2 *Legal estates and interests affecting title*   In accordance with the principle of universal enforceability, the purchaser is bound by any other existing legal estates and interests (as listed in the Law of Property Act 1925, s.1(1), (2)) irrespective of whether or not he had notice of the interest at the time of the conveyance. Thus a purchaser would take subject to an existing legal lease and any legal easement over the land. As will be seen, there is one exception this principle: a (legal) puisne mortgage is treated as an equitable interest. The universal enforceability of legal interests is justified on the ground that such interests are normally discoverable on an inspection of the land.

3.1.3 *Equitable interests affecting title*   The enforceability of existing equitable interests is no longer determined exclusively or even primarily by the doctrine of notice.

3.1.3.1 *Overreachable interests*   Interests under trusts (and certain other interests of an essentially financial nature) are normally overreached by a purchaser provided that he complies with the statutory requirements; in particular, the purchaser must pay the purchase money to at least two trustees or to a trust corporation.

3.1.3.2 *Interests registrable under the Land Charges Acts*   Those interests of an essentially commercial nature (for example, equitable easements, restrictive covenants, estate contracts (and (legal) puisne mortgages)) are subject to the system of registration of incumbrances introduced by the Land Charges Act 1925 (and replaced by the Land Charges Act 1972). The registration of such interests is deemed to constitute notice with the result that a purchaser is bound by any registered interest irrespective of whether or not he would have had notice under the equitable doctrine. Conversely, an interest that is registrable under the Act, but which is not registered, does not bind a purchaser of the land, again irrespective of whether he would have had notice under the equitable doctrine.

3.1.3.3 *Doctrine of notice*   Those interests which do not fall within either of the above categories (and potentially overreachable interests that have not been overreached because of non-compliance with the statutory requirements) continue to depend for their enforceability on the equitable doctrine of notice: see Law of Property Act 1925, s.199(1)(ii).

3.2 *Registered land*
In the context of registered land, the protection of interests does not centre on the dichotomy of legal and equitable interests, although the distinction is not wholly without significance.

3.2.1 *Title*   Under the Land Registration Act 1925, a separate register is established for each principal interest (title) affecting a particular plot of land. These principal interests are identified, by express reference to the Law of Property Act 1925, as the legal fee simple absolute in possession and the legal term of years absolute (provided that the term of years is granted for more than 21 years or, in the case of assignment, has more than 21 years unexpired). Since the register is effectively conclusive as to the entitlement of the person currently named as registered proprietor of the legal fee simple (or the legal term of years), the intending purchaser can verify the entitlement of the vendor by an inspection of the register. Assuming that the purchaser acquires the legal fee simple absolute in possession (or the legal term of years absolute), the Land Registration Act 1925 expressly provides that the purchaser takes subject to interests protected on the register relating to the relevant title and to overriding interests.

3.2.2 *Interests protected on the register*   The category of interests capable of protection on the register includes most third party interests, both legal and equitable; but the different forms of protection to some extent reflect the different categories of third party interests identified in the context of unregistered land. Thus legal leases, legal easements and legal mortgages, although entered on the register of the title affected, require to be created by registered disposition; (equitable) interests under trusts are entered on the register for the express purpose of ensuring that a purchaser complies with the statutory requirements for overreaching; and (equitable) commercial interests are entered for the purpose of binding the purchaser.

3.2.3 *Overriding interests*   Overriding interests are those interests which bind a purchaser even though they are not protected on the register and even though the purchaser has no notice of them. Many of the interests which may bind a purchaser as overriding interests are in practice entered on the register; but, in the absence of such entry, their status as overriding interests is justified on the basis that they are interests that would be discovered on an inspection of the land. However, the courts have adopted an expansive approach to overriding interests which permits interests that were apparently intended to be protected on the register to be protected instead as overriding interests.

3.2.4 *Doctrine of notice*   In principle, the doctrine of notice has no role in the context of registered land. However, the substance of the doctrine has on occasions been invoked by the courts: see *post*, p. 170.

3.3 *Machinery and substance*
Although it is sometimes asserted that conveyancing is concerned only with the creation, transfer and protection of interests in land and that both systems of conveyancing are superimposed on the same substantive law, it is unrealistic to suggest that the conveyancing process does not have an influence on the substantive law itself: see *post*, p. 159.

F. ACQUISITION OF OWNERSHIP RIGHTS IN LAND

This section considers briefly three matters relating to the acquisition of ownership rights in land. First, it outlines the most common method of acquisition, through documentary lifetime transfer by way of sale, normally a two-stage process involving contract and conveyance. Secondly, although the documentary transfer is effective to transfer the legal estate in the land to the transferee(s), it is sometimes necessary to consider as a separate matter the entitlement to the equitable ownership rights in the land. Thirdly, the section outlines the principles of the acquisition of ownership rights through adverse possession. Acquisition of ownership rights under the doctrine of proprietary estoppel is considered in Chapter 6.

1. Contract and conveyance

It is not within the scope of this book to examine in detail the various stages of the conveyancing process. Nonetheless, land law is inextricably linked with the principles of conveyancing; and it is therefore appropriate to outline the conveyancing process better to understand the principles of title deeds conveyancing and registered title conveyancing, which are the subject-matter of Chapters 2 and 3.

The documentary lifetime transfer of ownership rights in land, whether in the form of the legal fee simple in possession or a legal term of years, usually involves, first, a formal contract by which the vendor and purchaser commit themselves to the sale and purchase of the land and, secondly, the "completion" of that contract by a conveyance (in the case of unregistered land) or transfer (in the case of registered land) of the legal estate. As will be seen, in the case of registered land, there is a further requirement that the transfer be registered. Both the contract and the completion document must comply with certain formal requirements.

It is anticipated that over the next decade or so there will be a progressive move towards a system of electronic conveyancing, under which most transactions in land would be executed electronically by registration. Such a system would replace the above multi-stage process applicable to transactions in registered land with a single-stage process of registering the transaction; and, until registration, the transaction would have no effect. However, at this stage the Law Commission has only recommended that the Lord Chancellor be empowered to make rules to provide for the introduction of a system of electronic conveyancing: see Law Com. No. 254, *Land Registration for the Twenty-First Century* (1998); and see *post*, p. 262. It therefore remains necessary to consider the current process.

1.1 *Contract*

When the vendor and purchaser have agreed in principle to the sale and purchase, the purchaser will normally have to attend to a range of matters before committing himself to the purchase by the formal exchange of contracts. Apart from the essentially practical concerns of a structural survey of the property and the arrangement of mortgage finance, the purchaser will wish to obtain an appreciation of the "legal" matters affecting the property. Thus he will normally inspect the property to discover persons other than the vendor in occupation and evidence of third party rights affecting the property; he will address preliminary enquiries to the vendor on these and other matters such as disputes over the property and maintenance obligations (unless this information is provided unsolicited by the vendor under the voluntary National Conveyancing Protocol procedure); he will search the local land charges register to discover any relevant planning matters and will address further inquiries to the local authority in respect of such matters as drainage and planned new roads; and, where title to the property is not yet registered, he will make a preliminary search of the land charges register to discover any relevant third party interests affecting the land.

Assuming that these various inspections, inquiries and searches have not deterred the purchaser, the process moves to the stage at which the parties commit themselves to the sale and purchase by the exchange of contracts and the payment by the purchaser of a deposit (normally ten per cent of the purchase price). The contract itself may be "open", containing only the essential terms relating to the parties, the property and the price; but more usually it will incorporate, with or without modification, the detailed substantive and procedural provisions of the Standard Conditions of Sale.

However, irrespective of the substantive detail of the contract, all contracts for the sale or other disposition of interests in land must comply with certain formal requirements. In relation to contracts entered into before 27 September 1989 there were no formal requirements for *validity*; but section 40 of the Law of Property Act 1925, which continues to apply to such contracts, imposed formal requirements for *enforceability*. A person seeking to enforce a contract (or to establish its enforceability) had to be able to point either (i) to some written evidence of the principal terms of the contract signed by the person against whom enforcement was sought: *Tiverton Estates Ltd v. Wearwell Ltd* [1975] Ch. 146; or (ii) to some act of "part performance", that is some act which pointed to the existence of a contract between the parties, by the person seeking to enforce the contract: *Steadman v. Steadman* [1976] A.C. 536. Section 2 of the Law of Property (Miscellaneous Provisions) Act 1989 replaced section 40 in relation to contracts concluded on or after 27 September 1989. It imposes formal requirements for *validity*; and, if those requirements are satisfied, the valid contract is prima facie enforceable.

Law of Property (Miscellaneous Provisions) Act 1989, s.2

Contracts for sale etc. of land to be made by signed writing

2.—(1) A contract for the sale or other disposition of an interest in land can only be made in writing and only by incorporating all the terms which the parties have expressly agreed in one document or, where contracts are exchanged, in each.

(2) The terms may be incorporated in a document either by being set out in it or by reference to some other document.

(3) The document incorporating the terms or, where contracts are exchanged, one of the documents incorporating them (but not necessarily the same one) must be signed by or on behalf of each party to the contract.

(4) Where a contract for the sale or other disposition of an interest in land satisfies the conditions of this section by reason only of the rectification of one or more documents in pursuance of an order of a court, the contract shall come into being, or be deemed to have come into being, at such time as may be specified in the order.

(5) This section does not apply in relation to—

(a) a contract to grant such a lease as is mentioned in section 54(2) of the Law of Property Act 1925 (short leases);

(b) a contract made in the course of a public auction; or

(c) a contract regulated under the Financial Services Act 1986—

and nothing in this section affects the creation or operation of resulting, implied or constructive trusts.

(6) In this section—

"disposition" has the same meaning as in the Law of Property Act 1925;

"interest in land" means any estate, interest or charge in or over land. . .

(7) Nothing in this section shall apply in relation to contracts made before this section comes into force.

(8) Section 40 of the Law of Property Act 1925 (which is superseded by this section) shall cease to have effect.

NOTES:

1. For the background to the section, see Law Com. No. 164, *Transfer of Land: Formalities for Contracts for Sale etc. of Land* (1987), discussed at [1987] Conv. 313. However, the section as enacted is materially different from that contained in the draft Bill appended to the Law Commission report; and the report cannot, therefore, be regarded as a conclusive aid to the interpretation of the section. For discussion of the section and its implications, see Pettit [1989] Conv. 431; Annand (1989) 105 L.Q.R. 555; Howell [1990] Conv. 441; Hill (1990) 106 L.Q.R. 396; Bently and Coughan (1990) 10 Legal Studies 325; Jenkins [1993] Conv. 13; Davis (1993) 13 O.J.L.S. 99.

2. According to Hoffmann J. in *Spiro v. Glencrown Properties Ltd* [1991] Ch. 537, 541, "section 2 was intended to prevent disputes over whether the parties had entered into a binding agreement or over what terms they had agreed. It prescribes the formalities for recording their mutual consent"; according to Peter Gibson L.J. in *Firstpost Homes Ltd v. Johnson* [1995] 1 W.L.R. 1567, 1571, the Act introduced a "markedly different regime" which was intended to make "radical changes" to contracts for the sale of land so as to simplify the law and to avoid disputes; and, according to Neill L.J. in *McCausland v. Duncan Lawrie Ltd* [1997] 1 W.L.R. 38, 44, Parliament intended to introduce new *and strict* requirements.

3. The formal requirements of section 2 have been held to apply to (i) the grant of an option to purchase land: *Spiro v. Glencrown Properties Ltd* [1991] Ch. 537, noted at [1991] C.L.J. 236, [1991] Conv. 140; (ii) an agreement varying the terms of a contract: *McCausland v. Duncan Lawrie Ltd* [1997] 1 W.L.R. 38, noted at [1996] Conv. 366; and (iii) a contract to create an equitable mortgage: *United Bank of Kuwait plc v. Sahib* [1997] Ch. 107, *post*, p. 815. However, the requirements have been held not to apply to (i) the exercise of an option to purchase land: *Spiro v. Glencrown Properties Ltd*, *supra*; (ii) a collateral contract: *Record v. Bell* [1991] 1 W.L.R. 853, noted at [1991] C.L.J. 399, [1991] Conv. 471, (1992) 108 L.Q.R. 217; (iii) an executed supplementary agreement: *Tootal Clothing Ltd v. Guinea Properties Manufacturing Ltd* (1992) 64 P. & C.R. 452, noted at [1993] Conv. 89, (1993) 109 L.Q.R. 191; (iv) a lock-out agreement: *Walford v. Miles* [1992] 2 A.C. 128; *Pitt v. P.H.H. Asset Management Ltd* [1994] 1 W.L.R. 327, noted at [1993] C.L.J. 392, [1994] Conv. 58; and (v) a contract of disposition (as

distinct from an executory contract for the disposition) of an interest in land: *Target Holdings Ltd v. Priestley* (1999), *The Times*, May 13, 1999.

4. In *Cooper v. Critchley* [1955] Ch. 431 the Court of Appeal held that a contract for the sale of a beneficial interest under a trust for sale was within the terms of section 40 of the Law of Property Act 1925. Although that decision was contrary to the logic of the doctrine of conversion, according to which such interests were regarded as interests in the proceeds of sale of the land (see *post*, p. 300), the decision was expressly confirmed in section 2(6) of the 1989 Act as originally enacted. Under the regime of the Trusts of Land and Appointment of Trustees Act 1996 such interests are now to be regarded as interests in land: see *post*, p. 302; and they are clearly within the terms of section 2(1) of the 1989 Act.

5. The section has produced considerable uncertainty, largely in relation to the practical consequences of the new requirements for the conveyancing process. This uncertainty stems in part from the wording of the section and in part from the failure of the courts to take a consistent approach to the relevance of the earlier law and to the striking of the balance between the desirability of clear and workable rules and the undesirability of permitting the section to be used as a means of escaping from concluded agreements: see [1995] C.L.J. 503; [1995] Conv. 319, 364, 484; [1996] C.L.J. 192.

6. For present purposes the more important issue is the effect of a contract which complies with the section and is therefore valid.

According to the orthodox view, since the courts would normally compel the parties to complete the contract, and to that end would grant the equitable remedy of specific performance against the party refusing to complete, equity anticipates the completion of the contract and treats the contract alone as effective to transfer the equitable ownership of the land to the purchaser: see *Lysaght v. Edwards* (1876) 2 ChD. 499, where Jessel M.R. stated (at 506):

The effect of a contract for sale has been settled for more than two centuries; certainly it was completely settled before the time of Lord Hardwicke, who speaks of the settled doctrine of the court as to it. What is that doctrine? It is that the moment you have a valid contract for sale the vendor becomes in equity a trustee for the purchaser of the estate sold, and the beneficial [equitable] ownership passes to the purchaser, the vendor having a right to the purchase-money, a charge or lien on the estate for the security of that purchase-money, and a right to retain possession of the estate until the purchase-money is paid, in the absence of express contract as to the time of delivering possession.

However, analysis of the orthodox view demonstrates that the transfer of the equitable *ownership* in the property is subject to the payment of the purchase money, which does not normally occur until completion of the contract. Moreover, pending completion the vendor is entitled to remain in possession; he is entitled to any rents and profits accruing before completion; and he retains an "unpaid vendor's lien" over the property until the purchase price is paid in full. Consequently, the orthodox trust analysis has been questioned and, by way of refinement, it has been asserted that in the period between exchange of contracts and completion (or the earlier payment of the purchase money) the purchaser acquires an equitable interest "impressed upon" or "engrafted onto" rather than "carved out of" the vendor's legal estate: see *D.K.L.R. Holding Co. (No. 2) Pty Ltd v. Commissioner of Stamp Duties (N.S.W.)* (1982) 149 C.L.R. 431, 474 *per* Brennan J.; *Re Transphere Pty Ltd* (1986) 5 N.S.W.L.R. 309, 311 *per* McLelland J.; and see *Lloyds Bank plc v. Carrick* [1996] 4 All E.R. 630, 637 *per* Morritt L.J.

This doctrine, sometimes (strictly inaccurately) referred to as the doctrine in *Walsh v. Lonsdale*, applies to valid contracts to create or convey *any* legal estate or interest in land. It is considered further in the context of leases: see *post*, p. 389.

7. Even where an agreement fails to comply with the requirements of section 2, the Court of Appeal has held that the agreement may be enforceable through the doctrine of constructive trust in circumstances where the doctrines of part performance and/or proprietary estoppel might previously have been relied upon: *Yaxley v. Gotts* (1999), *The Times*, July 8, 1999. On the applicability of the doctrine of proprietary estoppel in such circumstances, see Davis (1993) 13 O.J.L.S. 99.

1.2 *Conveyance/transfer*

Following the conclusion of a valid contract, normally by the "exchange of contracts" between vendor and purchaser, the purchaser completes his formal investigations of the title of the vendor, ensuring that the vendor will be in a position to transfer what he has contracted to transfer. As will be seen, the nature of the investigations differs according to whether the title to the land is registered or unregistered. However, provided that the purchaser is satisfied as to the title, the parties proceed to the second stage of the transaction, the formal deed of conveyance or document of transfer. The completion document must also comply with certain formal requirements.

Law of Property Act 1925, s.52

Conveyances to be by deed

(1) All conveyances of land or of any interest therein are void for the purpose of conveying or creating a legal estate unless made by deed.

NOTES:

1. The requirements as to the content and execution of deeds are now contained in section 1 of the Law of Property (Miscellaneous Provisions) Act 1989:

Deeds and their execution

1.—(1) Any rule of law which—
(a) restricts the substances on which a deed may be written:
(b) requires a seal for the valid execution of an instrument as a deed by an individual; or

(c) requires authority by one person to another to deliver an instrument as a deed on his behalf to be given by deed,

is abolished.

(2) An instrument shall not be a deed unless—

(a) it makes it clear on its face that it is intended to be a deed by the person making it or, as the case may be, by the parties to it (whether by describing itself as a deed or expressing itself to be executed or signed as a deed or otherwise); and

(b) it is validly executed as a deed by that person or, as the case may be, one or more of those parties.

(3) An instrument is validly executed as a deed by an individual if, and only if—

(a) it is signed—

   (i) by him in the presence of a witness who attests the signature; or

   (ii) at his direction and in his presence and the presence of two witnesses who each attest the signature; and

(b) it is delivered as a deed by him or a person authorised to do so on his behalf.

2. There are a number of exceptions to the requirement of a deed: see Law of Property Act 1925, ss.52(2), 54(2), 55. These exceptions include certain short leases: *ibid.* s.54(2); and see *post*, p. 387.

3. A conveyance or transfer that fails to comply with the formal requirements and is thus ineffective to convey or transfer the legal estate may nonetheless be treated as a contract for the conveyance or transfer; and, if the deemed contract satisfies the requirements for a valid and enforceable contract, it may be effective to transfer an equitable interest pursuant to the doctrine outlined above. This doctrine is considered further in the context of leases: see *post*, p. 388.

2. Acquisition of equitable ownership rights

There is rarely any doubt as to the ownership of the legal estate in land. Subject to the possibility of acquisition of ownership rights by adverse possession (*infra*, p. 79), ownership of the legal estate is documented, by the most recent conveyance (in the case of unregistered land) or by the register (in the case of registered land). However, it is sometimes necessary to consider as a separate matter the entitlement to the equitable ownership rights in the land.

It has already been seen that in some circumstances the owner of the legal estate in land is not the owner of the equitable ownership rights in that land. However, the present concern is not with those cases where the owner of the legal estate is a trustee holding land on trust for a succession of persons. Rather the concern is with those situations, exemplified by ownership of the matrimonial or family home, where it is claimed that the equitable ownership rights comprising the equitable fee simple in the land are owned concurrently by two persons, although the legal estate in the property may have been transferred to only one of those persons: see, *e.g. Caunce v. Caunce* [1969] 1 W.L.R. 286, *supra*, p. 39; *Kingsnorth Finance Co. Ltd v. Tizard* [1986] 1 W.L.R. 783, *supra*, p. 42.

In fact it is becoming more common for documentary transfers of land to include an express declaration as to the equitable ownership of the land; and in the absence of fraud or mistake, such a declaration (of trust) will generally be conclusive: *Pettitt v. Pettitt* [1970] A.C. 777, 813 *per* Lord Upjohn; *Goodman v. Gallant* [1986] Fam. 106, 117 *per* Slade L.J.; *Hembury v. Peachey* (1996) 72 P. & C.R. D46. However, the House of Lords did not apply the rule where the claimant to a share in the equitable ownership had contributed to the purchase price but was not a party to the transfer: *City of London Building Society v. Flegg* [1988] A.C. 54, *post*, p. 297. Moreover, the Court of Appeal has held that a transfer of the legal title to the property into the joint names of the parties does not constitute an express declaration of trust: *Springette v. Defoe* (1992) 65 P. & C.R. 1; nor does a declaration that the survivor can give a valid receipt for capital monies arising on a disposition of the property: *Harwood v. Harwood* [1991] 2. F.L.R. 274; *Huntingford v. Hobbs* [1993] 1 F.L.R. 736; *Evans v. Hayward* [1995] 2 F.L.R. 511.

Consequently, there are a significant number of cases where there is no express declaration of trust, either contained in the document transferring the legal estate or otherwise evidenced in writing (see Law of Property Act 1925, s.53(1)(b)), nor a valid and enforceable contract (see Law of Property (Miscellaneous Provisions) Act 1989, s.2, *supra*); and in such cases a person who is not also a transferee of the legal estate may nonetheless be able to establish that he or she is entitled to a share in the equitable ownership rights.

The starting point is the traditional or strict doctrine of resulting trusts. According to that doctrine, there is an equitable presumption that a person who contributes to the purchase price of land intends to acquire an interest in that land, proportional to the value of the contribution (although the presumption can be rebutted by evidence of an actual intention to the contrary); and to give effect to the presumption, the legal owner of the land holds the land on (resulting) trust for the contributors: see, *e.g. Dyer v. Dyer* (1788) 2 Cox Eq. Cas. 92, 93 *per* Eyre C.B.; *Pettitt v. Pettitt* [1970] A.C. 777, 814 *per* Lord Upjohn; *Springette v. Defoe* [1992] 2 F.L.R. 388, 391 *per* Dillon L.J. Thus, where A and B provide the purchase price of land, which is transferred into the name of A alone, pursuant to the presumption A holds the land on resulting trust for A and B; and their respective shares in the equitable interest are proportional to their contributions to the purchase price. However, that simple model is rarely applicable or even appropriate in the more complex factual circumstances that surround the acquisition of the family home. The traditional resulting trust has therefore been developed, supplemented and arguably replaced by the constructive trust and related doctrines.

The foundations of the current law were laid down in the cases of *Pettitt v. Pettitt* [1970] A.C. 777 and *Gissing v. Gissing* [1971] A.C. 886. In those cases the House of Lords rejected an emerging doctrine of "family assets", according to which the parties would become jointly entitled in equity to any land (or other property) acquired by either party for their joint use (see, *e.g. Rimmer v. Rimmer* [1953] 1 Q.B. 63, 76 *per* Romer L.J.; *Fribance v. Fribance* [1957] 1 W.L.R. 384, 387 *per* Denning L.J.); and their Lordships firmly re-established the requirement that any claim to an equitable interest in land must be based strictly on the principles of the law relating to resulting, implied or constructive trusts. In *Gissing v. Gissing* Lord Diplock stated (at 905–910):

Any claim to a beneficial interest in land by a person, whether spouse or stranger, in whom the legal estate in the land is not vested must be based upon the proposition that the person in whom the legal estate is vested holds it as trustee upon trust to give effect to the beneficial interest of the claimant as cestui que trust. The legal principles applicable to the claim are those of the English law of trusts and in particular, in the kind of dispute between spouses that comes before the courts, the law relating to the creation and operation of "resulting, implied or constructive trusts." Where the trust is expressly declared in the instrument by which the legal estate is transferred to the trustee or by a written declaration of trust by the trustee, the court must give effect to it. But to constitute a valid declaration of trust by way of gift of a beneficial interest in land to a cestui que trust the declaration is required by section 53(1) of the Law of Property Act 1925 to be in writing. If it is not in writing it can only take effect as a resulting, implied or constructive trust to which that section has no application.

A resulting, implied or constructive trust—and it is unnecessary for present purposes to distinguish between these three classes of trust—is created by a transaction between the trustee and the cestui que trust in connection with the acquisition by the trustee of a legal estate in land, whenever the trustee has so conducted himself that it would be inequitable to allow him to deny to the cestui que trust a beneficial interest in the land acquired. And he will be held so to have conducted himself if by his words or conduct he has induced the cestui que trust to act to his own detriment in the reasonable belief that by so acting he was acquiring a beneficial interest in the land.

This is why it has been repeatedly said in the context of disputes between spouses as to their respective beneficial interests in the matrimonial home, that if at the time of its acquisition and transfer of the legal estate into the name of one or other of them an express agreement has been made between them as to the way in which the beneficial interest shall be held, the court will give effect to it—notwithstanding the absence of any written declaration of trust. Strictly speaking this states the principle too widely, for if the agreement did not provide for anything to be done by the spouse in whom the legal estate was not to be vested, it would be a merely voluntary declaration of trust and unenforceable for want of writing. But in the express oral agreements contemplated by these dicta it has been assumed sub silentio that they provide for the spouse in whom the legal estate in the matrimonial home is not vested to do something to facilitate its acquisition, by contributing to the purchase price or to the deposit or the mortgage instalments when it is purchased upon mortgage or to make some other material sacrifice by way of contribution to or economy in the general family expenditure. What the court gives effect to is the trust resulting or implied from the common intention expressed in the oral agreement between the spouses that if each acts in the manner provided for in the agreement the beneficial interests in the matrimonial home shall be held as they have agreed.

An express agreement between spouses as to their respective beneficial interests in land conveyed into the name of one of them obviates the need for showing that the conduct of the spouse into whose name the land was conveyed was intended to induce the other spouse to act to his or her detriment upon the faith of the promise of a specified beneficial interest in the land and that the other spouse so acted with the intention of acquiring that beneficial interest. The agreement itself discloses the common intention required to create a resulting, implied or constructive trust.

But parties to a transaction in connection with the acquisition of land may well have formed a common intention that the beneficial interest in the land shall be vested in them jointly without having used express words to communicate this intention to one another; or their recollections of the words used may be imperfect or conflicting by the time any dispute arises. In such a case—a common one where the parties are spouses whose marriage has broken down—it may be possible to infer their common intention from their conduct.

As in so many branches of English law in which legal rights and obligations depend upon the intentions of the parties to a transaction, the relevant intention of each party is the intention which was reasonably understood by the other party to be manifested by that party's words or conduct notwithstanding that he did not consciously formulate that intention in his own mind or even acted with some different intention which he did not communicate to the other party. On the other hand, he is not bound by any inference which the other party draws as to his intention unless that inference is one which can reasonably be drawn from his words or conduct. It is in this sense that in the branch of English law relating to constructive, implied or resulting trusts effect is given to the inferences as to the intentions of parties to a transaction which a reasonable man would draw from their words or conduct and not to any subjective intention or absence of intention which was not made manifest at the time of the transaction itself. It is for the court to determine what those inferences are.

In drawing such an inference, what spouses said and did which led up to the acquisition of a matrimonial home and what they said and did while the acquisition was being carried through is on a different footing from what they said and did after the acquisition was completed. Unless it is alleged that there was some subsequent fresh agreement, acted upon by the parties, to vary the original beneficial interests created when the matrimonial home was acquired, what they said and did after the acquisition was completed is relevant if it is explicable only upon the basis of their having manifested to one another at the time of the acquisition some particular common intention as to how the beneficial interest should be held. But it would in my view be unreasonably legalistic to treat the relevant transaction involved in the acquisition of a matrimonial home as restricted to the actual conveyance of the fee simple into the name of one or other spouse. Their common intention is more likely to have been concerned with the economic realities of the transaction than with the unfamiliar technicalities of the English law of legal and equitable interests in land. The economic reality which lies behind the conveyance of the fee simple to a purchaser in return for a purchase price the greater part of which is advanced to the purchaser upon a mortgage repayable by instalments over a number of years, is that the new freeholder is purchasing the matrimonial home upon credit and that the purchase price is represented by the instalments by which the mortgage is repaid in addition to the initial payment in cash. The conduct of the spouses in relation to the payment of the mortgage instalments may be no less relevant to their common intention as to the beneficial interests in a matrimonial home acquired in this way than their conduct in relation to the payment of the cash deposit.

It is this feature of the transaction by means of which most matrimonial homes have been acquired in recent years that makes difficult the task of the court in inferring from the conduct of the spouses a common intention as to how the beneficial interest in it should be held. Each case must depend upon its own facts but there are a number of factual situations which often recur in the cases.

Where a matrimonial home has been purchased outright without the aid of an advance on mortgage it is not difficult to ascertain what part, if any, of the purchase price has been provided by each spouse. If the land is conveyed into the name of a spouse who has not provided the whole of the purchase price, the sum contributed by the other spouse may be explicable as having been intended by both of them either as a gift or as a loan of money to the spouse to whom the land is conveyed or as consideration for a share in the beneficial interest in the land. In a dispute between living spouses the evidence will probably point to one of these explanations as being more probable than the others, but if the rest of the evidence is neutral the prima facie inference is that their common intention was that the contributing spouse should acquire a share in the beneficial interest in the land in the same proportion as the sum contributed bore to the total purchase price. This prima facie inference is more easily rebutted in favour of a gift where the land is conveyed into the name of the wife: but as I understand the speeches in *Pettitt v. Pettitt* four of the members of your Lordships' House who were parties to that decision took the view that even if the "presumption of advancement" as between husband and wife still survived today, it could seldom have any decisive part to play in disputes between living spouses in which some evidence would be available in addition to the mere fact that the husband had provided part of the purchase price of property conveyed into the name of the wife.

Similarly when a matrimonial home is not purchased outright but partly out of moneys advanced on mortgage repayable by instalments, and the land is conveyed into the name of the husband alone, the fact that the wife made a cash contribution to the deposit and legal charges not borrowed on mortgage gives rise, in the absence of evidence which makes some other explanation more probable, to the inference that their common intention was that she should share in the beneficial interest in the land conveyed. But it would not be reasonable to infer a common intention as to what her share should be without taking account also of the sources from which the mortgage instalments were provided. If the wife also makes a substantial direct contribution to the mortgage instalments out of her own earnings or unearned income this would be prima facie inconsistent with a common intention that her share in the beneficial interest should be determined by the proportion which her original cash contribution bore either to the total amount of the deposit and legal charges or to the full purchase price. The more likely inference is that her contributions to the mortgage instalments were intended by the spouses to have some effect upon her share.

Where there has been an initial contribution by the wife to the cash deposit and legal charges which points to a common intention at the time of the conveyance that she should have a beneficial interest in the land conveyed to her husband, it would be unrealistic to regard the wife's subsequent contributions to the mortgage instalments as without significance unless she pays them directly herself. It may be no more than a matter of convenience which spouse pays particular household accounts, particularly when both are earning, and if the wife goes out to work and devotes part of her earnings or uses her private income to meet joint expenses of the household which would otherwise be met by the husband, so as to enable him to pay the mortgage instalments out of his moneys this would be consistent with and might be corroborative of an original common intention that she should share in the beneficial interest in the matrimonial home and that her payments of other household expenses were intended by both spouses to be treated as including a contribution by the wife to the purchase price of the matrimonial home.

Even where there has been no initial contribution by the wife to the cash deposit and legal charges but she makes a regular and substantial direct contribution to the mortgage instalments it may be reasonable to infer a common intention of the spouses from the outset that she should share in the beneficial interest or to infer a fresh agreement reached after the original conveyance that she should acquire a share. But it is unlikely that the mere fact that the wife made direct contributions to the mortgage instalments would be the only evidence available to assist the court in ascertaining the common intention of the spouses.

Where in any of the circumstances described above contributions, direct or indirect, have been made to the mortgage instalments by the spouse into whose name the matrimonial home has not been conveyed, and the court can infer from their conduct a common intention that the contributing spouse should be entitled to *some* beneficial interest in the matrimonial home, what effect is to be given to that intention if there is no evidence that they in fact reached any express agreement as to what the respective share of each spouse should be? I take it to be clear that if the court is satisfied that it was the common intention of both spouses that the contributing wife should have a share in the beneficial interest and that her contributions were made on this understanding, the court in the exercise of its equitable jurisdiction would not permit the husband in whom the legal estate was vested and who had accepted the benefit of the contributions to take the whole beneficial interest merely because at the time the wife made her contributions there had been no express agreement as to how her share in it was to be quantified. In such a case the court must first do its best to discover from the conduct of the spouses whether any inference can reasonably be drawn as to the probable common understanding about the amount of the share of the contributing spouse on which each must have acted in doing what each did, even though that understanding was never expressly stated by one spouse to the other or even consciously formulated in words by either of them independently. It is only if no such inference can be drawn that the court is driven to apply as a rule of law, and not as an inference of fact, the maxim "equality is equity", and to hold that the beneficial interest belongs to the spouses in equal shares. The same result however may often be reached as an inference of fact. The instalments of a mortgage to a building society are generally repayable over a period of many years. During that period, as both must be aware, the ability of each spouse to contribute to the instalments out of their separate earnings is likely to alter, particularly in the case of the wife if any children are born of the marriage. If the contribution of the wife in the early part of the period of repayment is substantial but is not an identifiable and uniform proportion of each instalment, because her contributions are indirect or, if direct, are made irregularly, it may well be a reasonable inference that their common intention at the time of acquisition of the matrimonial home was that the beneficial interest should be held by them in equal shares and that each should contribute to the cost of its acquisition whatever amounts each could afford in the varying exigencies of family life to be expected during the period of repayment. In the social conditions of today this would be a natural enough common intention of a young couple who were both earning when the house was acquired but who contemplated having children whose birth and rearing in their infancy would necessarily affect the future earning capacity of the wife. The relative size of their respective contributions to the instalments in the early part of the period of repayment, or later if a subsequent reduction in the wife's contribution is not to be accounted for by a reduction in her earnings due to motherhood or some other cause from which the husband benefits as well, may make it a more probable inference that the wife's share in the beneficial interest was intended to be in some proportion other than one-half. And there is nothing inherently improbable in their acting on the understanding that the wife should be entitled to a share which was not to be quantified immediately on the acquisition of the home but should be left to be determined when the mortgage was repaid or the property disposed of, on the basis of what would be fair having regard to the total contributions, direct or indirect, which each spouse had made by that date. Where this was the most likely inference from their conduct it would be for the court to give effect to that common intention of the parties by determining what in all the circumstances was a fair share. Difficult as they are to solve, however, these problems as to the amount of the share of a spouse in the beneficial interest in a matrimonial home where the legal estate is vested solely in the other spouse, only arise in cases where the court is satisfied by the words or conduct of the parties that it was their common intention that the beneficial interest was not to belong solely to the spouse in whom the legal estate was vested but was to be shared between them in some proportion or other.

Where the wife has made no initial contribution to the cash deposit and legal charges and no direct contribution to the mortgage instalments nor any adjustment to her contribution to other expenses of the household which it can be inferred was referable to the acquisition of the house, there is in the absence of evidence of an express agreement between the parties no material to justify the court in inferring that it was the common intention of the parties that she should have any beneficial interest in a matrimonial home conveyed into the sole name of the husband, merely because she continued to contribute out of her own earnings or private income to other expenses of the household. For such conduct is no less consistent with a common intention to share the day-to-day expenses of the household, while each spouse retains a separate interest in capital assets acquired with their own moneys or obtained by inheritance or gift. There is nothing here to rebut the prima facie inference that a purchaser of land who pays the purchase price and takes a conveyance and grants a mortgage in his own name intends to acquire the sole beneficial interest as well as the legal estate: and the difficult question of the quantum of the wife's share does not arise.

Following a period during which the Court of Appeal (presided over by Lord Denning M.R.) interpreted and applied the above principles very broadly (see, *e.g. Cooke v. Head* [1972] 1 W.L.R. 518, 520; *Hall v. Hall* [1982] 3 F.L.R. 379, 381), the stricter and more orthodox version of the principles was restated by the Court of Appeal in *Burns v. Burns* [1984] Ch. 317 and in *Grant v. Edwards* [1986] Ch. 638. The most recent decision of the House of Lords in *Lloyds Bank plc v. Rosset* [1991] 1 A.C. 107, where the relevant principles were summarised and applied by Lord Bridge, may be seen to represent a consolidation of that stricter approach.

Lloyds Bank plc v. Rosset [1991] 1 A.C. 107

(HL, Lord Bridge, Lord Griffiths, Lord Ackner, Lord Oliver, Lord Jauncey)

The defendants were husband and wife. In 1982 they decided to purchase and renovate a semi-derelict farmhouse. The purchase was to be funded by money from the husband's family trust, on the condition that the husband was the sole owner of the legal estate. However, the defendants intended that the renovation should be a joint project and that the farmhouse should be the family home. Even before contracts were exchanged, the vendors permitted builders employed by the defendants to start work on the property; and for six weeks prior to the transfer, the builders and the wife were working on the property. In the course of subsequent litigation (see *post*, p. 211), the trial judge found that the wife had acquired a share in the equitable ownership of the farmhouse. That finding was upheld by the Court of Appeal but reversed by the House of Lords.

LORD BRIDGE:
The case pleaded and carefully particularised by Mrs Rosset in support of her claim to an equitable interest in the property was that it had been expressly agreed between her and her husband in conversations before November 1982 that the property was to be jointly owned and that in reliance on this agreement she had made a significant contribution in kind to the acquisition of the property by the works she had personally undertaken in the course of the renovation of the property which was sufficient to give rise to a constructive trust in her favour.

There was a conflict of evidence between Mr and Mrs Rosset on the vital issue raised by this pleading. The question the judge had to determine was whether he could find that before the contract to acquire the property was concluded they had entered into an agreement, made an arrangement, reached an understanding or formed a common intention that the beneficial interest in the property would be jointly owned. I do not think it is of importance which of these alternative expressions one uses. Spouses living in amity will not normally think it necessary to formulate or define their respective interests in property in any precise way. The expectation of parties to every happy marriage is that they will share the practical benefits of occupying the matrimonial home whoever owns it. But this is something quite distinct from sharing the benefical interest in the property asset which the matrimonial home represents. These considerations give rise to special difficulties for judges who are called on to resolve a dispute between spouses who have parted and are at arm's length as to what their common intention or understanding with respect to interests in property was at a time when they were still living as a united family and acquiring a matrimonial home in the expectation of living in it together indefinitely.

Since Mr Rosset was providing the whole purchase price of the property and the whole cost of its renovation, Mrs Rosset would, I think, in any event have encountered formidable difficulty in establishing her claim to joint beneficial ownership. The claim as pleaded and as presented in evidence was, by necessary implication, to an equal share in the equity. But to sustain this it was necessary to show that it was Mr Rosset's intention to make an immediate gift to his wife of half the value of a property acquired for £57,500 and improved at a further cost of some £15,000. What made it doubly difficult for Mrs Rosset to establish her case was the circumstance, which was never in dispute, that Mr Rosset's uncle, who was trustee of his Swiss inheritance, would not release the funds for the purchase of the property except on terms that it was to be acquired in Mr Rosset's sole name. If Mr and Mrs Rosset had ever thought about it, they must have realised that the creation of a trust giving Mrs Rosset a half share, or indeed any other substantial share, in the beneficial ownership of the property would have been nothing less than a subterfuge to circumvent the stipulation which the Swiss trustee insisted on as a condition of releasing the funds to enable the property to be acquired.

In these circumstances, it would have required very cogent evidence to establish that it was the Rossets' common intention to defeat the evident purpose of the Swiss trustee's restriction by acquiring the property in Mr Rosset's name alone but to treat it nevertheless as beneficially owned jointly by both spouses. I doubt whether the evidence would have sustained a finding to that effect. But the judge made no such finding. On the contrary, his judgment on this point amounts to a clear rejection of Mrs Rosset's pleaded case....

Even if there had been the clearest oral agreement between Mr and Mrs Rosset that Mr Rosset was to hold the property in trust for them both as tenants in common, this would, of course, have been ineffective since a valid declaration of trust by way of gift of a beneficial interest in land is required by section 53(1) of the Law of Property Act 1925 to be in writing. But if Mrs Rosset had, as pleaded, altered her position in reliance on the agreement this could have given rise to an enforceable interest in her favour by way either of a constructive trust or of a proprietary estoppel.

Having rejected the contention that there had been any concluded agreement or arrangement or any common intention formed before contracts for the purchase of the property were exchanged on 23 November 1982 that Mrs Rosset should have any beneficial interest, the judge concentrated his attention on Mrs Rosset's activities in connection with the renovation works as a possible basis from which to infer such a common intention.

[His Lordship listed the contributions of the wife as found by the judge, which included assisting the planning of the renovation work; co-ordinating the activities of the builders; obtaining materials from builders' merchants; and painting and decorating. He continued:]

It is clear ... that the judge based his inference of a common intention that Mrs Rosset should have a beneficial interest in the property under a constructive trust essentially on what Mrs Rosset did in and about assisting in the renovation of the property between the beginning of November 1982 and the date of completion on 17 December 1982. Yet by itself this activity, it seems to me, could not possibly justify any such inference. It was common ground that Mrs Rosset was extremely anxious that the new matrimonial home should be ready for occupation before Christmas if possible. In these circumstances it would seem the most natural thing in the world for any wife, in the absence of her husband abroad, to spend all the time she could spare and to employ any skills she might have, such as the ability to decorate a room, in doing all she could to accelerate progress of the work quite irrespective of any expectation she might have of enjoying a beneficial interest in the property. The judge's view that some of this work was work "upon which she could not reasonably have been expected to embark unless she was to have an interest in the house" seems to me, with respect, quite untenable. The impression that the judge may have thought that the share of the equity to which he held Mrs Rosset to be entitled had been "earned" by her work in connection with the renovation is emphasised by his reference in the concluding sentence of his judgment to the extent to which her "qualifying contribution" reduced the cost of the renovation.

On any view the monetary value of Mrs Rosset's work expressed as a contribution to a property acquired at a cost exceeding £70,000 must have been so trifling as to be almost de minimis. I should myself have had considerable doubt whether Mrs Rosset's contribution to the work of renovation was sufficient to support a claim to a constructive trust in the absence of writing to satisfy the requirements of section 53 of the Law of Property Act 1925 even if her husband's intention to make a gift to her of half or any other share in the equity of the property had been clearly established or if he had clearly represented to her that that was what he intended. But here the conversations with her husband on which Mrs Rosset relied, all of which took place before November 1982, were incapable of lending support to the conclusion of a constructive trust in the light of the judge's finding that by that date there had been no decision that she was to have any interest in the property. The finding that the discussions "did not exclude the possibility" that she should have an interest does not seem to me to add anything of significance.

These considerations lead me to the conclusion that the judge's finding that Mr Rosset held the property as constructive trustee for himself and his wife cannot be supported and it is on this short ground that I would allow this appeal. In the course of the argument your Lordships had the benefit of elaborate submissions as to the test to be applied to determine the circumstances in which the sole legal proprietor of a dwelling house can properly be held to have become a constructive trustee of a share in the beneficial interest in the house for the benefit of the partner with whom he or she has cohabited in the house as their shared home. Having in this case reached a conclusion on the facts which, although at variance with the views of the courts below, does not seem to depend on any nice legal distinction and with which, I understand, all your Lordships agree, I cannot help doubting whether it would contribute anything to the illumination of the law if I were to attempt an elaborate and exhaustive analysis of the relevant law to add to the many already to be found in the authorities to which our attention was directed in the course of the argument. I do, however, draw attention to one critical distinction which any judge required to resolve a dispute between former partners as to the beneficial interest in the home they formerly shared should always have in the forefront of his mind.

The first and fundamental question which must always be resolved is whether, independently of any inference to be drawn from the conduct of the parties in the course of sharing the house as their home and managing their joint affairs, there has at any time prior to acquisition, or exceptionally at some later date, been any agreement, arrangement or understanding reached between them that the property is to be shared beneficially. The finding of an agreement or arrangement to share in this sense can only, I think, be based on evidence of express discussions between the partners, however imperfectly remembered and however imprecise their terms may have been. Once a finding to this effect is made it will only be necessary for the partner asserting a claim to a beneficial interest against the partner entitled to the legal estate to show that he or she has acted to his or her detriment or significantly altered his or her position in reliance on the agreement in order to give rise to a constructive trust or a proprietary estoppel.

In sharp contrast with this situation is the very different one where there is no evidence to support a finding of an agreement or arrangement to share, however reasonable it might have been for the parties to reach such an arrangement if they had applied their minds to the question, and where the court must rely entirely on the conduct of the parties both as the basis from which to infer a common intention to share the property beneficially and as the conduct relied on to give rise to a constructive trust. In this situation direct contributions to the purchase price by the partner who is not the legal owner, whether initially or by payment of mortgage instalments, will readily justify the inference necessary to the creation of a constructive trust. But, as I read the authorities, it is at least extremely doubtful whether anything less will do.

The leading cases in your Lordships' House are *Pettitt v. Pettitt* [1970] A.C. 777 and *Gissing v. Gissing* [1971] A.C. 886. Both demonstrate situations in the second category to which I have referred and their Lordships discuss at great length the difficulties to which these situations give rise. The effect of these two decisions is very helpfully analysed in the judgment of Lord MacDermott L.C.J. in *McFarlane v. McFarlane* [1972] N.I. 59.

Outstanding examples on the other hand of cases giving rise to situations in the first category are *Eves v. Eves* [1975] 1 W.L.R. 1338 and *Grant v. Edwards* [1986] Ch. 638. In both these cases, where the parties who had cohabited were unmarried, the female partner had been clearly led by the male partner to believe, when they set up home together, that the property would belong to them jointly. In *Eves v. Eves* the male partner had told the female partner that the only reason why the property was to be acquired in his name alone was because she was under 21 and that, but for her age, he would have had the house put into their joint names. He admitted in evidence that this was simply an "excuse". Similarly in *Grant v. Edwards* the female partner was told by the male partner that the only reason for not acquiring the property in joint names was because she was involved in divorce proceedings and that, if the property were acquired jointly, this might operate to her prejudice in those proceedings. As Nourse L.J. put it, at p. 649:

> "Just as in *Eves v. Eves* [1975] 1 W.L.R. 1338, these facts appear to me to raise a clear inference that there was an understanding between the plaintiff and the defendant, or a common intention, that the plaintiff was to have some sort of proprietary interest in the house: otherwise no excuse for not putting her name on to the title would have been needed."

The subsequent conduct of the female partner in each of these cases, which the court rightly held sufficient to give rise to a constructive trust or proprietary estoppel supporting her claim to an interest in the property, fell far short of such conduct as would by itself have supported the claim in the absence of an express representation by the male partner that she was to have such an interest. It is significant to note that the share to which the female partner in *Eves v. Eves* and *Grant v. Edwards* were held entitled were one quarter and one half respectively. In no sense could these shares have been regarded as proportionate to what the judge in the instant case described as a "qualifying contribution" in terms of the indirect contributions to the acquisition or enhancement of the value of the houses made by the female partners.

I cannot help thinking that the judge in the instant case would not have fallen into error if he had kept clearly in mind the distinction between the effect of evidence on the one hand which was capable of establishing an express agreement or an express representation that Mrs Rosset was to have an interest in the property and evidence on the other hand of conduct alone as a basis for an inference of the necessary common intention.

NOTES:

1. For comment, see (1990) 106 L.Q.R. 539; [1990] Conv. 314; [1991] C.L.J. 38; (1991) 54 M.L.R. 126; (1996) 16 *Legal Studies* 325; and see Moffat, *Trusts Law: Text and Materials* (2nd ed., 1994), pp. 432–480, especially at pp. 449–468.

2. Lord Bridge identifies and clearly distinguishes two alternative means by which the non-legal owner (the claimant) may establish a share in the equitable interest.

3. *Express agreement or arrangement*

(1) The court must find, on the basis of evidence of express discussions between the parties, that they had some agreement, arrangement or understanding that the claimant had acquired or would acquire an equitable interest. Such an agreement was found in *Eves v. Eves* [1975] 1 W.L.R. 1338 and in *Grant v. Edwards* [1986] Ch. 638 on the reasoning indicated by Lord Bridge, that the stated excuse for not transferring the legal estate into the joint names of the parties was unnecessary unless, and thus provided evidence that, the parties intended that they were both to acquire a share in the equitable interest. Although that reasoning has been criticised (see Clarke (1992) Fam. Law 72; Gardner (1993) 109 L.Q.R. 263, 265), the finding of an agreement in *Hammond v. Mitchell* [1991] 1 W.L.R. 1127 was based, at least in part, on similar reasoning. For comment, see [1992] Conv. 218, (1993) 56 M.L.R. 224. However, in *Lloyds Bank plc v. Rosset* Lord Bridge held that, even though there was the clearest understanding between the parties that the renovation of the house was a joint venture and that the house was subsequently to be occupied as a family home, that was not sufficient to constitute an agreement in respect of the (equitable) *ownership* of the house.

(2) The claimant must establish detrimental reliance on the express agreement. This requirement was held to be satisfied where the claimant had made substantial financial contributions to the household expenses (*Grant v. Edwards*); where the claimant had undertaken an abnormal level of manual labour in the house (*Eves v. Eves*); and where the claimant had agreed to postpone her (putative) interest in the house to the interest of the bank which had provided finance for her partner's business ventures and where she had fulfilled the role(s) of "mother/helper/unpaid assistant and at times financial supporter to the family prosperity" (*Hammond v. Mitchell*). However, the courts have not provided any formulation of the necessary "link" between the terms of the agreement and the conduct alleged to constitute the detrimental reliance. In *Grant v. Edwards* Browne-Wilkinson V.-C. posed (at 656), but did not answer, a number of questions:

Does there have to be positive evidence that the claimant did the acts in conscious reliance on the common intention? Does the court have to be satisfied that she would not have done the acts relied on but for the common intention, *e.g.* would not the claimant have contributed to the household expenses out of affection for the legal owner and as part of their joint life together even if she had no interest in the house? Do the acts relied on as detriment have to be inherently referable to the house, *e.g.* contribution to the purchase or physical labour on the house?

(3) Where there is express agreement on the issue of quantification, the agreement will conclusively determine the shares of the parties: *Savill v. Goodall* [1993] 1 F.L.R. 755; *Clough v. Killey* (1996) 72 P. & C.R. D22; but such cases are very much the exception. Otherwise, the courts appear to have a wide discretion to act fairly in the quantification of any share acquired through detrimental reliance on an express agreement: see *Grant v. Edwards, supra,* at 657 *per* Browne-Wilkinson V.-C. In particular, the share acquired by the claimant is not necessarily limited by the precise value of the financial

contributions; thus in *Eves v. Eves* the claimant was held to have acquired a quarter share; and in *Grant v. Edwards* and *Hammond v. Mitchell* the claimants were held to have acquired half shares.

(4) Lord Bridge stated that detrimental reliance on an express agreement gives rise to a constructive trust *or to a proprietary estoppel*. The substance of this assimilation was evident in the classic statement of Lord Diplock in *Gissing v. Gissing* [1971] A.C. 886 at 905:

A resulting, implied or constructive trust—and it is unnecessary for present purposes to distinguish between these three classes of trust—is created by a transaction between the trustee and the cestui que trust in connection with the acquisition by the trustee of a legal estate in land, whenever the trustee has so conducted himself that it would be inequitable to allow him to deny to the cestui que trust a beneficial interest in the land acquired. And he will be held so to have conducted himself if by his words or conduct he has induced the cestui que trust to act to his own detriment in the reasonable belief that by so acting he was acquiring a beneficial interest in the land.

And the assimilation was endorsed in express terms by Browne-Wilkinson V.-C. in *Grant v. Edwards*, where he stated (at 656):

I suggest that in other cases of this kind, useful guidance may in the future be obtained from the principles underlying the law of proprietary estoppel which in my judgment are closely akin to those laid down in *Gissing v. Gissing* [1971] A.C. 886. In both, the claimant must to the knowledge of the legal owner have acted in the belief that the claimant has or will obtain an interest in the property. In both, the claimant must have acted to his or her detriment in reliance on such belief. In both, equity acts on the conscience of the legal owner to prevent him from acting in an unconscionable manner by defeating the common intention. The two principles have been developed separately without cross-fertilisation between them; but they rest on the same foundation and have on all other matters reached the same conclusions.

On the other hand, the Court of Appeal has denied that the assimilation is complete: see *Stokes v. Anderson* [1991] 1 F.L.R. 391, 399 *per* Nourse L.J.; and see Lawson (1996) 16 *Legal Studies* 218.

For discussion of the doctrine of proprietary estoppel and its relationship with constructive trusts, see *post*, pp. 534. *et seq.*

4. *Inferred common intention*

(1) Where there is no evidence of an *express* agreement or arrangement that the claimant is to have a share in the equitable interest, the claimant must establish conduct (i) which provides the basis for inferring that the parties had an uncommunicated common intention that the claimant was to have a share in the equitable interest and (ii) which also constitutes the necessary detrimental reliance on the part of the claimant.

(2) According to Lord Bridge, he doubts whether this requirement is satisfied except by direct contributions to the purchase price of the land. That restriction seems to be inconsistent with the authorities, which have stated that *indirect* financial contributions are sufficient for the acquisition of an equitable interest, even in the absence of an express common intention

between the parties, provided that those contributions are *referable to the acquisition of the land*: see *Gissing v. Gissing* [1971] A.C. 886, 903 *per* Lord Pearson, 907–910 *per* Lord Diplock, *supra*. In *Burns v. Burns* [1984] Ch. 317 Fox L.J. summarised the position (at 328–329):

What is needed, I think, is evidence of a payment or payments . . . which it can be inferred was referable to the acquisition of the house. . . . If there is a substantial contribution to family expenses, and the house was purchased on a mortgage, [that] contribution is, indirectly, referable to the acquisition of the house since, in one way or another, it enables the family to pay the mortgage instalments. Thus, a payment could be said to be referable to the acquisition of the house if, for example, the payer either (a) pays part of the purchase price or (b) contributes regularly to the mortgage instalments or (c) pays off part of the mortgage *or (d) makes a substantial financial contribution to the family expenses so as to enable the mortgage instalments to be paid.* (Emphasis added.)

In *Burns v. Burns* the claimant relied upon non-substantial financial contributions to the household expenses, the performance of domestic work in the house and looking after the children of the relationship. The Court of Appeal held that none of those contributions, individually or collectively, was in the above terms referable to the acquisition of the house; and that there was therefore no basis for inferring the required common intention that she should have an equitable interest in the house. However, the restrictive statement of Lord Bridge in *Lloyds Bank plc v. Rosset* was applied by the Court of Appeal in *Ivin v. Blake* [1995] 1 F.L.R. 70, noted at [1996] Conv. 462.

(3) The cases reveal a wide range of approaches to the quantification of a share in the equitable ownership acquired pursuant to an inferred common intention. It is arguable that both the acquisition and the quantification of the shares should depend on an inferred common intention based on direct financial contributions. In *Springette v. Defoe* (1992) 65 P. & C.R. 1 (which the Court of Appeal treated as an orthodox resulting trust case) the quantification was determined strictly by reference to direct financial contributions; and in *Evans v. Hayward* [1995] 2 F.L.R. 511 the quantification was determined by reference to deemed direct financial contributions (*per* Dillon L.J.) or an inferred intention based on deemed direct financial contributions (*per* Staughton L.J.). However, even if the court is restricted to inferring a common intention from direct financial contributions, the quantification of qualifying contributions is by no means straightforward. For example, where the purchase of the land is financed in part by a mortgage loan, the question arises as to whether credit should be given on the basis of (i) the legal obligations of the parties under the mortgage, or (ii) any agreement between the parties as to the mortgage repayments, or (iii) the actual mortgage repayments: see *Huntingford v. Hobbs* [1993] 1 F.L.R. 736. If, on the other hand, the common intention as to the acquisition and/or the quantification of the shares can be inferred also from *indirect* financial contributions, the quantification of the share acquired by reason of such contributions becomes extremely complex and must almost inevitably be determined by what is fair in the circumstances: see *Gissing v. Gissing* [1971] A.C. 886, 909 *per* Lord Diplock; *Grant v. Edwards* [1986] Ch. 638, 657 *per*

Browne-Wilkinson V.-C. In some cases, the court has asserted that it has inferred that the parties intended their shares to be determined when the property was disposed of on the basis of what would be fair having regard to the total contributions, direct or indirect, which each party had made by that date: *Passee v. Passee* [1988] 1 F.L.R. 263; *Stokes v. Anderson* [1991] 1 F.L.R. 391. However, in two more recent cases, where the parties expressly stated that they had reached no agreement, the Court of Appeal was prepared to *impute* an intention as to quantification. In *Midland Bank plc v. Cooke* [1995] 4 All E.R. 562 the claimant was held to have made a direct financial contribution to the initial purchase price and thus to have acquired some share in the equitable ownership of the property. Turning to the issue of quantification Waite L.J. stated (at 574):

The general principle to be derived from *Gissing v. Gissing* and *Grant v. Edwards* can in my judgement be summarised in this way. When the court is proceeding in cases like the present where the partner without legal title has successfully asserted an equitable interest through direct contribution, to determine (in the absence of express evidence of intention) what proportions the parties must have intended for their beneficial ownership, the duty of the judge is to undertake a survey of the whole course of dealing between the parties relevant to their ownership and occupation of the property and their sharing of its burdens and advantages. That scrutiny will not confine itself to the limited range of acts or direct contribution of the sort needed to found a beneficial interest in the first place. It will take into consideration all conduct which throws light on the question what shares were intended. Only if that search proves inconclusive does the court fall back on the maxim "equity is equality".

... The court is not bound to deal with the matter on the strict basis of the trust resulting from the cash contribution to the purchase price, and is free to attribute to the parties an intention to share the beneficial interest in some different proportions.

For comment, see [1996] C.L.J. 194; (1996) 112 L.Q.R. 378; [1997] Conv. 66; (1997) 60 M.L.R. 420. In *Drake v. Whipp* [1996] 1 F.L.R. 826 the parties asserted that there had been no common intention and based their arguments on orthodox resulting trust principles. Notwithstanding, the Court of Appeal held that the evidence pointed to an inferred common intention; and, on the issue of quantification, the court adopted a broad approach similar to that in *Midland Bank plc v. Cooke*. For comment, see [1997] Conv. 467.

(4) Although there has been little consistency in the terminology adopted by the courts in this area over the last 30 years, the trust based on an inferred common intention and arising from (direct) financial contributions to the purchase price has generally been referred to as a resulting trust. However, the *Gissing v. Gissing* type of resulting trust imposed by the courts in family home cases seems to be distinguishable from the traditional or strict resulting trust explained above. While the latter has been imposed pursuant to an equitable presumption that a person who contributes to the purchase price of land intends to acquire an interest in that land (proportional to the value of the contribution), the former has been imposed on the basis of an actual (express or inferred) common intention to acquire an interest (not necessarily strictly proportional to the value of the contribution). On the other hand, in *Tinsley v. Milligan* [1994] 1 A.C. 340 Lord Browne-Wilkinson (at 371)

seemed prepared to accept that the *Gissing v. Gissing* type of trust is no more than a development of the old law of strict resulting trusts.

5. A husband or wife who makes a substantial contribution in money or money's worth to the improvement of land (or other property) in which either or both of them has an equitable interest may thereby acquire a share or an enlarged share in that equitable interest: Matrimonial Proceedings and Property Act 1970, s.37.

6. For a comprehensive "re-think" of family property, see Gardner (1993) 109 L.Q.R. 263; Moffat, *supra* note 4, pp. 468–480.

3. Adverse possession

Although title to land is normally acquired through documentary transfer from the existing title owner, it has been seen that title may be acquired (and the existing documentary title extinguished) through possession of the land: see *supra*, p. 24. The law relating to adverse possession and the limitation of actions seeks to regularise this phenomenon in a manner than balances the rights and expectations of the parties. In summary, the law specifies certain requirements as to the nature of the possession of the adverse possessor and it requires such possession to continue undisturbed for a specified period (generally 12 years). If, notwithstanding such adverse possession, the person with the existing (documentary) title fails to take action within the specified period to secure the eviction of the adverse possessor, he is barred from taking such action thereafter; he has no other means of asserting his title, which is therefore effectively extinguished; and the title of the adverse possessor becomes "impregnable, giving him a title superior to all others": *Buckinghamshire CC v. Moran* [1990] Ch. 623, 644 *per* Nourse L.J. See, generally, Dockray [1985] Conv. 272.

3.1 *The nature of adverse possession*

Buckinghamshire CC v. Moran [1990] Ch. 623

(CA, Slade, Nourse and Butler-Sloss L.JJ.)

In 1955 the plaintiff council purchased a plot of land. The land was intended for a proposed road diversion and was left undeveloped. In 1967 the predecessors in title of the defendant incorporated the plot into their adjoining property; and in 1971 the defendant purchased that property "together with ... all such rights estate title and interests as the vendors may have in or over [the plot]". The defendant continued to use the plot as part of his garden; and he prevented all means of access to the plot except through the garden. In correspondence with the plaintiff council in 1975, the defendant asserted his "firm understanding that the [plot] should be kept by the owner of the [adjoining property] if and until [the proposed road diversion was built]". In 1985 the plaintiff council brought proceedings to recover possession of the plot. Hoffman J. and the Court of Appeal held that the defendant had acquired title to the plot by adverse possession.

SLADE L.J.:
Section 15(1) of the Limitation Act 1980 provides:

> "No action shall be brought by any person to recover any land after the expiration of 12 years from the date on which the right of action accrued to him or, if it first accrued to some person through whom he claims, to that person."

Subject to certain irrelevant exceptions, section 17 of the Act of 1980 provides for the extinction of a person's title to land after the expiration of the relevant time limit.

As is stated in section 15(6), Part I of Schedule 1 to the Act of 1980 contains provisions for determining the date of accrual of rights of action to recover land in the cases there mentioned. Paragraph 1 of Schedule 1 provides:

> "Where the person bringing an action to recover land, or some person through whom he claims, has been in possession of the land, and has while entitled to the land been dispossessed or discontinued his possession, the right of action shall be treated as having accrued on the date of the dispossession or discontinuance."

It is clear that, under the Act of 1980 as under the previous law, the person claiming a possessory title must show either (1) discontinuance by the paper owner followed by possession, or (2) dispossession (or, as it is sometimes called "ouster") of the paper owner: compare *Treloar v. Nute* [1976] 1 W.L.R. 1295, 1300,

> "the difference between the dispossession and the discontinuance of possession might be expressed in this way—the one is where a person comes in and drives out the others from possession, the other case is where the person in possession goes out and is followed into possession by other persons: see *per* Fry J. in *Rains v. Buxton* (1880) 14 Ch.D. 537, 539–540."

In the present case the judge found that the council had never discontinued its possession of the plot, and this finding is not challenged on this appeal. The defendant's claim is that the council had been dispossessed of the plot by him more than 12 years before it instituted its proceedings.

If the law is to attribute possession of land to a person who can establish no paper title to possession, he must be shown to have both factual possession and the requisite intention to possess (animus possidendi). A person claiming to have "dispossessed" another must similarly fulfil both these requirements. However, a further requirement which the alleged dispossessor claiming the benefit of the Act of 1980 must satisfy is to show that his possession has been "adverse" within the meaning of the Act. Paragraph 8(1) of Schedule 1 defines "adverse possession" as follows:

> "No right of action to recover land shall be treated as accruing unless the land is in the possession of some person in whose favour the period of limitation can run (referred to below in this paragraph as 'adverse possession'); and where under the preceding provisions of this Schedule any such right of action is treated as accruing on a certain date and no person is in adverse possession on that date, the right of action shall not be treated as accruing unless and until adverse possession is taken of the land."

Paragraph 8(2) of Schedule 1 provides:

> "Where a right of action to recover land has accrued and after its accrual, before the right is barred, the land ceases to be in adverse possession, the right of action shall no longer be treated as having accrued and no fresh right of action shall be treated as accruing unless and until the land is again taken into adverse possession."

On this appeal Mr Douglas, on behalf of the council, has accepted that if the plot was in adverse possession of the defendant more than 12 years before action was brought (i.e., on 28 October 1973) it has not ceased to be in adverse possession since that time. Ultimately, therefore, the crucial question will be: was the defendant in adverse possession of the plot on 28 October 1973?

Possession is never "adverse" within the meaning of the Act of 1980 if it is enjoyed under a lawful title. If, therefore, a person occupies or uses land by licence of the owner with the paper title and his licence has not been duly determined, he cannot be treated as having been in "adverse possession" as against the owner with the paper title.

Before the passing of the Act of 1980, certain decisions of this court (in particular *Wallis's Cayton Bay Holiday Camp Ltd v. Shell-Mex and B.P. Ltd* [1975] Q.B. 94 and *Gray v. Wykeham Martin & Goode* (unreported), 17 January 1977; Court of Appeal (Civil Division) Transcript No. 10A of 1977) were thought to have established a general doctrine that in one special type of case there would be implied in favour of the would be adverse possessor, *without any specific factual basis for such implication*, a licence permitting him to commit the acts of possession upon which he sought to rely; the effect of implying such a licence would, of course, be to prevent the squatter's possession from being "adverse". That special type of case was broadly one where the acts of an intruder, however continuous and far-reaching, did not substantially interfere with any plans which the owners might have for the further use of undeveloped land.

The doctrine of implied licence, in my view, raised substantial conceptual difficulties as a matter of law for reasons which I stated in *Powell v. McFarlane* (1979) 38 P. & C.R. 452, 484, where I said:

"I do not find it easy to see how the words 'possession' or 'dispossess' can properly be given anything but their ordinary meaning in the context of the Act of 1939 and I doubt whether this has been done in any decisions before the *Wallis* case. I am not sure how one can justify the imputation of an implied or hypothetical licence for the purpose of applying or defeating the provisions of that Act in circumstances where the facts would not admit the imputation of a licence for any other purposes."

The doctrine has now been abrogated by paragraph 8(4) of Schedule 1 to the Act of 1980 which provides:

"For the purpose of determining whether a person occupying any land is in adverse possession of the land it shall not be assumed by implication of law that his occupation is by permission of the person entitled to the land merely by virtue of the fact that his occupation is not inconsistent with the latter's present or future enjoyment of the land. This provision shall not be taken as prejudicing a finding to the effect that a person's occupation of any land is by implied permission of the person entitled to the land in any case where such a finding is justified on the actual facts of the case."

In the light of this provision, it would at first sight appear that there is now no reason why the words "possess" and "dispossess" or similar expressions should not be given their ordinary legal meaning in the context of the Act of 1980. However, Mr Douglas, on behalf of the council, while accepting that the implied licence doctrine is now abrogated, nevertheless submits that paragraph 8(1) (I quote from his skeleton argument):

"leaves intact the special rule formulated by Bramwell L.J. in *Leigh v. Jack* (1879) 5 Ex.D. 264 and Sir John Pennycuick in *Treloar v. Nute* [1976] 1 W.L.R. 1295 that where land is acquired or retained by the owner for a specific future purpose, then acts of trespass which are not inconsistent with such purpose do not amount to dispossession."

The origin of the suggested "special rule" is said to be the often cited statement of Bramwell L.J. in *Leigh v. Jack* (1879) 5 Ex.D. 264, 273, where he said:

> "in order to defeat a title by dispossessing the former owner, acts must be done which are inconsistent with his enjoyment of the soil for the purposes for which he intended to use it: that is not the case here, where the intention of the plaintiff and her predecessors in title was not either to build upon or to cultivate the land, but to devote it at some future time to public purposes."

Superficial support for the existence of the "special rule" is to be found in a passage in the judgment of this court delivered by Sir John Pennycuick in *Treloar v. Nute* [1976] 1 W.L.R. 1295, 1300–1301, where he said:

> "The literal application of the statutory provisions has been adapted by this court to meet one special type of case. It sometimes happens that the owner of a piece of land retains it with a view to its utilisation for some specific purpose in the future and that meanwhile some other person has physical possession of it. When that state of affairs exists, the owner is not treated as dispossessed: see *Leigh v. Jack* (1879) 5 Ex.D. 264, where factory materials were placed upon a strip of land intended by the owner to be dedicated as a road ..."

Sir John Pennycuick went on to refer to the judgment of Cockburn C.J. in *Leigh v. Jack* (1879) 5 Ex.D. 264, 271, and cited the passage from Bramwell L.J.'s judgment, at p. 273, cited above. He also referred very briefly to the decision of this court in *Williams Brothers Direct Supply Ltd v. Raftery* [1958] 1 Q.B. 159.

All the observations of Sir John Pennycuick in *Treloar v. Nute* [1976] 1 W.L.R. 1295, to which I have referred, were obiter because they were made in the absence of any evidence of "special purpose" on the part of the plaintiff: see p. 1302E. The court below had found that the defendant's father took possession of the disputed land outside the limitation period, but that this possession was not adverse by reason that it caused no inconvenience to the plaintiff. The actual decision of this court was that, in the absence of any evidence of special purpose, the absence of inconvenience to the plaintiff was an irrelevant consideration, and that time began from the taking of possession by the father, whether or not the plaintiff suffered inconvenience from such possession.

The other members of this court in *Treloar v. Nute* were Ormrod L.J., who had been one of the majority in *Wallis's* case [1975] Q.B. 94, in which Lord Denning M.R. had introduced the doctrine of implied licence, and Stamp L.J., who had dissented in that case. In giving judgment, the court [1976] 1 W.L.R. 1295, 1302F, referred to the considerable disadvantage which it had suffered from the absence of any legal argument on behalf of the appellant. It was faced with a further difficulty that the ratio of the majority decision in *Wallis's* case, so far as that ratio extended, was binding on it, since the Act of 1980 had not been passed. I respectfully agree with the actual decision in *Treloar v. Nute*, but respectfully disagree with the obiter dicta to which I have referred.

On any footing, it must, in my judgment, be too broad a proposition to suggest that an owner who retains a piece of land with a view to its utilisation for a specific purpose in the future can never be treated as dispossessed, however firm and obvious the intention to dispossess, and however drastic the acts of dispossession of the person seeking to dispossess him may be. Furthermore, while it may well be correct to say that the implied licence doctrine (so long as it survived) itself involved the "adaptation" of the literal application of the statutory provisions "to meet one special type of case", I do not think it correct to suggest that the decisions in *Leigh v. Jack* (1879) 5 Ex.D. 264 or *Williams Brothers Direct Supply Ltd v. Raftery* [1958] 1 Q.B. 159 (or indeed any other decisions prior to *Wallis's* case [1975] Q.B. 94) authorise or justify an application of the statutory provisions otherwise than in accordance with their ordinary and natural meaning.

In the course of my judgment in *Powell v. McFarlane* (1979) 38 P. & C.R. 452, 472–474, I considered in some detail the decisions in *Leigh v. Jack* and *Williams Brothers Direct Supply Ltd v. Raftery* and *Tecbild Ltd v. Chamberlain* (1969) 20 P. & C.R. 633. I do not propose to embark on a similar analysis in this judgment, but would venture to repeat certain conclusions about these cases which I expressed, at pp. 484–485:

> "I incline to the view that the ratio decidendi of all the various judgments in cases such as *Leigh v. Jack*, the *Williams* case and *Tecbild Ltd v. Chamberlain* was either (a) that the necessary animus possidendi had not been shown or (b) that the acts relied on had been too trivial to amount to the taking of actual possession; some members of each court seem to have relied on the first ground and others on the second. I venture to think that all these three decisions are readily explicable, not so much on the basis of any imputed licence, but merely on the grounds that in circumstances where an owner has no present use for his land but has future plans for its use (for example by development or by dedication to the public as a highway), then the court will, on the facts, readily treat a trespasser, whose acts have not been inconsistent with such future plans, as having not manifested the requisite animus possidendi or alternatively, as not having acquired a sufficient degree of exclusive occupation to constitute possession."

On re-reading the relevant authorities, the view to which I then inclined has become a firm one. The statement of Bramwell L.J. in *Leigh v. Jack* (1879) 5 Ex.D. 264, 273, on which so much reliance has been placed on this appeal was made in the context of a case in which, it would appear, the defendant would have had knowledge of the intention of the owner to dedicate it to the public as a highway. (It was marked as a street on a plan of his estate, which he hung up in his estate office and this fact was presumably common knowledge among those interested in the property.) If in any given case the land in dispute is unbuilt land and the squatter is aware that the owner, while having no present use for it, has a purpose in mind for its use in the future, the court is likely to require very clear evidence before it can be satisfied that the squatter who claims a possessory title has not only established factual possession of the land, but also the requisite intention to exclude the world at large, including the owner with the paper title, so far as is reasonably practicable and so far as the processes of the law will allow. In the absence of clear evidence of this nature, the court is likely to infer that the squatter neither had had nor had claimed any intention of asserting a right to the possession of the land.

I agree entirely with the following passage from the dissenting judgment of Stamp L.J. in *Wallis's* case [1975] Q.B. 94, 109–110:

> "Reading the judgments in *Leigh v. Jack* ... and *Williams Brothers Direct Supply Ltd v. Raftery* [1958] 1 Q.B. 159, I conclude that they establish that in order to determine whether the acts of user do or do not amount to dispossession of the owner the character of the land, the nature of the acts done upon it and the intention of the squatter fall to be considered. Where the land is waste land and the true owner cannot and does not for the time being use it for the purpose for which he acquired it, one may more readily conclude that the acts done on the waste land do not amount to dispossession of the owner. But I find it impossible to regard those cases as establishing that so long as the true owner cannot use his land for the purpose for which he acquired it the acts done by the squatter do not amount to possession of the land. One must look at the facts and circumstances and determine whether what has been done in relation to the land constitutes possession."

In the present case, the defendant was well aware that the council had acquired the plot in order to construct a road on it at some time in the future and meantime had no present use for the land. This factor, which Mr Douglas naturally stressed in the course of his argument, should make the court the more cautious before holding that the defendant had had both a factual possession and animus possidendi sufficient to confer on him a possessory title. Nevertheless, every *Leigh v. Jack* type of case such as this must involve questions of fact and degree. I would, for my part, reject the submission that since the Act of 1980 there remains any "special rule" which requires the words "possessed" and "dispossessed" or similar words to be given anything other than their natural and ordinary meaning in the *Leigh v. Jack* type of case.

Thus far, therefore, I conclude that (1) if by 28 October 1973 the defendant had taken possession of the plot, his possession must have been adverse to the council; (2) the question whether or not the defendant had taken possession of the plot by 28 October 1973 falls to be decided by reference to conventional concepts of possession and dispossession and not by departing from the ordinary and natural meaning of the relevant statutory provisions merely because this is a *Leigh v. Jack* type of case.

I turn then to consider the first of the two requisite elements of possession. First, as at 28 October 1973 did the defendant have factual possession of the plot? I venture to repeat what I said in *Powell v. McFarlane* (1979) 38 P. & C.R. 452, 470–471:

> "Factual possession signifies an appropriate degree of physical control. It must be a single and [exclusive] possession ... Thus an owner of land and a person intruding on that land without his consent cannot both be in possession of the land at the same time. The question what acts constitute a sufficient degree of exclusive physical control must depend on the circumstances, in particular the nature of the land and the manner in which land of that nature is commonly used or enjoyed."

On the evidence it would appear clear that by 28 October 1973 the defendant had acquired complete and exclusive physical control of the plot. He had secured a complete enclosure of the plot and its annexation to Dolphin Place. Any intruder could have gained access to the plot only by way of Dolphin Place, unless he was prepared to climb the locked gate fronting the highway or to scramble through one or other of the hedges bordering the plot. The defendant had put a new lock and chain on the gate and had fastened it. He and his mother had been dealing with the plot as any occupying owners might have been expected to deal with it. They had incorporated it into the garden of Dolphin Place. They had planted bulbs and daffodils in the grass. They had maintained it as part of that garden and had trimmed the hedges. I cannot accept Mr Douglas's submission that the defendant's acts of possession were trivial. It is hard to see what more he could have done to acquire complete physical control of the plot by October 1973. In my judgment, he had plainly acquired factual possession of the plot by that time.

However, as the judge said, the more difficult question is whether the defendant had the necessary animus possidendi. As to this, Mr Douglas accepted the correctness of the following statement (so far as it went) which I made in *Powell v. McFarlane* (1979) 38 P. & C.R. 452, 471–472:

> "the animus possidendi involves the intention, in one's own name and on one's own behalf, to exclude the world at large, including the owner with the paper title if he be not himself the possessor, so far as is reasonably practicable and so far as the process of the law will allow."

At least at first sight the following observations of Lord Halsbury L.C. in *Marshall v. Taylor* [1895] 1 Ch. 641, 645, which were referred to by Hoffmann J. in his judgment, are very pertinent to the present case:

> "The true nature of this particular strip of land is that it is enclosed. It cannot be denied that the person who now says he owns it could not get to it in any ordinary way. I do not deny that he could have crept through the hedge, or, if it had been a brick wall, that he could have climbed over the wall; but that was not the ordinary and usual mode of access. That is the exclusion—the dispossession—which seems to me to be so important in this case."

As a number of authorities indicate, enclosure by itself prima facie indicates the requisite animus possidendi. As Cockburn C.J. said in *Seddon v. Smith* (1877) 36 L.T. 168, 169: "Enclosure is the strongest possible evidence of adverse possession". Russell L.J. in *George Wimpey & Co. Ltd v. Sohn* [1967] Ch. 487, 511A, similarly observed: "Ordinarily, of course, enclosure is the most cogent evidence of adverse possession and of dispossession of the true owner". While Mr Douglas pointed out that the plot was always accessible from the north where no boundary demarcation existed, it was only accessible from the defendant's own property, Dolphin Place. In my judgment, therefore, he must be treated as having enclosed it.

Mr Douglas, however, submitted that even if enclosure had occurred, the defendant's intention must be assessed in the light of the particular circumstances of this case. The defendant knew that the council had acquired and retained the plot with the specific intention of building a road across it at some future time. The council had no use for the land in the interim. It was for all practical purposes waste land. None of the defendant's acts, he submitted, were inconsistent with the council's known future intentions. He invoked, inter alia, the words of Cockburn C.J. in *Leigh v. Jack* (1879) 5 Ex.D. 264, 271, which he submitted, applied in the present case:

> "I do not think that any of the defendant's acts were done with the view of defeating the purposes of the parties to the conveyances; his acts were those of a man who did not intend to be a trespasser, or to infringe upon another's right. The defendant simply used the land until the time should come for carrying out the object originally contemplated."

If the defendant had stopped short of placing a new lock and chain on the gate, I might perhaps have felt able to accept these submissions. Mr Douglas submitted that this act did not unequivocally show an intention to exclude the council as well as other people. (It is well established that it is no use for an alleged adverse possessor to rely on acts which are merely equivocal as regards the intention to exclude the true owner: see for example *Tecbild Ltd v. Chamberlain* (1969) 20 P. & C.R. 633, 642, *per* Sachs L.J.) In my judgment, however, the placing of the new lock and chain and gate did amount to a final unequivocal demonstration of the defendant's intention to possess the land. I agree with the judge in his saying (1988) 86 L.G.R. 472, 479:

> "... I do not think that if the council, on making an inspection, had found the gate newly padlocked, they could have come to any conclusion other than that [the defendant] was intending to exclude everyone, including themselves, from the land."

The other main point which Mr Douglas has argued in support of this appeal has caused me slightly more difficulty. In his submission there can be no sufficient animus possidendi to constitute adverse possession for the purpose of the Act of 1980 unless there exists the intention to exclude the owner with the paper title in *all* future circumstances. The defendant's oral statements to Mr Harris in the conversation of 10 November 1975, as recorded in the attendance note, do appear to have constituted an implicit acknowledgement by the defendant that he would be obliged to leave the plot if in the future the council required it for the purpose of constructing the proposed new road. The letter of 18 December 1975, which I have concluded should be admitted in evidence, contains an express acknowledgement of this nature. If the intention to exclude the owner with the paper title in all future circumstances is a necessary constituent of the animus possidendi, the attendance note and the letter of 18 December 1975 show that this constituent was absent in the present case.

There are some dicta in the authorities which might be read as suggesting that an intention to *own* the land is required. Sir Nathaniel Lindley M.R., for example, in *Littledale v. Liverpool College* [1900] 1 Ch. 19, 23, referred to the "acts of ownership" relied upon by the plaintiffs. Russell L.J. in *George Wimpey & Co. Ltd v. Sohn* [1967] Ch. 487, 510, said:

"... I am not satisfied that the actions of the predecessors in bricking up the doorway and maintaining a lock on the gate to the roadway were necessarily referable to an intention to occupy the [land] as their own absolute property."

At one point in my judgment in *Powell v. McFarlane* (1979) 38 P. & C.R. 452, 478, I suggested:

"any objective informed observer might probably have inferred that the plaintiff was using the land simply for the benefit of his family's cow or cows, during such periods as the absent owner took no steps to stop him, without any intention to appropriate the land as his own."

Nevertheless, I agree with the judge that "what is required for this purpose is not an intention to own or even an intention to acquire ownership but an intention to possess"—that is to say, an intention for the time being to possess the land to the exclusion of all other persons, including the owner with the paper title. No authorities cited to us establish the contrary proposition. The conversation with Mr Harris, as recorded in the attendance note and the letter of 18 December 1975, to my mind demonstrate the intention of the defendant for the time being to continue in possession of the plot to the exclusion of the council unless and until the proposed by-pass is built. The form of the conveyance to the defendant and of the contemporaneous statutory declaration which he obtained from Mr and Mrs Wall, are, of course entirely consistent with the existence of an intention on his part to take and keep adverse possession of the plot, at least unless and until that event occurred.

In the light of the line of authorities to which we have been referred, beginning with *Leigh v. Jack* (1879) 5 Ex.D. 264, I have already accepted that the court should be slow to make a finding of adverse possession in a case such as the present. However, as the judge pointed out, in none of those earlier cases, where the owner with the paper title successfully defended his title, was there present the significant feature of complete enclosure of the land in question by the trespasser. On the evidence in the present case he was, in my judgment, right in concluding that the defendant had acquired adverse possession of the plot by 28 October 1973 and had remained in adverse possession of it ever since. There is no evidence that any representative of the council has even set foot on the plot since that date.

This appeal, which has been well argued on both sides, should in my judgment be dismissed.

NOURSE L.J.:

I agree. I add some views of my own on the substantive issue. Under most systems of law a squatter who has been in long possession of land can acquire title to it in the place of the true owner. The Scots and continental systems, more faithful to the Roman law, have opted for prescription, a doctrine founded on the fiction that the land has been granted to the squatter. In England, prescription, although a shoot well favoured by the common law, was stunted in its lateral growth by the statutes of limitation, being confined in its maturity to the acquisition of easements and profits à prendre over another's land. Limitation, so far from being founded on some fictional grant, extinguishes the right of the true owner to recover the land, so that the squatter's possession becomes impregnable, giving him a title superior to all others.

The essential difference between prescription and limitation is that in the former case title can be acquired only by possession as of right. That is the antithesis of what is required for limitation, which perhaps can be described as possession as of wrong. It can readily be understood that with prescription the intention of the true owner may be of decisive importance, it being impossible to presume a grant by someone whose intention is shown to have been against it. But with limitation it is the intention of the squatter which is decisive. He must intend to possess the land to the exclusion of all the world, including the true owner, while the intention of the latter is, with one exception, entirely beside the point.

In order that title to land may be acquired by limitation, (1) the true owner must either (a) have been dispossessed, or (b) have discontinued his possession, of the land; and (2) the squatter must have been in adverse possession of it for the statutory period before action is brought. Adopting the distinction between dispossession and discontinuance which was suggested by Fry J. in *Rains v. Buxton* (1880) 14 Ch.D. 537, 539, I take the first case to be one where the squatter comes in and drives out the true owner from possession and the second to be one where the true owner goes out of possession and is followed in by the squatter. In the light of that distinction, a very fine one, it is sometimes said that the intention of the true owner may be material in this way. If he intends to use the land for a particular purpose at some future date, a discontinuance of possession can be prevented by the slightest acts of ownership on his part, even by none at all. That no doubt is perfectly correct, but nothing follows from it except that the case becomes one where the true owner must be dispossessed before his title can be lost. He can only be dispossessed if the squatter performs sufficient acts and has a sufficient intention to constitute adverse possession. Those acts and that intention are no different from those which are required in a case of discontinuance, there being no practical distinction between what is necessary to exclude all the world in a case where the true owner has retained possession and in one where he has discontinued it.

By this route I have come to a belief that the intention of the true owner, although it may have some influence in theory, is irrelevant in practice. To that I would make one exception. If an intention on the part of the true owner to use the land for a particular purpose at some future date is known to the squatter, then his knowledge may affect the quality of his own intention, reducing it below that which is required to constitute adverse possession. To say that is only to emphasise that it is adverse possession on which everything depends. I think it very doubtful whether the distinction between dispossession and a discontinuance of possession can ever have decisive consequences, a consideration which is perhaps confirmed by the confusion between them which is found in some of the decided cases.

For over a hundred years the leading case on adverse possession in English law has been the decision of this court in *Leigh v. Jack* (1879) 5 Ex.D. 264, where Bramwell L.J. said, at p. 273:

> "I do not think that there was any dispossession of the plaintiff by the acts of the defendant: acts of user are not enough to take the soil out of the plaintiff and her predecessors in title and to vest it in the defendant; in order to defeat a title by dispossessing the former owner, acts must be done which are inconsistent with his enjoyment of the soil for the purposes for which he intended to use it: that is not the case here, where the intention of the plaintiff and her predecessors in title was not either to build upon or to cultivate the land, but to devote it at some future time to public purposes."

These observations suppose that the intention of the true owner may, in the circumstances stated, defeat what would, without the intention, constitute adverse possession. They would, for example, allow a true owner to recover land, even against a squatter who had enclosed it for a garden with the intention of excluding all the world, by claiming that that use was not inconsistent with the future residential development which he had always intended.

For the reasons already expressed, I cannot accept Bramwell L.J.'s observations to have been a correct statement of the law. Moreover, the decision in *Leigh v. Jack* can be satisfactorily explained on the grounds that there was no enclosure of the land by the defendant, that his acts of possession were trivial and, more significantly, that his knowledge of the plaintiff's intention prevented him from having a sufficient intention himself. . . .

In *Williams Brothers Direct Supply Ltd v. Raftery* [1958] 1 Q.B. 159, 169, Hodson L.J. rejected a submission by counsel that in *Leigh v. Jack*:

"... Bramwell L.J. was striking out on his own, unsupported by the other members of the court, when he spoke of acts having to be done inconsistent with the enjoyment of the soil for the purposes for which the plaintiff intended to use it."

For myself, I respectfully think that the submission was correct. However, it is not clear how far Hodson L.J. or the other members of the court (Morris and Sellers L.JJ.) relied on Bramwell L.J.'s dictum for the purpose of making a decision in that case. Again it can be satisfactorily explained on the grounds that there was no enclosure of the land, that the defendant's acts of possession were trivial and that he did not have a sufficient animus possidendi.

The decision in *Williams Brothers Direct Supply Ltd v. Raftery* was given at a time when many plots of waste land had been brought under the spade in digging for victory during the Second World War and afterwards. The problem was a very familiar one and this court's endorsement of Bramwell L.J.'s dictum gave county court judges all round the country a simple and straightforward basis for rejecting unmeritorious claims to squatters' titles, even, we may be sure, where the land had been enclosed. By 1976 the dictum had assumed the dignity of a special rule, although it was recognised by this court that it carried with it an adaptation of the literal application of the statutory provisions in order to meet a special type of case: see *Treloar v. Nute* [1976] 1 W.L.R. 1295, 1300. Before that, it had been effectively rejected in the dissenting judgment of Stamp L.J. in *Wallis's Cayton Bay Holiday Camp Ltd v. Shell-Mex and B.P. Ltd* [1975] Q.B. 94, 109–110, a case in which Lord Denning M.R. propounded an original heresy of his own, the implied licence theory. That has now been put to rest by paragraph 8(4) of Schedule 1 to the Limitation Act 1980, a provision which did not have any wider effect. The argument of Mr Douglas on behalf of the council has shown us that the dictum of Bramwell L.J. rides on.

The whole of this troubled subject was carefully considered by Slade J. in *Powell v. McFarlane* (1979) 38 P. & C.R. 452. In my opinion that judgment accurately stated the law in all material respects and I speak from my own experience in saying that it has consistently been treated as having done so. There can be no doubt that the view of the difficult cases from *Leigh v. Jack* (1879) 5 Ex.D. 264 onwards to which Slade J. inclined, at pp. 484–485, is correct. Those authorities can be satisfactorily explained on conventional grounds without reliance on the dictum of Bramwell L.J. We should now say that it must no longer be followed, so that the decision of these cases can be returned to the paths of orthodoxy, without, I am confident, any increase in the success rate amongst unmeritorious claims.

For these reasons I am of the opinion that Hoffmann J. was right to approach this case, albeit that it is in the classical *Leigh v. Jack* mould, by looking no further than the principles stated in *Powell v. McFarlane*. He correctly applied those principles to the facts which he found. I would affirm his decision accordingly. On this part of the case I do not wish to add anything to the judgment of Slade L.J., with which I am in complete agreement.

NOTES:

1. For comment, see [1988] Conv. 359; [1989] Conv. 211; [1990] C.L.J. 23. See also Jackson (1980) 96 L.Q.R. 333; Dockray [1982] Conv. 256, 345.

2. The requirement of factual possession is normally satisfied by dispossession on the part of the adverse possessor. The alternative requirement of discontinuance of possession by the documentary owner (followed by adverse possession) is readily found to have been negatived by "the slightest acts done by or on behalf of" the documentary owner. For instances of established discontinuance, see *Red House Farms (Thorndon) Ltd v. Catchpole*

[1977] 2 E.G.L.R. 125; *Hounslow LBC v. Minchinton* (1997) 74 P. & C.R. 221.

3. There can be no adverse possession by a person in possession of land pursuant to the grant of a lease or licence: *Colchester BC v. Smith* [1991] Ch. 448, 464, 489 *per* Ferris J., noted at [1991] C.L.J. 234; [1991] Conv. 397; [1992] C.L.J. 420; but, on the expiry of the lease/licence, the leaseholder/licensee may become an adverse possessor: *ibid.* However, in *B.P. Properties Ltd v. Buckler* (1987) 55 P. & C.R. 337 the Court of Appeal held that adverse possession ceased to be "adverse" where the documentary owner gave the adverse possessor unsolicited permission to remain in possession: *ibid.* 345–347 *per* Dillon L.J. For criticism that the decision is inconsistent with the general tenor of the law of adverse possession, see Wallace [1994] Conv. 196. Adverse possession may also cease to be adverse if the adverse possessor acknowledges by signed writing the claim of the documentary owner (Limitation Act 1980, s.29); or if the documentary owner obtains (even if he does not enforce) an order for possession against the adverse possessor: *B.P. Properties Ltd v. Buckler, supra,* 344–345 *per* Dillon L.J.; but a mere demand for possession is not sufficient: *Mount Carmel Investments Ltd v. Peter Thurlow Ltd* [1988] 1 W.L.R. 1078, 1085–1086 *per* Nicholls L.J. Where adverse possession ceases to be adverse, any subsequent dispossession will be a new adverse possession for which the limitation period will begin to run again.

4. In *Prudential Assurance Co. Ltd v. Waterloo Real Estate Inc* [1999] 17 E.G. 131 the Court of Appeal stressed the requirement that, where a claimant seeks to rely on his conduct to establish the necessary intention to possess the land, that conduct has to be unequivocal in the sense that the intention to possess to the exclusion of the documentary owner has been made plain to the world.

5. Although adverse possessors are sometimes referred to as "squatters", that expression is frequently understood to mean persons who take possession of land as a hostile act of protest. In practice, adverse possession by such persons rarely continues long enough to extinguish the title of the person dispossessed. Far more common are situations where adverse possession is taken knowingly but without any "hostile intent": see, *e.g. Buckinghamshire CC v. Moran*; or where adverse possession is consequent upon defective conveyancing or is otherwise innocent.

6. Justifications for the recognition of adverse possession (and the law of limitation) as a basis of entitlement to land tend to be more or less persuasive according to the circumstances. Justifications include the protection of factual possession against stale claims and the encouragement to documentary owners to assert their rights; the concurrence of documentary ownership and the reality of possession; and the facilitation of conveyancing, in particular the investigation and acquisition of title. However, as the Law Commission has argued, while the last consideration may be regarded as the strongest justification for adverse possession, it normally has no application to registered land. The Law Commission has therefore provisionally recommended

fundamental reform of the law on adverse possession as it relates to registered land: see *infra*, p. 101.

3.2 *Limitation of actions*

3.2.1 *Adverse possession against the freehold owner*

3.2.1.1 *Unregistered land* In the case of unregistered land, the effect of section 17 of the Limitation Act 1980 is to extinguish the title of the dispossessed owner: *Tichborne v. Weir* (1892) 67 L.T. 735, 736–737 *per* Kay L.J.; and to create a new title in the adverse possessor. There is no "Parliamentary conveyance" of the former title: *ibid.; Fairweather v. St Marylebone Property Co. Ltd* [1963] A.C. 510, 535 *per* Lord Radcliffe. However, the new title remains subject to third party rights affecting the land, since the Act operates to extinguish only the rights of those persons who were entitled but failed to assert their ownership rights. Moreover, an adverse possessor cannot claim to be a bona fide *purchaser*: see *Re Nisbet and Potts' Contract* [1906] 1 Ch. 386, 402–403 *per* Collins M.R., *supra*, p. 35.

Where a leaseholder has adversely possessed land other than the land comprised in the lease, there is a (rebuttable) presumption that he has done so on behalf of his freeholder and not for his own benefit so that, on the termination of the lease, the freeholder becomes owner of the land acquired by adverse possession: *Kingsmill v. Millard* (1855) 11 Exch. 313; *Long v. Tower Hamlets LBC* [1998] Ch. 197, 203–204 *per* James Munby Q.C. However, it appears that the presumption does not apply where the adversely possessed land is too remote from the land comprised in the lease: *Smirk v. Lyndale Developments Ltd* [1975] Ch. 317, 328 *per* Pennycuick V.-C.

3.2.1.2 *Registered land* According to section 75(1) of the Land Registration Act 1925, the Limitation Act 1980 applies to registered land "in the same manner and to the same extent" as it applies to unregistered land. However, in the case of registered land, the registered title of the dispossessed owner is not automatically extinguished at the end of the limitation period: the dispossessed owner holds the title on trust for the adverse possessor until the adverse possessor is registered as proprietor.

The precise effect of the trust imposed by section 75(1) of the Land Registration Act 1925 is uncertain. The section does not make clear the relationship between the title of the registered proprietor and the distinct possessory title of the adverse possessor, in particular whether the adverse possessor is subsequently registered as proprietor of the former title or his possessory title. The wording of section 75 would seem to favour the former view and the "Parliamentary conveyance" theory of adverse possession: and see *Spectrum Investment Co. v. Holmes* [1981] 1 W.L.R. 221, 230 *per* Browne-Wilkinson J.; *Central London Commercial Estates Ltd v. Kato Kaguka Ltd* [1998] 4 All E.R. 948, *infra*, p. 92. On the other hand, in *Fairweather v. St Marylebone Property Co. Ltd* [1963] A.C. 510, 542, Lord Radcliffe seemed to favour the latter view. However, there has been a more general tendency on the part of the courts to treat the section 75(1) trust as no more than machinery to apply the Limitation Acts to registered land: see *Fairweather v. St Marylebone Property Co. Ltd, supra,* 548 *per* Lord Denning; *Jessamine Investment Co. v. Schwartz* [1978] Q.B. 264, 275 *per* Sir John Pennycuick; *Mount Carmel Investments Ltd v. Peter Thurlow Ltd* [1988] 1 W.L.R. 1078, 1089 *per* Nicholls L.J.; and on this basis the Law Commission has suggested that the trust should be treated as denoting nothing more than an obligation on the part of the registered proprietor to give effect to the rights of the adverse possessor and submit to that person's registration as proprietor: Law Com. No. 254, *Land Registration for the Twenty-First Century* (1998), para. 10.34.

For discussion, see Wade (1962) 78 L.Q.R. 541; Cooke (1994) 14 *Legal Studies* 1; Law Com. No. 254, *Land Registration for the Twenty-First Century* (1998), paras 10.27–10.34.

3.2.2 *Adverse possession against the leasehold owner*

3.2.2.1 *Unregistered land*   Adverse possession against a leasehold owner extinguishes the title of the leasehold owner *as against the adverse possessor*. On the other hand, the leasehold title continues *as against the freehold owner*; and the right of the freehold owner to take action to recover the land from the adverse possessor does not accrue (and the limitation period in respect of any adverse possession against the freehold owner does not begin to run) until the expiry of the agreed term of the lease: Limitation Act 1980, s.15(1),(6), Sched. 1, para. 4; *Tichborne v. Weir* (1892) 67 L.T. 735, 736–737 *per* Kay L.J.; *Fairweather v. St Marylebone Property Co. Ltd* [1963] A.C. 510, 535–537 *per* Lord Radcliffe, 543–544, *per* Lord Denning.

Moreover, the freehold owner cannot enforce any covenants in the lease directly against the adverse possessor, who is not an assignee of the lease: *ibid.* However, the freehold owner may forfeit the lease for non-performance of the covenants *as against the dispossessed leasehold owner* and the adverse possessor would have no right to apply for relief against forfeiture: *Tickner v. Buzzacott* [1965] Ch. 426, 434 *per* Plowman J.

It has also been held by the House of Lords that a leaseholder whose title has been barred by adverse possession may nonetheless surrender the lease to the freeholder so as to confer on the freeholder an immediate right to possession against the adverse possessor: *Fairweather v. St Marylebone Property Co. Ltd, supra,* 537–541 *per* Lord Radcliffe, 544–548 *per* Lord Denning. (The decision may be seen as unsatisfactory because there was some doubt as to whether the leasehold title was registered at the relevant time, although, on the evidence that was admitted, the Court of Appeal and the House of Lords found that the title was not registered. However, the House of Lords took the tentative view that the decision would have been no different.) The decision has been criticised: see, in particular, Wade (1962) 78 L.Q.R. 541 (although, for a contrary view, see Cooke (1994) 14 *Legal Studies* 1); and its correctness has been left open by the Privy Council: *Chung Ping Kwan v. Lam Island Development Co. Ltd* [1997] A.C. 38, 47 *per* Lord Nicholls, who referred to Professor Wade's "powerful critique". See also Hopkins [1996] Conv. 284.

3.2.2.2 *Registered land*   The position on the same issue in the context of registered land has been rendered uncertain by the difficulties surrounding section 75 of the Land Registration Act 1925: see *supra* p. 90. In *Spectrum Investment Co. v. Holmes* [1981] 1 W.L.R. 221 the defendant had been in adverse possession of land subject to a registered lease and was registered as proprietor of the leasehold interest. The former leasehold owner later purported to surrender the lease to the freehold owner, who then sought to have the defendant's title deleted from the register, pursuant to the principle applied in *Fairweather v. St Marylebone Property Co. Ltd* However, Browne-Wilkinson J. dismissed the claim, holding that, following registration, the title of the former leasehold owner was vested in the defendant and the former leasehold owner had no lease to surrender to the freehold owner. For comment, see [1981] Conv. 157; [1982] Conv. 201; Cooke (1994) 14 *Legal Studies* 1; Law Com. No. 254, *Land Registration for the Twenty-First Century* (1998), paras 10.35–10.39.

On the basis that the title of the dispossessed leasehold owner is transferred to the adverse possessor, it is arguable that the freehold owner can enforce any covenants in the lease directly against the adverse possessor.

Browne-Wilkinson J. expressly left open the position during the period between the date when the adverse possessor acquires title by adverse possession and the date when he is registered as proprietor of the leasehold estate. That issue was considered in *Central London Commercial Estates Ltd v. Kato Kaguka Ltd* [1998] 4 All E.R. 948, where Sedley J. reviewed the authorities referred to above.

Central London Commercial Estates Ltd v. Kato Kaguka Ltd [1998] 4 All E.R. 948

(Ch D., Sedley J.)

In 1935 the registered freehold owner granted a long lease of land forming part of Bush House in London. In 1942 the leasehold title, subject to a sub-lease, was assigned to Axa. In 1996 Axa purported to surrender the leasehold title to Central, who had acquired the freehold title in 1989. The Land Registry closed the title to the lease and re-registered the freehold title subject only to the sub-lease. However, for more than 12 years prior to the purported surrender in 1996, Kato had been in adverse possession of part of the land comprised in the lease (and excluded from the sub-lease). Central sought to recover possession from Kato.

SEDLEY J.:
The issue
There is before the court a preliminary issue raising a vexed but unresolved question of real property law: whether, after more than 12 years' adverse possession by a

trespasser, the registered leaseholder of land can by surrendering the remainder of his term to the freeholder give the latter a right to immediate possession against the erstwhile squatter. In relation to unregistered land the answer, on House of Lords authority, is Yes. The issue is whether the provisions of the Land Registration Act 1925, centrally s. 75, produce a different outcome in registered conveyancing.

...

The law

Unless at some future date their Lordships' House, pursuant to its 1966 practice statement (*Note* [1966] 1 W.L.R. 1234), revisits the issue, the law of unregistered conveyancing makes a surrender in equivalent circumstances to the foregoing effective to defeat any possessory right or title in the squatter.

The starting point is the decision of the Court of Appeal in *Tichborne v. Weir* (1892) 67 L.T. 735 on the Real Property Limitation Act 1833, which provided that after 20 years of adverse possession "the Right and Title" to the land "shall be extinguished" (ss.2 and 34). The Court of Appeal explained that by barring the remedy and extinguishing the title of the person out of possession the Act did not create a new title in the disseisor or convey the dispossessed person's title to him. A decade earlier in *Rosenberg v. Cook* (1881) 8 Q.B.D. 162 at 165 Jessel M.R. had spelt out clearly that a squatter's title is a freehold. By the date of these decisions, however, Parliament had legislated, by s.21 of the Land Transfer Act 1875, to protect a registered proprietor from the acquisition of an adverse title by adverse possession of whatever duration. This was modified by s.12 of the Land Transfer Act 1897, which provided that rectification of the register was to be available to a disseisor who would have obtained a title by possession to registered land but for the statutory block upon it. The limitation period for real property had been brought down to 12 years by s.1 of the Real Property Limitation Act 1874. The law of adverse possession of registered land was again recast by s.173 of the Law of Property Act 1922, which substituted for s.12 of the 1897 Act the trusteeship provisions which now appear, by way of consolidation, in s.75 of the Land Registration Act 1925. Legislative history is not an aid to the construction of a consolidating statute, except in extremis, but it is not irrelevant that the history of s.75 is no more than a history of varying policy approaches to the combined effects of the Limitation Acts and the squatter's common law freehold upon registered leasehold land.

At the time when the 1925 Act (like its immediate predecessor) was passed, the law was believed to be as stated by the Divisional Court in *Walter v. Yalden* [1902] 2 K.B. 304, namely that the surrender of a lease by a lessee whose right and title to possession had been extinguished by effluxion of time gave the leaseholder no right of re-entry during the remainder of the term. It was in the leading case of *Fairweather v. St Marylebone Property Co. Ltd* [1963] A.C. 510 that the House of Lords by a majority, indorsing the decision ([1962] 1 Q.B. 498) of a majority of the Court of Appeal, held that *Walter v. Yalden* had been wrongly decided and that, in the case of unregistered land, a surrender after the running of 12 years' adverse possession against a leaseholder was effective to give the fee simple owner a right of re-entry against the disseisor. Lord Radcliffe who, with Lord Denning, spoke for the majority, explained ([1963] A.C. 510 at 535–536) that a squatter does not succeed to the title which he has disturbed: by sufficiently long adverse possession he obtains a title of his own, but "his possession only defeats the rights of those to whom it has been adverse". It follows that—

> "the effect of the 'extinguishment' sections of the Limitation Acts is not to destroy the lessee's estate as between himself and the lessor; and that it would be incorrect to say that if he offers a surrender to the lessor he has nothing to surrender to him in respect of the land in the possession of the squatter ... What the lessee surrendered in this case was the incumbrance on the fee simple in possession which was represented by the term of years ... Now ... if the landlord then goes to the lessee and gets him to surrender the outstanding term, which incumbers his fee

simple in possession, then the squatter's defence against the landlord disappears and, since he has not completed adverse possession against the landlord, he must give up to the rightful owner's claim to the land." (see [1963] A.C. 510 at 540–541.)

Lord Denning ([1963] A.C. 510 at 545) agreed that "the title of the leaseholder ... is extinguished *as against the squatter*, but remains good *as against the freeholder*" (Lord Denning's emphasis). He added ([1963] A.C. 510 at 547):

"The only reason, it seems to me, which can be urged against this conclusion is that it means that a squatter's title can be destroyed by the leaseholder and freeholder putting their heads together. It is said that they can by a surrender—or by a surrender and regrant—destroy the squatter's title completely and get rid of him. So be it. There is no way of preventing it."

This being the effect of limitation on the law of unregistered conveyancing, how does it differ, if at all, from registered conveyancing? The current limitation provision (replicating that made by the Limitation Act 1939 at the time when *Fairweather*'s case was decided) is in ss.15 and 17 of the Limitation Act 1980:

"**15.**—(1) No action shall be brought by any person to recover any land after the expiration of twelve years from the date on which the right of action accrued to him or, if it first accrued to some person through whom he claims, to that person ...
17. Subject to—(a) section 18 of this Act; and (b) section 75 of the Land Registration Act 1925; at the expiration of the period prescribed by this Act for any person to bring an action to recover land (including a redemption action) the title of that person to the land shall be extinguished."

Section 75 of the Land Registration Act 1925 provides:

"(1) The Limitation Acts shall apply to registered land in the same manner and to the same extent as those Acts apply to land not registered, except that where, if the land were not registered, the estate of the person registered as proprietor would be extinguished, such estate shall not be extinguished but shall be deemed to be held by the proprietor for the time being in trust for the person who, by virtue of the said Acts, has acquired title against any proprietor, but without prejudice to the estates and interests of any other person interested in the land whose estate or interest is not extinguished by those Acts.
(2) Any person claiming to have acquired a title under the Limitation Acts to a registered estate in the land may apply to be registered as proprietor thereof.
(3) The registrar shall, on being satisfied as to the applicant's title, enter the applicant as proprietor either with absolute, good leasehold, qualified, or possessory title, as the case may require, but without prejudice to any estate or interest protected by any entry on the register which may not have been extinguished under the Limitation Acts, and such registration shall, subject as aforesaid, have the same effect as the registration of a first proprietor; but the proprietor or the applicant or any other person interested may apply to the court for the determination of any question arising under this section."

By virtue of ss.17(2)(a) and 22(1) of and Sched. 2, para 3, to the Interpretation Act 1978, the reference in the 1925 Act to the earlier Limitation Acts becomes a reference to the current Limitation Act.

Section 70(1) (subject to contradiction by the register) deems registered land to be subject to any subsisting overriding interests in the form of, inter alia, "(f) Subject to the provisions of this Act, rights acquired or in course of being acquired under the Limitation Acts".

Section 23(1)(c) makes any disposition of a leasehold estate subject (unless the register shows otherwise) to any overriding interest affecting the estate.

An overview of the scheme of the Act in relation to prescription can be found in Ruoff and Roper *Registered Conveyancing* para. 29–02 (though they are surely wrong to describe the squatter's title as equitable, or to suggest that there can be only one legal estate in a piece of land), and (albeit overtly critical of *Fairweather*'s case) in *Megarry and Wade's The Law of Real Property*, 5th ed. (1984). The Act has not had a good press. *Megarry and Wade,* at p. 196, speak of its "deficiencies" and characterise it as "legislation of exceptionally low quality", a description quoted without dissent by Nourse L.J. in *Clark v. Chief Land Registrar* [1994] Ch. 370, at 378, 385.

Section 75 came into *Fairweather*'s case in an unsatisfactory way: registration had not been argued in the county court, probably for good legal reason; and although it was allowed to be raised in the Court of Appeal, leave was refused to adduce evidence of the date of registration. The report ([1963] A.C. 510 at 519–520, 527–528, 532–533) shows that serious attention was devoted to it in argument before the House, and both Lord Radcliffe and Lord Denning considered it, although inconclusively. Lord Radcliffe ([1963] A.C. 510 at 541–543) mentioned the procedural history and went on:

"As I think that the true meaning of s.75(1) is not at all easy to discover and may have to be fully considered on some other occasion, I think it best on this occasion to say as little about it as possible. Briefly, s.75(1) appears to set out with the purpose of applying the Limitation Acts and therefore the statutory consequences of adverse possession to registered land but then goes on to provide that where the estate of a person registered as proprietor would be extinguished, '... such estate shall not be extinguished but shall be deemed to be held by the proprietor for the time being in trust for the person who ... has acquired title against [the] proprietor'. It therefore succeeds in making a provision at the end of the subsection which is wholly inconsistent with the conceptions of the Limitation Acts as previously understood and achieves just that "parliamentary conveyance" (through the medium of trustee and cestui que trust) which was denied by the decision in *Tichborne v. Weir* ((1892) 67 L.T. 735). It would certainly be very satisfactory for the appellant if this is what the Act of 1925 has really done, because it would give him just that beneficial interest in the lessee's term which, in my view, he lacks under the Limitation Acts themselves ... I only wish to add that at present I am not at all satisfied that s.75(1) does create a trust interest in the squatter of the kind that one would expect from the words used. So to hold would raise difficulties which I do not now explore; and the trust of the dispossessed owner's title under sub-s.(1) must somehow be reconciled with the provision under sub-s.(2) for the squatter to apply to register his own title, which would presumably be his independent possessory title acquired by the adverse possession."

Lord Denning concluded his speech ([1963] A.C. 510 at 548):

"... I doubt if [s.75(1)] puts registered land on a very different footing from unregistered land. It is machinery so as to apply the Limitation Acts to registered land but it does not alter the substantive position very materially. The registered leaseholder clearly remains liable on the covenants and subject to the conditions of the lease, including the proviso for re-entry: and I do not see why, on a surrender, the freeholder should not recover possession from a squatter, just as he can on a forfeiture. The freeholder has no notice of the trust in favour of the squatter and his interests are not to be prejudiced by the fact that the leasehold is registered."

The insidious problems identified by Lord Radcliffe emerged more starkly in *Spectrum Investment Co. v. Holmes* [1981] 1 W.L.R. 221. The plaintiff company had in 1957 acquired the freehold of a house and registered itself as proprietor. The house was already demised on a long lease. The leaseholder had sublet to the defendant, who, by continuous non-payment of rent, had by 1963 acquired a prescriptive title against her. In 1968 the defendant sought registration as proprietor of the leasehold interest and in the absence of any response from the leaseholder's solicitors to the notice which they received, the Land Registry closed the registration of the latter's title and opened a new registration of the defendant's title, describing the property as leasehold land held on the terms of the 1902 lease. Seven years later, in 1975, the leaseholder sought to defeat the defendant's title by executing a deed of surrender to the freeholder (a company controlled by her own family). Browne-Wilkinson J. held that the device, as it was admitted to be, failed. He said ([1981] 1 W.L.R. 221 at 230):

> "To my mind the words [of s.75(1)] are clear and unequivocal: the squatter claims to have acquired a title to 'a registered estate in the land' (*i.e.* the leasehold interest) and applies to be registered as a proprietor *'thereof'*. Therefore, under s.75(2), references to the squatter having acquired title to a registered estate must include the rights which under the Limitation Act 1939 the squatter acquires in relation to leasehold interests. Subsection (2) then refers to the squatter applying to be registered as proprietor 'thereof'. This word can, in my judgment, only refer back to the registered estate in the land against which the squatter has acquired title under the 1939 Act, i.e. the leasehold interest. The clear words of the Act therefore seem to require that, once the 12 years have run, the squatter is entitled to be registered as proprietor of the lease itself, and is bound to be so registered if he applies for registration. It follows that in my judgment [the defendant] (as the squatter) is correctly registered as proprietor of the lease itself in accordance with the clear requirements of s.75 ... If that is right, [the leaseholder] cannot be entitled to rectification of the register as against [the defendant], and she can therefore never get into a position in which she is competent to surrender the lease to [the plaintiff]." (Browne-Wilkinson J.'s emphasis.)

It is to be observed that Browne-Wilkinson J.'s construction of s.75(2) controverts Lord Radcliffe's provisional view (in *Fairweather*'s case [1963] A.C. 510 at 543) that s.75(2) relates not to the usurped leasehold title but to the independent prescriptive title acquired by adverse possession. In the present case counsel for all three parties, for their own independent reasons, have in the end united behind Browne-Wilkinson J.'s reading, from which I would not in any case have felt justified in departing. It eliminates the possible view that while s.75(1) creates a trust of the leasehold interest for the squatter, s.75(2) allows registration of the squatter's own prescriptive title. Instead, a squatter on registered land is deprived by s.75(1) of his own prescriptive title ("such estate shall not be extinguished") and is furnished instead with the right to acquire and register as his own the usurped leasehold title. What this does to the opening words of sub-s.(2) may have to be considered on another occasion.

It is also common ground before me that s.75 includes leasehold interests. Mr Romie Tager Q.C. for Central concedes it only because registration "with good leasehold title" is spelt out as a possibility in sub-s.(3); but Mr Christopher Nugee Q.C. for Kato points out that the saving at the end of sub-s.(1) for unextinguished estates or interests of others in the land must also be designed to bring leasehold interests within the section.

The critical difference between this case and the *Spectrum* case is that the possibility of Kato's becoming registered as proprietor of the leasehold interest under s.75 has been pre-empted by the surrender of the headlease and the consequent reregistration of the plaintiff's freehold title subject only to the underlease. Browne-Wilkinson J. ([1981] 1 W.L.R. 221 at 231) was careful to distinguish this situation from that which faced him:

> "... I am not deciding anything as to the position during the period between the date when the squatter obtains his title by adverse possession and the date on which he obtains registration of it. This is the period covered by sub-s.(1) of s.75 which is the subsection on which Lord Radcliffe ([1963] A.C. 510 at 542) and Sir John Pennycuick [in *Jessamine Investment Co. v. Schwartz* ([1978] Q.B. 264 at 275)] were commenting. It may well be, as their dicta suggest, that during the period preceding any registration of the squatter's rights, the documentary lessee (as registered proprietor of the lease) and the freeholder can deal with the legal estate with

reference to a person whose rights are not recorded on the register. But once the Act provides for registration of the squatter's title, it must in my judgment follow that the squatter's rights (once registered) cannot be overridden."

The Court of Appeal had decided the *Jessamine* case, contrary to the approach of the trial judge, without reliance upon s.75; but Sir John Pennycuick had added ([1978] Q.B. 264 at 275):

"I should be very reluctant to introduce a substantive distinction in the application of a provision of the Limitation Act 1939 to registered and unregistered land respectively, based on what is plainly a conveyancing device designed to adapt that provision to the former class of land."

Browne-Wilkinson J., guided by the opening words of s.75(1), took the same approach in the *Spectrum* case. But, given the decision of the House of Lords in *Williams & Glyn's Bank Ltd v. Boland* [1981] A.C. 487, to the effect that "if the words of the Land Registration Act 1925 are clear, they are to be given their natural meaning and not distorted so as to seek to produce uniformity in the substantive law as between registered and unregistered land", he concluded ([1981] 1 W.L.R. 221 at 230):

"I therefore approach this question on the basis that one would expect that substantive legal rights would be the same whether the land is registered or unregistered but that clear words in the 1925 Act must be given their natural meaning even if this leads to a divergence."

Since this was enough to conclude the case in the defendant's favour Browne-Wilkinson J. went no further into her counsel's submission "that the whole scheme of the Land Registration Act 1925 shows that the position of the squatter on registered land is totally different from that of a squatter on unregistered land". He was, he said, leaving it to others to resolve the more fundamental questions. This is the lot which has fallen to me.

The arguments

No summary will do justice to the able arguments addressed to me by counsel for the three active parties, but in essence they are these.

Mr Nugee, while reserving his position on the correctness of the decision in *Fairweather*'s case, argues that the position in registered conveyancing is fundamentally different from that in unregistered conveyancing. From the common starting point for registered and unregistered land dictated by the opening words of s.75(1), the section goes on to create for the former a tangibly different regime. How different is not to be quantified by the characterisation of the section (*e.g.* by the Court of Appeal in *Mount Carmel Investments Ltd v. Peter Thurlow Ltd* [1988] 1 W.L.R. 1078 at 1089) as machinery but (since machinery itself can have important effects: see *Williams & Glyn's Bank Ltd v. Boland* [1981] A.C. 487 at 504, 511) is to be ascertained by following the ordinary principles of construction and seeing where they lead. They lead, Mr Nugee submits, after 12 years' adverse possession of leasehold land, to a situation in which the disseisor can secure registration as surrogate proprietor of the leasehold interest or estate under s.75(2), in which case, barring rectification, the decision in the *Spectrum* case concludes matters in his favour. In the interim between the extinction of the lessee's title vis-à-vis the squatter and the registration of the squatter as proprietor of the lessee's leasehold interest, the statutory trust comes into operation under s.75(1). The answer to the still open question whether in this period the leaseholder can arrange with the freeholder to defeat the squatter's title by merging the leasehold and freehold estates is given, Mr Nugee submits, by the statute itself: Axa has since the expiry of the limitation period held the leasehold estate on trust for Kato, whose rights are overriding interests under ss.70(1)(f) and 23(1)(c) of the 1925 Act, placing Axa and Central in a position no different from that found in the *Spectrum* case. The relativity of titles in unregistered land cannot survive in a system of registration which makes a registered title good against the world. As Harman J. said in *Bridges v. Mees* [1957] Ch. 475 at 483, "this being registered land, the defendant gets the title which the register gives him."

It will follow that any disposition by Axa, surrender included, is incapable of extinguishing Kato's rights; or, at worst, will afford Kato a remedy against Axa for breach of trust.

To this scheme Mr Tager and (for Axa) Mr Terence Etherton Q.C. advance different but complementary answers. Mr Tager, starting from the accepted fact that all that distinguishes the present case from *Fairweather*'s case is the registration of the headlease, and reserving his position on the *Spectrum* case, argues that in a case like the present the s 75(1) exception has nothing to bite on because the barring of Axa's right and title as against Kato did nothing to extinguish the relationship or estate between Axa and the freeholder, with the result that the condition for the operation of the exception, the extinction of the estate of the person registered as proprietor, is not met. This is because, in Mr Tager's submission, title (which is all that s.17 of the Limitation Act 1980 extinguishes) and estate (which is what s.75(1) focuses on) are different things, at least in the case of leasehold land; and the extinction of the leaseholder's possessory title by 12 years' adverse possession does not extinguish the estate which he has of the freeholder. Mr Etherton reaches the same destination by a less semantic route. The House of Lords in *Fairweather*'s case [1963] A.C. 510 at 540, 545 has determined as part of its ratio decidendi that the freeholder's title to the leasehold interest in unregistered land is not extinguished by adverse possession against the leaseholder and is capable of being surrendered. This being so, he submits, a tripartite relationship such as the present does not enter the statutory exception under which a trust comes into being; only the limited element of it which relates leaseholder to squatter, if jeopardised by the leaseholder, does so. The statutory purpose is to protect the sanctity of registered title, but nothing more.

Both Mr Etherton and Mr Tager accept, indeed assert, that everything depends on whether the squatter can register his title or estate before the leaseholder extinguishes it by merger. If, therefore, Kato had obtained registration under s.75(2) before the date of Axa's surrender, it would have succeeded in protecting its acquired leasehold interest from the effect of the surrender; but absent such registration, the surrender vested in the freeholder a title absolute to the courtyard unencumbered save for the underlease.

Alternatively Mr Tager relies on s.74 of the 1925 Act:

"Subject to the provisions of this Act as to settled land, neither the registrar nor any person dealing with a registered estate or charge shall be affected with notice of a trust express implied or constructive, and references to trusts shall, so far as possible, be excluded from the register."

As to the remedies, if any, available to Kato against Axa if Axa's surrender is held to have injured Kato's rights, Kato's primary position is that the issue does not arise since the estate surrendered to Central was and remains impressed with the statutory trust in Kato's favour. If, however, this is not so, Mr Nugee asserts and Mr Etherton denies that Kato have a cause of action against Axa for breach of trust. Plainly this cannot arise if—as both Central and Axa contend—no trust came into being, but if (contrary to their contention) it did, and if (contrary to Kato's primary contention) it was violated by the surrender, then Mr Etherton submits that no cause of action arises. The s.75(1) trust is a legal oddity, not a true private trust but simply machinery permitting transfer one way (to the squatter) but not precluding transfer the other way (for example by surrender to the freeholder). Mr Nugee contends that a trust, however created, carries at least an obligation enforceable by injunction to carry out the purpose of the trust and an obligation to account to the beneficiary for any profit improperly made by acting in breach of trust. Both would afford a cause of action.

Conclusions

I approach the construction of s.75(1) in the same way as Browne-Wilkinson J. in the *Spectrum* case, by regarding it as creating a specified exception to a general rule that limitation should affect registered and unregistered land similarly. The ordinary principle that legislation alters the general law is inverted by the opening words of s.75(1). If therefore the effect of limitation on unregistered land has turned out, on authority, to be other than it was believed to be at the time of enactment, then (as Mr Tager says) it is the construction of the statute and not the general law which must give way. I do not consider, however, that any other assumptions should be brought to bear on the exercise. In particular, in spite of the regard paid in places by Lord Radcliffe and Lord Denning to the potential factual merits of the rival submissions in *Fairweather*'s case, the law seems to me to adopt and in turn to demand a stance of neutrality as between disseisor and disseised. Parliament has prescribed the effects of a sufficient period of adverse possession without reference to circumstances, and enough examples have been canvassed in the course of the submissions to demonstrate that the deserving and the undeserving alike may be caught or spared by the operation of the Limitation Acts. The law, correspondingly, leans neither towards nor against the extinction of titles by prescription: for policy reasons it simply provides for it to happen in certain situations (see Ruoff and Roper *Registered Conveyancing*, para. 29–03 and *Megarry and Wade's The Law of Real Property*, 5th ed. (1984), p. 1030). This is why, for example, I have received no evidence about how Kato came to occupy the car park.

The situation before the court for the purposes of the exception in s.75(1) is that, were the leasehold estate in the courtyard unregistered, s.17 of the Limitation Act 1980 would by now have extinguished as much of the leasehold estate as entitles Axa to exclude Kato, but not as much of it as was held of the freeholder and has now been surrendered: see *Fairweather*'s case. Is the element of the estate which would otherwise be extinguished all that the statute saves, or is the estate indivisible for the purposes of the exception and so wholly subject to the trust?

I do not consider that Mr Tager's distinction between estate and title is material here, though it may be elsewhere. If estate were not synonymous with title in s.75 (as both Lord Radcliffe and Lord Denning in *Fairweather*'s case clearly thought it was), the linkage of the Limitation Acts to the extinction of estates would be meaningless, since the Limitation Acts speak not of estates but of titles. In the bipartite situation of freeholder and disseisor, it is common ground that to bar the title is to bar the estate. The two must mean the same in the present context.

What then is the estate or title which, but for the disapplication of the effects of the Limitation Acts on registered land, "would be extinguished" on the expiry of 12 years' adverse possession? The relevant unit of registration is "the land", which by s.3(viii) includes land of any tenure—in a case like the present, the leasehold estate. Such an estate is divisible for many purposes, but nothing in s.75 suggests to me that it is divisible for the statutory purpose: on the contrary, what is evidently contemplated is the substitution of one registered proprietor for another without more, placing the second in the same relationship to the freeholder as had been enjoyed by the first. In the state of the decided cases in 1922 and 1925, this is unsurprising. The difficulty is to fit the statute to the post-*Fairweather* situation.

To split the leasehold interest after 12 years' adverse possession into an element related entirely to the freehold and another related solely to the squatter, as is now known to happen with unregistered land, does not seem to me to marry up with either the purpose or the operation of s.75(1). The squatter, unlike an underlessee, has no legal relationship at all with the leaseholder during the 12 initial years of trespass (except in the negative sense that the leaseholder may at any time evict him and claim damages); and at the end of the 12 years by operation of law the leaseholder's right and title to do even this are extinguished wherever the Limitation Acts apply. At law the squatter is then in a position to make a good title, independent of the lease although always subject to the freeholder's eventual reversion. In relation to a registered leasehold, however, s.75 lifts the extinguishing effect of the Limitation Act and substitutes a trust of the leasehold interest, benefits and burdens alike, from the moment of extinction of the leasehold title. The squatter becomes entitled, without regard to merits, to be placed in the same relationship with the freeholder as had previously been enjoyed by the leaseholder. The trust preserves not the squatter's common law title but a new statutory right to be substituted by registration for the leaseholder—carrying with it, as Mr Nugee accepts, an obligation to indemnify the leaseholder against outgoings. This is to all appearances a statutory conveyance of the entire leasehold interest.

There is apparent force in Mr Nugee's submission that Mr Etherton's ostensibly equally straightforward construction has hidden traps in it. Because Mr Etherton seeks to construe "where" as focusing on the facts of a particular transaction, it is only when subsequent events are known that it becomes possible to say whether a statutory trust exists: if the leaseholder sues the squatter for possession, the trust intervenes; if the leaseholder surrenders to the freeholder, no trust arises (as distinct from there being no breach of trust). But it may be that in the end this does no more than carry into effect the dichotomy of the leasehold interest which Axa and Central assert characterises registered as it does unregistered land. The real question is whether, as Mr Tager and Mr Etherton argue, the material estate for the present statutory purpose is as much of the whole estate as would not be extinguished if the land were not registered—that is to say the leasehold interest shorn of the right to possession. If it is, then there is no doubt that it falls outside the exception, so that surrendering it extinguishes the squatter's title.

I appreciate that the search for the true meaning of a statute, especially the Land Registration Act 1925, is not the same thing as a search for simplicity. But it is realistic, I think, to see in s.75 the relatively straightforward purpose which I have described. Such a purpose becomes unattainable if the leasehold estate is split up into two tranches, one the right to possession which after 12 years passes to the squatter; the other the interest held of the freeholder, which can be disposed of so as to frustrate the right to possession—unless the disseisor, following the giving of the necessary notices by the Registrar, first succeeds in obtaining registration in lieu of the leaseholder. The conceded fact that what the disseisor in the latter case obtains by virtue of s.75(2) is the entirety of the leasehold interest seems to me a strong indicator that this is the estate intended to be preserved from extinction by the exception contained in s.75(1). So is the fact that the s.75(1) exception begins by nullifying the squatter's common law freehold if the land is registered: why should registration be given this effect unless the loss is to be made good by another means? By contrast, a trust of a bare right not to be evicted seems almost pointless. I accept the submission of Mr Tager and Mr Etherton that the race to register which their case entails is not unthinkable or unique; but when the result is less like a race than like a game of double or quits, one has to ask if it can be what Parliament meant to happen. I am persuaded that it is not.

If, as I hold, the leasehold interest was impressed by 1996 with the statutory trust, it must follow that the trusteeship passed to the freeholder upon the merger of the leasehold with the freehold interest by surrender. The full incidents of this trust, which are far from clear, do not fall for decision by me. It is sufficient to hold, as I do, that the beneficial interest of Kato under s.75 was an overriding interest under s.70(1)(f) or (g) or both, and that by virtue of ss.23(1)(c) and 69 it now binds Central. Section 74 cannot intervene: see *Williams & Glyn's Bank Ltd v. Boland* [1981] A.C. 487 at 508.

NOTE:

1. For comment, see [1999] C.L.J. 30; [1999] Conv. 136; (1999) 115 L.Q.R. 187.

3.2.3 *Adverse possession in relation to land held on trust*   The effect of adverse possession in relation to land held in trust for successive interests is analogous to the effect where land is subject to a lease. Adverse possession for 12 years extinguishes only the equitable interest in possession; an interest in remainder will be extinguished only after adverse possession for 12 years or six years after the interest in remainder falls into possession, whichever is the later: Limitation Act 1980, s.15(2).

3.2.4 *Successive adverse possessors*   As has been seen, even before the expiry of the limitation period the adverse possessor acquires a title to the land that is good against everyone except the person whom he has dispossessed; that that title can be transferred; and that the limitation period continues to run as against the person dispossessed: see *Asher v. Whitlock* (1865) L.R. 1 Q.B. 1, *supra*, p. 24. The same principle applies where the adverse possessor is himself dispossessed before the expiry of the limitation period. Provided that the periods of adverse possession by the two (or more) adverse possessors are continuous and together exceed the limitation period, the title of the documentary owner is extinguished: Limitation Act 1980, s.15(1), Sched. 1, para. 8(2); *Willis v. Earl Howe* [1893] 2 Ch. 545, 553–554 *per* Kay L.J.; *Mount Carmel Investments Ltd v. Peter Thurlow Ltd* 1087–1088 *per* Nicholls L.J. However, the first adverse possessor will be able to recover the land from the second adverse possessor unless the latter can establish 12 years of adverse possession as against the former: *ibid.* 1086 *per* Nicholls L.J.

3.2.5 *Proposals for reform*   As part of its blueprint for conveyancing in the twenty-first century, the Law Commission has provisionally recommended fundamental reform of the law relating to adverse possession and the limitation of actions in so far as it relates to registered land. The broad approach is that the law should reflect the principles of land registration and that, in striking the balance between registered proprietors and adverse possessors, the law should restrict the circumstances in which the registered title can be extinguished to those cases where it is essential to ensure the marketability of land or to prevent unfairness: Law Com. No. 254, *Land Registration for the Twenty-First Century* (1998), para. 10.19.

The Law Commission has further provisionally recommended a new mechanism for applying the relevant principles of adverse possession to registered land; and those recommendations would apply either to the existing principles or to the recommended new principles.

Law Com. No. 254, Land Registration for the Twenty-First Century (1998)

Adverse possession

The proposed scheme of adverse possession for registered land

12.68 We provisionally recommend that—
    (1) adverse possession should no longer of itself bar the title of a registered proprietor;

(2) only the closure of that proprietor's title on the register would have that effect, and it would do so for all purposes; and

(3) the principles of adverse possession applicable to registered land should be as set out in the following paragraphs.

12.69 First, there should be a new system to enable an adverse possessor to seek registration as proprietor, and it should operate as follows—

(1) Where a person had been in adverse possession of land with a registered title for more than 10 years, he or she would be entitled to apply to be registered as proprietor of that land.

(2) On receipt of that application, the Registry would be required to serve a notice on the registered proprietor, any proprietor of a registered charge affecting the title in question, and any person who, from any entry on the register, appears to have a right to possession of the land, informing each of them of the application for registration.

(3) If the registered proprietor, chargee or person entitled to possession failed to object within two months of service of the notice, the registrar would register the adverse possessor as registered proprietor and would close the title of the existing proprietor.

(4) If the registered proprietor or chargee objected to the registration, the application would be dismissed unless the adverse possessor could show that—

(a) the proprietor was estopped by his or her conduct from objecting to his or her registration;

(b) he or she had some independent right to the land that entitled him or her to be registered as proprietor; or

(c) he or she had entered into adverse possession under a mistaken belief, reasonably held, as to his or her rights.

(5) If the adverse possessor raised any of these matters, the issue would be resolved by the registrar, unless he referred it to the court at any time prior to his making a final adjudication. There would be a right of appeal from his decision.

(6) If the adverse possessor established that he or she had entered under a mistaken belief as to his or her rights (above, (4)(c)), the court or registrar would order that the adverse possessor be registered as proprietor of the land unless in the circumstances it was inequitable or otherwise inappropriate to do so. Where the court or registrar ordered such registration, it would be on such terms, if any, whether as to payment or otherwise, as were equitable between the parties having regard to all the circumstances. In particular, the squatter could be required to grant the former registered proprietor an easement over his or her land, or to enter into a positive or restrictive covenant for his or her benefit.

(7) Where the adverse possessor's application to be registered was rejected and he or she subsequently remained in adverse possession for two years from the date of that rejection, he or she could re-apply to be registered as proprietor of the land.

(8) On such re-application, the registrar would, on being satisfied of the facts set out in (7), register the adverse possessor as proprietor of the land and close the title of the registered proprietor. The registered proprietor would remain as such unless and until such an application were made. He or she could therefore deal with the land, but subject to any overriding interest (if any) as the adverse possessor might have, and subject to that person's rights to bring a claim in damages for trespass.

12.70 Secondly, corresponding provision should be made for the situation where a registered proprietor sought possession in legal proceedings against the adverse possessor.

(1) Where a registered proprietor brought proceedings for possession against a person who had been in adverse possession of the proprietor's land for more than 10 years, the proprietor would be entitled to recover the land unless the adverse possessor could show that—

   (a) the proprietor was estopped by his or her conduct from objecting to his or her registration;

   (b) he or she had some independent right to the land that entitled him or her to be registered as proprietor; or

   (c) he or she had entered into adverse possession under a mistaken belief, reasonably held, as to his or her rights.

(2) If the adverse possessor established (a) or (b), the court would order that the claim for possession should be dismissed and that he or she should be registered as proprietor of the land. If (c) were established, the court would dismiss the claim unless circumstances made it inequitable or otherwise inappropriate to do so, and would order that the adverse possessor be registered as proprietor. Such an order would be on such terms, if any, whether as to payment or otherwise, as were equitable between the parties having regard to all the circumstances, as explained above, at paragraph 12.69(6).

(3) Where the registered proprietor failed either to enforce the judgment or to commence new proceedings for possession within two years of its being given, he or she would thereafter be unable to recover the land from the adverse possessor, who would be entitled to be registered as proprietor of the land. Unless and until that happened, the registered proprietor would remain as such, and could deal with the land, but subject both to any overriding interest (if any) as the adverse possessor might have, and to that person's rights to bring a claim in damages for trespass.

12.71 The scheme which we propose above would not apply—

(1) in a case of adverse possession against a short lease which was an overriding interest (which would be subject to the same principles as if it were unregistered land); or

(2) to an adverse possessor who could show that he or she had barred the rights of a registered proprietor before any legislation implementing that scheme was brought into force.

. . .

The machinery for giving effect to adverse possession where title is registered

12.73 [We provisionally recommend that—]

(1) the trust should no longer be used as a means of giving effect to the rights of an adverse possessor who has barred the estate of the registered proprietor;

(2) where an adverse possessor is entitled to be registered as proprietor, he or she should be registered with an absolute, possessory or qualified title;

(3) where the title barred is that of a tenant under a lease or a life tenant under a settlement or trust of land—

   (a) the adverse possessor should normally be registered with a qualified freehold title;

    (b) the qualification should be that he or she takes subject to the estate or interest of any person or persons entitled on the termination of the lease or the life interest; and

(4) where the title barred is that of a tenant under a lease, the freehold (or other) title of any person entitled to the reversion on that or any superior lease should not be closed or otherwise affected by the registration of the adverse possessor with a freehold title.

NOTES:

1. Since the title of the registered proprietor would not be extinguished unless and until it was formally closed by the Land Registry, until such time and irrespective of the duration of the adverse possession, the registered proprietor would be able to object to an application by the adverse possessor or take proceedings to recover possession of the land. Moreover, if the adverse possessor abandoned possession prior to his application to be registered as proprietor, the adverse possession would cease.

2. If an adverse possessor were registered with a new title, and the title of the former registered proprietor were closed, the estate of the latter would cease to exist for all purposes, although contractual obligations might continue.

3. Where an adverse possessor makes an application to be registered as proprietor and the application is rejected, but the registered proprietor takes no proceedings to recover possession or to regularise the position of the adverse possessor, provided that the adverse possessor remains in possession for a further two years, he would be entitled to apply to be registered as proprietor and in the meantime he would have a complete defence to any proceedings brought by the registered proprietor.

2

TITLE DEEDS CONVEYANCING

A. Introduction

The purpose of this chapter (and the following chapter) is to examine the principles of conveyancing in so far as they affect the investigation of title by the purchaser and the enforceability of third party interests against the purchaser. The basic principles have been summarised; and some of those principles have already been further considered in the previous chapter.

B. Investigation of Title

It has been seen that, except where the vendor and purchaser (or their legal representatives) have agreed to adopt the National Conveyancing Protocol procedure, the purchaser of land is not entitled formally to investigate title to the land until he has already exchanged contracts with the vendor and committed himself to the purchase. This may seem somewhat paradoxical but, in practice, it creates few difficulties, since the purchaser will normally be able to withdraw from the contract if the subsequent investigation reveals defects in the title which were not disclosed by the vendor during the pre-contract negotiations: see *Re Nisbet and Potts' Contract* [1906] 1 Ch. 386, *ante*, p. 35; and see *infra*, p. 116.

It has been seen that under the title deeds system of conveyancing that applies to unregistered land the purchaser (and any mortgagee which is lending money to the purchaser to finance the purchase) will need to investigate the title to the land; but that, in the absence of any centralised record of land ownership, their investigation is necessarily based on documentary evidence of previous dealings in the land. To that end, and assuming that the relevant title is the legal fee simple, the vendor is required to provide an "abstract of title", detailing documentary evidence of his entitlement to the legal fee simple that he is purporting to sell to the purchaser. This evidence would normally comprise the document by which he acquired the fee simple and the documents by which each preceding owner acquired the fee simple; the evidence will also include documents relating to mortgages and certain other dealings in the land. However, in the absence of any contrary agreement between the vendor and purchaser, statute specifies the period to be covered by the abstract of title; and the current period is 15 years: Law of Property Act 1925, s.44(1), as amended by the Law of Property Act 1969, s.23. In practice this means that the vendor must identify the person who owned the fee simple 15 years ago; and he must provide documentary evidence of the conveyance to that person (the so-called "root of title") together with evidence of all subsequent conveyances of, and dealings affecting, the fee simple.

The purchaser is entitled to "make requisitions on title" in order to satisfy himself so far as possible that the title is complete and that there are no defects in title that may emerge after the purchaser has purchased the land. However, assuming that the purchaser is so satisfied, and subject to the investigation of third party interests discussed below, the transaction proceeds to the completion stage and the formal conveyance.

C. Enforceability of Third Party Interests

Assuming that the purchaser acquires the legal fee simple, the second question relates to the continued enforceability of third party interests that affected the land in the ownership of the vendor.

1. Legal interests

In accordance with the principle of universal enforceability, the purchaser is bound by any other existing legal estates and interests (as listed in section 1(1) and (2) of the Law of Property Act 1925) irrespective of whether or not he has notice of the interest at the time of the conveyance. For example, a purchaser of land would acquire the land subject to any existing legal leases and any legal easements over the land. As will be seen, there is one exception the principle of the universal enforceability of legal interests: a (legal) puisne mortgage is registrable as a land charge under the Land Charges Act and is subject to the principles of the land charges system.

2. Equitable interests: the underlying dichotomy

Prior to 1926 the enforceability of equitable third party interests depended almost exclusively upon the doctrine of notice: see *ante*, p. 31. The 1925 legislation largely sought to replace that doctrine; but it did not substitute a single device. Rather it distinguished different types of equitable interest, what have been termed "family" and "commercial" interests. Although such terminology has no statutory basis, the substance of the distinction seems to be reflected in the 1925 legislation. Thus, very broadly, in the context of title deeds conveyancing the doctrine of notice was replaced by *overreaching* in the case of *family* interests and by the *registration of land charges under the Land Charges Act* in the case of *commercial* interests.

3. Overreachable interests

The function of the doctrine of overreaching in the context of the 1925 legislation has been discussed above; and the operation of the doctrine has been outlined. In summary, the doctrine operates to confer on the purchaser of land a title to that land free from certain equitable interests which affected the land prior to the purchase. Those interests are commuted into equivalent interests in the proceeds of sale.

The principal statutory provision on overreaching is section 2 of the Law of Property Act 1925.

Law of Property Act 1925, s.2

Conveyances overreaching certain equitable interests and powers

2.—(1) A conveyance to a purchaser of a legal estate in land shall overreach any equitable interest or power affecting that estate, whether or not he has notice thereof, if—

 (i) the conveyance is made under the powers conferred by the Settled Land Act 1925, or any additional powers conferred by a settlement, and the equitable interest or power is capable of being overreached thereby, and the statutory requirements respecting the payment of capital money arising under the settlement are complied with;

 (ii) the conveyance is made by trustees of land and the equitable interest or power is at the date of the conveyance capable of being overreached by such trustees under the provisions of subsection (2) of this section or independently of that subsection, and the requirements of section 27 of this Act respecting the payment of capital money arising on such a conveyance are complied with;

 (iii) the conveyance is made by a mortgagee or personal representative in the exercise of his paramount powers, and the equitable interest or power is capable of being overreached by such conveyance, and any capital money arising from the transaction is paid to the mortgagee or personal representative;

 (iv) the conveyance is made under an order of the court and the equitable interest or power is bound by such order, and any capital money arising from the transaction is paid into, or in accordance with the order of, the court.

(1A) An equitable interest in land subject to a trust of land which remains in, or is to revert to, the settlor shall (subject to any contrary intention) be overreached by the conveyance if it would be so overreached were it an interest under the trust.

(2) Where the legal estate affected is subject to a trust of land, then if at the date of a conveyance made after the commencement of this Act by the trustees, the trustees (whether original or substituted) are either—

 (a) two or more individuals approved or appointed by the court or the successors in office of the individuals so approved or appointed; or

 (b) a trust corporation,

any equitable interest or power having priority to the trust shall, notwithstanding any stipulation to the contrary, be overreached by the conveyance, and shall, according to its priority, take effect as if created or arising by means of a primary trust affecting the proceeds of sale and the income of the land until sale.

(3) The following equitable interests and powers are excepted from the operation of subsection (2) of this section, namely—

 (i) Any equitable interest protected by a deposit of documents relating to the legal estate affected;

 (ii) The benefit of any covenant or agreement restrictive of the user of land;

   (iii) Any easement, liberty, or privilege over or affecting land and being merely an equitable interest (in this Act referred to as an "equitable easement");

   (iv) The benefit of any contract (in this Act referred to as an "estate contract") to convey or create a legal estate, including a contract conferring either expressly or by statutory implication a valid option to purchase, a right of pre-emption, or any other like right;

   (v) Any equitable interest protected by registration under the Land Charges Act 1925 other than—

      (a) an annuity within the meaning of Part II of that Act;

      (b) a limited owner's charge or a general equitable charge within the meaning of that Act.

(4) Subject to the protection afforded by this section to the purchaser of a legal estate, nothing contained in this section shall deprive a person entitled to an equitable charge of any of his rights or remedies for enforcing the same.

(5) So far as regards the following interests, created before the commencement of this Act (which accordingly are not within the provisions of the Land Charges Act 1925), namely—

      (a) the benefit of any covenant or agreement restrictive of the user of the land;

      (b) any equitable easement;

      (c) the interest under a puisne mortgage within the meaning of the Land Charges Act 1925, unless and until acquired under a transfer made after the commencement of this Act;

      (d) the benefit of an estate contract, unless and until the same is acquired under a conveyance made after the commencement of this Act;

a purchaser of a legal estate shall only take subject thereto if he has notice thereof, and the same are not overreached under the provisions contained or in the manner referred to in this section.

NOTES:

1. Section 2(1) enumerates four categories of conveyance that may have overreaching effect. The first two categories concern conveyances of land subject to different types of trust, the strict settlement and the trust of land: see *post*, p. 332. The third category concerns conveyances by a mortgagee pursuant to his statutory power of sale: see *post*, p. 894. The fourth category concerns conveyances made under court orders: it is not considered further.

2. Further provisions on overreaching in the context of strict settlements are found in the Settled Land Act 1925: see, especially, section 18 (for the requirement that any capital money arising on the conveyance (whether purchase money or mortgage loan) must be paid to, and receipted by, at least two trustees or a trust corporation (or paid into court)) and section 72 (for the detailed effect of the conveyance).

3. The corresponding provisions on overreaching in the context of trusts of land are found in the Law of Property Act 1925: see, especially, section 2(2), *supra* (for the requirement that the purchaser must deal with at least two trustees or a trust corporation), section 27 (for the requirement that any purchase money or mortgage loan arising on the conveyance must be paid to, and receipted by, at least two trustees or a trust corporation) and section 2(3)–(5), *supra* (for the detailed effect of the conveyance). For further discussion of overreaching in the context of co-ownership trusts for sale (now replaced by trusts of land), see *City of London Building Society v. Flegg* [1988] A.C. 54, *post*, p. 197.

4. In the context of the first two categories of conveyance, the equitable interests of the beneficiaries under the trust are converted into equivalent interests in the capital fund representing the proceeds of sale of the land or the mortgage loan. Thus, where land is held on trust for a succession of persons, the owner of each successive life interest in the land would become entitled to lifetime enjoyment of the capital fund representing the proceeds of sale, which in practical terms means the income or interest earned by the investment of the fund during his lifetime; and, when the ultimate equitable fee simple falls into possession, the owner of that interest would become entitled to the capital fund itself.

5. For detailed analysis of the doctrine of overreaching, see Harpum [1990] C.L.J. 277.

6. According to the orthodoxy, overreaching operates irrespective of the consent of the owners of the equitable interests; but that orthodoxy has been questioned in the context of co-ownership trusts: see *post*, p. 204. The Law Commission recommended that a conveyance of a legal estate should not have the effect of overreaching the interest of anyone of full age and capacity who is entitled to a beneficial interest in the land and who has a right to occupy it and is in actual occupation of it at the date of the conveyance, unless that person consents (although it was also recommended that the court should have a discretionary power to dispense with the consent requirement): Law Com. No. 188, *Transfer of Land: Overreaching: Beneficiaries in Occupation* (1989), paras 4.3, 4.19. It is arguable that the Trusts of Land and Appointment of Trustees Act 1996 has had the effect of implementing a version of the Law Commission's recommendation: see *post*, p. 336; but in March 1998 the Government announced that it had decided not to implement the (remaining) recommendations in the Report: *Hansard* HL, March 19, 1998, Written Answers 213.

7. A purchaser of land will normally know when the land is subject to a trust and will accordingly comply with the statutory requirement that the purchase money be paid to at least two trustees. However, where a purchaser does not know that he is purchasing land subject to a trust, and does not therefore comply with the statutory requirement, the conveyance will not overreach the equitable interests under the trust. In those circumstances, the purchaser may be held to have constructive notice of, and to hold the land subject to, the equitable interests under the trust: see *post*, p. 332.

8. In most instances overreaching takes place on a conveyance or mortgage where capital money is paid to and receipted by the trustees and the equitable interests of the beneficiaries under the trust are transformed into corresponding interests in that capital money. However, as Harpum [1990] C.L.J. 277 argued, the Court of Appeal has recently held that overreaching may simply involve the subordination of the beneficiaries' equitable interests to the purchaser's interest. Such subordination, without the transformation of the beneficiaries' interests into interests in the capital money, will be the effect where the trustees exercise a power of disposition that does not give rise to any capital money: *State Bank of India v. Sood* [1997] Ch. 276, *infra*.

State Bank of India v. Sood [1997] Ch. 276

(CA, Hirst, Peter Gibson and Pill L.JJ.)

The first and second defendants held a dwelling-house on trust (for sale) for themselves and for the third to seventh defendants. They created a legal charge over the house in order to secure the discharge on demand of their existing and future indebtedness to the Punjab National Bank. No money was advanced to the first and second defendants at the time of the creation of the charge. The charge was later assigned to the plaintiff bank. When the level of indebtedness exceeded £1 million and the first and second defendants failed to meet demands for repayment, the plaintiff sought possession of the house. The third to seventh defendants claimed that they had equitable interests in the house, that those interests had not been overreached by the legal charge and that those interests were binding on the plaintiff. The plaintiff applied to have the claims of the defendants struck out.

PETER GIBSON L.J.:

Before I turn to the statutory provisions, I would make a few general observations on overreaching. As is explained by Charles Harpum in his illuminating article, "Overreaching, Trustees' Powers and the Reform of the 1925 Legislation" [1990] C.L.J. 277, overreaching is the process whereby existing interests are subordinated to a later interest or estate created pursuant to a trust or power. Mr Harpum arrived at that statement of the true nature of overreaching by a consideration of the effect of the exercise of powers of disposition in a settlement, referring to *Sugden on Powers*, 8th ed. (1861), pp. 482, 483. He argued cogently that a transaction made by a person within the dispositive powers conferred upon him will overreach equitable interests in the property the subject of the disposition, but ultra vires dispositions will not, and the transferee with notice will take the property subject to those interests. Mr Harpum expressed the view that the exercise intra vires of a power of disposition which does not give rise to any capital money, such as an exchange of land, overreaches just as much as a transaction which does. There is every reason to think that the draftsman of the 1925 property legislation fully appreciated the true nature of overreaching. A principal objective of the 1925 property legislation was to simplify conveyancing and the proof of title to land. To this end equitable interests were to be kept off the title to the legal estate and could be overreached on a conveyance to a purchaser who took free of them.

The statutory provision governing overreaching is section 2 of the Law of Property Act 1925...

The opening words of section 2(1) and paragraph (ii) are the provisions most material to the appeal. The term "conveyance" is given a wide meaning in section 205(1)(ii) of the Law of Property Act 1925. It includes "a mortgage, charge, lease, assignment, vesting declaration, disclaimer, release and every other assurance of property or of an interest therein by any instrument, except a will." Plainly therefore the legal charge is such a conveyance. The term "purchaser" is defined as meaning for the relevant part of the Act "a person who acquires an interest in or charge on property for money's worth" and in reference to a legal estate includes a charge by way of legal mortgage: section 205(1)(xxi) of the Law of Property Act 1925. Although the legal charge does not expressly state the consideration passing to the first and second defendants, Mr Havey and Mr Williams [counsel for the defendants] rightly do not suggest that the Punjab National Bank was not a purchaser. It is not in issue that the first and second defendants are trustees for sale.

The term "capital money" is by section 205(1)(xxvi) of the Law of Property Act 1925 to have the same meaning as in the Settled Land Act 1925. ...

There is no dispute that the equitable interests of the third to seventh defendants were at the date of the legal charge capable of being overreached. That condition of section 2(1)(ii) was therefore satisfied. Most of the argument has turned on the final condition of that paragraph relating to compliance with the statutory requirements respecting the payment of capital money. Section 27(2) of the Law of Property Act 1925 (as amended by the Law of Property (Amendment) Act 1926) provides (so far as material):

> "the proceeds of sale or other capital money shall not be paid to or applied by the direction of fewer than two persons as trustees for sale, except when the trustee is a trust corporation ..."

It is common ground that this provision contains the statutory requirements regulating the payment of capital money which are referred to in section 2(1)(ii).

...

The case of the third to seventh defendants has always been that their beneficial interests in respect of the property ... were not overreached by the legal charge because no capital money arose thereunder contemporaneously therewith and that accordingly their interests bound the plaintiff and take priority over its interests under the legal charge. The plaintiff's case has always been that the equitable interests of the third to seventh defendants were overreached by the legal charge, there being no statutory requirement that capital money should arise contemporaneously with the disposition.

...

I accept that a novel and important point of law is raised by this appeal. Lending institutions regularly take security from businessmen in the form of a legal charge on property (which very frequently means that the matrimonial home is charged) to secure existing and future indebtedness, and very commonly that property will be registered land held by two registered proprietors on trust for sale with no restriction registered in respect of their power to transfer or mortgage that property. It was not suggested that it had ever been the practice of mortgagees to make inquiries of occupiers of the property as to any claimed rights. Yet if the third to seventh defendants are right, that is what the mortgagees must do if they are not to take subject to the beneficial interests of the occupiers.

It is remarkable that the point of law taken by those defendants does not appear to have arisen before in any reported case. We were taken by counsel to only two cases: *Williams & Glyn's Bank Ltd v. Boland* [1979] Ch. 312; [1981] A.C. 487 in the Court of Appeal and in the House of Lords and *City of London Building Society v. Flegg* [1986] Ch. 605; [1988] A.C. 54 in the Court of Appeal and in the House of Lords. In the *Boland* case it was common ground between the parties that there was no overreaching. Money was raised on mortgage of registered land and paid to a single trustee holding the land on trust for sale. ... In the present case, as in the *Flegg* case, the registered proprietors were two in number. But in the *Flegg* case it was held that where money was raised on mortgage of registered land to discharge an existing incumbrance (and so in exercise of the power conferred by section 28(1) of the Law of Property Act 1925 by reference to section 71(1)(i) of the Settled Land Act 1925) and paid to two trustees for sale, the rights of occupying beneficiaries were overreached. In the present case the legal charge was not entered into to raise money for the discharge of an existing incumbrance nor was any money raised contemporaneously with the legal charge. No less surprising is the fact that counsel were not able to point to a single textbook for assistance nor to any other academic writing, though the court drew counsel's attention to Mr Harpum's article to which I have already referred.

...

The crucial issue is the true construction of the final condition of section 2(1)(ii) relating to compliance with statutory requirements respecting the payment of capital money. There is no dispute that if capital money does arise under a conveyance by trustees for sale to a purchaser it must be paid to or applied as section 27(2) dictates. But for overreaching to occur, does capital money have to arise on and contemporaneously with the conveyance?

The judge appears to have assumed that there could be no overreaching if no capital money arose.

He said:

> "we have to look to see whether capital money was paid [to] or applied by the direction of the two trustees. If it was, then the defendants have no defence; if it was not, then the bank cannot overreach and they have an arguable defence on the evidence."

Mr Havey and Mr Williams submitted that was indeed the position and they said that the arising of capital money on the conveyance was the assumption on which section 2(1)(ii) was drafted. Mr Crawford's [counsel for the plaintiff] initial submission accorded with that view, but he sought to escape the consequences by contending that capital money arose whenever the Punjab National Bank advanced money, even if before the legal charge was executed. However, I cannot accept that what was done prior to the legal charge has any relevance to the condition that "the statutory requirements respecting the payment of capital money arising under a disposition upon trust for sale are complied with". Nor can I accept Mr Crawford's further submission that the debt existing at the date of the legal charge was not materially different from the secured debt which existed at the date of the mortgage in *Flegg* and was discharged in that case out of the money raised. The circumstances are wholly different.

Mr Crawford however had recourse to a further submission, adopting a point suggested by the court, that the relevant condition in section 2(1)(ii) should be construed as applying only to those cases where there was capital money arising under a disposition upon trust for sale, the statutory requirements of section 27(2) being simply irrelevant to a transaction under which no capital money arises. There are several types of conveyance to a purchaser (within the statutory meanings of those terms) other than a charge to secure existing and future debt which do not give rise to capital money, for example, an exchange or a lease not at a premium. Why should the legislature have intended to exclude such conveyances from having an overreaching effect? It is interesting to note that the precursor of section 2(1), viz. section 3(2)(ii) of the Law of Property Act 1922, used as one of the conditions for overreaching to occur the formula "If any capital money arises from the transaction ... the requirements of this Act respecting the payment of capital money arising under a trust for sale ... are complied with." However the form of section 3(2) differed in a number of respects from section 2(1) of the Act of 1925 and it may not be safe to infer that the later provision was intended to re-enact the substance of the earlier provision. But it points to the relevant condition of section 2(1) being worded in surprisingly oblique fashion if what was intended was that capital money must arise so that the statutory requirements can be complied with. Mr Havey drew attention to the word "any" in connection with "capital money" in section 2(1)(iii) and (iv) and suggested that its omission from the reference to "capital money" in section 2(1)(i) and (ii) was significant. But the structure of those paragraphs is quite different from section 2(1)(iii) and (iv) and the draftsman could not have achieved the effect of section 3(2) of the Act of 1922 by adding "any" before "capital money" in section 2(1)(i) or (ii).

The relevant condition in section 2(1)(ii) is the same as that in section 2(1)(i). The overreaching powers conferred by the Settled Land Act 1925 include power to convey by an exchange or lease as well as by a mortgage or charge where capital money may not arise (see section 72 of that Act). The statutory requirements governing capital money (to be paid to or applied by the direction of not less than two individuals or a trust corporation: sections 94 and 95 of that Act) can only apply to those conveyances giving rise to capital money. The same interpretation must apply to the condition in section 2(1)(i) as it does to the conveyancing condition in section 2(1)(ii).

A more substantial argument of policy advanced on behalf of the third to seventh defendants is that if overreaching occurs where no capital money arises, the beneficiaries' interests may be reduced by the conveyance leaving nothing to which the interests can attach by way of replacement save the equity of redemption, and that may be or become valueless. I see considerable force in this point, but I am not persuaded that it suffices to defeat what I see to be the policy of the legislation, to allow valid dispositions to overreach equitable interests. In my judgment on its true construction section 2(1)(ii) only requires compliance with the statutory requirements respecting the payment of capital money if capital money arises. Accordingly I would hold that capital money did not have to arise under the conveyance.

. . .

Both Mr Havey and Mr Williams supported the judge's conclusion that some capital money must arise contemporaneously with the conveyance for there to be overreaching. They said that if a conveyance provided only for deferred payment, that would not suffice. They further submitted that provided some capital money arose contemporaneously with the conveyance and section 27(2) was complied with, overreaching would occur even though other money was subsequently advanced under the conveyance. Thus if a £1m. facility was secured by a mortgage and in the course of time was fully drawn on but at the time of the mortgage only £100 was advanced, there would nevertheless be overreaching in respect of the whole £1m. thereby secured, whereas if the £100 had not been advanced at the time of the mortgage, there would have been no overreaching. I do not believe that the statutory language supports a requirement producing such a surprising and illogical result. Mr Havey drew our attention to a large number of provisions in the Settled Land Act 1925 which, he said, showed that money arising from a transaction must be received or applied at the same time as the transaction. I cannot agree, though I of course accept that to be paid or applied, capital money must be in hand. If and to the extent that capital money arises after the conveyance, section 27(2) must be complied with for the mortgagee to obtain a good receipt. If it is not, for example if an advance is made after a mortgage has been executed but under a facility provided for by the mortgage but is not paid to or at the direction of two or more trustees or a trust corporation, that would not affect the overreaching which would have occurred on the mortgage.

I take the following statement in *Snell's Equity*, 29th ed. (1990), p. 63, to be correct:

"A conveyance to a purchaser of a legal estate for money or money's worth will overreach ... any equitable interest or power affecting the estate whether or not the purchaser has notice of it, if the conveyance is made ... (ii) by trustees for sale ... provided that the ... equitable interest or power is one of those which are capable of being overreached by the conveyance, and that *any* capital money arising from the transaction is paid—in case ... (ii) to the trustees, who must be at least two in number, or a trust corporation ..." (My emphasis.)

The correct analysis of the position in the present case is that on the execution of the legal charge, the interests of the third to seventh defendants were overreached and attached to the equity of redemption. The legal estate in the property was by the legal charge made subject to the rights thereunder of the Punjab National Bank which were subsequently assigned to the plaintiff, including the right to sell the property. The value of the equity of redemption on the execution of the legal charge would reflect the then existing liabilities thereby secured. That value would be further reduced as further liabilities arose and were secured under the legal charge....

Much though I value the principle of overreaching as having aided the simplification of conveyancing, I cannot pretend that I regard the resulting position in the present case as entirely satisfactory. The safeguard for beneficiaries under the existing legislation is largely limited to having two trustees or a trust corporation where capital money falls to be received. But that is no safeguard at all, as this case has shown, when no capital money is received on and contemporaneously with the conveyance. Further, even when it is received by two trustees as in *City of London Building Society v. Flegg* [1986] Ch. 605; [1988] A.C. 54, it might be thought that beneficiaries in occupation are insufficiently protected. Hence the recommendation for reform in the Law Commission's report, "Transfer of Land, Overreaching: Beneficiaries in Occupation (1989)" Law Com. No. 188, that a conveyance should not overreach the interest of a sui juris beneficiary in occupation unless he gives his consent. Mr Harpum in the article to which reference has been made proposed an alternative reform, limiting the power of trustees to mortgage. Whether the legislature will reform the law remains to be seen. I should add for completeness that we were assured by counsel that the recent Trusts of Land and Appointment of Trustees Act 1996 was of no assistance and we have not considered its effect.

Despite the dissatisfaction with the existing law which I have voiced, for the reasons which I have given I would allow this appeal ....

NOTES:

1. For comment, see [1997] C.L.J. 494; [1997] Conv. 134.

2. As Peter Gibson L.J. points out, overreaching without the transformation of the beneficiaries' interests into interests in the capital money provides very limited protection for the beneficiaries. In the instant case the interests of the third to seventh defendants attached to the equity of redemption held by the first and second defendants; but the implication seems to have been that the equity of redemption (in monetary terms, the value of the house less the amount of the indebtedness) was probably valueless.

3. As Peter Gibson L.J. also points out, the position of beneficiaries in the not uncommon circumstances exemplified by the instant case provides further grounds for supporting the recommendations in Law Com. No. 188, Transfer of Land: Overreaching: Beneficiaries in Occupation (1989), *supra*, p. 109.

4. The case in fact involved land with *registered* title. That factor did not affect the question of overreaching; but, according to the argument of the third to seventh defendants, if the court had held that their interests had *not* been overreached, it would have provided the basis for their claim that those interests were binding on the plaintiff: see *post*, p. 197.

5. The Trusts of Land and Appointment of Trustees Act 1996, referred to in the penultimate paragraph of the judgment of Peter Gibson L.J., has replaced the trust for sale with the trust of land as the machinery for co-ownership of land: see *post*, p. 294. However, the amended section 2 of the Law of Property Act 1925 (*supra*, p. 107) applies the doctrine of overreaching to trusts of land.

4. Registration of land charges under the Land Charges Act 1972

Notwithstanding the terminology of "registration", the system of registration of land charges under the Land Charges Act 1972 (replacing the Land Charges Act 1925) is a constituent element of *title deeds conveyancing*. Pending the complete replacement of that system by registration of title, the Land Charges Act 1925 was intended to reduce the scope of operation of the doctrine of notice with all its uncertainties for both purchasers of land and owners of third party interests affecting that land. The fundamental idea behind the registration of interests under the Land Charges Act was to replace the equitable doctrine of notice with what has been termed "statutory notice". Registration is deemed to constitute "actual notice ... to all persons and for all purposes" (Law of Property Act 1925, s.198(1)) so that a duly registered third party interest is enforceable against a purchaser irrespective of whether or not that purchaser would have had notice under the equitable doctrine.

In fact there are five separate registers maintained under the Land Charges Act 1972: land charges; pending actions; writs and orders affecting land; deeds of arrangement affecting land; and annuities (now effectively obsolete). However, the register of land charges is the most important and it alone is examined in detail.

4.1 *Principles of registration of land charges*

4.1.1 *Register of names*   In contrast with the registered title system, under which third party interests affecting land are entered on the register relating to the land (or title) in question, interests under the Land Charges Act are required to be registered against the name of the person who is the "estate owner" of the land in question and "whose estate is intended to be affected": Land Charges Act 1972, s.3(1). Thus the person entitled to the relevant interest will normally register it as a land charge against the name of the estate owner who created it.

However, the relevant date for registration purposes is the date of registration (not the date of creation) of the land charge; and problems could therefore arise where the estate owner created a registrable land charge but died before the land charge was registered. Registration against the name of a deceased person, where the person seeking to register the land charge did not know of the death, was almost certainly ineffective; but, even where the person seeking to register the land charge did know of the death, it could be difficult to discover the existence and identity of the persons in whom the land was currently vested: see Prichard [1979] Conv. 249; Law Com. No. 184, *Property Law: Title on Death* (1989), paras 2.2–2.9, noted at [1990] Conv. 69.

It is now provided that in the circumstances under discussion, the land charge remains registrable against the deceased estate owner: Land Charges Act 1972, s.3(1A), inserted by the Law of Property (Miscellaneous Provisions) Act 1994, s.15(1),(2), noted at [1995] Conv. 476.

Further problems of a names-based register are considered below.

4.1.2 *Effect of registration*

Law of Property Act 1925, s.198(1)

Registration under the Land Charges Act 1972 to be notice

198.—(1) The registration of any instrument or matter in any register kept under the Land Charges Act 1972 or any local land charges register, shall be deemed to constitute actual notice of such instrument or matter, and of the fact of such registration, to all persons and for all purposes connected with the land affected, as from the date of registration or other prescribed date and so long as the registration continues in force.

NOTES:

1. See generally Wade [1956] C.L.J. 216.

2. The statutory effect of registration of a land charge against the freeholder extends to a leaseholder. As has been seen (*ante*, p. 38), after 1925 a prospective purchaser of a leasehold estate is not entitled to investigate the relevant freehold title: Law of Property Act 1925, s.44(2); and, accordingly, he is not deemed to have (equitable) notice of those equitable interests that he would have discovered if he had investigated it: *ibid*. s.44(5), abolishing the contrary rule in *Patman v. Harland* (1881) 17 Ch.D. 353, 359 *per* Jessel M.R. However, it has been held that section 44(5) has no application to statutory notice under section 198(1): *White v. Bijou Mansions Ltd* [1937] Ch. 610, 619 *per* Simonds J. Moreover, leaseholders are excluded from the compensation scheme introduced by the Law of Property Act 1969: see *infra*, note 4.

3. The statutory effect of registration of a land charge no longer applies to a purchaser who has entered into but not yet completed a contract for the sale and purchase of land. Where a purchaser has contracted to purchase land and only then discovers an incumbrance which is inconsistent with or prejudicial to his intended use of the land, but which will be enforceable if he proceeds with the purchase, as a matter of contract he would be entitled to withdraw from the contract on the ground that the vendor could not show good title, *provided that the purchaser did not know of the incumbrance at the time of the contract*: see *Re Nisbet and Potts' Contract* [1906] 1 Ch. 386, *ante*, p. 35. (The position would be different if the purchaser knew of the incumbrance at the time of the contract, unless the vendor had contracted to sell the land free from incumbrances: see *Re Gloag and Miller's Contract* (1883) 23 Ch.D. 320, 327 *per* Fry J.; *McGrory v. Alderdale Estate Co. Ltd* [1918] A.C. 503, 508 per Lord Finlay L.C.) The difficulty posed by section 198(1) for contracts entered into after 1925 was that, where the incumbrance had been duly registered under the Land Charges Act, the purchaser was deemed to have had notice of the incumbrance *at the time of the contract*; and it made no difference that the contract provided for the sale to be free from incumbrances: see *Re Forsey and Hollebone's Contract* [1927] 2 Ch. 279. For trenchant criticism of the decision, see Wade [1954] C.L.J. 89; and see Law Com. No. 18, *Transfer of Land: Report on Land Charges Affecting Unregistered Land* (1969), para. 29. Section 24(1) of the Law of Property Act 1969 now provides:

Contracts for purchase of land affected by land charge, etc.

24.—(1) Where under a contract for the sale or other disposition of any estate or interest in land the title to which is not registered under the Land Registration Act 1925 or any enactment replaced by it any question arises whether the purchaser had knowledge, at the time of entering into the contract, of a registered land charge, that question shall be determined by reference to his actual knowledge and without regard to the provisions of section 198 of the Law of Property Act 1925 (under which registration under the Land Charges Act 1972 or any enactment replaced by it is deemed to constitute actual notice).

However, if the purchaser proceeds with the purchase, he will be bound by the land charge.

The principle in *Re Forsey and Hollebone's Contract* still applies in the context of *local* land charges; but in *Rignall Developments Ltd v. Halil* [1988] Ch. 190, 199–203, Millett J. questioned the assimilation of "notice" in section 198(1) with "knowledge" for the purposes of the common law rule. For comment, see [1987] Conv. 291; [1988] C.L.J. 18.

4. In certain circumstances, compensation may be available where a purchaser suffers loss by reason of the statutory effect of the registration of land charges. The problem is caused by the combination of a names-based register, the continued operation of the land charges system that was intended as a temporary expedient only (pending the completion of registration of title) and the reduction in the statutory period for the investigation of title. As a consequence of those factors, it is increasingly possible that a purchaser will investigate the names of estate owners revealed by the abstract of title covering the statutory period of 15 years but that the abstract of title will not reveal the names of the earlier post-1925 estate owners of the land. Yet, according to section 198(1) the registration of any land charges against the names of those persons is deemed to constitute actual notice to the purchaser and the registered interests are enforceable against him. Although the "undiscoverable" registered land charge has been described as "an entirely academic creation", on the ground that "active" incumbrances are almost invariably referred to in successive conveyances, the problem was acknowledged by the Law Commission: see Law Com. No. 18, *Transfer of Land: Report on Land Charges Affecting Unregistered Land* (1969), paras 30–42. Section 25 of the Law of Property Act 1969 now provides:

Compensation in certain cases for loss due to undisclosed land charges

25.—(1) Where a purchaser of any estate or interest in land under a disposition to which this section applies has suffered loss by reason that the estate or interest is affected by a registered land charge, then if—
(a) the date of completion was after the commencement of this Act; and
(b) on that date the purchaser had no actual knowledge of the charge; and
(c) the charge was registered against the name of an owner of an estate in the land who was not as owner of any such estate a party to any transaction, or concerned in any event, comprised in the relevant title;
the purchaser shall be entitled to compensation for the loss.

(2) For the purposes of subsection (1)(b) above, the question whether any person had actual knowledge of a charge shall be determined without regard to the provisions of section 198 of the Law of Property Act 1925 (under which registration under the Land Charges Act 1972 or any enactment replaced by it is deemed to constitute actual notice).

5. The statutory effect of registration may not apply where the registration is not made against the "correct" name of the estate owner: see *infra*, p. 133.

6. The statutory effect of registration of a right of pre-emption is suspended until the right becomes exercisable: see *infra*, p. 139.

4.1.3 *Effect of non-registration*   In principle an interest which is capable of registration under the Land Charges Act, but which is not registered, is void as against a purchaser of the land. The Act defines "purchaser" as "any person (including a mortgagee or lessee) who, for valuable consideration, takes any interest in land ...": *ibid.* s.17(1). However, the Act differentiates between two categories of land charge and between two categories of purchaser. Land charges of classes A, B, C(i), C(ii), C(iii) and F, if unregistered, are void as against a purchaser of *any interest in the land: ibid.* s.4(2), (5), (8); land charges of classes C(iv), D(i), D(ii) and D(iii), if unregistered, are void only as against a purchaser *for money or money's worth of a legal estate in the land: ibid.* s.4(6). An unregistered land charge that is not void under the terms of section 4 remains enforceable. For example, an unregistered class C(iv) land charge is enforceable against a purchaser of an equitable interest in the land in question: see *McCarthy and Stone Ltd v. Hodge* [1971] 1 W.L.R. 1547, 1555 *per* Foster J., noted at [1972A] C.L.J. 34; and an unregistered land charge of any class is enforceable against a donee of the land in question.

Despite the apparently unambiguous terms of section 4, various arguments have been advanced in attempts to avoid its stated consequences.

4.1.3.1 *Actual occupation*   First, it has been argued that a registrable but unregistered interest should not be void where the person claiming that interest is in possession or actual occupation of the land in question. The argument is based on section 14 of the Law of Property Act 1925, which provides that "Part I of this Act shall not prejudicially affect the interest of any person in possession or in actual occupation of land to which he may be entitled in right of such possession or occupation." Although the ambit of the section "has puzzled conveyancers ever since the Law of Property Act was enacted" (*City of London Building Society v. Flegg* [1988] A.C. 54, 80 *per* Lord Oliver), such an argument would certainly be consistent with the protection afforded to persons in actual occupation of registered land: see Land Registration Act 1925, s.70(1)(g), *post*, p. 187; and see *Lloyds Bank plc v. Carrick* [1996] 4 All E.R. 630, 642 *per* Morritt L.J., *infra*, p. 126. However, any such argument seems to be precluded by the opening words of the section. The provisions detailing the prejudicial effect of non-registration are contained not in Part I of the Law of Property Act 1925 but in the Land Charges Act 1972. It is correctly pointed out that all the relevant provisions were contained in the same part of the Law of Property Act 1922 and it is asserted that they were accidentally separated in the 1925 consolidation: see Friend and Newton [1982] Conv. 213, 215–217; but it might be argued that Parliament has had ample opportunity to remedy the allegedly unintended consequence of that consolidation.

4.1.3.2 *Actual notice*   Secondly, it has been argued that a registrable but unregistered interest should not be void where the person claiming that the interest is unenforceable had *actual* notice of it. This argument seemed to have been addressed specifically by the 1925 legislation. For section 199(1)(i) of the Law of Property Act 1925 provides:

> **199.**—(1) A purchaser shall not be prejudicially affected by notice of—
> (i)   any instrument or matter capable of registration under the provisions of the Land Charges Act 1972, or any enactment which it replaces, which is void or not enforceable as against him under that Act or enactment, by reason of the non-registration thereof; ...

However, the argument has been advanced on a number of occasions and it was pursued all the way to the House of Lords in *Midland Bank Trust Co. Ltd v. Green* [1981] A.C. 513.

Midland Bank Trust Co. Ltd v. Green [1981] A.C. 513

(HL, Lord Wilberforce, Lord Edmund-Davies, Lord Fraser, Lord Russell, Lord Bridge)

[The facts are stated in the speech of Lord Wilberforce.]

LORD WILBERFORCE:

My Lords, this appeal relates to a 300-acre farm in Lincolnshire called "Gravel Hill Farm". It was owned by Walter Stanley Green ("Walter") and since 1954, let to his son Thomas Geoffrey Green ("Geoffrey") who farmed it as tenant. Walter owned another larger farm which he farmed jointly with another son Robert Derek Green ("Robert"), the appellant. In 1960 Walter sold this other farm to Robert at £75 per acre.

On March 24, 1961, Walter granted to Geoffrey an option to purchase Gravel Hill Farm, also at £75 per acre. The option was granted for the consideration of £1, and so was contractually binding upon Walter. It was to remain open for ten years. It seems that the reason why this transaction was entered into rather than one of sale to Geoffrey, was to save estate duty on Walter's death.

This option was, in legal terms, an estate contract and so a legal charge, class C, within the meaning of the Land Charges Act 1925. The correct and statutory method for protection of such an option is by means of entering it in the Register of Land Charges maintained under the Act. If so registered, the option would have been enforceable, not only (contractually) against Walter, but against any purchaser of the farm.

The option was not registered, a failure which inevitably called in question the responsibility of Geoffrey's solicitor. To anticipate, Geoffrey in fact brought proceedings against his solicitor which have been settled for a considerable sum, payable if the present appeal succeeds.

In 1967 there appears to have been some family disagreement. We do not know the nature of it, nor the merits. I am not prepared to assume, in the absence of any evidence, that either side was in the wrong. All we know is that Walter formed the intention, contrary to what he had planned in 1961, to defeat Geoffrey's option and to make Gravel Hill Farm available for the family. He instructed solicitors to prepare a conveyance of it to his wife Evelyne: this the solicitors did after verifying that the option was not registered as a land charge.

On or about August 17, 1967, Walter executed a conveyance of Gravel Hill Farm to

Evelyne for a consideration of £500. The judge found that this sum was paid by Evelyne to Walter. It was of course far less than the value of the farm, which was then worth about £40,000. The conveyance was also a breach of contract by Walter for which Walter or his estate was liable to Geoffrey in damages.

Later, Evelyne made a will in which she left the farm, subject to Walter's life interest, to her five children—including Geoffrey. On September 5, 1967, Geoffrey, who had learnt of the conveyance, caused the option to be registered as an estate contract, and on October 6, 1967, gave notice exercising the option. Finally, on January 27, 1970, Geoffrey issued a writ against Walter and Evelyne's executors (she had died in 1968) claiming that the option was still binding, specific performance of the contract arising from its exercise and damages. This was later amended so as to claim damages for conspiracy by Walter and Evelyne.

Most of the principals involved in the above transactions are dead. The place of Geoffrey is taken by the present respondents as his executors; that of Evelyne by the appellant, as her sole surviving executor; the place of Walter was taken by Beryl Rosalie Kemp as his executrix, but her defence was struck out by order dated October 7, 1975. The issue therefore effectively is between the appellant, as representing the estate of Evelyne, and the respondents as representing the estate of Geoffrey.

The trial took place before Oliver J. in 1977. A number of issues arose which are no longer relevant. The learned judge, in an admirable judgment with which I wholly agree, decided (i) that the sale and conveyance to Evelyne was not a sham and was a genuine sale by the vendor to a "purchaser", as defined by the Land Charges Act 1925 for money or money's worth, and accordingly that the option was not specifically enforceable; (ii) that Walter's estate had no answer to a claim for damages, and that an inquiry as to damages must be made; (iii) that any claim for damages against the estate of Evelyne was statute-barred by virtue of the Law Reform (Miscellaneous Provisions) Act 1934.

An appeal was brought to the Court of Appeal which, by a majority, reversed the judge's decision on point (i), and declared the option specifically enforceable. The ground of this decision appears to have been that the sale in 1967 was not for "money or money's worth", within the meaning of section 13 of the Land Charges Act 1925. In addition Lord Denning M.R. was prepared to hold that the protection of the Act was not available in a case of fraud meaning thereby "any dishonest dealing done so as to deprive unwary innocents of their rightful dues." The respondents, however, did not seek to support this except to the extent that they relied upon lack of good faith on the part of Evelyne.

My Lords, section 13(2) of the Land Charges Act 1925 reads as follows:

> "A land charge of class B, class C or class D, created or arising after the commencement of this Act, shall (except as hereinafter provided) be void as against a purchaser of the land charged therewith ... unless the land charge is registered in the appropriate register before the completion of the purchase: Provided that, as respect of land charge of class D and an estate contract created or entered into after the commencement of this Act, this subsection only applies in favour of a purchaser of a legal estate for money or money's worth."

As regards the word "purchaser" section 20(8) of the same Act reads: " 'Purchaser' means any person ... who, for valuable consideration, takes any interest in land ..."

Thus the case appears to be a plain one. The "estate contract", which by definition (section 11) includes an option of purchase, was entered into after January 1, 1926; Evelyne took an interest (in fee simple) in the land "for valuable consideration"—so was a "purchaser": she was a purchaser for money—namely £500: the option was not registered before the completion of the purchase. It is therefore void as against her.

In my opinion this appearance is also the reality. The case is plain: the Act is clear and definite. Intended as it was to provide a simple and understandable system for the protection of title to land, it should not be read down or glossed: to do so would destroy the usefulness of the Act. Any temptation to remould the Act to meet the facts of the present case, on the supposition that it is a hard one and that justice requires it, is, for me at least, removed by the consideration that the Act itself provides a simple and effective protection for persons in Geoffrey's position—viz.—by registration.

The respondents submitted two arguments as to the interpretation of section 13(2): the one sought to introduce into it a requirement that the purchaser should be "in good faith"; the other related to the words "in money or money's worth".

The argument as to good faith fell into three parts: first, that "good faith" was something required of a "purchaser" before 1926; secondly, that this requirement was preserved by the 1925 legislation and in particular by section 13(2) of the Land Charges Act 1925. If these points could be made good, it would then have to be decided whether the purchaser (Evelyne) was in "good faith" on the facts of the case.

My Lords, the character in the law known as the bona fide (good faith) purchaser for value without notice was the creation of equity. In order to affect a purchaser for value of a legal estate with some equity or equitable interest, equity fastened upon his conscience and the composite expression was used to epitomise the circumstances in which equity would or rather would not do so. I think that it would generally be true to say that the words "in good faith" related to the existence of notice. Equity, in other words, required not only absence of notice, but genuine and honest absence of notice. As the law developed, this requirement became crystallised in the doctrine of constructive notice which assumed a statutory form in the Conveyancing Act 1882, section 3. But, and so far I would be willing to accompany the respondents, it would be a mistake to suppose that the requirement of good faith extended only to the matter of notice or that when notice came to be regulated by statute, the requirement of good faith became obsolete. Equity still retained its interest in and power over the purchaser's conscience. The classic judgment of James L.J. in *Pilcher v. Rawlins* (1872) L.R. 7 Ch.App. 259, 269 is clear authority that it did: good faith there is stated as a separate test which may have to be passed even though absence of notice is proved. And there are references in cases subsequent to 1882 which confirm the proposition that honesty or bona fides remained something which might be inquired into (see *Berwick & Co. v. Price* [1905] 1 Ch. 632, 639; *Taylor v. London and County Banking Co.* [1901] 2 Ch. 231, 256; *Oliver v. Hinton* [1899] 2 Ch. 264, 273).

But did this requirement, or test, pass into the property legislation of 1925?

My Lords, I do not think it safe to seek the answer to this question by means of a general assertion that the property legislation of 1922–25 was not intended to alter the law, or not intended to alter it in a particular field, such as that relating to purchases of legal estates. All the Acts of 1925, and their precursors, were drafted with the utmost care, and their wording, certainly where this is apparently clear, has to be accorded firm respect. As was pointed out in *Grey v. Inland Revenue Commissioners* [1960] A.C. 1, the Acts of 1922–4 effected massive changes in the law affecting property and the House, in consequence, was persuaded to give to a plain word ("disposition") its plain meaning, and not to narrow it by reference to its antecedents. Certainly that case should firmly discourage us from muddying clear waters. I accept that there is merit in looking at the corpus as a whole in order to produce if possible a consistent scheme. But there are limits to the possibilities of this process: for example it cannot eliminate the difference between registered and unregistered land, or the respective charges on them.

As to the requirement of "good faith" we are faced with a situation of some perplexity. The expression "good faith" appears in the Law of Property Act 1925 definition of "purchaser" ("a purchaser in good faith for valuable consideration"), section 205(1)(xxi); in the Settled Land Act 1925, section 117(1)(xxi) (ditto); in the Administration of Estates Act 1925, section 55(1)(xviii) (" 'Purchaser' means a lessee, mortgagee or other person who in good faith acquires an interest in property for valuable consideration") and in the Land Registration Act 1925, section 3(xxi) which does not however, as the other Acts do, include a reference to nominal consideration. So there is certainly some indication of an intention to carry the concept of "good faith" into much of the 1925 code. What then do we find in the Land Charges Act 1925? We were taken along a scholarly peregrination through the numerous Acts antecedent to the final codification and consolidation in 1925—the Land Charges Registration and Searches Act 1888, the Law of Property Act 1922, particularly Schedule 7, the Law of Property (Amendment) Act 1924 as well as the Yorkshire and Middlesex Deeds Registration Acts. But I think, with genuine respect for an interesting argument, that such solution as there is of the problem under consideration must be sought in the terms of the various Acts of 1925 themselves. So far as concerns the Land Charges Act 1925, the definition of "purchaser" quoted above does not mention "good faith" at all. "Good faith" did not appear in the original Act of 1888, not in the extension made to that Act by the Act of 1922, Schedule 7, nor in the Act of 1924, Schedule 6. It should be a secure assumption that the definition of "purchaser for value" which is found in section 4 of the Act of 1888 (... "person who for valuable consideration takes any interest in land") together with the limitation which is now the proviso to section 13(2) of the Act of 1925, introduced in 1922, was intended to be carried forward into the Act of 1925. The expression "good faith" appears nowhere in the antecedents. To write the word in, from the examples of contemporaneous Acts, would be bold. It becomes impossible when it is seen that the words appear in section 3(1) and in section 7(1), in each case in a proviso very similar, in structure, to the relevant proviso in section 13(2). If canons of constructions have any validity at all, they must lead to the conclusion that the omission in section 13(2) was deliberate.

My Lords, I recognise that the inquiring mind may put the question: why should there be an omission of the requirement of good faith in this particular context: I do not think there should be much doubt about the answer. Addition of a requirement that the purchaser should be in good faith would bring with it the necessity of inquiring into the purchaser's motives and state of mind. The present case is a good example of the difficulties which would exist. If the position was simply that the purchaser had notice of the option, and decided nevertheless to buy the land, relying on the absence of notification, nobody could contend that she would be lacking in good faith. She would merely be taking advantage of a situation, which the law has provided, and the addition of a profit motive could not create an absence of good faith. But suppose, and this is the respondents' argument, the purchaser's motive is to defeat the option, does this make any difference? Any advantage to oneself seems necessarily to involve a disadvantage for another: to make the validity of the purchase depend upon which aspect of the transaction was prevalent in the purchaser's mind seems to create distinctions equally difficult to analyse in law as to establish in fact: avarice and malice may be distinct sins, but in human conduct they are liable to be intertwined. The problem becomes even more acute if one supposes a mixture of motives. Suppose—and this may not be far from the truth—that the purchaser's motives were in part to take the farm from Geoffrey, and in part to distribute it between Geoffrey and his brothers and sisters, but not at all to obtain any benefit for herself, is this acting in "good faith" or not? Should family feeling be denied a protection afforded to simple greed? To eliminate the necessity for inquiries of this kind may well have been part of the legislative intention. Certainly there is here no argument for departing—violently—from the wording of the Act.

Before leaving this part of the case, I must comment on *In re Monolithic Building Co.* [1915] 1 Ch. 643, which was discussed in the Court of Appeal. There was a case arising under section 93 of the Companies (Consolidation) Act 1908 which made an unregistered mortgage void against any creditor of the company. The defendant Jenkins was a managing director of the company, and clearly had notice of the first unregistered mortgage: he himself subsequently took and registered a mortgage debenture and claimed priority over the unregistered mortgage. It was held by the Court of Appeal, first that this was not a case of fraud: "it is not fraud to take advantage of legal rights, the existence of which may be taken to be known to both parties" (*per* Lord Cozens-Hardy M.R., p. 663), secondly that section 93 of the Act was clear in its terms, should be applied according to its plain meaning, and should not be weakened by infusion of equitable doctrines applied by the courts during the 19th century. The judgment of Lord Cozens-Hardy M.R. contains a valuable critique of the well known cases of *Le Neve v. Le Neve* (1748) 3 Atk. 646 and *Greaves v. Tofield* (1880) 14 Ch.D. 563 which, arising under the Middlesex Registry Act 1708 and other enactments, had led the judges to import equitable doctrines into cases of priority arising under those Acts and establishes that the principles of those cases should not be applied to modern Acts of Parliament.

My Lords, I fail to see how this authority can be invoked in support of the respondents' argument, or of the judgments of the majority of the Court of Appeal. So far from supporting them, it is strongly the other way. It disposes, for the future, of the old arguments based, ultimately, upon *Le Neve v. Le Neve* (1748) 3 Atk. 643 for reading equitable doctrines (as to notice, etc.) into modern Acts of Parliament: to make it clear that it is not "fraud" to rely on legal rights conferred by Act of Parliament: it confirms the validity of interpreting clear enactments as to registration and priority according to their tenor.

The judgment of Phillimore L.J. in *In re Monolithic Building Co.* [1915] 1 Ch. 643, 669, 670 does indeed contain a passage which appears to favour application of the principle of *Le Neve v. Le Neve* (1748) 3 Atk. 646 and to make a distinction between a transaction designed to obtain an advantage, and one designed to defeat a prior (unregistered) interest. But, as I have explained, this distinction is unreal and unworkable: this whole passage is impossible to reconcile with the views of the other members of the Court of Appeal in the case, and I respectfully consider that it is not good law.

My Lords, I can deal more shortly with the respondents' second argument. It relates to the consideration for the purchase. The argument is that the protection of section 13(2) of the Land Charges Act 1925 does not extend to a purchaser who has provided only a nominal consideration and that £500 is nominal. A variation of this was the argument accepted by the Court of Appeal that the consideration must be "adequate"—an expression of transparent difficulty. The answer to both contentions lies in the language of the subsection. The word "purchaser," by definition (section 20(8)), means one who provides valuable consideration—a term of art which precludes any inquiry as to adequacy. This definition is, of course, subject to the context. Section 13(2), proviso, requires money or money's worth to be provided: the purpose of this being to exclude the consideration of marriage. There is nothing here which suggests, or admits of, the introduction of a further requirement that the money must not be nominal.

The argument for this requirement is based upon the Law of Property Act 1925 which, in section 205(1)(xxi) defining "purchaser" provides that "valuable consideration" includes marriage but does not include a "nominal consideration in money." The Land Charges Act 1925 contains no definition of "valuable consideration," so it is said to be necessary to have resort to the Law of Property Act definition: thus "nominal consideration in money" is excluded. An indication that this is intended is said to be provided by section 199(1)(i). I cannot accept this. The fallacy lies in supposing that the Acts—either of them—set out to define "valuable consideration"; they do not: they define "purchaser," and they define the word differently (see the first part of the argument). "Valuable consideration" requires no definition: it is an expression denoting an advantage conferred or detriment suffered. What each Act does is, for its own purposes, to exclude some things from this general expression: the Law of Property Act includes marriage but not a nominal sum in money; the Land Charges Act excludes marriage but allows "money or money's worth." There is no coincidence between these two; no link by reference or necessary logic between them. Section 199(1)(i) by refering to the Land Charges Act 1925, necessarily incorporates—for the purposes of this provision—the definition of "purchaser" in the latter Act, for it is only against such a "purchaser" that an instrument is void under that Act. It cannot be read as incorporating the Law of Property Act definition into the Land Charges Act. As I have pointed out the land charges legislation has contained its own definition since 1888, carried through, with the addition of the reference to "money or money's worth" into 1925. To exclude a nominal sum of money from section 13(2) of the Land Charges Act would be to rewrite the section.

This conclusion makes it unnecessary to determine whether £500 is a nominal sum of money or not. But I must say that for my part I should have great difficulty in so holding. "Nominal consideration" and a "nominal sum" in the law appear to me, as terms of art, to refer to a sum or consideration which can be mentioned as consideration but is not necessarily paid. To equate "nominal" with "inadequate" or even "grossly inadequate" would embark the law upon inquires which I cannot think were contemplated by Parliament.

I would allow the appeal.

NOTES:

1. The House of Lords thus endorsed the strict application of the terms of the Land Charges Act. That approach had also been adopted at first instance, where Oliver J. stated ([1980] Ch. 590, 614):

... as it seems to me Geoffrey had a clear legal right which was deliberately frustrated by his parents in breach of the contract created by the option. Nevertheless I cannot, with the best will in the world, allow my subjective moral judgment to stand in the way of what I apprehend to be the clear meaning of the statutory provisions.

By contrast a majority of the Court of Appeal had held that Evelyne could not rely on section 13(2) of the Land Charges Act 1925 (now section 4(6) of the Land Charges Act 1972). Lord Denning M.R. held ([1980] Ch. 590, 624) that she was not a purchaser *for money or money's worth* because she had not given "fair and reasonable value"; and (at 624–625) that in any event her fraud (in the sense of "dishonest dealing done so as to deprive unwary innocents of their rightful dues") precluded her from relying on section 13(2). Eveleigh L.J. held (at 628) that the consideration of £500 expressed in the conveyance to Evelyne was a "sham" so that the conveyance to Evelyne was in reality a gift. Sir Stanley Rees disagreed both with the interpretation of section 13(2) and with the view that there had been any vitiating fraud. On his view of the evidence, although Evelyne and Walter intended to take advantage of the non-registration of the option, they had been motivated by a wish to distribute the family assets among all their children.

2. For discussion see (1980) 96 L.Q.R. 8; [1981] C.L.J. 213; [1981] Conv. 361; (1981) 97 L.Q.R. 518; and see generally Thompson [1985] C.L.J. 280.

3. In *Hollington Bros. Ltd v. Rhodes* [1951] 2 T.L.R. 691 the defendants were lessees of an office block. They agreed to sub-let part of the premises to the plaintiffs for seven years; and the plaintiffs were let into possession. However, the sub-lease was never executed and the agreement was never registered as a class C(iv) land charge. The defendants later assigned the headlease "subject to and with the benefit of such tenancies as may affect the premises"; but the assignees gave the plaintiffs notice to quit. In litigation between the plaintiffs and the defendants, Harman J. held that the unregistered estate contract was not enforceable against the assignees even though the assignees knew of the interest of the plaintiffs and took the assignment expressly subject to that interest. He stated (at 695–696):

It seems to me ... that this argument cannot prevail having regard to the words in section 13(2) of the Land Charges Act 1925 ... The fact is that it was the policy of the framers of the 1925 legislation to get rid of equitable rights of this sort unless registered ... [A]s under section 13 of the Land Charges Act ... an unregistered estate contract is void, and under section 199 of the Law of Property Act 1925 the purchaser is not to be prejudicially affected by it, I do not see how that which is void and which is not to prejudice the purchaser can be validated by some equitable doctrine.

The case provides a particularly striking example of the effect of non-registration since the plaintiffs were in a position to argue both actual occupation on their part and actual notice on the part of the purchasers. For comment, see Wade [1956] C.L.J. 216, 226–228.

4. In 1987 the Law Commission expressed the view, albeit in the context of registered land, that the consequence of omitting the element of good faith on the part of a person claiming to take free of an unregistered interest was not acceptable; and reference was made to the decision in *Midland Bank Trust Co. Ltd v. Green*: see Law Com. No. 158, *Property Law: Third Report on Land Registration* (1987), para. 4.15. However, in its most recent consideration of the issue, albeit again in the context of registered land, the Law Commission has resiled from that position and has provisionally recommended that there should be no requirement of good faith on the part of a purchaser claiming to take free of an unregistered interest: Law Com. No. 254, *Land Registration for the Twenty-First Century* (1998), paras 3.39–3.50; and see *post*, p. 177.

5. For the successful actions by Geoffrey's estate against his solicitor for failing to register the option, see *Midland Bank Trust Co. Ltd v. Hett, Stubbs and Kemp* [1978] Ch. 384; and against Walter's estate for conspiracy, see *Midland Bank Trust Co. Ltd v. Green (No. 3)* [1982] Ch. 529.

4.1.3.3 *Estoppel*   In certain circumstances it may be argued that a purchaser is estopped (prevented) from relying on the non-registration of a registrable land charge. If the purchaser of land represents, expressly or by implication, to the owner of a registrable but unregistered land charge that it is enforceable, intending that the owner should rely on that representation, and if the owner acts to his detriment in reliance on the representation, the purchaser may be estopped from denying the substance of his representation: see *E.R. Ives Investment Ltd v. High* [1967] 2 Q.B. 379, *infra*, p. 142, *Taylors Fashions Ltd v. Liverpool Victoria Trustees Co. Ltd* [1982] Q.B. 133, *post*, p. 535.

4.1.3.4 *Independent interest enforceable against the purchaser*   In *Lloyds Bank plc v. Carrick* [1996] 4 All E.R. 630 it was argued that, despite the non-registration of a registrable land charge, rendering the relevant interest unenforceable against the purchaser, the claimant may be able to identify a separate and distinct interest, not registrable as a land charge but enforceable against the purchaser by virtue of the doctrine of notice.

Lloyds Bank plc v. Carrick [1996] 4 All E.R. 630

(CA, Beldam, Morritt and Ralph Gibson L.JJ.)

Mrs Carrick (the second defendant) was the widowed sister-in-law of Mr Carrick (the first defendant). Pursuant to an agreement that Mrs Carrick should purchase a maisonette held by Mr Carrick on a long lease, Mrs Carrick sold her house, paid the proceeds of £19,000 to Mr Carrick and moved into the maisonette. Thereafter, she paid all the outgoings and she also paid for various substantial improvements. However, there was no formal conveyance of the lease, which remained in the name of Mr Carrick; nor was the estate contract between the defendants registered as a Class C(iv) land charge. Mr Carrick subsequently mortgaged the lease to the plaintiff bank. He signed a form stating that no persons other than himself would occupy the maisonette and the bank made no further inquiries. When Mr Carrick defaulted on the repayments of the mortgage loan, the bank brought proceedings for possession. The county court judge dismissed the claim. Although the estate contract was void against the bank for want of registration, he held that Mr Carrick held the property on trust for Mrs Carrick and that her interest under the trust was enforceable against the bank under the doctrine of constructive notice. The bank appealed.

MORRITT L.J.:

First, it is accepted by Mrs Carrick that if her only interest in the maisonette was derived from the contract which she accepts is void as against the bank as an unregistered estate contract then the appeal succeeds. Second, Mrs Carrick accepts that the original contract between her and Mr Carrick, as found by the recorder, was a valid open contract for the purchase of the maisonette; that it became enforceable by her when she partly performed it by entering into possession and paying the whole of the purchase price but that it remained executory, that is to say uncompleted, at the time of the legal charge to the bank granted in November 1986. Third, the bank accepts that if Mrs Carrick had an interest in the maisonette not arising from but separate and distinct from the unregistered contract, it was and is binding on the bank for, as found by the recorder, the bank had notice of it.

Thus the issue argued on this appeal was whether Mrs Carrick had an interest in the maisonette separate and distinct from that which arose under the unregistered estate contract which was capable of binding the bank as successor in title to Mr Carrick. For Mrs Carrick it was submitted that she did. It was contended that she was entitled to such an interest under a bare trust, a constructive trust and by virtue of a proprietary estoppel.

I shall consider each of these points in due course. But before doing so it is necessary to consider the position of Mr Carrick and Mrs Carrick before the charge to the bank was executed. At the time it was made the contract was valid but, as provided by s.40 of the Law of Property Act 1925, unenforceable for want of a memorandum in writing or part performance. It became enforceable when in or about November 1982 Mrs Carrick paid the purchase price to Mr Carrick and went into possession. One consequence of the contract becoming enforceable was that it was specifically enforceable at the suit of Mrs Carrick. Accordingly Mr Carrick became a trustee of the maisonette for Mrs Carrick. Normally such trusteeship is of a peculiar kind because the vendor himself has a beneficial interest in the property as explained in *Megarry and Wade, The Law of Real Property*, 5th ed. (1984), p. 602. But in this case as Mrs

Carrick had paid the whole of the purchase price at the time the contract became enforceable Mr Carrick as the vendor had no beneficial interest. Thus he may properly be described as a bare trustee (cf. *Bridges v. Mees* [1957] Ch. 475 at 485). It follows that at all times after November 1982 Mrs Carrick was the absolute beneficial owner of the maisonette and Mr Carrick was a trustee of it without any beneficial interest in it.

The argument for Mrs Carrick relied on the relative position at law and in equity as I have described it to found the argument that such an absolute equitable interest was not itself registrable but bound the bank as they had constructive notice of it. Counsel for Mrs Carrick accepted that such interest came or started from the contract but, he contended, it matured into an interest separate and distinct from the contract as soon as the purchase price was paid in full.

For my part I am unable to accept this analysis. The payment of £19,000 by Mrs Carrick to Mr Carrick did not as such and without more give her any interest in the maisonette. Nor, prior to the conclusion of the contract, were the circumstances such that Mrs Carrick could assert that her brother-in-law held the maisonette on any trust for her benefit. The source and origin of the trust was the contract; the payment of the price by Mrs Carrick served only to make it a bare trust by removing any beneficial interest of Mr Carrick. Section 4(6) of the 1972 Act avoids that contract as against the bank. The result, in my judgment, must be that Mrs Carrick is unable to establish the bare trust as against the bank for it has no existence except as the equitable consequence of the contract. Accordingly I reject the contention founded on the bare trust.

The second contention for Mrs Carrick was to the effect that she was entitled to the whole beneficial interest in the maisonette arising under a constructive trust and that that interest was not registrable so that the bank, having had constructive notice of it, took subject to it. For this proposition her Counsel relied on the speech of Lord Bridge of Harwich in *Lloyds Bank plc v. Rosset* [1991] 1 A.C. 107. That case was concerned with the question of what must be established to entitle a wife to an equitable interest in registered land the title to which is registered in the sole name of her husband. Lord Bridge of Harwich said:

"The first and fundamental question which must always be resolved is whether, independently of any inference to be drawn from the conduct of the parties in the course of sharing the house as their home and managing their joint affairs, there has at any time prior to acquisition, or exceptionally at some later date, been any agreement, arrangement or understanding reached between them that the property is to be shared beneficially. The finding of an agreement or arrangement to share in this sense can only, I think, be based on evidence of express discussions between the partners, however imperfectly remembered and however imprecise their terms may have been. Once a finding to this effect is made it will only be necessary for the partner asserting a claim to a beneficial interest against the partner entitled to the legal estate to show that he or she has acted to his or her detriment or significantly altered his or her position in reliance on the agreement in order to give rise to a constructive trust or a proprietary estoppel." (see [1991] 1 A.C. 107 at 132.)

Counsel recognised that in this case the contract between Mr Carrick and Mrs Carrick was entered into after Mr Carrick had taken an assignment of the lease into his own name. But he submitted that the same principle applied and for that purpose relied on the statement of Lord Oliver of Aylmerton in giving the opinion of the Privy Council in *Austin v. Keele* (1987) 61 A.L.J.R. 605 at 609, where he said

"Although Lord Diplock [in *Gissing v. Gissing* [1971] A.C. 886 at 905] referred to the formation of a common intention 'at the time of acquisition', the Court of Appeal expressed the view, with which their Lordships agree, that although it may be more difficult to prove the requisite intention in relation to property already held beneficially by the trustee, there is no reason in principle why the doctrine should be limited to an intention formed at the time of the first acquisition of the property—an opinion echoed by Mustill L.J. in his judgment in *Grant v. Edwards* ([1986] Ch. 638 at 651). In essence the doctrine is an application of proprietary estoppel and there is no reason in principle why it should be confined to the single event of acquisition of the property by the owner of the legal estate."

Counsel for Mrs Carrick submitted that if there had been no contract then on the proper application of these principles there would have been a constructive trust in favour of Mrs Carrick. From this he argued that Mrs Carrick should not be in any worse position just because there was a contract.

In this case there was a trust of the maisonette for the benefit of Mrs Carrick precisely because there had been an agreement between her and Mr Carrick which, for her part, she had substantially if not wholly performed. As between her and Mr Carrick such trust subsisted at all times after November 1982. I agree with counsel for the bank that there is no room in those circumstances for the implication or imposition of any further trust of the maisonette for the benefit of Mrs Carrick. In *Lloyds Bank plc v. Rosset* there was no contract which conferred any interest in the house on the wife. As with all such statements of principle the speech of Lord Bridge of Harwich must be read by reference to the facts of the case. So read there is nothing in it to suggest that where there is a specifically enforceable contract the court is entitled to superimpose a further constructive trust on the vendor in favour of the purchaser over that which already exists in consequence of the contractual relationship.

It is true that on this footing the ultimate position of Mrs Carrick with the benefit of a specifically enforceable contract may be worse than it would have been if there had been no contract. But that is because she failed to do that which Parliament has ordained must be done if her interest is to prevail over that of the bank, namely to register the estate contract. Her failure in that respect cannot, in my view, justify the implication or imposition of a trust after the execution of the charge when the dealings between Mr Carrick and Mrs Carrick before such execution did not. For these reasons I would reject the second point on which Mrs Carrick relied.

The third contention was that Mrs Carrick is entitled to the benefit of a proprietary estoppel. Counsel on her behalf submitted by reference to the principles set out in *Snell's Equity*, 29th ed. (1990), pp. 574–576 that such an estoppel arose in her favour by virtue of the facts pleaded in her defence. He submitted that Mrs Carrick had paid the purchase price and carried out the improvements to the maisonette in the belief common to both her and Mr Carrick and to that extent encouraged by him that she either did or would own it. Reliance was placed on the decisions of this court in *Inwards v. Baker* [1965] 2 Q.B. 29 and *E.R. Ives Investments Ltd v. High* [1967] 2 Q.B. 379 as establishing that such an estoppel gives rise to an interest in land capable of binding a successor in title with notice.

This was disputed by counsel for the bank. She submitted that such principles could not be applied to cases in which there was no belief or expectation of having or acquiring an interest in someone else's land. In this context she relied on *Western Fish Products Ltd v. Penwith D.C.* [1981] 2 All E.R. 204. ... In addition she submitted that such an estoppel cannot give rise to an interest in land capable of binding successors in title with notice.

I would observe at the outset that it is a matter of some doubt whether the principles of proprietary estoppel differ from those of that species of constructive trust which was referred to by Lord Bridge of Harwich in *Lloyds Bank plc v. Rosset*. In the passage from his speech which I have already quoted he treated the two labels as interchangeable. To the like effect is the passage in the advice of the Privy Council in *Austin v. Keele* (1987) 61 A.L.J.R. 605 given by Lord Oliver of Aylmerton, which I have also quoted. However that may be, the case under this head was put somewhat differently and should be considered on its own merits.

...

In my judgment the claim of Mrs Carrick fails on a number of grounds. First, as in the case of the constructive trust, I do not see how there is any room for the application of the principles of proprietary estoppel when at the time of the relevant expenditure there was already a bare trust arising in consequence of an enforceable contract to the same effect as the interest sought pursuant to the proprietary estoppel. As the evidence showed Mrs Carrick knew of the need for a conveyance and was content that it should be deferred. Thus at the time that she paid the price and committed herself to the expenditure on the subsequent improvements she believed, rightly, that she was spending the money in respect of her own property, albeit under an uncompleted contract. In this respect I see no relevant distinction between this case and that of *Western Fish Products Ltd v. Penwith D.C.*

Second, this is not a case in which the expectations of Mrs Carrick have been defeated by Mr Carrick seeking to resile from the position he had encouraged her to expect. As far as he is concerned he has always accepted that she had contracted to buy the maisonette and had paid the price in full. As against him the contract is still binding and enforceable although, as he is unable to redeem the mortgage, he is in breach of contract for having charged the maisonette and in breach of trust for failing to account to Mrs Carrick for the money raised on the security of the maisonette. Mrs Carrick's expectations have been defeated because the contract was not registered at any time before the charge was granted and Parliament has decreed that in those circumstances the contract is void against the bank.

Third, it was common ground that the right arising from a proprietary estoppel cannot exceed that which the party sought to be estopped encouraged the other to believe that she had or would acquire. The party sought to be estopped is Mr Carrick. In so far as he encouraged Mrs Carrick to believe that she was or would become the beneficial owner of the maisonette there is no further right to be obtained for she was, and, subject to the charge, still is. But counsel for Mrs Carrick submits that Mr Carrick went further and encouraged her in the belief that she was or would become the legal owner of the maisonette. Apart from the fact that this was never alleged in the defence of Mrs Carrick nor explored in evidence at the trial I do not think that it could avail Mrs Carrick. Section 4(6) of the 1972 Act invalidates, as against the bank, any unregistered contract by the estate owner for the conveyance of the legal estate. It cannot be unconscionable for the bank to rely on the non-registration of the contract. I do not see how it could be right to confer on Mrs Carrick indirectly, and by means of a proprietary estoppel binding on the bank, that which Parliament prevented her from obtaining directly by the contract it has declared to be void. To avoid any future misunderstanding I would emphasise that there was and is a valid and enforceable contract as against the vendor. Accordingly this case is quite unlike those which may become more prevalent where there is no contract at all, not because there was no agreement but because the agreement was not in writing as now required by s.2 of the Law of Property (Miscellaneous Provisions) Act 1989.

In my judgment, the claim based on proprietary estoppel fails. In the circumstances it is unnecessary to consider further the submission of counsel for the bank to the effect that a proprietary estoppel cannot give rise to an interest in land capable of binding successors in title. This interesting argument will have to await another day, though it is hard to see how in this court it can surmount the hurdle constituted by the decision of this court in *E.R. Ives Investments Ltd v. High* [1967] 2 Q.B. 379.

For all these reasons I consider that the recorder was wrong to have held that Mrs Carrick had any interest valid against the bank sufficient to constitute a defence to the claim against her for possession of the maisonette. I would allow this appeal.

This result seems to me to be inevitable in the light of the provisions of the 1972 Act and of the Law of Property Act 1925.... However, it should be noted that the result would have been different if the title to the maisonette had been registered. In such a case the interest of Mrs Carrick, who was in possession of the maisonette and of whom no enquiry had been made, would have been an overriding interest under s.70(1)(g) of the Land Registration Act 1925. As such it would have been binding on the bank.

As the authors of *Megarry and Wade, The Law of Real Property* point out at pp. 186–187 the same position would have been achieved under the Law of Property Act 1922, for what is now s.14 of the Law of Property Act 1925 was then in a part which also contained the legislation which subsequently became the Land Charges Act 1925.

In my view it is beyond doubt that s.14 of the Law of Property Act 1925 does not achieve for unregistered land that which s.70(1)(g) of the Land Registration Act 1925 achieves for registered land, but whether that was originally intended or is a quirk of the process of breaking up the Law of Property Act 1922 into, amongst others, the Law of Property Act 1925 and the Land Charges Act 1925 is unclear. What is certain is that it must be for others to consider and for Parliament to decide whether this distinction between registered and unregistered land should continue, particularly as the system for the registration of incumbrances in the case of unregistered land is by no means complete, as shown by *Inwards v. Baker* [1965] 2 Q.B. 29, *E.R. Ives Investments Ltd v. High* [1967] 2 Q.B. 379 and *Shiloh Spinners Ltd v. Harding* [1973] A.C. 691.

NOTES:

1. For discussion, see [1996] Conv. 295; (1996) 112 L.Q.R. 549; [1997] C.L.J. 32; (1998) 61 M.L.R. 486.

2. The case seems to reflect a strict approach to the enforcement of the policy and regime of the Land Charges Act; but it is arguable that the approach was unnecessarily strict (i) in adopting a construction of the agreement as a traditional estate contract for the disposal of a legal estate rather than the equally plausible construction as a contract for the creation of an equitable interest: see (1996) 112 L.Q.R. 549, 551; [1997] C.L.J. 32, 34; and (ii) in holding that the existence of the estate contract precluded the implication of a constructive trust under the principles of *Lloyds Bank plc v. Rosset* (which themselves circumvent the formality requirements for the declaration of trusts of land): see (1996) 112 L.Q.R. 549, 551–552.

3. As Morritt L.J. points out in the final paragraphs of his judgment, the decisive finding of a valid and enforceable estate contract was based on the then existing law (Law of Property Act 1925, s.40). Under the current requirements for a valid contract for the disposition of an interest in land (Law of Property (Miscellaneous Provisions) Act 1989, s.2, *ante*, p. 61), there would have been no contract on the facts of the present case and no consequent obstacle to reliance on the trust-based interest.

4. As Morritt L.J. also points out, the case illustrates that the principles of unregistered land may produce different consequences from those produced by the principles of registered land when applied to the same facts.

5. The capacity of a claim based on proprietary estoppel to bind a successor in title is discussed *post*, p. 602.

6. The relationship between constructive trusts and proprietary estoppel is discussed *post*, p. 607.

4.1.3.5 *Contractual obligations statutorily annexed to land*   In *Taylors Fashions Ltd v. Liverpool Victoria Trustees Co. Ltd* [1982] Q.B. 133 it was argued that certain contractual obligations (including the burden of an option to renew a lease) were outside the land charges scheme; and that such obligations were statutorily annexed to the land so as to be binding on a purchaser, irrespective of registration and irrespective of notice. Oliver J. considered (but rejected) the argument at 142–143:

Mr Scott puts the case thus. The Land Charges Act 1925 (which was the statute in force at the material time) was concerned with the registration of interests in land or equitable burdens on land and was designed to substitute registration as a land charge for the equitable doctrine of notice in those cases where, prior to 1925, the binding effect of the interest on a subsequent purchaser depended upon notice. The Act, of course, also applies to certain statutory or legal interests (for instance, a puisne mortgage) but the important point for Mr Scott is that it applies to interests in land, not to merely contractual rights, or, in those cases where it does apply to merely contractual burdens, it applies only to those which, prior to 1925, depended for their enforceability against subsequent purchasers on the doctrine of notice (*e.g.* restrictive covenants). The Act provides, in section 10, that interests or obligations of this sort may be registered as land charges of the appropriate class and class C defines estate contracts as including "a valid option to purchase, a right of pre-emption or any other like right." Section 13(2) provides that a land charge of this type

"shall be void as against a purchaser of the land charged therewith, or of any interest in such land, unless the land charge is registered in the appropriate register before the completion of the purchase."

That means, Mr Scott submits, that it is void as a land charge, that is, as an interest in or incumbrance on the land, even if the purchaser has notice of the interest, and one sees this reflected in sections 198 and 199 of the Law of Property Act 1925 which provide respectively that registration shall constitute actual notice and that a purchaser shall not be prejudicially affected by notice of a registrable charge if it is not registered. But, Mr Scott submits, none of this touches contractual obligations which, by statute and quite independently of any equitable doctrine of notice, bind a purchaser as an integral part of the land purchased. The obligation resting on a reversioner under an option to renew in a lease is one of the obligations which, ever since the statute 32 Hen. 8 c. 34 [Grantees of Reversions Act 1540], has run with the land and remained binding at law quite regardless of any question of notice. It binds the reversioner not because it is an interest in land, although it may incidentally create one, but because it is a contractual obligation statutorily annexed to the land to which the Land Charges Act 1925 has no application. Indeed it is expressly provided in section 6 of the Law of Property Act 1925 that nothing in Part I of the Act (and this must I think be referring particularly to the provisions of section 1(3)) affects prejudicially the right to enforce (inter alia) lessor's covenants the burden of which runs with the reversion.

There is, I think, a logic in Mr Scott's submissions, which accord with the view of the original authors of *Wolstenholme and Cherry's Conveyancing Statutes*, with what Harman J. thought was the policy of the legislation in *Hollington Brothers Ltd v. Rhodes* [1951] 2 All E.R. 578 and with the practice of the legal profession up to 1960. This view of the matter moreover derives some support from the analysis of the anomalous nature of covenants running with the land contained in the judgment of Farwell J. in *Muller v. Trafford* [1901] 1 Ch. 54, 61. They are not executory in nature but bind the land from their inception and "pass with it in much the same way as title deeds." But whatever might have been my view of the matter if it were still res integra, it is not so in fact and the judgment of Buckley J. in *Beesly v. Hallwood Estates Ltd* [1960] 1 W.L.R. 549 is direct authority for the proposition that an unregistered option for renewal in a lease is void and unenforceable against a purchaser for money or money's worth of the reversion. That case is no less an authority because the actual decision in favour of the plaintiff was based on an entirely different point and was affirmed by the Court of Appeal [1961] Ch. 105 on that ground. It has been adopted as correct, although apparently without argument, by the Court of Appeal in *Greene v. Church Commissioners for England* [1974] Ch. 467 and *Kitney v. MEPC Ltd* [1977] 1 W.L.R. 981, although in neither case was Mr Scott's point argued. Nor indeed is it clear that the case before Buckley J. was argued in this way. Mr Scott submits that I am not bound by *Beesly's* case, and that, on the authority of *National Enterprises Ltd v. Racal Communications Ltd* [1975] Ch. 397 the existence of two Court of Appeal decisions where the specific point was not argued does not preclude me from declining to follow it. That may be so, but nevertheless *Beesly's* case was a considered judgment on a difficult point of statutory interpretation and it has been followed and acted upon for the past 18 years. Quite apart from judicial comity and from the respect that I would feel for any decision from that source, I am mindful of the remarks of Maugham J. in *In re Smith* [1930] 1 Ch. 88, 90, remarks, I should add, which were also made in the context of the 1925 property legislation. He said:

> "I take this opportunity of repeating what I have said on previous occasions, that where a learned judge, after consideration, has come to a definite decision on a matter arising out of this exceedingly complicated and difficult legislation, it is very desirable that the court should follow that decision, and accordingly I should be strongly inclined, whatever my own view was, to follow what I take to be the positive decision of Tomlin J."

In my judgment, *Beesly's* case [1961] Ch. 105 must be taken as representing the law and I would not feel at liberty, at this level, to depart from it now, even were I so minded to do.

4.2 *Searching the register*

As has been seen, the title deeds conveyancing system does not formally entitle the purchaser to make a complete search of the land charges register until after he has committed himself to the purchase by the exchange of contracts. However, as noted above, any paradox in this procedure is largely removed by the fact that the purchaser will probably be able to withdraw from the contract if the purchaser only discovers at that stage registered land charges which the vendor has failed to disclose at an earlier stage of the negotiations: see *supra*, p. 116. Moreover, in practice, the existence of interests adversely affecting the land will normally be disclosed by the vendor prior to the exchange of contracts.

Following exchange of contracts, the vendor provides the abstract of title which should disclose the names of previous estate owners. Because the land charges register is a register of names, and any registered land charge will have been registered against the name of the estate owner at the time when the interest was created, the purchaser must search against each of the names disclosed by the abstract of title. For the problems of land charges registered against names not included in the period covered by the abstract of title, see *supra*, p. 117.

A purchaser may make a personal search of the land charges register: Land Charges Act 1972, s.9; but personal searches are discouraged: see *Oak Co-operative Building Society v. Blackburn* [1968] Ch. 730, 743–744 *per* Russell L.J. Moreover, an official search by the staff of the registry and the issue of an official search certificate has a number of advantages. First, provided that the application for the official search correctly identifies the relevant persons and land (see *infra*), the certificate is conclusive, even if it fails to disclose a registered land charge: Land Charges Act 1972, s.10(4). In such circumstances, the undisclosed interest is defeated but the owner may have an action in negligence against the responsible public authority to recover damages for any loss suffered: see *Ministry of Housing and Local Government v. Sharp* [1970] 2 Q.B. 223. Secondly, the certificate provides a period of protection for the purchaser: provided that the conveyance is completed within 15 working days after the issue of the certificate, the purchaser is not affected by any interest registered within that period: Land Charges Act 1972, s.11(5). There is an exception to the rule where any such interest is registered pursuant to a priority notice entered on the register before the certificate was issued: *ibid.*; but in those circumstances the priority notice should have appeared on the official search certificate issued to the purchaser.

The names-based register provides potential scope for error both at the time of registration and at the time of search.

Oak Co-operative Building Society v. Blackburn [1968] Ch. 730

(CA, Harman, Russell and Sachs L.JJ.)

The first defendant was the fee simple owner of a house, conveyed to him in his full name of Francis David Blackburn. He agreed to sell the property to the third defendant, the purchase price to be paid over a period of 15 years. The third defendant moved into the house and registered the estate contract as a class C(iv) land charge against the name of *Frank* David Blackburn. The first defendant subsequently mortgaged the property to the plaintiffs to secure the repayment of a loan. The plaintiffs had requisitioned an official search against the name of Francis *Davis* Blackburn, which failed to disclose the interest of the third defendant. When the first defendant became bankrupt, the plaintiffs sought possession of the property against the third defendant. Ungoed-Thomas J. held ([1967] Ch. 1169) that both the registration and search were ineffective; and he ordered the third defendant to give up possession. The Court of Appeal allowed her appeal.

RUSSELL L.J.:
The real problem is, what is meant by the name or the names of the estate owner in this legislation?

As a matter of theoretical approach it is obvious that it is intended or hoped by the legislation that every registered land charge will be safeguarded by registration because due diligence in search will reveal it: and correspondingly that every duly diligent search will reveal every registered land charge affecting the land to be purchased. It is realised that if an official search certificate is issued there may be a blunder for which some innocent person must suffer, and section 17(3) provides, for example, that if a nil certificate is given the owner of the land charge suffers, however valid his registration. But it would be supposed that it would be intended to reduce error to a minimum. What then is meant by the requirement that the name—surname and Christian names—of the estate owner be given when requisitioning a search? People use different names at different times and for different purposes. But the matter now under consideration relates to two things: first, the investigation into the soundness of the paper title of a proposed vendor by a proposed purchaser: second, the attempt to prevent by registration the disposal by the owner of that paper title of the legal estate in a manner which will override the interest of the owner of the land charge.

In the case of a request for an official search, which of course takes place before completion after title examined, we can only think that the name or names referred to in the request should be that or those appearing on the title. A nil certificate here as to Francis Davis *Blackburn* would not have served to override the third defendant's land charge had it been registered in the name Francis Davi*d Blackburn*, though it *could* have been issued.

In most cases of contracts to purchase land nowadays many of the formalities precede exchange of contracts, and indeed those acting for the vendor would have used in the contract the name of the proposed vendor as appearing on the title. But of course there are other cases, such as the present, where the contract is much less formally arrived at, and the purchaser has no ready means of ascertaining the "title" names of the vendor. It would seem to be a great hardship on a purchaser registering in the name by which the vendor ordinarily passed that his registration should be entirely without operation, which is of course the submission of the plaintiffs in this case. We have said earlier that if in this case the search had been against "Francis David Blackburn" and the certificate *had* referred to the fact that an estate contract was registered against "Frank David Blackburn" in respect of this property, the proposed mortgage transaction would have been blown sky-high. But if the plaintiffs' contention is correct the registration would be no registration at all, and by force of sections 199 of the Law of Property Act 1925 and 13(2) of the Land Charges Act 1925 the plaintiffs could have carried through the mortgage ignoring the estate contract though in fact aware of its existence. Indeed, if the plaintiffs had contracted to grant a mortgage loan subject to getting good title they would have been in breach of their contract by refusing to grant it.

We have come to the conclusion that the registration on this occasion ought not to be regarded as a nullity simply because the formal name of Blackburn was Francis and not Frank, and notwithstanding that Frank as a name is not merely an abbreviation or version of Francis but also a name in its own right, as are also for example Harry and Willie. We are not led to this conclusion by the fact that initials would seem to suffice for registration of a lis pendens: see *Dunn v. Chapman* [1920] 2 Ch. 474—at least under the then legislation and rules: for presumably a request for search under a full name having the same initials should throw up all entries under those initials. We take a broader view that so far as possible the system should be made to work in favour of those who seek to make use of it in a sensible and practical way. If a proposing purchaser here had requested a search in the correct full names he would have got a clean certificate and a clear title under section 17(3) of the Land Charges Act 1925 and would have suffered no harm from the fact that the registration was not in such names: and a person registering who is not in a position to satisfy himself what are the correct full names runs that risk. But if there be registration in what may be fairly described as a version of the full names of the vendor, albeit not a version which is bound to be discovered on a search in the correct full names, we would not hold it a nullity against someone who does not search at all, or who (as here) searches in the wrong name.

There is one objection to this approach, and that is that provision is made for personal as distinct from official search: a personal searcher in the full correct name in the present case would, it seems, not have encountered the registration in the present case: he would not have had the benefit of an official certificate under section 17(3) and on the contrary would have been affected by a deemed actual notice of the estate contract under section 198 of the Law of Property Act 1925. But we think that anyone who nowadays is foolish enough to search personally deserves what he gets: and if the aim of the statute is to arrive at a sensible working system that aim is better furthered by upholding a registration such as this than by protecting a personal searcher from his folly.

NOTES:

1. For comment, see (1967) 31 Conv. 276; (1968) 32 Conv. 284; (1968) 84 L.Q.R. 303; (1968) 31 M.L.R. 705.

2. It is now clearly established that for the purposes of registration and search, the correct name of the estate owner is his name *as it appears on the conveyance to him*, even where that name is different from his full name: *Diligent Finance Co. Ltd v. Alleyne* (1972) 23 P. & C.R. 346, 349 *per* Foster J.; *Standard Property Investment plc v. British Plastics Federation* (1985) 53 P. & C.R. 25, 30 *per* Walton J., noted at [1989] Conv. 135.

3. Where the correct name is used by the person registering the interest, the interest will bind a person who searches against the incorrect name and receives a clear certificate: *Standard Property Investment plc v. British Plastics Federation, supra,* 35 *per* Walton J.; and where the incorrect name is used by the person registering the interest, the interest will not bind a person who searches against the correct name and receives a clear certificate: *Diligent Finance Co. Ltd v. Alleyne, supra,* 349–350 *per* Foster J.

4. Although searches are made against the names of estate owners of the land, a requisition for an official search must not give any reasonable scope for misunderstanding by reason of lack of clarity in the description of the land: see *Du Sautoy v. Symes* [1967] Ch. 1146, 1166–1168 *per* Cross J.

5. For discussion of the problem of defective registrations and defective searches, and for the conclusion that there is nothing (substantial) that can be done about it, see Law Com. No. 18, *Transfer of Land: Report on Land Charges Affecting Unregistered Land* (1969), paras 43–48.

4.3 *Vacating the register*

A land charge is normally registered without any investigation as to the validity of the interest protected. The court therefore has both inherent and statutory jurisdiction to vacate an unsubstantiated or spent entry on the register: see, respectively, *Calgary and Edmonton Land Co. Ltd v. Dobinson* [1974] Ch. 102, 110 *per* Megarry J.; Land Charges Act 1972, s.1(6).

4.4 *Land charges registrable under the Land Charges Act 1972*

Land Charges Act 1972, s.2

The register of land charges

2.—(1) If a charge on or obligation affecting land falls into one of the classes described in this section, it may be registered in the register of land charges as a land charge of that class.

(2) A Class A land charge is—

(a) a rent or annuity or principal money payable by instalments or otherwise, with or without interest, which is not a charge created by deed but is a charge upon land (other than a rate) created pursuant to the application of some person under the provisions of any Act of Parliament, for securing to any person either the money spent by him or the costs, charges and expenses incurred by him under such Act, or the money advanced by him for repaying the money spent or the costs, charges and expenses incurred by another person under the authority of an Act of Parliament; or

(b) a rent or annuity or principal money payable as mentioned in paragraph (a) above which is not a charge created by deed but is a charge upon land (other than a rate) created pursuant to the application of some person under any of the enactments mentioned in Schedule 2 to this Act.

(3) A Class B land charge is a charge on land (not being a local land charge) of any of the kinds described in paragraph (a) of subsection (2) above, created otherwise than pursuant to the application of any person.

(4) A Class C land charge is any of the following (not being a local land charge), namely—

(i) a puisne mortgage;
(ii) a limited owner's charge;
(iii) a general equitable charge;
(iv) an estate contract;

and for this purpose—

(i) a puisne mortgage is a legal mortgage which is not protected by a deposit of documents relating to the legal estate affected;
(ii) a limited owner's charge is an equitable charge acquired by a tenant for life or statutory owner under the Inheritance Tax Act 1984 or under any other statute by reason of the discharge by him of any inheritance tax or other liabilities and to which special priority is given by the statute;
(iii) a general equitable charge is any equitable charge which—

  (a) is not secured by a deposit of documents relating to the legal estate affected; and
  (b) does not arise or affect an interest arising under a trust of land or a settlement; and
  (c) is not a charge given by way of indemnity against rents equitably apportioned or charged exclusively on land in exoneration of other land and against the breach or non-observance of covenants or conditions; and
  (d) is not included in any other class of land charge:

(iv) an estate contract is a contract by an estate owner or by a person entitled at the date of the contract to have a legal estate conveyed to him to convey or create a legal estate, including a contract conferring either expressly or by statutory implication a valid option to purchase, a right of pre-emption or any other like right.

(5) A Class D land charge is any of the following (not being a local land charge), namely—

(i) an Inland Revenue charge;
(ii) a restrictive covenant;
(iii) an equitable easement;

and for this purpose—

(i) an Inland Revenue charge is a charge on land, being a charge acquired by the Board under the Inheritance Tax Act 1984;
(ii) a restrictive covenant is a covenant or agreement (other than a covenant or agreement between a lessor and a lessee) restrictive of the user of land and entered into on or after 1st January 1926;
(iii) an equitable easement is an easement, right or privilege over or affecting land created or arising on or after 1st January 1926, and being merely an equitable interest.

(6) A Class E land charge is an annuity created before 1st January 1926 and not registered in the register of annuities.

(7) A Class F land charge is a charge affecting any land by virtue of Part IV of the Family Law Act 1996.

(8) A charge or obligation created before 1st January 1926 can only be registered as

a Class B land charge or a Class C land charge if it is acquired under a conveyance made on or after that date.

NOTES:

1. In 1956 the Roxburgh Committee recommended the abolition of class C(iii) land charges (with the exception of equitable mortgages, which would have become registrable as class C(i) land charges): *Report of the Committee on Land Charges* (1956), para. 13; it recommended that options to renew leases should cease to be registrable as class C(iv) land charges: *ibid.* para. 15; and it recommended the abolition of class D(iii) land charges: *ibid.* para. 16. For discussion, see Wade [1956] C.L.J. 216. The Law Commission subsequently recommended the continuation of the existing range of registrable land charges: see Law Com. No. 18, *Transfer of Land: Report on Land Charges Affecting Unregistered Land* (1969), paras 63–65.

2. Certain categories of land charge require further consideration.

4.4.1 *Puisne mortgages* Puisne mortgages (class C(i)) are second or subsequent *legal* mortgages. A mortgagor of unregistered land is normally required to deposit the title deeds relating to the land with the first mortgagee, thereby providing the first mortgagee with some protection against further dealings with the land that might prejudice the security of the mortgage. Since that form of protection is normally therefore no longer available to a subsequent mortgagee, registration of the subsequent mortgage provides a convenient alternative form of protection. Moreover, although puisne mortgages are legal interests, the principles of registration under the Land Charges Act and the consequences of non-registration are the same as for registrable equitable interests. For substantive discussion of mortgages, see *post*, Chapter 9.

4.4.2 *General equitable charges* General equitable charges (class C(iii)) constitute a (restricted) residual class of land charges. The class includes an equitable mortgage of a legal estate and an unpaid vendor's lien over the land sold.

4.4.3 *Estate contracts* Estate contracts (class C(iv)) include contracts to convey or create any legal estate or interest made by the current owner and also "sub-contracts" of a similar nature made by a person entitled under an estate contract. Thus, where A contracts to sell the fee simple in land to B, even before the conveyance to B, B may contract to sell the fee simple to C; both contracts are estate contracts within the meaning of the section. However, in such circumstances, *both* estate contracts are registrable against the name of A since he is the estate owner at the relevant time: *Barrett v. Hilton Developments Ltd* [1975] Ch. 237, 242–244 *per* Russell L.J.; *Property Discount Corp. Ltd v. Lyon Group Ltd* [1981] 1 W.L.R. 300, 306–307 *per* Goulding J.

An estate contract must in its terms bind the estate owner (or other person entitled) to convey or create a legal estate (although there is no requirement that the grantee must be named or identified in the contract): *Thomas v. Rose* [1968] 1 W.L.R. 1797, 1804–1805 *per* Megarry J. Thus a contract of agency that merely provides machinery whereby such an obligation may be created by another transaction is not an estate contract within the meaning of the section.

Estate contracts also include options to purchase land and rights of pre-emption. An option to purchase entitles but does not require the grantee to demand that the grantor convey to the grantee the agreed interest in the land, provided that the grantee makes the demand within the specified period and satisfies all the other terms of the option: see, *e.g. Midland Bank Trust Co. Ltd v. Green* [1981] A.C. 513, *supra*, p. 119. Thus the mere grant of the option imposes no obligation on the grantee to exercise the option or to accept the conveyance contemplated by the option: see *United Dominions Trust (Commercial) Ltd v. Eagle Aircraft Services Ltd* [1968] 1 W.L.R. 74, 84 *per* Diplock L.J. Nor, if the grantee elects not to exercise the option, or fails to do so, within the specified period, does the grant of the option impose any positive obligation on the grantor. On the other hand, during the currency of the option and pending its exercise (if any), the grantor is under a negative obligation not to do anything that will prevent him from fulfilling the obligation to execute the conveyance that will arise if the grantee does elect to exercise the option: *ibid.* 83. It is the fact that the conveyance can be demanded at the election of the grantee, and that the grantor, by binding himself to comply with any such demand, has placed the disposition of his land beyond his control, which justifies the conclusion that, from the time of the grant of the option, the grantee has an equitable interest in the land of the grantor: *London and South Western Railway Co. v. Gomm* (1882) 20 Ch.D. 562, 581 *per* Jessel M.R.; *First National Securities Ltd v. Chiltern DC* [1975] 1 W.L.R. 1075, 1079–1080 *per* Goulding J.; *London & Blenheim Estates Ltd v. Ladbroke Retail Parks Ltd* [1992] 1 W.L.R. 1278, 1282 *per* Judge Paul Baker Q.C. However, the grantee does not acquire equitable *ownership* of the land at least until he exercises the option, thereby creating between the parties the relationship of vendor and purchaser and the rights and obligations of an ordinary contract for the sale and purchase of land: *Raffety v. Schofield* [1897] 1 Ch. 937, 942–944 *per* Romer J.; *Mountford v. Scott* [1975] Ch. 259, 264 *per* Russell L.J.; and equitable ownership probably does not pass until the purchase money has been paid: see *ante*, p. 63. Of course, the grantee does not acquire legal ownership until the execution of the conveyance. See generally Prichard (1974) 38 Conv. 8; Tromans [1984] C.L.J. 55; and see *Spiro v. Glencrown Properties Ltd* [1991] Ch. 537, noted at [1991] C.L.J. 236, [1991] Conv. 140.

The scheme of the Land Charges Act 1972 applies without distinction to options in gross and to options contained in leases; and to options to purchase the freehold or leasehold interest of the grantor and to options to renew a lease: see *Taylors Fashions Ltd v. Liverpool Victoria Trustees Co. Ltd* [1982] Q.B. 133, 142–143, *supra*, p. 130; *Phillips v. Mobil Oil Co. Ltd* [1989] 1 W.L.R. 888; but see Howell [1990] Conv. 168, 250. However, there is no requirement that the contract resulting from the exercise of a duly registered land option must itself be protected by further registration: *Armstrong & Holmes Ltd v. Holmes and Dodds* [1993] 1 W.L.R. 1482, noted at [1994] Conv. 483.

A right of pre-emption (sometimes referred to as a right of first refusal) differs from an option in that the grantee cannot demand that the grantor convey the agreed interest in the land *unless and until the grantor indicates his willingness to sell*; but, if and when the grantor does indicate that willingness, the right of pre-emption becomes in effect an option to purchase. However, although a right of pre-emption is registrable as a class C(iv) land charge as soon as it is granted, in *Pritchard v. Briggs* [1980] Ch. 338 a majority of the Court of Appeal expressed the view that the grantee obtains an equitable interest in the land of the grantor only when the grantor indicates his willingness to sell; and that until that time registration is dormant and cannot confer any priority on the right. The decision in *Pritchard v. Briggs* is conveniently summarised in *Kling v. Keston Properties Ltd* (1983) 49 P. & C.R. 212, where Vinelott J. stated (at 215–217):

The question whether a right of pre-emption or first refusal over land creates an equitable interest in the land capable of binding a purchaser was for many years a controversial one. It was settled so far as this court is concerned by the decision of the Court of Appeal in *Pritchard v. Briggs* [1980] Ch. 338. In that case, the owners of a piece of land granted the defendants' predecessor in title a right of first refusal. It was granted in the form of a negative stipulation

"that so long as the [grantee] shall live and the [owners] or the survivors of them shall also be alive the [owners] will not nor will either of them sell or concur in selling all or any part of the [land] without giving to the [grantee] the option of purchasing [the land]"

—at a stated price. Later the owners granted a lease to the plaintiff and the lease contained an option giving the plaintiff the right to purchase the land on three months' notice after the death of the survivor of the owners, again at a fixed price. A further lease was subsequently granted and the option was repeated in it. Both the right of pre-emption and the option were registered as estate contracts under the Land Charges Act 1925. Under that Act, and under the Land Charges Act 1972 (which is a consolidating Act) the contracts registrable as estate contracts expressly include a contract conferring "a valid option or right of pre-emption or any other like right." The survivor of the owners, a Major Lockwood, in fact sold the land to the defendants, purportedly in pursuance of the right of pre-emption. After the death of Major Lockwood, the plaintiff gave notice exercising the option. Goff L.J. was of the opinion that the right of pre-emption created a merely personal right and did not create an interest in land even after the conditions for its exercise had been satisfied. Accordingly the defendants could not claim priority over the plaintiff's option. In his opinion the Land Charges Act 1972, in so far as it provided for registration of a right of pre-emption as an estate contract, proceeded on a wrong view of the law. However, Templeman and Stephenson L.JJ. took a different view of the nature and effect of a right of pre-emption. Templeman L.J. explained the effect of a right of pre-emption in a passage which I should, I think, cite in full. He said (at p. 418):

"Rights of option and rights of pre-emption share one feature in common; each prescribes circumstances in which the relationship between the owner of the property which is the subject of the right and the holder of the right will become the relationship of vendor and purchaser. In the case of an option, the evolution of the relationship of vendor and purchaser may depend on the fulfilment of certain specified conditions and will depend on the volition of the option holder. If the option applies to land, the grant of the option creates a contingent equitable interest which, if registered as an estate contract, is binding on successors in title of the grantor and takes priority from the date of its registration. In the case of a right of pre-emption, the evolution of the relationship of vendor and purchaser depends on the grantor, of his own volition, choosing to fulfil certain specified conditions and thus converting the pre-emption into an option. The grant of the right of pre-emption creates a mere spes which the grantor of the right may either frustrate by choosing not to fulfil the necessary conditions or may convert into an option and thus into an equitable interest by fulfilling the conditions. An equitable interest thus created is protected by prior registration of the right of pre-emption as an estate contract but takes its priority from the date when the right of pre-emption becomes exercisable and the right is converted into an option and the equitable interest is then created. The holder of a right of pre-emption is in much the same position as a beneficiary under a will of a testator who is still alive, save that the holder of the right of pre-emption must hope for some future positive action by the grantor which will elevate his hope into an interest. It does not seem to me that the property legislation of 1925 was intended to create, or operated to create an equitable interest in land where none existed."

Accordingly the plaintiff's claim succeeded, for (at p. 421):

"After the grant of Mr Pritchard's option, Major Lockwood was not in a position to make an offer to Mr and Mrs Briggs or to grant an option to them pursuant to their right of pre-emption or at all save subject to Mr Pritchard's option. After the registration of Mr Pritchard's option, Mr and Mrs Briggs could not accept an offer or exercise an option granted by Major Lockwood pursuant to the right of pre-emption or at all save subject to Mr Pritchard's option. In short Major Lockwood could only sell and the Briggs could only purchase subject to Mr Pritchard's option..."

Stephenson L.J. said (at p. 423):

"The 1944 conveyance—(which created the right of pre-emption)—refers to giving the option of purchasing but as a future act, not as a present right; and Mr Scott has satisfied me that what is granted as a right of pre-emption, on the true construction of the grant, is only properly called an option when the will of the grantor turns it into an option by deciding to sell and thereby binding the grantor to offer it for sale to the grantee. That it thereby becomes an interest in land is a change in the nature of the right to which, unlike Goff L.J., I see no insuperable objection in logic or in principle. And, as I understand his opinion on this point, its consequence would be that a right of pre-emption could never be enforceable against a successor in title whether it is registered or not.
I accordingly prefer the opinion of Templeman L.J. on this point."

On the particular facts of *Pritchard v. Briggs* the right of pre-emption would have become exercisable (and would have been converted into an option to purchase and an equitable interest in land) only when the grantor indicated a willingness to sell *during his lifetime*. That conversion was not effected by the grant of the option to purchase *after the death of the grantor* and it therefore followed that the option had priority over the right of pre-emption. The decision leaves uncertain the position where a later option is exercisable during the currency of the right of pre-emption. For discussion, see [1978] C.L.J. 213; [1980] C.L.J. 35; [1980] Conv. 433; (1980) 96 L.Q.R. 488.

More generally, there was no previous authority for the observations of the

Court of Appeal in *Pritchard v. Briggs* and what has been termed "this strange doctrine of delayed effectiveness" ((1980) 96 L.Q.R. 488, 489). Indeed, earlier decisions reflected differing views. In *Birmingham Canal Co v. Cartwright* (1879) 11 ChD. 421 it was held that a right of pre-emption created an equitable interest in land from the time of its creation, whereas in *Murray v. Two Strokes Ltd* [1973] 1 W.L.R. 825, noted at [1974] C.L.J. 57, it was held that a right of pre-emption remained a purely contractual right and could never be an interest in land. On the other hand, certain statutory provisions seem to presuppose that a right of pre-emption creates an interest in land: see, for example, Law of Property Act 1925, s.186; Land Charges Act 1972, s.2(4)(iv).

The approach in *Pritchard v. Briggs* has subsequently been applied (*Kling v. Keston Properties Ltd* (1983) 49 P. & C.R. 212 and cited without express disapproval (*London and Blenheim Estates Ltd v. Ladbroke Retail Parks Ltd* [1992] 1 W.L.R. 1278, 1282 *per* Judge Paul Baker Q.C.; [1994] 1 W.L.R. 31, 35–38 *per* Peter Gibson L.J.; *Homsy v. Murphy* (1996) 73 P. & C.R. 26, 38–39 *per* Beldam L.J.). However, it has been the subject of academic criticism: see especially (1980) 96 L.Q.R. 488; and that criticism has been judicially noted (*London and Blenheim Estates Ltd v. Ladbroke Retail Parks Ltd* [1994] 1 W.L.R. 31, 38 *per* Peter Gibson L.J.)

The Law Commission has concluded that the status of rights of pre-emption cannot be regarded as finally settled, especially since the observations in *Pritchard v. Briggs* were made obiter. More particularly, it has expressed the view that the approach in *Pritchard v. Briggs* could produce unfortunate effects: for example, the potential uncertainty as to the precise time when a right of pre-emption acquires the status of an interest in land and the general undesirability that a properly registered right may be defeated by a purchaser who knows of that right. The Law Commission has therefore provisionally recommended, albeit in the context of *registered* land, that, for the purposes of determining priorities, a right of pre-emption should take effect as an interest in land *from the time when it is created*: Law Com. No. 254, *Land Registration for the Twenty-First Century* (1998), paras 3.28–3.32. It is clearly arguable that such a recommendation should be extended to unregistered land while it continues to exist.

There seems to be a general willingness on the part of the courts to endorse the registration of conditional contracts other than options and rights of pre-emption, for example contracts made subject to the grant of planning permission: see *Haslemere Estates Ltd v. Baker* [1982] 1 W.L.R. 1109, 1118–1119 *per* Megarry V.-C., noted at [1983] Conv. 69; and see [1988] Conv. 10.

4.4.4 *Restrictive covenants*   Restrictive covenants relating to freehold land (class D(ii)) are registrable only if they are entered into after 1925; the enforceability of pre-1926 covenants depends upon the equitable doctrine of notice: see *infra*, p. 153. See generally Rowley (1956) 20 Conv. 370. For substantive discussion of covenants affecting freehold land, see *post*, Chapter 8.

4.4.5 *Equitable easements*   Equitable easements (class D(iii)) are registrable only if they are created or arose after 1925; the enforceability of pre-1926 equitable easements depends upon the equitable doctrine of notice: see *infra*, p. 153. However, there is some controversy over the precise scope of registrable equitable easements.

E.R. Ives Investment Ltd v. High [1967] 2 Q.B. 379

(CA, Lord Denning M.R., Danckwerts, Winn L.JJ.)

The defendant and Westgate were in the early stages of building a house and a block of flats respectively on adjoining sites. The defendant discovered that the foundations of the flats encroached upon his land; but the parties agreed that Westgate could maintain the foundations where they were and that in return the defendant could have a right of access across Westgate's yard to a garage that the defendant intended to build at the rear of his house. Both parties acted on the agreement. In particular, the defendant built his house in such a way that the only practicable vehicular access to the proposed garage was across Westgate's yard. Westgate sold the flats to the Wrights, who knew of the arrangement between the defendant and Westgate, although it was not referred to in the conveyance and it had not been protected by registration under the Land Charges Act 1925. The Wrights made no objection when the defendant continued to use the access and built his garage; and they accepted from him a contribution towards the resurfacing of the yard. The Wrights sold the flats to the plaintiffs, expressly subject to the rights "if any" of the defendant. The plaintiffs brought an action for trespass, claiming that, even if the defendant had acquired an equitable easement from Westgate, it was void against the plaintiffs for want for registration by virtue of section 13(2) of the Land Charges Act 1925 (now section 4(6) of the Land Charges Act 1972); the defendant counterclaimed, if the plaintiffs succeeded, for a mandatory injunction requiring the removal of the foundations of the flats.

LORD DENNING M.R.:
Now here is the point. The right of way was never registered as a land charge. The purchasers, the plaintiffs, say that it should have been registered under Class C(iv) as an estate contract, or under Class D(iii) as an equitable easement: and that, as it was not registered, it is void against them, the purchasers. Even though they had the most explicit notice of it, nevertheless they say that it is void against them. They claim to be entitled to prevent Mr High having any access to his garage across their yard: and thus render it useless to him. They have brought an action for an injunction to stop him crossing the yard at all.

One thing is quite clear. Apart from this point about the Land Charges Act 1925, Mr High would have in equity a good right of way across the yard. This right arises in two ways:

1. Mutual benefit and burden

The right arises out of the agreement of November 2, 1949, and the subsequent action taken on it: on the principle that "he who takes the benefit must accept the burden." When adjoining owners of land make an agreement to secure continuing rights and benefits for each of them in or over the land of the other, neither of them can take the benefit of the agreement and throw over the burden of it. This applies not only to the original parties, but also to their successors. The successor who takes the continuing benefit must take it subject to the continuing burden. This principle has been applied to neighbours who send their water into a common drainage system: see *Hopgood v. Brown* [1955] 1 W.L.R. 213; and to purchasers of houses on a building estate who had the benefit of using the roads and were subject to the burden of contributing to the upkeep: see *Halsall v. Brizell* [1957] Ch. 169. The principle clearly applies in the present case. The owners of the block of flats have the benefit of having their foundations in Mr High's land. So long as they take that benefit, they must shoulder the burden. They must observe the condition on which the benefit was granted, namely, they must allow Mr High and his successors to have access over their yard: cf. *May v. Belleville* [1905] 2 Ch. 605. Conversely, so long as Mr High takes the benefit of the access, he must permit the block of flats to keep their foundations in his land.

2. Equity arising out of acquiescence

The right arises out of the expense incurred by Mr High in building his garage, as it is now, with access only over the yard: and the Wrights standing by and acquiescing in it, knowing that he believed he had a right of way over the yard. By so doing the Wrights created in Mr High's mind a reasonable expectation that his access over the yard would not be disturbed. That gives rise to an "equity arising out of acquiescence." It is available not only against the Wrights but also their successors in title. The court will not allow that expectation to be defeated when it would be inequitable so to do. It is for the court in each case to decide in what way the equity can be satisfied: see *Inwards v. Baker* [1965] 2 Q.B. 29; *Ward v. Kirkland* [1966] 1 W.L.R. 601 and the cases cited therein. In this case it could only be satisfied by allowing Mr High and his successors to have access over the yard so long as the block of flats had its foundations in his land.

The next question is this: was that right a land charge such as to need registration under the Land Charges Act 1925? For if it was a land charge, it was never registered and would be void as against any purchaser: see section 13 of the Act. It would, therefore, be void against the plaintiffs, even though they took with the most express knowledge and notice of the right.

It was suggested that the agreement of November 2, 1949, was "an estate contract" within Class C(iv). I do not think so. There was no contract by Mr Westgate to convey a legal estate of any kind.

It was next suggested that the right was an "equitable easement" within Class D(iii). This class is defined as "any easement right or privilege over or affecting land created or arising after the commencement of this Act, and being merely an equitable interest". Those words are almost identical with section 2(3)(iii) of the Law of Property Act 1925 and should be given the same meaning. They must be read in conjunction with sections 1(2)(a), 1(3) and 4(1) of the Law of Property Act 1925. It then appears that an "equitable easement" is a proprietary interest in land such as would before 1926 have been recognised as capable of being conveyed or created *at law*, but which since 1926 only takes effect as an equitable interest. An instance of such a proprietary interest is a profit à prendre for life. It does not include a right to possession by a requisitioning authority: see *Lewisham Borough Council v. Maloney* [1948] 1 K.B. 50. Nor does it include a right, liberty or privilege arising in equity by reason of "mutual benefit and burden," or arising out of "acquiescence," or by reason of a contractual licence: because none of those before 1926 were proprietary interests such as were capable of being conveyed or created *at law*. They only subsisted *in equity*. They do not need to be registered as land charges, so as to bind successors, but take effect in equity without registration: see an article by Mr C. V. Davidge on "Equitable Easements" in (1937) 59 Law Quarterly Review, p. 259 and by Professor H. W. R. Wade in [1956] Cambridge Law Journal, pp. 225–226.

The right of Mr High to cross this yard was not a right such as could ever have been created or conveyed at law. It subsisted only in equity. It therefore still subsists in equity without being registered. Any other view would enable the owners of the flats to perpetrate the grossest injustice. They could block up Mr High's access to the garage, whilst keeping their foundations in his land. That cannot be right.

I am confirmed in this construction of the statute when I remember that there are many houses adjoining one another which have drainage systems in common, with mutual benefits and burdens. The statute cannot have required all these to be registered as land charges.

I know that this greatly restricts the scope of Class D (iii) but this is not disturbing. A special committee has already suggested that Class D (iii) should be abolished altogether: see the report of the Committee on Land Charges ((1956) Command Paper 9825, para. 16).

In these circumstances it is not necessary to consider the counterclaim. I would only say that I do not think that the owners of the block of flats have acquired a "squatter's title" to the space occupied by the foundations. They were only licensees and cannot acquire a title by limitation. If they were entitled to block up Mr High's access over their yard, he would, I think, be entitled to require them to remove the foundations from his land. But, fortunately for them, no such consequence will befall them. They can keep their foundations there, but they must not block up or impede his access across their yard, with or without vehicles.

DANCKWERTS L.J.:

It is necessary, in connection with Mr High's case, to consider the effect of the Land Charges Act 1925 and section 199 of the Law of Property Act 1925. The effect of the provisions of the Land Charges Act 1925, ss.10 and 13, is to make Mr High's right of way, so far as it ought to have been registered as an estate contract or an equitable easement, either void or unenforceable, and section 199 of the Law of Property Act 1925 prevents express notice of Mr High's rights being effective in any way, though the plaintiffs bought subject to the right of way and had the most positive notice of it.

But that is not the end of the matter. There is another equitable ground on which Mr High's rights may be protected, which has nothing whatever to do with the Land Charges Act. It is discussed in Snell's EQUITY (26th ed. 1966), pp. 629–633, under the name "proprietary estoppel," and the comment is made (p. 633) that "the doctrine thus displays equity at its most flexible." There are two aspects in which this equitable principle applies in the present case. Firstly, in the present case Mr High, in reliance on the arrangement made with Mr Westgate, allowed the encroaching foundations to remain on his land and built his house without proper access except over the yard, and finally built his garage in such a way that it was useless unless access to it and from it could be had over the yard. Mr Westgate acquiesced in the use of the yard for access, and the Wrights stood by and, indeed, encouraged Mr High to build his garage in these conditions and for these purposes. Could anything be more monstrous and inequitable afterwards than to deprive Mr High of the benefit of what he has done?

Secondly, the Wrights had continued to enjoy the benefit of the encroaching foundations on Mr High's land. It would no doubt be quite an expensive job to remove the encroaching foundations and provide other support for the building. Equity does not allow a person who takes advantage of such a situation to deny to the other party the corresponding benefits which were the consideration for allowing the foundations to remain.

The plaintiffs bought the property subject to Mr High's equitable rights and the property was so conveyed to them. They had full knowledge of the situation, yet they continue to enjoy the benefits of the situation and wish to deny to Mr High the benefit of what he was induced to do in reliance on the mutual arrangement. As long as the plaintiffs continue to enjoy the foundations, they must accept the terms of that enjoyment.

This is not a registrable charge, and section 199 of the Law of Property Act 1925 has no application.

I will now refer to the authorities in which support for these principles can be found.

Inwards v. Baker [1965] 2 Q.B. 29 (a decision of this court) is a modern example of the protection of equity which is given to a person who is induced to expend money on land on reliance on representations by another. I would like to refer to my observations in that case (at p. 38):

> "In my view the case comes plainly within the proposition stated in the cases. It is not necessary, I think, to imply a promise. It seems to me that this is one of the cases of an equity created by estoppel, or equitable estoppel, as it is sometimes called, by which the person who has made the expenditure is induced by the expectation of obtaining protection, and equity protects him so that an injustice may not be perpetrated."

Those words apply to the present case.

The principle there stated is not new. It goes back at least as far as the observations of Lord Kingsdown in *Ramsden v. Dyson* (1866) L.R. 1 H.L. 129, which were approved by the Privy Council in *Plimmer v. Wellington Corporation* (1884) 9 App.Cas. 699.

In the same case (*Inwards v. Baker*) Lord Denning M.R. pointed out (at p. 37) that any purchaser who took with notice would clearly be bound by the equity. The same principles were applied by Thomas J. in *Ward v. Kirkland* [1966] 1 W.L.R. 601.

Examples of the principle that a party cannot enjoy the benefits of an arrangement without giving effect to the burdens imposed on such benefits are to be found in *Hopgood v. Brown* [1955] 1 W.L.R. 213 (a decision of this court relating to the use of drainage) and *Halsall v. Brizell* [1957] Ch. 169 (a decision of Upjohn J. holding that a successor in title could not use roads without bearing the burden of the contributions to upkeep imposed under the original terms).

WINN L.J.:

In the county court proceedings and before this court the dispute has centred upon the effect in law of the agreement and the extent to which, if at all, it can operate to secure for Mr High the continued user of the right of way for which he so bargained, due regard being had to the provisions of the Land Charges Act 1925 and of section 199 of the Law of Property Act 1925 in the light of the changes in ownership of the land formerly owned by Mr Westgate which have occurred since 1949, the conduct of the parties who have held and now hold the title to that land, and the fact that the footings are still in the same position, where the plaintiffs in the present action assert that they are entitled to have them left undisturbed. The argument has involved many niceties of a somewhat technical and esoteric character.

The substance of the dispute is whether Mr High's claim to be entitled to cross the yard behind the plaintiffs' block of flats, called Francis Court, on foot and in a car, which the plaintiffs sought by their claim in this action to deny and destroy, and the claim of the plaintiffs to be free in law to maintain the footings of the west wall of their flats in Mr High's land, are interdependent or, by contrast, so mutually separate and independent, in fact or in law, that the plaintiffs can both maintain their claim and bar that of Mr High. There is a subsidiary but important question whether Mr High's claim, if valid, is only a personal right; this does not now fall to be decided.

I have found it simple to decide in my own mind that Mr High and Mr Westgate intended and mutually communicated by words or conduct the intention that Mr High's plot of land should for an indefinite time (a) enjoy the adjunct of a right of way 8 feet wide, for use on foot or in a car to and from Belvoir Street and the eastern boundary of the plot, (b) be subject to the detriment of the presence in the plot of such footings as existed there in November 1949; further, such intention, by necessary inference, fixed as the event upon which this arrangement would terminate any future removal of the protruding footings. It would have been wholly inconsistent with their intention, on the traditional "officious bystander" test, that it should have been left to the choice or whim of Mr High or any successor in title to his plot to require at any time the removal of the footings, even upon simultaneously abandoning any claim to the right of way.

It is, however, far from a simple matter to have to envisage, as I think one must, in terms of legal concepts what effect was produced by the arrangement made with that intention. On the one hand, I accept [counsel for the plaintiffs'] submission that it comprised a contract by Mr Westgate to grant a legal easement, which was equivalent in equity to an equitable easement, and his further submission that such contract or easement was by force of section 13(2) of the Land Charges Act 1925 void against any subsequent purchaser for value of Mr Westgate's property, if unregistered, despite any notice of it which such purchaser might have had before purchasing. On the other hand, I am unable to accept his submission that a tenancy at will arose in favour of Mr Westgate in respect of the subterranean space occupied by the footings. Some legal fictions are valuable and may conveniently be used, but properly only constructively to make good lacunae in imperfectly comprehended arrangements: to impose an effect in law inconsistent with that mutually intended by the parties is, in my opinion, a function of such a device which cannot, or at least should not, if avoidable, be tolerated. In determining whether any, and if so what, tenancy has come into existence, the intention of the suggested parties is of paramount importance: cf. per Denning L.J. in *Errington v. Errington and Woods* [1952] 1 K.B. 290, 296:

> "in my opinion it is of the essence of a tenancy at will that it should be determinable by either party on demand, and it is quite clear that the relationship of these parties was not so determinable.... It was therefore not a tenancy at will." And, quoting Lord Greene M.R. in *Booker v. Palmer* [1942] 2 All E.R. 674, 677: "To suggest there is an intention there to create a relationship of landlord and tenant appears to me to be quite impossible. There is one golden rule which is of very general application, namely, that the law does not impute intention to enter into legal relationships where the circumstances and the conduct of the parties negative any intention of the kind."

Mr Westgate would certainly not have been willing to rely on a tenancy at will. For my part I do not envisage any tenancy of the subterranean space, but supposing, arguendo, that one is to be deemed, I would think that a tenancy at sufferance would more nearly fit the reality of the arrangement. For this reason I reject the submission that a limitation period of 12 years, running from the expiry of the first year of a tenancy at will, now bars a claim for trespass by the protruding footings; if there was a tenancy by sufferance, it was not terminated before Mr High's alleged trespass or in anticipation of the present action.

Licence to maintain the footings is, to my mind, the concept which is far preferable: whilst recognising that a licence could not run with the land of either licensor or licensee, I have no difficulty in supposing that both intended that the licence should be, or that it was, periodically renewable and renewed between the persons from time to time concerned that it should apply. In my judgment the protrusion of the footings was permitted by licence until but not after the counterclaim in this action was filed.

During the 12 years from 1950 to 1962 purchasers from Mr Westgate of his plot of land, a Flt. Lt. Wright and his wife, managed and from time to time resided in Francis Court. They not only licensed Mr High, as had Mr Westgate, to pass over the yard, probably motivated by their knowledge that their footings protruded, but allowed and even encouraged him when he proposed to build himself a garage on his eastern boundary so that, after he first bought a car in about 1960, he could drive it in and across their yard; they also accepted a contribution from him to the cost of resurfacing that yard. Thus they represented to him that he had a right so to do. A very clear equity and also an estoppel thus arose against them preventing them from denying Mr High use of the right of way: cf. *per* Upjohn J. in *Halsall v. Brizell* [1957] Ch. 169, 182. It is, however, to be observed that that case related more specifically to benefits and burdens arising under a deed and held that such benefits could not be taken without assuming also the burdens: cf. also *Inwards v. Baker* [1965] 2 Q.B. 29, a case of standing by with knowledge that expenditure was being incurred in reliance upon conduct of the party against whom an equity was therefore held to arise. Notice of this equity, which amounted to an equitable easement, was given in paragraph 9 of the particulars of the auction at which the plaintiffs bought Francis Court, and the land on which it stood, and by the draft of the conveyance of the property.

In my opinion the plaintiffs as successors in title are bound by that estoppel. I do not regard myself as thereby saying anything contradictory of the proposition submitted to the court that the said equity or equitable easement, as distinct from the estoppel, was rendered void as against the plaintiffs by the statutes to which I have referred. Estoppels arising from representations made by owners of land that rights exist affecting their land will, unless in form they are limited to the duration of the interest of the representor, bind successors to his title. It is no anomaly that a person should have a legally valid answer to a claim and yet be estopped from asserting that answer against the claimant; citation of examples would be otiose and one should suffice: a tenant under a lease, in occupation, is estopped from setting up against his lessor, or an assignee, when sued by him for, e.g. rent, any denial that the lessor had an estate in the demised premises entitling him to grant that lease. Where estoppel applies, the person entitled to wield it as a shield has, ex hypothesi, suffered a past detriment or other change of position; he is not asserting any positive right but is invoking law or equity to afford him procedural protection to avert injustice.

Such equities as arise from merely standing by whilst expenditure is incurred under a mistake of fact or law, or from attempts both to approbate and reprobate a deed, always supposing them to be capable of registration, which is, I think, on the whole an open question, may not survive the lethal effect of the Land Charges Act unless they have been registered. On the other hand, I cannot see that the statute has any impact upon an estoppel, nor do I think that an estoppel could be registrable under its provisions.

NOTES:

1. For discussion, see Crane (1967) 31 Conv. 332; (1967) 30 M.L.R. 580; Battersby (1995) 58 M.L.R. 637.

2. In view of the increasing importance of estoppel as a mechanism for the informal creation of rights over land (see *post*, p. 534), the Law Commission has considered it desirable, in the context of its blueprint for land registration in the next century, to clarify the status of an equity arising by estoppel before it has been given effect by a court order. It has provisionally recommended that such an "inchoate equity" should be regarded *from the time at which it arises* as a minor interest capable of protection by an appropriate entry on the register (or as an overriding interest where the person having the benefit of it is in actual occupation): Law Com. No. 254, *Land Registration for the Twenty-First Century* (1998), paras 3.33–3.36. Again, it is clearly arguable that such a recommendation should be extended to unregistered land while it continues to exist and that inchoate equities arising by estoppel should be capable of registration under the Land Charges Act.

3. *Poster v. Slough Estates Ltd* [1968] 1 W.L.R. 1515 concerned the registrability and enforceability of a lessee's right to remove fixtures at the end of the contractual term against a sublessee whose sublease had been extended

by virtue of the Landlord and Tenant Act 1954. Cross J. stated (at 1520–1521):

Turning now to the question of registration, it has always been a moot point what rights—not being legal estates or interests—are included in those "easements, liberties or privileges" or "easements, rights or privileges" over or affecting land and being merely equitable interests which are defined as "equitable easements" in section 2(3) of the Law of Property Act 1925 and section 10(1) Class D(iii) of the Land Charges Act 1925.

In *Lewisham Borough Council v. Maloney* [1948] 1 K.B. 50, it was decided that a right conferred on a local authority by the defence regulations to requisition property was not an "equitable easement," but that does not carry one very far because a right to requisition is a right to take possession of the property and so is not at all analogous to an incorporeal right such as an easement or profit. In the recent case *E.R. Ives Investment Ltd v. High* [1967] 2 Q.B. 379 Lord Denning M.R. and Danckwerts L.J. held that equities arising out of the principle that "he who takes the benefit must accept the burden" and equities arising out of acquiescence were not "equitable easements" and Winn L.J., though he thought that the question whether such equities were registrable was doubtful, held that an ordinary estoppel was not registrable. But, again, the rights which fell to be considered in that case are very different from an express grant of a right to enter on land in the possession of another for the purpose of removing a fixture. Such a right may certainly be said to be analogous to such an incorporeal right as a profit in gross. And *Megarry and Wade* (*Law of Real Property*, 3rd ed. (1966), 723) suggest that it may be registrable; on the other hand, Guest and Lever, in an article in the Conveyancer and Property Lawyer (N.S. Vol. 27, pp. 30, 33) take the view that it is not registrable. But Lord Denning, however, based his decision in the *Ives* case, that the equities which he was considering were not equitable easements, on a wide ground which would exclude even such an equitable right as this from the category of "equitable easements," for he adopted the view advocated by C.V. Davidge in an article in 53 L.Q.R. 259 that "equitable easements" comprise only those equitable interests which, before 1926, could have subsisted as legal estates in easements or profits. There is nothing in the judgments of Danckwerts L.J. and Winn L.J. to suggest that they agreed with this view, and to accept it would, as Lord Denning recognised, limit the ambit of the words "equitable easement" considerably. Nevertheless, even if Lord Denning's view is not strictly binding on me I would, naturally, follow it, unless I was clearly of opinion that it was wrong—and in this field I am not clear about anything.

Therefore, if I had been in favour of the plaintiffs on the construction and effect of the Act I would have held that they could enforce the right in question against the second defendants, although it was not registered under the Land Charges Act.

Before parting with the case I would, however, like to refer briefly to some consequences which may flow from the acceptance of Davidge's view. So long as one is dealing with unregistered land, all is plain sailing, for the judge can apply the doctrine of notice to the unregistrable equities in question. This may enable him to arrive at a fairer result in the particular case than he could have reached had the equity been registrable but unregistered. But if he is dealing with registered land the position may be different. The general principle of the Land Registration Act is that a purchaser of registered land takes free from any unregistered rights which are not "overriding interests". The sort of right with which we are concerned in this case is not an overriding interest, and the result of holding that it is not registrable as an equitable easement may, in the case of registered land, be that there is no way of making it bind a purchaser. This would be unfortunate. On the whole, the modern law of real property works well, but "equitable easements" seem to be a weak spot in it which might with advantage receive the attention of the Law Commission.

4. *Shiloh Spinners Ltd v. Harding* [1973] A.C. 691 concerned the registrability and enforceability of a right of re-entry for breach of covenants entered into on the assignment of a lease. Lord Wilberforce stated (at 718–721):

The right of entry, it is said, is unenforceable against the respondent, although he took with actual notice of it, because it was not registered as a charge under the Land Charges Act 1925. There is no doubt that if it was capable of registration under that Act, it is unenforceable if not registered: the appellants deny that it was so capable either (i) because it was a legal right, not an equitable right, or (ii) because, if equitable, it does not fall within any of the classes or descriptions of charges registration of which is required.

I consider first whether the right of entry is legal in character or equitable, using these adjectives in the technical sense in which they are used in the 1925 property legislation. The question is purely one of statutory definition, the ingredients of which are found in sections 1 and 205(1)(x) of the Law of Property Act 1925. The contention that the right is legal was not accepted by Burgess V.-C. or advanced in the Court of Appeal below, nor was it contained in the printed case signed by eminent counsel, though if it were upheld it would be decisive of the case. The appellants were, however, permitted to lodge an amended case raising the point. I set out for convenience section 1(1), (2) and (3) of the Act. The definition section 205(1)(x) uses the same verbiage and adds nothing to the argument.

"(1) The only estates in land which are capable of subsisting or of being conveyed or created at law are—(a) An estate in fee simple absolute in possession; (b) A term of years absolute. (2) The only interests or charges in or over land which are capable of subsisting or of being conveyed or created at law are—... (e) Rights of entry exercisable over or in respect of a legal term of years absolute, or annexed, for any purpose, to a legal rentcharge. (3) All other estates, interests, and charges in or over land take effect as equitable interests."

The right of entry in this case is not contained in a lease, so as to be annexed to a reversion, nor is it exercisable for a term of years, or (comparably with a fee simple) indefinitely. Its duration is limited by a perpetuity period. Whether it can be said to be "exercisable over or in respect of a legal term of years absolute" appears obscure. It is not exercisable for a legal term of years (whether that granted by the lease or any other term): it is not so exercisable as to determine a legal term of years. To say that a right of entry is exercisable in respect of a legal term of years appears to me, with respect, to be without discernible meaning. The effect of this right of entry is to cause a legal term of years to be divested from one person to another upon an event which may occur over a perpetuity period. It would, I think, be contrary to the whole scheme of the Act, which requires the limiting and vesting of legal estates and interests to be by reference to a fee simple or a term of years absolute, to allow this to rank as a legal interest. In my opinion it is clearly equitable.

So I pass, as did the Court of Appeal, to the Land Charges Act 1925. The original contention of the respondents was that the equitable right of entry was capable of registration under Class D(iii) of the Act. In the Court of Appeal an alternative contention was raised, apparently at the court's suggestion, that it might come within Class C(iv). In my opinion this is unmaintainable. Class C(iv) embraces:

"Any contract by an estate owner or by a person entitled at the date of the contract to have a legal estate conveyed to him to convey or create a legal estate, including a contract conferring either expressly or by statutory implication a valid option of purchase, a right of pre-emption or any other like right (in this Act referred to as 'an estate contract')."

The only words capable of including a right of entry are "any other like right", but, in my opinion, no relevant likeness can be found. An option or right of pre-emption eventuates in a contract for sale at a price; this is inherent in "purchase" and "pre-emption"; the right of entry is penal in character and involves the revesting of the lease, in the event of default, in a previous owner. There is no similarity in law or fact between these situations.

Class D(iii) reads:

> "A charge or obligation affecting land of any of the following kinds, namely:—...
> (iii) Any easement right or privilege over or affecting land created or arising after the commencement of this Act, and being merely an equitable interest (in this Act referred to as an 'equitable easement')."

The argument for inclusion in this class falls into two parts. First it is said that a right of entry falls fairly within the description, or at least that, if the words do not appear to include it, they are sufficiently open in meaning to admit it. Secondly it is said that the provisions of the Law of Property Act as to "overreaching" compel the conclusion that a right of entry must fall under some class or sub-class of the Land Charges Act, and since this is the only one whose words can admit it, they should be so interpreted as to do so. Thus the argument depends for its success upon a combination of ambiguity, or openness of Class D(iii) with compelling consideration brought about in the overreaching provisions. In my opinion it fails under both limbs: Class D(iii) cannot be interpreted so as to admit equitable rights of entry, and no conclusive, compelling, or even clear conclusions can be drawn from the overreaching provisions which can influence the interpretation of Class D(iii).

Dealing with Class D(iii), I reject at once the suggestion that any help (by way of enlarging the content of this class) can be derived either from the introductory words, for they limit themselves to the "following kinds," or from the words "and being merely an equitable interest," for these are limiting, not enlarging, words. I leave out of account the label at the end—though I should think it surprising if so expert a draftsman had attached that particular label if the class included a right of entry. To include a right of entry in the description of "equitable easement" offends a sense both of elegance and accuracy. That leaves "easement right or privilege over or affecting land." If this were the only place where the expression occurred in this legislation, I should find it difficult to attribute to "right" a meaning so different in quality from easement and privilege as to include a right of entry. The difference between a right to use or draw profit from another man's land, and a right to take his land altogether away, is one of quality, not of degree. But the words are plentifully used both in the Law of Property Act and elsewhere in the 1925 legislation, so are the words "rights of entry," and I find it impossible to believe that in this one context the one includes the other. The two expressions are even used by way of what seems deliberate contrast in two contexts: first in section 1 of the Law of Property Act, where subsection (2)(a) mentions "An easement, right, or privilege in or over land" and paragraph (e) of the same subsection "Rights of entry": secondly, in section 162(1)(d) which mentions both. An argument, unattractive but perhaps just palatable, can be devised why it might have been necessary in section 1 of the Law of Property Act to mention both easements, rights or privileges and the particular rights of entry described in subsection (2)(e), but no explanation can be given why, if the latter are capable of being included in the former, they should be mentioned with such a degree of separation. I do not further elaborate this point because a reading of their judgments leaves little doubt that the Lords Justices would themselves have read Class D(iii) as I can only read it but for the influence of the overreaching argument.

So I turn to the latter. This, in my opinion, only becomes compelling if one first accepts the conclusion that all equitable claims relating to land are either registrable under the Land Charges Act, or capable of being overreached under section 2 of the Law of Property Act; i.e., are capable by use of the appropriate mechanism of being transferred to the proceeds of sale of the land they affect. If this dilemma could be made good, then there could be an argument for forcing, within the limits of the possible, an equitable right of entry into one of the registrable classes, since it is obviously not suitable for overreaching. But the dilemma cannot be made good. What may be overreached is "any equitable interest or power affecting that estate": yet "equitable interest" (for powers do not enter into the debate) is a word of most uncertain content. The searcher after a definition has to be satisfied with section 1(8) "Estates, interests, and charges in or over land which are not legal estates are in this Act referred to as 'equitable interests' "—a tautology rather than a definition. There is certainly nothing exhaustive about the expression "equitable interests"—just as certainly it has no clear boundaries. The debate whether such rights as equity, over the centuries, has conferred against the holder of the legal estate are truly proprietary in character, or merely rights in personam, or a hybrid between the two, may have lost some of its vitality in the statutory context but the question inevitably rises to mind whether the "curtain" or "overreaching" provisions of the 1925 legislation extend to what are still conveniently called "equities" or "mere equities," such as rights to rectification, or to set aside a conveyance. There is good authority, which I do not presume to doubt, for a sharp distinction between the two—I instance Lord Upjohn in *National Provincial Bank Ltd v. Hastings Car Mart Ltd* [1965] A.C. 1175, 1238 and *Snell's Principles of Equity*, 25th ed. (1960), p. 38. I am impressed by the decision in *E.R. Ives Investment Ltd v. High* [1967] 2 Q.B. 379 in which the Court of Appeal held that a right by estoppel—producing an effect similar to an easement—was not registrable under Class D(iii). Lord Denning M.R. referred to the right as subsisting only in equity. Danckwerts L.J. thought it was an equity created by estoppel or a proprietary estoppel: plainly this was not an equitable interest capable of being overreached, yet no member of the court considered that the right—so like an easement—could be brought within Class D(iii). The conclusion followed, and the court accepted it, that whether it was binding on a purchaser depended on notice. All this seems to show that there may well be rights, of an equitable character, outside the provisions as to registration and which are incapable of being overreached.

That equitable rights of entry should be among them is not in principle unacceptable. First, rights of entry, before 1925, were not considered to confer an interest in the land. They were described as bare possibilities (*Challis's Real Property*, (3rd ed. 1911), p. 76) so that it is not anomalous that equitable rights of entry should not be treated as equitable interests. Secondly, it is important that section 10 of the Land Charges Act 1925 should be given a plain and ordinary interpretation. It is a section which involves day to day operation by solicitors doing conveyancing work: they should be able to take decisions and advise their clients upon a straightforward interpretation of the registration classes, not upon one depending upon a sophisticated, not to say disputable, analysis of other statutes. Thirdly, the consequence of equitable rights of entry not being registrable is that they are subject to the doctrine of notice, preserved by section 199 of the Law of Property Act. This may not give complete protection, but neither is it demonstrable that it is likely to be less effective than the present system of registration against names. I am therefore of opinion that Class D(iii) should be given its plain prima facie meaning and that so read it does not comprise equitable rights of entry. It follows that non-registration does not make the appellant's right unenforceable in this case.

For comment, see [1971] C.L.J. 258, [1973] C.L.J. 218; (1974) 37 M.L.R. 87.

5. For further discussion of the nature and scope of equitable easements, see Cross (1935) 15 Bell Yard 18; Davidge (1937) 58 L.Q.R. 259; Wade (1948) 64 L.Q.R. 57, 58 (note 6); Garner (1967) 31 Conv. 394, 394–397; Jackson (1969) 33 Conv. 135; Thompson [1986] Conv. 31, 34–37; Barnsley (1999) 115 L.Q.R. 89.

6. For substantive discussion of easements, see *post*, Chapter 7; of the doctrine of mutual benefit and burden, see *post*, p. 723; and of the doctrine of proprietary estoppel, see *post*, p. 534.

4.4.6 Matrimonial home rights under the Family Law Act 1996   The category of class F land charges was created by the Matrimonial Homes Act 1967. At common law a wife has a personal right to occupy the matrimonial home by reason of her status as a wife: *Hall v. King* (1987) 55 P. & C.R. 307, 310 *per* Lord Donaldson M.R.; and for the suggestion that the right must now extend to a husband, see *Harman v. Glencross* [1985] Fam. 49, 58 *per* Ewbank J. During the 1950s the Court of Appeal developed the doctrine of the "deserted wife's equity", according to which the common law rights of the wife were afforded protection against a purchaser of the matrimonial home from the husband (other than a bona fide purchaser for value without notice): see *Bendall v. McWhirter* [1952] 2 Q.B. 466; *Ferris v. Weaven* [1952] 2 All E.R. 233; *Lee v. Lee* [1952] 2 Q.B. 489; *Street v. Denham* [1954] 1 W.L.R. 624; *Jess B. Woodcock & Sons Ltd v. Hobbs* [1955] 1 W.L.R. 152; *Westminster Bank Ltd v. Lee* [1956] Ch. 7; *National Provincial Bank Ltd v. Hastings Car Mart Ltd* [1964] Ch. 665; and see Megarry (1952) 68 L.Q.R. 379; Crane (1955) 19 Conv. 343; Crane (1965) 29 Conv. 254, 464. The doctrine was rejected by the House of Lords in *National Provincial Bank Ltd v. Ainsworth* [1965] A.C. 1175; and their Lordships reasserted the personal nature of the wife's right to occupy the matrimonial home: see [1965] C.L.J. 216; Crane (1965) 29 Conv. 254, 464; (1965) 81 L.Q.R. 353; (1966) 29 M.L.R. 74. However, the decision of the House of Lords prompted the enactment of the Matrimonial Homes Act 1967. The relevant statutory provisions are now contained in Part IV of the Family Law Act 1996.

The Act confers statutory rights of occupation in the matrimonial home on a spouse who is not on the legal title: the right not to be evicted or excluded from the matrimonial home and, if not in occupation, the right with the leave of the court to enter into and occupy the matrimonial home: Family Law Act 1996, s.30. These "matrimonial home rights," which are subject to regulation by the court, constitute a charge on the interest of the other spouse; and, if protected by registration as a class F land charge, they are enforceable against a purchaser from the other spouse. For discussion of the earlier version of the legislation, see *Wroth v. Tyler* [1974] Ch. 30, 43–46 *per* Megarry J.

It is important to stress that the matrimonial home rights are quite distinct from any contribution-based equitable ownership rights of the spouse; and that the two rights should be considered separately. For example, a wife may have failed to register a class F land charge in respect of her matrimonial home rights, with the consequence that those rights are unenforceable against a purchaser from the husband. However, it is an entirely separate matter to consider whether the wife acquired equitable ownership rights by reason of any contribution to the purchase price and whether that interest has been overreached or remains enforceable against the purchaser pursuant to the doctrine of notice: see *infra*, p. 153.

5. Doctrine of notice

It will be apparent that, even after 1925, in certain circumstances the equitable doctrine of notice continues to determine the question of enforceability of equitable interests against a purchaser of land under the title deeds conveyancing system. The principal interests to which the doctrine still applies may be summarised as follows:

(i) Equitable interests excluded by statute from the operation of the doctrine of overreaching and from the registration system of the Land Charges Act 1972. This category mainly comprises restrictive covenants entered into before 1926 and equitable easements created or arising before 1926: see Law of Property Act 1925, s.2(3), (5); Land Charges Act 1972, s.2(5)(ii), (iii).

(ii) Equitable interests excluded by the interpretation of the courts from the operation of the doctrine of overreaching and from the registration system of the Land Charges Act 1972: see *E.R. Ives Investment Ltd v. High* [1967] 2 Q.B. 379, *per* Lord Denning M.R., *supra*, p. 142; *Poster v. Slough Estates Ltd* [1968] 1 W.L.R. 1515, *supra*, p. 149; *Shiloh Spinners Ltd v. Harding* [1973] A.C. 691, *supra*, p. 147.

(iii) Equitable interests which are in principle subject to the registration system of the Land Charges Act 1972, which are void for non-registration but which the courts have nonetheless been prepared to declare enforceable against a purchaser because, pursuant to the principle of estoppel, the purchaser is not permitted to rely on the absence of registration: *E.R. Ives Investment Ltd v. High* [1967] 2 Q.B. 379, *supra*, p. 142; *Taylors Fashions Ltd v. Liverpool Victoria Trustees Co. Ltd* [1982] Q.B. 133, *post*, p. 535.

(iv) Equitable interests which are in principle subject to overreaching but which have not been overreached because the purchaser has failed to comply with the statutory requirement that the purchase money be paid to at least two trustees: see *Caunce v. Caunce* [1969] 1 W.L.R. 286, *ante*, p. 39; *Kingsnorth Finance Co Ltd v. Tizard* [1986] 1 W.L.R. 783, *ante*, p. 42; and see *post*, p. 332.

6. Other matters registrable under the Land Charges Act 1972

6.1 *Pending actions*

Pending actions include pending land actions and petitions in bankruptcy: Land Charges Act 1972, s.5(1). Pending land action is defined as "any action or proceeding pending in court relating to land or any interest in or charge on land": *ibid.* s.17(1). The definition has been construed as restricted to actions asserting an existing *proprietary* interest in land or claiming such an interest: *Calgary and Edmonton Land Co. Ltd v. Dobinson* [1974] Ch. 102, 105–107 *per* Megarry J.; *Whittingham v. Whittingham* [1979] Fam. 9, 13–14 *per* Balcombe J., 21–24 *per* Stamp L.J.; *Perez-Adamson v. Perez-Rivas* [1987] Fam. 89, 94–96 *per* Dillon L.J., 97 *per* Nicholls L.J.; *13–20 Embankment Gardens Ltd v. Coote* (1997) 74 P. & C.R. D6 *per* Millett L.J. For example, pending land actions may be registered in relation to claims for property transfer orders on divorce (*Perez-Adamson v. Perez-Rivas, supra*) and estoppel-based claims, provided that the claim is for an established property right (*Haslemere Estates Ltd v. Baker* [1982] 1 W.L.R. 1109, 1119–1120 *per* Megarry V.-C.). Moreover, applications for access orders under the Access to Neighbouring Land Act 1992 are expressly made registrable as pending land actions: Access to Neighbouring Land Act 1992, s.5(6).

The effect of registration of a pending land action is that any purchaser of the land in question is deemed to have notice of the action and will be bound by any interest in the land successfully asserted or claimed in the action: see Law of Property Act 1925, s.198(1); *Perez-Adamson v. Perez-Rivas, supra*, 96 *per* Dillon L.J., 97 *per* Nicholls L.J. The consequences of non-registration are less drastic than in the case of land charges. An unregistered pending land action will still bind a purchaser who has express notice of it: Land Charges Act 1972, s.5(7); and an unregistered petition in bankruptcy will bind a purchaser unless he is purchaser of a legal estate in good faith for money or money's worth: *ibid.* s.5(8).

For discussion of the relationship between section 5 of the Land Charges Act 1972 and the common law doctrine of *lis pendens*, see Howell [1995] Conv. 309.

6.2 *Writs and orders*
Writs and orders affecting land are restricted to writs and orders *enforcing* judgments and orders of the court. The category includes charging orders, orders appointing a receiver or sequestrator of land, bankruptcy orders and access orders under the Access to Neighbouring Land Act 1992: Land Charges Act 1972, s.6(1). Any such order that is not registered is void as against a purchaser of the land, although in the case of bankruptcy orders only against a purchaser of a legal estate *in good faith* for money or money's worth: *ibid.* s.6(4), (5), (6).

6.3 *Deeds of arrangement*
Deeds of arrangement affecting land include any document conferring control over a debtor's land for the benefit of his creditors. An unregistered deed is void as against a purchaser of the land: *ibid.* s.7(2).

Registration of any of the above matters lapses after five years but is renewable: *ibid.* s.8.

7. Registration of local land charges

A wide range of matters may be registered in the local land charges register maintained by the local authority under the Local Land Charges Act 1975.

Such matters are for the most part public matters such as charges for highway or sewerage works and planning conditions and restrictions. Unlike searches of the land charges register, searches of the *local* land charges register normally take place before exchange of contracts. Unregistered local land charges remain enforceable; but a purchaser of land who suffers any consequential loss is normally entitled to compensation: Local Land Charges Act 1975, s.10.

3

REGISTRATION OF TITLE

A. Introduction

1. The aim of registration of title

The title deeds system of conveyancing required the "wearisome and intricate task of examining title": *Williams & Glyn's Bank Ltd v. Boland* [1981] A.C. 487, 511 *per* Lord Scarman; and proof of title depended upon a collection of title deeds which were "difficult to read, impossible to understand and disgusting to touch": Lord Westbury L.C., quoted in Dowson and Sheppard, *Land Registration* (2nd ed., 1956), p. 11. There was no comprehensive official record of dealings in land because the documents which both created and recorded rights in relation to the land were prepared and retained by the parties. Thus the system was time-consuming and expensive because the same title had to be examined on each successive conveyance, irrespective of the time that had elapsed since the previous conveyance.

The fundamental aim of any system of registration of title is to eliminate reliance on title deeds and to remove the need for the repeated examination of the same title; and to do so by establishing and maintaining an official register which accurately records all the current details relevant to any parcel of land from a conveyancing viewpoint. Once the title to a parcel of land has been investigated and verified, it is recorded in the register; and the registered title thereby created effectively constitutes a new title which replaces and supersedes the previous documentary title. It provides the basis for all subsequent transactions relating to the land, which are effected by making appropriate alterations to the register. As a result, the register provides a prospective purchaser of land with an accurate record of the relevant details relating to that land. In particular, an examination of the register will indicate (i) whether the vendor is entitled to sell the land and (ii) subject to certain exceptions, what third party interests affect the land.

2. The Land Registration Act 1925

In England and Wales some registration of title took place on a voluntary basis pursuant to the Land Registry Act 1862 and the Land Transfer Act

1875; and the Land Transfer Act 1897 introduced compulsory registration of title in respect of dealings in land in London. However, the current system is based on the Land Registration Act 1925, supplemented by the Land Registration Rules 1925.

Law Commission Report No. 125, Property Law: Land Registration (1983), para. 1.5

(1) The system of land registration is a statutory one governed by the Land Registration Acts ... and subordinate legislation ...
(2) The system was primarily designed to simplify the process of land transfer rather than to alter the substantive law relating to land, though some aspects of the substantive law are affected by the system.
(3) The foundation of the system [of land registration] is the registration of title to freehold and long leasehold estates, the legal title being established by an official register rather than by the assemblage of deeds and documents upon which unregistered titles are based ...

      . . .

(5) In addition to the registration of title to freehold and leasehold estates the 1925 Act provides for the registration of legal mortgages or charges upon such estates, so that title to these mortgages and charges is established by the register. The many other rights and interests in land such as restrictive covenants, easements and various kinds of financial burden are not susceptible of substantive registration: they are however capable of protection by entry on the registers of the titles which they affect, and a limited class of interests (known as "overriding interests") is protected even though they are not entered on the register.
(6) The register is backed by a kind of "state guarantee", through the use of powers of rectification and indemnity. If there is some error or omission in the register the register may be rectified, though the possibility of rectifying a registered title against the proprietor when he is in possession is restricted. If an error or omission, or its rectification, results in loss, indemnity for that loss is payable out of public funds. For example where a registered title is found to contain more land than the vendor had to convey, if the registered proprietor is not in possession it may be rectified by the removal of the land from the title and the proprietor indemnified, and if the registered proprietor is in possession the rightful owner of the land registered in error may be indemnified.

NOTES:
   1. For an account of the nineteenth century campaigns for the introduction of land registration, see Wilkinson (1972) 36 Conv. 390. For early discussions of the Land Registration Act 1925, see Potter (1949) 12 M.L.R. 205; Hargreaves (1949) 12 M.L.R. 477.
   2. Despite its title, the Land Registration Act 1925 provides for a system of registration of titles, not registration of land. Registration of land would involve a single register for each parcel of land, recording all the interests affecting that land together with other information relevant to that land from a conveyancing viewpoint. By contrast, registration of title involves a separate register for each principal interest (title) affecting a particular piece of land. Thus, where the fee simple owner of Blackacre has granted a 25-year lease over the land, there are two titles affecting Blackacre, the fee simple and the

lease: each will have a separate register and each will have its own title number.

3. As indicated in subparagraph (2) above, the system of registration of title contained in the Land Registration Act 1925 was not seen as introducing new principles of substantive law. It was seen as simply introducing new machinery for the creation, transfer and protection of the same estates and interests in land that were the subject-matter of title deeds conveyancing. In that respect the Act did not differ from the earlier legislation on registration of title (summarised in Stewart-Wallace, *Principles of Land Registration* (1937), p. 33):

[The members of the 1857 Royal Commission on the Registration of Title with reference to the Sale and Transfer of Land] decided, and the wisdom of their decision has never been challenged, that the Act introducing registration of title should be confined to making changes in the machinery of conveyancing merely. The alternative of introducing substantive changes applicable to registered land only, so that the substantive law affecting registered land would differ from that affecting unregistered land, was rejected. They adopted the root principle that the register should be a substitute for title deeds and nothing more than a substitute; that the register should reveal what was revealed in the title deeds, but that nothing not shown in the deeds should be shown by the register.

The same view was endorsed by the House of Lords: see, *e.g. National Provincial Bank Ltd v. Ainsworth* [1965] A.C. 1175, 1260–1261 *per* Lord Wilberforce. It was also the view taken in the early publications of the Law Commission: see Law Commission Working Paper No. 32, *Transfer of Land: Land Registration (First Paper)* (1970), para. 6; Law Commission Working Paper No. 45, *Transfer of Land: Land Registration (Third Paper)* (1972), para. 73. For a wide-ranging critical discussion of (i) the failure of the Land Registration Act to make clear the relationship between the land registration scheme and the pre-existing substantive law, and (ii) the constant reference by the courts to unregistered land principles in a registered land context, see Jackson (1972) 88 L.Q.R. 93. However, the Law Commission has since become progressively more "registration minded" (Jackson (1978) 94 L.Q.R. 239, 254) and no longer feels contrained by the fact that its reforms might create or perpetuate differences between the substantive law applicable to registered and unregistered land respectively: Law Com. No. 158, *Property Law: Third Report on Land Registration* (1987), para. 2.5; Law Com. No. 254, *Land Registration for the Twenty-First Century* (1998), paras 1.5–1.6. Indeed, the computerisation of the register and the proposed move to electronic conveyancing provide opportunities for improvements in the law that *cannot* be achieved within the system of conveyancing applicable to unregistered land: *ibid.* para. 1.6; and see *infra*, p. 261.

The current reality seems to be that, although the substantive estates and interests are the same in both registered and unregistered land, the Land Registration Act 1925 introduced a different classification of those estates and interests and different machinery for their creation, transfer and protection; and it has become clear that the operation of the different machinery of registered land may produce consequences different from those produced by the operation of the machinery of unregistered land on the same facts: *Williams & Glyn's Bank Ltd v. Boland* [1981] A.C. 487, 511 *per* Lord Scarman; and see Riddall (1977) 41 Conv. 405.

4. Although transactions continue to be executed by the parties, the effectiveness of transactions in registered land depends upon registration: Land Registration Act 1925, ss.19, 22. Moreover, the conclusiveness of registration (*ibid.* s.69(1)) means that, even where the transaction is substantively void, the registration of that transaction confers validity, although the register may subsequently be rectified: *Argyle Building Society v. Hammond* (1985) 49 P. & C.R. 153. For discussion of the effect of forged transfers, see Smith (1985) 101 L.Q.R. 79, 86–95.

5. It is asserted that the system of registration of title introduced by the Land Registration Act 1925 reflects three principles: the mirror principle, the insurance principle and the curtain principle:

(a) Pursuant to the so-called "mirror principle", the register should be an accurate and conclusive reflection of relevant interests affecting the land in question. However, it was never contemplated that the system of registration of title introduced by the Land Registration Act 1925 would involve the recording on the register of *all* interests affecting the land in question. The Report of the 1857 Royal Commission stated (at para. 63):

The register will be a substitute for the documentary or parchment title. But the registered ownership ... will remain subject, as the fee simple now is, ... to such other rights as are not usually included in the abstract of title ... These are rights which are commonly evidenced by known usage or continued enjoyment or may be ascertained on the spot by inspection or enquiry; and the title to them is generally so independent of the documentary title to the property that they will necessarily form a partial exception to that which will constitute the registered ownership.

Although the register is not confined to proof of title in the narrow sense, the Land Registration Act 1925 provides for a category of overriding interests which are enforceable against the land affected even though they are not mentioned in the register: see *infra*, p. 180.

(b) Pursuant to the so-called "insurance principle", the accuracy of the register should be guaranteed in the sense that, if the register is found to be inaccurate, any person adversely affected by the rectification or non-rectification of the register, should be entitled to be indemnified. However, overriding interests, which constitute an exception to the "mirror principle" are also an exception to the "insurance principle" in that no indemnity is payable where the register is rectified in order to give effect to an overriding interest: see *infra*, p. 254.

(c) Pursuant to the so-called "curtain principle", a purchaser of land is not concerned with matters behind the entries on the register. In particular, the details (as opposed to the implied existence) of trusts affecting registered land should not be entered on the register. In this more restricted sense, the principle is not exclusive to registered title conveyancing: trust documentation in the context of title deeds conveyancing is normally so arranged that a purchaser sees only that information which is necessary to enable him effectively to overreach the beneficial interests under the trust.

However, it will become apparent that the Land Registration Act 1925 to a significant degree fails to incorporate all these principles.

3. The Land Register

The Land Register is under the administrative control of the Chief Land Registrar, who is based in London. However, the operation of the system is decentralised in 24 district land registries. Computerisation of the register is nearing completion: all registered titles are on the computer and digital plans are currently being added.

It will already be apparent that the term "register" is used in different senses. It is used to denote, first, the whole register maintained by the Land Registry, secondly, the record of each individual title and, thirdly, the subdivisions of each individual title—the property register, the proprietorship register and the charges register. The *property register* contains a verbal description of the land and a description by reference to a plan; it identifies the particular estate comprised in the title; and it notes any appurtenant rights which benefit the land, for example easements and covenants: Land Registration Rules 1925, r.3. Furthermore, if the title is leasehold, there will be a note of the principal terms of the lease: *ibid*. r.5. The *proprietorship register* includes the name and address of the registered proprietor of the relevant title, the date of registration and the nature of the title (absolute, good leasehold, qualified or possessory: see *infra*). It also notes any cautions, restrictions or inhibitions which may affect the right of the registered proprietor to dispose of or otherwise deal with the land: *ibid*. r.6. The *charges register* contains notices and entries relating to matters which adversely affect the land, for example, charges, leases, easements, restrictive covenants: *ibid*. r.7.

For many years, there was no general right of access to the register, although with the authority of the registered proprietor a prospective purchaser could inspect the register relating to the land in question. However, under the Land Registration Act 1988, on payment of the prescribed fee any person may now inspect entries on the register and any documents (except leases and charges) referred to in the register: Land Registration Act 1925, s.112(1).

4. Classification of interests under the Land Registration Act 1925

As indicated above, although the substantive estates and interests are the same in both registered and unregistered land, the Land Registration Act 1925 introduced a different classification of those estates and interests. In the context of unregistered land, five categories of interest were identified: (i) legal estates; (ii) legal interests; (iii) (family) equitable interests capable of being overreached on a conveyance of the land; (iv) (commercial) equitable interests capable of registration under the Land Charges Act 1972; and (v) equitable interests which depend on the doctrine of notice for their enforceability. In the context of registered land, there are four categories of interest: (i) registrable interests; (ii) registered charges; (iii) minor interests; (iv) overriding interests.

B. REGISTRABLE INTERESTS AND REGISTERED CHARGES

1. Registrable interests

Registrable interests are those principal interests in land which are capable of substantive registration in the sense that they generate separate titles, each with its individual register. The interests in this category correspond closely to those interests that are capable of existing as legal estates: Land Registration Act 1925, s.2. In accordance with section 1(1) of the Law of Property Act 1925, this category therefore comprises the legal fee simple absolute in possession and the legal term of years absolute, although a term of years is not capable of substantive registration unless it exceeds 21 years: Land Registration Act 1925, s.8(1). However, the Law Commission has raised for consultation the question as to whether substantive registration should be required or permitted in relation to shorter leases: Law Com. No. 254, *Land Registration for the Twenty-First Century* (1998), paras 3.7–3.12. Legal leases that are not required to be registered substantively take effect as overriding interests: see *infra*, p. 232.

1.1 *Application for first registration*

1.1.1 *Compulsory registration*   Compulsory registration of title was progressively extended to more and more areas of the country and since 1990 it has applied to the whole country. However, that is not to say that all title to land is now registered. Where title to land has not previously been registered, there is no requirement to register until there has been a disposition affecting the legal title; and even then not every such disposition triggers the requirement. Until recently, registration of title was only compulsory (within an area of compulsory registration) following a conveyance on sale of the fee simple, the grant of a lease for a term exceeding 21 years or the assignment of a lease with more than 21 years to run. The Land Registration Act 1997 extended the list of dispositions triggering compulsory registration by adding (i) conveyances, grants and assignments by way of gift or pursuant to a court order; (ii) dispositions of a fee simple or lease with more than 21 years to run effected by assent, vesting assent or vesting deed; and (iii) first legal mortgages protected by the deposit of documents of a fee simple or lease with more than 21 years to run: Land Registration Act 1925, s.123. The list is still not comprehensive but the Act provides for the list of dispositions triggering compulsory registration to be further extended by statutory instrument: *ibid.* s.123(4). On the other hand, primary legislation would be necessary to require registration in the absence of any disposition. As a result, there is no immediate prospect of bringing on to the register land owned, for example, by companies, which can remain in the same ownership and unmortgaged for many years.

The Land Registration Act 1997 also sought to clarify the effect of failure to comply with the requirement of compulsory first registration. Pending application for registration, the disposition operates to transfer or grant a legal estate; but if the application is not made within two months of the disposition, the disposition becomes void. In the case of purported transfers, the legal estate reverts to the transferor, who holds it on bare trust for the transferee; in the case of purported grants or mortgages, the disposition takes effect as a contract for the disposition in question. The effect is the same where the Registrar grants an extension of the two-month time limit, although, if the extension is granted *after* the original two months, it is not clear whether the renewed effectiveness of the disposition is retrospective: see Tee [1997] C.L.J. 241.

The above provisions do not preclude voluntary registration at any time; but, despite provisions for the waiver or reduction of fees (Land Registration Act 1925, s.145(3),(4)), there is no real incentive to incur the other costs involved.

1.1.2 *Cautions against first registration*   Any person who has or claims to have an interest in unregistered land that would entitle him to object to a disposition of the relevant legal estate without his consent and who claims that his interest would be adversely affected by the substantive registration of title to the land is entitled to lodge a caution against first registration: Land Registration Act 1925, s.53. If an application for first registration is subsequently made, the cautioner will be given the opportunity to substantiate his claim.

1.1.3 *Effect of first registration*   The first registration of title marks the break with the past. A new statutory title is conferred on the registered proprietor and that title constitutes the basis for subsequent dealings affecting the relevant interest. In *Kitney v. MEPC Ltd* [1977] 1 W.L.R. 981 it was contended that "registration under the Land Registration Act 1925 wipes the slate of history clean and makes a new start; or to change the metaphor ... lowers an impenetrable curtain beyond which one may not look to ascertain the proprietor's title". Buckley L.J. responded (at 993):

To a certain extent at least it is true that the first registration under the Land Registration Act 1925 creates a new root of title and it defines the estate vested in the registered proprietor, whether that estate is identical with the estate which was vested in him before registration or not.

This more guarded admission was intended to leave open the possibility of removing entries in relation to invalid claims. The rather more heretical proposition that the common law estates have been replaced by statutory estates was asserted in *Chowood Ltd v. Lyall (No. 2)* [1930] 2 Ch. 145, 163 *per* Lord Hanworth M.R.; but, not surprisingly, this provoked considerable controversy: see Connell (1947) 11 Conv. 184, 232; Potter (1949) 12 M.L.R. 205; Hargreaves (1949) 12 M.L.R. 477; and see, generally, Palk (1974) 38 Conv. 236.

1.1.4 *Classes of title*

1.1.4.1 *Absolute title and good leasehold title*   The first registered proprietor of the freehold will normally be registered with *absolute* title. This vests in him the fee simple in possession together with the benefit of appurtenant rights such as easements but subject to (i) interests entered on the register, (ii) overriding interests affecting the land (unless the contrary is expressed on the register) and (iii) where the registered proprietor is a trustee, minor interests of which he has notice: Land Registration Act 1925, s.5.

It is possible for the first registered proprietor of a leasehold interest to be registered with absolute title; and, when he is so registered, he takes the interest together with all express and implied appurtenant rights and subject to all express and implied covenants, obligations and liabilities incident to the registered land, in addition to those matters which affect a freehold title on first registration: *ibid.* s.9. However, registration of a leasehold interest with absolute title is only possible where the registrar is also satisfied with the freehold title: *ibid.* s.8. There is no difficulty where the freehold title is already registered; but where it is not, the lessee will not be in a position to provide the necessary evidence unless he has so stipulated in his contract: Law of Property Act 1925, s.44. Where registration with absolute title is not possible, the applicant for first registration of a leasehold title is registered with *good leasehold title*, which does not guarantee the right of the lessor to grant the lease: Land Registration Act 1925, s.10.

1.1.4.2 *Qualified title*   Where the registrar is unable to register an absolute title in relation to a freehold or leasehold interest, or good leasehold title, because of some defect in the title, he may register a *qualified* title, which has the same effect as registration with absolute or good leasehold title except that the title is also subject to the specified defect: Land Registration Act 1925, ss.7, 12.

1.1.4.3 *Possessory title*   A person who cannot establish his claim to land by documentary evidence but who relies upon possession (or receipt of rent and profits) may apply for registration with *possessory* title. Although it is possible that the registrar will still register an absolute or good leasehold title in these circumstances, where a possessory title is registered the title is guaranteed in relation to dealings following registration but remains subject to all adverse interests existing at the date of registration: Land Registration Act 1925, ss.6, 11.

1.1.4.4 *Conversion of title* Where the first registered proprietor has not been registered with absolute title, the title may subsequently be converted to the relevant superior class of title if the defect (explicit or implicit) in the original title is cured: Land Registration Act 1925, s.77.

1.2 *Land certificate*

On the first registration of a freehold or leasehold estate, the Registry prepares a land certificate, which includes all the details on the register relating to the title in question. The land certificate is available to the registered proprietor as his document of title: Land Registration Act 1925, s.63. However, where the freehold or leasehold is mortgaged, the land certificate is retained by the Registry: *ibid.* s.65. In any event, it is the register, and not the land certificate, which constitutes the definitive proof of title.

1.3 *Subsequent dealings in registered land*

Following first registration, the registered proprietor may deal with, and create interests in the land, in the same way as if the title to the land were not registered; but he must do so in accordance with the requirements of the Land Registration Act 1925.

1.3.1 *Dispositions of registrable interests* A subsequent *inter vivos* disposition of a registrable interest is effected by lodging a simple form of transfer and the relevant land certificate at the appropriate district land registry. In theory there is no transfer until the appropriate amendments are made to the register: Land Registration Act 1925, ss.19(1), 22(1); but registration is treated as having taken place on the date when the documents were lodged: Land Registration Rules, r.83(2). The effect of a subsequent disposition for value of a freehold title is to vest in the transferee the registered title together with the benefit of appurtenant rights but subject to interests entered on the register and overriding interests affecting the land (unless the contrary is expressed on the register): Land Registration Act 1925, s.20. A disposition for value of a leasehold title takes effect subject in addition to all express and implied covenants, obligations and liabilities incident to the estate transferred or created: *ibid.* s.23. Moreover, where a disposition is made without valuable consideration, the transferee takes subject to those unprotected minor interests that affected the transferor: *ibid.* ss.20(4), 23(5).

If the disposition is not registered, the transferor holds the legal estate on trust for the transferee, although the transferee, who thus has only an equitable interest in the land, may acquire an overriding interest enforceable against a subsequent purchaser: see *infra*, p. 196. In the meantime (that is, during the "registration gap" between the disposition and its registration), as between the parties to the transaction, the disposition may be regarded as effective in equity, provided that the transferor has done all that he is required to do to effect the disposition: *Mascall v. Mascall* (1984) 50 P. & C.R. 119; but, in relation to third parties, only the strict legal position is relevant: *Brown & Root Technology Ltd v. Sun Alliance and London Assurance Co. Ltd* (1996) 75 P. & C.R. 223. However, the practical consequences of this decision in the context of the assignment of leases are potentially serious; and the Law Commission has raised the issue for consultation: Law Com. No. 254, *Land Registration for the Twenty-First Century* (1998), paras 11.26–11.29.

1.3.2 *Other registered dispositions*   In addition to the disposition of the two legal estates in land, certain other transactions in relation to registered land constitute "dispositions": Land Registration Act 1925, ss.18, 21. Such transactions, which include the express grant of a legal easement (*ibid.* ss.18(1)(c), 21(1)(b)) do not generate interests capable of substantive registration in the sense discussed above; but they must be "completed by registration": *ibid.* ss.19(2), 22(2). In the case of legal easements, the easement should be noted in the property register of the land benefiting from the easement and in the charges register of the land burdened by the easement. However, where the grant of a legal easement is not completed by registration, the resulting equitable easement may still be enforceable against a purchaser of the burdened land as an overriding interest: see *infra*, p. 182.

The Law Commission has raised for consultation the question whether the range of registered dispositions should be extended to the creation or transfer of any other rights or interests in land which do not currently have that status: Law Com. No. 254, *Land Registration for the Twenty-First Century* (1998), paras 3.24–3.27.

2. Registered charges

The standard method of creating a legal mortgage over registered land is by registered charge: see *post*, p. 814. A registered charge is not a registrable interest capable of substantive registration in the sense discussed above. However, it constitutes a "disposition": Land Registration Act 1925, ss.18(4), 21(4); and it must therefore be completed by registration: *ibid.* ss.19(2), 22(2). The charge is registered when an entry showing the charge and the name of its proprietor is made in the charges register of the title to which the charge relates. The proprietor of the charge is issued with a charge certificate; and during the subsistence of the charge, the land certificate relating to the title affected is retained in the Land Registry: *ibid.* ss.63, 65.

C. Minor Interests

1. The category of minor interests

Land Registration Act 1925, s.3

Interpretation

(xv) "Minor interests" mean the interests not capable of being disposed of or created by registered dispositions and capable of being overridden (whether or not a purchaser has notice thereof) by the proprietors unless protected as provided by this Act, and all rights and interests which are not registered or protected on the register and are not overriding interests, and include—

(a) in the case of land subject to a trust of land, all interests and powers which are under the Law of Property Act 1925 capable of being overridden by the trustees, whether or not such interests and powers are so protected; and

(b) in the case of settled land, all interests and powers which are under the Settled Land Act 1925 and the Law of Property Act 1925, or either of them, capable of being overridden by the tenant for life or statutory owner, whether or not such interests and powers are so protected as aforesaid;

NOTES:

1. Minor interests thus constitute a residual category comprising all interests in registered land other than registrable interests, registered charges and overriding interests: Land Registration Act 1925, s.3(xv). However, in view of the judicial interpretation of the category of overriding interests, it is convenient to consider minor interests first.

2. The category of minor interests largely comprises equitable interests. The principal minor interests include: those interests which, in the context of unregistered land, are capable of protection by registration under the Land Charges Act 1972; interests of beneficiaries under trusts of land or strict settlements, which are capable of being overreached on a sale of the land; any other equitable interests or rights under the general law in or over land; and interests or rights acquired under authorised dispositions by the registered proprietor which have not yet been registered: see Law Com. No. 158, *Property Law: Third Report on Land Registration* (1987), para. 4.12; Law Com. No. 254, *Land Registration for the Twenty-First Century* (1998), para. 2.19. The remaining minor interests under the current law are leases containing an absolute prohibition on assignment and sub-letting (except where registered under the Land Registration Act 1986, s.3(2)) and leases granted in consideration of a premium for a term of 21 years or less, if created prior to the commencement of the Land Registration Act 1986.

2. The protection of minor interests

2.1 *Methods of protection*

It appeared to have been the policy of the Land Registration Act 1925 that all minor interests should be protected (and thereby made enforceable against a purchaser of the land) by an appropriate entry on the register relating to the title affected by the interest. However, in contrast with interests that are the subject of registered dispositions, the land registration system does not guarantee the validity of minor interests. Thus, an entry on the register does not validate an intrinsically invalid interest.

2.1.1 *Notice*   A notice on the charges register of the relevant title is the preferred form of entry for the protection of those interests which, in the context of unregistered land, are capable of protection by registration under the Land Charges Act 1972: Land Registration Act 1925, ss.49, 50. A notice is also the appropriate entry for noting a substantively registered lease on the register relating to the freehold title: *ibid.* s.48. As indicated above, the entry of a notice does not otherwise validate the interest protected by it; and a subsequent registered proprietor will not be bound by a notice entered in respect of an intrinsically invalid interest: *ibid.* s.52; and see *Kitney v. MEPC Ltd* [1977] 1 W.L.R. 981, noted at (1977) 41 Conv. 356; [1978] C.L.J. 13; but a notice will only be cancelled after an investigation of the merits of the claim. Subject to that qualification, the effect of a notice is that any subsequent registered disposition of the land takes effect subject to the interest protected by the notice: Land Registration Act 1925, ss.20(1), 23(1), 52. With certain exceptions, a notice cannot be entered unless the relevant land certificate is produced. Consequently, unless the land certificate is already lodged with the Registry (because the land is mortgaged), the entry of a notice requires the co-operation of the registered proprietor: Land Registration Act 1925, s.64. The exceptions include notices to protect matrimonial home rights under the Family Law Act 1996: *ibid.* s.64(5).

2.1.2 *Restriction*   The purpose of a restriction is to note on the register any limitations on the powers of disposition of the registered proprietor. In particular, a restriction is the preferred form of entry for the protection of interests of beneficiaries under trusts of land or strict settlements. A restriction is entered on the proprietorship register of the relevant title and, by providing that no disposition is to be registered unless the capital money is paid to two trustees or to a trust corporation, it should ensure that any disposition of land subject to a trust of land or strict settlement is effective to overreach the beneficial interests. Thus, a restriction does not render the protected interest binding on a purchaser of the land: rather it provides a purchaser with the means of ensuring that the protected interest does *not* bind him. In addition, a restriction may provide that no disposition is to be registered unless required consents have been obtained: Land Registration Act 1925, s.58. A restriction, like a notice, cannot be entered unless the relevant land certificate is produced: *ibid.* s.64(1)(c).

2.1.3 *Caution*   Where a notice or restriction would be the preferred form of entry but the registered proprietor disputes the interest claimed and refuses to make the land certificate available, it will be necessary for the claimant instead to enter a caution (against dealings): Land Registration Act 1925, s.54; and, more generally, a caution would seem to be the appropriate entry for the protection of claims to any other equitable rights under the general law in or over land. The effect of a caution, which is entered on the proprietorship register of the relevant title, is that no dealings in the land should be registered without the consent of the cautioner or without the cautioner being given the opportunity to substantiate his claim: *ibid.* s.55. If the cautioner fails to substantiate his claim, the caution is removed from ("warned off") the register; but if the claim is substantiated, the caution is replaced by the entry of a notice or restriction; and any subsequent dealing in the land takes effect subject to the interest so protected: *ibid.* ss.20(1), 23(1). It is important to note that the entry of a caution on the register does not confer any priority on the protected interest. Thus, it has been held that, even where the Land Registry failed to notify the cautioner of an application to register a charge over the land in question and failed to follow the "warning off" procedure, the entry of a caution did not give the protected interest priority over the subsequently registered charge: *Clark v. Chief Land Registrar; Chancery plc v. Ketteringham* [1994] Ch. 370.

2.1.4 *Inhibition*   An inhibition entered on the proprietorship register of the relevant title prevents any registered dealing in the land or entry on the register for a specified period or until further order: Land Registration Act 1925, s.57; but an inhibition is normally only entered where the land certificate has been stolen from the registered proprietor. A "bankruptcy inhibition" is entered automatically on the bankruptcy of the registered proprietor: *ibid.* s.61(3).

2.1.5 *Recommendations for reform*   The Law Commission has identified two principal defects in the current system for the protection of minor interests on the register. First, it is unnecessarily complex, and, secondly, the entry of a caution confers no priority and thus provides inadequate protection for any interest to which it relates and which is subsequently substantiated.

The Law Commission has provisionally recommended the replacement of notices and cautions with a new form of notice. The notice would be the method of protection for all minor interests (except an interest under a trust, which would continue to be protected by the entry of a restriction). A notice would take one of two forms, the "consensual notice", made with the consent of the registered proprietor, and the "unilateral notice", made without such consent. A unilateral notice, which could only be entered if it could be established that the right claimed is capable of being a minor interest, would be subject to the warning-off procedure. The real significance of the new form of notice would be that, irrespective of whether it was consensual or unilateral, it would preserve the priority of any substantiated interest to which it related: Law Com. No. 254, *Land Registration for the Twenty-First Century* (1998), paras 6.48–6.54.

The Law Commission has also provisionally recommended that restrictions should perform the function currently performed by inhibitions and that the latter form of entry should be abolished.

2.2 *Searching the register*
As in the case of searches of the Land Charges Register in the context of title deeds conveyancing, the purchaser of registered land will normally requisition an official search of the register shortly before the anticipated date of completion of the transfer. The purchaser thereby acquires the benefit of a 30-day priority period; and, provided that the application for registration of the transfer is made within that period, the purchaser will not be affected by entries made during that period: see Land Registration (Official Searches) Rules 1993. If the application for registration is not made within the priority

period, the purchaser loses the protection of the official search certificate: see *Watts v. Waller* [1973] 1 Q.B. 153.

2.3 *Failure to protect a minor interest*
Irrespective of the wide range of minor interests and the different forms of protection, it was the apparent intention of the legislation that all minor interests should be protected by entry on the register. More specifically, it was the apparent intention that what have been termed "family" interests should be protected in the sense that the entry of a restriction (or caution) would ensure that such interests would be overreached on a subsequent transfer of the land; and that what have been termed "commercial" interests should be protected in the sense that the entry of a notice (or caution) would ensure that such interests would actually prevail and be enforceable against a subsequent transferee.

Conversely, in common with all systems of registration of title, the Land Registration Act 1925 purports to leave no doubt that a minor interest which is not protected by the appropriate entry on the register will not be enforceable against a subsequent transferee for value: Land Registration Act 1925, ss.20(1), 59(6), 74. However, this fundamental principle of registration has been compromised by the courts. First, in *Peffer v. Rigg* [1977] 1 W.L.R. 285 Graham J. effectively relied on the doctrine of notice in holding that an unprotected minor interest was enforceable against a subsequent transferee of the land: see *infra*. Secondly, the courts have been prepared to permit interests which were clearly intended to be protected as minor interests, but which were not so protected, to prevail against a subsequent transferee of the land as overriding interests: see *infra*, p. 193.

Peffer v. Rigg [1977] 1 W.L.R. 285

(Ch D., Graham J.)

The plaintiff and the first defendant were married to two sisters. They decided to purchase a house, initially to accommodate their mother-in-law but also as an investment. Although the first defendant was registered as sole proprietor, the plaintiff had contributed to the purchase price. Consequently, the first defendant held the property on trust for sale for himself and the plaintiff; and this was confirmed by a subsequent trust deed. However, the plaintiff failed to protect his beneficial interest by any entry on the register. When the first and second defendants were divorced, the first defendant purported to transfer the house to the second defendant as part of the financial arrangements. The transfer was expressed to be in consideration of one pound, although it seems that the second defendant assumed (partial) responsibility for the repayment of the mortgage loan. When the plaintiff sought a declaration that the second defendant held the house on trust, as to one half for the plaintiff, the second defendant, who had been perfectly well aware of the trust, nonetheless claimed that the unprotected interest of the plaintiff was no longer enforceable against her and that she was entitled to the property absolutely.

GRAHAM J.:

It was argued by Mr Banks, for the second defendant, that the property was transferred to her for valuable consideration as part of the divorce agreement and that, therefore, the combined effect of sections 20 and 59 of the Land Registration Act 1925 protected the second defendant against any claim or interest of the plaintiff because there is no entry on the register in his favour prior to the transfer to the second defendant. This argument would be convincing if it were not for my finding that the second defendant at the time knew perfectly well that the first defendant could not transfer to her more than a half share of the property. It is this knowledge which seems to me to cause great difficulty to her and prevents her argument succeeding for a number of different reasons put forward by Mr Poulton for the plaintiff at the second hearing. He argues first that the purported transfer from the first defendant to the second defendant of the beneficial interest of the whole of the property of 103, Leighton Road was expressed to be for the consideration of £1. This is a nominal consideration and not valuable consideration and it follows that the second defendant is not protected by section 20 of the Land Registration Act 1925. In accordance with the provisions of section 20(4) she can only take subject to any minor interests subject to which the first defendant held the same. He was party to the trust deed of May 30, 1968, and clearly had notice of the plaintiff's half interest in the property. The second defendant can therefore only take subject to the minor interest of the plaintiff in the property subject to which the first defendant held it.

The argument to the contrary is that the transfer was only part of the whole agreement entered into by the first and second defendants on the occasion of the divorce and it is not therefore right to limit the consideration for the transfer to the £1 expressed to be therefor. The consideration, there, was a great deal more and included all the obligations undertaken by the second defendant. Such consideration was therefore not nominal but valuable within section 20 and the second defendant received the protection of the section. I do not see why, when the parties have chosen to express a transfer as being for a nominal consideration, the court should seek to hold that the consideration was in fact otherwise than as agreed and stated. If, however, the proper view is that there was valuable consideration for the transfer here, then it is argued as follows. There is a contrast between sections 20 and 59 of the Act. Section 20(1) protects any "transferee" for valuable consideration. By section 18(5) "transfer" and "transferee" in relation to freehold land have very wide meanings but are not specifically defined in section 3. It is to be noted, however, that section 20, though it mentions valuable consideration, does not mention "good faith" as being necessary on the part of the transferee, nor does it mention notice. It can be argued therefore that the section seems to be saying that a transferee whether he has good faith or not, and whether he has notice or not, takes free of all interests (other than overriding interests) provided he has given valuable consideration.

This at first sight seems a remarkable proposition and though undoubtedly the property legislation of 1925 was intended to simplify such matters of title as far as possible, I find it difficult to think that section 20 of this Act can have been intended to be as broad in scope as this. Similar doubt is expressed in *Brickdale & Stewart-Wallace's Land Registration Act 1925*, 4th ed. (1939), p. 107, note (1). The provisions for rectification in section 82 as against a proprietor in possession who has been a party to a fraud, mistake or an omission in consequence of which rectification of the register is sought also seems to me to show that section 20 must be read with some limitations: see also *Ruoff & Roper, Registered Conveyancing*, 3rd ed. (1972), p. 417. Section 59(6) on the other hand speaks of a "purchaser" not being affected by matters which are not protected by a caution or other entry on the register. By definition, however (see section 3(xxi)), "purchaser" means a purchaser in good faith for valuable consideration. It seems clear therefore that as a matter of construction a purchaser who is not in fact one "in good faith" *will* be concerned with matters not protected by a caution or other entry on the register, at any rate, as I hold, if he has notice thereof. If these sections 20 and 59 are read together in the context of the Act they can be reconciled by holding that if the "transferee" spoken of in section 20 is in fact a "purchaser" he will only be protected if he has given valuable consideration and is in good faith. He cannot in my judgment be in good faith if he has in fact notice of something which affects his title as in the present case. Of course if he and, *a fortiori*, if a purchaser from him has given valuable consideration and in fact has no notice he is under no obligation to go behind the register, and will in such a case be fully protected. This view of the matter seems to me to enable the two sections to be construed consistently together without producing the unreasonable result of permitting a transferee purchaser to take advantage of the Act, and divest himself of knowledge of defects in his own title, and secure to himself a flawless title which he ought not in justice to be allowed to obtain. This view of the Act produces a result which is also produced by applying the principles applicable in the case of a constructive trust, which I will now consider.

On the evidence in this case I have found that the second defendant knew quite well that the first defendant held the property on trust for himself and the plaintiff in equal shares. The second defendant knew this was so and that the property was trust property when the transfer was made to her, and therefore she took the property on a constructive trust in accordance with general equitable principles: see *Snell's Principles of Equity*, 27th ed. (1973), pp. 98–99. This is a new trust imposed by equity and is distinct from the trust which bound the first defendant. Even if, therefore, I am wrong as to the proper construction of sections 20 and 59, when read together, and even if section 20 strikes off the shackles of the express trust which bound the first defendant, this cannot invalidate the new trust imposed on the second defendant.

On this assumption it seems to me that the ground is properly laid for granting rectification of the register under section 82. The second defendant, even though in possession, comes within the exceptions of subsection (3) and this would in my judgment be a case where rectification could properly be ordered against her. Mr Reid, for the first defendant, supported the propositions of Mr Poulton and adopted his argument. In addition he referred to *Jones v. Lipman* [1962] 1 W.L.R. 832, which, he submitted, could only have been decided on the basis that the company in that case could not escape from, or divest itself of, its knowledge by reason of sections 20 and 59. It seems that this must be so, and Russell J. mentions and rejects the argument at p. 837.

...

It follows that in my judgment the second defendant holds the property in question in trust for herself and the plaintiff and that the latter is entitled to appropriate relief.

The court granted a declaration that the second defendant held the property of trust for herself and the plaintiff in equal shares; and the court made an order for sale and division of the proceeds.

NOTES:

1. If it is accepted the transfer was not for valuable consideration, it is clear that the second defendant would have taken the house subject to the trust and the equitable interest of the plaintiff: Land Registration Act 1925, s.20(4). However, an express statement in a transfer as to the amount of consideration is not conclusive and parol evidence of greater consideration is admissible: *Turner v. Forwood* [1951] 1 All E.R. 746, applying *Clifford v. Turrell* (1845) 14 H.L.Ch. 390 and *Frith v. Frith* [1906] A.C. 254.

2. Whatever the merits of the actual decision in *Peffer v. Rigg*, the reasoning of Graham J. has been severely criticised. Those criticisms are considered below.

2.3.1 *Requirement of good faith on the part of a transferee/purchaser*　The insistence that a transferee who is also a purchaser must satisfy the implicit conditions of both section 20(1) and section 59(6) in order to take free of the unprotected minor interest is questioned by Hayton [1977] C.L.J. 227 and by Anderson (1977) 40 M.L.R. 602, who doubts the strict relevance of section 59(6) to the enforceability of interests under trusts. Hayton [1977] C.L.J. 227, Anderson (1977) 40 M.L.R. 602 and Smith (1977) 93 L.Q.R. 341 criticise the insertion of any good faith requirement in section 20(1) and question whether its insertion in section 59(6) is appropriate: the definition of "purchaser" in section 3(xxi) applies "unless the context otherwise requires".

2.3.2 *Good faith negatived by notice*　On the basis that section 59(6) incorporates the good faith requirement, the section provides that a "purchaser [in good faith] ... shall not be concerned with [an unprotected minor interest], whether he has or has not notice thereof ...". It follows that the subsection clearly contemplates that a purchaser in good faith may have notice; and that notice *per se* does not therefore negative good faith: see Hayton [1977] C.L.J. 227; Anderson (1977) 40 M.L.R. 602; Smith (1977) 93 L.Q.R. 341; Crane (1977) 41 Conv. 207.

Graham J. does not refer to the Land Registration Act 1925, s.74, which provides that a person dealing with a registered estate "shall [not] be affected with notice of a trust".

More fundamentally, in holding that an unprotected minor interest is binding on a registered proprietor on the basis of actual notice, Graham J. ignored the considered and deliberate decision that notice should be irrelevant in the context of registered land: see *Second Report of the Real Property Commissioners* (1830), pp. 36–37; *Report of the Royal Commission on the Registration of Title with reference to the Sale and Transfer of Land* (1857), para. lxxii; *Report of the Royal Commission on the Land Transfer Acts* (1911), Cd. 5483, para. 79; *Report of the Acquisition and Valuation of Land Committee* (1919), Cmd. 424, para. 32; and see Howell [1997] Conv. 431. Moreover, Graham J. referred to none of the cases which have emphasised the irrelevance of notice. Thus in *Strand Securities Ltd v. Caswell* [1965] Ch. 373 Cross J. stated (at 390): "It is vital to the working of the land registration system that notice of something which is not on the register of the title in question shall not affect a transferee unless it is an overriding interest"; and in *Parkash v. Irani Finance Ltd* [1970] Ch. 101 Plowman J. stated (at 109): "One of the essential features of registration of title is to substitute a system of registration of rights for the doctrine of notice"; and see also *Hodges v. Jones* [1935] 1 Ch. 657, 671 *per* Luxmoore J.; *Strand Securities Ltd v. Caswell* [1965] Ch. 958, 987 *per* Russell L.J.; *De Lusignan v. Johnson* (1973) 230 E.G. 499 *per* Brightman J. More recently, in *Williams & Glyn's Bank Ltd v. Boland* [1981] A.C. 487, Lord Wilberforce stated (at 503): "Above all, the [Land Registration Act] system is designed to free the purchaser from the hazards of notice—real or constructive—which, in the case of unregistered land, involved him in enquiries, often quite elaborate, failing which he might be bound by equities." See, generally, Thompson [1985] C.L.J. 280.

Nonetheless, in recent years a number of commentators have expressed the view that a purchaser with actual notice (but not merely constructive notice) of an unprotected minor interest should be bound by that interest: see Battersby (1995) 58 M.L.R. 637, 655–656; Howell [1996] Conv. 34, 40–43. Smith ("Land Registration: Reform at Last" in *The Reform of Property Law* (Jackson and Wilde eds., 1997), pp. 129, 135–137) acknowledges the instinctive support for that view but he argues that the difficulty of distinguishing clearly between actual and constructive notice would create problems in the application of a test based on actual notice *per se*; he suggests that those problems would be avoided if actual notice were to be regarded as merely indicative evidence of bad faith in the context of a test based on the requirement of good faith.

2.3.3 *Constructive trust*   The imposition of a constructive trust—distinct from the express trust—"in accordance with general equitable principles" may provide a basis for overriding the clear provisions of the Land Registration Act 1925, although the imposition of such a trust expressly and exclusively on the basis of actual notice (as in *Peffer v. Rigg*) is subject to the criticism referred to above.

The application of general equitable principles was restricted by the 1925 legislation. Thus, in *Miles v. Bull (No. 2)* [1969] 3 All E.R. 1585, Bridge J., referring to the registration of statutory rights of occupation under the Matrimonial Homes Act 1967 (now matrimonial home rights under Part IV of the Family Law Act 1996), stated (at 1590):

[W]hen an Act contains provisions which make it perfectly clear what steps are to be taken in order that [an interest] shall be appropriately protected if the property comes into the hands of third parties, it does not seem to me that it is for the court to say that Parliament really did not mean what it said, that Parliament has not provided adequate or effective protection, or that the old equitable doctrines can be introduced for the purpose in effect of widening the protection to extend it to those who have not protected themselves by taking the appropriate statutory steps.

Nonetheless, it is clear that a registered proprietor who is fraudulent in seeking to defeat an unprotected minor interest will not be able to rely on section 20(1) and section 59(6): but it is not certain what precisely constitutes fraud for these purposes. In *Jones v. Lipman* [1962] 1 W.L.R. 832 an unprotected estate contract entered into with the transferor of the relevant land was held to be binding on the transferee, a company which was controlled by the transferor and to which the land had been transferred in an attempt to defeat the interest. In *Du Boulay v. Raggett* (1988) 58 P. & C.R. 138 there was an arrangement that the first defendant would purchase land, which would then be divided among the parties to the arrangement; but no entry was made on the register in respect of the arrangement. The land was in fact transferred into the joint names of the first and second defendants. It was held that the second defendant, who was aware that the first defendant had purchased as agent, could not rely on section 20(1) to defeat the interests of the principals.

Arguably more controversial was the imposition of a constructive trust in *Lyus v. Prowsa Developments Ltd* [1982] 1 W.L.R. 1044.

Lyus v. Prowsa Developments Ltd [1982] 1 W.L.R. 1044

(Ch D., Dillon J.)

A development company was the registered proprietor of land which was mortgaged to a bank. The company contracted with the plaintiffs to build a house on part of the land (plot 29) and then sell it to them: the plaintiffs protected the contract by the entry of a caution. However, before the house was completed the company became insolvent. In the exercise of its statutory power as mortgagee, the bank contracted to sell plot 29 to Prowsa Developments, the first defendant, "subject to and with the benefit of" the plaintiffs' contract (clause 11); but the transfer itself did not mention the contract and the caution was apparently cancelled pursuant to section 34(4) of the Land Registration Act 1925. Prowsa Developments then contracted to sell plot 29 to the second defendant, subject to the plaintiffs' contract "so far, if at all, as it may be enforceable against [Prowsa Developments]" (condition (b)). The second defendants became registered proprietors of plot 29 but the transfer did not mention the plaintiffs' contract. The plaintiffs sought a declaration that their contract was binding on the first and second defendants and an order for specific performance of the contract. Dillon J. found that the bank had been under no obligation to the plaintiffs; that clause 11 of the agreement between the bank and the first defendant was not inserted for the protection of the bank as vendor; but that it constituted an undertaking by the first defendant to complete the plaintiffs' contract. He continued (at 1053):

If that is correct, it would follow, in my judgment, from the judgment of Scott L.J. in *Bannister v. Bannister* [1948] 2 All E.R. 133 and from the judgment in *Binions v. Evans* [1972] Ch. 359 of Lord Denning M.R. at p. 368, unless the Land Registration Act 1925 requires a different conclusion, that the first defendant, having accepted the land under the agreement of October 18, 1979, and the consequent transfer, holds Plot 29 on a constructive trust in favour of the plaintiffs to give effect to the plaintiffs' contract. That trust is also imposed on the second defendants by virtue of condition (b) of their agreement with the first defendant.
...
   This does not, however, conclude the matter since I also have to consider the effect of the provisions of the Land Registration Act 1925, Plot 29 having at all material times, as I have mentioned, been registered land. In the course of the argument, emphasis was laid on the effect of section 34(4) of the Land Registration Act 1925, which is concerned with the effect on subsequent interests of a transfer of registered land by a mortgagee. Section 34 has, however, to be read with section 20, which is concerned with the effect of the registration of a transfer of registered land by the registered proprietor. The protection conferred by section 34 on a transfer by a mortgagee is thus additional to the protection which is conferred by section 20 on registration of a transfer by a registered proprietor.
   It has been pointed out by Lord Wilberforce in *Midland Bank Trust Co. Ltd v. Green* [1981] A.C. 513, 531, that it is not fraud to rely on legal rights conferred by Act of Parliament. Under section 20, the effect of the registration of the transferee of a

freehold title is to confer an absolute title subject to entries on the register and overriding interests, but, "free from all other estates and interests whatsoever, including estates and interests of His Majesty ..." In *Miles v. Bull (No. 2)* [1969] 3 All E.R. 1585, Bridge J. expressed the view that the words which I have quoted embraced, prima facie, not only all kinds of legal interests, but all kinds of equitable interests: see p. 1589. He therefore held, at p. 1590, as I read his judgment, that actual or constructive notice on the part of a purchaser of an unregistered interest would not have the effect of imposing a constructive trust on him. The interest in *Miles v. Bull (No. 2)* was the interest in the matrimonial home of a deserted wife who had failed to protect her interest by registration under the Matrimonial Homes Act 1967. The contract for sale between the husband, who was the registered proprietor, and the purchaser provided that the house concerned was sold subject to such rights of occupation as might subsist in favour of the wife, with a proviso that this was not to imply that the wife had, or would after completion have any such rights as against the purchaser. Plainly, therefore, the clause was only included in the contract for the protection of the husband who was the vendor. The wife was to get no fresh rights, and it was not in *Miles v. Bull (No. 2)* a stipulation of the bargain between the vendor and the purchaser that the purchaser should give effect to the rights as against the vendor of the deserted wife. *Miles v. Bull (No. 2)* is thus distinguishable from the facts of the present case as I interpret those facts.

It seems to me that the fraud on the part of the defendants in the present case lies not just in relying on the legal rights conferred by an Act of Parliament, but in the first defendant reneging on a positive stipulation in favour of the plaintiffs in the bargain under which the first defendant acquired the land. That makes, as it seems to me, all the difference. It has long since been held, for instance, in *Rochefoucauld v. Boustead* [1897] 1 Ch. 196, that the provisions of the Statute of Frauds 1677 (29 Car. 2 c. 3), now incorporated in certain sections of the Law of Property Act 1925, cannot be used as an instrument of fraud, and that it is fraud for a person to whom land is agreed to be conveyed as trustee for another to deny the trust and relying on the terms of the statute to claim the land for himself. *Rochefoucauld v. Boustead* was one of the authorities on which the judgment in *Bannister v. Bannister* [1948] 2 All E.R. 133 was founded.

It seems to me that the same considerations are applicable in relation to the Land Registration Act 1925. If, for instance, the agreement of October 18, 1979, between the bank and the first defendant had expressly stated that the first defendant would hold Plot 29 upon trust to give effect for the benefit of the plaintiffs to the plaintiffs' agreement with the vendor company, it would be difficult to say that that express trust was overreached and rendered nugatory by the Land Registration Act 1925. The Land Registration Act 1925 does not, therefore, affect the conclusion which I would otherwise have reached in reliance on *Bannister v. Bannister* and the judgment of Lord Denning M.R. in *Binions v. Evans* [1972] Ch. 359 had Plot 29 been unregistered land.

The plaintiffs are, therefore, entitled to succeed in this action. The appropriate relief in that event is that specific performance should be ordered as against the second defendants of the sale to the plaintiffs of Plot 29, with the completed house thereon, on the terms of the agreement of January 30, 1978, made between the plaintiffs and the vendor company.

NOTES:

1. For generally critical comment, see Harpum [1983] C.L.J. 54; Jackson [1983] Conv. 64; and see *Ashburn Anstalt v. Arnold* [1989] 1 Ch. 1, *post*, p. 522.

2. Although there seems to be general agreement that in appropriate circumstances it is prima facie legitimate to invoke general equitable principles to override the provisions of the Land Registration Act 1925, there is also

agreement that there should be (statutory) clarification of the scope of the equitable jurisdiction and its relationship to registered land principles: see Jackson (1978) 94 L.Q.R. 239; Martin [1978] Conv. 52; Clarke [1982] All E.R.Rev. 165; Kenny (1983) 46 M.L.R. 96; contrast Bennett (1984) 47 M.L.R. 476, who argues that intervention based on bad faith is already provided for in the Land Registration Act 1925.

3. However, it is also argued that in the context of registration of title the jurisdiction to intervene on the basis of general equitable principles is already provided for in the rectification provisions of the Land Registration Act 1925: see *infra*.

2.3.4 *Rectification*   In *Peffer v. Rigg* Graham J. would have been prepared to order rectification of the register so that the register accurately reflected his decision that the second defendant held the house on trust for the plaintiff; but the argument referred to in the preceding section is that, in order to preserve the integrity of the protection afforded by section 20(1), cases like *Peffer v. Rigg* and *Lyus v. Prowsa Developments Ltd* should be decided by reference to rectification alone: see Hayton [1977] C.L.J. 227; Smith (1977) 93 L.Q.R. 341; Jackson (1978) 94 L.Q.R. 239; Harpum [1983] C.L.J. 54. However, it is further argued that rectification should not be ordered except in accordance with the principles of the land registration scheme; and that the Court of Appeal in *Orakpo v. Manson Investments Ltd* [1977] 1 W.L.R. 347 was wrong to contemplate rectification under section 82(1)(a) of the Land Registration Act 1925 in order to give effect to an interest which, though enforceable under unregistered land principles, was unenforceable under the registered land principles contained in section 20(1): see Crane (1977) 41 Conv. 210; Jackson (1978) 94 L.Q.R. 239.

The grounds for rectification are considered below: see *infra*, p. 237.

2.3.5 *Internal coherence of the land registration system*   Jackson (1978) 94 L.Q.R. 239 argues that the enforcement of unprotected minor interests (*Peffer v. Rigg*; *Lyus v. Prowsa Developments Ltd*; *Orakpo v. Manson Investments Ltd*) and rectification (*Orakpo v. Manson Investments Ltd*) both constitute threats to the indefeasibility of registered title; that the two issues should therefore be approached, not independently, but in the context of the registered land system as a whole; that the approach should reject the subordination of registered land principles to unregistered land principles; and that the courts and the legislature must take up the challenge to become more "registration minded". For a more wide-ranging critical discussion of (i) the failure of the Land Registration Act to make clear the relationship between the land registration system and the pre-existing substantive law, and (ii) the constant reference by the courts to unregistered land principles in a registered land context, see Jackson (1972) 88 L.Q.R. 93.

2.3.6 *Recommendations for reform*   The legal response to the problem of unprotected minor interests provides an important indication of the level of commitment to the principles of land registration. The case of *Peffer v. Rigg* highlights the issues and it is generally regarded as involving a "fair" decision reached on grounds that are difficult to reconcile with the relevant provisions of the Land Registration Act 1925. That seems to have been the assessment of the Law Commission but the change in its recommendations between 1987 and 1998 seems to reflect a significant increase in its commitment to the fundamental principles of a land registration system.

In 1987, the Law Commission recommended that a purchaser or transferee for valuable consideration should take free of an unprotected minor interest only if he were in good faith, although, contrary to the apparent approach of Graham J. in *Peffer v. Rigg*, a purchaser or transferee would not be regarded as lacking good faith merely because he had actual knowledge of the interest in question: Law Com. No. 158, *Property Law: Third Report on Land Registration* (1987), paras 4.15–4.16. In the view of the Law Commission, the consequences of omitting the element of good faith were not acceptable (and there was implicit criticism of the decision in *Midland Bank Trust Co. Ltd v. Green* [1981] A.C. 513, *ante*, p. 119, where, in the context of unregistered land, the House of Lords declined to import a requirement of good faith into the provisions of the Land Charges Act 1972).

However, in its latest report the Law Commission has signalled its commitment to the development of the land registration system in accordance with principles that fully reflect the nature and potential of land registration: Law Com. No. 254, *Land Registration for the Twenty-First Century* (1998), see *infra*, p. 261. Consistent with that approach the Law Commission has now rejected the 1987 recommendation and has provisionally recommended that issues of good faith, knowledge and notice should have no application to dealings in registered land: *ibid.* paras 3.39–3.50.

The later Report identifies a number of objections to the earlier recommendation. It is argued, first, that the element of "good faith" in the definition of "purchaser" was a legislative accident during the consolidation process of the 1925 property legislation: the Land Registration Act should have adopted the definition in the Land Charges Act, which makes no reference to "good faith"; and, secondly, that the inclusion of "good faith" within the definition, with the consequent investigations into the motives of the parties to a transaction, could introduce uncertainty and could thereby undermine the indefeasibility of registered title.

The Report concludes that there should in general be no place for the concepts of knowledge or notice in registered land; and it details a number of reasons for that conclusion. First, it was intended that the system of registration should displace the doctrine of notice. Secondly, there is little evidence that the absence of the doctrine of notice in dealings in registered land has caused any injustice in practice. Thirdly, the ethical argument loses force if the issue of the unregistered interest is considered in relation to the proposed guiding principles for the development of land registration—that registration should be regarded as an integral part of the process of creating and transferring interests in registered land. Fourthly, if an unregistered interest were enforceable because a purchaser had *actual* knowledge of it, it would be very difficult to prevent the introduction by judicial interpretation of the doctrine of *constructive* notice. Finally, the mere fact that a purchaser could be bound by an unregistered interest on the basis of actual knowledge would weaken the security of title provided by the land registration system.

The Law Commission acknowledges the need for a "safety valve" in the system, for cases where a person cannot reasonably be expected to register his rights; but, in its view, that requirement is substantially met by the category of overriding interests. Moreover, the law also provides a wide range of *personal* remedies against improper behaviour: the purchaser may not be bound by the third party interest but may be personally liable for the loss suffered by the third party or may be subject to some personal equity that enables the transaction to be set aside.

In summary, the Report provisionally recommends (i) that the proposed legislation should define "purchaser" to mean "any person (including a mortgagee or lessee) who for valuable consideration takes an interest in land or in a charge on land"; and (ii) that it should be made clear in the legislation that (subject to express exceptions) the doctrine of notice should not apply to dealings with registered land.

3. Priority between minor interests

The above discussion was concerned with the protection of minor interests against a transferee under a subsequent registered disposition; and it has been seen that a duly protected minor interest will bind (or have priority over) the subsequent registered disposition. It remains to consider the question of priority *between* minor interests. Although minor interests generally take effect as equitable interests (Land Registration Act 1925, ss.2(1), 101(3)), it might have been thought that, under a system of registration of title which provides for the protection of such interests on the register, priority would be determined in accordance with the date of entry on the register. However, despite some support for such an approach (*Re White Rose Cottage* [1965] Ch. 940, 949 *per* Lord Denning M.R.), the Court of Appeal subsequently decided that priority is governed by the pre-1926 principles and is therefore prima facie determined in accordance with the date of creation of the interests: *Barclays Bank v. Taylor* [1974] Ch. 137; and see (1972) 36 Conv. 272, (1972) 88 L.Q.R. 476; (1973) 37 Conv. 203, (1973) 89 L.Q.R. 170. The fundamental principle of that decision has been confirmed and applied by the Court of Appeal: see *Mortgage Corp. Ltd v. Nationwide Credit Corp. Ltd* [1994] Ch. 49; *Clark v. Chief Land Registrar* [1994] Ch. 370. It had been argued that *Barclays Bank v. Taylor* only provided authority on the question of priority between interests protected by *caution* and that priority between interests protected by *notice* was indeed determined in accordance with the date of entry on the register: see Smith (1977) 93 L.Q.R. 541. However, the argument did not receive general acceptance; and the Court of Appeal has held that the entry of a notice does not give the interest protected priority over any existing interest, even if that interest has not been protected: *Mortgage Corp. Ltd v. Nationwide Credit Corp. Ltd*, *supra*, noted at [1993] Conv. 224.

However, it should be noted that the issue of priority is normally of practical relevance only where two or more minor interests are in competition: and such competition does not normally arise except where financial charges are involved. Further discussion is therefore postponed to the chapter on mortgages: see *post*, p. 959.

In Law Com. No. 158, *Property Law: Third Report on Land Registration* (1987) the Law Commission recommended that priority between minor interests should be determined according to the date of entry on the register: para. 4.97. However, the current position of the Law Commission has been influenced by the proposed move to a system of electronic conveyancing. Under such a system registration would become an essential part of the process of creating most interests over land and would therefore as a matter of fact introduce a system of priorities according to the date of registration. On grounds of fairness and simplicity, the Law Commission has expressed a strong preference for leaving the present law unchanged pending the introduction of electronic conveyancing: Law Com. No. 254, *Land Registration for the Twenty-First Century* (1998), paras 7.28–7.34; and see *infra*, p. 261.

D. Overriding Interests

Overriding interests are defined by section 3(xvi) of the Land Registration Act 1925 as "all the incumbrances, interests, rights and powers not entered on the register but subject to which registered dispositions are...to take effect"; and section 70(1) contains a list of overriding interests, which includes, *inter alia*, easements not being equitable easements required to be protected by notice on the register, rights acquired or in the course of being acquired under the Limitation Acts, rights of persons in actual occupation of the land and leases granted for a term not exceeding 21 years. Such interests are enforceable against the land affected even though they are not mentioned in the register and even though the registered proprietor of the land has no notice of them. Although this category of interests obviously represents a significant exception to the mirror principle (and thus reduces the comprehensiveness and reliability of the register), as indicated above, it was never contemplated that the system of registration of title introduced by the Land Registration Act 1925 would involve the recording on the register of *all* interests affecting the land in question. By way of practical justification, it is argued that registration of some interests is either "unnecessary, impracticable or undesirable": Law Commission Working Paper No. 37, *Transfer of Land: Land Registration (Second Paper)* (1971), para. 4; and that such interests are usually discoverable in the course of the inspection of the land and the inquiries of the vendor of the kind which are carried out in the context of unregistered conveyancing. In *National Provincial Bank Ltd v. Hastings Car Mart Ltd* [1964] Ch. 9 Cross J. stated (at 15):

Overriding interests are, speaking generally, matters which are not usually shown on title deeds or mentioned in abstracts of title and as to which, in consequence, it is not possible to form a trustworthy record on the register. As to such matters, persons dealing with registered land must obtain information outside the register in the same manner and from the same sources as people dealing with unregistered land would obtain it.

On the other hand, despite this proffered justification, there is provision for intersts included in the list of overriding interests to be entered on the register. First, although easements are included in the list in section 70(1), under section 70(2) of the Land Registration Act 1925 the registrar is required to enter on the register relating to a newly-created registered title a note of legal easements expressly granted over that land before the title was registered: see *Re Dances Way, West Town, Hayling Island* [1962] Ch. 490. Secondly, as has been seen, the express grant of a legal easement over registered land constitutes a disposition which, under sections 19(2) and 22(2), is required to be completed by registration. Thirdly, and more generally, where the registrar is satisfied that an overriding interest of any category exists, he may enter a notice of that interest on the register pursuant to section 70(3).

This initial picture of the category of overriding interests, narrow in range and justifiable in content, no longer represents the reality. The courts have extended the range of overriding interests, in particular by permitting unprotected minor interests to take effect as overriding interests: see, *e.g. Williams & Glyn's Bank Ltd v. Boland* [1981] A.C. 487, *infra*, p. 193. Moreover, some overriding interests may not be discovered by a purchaser, even after the most careful inspection and inquiry: yet, by contrast with the position in unregistered land, such interests may be enforceable in the absence of notice: *ibid.* at 504 *per* Lord Wilberforce; *Kling v. Keston Properties Ltd* (1983) 49 P. & C.R. 212, 221–222 *per* Vinelott J., *infra*, p. 216.

However, the Law Commission remains of the view that the concept of overriding interests should be retained as a means of protection for rights that a person cannot reasonably be expected to register; but that the number and scope of such interests should be kept to the minimum precisely because they compromise the conclusiveness of the register: see *infra*, p. 263.

1. Categories of overriding interests

1.1 *The statutory list*

Land Registration Act 1925, s.70(1)

Liability of registered land to overriding interests

70.—(1) All registered land shall, unless under the provisions of this Act the contrary is expressed on the register, be deemed to be subject to such of the following overriding interests as may be for the time being subsisting in reference thereto, and such interests shall not be treated as incumbrances within the meaning of this Act, (that is to say):—

(a) Rights of common, drainage rights, customary rights (until extinguished), public rights, profits à prendre, rights of sheepwalk, rights of way, water-courses, rights of water, and other easements not being equitable easements required to be protected by notice on the register;

(b) Liability to repair highways by reason of tenure, quit-rents, crown rents, heriots, and other rents and charges (until extinguished) having their origin in tenure;

(c) Liability to repair the chancel of any church;

(d) Liability in respect of embankments, and sea and river walls;

(e) Payments in lieu of tithe, and charges or annuities payable for the redemption of tithe rentcharges;

(f) Subject to the provisions of this Act, rights acquired or in course of being acquired under the Limitation Acts;

(g) The rights of every person in actual occupation of the land or in receipt of the rents and profits thereof, save where enquiry is made of such person and the rights are not disclosed;

(h) In the case of a possessory, qualified, or good leasehold title, all estates, rights, interests, and powers excepted from the effect of registration;

(i) Rights under local land charges unless and until registered or protected on the register in the prescribed manner;

(j) Rights of fishing and sporting, seignorial and manorial rights of all descriptions (until extinguished), and franchises;

(k) Leases granted for a term not exceeding twenty-one years;

(l) In respect of land registered before the commencement of this Act, rights to mines and minerals, and rights of entry, search, and user, and other rights and reservations incidental to or required for the purpose of giving full effect to the enjoyment of rights to mines and minerals or of property in mines or minerals, being rights which, where the title was first registered before the first day of January, eighteen hundred and ninety-eight, were created before that date, and where the title was first registered after the thirty-first day of December, eighteen hundred and ninety-seven, were created before the date of first registration;

(m) any interest or right which is an overriding interest by virtue of paragraph 1(1) of Schedule 9 to the Coal Industry Act 1994:

Provided that, where it is proved to the satisfaction of the registrar that any land registered or about to be registered is exempt from land tax, or tithe rentcharge or payments in lieu of tithe, or from charges or annuities payable for the redemption of tithe rentcharge, the registrar may notify the fact on the register in the prescribed manner.

NOTES:

1. For the assertion that section 70(1) does not constitute an exhaustive list of overriding interests, see *Abbey National Building Society v. Cann* [1991] 1 A.C. 56, 85 *per* Lord Oliver.

2. See the recommendations of the Law Commission for the rationalisation of the categories of overriding interests: *infra*, p. 263.

3. Certain categories of overriding interest require more detailed consideration.

1.2 *Legal and equitable easements*

As already noted, the protection of legal easements is not entirely clear. On the one hand, the Land Registration Act 1925 provides that the grant of a legal easement is a registered disposition (sections 18(1)(c),(d), 21(1)(b),(c)) which must be completed by registration (sections 19(2), 22(2)); and that if such a disposition remains unregistered it takes effect as an unprotected minor interest, which is liable to be defeated by a transfer for value of the land in question: *ibid.* s.101. On the other hand, section 70(1)(a) includes easements in the category of overriding interests which by definition are *not* entered on the register. One solution of the apparent inconsistency would be that overriding status is restricted to those legal easements which are not expressly created but which arise by operation of law. However, the recognition of potential "dual status" for certain interests (see *infra*, p. 193) might permit expressly created legal easements to take effect as overriding interests.

Equitable easements raise a different problem. The final words of section 70(1)(a) are ambiguous (i) as to whether equitable easements are included in the category of overriding interests at all and (ii) if so, which equitable easements are included. As to the first question, one construction is that equitable easements are not included in the category of overriding interests but require to be protected as minor interests by the entry of a notice or caution on the register of the burdened land. An alternative construction is that some equitable easements require to be protected on the register but others may take effect as overriding interests. This latter construction then raises the second question identified above. These questions received some consideration in *Celsteel Ltd v. Alton House Holdings Ltd* [1985] 1 W.L.R. 204.

Celsteel Ltd v. Alton House Holdings Ltd [1985] 1 W.L.R. 204

(Ch D., Scott J.)

The first defendants (Alton House Holdings) were the registered freehold proprietors of a block of flats and garages and a petrol filling station. The third plaintiff occupied one of the flats and a garage under a contract for a 120-year lease from the predecessor in title of the first defendants, the contract also providing for access from the public highway to the garage; but the lease was never executed and the right of way was never protected by any entry on the register. In 1982 the first defendants granted to the second defendants (Mobil) a lease of the petrol filling station and of part of the driveway that provided access to the garages. When the plaintiffs sought to prevent the second defendants from constructing an automatic car-wash that would significantly reduce the width of the driveway, one question was whether the second defendants were bound by any right of way of the third plaintiff.

SCOTT J.:
I now turn to the title of the third plaintiff in respect of garage 52. I have already read paragraphs 11A, 11B and 11C of the re-amended statement of claim. Those facts entitled the third plaintiff as against Calflane Ltd, the original freeholders, to be regarded as lessee of garage 52 on the terms of the lease contracted to be granted. Ever since February 1980 the third plaintiff has been in actual occupation of garage 52 and has been exercising the easements to which he was entitled under the lease of garage 52 that Calflane Ltd had contracted to grant. However, the third plaintiff's rights in that respect were not protected by any notice, caution or other entry against the registered freehold title.

In due course the first defendants became registered holders of the freehold title. They acquired the property subject, inter alia, to "the rights of every person in actual occupation of the land ... save where enquiry is made of such person and the rights are not disclosed": section 70(1)(g) of the Land Registration Act 1925. No such inquiry was directed to the third plaintiff and accordingly the first defendants took the property subject to the rights of the third plaintiff to be treated as lessee of garage 52 on the terms of the lease contracted to be granted to him by Calflane Ltd. [Counsel for the defendants] has not argued the contrary.

It follows that, as against the first defendants, the third plaintiff is entitled to the rights of way which would have been contained in the lease of garage 52.

The position of the second defendants is, however, different. The premises demised to the second defendants by the lease dated 27 October 1982 included the part of the rear driveway intended as the site of the car wash. The rear driveway was subject to the rights of way of the third plaintiff in respect of garage 52 but these rights were not protected by any entry on the register. In due course the second defendants registered at Her Majesty's Land Registry their leasehold title under the said lease. They thereby became registered proprietors thereof. It is rightly accepted by [counsel for the plaintiffs] that unless the third plaintiff's right as lessee of garage 52 to easements over the part of the rear driveway comprised in Mobil's lease, represented an overriding interest for the purposes of section 70(1) of the Land Registration Act 1925, Mobil hold their premises free of that right. It is plain, also, that the third plaintiff, although in actual occupation of garage 52, was not in actual occupation of any part of the rear driveway. He cannot therefore protect his easement over the rear driveway under paragraph (g) of section 70(1) and the only paragraph of section 70(1) under which, arguably, he might protect that easement as an overriding interest is paragraph (a).

Paragraph (a) of section 70(1) protects as overriding interests the following rights:

"Rights of common, drainage rights, customary rights (until extinguished), public rights, *profits à prendre*, rights of sheepwalk, rights of way, watercourses, rights of water, and other easements not being equitable easements required to be protected by notice on the register."

The rights over the rear driveway which the third plaintiff acquired by virtue of the facts pleaded in the paragraphs of the statement of claim which I have mentioned were certainly rights of way. If they were legal rights of way then the second defendants are bound by them. If they were only equitable rights of way then I must decide whether or not they are excepted from paragraph (a) by the phrase "not being equitable easements required to be protected by notice on the register."

The third plaintiff's entitlement to the easements comprised in the intended lease of garage 52 for the intended 120 year term is an *equitable* entitlement. It could only become a *legal* entitlement by the grant to him of the lease contracted to be granted and the registration of that lease at Her Majesty's Land Registry. But the meaning and scope of the provision "equitable easements required to be protected by notice on the register" is somewhat obscure. In *E. R. Ives Investment Ltd v. High* [1967] 2 Q.B. 379 it was held by the Court of Appeal that easements acquired in equity by proprietary estoppel were not equitable easements for the purposes of section 10(1) Class D(iii) of the Land Charges Act 1925 (15 & 16 Geo. 5, c. 22). Lord Denning M.R. expressed the view that "equitable easements" referred simply to that limited class of rights which before the 1925 property legislation were capable of being conveyed or created at law but thereafter were capable of existing only in equity: see p. 395. In *Poster v. Slough Estates Ltd* [1969] 1 Ch. 495 Cross J. declined, at pp. 506–507, to disagree with Lord Denning M.R.'s view of the meaning of the expression and held that a right to re-enter premises after termination of a lease and to remove fixtures therefrom was not an "equitable easement" for the purposes of the Land Charges Act 1925. These authorities might be thought to suggest by analogy that equitable easements in section 70(1)(a) should be given a similarly limited meaning. I am, however, reluctant to do that because in general the clear intention of the Land Registration Act 1925 is that equitable interests should be protected either by entry on the register or as overriding interests and, if equitable easements in general are not within the exception in paragraph (a), it would follow that they would rank as overriding interests and be binding upon registered proprietors of servient land even though such proprietors did not have and could not by any reasonable means have obtained any knowledge of them. That result could not possibly be supported. In my view, therefore, the dicta in the two cases are not applicable to the construction of "equitable easements" in paragraph (a) of section 70(1).

[Counsel for the plaintiffs] submitted that the exception expressed in section 70(1)(a) applied only to those equitable easements in respect of which a positive requirement that they be protected by notice on the register could be found in the Act. He submitted further that the Act contained no such requirement and that accordingly the expression covered nothing. It seems, however, from paragraph (c) of the proviso to section 19(2) of the Act that the draftsman assumed that easements would require to be protected either by registration as appurtenant to registered land or by entry of notice against the registered title of the servient land. I do not, therefore, feel able to accept these submissions.

In my opinion, the words "required to be protected" in paragraph (a) should be read in the sense "need to be protected." The exception in the paragraph was, in my view, intended to cover all equitable easements other than such as by reason of some other statutory provision or applicable principle of law, could obtain protection otherwise than by notice on the register. The most obvious example would be equitable easements which qualified for protection under paragraph (g) as part of the rights of a person in actual occupation. In my view I must examine the easement claimed by the third plaintiff and consider whether there is any statutory provision or principle of law which entitles it to protection otherwise than by entry of notice on the register.

The matter stands in my opinion thus. At the time when Mobil acquired its registered leasehold title the third plaintiff's right to an easement of way for the benefit of garage 52 over a part of the property enjoyed under that leasehold title was an equitable and not a legal right. It was, in ordinary conveyancing language, an equitable easement. It was not protected by any entry on the register. On the other hand, it was at the relevant time openly exercised and enjoyed by the third plaintiff as appurtenant to garage 52. Section 144 of the Land Registration Act 1925 contains power for rules to be made for a number of specified purposes. The Land Registration Rules 1925 (S.R. & O. 1925 No. 1093) were accordingly made and rule 258 provides:

"Rights, privileges, and appurtenances appertaining or reputed to appertain to land or demised, occupied, or enjoyed therewith or reputed or known as part or parcel of or appurtenant thereto, which adversely affect registered land, are overriding interests within section 70 of the Act, and shall not be deemed incumbrances for the purposes of the Act."

The third plaintiff's equitable right of way over the rear driveway was, in my view, at the time when Mobil acquired its registered leasehold title, a right enjoyed with land for the purposes of this rule. It was plainly a right which adversely affected registered land including the part of the rear driveway comprised in Mobil's lease. Rule 258 categorises such a right as an overriding interest. Section 144(2) of the Act provides that "Any rules made in pursuance of this section shall be of the same force as if enacted in this Act." Accordingly, in my judgment, the third plaintiff's right ranks as an overriding interest, does not need to be protected by entry of notice on the register and is binding on Mobil.

Mr Davidson submitted that there was no power under section 144(1) for rules to add to the overriding interests specified in the various paragraphs of section 70(1). He submitted that rule 258 was ultra vires and of no effect. I do not agree. Sub-paragraph (xxxi) of section 144(1) enables rules to be made, "for regulating any matter to be prescribed or in respect of which rules are to or may be made under this Act and any other matter or thing, whether similar or not to those above mentioned, in respect of which it may be expedient to make rules for the purpose of carrying this Act into execution."

This is a power in very wide terms. In my view, it is in terms wide enough to justify rule 258 and I see no reason why it should be given a limited effect.

Accordingly, for these reasons, the third plaintiff's equitable right of way over the rear driveway enjoyed with garage 52 was and is, in my judgment, binding on Mobil.

NOTES:

1. For comment, see Thompson [1986] Conv. 31.

2. The decision of Scott J. on the interpretation of section 70(1)(a), and the inclusion of certain equitable easements within that paragraph, was subsequently approved and applied by the Court of Appeal in *Thatcher v. Douglas* (1995) 146 N.L.J. 282.

3. Greed [1999] Conv. 11 examines the legislative history of rule 258 of the Land Registration Rules 1925 and argues that the enforceability of unregistered equitable easements by virtue of the rule was intended to depend on the doctrine of notice. However, the implication that such easements should be discoverable is arguably met by the express requirement in rule 258 that the easement must be "reputed" to appertain to land and by the (necessary) finding in *Celsteel Ltd v. Alton House Holdings Ltd* and in *Thatcher v. Douglas* that the easement was "openly exercised and enjoyed".

4. For detailed discussion of the continuing uncertainty as to the meaning and scope of equitable easements, see Barnsley (1999) 115 L.Q.R. 89.

5. The Law Commission has provisionally recommended (i) that all easements should be overriding interests except (a) legal easements that have been expressly granted; and (b) equitable easements arising from contracts to grant such easements expressly; (ii) that, without prejudice to the generality of (i) above, the following easements should be overriding interests unless and until noted on the register of the burdened land: (a) easements arising by implied grant or reservation (including easements arising by operation of section 62 of the Law of Property Act 1925); (b) easements acquired or in the course of being acquired by prescription; (c) legal easements to which a property was subject at the time of first registration but which were not noted on the register; and (d) easements appurtenant to an overriding interest; and (iii) that rule 258 of the Land Registration Rules 1925 should be abolished: Law Com. No. 254, *Land Registration for the Twenty-First Century* (1998), paras 5.2–5.24. Implementation of the recommendation would prospectively reverse the decision in *Celsteel Ltd v. Alton House Holdings Ltd*: see Prichard [1987] Conv. 328; but the Law Commission has recommended transitional provisions so that existing easements which are overriding interests at the time when the principal recommendation comes into force would retain that status.

1.3 *Rights acquired through adverse possession*

In principle, the law relating to adverse possession and the limitation of actions applies to registered land "in the same manner and to the same extent" as it applies to unregistered land, although the mechanism by which the rules are made to apply to registered land is different: Land Registration Act 1925, s.75; and see *ante*, p. 90. As the law currently stands, the rights of the adverse possessor, both before and (pending substantive registration) after the expiration of the limitation period, are binding on a transferee of the land as an overriding interest under section 70(1)(f): see *Bridges v. Mees* [1957] Ch. 475. Moreover, this is so even where the adverse possessor abandons the land after the expiration of the limitation period (provided that the rights of the adverse possessor are not themselves barred by a subsequent adverse possessor).

The Law Commission has provisionally recommended that the law relating to adverse possession as it applies to registered land should be recast to reflect the principles of registration of title: see *ante*, p. 101. However, independently of that recommendation but pursuant to the same principles, the Law Commission has also recommended that section 70(1)(f) should be repealed and that the rights of adverse possessors should only qualify as overriding interests (under section 70(1)(g)) where the adverse possessor is in actual occupation of the land in question: Law Com. No. 254, *Land Registration for the Twenty-First Century* (1998), paras 5.42–5.55.

1.4 *Rights of every person in actual occupation*

The Law Commission traces the origin of section 70(1)(g) to the Report of the Royal Commission on the Land Transfer Acts. The Report (Cd. 5483 (1911)) recommended (at para. 81):

There should be provision that the rights of parties actually in occupation or receipt of rent and profits of the land at the time of first registration should not be affected by the registration; and that these rights should be protected as against all transferees so long as the parties or their successors in title remain in such occupation or receipt. This is in accordance with the ordinary law applicable to sales of land.

The judicial interpretation and application of section 70(1)(g) has been controversial: in particular, it has led to the significant extension of the range of overriding interests referred to above. However, the Law Commission takes the view that the rationale for retaining the category of overriding interests generally is particularly applicable to the rights referred to in section 70(1)(g). Section 70(1)(g) includes within its scope rights that are created informally (but nonetheless recognised by the law) and in circumstances where the owners of those rights are often unlikely to appreciate the need for registration: Law Com. No. 254, *Land Registration for the Twenty-First Century* (1998), para. 5.61.

The purpose of section 70(1)(g) was explained by Lord Denning M.R. in *Strand Securities Ltd v. Caswell* [1965] Ch. 958. He stated (at 979):

Fundamentally, its object is to protect a person in actual occupation of land from having his rights lost in the welter of registration. He can stay there and do nothing. Yet he will be protected. No one can buy the land over his head and thereby take away or diminish his rights. It is up to every purchaser before he buys to make inquiry on the premises. If he fails to do so, it is at his own risk. He must take subject to whatever rights the occupier may have. Such is the doctrine of *Hunt v. Luck* [1901] 1 Ch. 45 for unregistered land. Section 70(1)(g) carries the same doctrine forward into registered land but with this difference. Not only is the actual occupier protected, but also the person from whom he holds. It is up to the purchaser to inquire of the occupier, not only about the occupier's own rights, but also about the rights of his immediate superior. The purchaser must ask the occupier "To whom do you pay your rent?" And the purchaser must inquire what the rights of that person are. If he fails to do so, it is at his own risk for he takes subject to "the rights of every person in actual occupation of the land or in receipt of the rents and profits thereof".

The comparison with the rule in *Hunt v. Luck* has frequently been repeated in the case law; but such comparisons may be misleading. In particular, under the rule the rights of occupiers are enforceable against a purchaser through the doctrine of constructive notice: by contrast, in the context of registered land, the wording of section 70(1)(g) would appear to provide for the enforceability of the rights of persons in actual occupation *irrespective of notice on the part of the purchaser*. This issue is discussed *infra*, p. 205.

It is important to understand the effect of section 70(1)(g). It affords overriding status (and thus makes enforceable against a purchaser of the land in question) the *rights* of every person in actual occupation of the land (or in receipt of the rents and profits: see *infra*, p. 231) at the relevant time: see *infra*, p. 218. It is the *rights* of the person in actual occupation which, when combined with that actual occupation, constitute the overriding interests. Occupation without rights does not create an overriding interest: *City of London Building Society v. Flegg* [1988] A.C. 54, 74 *per* Lord Oliver. The actual occupation is the catalyst which transforms rights into overriding interests in the same way that the entry of a notice transforms a minor interest into an enforceable interest. Without the actual occupation the rights would not be enforceable as overriding interests: with actual occupation they become enforceable as such.

1.4.1 *Qualifying rights under section 70(1)(g)*

1.4.1.1 *Proprietary and personal rights*   All categories of overriding interests are qualified by the opening words of section 70(1), which require the interests to be "subsisting in reference [to registered land]" and by the wording of sections 20(1)(b) and 23(1)(c), which refer to overriding interests "affecting the estate transferred or created". In *National Provincial Bank Ltd v. Hastings Car Mart Ltd* [1964] Ch. 665 Russell L.J. stated (at 696):

[S]ection 70 in all its parts is dealing with rights in reference to land which have the quality of being capable of enduring through different ownerships of land, according to normal conceptions of title to real property.

This view was confirmed by the House of Lords. In *National Provincial Bank Ltd v. Ainsworth* [1965] A.C. 1175 Lord Wilberforce stated (at 1261):

To ascertain what "rights" come within this provision, one must look outside the Land Registration Act and see what rights affect purchasers under the general law. To suppose that the subsection makes any right, of howsoever a personal character, which a person in occupation may have, an overriding interest by which a purchaser is bound, would involve two consequences: first that this Act is, in this respect, bringing about a substantive change in real property law by making personal rights bind purchasers; second, that there is a difference *as to the nature of the rights by which a purchaser may be bound* between registered and unregistered land; for purely personal rights including the wife's right to stay in the house (if my analysis of this is correct) cannot affect purchasers of unregistered land even with notice. One may have to accept that there is a difference between unregistered land and registered land as regards what kind of notice binds a purchaser, or what kind of inquiries a purchaser has to make. But there is no warrant in the terms of this paragraph or elsewhere in the Act for supposing that the nature of the rights which are to bind a purchaser is to be different, excluding personal rights in one case, including them in another. The whole frame of section 70, with the list that it gives of interests, or rights, which are overriding, shows that it is made against a background of interests or rights whose nature and whose transmissible character is known, or ascertainable, aliunde, i.e., under other statutes or under the common law.

Although this formulation has been interpreted to mean that the rights of persons in actual occupation must be proprietary rights in order to qualify as overriding interests, it seems to have given the courts considerable flexibility.

Certain undoubted proprietary rights have been held to qualify: an estate contract in relation to a freehold interest: *Bridges v. Mess* [1957] Ch. 475; an estate contract in relation to a leasehold interest: *Woolwich Equitable Building Society v. Marshall* [1952] 1 Ch. 1; *Grace Rymer Investments Ltd v. Waite* [1958] Ch. 831; *Homsy v. Murphy* (1996) 73 P. & C.R. 26, 35 *per* Beldam L.J.; an option to purchase a freehold interest: *Webb v. Pollmount* [1966] Ch. 584; a right of pre-emption/option to purchase a leasehold interest: *Kling v. Keston Properties Ltd* (1983) 49 P. & C.R. 212; an unpaid vendor's lien: *London and Cheshire Insurance Co. Ltd v. Laplagrene Property Co. Ltd* [1971] Ch. 499; *Nationwide Anglia Building Society v. Ahmed* (1995) 70 P. & C.R. 381, 387 *per* Aldous L.J.; *U.C.B. Bank plc v. French* [1995] N.P.C. 144, noted at [1996] Conv. 44; and an equitable fee simple under a bare trust: *Hodgson v. Marks* [1971] Ch. 892. In addition, the House of Lords has held that an equitable interest under an implied trust for sale is a right subsisting in reference to registered land for the purposes of section 70(1)(g): *Williams & Glyn's Bank Ltd v. Boland* [1981] A.C. 487, *infra*, p. 193. However, in that case the purchaser/mortgagee had not overreached the interest; contrast the position where the equitable interest has been overreached: *City of London Building Society v. Flegg* [1988] A.C. 54, *infra*, p. 197; *State Bank of India v. Sood* [1997] Ch. 276. In *National Provincial Bank Ltd v. Hastings Car Mart Ltd* [1964] Ch. 665 Lord Denning M.R. expressed the view (at 689) that the rights of a tenant under a statutory tenancy were qualifying rights; that view does not appear to have been questioned by the Court of Appeal in *Woolwich Building Society v. Dickman* [1996] 3 All E.R. 204; but the point was not regarded as incontrovertible in *Barclays Bank plc v. Zaroovabli* [1997] Ch. 321, 328–329 *per* Scott V.-C., noted at [1997] C.L.J. 496.

On the other hand, the House of Lords has held that the common law right of a wife to occupy the matrimonial home provided by her husband is a personal right and incapable of constituting an overriding interest under section 70(1)(g): *National Provincial Bank Ltd v. Ainsworth* [1965] A.C. 1175, 1261 *per* Lord Wilberforce; and, although matrimonial home rights under Part IV of the Family Law Act 1996 are capable of binding third parties if protected on the register, the Act expressly excludes those rights from the category of overriding interests: Family Law Act 1996, s.31(10)(b). It is clear that bare licences do not constitute qualifying interests: *Strand Securities Ltd v. Caswell* [1965] Ch. 958, 980 *per* Lord Denning M.R.; it is also the case that contractual licences do not constitute qualifying interests: *National Provincial Bank Ltd v. Ainsworth* [1965] A.C. 1175, 1239–1240 *per* Lord Upjohn, 1251–1252 *per* Lord Wilberforce; *Ashburn Anstalt v. Arnold* [1989] Ch. 1, 24 *per* Fox L.J.; *Nationwide Anglia Building Society v. Ahmed* (1995) 70 P. & C.R. 381, 389 *per* Aldous L.J.; and see *post*, p. 522. The capacity of "estoppel licences" to bind purchasers is less clear: *Habermann v. Koehler* (1996) 73 P. & C.R. 515, 520 *per* Evans L.J., 522–523 *per* Peter Gibson L.J.; and see *post*, p. 602; but there is recent judicial support for the view that such licences are not and should not be differentiated in this respect from contractual licences: *Canadian Imperial Bank of Commerce v. Bello* (1992) 64 P. & C.R. 48, 52 *per* Dillon L.J.; *United Bank of Kuwait plc v. Sahib* [1997] Ch. 107, 141–142 *per* Peter Gibson L.J.

The dividing line between proprietary and personal rights, and between qualifying and non-qualifying rights, was considered in *Blacklocks v. J.B. Developments (Godalming) Ltd* [1982] Ch. 183.

Blacklocks v. J. B. Developments (Godalming) Ltd [1982] Ch. 183

(Ch D., Judge Mervyn Davies Q.C.)

The plaintiff had sold some farmland but the registered title of the purchaser mistakenly included an additional plot of land. The purchaser subsequently sold the farmland (including the plot) to the defendant; and only then was the mistake discovered. The plaintiff was found to have remained in actual occupation of the plot at all relevant times on the basis of the fact that he had erected a barn there. It was held that the right to have the contract and conveyance rectified in equity on the ground of mistake was a right subsisting in reference to registered land for the purposes of section 70(1)(g). Judge Mervyn Davies Q.C. stated (at 195–196):

The right to rectify is often described as a mere equity; see, for example, *Williams on Vendor and Purchaser* 4th ed. (1936), vol. 2, p. 791 and *Snell's Principles of Equity* 27th ed. (1973), p. 53. So the question is, does the right to rectify (or mere equity) have "the quality of being capable of enduring through different ownerships of land, according to the normal conceptions of title to real property?" In *National Provincial Bank Ltd v. Ainsworth* [1965] A.C. 1175, at 1238, Lord Upjohn considered that a mere equity might be either "naked and alone" or ancillary to or dependent upon an equitable estate or interest in land, and in *Latec Investments Ltd v. Hotel Terrigal Pty Ltd (In Liquidation)* (1965) 113 C.L.R. 265, 277, Kitto J. made a distinction between an equity which is and an equity which is not accompanied by an equitable interest. It is plain that the wife's equity in *National Provincial Bank Ltd v. Ainsworth* was naked and alone and had not the enduring quality that might render it capable of being a right under section 70. But was the mere equity possessed by the plaintiff of the same kind, or was it an equity ancillary to an interest in land? If the equity was of the latter kind if may be transmissible and so have the "quality of being capable of enduring" spoken of by Russell L.J.

. . .

The *Latec* case shows that a right or equity to set aside a conveyance of Blackacre is, when in competition with other interests in Blackacre, likely to be regarded as a mere personal claim rather than as a right ancillary to an equitable interest then subsisting: see *per* Taylor J., at pp. 280 *et seq.*, and *per* Menzies J., at p. 290. No doubt that is so when the rules as to the priority of equitable interests have to be applied. But in this case those rules do not fall to be applied. Here what one has to decide is whether or not a right to rectify is of the enduring character explained by Russell L.J. in *National Provincial Bank Ltd v. Hastings Car Mart Ltd* [1964] Ch. 665, 696. In the light of *Stump v. Gaby* (1852) 2 De G.M. & G. 623 and the other authorities I have mentioned, I regard the right to rectify as having that character. The plaintiff had an equity that was ancillary to an interest in land, being an equity and an ancillary interest that was transmissible. It follows that he had a right within section 70(1)(g) of the Land Registration Act 1925. The right is not itself an overriding interest but it has been accompanied at all times by actual occupation. The association of the right with actual occupation constitutes an overriding interest that is binding on the land in the hands of the defendant: see *Williams & Glyn's Bank Ltd v. Boland* [1981] A.C. 487, 510–511.

NOTES:

1. For controversy as to whether it was the right to have a contract and conveyance rectified or the right to have the register rectified which, in association with actual occupation, constituted the overriding interest, see [1983] Conv. 169, 257; Barnsley [1983] Conv. 361.

2. In *D.B. Ramsden and Co. Ltd v. Nurdin & Peacock plc* [1998] E.G.C.S. 123 Neuberger J. expressly approved the decision of Judge Mervyn Davies Q.C. In *Ramsden* a landlord claimed the right to rectify the rent provisions in a lease as against the assignee of the lease. On the facts, there was held to be no right to rectify, but Neuberger J. endorsed the view that such a right could be an overriding interest within section 70(1)(g). He delivered a robust defence of the decision in *Blacklocks* and expressly addressed the criticisms of Barnsley [1983] Conv. 361; in particular, he was in no doubt that the qualifying right in *Blacklocks* was the right to rectify the contract and conveyance and that the right to rectify the register was ancillary. However, there appears to be a point of distinction between *Blacklocks* and *Ramsden*. In *Blacklocks* the rectification of the conveyance and the register resulted in the restoration to the plaintiff of the legal title to land mistakenly transferred to the predecessor in title of the defendant (and in *Latec Investments Ltd v. Hotel Terrigal Pty Ltd* (1965) 113 C.L.R. the setting aside of the sale by the mortgagee would have resulted in the restoration to the mortgagors of the equity of redemption; by contrast, in *Ramsden* the rectification of the lease would not have resulted in any such "restoration" of an interest in land. To that extent, Neuberger J. seems to have adopted a more liberal approach to the requirement that the qualifying right must be an "equity ancillary to an

interest in land" (as opposed to a "mere equity") and thus extended still further the scope of section 70(1)(g).

Tee [1998] C.L.J. 328 catalogues the rights that have been held to be qualifying rights within section 70(1)(g) and concludes that, in seeking to apply the tests expounded in *National Provincial Bank Ltd v. Ainsworth*, the courts have generated a case law that is "confused and incoherent". She argues that the interests of certainty, fairness and comprehensiveness would be served by expanding the category of qualifying rights to include *all* rights except those which are wholly unrelated to the land or its occupation and those which involve personal skill and confidence in their exercise. (However, she proposes that this expansion in the scope of section 70(1)(g) should be offset to some extent by requiring that the person entitled to the right should be in actual *and apparent* occupation: see *infra*, p. 216.)

The Law Commission has provisionally recommended, in relation to the category of overriding interests generally, that only proprietary rights and interests in or over land should be capable of subsisting as overriding interests: Law Com. No. 254, *Land Registration for the Twenty-First Century* (1998), para. 4.36.

1.4.1.2 *The extent of qualifying rights*   As with minor interests, the protection of rights as overriding interests by association with actual occupation cannot enlarge the rights of the occupier.

Paddington Building Society v. Mendelsohn (1985) 50 P. & C.R. 244

(CA, Donaldson M.R., Browne-Wilkinson L.J.)

The claimant of a contribution-based equitable interest in property knew that the purchase of the property was to be financed in part by a mortgage loan. Following the decision of the Court of Appeal in *Bristol and West Building Society v. Henning* [1985] 1 W.L.R. 778, which raised the same legal issue in the context of unregistered land, Browne-Wilkinson L.J. concluded that, in the absence of other evidence, the claimant must have intended that the rights of the mortgagee should take priority over her own rights. Applying that principle in the context of registered land, he continued (at 248):

Section 70(1) deems the registered land to be subject to certain rights which "override" the rights appearing on the register. The rights referred to in paragraph (g) are "the rights of every person in occupation." There is no doubt therefore that the registered land is subject to the rights of such person. But the essential question remains to be answered. "What are the rights of the person in actual occupation?" If the rights of the person in actual occupation are not under the general law such as to give any priority over the holder of the registered estate, there is nothing in section 70 which changes such rights into different and bigger rights. Say, in the present case, before the acquisition of the flat a trust deed had been executed declaring that the flat was held in trust for the mother but expressly subject to all the rights of the society under the proposed legal charge. The effect of section 70(1)(g) could not in my judgment have been to enlarge the mother's rights so as to give her rights in priority to the society when, under the trust deed, her rights were expressly subject to those of the society. Her rights would be "overriding interests" in that the society would have to give effect to them, but the inherent quality of the mother's rights would not have been such as to give them priority over the society's rights. So in the present case, once it is established that the imputed intention must be that the mother's rights were to be subject to the mortgage, there is nothing in section 70 of the Registration Act 1925 which enlarges those rights into any greater rights.

NOTE:
1. See also E.S. *Schwab & Co. Ltd v. McCarthy* (1976) 31 P. & C.R. 196, 205 *per* Oliver J.; *City of London Building Society v. Flegg* [1988] A.C. 54, 88 *per* Lord Oliver; *Abbey National Building Society v. Cann* [1991] 1 A.C. 56, 87 *per* Lord Oliver, 95 *per* Lord Jauncey.

1.4.1.3 *Rights having "dual status"* It will be apparent that the category of qualifying rights includes interests which are capable of protection as minor interests. Against the background of the scheme of the Land Registration Act 1925, and in particular the classification of interests and the apparent requirement for minor interests to be protected by entry on the register, it would have been reasonable to suppose that there was no overlap between minor interests and overriding interests. Yet in 1980 the House of Lords confirmed that it was possible for an interest, which was apparently intended to take effect as a minor interest but which had not been protected by entry on the register, to take effect as an overriding interest under section 70(1)(g) and thereby to bind a subsequent purchaser of the land affected.

Williams & Glyn's Bank Ltd v. Boland [1981] A.C. 487

(HL, Lord Wilberforce, Viscount Dilhorne, Lord Salmon, Lord Scarman, Lord Roskill)

The husband was the sole registered proprietor of the matrimonial home; but since the wife had contributed to the purchase price, the husband held the property on trust for sale for himself and the wife. However, the wife failed to protect that interest as a minor interest by the entry of a restriction or caution on the proprietorship register. The husband subsequently mortgaged the property to the bank by way of security for the repayment of a loan. When he subsequently defaulted on the repayments, the bank sought possession of the property. The question for consideration was whether the contribution-based interest of the wife, if combined with actual occupation on the part of the wife, was capable of constituting an overriding interest under section 70(1)(g) of the Land Registration Act 1925.

LORD WILBERFORCE:
This brings me to the second question, which is whether such rights as a spouse has under a trust for sale are capable of recognition as overriding interests—a question to my mind of some difficulty. The argument against this is based upon the structure of the Land Registration Act 1925 and upon specific provisions in it.
As to structure, it is said that the Act recognises three things: (a) legal estates, (b)

minor interests, which take effect in equity, (c) overriding interests. These are mutually exclusive: an equitable interest, which is a minor interest, is incapable of being at the same time an overriding interest. The wife's interest, existing under or behind a trust for sale, is an equitable interest and nothing more. To give it the protection of an overriding interest would, moreover, contradict the principle according to which such an equitable interest can be overreached by an exercise of the trust for sale. As to the provisions of the Act, particular emphasis is placed on section 3(xv) which, in defining "minor interests" specifically includes in the case of land held on trust for sale "all interests and powers which are under the Law of Property Act 1925 capable of being overridden by the trustees for sale" and excludes, expressly, overriding interests. Reliance is also placed on section 86, which, dealing analogously, so it is said, with settled land, prescribes that successive or other interests created by or arising under a settlement take effect as minor interests and not otherwise, and on section 101 which, it is argued, recognises the exclusive character of minor interests, which in all cases can be overridden.

My Lords, I find this argument formidable. To reach a conclusion upon it involves some further consideration of the nature of trusts for sale, in relation to undivided shares. The trusts upon which, in this case, the land is to be held are defined—as "statutory trusts"—in section 35 of the Law of Property Act 1925, *i.e.*:

> "... upon trust to sell the same and to stand possessed of the net proceeds of sale, after payment of costs, and of the net rents and profits until sale after payment of rates, taxes, costs of insurance, repairs, and other outgoings, upon such trusts, and subject to such powers and provisions, as may be requisite for giving effect to the rights of the persons...interested in the land."

In addition to this specific disposition, the general provisions as to trusts for sale in sections 23 to 31, where not inconsistent, appear to apply. The right of occupation of the land pending sale is not explicitly dealt with in these sections and the position as to it is obscure. Before the Act the position was that owners of undivided shares (which could exist at law) had concurrent rights of occupation. In *Bull v. Bull* [1955] 1 Q.B. 234, it was held by the Court of Appeal, applying *In re Warren* [1932] 1 Ch. 42, that the conversion of these legal estates into equitable interests by the Law of Property Act 1925 should not affect the mutual rights of the owners. Denning L.J., in a judgment which I find most illuminating, there held, at p. 238 in a factual situation similar to that of the instant cases, that "when there are two equitable tenants in common, then, until the place is sold, each of them is entitled concurrently with the other to the possession of the land and to the use and enjoyment of it in a proper manner." And he referred to section 14 of the Law of Property Act 1925 which provides that the Act "shall not prejudicially affect the interest of any person in possession or in actual occupation of land to which he may be entitled in right of such possession or occupation."

How then are these various rights to be fitted into the scheme of the Land Registration Act 1925? It is clear, at least, that the interests of the co-owners under the "statutory trusts" are minor interests—this fits with the definition in section 3(xv). But I can see no reason why, if these interests, or that of any one of them, are or is protected by "actual occupation" they should remain merely as "minor interests." On the contrary, I see every reason why, in that event, they should acquire the status of overriding interests. And, moreover, I find it easy to accept that they satisfy the opening, and governing, words of section 70, namely, interests subsisting in reference to the land. As Lord Denning M.R. points out, to describe the interests of spouses in a house jointly bought to be lived in as a matrimonial home as merely an interest in proceeds of sale, or rents and profits until sale, is just a little unreal: see also *Elias v. Mitchell* [1972] Ch. 652, *per* Pennycuick V.-C. with whose analysis I agree; and contrast *Cedar Holdings Ltd v. Green* [1981] Ch. 129 (which I consider to have been wrongly decided).

There are decisions, in relation to other equitable interests than those of tenants in common, which confirm this line of argument. In *Bridges v. Mees* [1957] Ch. 475, Harman J. decided that a purchaser of land under a contract for sale, who had paid the price and so was entitled to the land in equity, could acquire an overriding interest by virtue of actual occupation, and a similar position was held by the Court of Appeal to arise in relation to a resulting trust: *Hodgson v. Marks* [1971] Ch. 892. These decisions (following the law as it undoubtedly existed before 1925—see *Barnhart v. Greenshields* (1853) 9 Moo.P.C.C. 18, 32, *Daniels v. Davison* (1809) 16 Ves.Jun. 249, *Allen v. Anthony* (1816) 1 Mer. 282, 284 *per* Lord Eldon L.C.) provide an answer to the argument that there is a firm dividing line, or an unbridgeable gulf, between minor interests and overriding interests, and, on the contrary, confirm that the fact of occupation enables protection of the latter to extend to what without it would be the former. In my opinion, the wives' equitable interests, subsisting in reference to the land, were by the fact of occupation, made into overriding interests, and so protected by section 70(1)(g). I should add that it makes no difference to this that these same interests might also have been capable of protection by the registration of a caution: see *Bridges v. Mees* [1957] Ch. 475, 487 and Land Registration Act 1925, section 59(6).

There was finally an argument based upon section 74 of the Land Registration Act 1925. The section provides:

"Subject to the provisions of this Act as to settled land, neither the registrar nor any person dealing with a registered estate or charge shall be affected with notice of a trust express implied or constructive, and references to trust shall, so far as possible, be excluded from the register."

The argument was that if the overriding interest sought to be protected is, under the general law, only binding on a purchaser by virtue of notice, the section has the effect of denying the protection. It is obvious—and indeed conceded—that if this is right, *Hodgson v. Marks* and *Bridges v. Mees* must have been wrongly decided.

I am of the opinion that this section has no such effect. Its purpose is to make clear, as I have already explained, that the doctrine of notice has no application to registered conveyancing, and accordingly to establish, as an administration measure, that entries may not be made in the register which would only be appropriate if that doctrine were applicable. It cannot have the effect of cutting down the general application of section 70(1).

NOTES:

1. Lord Scarman stated (at 511–512):

The critically important right of the wife, so far as these appeals are concerned, is the right of occupation of the land [in consequence of her equitable interest under the trust for sale]. This right, if unaccompanied by actual occupation, is clearly within the definition of a minor interest: section 3(xv). It is not, therefore, itself an overriding interest. But, once it is associated with actual occupation, the association is an overriding interest. I agree with the appellants that overriding interests and minor interests are, as categories, exclusive of each other. But there is no logical difficulty in the association of a minor interest with another factor (*i.e.* actual occupation) being, *qua* association, an overriding interest. And this is, in my judgment, the effect of section 70(1)(g).

See also *City of London Building Society v. Flegg* [1988] A. C. 54, 89–90 *per* Lord Oliver; *Abbey National Building Society v. Cann* [1991] 1 A.C. 56, 84–85 *per* Lord Oliver, 95 *per* Lord Jauncey.

2. The issue whether the beneficial interest of the wife under the trust for sale constituted an interest "subsisting in reference to registered land" and thus whether it was a qualifying right under section 70(1)(g) was discussed at

greater length by the Court of Appeal. However, the replacement of the trust for sale by the trust of land, pursuant to the Trusts of Land and Appointment of Trustees Act 1996, has rendered that issue obsolete.

3. "Dual status" had been expressly accepted in relation to estate contracts and options to purchase land: see *Bridges v. Mees* [1957] Ch. 475, 487 *per* Harman J.; *Webb v. Pollmount* [1966] Ch. 584, 599–603 *per* Ungoed-Thomas J.; *Kling v. Keston Properties Ltd* (1985) 49 P. & C.R. 212, 221 *per* Vinelott J.; *Ashburn Anstalt v. Arnold* [1989] Ch. 1, 28 *per* Fox L.J.; *Habermann v. Koehler* (1996) 73 P. & C. R. 515, 520 *per* Evans L.J. The potential of "dual status" would seem to extend to any minor interest created in favour of a person already in actual occupation of the land affected or in favour of a person who may go into actual occupation as a result. Moreover, "dual status" has been held to extend also to interests capable of substantive registration but not (yet) registered: see *Strand Securities Ltd v. Caswell* [1965] Ch. 958, 979–981 *per* Lord Denning M.R.

4. Dual status has been excluded in the case of certain interests where statute provides that the interest cannot take effect as an overriding interest: section 86(2) of the Land Registration Act 1925 excludes the rights of beneficiaries under a strict settlement, although the Law Commission has provisionally recommended that such rights should be capable of existing as overriding interests under section 70(1)(g): Law Com. No. 254, *Land Registration for the Twenty-First Century* (1998), para. 5.63; section 20(6) of the Landlord and Tenant (Covenants) Act 1995 excludes "overriding leases" under the 1995 Act; and section 31(10)(b) of the Family Law Act 1996 excludes matrimonial home rights under Part IV of the 1996 Act.

5. The Law Commission recommended "a *registration requirement* whereby an equitable co-ownership interest (including the rights which flow from it) is enforceable against a purchaser or lender if, but only if, the interest is registered in the appropriate manner": Law Com. No. 115, *Property Law: The Implications of Williams & Glyn's Bank Ltd v. Boland* (1982), para. 83; for critical comment, see [1982] Conv. 393, Murphy [1983] 46 M.L.R. 330. In 1985 the Land Registration and Law of Property Bill was introduced in the House of Lords. It was intended to give statutory effect to the decision in *Williams & Glyn's Bank Ltd v. Boland* but to confine the protection of that decision to the spouse of the vendor/mortgagor. However, the preferential treatment of spouses provoked considerable opposition and the Bill was withdrawn.

6. The recognition of "dual status" increases the potential scope for different results on similar facts according to whether title to the land in question is registered or unregistered. For example, in the context of registered land an estate contract/equitable lease not protected as a minor interest by entry on the register may nonetheless be enforceable against a purchaser if the equitable lessee is in actual occupation of the land: see *Grace Rymer Investments Ltd v. Waite* [1958] Ch. 831; by contrast, in the context of unregistered land an estate contract/equitable lease not protected by registration in the Land Charges Register will be unenforceable notwithstanding the actual occupation of the equitable lessee (and the actual notice of the purchaser): *Hollington Bros. Ltd v.*

Rhodes (1951) 2 T.L.R. 691; *Midland Bank Trust Co. Ltd v. Green* [1981] A.C. 512, *ante*, p. 119.

1.4.1.4 *Overreached interests as overriding interests*   In *Williams & Glyn's Bank v. Boland* the issue of the status and enforceability of the wife's contribution-based equitable interest arose because the bank had failed to pay the loan to two trustees and had therefore failed to overreach that interest. Although it was questioned whether the decision of the House of Lords had undermined the orthodox doctrine of overreaching, it was generally concluded by commentators that a purchaser of land held on trust for sale who paid the purchase money to two trustees would take free of the beneficial interests, even though the beneficiaries were in actual occupation of the land at the relevant time: see Martin [1980] Conv. 361; Sydenham [1980] Conv. 427; Martin [1981] Conv. 219. However, in *City of London Building Society v. Flegg* [1986] Ch. 605 the Court of Appeal held that the reasoning of *Williams & Glyn's Bank Ltd v. Boland* applied even on such facts; but the orthodoxy was restored by the House of Lords.

City of London Building Society v. Flegg [1988] A.C. 54

(HL, Lord Bridge, Lord Templeman, Lord Mackay, Lord Oliver, Lord Goff)

In 1977 Mr and Mrs Maxwell-Brown became registered proprietors of Bleak House under a transfer which declared them to be beneficial joint tenants and to have the mortgaging powers of an absolute owner. However, while the Maxwell-Browns had raised £16,000 of the purchase price of £34,000 by a loan secured by a legal charge over the property, the balance of £18,000 was provided by the respondents (Mr and Mrs Flegg), the parents of Mrs Maxwell-Brown, who occupied the property with the Maxwell-Browns. It was therefore held that, notwithstanding the express trust set out in the conveyance, the property was held by the Maxwell-Browns on trust for sale for themselves *and the respondents*. However, the respondents did not protect their interest by any entry on the register of the property. The Maxwell-Browns subsequently created two further charges over the property without the knowledge or consent of the respondents; and they created a final charge in favour of the appellants to secure a loan with which they repaid the earlier charges. When the Maxwell-Browns defaulted on the repayments, the appellants sought possession of the property. The respondents, relying on the decision of the House of Lords in *William & Glyn's Bank Ltd v. Boland*, claimed that they had overriding interests under section 70(1)(g) and that those interests took priority over the appellants' charge. The respondents also sought to rely on section 14 of the Law of Property Act 1925.

LORD TEMPLEMAN:
The respondents resist the claim of the appellants to possession of Bleak House and rely on section 14 of the Law of Property Act 1925. Sections 27 and 28 of that Act

which overreach the interests of the respondents under the trust for sale of Bleak House are to be found in Part I of the Act. Section 14 provides:

"This Part of this Act shall not prejudicially affect the interest of any person in possession or in actual occupation of land to which he may be entitled in right of such possession or occupation."

The respondents were in actual occupation of Bleak House at the date of the legal charge. It is argued that their beneficial interests under the trust for sale were not overreached by the legal charge or that the respondents were entitled to remain in occupation after the legal charge and against the appellants despite the overreaching of their interests.

My Lords, the respondents were entitled to occupy Bleak House by virtue of their beneficial interests in Bleak House and its rents and profits pending the execution of the trust for sale. Their beneficial interests were overreached by the legal charge and were transferred to the equity of redemption held by the Maxwell-Browns and to the sum advanced by the appellants in consideration of the grant of the legal charge and received by the Maxwell-Browns. After the legal charge the respondents were only entitled to continue in occupation of Bleak House by virtue of their beneficial interests in the equity of redemption of Bleak House and that equity of redemption is subject to the right of the appellants as mortgagee to take possession. Sections 27 and 28 did not "prejudicially" affect the interests of the respondents who were indeed prejudiced but at the subsequent failure of the trustees for sale to account to their beneficiaries for capital money received by the trustees. A beneficiary who is entitled to share in the proceeds of sale of land held on trust for sale relies on the trustees. Section 26(3) of the Act (as amended) requires trustees for sale to consult their beneficiaries and to give effect to the wishes of the majority of the beneficiaries "but a purchaser shall not be concerned to see that the provisions of this subsection have been complied with." If the argument for the respondents is correct, a purchaser from trustees for sale must ensure that a beneficiary in actual occupation is not only consulted but consents to the sale. Section 14 of the Law of Property Act 1925 is not apt to confer on a tenant in common of land held on trust for sale, who happens to be in occupation, rights which are different from and superior to the rights of tenants in common, who are not in occupation on the date when the interests of all tenants in common are overreached by a sale or mortgage by trustees for sale.

. . .

In my view the object of section 70 was to reproduce for registered land the same limitations as section 14 of the Law of Property Act 1925 produced for land whether registered or unregistered. The respondents claim to be entitled to overriding interests because they were in actual occupation of Bleak House on the date of the legal charge. But the interests of the respondents cannot at one and the same time be overreached and overridden and at the same time be overriding interests. The appellants cannot at one and the same time take free from all the interests of the respondents yet at the same time be subject to some of those interests. The right of the respondents to be and remain in actual occupation of Bleak House ceased when the respondents' interests were overreached by the legal charge save in so far as their rights were transferred to the equity of redemption. As persons interested under the trust for sale the respondents had no right to possession as against the appellants and the fact that the respondents were in actual occupation at the date of the legal charge did not create a new right or transfer an old right so as to make the right enforceable against the appellants.

One of the main objects of the legislation of 1925 was to effect a compromise between on the one hand the interests of the public in securing that land held in trust is freely marketable and, on the other hand, the interests of the beneficiaries in preserving their rights under the trusts. By the Settled Land Act 1925 a tenant for life may convey the settled land discharged from all the trusts powers and provisions of the settlement. By the Law of Property Act 1925 trustees for sale may convey land held on trust for sale discharged from the trusts affecting the proceeds of sale and rents and profits until sale. Under both forms of trust the protection and the only protection of the beneficiaries is that capital money must be paid to at least two trustees or a trust corporation. Section 14 of the Law of Property Act 1925 and section 70 of the Land Registration Act 1925 cannot have been intended to frustrate this compromise and to subject the purchaser to some beneficial interests but not others depending on the waywardness of actual occupation. The Court of Appeal took a different view, largely in reliance on the decision of this House in *Williams & Glyn's Bank Ltd v. Boland* [1981] A.C. 487. In that case the sole proprietor of registered land held the land as sole trustee upon trust for sale and to stand possessed of the net proceeds of sale and rents and profits until sale upon trust for himself and his wife as tenants in common. This House held that the wife's beneficial interest coupled with actual possession by her constituted an overriding interest and that a mortgagee from the husband, despite the concluding words of section 20(1), took subject to the wife's overriding interest. But in that case the interest of the wife was not overreached or overridden because the mortgagee advanced capital moneys to a sole trustee. If the wife's interest had been overreached by the mortgagee advancing capital moneys to two trustees there would have been nothing to justify the wife in remaining in occupation as against the mortgagee. There must be a combination of an interest which justifies continuing occupation plus actual occupation to constitute an overriding interest. Actual occupation is not an interest in itself.

For these reasons and for the reasons to be given by my noble and learned friend, Lord Oliver of Aylmerton, I would allow this appeal and restore the order of Judge Thomas who ordered the respondents to deliver up Bleak House to the appellants.

LORD OLIVER:

In the Court of Appeal in the instant case Dillon L.J. held that, quite apart from the provisions of the Land Registration Act 1925, the respondents had an equitable interest in the property protected by occupation which took priority over the appellants' mortgage by virtue of section 14 of the Law of Property Act 1925. My Lords, the ambit of section 14 is a matter which has puzzled conveyancers ever since the Law of Property Act was enacted. ... For my part, I think that it is unnecessary for present purposes to seek to resolve the conundrum. What section 14 does not do, on any analysis, is to enlarge or add to whatever interest it is that the occupant has "in right of his occupation" and in my judgment the argument that places reliance upon it in the instant case founds itself upon an assumption about the nature of the occupying co-owners' interest that cannot in fact be substantiated. The section cannot of itself create an interest which survives the execution of the trust under which it arises or answer the logically anterior question of what, if any, interest in the land is conferred by the possession or occupation. It is suggested in *Wolstenholme and Cherry's Conveyancing Statutes*, 13th ed. (1972), vol. 1, p. 69, that section 14 was designed to preserve the principle, exemplified by *Hunt v. Luck* [1902] 1 Ch. 428, that a purchaser will have constructive notice of any rights reasonably discoverable from inspection of the property and, in particular, from inquiry of any occupier as to his interest and the terms on which he holds it. With that I respectfully agree. Leaving aside, however, the question whether the words "in right of such possession or occupation" have, as the judge thought and as the appellants have argued before your Lordships, the effect of limiting the interests to which the section applies to those which are conferred by the preceding fact of possession or occupation or whether, as the Court of Appeal held in effect, they mean merely "in respect of" or "associated with" possession or occupation, the section cannot, in my judgment, have the effect of preserving, as equitable interests in the land, interests which are overreached by the exercise of the trustees' powers or of bringing onto the title which the purchaser from trustees for sale is required to investigate the equitable interest of every beneficiary who happens to be in occupation of the land. That would be to defeat the manifest purpose of the legislature in enacting the sections to which reference has already been made. Looking at the interest of the tenant in common in actual occupation and considering for the moment only the position in relation to unregistered land, one has, as it seems to me, to bear in mind always the distinction between his rights as against his co-beneficiaries or against the trustee or trustees in whom the legal estate is vested and his rights against a purchaser of the legal estate from the trustees for sale. His interest is overreached and the purchaser is absolved from inquiry only if the statutory requirements respecting the payment of capital money arising under a disposition upon trust for sale are complied with: sections 2(1)(ii) and 27. Until that occurs, he remains entitled to assert against the trustees and, indeed, against any purchaser from the trustees who has not complied with the statutory requirements all the incidents of his beneficial interest in the proceeds of sale of the property and in the net rents and profits until the sale. One of the incidents of that beneficial interest is, or may be according to the agreement between the beneficiaries or to the purpose for which the trust was originally created, the enjoyment of the property in specie either alone or concurrently with other beneficiaries. But the enjoyment in specie, whilst it may serve to give notice to third parties of the occupier's interest under the trust, is not a separate and severable right which can be regarded as, as it were, free standing. It is and has to be referable to the trust from which, and from which alone, it arises. It is the beneficial interest in the rents and profits pending sale that is the foundation of that enjoyment and there is nothing in the statute or in the cases—leaving aside, for the moment, the *Boland* case [1981] A.C. 487 which I shall have to come to a little later—to suggest that the enjoyment of the property in specie of itself confers some independent right which will survive the operation of the overreaching provisions of the Law of Property Act 1925. Indeed, the framers of that legislation would, I think, have been shocked and surprised to hear it asserted that a purchaser in proper form from the trustees of the statutory trusts was required to investigate the purposes for which the trust property had been acquired by the trustees or the terms of some private and unwritten agreement or understanding between the beneficiaries inter se or between one or more of the beneficiaries and the trustees. ...

If this is right, as I believe that it is, the reason why a purchaser of the legal estate (whether by way of outright sale or by way of mortgage) from a single proprietor takes subject to the rights of the occupying beneficiary is not because section 14 of the Act confers upon the latter some interest in land which is incapable of being overreached but because, having constructive notice of the trust as a result of the beneficiary's occupation, he steps into the shoes of the vendor or mortgagor and takes the estate subject to the same equities as those to which it was subject in the latter's hands, those equities and their accompanying incidents not having been overreached by the sale under the provisions of section 2(1) and section 27 of the Act. Where the purchase has taken effect in accordance with those provisions, it is quite clear from the terms of the statute both that the purchaser, even with express notice, is not concerned with the beneficiary's interest in the proceeds of sale or the net rents and profits until sale and that that interest is overreached. The beneficiary's possession or occupation is no more than a method of enjoying in specie the rents and profits pending sale in which he is entitled to share. It derives from and is, as [counsel for the appellants] has graphically put it, fathered by the interests under the trust for sale. Once that goes, as it does on the execution of the trust for sale, then the foundation of the occupation goes and the beneficiary has no longer any "interest ... to which he may be entitled in right of such ... occupation." We are, or course, concerned here not with the execution of the trust by a sale of the land by the trustees, but with the exercise by the trustees of their power to raise capital money by creating a charge on the land. But the same principle must, in my judgment, apply, the "overreaching" in this case consisting in the creation by the trustees of a legal estate and of powers incidental thereto (including the mortgagee's power of sale) which have an absolute priority over the beneficial interests, although, no doubt, those beneficial interests and their accompanying incidents continue as against the equity of redemption which remains vested in the trustees. If I may say so respectfully, the reasoning of the Court of Appeal in the instant case starts at the wrong end by assuming that there is an interest conferred by occupation which, were it not for section 14, would be in some way prejudiced by the provisions of Part I of the Act, whereas in fact the occupier's interest in this instance is one which stems from, depends upon and is co-terminous with the interest in the rents and profits arising under those very provisions and which is displaced by the execution of the trust or the exercise of the trustees' powers to the same extent as that interest. For my part, I have found myself unable to accept the reasoning in this part of the judgment of Dillon L.J. If this were a case concerned solely with unregistered land, I am of opinion that the appellants' charge would take effect in priority to the respondents' interest which would be pro tanto overreached and which, so far as it can properly be considered as an equitable interest in land, would continue to subsist only in the equity of redemption.

So to conclude, however, resolves only part of the question, for the land concerned was at the material time registered land and there remain to be considered two questions, viz: first, how do the provisions of the Land Registration Act 1925 fit with the provisions of the Law of Property Act 1925 and, secondly, does the decision of this House in *Boland*'s case [1981] A.C. 487, which was concerned with a transaction between a mortgagee and a sole individual trustee, falsify or otherwise affect the conclusion just stated?

. . .

The respondents' submission, which succeeded in the Court of Appeal, is a very simple one. What is said is that the decision of this House in *Boland*'s case [1981] A.C. 487 established the proposition that the interest of a tenant in common in occupation of registered land is, by reason of such occupation, an interest incapable of being overreached by a sale or other disposition of the land, save with the consent of the occupier; that section 70 makes that interest an overriding one; and that, accordingly, the disposition by the registered proprietors in favour of the appellants takes effect subject to the right of the respondents to remain in occupation of the house indefinitely notwithstanding that (a) the appellants were specifically exonerated from inquiry into the trusts affecting the rents and profits of land pending sale by section 27 of the Law of Property Act 1925 and (b) the capital moneys raised by the registered proprietors were paid to two trustees in accordance with section 27(2). My Lords, if the first step in this composite proposition be correct, then the remainder follows as a matter of unassailable logic. The Court of Appeal concluded that it was correct by reference to an analysis of the speech of Lord Wilberforce in *Boland*'s case. Dillon L.J. accepted that Lord Wilberforce's observations were made in the context of a case where the dealing which was claimed as being subject to an overriding interest in the occupying beneficiary was with a single trustee and would not therefore overreach the beneficiary's interest. But in his view the reasoning did not depend upon the fact that in *Boland* there was only one registered proprietor of the land and therefore only one trustee for sale. It concentrated simply on the distinction between a minor interest and an overriding interest, the mere fact of occupation converting what would otherwise be a minor interest into an overriding interest. Thus he found the instant case indistinguishable from *Boland*'s case in any material respect. The proposition is encapsulated in the following short passage from his judgment [1986] Ch. 605, 617:

> "the reasoning of Lord Wilberforce concentrates on the distinction between the minor interest and the overriding interest. This necessarily covers the case where there are two registered proprietors and so two trustees for sale, because the wording in the definition of 'minor interests' in section 3(xv): 'in the case of land held on trust for sale, all interests and powers which are under the Law of Property Act 1925 capable of being overridden by the trustees for sale ...' must refer to the case where there are two trustees for sale; indeed, only where there are two (or three or four) trustees for sale would the interests of the beneficiaries be overridden under the Law of Property Act 1925. On a sale, what would otherwise have been a minor interest capable of being overridden under the Law of Property Act 1925 by two

trustees for sale is, if protected by the fact of actual occupation of the land, elevated to the status of an overriding interest. In my judgment, therefore, the reasoning in *Boland*'s case covers entirely the position of the parents in the present case. As no inquiry was made of the parents before the plaintiffs took their mortgage on the property, the parents have an overriding interest in the property which binds the plaintiffs."

The fundamental criticism of this advanced by the appellants is that it fails to analyse the incidents of and limitations upon the interest which the court held to override the interest of the appellants. What section 70(1)(g) does is to define as an overriding interest the rights (whatever they may be) of every person in actual occupation and to subject the registered land to such overriding interests "as may be for the time being subsisting in reference thereto." It does not create or enlarge rights but merely operates, to use the words of Lord Wilberforce in *National Provincial Bank Ltd v. Hastings Car Mart Ltd* [1965] A.C. 1175, 1260–1261:

"to adapt the system of registration, and the modified form of inquiry which is appropriate to that system, to the same kind of right as under the general law would affect a purchaser finding a person in occupation of his land."

One may, quoting again from the speech of Lord Wilberforce, in the same case, at p. 1261:

"have to accept that there is a difference between unregistered land and registered land as regards what kind of notice binds a purchaser, or what kind of inquiries a purchaser has to make. But there is no warrant in the terms of this paragraph or elsewhere in the Act for supposing that the nature of the rights which are to bind a purchaser is to be different, excluding personal rights in one case, including them in another. The whole frame of section 70, with the list that it gives of interests, or rights, which are overriding, shows that it is made against a background of interests or rights whose nature and whose transmissible character is known, or ascertainable, aliunde, i.e., under other statutes or under the common law."

With this preliminary caution in mind, therefore, I turn to consider whether, in fact, the decision of this House in *Boland* [1981] A.C. 487 does lead to the conclusion that the occupying co-owner's interest under the statutory trusts is, by reason of his occupation, one which is incapable of being overreached. It has, I think, to be borne in mind when reading both the judgments in the Court of Appeal in that case and the speeches in this House that they were prepared and delivered against a background of fact which precluded any argument that the interests of Mrs Boland and Mrs Brown had been overreached under the provisions of the Law of Property Act 1925. Equally, the holding, contrary to the argument of the mortgagees, that Mrs Boland and Mrs Brown were in actual occupation ruled out any question of the mortgagees having taken their interest without notice of the occupier's rights, whatever those rights were. The mortgagees in that case were, therefore, quite simply purchasers from the owner of the legal estate with notice of the existence of whatever equitable rights the occupier was entitled to claim. Their claim to take free from them accordingly rested simply and solely on the fact that the land charged happened to be registered land, a feature which enabled them to claim, if they could substantiate it, that the beneficiaries' interests were minor interests and so overridden by a disposition by the registered proprietor. Thus, in the argument for the mortgagees before the Court of Appeal, it was contended that the argument for the appellants involved the proposition that even if two trustees or a trust corporation received the purchase money there would still be an overriding interest: [1979] Ch. 312, 319. In the argument in reply this was countered by counsel for the appellants who pointed out that the rights of beneficiaries are not overreached by a sale by one trustee. In such a case, section 199 of the Law of Property Act 1925 (relating to notice) applies. Counsel emphasised in this context that there was no inconsistency between the Law of Property Act and the Land Registration Act and went on to point out that the powers of management in section 28 of the Law of Property Act (and, in particular, the power to mortgage contained in section 71 of the Settled Land Act 1925) do not apply to one trustee who would have no power to borrow money. It is in the light of these arguments that one finds in the judgments of the Court of Appeal specific references to the fact that the transactions there in question were transactions in which the capital money was received by one trustee only so that the beneficiaries' rights were not overreached: see pp. 330B-E *per* Lord Denning M.R.; pp. 334B-D, 337G *per* Ormrod L.J. and pp. 340A-B, 341B-C *per* Browne L.J. Dillon L.J. in the Court of Appeal regarded these references as merely part of the narrative but I am, for my part, unable to agree. They were, as it seems to me, an essential part of the reasoning upon which the judgments were based, for it was a critical feature of the appellants' argument that their interests were not overreached but were kept alive as against the purchaser, by notice in the case of unregistered land or by being overriding interests in the case of registered land. In the argument before your Lordships' House, one finds the same underlying thesis [1981] A.C. 487, 498D-E, 499D-E, 499C-D in the respondents' argument and at p. 501D-E in the appellants' argument in reply. It was, indeed, this feature, namely that in each case the mortgage was effected by a single registered proprietor, which compelled the mortgagees to argue that the beneficiaries' interests in that case fell within the definition of minor interests, that "minor interests" and "overriding interests" were mutually exclusive categories and that an interest under a trust for sale was incapable of constituting an overriding interest. They could not deny that they had constructive notice, so that if they were to succeed at all it could only be because the land was registered land and the provisions of section 20(1) of the Act enabled them to take free from minor interests. It is this argument to which the relevant part of Lord Wilberforce's speech was directed and he pointed out at the inception, in considering whether the provisions of section 70(1)(g) could afford protection to the interests of the tenant in common in equity, that the effect of a disposition by two trustees or a trust corporation would be to overreach the trusts with the result that a purchaser would take free from them, whether or not he had notice: see p. 503D-E. Thus, the only question, it being common ground that there had not, in fact, been any overreaching, was whether the respondents' interests, although capable of being overreached by appropriate machinery and so within the definition of minor interests, could also be overriding interests by reason of the beneficiaries' occupation of the land. That question is answered by Lord Wilberforce in the following passage in his speech, at p. 507:

> "How then are these various rights to be fitted into the scheme of the Land Registration Act 1925? It is clear, at least, that the interests of the co-owners under the 'statutory trusts' are minor interests—this fits with the definition in section 3(xv). But I can see no reason why, if these interests, or that of any one of them, are or is protected by 'actual occupation' they should remain merely as 'minor interests.' On the contrary, I see every reason why, in that event, they should acquire the status of overriding interests. And, moreover, I find it easy to accept that they satisfy the opening, and governing, words of section 70, namely, interests subsisting in reference to the land."

My Lords, if I may respectfully say so, this is plainly right, but it has to be read in the context of the facts in *Boland*'s case. Quite clearly the interests of the respondents in that case were subsisting. Nothing had occurred which had the effect of overreaching them. I cannot, however, for my part, read Lord Wilberforce's words as applying to a case which was not before the House where the effect of the transaction in question was precisely that to which he himself had alluded in his outline of the legal framework within which the appeals before the House fell to be decided, that is to say a conveyance by two trustees involving the consequence that the purchaser took free from the trusts regardless of notice.

Considered in the context of a transaction complying with the statutory requirements of the Law of Property Act 1925 the question of the effect of section 70(1)(g) of the

Land Registration Act 1925 must, in my judgment, be approached by asking first what are the "rights" of the person in occupation and whether they are, at the material time, subsisting in reference to the land. In the instant case the exercise by the registered proprietors of the powers conferred on trustees for sale by section 28(1) of the Law of Property Act 1925 had the effect of overreaching the interests of the respondents under the statutory trusts upon which depended their right to continue in occupation of the land. The appellants took free from those trusts (section 27) and were not, in any event, concerned to see that the respondents' consent to the transaction was obtained (section 26). If, then, one asks what were the subsisting rights of the respondents referable to their occupation, the answer must, in my judgment, be that they were rights which, *vis-à-vis* the appellants, were, eo instante with the creation of the charge, overreached and therefore subsisted only in relation to the equity of redemption. I do not, for my part, find in *Boland*'s case [1981] A.C. 487 anything which compels a contrary conclusion. Granted that the interest of a co-owner pending the execution of the statutory trust for sale is, despite the equitable doctrine of conversion, an interest subsisting in reference to the land the subject matter of the trust and granted also that *Boland*'s case establishes that such an interest, although falling within the definition of minor interest and so liable to be overriden by a registered disposition, will, so long as it subsists, be elevated to the status of an overriding interest if there exists also the additional element of occupation by the co-owner, I cannot for my part accept that, once what I may call the parent interest, by which alone the occupation can be justified, has been overreached and thus subordinated to a legal estate properly created by the trustees under their statutory powers, it can, in relation to the proprietor of the legal estate so created, be any longer said to be a right "for the time being subsisting." Section 70(1)(g) protects only the rights in reference to the land of the occupier whatever they are at the material time—in the instant case the right to enjoy in specie the rents and profits of the land held in trust for him. Once the beneficiary's rights have been shifted from the land to capital moneys in the hands of the trustees, there is no longer an interest in the land to which the occupation can be referred or which it can protect. If the trustees sell in accordance with the statutory provisions and so overreach the beneficial interests in reference to the land, nothing remains to which a right of occupation can attach and the same result must, in my judgment, follow *vis-à-vis* a chargee by way of legal mortgage so long as the transaction is carried out in the manner prescribed by the Law of Property Act 1925, overreaching the beneficial interests by subordinating them to the estate of the chargee which is no longer "affected" by them so as to become subject to them on registration pursuant to section 20(1) of the Land Registration Act 1925. In the instant case, therefore, I would, for my part, hold that the charge created in favour of the appellants overreached the beneficial interests of the respondents and that there is nothing in section 70(1)(g) of the Land Registration Act 1925 or in *Boland*'s case which has the effect of preserving against the appellants any rights of the respondents to occupy the land by virtue of their beneficial interests in the equity of redemption which remains vested in the trustees.

NOTES:

1. The rejection of the orthodoxy by the Court of Appeal in *City of London Building Society v. Flegg* was generally criticised: see [1986] C.L.J. 202; [1986] Conv. 131; (1986) 102 L.Q.R. 349; (1986) 49 M.L.R. 519; and the reinstatement of the orthodoxy by the House of Lords was generally applauded: see [1987] C.L.J. 392; (1987) 103 L.Q.R. 520; (1988) 51 M.L.R. 565. However, Swadling [1986] Conv. 379, [1987] Conv. 451 sought to justify the decision of the Court of Appeal on the ground that the informal creation of equitable co-ownership under a resulting trust did not involve the trust for sale machinery and that the interests of the beneficiaries were thus incapable of being overreached: see *post*, p. 297. Moreover, the support for

the overreaching orthodoxy was to some extent tempered by concern as to the effect on the occupational and other rights that were acknowledged as incidents of equitable co-ownership where the land was purchased for occupation by the beneficiaries: see *post*, p. 301. Some commentators therefore favoured reliance on section 14 of the Law of Property Act 1925 to prevent the operation of the overreaching provisions where they would prejudice such occupational rights: see Thompson (1986) 6 *Legal Studies* 140; Smith (1987) 103 L.Q.R. 520.

2. The House of Lords discounted other arguable difficulties raised by the facts of the case: (i) that the appellants' charge was not registered: see Thompson [1988] Conv. 108; (ii) that the appellants, having obtained an official search certificate, failed to apply for registration of the charge within the priority period and in the meantime the respondents lodged a caution: see Sparkes [1988] Conv. 141; and (iii) that the Maxwell-Browns had no mortgaging power under the statutory (as opposed to the express) trust for sale: see Clayton [1981] Conv. 19; Smith (1986) 49 M.L.R. 519; Harpum [1987] C.L.J. 392; Ferris and Battersby [1998] Conv. 168, 185–186.

3. The reasoning in *Flegg* was applied in *State Bank of India v. Sood* [1997] Ch. 276, noted at [1997] C.L.J. 494; [1997] Conv. 134. For consideration of the prior question as to whether the interests of the beneficiaries had been overreached, see *ante*, p. 110.

4. The Law Commission recommended that a conveyance of a legal estate should not have the effect of overreaching the interest of anyone of full age and capacity who is entitled to a beneficial interest in the land and who has a right to occupy it and is in actual occupation of it at the date of the conveyance, unless that person consents (although it was also recommended that the court should have a discretionary power to dispense with the consent requirement): Law Com. No. 188, *Transfer of Land: Overreaching: Beneficiaries in Occupation* (1989), paras 4.3, 4.19. The Law Commission expressed the view that implementation of its recommendation would not necessitate changes in conveyancing practice beyond those changes that had already been adopted in response to the decision in *Williams & Glyn's Bank Ltd v. Boland*. It is arguable that the Trusts of Land and Appointment of Trustees Act 1996 has had the effect of implementing a version of the Law Commission's recommendation: see *post*, p. 336; but in March 1998 the Government announced that it had decided not to implement the (remaining) recommendations in the Report: *Hansard*, HL, March 19, 1998, Written Answers 213.

1.4.2 *Actual occupation*

1.4.2.1 *The meaning of "actual occupation"*

Williams & Glyn's Bank Ltd v. Boland [1981] A.C. 487

(HL, Lord Wilberforce, Viscount Dilhorne, Lord Salmon, Lord Scarman, Lord Roskill)

For the facts, see *supra*, p. 193.

LORD WILBERFORCE:

The system of land registration, as it exists in England, which long antedates the Land Registration Act 1925, is designed to simplify and to cheapen conveyancing. It is intended to replace the often complicated and voluminous title deeds of property by a single land certificate, on the strength of which land can be dealt with. In place of the lengthy and often technical investigation of title to which a purchaser was committed, all he has to do is to consult the register; from any burden not entered on the register, with one exception, he takes free. Above all, the system is designed to free the purchaser from the hazards of notice—real or constructive—which, in the case of unregistered land, involved him in enquiries, often quite elaborate, failing which he might be bound by equities. The Law of Property Act 1925 contains provisions limiting the effect of the doctrine of notice, but it still remains a potential source of danger to purchasers. By contrast, the only provisions in the Land Registration Act 1925 with regard to notice are provisions which enable a purchaser to take the estate free from equitable interests or equities whether he has notice or not. (See, for example, section 3(xv) s.v. "minor interests"). The only kind of notice recognised is by entry on the register.

The exception just mentioned consists of "overriding interests" listed in section 70. As to these, all registered land is stated to be deemed to be subject to such of them as may be subsisting in reference to the land, unless the contrary is expressed on the register. The land is so subject regardless of notice actual or constructive. In my opinion therefore, the law as to notice as it may affect purchasers of unregistered land, whether contained in decided cases, or in a statute (the Conveyancing Act 1882, section 3, Law of Property Act, section 199) has no application even by analogy to registered land. Whether a particular right is an overriding interest, and whether it affects a purchaser, is to be decided upon the terms of section 70, and other relevant provisions of the Land Registration Act 1925, and upon nothing else.

In relation to rights connected with occupation, it has been said that the purpose and effect of section 70(1)(g) of the Land Registration Act 1925 was to make applicable to registered land the same rule as previously had been held to apply to unregistered land: see *per* Lord Denning M.R. in *National Provincial Bank Ltd v. Hastings Car Mart Ltd* [1964] Ch. 665, 689, and in this House [1965] A.C. 1175, 1259.

I adhere to this, but I do not accept the argument which learned counsel for the appellant sought to draw from it. His submission was that, in applying section 70(1)(g), we should have regard to and limit the application of the paragraph in the light of the doctrine of notice. But this would run counter to the whole purpose of the Act. The purpose, in each system, is the same, namely, to safeguard the rights of persons in occupation, but the method used differs. In the case of unregistered land, the purchaser's obligation depends upon what he has notice of—notice actual or constructive. In the case of registered land, it is the fact of occupation that matters. If there is actual occupation, and the occupier has rights, the purchaser takes subject to them. If not, he does not. No further element is material.

I now deal with the first question. Were the wives here in "actual occupation"? These words are ordinary words of plain English, and should, in my opinion, be interpreted as such. Historically they appear to have emerged in the judgment of Lord Loughborough L.C. in *Taylor v. Stibbert* (1794) 2 Ves.Jun. 437, 439–440, in a passage which repays quotation:

"... whoever purchases an estate from the owner, knowing it to be in possession of tenants, is bound to inquire into the estates those tenants have. It has been determined that a purchaser being told particular parts of the estate were in possession of a tenant, without any information as to his interest, and taking it for granted it was only from year to year, was bound by a lease that tenant had, which was a surprise upon him. That was rightly determined; for it was sufficient to put the purchaser upon inquiry, that he was informed the estate was not in the *actual possession* of the person with whom he contracted; that he could not transfer the ownership and possession at the same time; that there were interests, as to the extent and terms of which it was his duty to inquire."

They were taken up in the judgment of the Privy Council in *Barnhart v. Greenshields* (1853) 9 Moo. P.C.C. 18. The purpose for which they were used, in that case, was evidently to distinguish the case of a person who was in some kind of legal possession, as by receipt of the rents and profits, from that of a person actually in occupation as tenant. Given occupation, i.e., presence on the land, I do not think that the word "actual" was intended to introduce any additional qualification, certainly not to suggest that possession must be "adverse": it merely emphasises that what is required is physical presence, not some entitlement in law. So even if it were necessary to look behind these plain words into history, I would find no reason for denying them their plain meaning.

Then, were the wives in actual occupation? I ask: why not? There was physical presence, with all the rights that occupiers have, including the right to exclude all others except those having similar rights. The house was a matrimonial home, intended to be occupied, and in fact occupied by both spouses, both of whom have an interest in it: it would require some special doctrine of law to avoid the result that each is in occupation. Three arguments were used for a contrary conclusion. First, it was said that if the vendor (I use this word to include a mortgagor) is in occupation, that is enough to prevent the application of the paragraph. This seems to be a proposition of general application, not limited to the case of husbands, and no doubt, if correct, would be very convenient for purchasers and intending mortgagees. But the presence of the vendor, with occupation, does not exclude the possibility of occupation of others. There are observations which suggest the contrary in the unregistered land case of *Caunce v. Caunce* [1969] 1 W.L.R. 286, but I agree with the disapproval of these, and with the assertion of the proposition I have just stated by Russell L.J. in *Hodgson v. Marks* [1971] Ch. 892, 934. Then it was suggested that the wife's occupation was nothing but the shadow of the husband's—a version I suppose of the doctrine of unity of husband and wife. This expression and the argument flowing from it was used by Templeman J. in *Bird v. Syme-Thomson* [1979] 1 W.L.R. 440, 444, a decision preceding and which he followed in the present case. The argument was also inherent in the judgment in *Caunce v. Caunce* [1969] 1 W.L.R. 286 which influenced the decisions of Templeman J. It somewhat faded from the arguments in the present case and appears to me to be heavily obsolete. The appellant's main and final position became in the end this: that, to come within the paragraph, the occupation in question must be apparently inconsistent with the title of the vendor. This, it was suggested, would exclude the wife of a husband-vendor because her apparent occupation would be satisfactorily accounted for by his. But, apart from the rewriting of the paragraph which this would involve, the suggestion is unacceptable. Consistency, or inconsistency, involves the absence, or presence, of an independent right to occupy, though I must observe that "inconsistency" in this context is an inappropriate word. But how can either quality be predicated of a wife, simply qua wife? A wife may, and everyone knows this, have rights of her own; particularly, many wives have a share in a matrimonial home. How can it be said that the presence of a wife in the house, as occupier, is consistent or inconsistent with the husband's rights until one knows what rights she has? And if she has rights, why, just because she is a wife (or in the converse case, just because an occupier is the husband), should these rights be denied protection under the paragraph? If one looks beyond the case of husband and wife, the difficulty of all these arguments stands out if one considers the case of a man living with a mistress, or of a man and a woman—or for that matter two persons of the same sex— living in a house in separate or partially shared rooms. Are these cases of apparently consistent occupation, so that the rights of the other person (other than the vendor) can be disregarded? The only solution which is consistent with the Act (section 70(1)(g)) and with common sense is to read the paragraph for what it says.

Occupation, existing as a fact, may protect rights if the person in occupation has rights. On this part of the case I have no difficulty in concluding that a spouse, living in a house, has an actual occupation capable of conferring protection, as an overriding interest, upon rights of that spouse.

NOTES:

1. Lord Scarman said (at 511):

[Overriding] interests take effect under the section without registration and whether or not a purchaser has notice of them. I do not, therefore, read the Act of 1925 as requiring the courts to give the words "actual occupation" in section 70(1)(g) the special meaning for which the appellants contend, namely an occupation, which by its nature necessarily puts a would-be purchaser (or mortgagee) upon notice of a claim adverse to the registered owner. On the contrary, I expect to find—as I do find—that the statute has substituted a plain factual situation for the uncertainties of notice, actual or constructive, as the determinant of an overriding interest.

2. What constitutes "actual occupation" of land must depend on the nature and condition of the land which is claimed to be occupied: *Lloyds Bank plc v. Rosset* [1989] Ch. 350, 377 *per* Nicholls L.J., 394 *per* Mustill L.J.; *Abbey National Building Society v. Cann* [1991] 1 A.C. 56, 93 *per* Lord Oliver. Actual occupation cannot be equated with residence in the context of business or agricultural premises: see *Epps v. Esso Petroleum Co. Ltd* [1973] 1 W.L.R. 1071, *infra*, p. 255; *Blacklocks v. J.B. Developments (Godalming) Ltd* [1982] Ch. 183, *supra*, p. 190; nor in the context of a semi-derelict house in the course of renovation: *Lloyds Bank plc v. Rosset, infra*, p. 211. There is no need for continued and uninterrupted physical presence on the part of the person claiming to be in actual occupation nor for the person to be physically present at the relevant time, provided that he has already established a presence involving some degree of permanence and continuity (and not a mere "fleeting presence") and provided that he intends to return: *Chhokar v. Chhokar* [1984] F.L.R. 313; and see *Kingsnorth Finance Co. Ltd v. Tizard* [1986] 1 W.L.R. 783, *ante*, p. 42. In *Stockholm Finance Ltd v. Garden Holdings Inc.* [1995] N.P.C. 162 the claimant, who was absent from her fully-furnished London home for 14 months while living abroad with her mother, was held not to be in actual occupation. Robert Walker J. said:

Whether a person's intermittent presence at a house which is fully furnished, and ready for almost immediate use, should be seen as continuous occupation marked (but not interrupted) by occasional absences, or whether it should be seen as a pattern of alternating periods of presence and absence, is a matter of perception which defies deep analysis. Not only the length of any absence, but also the reason for it, may be material. (A holiday or a business trip may be easier to reconcile with continuing and unbroken occupation than a move to a second home, even though the duration of the absence is the same in each case.) But there must come a point at which a person's absence from his house is so prolonged that the notion of his continuing to be in actual occupation of it becomes unsupportable.

On the other hand, the mere taking of preparatory steps leading to the assumption of actual residential occupation is not sufficient: *Abbey National Building Society v. Cann, infra*, p. 215.

Moreover, actual occupation does not necessarily involve the personal presence of the person claiming to occupy: occupation through an agent such as a caretaker or employee may suffice provided that the agent is in occupation for the purposes of the principal and not merely as his licensee. In *Strand Securities Ltd v. Caswell* [1965] Ch. 958 the first defendant had been granted, in 1952, a 39-year sub-lease of a flat in London; but at the material time the sub-lease was neither substantively registered nor was any notice of it entered against the registered title of the head-lease. From 1961 the first defendant, who had subsequently moved to the country, permitted his step-daughter, the second defendant, and her children to live in the flat rent-free. However, some of the furniture in the flat belonged to the first defendant, who occasionally used the flat for family meetings and as a place to change when he wished to go out in the evening in London. In March 1962 the plaintiffs purchased the head-lease and in April 1962 the transfer was registered. *Inter alia*, the question arose as to whether the first defendant was in actual occupation of the flat. Russell L.J. stated (at 983–985):

On the facts, was the first defendant, at April 24, 1962, a person in actual occupation, though he was not in any ordinary sense residing there or treating it as his home, and the second defendant and her family were allowed by him to reside there? As a matter of the ordinary use of language I would not consider the first defendant to be such. For him it was argued that the phrase "in actual occupation" derives from cases in which "actual occupation" and "actual possession" are used indifferently to describe a condition of enjoyment of the land itself, and that the phrase "actual occupation" here involves that form of the legal concept of possession as distinct from the other or notional forms of that concept consisting of the receipt of money payments derived from land, or of the right to possession though the land be vacant. And it was argued that "actual possession" was avoided by the draftsman as a phrase because of the difficulty which would flow from the definition of "possession" in section 3(xviii) of the Land Registration Act 1925. Reference was made to a number of authorities, including cases in the fields of rating, poor law, and landlord and tenant, with a view to showing that possession, and therefore occupation, may be had through the medium of another. Suppose, it was said, that the first defendant employed a resident caretaker to look after the flat in question, would the first defendant not be a person in actual occupation? I think that is correct. Then, it was argued, that is because the caretaker would be his licensee, bound to go at his will, and that was the position of the second defendant. But I think that here is the distinction between occupation by the caretaker as a matter of duty on behalf of the first defendant and the occupation of the second defendant on her own behalf; both were licensees, but the former, by her occupation for which she was employed, was the representative of the first defendant and her occupation may therefore be regarded as his. The proposition that in each case the first defendant was in actual occupation because neither the caretaker nor the second defendant had a right to occupy independently of him seems to me too broadly stated and to ignore that distinction. I do not say that a contract of employment or agency with the person residing there is essential to actual occupation by the other person. I think that it might well be that if a house was used as a residence by a wife, separated from the tenant, her husband (whether or not in desertion), he could also be regarded as in actual occupation through her; the question whether the husband was also a person in actual occupation did not, of course, arise in *National Provincial Bank Ltd v. Hastings Car Mart Ltd* [1964] Ch. 665. But this conception, even if valid, could not extend to the relationship in the present case.

Nor, it seems to me, can the presence on the premises of some of the first defendant's furniture, nor the previously mentioned use by him and others of the family of the flat, nor the fact, which I am prepared to assume though it was not proved, that he had a key, nor a combination of those matters, constitute actual occupation by him.

See also *ibid.* 981 *per* Lord Denning M.R.; *Lloyds Bank plc v. Rosset* [1989] Ch. 350, 377–378 *per* Nicholls L.J., 397 *per* Mustill L.J., 405 *per* Purchas L.J.; *Abbey National Building Society v. Cann* [1991] 1 A.C. 56, 93 *per* Lord Oliver.

3. In *Hypo-Mortgage Services Ltd v. Robinson* [1997] 2 F.L.R. 71 the Court of Appeal held that minor children (living with their parent(s)) who had beneficial interests in property could not be "in actual occupation" of that property for the purposes of section 70(1)(g). Nourse L.J. (with whom Sir John May agreed) stated (at 72):

In *Bird and Another v. Syme-Thomson and Another* [1979] 1 W.L.R. 440 Templeman J., following *Caunce v. Caunce and Others; Lloyds Bank Ltd v. Caunce and another* [1969] 1 W.L.R. 286 (a case on unregistered land), held that the spouse of a sole legal owner was not in actual occupation of the matrimonial home within s.70(1)(g). At 444E he said:

> "It seems to me that when husband and wife are in occupation of premises and the legal title is in one of them, actual occupation for the purposes of section 70 belongs to that one and the other is not in actual occupation but only there as a shadow of occupation of the owner."

Although both those decisions were effectively disapproved so far as spouses are concerned in *Williams & Glyn's Bank v. Boland* [1981] A.C. 487, I regard it as axiomatic that minor children of the legal owner are not in actual occupation within s.70(1)(g). That seems to have been assumed without discussion by Templeman J. in *Bird v Syme-Thomson* in a sentence immediately preceding the passage I have read. The minor children are there because their parent is there. They have no right of occupation of their own. As Templeman J. put it, they are only there as shadows of occupation of their parent. Moreover, as Mr Marks submits, it cannot have been intended that s.70(1)(g) should operate as the second defendant suggests. No inquiry can be made of minor children or consent obtained from them in the manner contemplated by that provision, especially when they are, as here, of tender years at the material date. If the second defendant was right, lenders would never be protected. Their security could always be frustrated by simple devices.

4. Baughen [1991] Conv. 116 suggests that, although actual occupation protects all the qualifying rights of the occupier, the actual occupation must be referable to a proprietary right. He thus suggests that the finding in *Abbey National Building Society v. Cann*, that the equitable owner was not in actual occupation, could be explained on the ground that any occupation prior to completion was enjoyed as a licensee of the vendor and not pursuant to any interest based on her contribution to the purchase price.

5. Hayton, *Registered Land* (3rd ed., 1981), p. 87, identifies two views of actual occupation. According to the "absolutist" view, actual occupation is a question of pure fact and a purchaser may be bound by the rights of a person in actual occupation even though the purchaser could not discover the occupation and/or the rights. However, this view, which reflects the evidence of Brickdale, the then Registrar, to the Royal Commission on the Land

Transfer Acts, and which was adopted by Lord Wilberforce and Lord Scarman in *Williams & Glyn's Bank Ltd v. Boland*, has not been consistently adopted. In some cases, in particular those discussed above involving marginal physical occupation, the courts have adopted a "constitutionalist" view of actual occupation, according to which the purchaser is bound only where there is an element of discoverability in the actual occupation/interest of the occupier; such a view has undertones of the doctrine of constructive notice. It is not really surprising that there are these different views. The traditional judicial explanation of section 70(1)(g) is that it is "a statutory application to registered land of the well-known rule protecting the rights of persons in actual occupation": *National Provincial Bank Ltd v. Ainsworth* [1965] A.C. 1175, 1259 *per* Lord Wilberforce; see also *Woolwich Equitable Building Society v. Marshall* [1952] 1 Ch. 1, 9 *per* Danckwerts J.; *Mornington Permanent Building Society v. Kenway* [1953] Ch. 382, 386 *per* Vaisey J.; *Grace Rymer Investments Ltd v. Waite* [1958] Ch. 831, 849 *per* Lord Evershed M.R.; *National Provincial Bank Ltd v. Hastings Car Mart Ltd* [1964] Ch. 665, 689 *per* Lord Denning M.R.; *Williams & Glyn's Bank Ltd v. Boland* [1979] Ch. 312, 335 *per* Ormrod L.J.; *City of London Building Society v. Flegg* [1988] A.C. 54, 80 *per* Lord Oliver; *Lloyds Bank plc v. Rosset* [1989] Ch. 350, 372 *per* Nicholls L.J., 394–397 *per* Mustill L.J., 403 *per* Purchas L.J.; *Abbey National Building Society v. Cann* [1991] 1 A.C. 56, 87–88 *per* Lord Oliver. This is a reference to the rule in *Hunt v. Luck* [1902] 1 Ch. 428, according to which a purchaser of unregistered land had constructive notice of any interest of an occupier that might be discovered by making reasonable enquiry of that occupier. There are difficulties in equating section 70(1)(g) with the rule in *Hunt v. Luck*, in particular its very association with the doctrine of constructive notice: see Law Com. No. 158, *Property Law: Third Report on Land Registration* (1987), para. 2.61. Sparkes [1989] Conv. 342 notes that the rule in *Hunt v. Luck* "has come to symbolise different levels of the doctrine of constructive notice. At one level it is simply a synonym for the general doctrine". He asserts that section 70(1)(g) was intended to incorporate in the registered land system the rule that occupation gives notice to a purchaser of the occupier's rights so that the purchaser is bound by those rights; but that it was not intended to incorporate the general duty of inquiry, that is, the duty to make all those inquiries that a prudent purchaser would make in the circumstances.

There is now considerable support both in principle and as a matter of policy for rejecting the absolutist view of section 70(1)(g): see *Lloyds Bank plc v. Rosset, infra*; see also *Abbey National Building Society v. Cann, supra*, 88 *per* Lord Oliver.

Lloyds Bank plc v. Rosset [1989] Ch. 350

(CA, Nicholls, Mustill and Purchas L.JJ.)

The defendants were husband and wife. In 1982 they decided to purchase and renovate a semi-derelict farmhouse. The purchase was to be funded by money from the husband's family trust, on the condition that the husband was the sole registered proprietor. However, the defendants intended that the renovation should be a joint project and that the farmhouse should be the family home. Even before contracts were exchanged, the vendors permitted builders employed by the defendants to start work on the property; and for six weeks prior to the transfer, during November and December, the builders and the wife were working on the property. On 17 December completion of the purchase took place and, without the knowledge of the wife, the husband charged the property in favour of the plaintiff bank to secure a short-term loan. The transfer and the charge were duly registered on 3 February 1983. Following matrimonial difficulties, the husband defaulted on the repayment of the loan. When the plaintiff bank sought possession of the property, the wife claimed that she had an overriding interest under section 70(1)(g) which took priority over the plaintiffs' charge.

The Court of Appeal held that the wife was entitled to a beneficial interest in the property: but see note 3, *infra*; and that it was necessary for her to establish that she was in actual occupation at the date of completion of the purchase: see *infra*, p. 218. The question therefore was whether the wife was "in actual occupation" at that date.

MUSTILL L.J.:

Accordingly, I must now turn to the question whether the judge was right to hold that on 17 December 1982 the wife was not in "actual occupation" of Vincent Farmhouse within the meaning of section 70(1)(g) of the Land Registration Act 1925. This expression is nowhere defined and its meaning must therefore be ascertained by considering the ordinary meaning of the words, if in fact they have one; the context in which they are used; and the judicial history of this aspect of land law.

As to the word "occupation" all are agreed that no conclusive guidance can be obtained from reported cases in other branches of the law, since it has different meanings in different contexts. The addition of the epithet "actual" does, however, provide a clue. It must have been included for a purpose. That purpose must, as it seems to me, have been to distinguish the person who is in fact there, occupying the property, from someone who is not in fact occupying it, but who stands in such a relation to the property that for the purpose of exercising certain rights or being subjected to certain duties, he is treated in law as if he were the occupier.

The context in which the words appear also yields some guidance. In the first place, the miscellaneous interests listed in section 70(1) of the Act of 1925 have this in common, that they are all interests which bind persons with a legal interest in land, even though they are not entered in the register, and even if the proprietor is a bona fide purchaser without notice. (I omit for the moment the special situation contemplated by the concluding words of section 70(1)(g).) These rights can bear harshly on the purchaser, if they are given too wide a scope, and the words under consideration must be construed on the assumption that, when Parliament decided in 1925 to add paragraph (g) to the list of overriding interests in registered land already created by the Land Transfer Act 1875 (38 & 39 Vict. c. 87) and the amending Land Transfer Act 1897 (60 & 61 Vict. c. 65), it intended to produce a result which did reasonable justice to the bona fide purchaser.

Second, the reference to "every person" in paragraph (g) of section 70(1) shows that the notion of actual occupation is wide enough to embrace a situation where more than one person is in occupation at the same time.

Third, the inclusion in the list of overriding interests of a specific reference to a person in receipt of the rents and profits of the land, an amendment which brought about a change in the law, see *post*, demonstrates that the occupation of land pursuant to a contract by one person does not by itself suffice to put the other party in actual occupation.

Fourth, the concept of actual occupation as an ingredient in an overriding interest seems, to my mind at least, to involve some notion of continuity. The interest can hardly override the legal estate intermittently, according to momentary changes in the proprietor's degree of actual physical connection with the land.

Fifth, paragraph (g) cannot be read as if Parliament had simply enacted the section with some other formula, such as "in residence at" in place of "in actual occupation of:" for the paragraph applies to all types of land, and the acts which constitute actual occupation of a dwelling house, a garage or woodland cannot all be the same.

Finally, although the paragraph does not actually say that the acts constituting actual occupation must be such that a purchaser who went to the land and investigated would discover the fact of occupation and thereby be put on inquiry, the closing words of the paragraph are at least a hint that this is what Parliament principally had in mind.

Note may also be taken of section 14 of the Law of Property Act 1925, which preserves the interest of "any person in possession or in actual occupation" of land to which he may be entitled in right of such possession or occupation. It is legitimate to assume that, when the list of overriding interests was extended by the other Act of 1925, the Land Registration Act, actual occupation was not intended to be synonymous with the kind of constructive occupation denoted by the concept of possession.

These fragments of guidance must be set against the judicial history of the legislation. As Lord Wilberforce observed in *Williams & Glyn's Bank Ltd v. Boland* [1981] A.C. 487, the word "actual" in conjunction with "possession" appears in the judgment of Lord Loughborough in *Taylor v. Stibbert* (1794) 2 Ves. Jun. 437, 439–440, one of the earliest in a line of cases which determined that notice of the presence of a person on the land is notice of his interests, but not of the interests of another person from whom that occupation is derived: so that, in particular, notice of the presence of a tenant on the land is not notice of the landlord's rights. These cases were rehearsed in *Barnhart v. Greenshields* (1853) 9 Moo. P.C. 18, where the appellant's land was managed for him by his father, who for a time put in tenants and received rents, and then went into occupation himself. It was held that a mortgagee who acquired his interest at a time when a tenant was on the land did so free of the appellant's rights. Delivering the judgment of the Board, Mr Pemberton Leigh, afterwards Lord Kingsdown, said, at pp. 32–33:

> "With respect to the effect of possession merely, we take the law to be that if there be a tenant in possession of land, a purchaser is bound by all the equities which the tenant could enforce against the vendor ... the principle being ... that the possession of the tenant is notice that he has some interest in the land, and that a purchaser having notice of that fact is bound, according to the ordinary rule, either to inquire what that interest is, or to give effect to it, whatever it may be."

There was then citation of the line of cases of which *Taylor v. Stibbert* (1794) 2 Ves. Jun. 437 formed part, and the judgment continued, at p. 34:

> "In all the cases to which we have referred, it will be observed that the possession relied on was the actual occupation of the land; and that the equity sought to be enforced was on behalf of the party so in possession."

Then, in the course of a discussion of the facts, Mr Pemberton Leigh said, at pp. 35–36.

> "There is not the least pretence for saying that the appellant was ever in the actual possession of the land.... It is sufficient to say that in any view of the case there was no possession of the land which could in any manner affect the respondent with notice of the appellant's title."

Next, there was *Hunt v. Luck* [1901] 1 Ch. 45. The contest was between the personal representatives of a Dr Hunt and the mortgagees of a group of houses let on weekly tenancies. The rents of these houses had for a substantial time been collected by an agent named Woodrow and remitted by them to Dr Hunt. A document subsequently came to light purporting to be a conveyance of the properties for value by Hunt to one Gilbert, who subsequently raised a loan using a deposit of the title deeds as security. The case is not easy to follow, because the prime issue of fact at the trial was whether the conveyance was invalid, as being either a forgery or procured dishonestly by Gilbert at a time when Dr Hunt was incapable. The judge found that fraud and incapacity were not established, and one might have thought this to be the end of the case. There was, however, argument both before Farwell J. and the Court of Appeal [1902] 1 Ch. 428 on the question whether the mortgagees had constructive notice of the alleged defects in Gilbert's title, because they knew that the tenants were paying their rents to Woodrow, a stranger to the paper title. The argument for the personal representatives was to the following effect [1901] 1 Ch. 45, 47:

> "it is clear that a purchaser has constructive notice of the rights of the tenant: *Holmes v. Powell* (1856) 8 De G.M. & G. 572; and this rule is not limited to the terre-tenant, who is in the actual occupation, but it extends also to the person who is known to receive the rents from the occupier of the land."

At first instance, Farwell J. rejected this contention, holding that a tenant's occupation is notice of all that tenant's rights, but not of his lessor's tenants or rights. This view was endorsed by Vaughan Williams L.J. [1902] 1 Ch. 428, delivering the leading judgment in the Court of Appeal, and was explained as meaning, at p. 433:

> "if a purchaser or a mortgagee has notice that the vendor or mortgagor is not in possession of the property, he must make inquiries of the person in possession—of the tenant who is in possession—and find out from him what his rights are, and, if he does not choose to do that, then whatever title he acquiries as purchaser or mortgagee will be subject to the title or right of the tenant in possession."

Vaughan Williams L.J. continued, at p. 434:

> "I do not think that there is, for the purpose of ascertaining the title of the vendor, any obligation on the purchaser to make inquiries of the tenant in reference to anything but protection against the rights of the tenant."

These decisions formed the background to the addition by the Land Registration Act 1925 of paragraph (g) to the existing list of overriding interests. A person coming to the legislation without the benefit of subsequent authority might, I believe, have been justified in arriving at the following tentative conclusions. (1) The reversal of the previous law brought about by the addition of the lessor's rights to the list of overriding interests shows that the question is no longer one of a reasonable opportunity to make inquiry, as it had been under *Hunt v. Luck* [1902] 1 Ch. 428. (2) Equally, the fact that the overriding character of the occupier's rights is taken away only if the purchaser actually makes fruitless inquiry of the occupier, and not where he does not even try to inquire, shows that we are no longer in the realm of constructive notice. (3) At the same time, the reference to the person in receipt of rents shows, as previously suggested, that the physical presence of one person on the land pursuant to a contract with another does not give the latter's rights an overriding character, for otherwise the reference would be unnecessary. (4) The choice of the expression "actual occupation," appearing as it had done in the earlier cases, was not accidental, and this consideration, taken together with the retention of a reference to inquiry, which would be meaningless if actual occupier embraced those whose existence it would be impractical to detect, and in respect of whom attempts at inquiry would be fruitless, supports the view that, even if constructive notice no longer applies in this field, the old law still gives a flavour to the new words of the section, section 70(1). (5) If the words are not given this flavour, there will be a marked, and it may be said unacceptable, contrast with the workmanlike solution arrived at for unregistered land in cases such as *Caunce v. Caunce* [1969] 1 W.L.R. 286. (On this aspect, see the discussion by Mr Ian Leeming in *The Conveyancer and Property Lawyer* (1971), vol. 35 (N.S.), p. 255, and also the brief comments in *Brickdale & Stewart-Wallace's Land Registration Act 1925*, 4th ed. (1939), p. 193.) (6) For want of a better synonym, the person in occupation could be identified as the person who is "there" on the property: although what this entails will be dependent on the nature of the property, and the circumstances of the individual case.

NOTES:

1. Purchas L.J. was rather clearer in his assimilation of section 70(1)(g) with constructive notice. He stated (at 403–404):

The provisions of [section 70(1)(g)] clearly were intended to import into the law relating to registered land the equitable doctrine of constructive notice ... In order for the wife's interest in the property to qualify as an overriding interest under section 70(1)(g) two things must be established: (a) was she in actual occupation? and (b) would appropriate inquiries made by the bank have elicited the fact of her interest?

2. Nicholls L.J. (at 378–379) and Purchas L.J. (at 404–406) held that the wife was in actual occupation, both in her own right and through the agency of the builders; and that reasonable inquiries by the bank would have revealed her interest. Mustill L.J. (at 397–399), dissenting, held that the presence of the wife and that of the builders did not constitute sufficient continuity of presence to mean that the wife was "there" on the property; their presence indicated no more than that the wife was preparing the property for occupation. However, since Mustill L.J. agreed that actual occupation of a semi-derelict house is possible, it is not clear what more would have been required.

3. The meaning of actual occupation was not discussed in the House of Lords since it was held that the wife did not have a beneficial interest in the property: see *ante*, p. 71.

4. In *Abbey National Building Society v. Cann* [1989] 2 F.L.R. 265 the defendant based her claim to have been in actual occupation on a period of 35 minutes, during which time carpet layers started laying carpets and her son started unloading her furniture and personal belongings. Ralph Gibson L.J. stated (at 278):

The concept of "the rights of every person in actual occupation of the land, or in receipt of the rents and profits thereof, save where inquiry is made of such person and the rights are not disclosed", contained in s.70(1)(g), is, as I understand it, based upon the notion that the purchaser could if he made proper inquiries and/or inspection of the property, discover the presence of a person in actual occupation or indications of that occupation which would at least put him on inquiry: see the passage in the judgment of Nicholls L.J. in *Rosset*. Where, as in this case, the only occupation of Mrs Cann was what appears to have been in the normal course of taking possession on completion it is difficult to see how the plaintiffs, acting reasonably and as they might be expected to act, could have detected the presence of Mrs Cann as an occupier who might have rights to which the plaintiff's legal estate would be subject.

In *Rosset* the wife and husband had been in occupation of the property for some weeks before completion of the mortgage. .... *Rosset* establishes that the time at which "actual occupation of the land" is required for the purposes of s.70(1)(*g*) is at completion. It seems to me that there is both good sense and fairness in the view expressed by Judge Thomas that the acts done on 13 August 1984—at least so far as concerns any acts which had in probability been done by the time of completion at 12.20 p.m.—did not amount to actual occupation at completion by Mrs Cann for the purposes of s.70(1)(*g*). If the plaintiff had had a competent observer present to inspect the house before completion and to watch the process of completion so far as it took place at the premises, with knowledge of the expected working of completion by post in the circumstances of this case, he would have supposed, I think, that there was in progress the departure of Mr Watson and the arrival to take up occupation of the purchaser pursuant to and by reason of that completion. Such an observer would not, I think, have supposed that there was "actual occupation" by the owner of such of the carpets and furniture as had been moved into the house prior to completion. ....

5. The argument in favour of the constitutionalist approach, in particular in cases involving marginal physical occupation, is well-stated in *Kling v. Keston Properties Ltd* (1983) 49 P. & C.R. 212, where Vinelott J., assuming the absolutist approach to be required, stated (at 222):

It is quite clear that there can be cases where a purchaser may make the most searching inquiries without discovering that the land in question is in the actual occupation of a third party. It is disquieting that the system of land registration which is being steadily extended should be so framed that a person acquiring an interest in registered land may find his interest subject to an option or right of pre-emption which has not been registered and notwithstanding that there is no person other than the vendor in apparent occupation of the property and that careful inspection and inquiry has failed to reveal anything which might give the purchaser any reason to suspect that someone other than the vendor had any interest in or rights over the property.

See also the argument of Ungoed-Thomas J. in *Hodgson v. Marks* [1971] Ch. 892, 913–917.

6. Sparkes [1989] Conv. 342 argues that the assertion of the "absolutist" view in *Williams & Glyn's Bank Ltd v. Boland* has been overstated and that "discoverability" (and hence the "constitutionalist" view) is an inherent assumption in the formulation and application of section 70(1)(g). For critical comment on the language of "discoverability" and its association with constructive notice as a *generally applicable* element of the concept of actual occupation, see Thompson [1988] Conv. 453; Smith (1988) 104 L.Q.R. 507, (1990) 106 L.Q.R. 32.

7. Tee [1998] C.L.J. 328 argues that section 70(1)(g) should be amended to require actual *and apparent* occupation.

8. In 1987 the Law Commission considered and rejected the requirement of actual *and apparent* occupation on the ground that it would introduce the doctrine of notice into land registration: Law Com. No. 158, *Property Law: Third Report on Land Registration* (1987), paras 2.60–2.62. In its latest report the Law Commission endorses the view that the doctrine of notice should have no part in the land registration system but disagrees that a requirement of apparent occupation would have that effect. It is argued that the principles, well known to conveyancers, behind the dichotomy of latent and patent defects in title provide a potential solution. In the context of

section 70(1)(g) the test would be whether the right is apparent on a reasonable inspection of the land, not whether the right would have been discovered if the purchaser had made all the inquiries that ought reasonably to have been made. The Law Commission has therefore provisionally recommended that persons would be in actual occupation of land only if they were physically present on the land and their occupation was patent, that is, apparent on a reasonable inspection of the land: Law Com. No. 254, *Land Registration for the Twenty-First Century* (1998), paras 5.71–5.73.

1.4.2.2 *Occupation of part*   In most cases the person claiming an overriding interest under section 70(1)(g) has been in occupation of the whole of the land over which the interest is claimed. However, the claimant may be in occupation of only part of the land over which the interest is claimed. In such circumstances, the question arises as to whether actual occupation of part is sufficient to generate an overriding interest over the whole. That question was addressed briefly in *Ashburn Anstalt v. Arnold* [1989] Ch. 1, where the Court of Appeal expressed the view that the overriding interest extended only to the land actually occupied by the claimant. The question was considered more fully in *Ferrishurst Ltd v. Wallcite Ltd* [1999] 2 W.L.R. 667. The claimants occupied some offices under a sub-underlease. The sub-underlease contained an option to purchase the underlease, which also included a garage occupied by a third party under a separate sub-underlease. The option had not been protected on the register but the claimants argued that it was enforceable as an overriding interest under section 70(1)(g). The Court of Appeal held that the claimants were entitled to exercise the option in respect of the entire property comprised in the underlease. Robert Walker L.J. stated (at 681–682):

It is necessary to see what principles as to the meaning and effect of the Act emerge from *Boland* [1981] A.C. 487 and authorities approved in *Boland*. If, contrary, it seems, to the view of the Law Commission, the application of those principles leads to unacceptable anomalies in practice, that would be a matter for Parliament no doubt after further consideration by the Law Commission.

  Having already discussed the authorities at length I will set out quite shortly the principles which can in my view be extracted from them.

  (1) The function of overriding interests in registered conveyancing is comparable to that of notice (actual, constructive or imputed) in unregistered conveyancing, but there are significant differences and the burden on a purchaser to make enquiries is now heavier than before.

  (2) The rights of an occupier of registered land are to be distinguished from the fact of his occupation. The capacity in which a person occupies, for instance as a tenant, need not be indicative of the right which he claims, for instance an option to purchase the freehold reversion or an unpaid vendor's lien.

  (3) The occupier need not, in order to rely on section 70(1)(g), be in actual occupation of the whole of the land comprised in a registered disposition, whether that disposition is from the registered proprietor's point of view a transfer of the whole, or a transfer of part, or a demise or other disposition taking effect in relation to the whole or part.

  Having anxiously read and reread the penultimate paragraph of the main judgment in *Ashburn* [1989] Ch. 1, 28E-G, I feel satisfied that had the court been referred to the

House of Lords authority which now establishes those points, it would not have decided the case as it did. Instead it would have put together the three points set out above and extracted a fourth point as a conclusion, that a person in actual occupation of a part of the land comprised in a registered disposition can enforce against the new registered proprietor any overriding interest which he has either in the land, or part of the land, occupied by him or in the remainder, or part of the remainder, of the land comprised in the registered disposition in question.

For comment, see [1999] Conv. 144.

In 1987 the Law Commission had recommended that legislation should make explicit the view expressed in *Hodgson v. Marks* [1971] Ch. 892, 916 *per* Ungoed-Thomas J., 931 *per* Russell L.J., that "the rights of every person in actual occupation of the land" included the case where the person was in occupation of *part* of the land to which his rights related: Law Com. No. 158, *Property Law: Third Report on Land Registration* (1987), para. 2.55. In its subsequent report, the Law Commission has provisionally recommended that where a person is in occupation of part only of the property in or over which he has rights, his rights should be an overriding interest within section 70(1)(g) *but only as regards the part of the land which he occupies*: Law Com. No. 254, *Land Registration for the Twenty-First Century* (1998), para. 5.70.

1.4.2.3 *The relevant time for actual occupation*   Very much linked with the meaning of actual occupation is the question as to the time at which actual occupation is required if the rights of the occupier are to bind a purchaser as overriding interests under section 70(1)(g). The orthodox view, based on a dictum of Wilberforce J. in *Re Boyle's Claim* [1961] 1 W.L.R. 339, 344, was that a purchaser would be bound by an overriding interest within section 70(1)(g) if the claimant was in actual occupation at the (deemed) date of registration of the transaction; see also *E.S. Schwab & Co. Ltd v. McCarthy* (1976) 31 P. & C.R. 196, 204 *per* Oliver J. Acceptance of the orthodox view created the "registration gap", which caused potential problems for mortgagees. For, even if the mortgagee inspected the property before the mortgage was executed and the money was advanced, the mortgage might still be subject to the rights of persons who entered into occupation after execution of the mortgage but before the (deemed) date of registration. The problem was considered by the Law Commission in the context of its consideration of the implications of *Williams & Glyn's Bank v. Boland*; but no change was recommended, since it was of the view that the perceived problems would be effectively met by the recommended registration requirement (see *supra*, p. 196: Law Com. No. 115 *Property Law: The Implications of Williams & Glyn's Bank v. Boland* (1982), Appendix 2, paras 4–12. (The Law Commission subsequently recommended that the relevant date for determining the existence of all overriding interests should be the date of the relevant transaction: Law Com. No. 158, *Property Law: Third Report on Land Registration* (1987), paras 2.76–2.77; but that recommendation has now itself been superseded: see *infra*, p. 219.) The orthodox view was questioned in *Paddington Building Society v. Mendelsohn* (1985) 50 P. & C.R. 244, 247 *per* Browne-Wilkinson L.J.; and the Court of Appeal in *Lloyds Bank plc v. Rossett* decided that, although all overriding interests crystallise at the date of registration of a transaction, a purchaser would not be bound by an overriding interest within section 70(1)(g) unless the claimant was in actual occupation at the date of completion of the transaction. The latter view has now been affirmed by the House of Lords in *Abbey National Building Society v. Cann.*

Abbey National Building Society v. Cann [1991] 1 A.C. 56

(HL, Lord Bridge, Lord Griffiths, Lord Ackner, Lord Oliver, Lord Jauncey)

In May 1984 the first defendant applied to the plaintiff building society for a loan of £25,000 to be secured by a mortgage of a leasehold property which he proposed to purchase. He was to be the sole registered proprietor and he stated that the property was for his sole occupation, although he intended that it should be occupied by his mother and her future husband, the second and third defendants. The purchase was financed by £4,000 of the loan and by the proceeds of sale of another property occupied by the second defendant: and it was accepted that she had an equitable interest in the property. Completion of the purchase and of the charge took place on 13 August when the second defendant was abroad. However, some 35 minutes prior to the actual time of completion, with the consent of the vendor, carpet-layers went into the house and started laying carpets; and the first and third defendants started unloading the furniture and personal belongings of the second defendant. The second defendant moved into the property before the transfer and charge were registered at the Land Registry.

LORD OLIVER:
First in logical order is the question of the appropriate date for ascertaining the existence of overriding interests under the Land Registration Acts. Curiously enough the point appears never to have arisen directly for decision in any reported case prior to *Rosset*, save in one case in 1985 in the Bristol County Court which was decided on appeal on a different point (*Paddington Building Society v. Mendelsohn* (1985) 50 P. & C.R. 244). In *In re Boyle's Claim* [1961] 1 W.L.R. 339, 344, Wilberforce J. expressed the view that the relevant date was the date of acquisition of the registered title, but the issue in that case was quite a different one and the point does not appear to have been argued. That case has, however, been used as the basis for statements in a number of leading conveyancing textbooks that that is the date at which occupation for the purposes of section 70(1)(g) has to be ascertained: see, *e.g., Wolstenholme and Cherry's Conveyancing Statutes*, 13th ed., (1972), vol. 6, p. 65; *Emmet on Title*, 19th ed., (1986), para. 5. 197). The question arose directly in *Rosset* in which the Court of Appeal [1989] Ch. 350 decided unanimously that the relevant date was the date of completion of the purchase and not that of registration. Your Lordships are now invited to overrule that decision.

My Lords, the conclusion at which the Court of Appeal arrived makes good conveyancing sense and, speaking for myself, I should be extremely reluctant to overrule it unless compulsively driven to do so, the more so because it produces a result which is just, convenient and certain, as opposed to one which is capable of leading to manifest injustice and absurdity. It has, I think, to be acknowledged that the interrelation between the provisions of sections 3(xvi), 20 and 23, 37, 69 and 70(1) is not altogether easy to understand, particularly in relation to the position of a chargee whose charge is created by a purchaser of land who is not yet himself the registered proprietor. The solution propounded by the trial judge and by counsel for the bank in *Rosset* depends upon the words "affecting the estate transferred or created" in section 20(1)(b) and 23(1)(c) and construes them as if there were added the words "at the time at which it was transferred or created," thus excluding from the category of interests affecting the estate the rights of a person entering into occupation after the transfer or creation of the estate effected by completion of the transaction. It will be convenient to refer to this as "the judge's construction."

This is an attractive solution because it is, as Nicholls L.J. observed in the course of his judgment in *Rosset*, at p. 373, a conveyancing absurdity that, for instance, a mortgagee should, after completion and after having made all possible inquiries and parted with his money, be bound by the interest asserted by a newly-arrived occupant coming in between completion and the registration of his charge. So far as registered interests are concerned the chargee can protect himself by an official search which will preserve his priority over any further registered entries during a priority period well sufficient to enable him to have his charge stamped and lodged for registration: see rules 3 and 5 of the Land Registration (Official Searches) Rules 1981 (S.I. 1981 No. 1135). There is, however, no similar protection against overriding interests which are not recorded on the register and whose existence can be ascertained only by inquiry and there is, accordingly, good sense in so construing sections 20(1) and 23(1) as to preserve the priority of the purchaser or chargee as from the date of completion when both are irrevocably committed to the transaction, which only awaits the formal step of registration in order to vest the legal estate.

In *Rosset*, however, the Court of Appeal found some difficulty in accepting that the solution could be found simply in construing sections 20(1) and 23(1) in the manner suggested. Nicholls L.J. pointed out, at p. 371, that it was common ground that paragraph (a) of section 20(1) (paragraph (b) of section 23(1)), which subjects the land transferred to entries appearing on the register, undoubtedly refers to entries so appearing at the date of registration. This appears to me to be beyond doubt. One would, therefore, expect that the paragraph subjecting the land to overriding interests would be related to the same date. Nicholls L.J. reached, in relation to overriding interests within section 70(1)(g), the same result as that produced by the judge's construction but by reference to the words "for the time being subsisting" in section 70(1) and by holding that, in relation to paragraph (g) specifically, an interest was not a subsisting interest except in a case in which the claimant was in occupation of the land prior to and at the date of completion of the purchase.

I share the difficulty that Nicholls L.J. felt in accepting the attractive solution of the judge's construction and I agree with him that the key to the problem lies in the words of section 70(1) rather than in the reference to the interests affecting the estate transferred or created in sections 20(1) and 23(1). The Act of 1925 displays a degree of circularity in its general definition of what an overriding interest is. Section 3(xvi) defines it as an unregistered encumbrance "subject to which registered dispositions take effect," but when one turns to inquire to what unregistered encumbrances a disposition is subject, sections 20(1) and 23(1) merely specify that they are "overriding interests, if any, affecting the estate transferred or created". As a definition, therefore, this is a little less than satisfactory, for it simply means "overriding interests" are "overriding interests." It does, however, involve this consequence, that if the judge's construction is correct, no interest which does not affect the estate or interest at the time when a relevant disposition is effected by transfer, grant or charge can be an overriding interest. That, of course, does not demonstrate that the judge's construction is erroneous, but it might be thought to be a surprising result when consideration is given to the remaining words in sections 20 and 23 and to the terms of sections 69 and 70.

I turn to those sections, because the circularity of the definition so far compels a reference to other provisions of the Act of 1925 in order to ascertain the nature of the interests which are to override. They are, to begin with, not "minor interests" (section

3(xv)), that is to say, interests not capable of being disposed of or created by registered dispositions and interests created by unregistered dealings and subsisting only in equity. Unless protected by notice, caution, inhibition or restriction entered on the register, these will be overriden by registered dispositions for valuable consideration. Specifying what overriding interests are not does not, however, assist in determining what they are and, moreover, it is clear from *Williams & Glyn's Bank Ltd v. Boland* [1981] A.C. 487 that a minor interest may become an overriding interest if the claimant is in actual occupation. Section 69 is of some assistance in that it demonstrates that the list of miscellaneous overriding interests contained in section 70(1) is not exhaustive, since the legal estate is vested in the registered proprietor under this section subject to

> "the overriding interests ... including any ... charge by way of legal mortgage created ... under ... this Act or otherwise which has priority to the registered estate:" subsection (1)."

Section 70(1) contains no reference to a mortgage or charge as an overriding interest, but section 69(1) necessarily implies that it is one so long as it has priority to the registered estate.

When regard is had to the list of overriding interests in section 70(1) it is apparent that all of them are interests which can come into being at any time, and some of them may arise without any volition on the part of the registered proprietor or anyone else seized of an estate in the land. A right of way or a profit à prendre may be acquired by a neighbouring landowner by prescription. A third party may acquire title to the land by adverse possession. A local land charge may be imposed on the land at any time under a variety of different statutes. A lease at a rent for a term not exceeding 21 years may be granted at any time. Yet on the judge's construction, a purchaser would, on registration, take free from any such interests arising after completion of his purchase (in the sense of payment of the price against delivery of the executed transfer) even though, if the land were unregistered land, he would clearly be subjected to them. This necessarily follows, if the judge's construction is right, from the words which immediately follow paragraph (b) of section 20(1) (paragraph (c) of section 23(1))—"but free from all other estates and interests whatsoever ..." It also involves, I think, a conflict between sections 20(1) and 23(1) on the one hand, and sections 69(1) and 70(1) on the other. Section 69, as it seems to me, is looking at the continuous position of the registered proprietor and providing that the legal estate is deemed to be vested in him subject to such overriding interests as shall from time to time subsist during his proprietorship, whereas, if the judge's construction is correct, it is indeed subject to all such interests but with the exception of those which come into being between the date when he took his transfer and the date when he became registered. Moreover it would also follow that the effect of registration of the transferee would be to free him even from overriding interests which he himself had created in the interval between completion and registration.

That cannot, I think, have been the intention of the legislature. ...

I conclude, therefore, like Nicholls L.J., that the relevant date for determining the existence of overriding interests which will "affect the estate transferred or created" is the date of registration. This does, of course, give rise to the theoretical difficulty that since a transferor remains the registered proprietor until registration of the transfer, it would be possible for him, in breach of trust, to create overriding interests, for instance, by grant of an easement or of a lease, which would be binding on the transferee and against which the transferee would not be protected by an official search. That would, of course, equally be the case in a purchase of unregistered land where the purchaser pays the price in advance of receiving a conveyance. I cannot, however, find in the theoretical possibility of so improbable an event a context for preferring the judge's construction.

The question remains, however, whether the date of registration is also the relevant date for determining whether a claimant to a right is in actual occupation. It is to be noted that it is not the actual occupation which gives rise to the right or determines its existence. Actual occupation merely operates as the trigger, as it were, for the treatment of the right, whatever it may be, as an overriding interest. Nor does the additional quality of the right as an overriding interest alter the nature or quality of the right itself. If it is an equitable right it remains an equitable right. As was observed in *Williams & Glyn's Bank Ltd v. Boland* [1981] A.C. 487, 504, the purpose of section 70(1)(g) was to make applicable to registered land the same rule for the protection of persons in actual occupation as had been applied in the case of unregistered land in, for instance, *Hunt v. Luck* [1902] 1 Ch. 428. In relation to legal rights it does nothing, for it is not easy to conceive of a legal right in the land which would not already be an overriding interest under some other head, as, for instance, paragraphs (a) or (k). Again, as regards equitable rights in an occupier which arise before completion and are supported by occupation at that date there is no difficulty. A chargee who advances money and so acquires an equitable charge prior to the creation of the occupier's right does not lose his priority because the occupier's right becomes an overriding interest. That interest remains what it always was, an interest subject to the prior equity of the chargee which, on registration, is fortified by the legal estate. Equally, a chargee advancing his money after the creation of the occupier's equitable right is, as one would expect, subject to such right.

The case which does give rise to difficulty if the date of registration is the relevant date for determining whether there is a claimant in actual occupation is one in which the sequence of events is that the right, unaccompanied by occupation, is created before completion and before the chargee has advanced his money and then subsequently the claimant enters into actual occupation after completion and remains in occupation up to the date when the registration of the charge is effected. The chargee in that event would have no possibility of discovering the existence of the claimant's interest before advancing his money and taking his charge, but would nevertheless be subject, on registration, to the claimant's prior equitable interest which, ex hypothesi, would not have been subject to the charge at its creation.

This does indeed produce a conveyancing absurdity and there is, as Nicholls L.J. observed [1989] Ch. 350, 374B—C, an internal context for supposing that the legislature, in enacting paragraph (g), must have been contemplating an occupation which preceded and existed at completion of a transfer or disposition. Not only was the paragraph clearly intended to reflect the rule discussed in *Hunt v. Luck* with regard to unregistered conveyancing, but the reference to inquiry and failure to disclose cannot make any sense unless it is related to a period in which such inquiry could be other than otiose. That absurdity can, I think, be avoided only by the route which the Court of Appeal adopted and by referring the "actual occupation" in paragraph (g) to the date of completion of the transaction by transfer and payment of the purchase money. Section 70(1) refers to such interests "as may be for the time being subsisting" and in order to affect "the estate transferred or created" on registration such interests would no doubt require to be subsisting on that date. But I see no insuperable difficulty in holding that the actual occupation required to support such an interest as a subsisting interest must exist at the date of completion of the transaction giving rise to the right to be registered, for that is the only date at which the inquiry referred to in paragraph (g) could, in practice, be made and be relevant. I agree, therefore, with the conclusion of the Court of Appeal in *Rosset* [1989] Ch. 350 that it is at that moment that it falls to be determined whether there is an actual occupation for the purposes of paragraph (g). I do not think that I can improve upon Nicholls L.J.'s analysis when he said, in the course of his judgment in *Rosset*, at p. 374:

"If this is right, the pieces of the jigsaw fit together reasonably well. A purchaser or mortgagee inspects and inquires before completion, in the established fashion. Or he fails to do so, at his own risk. He then completes the transaction, taking an executed transfer or mortgage. Whether or not an overriding interest under paragraph (g) subsists so far as his freehold or mortgage is concerned falls to be determined at that moment. If an overriding interest does subsist, then his estate when registered takes subject to that interest. If it does not, then subsequent entry of a person into occupation before the transfer or mortgage has been registered, and 'completed' for the purposes of section 19, does not have the consequences of creating an overriding interest under paragraph (g) in relation to that freehold or mortgage."

NOTES:

1. Lord Griffiths, Lord Ackner and Lord Jauncey agreed that the requirement of actual occupation at the date of the transaction in the context of section 70(1)(g) is an exception to the general rule that the relevant date for determining the existence of overriding interests is the date of registration; by contrast Lord Bridge (at 76) considered the date of the transaction as the general rule subject to the exception of the date of registration in the context of section 70(1)(i) (local land charges).

2. It seems to be implicit that the claimant must still be in actual occupation at the date of registration, although only Lord Jauncey (at 104) expressly asserted that requirement.

3. The view of the majority was adopted in *Barclays Bank plc v. Zaroovabli* [1997] Ch. 321, *infra*, p. 232.

4. Smith (1988) 104 L.Q.R. 507, (1990) 106 L.Q.R. 32 argues that the adoption of the date of the transaction as the relevant date for actual occupation involves the downgrading of the role of registration; but that once the date of registration is abandoned it would be more appropriate to require actual occupation at the date of the official search certificate. Provided that the purchaser/mortgagee applies for registration within the priority period, he would be protected against intervening entries of minor interests *and intervening overriding interests*.

5. Once an overriding interest has crystallised on the registration of the disposition, it remains binding on the transferee under that disposition, even if the owner of the interest ceases to be in actual occupation: *London and Cheshire Insurance Co. Ltd v. Laplagrene Property Co. Ltd* [1971] Ch. 499, 505, 509 *per* Brightman J.; and see (1971) 35 Conv. 188.

6. In its most recent report, the Law Commission has provisionally recommended that the decision in *Abbey National Building Society v. Cann* should be codified, so that (i) overriding interests that are in existence at the date of registration would bind any transferee; and (ii) where the overriding interest claimed is the right of an occupier that person would have to be in occupation at the date of the execution of the transfer or disposition of the registered land: Law Com. No. 254, *Land Registration for the Twenty-First Century* (1998), paras 5.112–5.113. The Law Commission takes the view that those rules would achieve a fair balance between the principles of registration and the interests of encumbrancers on the one hand and the need to ensure security for the interests of purchasers and mortgagees on the other hand. In any event, the introduction of electronic conveyancing would eliminate the registration gap.

1.4.3 Williams & Glyn's Bank Ltd v. Boland *and its aftermath*   The decision in *Williams & Glyn's Bank Ltd v. Boland* generated a significant volume of periodical literature: see, on the first instance decisions, Prichard

[1979] C.L.J. 23, Crane [1979] Conv. 72; on the decision of the Court of Appeal, Prichard [1979] C.L.J. 254, Crane [1979] Conv. 377, Smith (1979) 95 L.Q.R. 501, Murphy (1979) 42 M.L.R. 567; and, on the decision of the House of Lords, Prichard [1980] C.L.J. 243, Martin [1980] Conv. 361, Smith (1981) 97 L.Q.R. 12, Freeman (1980) 43 M.L.R. 692.

Much of the initial concern expressed on behalf of purchasers and mortgagees following the decision has proved to be an overreaction. In theory a purchaser or mortgagee of registered land is bound by the interest of any person in actual occupation of the land at the time of the purchase or mortgage. In practice, the decision is unlikely to create significant problems for purchasers, since normally the occupier will acquiesce in the sale or the claims of the occupier will deter the purchaser: but see *Hodgson v. Marks* [1971] Ch. 892; *Chhokar v. Chhokar* [1984] F.L.R. 313. However, the decision seemed to create potentially very significant problems for mortgagees in relation to undocumented contribution-based ownership rights in the mortgaged land, which essentially means the beneficial interest under a trust for sale of an equitable co-owner who is not also a legal owner.

On the one hand, where the interest is known to the mortgagee, he will insist that the mortgage is executed, and a receipt for the mortgage loan is signed, by at least two trustees: in that way the mortgagee will not be concerned with the equitable interests under the trust, which will be overreached. On the other hand, such interests have the potential to bind the mortgagee where the mortgagee has no actual knowledge of them and does not comply with the requirements for overreaching: for the interest may bind the mortgagee as an overriding interest if the equitable owner is in actual occupation of the mortgaged land at the relevant time.

1.4.3.1 *Express consent to postpone overriding interests under section 70(1)(g)* Against that background, a mortgagee would normally seek to secure priority over any (potential) overriding interest under section 70(1)(g) by requiring any (potential) occupier to sign a written consent to the postponement of his interest to that of the mortgagee. The paucity of reported cases in which such express consents have been challenged may provide some evidence of their effectiveness; and, where express consents have been challenged, the courts have generally confirmed their effectiveness: see, *e.g. Gracegrove Estates Ltd v. Boateng* [1997] E.G.C.S. 103. *Woolwich Building Society v. Dickman* [1996] 3 All E.R. 204 provides an exception, albeit of limited application; but the case purports to explain the basis of an effective consent.

Woolwich Building Society v. Dickman [1996] 3 All E.R. 204

(CA, Butler-Sloss, Waite and Morritt L.JJ.)

The respondent, Dickman, owned a leasehold flat with registered title. He granted a tenancy of the flat to his parents-in-law (the Todds), who became protected tenants under the Rent Act 1977. Dickman subsequently mortgaged the property to the appellant building society to secure the repayment of a loan. Although the building society's valuer noted the tenancy, the building society proceeded on the basis that the Todds had no formal legal title but that they might have some other interest in the property. The Todds willingly signed forms in which they agreed that their rights of occupation were postponed to the rights of the building society as mortgagee. When Dickman defaulted on the repayments, the Todds resisted the building society's action for possession of the flat on the ground that their consents were ineffective. In particular, they argued that their protected tenancy could be determined only in accordance with the provisions of the Rent Act 1977. The district judge held that the consents were effective to postpone the rights of the Todds but that decision was reversed on appeal to the county court. The building society appealed.

WAITE L.J.:

The arguments in the appeal

Mr Nurse's argument, on behalf of the appellant society, is that the consents took clear effect according to their tenor, and that a transaction by which a mortgagee is induced to lend money on the security of property subject to a tenancy, by a written agreement on the part of the tenant that his right of occupancy is to be postponed to the rights of the mortgagee under the mortgage, is a clear and unequivocal bargain, supported by writing and consideration, to which the courts will give effect. If it is necessary to go further, and analyse the transaction more widely than the effect stated on the face of the documents themselves, he invokes the principle of estoppel stated by Sir Christopher Slade in *Skipton Building Society v. Clayton* (1993) 66 P. & C.R. 223 at 228–229, as follows:

> "Recent authorities such as *Abbey National Building Society v. Cann* [1991] 1 A.C. 56 and *Bristol and West Building Society v. Henning* [1985] 1 W.L.R. 778 demonstrate that in a case where A, the holder of the legal estate in land, has executed a mortgage of the land in favour of B ... which will have priority to C's interest, then C will be estopped from asserting that his interest has priority to B's charge ..."

Miss Kennedy-McGregor, for the Todds, submits that the proper view of the consents is that they were wholly inapposite for the purpose now relied on by the society. They were issued in the erroneous belief (engendered by the failure of the society's left hand to know what its right hand was doing) that the Todds were mere occupiers; and were incapable of affecting the Todds' rights as tenants.

As regards the issues under the Rent Acts and the consequence of the flat being registered land, Miss Kennedy-McGregor submits that even if (contrary to her first submission) the consents were effective prima facie to postpone interests under a tenancy, they were in fact ineffective because: (i) s.98(1) of the 1977 Act expressly prohibits the making of a possession order, except in specified circumstances (none of which is relied on in this case); and (ii) the leasehold title to the flat is registered under the Land Registration Act 1925, and subject as such to the provisions of s.70(1)(g) of that Act.

Mr Nurse replies that the effect of the consents was to supplant the occupancy rights of the Todds for all purposes, including those of rent control and land registration, with the result that the Todds fall to be treated—vis-à-vis the society—as trespassers, whose occupation is protected neither by the Rent Acts nor by the 1925 Act.

The meaning of the consents

On this issue Mr Nurse's submission, in my judgment, succeeds. The consents were carefully drawn, and clearly relied on by the society as an essential pre-condition to the grant of the mortgage. The fact that they were obtained at a time when the society was labouring under a misapprehension (through error in its own office) as to the precise nature of the Todds' occupation provides no ground, in my judgment, for depriving them of legal effect. Once they are given effect, they cannot sensibly be read as anything other than an express agreement that the Todds' rights of occupation of the flat—whensoever and howsoever derived—are to be subjected to the possessory rights of the society. The district judge was right to regard them as apt to cover rights of occupancy arising under a tenancy as well as occupancy rights derived from a licence or beneficial interest. The judge appears to have taken the view that the consents would not be valid unless their full import was fully explained to the Todds. In the absence of any defence of undue influence, that finding was not, in my judgment, open to him. In ... his judgment ... he refers to extracts from the judgment in the *Skipton* case dealing with the extent to which the occupiers of the mortgaged property in that case were aware of the implications of a mortgage being granted to the mortgagor. If, as that would suggest, he was relying upon a supposed analogy between the facts of this case and those under consideration in the *Skipton* case, he was in my view mistaken. *Skipton* involved an investigation of circumstances in which no express consent had been obtained from the occupiers regarding the subordination of their rights to those of the mortgagee, for the purpose of determining whether any such consent could be inferred; and the passages quoted by the judge were part of the court's reasons for holding that it could not. The present case, by contrast, involves an express consent, and the only issue is its meaning.

The effect of the Rent and Land Registration Acts

Section 98(1) of the 1977 Act contains a prohibition expressed in the most general terms:

"... a court shall not make an order for possession of a dwelling-house which is for the time being let on a protected tenancy ... unless the court considers it reasonable to make such an order and ... [certain specified conditions are satisfied]"

Its statutory predecessor (in identical terms) was considered by this court in *Dudley and District Benefit Building Society v. Emerson* [1949] Ch. 707 in the context of a case where, after the grant of a mortgage explicitly excluding any power of leasing by the mortgagor without the consent of the mortgagee (which had not been obtained) the mortgagor had granted a weekly tenancy of the premises to the second defendant. That tenancy was protected, as between the defendant and the mortgagor, by the Rent Acts. The court held that the prohibition in s.98(1), despite the generality of its language, must be construed as limited to the class of possession claimant with whose rights it was the purpose of the legislation to interfere—that is to say landlords. Note was taken of the definition of "landlord" (in what is now s.152(1) of the 1977 Act) as including "any person from time to time deriving title under the original landlord" and "any person other than the tenant who is ... entitled to possession of the dwelling-house". This definition, it was held, controls the context of the prohibition in s.98(1). So construed, it does not apply to a mortgagee asserting rights of possession against a tenant of the mortgagor whose tenancy is unlawful as against the mortgagee because it was granted without the latter's consent. Evershed M.R. expressed it in this way ([1949] Ch. 707 at 718):

"... the mortgagees, asserting their title paramount, can properly resist the claim of the tenant to protection under [the Rent and Mortgage Restrictions (Amendment) Act 1933] by denying, as they can deny, any contractual right which binds them, or any estate or interest in the land on the part of the tenant which affects the mortgagees' title."

Mr Nurse acknowledges that the circumstances of the present case are different from those under consideration in the *Dudley Building Society* case, in that the tenancy in this case was already in existence at the date of grant of the mortgage and took effect (under the enactments already mentioned) as a sub-demise under the notional term of years conferred by the mortgage on the society. But the effect, he contends, of the consents was to subordinate the tenant rights of the Todds, for all purposes connected with the mortgage, to the possessory rights of the society. Between the Todds and the society it is as though the tenancy had never existed or as though (just as in the *Dudley Building Society* case) it had been granted unlawfully so as not to bind the mortgagee. The effect, in short, of the consents was to place the society in the position of a mortgagee asserting title paramount, in the sense in which that term was used by Evershed M.R.

I cannot accept that submission. It seems to me to be inescapable that the society derives its right to claim possession of the flat from the mortgage (including the demise from Mr Dickman which it notionally incorporated). The society does not, therefore, enjoy the advantage that was available to the mortgagees in the *Dudley Building Society* case of being able (again adopting Evershed M.R.'s terms) to deny any contractual right in the Todds which binds them or any interest in the Todds which affects their title. The reliance which Miss Kennedy-McGregor places upon s.70 of the 1925 Act is well-founded. However effective the consents may otherwise have been to override the rights of the Todds as persons in actual occupation of the flat, they could have no effect upon the mandatory rights they enjoyed under s.70(1)(g) unless a provision to that effect was "expressed on the register". No such provision is there expressed. In that respect I agree entirely with the views of Morritt L.J., whose judgment I have had an opportunity of seeing in draft.

I would dismiss the appeal.

MORRITT L.J.:
...

Two questions arise. First, did the form of consent signed by the Todds extend to their interest as weekly tenants of the flat? Second, if it did, was the court precluded from giving effect to the claim of the building society to possession of the flat by s.98(1) of the Rent Act 1977? The district judge answered the first question in the affirmative and the second in the negative. The country court judge answered the first question in the negative, and in those circumstances the second did not arise.

With respect to the first question, I agree entirely with the analysis and conclusion of Waite L.J. In short it seems to me that the question depends on the construction of the letters of consent. I see no basis on which those letters can be restricted to some only of the rights or interests giving to the holder a right of occupation of the flat. There is nothing in their wording or in the surrounding circumstances to warrant the exclusion of a tenancy. If that were the only question I would allow the appeal. But it is not, for if the Todds are right on the second question, then the court did not have jurisdiction to make an order for possession in favour of the building society except as permitted by s.98(1) of the 1977 Act, the terms of which, as is common ground, were not satisfied.

...

There can be no doubt that, subject only to the consent letters, s.98(1) would apply. The building society would undoubtedly derive title under the original landlord, Mr Dickman, so as to fall within the definition of landlord contained in s. 152(1). Further, the conveyancing machinery applied by s.27(1) of the Land Registration Act 1925 and s.87(1)(b) of the Law of Property Act 1925 would create in the building society a lease of the same duration, less one day, as that vested in Mr Dickman, and interpose it between that of Mr Dickman and the tenancy of the Todds. Thus, the building society would be entitled to the reversion immediately expectant on the Todds' tenancy and the relationship of landlord and tenant would subsist between them so long as the mortgage was neither redeemed nor enforced by sale.

For the building society, it is contended that this relationship never arose, for the letters of consent put the Todds in the position of persons to whom the property is let after the charge is executed. It is suggested that the effect of the letters is to deem the tenancy not to exist at the time of the execution of the charge. This analysis, if correct, supports the contention that the case is not one of trying to contract out of the Rent Acts or an agreement to surrender a protected tenancy at some future date, which are impermissible (see *A.G. Securities v. Vaughan, Antoniades v. Villiers* [1990] 1 A.C. 417 at 458 and *R v. Bloomsbury and Marylebone County Court, ex p. Blackburne* [1985] 2 E.G.L.R. 157), but one where, in accordance with its terms, the Act never applies at all, as in *Dudley and District Benefit Building Society.*

For my part, I am unable to accept the analysis. At all material times before 15 September 1986 the Todds were tenants of Mr Dickman. On 15 September 1986 they did not surrender their tenancy, they did not charge it to the building society as further security for the loan and they did not vacate the flat. The building society never asked them to do any of those things. Thereafter, the building society did not receive the rent or formally recognise the tenancy of the Todds, but it was quite content that they should remain in occupation of the flat and in enjoyment of such rights as entitled them to do so unless and until the building society sought to exercise their rights as mortgagee. From 15 September 1986 to 12 July 1993, when these proceedings were commenced, the Todds remained in occupation of the flat with the knowledge and consent of the building society.

In this case we are not concerned with how an estoppel of the nature for which the building society contends works in the case of unregistered land so as to alter the priorities between the tenants and the mortgagee. This case concerns registered land and overriding interests within s.70(1) of the Land Registration Act 1925. That section provides, so far as relevant:

"(1) All registered land shall, unless under the provisions of this Act the contrary is expressed on the register, be deemed to be subject to such of the following overriding interests as may be for the time being subsisting in reference thereto, and such interests shall not be treated as incumbrances within the meaning of this Act, (that is to say) ... (g) The rights of every person in actual occupation of the land or in receipt of the rents and profits thereof, save where enquiry is made of such person and the rights are not disclosed ... (k) Leases granted for a term not exceeding twenty-one years ..."

Nothing to "the contrary [was] expressed on the register" in relation to the letters of consent, so as to exclude the deeming effect of that section. In my view it must follow that whatever the result of the letters as between the building society and the Todds as persons, they had no effect on the property or charges register in the Land Registry so as to preclude the Todds' tenancy being an overriding interest. Accordingly, the property was subject to that overriding interest at the time of the charge and was an interest subject to which the charge was granted and took effect, for no estoppel between the building society and the Todds could exclude the effect of s.70(1).

In the case of registered land other than a dwelling house subject to a protected or statutory tenancy it will not matter whether the effect of the estoppel is to remove an overriding interest or merely to set up a bar as between the parties to the estoppel so as to prevent the one relying on that interest as against the other. But in the case of a dwelling house let on a protected or statutory tenancy it does.

In my view, the Todds' tenancy remained an overriding interest notwithstanding the letters of consent. Thus, the charge to the building society took effect subject to it. It follows that the relationship of landlord and tenant between the building society and the Todds, which would clearly have arisen in the absence of those letters, came in to existence on 15 September 1986 in spite of them. Therefore, the claim of the building society to possession of the flat falls within s.98(1) of the 1977 Act and no amount of estoppel can take it out.

It follows that, in my view, the building society fails on the second question and this appeal should be dismissed. The result will be that the security for the debt of Mr Dickman is encumbered by the tenancy of the Todds and the building society is unable to realise the higher purchase price normally realised on a sale with vacant possession. It should not be overlooked that one reason for that result is that the building society failed to follow its own policy not to lend on the security of residential property with a sitting tenant.

BUTLER-SLOSS L.J.:
I agree with both judgments.

NOTES:

1. The reasoning of the Court of Appeal is not entirely clear. The court seemed concerned to safeguard the position of the Todds, whose tenancy pre-dated the mortgage, as protected tenants under the Rent Act; but that could have been achieved with greater transparency by holding that the consents were an attempt to contract out of the Rent Act and to that extent were ineffective: see Tee [1997] C.L.J. 37. Morritt L.J. came close to deciding the case on that basis; but like Waite L.J. (and Butler-Sloss L.J., who agreed with both judgments), he sought to rationalise the decision by reference to section 70(1) itself, relying in particular on the proviso that land is subject to overriding interests "unless ... the contrary is expressed on the register". However, he proceeded to suggest that, in relation to rights not enjoying special statutory protection, an occupier would lose his overriding interest, or would be estopped from asserting its priority, even where his consent was not entered on the register.

2. Express consent was effective to postpone any overriding interests in *Gracegrove Estates Ltd v. Boateng* [1997] E.G.C.S. 103, although there was no entry on the register as to that postponement.

3. The Law Commission argues that the references to a requirement of an entry on the register are misleading and that such entries are made not to postpone an overriding interest but to note the discharge of an overriding interest. The Law Commission has therefore recommended that it should not be possible (nor, *a priori*, necessary) to make any entry on the register in respect of a waiver of priority by a person having the benefit of an overriding interest: Law Com. No. 254, *Land Registration for the Twenty-First Century* (1998), paras 5.109–5.111.

4. It may be questioned whether the reasoning is consistent with that in *Paddington Building Society v. Mendelsohn* (1985) 50 P. & C.R. 244, *supra* p. 192, where it was stated that "once it is established that the imputed intention must be that the ... rights were to be subject to the mortgage, there is nothing in [section 70] which enlarges those rights into any greater rights": see Tee [1997] C.L.J. 37; Morgan [1997] Conv. 402. The response may be that the statutory rights of the Todds as Rent Act protected tenants prima facie took priority over the subsequent mortgagee and could never be made subject to the mortgage because that would involve interference with the jurisdiction of the court under the Rent Act.

5. For a similar approach to Rent Act protected tenancies in the context of section 70(1)(k), see *Barclays Bank plc v. Zaroovabli* [1997] Ch. 321, *infra*, p. 232.

6. For cases on inferred consent to postponement, see *infra*.

7. For cases on undue influence and misrepresentation, see *post*, p. 856.

1.4.3.2 *Retreat from* Boland   Much of the initial concern of mortgagees in the immediate aftermath of the decision in *Boland* proved to be unnecessary. A series of case law developments, most of which have been referred to above, has ensured that in most circumstances, at least in the context of acquisition mortgages, the mortgagee will take priority over any such claims to the mortgaged land. First, where a claimant knows or is deemed to know that the purchase is to be financed in whole or in part by a mortgage loan, the claimant will be estopped from asserting priority and his interest will be postponed to that of the mortgagee: *Paddington Building Society v. Mendelsohn* (1985) 50 P. & C.R. 244. This principle was adopted in the context of acquisition mortgages but it would seem to extend to post-acquisition mortgages; and similar reasoning has been applied in relation to a subsequent remortgage, at least to the extent of the original mortgage loan: *Equity and Law Home Loans Ltd v. Prestidge* [1992] 1 W.L.R. 137. Secondly, the decision in *Abbey National Building Society v. Cann* [1991] 1 A.C. 56, that the claimant must be in actual occupation at the time of the *completion* of the transaction, precludes a claim based on actual occupation which commences in the "registration gap" between completion and registration. Thirdly, and more fundamentally, *Abbey National Building Society v. Cann* decided that in the context of acquisition mortgages the acquisition of the legal title by the purchaser and the creation of the mortgage are "indissolubly bound together": *ibid.* 89–93 *per* Lord Oliver, overruling *Church of England Building Society v. Piskor* [1954] Ch. 553. That aspect of the decision means that any contribution-based equitable ownership rights that affect the legal title of the purchaser affect a legal title *already encumbered by the mortgage* and are therefore postponed to the mortgage. However, this principle would appear not to operate to postpone contribution-based equitable ownership rights to a post-acquisition mortgage. It would seem to follow that a mortgage will have priority over contribution-based equitable ownership rights except where the mortgage is a post-acquisition mortgage of which the claimant has no knowledge. These developments are discussed further in the chapter on mortgages, *post*, p. 880.

Finally, although an overriding interest under section 70(1)(g) may provide a defence to an action for possession by a mortgagee, it has been held that, where a mortgagee has already recovered possession, an overriding interest cannot prevent an application to the court for an order for sale under section 14 of the Trusts of Land and Appointment of Trustees Act 1996 (formerly section 30 of the Law of Property Act 1925); nor is the overriding interest in itself an obstacle to an order for sale: *Bankers Trust Company v. Namdar* [1997] N.P.C. 22; *Bank of Baroda v. Dhillon* [1998] 1 F.L.R. 524, noted at [1998] Conv. 415; *Halifax Mortgage Services Ltd v. Muirhead* (1997) 76 P. & C. R. 418; see *post*, p. 317.

1.4.4 *Protection for persons in receipt of rent and profits*   Section 70(1)(g) also affords the status of overriding interests to the rights of persons who are in receipt of rent and profits from the land in question, even though those persons are not in actual occupation.

However, there is a divergence of views as to whether the non-residential landlord seeking to rely on section 70(1)(g) must be able to demonstrate the actual receipt of rent and not merely the right to receive rent. In *Strand Securities Ltd v. Caswell* [1965] Ch. 958, *supra*, p. 209, Russell L.J. (at 983) seemed to indicate that it is sufficient that the landlord *demands* rent; but Lord Denning M.R. (at 981) seemed to require actual payment and receipt. The latter view is expressly preferred in *E.S. Schwab & Co. Ltd v. McCarthy* (1975) 31 P. & C.R. 196, 213 *per* Sir John Pennycuick, 215 *per* Buckley L.J.

The Law Commission has provisionally recommended that receipt of rent and profits should no longer be sufficient to afford the status of overriding interest under section 70(1)(g). Although there are arguments for and against the removal of overriding status, the anticipated introduction of a system of electronic conveyancing, under which it would be impossible to create a lease except by registration, is seen to tip the balance in favour of the recommendation: Law Com. No. 254, *Land Registration for the Twenty-First Century* (1998), paras 5.64–5.68.

1.4.5 *Inquiry under section 70(1)(g)*   According to the proviso to section 70(1)(g), the rights of every person in actual occupation of the land or in receipt of the rents and profits thereof constitute overriding interests binding on the purchaser "save where enquiry is made of such person and the rights are not disclosed".

Although it is clearly fair that a purchaser should not be bound where a claimant to rights has failed to disclose those rights in response to an enquiry from the purchaser, the requirements of the proviso appear to be rather precise. First, in order to be able to rely on the proviso to negative an overriding interest, the purchaser must address the enquiry to the person claiming that particular interest (or his solicitor: *Winkworth v. Edward Baron Development Co. Ltd* (1986) 52 P. & C.R. 67, 77 *per* Nourse L.J.) since "reliance on the untrue *ipse dixit* of the vendor will not suffice": *Hodgson v. Marks* [1971] Ch. 892, 932 *per* Russell L.J. Secondly, the enquiry must relate to the rights of the occupier generally; for a specific enquiry as to a particular right of the occupier will not constitute sufficient enquiry as to other rights of the occupier: *Winkworth v. Edward Baron Development Co. Ltd, supra; D.B. Ramsden and Co. Ltd v. Nurdin & Peacock plc* [1998] E.G.C.S. 123. Thirdly, although the relevant enquiry need not be made by the purchaser personally, it must be made "by or on behalf of the intending transferee or grantee for the purposes of the intended disposition": *London and Cheshire Insurance Co. Ltd v. Laplagrene Property Co. Ltd* [1971] Ch. 499, 505 *per* Brightman J.

It is clearly arguable that the proviso constitutes further evidence that section 70(1)(g) requires the occupation and/or rights of the claimant to be discoverable since the proviso contemplates an enquiry and must sensibly be based on the assumption that such enquiry is possible: see *Lloyds Bank plc v.*

Rosset [1989] Ch. 350, 374 *per* Nicholls L.J., 394 *per* Mustill L.J.; see also Sparkes [1989] Conv. 342.

The Law Commission has provisionally recommended that there should be a general provision to the effect that no overriding interest should prevail against a purchaser in cases of fraud or estoppel. However, the Law Commission rejects the view in an earlier Report (Law Com. No. 158, *Property Law: Third Report on Land Registration* (1987), para. 2.59) that the proviso as to inquiry performs no useful function. It is argued that the proviso provides a "clear and certain test by which a purchaser can tell whether a person who is in actual occupation has an overriding interest"; but it recommends that it should be made explicit that the inquiry that is required is that which is reasonable in the circumstances: Law Com. No. 254, *Land Registration for the Twenty-First Century* (1998), para. 5.69.

1.5 Leases not exceeding twenty-one years

Section 70(1)(k) applies to *legal* leases only: *City Permanent Building Society v. Miller* [1952] Ch. 840, 853 *per* Jenkins L.J.; but there is no requirement that the lessee should be in actual occupation of the land. Moreover, the paragraph no longer excludes leases granted in return for the payment of a fine (capital sum): Land Registration Act 1986, s.4.

The Law Commission has provisionally recommended that reversionary leases granted for a term of 21 years or less should cease to be protected as overriding interests (and would therefore have to be protected as minor interests) unless they take effect within three months of the grant: Law Com. No. 254, *Land Registration for the Twenty-First Century* (1998), para. 5.91. Smith [1987] Conv. 334 criticised the earlier recommendation that would have restricted section 70(1)(k) to reversionary leases taking effect within one month on the ground that the requirement would have created a potential trap where a lease was renewed in advance of the expiry of the existing term. Furthermore, if, as a result of the consultation process, the length of leases capable of substantive registration were reduced (see *supra* p. 162), there would have to be a commensurate reduction in the length of leases taking effect as overriding interests under section 70(1)(k).

A statutory tenancy that comes into being on the termination of a contractual tenancy has been held to be enforceable as an overriding interest under section 70(1)(k): *Barclays Bank plc v. Zaroovabli* [1997] Ch. 321.

Barclays Bank plc v. Zaroovabli [1997] Ch. 321

(Ch D., Sir Richard Scott V.-C.)

In May 1988 the defendants, registered proprietors of a residential property, mortgaged the property to the plaintiff bank as security for the repayment of a loan. However, the bank failed to register the charge until August 1994. In July 1988, contrary to the express terms of the mortgage, the defendants granted to Mrs Pourdanay a six-month tenancy, which, as a Rent Act protected tenancy, became a statutory tenancy. The question arose as to whether the statutory tenancy was enforceable against the bank.

SIR RICHARD SCOTT V.-C.:

It is common ground that where a protected tenancy or a statutory tenancy is in existence at the time a mortgage of the property is granted, the mortgagee takes subject to the tenancy: see e.g. *Woolwich Building Society v. Dickman* [1996] 3 All E.R. 204, 211, *per* Waite L.J. In *Dudley and District Benefit Building Society v. Emerson* [1949] Ch. 707, however, the grant of the tenancy post-dated the grant of the mortgage. The mortgage had contained an express provision excluding the mortgagor's statutory power of leasing under section 99(1) of the Law of Property Act 1925. The mortgagee had not consented to the grant by the mortgagor of the tenancy. In the circumstances, the Court of Appeal held that, although the tenant was entitled to Rent Act protection as against the mortgagor, the tenant was not entitled to that protection against the mortgagee. The mortgagee, it was held, was entitled by virtue of its paramount title to resist the tenant's claim under the Rent Acts to remain in possession. ... The Court of Appeal left open the question whether, if the tenant had been a statutory and not a contractual tenant of the mortgagor at the time the proceedings for possession were taken, the answer would have been the same. But this question was answered in the affirmative in *Britannia Building Society v. Earl* [1990] 1 W.L.R. 422. McCowan L.J., with whose judgment Butler-Sloss L.J. concurred, approved and applied an obiter passage from the judgment of Templeman L.J. in *Quennell v. Maltby* [1979] 1 W.L.R. 318. Templeman L.J. had said, at p. 323:

> "The lease to the statutory tenant was made by the landlord after the date of the mortgage without the consent of the bank and was therefore in breach of the landlord's covenant contained in the mortgage. That lease was binding on the landlord but void against the bank. On expiry of the lease the tenant became a statutory tenant as against the landlord but not as against the bank."

Mr Wolfson, for the bank, relies strongly on *Dudley and District Benefit Building Society v. Emerson* [1949] Ch. 707. That case, however, turned on the title paramount of the building society. The mortgagor had granted the building society a legal mortgage. The mortgagor's statutory power of leasing having been excluded, the mortgagor had no power to make a subsequent grant of a tenancy with priority over the mortgage. But the facts of the present case do not, in my opinion, permit this title paramount approach to be applied.

The legal charge executed on 25 May 1988 did not vest a legal estate in the bank. If title to the property had been unregistered, the legal charge would have done so; but [the property] was registered land. It is fundamental to registered land conveyancing that, whereas in unregistered conveyancing a deed takes effect from execution, a registrable disposition must be completed by registration ... Pending registration, the estates and rights created by a registrable deed may be enforceable as between the parties to the deed and can take effect as minor interests, but they will not take effect in rem. They will take effect in rem only upon registration. Minor interests can be protected by suitable entries on the register but "take effect only in equity:" section 101(3) of the Land Registration Act 1925.

Needless to say, over the period from 25 May 1988, when the bank's legal charge was executed, to 23 August 1994, when registration took place, there was no entry on the register protecting the interests of the bank under the unregistered legal charge. Section 18(1) of the Land Registration Act 1925 provides, inter alia, that the registered proprietor "subject to any entry in the register to the contrary, may in the prescribed manner ... (*e*) grant ... a lease of the registered land ..." And under section 19 of the Act, although in general dispositions have to be completed by registration, a lease granted for a term not exceeding 21 years cannot be registered and takes effect "as if it were a registered disposition immediately on being granted".

The clear effect of these provisions and the facts of this case, is, in my opinion, that the grant of the tenancy to Mrs Pourdanay on 28 July 1988 vested in her a contractual tenancy that was not subject to any rights of the bank under its unregistered legal charge: see section 20(1) of the Land Registration Act 1925. The grant of the tenancy may well have been a breach by Mr and Mrs Zaroovabli of the terms of the legal charge. But that was of no concern to Mrs Pourdanay. To express the point in *Dudley and District Benefit Building Society v. Emerson* [1949] Ch. 707 terms, at the date of grant of the tenancy the bank did not have a paramount title but had merely equitable rights ranking as minor interests and unprotected by any entry on the register.

The conclusion that when the contractual tenancy was granted to Mrs Pourdanay it was binding on the bank is accepted by Mr Wolfson. He accepts, also, that her contractual tenancy and its statutory tenancy successor remained binding on the bank up to the time, 23 August 1994, when the bank's legal charge was registered. He contends, however, that the effect of registration on 23 August 1994 was to overreach the statutory tenancy, and would have been to overreach the contractual tenancy if the contractual tenancy had still been in existence.

This contention requires a careful look to be taken at Lord Oliver of Aylmerton's speech in *Abbey National Building Society v. Cann* [1991] 1 A.C. 56. The case raised the question whether equitable rights which had been acquired after the date of execution of a charge but before its registration were binding on the registered chargee. The claimant was in actual occupation of the property at the time of registration of the charge and claimed priority over the chargee by virtue of section 70(1)(g) of the Land Registration Act 1925.

Lord Oliver, with whose speech Lord Griffiths and Lord Ackner agreed, posed the question whether the date for ascertaining the existence of overriding interests under the Land Registration Acts should be taken to be the date of registration or the earlier date on which the transaction between the parties was completed. Having considered the question in the round, and with particular attention to local land charges and section 70(1)(i), Lord Oliver expressed the conclusion, at p. 87, that "the relevant date for determining the existence of overriding interests which will 'affect the estate transferred or created' is the date of registration". He went on, however, to hold, at p. 88, that for the purposes of section 70(1)(g) the requisite "actual occupation" had to exist at the date of completion of the transaction that had given rise to the registrable disposition.

Mr Wolfson submitted that the ratio of the case should be confined to a decision that section 70(1)(g) rights should be ascertained by reference to their existence at the date of registration but on the footing that the requisite "occupation" had to exist at the date of completion. Everything said about the date at which other overriding interests should be ascertained was, he submitted, merely obiter. I decline to carve up Lord Oliver's reasoning in that fashion. His conclusion, expressed in the passage at p. 87 that I have already cited, was clearly, in my opinion, part of the ratio decidendi and constitutes an authoritative statement of the law.

Under section 70(1)(k), the overriding interests to which registered land is deemed to be subject include "leases granted for a term not exceeding 21 years." It follows, in my opinion, from *Abbey National Building Society v. Cann* [1991] 1 A.C. 56 that if Mrs Pourdanay's contractual tenancy had been still subsisting when the bank's charge was registered, the registered charge would have been subject to that tenancy.

But, at some point in the period between grant of the contractual tenancy and registration of the bank's charge, the contractual tenancy had terminated—or so I must assume. Mrs Pourdanay's occupation had, on that assumption, continued by virtue of a statutory tenancy. Mr Wolfson submits, rightly, that a statutory tenancy cannot be an overriding interest under section 70(1)(k). It is not a lease "granted for a term not exceeding 21 years." It is possible that the rights of a statutory tenant should be regarded as capable of being protected under section 70(1)(g). In *National Provincial Bank Ltd v. Hastings Car Mart Ltd* [1964] Ch. 665, 689 Lord Denning M.R. gave "the right of a statutory tenant to be in possession" as an example of non-proprietary rights that could qualify for protection under section 70(1)(*g*). In view of the decision in *Abbey National Building Society v. Cann* [1991] 1 A.C. 56, however, Mrs Pourdanay cannot claim priority over the bank's registered charge via the section 70(1)(*g*) route. She was not in occupation on 25 May 1988 when the transaction between Mr and Mrs Zaroovabli and the bank was completed by execution of the legal charge. But her inability to obtain protection for her statutory tenancy rights via section 70(1)(*g*) is not, in my opinion, the end of the matter. Whether or not Lord Denning was right in holding that the rights of a tenant under a statutory tenancy were rights which could fall within section 70(1)(*g*), the rights are of an anomalous character if measured against the general quality of rights to which registered land may, under section 70(1), be subject. In *Jessamine Investment Co. v. Schwartz* [1978] Q.B. 264, Sir John Pennycuick said, at p. 270, that "the statutory tenant has no estate as tenant, but a personal right to retain the property" and, at pp. 272–273, that a statutory tenancy carries with it a "status of irremovability, that status being enjoyed upon terms analogous to those of a tenancy:" see also *per* Stephenson L.J., at p. 276.

The statutory status of irremovability that adheres to a tenant under a statutory tenancy cannot bind someone who claims through title paramount: see *Dudley and District Benefit Building Society v. Emerson* [1949] Ch. 707. But whether a claimant does or does not have a title paramount must, in my opinion, be judged by comparing the title in question with the contractual tenancy from which sprang the statutory tenancy. If, as here, the contractual tenancy was entitled to priority over the title on which the claimant, in this case the bank, relies, it would, it seems to me, be inconsistent with the statutory protection intended to be afforded to statutory tenants under the Rent Acts to hold that the translation of the contractual tenancy into a statutory tenancy has the result of depriving the tenant of that priority. There are obvious reasons why neither a protected contractual tenancy nor a statutory tenancy should be binding on a claimant who can show a title that was at the date of grant of the contractual tenancy paramount to the title of the landlord who granted the tenancy. *Dudley and District Benefit Building Society v. Emerson* was such a case. So was *Britannia Building Society v. Earl* [1990] 1 W.L.R. 422. But if a protected contractual tenancy is, when granted, binding on a mortgagee, a statutory tenancy that comes into existence on the termination of the contractual tenancy is, in my opinion, also binding on that mortgagee.

Mr Wolfson argued that a conclusion in favour of Mrs Pourdanay on this issue would gravely prejudice mortgagees and place a damaging obstacle in the way of attempts to use residential property as security for loans. There is, he said, bound to be a period between the date on which a mortgage or sale is completed and the date on which registration of the disposition can be obtained. If, in that period, tenancies can be created which bind the mortgagee or purchaser, as the case may be, great problems may be caused. I follow the point. It is, in my opinion, an inevitable consequence of the ruling in *Abbey National Building Society v. Cann* [1991] 1 A.C. 56 that overriding interests in existence at the date of registration of a disposition bind the registered property. I am not, however, persuaded that the problem is a serious one. It is to be expected that in general a mortgagee or purchaser would promptly lodge for registration the charge or transfer. It is inexplicable why the bank in the present case did not do so. I am told by counsel that the date of registration of a disposition is taken to be the date on which the application for registration was made. So the period between completion and registration ought to be a very short one. It would, moreover, be possible, at least for mortgagees such as banks and building societies, to decline to release any funds until registration had been effected. Moreover, Mr Wolfson's cri de coeur on behalf of mortgagees echoes similar Cassandra-like prophecies of disaster made to the court when *Williams & Glyn's Bank Ltd v. Boland* [1981] A.C. 487 was decided and, again, when *Barclays Bank Plc v. O'Brien* [1994] 1 A.C. 180 was decided. These prophecies have not been fulfilled. I am not persuaded that the fears

Mr Wolfson expresses have any real substance or are any more likely to be well founded than their predecessors.

In any event, for the reasons I have given, the bank is not, in my judgment, entitled to an order for possession against Mrs Pourdanay.

NOTES:

1. For comment, see [1997] C.L.J. 496, (1997) 113 L.Q.R. 390.

2. The decision provides a graphic illustration of the potential consequences of the "registration gap" and the importance of prompt (application for) registration. As noted above *supra*, p. 232, the Law Commission has endorsed the current law on the ground that it achieves a fair balance between the principles of registration and the interests of encumbrancers on the one hand and the need to ensure security for the interests of purchasers and mortgagees on the other hand. In any event, the introduction of electronic conveyancing would eliminate the registration gap.

An equitable lease may constitute an overriding interest under section 70(1)(g), provided that the lessee is in actual occupation of the land at the relevant time or in receipt of the rents and profits: see *Strand Securities Ltd v. Caswell* [1965] Ch. 958, *supra*, p. 209.

E. RECTIFICATION AND INDEMNITY

The operation of any system of registration of title requires a position as to the conclusiveness of the register. The idea of indefeasibility of title following investigation by the Land Registry is clearly attractive in theory; and when registration of title was introduced into England and Wales by the Land Registry Act 1862 the scheme of that legislation adopted an extremely strict version of indefeasibility: the register could be amended (or "rectified") only in very exceptional circumstances on the ground of fraud. However, the operation of that scheme demonstrated the significant practical argument against a strict version of indefeasibility. If registration was to be conclusive, the Land Registry needed to be absolutely certain as to the validity of any title that it registered: no title could be safely registered without the most extensive and therefore expensive investigation. The result was that, under the voluntary scheme of the 1862 Act, very few titles were registered. Under the Land Transfer Act 1875 the requirements for registration became less rigorous; but, although the powers of rectification were extended to include certain cases not involving fraud, rectification was not available if it would affect rights acquired by registration. In practice, therefore, the principle of indefeasibility was retained. The Land Transfer Act 1897 extended the power of the courts to rectify the register, so that a registered proprietor could be deprived of his title. However, in order to compensate for the consequent lesser degree of security, the legislation introduced a system of insurance: it provided for financial compensation (or "indemnity") for loss suffered where the register was rectified and, in certain circumstances, where the register was *not* rectified. The grounds of rectification were further extended by the Land

Registration Act 1925; but the Act sought to preserve an element of indefeasibility by affording some measure of protection against rectification for registered proprietors in possession. The provisions of the Land Registration Act 1925 dealing with rectification and indemnity are sections 82 and 83. Both sections have been amended since 1925 to remove elements of unfairness in the original provisions; and the Land Registration Act 1997 substituted a new section 83, which was intended to remove some of the anomalies in the indemnity provisions and in their relationship with the rectification provisions.

1. Rectification

1.1 *Grounds of rectification*

Land Registration Act 1925, s.82(1)

Rectification of the register

82.—(1) The register may be rectified pursuant to an order of the court or by the registrar, subject to an appeal to the court, in any of the following cases, but subject to the provisions of this section:—

(a) Subject to any express provisions of this Act to the contrary, where a court of competent jurisdiction has decided that any person is entitled to any estate right or interest in or to any registered land or charge, and as a consequence of such decision such court is of opinion that a rectification of the register is required, and makes an order to that effect;

(b) Subject to any express provision of this Act to the contrary, where the court, on the application in the prescribed manner of any person who is aggrieved by any entry made in, or by the omission of any entry from, the register, or by any default being made, or unnecessary delay taking place, in the making of any entry in the register, makes an order for the rectification of the register;

(c) In any case and at any time with the consent of all persons interested;

(d) Where the court or the registrar is satisfied that any entry in the register has been obtained by fraud;

(e) Where two or more persons are, by mistake, registered as proprietors of the same registered estate or of the same charge;

(f) Where a mortgagee has been registered as proprietor of the land instead of as proprietor of a charge and a right of redemption is subsisting;

(g) Where a legal estate has been registered in the name of a person who if the land had not been registered would not have been the estate owner; and

(h) In any other case where, by reason of any error or omission in the register, or by reason of any entry made under a mistake, it may be deemed just to rectify the register.

NOTES:

1. The Land Registration Rules 1925 provide additional grounds for rectification but they largely concern clerical or technical errors.

2. The statutory power of rectification is unrelated to the equitable remedy of rectification, although both "remedies" may arise on the same facts: see *Blacklocks v. J.B. Developments (Godalming) Ltd* [1982] Ch. 183, *supra*, p. 190; *D.B. Ramsden and Co. Ltd v. Nurdin & Peacock plc* [1998] E.G.C.S. 123 *supra*, p. 191.

3. There has been a tendency in recent years for the courts to construe the grounds for rectification very widely, in effect assuming a general discretion to order rectification, so that "if the present entries on the register do not reflect the true position, the register is open to rectification": *Orakpo v. Manson Investments Ltd* [1977] 1 W.L.R. 347, 360 *per* Buckley L.J.; and see also *Peffer v. Rigg* [1977] 1 W.L.R. 285, 294 *per* Graham J.; *Argyle Building Society v. Hammond* (1984) 49 P. & C.R. 148, 158 *per* Slade L.J.; *Proctor v. Kidman* (1985) 51 P. & C.R. 67, 72 *per* Croom-Johnson L.J. The Law Commission has commented that section 82(1)(h) has not infrequently been relied upon "with very little judicial heart searching or even discussion", citing *Freer v. Unwins Ltd* [1976] Ch. 288; *Epps v. Esso Petroleum Co. Ltd* [1973] 1 W.L.R. 1071, *Orakpo v. Manson Investments Ltd* [1977] 1 W.L.R. 347: Law Com. No. 158, *Property Law: Third Report on Land Registration* (1987), para. 3.7.

4. The Court of Appeal in *Norwich and Peterborough Building Society v. Steed* [1993] Ch. 116 adopted an approach to section 82(1) which appears at first sight to be rather more disciplined. In particular, it was stressed that neither the court nor the registrar has power to order rectification unless one of the specified grounds is established: *ibid.* at 132. However, the availability of rectification may not be significantly curtailed.

Norwich and Peterborough Building Society v. Steed [1993] Ch. 116

(CA, Purchas, Butler-Sloss and Scott L.JJ.)

The defendant was the former registered proprietor of a property in London. While he was living abroad, the property was occupied by his mother, and his sister and brother-in-law, the Hammonds. At the instigation of his sister, the defendant executed a power of attorney in favour of his mother, empowering her to sell the property, although she was apparently unaware of the power. Under a purported transfer on sale apparently signed by the mother, the Hammonds became registered proprietors of the property; and under a charge created by the Hammonds to secure a loan (purportedly to finance the purchase), the plaintiff building society (then the Argyle Building Society) became registered chargees of the property. When the Hammonds fell into arrears on the repayment of the loan and the plaintiffs obtained a possession order, the defendant applied to be joined as a party to the proceedings and claimed rectification of the register. On the assumption that the transfer apparently signed by the mother was a forgery, the Court of Appeal held that section 82(2) empowered rectification of the register both against the Hammonds (so that the defendant would be restored as registered proprietor) and against the plaintiffs (so that the charge would be removed from the register): see *Argyle Building Society v. Hammond* (1984) 49 P. & C.R. 148.

The action was transferred to the Chancery Division for the determination of the facts regarding the transfer to the Hammonds. The allegation of forgery was abandoned; and both Knox J. and the Court of Appeal rejected further arguments that the transfer was void: the mother could not rely on the doctrine of *non est factum* in respect of the transfer nor was the transfer *ultra vires* the power of attorney. Although the transfer had been obtained by fraud and was voidable, so that the defendant had grounds for rectification against the Hammonds, the question was whether rectification was available against the plaintiffs, who had become registered charges before the transfer had been avoided.

On the basis of *Argyle Building Society v. Hammond* Knox J. assumed that the court had jurisdiction to order rectification against the plaintiffs; but as a matter of discretion he declined to do so. The defendant appealed to the Court of Appeal.

SCOTT L.J.:

If an order of rectification is to be made the case must be brought within at least one of paragraphs (a) to (h) of section 82(1). The dispute in the present case is as to the breadth of the power conferred by paragraphs (a) and (b) and, to a lesser extent, (d) and (h). There is no doubt but that, if Mrs Steed's signature had been forged or if the non est factum plea had been made good, the case would have fallen squarely within paragraph (g). In neither case, if the land had been unregistered, would the Hammonds or the building society have obtained a legal estate. I cannot see any reasonable basis on which an order of rectification could have been withheld. If, however, as is the case, the transfer is only voidable, paragraph (g) does not apply. It is plain that, if title to the property had been unregistered, Mr Steed would have had no remedy against the building society. He would have recovered the property from the Hammonds but the property would have remained subject to the charge. It is submitted, however, that paragraphs (a), (b), (d) or (h) can, since title is registered, be prayed in aid. This submission is made on the footing that, under one or more of these paragraphs, the court is given a general discretion to order rectification in any case in which it may be thought just to do so. If the submission is right, then section 82, or its statutory predecessors, achieved a remarkable and unnoticed change in the substantive law. If the discretion can be exercised where there has been a fraudulent misrepresentation, as in the present case, it must be exercisable also where a merely innocent misrepresentation has been made. It would, as Mr Lloyd [counsel for the defendant] conceded, be exercisable also in a case where no misrepresentation inducing the transaction could be pointed to but where a registered proprietor had entered into a transaction under a misapprehension for which the other party to the transaction was not responsible, a misapprehension as to the value of the property, for example. Mr Lloyd said that in such a case the discretion to order rectification against a bona fide purchaser, such as the building society in the present case, would be very unlikely ever to be exercised. But the proposition that the discretionary power contended for can be spelled out of the statutory language is, to me, so startling as to require the premise of the proposition to be very carefully examined.

There is a sense in which the power to rectify under section 82 is undoubtedly discretionary. The words in subsection (1) are "may be rectified." Section 83(2) shows that rectification is not automatic. The power to rectify may, in a particular case, be present but, nonetheless, there is a general discretion to refuse rectification. It does not follow, however, that there is, in every case, a general discretion to grant rectification. The power to grant rectification is limited in subsection (1) to "any of the following cases." The power to order rectification must, therefore, be found within one or other of the subsection (1) paragraphs and cannot be spelled out of the words "may be rectified."

Paragraphs (a) and (b) provide a power to rectify that can only be exercised by the court. The power conferred by the other paragraphs can be exercised either by the registrar or by the court. Paragraph (a) enables an order of rectification to be made where the court "has decided that any person is entitled to any estate right or interest in or to any registered land or charge ..." This, in my judgment, is a clear reference to an entitlement under the substantive law. An example would be a case, such as Mr Steed's case against the Hammonds, for the setting aside of a transaction on the ground of misrepresentation or some other sufficient cause. Another example would be the successful assertion of a possessory title. A third example might be the assertion of a right by a beneficiary under a trust who had become absolutely entitled to the land. In each of these cases, once the entitlement had been established the court would have power under paragraph (a) to order the register to be rectified so as to reflect the entitlement. But paragraph (a) does not, in my judgment, give any substantive cause of action where none before existed. It does not enable a voidable transaction to be set aside as against a bona fide purchaser who has acquired by registration a legal estate. And if no entitlement as against such a purchaser can be established, paragraph (a) does not, in my judgment, enable the register to be rectified as against such a purchaser. Paragraph (a) does not assist Mr Steed in his rectification claim against the building society.

Paragraph (b) is the paragraph on which Mr Lloyd pinned his main hopes. It applies, he submitted, whenever any person is "aggrieved" by an entry on the register. Paragraph (b) is something of a puzzle, not least because the form of the "application." is not "prescribed" by any rules made under the Act. The same language was used in section 96 of the Act of 1875, but there, too, no form of application was "prescribed." The legislative intention underlying paragraph (b) and its statutory predecessor is difficult to identify with clarity. The reference to "the application in the prescribed manner" makes me believe that it was contemplated that some form of summary process would be prescribed in order to enable speedy relief to be given in clear cases. Be that as it may, the real question at issue is whether the provision was intended simply to provide a remedy in respect of proprietary rights that either entitled the proprietor to have some entry made on the register or entitled the proprietor to have some entry removed from the register or whether the provision should be construed as creating a new cause of action entitling the court to make rectification orders as it might in its discretion think fit in favour of persons who would not under substantive law, apart from paragraph (b), have any proprietary rights which they could assert against the registered proprietor or chargee. In my judgment, the question has only to be put for the answer to be apparent. Parliament could not have intended paragraph (b) to produce new substantive rights in respect of registered land, enabling registered dispositions to be set aside and removed from the register in circumstances where, if the land had not been registered, no cause of action would have existed. In my judgment, paragraph (b), like paragraph (a), provides a remedy but does not create any new substantive rights or causes of action.

The scope of paragraph (c) is self-evident and not relevant in the present case.

Paragraph (d) too was relied on by Mr Lloyd. He contended that since the transfer had been induced by the Hammonds' fraud, both the registration of the Hammonds as proprietors and the registration of the building society's legal charge could be described as having been "obtained by fraud." In my judgment, this is a misreading of the paragraph. The paragraph is directed, in my opinion, to fraud practised upon the Land Registry in order to obtain the entry in question. No fraud was used to obtain the entry on the charges register of the building society's legal charge.

This construction of paragraph (d) derives support from the language used in section 174(1)(c) of the Law of Property Act 1922, the statutory predecessor of paragraph (d). Section 174(1)(c) enabled the register to be rectified:

"Where the court or the registrar is satisfied that the registration of ... a charge, mortgage, or other entry in the register ... has been obtained by fraud, by annulling the registration, notice or other entry ..."

This provision was reduced to its present succinct form in the Law of Property (Amendment) Act 1924: see section 8 and Schedule 8, paragraph 16. It is the *registration* that must be obtained by fraud.

The registration of a forged transfer could, in my opinion, at least if the application for registration had been made by the forger, be annulled under paragraph (d). The entry would have been obtained by fraud in the presenting of a forged transfer for registration. But if a voidable disposition were registered before being avoided, I would doubt whether the register could be rectified under paragraph (d), even if the disposition were voidable on account of fraud. In such a case the entry on the register would not, it seems to me, have been obtained by fraud. Rectification could, of course, in such a case be obtained under paragraph (a) or paragraph (b). Whether or not that is right, and it need not be decided in this case, a registered disposition made by the fraudster to a bona fide purchaser cannot in my judgment be removed from the register under paragraph (d). The registration would not have been obtained by fraud. So paragraph (d) cannot in my judgment assist Mr Steed as against the building society.

Paragraphs (e) and (f) are self-explanatory and are of no relevance to this case.

Paragraph (g) does not, in the event that the transfer is voidable, assist Mr Steed as against the building society. It is, however, an important paragraph so far as an understanding of the scheme of section 82(1) is concerned.

In my opinion the scheme is reasonably clear. Paragraphs (a) and (b) give power to the court to make orders of rectification in order to give effect to property rights which have been established in an action or which are clear. Paragraph (c) enables orders to be made by consent. The remaining paragraphs, (d) to (h), are intended to enable errors to be corrected. Paragraph (d), paragraph (e), paragraph (f) and paragraph (g) each deals with an error of a particular character. But, since these paragraphs might not cover comprehensively all errors, paragraph (h) was added as a catch-all provision to cover any other errors. The breadth of the catch-all provision was, I imagine, the reason why it was thought appropriate to make the power exercisable "where ... it may be deemed just to rectify the register". There are no comparable words in any of the other paragraphs.

Paragraph (h) is relied on by Mr Lloyd. But in order for the paragraph to be applicable some "error or omission in the register" or some "entry made under a mistake" must be shown. The entry in the charges register of the building society's legal charge was not an error and was not made under a mistake. The legal charge was executed by the Hammonds, who were at the time transferees under a transfer executed by Mrs Steed as attorney for the registered proprietor. The voidable transfer had not been set aside. The registration of the Hammonds as proprietors took place at the same time as the registration of the legal charge. Neither registration was an error. Neither entry was made under a mistake. So the case for rectification cannot be brought under paragraph (h).

As a matter of principle, if, as I think, the defendant's case for rectification as against the building society cannot be brought under any of the paragraphs of section 82(1), I would conclude that that must be an end to the rectification claim. Mr Lloyd, however, has relied strongly on passages in the judgment of Slade L.J. in *Argyle Building Society v. Hammond* (1984) 49 P. & C.R. 148. Before I come to those passages, it is convenient to refer to such earlier authority as there is.

Chowood Ltd v. Lyall (No. 2) [1930] 2 Ch. 156 concerned a strip of land which had, on first registration, been included in a registered title notwithstanding that it was in the possession of an adjoining owner. The register was rectified under paragraph (h) on an application made by the adjoining owner, the defendant. In the Court of Appeal Lawrence L.J. said, at pp. 168–169:

"I see no reason to limit the word 'mistake' in that section to any particular kind of mistake. ... I further agree ... that the rectification might also be made under clauses (a) and (g) of subsection (1). Moreover I am not satisfied that the defendant's application for rectification would not come under clause (b) as being made by a person who is aggrieved by an entry in the register. Mr Armitage [junior counsel for the plaintiff] suggested that clause (b) applies only to a mistake made by the officials in the Registry and not to a mistake made or induced by one or other of the parties. I prefer not to express any concluded opinion on this point ..."

Underlying this passage, as it seems to me, is Lawrence L.J.'s acceptance of the importance of bringing the rectification case within one or other of the paragraphs of section 82(1).

Calgary & Edmonton Land Co. Ltd v. Discount Bank (Overseas) Ltd [1971] 1 W.L.R. 81 concerned cautions which had been entered on the register in order to protect interests claimed in a pending action. The action had been struck out at first instance, an appeal to the Court of Appeal had failed but a petition for leave to appeal to the House of Lords was still pending. On an interlocutory notice of motion Brightman J. ordered that the register be rectified by vacating the cautions. He held that he had power to make the order either under paragraph (a) or under paragraph (b) and that "it matters not whether the order is expressly made under paragraph (a) or paragraph (b) ..." I would respectfully accept that the order was justified under paragraph (a) but would regard the case as a classic example of the sort of case for which paragraph (b) was designed.

In *In re Leighton's Conveyance* [1936] 1 All E.R. 667 a non est factum case was raised. The plaintiff sought rectification first, against her daughter, who had fraudulently induced the plaintiff to sign a transfer leading to the daughter's registration as proprietor and, secondly, against chargees who, without any notice of the daughter's fraud, had advanced money to the daughter on the security of registered charges. The case was, therefore, very similar to the present case. Luxmoore J. ordered rectification as against the daughter but, having concluded that the non est factum plea failed, he dismissed the rectification claim against the chargees. He said, at p. 673:

"I am satisfied that there are no grounds on which I can say that these charges are bad, but with regard to the equity of redemption I am satisfied on the evidence that what Mrs Wardman did was at the request of and in reliance on her daughter, and under her influence. ... It follows that the conveyance to Mrs Bergin can have no effect as against Mrs Wardman, and she is still entitled to the equity of redemption in the property. ... With regard to the charges register, there is no ground for interfering with it and directing any rectification. They are good charges and remain enforceable against the property."

It was not stated in the judgment which paragraph or paragraphs of section 82(1) Luxmoore J. regarded as applicable, but the report of the argument of counsel and an editorial note at p. 667 suggest that the judge was invited to act under paragraph (d). It appears also from the report of argument that rectification as against the daughter was conceded and that the only issue in the case against the chargees was the non est factum issue. In my opinion, paragraph (a), rather than paragraph (d), provided the power to rectify as against the daughter. If the non est factum case had succeeded, paragraph (g) also would have been in point, both against the daughter and against the chargees. It was not suggested by counsel for the mother that, if the non est factum plea failed, she might nonetheless be entitled to rectification against the chargees. And there is nothing in the judgment of Luxmoore J. to indicate that, having rejected the non est factum plea, he thought that he had any discretionary power to order rectification of the charges register.

I now come to the judgment of Slade L.J. in *Argyle Building Society v. Hammond* (1984) 49 P. & C.R. 148. For the purposes of his judgment Slade L.J. assumed that the allegation of forgery would succeed. He assumed nothing else. References to the "assumed facts" are references to the facts regarding the forgery. At p. 157, having set out the text of section 82(1), he said:

"First, registers of title made pursuant to the Act of 1925 consist of three parts, namely the property register, the proprietorship register and the charges register. The jurisdiction to rectify under the subsection plainly extends to all or any of these parts. Secondly, on the assumed facts in the present case, the court would, in our judgment, have clear jurisdiction to rectify the proprietorship register of the house by substituting the name of the appellant for that of Mr and Mrs Hammond, since the case would fall within all or any of sub-paragraphs (a), (b), (d), (g) and (h) of section 82(1). The present argument relates to the possibility or otherwise of rectification of the charges register."

At p. 158 he made clear the opinion of the court that, on the assumed facts, the court would have power to rectify the charges register against the mortgagees as well as the proprietorship register against the Hammonds. I would respectfully agree, save that, for the reasons I have given, I do not think the case would come within paragraph (d). It would come, in my opinion, within paragraphs (a), (b), (g) and, perhaps, (h).

Slade L.J. then referred to *In re Leighton's Conveyance* [1936] 1 All E.R. 667, cited the passage from the judgment of Luxmoore J. that I have cited and continued, at p. 160:

"Reverting to the decision at first instance in the *Leighton* case, the report of the argument shows that the provisions of section 82(1) and (2) of the Act of 1925 were drawn to the attention of Luxmoore J. We feel no doubt that he would have appreciated that, even in the absence of a successful plea of forgery or non est factum, the section would in terms have conferred a discretion on the court to rectify the charges register, even as against the innocent chargees. Nevertheless, it is readily intelligible that Luxmoore J. should have considered that, when the discretion fell to be exercised, the equities were all on one side—that is to say in favour of the chargees, who had acted on the faith of a document of transfer which the mother had herself executed after having failed to make inquiries which would have revealed that the document related to the property. If the title to the land had not been registered, the title of the daughter would, at worst, have been voidable, not void; and under general principles of equity, mortgagees from the daughter in good faith and for value, without notice of the facts giving rise to the voidability, would have acquired a good title to their mortgages. We can see no reason why the court in the *Leighton* case should have regarded the equities as being any different, as between the mother and the chargees, merely because the land happened to be registered land."

In my respectful opinion, this analysis of *In re Leighton's Conveyance* is not justified by Luxmoore J.'s judgment. There is nothing in the judgment or in the report of counsel's argument to suggest that the possibility of rectification against the chargees, in the absence of a successful plea of forgery or non est factum, was ever considered. At p. 162 of his judgment Slade L.J. commented:

"in a case where one or more of the conditions of section 82(1) are fulfilled, the court always has at least theoretical discretion to rectify any part of the register, even as against innocent third parties. . ."

I would respectfully agree with this comment, based as it is on the premise that the case can be brought within one or other of the paragraphs of section 82(1). But Slade L.J. then went on to distinguish the case of a party "deprived of his title as a result of a forged document which he did not execute" from the case where the party "has been deprived as a result of a document which he himself executed, albeit under a mistake induced by fraud" and commented that "when the court comes to exercise its discretion, different considerations may well apply." The paragraph of section 82(1) under which the latter case could be brought was not identified. On the true construction of section 82(1) there is not, in my opinion, any paragraph under which the latter case could be brought.

Mr Lloyd's argument that the court has a general discretionary power to order rectification of the register was based on the passages from Slade L.J.'s judgment to which I have referred. The passages were not part of the ratio of the decision by which we are bound and with which I respectfully agree. A voidable transfer was not part of the "assumed facts" on which the ratio was based. In my judgment, the obiter passages, regarding voidable transfers and innocent third parties claiming thereunder, were based on an incorrect construction of section 82(1) and should not be followed.

In my opinion, if the defendant's non est factum case is rejected, the court has no power under section 82(1) to order rectification as against the building society.

It is strictly unnecessary for me to deal with the issue of discretion which only arises if the court has power to rectify. Knox J. refused rectification as a matter of discretion. He held that as between the defendant and the building society "all the equities are on the building society's side." This would certainly be so if the land were unregistered. But under section 83(1) the building society, if rectification were ordered, would have what seems to me to be an unimpeachable statutory right to an indemnity against the loss it would thereby suffer. On the other hand, if rectification were refused, the defendant would not be able to claim an indemnity under section 83(2). Mr Lloyd accepted, rightly, that, since the registration of the building society's charge was not an "error or omission," the case would not come within section 83(2). The financial consequences to the parties of ordering or refusing rectification make it difficult to weigh the "equities." If rectification were ordered, the loss would fall not upon the building society but upon the public purse. If rectification were refused, the public purse would be saved the burden of paying an indemnity. I mention these matters not in order to indicate any disagreement with Knox J.'s conclusions on discretion but because the indemnity provisions in section 83 seem to me to underline that the legislature did not contemplate the power of rectification being exercisable under section 82 except in cases either where an error or omission had occurred in the register, *i.e.* paragraphs (d) to (h), or where a substantive cause of action against the registered proprietor required the register to be rectified, *i.e.* paragraphs (a) and (b).

In "error or omission" cases, *i.e.* in cases coming within paragraphs (d) to (h), an indemnity would, if rectification were refused, be available under section 83(2), subject always to section 83(5)(a). In cases within paragraphs (a) and (b) but not within any of paragraphs (d) to (h), *e.g.* cases in which voidable transactions are set aside and, as a consequence, rectification of the register is required, it is difficult to construct any scenario in which rectification could be withheld. The construction of section 82(1) that I have suggested seems to me to mesh with and to explain the scheme of indemnity contained in section 83. The "general discretion" approach to section 82(1) does not.

For the reasons I have given I would dismiss this appeal.

NOTES:

1. In restating the grounds of rectification, Scott L.J. has rejected the view evident in some recent cases that section 82(1) confers a general discretion to order rectification: see generally Davis [1992] Conv. 293; Smith (1993) 109 L.Q.R. 187.

2. Paragraphs (a) and (b) do not confer a general discretion to rectify but permit the court to order rectification only where the applicant can establish "an entitlement under the substantive law". The Law Commission asserts that this is a reference to the principles of real property law *as they apply to registered land* (Law Com. No. 254, *Land Registration for the Twenty-First Century* (1998), paras 8.7, 8.11); and it questions the view of some commentators that the courts have looked to entitlement according to unregistered land principles rather than entitlement according to the registered land rules for the classification and protection of interests in land: see, *e.g.* Jackson (1978) 94 L.Q.R. 239, 254; Smith (1993) 109 L.Q.R. 187, 188.

Although rectification remains discretionary in principle, as Scott L.J. notes, where the grounds in paragraphs (a) and (b) are established, "it is difficult to construct any scenario in which rectification could be withheld".

3. The interpretation of paragraph (d), which requires the fraud to be practised on the *registrar*, imposes a significant restriction which is inconsistent with the earlier interpretation, according to which the paragraph covered the more usual case of fraud practised on the transferor: see *Re Leighton's Conveyance* [1936] 1 All E.R. 667; *Argyle Building Society v. Hammond* (1984) 49 P. & C.R. 148.

4. Paragraph (g) deals with the situation where the transfer that constitutes the registered disposition would, if title to the land were unregistered, be wholly ineffective to convey the legal estate. That is the situation if the transfer is a forgery. Similarly, there is jurisdiction to order rectification where a registered disposition includes a parcel of land but where the transferor has already disposed of that land or where the title of the transferor to that land has been extinguished by adverse possession: see *Chowood Ltd v. Lyall (No. 2)* [1930] 2 Ch. 156. However, the most common situation covered by this paragraph is where the registered title includes more land than was actually included in the transfer: Law Com. No. 254, *Land Registration for the Twenty-First Century* (1998), para. 8.19. The express reference in paragraph (g) to unregistered land has been criticised on the ground that it could involve the wholesale incorporation of unregistered land principles, including the doctrine of notice and the registration of land charges, which the registered land system was intended to supersede: Jackson (1978) 94 L.Q.R. 239, 243–244; Hayton, *Registered Land* (3rd ed., 1981), pp.169–170; Smith (1993) 109 L.Q.R. 187, 188. It is argued that such continued adherence to unregistered land principles "subordinates registered to unregistered land without any provision in the statute to support the subordination": Jackson (1978) 94 L.Q.R. 239, 254. However, according to the Law Commission, such concerns have not materialised.

5. The wide interpretation of paragraph (h) in earlier cases is clearly rejected by the Court of Appeal in *Norwich and Peterborough Building Society v. Steed*. Although the jurisdiction to rectify asserted in those earlier cases could probably be based instead on paragraphs (a) and (b), those grounds are available only to the court and not to the registrar.

6. The Court of Appeal in *Norwich and Peterborough Building Society v. Steed* has made it clear that grounds for rectification must be established against each person to be affected adversely. By contrast, it is arguable that the Court of Appeal in *Argyle Building Society v. Hammond* had asserted jurisdiction to order "secondary" rectification: so that where grounds for rectification are established against the registered proprietor, rectification may also be ordered against an innocent registered chargee without any need to establish any independent ground of rectification. Moreover, in *Norwich and Peterborough Building Society v. Steed* the Court of Appeal made it clear that, while independent grounds for rectification against the innocent chargees could almost certainly be established on the *assumed* facts in *Argyle Building Society v. Hammond* (that the transfer to the Hammonds was a forgery and

thus void), section 82(1) did not provide grounds for rectification against the innocent chargees where the transfer was merely voidable. See also *Re Leighton's Conveyance, supra.*

7. Although *Norwich and Peterborough Building Society v. Steed* involved an application to delete entries from the register, Davis [1992] Conv. 293 argues that the requirement of independent grounds for rectification should apply also where the application seeks a positive entry relating to some interest that will bind third parties as well as the registered proprietor.

8. For discussion of the availability of rectification of forged transfers, see Smith (1985) 101 L.Q.R. 79, 81–86.

1.2 *Effect of rectification*

Land Registration Act 1925, s.82(2)

(2) The register may be rectified under this section, notwithstanding that the rectification may affect any estates, rights, charges, or interests acquired or protected by registration, or by any entry on the register, or otherwise.

NOTES:

1. Section 82(2) reflects the abandonment of indefeasibility of title, which had been retained in the earlier legislation and according to which rectification was only permissible if it did not affect estates and rights acquired by registration. Moreover, it is clear from section 82(2) that rectification can take different forms. Most significantly, it involves the substitution of the registered proprietor: see, *e.g. Chowood Ltd v. Lyall (No. 2)* [1930] 2 Ch. 156; but it may also involve the entry of a notice of an interest affecting the registered land, whether such notice was omitted from the register or relates to an interest currently taking effect as an overriding interest: see, *e.g. Freer v. Unwins Ltd* [1976] Ch. 288; or the removal of an entry on the register: see, *e.g. Calgary & Edmonton Land Co. Ltd v. Discount Bank (Overseas) Ltd* [1971] 1 W.L.R. 81.

2. A second question relates to the effect of rectification on interests created or arising between the date of registration of the title which has been rectified and the date of rectification.

Freer v. Unwins Ltd [1976] Ch. 288

(Ch D., Walton J.)

The plaintiff had purchased a tobacconist shop together with the benefit of a covenant that the neighbouring shops would not be used for the sale of tobacco. Title to the properties was unregistered and the plaintiff registered the restricted covenant under the Land Charges Act. However, when the title to one of the neighbouring shops was registered, no notice of the restrictive covenant was entered on the register. In 1969 the freehold owners of the neighbouring shop granted a 21-year lease of the shop and in 1974 the lease was assigned to the defendants. The defendants searched the register of the freehold title and the search revealed no entry relating to the restrictive covenant. When the defendants started selling tobacco in the shop, the plaintiff obtained rectification of the register of the freehold title by the entry of a notice of the restrictive covenant; he then sought an injunction against the defendants.

WALTON J.:

The register having been rectified in that way, the question arises whether that rectification is binding on the defendants, in the sense that they are now bound by the restrictive covenant. It has been agreed, I think, by both [counsel] that either way round there is something of an anomaly, because if the defendants are not bound, then there does not appear to be any way in which, since the register has now been rectified, the plaintiff can obtain any benefit or compensation, or has any other remedy against any other person, notwithstanding that until the expiry of the lease the defendants will be able to act in breach of that restrictive covenant. On the other hand, so far as the defendants are concerned, they have done everything that they possibly could in order to ensure that they were entitled to use the property for the purposes for which they wished to use it, and it is hard to see what else they could have done; and further, they were not given any notice of the proposal to rectify, so that they were unable to make any submissions to the Chief Land Registrar about it. So that if the plaintiff wins, the defendants will then feel that they have been stabbed in the back, without any opportunity to turn round and face their attacker, although, of course, there would be no doubt that under the wide words of section 83(1) of the Land Registration Act 1925 they would be within the category of "any person suffering loss by reason of any rectification of the register," and therefore entitled to an indemnity.

That has led [counsel for the plaintiff] to submit to me that rectification and indemnity are complementary, the one being the mirror of the other, and that it must follow, since his client cannot get any indemnity against the defendants if they take free of the restrictive covenant for the duration of the lease, that that cannot be the right solution: whereas the fact that the defendants will be entitled to indemnity points to the fact that they are subject to the restrictive covenant. I see the force of that as an argument, but I think one is bound to take the Act as one finds it, and one of the odd things about rectification is that there is no provision in section 82—which is the section which deals with rectification—which states in terms or by implication what date is to be inserted against any entry which is inserted pursuant to rectification. One would perhaps have expected to have found some guidance as to the date, but no guidance whatsoever is given. It merely says "The register may be rectified," and then, apart from setting out the provision, the circumstances under which it may be rectified, and making certain qualifications as to when it may be and when it shall not be rectified, it does not, I think, tell one anything more about the date as from which the restriction takes effect.

Now, of course, if one were dealing with the ordinary sort of rectification with which courts of equity are accustomed to deal in relation to documents, that always correspondingly, the rights of all parties who have in the meantime gained interests on the faith of the unrectified document for value without notice are strenuously protected. So that I do not think that one can, having regard to the rather different provisions of the Land Registration Act 1925, really equate a rectification in equity with rectification under the Act.

So I turn to the effect of registration of dispositions of freeholds, bearing in mind for the moment, of course, that the lease which was granted and which the defendants now hold was not a lease which was registered, or indeed could be registered. But section 19(2) says:

"All interests transferred or created by dispositions by the proprietor, other than a transfer of the registered estate in the land, or part thereof, shall, subject to the provisions relating to mortgages, be completed by registration in the same manner and with the same effect as provided by this Act with respect to transfers of registered estates and notice thereof shall also be noted on the register: Provided that nothing in this subsection—(a) shall authorise the registration of a lease granted for a term not exceeding 21 years ...", and then it goes on to say: "Every such disposition shall, when registered, take effect as a registered disposition, and a lease made by the registered proprietor ... which is not required to be registered ... shall nevertheless take effect as if it were a registered disposition immediately on being granted."

Therefore, one must take it that for the purposes of the general scheme of the Act of 1925 the lease of December 8, 1969, must be taken to have taken effect as if it were a registered disposition immediately upon being granted. That being so, it is subject to the incumbrances and other entries appearing on the register and to overriding interests, if any, affecting it, but free from all other estates and interests whatsoever, and that is the language of section 20(1).

So, prima facie, one must look at what the position was on December 8, 1969, when the lease was granted, and see what was on the register then, and, of course, it is common ground that on that date there was nothing on the register in relation to the restrictive covenant. Now, what should have been on the register in relation to the restrictive covenant which the plaintiff now relies on? That is stated in section 50, which provides:

"(1) Any person entitled to the benefit of a restrictive covenant ... may apply to the register to enter notice thereof on the register ... (2) When such a notice is entered the proprietor of the land and the persons deriving title under him (except incumbrancers or other persons who at the time when the notice is entered may not be bound by the covenant or agreement) shall be deemed to be affected with the notice of the covenant or agreement as being an incumbrance on the land."

Then section 52(1):

"A disposition by the proprietor shall take effect subject to all estates, rights, and claims which are protected by way of notice on the register at the date of the registration or entry of notice of the disposition ..."

and then there is a proviso with which I am not concerned.

It seems to me that the scheme of the Act requires one to look in every case at the date of the notice of the restrictive covenant on the register. Section 50(2) provides:

"When such a notice is entered"—and that, I think, must mean when the notice is entered and not from any earlier date—"the proprietor of the land and the persons deriving title under him ..."—and then there is the exception which I will come back to in a moment—"shall be deemed to be affected with notice of the covenant or agreement as being an incumbrance on the land."

But there is excepted in clear language:

"... (except incumbrancers or other persons who at the time when the notice is entered may not be bound by the covenant or agreement) ..."

What Mr Jackson has submitted to me is that those words are inconsistent with the general scheme of the Land Registration Act 1925 and should therefore be given a very narrow ambit. I am not myself persuaded in any way that those words are inconsistent with the general scheme of the Act. It appears to me that the general scheme of the Act is that one obtains priority according to the date of registration, and one is subject, or not subject, to matters appearing on the register according to whether they were there before or after one took one's interest, whatever that interest might be. That seems to me to be the only sensible way in which the provisions of the Act can all be made to mesh together. For example, supposing that now, for the first time, the defendants' landlords, the registered proprietors, were to impose a restrictive covenant on the land, which they are fully entitled to do, that restrictive covenant would then have to be protected by notice on the register, and it would have the effect stated in section 50(2):

"When such a notice is entered the proprietor of the land and the persons deriving title under him (except incumbrances or other persons who at the time when the notice is entered may not be bound by the covenant or agreement) ..."

and that exception surely must include a lessee who was not a party to the covenant or agreement and who had taken his lease prior to the date when the notice was entered.

So it seems to me that so far from it being an exception to the scheme of the Act, those words are fully consistent with it and especially in view of the extremely simple example that I have given, which all must concede, I think, could not possibly result in the lessee being bound by the subsequent restrictive covenant. The words "other persons" in the exception in section 50(2) must surely include "lessees" and indeed I think there are many places in the Act in which "leases" are referred to as "incumbrances," so that, possibly, even without that, one might be driven to including "lessees" in the first exception, "incumbrancers," but certainly they are "other persons who at the time when the notice is entered may not be bound by the covenant or agreement." Of course, if it is contemplated that they may be bound for example if the defendants joined with their landlords in granting a restrictive covenant, then they would be bound—and of course the exception caters for that—but in general they would not be bound.

So, in my view at the end of the day, the matter comes down to the fact that, for better or for worse, the date which is given in the charges register for the entry of this notice of the restrictive covenant is April 28, 1975. [Counsel for the defendants] was quite content to take that date for the purposes of the present case, although of course, so far as he was concerned, it might be that date or any later date, so long as it was not any earlier date, and, of course, just to complete this—because this is a matter which puzzled me at the beginning—the charges register notes that the date at the beginning of each entry is the date on which the entry was made on this edition of the register. The result of course is that a large number of things are dated as of April 28, 1975, but all such matters appeared on the first edition of the register to which one could refer in order to discover whether they were on the first edition at the date of any particular disposition. It is not disputed that in the present case there was no such entry on the charges register on the first edition prior to April 28, 1975, and that therefore is the earliest date to which one can backdate the entry of this notice. The entry of the notice being subsequent to the date of the lease of December 8, 1969, in my judgment Shaws Laundries Ltd took free from that notice, therefore free from the restrictive covenant to which it related, and their assignees, the defendants, are in an exactly similar position. Therefore, it appears to me that the plaintiff, for whom I have the greatest possible sympathy, in fact is not entitled to enforce this covenant quoad the defendants. I realise that this is a very curious result, in that it appears that the plaintiff would have no claim to any indemnity against anybody because of the fact that he cannot enforce this restrictive covenant against the defendants, but it seems to me that if that is the position, that is a defect in the Act, and that the Act is clear in its general outlines and specific provisions, under which it is only matters that are actually registered at the time that the disposition is made which affect the person who derives title under the registered proprietor. Of course, I should like to make it clear that in other cases that may not be the end of the story. In the present case one is dealing with a lease which is not registrable, and therefore has not been registered, and therefore there is no proprietorship register in relation to it because it is not separately registered as leasehold land with a title of its own. But if there were to be a lease of that nature, then it might very well be that rectification would be available against that title, as well as the title of the freehold; but, of course, equally in that case the provisions of section 82(3)(c) would apply, and I cannot, as at present advised, think that a lessee who has taken every precaution to see that he is entitled to use the land for the purpose for which he wishes to use it, so far as he can see, would have the title rectified against him, because so far from it being unjust not to rectify the register against him—at any rate, in the usual case which is likely to happen—it seems to me that it would be most unjust to rectify the register against him. Vigilantibus non dormientibus servit aequitas; "Equity aids the vigilant and not the indolent," and here the defendants have been very vigilant—although I am not ascribing to the plaintiff any sleeping on his rights. But the defendants having been vigilant, even if they had had a separate registered title, I do not think there would have been any prospect of rectification as against them.

NOTES:

1. On the basis that the freehold owners were registered proprietors in possession by reason of their receipt of rent (see *infra*), Walton J. (at 295) expressed "very great surprise" that rectification had been ordered: but see Hayton [1976] C.L.J. 215; Crane (1976) 40 Conv. 304; Smith (1976) 92 L.Q.R. 338.

2. In *Clark v. Chief Land Registrar* [1993] Ch. 294 Ferris J. referred to the observations of Walton J. in *Freer v. Unwins* and doubted whether section 82 conferred on the court jurisdiction to order rectification with *retrospective* effect: *ibid.* 317–318. In neither case did the court consider section 82(2); but the Law Commission considers that rectification cannot be made retrospective by virtue of that provision or otherwise: Law Com. No. 254, *Land Registration for the Twenty-First Century* (1998), paras 8.32–8.33.

3. It has been seen that in *Argyle Building Society v. Hammond* Slade L.J. relied on section 82(2) in asserting that the jurisdiction of the court to order rectification is exercisable against innocent persons claiming through a registered proprietor. However, in so far as he relied on section 82(2) as authority for what has been termed "secondary" rectification, that interpretation has been rejected by the Court of Appeal in *Norwich and Peterborough Building Society v. Steed*.

1.3 *Protection of the registered proprietor in possession*
Despite the wider range of grounds for rectification introduced in the Land Registration Act 1925, the attraction of indefeasibility of title continued to be reflected in the protection afforded to the registered proprietor in possession.

Land Registration Act 1925, s.82(3)

(3) The register shall not be rectified, except for the purpose of giving effect to an overriding interest or an order of the court, so as to affect the title of the proprietor who is in possession—
   (a) unless the proprietor has caused or substantially contributed to the error or omission by fraud or lack of proper care; or
   (c) unless for any other reason, in any particular case, it is considered that it would be unjust not to rectify the register against him.

NOTES:

1. There is some uncertainty as to the meaning of "proprietor who is in

possession" for the purposes of section 82(3), although it is accepted that the protection cannot extend to *all* registered proprietors: see Law Com. No. 254, *Land Registration for the Twenty-First Century* (1998), paras 8.24–8.26. First, section 82(4) provides that a person who is "in possession of registered land in right of a minor interest" (for example, a beneficiary under a trust of land or a person in possession pursuant to an agreement for a lease) is, for the purposes of section 82, deemed to be in possession as agent for the proprietor. That provision would be redundant if the protection of section 82(3) extended to all registered proprietors. Secondly, "possession" is defined by section 3(xviii) as including "receipt of rents and profits or the right to receive the same". Although that definition applies only "unless the context otherwise requires", and although in this context it has been argued that the protection extends only to those registered proprietors who are themselves in *physical* possession of the relevant land, in *Freer v. Unwins Ltd* [1976] Ch. 288 Walton J. expressed the view (at 294) that the protection afforded by section 82(3) extended to registered proprietors actually in receipt of rents and profits. It is therefore argued that the protection does not extend to registered proprietors merely on the basis of their right to receive rent and profits, again because that would embrace all registered proprietors. That would be consistent with the protection afforded to persons in receipt of rents and profits under section 70(1)(g): see *supra*, p. 231.

2. The removal of the protection where rectification is sought to give effect to an overriding interest is supposedly justified on the basis that a transferee of registered land takes subject to overriding interests and he is therefore not adversely affected by the rectification of the register which merely reflects the existing position. On the other hand, the category of overriding interests has been significantly extended by the judicial interpretation, in particular, of section 70(1)(g) of the Land Registration Act 1925: see *supra*, p. 187.

3. The exception permitting rectification to give effect to an order of the court was introduced by the Administration of Justice Act 1977. Its purpose has remained unclear. To the extent that it includes a court order made under section 82(1) itself, it could entirely remove the protection of the registered proprietor. On the other hand, it has been suggested that the provision was indeed intended to ensure that there were no restrictions on the powers of the court to order rectification on the grounds in section 82(1)(a) and (b), where the order gives effect to the substantive rights and entitlements of the parties: Law Com. No. 254, *Land Registration for the Twenty-First Century* (1998), para. 8.29. It had previously been suggested that the provision was intended to remove the protection of the registered proprietor where rectification was sought to give effect to an order of the court setting aside a transfer designed to defeat the rights of a trustee in bankruptcy: see Law Com. No. 158, *Property Law: Third Report on Land Registration* (1987), para. 3.13.

4. As originally enacted, section 82(3)(a) was interpreted, albeit reluctantly, as removing the protection of the registered proprietor where he had *innocently* caused or contributed to the error in the register by lodging defective documents on an application for first registration: see *Re 139 Deptford High Street* [1951] Ch. 884, 891–892 *per* Wynn-Parry J.; *Re Sea*

View Gardens [1967] 1 W.L.R. 134, 141 *per* Pennycuick J., noted at (1967) 31 Conv. 56. Such an interpretation arguably rendered illusory the protection for a first registered proprietor: Law Commission Working Paper No. 45, *Transfer of Land: Land Registration (Second Paper)* (1972), para. 79. The amended version, introduced by the Administration of Justice Act 1977, has not been litigated; but it is suggested that "lack of proper care" probably covers the failure to carry out usual conveyancing inquiries and inspections.

5. Section 82(3)(c) seems to provide an extremely wide discretion for the courts to deny the prima facie protection of the registered proprietor. Thus, in *Chowood v. Lyall (No. 2)* [1930] 1 Ch. 426 Luxmoore J. expressed the view that it would be unjust not to rectify where registration had deprived an innocent person of land to which he was entitled immediately before that registration. Such an approach effectively treats the registered land system as no more than a method of recording the substantive principles of unregistered land. In *Epps v. Esso Petroleum Co. Ltd* [1973] 1 W.L.R. 1071, 1080–1083, Templeman J. adopted a more balanced approach to the paragraph: see *infra*, p. 255. In *Hounslow LBC v. Hare* (1992) 24 H.L.R. 9, noted at [1993] Conv. 224, Knox J. declined to order rectification against a registered proprietor in possession under what turned out to be a void lease: the proprietor had been a tenant of the property for many years and could not possibly have known that the transfer to him was *ultra vires* the transferor.

6. Where the protection of the registered proprietor is removed, rectification is not automatic: rather the discretion conferred by section 82(1) is restored: see *Re Sea View Gardens,* [1967] W.L.R. 134, 141 *per* Pennycuick J.; *Epps v. Esso Petroleum Co. Ltd, supra,* 1078–1079 *per* Templeman J.; contrast *Re 139 Deptford High Street,* [1951] Ch. 884, where Wynn-Parry J. (at 889) appears to have considered that rectification must inevitably follow in such circumstances. In practice, there seems to be a presumption in favour of rectification; and rectification is probably inevitable where the protection is removed by reason of section 82(3)(c).

2. Indemnity

In principle, indemnity is available to compensate for loss caused by rectification (and since 1997 loss caused *despite* rectification) or for loss caused by an error or omission which is not rectified.

Land Registration Act 1925, s.83(1),(2)

Indemnity for errors or omissions in the register

83.—(1) Where the register is rectified under this Act, then, subject to the provisions of this Act—
  (a) any person suffering loss by reason of the rectification shall be entitled to be indemnified; and
  (b) if, notwithstanding the rectification, the person in whose favour the register is rectified suffers loss by reason of an error or omission in the register in respect of which it is so rectified, he also shall be entitled to be indemnified.

(2) Where an error or omission has occurred in the register, but the register is not rectified, any person suffering loss by reason of the error or omission shall, subject to the provisions of this Act, be entitled to be indemnified.

NOTES:

1. If rectification and indemnity were truly complementary, subsections (1)(a) and (2) would operate as follows. Suppose two neighbouring properties, Blackacre and Whiteacre, separated by a strip of land, the "disputed land". Prior to registration of title, the disputed land constitutes part of Blackacre. However, when the properties are sold to B and W respectively, the transfer of Whiteacre mistakenly includes the disputed strip and W becomes registered proprietor. If B successfully claims rectification of the register, he will recover the disputed strip; but W will be deprived of land which the register previously credited to him. In such circumstances, W should be entitled to indemnity under subsection (1). On the other hand, if the court declines to order rectification in favour of B, W will retain the land which the register credits to him; but B will be deprived of the land to which he may fairly claim to be entitled. In such circumstances, B should be entitled to indemnity under subsection (2).

2. It appears, therefore, that neither B nor W can lose: for, leaving aside the use-value of the land, one party recovers/retains the land and the other party receives compensation. However, this apparent equality is distorted. First, section 83(8) provides for different levels of compensation. Where rectification is ordered, the maximum compensation payable to W (whose claim to the disputed land is based solely on the mistake in the transfer) is the value of the land immediately before rectification: section 83(8)(b); but where rectification is not ordered, the maximum compensation payable to B (who has been deprived of the disputed land solely by reason of the mistake in the transfer) is the value of the land when the error which caused the loss was made: section 83(8)(a); and see *Hounslow LBC v. Hare* (1992) 24 H.L.R. 9, 25 *per* Knox J. Against the traditional background of rising property values, B may thus receive by way of compensation considerably less than the current value of the land. Despite an earlier recommendation that compensation should be assessed in all cases by reference to the value of the land at the time of the decision as to rectification (Law Com. No. 158, *Property Law: Third Report on Land Registration* (1987), paras. 3.30–3.32), the differentiation has been preserved in the new section 83. It was argued (i) that, where the claim relates to loss suffered by reason of an error or omission which is not rectified, it would be inappropriate for compensation to cover alterations to the land that might have taken place since the error or omission; and (ii) that an award of indemnity includes interest from the time of the error or omission: Law Com. No. 235, *Transfer of Land: Land Registration* (1995), para. 4.6. On the first point, appropriate provision could have been made to prevent undeserved windfalls; on the second point, interest rates have usually been significantly lower than the rate of increase in property values: see Tee [1996] C.L.J. 241, 247. However, the Land Registration Act 1997 has removed what was an additional potential disadvantage for B. Under section 83 as originally

enacted, a claim to indemnity based on loss suffered by reason of an error that was not rectified was statute-barred after six years from the date of the error, *whether or not the claimant knew of the error at the time it was made.* The new section 83(12) applies the more usual limitation principle that the cause of action is deemed to arise only when the claimant knows, or but for his own default might have known, of the existence of his claim.

3. A lacuna in the indemnity provisions was revealed in the case of *Freer v. Unwins Ltd* [1976] Ch. 288, where the defendant suffered loss *despite* rectification because of the limited effect afforded to that rectification: see *supra*, p. 246. However, that lacuna would seem to have been filled by the new section 83(1)(b).

4. No indemnity is payable in respect of rectification to give effect to an overriding interest. This exception is not expressly mentioned in the Act but it is justified on the ground that a transferee of registered land takes subject to overriding interests and he therefore suffers no loss when the register is rectified so as to reflect the existing position: see *Re Chowood's Registered Land* [1933] Ch. 574. A recommendation from the Law Commission that indemnity should be payable where the register is rectified to give effect to an overriding interest (Law Com. No. 158, *Property Law: Third Report on Land Registration* (1987), paras 2.10–2.14) was contrary to its earlier proposal (Law Commission Working Paper No. 45, *Transfer of Land: Land Registration (Third Paper)* (1972), para. 101) and has now been abandoned: Law Com. No. 254, *Land Registration for the Twenty-First Century* (1998), paras 4.19–4.20. The Law Commission endorses the justification in *Re Chowood's Registered Land* and also notes the potential open-ended financial liability of paying indemnity in such circumstances.

5. Section 83 excludes or restricts the payment of indemnity where there is fraud or lack of proper care on the part of the applicant or any person from whom he derives title (otherwise than under a disposition for valuable consideration which is registered or protected on the register). Indemnity is excluded where the loss is suffered wholly or partly as a result of the fraud, or wholly as a result of the lack of proper care, of such a person. Where the loss is suffered partly as a result of his lack of proper care, any indemnity is reduced to such an extent as is just and equitable having regard to his share in the responsibility for the loss: section 83(5)–(7).

6. There are a number of cases which suggest that the availability or non-availability of indemnity is a relevant consideration in the exercise of the discretion to order rectification: *Epps v. Esso Petroleum Co. Ltd* [1973] 1 W.L.R. 1071, 1081–1083 *per* Templeman J.; *Argyle Building Society v. Hammond* (1984) 49 P. & C.R. 148, 162 *per* Slade L.J.; *Norwich and Peterborough Building Society v. Steed* [1993] Ch. 116, 138–139 *per* Scott L.J. However, it is clearly not a decisive factor. In *Epps v. Esso Petroleum Co. Ltd* indemnity would have been available to the defendants if rectification had been ordered in favour of the plaintiffs, whereas indemnity would not have been available to the plaintiffs if rectification had been refused; but Templeman J. refused to order rectification: see *infra*. Moreover, in *Norwich and Peterborough Building Society v. Steed* it seems that Scott L.J. would have

refused rectification against the plaintiffs notwithstanding that the defendant would not be entitled to indemnity.

3. Rectification and indemnity in operation

Epps v. Esso Petroleum Co. Ltd [1973] 1 W.L.R. 1071

(Ch D., Templeman J.)

Clifford was the fee simple owner of two adjoining properties, 4 Darland Avenue (the house) and Darland Garage; but both properties were leased to Jones. In 1955, when the titles to both properties were still unregistered, the house was conveyed to Jones' wife; the conveyance included "the disputed strip" between the house and Darland Garage, on which Mrs Jones intended to build a private garage; and Mrs Jones covenanted to erect a wall so as to separate the disputed strip from Darland Garage. In fact Mrs Jones neither built a garage nor erected a wall, so that the disputed strip was not clearly identifiable. In 1959, by which time the area was an area of compulsory registration, Darland Garage was transferred to Ball, subject to Jones' lease. Ball became first registered proprietor of Darland Garage and the disputed strip, which had mistakenly been included in the transfer. In 1964, after Jones' lease had expired, the defendants became registered proprietors of Darland Garage and the disputed strip (and by virtue of section 110 of the Land Registration Act 1925 they had no opportunity of discovering the double conveyance). In 1968 the plaintiffs became first registered proprietors of the house. Both before and after the transfer there had been inconclusive discussions between the plaintiffs and the defendants in which both parties assumed entitlement to the disputed strip; and the plaintiffs had erected a fence on the boundary between the disputed strip and Darland Garage. However, the registered title of the plaintiffs excluded the disputed strip and they sought rectification of the register.

TEMPLEMAN J.:
Mr Cullen, for the plaintiffs, submitted that when Mrs Jones was deprived of her legal estate in fee simple by the mistaken registration of Mr Ball as proprietor, Mrs Jones retained or acquired, and her successors in title, down to and including the plaintiffs, acquired an equitable interest in fee simple. The registered proprietor, first Mr Ball and now the defendants, acquired the legal estate, subject to the equitable interest of Mrs Jones and her successors. Effect should be given to that equitable interest by rectification. The limitation on the exercise of the power of rectification, which is to be found in section 82(3), does not apply where rectification is required to give effect to an overriding interest. The equitable interest of Mrs Jones and her successors in title is an overriding interest.

By section 70(1)(g) overriding interests include the rights of every person in actual occupation of the land or in receipt of the rents and profits thereof, save where inquiry is made of such person and the rights are not disclosed. Mrs Jones and her successors in title were in actual occupation, because Mr Jones, and later the plaintiffs, parked a car on the disputed strip. Mr Ball and the defendants acquired the disputed strip subject to the overriding interests of Mrs Jones and her successors constituted by an equitable interest protected by actual occupation. The defendants never were in possession or, at any rate, ceased to be in possession when the plaintiffs erected their fence in 1968. Thus far Mr Cullen.

In considering this case I propose to ignore the fence erected by the plaintiffs in 1968 after they had entered into amicable discussions with the defendants. Even if section 82(3) referred to de facto possession as at the date of the trial of these proceedings, I would have restored the position by ignoring the fence when considering the exercise of the general discretion conferred by section 82(1). It does not seem to me that in order to secure the protection given by the statute the defendants were bound forcibly to re-enter and tear down the fence or to get an injunction pending trial.

The claim put forward by Mr Cullen on behalf of the plaintiffs to an overriding interest depends on whether Mr Jones was in actual occupation of the disputed strip when the defendants became the registered proprietor of the disputed strip in 1964. The contention put forward by Mr Cullen that the defendants were not in possession depends on whether they went into possession of the disputed strip when they became the registered proprietor and remained in possession until after the plaintiffs completed their purchase in 1968. Mr Brodie for the defendants took up a position at the opposite pole. He submitted that even if Mr Jones was in actual occupation he occupied in his capacity as tenant of Mr Ball. Alternatively, the occupation of Mr Jones could not protect any equitable interest vested in the probate judge at the date when the defendants became the registered proprietors of the disputed strip in 1964.

I reject these submissions of Mr Brodie. If Mr Jones was in actual occupation when the defendants completed their purchase of the disputed strip then his occupation in the present circumstances sufficed to assert and protect any equitable interest of Mrs Jones and her estate so as to constitute an overriding interest, and sufficed also to defeat the claim by the defendants to be in possession.

Mr Brodie also submitted that where rectification is sought, not against the first registered proprietor, in this case Mr Ball, but against the subsequent transferee for value, in this case the defendants, the subsequent transferee must be treated as a bona fide purchaser for value without notice, and he will not be compelled to suffer rectification save in exceptional circumstances. For this proposition he cited *In re Leighton's Conveyance* [1936] 1 All E.R. 667 where a transfer was procured from a registered proprietor by fraud, and the original registered proprietor was held to be bound by a charge executed by the fraudulent transferee in favour of an innocent mortgagee.

That case is, however, only an illustration of an estoppel operating in certain circumstances against a person who executes a document relied upon by an innocent third party, and does not assist me in the present case.

In my judgment, the fact that the defendants were not the original proprietors, but subsequent transferees, is only one element to be considered in the exercise of the discretion conferred by section 82(1) and section 82(3)(c) of the Land Registration Act 1925. In the confrontation envisaged by section 82(1) and in particular by section 82(1)(g), between, on the one hand, the registered proprietor, who is a victim of double conveyancing, and the first purchaser or his successors, deprived of the legal estate by registration, the court must first determine whether the registered proprietor is in possession. If the registered proprietor is not in possession then section 82(3) does not apply, and the court will normally grant rectification: see *Chowood Ltd v. Lyall (No. 2)* [1930] 2 Ch. 156. A fortiori if the registered proprietor is not in possession but the applicant has an overriding interest constituted by an equitable interest protected by actual occupation, the court will grant rectification: see *Bridges v. Mees* [1957] 1 Ch. 475, 486. However, the power of rectification given by section 82(1) never ceases to be discretionary, so that where section 82(3) does not apply there may still be circumstances which defeat the claim for rectification.

If the registered proprietor is in possession, the applicant for rectification will not normally be in actual occupation, and one of the conditions specified in section 82(3) must be satisfied if rectification is to be granted. If the registered proprietor is the first registered proprietor and has caused or contributed to the mistake in registration then section 82(3)(a) applies and rectification will normally be granted: see *In re No. 139 Deptford High Street, Ex parte British Transport Commission* [1951] Ch. 884. But where the applicant has, for example, allowed the registered proprietor to build on the land, then, even though the conditions in section 82(3)(a) have been satisfied, the court taking the hint from section 82(3)(c) and exercising the discretion conferred by section 82(1) may refuse to rectify: see *Claridge v. Tingey* [1967] 1 W.L.R. 134.

If the proprietor is not the first registered proprietor but is a subsequent transferee he will not normally be responsible for the mistake in registration in any way at all. So that the conditions specified in section 82(3)(a) will not be satisfied, and to this limited extent a subsequent transferee is in a better position than the first registered proprietor. But whether the proprietor be the first registered proprietor or a subsequent transferee rectifications will still be granted under section 82(3)(c) if for any reason in any particular case it is considered that it would be unjust not to rectify the register against the registered proprietor.

It follows that the crucial questions in the present case are, first, whether Mr Jones was in actual occupation of the disputed strip when the defendants completed purchase in 1964; secondly, whether the defendants were in possession at the date when the plaintiffs completed their purchase of 4 Darland Avenue in 1968; and if those questions are decided in favour of the defendants, thirdly, whether it would be unjust not to rectify against them.

In *Hodgson v. Marks* [1971] Ch. 892, 931, Russell L.J. said, on actual occupation as an ingredient of an overriding interest, that he was prepared for the purpose of that case to assume, without necessarily accepting, that section 70(1)(g) of the Land Registration Act 1925 is designed only to apply to a case in which the occupation is such in point of fact as would in the case of unregistered land affect a purchaser with constructive notice of the rights of the occupier. Then Russell L.J. said, at p. 932:

"I do not think it desirable to attempt to lay down a code or catalogue of situations in which a person other than the vendor should be held to be in occupation of unregistered land for the purpose of constructive notice of his rights, or in actual occupation of registered land for the purposes of section 70(1)(g). It must depend on the circumstances, and a wise purchaser or vendor will take no risks. Indeed, however wise he may be he may have no ready opportunity of finding out; but, nevertheless, the law will protect the occupier."

In my judgment Mr Jones was not in actual occupation of the disputed strip when the defendants completed their purchase of Darland Garage and was not thereafter in actual occupation.

Mr Jones gave evidence that every night he parked his car on the disputed strip, and sometimes the car was there during the day. Mr Jones's recollection, not unnaturally, was not very reliable, and I find that he sometimes parked his car on the disputed strip, but how often and when no one can now determine with any certainty. But even if Mr Jones regularly parked his car on the disputed strip I do not consider that this constituted actual occupation of the disputed strip in the circumstances of the present case. I reach this conclusion for the following reasons: first, the parking of a car on a strip 11 feet wide by 80 feet long does not actually occupy the whole, or a substantial, or any defined part of that disputed strip for the whole or any defined time. Secondly, the parking of a car on an unidentified piece of land, apparently comprised in garage premises, is not an assertion of actual occupation of anything.

In addition to these two reasons there are circumstances which show that, not only was Mr Jones not in actual occupation, but on the contrary that the defendants were. First, there is no evidence that Mr Ball or the defendants were ever aware that Mr Jones parked his car on the disputed strip. The fact that the defendants completed their purchase after stipulating for vacant possession is an indication that both Mr Ball and the defendants considered that vacant possession was in fact given and taken on completion. Secondly, the brick wall 4 feet from the house, 4 Darland Avenue, was an assertion that the occupier of Darland Garage occupied land up to that wall, and was just as much in possession of the disputed strip as of any other part of the apparent Darland Garage premises. Thirdly, as appears from the defendants' photographs, there was no method of driving on to the strip from Darland Avenue without trespassing on to the garage premises unless the car in question was bounced up the kerb and steered between a stop sign and a tree. These difficulties could, no doubt, be overcome, but they added force to the apparent assertion by all the indications on the ground that the disputed strip was part and parcel of Darland Garage and was occupied and possessed therewith, and that the claim and title of 4 Darland Avenue ceased where the brick wall ceased. In the result Mr Jones and the plaintiffs were, in my judgment, never at any material time in actual occupation of the disputed strip, and the defendants were at all material times in possession of the disputed strip. The defendants claimed that they occupied the disputed strip by depositing waste materials on the strip as part of the garage land. Precise evidence of this was, not unnaturally, impossible to obtain. I accept, however, that the defendants did treat the disputed strip just in the same way that they treated any other part of the garage land and premises.

In my judgment, therefore, section 82(3) does apply because the Jones's and the plaintiffs had no overriding interest protected by actual occupation and because the defendants were in possession. There remains the question, under condition (c) of section 82(3) whether it would be unjust not to rectify against the defendants.

In my judgment, justice in the present case lies wholly with the defendants and not with the plaintiffs. There was nothing on the register or on the ground on or before the date when the defendants became the registered proprietors of the disputed strip which put the defendants on inquiry. On the contrary, both the register and the appearance on the ground proclaimed title to and possession of the disputed strip, and the garage premises were one and indivisible. No reasonable requisition by the defendants from the vendor, Mr Ball, would in the circumstances have disclosed the existence, let alone any claim to the disputed strip. The absence of any indication on the ground was due to the default of the plaintiffs' predecessor in title in not complying with her covenant to build a boundary wall which would mark out the disputed strip. On the other hand, the plaintiffs, even without hindsight, were taking a gamble. The title disclosed to them showed the obligation of Mrs Jones to build a boundary wall. Inspection of the site disclosed that the only wall in existence was the original wall 4 feet from the side of the house. It was possible that the frontage of 39 feet mentioned in the 1955 conveyance was a mistake; whether it was a mistake or not it was possible that the true 1955 boundary between 4 Darland Avenue and Darland Garage was the line of the original wall. If the true 1955 boundary was not the existing wall but a new wall to be constructed on the northern boundary of the disputed strip it was possible that because of the failure to build the wall or to mark out the disputed strip, title to the disputed strip had been lost by adverse possession, or, as in fact happened, by a natural mistake on registration.

The plaintiffs must have realised that there might be some difficulty over the boundary between 4 Darland Avenue and Darland Garage; hence Mr Epps's letter dated July 31, 1968. The inquiries made in that letter after completion could have been made, and ought to have been made, before completion. The plaintiffs or their legal advisers, if properly instructed, ought to have required their vendor, Mr Jones, to prove that the boundary between the disputed strip and Darland Garage was 11 feet from the brick wall, and was known to and acknowledged by the owner of Darland Garage to be that un-marked boundary and not the apparent boundary constituted by the brick wall 4 feet from the side wall of the house. The plaintiffs or their legal advisers, if properly instructed, ought to have realised that without further inquiries to their vendor, and inquiries by their vendor to the defendants, it had not been established that the vendor was in a position to give a good title or in a position to give possession of the disputed strip to the plaintiffs.

In my judgment, whereas the defendants bought the disputed strip, the plaintiffs bought a law suit, thanks to the default of their vendor in not taking steps to assert ownership and possession of the disputed strip, and thanks to the failure of the plaintiffs to make before completion the inquiries which they made immediately after completion.

Mr Cullen put forward one additional circumstance which he argued, with some force, tilted the balance of justice in favour of rectification. That circumstance, he submitted, was that if the register is rectified the defendants can recover compensation based on the 1973 value of the disputed strip, but if the register is not rectified the plaintiffs cannot recover compensation. This argument is founded on section 83 of the Land Registration Act 1925 which deals with compensation. Section 83(1) provides that, subject to the provisions of the Act to the contrary, any person suffering loss by reason of any rectification of the register under the Act shall be entitled to be indemnified. That will be the position of the defendants if I rectify. Section 83(2) provides that where an error or omission has occurred in the register but the register is not rectified, any person suffering loss by reason of such error or omission shall, subject to the provisions of the Act, be entitled to be indemnified. That is the position of the plaintiffs, if I do not rectify.

By section 83(6) where indemnity is paid in respect of the loss of an estate or interest in or charge on land the amount so paid shall not exceed (a), where the register is not rectified the value of the estate interest or charge at the time when the error or omission which caused the loss was made. In other words, if I do not rectify then the plaintiffs' indemnity is reduced to the value of the disputed strip as at 1959 when the error was made. Subsection (6)(b), on the other hand, says that where the register is rectified the indemnity is not to exceed the value if there had been no rectification of the estate, interest or charge immediately before the time of rectification. This would apply to the defendants. So that the legislature provides 1959 values for the plaintiffs and 1973 values for the defendants. The matter does not end there, however, because by subsection (11) there is a further limitation on indemnity. Subsection (11) provides that a liability to pay indemnity under the Act shall be deemed a simple contract debt and for the purposes of the Limitation Act the cause of action shall be deemed to arise at the time when the claimant knows or, but for his own default, might have known of the existence of his claim. Whether or not that applies to the plaintiffs, it clearly does not affect the defendants; first, because they are not claimants; and, secondly, because they must have been in complete innocence of anything wrong until the plaintiffs came on the scene and raised the question of where the true boundary lay. Then there is a proviso:

> "Provided that, when a claim to indemnity arises in consequence of the registration of an estate in land with an absolute or good leasehold title, the claim shall be enforceable only if made within six years from the date of such registration, except in the following cases..."

and then it sets out cases involving infants or settled land, which plainly do not apply. Clearly, that proviso operates to deprive the plaintiffs of compensation, because their claim to indemnity is made more than six years from the date of the 1959 registration. Mr Cullen submits that it does not apply to the defendants. First, he says that the proviso only applies to section 83(2); and, secondly, he says that the claim to indemnity will only arise so far as the defendants are concerned in consequence of the registration which will follow upon any order for rectification.

Mr Brodie, on the other hand, submits that the proviso applies to the defendants and that if it does not, the matter is obscure, and any decision I make on it will not be binding, and the defendants should not be left in the uncertainty of knowing whether that decision is right.

I can only peer through my own spectacles and, in my judgment, the proviso does not apply to the defendants. It is intended only to apply to a claimant who has the means and opportunity of finding out and asserting his claim, and therefore there is no reason why the six-year period should not operate. In the case of the defendants, however, who are in possession and who have got the title, I do not consider that the proviso applies; they will not suffer and their claim to indemnity will not arise unless and until an order for rectification is made. Accordingly, the foundation for Mr Cullen's submission is established. This is a case, in my judgment, in which if an order for rectification is made the defendants will be entitled to indemnity on 1973 values, and if the claim for rectification is refused then they will keep the land, but the plaintiffs will not get compensation.

The question I have to determine is whether that is sufficient to upset the justice of the defendants' claim that there should not be rectification in the present instance. Is it sufficient—and this is the test—to make it unjust not to rectify the register against the defendants? Mr Cullen pointed out that as far as the defendants are concerned the disputed strip formed, he calculated, 4 per cent of the garage premises. He said it could not make a lot of difference to the defendants' garage; on the other hand, it was of importance to 4 Darland Avenue because it provided a private garage, an asset which is important in commuter territory.

In my judgment, however, this cannot be solved merely on the question of money. The defendants bought the land; they bought it to exploit for their commercial purposes; they did not buy it in order to sell a strip for a 1973 value, which in real terms will not, in my judgment, adequately indemnify them. Although the strip is at the back of the garage, in the same way as it could be used as a private garage for 4 Darland Avenue, so it could be used by the defendants for commercial purposes, and in fact they say now they intend to use it in connection with a car wash; if they are deprived of it they will be in considerable difficulty, and will not have all the facilities which a modern garage requires. I think that may be putting it a bit high, but the fact of the matter is that this strip is worth more to the defendants than the pounds, shillings and pence which they will receive by indemnity, even on a 1973 basis.

Accordingly, in my judgment, that argument is not sufficient to overturn all the other arguments in favour of the defendants, and I decline to order rectification of the register.

NOTE:

1. For comment, see (1973) 37 Conv. 284; [1974] C.L.J. 60.

F. REFORM

1. Introduction

Land registration has been on the agenda of the Law Commission since the Commission was established in 1965. In the 1970s the Commission produced four Working Papers: Law Commission Working Paper No. 32, *Transfer of Land: Land Registration (First Paper)* (1970) on registration of leasehold interests and public access to the register; Law Commission Working Paper No. 37, *Transfer of Land: Land Registration (Second Paper)* (1971) on overriding interests and the minor interests index; Law Commission Working Paper No. 45, *Transfer of Land: Land Registration (Third Paper)* (1972) on identity and boundaries and rectification and indemnity; Law Commission Working Paper No. 67, *Transfer of Land: Land Registration (Fourth Paper)* (1976) on protection and priority of derivative interests. Following consultation, the Commission produced four Reports. The first two Reports made recommendations in relation to specific matters which, though not insignificant, did not touch upon the fundamental principles of the system: Law Com. No. 125, *Property Law: Land Registration* (1983) dealt with identity and boundaries, conversion of title, the treatment of leases and the abolition of the minor interests index; and Law Com. No. 148, *Property Law: Second Report on Land Registration* (1985) dealt with inspection of the register. The recommendations contained in those Reports were implemented by the Land Registration Acts of 1986 and 1988 respectively.

By contrast the third and fourth Reports dealt with the fundamental features of the land registration system: minor interests, overriding interests and rectification and indemnity. Law Com. No. 158, *Property Law: Third Report on Land Registration* (1987) dealt with the substance of these three topics. Law Com. No. 173, *Property Law: Fourth Report on Land Registration* (1988) contained a draft new Land Registration Bill which incorporated the various Law Commission proposals and sought to simplify and restate the law on land registration as reformed in accordance with those proposals. However, the recommendations of the third and fourth Reports remained unimplemented.

In 1994 a Joint Working Group, comprising representatives of the Law Commission, the Land Registry and the Lord Chancellor's Department, was established to consider ways in which any parts of the third and fourth Reports might be implemented (with or without modifications). The Joint Working Group produced its First Report (Law Com. No. 235, *Transfer of Land: Land Registration*) in 1995. The recommendations contained in that report, which concerned the extension of the list of transactions that trigger compulsory first registration, provision for fee concessions to encourage voluntary registration and amendments to the provisions on indemnity, were implemented by the Land Registration Act 1997.

2. Land registration for the twenty-first century

In 1998 the Joint Working Group produced its Second Report (Law Com. No. 254, *Land Registration for the Twenty-First Century*) ("the Report"). The Report, which purports to offer "a blueprint for the development of conveyancing ... over the next quarter of a century or so", takes the form of a consultation document on provisional recommendations and it is intended that draft legislation will be drafted in the light of the responses and will be published in 1999.

In the light of actual and potential developments, the Joint Working Group considered that its remit should not be limited to the issues discussed in the third and fourth Reports. First, experience of the operation of the registered land system has revealed a number of practical difficulties that should be remedied. Secondly, the prevalence of the land registration system has reached the point where it is no longer appropriate to continue to inhibit the development of the principles of property law by reference to the unregistered land system. Rather the land registration system should develop in accordance with principles that fully reflect the nature and potential of land registration. These factors would be sufficient in themselves to justify the wholesale replacement of the current legislation with a new statute that simplifies and clearly articulates the principles of land registration. They also explain why many of the recommendations of the Joint Working Group differ significantly from, and go much further than, the proposals in the third and fourth Reports of the Law Commission. However, the most significant factor informing the Report is the central assumption that electronic conveyancing will be introduced in the medium-term future. It is appropriate to consider that factor first.

2.1 *Electronic conveyancing*

The Report is inevitably vague on the detailed operation of electronic conveyancing, although the eventual aim is reasonably clear. A system of electronic conveyancing would eliminate the current three-stage process applicable to any transaction in registered land, involving the execution of a formal document, its lodgement with the Registry and then the registration itself. Instead, most transactions (the creation or transfer of registrable interests, other registered dispositions and the protection of minor interests) would be executed electronically by registration. The transaction would be effected, and the intended interest created or transferred, only by the single-stage process of registering the transaction; and, until registration, the transaction would have no effect. However, certain transactions would continue to take effect as they do at present: these would include the acquisition of rights that can arise without an express grant, dispositions taking effect by operation of law, the creation of interests under trusts and the creation and assignment of leases that are not capable of substantive registration.

The Report identifies certain benefits that should result from such a system: the emergence of a register that provides a more complete record of the rights and interests affecting the land in question, including a clearer record of the priority of minor interests; quicker and substantially cheaper conveyancing transactions (a claim also made in relation to the Land Registration Act 1925), with a reduced risk of error; and the elimination of the "registration gap" and its consequences.

At this stage, the Report only recommends that the Lord Chancellor be empowered to make rules to provide for the introduction of a system of electronic conveyancing, more specifically to provide for the transfer of title to registered land and the creation of rights over registered land without the need for a written instrument.

2.2 A *"culture" of registration*

In the meantime the Joint Working Group is seeking to create a "culture" of registration in advance of the introduction of electronic conveyancing—so that registration is perceived to be an integral part of the creation of rights in or over registered land. To that end the recommendations in the Report are intended to ensure that registration provides better protection for rights and interests, to facilitate the process of registration and to restrict so far as possible the range of rights that can be protected outside the register.

2.3 *Summary of recommendations*

The following list of the most important recommendations (taken from the executive summary of the Report) is intended to provide an overview of the scope of the Report. The commentary highlights those recommendations relevant to the major issues that are discussed in this and other chapters.

(a) *that there should be in place a legal framework (in the form of a rule-making power) that will enable a system of electronic conveyancing to be introduced*

See *supra*, p. 262.

(b) *that there should be new rules on the acquisition of title to registered land by adverse possession that would considerably strengthen the protection enjoyed by those who have registered title: registration would itself protect a landowner against the claims of squatters*

The recommendations are intended to ensure that registration provides better protection for the registered proprietor and that his title should be capable of being overridden by adverse possession only where it is essential to ensure the marketability of the land or to prevent unfairness. Most significantly, it is recommended that adverse possession should no longer in itself bar the title of a registered proprietor. For a summary of the proposed scheme, see *ante*, p. 101.

(c) *that the methods of protecting rights in or over land (such as easements, restrictive covenants and options) by entry on the register should be simplified and the strength of that protection greatly enhanced*

The Report recommends that the current range of different methods of protection on the register for minor interests should be rationalised and that in most cases an entry on the register should afford protection and priority to the interest in question: see *supra*, pp. 169, 180. Pursuant to the same principle that registration should be encouraged, the Report recommends that a purchaser for valuable consideration should take the land free of *unprotected* minor interests and that in general there should be no place for the concepts of good faith, knowledge or notice in registered land: see *supra*, p. 177.

(d) *that the number and scope of overriding interests should be reduced, thereby increasing the security of registered titles*

The Report recommends that the concept of overriding interests should be retained but that the number and scope of such interests should be kept to the minimum precisely because they compromise the conclusiveness of the register. The Report endorses the two principles adopted in the third Report: that, in the interests of certainty and simplifying conveyancing, the class of rights which might bind a purchaser other than as a result of an entry on the register should be as narrow as possible; and that the only overriding interests should be those where protection against purchasers is needed, yet it is either not reasonable to expect nor sensible to require any entry on the register.

The Report acknowledges the difficulties in abolishing the overriding interest status of existing interests, not least the potential contravention of the European Convention on Human Rights. However, the Report recommends that new legislation should define more clearly and accurately the existing categories of overriding interest, should encourage the entry on the register of existing overriding interests and should prospectively redefine the scope of specific overriding interests so as to exclude rights that ought to be protected on the register. It is pointed out that the introduction of electronic conveyancing should significantly reduce the number of overriding interests because it would not be possible to create many rights except by registration.

The Report recommends the redefinition of a number of categories of overriding interest, in particular: easements: see *supra*, p. 186; the rights of occupiers: see *supra*, p. 192; and leases not exceeding 21 years: see *supra*, p. 232. It recommends that the rights of adverse possessors should no longer constitute a separate category of overriding interests but should be subsumed under the rights of occupiers: see *supra*, p. 187.

The Report recommends that all overriding interests should be subject to the application of any rule of law relating to fraud or estoppel and that it should not be possible (nor, *a priori*, necessary) to make any entry on the register in respect of a waiver of priority by a person having the benefit of an overriding interest: see *supra*, p. 229.

Finally, the Report endorses the decision of the majority in the House of Lords in *Abbey National Building Society v. Cann* [1991] 1 A.C. 56, that the relevant date for ascertaining the existence of an overriding interest should be the date of registration of the relevant disposition but that, where the overriding interest claimed is the right of an occupier, the person should be in occupation at the date of the transaction: see *supra*, p. 223.

(e) *that the circumstances in which the register can be rectified to correct an error or omission should be clarified and simplified*

The Joint Working Group expresses the view that the rectification provisions require clarification rather than fundamental change. The Report recommends that "rectification" should be understood in the restricted sense of the remedying of errors and omissions (and that the availability of indemnity should be limited accordingly). Consequently, it recommends that, in the absence of any error or omission in the register, where a court makes a determination of substantive rights in or over registered land (see the Land Registration Act 1925, s.82(1)(a),(b), *supra*, p. 244), it should do so in accordance with the principles of registered land and not the principles of unregistered land; and that the register should be *amended* (as opposed to being rectified) to reflect the determination. The Report recommends the continuation of the protection afforded to the registered proprietor in possession (but raises for consultation the precise scope of that concept): see *supra*, p. 250. Finally, the Report recommends that rectification should not have retrospective effect, although it may affect for the future any interest protected by registration or entry on the register or any overriding interest: see *supra*, p. 246.

(f) *that the rules governing the competing priorities of estates, rights and interests in registered land should be clearly defined*

The Report endorses the principle that the priority of minor interests should be determined in accordance with the date of the appropriate entry on the register (whereas under the present law priority is determined in accordance with the date of creation: see *supra*, p. 179). However, it argues that the simplest and fairest method of implementing the preferred principle would be to await the introduction of electronic conveyancing: most rights in or over registered land would only be created by registration and thus as a matter of course the date of registration would become the only relevant date for determining priorities.

The Report recommends retention but clarification of the current rules relating to the priority of overriding interests.

(g) *that, to provide better protection for those who purchase land, there should be just one method of acquiring easements and analogous rights by prescription, and not as at present three*

See *post*, p. 674.

(h) *that the status and definition of certain estates, rights and interests in registered land should be reviewed and, where necessary, clarified*

The Report raises for consultation the current rule that only leases granted for a term exceeding 21 years are capable of substantive registration: see *supra*, p. 162.

The Report also recommends that certain rights whose current status is uncertain should be declared to be interests in registered land and to be capable of taking effect as minor interests or overriding interests according to the circumstances. The rights in question are: rights of pre-emption: see *ante*, p. 141; rights arising by estoppel: see *post*, p. 604; and inchoate rights arising under the Prescription Act 1832: see *post*, p. 674.

(i) *that the existing requirements as to the proof of title that has to be shown by a seller of registered land should be relaxed*

The recommendations as to proof of title are largely a reflection of changes in circumstances consequent upon the increasing prevalence of the land registration system and developments in the operation of that system.

4

TRUSTS OF LAND

A. INTRODUCTION

The trust has been encountered in general terms as the machinery which accommodates multiple ownership of land and family interests in land. The essence of the trust is the division of the ownership rights in land into (i) bare legal ownership, which confers on the trustee(s) no enjoyment rights but rather fiduciary duties and powers of management and disposition; and (ii) equitable ownership, which confers on the beneficiaries of the trust the actual enjoyment rights in the land.

At this point it is necessary to be more specific and to make certain distinctions. First, the trust machinery is used to give effect to both successive and concurrent enjoyment rights in land. Secondly, the trust machinery may be created expressly or it may arise by operation of law.

1. Successive and concurrent ownership rights

As to the first distinction, it has been seen that the ownership rights in land may be divided into estates and that different estates confer the enjoyment rights for a particular period of time. In the cases considered, the owners of the respective estates were entitled to successive rights to enjoy the land in question (for example, a grant of Blackacre to A for life, then to B for life, then to C in fee simple), although the doctrine of estates means that from the outset the present right of enjoyment of A and the future rights of enjoyment of B and C are in each case the content of a present interest in the land. Such arrangements, involving a succession of interests in land, have traditionally been referred to generally as "settlements"; but, in this general sense, the term "settlement" included both "strict settlements" and "trusts for sale".

In the 1925 property legislation, strict settlements were governed by the provisions of the Settled Land Act 1925 while trusts for sale were governed by provisions in the Law of Property Act 1925. However, these two forms of machinery for giving effect to successive interests in land have now been replaced by a single form of machinery, the *trust of land*. As a consequence of the Trusts of Land and Appointment of Trustees Act 1996, which came into force at the beginning of 1997, any newly-created arrangement involving the fragmentation of the freehold ownership of land takes effect under a trust of land. Existing trusts for sale have been converted into trusts of land; but the Act provides that existing strict settlements continue in that form.

However, formal arrangements creating successive ownership rights in land are rather rare in modern times. They are more a feature of a society and times in which greater emphasis was placed on the transfer of land (as the most important form of wealth) from generation to generation. Substantial landholding brought economic and political power; and the perpetuation of family wealth thereby served to perpetuate the family influence. Land was retained in the family by conferring limited interests on certain family members and effecting a resettlement every generation so that no individual member of the family ever had unrestricted control of the land, or the wealth that it represented. Such formal arrangements for successive ownership that give rise to litigation today tend to be arrangements made many years ago: see, *e.g. Hambro v. Duke of Malborough* [1994] Ch. 158, noted at [1994] Conv. 492.

Far more common is concurrent ownership (or co-ownership) of land, where two or more persons are simultaneously entitled to the enjoyment rights in a single parcel of land. Concurrent ownership, which is manifested most obviously in the context of the family home, also involved the trust for sale machinery. However, as with successive interest trusts for sale, the Trusts of Land and Appointment of Trustees Act 1996 now provides that any existing or future arrangement of co-ownership must take effect under a trust of land.

2. Trusts expressly created and trusts arising by operation of law

It will be apparent from the above summary that, while the strict settlement was (and, in the case of strict settlements already in existence when the Trusts of Land and Appointment of Trustees Act 1996 came into force, remains) a form of trust dealing only with successive ownership, the trust for sale machinery was used to accommodate both successive ownership and concurrent ownership.

In the context of successive ownership, trusts for sale could only be created expressly by the use of appropriate terminology, for example "Blackacre to trustees *on trust for sale* for A for life, then for B in fee simple". If the settlor purported to create successive interests in land without such terminology, for example a simple grant of "Blackacre to A for life, then to B in fee simple", the arrangement took effect as a strict settlement by default. Moreover, strict settlements were sometimes held to have been created by informal "family" arrangements relating primarily to the *occupation* of land: see *infra*, p. 271.

In the context of concurrent ownership, trusts for sale arose either expressly or by operation of law. If the settlor did not use the appropriate terminology or if he did not even purport to create the trust machinery, statute imposed the trust for sale machinery. Thus in a number of cases discussed in earlier chapters the legal title to the matrimonial home had been transferred to the husband alone and there was no express creation of a trust for sale. However, the wife had contributed to the purchase price of the house, as a result of which she had acquired a share in the equitable ownership. The husband and wife were therefore concurrent owners; and, in the absence of an express trust for sale, statute imposed the trust for sale machinery: see *Caunce v. Caunce* [1969] 1 W.L.R. 286, *ante*, p. 39; *Kingsnorth Finance Co. Ltd v. Tizard* [1986] 1 W.L.R. 783, *ante*, p. 42; *Williams & Glyn's Bank Ltd v. Boland* [1981] A.C. 487, *ante*, p. 193.

In so far as the Trusts of Land and Appointment of Trustees Act 1996 now requires that any arrangement of co-ownership must take under a trust of land, statute will impose a trust of land wherever the parties do not create one expressly.

3. Bare trusts

Whereas strict settlements and trusts for sale involved multiple ownership of the equitable ownership rights in land, whether in the form of successive interests or concurrent interests, a *bare* trust arises where land is held on trust for a sole beneficiary (of full age and of sound mind) absolutely, *i.e.* where the trustee owns the legal fee simple absolute in possession and the sole beneficiary owns the equitable fee simple absolute in possession. Such trusts, which may be created expressly or arise by operation of law, are also brought under the regime of the Trusts of Land and Appointment of Trustees Act 1996 and take effect as trusts of land.

B. Successive Ownership

Since the incidence of successive ownership is relatively rare, the following discussion is intended to provide an outline only, largely as an introduction to the examination of the Trusts of Land and Appointment of Trustees Act 1996 and the new all-embracing trust of land: see *infra*, p. 298. For detailed treatment of successive ownership, see Burn, *Cheshire and Burn's Modern Law of Real Property* (15th ed., 1994), pp. 67–78, 175–202; Gray, *Elements of Land Law* (2nd ed., 1993), pp. 608–644; Megarry and Wade, *The Law of Real Property* (5th ed., 1984), pp. 311–416.

1. Strict settlements

Strict settlements are governed by the provisions of the Settled Land Act 1925. The definition of strict settlements is contained in section 1.

Settled Land Act 1925, s.1(1)

What constitutes a settlement

1.—(1) Any deed, will, agreement for a settlement or other agreement, Act of Parliament, or other instrument, or any number of instruments, whether made or passed before or after, or partly before and partly after, the commencement of this Act, under or by virtue of which instrument or instruments any land, after the commencement of this Act, stands for the time being—

   (i)   limited in trust for any persons by way of succession; or

  (ii)   limited in trust for any person in possession—

      (a) for an entailed interest whether or not capable of being barred or defeated;

      (b) for an estate in fee simple or for a term of years absolute subject to an executory limitation, gift, or disposition over on failure of his issue or in any other event;

      (c) for a base or determinable fee or any corresponding interest in leasehold land;

      (d) being an infant, for an estate in fee simple or for a term of years absolute; or

 (iii)   limited in trust for any person for an estate in fee simple or for a term of years absolute contingently on the happening of any event; or

  (v)   charged, whether voluntarily or in consideration of marriage or by way of family arrangement, and whether immediately or after an interval, with the payment of any rentcharge for the life of any person, or any less period, or of any capital, annual or periodical sums for the portions, advancement, maintenance, or otherwise for the benefit of any persons, with or without any term of years for securing or raising the same;

creates or is for the purposes of this Act a settlement and is in this Act referred to as a settlement, or as the settlement, as the case requires:

Provided that, where land is the subject of a compound settlement, references in this Act to the settlement shall be construed as meaning such compound settlement, unless the context otherwise requires. ...

NOTES:

   1. The arrangements covered by the term "settlement" (which more accurately denotes the document or documents creating those arrangements) fall into two broad categories: first, where the settlor expressly or impliedly creates a succession of interests in the land, but does not create a trust for sale of the land: Settled Land Act 1925, s.1(1)(i), (ii)(a)–(c), (iii); and, secondly, where the settlor purports to grant an absolute interest in land to a person who is subject to some legal liability: *ibid.* s.1(1)(v); or to a person who, by reason of his legal disability, is not a permissible grantee, most obviously a person under the age of 18: *ibid.* s.1(1)(ii)(d). In both categories of strict settlement, the settled land is held on trust and the relevant substantive interests of the beneficiaries take effect in equity.

   2. Given the general structure of the trust, it might be expected that the legal estate of land subject to a strict settlement would be held by trustees in the normal manner. However, as noted above, the strict settlement, at least in its more common form involving actual successive ownership, was primarily concerned with preserving land within the family, to be enjoyed by successive generations. It was therefore regarded as more convenient for the legal estate, with the concomitant powers of management and disposition, to be vested in the person currently entitled to the enjoyment of the land. That person could be expected to manage the property responsibly since he was the person who would derive the immediate benefit from doing so. Thus under a strict settlement the legal estate of the land is vested, not in the trustees, but in the "tenant for life", who is defined as "the person of full age who is for the time being beneficially entitled under a settlement to possession of settled land for his life": *ibid* s.19. In the absence of a tenant for life within the section 19 definition, section 20

provides a list of persons who may have the powers of a tenant for life. Of course, this arrangement cannot apply where the person currently entitled to the enjoyment of the land is a minor since *ex hypothesi* such a person cannot own the legal estate and the powers of management and disposition. In such cases, until the minor reaches full age, the legal estate and the concomitant powers are vested in the "statutory owner(s)", person(s) nominated by the settlor or, in default of such nomination, the trustees of the settlement: *ibid.* s.23.

3. Notwithstanding that the legal estate is vested in the current beneficiary rather than in trustees, strict settlements still require trustees; and section 30 provides, in descending order of priority, a list of persons who may act as trustees. In particular, the trustees are required to step in whenever there is a potential conflict between the interests of the tenant for life as beneficiary in possession and the duties of the tenant for life as owner of the legal estate and thus trustee for the beneficiaries in remainder: see *ibid.* s.107. Thus, if the tenant for life exercises his power to sell or lease the settled land, any purchase money must be paid to the trustees. Indeed, a purchaser of the settled land would be required to pay the purchase money to at least two trustees, except where the trustee is a trust corporation, in order to overreach the beneficial interests under the settlement: Law of Property Act 1925, s.2(1)(i), Settled Land Act 1925, s.18(1). Moreover, certain powers of the tenant for life cannot be exercised unless the tenant for life gives the trustees notice of his intention to exercise them (powers to sell, exchange, lease, mortgage, charge or grant options: Settled Land Act 1925, s.101) or, in some instances, unless the trustees consent to their exercise (for example, the power to dispose of the principal mansion house: *ibid.* s.65).

4. As noted above, informal "family" arrangements relating primarily to the *occupation* of land have sometimes been held to create a succession of interests in the land and thus strict settlements subject to the full regime of the Settled Land Act 1925: see *Bannister v. Bannister* [1948] 2 All E.R. 133; *Binions v. Evans* [1972] Ch. 359; *Ungurian v. Lesnoff* [1990] Ch. 206; *Costello v. Costello* (1994) 70 P. & C.R. 297; but see *Dent v. Dent* [1996] 1 All E.R. 659; and, for discussion, see Hornby (1977) 93 L.Q.R. 561; Hill (1991) 107 L.Q.R. 596; Thompson [1994] Conv. 391. The inconvenience of this conclusion and its avoidance are considered further, *post*, pp. 520, 562; but the problem no longer arises in relation to arrangements made after the coming into force of the Trusts of Land and Appointment of Trustees Act 1996.

As noted above, the Trusts of Land and Appointment of Trustees Act 1996 preserves existing strict settlements; and it even permits the creation of new settlements, by the resettlement of an existing settlement or by the exercise of a power of appointment contained in an existing settlement, although in each case the new settlement may take effect as a trust of land: *ibid.* s.2.

2. Trusts for sale

In contrast with the strict settlement, which had its rationale in the desire to retain land within the family, the trust for sale operated on the premise that the property subject to the trust simply represented a capital fund of money and the trust provided a means for its distribution among specified beneficiaries. (In the present context the concern is with the distribution of income generated by the fund (and ultimately the capital fund itself) to a *succession* of beneficiaries. The use of the trust for sale machinery in the context of *concurrent ownership* is considered below.) The different rationale of the trust for sale meant that, in the case of successive interest trusts for sale, there was no need for the special arrangements as to the legal estate which were devised for the strict settlement. The legal estate was therefore vested in the trustees for sale; and it was they who had the powers of management and disposition, although certain powers of management could be delegated to any beneficiary currently entitled in possession under the terms of the trust for sale.

The definition of trust for sale is contained in section 205(1)(xxix) of the Law of Property Act 1925.

Law of Property Act 1925, s.205(1)

General definitions

(xxix) "Trust for sale", in relation to land, means an immediate trust for sale, whether or not exercisable at the request or with the consent of any person, ...

NOTES:

1. Trusts for sale and strict settlements were mutually exclusive arrangements: Settled Land Act 1925, s.1(7). However, it was not uncommon for a settlor to create the two arrangements in tandem. For example, a grant of Blackacre "to A for life, then to B and C on trust for sale" created a strict settlement during the lifetime of A and a trust for sale on his death.

2. There was no trust for sale unless the trustees were under a duty to sell the trust property and that duty had to arise immediately and not merely in the future. Thus in the above example there was no immediate duty to sell, and therefore no trust for sale, until A died. The duty to sell was not negatived by a provision in the trust deed that the sale was to take place only at the request of, or with the consent of, any person, even if such request or consent was unlikely to be forthcoming: see *Re Inns* [1947] 1 Ch. 576; *Re Herklot's Will Trusts* [1964] 2 All E.R. 66. There was no requirement that the sale should take place immediately, only that the duty to sell should arise immediately. Hence there was no paradox in the fact that "unless the contrary intention appears" a power to postpone sale was implied in every trust for sale: Law of Property Act 1925, s.25(1).

3. Despite statements above to the effect that the trust for sale has been abolished as a concept and replaced by the trust of land, it is still possible for a settlor expressly to impose a duty to sell on the trustees. However, that duty is subject to an implied power to postpone sale that cannot be excluded by the settlor: Trusts of Land and Appointment of Trustees Act 1996, s.4(1);

and, more generally, such trusts are subject to the full regime of the 1996 Act.

4. Pettit (1997) 113 L.Q.R. 207 argues that express trusts for sale have not been abolished (and that existing *express* trusts for sale continue as trusts for sale); but, although section 205(1)(xxix) of the Law of Property Act 1925 still provides a definition (albeit an amended definition) of "trust for sale", it is not clear that he would disagree with the substance of the preceding note.

3. Trusts of land

There are no specific provisions in the Trusts of Land and Appointment of Trustees Act 1996 dealing with trusts of land that create successive interests in land. The regime of the 1996 Act appears to apply to all trusts of land, although some aspects of the regime are likely to have a particular application to arrangements involving successive interests. For example, the discretion conferred on the trustees by section 9 of the 1996 Act to delegate their functions to the beneficiaries is more likely to be exercised in the context of successive interests where the trustees consciously wish to reproduce the functional equivalent of a strict settlement. The principal difference is that, although the trustees may delegate the power to dispose of the legal estate in the land, the legal title remains in the trustees and any transfer must be formally executed by them.

C. Concurrent Ownership

Concurrent ownership (or co-ownership) of land exists where two or more persons are simultaneously entitled to the ownership rights in a single parcel of land. However, at the time when the provisions of the Law of Property Act 1925 relating to co-ownership were settled, co-ownership was much less prevalent than it is now. As the incidence of co-ownership rapidly increased, particularly in the context of the family home, the law proved to be less than satisfactory in accommodating the modern circumstances of co-ownership. The Trusts of Land and Appointment of Trustees Act 1996 has sought to address the problems that emerged but it has not altered the fundamental nature and structure of co-ownership.

1. Nature and classification of co-ownership

Although there are different types of co-ownership, the basic feature common to all is that each co-owner is simultaneously entitled to possession of the whole land: *Wiseman v. Simpson* [1988] 1 W.L.R. 35, 42 *per* Ralph Gibson L.J.; and no co-owner is entitled to exclusive possession of any specific part: *Meyer v. Riddick* (1990) 60 P. & C.R. 50, 54 *per* Fox L.J. It is this feature, the so-called "unity of possession", that distinguishes co-ownership of a single parcel of land from individual ownership of separate parcels of land.

English law has known four types of co-ownership; but only joint tenancies and tenancies in common remain of practical significance. The other types of co-ownership were tenancies by entireties and co-parcenary. Tenancies by entireties were an unseverable form of joint tenancy between husband and wife. Their creation was prohibited by the Married Women's Property Act 1882, ss.1, 5; and any remaining such tenancies were converted into joint tenancies by the Law of Property Act 1925, Sched. 1, Pt. VI. Co-parcenary was a hybrid form of co-ownership arising where a person died intestate leaving two or more daughters and no sons. Co-parcenary can still arise in the very exceptional circumstances where real property still descends to an "heir"; but where it existed at the end of 1925, it was converted into tenancy in common by the Law of Property Act 1925, Sched. 1, Pt. IV.

In this context the term "tenancy" simply denotes a holding of land. There can be co-ownership of both freehold and leasehold interests in land.

1.1 *Joint tenancies*

The essential characteristic of joint tenancy is that each of the co-owners is wholly entitled to the whole of a single interest in the land. A transfer of land to two or more persons as joint tenants "operates so as to make them, *vis-à-vis* the outside world, one single owner": *Hammersmith and Fulham LBC v. Monk* [1992] 1 A.C. 478, 492 *per* Lord Browne-Wilkinson. There is no sense in which the joint tenants can be said to have specific shares in the land. It has been seen that, in accordance with the principle of unity of possession, no co-owner can claim to be entitled to exclusive possession of a specific *physical* part of the land; and in the case of joint tenancies (and this provides a point of distinction from tenancies in common) it is also true that no co-owner can claim to be entitled to a specific *arithmetical or proportional* share of the land or its value.

This essential characteristic is reflected in the principal features of joint tenancies: the right of survivorship and the four unities.

1.1.1 *Right of survivorship*

On the death of one joint tenant, the remaining joint tenant(s) continue to be entitled to the whole of the interest that was the subject-matter of the original joint tenancy. The deceased joint tenant never had any "share" capable of disposition on his death: he therefore simply drops out of the picture and the joint tenancy continues with one fewer joint tenants. This process is repeated on the death of the remaining joint tenants until there is only one survivor, who then becomes sole owner of the interest in the land. However, because the survivor was always entitled to the whole of the interest, he has no greater interest than when the joint tenancy was first created, except that he is no longer subject to the possibility that he might predecease the other joint tenants, thereby ceasing to be entitled to the interest.

Survivorship operates automatically at the moment of death of a joint tenant. Consequently, although, as will be seen, survivorship may be excluded (by severance of the joint tenancy and its conversion to a tenancy in common), exclusion must be effected before the death of the joint tenant. However, even where there has been no severance, survivorship may not operate where the surviving joint tenant is criminally responsible for the death of the deceased joint tenant: see *infra*, p. 280, or where a claim is made against the estate of the deceased joint tenant under the Inheritance (Provision for Family and Dependants) Act 1975 s.9(1).

1.1.2 *Four unities* The nature of joint tenancy as outlined above necessarily demands that the so-called "four unities" must be present if co-ownership is to take the form of a joint tenancy: *A.G. Securities v. Vaughan* [1990] 1 A.C. 417, 431 *per* Fox L.J. *Unity of possession* has already been explained. *Unity of interest* reflects the requirement that each joint tenant is wholly entitled to the one interest in the land: thus there can be no joint tenancy between persons who own interests different in nature (freehold/leasehold), in duration (fee simple/life interest) or in time (in possession/in remainder). *Unity of title* and *unity of time* effectively reinforce the unity of interest: all the joint tenants must derive their entitlement to the land from the same document (for example, a conveyance/transfer or will) or from the same act (for example, adverse possession); and normally all joint tenants must become entitled at the same time.

1.2 *Tenancies in common*
Tenancies in common tend to be explained by reference to the similarities with, and differences from, joint tenancies. Thus, like joint tenancies, tenancies in common necessarily involve unity of possession since that characteristic distinguishes co-ownership of a single parcel of land from individual ownership of separate parcels of land. However, unlike individual joint tenants, each tenant in common can claim to be entitled to a specific arithmetical or proportional share of the land or its value. This explanation of tenancies in common—arithmetical shares in land that has not been physically divided—is reflected in the statutory terminology which refers to the interests of tenants in common as "undivided shares" in land.

These characteristics of tenancies in common are reflected in the fact that the doctrine of survivorship does not operate on the death of a tenant in common; his share devolves upon the person entitled under his will or on his intestacy, who thus replaces the deceased as tenant in common with the surviving original tenants in common. Moreover, of the four unities only unity of possession is required between tenants in common. The absence of any need for the unities of interest, title and time is illustrated by the following not uncommon situation. Suppose three tenants in common (A, B and C), each entitled to a one-third share in the land; A dies, leaving his share to B. B and C continue as tenants in common, notwithstanding that their respective shares in the land are now two-thirds and one-third and notwithstanding that B acquired his additional one-third share from a different document (the will of A) and at a different time (the death of A) from the creation of the original tenancy in common.

1.3 *Severance*
The fundamental distinction between joint tenancies and tenancies in common is the doctrine of survivorship, which applies only to the former. That

doctrine creates obvious uncertainty. One of two joint tenants can become sole owner of the land in question provided he survives the other joint tenant; but equally he (or his estate) can lose all entitlement to the land if he predeceases the other joint tenant. In order to mitigate such uncertainty, it has always been possible for a joint tenant to sever the joint tenancy and thereby to convert it into a tenancy in common; the doctrine of survivorship ceases to be applicable and each co-owner has a guaranteed share in the property or its value.

The availability of severance means that, despite the theory of joint tenancy, in practice joint tenants are frequently treated as having potentially distinct shares in the co-owned land.

Further consideration of severance is postponed until after the examination of the structure of co-ownership: see *infra*, p. 278.

2. Structure of co-ownership

Consistently with the position in relation to successive interests in land, prior to 1926 co-ownership of land could be created with or without the trust machinery. Thus a fee simple owner (F) could simply transfer the fee simple in Blackacre to A and B so that A and B became co-owners of the combined legal and equitable fee simple. Alternatively, F could transfer the fee simple in Blackacre to A and B to hold on trust for C and D so that A and B became co-owners of the legal fee simple as trustees and C and D became co-owners of the equitable fee simple. However, even before 1926 co-ownership without the trust machinery was relatively uncommon.

After 1925, again consistently with the regime of the 1925 legislation applicable wherever there was a division of ownership rights in land, co-ownership of land could only exist under the trust machinery, that is where the legal estate in the land is vested in the trustees, who hold the land on trust for the co-owners of the equitable interest.

It is, of course, important always to remember that ownership of the bare legal title, which imposes duties and powers of management but which confers none of the actual enjoyment rights over the land, is to that extent relatively unimportant. Nonetheless, it is vital to an understanding of post-1925 co-ownership to maintain a clear distinction between co-ownership *at law* and co-ownership *in equity*, that is between the co-ownership of the legal estate of the trustees and the co-ownership of the equitable interest of the beneficiaries under the trust. Otherwise it is not readily understandable that two persons may be both joint tenants of the legal estate in land and tenants in common of the equitable interest in that land.

It is therefore necessary to consider the attitudes to co-ownership adopted by the common law and equity respectively.

2.1 Co-ownership at law: co-ownership of the legal estate
The common law traditionally preferred joint tenancy to tenancy in common. This preference was at first explained on the ground that the doctrine of survivorship inherent in joint tenancy tended towards sole ownership, which

in turn facilitated the enforcement of the feudal incidents attached to tenure. More recently, the preference has been based on the simplification of conveyancing (and the free alienability of land) consequent upon the simplification of title to land where ownership rights are not fragmented. The common law therefore operated a presumption that co-ownership took the form of joint tenancy except in two situations: first, where one of the four unities was absent; and, secondly, where the transfer to the co-owners incorporated so-called "words of severance", such as "to be divided between", "in equal shares", or "equally": such words were deemed to indicate an intention, characteristic of tenancies in common, that the co-owners should have specific (albeit undivided) shares in the land.

Bearing in mind the reason for the common law preference and bearing in mind also that the 1925 legislation was intended to further the same objective, it is no surprise that the Law of Property Act 1925 extended the common law presumption to its logical conclusion. The Act therefore provided that it was no longer possible to create a tenancy in common of a *legal* estate in land directly: Law of Property Act 1925, s.1(6); nor was it possible to create a legal tenancy in common indirectly through severance: *ibid.* s.36(2), *infra*, p. 279.

The post-1925 position is therefore that co-ownership necessarily involves the trust machinery and the co-ownership of the legal estate by the trustees necessarily takes the form of a joint tenancy. Since the form of co-ownership of the legal estate is now fixed, it follows that the joint tenancy/tenancy in common dichotomy is only relevant in the context of the equitable interest of the beneficiaries under the trust.

2.2 Co-ownership in equity: co-ownership of the equitable interest

In contrast with the attitude of the common law, equity has always preferred tenancy in common as the form of co-ownership of equitable interests, on the ground of the supposed certainty and fairness of fixed interests rather than the supposed uncertainty and arbitrariness of the doctrine of survivorship inherent in joint tenancy. Equity therefore continues to lean in favour of tenancy in common when determining whether in any particular case co-ownership of the equitable interest takes the form of a joint tenancy or a tenancy in common. First, equity follows the pre-1926 common law approach in those circumstances where the common law accepted the existence of a tenancy in common, that is where one of the four unities is absent or where the transfer to the co-owners incorporates words of severance. Secondly, in certain circumstances, irrespective of the attitude of the common law, equity presumes that co-ownership takes the form of a tenancy in common. In the first three situations outlined below, equity presumes that the equitable co-ownership takes the form of a tenancy in common because a joint tenancy, with the inherent doctrine of survivorship, would be regarded as incompatible with the essentially commercial nature of the relevant transaction. However, it should be stressed that the circumstances in question create a presumption only and that the presumption may be rebutted by evidence of a contrary intention.

2.2.1 *Partnership assets*   Where two or more business partners acquire land as part of their partnership assets, although they necessarily hold the legal estate as joint tenants, *as between themselves* they are presumed to be tenants in common of the equitable interest: *Lake v. Craddock* (1732) 3 P.Wms. 158.

2.2.2 *Joint mortgages*   Where two or more persons lend money on the security of a legal mortgage, the mortgage is necessarily granted to them as joint tenants: Law of Property Act 1925, s.111; but *as between themselves* they are presumed to be tenants in common in equity: *Re Jackson* (1887) 34 Ch D. 732.

2.2.3 *Lessees of business premises*   Where two or more persons are granted a lease of business premises, which they use for their several individual business purposes, they necessarily hold the lease as joint tenants at law; but *as between themselves* they are presumed to be tenants in common in equity: *Malayan Credit Ltd v. Jack Chia-MPH Ltd* [1986] A.C. 549.

2.2.4 *Unequal contributions to purchase price*   It has been seen that, irrespective of any share in the legal estate, contributions to the purchase price of land may give the contributors shares in the beneficial or equitable ownership of that land by virtue of the doctrines of resulting and constructive trusts: see *ante*, pp. 65 *et seq*. In the present context, it should be noted that, where the contributors provide the purchase money in *unequal* shares, equity presumes that they hold the equitable interest in the land as tenants in common.

2.3 *Structure of co-ownership: the current position*
In summary, co-ownership involves the trust machinery. Whenever land is subject to co-ownership, the land is held on trust. The trustees necessarily hold the legal estate as joint tenants; the beneficiaries (who may or may not be the same persons as the trustees) hold the equitable interest either as joint tenants or as tenants in common according to the principles discussed above. Bandali (1977) 41 Conv. 243 and Thompson [1987] Conv. 29, 275 argue that the problems of equitable joint tenancies (primarily the uncertainties relating to severance and the operation of survivorship) outweigh the advantages; and that equitable joint tenancies should therefore be abolished. For a different view of the balance, see Prichard [1987] Conv. 273.

3. Severance of joint tenancies

3.1 *Nature of severance*
Reference has already been made to the possibility of the severance of a joint tenancy and its conversion into a tenancy in common. The purpose of severance is usually to exclude the operation of survivorship on the death of a joint tenant and the consequent loss of entitlement of the deceased's estate to any share in the co-owned land. In *Harris v. Goddard* [1983] 1 W.L.R. 1203 Dillon L.J. stated (at 1210):

Severance ... is the process of separating off the share of a joint tenant, so that the concurrent ownership will continue but the right of survivorship will no longer apply. The parties will hold separate shares as tenants in common.

Since 1925 severance has operated only on equitable co-ownership. As has been seen, the Law of Property Act 1925 prohibited both the direct creation of legal tenancies in common and their indirect creation through the severance of legal joint tenancies; but the Act did not affect the right to sever *equitable* joint tenancies.

Law of Property Act 1925, s.36(2)

(2) No severance of a joint tenancy of a legal estate, so as to create a tenancy in common in land, shall be permissible, whether by operation of law or otherwise, but this subsection does not affect the right of a joint tenant to release his interest to the other joint tenants, or the right to sever a joint tenancy in an equitable interest whether or not the legal estate is vested in the joint tenants:

Provided that, where a legal estate (not being settled land) is vested in joint tenants beneficially, and any tenant desires to sever the joint tenancy in equity, he shall give to the other joint tenants a notice in writing of such desire or do such other acts or thing as would, in the case of personal estate, have been effectual to sever the tenancy in equity, and thereupon the land shall be held in trust on terms which would have been requisite for giving effect to the beneficial interests if there had been an actual severance.

NOTES:

1. Severance can only be effected before the doctrine of survivorship operates at the moment of death of the joint tenant: it can therefore only be effected during the lifetime of the joint tenant and cannot be effected by his will.

2. The burden of proof is on the person seeking to establish that the joint tenancy has been severed: *Greenfield v. Greenfield* (1979) 38 P. & C.R. 570, 578 *per* Fox J.; *Barton v. Morris* [1985] 1 W.L.R. 1257, 1260 *per* Nicholls J. "Without prejudice" correspondence was admissible in evidence where severance of a joint tenancy as a result of that correspondence was sought to be established as an independent fact: see *McDowell v. Hirschfield Lipson & Rumney* [1992] 2 F.L.R. 126, 131–132 *per* Judge Eric Stockdale.

3. Section 36(2) provides for severance by notice in writing to the other joint tenant(s) or by those pre-1926 methods of severance applicable to personalty; the reference to pre-1926 methods of severance is interpreted as a reference to the methods listed in *Williams v. Hensman* (1861) 1 J. & H. 546 (the "*Williams v. Hensman* catalogue"): see *Harris v. Goddard* [1983] 1 W.L.R. 1203, 1208–1209 *per* Lawton L.J.

In *Williams v. Hensman* Page Wood V.-C. stated (at 557):

A joint tenancy may be severed in three ways: in the first place, an act of any one of the persons interested operating upon his own share may create a severance as to that share. ... Secondly, a joint tenancy may be severed by mutual agreement. And, in the third place, there may be a severance by any course of dealing sufficient to intimate that the interests of all were mutually treated as constituting a tenancy in common.

It will become apparent from the following discussion that there is some degree of overlap between the various methods of severance.

4. In *Bedson v. Bedson* [1965] 2 Q.B. 666 Lord Denning M.R. asserted (at 678) that where land is held by spouses as beneficial joint tenants and at least one of them is in possession of the land neither spouse can sever the joint tenancy so as to convert it into a tenancy in common. That proposition was thought by Russell L.J. (at 690) to be "without the slightest foundation in law or in equity"; and it has been consistently rejected in subsequent cases: see *Re Draper's Conveyance* [1969] 1 Ch. 486, 494 *per* Plowman J.; *Cowcher v. Cowcher* [1972] 1 W.L.R. 425, 430 *per* Bagnall J.; *Harris v. Goddard* [1983] 1 W.L.R. 1203, 1208 *per* Lawton L.J.; and see Megarry (1966) 82 L.Q.R. 29.

5. As to the effect of severance, in *Bedson v. Bedson, supra,* Russell L.J. stated (at 689):

[O]n severance the beneficial joint tenancy becomes a beneficial tenancy in common in undivided shares and right by survivorship no longer obtains. If there be two beneficial joint tenants, severance produces a beneficial tenancy in common in two equal shares. If there be three beneficial joint tenants and one only severs, he is entitled to a one-third undivided share and there is no longer survivorship between him and the other two, though the other two may remain *inter se* beneficial joint tenants of the other two-thirds.

See also *Nielson-Jones v. Fedden* [1975] Ch. 222, 228 *per* Walton J.

6. It appears that on severance each joint tenant as a general rule takes an equal share in the land or its value, *irrespective of the contributions of the joint tenants to the original purchase price: Goodman v. Gallant* [1986] Fam. 106, 118–119 *per* Slade L.J. However, unequal shares may be stipulated for in an agreement between the parties: *Barton v. Morris* [1985] 1 W.L.R. 1257, 1262 *per* Walton J.; or in a declaration of trust: *Goodman v. Gallant* [1986] Fam. 106, 119 *per* Slade L.J.; and, in the context of financial provision on divorce, the court may order a sale and distribution of the proceeds in unequal shares: see Matrimonial Causes Act 1973, ss.24, 24A. In *Hunter v. Babbage* (1994) 69 P. & C.R. 548 the joint tenants of property had been in the process of negotiating, but had not finalised, a financial settlement involving unequal division of the proceeds of sale of the property. The court held that the joint tenancy had been severed but that, in the absence of a final agreement as to the division of the proceeds of sale, the parties were entitled to equal shares.

7. For comprehensive and detailed analysis of severance, see McClean (1979) 57 Can.Bar.Rev. 1; Butt (1982) 9 Sydney L.R. 568; Tee [1995] Conv. 105; and see the discussion in the Australian High Court in *Corin v. Patton* (1990) 169 C.L.R. 540.

8. Under the so-called "forfeiture rule" a person who has unlawfully killed another person is prima facie precluded from acquiring a benefit in consequence of the killing: Forfeiture Act 1982, s.1(1). In *Re K.* [1985] Ch. 85 (affirmed by the Court of Appeal ([1986] Ch. 180)) the killer and her victim were joint tenants of the matrimonial home; and Vinelott J. held that it had been rightly conceded that the forfeiture rule operated in effect to sever the

equitable joint tenancy, with the result that (subject to relief under the Forfeiture Act 1982) the killer held the legal estate on trust for sale for herself and the deceased's estate as tenants in common. See Youdan (1973) 89 L.Q.R. 235; Earnshaw and Pace (1974) 37 M.L.R. 481.

3.2 *Methods of severance*

3.2.1 *Notice in writing*

Harris v. Goddard [1983] 1 W.L.R. 1203

(CA, Lawton, Kerr and Dillon L.JJ.)

A husband and wife were joint tenants of the matrimonial home. The marriage broke down and the wife petitioned for divorce. The prayer of the petition asked "that such order may be made [pursuant to section 24 of the Matrimonial Causes Act 1973] by way of transfer of property and/or settlement of property and/or variation of settlement as may be just". Three days before the hearing of the petition, the husband was injured in a car accident and he died a few weeks later. The husband's executors sought a declaration that the prayer of the divorce petition had been effective to sever the joint tenancy of the matrimonial home, which was therefore held on trust for sale for the wife and the husband's estate as tenants in common.

LAWTON L.J.:
Since in this case severance is said to have come about by a notice in writing the sole question is whether that which is said to be the notice did show that Mrs Harris desired to sever the joint tenancy.
    In *Williams v. Hensman* (1861) 1 Johns & Hem. 546, 557, Page-Wood V.-C. said that a joint tenancy could be severed in three ways, that is, by disposal of one of the interests, by mutual agreement and "by any course of dealing sufficient to intimate that the interests of all were mutually treated as constituting a tenancy in common." The words in section 36(2) "do such other acts or things as would ... have been effectual to sever the tenancy" put into statutory language the other ways of effecting severance to which Page-Wood V.-C. referred in *Williams v. Hensman*. The words "and any tenant desires to sever the joint tenancy in equity, he shall give to the other joint tenants a notice in writing of such desire" operate to extend the mutual agreement concept of severance referred to in *Williams v. Hensman*. Unilateral action to sever a joint tenancy is now possible. Before 1925 severance by unilateral action was only possible when one joint tenant disposed of his interest to a third party. When a notice in writing of a desire to sever is served pursuant to section 36(2) it takes effect forthwith. It follows that a desire to sever must evince an intention to bring about the wanted result immediately. A notice in writing which expresses a desire to bring about the wanted result at some time in the future is not, in my judgment, a notice in writing within section 36(2). Further the notice must be one which shows an intent to bring about the consequences set out in section 36(2), namely, that the net proceeds of the statutory trust for sale "shall be held upon the trusts which would have been requisite for giving effect to the beneficial interests if there had been an actual severance." I am unable to accept [counsel for the executors'] submission that a notice in writing which shows no more than a desire to bring the existing interest to an end is a good notice. It must be a desire to sever which is intended to have the statutory consequences.

Paragraph 3 of the prayer to the petition does no more than invite the court to consider at some future time whether to exercise its jurisdiction under section 24 of the Act of 1973, and if it does, to do so in one or more of three different ways. Orders under section 24(1)(a) and (b) could bring co-ownership to an end by ways other than by severance. It follows, in my judgment, that paragraph 3 of the prayer of the petition did not operate as a notice in writing to sever the joint tenancy in equity. This tenancy had not been severed when Mr Harris died with the consequence that Mrs Harris is entitled to the whole of the fund held by the first and second defendants as trustees. I wish to stress that all I am saying is that paragraph 3 in the petition under consideration in this case did not operate as a notice of severance.

Perhaps this case should be a cautionary tale for those who draft divorce petitions when the spouses hold property as joint tenants in equity. The decision of Plowman J. in *In re Draper's Conveyance* [1969] 1 Ch. 486 is an example of how starting legal proceedings can sever a joint tenancy. In that case a wife, after a decree nisi but before a decree absolute, issued a summons under section 17 of the Married Women's Property Act 1882 asking for an order that a house in the joint names of herself and her husband be sold and the proceeds of sale distributed in accordance with the parties' respective interests therein. An affidavit sworn by the wife in support of the summons contained this paragraph:

> "In the premises I humbly ask that the said property may be sold and that the proceeds of sale thereof may be distributed equally; alternatively that the respondent pay me one half of the value of the said property with vacant possession. ..."

Plowman J. adjudged that the summons and the affidavit together effected a severance during the lifetime of the husband. I agree that it did; but it is not clear from the judgment whether the judge regarded the summons or the affidavit or both as notices in writing or whether the service of the summons and the filing of the affidavit were acts which were effectual to sever the joint tenancy. I do not share the doubts about the correctness of this judgment on this point which Walton J. expressed in *Nielson-Jones v. Fedden* [1975] Ch. 222, 236 relying on *In re Wilks* [1891] 3 Ch. 59. The fact that the wife in *In re Draper's Conveyance* [1969] 1 Ch. 486 could have withdrawn the summons is a factor which could have been taken into account in deciding whether what was done was effectual to sever the joint tenancy in equity. The weight of that factor would have depended upon all the other circumstances and was in that case clearly negligible.

NOTES:

1. For a similar conclusion, albeit reached with reluctance, see *Hunter v. Babbage* (1994) 69 P. & C.R. 248.

2. For an appropriate form of words indicating the required intention to sever immediately, see *Goodman v. Gallant* [1986] Fam. 106, 109:

I hereby give you notice of my desire to sever as from this day the joint tenancy and equity of and in [Blackacre] now held by you and me as joint tenants both at law and in equity so that the said property shall henceforth belong to you and me in equal shares.

3. The basis and the status of the decision in *Re Draper's Conveyance* [1969] 1 Ch. 486 is not entirely clear. Plowman J. stated (at 490):

Mr Cooke, on behalf of the defendants, submits that the joint tenancy was severed, and he puts the matter in two ways, either that it was severed by notice in writing, or it was severed by conduct ... First, he submits that the wife's conduct was such as to effect a severance of the joint tenancy, and in relation to that matter he relies on the summons of February 11, 1966, in the Probate, Divorce and Admiralty Division, coupled with the orders which were made by that court, coupled with the plaintiff's solicitor's letter of June 7, 1966. And he says, either as a result of those three matters or as a result of any of them, the joint tenancy became severed by conduct, and he referred me to the decision of Havers J. in *Hawkesley v. May* [1956] 1 Q.B. 304.

. . .

From that case I derive this; a declaration by one of a number of joint tenants of his intention to sever operates as a severance. Mr Cooke also, as I have said, relied upon the notice in writing which under section 36(2) of the Law of Property Act 1925 is allowed in the case of a joint tenancy in land, although not in personalty, and he submits that the summons to which I have already referred, although not signed, amounted to a notice in writing on the part of the wife that she desired to sever the joint tenancy in equity. I say "although not signed by the wife or by anybody on her behalf" because there is no requirement in the subsection of a signature.

Dealing with the matter there, and ignoring for a moment certain matters which were submitted by Mr McCulloch, it seems to me that Mr Cooke's submissions are right whether they are based on the new provision in section 36(2) of the Law of Property Act 1925 or whether they are based on the old law which applied to severing a joint tenancy in the case of a personal estate. It seems to me that that summons, coupled with the affidavit in support of it, clearly evinced an intention on the part of the wife that she wished the property to be sold and the proceeds distributed, a half to her and a half to the husband. And if that is right then it seems to me that that is wholly inconsistent with the notion that a beneficial joint tenancy in that property is to continue, and therefore, apart from these objections to which I will refer in a moment, I feel little doubt that in one way or the other this joint tenancy was severed in equity before the end of February 1966 as a result of the summons which was served on the husband and as a result of what the wife stated in her affidavit in support of the summons.

[His Lordship rejected the argument (based on the judgment of Lord Denning M.R. in *Bedson v. Bedson* [1965] 2 Q.B. 666) that a spouse cannot sever a joint tenancy where at least one of the spouses is still in possession of the land: see *supra.*, p. 228. He continued:]

Then Mr McCulloch took another point. Mr Cooke, in argument, having indicated that he relied not only on the summons as operating to sever the joint tenancy but on the orders as well, Mr McCulloch submitted on the authority of *Bedson v. Bedson* [1965] 2 Q.B. 666 that there was no power in the court by an order made under the Married Women's Property Act 1882 to sever a beneficial joint tenancy. He submitted that the power of the court was to declare what the rights of the parties were and not to alter those rights. That may well be so—for the purposes of my judgment I am prepared to assume that Mr McCulloch is right about that—but the view I take is that the question does not arise here. The severance, in my judgment, is effected by the summons and the affidavit not by any order that was made. Accordingly, in my judgment, the beneficial joint tenancy was severed by the wife in the lifetime of the husband, and I propose to declare that on the true construction of the conveyance and section 36 of the Law of Property Act 1925, and in the events which have happened, the wife, as trustee, holds the beneficial interest in any proceeds of sale of the property after discharge of encumbrances and costs for herself and the estate of the husband as tenants in common in equal shares.

In so far as the decision was based on notice in writing (comprising the summons and affidavit *but not the court order*), it was criticised on the ground that for the purposes of section 36(2) the notice must be irrevocable whereas, until any order had been made by the court, the proceedings could have been withdrawn: *Nielson-Jones v. Fedden* [1975] Ch. 222, 237 *per* Walton J.; and see Baker (1968) 84 L.Q.R. 462. However, the view of

Plowman J. has subsequently been endorsed: see *Burgess v. Rawnsley* [1975] Ch. 429, 439–440 *per* Lord Denning M.R., 447 *per* Sir John Pennycuick; *Harris v. Goddard* [1983] 1 W.L.R. 1203, 1209–1210 *per* Lawton L.J., 1210 *per* Dillon L.J.; and see [1984] Conv. 148; (1984) 100 L.Q.R. 161. For the alternative basis of the decision, see *infra*, p. 286.

4. In *Gore and Snell v. Carpenter* (1990) 60 P. & C.R. 456 a husband and wife were involved in protracted negotiations following the breakdown of their marriage. Judge Blackett-Ord stressed (at 462) the importance of intention to the issue of severance; and he held that an express reference to severance as part of a package of proposals contained in a draft separation agreement that was never accepted did not constitute a notice in writing effective to sever the joint tenancy. See also *McDowell v. Hirschfield Lipson & Rumney* [1992] 2 F.L.R. 126.

5. In *Burgess v. Rawnsley* [1975] Ch. 429 Lord Denning M.R. seemed to express the view (at 440) that the proviso to section 36(2) was declaratory of the pre-1926 law and that it did not introduce any new method of severance confined to land. However, the predominant view is that severance by notice in writing was an entirely new method, although there remains disagreement and/or uncertainty as to whether it is confined to land: see *Re Draper's Conveyance* [1969] 1 Ch. 486, 491–492 *per* Plowman J.; *Nielson-Jones v. Fedden* [1975] Ch. 222, 229 *per* Walton J.; and see Prichard [1975] C.L.J. 28; Hayton [1976] C.L.J. 20; or whether it extends also to personal property: see *Burgess v. Rawnsley* [1975] Ch. 429, 444 *per* Browne L.J., 447 *per* Sir John Pennycuick.

6. It has been suggested that the wording of section 36(2) restricts the notice in writing method of severance to those cases where there is complete identity between the trustees and the beneficiaries: see Hayton [1976] C.L.J. 20, 25. However, since the argument is based on the opening words of the proviso ("where a legal estate ... is vested in joint tenants *beneficially*"), the argument, if correct, would seem to apply to severance generally; but no such general restriction is suggested.

7. Notice in writing may be effective to sever a joint tenancy even where the notice is not actually received by the other joint tenant(s). The courts have equated "giving notice" under section 36(2) with "serving notice" under section 196 of the Law of Property Act 1925. Thus, provided that the section 36(2) notice is delivered by hand or by ordinary post to the last known address of the other joint tenant(s), the notice is validly given: see section 196(3); *Kinch v. Bullard* [1998] 4 All E.R. 650. Moreover, where the notice is sent by registered post or recorded delivery service, there is no requirement that it should have been delivered at the relevant address; unless it is "returned by the post office undelivered", it is deemed to have been validly given: see section 196(4); *Re 88 Berkeley Road* [1971] Ch. 648. In each of the above cases, the notice had in fact been delivered to the relevant address where both joint tenants were living but it was intercepted by the person giving the notice (who wished to withdraw the notice) and was not actually received by the addressee. For comment, see [1999] Conv. 60.

3.2.2 *The* Williams v. Hensman *catalogue*   In *Williams v. Hensman* (1861) 1 J. & H. 546, Page Wood V.-C. stated (at 557):

A joint tenancy may be severed in three ways: in the first place, an act of any one of the persons interested operating upon his own share may create a severance as to that share. The right of each joint tenant is a right by survivorship only in the event of no severance having taken place of the share which is claimed under the *ius accrescendi*. Each one is at liberty to dispose of his own interest in such manner as to sever it from the joint fund—losing, of course, at the same time, his own right of survivorship. Secondly, a joint tenancy may be severed by mutual agreement. And, in the third place, there may be a severance by any course of dealing sufficient to intimate that the interests of all were mutually treated as constituting a tenancy in common. When severance depends on an inference of this kind without any express act of severance, it will not suffice to rely on an intention, with respect to the particular share, declared only behind the backs of the other persons interested. You must find in this class of cases a course of dealing by which the shares of all the parties to the contest have been [a]ffected, as happened in the cases of *Wilson v. Bell* (1843) 5 Ir.Eq.R. 501 and *Jackson v. Jackson* (1804) 9 Ves. Jun. 591.

NOTES:

1. For a detailed analysis of the decision in its historical context, see Luther (1995) 15 *Legal Studies* 219.
2. Gray, *Elements of Land Law* (2nd ed., 1993), states (at p. 489):

In general terms, in the context of a dealing between a joint tenant and a stranger the issue of severance tends to focus on whether the transaction in question has destroyed an essential unity of joint tenancy. Where, however, the context is that of a dealing of the joint tenants *inter se*, the more useful question seems to be whether any of the co-owners have evinced an intention which is clearly inconsistent with the future operation of the *ius accrescendi*.

It seems that dealings between the joint tenants may effect severance even before the four unities are destroyed: *Burgess v. Rawnsley* [1975] Ch. 429, 438 *per* Lord Denning M.R.

3. The three methods of severance referred to in the *Williams v. Hensman* catalogue are considered below.

3.2.2.1 *Act of one joint tenant "operating upon his own share"*   First, perhaps the most obvious act of severance under this heading is alienation by the joint tenant of his own potential share. Since in theory the share of the joint tenant does not exist until severance, the alienation operates both to realise the share and to transfer it. Thus, if A and B are joint tenants at law and in equity, and A transfers his share to X, the equitable joint tenancy between A and B is severed and replaced by an equitable tenancy in common between X and B; the act of severance does not affect the joint tenancy of the legal estate and A and B remain as trustees. If A, B and C are joint tenants at law and in equity, and A transfers his share to X, the equitable joint tenancy is severed in part: there is a tenancy in common between X (as to a one-third share) and B and C (as to the remaining two-thirds share); but *as between themselves* B and C remain joint tenants of that two-thirds share and the doctrine of survivorship continues to operate: see *Bedson v. Bedson* [1965] 2 Q.B. 666, 689 *per* Russell L.J., *supra*, p. 280. The same analysis should also apply where one joint tenant transfers his share to one of the other joint tenants.

Secondly, severance is effected under this heading where a joint tenant concludes a specifically enforceable contract to transfer his interest to a third party: *Brown v. Raindle* (1796) 3 Ves. 257; *Re Hewitt* [1894] 1 Ch. 362; or where he mortgages his share: *Bedson v. Bedson, supra*, at 690.

Thirdly, where one joint tenant purports to transfer or mortgage the entire property, by forging the signature of the other joint tenant(s), the effect of the transaction is normally to sever the equitable joint tenancy and to transfer/ mortgage the equitable interest of the first joint tenant: see *Ahmed v. Kendrick* (1987) 56 P. & C.R. 120, 126 *per* Slade L.J. (transfer); *First National Securities Ltd v. Hegerty* [1985] Q.B. 850, 854 *per* Bingham J., 862 *per* Sir Denys Buckley (mortgage). However, in *Penn v. Bristol and West Building Society* [1995] 2 F.L.R. 938 it was held that there was no severance and transfer of the equitable interest on the ground that the transferee was also a party to the forgery and that the transfer was therefore a sham and devoid of all effect.

Fourthly, severance may be effected by involuntary alienation. Thus the bankruptcy of a joint tenant severs the joint tenancy when the estate of the bankrupt vests in the trustee in bankruptcy. The precise time of such vesting may be crucial to the question of severance and the operation of the doctrine of survivorship. In *Re Dennis* [1993] Ch. 72, 74–76, Sir Donald Nicholls V.-C. decided that the relevant time was the date of adjudication; but the Court of Appeal reversed the decision on the ground that, pursuant to the doctrine of relation back, the vesting of the estate of the bankrupt in the trustee and thus severance occurred at the date of the first available act of bankruptcy: [1996] Ch. 80. In fact, this decision is now of historical interest only: the concept of "act of bankruptcy" was abolished and the doctrine of relation back became obsolete under the Insolvency Act 1986. Although the issue has not been litigated, the relevant date would now seem to be the date of the bankruptcy order: see Insolvency Act 1986, ss.278, 283. That would be consistent with the decision of the Court of Appeal that an insolvency administration order issued after the death of the debtor (one of two joint tenants) did not operate retrospectively so as to sever the joint tenancy; and that the doctrine of survivorship operated to exclude the interest of the debtor from his estate: *Re Palmer* [1994] Ch. 316, noted at [1995] C.L.J. 52; [1995] Conv. 68. The imposition of a statutory charge where a joint tenant recovers or preserves property in legally-aided litigation also seems to have the effect of severing the joint tenancy: see *Bedson v. Bedson, supra*, 690–691 *per* Russell L.J. Moreover, similar reasoning can probably be applied to the making of a charging order under the Charging Orders Act 1979.

Fifthly, as noted above, Plowman J. regarded this present method of severance as an alternative basis for his decision in *Re Draper's Conveyance* [1969] 1 Ch. 486. He based that conclusion almost exclusively on the proposition of Havers J. in *Hawkesley v. May* [1956] 1 Q.B. 304 that the first method of severance in the *Williams v. Hensman* catalogue "obviously includes a declaration of intention to sever by one party": *ibid.* 313. That aspect of the decision in *Re Draper's Conveyance* was criticised as decided *per incuriam* since the clearly contrary decision of Stirling J. in *Re Wilks* [1891] 3 Ch. 59 had not been not cited either to Plowman J. or to Havers J.: see *Nielson-Jones v. Fedden* [1975] Ch. 222, 233–237 *per* Walton J.; and see Baker (1968) 84 L.Q.R. 462; Hayton [1976] C.L.J. 20. The subsequent endorsement of the decisions in *Hawkesley v. May* and *Re Draper's Conveyance* and the criticism of the decisions in *Re Wilks* and *Nielson-Jones v. Fedden* failed to distinguish clearly between the different methods of severance: see *Burgess v. Rawnsley* [1975] 1 Ch. 429, 439–440 *per* Lord Denning M.R.; *Harris v. Goddard* [1983] 1 W.L.R. 1203, 1209–1210 *per* Lawton L.J., 1210 *per* Dillon L.J.

3.2.2.2 *"Mutual agreement" and "course of dealing"*

Burgess v. Rawnsley [1975] Ch. 429

(CA, Lord Denning M.R., Browne L.J., Sir John Pennycuick)

Honick, the plaintiff's father, and Rawnsley, the defendant, became friends. In 1967 they contributed in equal shares to the purchase of the fee simple of a house: Honick had been the tenant of the ground floor flat in the house and the first floor flat had become vacant. The property was conveyed to Honick and Rawnsley as joint tenants at law and in equity. However, the parties had different intentions as to their future relationship and Rawnsley never moved into the house. There was evidence that the parties orally agreed that Rawnsley would sell her share in the house to Honick for £750; but she later refused to agree to sell at that price. When Honick died, the plaintiff claimed that the house was held on trust for sale for Rawnsley and her father's estate in equal shares. The trial judge upheld that claim on two grounds: first, that there was a resulting trust for the parties because the supposed purpose behind the purchase of the house as joint tenants (that the parties would marry) had failed; and, secondly, that the joint tenancy had been severed. On appeal by the defendant, only Lord Denning M.R. was prepared to uphold the first ground; but all three judges in the Court of Appeal upheld the second ground.

LORD DENNING M.R.:
Secondly, was there a severance of the beneficial joint tenancy? The judge said:

"I hold that there has been a severance of the joint tenancy brought about by the conduct of the defendant is asking £750 for her share which was agreed to."

In making that statement the judge made a little slip. She did not ask £750. But it was a slip of no importance. The important finding is that there was an agreement that she would sell her share to him for £750. Almost immediately afterwards she went back upon it. Is that conduct sufficient to effect a severance?

Mr Levy [counsel for the defendant] submitted that it was not. He relied on the recent decision of Walton J. in *Nielson-Jones v. Fedden* [1975] Ch. 222, given subsequently to the judgment of the judge here. Walton J. held that no conduct is sufficient to sever a joint tenancy unless it is irrevocable. Mr Levy said that in the present case the agreement was not in writing. It could not be enforced by specific performance. It was revocable and was in fact revoked by Mrs Rawnsley when she went back on it. So there was, he submitted, no severance.

Walton J. founded himself on the decision of Stirling J. in *In re Wilks, Child v. Bulmer* [1891] 3 Ch. 59. He criticised *Hawkesley v. May* [1956] 1 Q.B. 304 and *In re Draper's Conveyance* [1969] 1 Ch. 486, and said that they were clearly contrary to the existing well-established law. He went back to *Coke upon Littleton*, 189a, 299b and to *Blackstone's Commentaries*. Those old writers were dealing with legal joint tenancies. *Blackstone* said, 8th ed. (1778), vol. II, pp. 180, 185:

> "The properties of a joint estate are derived from its unity, which is fourfold; the unity of interest, the unity of title, the unity of time, and the unity of possession: ... an estate in joint tenancy may be severed and destroyed ... by destroying any of its constituent unities."

and he gives instances of how this may be done. Now that is all very well when you are considering how a legal joint tenancy can be severed. But it is of no application today when there can be no severance of a legal joint tenancy; and you are only considering how a beneficial joint tenancy can be severed. The thing to remember today is that equity leans against joint tenants and favours tenancies in common.

Nowadays everyone starts with the judgment of Sir William Page Wood V.-C. in *Williams v. Hensman* (1861) 1 John. & Hem. 546, 557. ... In that passage Page Wood V.-C. distinguished between severance "by mutual agreement" and severance by a "course of dealing." That shows that a "course of dealing" need not amount to an agreement, expressed or implied, for severance. It is sufficient if there is a course of dealing in which one party makes clear to the other that he desires that their shares should no longer be held jointly but be held in common. I emphasise that it must be made clear to the other party. That is implicit in the sentence in which Page Wood V.-C. says:

> "it will not suffice to rely on an intention, with respect to the particular share, declared only behind the backs of the other persons interested."

Similarly it is sufficient if both parties enter on a course of dealing which evinces an intention by both of them that their shares shall henceforth be held in common and not jointly. As appears from the two cases to which Page Wood V.-C. referred of *Wilson v. Bell* (1843) 5 Ir.Eq.R. 501 and *Jackson v. Jackson* (1804) 9 Ves.June. 591.

I come now to the question of notice. Suppose that one party gives a notice in writing to the other saying that he desires to sever the joint tenancy. Is that sufficient to effect a severance? I think it is. It was certainly the view of Sir Benjamin Cherry when he drafted section 36(2) of the Law of Property Act 1925. It says in relation to real estates:

> "... where a legal estate (not being settled land) is vested in joint tenants beneficially, and any tenant desires to sever the joint tenancy in equity, he shall give to the other joint tenants <u>a notice in writing of such desire or do such other acts or things as would, in the case of personal estate, have been effectual</u> to sever the tenancy in equity, and thereupon under the trust for sale affecting the land the net proceeds of sale, and the net rents and profits until sale, shall be held upon the trusts which would have been requisite for giving effect to the beneficial interests if there had been an actual severance."

I have underlined the important words. The word "other" is most illuminating. It shows quite plainly that, in the case of personal estate one of the things which is effective in equity to sever a joint tenancy is "a notice in writing" of a desire to sever. So also in regard to real estate.

Taking this view, I find myself in agreement with Havers J. in *Hawkesley v. May* [1956] 1 Q.B. 304, 313–314, and of Plowman J. in *In re Draper's Conveyance* [1969] 1 Ch. 486. I cannot agree with Walton J. [1975] Ch. 222, 234–235, that those cases were wrongly decided. It would be absurd that there should be a difference between real estate and personal estate in this respect. Suppose real estate is held on a joint tenancy on a trust for sale and is sold and converted into personal property. Before sale, it is severable by notice in writing. It would be ridiculous if it could not be severed afterwards in like manner. I look upon section 36(2) as declaratory of the law as to severance by notice and not as a new provision confined to real estate. A joint tenancy in personal estate can be severed by notice just as a joint tenancy in real estate.

It remains to consider *Nielson-Jones v. Fedden* [1975] Ch. 222. In my view it was not correctly decided. The husband and wife entered upon a course of dealing sufficient to sever the joint tenancy. They entered into negotiations that the property should be sold. Each received £200 out of the deposit paid by the purchaser. That was sufficient. Furthermore there was disclosed in correspondence a declaration by the husband that he wished to sever the joint tenancy: and this was made clear by the wife. That too was sufficient.

I doubt whether *In re Wilks, Child v. Bulmer* [1891] 3 Ch. 59 can be supported. A young man who had just become 21 applied to the court to have one third of a joint fund paid out to him. He died just before the application was heard. Stirling J. held that, if he had died just after, there would have been a severance: but, as he died just before, there was not. Ironically enough too, the delay was not on his side. It was the delay of the court. Nowadays I think it should have been decided differently. The application was a clear declaration of his intention to sever. It was made clear to all concerned. There was enough to effect a severance.

It remains to apply these principles to the present case. I think there was evidence that Mr Honick and Mrs Rawnsley did come to an agreement that he would buy her share for £750. That agreement was not in writing and it was not specifically enforceable. Yet it was sufficient to effect a severance. Even if there was not any firm agreement but only a course of dealing, it clearly evinced an intention by both parties that the property should henceforth be held in common and not jointly.

On these grounds I would dismiss the appeal.

BROWNE L.J.:

I agree that this appeal should be dismissed, but only on the second of the two grounds on which the county court judge based his decision. ...

Whether or not there was an oral agreement between Mr Honick and Mrs Rawnsley was, of course, a question of fact. Unsatisfactory as the evidence seems to me, I have after much hesitation come to the conclusion that we should not be justified in upsetting the county court judge's finding of fact on this point.

Mr Levy conceded, as is clearly right, that if there had been an enforceable agreement by Mrs Rawnsley to sell her share to Mr Honick, that would produce a severance of the joint tenancy; but he says that an oral agreement, unenforceable because of section 40 of the Law of Property Act 1925, is not enough. Section 40 merely makes a contract for the disposition of an interest in land unenforceable by action in the absence of writing. It does not make it void. But here the plaintiff is not seeking to enforce by action the agreement by Mrs Rawnsley to sell her share to Mr Honick. She relies upon it as effecting the severance in equity of the joint tenancy. An agreement to sever can be inferred from a course of dealing (see Lefroy B, in *Wilson v. Bell* (1843) 5 Ir.Eq.R. 501, 507 and Stirling J. in *In re Wilks, Child v. Bulmer* [1891] 3 Ch. 59) and there would in such a case ex hypothesi be no express agreement but only an inferred, tacit agreement, in respect of which there would seldom if ever be writing sufficient to satisfy section 40. It seems to me that the point is that the agreement establishes that the parties no longer intend the tenancy to operate as a joint tenancy and that automatically effects a severance. I think the reference in *Megarry and Wade, The Law of Real Property*, 3rd ed. (1966), pp. 418, 419 to specifically enforceable contracts only applies where the suggestion is that the joint tenancy has been severed by an alienation by one joint tenant to a third party, and does not apply to severance by agreement between the joint tenants. I agree with Mr Mummery [counsel for the plaintiff] that section 40 ought to have been pleaded, but I should be very reluctant to decide this case on a pleading point.

The result is that I would uphold the country court judge's judgment on his second ground, namely, that the joint tenancy was severed by an agreement between Mrs Rawnsley and Mr Honick that she would sell her share to him for £750. In my view her subsequent repudiation of that agreement makes no difference. I would dismiss the appeal on this ground.

This conclusion makes it unnecessary to consider the important and difficult questions of what the effect of negotiations not resulting in an agreement or of a mere declaration would have been and, in particular, the problem raised by the decision of Plowman J. in *In re Draper's Conveyance* [1969] 1 Ch. 486, and Walton J. in *Nielson-Jones v. Fedden* [1975] Ch. 222. Further, if the evidence and the conclusion that there was an agreement in this case are rejected, I doubt whether there was enough evidence in this particular case as to a course of dealing to raise the question of the application of Page Wood V.-C.'s third category (1861) 1 John. & Hem. 546, 557. I therefore prefer not to express any final opinion on these points. Lord Denning M.R. has dealt with them in his judgment and I have the advantage of knowing what Sir John Pennycuick is going to say about that aspect of the case. I agree with both of them that Page Wood V.-C.'s third category is a separate category from his second category. I agree also that the proviso to section 36(2) of the Law of Property Act 1925 seems to imply that notice in writing would, before 1925, have been effective to sever a joint tenancy in personal property. It is clear that section 36(2), as Sir John Pennycuick is going to point out, made a radical alteration in the previous law by introducing the new method of severance by notice in writing, and that cases before 1925, in particular *In re Wilks, Child v. Bulmer* [1891] 3 Ch. 59, must now be read in the light of this alteration. I agree that an uncommunicated declaration by one joint tenant cannot operate as a severance.

In my judgment, the appeal should be dismissed on the second ground relied on by the county court judge.

SIR JOHN PENNYCUICK:

It is not in dispute that an agreement for severance between joint tenants effects a severance. This is the rule 2 propounded by Sir William Page Wood V.-C. in *Williams v. Hensman* (1861) 1 John. & Hem. 546, 557. The words he uses are contained in one sentence: "Secondly, a joint tenancy may be severed by mutual agreement." For a clear and full general statement as to severance of a joint tenancy: see *Halsbury's Laws of England* 3rd ed., vol. 32 (1960) p. 335. In the present case the judge found as a fact that Mr Honick and Mrs Rawnsley at the beginning of July 1968 agreed upon the sale by her to him of her share at the price of £750. The evidence upon which that finding was based appears to be rather weak and the judge misstated from whom the proposal originated. But the judge heard Mr Juniper [Honick's solicitor] and the evidence of Mr Honick's statement to him, which evidence was agreed to be admissible; and he heard Mrs Rawnsley herself. I do not think this court would be justified in holding that the judge's finding was so contrary to the weight of evidence that it should be set aside. Browne L.J. has reviewed the evidence in detail and I will not go over the ground again. Once that finding of facts is accepted, the case falls squarely within rule 2 of Page Wood V.-C. It is not contended that it is material that the parties by mutual consent did not proceed to carry out the agreement. Rule 2 applies equally, I think, whether the agreement between the two joint tenants is expressly to sever or is to deal with the property in a manner which involves severance. Mr Levy contended that in order that rule 2 should apply, the agreement must be specifically enforceable. I do not see any sufficient reason for importing this qualification. The significance of an agreement is not that it binds the parties; but that it serves as an indication of a common intention to sever, something which it was indisputably within their power to do. It will be observed that Page Wood V.-C. in his rule 2 makes no mention of specific enforceability. Contrast this position where severance is claimed under his rule 1 by reason of alienation by one joint tenant in favour of a third party. We were referred to a sentence in *Megarry and Wade, The Law of Real Property*, 3rd ed., p. 418, where, under the heading of "Alienation in equity", it is said:

"In equity, ... a specifically enforceable contract to alienate creates an equitable interest in the property even though the legal act of alienation has not taken place."

That statement has, I think, no application to an agreement between the two joint tenants themselves. The only other authority relied on by Mr Levy on this point is a sentence in the old Irish case of *Wilson v. Bell* (1843) 5 Ir.Eq.R. 501, 507, where it is said:

"... it is settled, that an agreement to sever will in equity amount to a severance: and as this is personal property, there is no doubt that even a parol agreement would be sufficient for that purpose."

I think that sentence is altogether inadequate to support Mr Levy's contention.

Mr Mummery advanced an alternative argument to the effect that even if there were no agreement by Mr Honick to purchase Mrs Rawnsley's share, nevertheless the mere proposal by Mr Honick to purchase her share would operate as a severance under rule 3 in *Williams v. Hensman* (1861) 1 John. & Hem. 546, 557. ...

I do not doubt myself that where one tenant negotiates with another for some rearrangement of interest, it may be possible to infer from the particular facts a common intention to sever even though the negotiations break down. Whether such an inference can be drawn must I think depend upon the particular facts. In the present case the negotiations between Mr Honick and Mrs Rawnsley, if they can be properly described as negotiations at all, fall, it seems to me, far short of warranting an inference. One could not ascribe to joint tenants an intention to sever merely because one offers to buy out the other for £X and the other makes a counter-offer of £Y.

We were referred to a long series of authorities going back to *Partriche v. Powlet* (1740) 2 Atk. 54 and culminating in the conflicting decisions of Plowman J. in *In re Draper's Conveyance* [1969] 1 Ch. 486; and Walton J. in *Nielson-Jones v. Fedden* [1975] Ch. 222. Once it has been determined that an agreement was made, as in the present case, anything more one may say on this line of authorities must necessarily be obiter; but I think it may be helpful to state very shortly certain views which I have formed in the light of the authorities.

(1) I do not think rule 3 in Page Wood V.-C.'s statement (1861) 1 John. & Hem. 546, 557, is a mere sub-heading of rule 2. It covers only acts of the parties, including, it seems to me, negotiations which, although not otherwise resulting in any agreement, indicate a common intention that the joint tenancy should be regarded as severed.

I do not overlook the words which I have read from Page Wood V.-C.'s statement, namely, that you must find a course of dealing by which the shares of all the parties to the contract have been affected. But I do not think those words are sufficient to import a binding agreement.

(2) Section 36(2) of the Law of Property Act 1925 has radically altered the law in respect of severance by introducing an entirely new method of severance as regards land, namely, notice in writing given by one joint tenant to the other.

(3) Pre-1925 judicial statements, in particular that of Stirling J. in *In re Wilks, Child v. Bulmer* [1891] 3 Ch. 59, must be read in the light of this alteration in the law; and, in particular, I do not see why the commencement of legal proceedings by writ or originating summons or the swearing of an affidavit in those proceedings, should not in appropriate circumstances constitute notice in writing within the meaning of section

36(2). The fact that the plaintiff is not obliged to prosecute the proceedings is I think irrelevant in regard to notice.

(4) Perhaps in parenthesis because the point does not arise, the language of section 36(2) appears to contemplate that even under the existing law notice in writing would be effective to sever a joint tenancy in personalty: see the words "such other act or thing". The authorities to the contrary are rather meagre and I am not sure how far this point was ever really considered in relation to personalty before 1925. If this anomaly does exist, and I am afraid I am not prepared to say positively that it does not exist, the anomaly is quite indefensible and should be put right as soon as possible.

(6) An uncommunicated declaration by one party to the other or indeed a mere verbal notice by one party to another clearly cannot operate as a severance.

(7) The policy of the law as it stands today, having regard particularly to section 36(2), is to facilitate severance at the instance of either party, and I do not think the court should be over zealous in drawing a fine distinction from the pre-1925 authorities.

(8) The foregoing statement of principles involves criticism of certain passages in the judgments of Plowman J. and Walton J. in the two cases cited. Those cases, like all other cases, depend on their own particular facts, and I do not myself wish to go on to apply these obiter statements of principle to the actual decisions in these cases.

Finally, I would say that if, contrary to my view, there was a resulting trust in this case, I should have no doubt that, on the particular facts in the case, the resulting trust would be for Mr Honick and for Mrs Rawnsley in equal shares. I was referred to *Robinson v. Preston* (1858) 4 Kay & J. 505. The circumstances of the present case are I think plainly such as to take this case out of the general principle laid down in that case as applicable apart from particular circumstances.

I would dismiss the appeal.

NOTES:

1. For comment see Crane (1975) 39 Conv. 443; Hayton [1976] C.L.J. 20; Garner (1976) 40 Conv. 77; Bandali (1977) 41 Conv. 243.

2. The precise relationship between the second and third methods in the *Williams v. Hensman* catalogue has given rise to differences of opinion. In *Nielson-Jones v. Fedden* [1975] Ch. 222 Walton J. referred (at 231) to a course of dealing "as merely being material from which an agreement is to be inferred"; by contrast, in *Burgess v. Rawnsley* [1975] Ch. 429 Lord Denning M.R. (at 439) asserted that a course of dealing "need not amount to an agreement, express or implied, for severance" and Sir John Pennycuick (at 447) expressed the view that the third method includes "negotiations which, although not otherwise resulting in any agreement, indicate a common intention that the joint tenancy should be regarded as severed". Subsequent cases have supported the view that mutual agreement and course of dealing are to be regarded as quite distinct methods of severance and that the latter is thus not "a mere sub-heading" of the former.

3. In *Nielson-Jones v. Fedden* [1975] Ch. 222 the plaintiff and her husband had separated and were contemplating divorce. They were joint tenants of the matrimonial home but they signed a memorandum in which they agreed that the husband should "use his entire discretion to sell [the matrimonial home] and employ the proceeds realised to provide a home for himself to live in". The husband negotiated a sale of the property and both parties received a share of the deposit. Moreover, in the course of protracted negotiations both parties indicated a desire to separate their financial affairs and the husband

expressed a wish to sever the joint tenancy of the property. Walton J. held (at 229) that the memorandum did not effect a severance of the joint tenancy; that it dealt solely with the *use* of the proceeds of sale and that agreement as to use is wholly ambiguous on the question of ownership. He further held (at 230) that the negotiations did not amount to a sufficient course of conduct as to lead to the implication of an agreement to sever, and hence a severance; and (at 230–237) that a mere declaration of an intention to sever does not effect a severance.

4. In *Greenfield v. Greenfield* (1979) 38 P. & C.R. 570 two brothers were joint tenants of a freehold property. The conversion of the house into two self-contained maisonettes and their separate occupation by the brothers and their respective families was held not to amount to a course of dealing effective to sever the joint tenancy.

5. In *Gore and Snell v. Carpenter* (1990) 60 P. & C.R. 456 a husband and wife were involved in protracted negotiations following the breakdown of their marriage. Judge Blackett-Ord stated (at 461–462):

The correspondence does not, in my judgment, show any such mutual agreement. It is suggested that there was an agreement between Mr and Mrs Carpenter before he produced his draft separation agreement in 1985. But I have said that I believe Mrs Carpenter's evidence as to the events leading up to the production of that agreement. There was not, in my judgment, any mutual agreement. Afterwards, when the discussion ranged more over the proposal that each party should take one house and that there should be a financial settlement, again there was no agreement reached. They were very near it—it was an agreement in principle—but I think each party reserved their rights and when the divorce proceedings had come on, if they had come on, it would have been open to them to have argued for some other provision.

Then, was there a course of dealing? There were negotiations, as I have said, but negotiations are not the same thing as a course of dealing. A course of dealing is where over the years the parties have dealt with their interests in the property on the footing that they are interests in common and are not joint. As, for instance, in the case of *Wilson v. Bell* (1843) 5 Ir.Eq.R. 501 which was referred to by Vice Chancellor Page Wood. But in the present case there were simply negotiations between the husband and the wife and again there was no finality and there was no mutuality. For severance to be effected by a course of dealing all the joint tenants must be concerned in such a course and in the present case there is no evidence that Mrs Carpenter was committing herself to accept a tenancy in common prior to the property division which would have been made in the divorce proceedings. Amongst the recent authorities (I am not going to refer to all of them) is *Burgess v. Rawnsley* [1975] Ch. 429 and I was pressed with the dictum of Sir John Pennycuick (at p. 447):

"I do not doubt myself that where one tenant negotiates with another for some rearrangement of interests, it may be possible to infer from the particular facts a common intention to sever, even though the negotiations break down. Whether such an inference can be drawn must, I think, depend upon the particular facts."

In the present case there was, of course, such negotiation, but I cannot infer from it a common intention to sever, because I do not think that Mrs Carpenter was prepared to commit herself at that stage. As Sir John Pennycuick said (at p. 448):

"An uncommunicated declaration by one party to the other, or indeed a mere verbal notice by one party to the other clearly cannot operate as a severance."

See also *McDowell v. Hirschfield Lipson & Rumney* [1992] 2 F.L.R. 126.

6. In *Hunter v. Babbage* (1994) 69 P. & C.R. 548 joint tenants of property had been in the process of negotiating, but had not finalised, a financial settlement involving unequal division of the proceeds of sale of the property. The court endorsed the statement of Sir John Pennycuick in *Burgess v. Rawnsley* [1975] Ch. 429, 446, that the significance of an agreement is not that it binds the parties but that it serves as an indication of a common intention to sever; and on that basis it was held that the joint tenancy had been severed. However, the court also held that, if there was no mutual agreement on the facts of the case, nor was there a course of dealing sufficient to effect severance.

7. Tee [1995] Conv. 105 suggests that an agreement to sever might be ineffective unless it complies with the requirements of section 2 of the Law of Property (Miscellaneous Provisions) Act 1989 (*ante*, p. 61). However, such a view is inconsistent with the broader approach taken in *Burgess v. Rawnsley* and *Hunter v. Babbage*.

3.3 *Reform of the law relating to severance*

As part of its consultation on trusts of land, the Law Commission identified three options for reform of the law relating to severance — the statutory codification of the current law, the removal of all methods of severance except written notice and the introduction of severance by will: Law Commission Working Paper No. 94, *Trusts of Land* (1985), paras. 16.11–16.14; and see Tee [1995] Conv. 105. However, the Law Commission subsequently postponed further consideration of severance: Law Com. No. 181, *Trusts of Land* (1989), para. 1.3.

4. Co-ownership: the statutory machinery

Under the general scheme of the 1925 legislation, co-ownership of land necessarily involved the trust machinery; but it has been seen that there were different forms of trust machinery. In order to promote the objectives of the 1925 legislation, in particular, the simplification of conveyancing, the protection of the purchaser and the protection of the owners of equitable interests, the assumed policy of the legislation was that all cases of co-ownership should operate under the trust for sale machinery; and that, if the transfer to the co-owners did not expressly create that machinery, statute would impose it. In that way, the sale of any land subject to co-ownership would attract the overreaching provisions of section 2(1)(ii) of the Law of Property Act 1925, thereby providing the necessary protection for both the purchaser and the equitable co-owners. The relevant statutory provisions were sections 34–36 of the Law of Property Act 1925.

However, since the coming into force of the Trusts of Land and Appointment of Trustees Act 1996, the trust for sale has been replaced by the trust of land and the 1996 Act provides a comprehensive code for the new form of trust. It defines the powers and duties of the trustees; it defines the rights of the beneficiaries; and it provides machinery and procedures for the resolution of disputes relating to those powers, duties and rights: see *infra*, p. 298.

On the other hand, it seems that the 1996 Act is not a completely self-contained code. Section 1 provides that any trust of property that consists of or includes land must take effect as a trust of land; but it does not expressly address the logically prior question as to whether there is a trust at all. The answer to that question is far from clear. It might be argued that there is an assumption that there is a trust whenever there is a fragmentation of the ownership rights in land; and that the 1996 Act simply operates on that assumption. However, if that is correct, it is difficult to see the reason for the retention (albeit in amended form) of sections 34(2) and 36(1) of the Law of Property Act 1925. As originally enacted, those provisions provided for the imposition of a trust for sale in the case of certain specified conveyances to co-owners. If those provisions operated on the supposed assumption (that there was a trust whenever there was a fragmentation of the ownership rights in land) and had the effect of imposing a trust for sale (as opposed to the bare trust that would have arisen in default), they would no longer have any role to play because, as noted above, the 1996 Act itself provides that any trust of property which consists of or includes land is a trust of land. Indeed, the Law Commission seems to have regarded what became section 1 of the 1996 Act as the necessary clarification that, wherever there is co-ownership of land, and a trust for sale would previously have been imposed, the land should now be held under a trust of land: Law Commission Working Paper No. 94, *Trusts of Land* (1985), para. 6.5; Law Com. No. 181, *Trusts of Land* (1989), para. 3.5. Yet sections 34(2) and 36(1) of the 1925 Act have been retained and amended to provide for the imposition of a trust of land in the same circumstances where those sections originally imposed a trust for sale. Whether or not those sections do more than refer to particular applications of the general statement in section 1 of the 1996 Act, it is surprising that they were not more comprehensively amended. Despite arguments to the contrary, it was generally assumed that it was the policy of the 1925 Act to impose a trust for sale in all cases of co-ownership; and, in order to give effect to that policy, the courts imposed trusts for sale in situations not strictly covered by the Act: see *infra*, p. 296.

Law of Property Act 1925, ss.34–36

Effect of future dispositions to tenants in common

34.—(1) An undivided share in land shall not be capable of being created except as provided by the Settled Land Act 1925 or as hereinafter mentioned.

(2) Where, after the commencement of this Act, land is expressed to be conveyed to any persons in undivided shares and those persons are of full age, the conveyance shall (notwithstanding anything to the contrary in this Act) operate as if the land had been expressed to be conveyed to the grantees, or, if there are more than four grantees, to the four first named in the conveyance, as joint tenants in trust for the persons interested in the land:

. . .

Joint tenancies

36.—(1) Where a legal estate (not being settled land) is beneficially limited to or held in trust for any persons as joint tenants, the same shall be held in trust, in like manner as if the persons beneficially entitled were tenants in common, but not so as to sever their joint tenancy in equity.

NOTES:

1. Where land is prima facie settled land within the meaning of the Settled Land Act 1925 and two or more persons are simultaneously entitled in possession, it is necessary to determine whether those persons are entitled as joint tenants or as tenants in common. Where they are joint tenants, then subject to special provisions where one or more are not of full age, they together constitute the tenant for life of the settled land: Settled Land Act 1925, s.19(2). However, where those entitled are tenants in common, the land ceases to be settled land governed by the provisions of the Settled Land Act 1925. The legal estate must be vested in the trustees of the (former) settlement to be held in trust for those entitled in equity: *ibid.* s.36.

2. The effect of sections 34–36 of the Law of Property Act 1925 is that where land (other than settled land) is purported to be granted to two or more persons as co-owners, and there is no *express* trust, a *statutory* trust, which, pursuant to section 1 of the Trusts of Land and Appointment of Trustees Act 1996, must be a trust of land, is superimposed on the grant. The transferees (up to a maximum of four) become trustees of the land, holding the legal estate as joint tenants; and the terms of the grant as to joint tenancy or tenancy in common determine the form of co-ownership of the equitable interest. Thus a purported grant of Blackacre "to A and B as tenants in common" operates as a transfer to A and B as trustees (as joint tenants of the legal estate) in trust for A and B as tenants in common of the equitable interest: Law of Property Act 1925 s.34(2). A purported grant of Blackacre "to A, B, C, D, E and F as tenants in common" operates as a transfer to A, B, C and D (assuming them all to be of full age and capacity) as trustees (as joint tenants of the legal estate) in trust for A, B, C, D, E and F as tenants in common of the equitable interest: *ibid.*; Trustee Act 1925 s.34(2). A purported grant of Blackacre "to A and B as joint tenants" operates as a transfer to A and B as trustees (as joint tenants of the legal estate) in trust for A and B as joint tenants of the equitable interest: Law of Property Act 1925, s.36(1). It will be appreciated that the imposition of the trust involves no inconsistency with the intention of the grantor since the substance of the grant operates in relation to the equitable ownership.

3. There were some situations for which the above provisions, as originally enacted, appeared not to provide. In particular, whereas section 36(1) of the Law of Property Act 1925 seemed to generate a trust for sale wherever the equitable interest in land was held by co-owners as joint tenants, the legislation did not appear to provide for the imposition of a trust for sale in every situation where the equitable interest in land was held by co-owners as tenants in common: see Friend and Newton [1982] Conv. 213; Swadling

[1986] Conv. 379. However, on the assumption that the policy of the legislation was that *all* cases of co-ownership of land should operate under the trust for sale machinery (but see note 4 *infra*), the courts imposed a trust for sale wherever there was co-ownership. Thus a grant of Blackacre "to A and B", in circumstances where equity presumes that A and B are tenants in common, was held to create a trust for sale with A and B holding as joint tenants of the legal estate and tenants in common of the equitable interest: *Re Buchanan-Wollaston's Conveyance* [1939] 1 Ch. 738. (The point was expressly decided by Farwell J. ([1939] 1 Ch. 217, 222); it was assumed *sub silentio* by the Court of Appeal, although the contrary was not argued.) Where land was expressly transferred to A and B as joint tenants at law *and in equity*, but where C and D had made a substantial contribution to the purchase price, the House of Lords took the view that A and B held the land on trust for sale for A and B on the one hand and C and D on the other hand as tenants in common of the equitable interest: *City of London Building Society v. Flegg* [1988] A.C. 54, 70 *per* Lord Templeman. The assumption that co-ownership always involved the trust for sale machinery had been taken even further in *Bull v. Bull* [1955] 1 Q.B. 234. In that case the Court of Appeal held that where land was transferred "to A", but where the purchase price of the land had been provided by A and B (in unequal shares), A held the land on trust for sale for A and B as tenants in common of the equitable interest: *ibid.* 237 *per* Denning L.J., relying on section 36(4) of the Settled Land Act 1925. However, the analysis was accepted by the House of Lords in *Williams & Glyn's Bank Ltd v. Boland* [1981] A.C. 487, 510 *per* Lord Scarman.

4. The assumption that it was the policy of the 1925 legislation that all cases of co-ownership should operate under the trust for sale machinery appeared to acquire the status of a rule: *Williams & Glyn's Bank Ltd v. Boland* [1981] A.C. 487, 503 *per* Lord Wilberforce; *City of London Building Society v. Flegg* [1988] A.C. 54, 77–78 *per* Lord Oliver. However, Swadling [1986] Conv. 379 argued that it was not the policy of the 1925 legislation to impose a trust for sale in all cases of co-ownership; that the policy was concerned merely to prevent the creation of legal tenancies in common; and that, accordingly, the imposition of trusts for sale was limited to those cases of co-ownership *expressly* covered by the above provisions of the Law of Property Act 1925. On that basis he argued that *Bull v. Bull, Williams & Glyn's Bank Ltd v. Boland* and *City of London Building Society v. Flegg* involved *bare* (resulting) trusts for the contributors. Harpum [1990] C.L.J. 277, 297–302, argued further that it was the intended policy of the 1925 legislation (i) that the existence of a trust for sale should be apparent from the documentary title; and (ii) that, in the absence of an equitable tenancy in common provided for under an express trust for sale or under a trust for sale imposed in the limited circumstances referred to in section 34, the adduction of evidence of an equitable tenancy in common should not be permitted. On that basis, *from the conveyancing point of view of the draftsman of the 1925 legislation*, he argued (i) that the co-owners in *Re Buchanan-Wollaston's Conveyance* should have been held to be joint tenants both at law *and in*

equity; and (ii) that in *Bull v. Bull, Williams & Glyn's Bank Ltd v. Boland* and *City of London Building Society v. Flegg* the equitable entitlement should have been limited to those persons on the legal title. However, he readily acknowledged that unanticipated changes in the pattern of land (co-) ownership after 1925 rendered such an approach unrealistic and unacceptable.

5. To the extent that the amendments made by the Trusts of Land and Appointment of Trustees Act 1996 to sections 34 and 36 only substitute references to trusts (of land) for references to trusts for sale, the lacunae in those provisions remain. On the other hand, there can be no doubt that, subject to the substitution of the trust of land, the assumption made in relation to the intended policy of the 1925 legislation has become the express basis of the 1996 Act. Where there is co-ownership of land, there is a trust of land.

5. Trusts of land: the regime of the Trusts of Land and Appointment of Trustees Act 1996

The Trusts of Land and Appointment of Trustees Act 1996 was designed to address three principal difficulties with the pre-existing law: the unnecessary complication of the dual system of strict settlements and trusts for sale to accommodate successive interests in land; the possibility that the complex mechanisms of the strict settlement could be triggered unintentionally; and the inappropriateness of the trust for sale as a mechanism for modern co-ownership of the family home: Law Com. No. 181, *Trusts of Land* (1989), para. 1.3. The solution to the first two difficulties, which relate to successive interests, has already been outlined: see *supra*, p. 269. This section examines the regime of the 1996 Act in more detail and, in particular, its solutions to the third difficulty with the pre-existing law identified by the Law Commission. For discussion of the Law Commission Report, see Pottage (1989) 52 M.L.R. 683; Smith [1990] Conv. 12. For overviews of the 1996 Act, see Hopkins [1996] Conv. 411; Clements (1998) 61 M.L.R. 56.

5.1 *The powers and duties of the trustees under a trust of land*

Trusts of Land and Appointment of Trustees Act 1996, s.6

General powers of trustees

6.—(1) For the purpose of exercising their functions as trustees, the trustees of land have in relation to the land subject to the trust all the powers of an absolute owner.

(2) Where in the case of any land subject to a trust of land each of the beneficiaries interested in the land is a person of full age and capacity who is absolutely entitled to the land, the powers conferred on the trustees by subsection (1) include the power to convey the land to the beneficiaries even though they have not required the trustees to do so; and where land is conveyed by virtue of this subsection—

(a) the beneficiaries shall do whatever is necessary to secure that it vests in them, and

(b) if they fail to do so, the court may make an order requiring them to do so.

(3) The trustees of land have power to purchase a legal estate in any land in England or Wales.

(4) The power conferred by subsection (3) may be exercised by trustees to purchase land—

(a) by way of investment,

(b) for occupation by any beneficiary, or

(c) for any other reason.

(5) In exercising the powers conferred by this section trustees shall have regard to the rights of the beneficiaries.

(6) The powers conferred by this section shall not be exercised in contravention of, or of any order made in pursuance of, any other enactment or any rule of law or equity.

(7) The reference in subsection (6) to an order includes an order of any court or of the Charity Commissioners.

(8) Where any enactment other than this section confers on trustees authority to act subject to any restriction, limitation or condition, trustees of land may not exercise the powers conferred by this section to do any act which they are prevented from doing under the other enactment by reason of the restriction, limitation or condition.

NOTES:

1. The powers of trustees for sale were limited to "the powers of a tenant for life and the trustees of a settlement under the Settled Land Act 1925": Law of Property Act 1925, s.28(1). Those powers were extensive but did not include all the powers of an absolute owner.

2. Subsection (2) authorises the trustees to terminate their trusteeship by transferring the legal title to the land to the beneficiaries, provided that the beneficiaries are of full age and capacity and absolutely entitled to the land. Subsections (3) and (4) extend and clarify the trustees' powers to purchase land.

3. Section 6 does not permit the trustees to act as if they are absolute owners. The section confers the powers of an absolute owner on the trustees "for the purpose of exercising their functions as trustees" (section 6(1)); the trustees are required to "have regard to the rights of the beneficiaries" (section 6(5)); the trustees must not exercise their powers "in contravention of, or of any order made in pursuance of, any other enactment or any rule of law or equity" (section 6(6)); and the trustees remain subject to restrictions on powers conferred by other enactments (section 6(8)). For an elaborate analysis of section 6, see Ferris and Battersby [1998] Conv. 168, who conclude that non-compliance with subsections (5), (6) or (8) would constitute a breach of trust and would render the purported exercise of the trustees' powers *ultra vires*; and that a disposition of land in contravention of any of those subsections would be ineffective to overreach the interests of the beneficiaries.

4. Section 6 is not an exhaustive statement of the powers of the trustees nor of the restrictions imposed on those powers.

Section 7 confers power on the trustees to effect a partition of the land, where the beneficiaries are of full age and absolutely entitled to the land: see *infra*, p. 336. Section 13 confers power to exclude, restrict or impose conditions on any right of the beneficiaries of the trust to occupy the land: see *infra*, p. 303. More generally, section 9 provides for the trustees jointly to

delegate any or all of their functions that relate to the land to any or all of
the beneficiaries, provided that the beneficiaries are of full age and entitled to
an interest in possession in the land. As noted above, delegation is of
particular significance in the context of successive interest trusts of land
because it enables the trustees to reproduce the functional equivalent of a
strict settlement.

Under section 8(2) a disposition creating a trust of land may include
provision requiring consent to be obtained to the exercise of any power
conferred by sections 6 and 7. Section 11 imposes on the trustees a general
duty of consultation except where a disposition creating a trust of land
includes a provision excluding that duty: see *infra*, p. 314. More generally, the
court has jurisdiction under section 14, on the application of any person who
has an interest in property subject to the trust (including any of the trustees),
to make orders relating to the exercise of the trustees' functions: see *infra*,
p. 314.

5. Where the trust is created by disposition, the person creating the trust
can exclude or restrict or qualify any of the powers (*ibid.* s.8), except for the
power to postpone a sale (*ibid.* s.4(1)). For discussion of the potentially
undesirable consequences of section 8 provisions, see Watt [1997] Conv. 263.

5.2 *A mechanism for modern co-ownership*
The trust for sale machinery was not designed for the realities of modern co-
ownership. Two specific problems were, first, the question of the rights of the
beneficiaries, in particular the right of occupation and, secondly, the question
of dealing with land subject to a trust for sale, in particular the decision to
sell or retain the land. The following discussion of those two issues first
considers briefly the position under the regime of the trust for sale and then
examines the position under the regime of the 1996 Act. It will be seen that
many of the pre-1997 cases probably remain relevant to the operation of the
1996 Act.

5.3 *The rights of beneficiaries*
In the context of the modern model of co-ownership, where two or more
persons contribute to the purchase price of residential property, the
fundamental purpose of the purchase is the provision of residential
accommodation. It would not be unreasonable to suppose that in such
circumstances the co-owners have a right to occupy the property in question.
However, the imposition of the trust for sale machinery did not inevitably
lead to that conclusion.

5.3.1 *The rights of beneficiaries under a trust for sale*

5.3.1.1 *The equitable doctrine of conversion*   Under the equitable doctrine
of conversion, where land was held on trust for sale, the interests of the
beneficiaries were deemed to be interests in the proceeds of sale of the land
rather than interests in the land itself; and this was so irrespective of whether
or not the land had actually been sold. The doctrine was said to follow

logically from the fact that *ex hypothesi* the trustees for sale were under a duty to sell the land, combined with the application of the principle that equity regards as done that which ought to be done. Such reasoning applied without distinction to all trusts for sale, whether they provided for successive interests or concurrent interests and, in the latter case, whether they were express or implied. It was also suggested that the doctrine was an essential element in the scheme of the 1925 legislation to protect purchasers against interests under trusts: *Irani Finance Ltd v. Singh* [1971] Ch. 59, 80 *per* Cross L.J.; *City of London Building Society v. Flegg* [1988] A.C. 54, 82–83 *per* Lord Oliver. However, it is suggested that the protection of purchasers was adequately provided for by overreaching at the time of sale: see Forrest [1978] Conv. 194, 206–207; Harpum [1990] C.L.J. 277, 278–279; and such a view would seem to be confirmed by the absence of the doctrine of conversion from the regime of the Trusts of Land and Appointment of Trustees Act 1996.

Anderson (1984) 100 L.Q.R. 86 argues that in the early case law so-called "conversion-logic" was rarely permitted to prevail where more practical considerations required that such interests should not be treated as mere personal property; and that the theory of "conversion-absolutism", according to which equitable interests under trusts for sale always fell outside rules concerning interests in land, was an invention of twentieth century commentators. However, the courts did on occasions refuse to apply the doctrine in the interpretation of particular statutory provisions: see Forrest [1978] Conv. 194; Warburton [1986] Conv. 415.

More significantly for present purposes, the imposition of the trust for sale machinery in all cases of co-ownership, highlighted by a significant increase in the incidence of co-ownership of the family home, presented a more fundamental basis for questioning the doctrine of conversion: see Boyle [1981] Conv. 108. For, in the context of the family home, a doctrine which postulated that co-owners of land in fact had interests only in the proceeds of sale of that land was highly artificial. The issue had been addressed in earlier cases: see, especially, *Bull v. Bull* [1955] 1 Q.B. 234. However, it was the judgments of the Court of Appeal in *Williams & Glyn's Bank Ltd v. Boland* [1979] Ch. 312, endorsed by the House of Lords ([1981] A.C. 487, 507 *per* Lord Wilberforce), which clearly signalled the demise of the doctrine in relation to implied trusts for sale: see [1979] C.L.J. 254, [1980] C.L.J. 243.

5.3.1.2 *Right of occupation*   Closely linked with the application *vel non* of the doctrine of conversion was the question whether the beneficiaries under a trust for sale had a right to occupy the land in question. For, if the interests of the beneficiaries were treated merely as interests in the proceeds of sale of the land, it was difficult to assert that the beneficiaries had a right to occupy the land itself. On the other hand, the demise of the doctrine referred to above made the assertion of a right of occupation more tenable.

There is pre-1925 authority for the proposition that the beneficiaries under trusts for sale had no right of occupation and that occupation was at best a privilege that the trustees might confer on the beneficiaries; but the relevant authorities involved express successive interest trusts: see *Re Bagot's*

Settlement [1894] 1 Ch. 177, 180–184 *per* Chitty J.; *Re Earl of Stamford and Warrington* [1925] Ch. 162, 171 *per* Russell J. On the other hand, while it is not disputed that prior to 1926 legal tenants in common had a right of occupation of the land, the effect of the imposition of a trust for sale was uncertain. *Re Warren* [1932] 1 Ch. 42 was cited by Denning L.J. in *Bull v Bull* [1955] 1 Q.B. 234 as authority for the view that equitable tenants in common had the same right to occupy the land as legal tenants in common used to have, whereas *Re Landi* [1939] Ch. 828 was frequently cited as authority for the view that equitable tenants in common could *not* claim possession as of right; but it is submitted that neither case was wholly unequivocal.

The issue was first addressed directly in *Bull v. Bull* [1955] 1 Q.B. 234, where Denning L.J. asserted that, pending a sale, equitable tenants in common are each "entitled concurrently with the other to the possession of the land and to the use and enjoyment of it". That decision was expressly endorsed by the House of Lords in *Williams & Glyn's Bank Ltd v. Boland* [1981] A.C. 487, 507 *per* Lord Wilberforce, 510 *per* Lord Scarman; and see *City of London Building Society v. Flegg* [1988] A.C. 54, 77–83, where Lord Oliver endeavoured to reconcile the right of occupation with the imposition of the trust for sale and the doctrine of conversion.

Barnsley [1998] C.L.J. 123 argues that, contrary to the view asserted by most commentators and endorsed by the Law Commission (Law Commission Working Paper 94, *Trusts of Land* (1985), para. 3.22; Law Com. No. 181, *Trusts of Land* (1989), para. 1.3), there was no uncertainty as to the post-1925 rights of occupation of equitable co-owners; and that those rights were unaffected by the imposition of the trust for sale and were in substance no different from the undisputed pre-1926 common law rights. See also Ross Martyn [1997] Conv. 254.

5.3.2 *The rights of beneficiaries under a trust of land*

5.3.2.1 *The equitable doctrine of conversion*   The Trusts of Land and Appointment of Trustees Act 1996 addressed the problems of the doctrine of conversion in two ways. First, the trust for sale (with its defining characteristic of the *duty* on the trustees to sell the trust property: see *supra*, p. 272) was replaced by the trust of land, under which the trustees have only a *power* to sell the trust property. As a result there is no duty to sell on which the doctrine of conversion can operate. Secondly, section 3 of the 1996 Act abolishes the doctrine of conversion in so far as it operates in the present context. It was necessary to include this provision because, as has been seen, it is still possible to "customise" a trust of land by imposing a duty to sell. The Act makes it clear that, even in such cases (but subject to certain transitional savings), the land is not to be regarded as personal property until it is actually sold.

5.3.2.2 *Right of occupation*   The 1996 Act seeks to clarify the question as to whether the beneficiaries have a right of occupation of land held on a trust of land. The relevant provisions are sections 12 and 13.

Trusts of Land and Appointment of Trustees Act 1996, ss.12, 13

The right to occupy

12.—(1) A beneficiary who is beneficially entitled to an interest in possession in land subject to a trust of land is entitled by reason of his interest to occupy the land at any time if at that time—
  (a) the purposes of the trust include making the land available for his occupation (or for the occupation of beneficiaries of a class of which he is a member or of beneficiaries in general), or
  (b) the land is held by the trustees so as to be so available.
(2) Subsection (1) does not confer on a beneficiary a right to occupy land if it is either unavailable or unsuitable for occupation by him.
(3) This section is subject to section 13.

Exclusion and restriction of right to occupy

13.—(1) Where two or more beneficiaries are (or apart from this subsection would be) entitled under section 12 to occupy land, the trustees of land may exclude or restrict the entitlement of any one or more (but not all) of them.
(2) Trustees may not under subsection (1)—
  (a) unreasonably exclude any beneficiary's entitlement to occupy land, or
  (b) restrict any such entitlement to an unreasonable extent.
(3) The trustees of land may from time to time impose reasonable conditions on any beneficiary in relation to his occupation of land by reason of his entitlement under section 12.
(4) The matters to which trustees are to have regard in exercising the powers conferred by this section include—
  (a) the intentions of the person or persons (if any) who created the trust,
  (b) the purposes for which the land is held, and
  (c) the circumstances and wishes of each of the beneficiaries who is (or apart from any previous exercise by the trustees of those powers would be) entitled to occupy the land under section 12.
(5) The conditions which may be imposed on a beneficiary under subsection (3) include, in particular, conditions requiring him—
  (a) to pay any outgoings or expenses in respect of the land, or
  (b) to assume any other obligation in relation to the land or to any activity which is or is proposed to be conducted there.
(6) Where the entitlement of any beneficiary to occupy land under section 12 has been excluded or restricted, the conditions which may be imposed on any other beneficiary under subsection (3) include, in particular, conditions requiring him to—
  (a) make payments by way of compensation to the beneficiary whose entitlement has been excluded or restricted, or
  (b) forgo any payment or other benefit to which he would otherwise be entitled under the trust so as to benefit that beneficiary.
(7) The powers conferred on trustees by this section may not be exercised—
  (a) so as [to] prevent any person who is in occupation of land (whether or not by reason of an entitlement under section 12) from continuing to occupy the land, or

(b) in a manner likely to result in any such person ceasing to occupy the land, unless he consents or the court has given approval.

(8) The matters to which the court is to have regard in determining whether to give approval under subsection (7) include the matters mentioned in subsection (4)(a) to (c).

NOTES:

1. The wording of section 12(1) suggests that the right of occupation depends upon the beneficiaries continuing to satisfy the conditions of that right: see Hopkins [1996] Conv. 411, 420.

2. The first condition (section 12(1)(a)) seems to reflect the developed pre-1997 law. Where the land is intended for occupation by the beneficiaries, there is a right of occupation: see *Bull v. Bull* [1955] 1 Q.B. 234; *Williams & Glyn's Bank Ltd v. Boland* [1981] A.C. 487, *supra*, p. 302. On the other hand, there will probably be no right of occupation where an express duty to sell the land is imposed on the trustees. In *Barclay v. Barclay* [1970] 2 Q.B. 677 the testator lived in a bungalow, where he was later joined by one of his sons, the defendant. By his will, the testator directed that the bungalow be sold and the proceeds be divided between his two surviving sons and three daughters-in-law. Nothing was done until 10 years later, when the plaintiff, one of the daughters-in-law, proceeded to administer the estate: in particular, she sought possession of the bungalow with the intention of selling it and dividing the proceeds. The county court judge held, following *Bull v. Bull*, that the defendant was an equitable tenant in common of the bungalow and was entitled to remain in possession. The Court of Appeal (Lord Denning M.R., Edmund-Davies and Megaw L.JJ.) allowed the plaintiff's appeal. Lord Denning M.R. said (at 684):

In *Bull v. Bull* the prime object of the trust was that the parties should occupy the house together. They were entitled to the possession of it in undivided shares. That made them, in equity, tenants in common. An equitable tenancy in common arises whenever two or more persons become entitled to the possession of property (or the rents and profits thereof) in undivided shares. They may become so entitled by agreement, or under a will, or by inference, as often happens when husband and wife acquire their matrimonial home. The legal owner holds the legal estate on trust for them as tenants in common.

The present case is very different. The prime object of the trust was that the bungalow should be sold. None of the five beneficiaries was given any right or interest in the bungalow itself. None of them was entitled to the possession of it. The testator, by his will, expressly directed that it was to be sold and the proceeds divided between them. In such a situation there was no tenancy in common of the bungalow itself, but at most in the proceeds of sale.

. . .

So we have the clear distinction. In *Bull v. Bull* [1955] 1 Q.B. 234 the prime object was that the house should be occupied by them both. So they were tenants in common of the house itself. In the present case, the prime object of the testator was that the bungalow should be sold and the proceeds divided. So the beneficiaries were not tenants in common of the bungalow, but only of the proceeds after it was sold.

Similarly, there will almost certainly be no right of occupation were the land is purchased solely as an investment or for other purposes that preclude occupation by the beneficiaries: see, for example, *Re Buchanan-Wollaston's Conveyance* [1939] 1 Ch. 738; and see *infra*, p. 307.

3. The purpose behind the second condition (section 12(1)(b)) and its relationship with the first condition is not clear, save that it reinforces the power of trustees to purchase land for occupation by the beneficiaries: see section 6(4)(b); and see Law Com. No. 181, *Trusts of land* (1989), para. 13.3.

4. The exclusion of the right of occupation on the basis of the "unavailability" or "unsuitability" of the land (section 12(2)) is also rather uncertain. "Unavailability" seems to add nothing to the conditions in section 12(1); and "unsuitability" of the *land* seems unlikely to arise as an issue in many cases.

5. Subject to various conditions, the trustees have discretion under section 13 to exclude or restrict the right of occupation of the beneficiaries under section 12 or to make the right of occupation subject to the payment of outgoings or compensation to any excluded beneficiaries. However, in most cases of co-ownership, there are no independent trustees: the trustees and the beneficiaries are the same persons. In practice, therefore, disputes over occupation and ancillary matters will not be resolved by section 13 but will require an application to the court under section 14: see *infra*, p. 314.

6. Barnsley [1998] C.L.J. 123 argues that sections 12 and 13, to the extent that they confer qualified rights of occupation, in their terms represent an erosion of the common law rights and a denial of the fundamental unity of possession; but that, because the 1996 Act in fact preserves the unity of possession together with the incidents attaching to it at common law, equitable co-owners may be able to resort to and enforce their common law rights of occupation where it would be advantageous to do so.

7. Ross Martyn [1997] Conv. 254 argues that sections 12 and 13 may generate practical problems by failing to distinguish between three kinds of entitlement to occupy under the pre-existing law, namely entitlement arising as a result of the exercise of the trustees' discretion; entitlement by virtue of being a co-owner; and entitlement based on the purpose for which the trust was created.

8. Independently of the right of occupation conferred by section 12, spouses may have rights of occupation under the provisions of Part IV of the Family Law Act 1996. The Act confers on a spouse who is not on the legal title the right not to be evicted or excluded from the matrimonial home and, if not in occupation, the right with the leave of the court to enter into and occupy the matrimonial home: Family Law Act 1996, s.30(1),(2); and these "matrimonial home rights" are subject to variation and regulation by the courts: *ibid.* s.33. Moreover, although "matrimonial home rights" are restricted to spouses, the Family Law Act 1996 also confers powers on the court to vary rights of occupation of (former) spouses, cohabitants and other "associated persons". Such powers are available where both parties have a right of occupation based on property rights (including a right of occupation under section 12 of the Trusts of Land and Appointment of Trustees Act 1996) and, to a limited extent, even where only one party or neither party has a right of occupation: *ibid.* ss.35–38.

5.4 *Dealing with co-owned land*

It is not uncommon for the co-owners of land to disagree as to whether the
land should be sold or retained. In particular, such disagreement may occur
where the property in question is a family home and the relationship between
the co-owners has broken down.

5.4.1 *The position under a trust for sale*

5.4.1.1 *Theory and practice*   In theory, the resolution of such disputes
where land was held under a trust for sale should have been straightforward.
Subject to any requirements as to consents and consultation, unless the
trustees for sale were unanimous in postponing the sale, the defining duty to
sell should have prevailed: see *Re Hilton* [1909] 2 Ch. 548, 551 *per* Neville J.
In practice, the mere existence of that obligation did not of itself guarantee
the necessary participation of all the trustees. In such circumstances, where
one or more trustees refused to co-operate in the sale, the other trustee(s)
could apply to the court under section 30 of the Law of Property Act 1925
for an order directing the recalcitrant trustee(s) to join in the sale; and the
court would normally be expected to exercise its discretion to "make such
order as it thinks fit" in accordance with the theoretical position: *Re Mayo*
[1943] 1 Ch. 302, 304 *per* Simonds J.

However, in practice, that basic principle was qualified and modified.
Relying on the terms of section 30, the courts assumed a wide discretion,
including a discretion to refuse to order a sale. The exercise of that discretion
involved the development of the "collateral (or secondary) purpose" doctrine,
according to which the defining duty to sell the land was displaced where the
property was in fact purchased for purposes that involved the *retention* of the
property.

On the other hand, section 30 of the Law of Property Act 1925 and the
potential application of the "collateral purpose" doctrine did not seem to
provide any assistance for a beneficiary who was not also a trustee and who
wished to resist a sale of the land. Leaving aside any requirements as to
express consents and consultation, the co-operation of a non-trustee
beneficiary seemed to be unnecessary for a sale of the land. However, the
retreat from the doctrine of conversion and the recognition that beneficiaries
under a trust for sale had rights of occupation were accompanied by
assertions that those beneficiaries had concomitant rights to resist a sale, at
least to the extent of compelling the trustee(s) to apply to the court under
section 30: see *Bull v. Bull* [1955] 1 Q.B. 234; *Waller v. Waller* [1967] 1
W.L.R. 451.

To the extent that the purpose behind a trust of land is relevant under the
1996 Act to the right of occupation of beneficiaries and the exercise of the
courts' powers under section 14, it is suggested that the cases on the
"collateral purpose" doctrine may provide valuable guidance to the resolution
of disputes under the 1996 Act: see Law Com. No. 181, *Trusts of Land*
(1989), para. 12.9. Those cases are therefore considered below.

5.4.1.2 The "collateral purpose" doctrine   In *Re Buchanan-Wollaston's Conveyance* [1939] 1 Ch. 738 the Court of Appeal considered an application under section 30 of the Law of Property Act 1925 by one of four co-owners. The applicant was seeking an order for sale but the application was resisted by the other three co-owners. Sir Wilfred Green M.R. stated (at 747):

[I]t seems to me that the court of equity, when asked to enforce the trust for sale, whether one created by a settlement or a will or one created by the statute, must look into all the circumstances of the case and consider whether or not, at the particular moment and in the particular circumstances when the application is made to it, it is right and proper that such an order shall be made. In considering a question of that kind ... the Court is bound ... to ask itself the question whether or not the person applying for execution of the trust for sale is a person whose voice should be allowed to prevail.

The reconciliation of this statement with the theoretical position outlined above was explained in *Jones v. Challenger* [1961] 1 Q.B. 176.

Jones v. Challenger [1961] 1 Q.B. 176

(CA, Ormerod and Devlin L.JJ., Donovan J.)

In 1956 a husband and wife purchased as joint tenants at law and in equity a lease (with about 10 years to run) of a house, which they occupied as the matrimonial home. Following the divorce of the parties in 1959, the wife moved out of the house and remarried; but the husband remained in possession. The wife wished to realise her share of the value of the lease; and, when the husband refused to sell, she applied to the court under section 30 of the Law of Property Act 1925. The county court judge concluded that he had a complete discretion to do what was reasonable in the circumstances; and he refused to order a sale. The Court of Appeal allowed the appeal.

DEVLIN L.J.:
There does not appear to be any case in which an order under section 30 has been made where the trust property consists of what was formerly the matrimonial home. The county court judge had no clear authority to guide him in arriving at his decision, and neither have we. After careful consideration of the authorities and some hesitation, I have come to the conclusion that the judge applied the wrong test, and that the question is not whether it is reasonable or unreasonable that the husband should be allowed to remain in the house.

At the front of his argument on behalf of the wife Mr ap Robert put *In re Mayo* [1943] Ch. 302. In this case Simonds J. said (at p. 304): "The trust for sale will prevail, unless all three trustees agree in exercising the power to postpone." If that dictum governs this case, Mr ap Robert must succeed. But he felt a difficulty in pushing his argument to this extent because of what was said by Lord Greene M.R. in *In re Buchanan-Wollaston's Conveyance* [1939] Ch. 738, where he laid down the principle more widely, and said (at p. 747) that the court must ask itself "whether or not the person applying for execution of the trust for sale is a person whose voice should be allowed to prevail."

The apparent difference between these two dicta is, I think, explained when the different facts in the two cases are considered. *In re Mayo* was a simple uncomplicated case of a trust for sale of freehold property, where the beneficiaries were brother and sister, and where there was no suggestion that either of them were intended to or even wished to occupy the property. Simonds J. was applying the simple and fundamental principle that in a trust for sale there is a duty to sell and a power to postpone; and, accordingly, one trustee may call upon the others to perform the duty, but all must be agreed if they are to exercise the power.

But this simple principle cannot prevail where the trust itself or the circumstances in which it was made show that there was a secondary or collateral object besides that of sale. Simonds J., in his judgment in *In re Mayo*, said that if there were mala fides, the position would be different. If it be not mala fides, it is at any rate wrong and inequitable for one of the parties to the trust to invoke the letter of the trust in order to defeat one of its purposes, whether that purpose be written or unwritten, and the court will not permit it. In *In re Buchanan-Wollaston's Conveyance* four owners, who each had separate but neighbouring properties, combined to buy a piece of land which they desired to keep as an open space. The land was conveyed to them as joint tenants and consequently a statutory trust for sale came into existence by virtue of section 35 of the Law of Property Act 1925. The parties then entered into a covenant in which they agreed in effect to preserve the land as an open space. One of the parties subsequently sold his property and then applied against the opposition of the others to have the piece of land sold. The application was refused and it is plain from the judgment that in such circumstances the court has a complete discretion to do what is right and proper, and will not allow the voice of the man who is in breach of his obligation to prevail.

Three other cases were cited as supporting this wider principle. In *In re Hyde's Conveyance* (1952) 102 L.J. 58 two brothers jointly purchased property for occupation by a company in which they were both interested, and for the erection of a factory thereon. Subsequently they quarrelled and one brother applied for an order under section 30 for the sale of the property. The company was still a going concern and the applicant had abandoned a petition for its winding up; he had also refused an offer from the other brother based on the full market value of the property as settled by an independent valuer. The application was refused. Danckwerts J. appears to have been satisfied that the applicant was acting out of spite, and said that he was endeavouring to use the trust for sale to defeat the purpose for which the land had been acquired.

In *Stevens v. Hutchinson* [1953] Ch. 299 a husband and wife held property, which was in fact the matrimonial home, on trust for sale as tenants in common in equal shares. A judgment creditor of the husband applied for an order under section 30, which was refused by Upjohn J. on the ground that the creditor was not a person interested. But the judge went on to say that the creditor could, in any event, have no better right than the husband, and that the husband could not have obtained an order which would have turned the wife out of the matrimonial home. This means, as [counsel for the husband] rightly submits, that the judge would clearly have exercised a discretion in favour of postponing the sale. The case shows, I think, that where property is acquired by husband and wife for the purpose of providing a matrimonial home, neither party has a right to demand the sale while that purpose still exists; that might defeat the object behind the trust, and the court must do what is right and proper in all the circumstances. The case is no authority for the view that the same wide discretion exists when the house is no longer the matrimonial home and the purpose has failed.

Bull v. Bull [1955] 1 Q.B. 234 is a case in which the joint occupation was not matrimonial. The house was owned jointly by a mother and son but the son had provided the greater part of the purchase price. The son gave his mother notice to quit, but this court held that as a tenant in common she could not be ejected. Denning L.J. said that the son could apply under section 30, and the court, in order that there might be a sale with vacant possession, could turn the mother out if it was right and proper to do so. I think that this dictum must be considered on the footing that the house was bought for the purpose of providing a home for mother and son and that, as the mother was still residing there, that purpose had not been brought to an end.

In each of these four cases, *In re Buchanan-Wollaston's Conveyance, In re Hyde's Conveyance, Stevens v. Hutchinson* and *Bull v. Bull*, there was a trust for sale because there was a joint tenancy, and the joint tenancy had been created for a particular purpose. In the first case this purpose was expressed, and in the other three cases the object of the joint tenancy was clear from the circumstances in which it was created. I see no inconsistency between these four cases and *In re Mayo*, in which no collateral purpose was manifest. There is, as I have said, something akin to *mala fides* if one trustee tries to defeat a collateral object in the trust by arbitrarily insisting on the duty of sale. He should have good grounds for doing so and, therefore, the court will inquire whether, in all the circumstances, it is right and proper to order the sale.

In the case we have to consider, the house was acquired as the matrimonial home. That was the purpose of the joint tenancy and, for so long as that purpose was still alive, I think that the right test to be applied would be that in *In re Buchanan-Wollaston's Conveyance*. But with the end of the marriage, that purpose was dissolved and the primacy of the duty to sell was restored. No doubt there is still a discretion. If the husband wanted time to obtain alternative accommodation, the sale could be postponed for that purpose, but he has not asked for that. If he was prepared to buy out the wife's interest, it might be proper to allow it, but he has not accepted a suggestion that terms of that sort should be made. In these circumstances, there is no way in which the discretion can properly be exercised except by an order to sell, because, since they cannot now both enjoy occupation of the property, that is the only way whereby the beneficiaries can derive equal benefit from their investment, which is the primary object of the trust.

It is said that it is hard on the husband that he should have to give up the house which it was his wife's choice and not his to abandon. So it is. But wherever there is a joint occupation, whether it is matrimonial or otherwise, and it is brought to an end, it may involve hardship and inconvenience on the person who would have preferred it to go on. If the wife had died and left her share under the trust to a stranger, I think that the house would obviously have had to be sold. The position is the same if the marriage is ended by divorce, for the court is not under section 30 concerned with the reasons for the ending of the marriage or the rights and wrongs of it; it can only take note that the object of the trust, so far as it required the preservation of the realty, has been fulfilled.

I think that the result must be the same whether the test to be applied is derived from the language used in *In re Mayo* or from that used in *In re Buchanan-Wollaston's Conveyance*. Let it be granted that the court must look into all the circumstances; if when the examination is complete, it finds that there is no inequity in selling the property, then it must be sold. The test is not what is reasonable. It is reasonable for the husband to want to go on living in the house, and reasonable for the wife to want her share of the trust property in cash. The true question is whether it is inequitable for the wife, once the matrimonial home has gone, to want to realise her investment. Nothing said in the cases which I have cited can be used to suggest that it is, and, in my judgment, it clearly is not. The conversion of the property into a form in which both parties can enjoy their rights equally is the prime object of the trust; the preservation of the house as a home for one of them singly is not an object at all. If the true object of the trust is made paramount, as it should be, there is only one order that can be made.

NOTES:

1. In *Rawlings v. Rawlings* [1964] P. 398 a majority of the Court of Appeal held that the collateral purpose of providing a matrimonial home ceased to operate where the marriage of the co-owners came to an end *in fact*, even though there had been no divorce; and a sale was ordered on the application of the "guilty" wife. For comment, generally supportive of the dissenting

judgment of Willmer L.J., see [1964] C.L.J. 210; (1964) 28 Conv. 399; (1964) 80 L.Q.R. 477.

2. In *Rawlings v. Rawlings* Salmon L.J. anticipated a much more important development when he stated (at 419):

If there were young children the position would be different. One of the purposes of the trust would no doubt have been to provide a home for them, and whilst that purpose still existed a sale would generally not be ordered. But when those children are grown up and the marriage is dead, the purposes of the trust have failed.

See *Williams v. Williams* [1976] Ch. 278, *infra*.

3. The "collateral purpose" doctrine has been applied where the purpose included the continued provision of housing for one co-owner after the death of the other co-owner, notwithstanding that the interest of the deceased had passed to a third party: *Jones (A.E.) v. Jones (F.W.)* [1977] 1 W.L.R. 438, 442 *per* Lord Denning M.R.; *Stott v. Radcliffe* (1982) 126 Sol.J. 319; *Harris v. Harris* (1995) 72 P. & C.R. 408; and see *Abbey National plc v. Moss* (1993) 26 H.L.R. 249, *infra*, p. 328.

Williams v. Williams [1976] Ch. 278

(CA, Lord Denning M.R., Roskill and Geoffrey Lane L.JJ.)

The parties were co-owners of the matrimonial home holding on trust for sale for themselves as equitable tenants in common. Following their divorce in 1971, the husband moved out of the house; but the wife remained in possession with the four children of the marriage. In 1973, when the youngest son was aged 12, the husband decided that he wished to realise his share of the value of the house; and he applied to the court under secton 30 of the Law of Property Act 1925. The county court judge made the order for sale; but the Court of Appeal allowed the appeal.

LORD DENNING M.R.:
The judge dealt with [the application under section 30] according to the old law of trusts. There was a trust for sale with power to postpone sale. He put the argument for the wife:

"It is said that I should postpone the sale so that he"—he is referring to the youngest boy, who was then 12 years of age—"can remain in the house and attend the school which he is now attending, and he wants to stay at that school and not move to another. Whether that would be the result of a sale one does not know, because one does not know what alternative accommodation the defendant"—that is, the wife— "will have."

Then he put the argument for the husband:

"But what I must look at is this: the whole of the original £7,000 was produced by the plaintiff to purchase this property. He has had nothing out of the property since he left it in December 1970, so that for nearly five years all the capital which he possesses in the world has been tied up in this property ... I for my part cannot see why the plaintiff must put up with having the only capital which he ever produced further tied up after so long a period as four years. ..."

So he ordered a sale in order that the husband should have his money even though it meant that the wife would have to leave. That is the old approach which was taken in *Jones v. Challenger* [1961] 1 Q.B. 176, where Devlin L.J. said, at pp. 183–184:

"The position is the same if the marriage had ended by divorce, for the court is not under section 30 concerned with the reasons for the ending of the marriage or the rights and wrongs of it; it can only take note that the object of the trust, so far as it required the preservation of the realty, has been fulfilled."

A similar approach was taken in *Burke v. Burke* [1974] 1 W.L.R. 1063, where Buckley L.J. said, at p. 1067:

"... it is not, I think, right to treat this case as though the husband was obliged to make provision for his children by agreeing to retain the property unsold. ... the trust for sale ... is the primary provision applicable to this property."

I must say that that approach is now outdated. When judges are dealing with the matrimonial home, they nowadays have great regard to the fact that the house is bought as a home in which the family is to be brought up. It is not treated as property to be sold nor as an investment to be realised for cash. That was emphasised by this court in the recent case of *Browne (formerly Pritchard) v. Pritchard* [1975] 1 W.L.R. 1366. The court, in executing the trust should regard the primary object as being to provide a home and not a sale. Steps should be taken to preserve it as a home for the remaining partner and children, but giving the outgoing partner such compensation, by way of a charge or being bought out, as is reasonable in the circumstances.

It seems to me that in this case the judge was in error in applying the old approach. He did not give proper effect to the modern view, which is to have regard to the needs of the family as a whole before a sale is ordered. We have here the wife and the four sons still in the house. The youngest son is only 13 years of age and still at school. It would not be proper at this stage to order the sale of the house, unless it were shown that alternative accommodation could be provided at a cheaper rate, and some capital released. That has not been shown here.

The truth is that the approach to these cases has been transformed since the Matrimonial Proceedings and Property Act 1970 and the Matrimonial Causes Act 1973 which have given the power to the court after a divorce to order the transfer of property. In exercising any discretion under section 30 of the Law of Property Act 1925, those Acts must be taken into account. The discretion should be exercised on the principles stated by this court in *Jackson v. Jackson* [1971] 1 W.L.R. 1539, 1543.

I would add this: An application about a matrimonial home should not be restricted to section 30 of the Law of Property Act 1925. In view of the wide powers of transfer and adjustment which are available under the new matrimonial property legislation it seems to me that the applications should be made to the Family Division under the relevant provisions. If taken out in another division, they should be transferred to a judge of the Family Division. In this very case it seems to me that the right course (which the wife's advisers ought to have taken before) is that they should now, and at once, take out the appropriate application under section 24 of the Matrimonial Causes Act 1973 for any necessary orders and so on to be made with regard to the house and the property. That application should be brought on together with an application under section 30.

I would therefore be in favour of allowing the appeal, setting aside the order for sale made by Foster J. and remitting the matter for further consideration by a judge of the Family Division when an application has been taken out under the matrimonial property legislation.

NOTES:

1. As Lord Denning M.R. indicated, where the dispute relating to the sale of co-owned property arose in the context of the divorce of the co-owners, it was more appropriate for the dispute to be resolved by the exercise of the powers of property transfer, adjustment and sale under the Matrimonial Causes Act 1973; and that approach doubtless still applies. However, where those powers were not available, because the parties were not seeking divorce, section 30 remained relevant.

2. Where the co-owners had never been married, section 30 provided the only procedure; but the courts applied the same guiding principles for the exercise of the discretion, including the broader notion of the "family home purpose" as influenced by the matrimonial legislation. In *Re Evers* [1980] 1 W.L.R. 1327 Ormrod L.J., having cited the authorities referred to above, stated (at 1332–1334):

This approach to the exercise of the discretion given by section 30 has considerable advantages in these "family" cases. It enables the court to deal with substance, that is reality, rather than form, that is, convenience of conveyancing; it brings the exercise of the discretion under this section, so far as possible, into line with exercise of the discretion given by section 24 of the Matrimonial Causes Act 1973; and it goes some way to eliminating differences between legitimate and illegitimate children in accordance with present legislative policy: see, for example Part II of the Family Law Reform Act 1969.

The relevant facts in the present case must now be examined. There is little or no dispute between the parties about them. Both the mother and the father have been married and divorced. The mother had two children of her marriage, both boys, now aged ten and eight. She met the father in May 1974. In August 1974, they began to live together at the father's former matrimonial home; the two boys remained in the care of their father, the mother visiting them regularly. Early in 1976 the mother became pregnant by the father and gave birth to the child, who is the subject of the wardship proceedings, on December 22, 1976. At about that time, the two older boys joined their mother and from then until the separation in August 1979 all five lived together, at first at the father's former matrimonial home, until in April 1978 the parties jointly acquired the cottage which is the subject of these proceedings. This property was purchased for £13,950, of which £10,000 was raised jointly on mortgage. The balance was provided as to £2,400 by the mother and as to £1,050 plus expenses by the father. The mother's contribution was derived from her share of her former matrimonial home. On April 28, 1978, the property was conveyed into their joint names as trustees upon a bare trust for sale with power to postpone the sale in trust for themselves as joint tenants.

The irresistible inference from these facts is that, as the judge found, they purchased this property as a family home for themselves and the three children. It is difficult to imagine that the mother, then wholly responsible for two children, and partly for the third, would have invested nearly all her capital in the purchase of this property if it was not to be available to her as a home for the children for the indefinite future. It is inconceivable that the father, when he agreed to this joint adventure, could have thought otherwise, or contemplated the possibility of an early sale without the consent of the mother. The underlying purpose of the trust was, therefore, to provide a home for all five of them for the indefinite future. Unfortunately, the relationship between the father and the mother broke down very soon, and the parties separated at the beginning of August 1979 in circumstances of great bitterness. This is clearly shown by two dates. On July 20, 1979, the mother issued her originating summons in the wardship proceedings; on August 2, 1979, the father issued his application under section 30 for an order for sale of the property.

...

It was argued that the father ought to be allowed to "take his money out" or "to realise his investment." In point of fact, his investment amounted to less than one-fifth of the purchase price of the property, and was smaller than the mother's investment. The major part of the purchase price was provided by the mortgagees, and the mother is prepared to accept full responsibility for paying the interest on the mortgage, and keeping up the capital re-payments. The father has a secure home with his mother. There is no evidence that he has any need to realise his investment. It is an excellent one, combining complete security with considerable capital appreciation in money terms. His share is now said to be worth about £5,000, i.e. it has more than doubled in value in two years. On the other hand, a sale of the property now would put the mother into a very difficult position because she cannot raise the finance to rehouse herself or meet the cost of borrowing money at present rates. So there is no justification for ordering a sale at the present time.

For these reasons the judge was right not to order an immediate sale but the form of his actual order is not satisfactory. Under section 30, the primary question is whether the court should come to the aid of the applicant at the "particular moment and in the particular circumstances when the application is made to it ...": see *In re Buchanan-Wollaston's Conveyance* [1939] 1 Ch. 738, 747. In the present case, at the present moment and in the existing circumstances, it would be wrong to order a sale. But circumstances may change unpredictably. It may not be appropriate to order a sale when the child reaches 16 years—a purely arbitrary date—or it may become appropriate to do so much sooner, for example on the mother's remarriage, or on it becoming financially possible for her to buy the father out. In such circumstances it will probably be wiser simply to dismiss the application while indicating the sort of circumstances which would, prima facie, justify a further application. The ensuing uncertainty is unfortunate but, under this section, the court has no power to adjust property rights or to re-draft the terms of the trust. Ideally, the parties should now negotiate a settlement on the basis that neither of them is in a position to dictate terms. We would therefore dismiss the father's appeal, but would vary the order to dismiss the application on the mother's undertaking to discharge the liability under the mortgage, to pay the outgoings and maintain the property, and to indemnify the father so long as she is occupying the property.

See also *Dennis v. MacDonald* [1982] Fam. 63; *Bernard v. Josephs* [1982] Ch. 391.

3. For the current relationship between the property law jurisdiction and the family law jurisdictions, see *infra*, p. 318.

5.4.2 *The position under a trust of land*

5.4.2.1 *Consent requirements* The rules relating to express consent requirements contained in the 1996 Act are similar to those formerly contained in section 26 of the Law of Property Act 1925. The disposition creating a trust of land may provide that the trustees must obtain the consent of any person to the exercise of any power (section 8(2)), although the court has jurisdiction under section 14 to relieve the trustees of their obligation to obtain such consent. Where the consent of a beneficiary is required, a failure on the part of the trustees to obtain that consent presumably constitutes a breach of trust. However, section 10(1) provides that, where the consent of more than two persons is required, the consent of any two is sufficient in favour of a purchaser.

The notion of an "implied consent" requirement as applied in *Bull v. Bull* [1955] 1 Q.B. 234 should now be obsolete. In so far as it was developed to protect the occupation of a beneficiary, the right of occupation conferred by section 12 should remove any need for it.

5.4.2.2 Consultation requirements   Section 11 of the 1996 Act provides that, subject to express exclusion, the trustees of land shall, in the exercise of any of their powers, *so far as practicable*, consult the beneficiaries of full age and beneficially entitled to an interest in possession in the land and, so far as consistent with the general interest of the trust, give effect to the wishes of those beneficiaries or (in the case of a dispute) of the majority (according to the value of their combined interests). However, the former consultation requirements (which did not apply to express trusts) were in similarly qualified terms and were of only limited practical value.

Moreover, the court has jurisdiction under section 14 to relieve the trustees of their obligation to consult; and section 16(1) re-enacts, in relation to *unregistered* land, the pre-1997 law that a purchaser need not be concerned to see that the consultation requirements have been complied with.

5.4.2.3 Powers of the court   Where the trustees disagree among themselves as to whether the land should be sold or where a beneficiary disagrees with a decision of the trustees, it will often be necessary for the court to resolve the dispute. This will certainly be the position where, as is so often the case, the trustees and the beneficiaries are the same persons.

Trusts of Land and Appointment of Trustees Act 1996, ss.14, 15

Applications for order

14.—(1) Any person who is a trustee of land or has an interest in property subject to a trust of land may make an application to the court for an order under this section.

(2) On an application for an order under this section the court may make any such order—

    (a) relating to the exercise by the trustees of any of their functions (including an order relieving them of any obligation to obtain the consent of, or to consult, any person in connection with the exercise of any of their functions), or

    (b) declaring the nature or extent of a person's interest in property subject to the trust,

as the court thinks fit.

(3) The court may not under this section make any order as to the appointment or removal of trustees.

(4) The powers conferred on the court by this section are exercisable on an application whether it is made before or after the commencement of this Act.

Matters relevant in determining applications

15.—(1) The matters to which the court is to have regard in determining an application for an order under section 14 include—

(a) the intentions of the person or persons (if any) who created the trust,

(b) the purposes for which the property subject to the trust is held,

(c) the welfare of any minor who occupies or might reasonably be expected to occupy any land subject to the trust as his home, and

(d) the interests of any secured creditor of any beneficiary.

(2) In the case of an application relating to the exercise in relation to any land of the powers conferred on the trustees by section 13, the matters to which the court is to have regard also include the circumstances and wishes of each of the beneficiaries who is (or apart from any previous exercise by the trustees of those powers would be) entitled to occupy the land under section 12.

(3) In the case of any other application, other than one relating to the exercise of the power mentioned in section 6(2), the matters to which the court is to have regard also include the circumstances and wishes of any beneficiaries of full age and entitled to an interest in possession in property subject to the trust or (in case of dispute) of the majority (according to the value of their combined interests).

(4) This section does not apply to an application if section 335A of the Insolvency Act 1986 (which is inserted by Schedule 3 and relates to applications by a trustee of a bankrupt) applies to it.

NOTES:

1. Section 14 replaces section 30 of the Law of Property Act 1925. Its terms would seem to indicate a wider jurisdiction than that conferred by section 30 in that it confers on the court jurisdiction to make orders "relating to the exercise of any of [the trustees'] functions" and to declare "the nature or extent of a person's interest in property subject to the trust". On the other hand, the original Bill drafted by the Law Commission also included jurisdiction to make orders "for the settlement any dispute which has arisen concerning the trust or the land subject to it": see Law Com. No. 181, *Trusts of Land* (1989), para. 12.6; clause 6.

2. The terms of the jurisdiction under section 14 raise a number of issues. First, although the section refers to orders "relating to the exercise of any of [the trustees'] *functions*", it seems that the jurisdiction is not limited to those trustees' powers included under that heading in the Act (general powers (section 6), partition (section 7) and delegation (section 9)). The section expressly refers to orders relieving the trustees of their obligations relating to consents and consultation; and section 15(2) expressly refers to applications relating to the exercise of the powers conferred on trustees by section 13. Secondly, even with that wider interpretation of the trustees' functions, it is not clear to what extent the jurisdiction of the court under section 14 is restricted by limitations imposed on those functions by the Act itself or by the disposition creating the trust. In particular, it is unclear whether the court has jurisdiction to exclude a beneficiary who is currently in occupation pursuant to his entitlement under section 12 in circumstances where the trustees are precluded from doing so: see section 13(7). On the same basis, it might be argued that the court has no jurisdiction to order the sale of land where a beneficiary is currently in occupation pursuant to his entitlement under section

12. However, if such a restricted interpretation of the jurisdiction of the court had been intended, it is arguable that the Act would have made the position rather clearer.

3. Section 15 sets out the criteria to be applied by the court in determining an application under section 14. Section 15(1)(b) reflects the "collateral purpose" doctrine developed by the courts in the context of the trust for sale: see *supra*, p. 307; and section 15(1)(a) adds little, especially where the "persons who created the trust" are also the trustees and the beneficiaries. Section 15(1)(c) provides clarification that the welfare of any children is a relevant consideration, although the pre-1997 "collateral purpose" doctrine had been extended to include the provision of a home for the children, at least in the absence of the bankruptcy of one of the parties. In broad terms, therefore, section 15(1)(a)-(c) seems to embrace the substance of the "collateral purpose" doctrine. Of course, that doctrine was developed by the courts in the context of the trust for sale and therefore against the background of a presumption of sale: as a matter of theory, the defining duty to sell should have prevailed unless the trustees were unanimous in exercising their power to postpone the sale: see *supra*, p. 306. By contrast, the trust of land involves a power of sale and a power to postpone sale; and, therefore, in the exercise of its jurisdiction under section 14, the court begins from a "neutral" position. Nonetheless, it is suggested that the earlier case law will continue to provide valuable guidance: Law Com. No. 181, *Trusts of Land* (1989), para. 12.9.

4. Section 15(1)(d) refers to the interests of any secured creditors of any beneficiary. Since section 15 does not apply to applications under section 14 made by a trustee in bankruptcy, it is necessary to consider this factor independently of the bankruptcy context, in which the courts have signalled that a sale will almost invariably be ordered in the absence of exceptional circumstances: see *infra*, p. 318. The cases involving trusts for sale and applications by secured creditors under section 30 of the Law of Property Act 1925 provide ambivalent guidance. In *Lloyds Bank plc v. Byrne and Byrne* (1991) 23 H.L.R. 472 the Court of Appeal ordered a sale on the application of a chargee under a charging order, holding that there was no difference in principle between the position of such a chargee and that of a trustee in bankruptcy. In *Abbey National plc v. Moss* (1993) 26 H.L.R. 249 Hirst L.J. held that the strict approach that applied in the context of bankruptcy cases should also be applied to the "almost identical position" of a mortgagee of the equitable interest of one co-owner. However, Peter Gibson L.J. (with whom Ralph Gibson L.J. agreed) held that the collateral purpose in that case was continuing and that, even in the absence of exceptional circumstances, the court should not therefore order a sale. In *Barclays Bank plc v. Hendricks* [1996] 1 F.L.R. 258 Laddie J. expressly endorsed the approach in *Lloyds Bank plc v. Byrne and Byrne* but also noted that the application of the majority view in *Abbey National plc v. Moss* would have produced the same result.

Academic opinion is also divided on the issue. Clarke [1994] Conv. 331 argued that the majority view in *Abbey National plc v. Moss* reflected an appropriately more flexible approach where the application was made by creditors who did not have the *duty* imposed on a trustee in bankruptcy to realise the assets of the bankrupt. However, Hopkins (1995) 111 L.Q.R. 72 argued that it was inappropriate to distinguish between different types of creditor; that in all such cases the courts should consider (i) whether there was a continuing collateral purpose and, if so, (ii) whether the vesting of a share of the ownership in the trustee in bankruptcy or the interest of the creditor was consistent with the continuance of that purpose; and that, where the second question received a negative answer, a sale should be ordered in the absence of exceptional circumstances.

It is arguable that section 15 has relaxed the strict "bankruptcy" approach to such cases. The interests of secured creditors is only one of the matters relevant in determining an application under section 14 and the section does not indicate any priority between the listed matters. In particular, it has been suggested that the interests of creditors may be given less weight if the welfare of children is seen as a factor to be considered independently of the interests of adult beneficiaries: Law Com. No. 181, *Trusts of Land* (1989), para. 12.10. Judicial comment on the question has been equivocal. In *TSB v. Marshall* [1998] 39 E.G. 208 the court expressly applied the principles established in the context of applications under section 30 of the Law of Property Act 1925 to an application under section 14 of the 1996 Act. However, in *Bankers Trust Co. v. Namdar* [1997] N.P.C. 22 the Court of Appeal intimated that the 1996 Act might engender a more sympathetic approach.

5. Where one co-owner purports to sell or mortgage the co-owned land, the purchaser or mortgagee may find that he has acquired land subject to the interest of a beneficiary under a trust. In such circumstances, the purchaser or mortgagee may wish to apply for an order for sale under section 14 in order to recover at least part of the purchase price or loan. In such circumstances it has been held that the purchaser or mortgagee is not precluded from making an application to the court for an order for sale: *Bankers Trust Co. v. Namdar* [1997] N.P.C. 22; *Bank of Baroda v. Dhillon* [1998] 1 F.L.R. 524, noted at [1998] Conv. 415; *Halifax Mortgage Services Ltd v. Muirhead* (1997) 76 P. & C.R. 418. Moreover, Martin [1980] Conv. 361, 375–379 suggests that in most cases the court would exercise its discretion in favour of a purchaser who purchased the property as a home, since he may otherwise be unable to purchase another property. However, in the rather unusual circumstances of *Chhokar v. Chhokar* [1984] F.L.R. 313 the Court of Appeal refused to order a sale. During matrimonial difficulties the husband had sold the jointly owned matrimonial home with the intention, as the purchaser knew, of defeating the interest of the wife. Although the court declined to set the transfer aside, the purchaser was bound by the equitable interest of the wife as an overriding interest. Moreover, the court also declined to order a sale: the husband and wife had resumed cohabitation and thus the family home purpose for which the property was originally acquired was still operating. The approach of the courts to applications by mortgagees has already been considered, *supra*, note 4.

6. The court is also required to have regard to the circumstances and wishes

of specified categories of beneficiaries in determining applications relating to particular powers of the trustees: section 15(2), (3).

7. Where the court declines to order a sale of the property and one co-owner remains in sole occupation (or where one co-owner has been in sole occupation for some period prior to a sale) the question may arise as to the payment of rent or other compensation by the occupier to the non-occupier. The court has jurisdiction under section 14 to order such payments as the trustees are empowered to require under section 13. However, it appears that the powers of the trustees and the jurisdiction of the court *under the 1996 Act* are prospective only; and that it may be necessary to examine the pre-1997 principles.

The general rule at common law was that, in the absence of agreement, a co-owner in sole occupation of the co-owned land was not liable to pay rent to the other co-owner(s) unless he had excluded the other co-owner(s): *M'Mahon v. Burchell* (1846) 2 Ph. 127, 134–135 *per* Lord Cottenham L.C.; *Henderson v. Eason* (1851) 17 Q.B. 701, 720 *per* Parke B.; and this rule was applied in *Jones (A.E.) v. Jones (F.W.)* [1977] 1 W.L.R. 438, 441–442 *per* Lord Denning M.R., noted at (1977) 41 Conv. 279; (1978) 41 M.L.R. 208. In *Dennis v. MacDonald* [1982] Fam. 63 the Court of Appeal held that rent was payable by the occupying co-owner, specifically because by reason of his violence he had effectively ousted the other co-owner: see [1982] Conv. 305; (1982) 98 L.Q.R. 519. However, in *Bernard v. Josephs* [1982] Ch. 391 the Court of Appeal adopted a less restrictive approach to the entitlement of the non-occupier to the payment of rent (or its equivalent); and the predominant view now seems to be that rent is payable where it is necessary to do equity between the parties: see *Chhokar v. Chhokar* [1984] F.L.R. 313, 332 *per* Cumming-Bruce L.J.; *Re Pavlou* [1993] 1 W.L.R. 1046, 1050 *per* Millett J.; and see Cooke [1995] Conv. 391. Moreover this approach is consistent with the greater willingness of the courts to require the payment of rent (or its equivalent) as an element in financial arrangements following marriage breakdown: see [1982] Conv. 305.

8. Although the jurisdiction under section 14 of the 1996 Act is wider than the former jurisdiction under section 30 of the Law of Property Act 1925 (and although the matters relevant to the exercise of that jurisdiction are more clearly spelt out), it seems that disputes as to the sale of property between spouses in the process of divorce will continue to be resolved by the exercise of the powers under the Matrimonial Causes Act 1973: see *supra*, p. 312. Moreover, disputes as to the occupation of property may be resolved under the jurisdiction now contained in Part IV of the Family Law Act 1996: see *supra*, p. 305. It remains to seen whether the jurisdiction contained in the Family Law Act 1996 in relation to unmarried cohabitants and "associated persons" will also be preferred to the property law jurisdiction under the 1996 Act.

5.4.2.4 *Intervention of the trustee in bankruptcy*   Disputes as to the sale or retention of co-owned property may arise where one of the co-owners is bankrupt. Where a person becomes bankrupt, his estate (defined to include property to which he is beneficially entitled: Insolvency Act 1986, s.283) vests in his trustee in bankruptcy: *ibid.* s.306. The trustee in bankruptcy is then under a duty to realise that property for the benefit of the bankrupt's creditors: *ibid.* s.305(2). Consequently, where the property includes co-owned land held on trust, and the non-bankrupt co-owner is unwilling to concur in a sale, the trustee in bankruptcy may apply to the court under section 14 of the 1996 Act (as a "person interested") for an order for the sale of that property: *Re Solomon (A Bankrupt)* [1967] Ch. 573, 586 *per* Goff J. (Even where the co-owners are spouses, the involvement of the trustee in bankruptcy precludes the matrimonial law jurisdiction: *Re Holliday (A Bankrupt)* [1981] Ch. 405, 419 *per* Goff L.J.)

The applicable principles in this context have developed through various stages. Prior to the Insolvency Act 1986, the courts at one time asserted that the test applied to resolve two-party disputes ("whose voice in equity ought to prevail") was equally applicable where a trustee in bankruptcy intervened and they insisted that the courts retained a discretion and that there was no presumption in favour of the trustee in bankruptcy: *Re Turner (A Bankrupt)* [1974] 1 W.L.R. 1556, 1558 *per* Goff J. However, that insistence was not maintained: the "collateral purpose" doctrine was sidelined and in case after case the interests of the creditors prevailed and a sale was ordered within a short period: *Re Solomon (A Bankrupt)* [1967] Ch. 573; *Re Turner (A Bankrupt)*, [1967] Ch. 573; Re *Densham (A Bankrupt)* [1975] 1 W.L.R. 1519; *Re Bailey (A Bankrupt)* [1977] 1 W.L.R. 278; *Re Lowrie (A Bankrupt)* [1981] 3 All E.R. 353; *Re Gorman (A Bankrupt)* [1990] 1 W.L.R. 616. The single exception to this pattern was *Re Holliday (A Bankrupt)*, [1981] Ch. 405, but the scope of that decision was strictly circumscribed in *Re Citro* (A Bankrupt) [1991] Ch. 142.

Re Citro (A Bankrupt) [1991] Ch. 142

(CA, Nourse and Bingham L.JJ., Sir George Waller)

In 1985 the Citro brothers, Domenico and Carmine, were adjudicated bankrupt, following the failure of a joint business venture. Their only substantial assets were their shares in their respective matrimonial homes. Domenico was separated from his wife but she continued to live in the house with the three children of the marriage; Carmine lived in his house with his wife and their three children. The trustee in bankruptcy applied under section 30 for orders for the sale of the two houses. In 1989 Hoffmann J. made the orders for possession and sale but postponed enforcement until the youngest child in each case had attained the age of 16 years (until 1994 and 1995 respectively). The Court of Appeal allowed the appeal of the trustee in bankruptcy.

NOURSE L.J.:
In the leading case of *Jones v. Challenger* [1961] 1 Q.B. 176 it was held by this court that on an application under section 30 of the Law of Property Act 1925 in relation to

property acquired jointly as a matrimonial home neither spouse has a right to demand a sale while that purpose still exists. That is now a settled rule of law, applicable to property owned jointly by joint occupants, whether married or unmarried. But its application depends on the whole of the beneficial interest being vested in the occupants. If one of them has become bankrupt, so that part of the beneficial interest is vested in his or her trustee, there arises a conflict between the interests of the occupants and the statutory obligation of the trustee to realise the bankrupt's assets for the benefit of the creditors.

In a series of bankruptcy decisions relating to matrimonial homes subsequent to *Jones v. Challenger* it has been held that the interest of the husband's creditors ought usually to prevail over the interests of the wife and any children and, with one exception, *In re Holliday (A Bankrupt), Ex parte Trustee of the Property of the Bankrupt v. Holliday* [1981] Ch. 405, a sale within a short period has invariably been ordered. It has also been assumed that no distinction ought to be made between a case where the property is still being enjoyed as the matrimonial home and one where it is not. That distinction, if it ought to be made, would be of significance on these appeals, which relate to the matrimonial homes of two bankrupt brothers, one of whom is still living there with his wife and the other of whom has been judicially separated and living elsewhere since 1984. It should be stated at the outset that section 336 of the Insolvency Act 1986 has no application to either case.

...

The judge was referred to two authorities, *In re Holliday (A Bankrupt)* [1981] Ch. 405 and *In re Lowrie (A Bankrupt), Ex parte Trustee of the Bankrupt v. The Bankrupt* [1981] 3 All E.R. 353. From the first of these he drew the guiding principle which Goff L.J. stated in these words, at p. 420:

> "So we have to decide having regard to all the circumstances, including the fact that there are young children ... whose voice, that of the trustee seeking to realise the debtor's share for the benefit of his creditors or that of the wife seeking to preserve a home for herself and the children, ought in equity to prevail."

In applying that principle to the facts which were before him, Hoffmann J. carefully considered the personal circumstances of each wife and her children. He observed that they had very little money coming in and that Mary Citro was not well. In evidence they had both said that their children's education would be upset if they had to move. The judge was clearly concerned, more so perhaps in the case of Mary Citro, that, if the houses had to be sold, the half shares of the proceeds received by the wives would not enable them to find proper accommodation for themselves and their families. He expressed his decision thus:

> "The balancing which one is required to do between the interests of the creditors and the interests of the wives and families—who are of course entirely innocent parties—is by no means an easy thing to do. The two interests are not in any sense commensurable. On the one hand, one has the financial interests of the Crown, some banking institutions and a few traders. On the other, one has personal and human interests of these two families. It is very hard to see how they can be weighed against each other, except in a way which involves some value judgment on the part of the tribunal.
>
> If one was considering the rights of these two wives to their matrimonial homes in the event of a breakdown of their marriages, I think that it would be accepted that, in so far as the Family Division did not order the interest of the husband to be transferred to the wife, it would be unlikely to make an order for the sale of the house to allow the husband to realise his share until at any rate such time as the youngest child of the marriage had attained the age of 16. It is of course true that the vesting of the husband's share in the trustee brings a new factor into the equation. It requires the interests of the creditors too to be taken into account. Nevertheless the normal practice in the Family Division seems to me a fair indication

of the way in which the court might deal with the husband's property rights as property rights, and it is after all to his property rights that the trustee has succeeded. It therefore appears to me that it would be wrong to refuse altogether to make an order for sale. That would be treating the wives as having a permanent right to reside in the houses and to prevent the husband or his trustee from realising their interests. That, in my view, would be inequitable. On the other hand, I think it would be equally wrong to make an immediate order for sale, having regard to the hardship which this would cause to the two families."

In order to see whether the judge's decision can be supported, it is necessary to give close consideration to the earlier authorities. So far as material, section 30 of the Law of Property Act 1925 provides:

"If the trustees for sale refuse to sell ... any person interested may apply to the court for a vesting or other order ... directing the trustees for sale to give effect thereto, and the court may make such order as it thinks fit."

One of the consequences of the 1925 property legislation is that the legal estate in any property which is beneficially owned jointly or in common is necessarily held on trust for sale and is thus subject to the jurisdiction of the court under section 30. From its inception the section was one of wide application. But it seems that before *Jones v. Challenger* [1961] 1 Q.B. 176 it had not been the means of making an order for the sale of a former matrimonial home: see p. 180. In that case Devlin L.J. considered the earlier authorities on the section and distinguished between those where the purpose behind the joint acquisition had been investment and no more and those where there had been a secondary or collateral purpose, either expressed or to be inferred from the circumstances. In the first category was *In re Mayo* [1943] Ch. 302 where, at p. 304, Simonds J. said: "The trust for sale will prevail, unless all three trustees agree in exercising the power to postpone." Chief amongst the authorities in the second category was *In re Buchanan-Wollaston's Conveyance* [1939] Ch. 738, 747, where Lord Greene M.R. said that the court must ask itself "whether or not the person applying for execution of the trust for sale is a person whose voice should be allowed to prevail." Devlin L.J. said, at pp. 183, 184:

"In the case we have to consider, the house was acquired as the matrimonial home. That was the purpose of the joint tenancy and, for so long as that purpose was still alive, I think that the right test to be applied would be that in *In re Buchanan-Wollaston's Conveyance*. But with the end of the marriage, that purpose was dissolved and the primacy of the duty to sell was restored. No doubt there is still a discretion. If the husband wanted time to obtain alternative accommodation, the sale could be postponed for that purpose ... If he was prepared to buy out the wife's interest, it might be proper to allow it. ... Let it be granted that the court must look into all the circumstances; if when the examination is complete, it finds that there is no inequity in selling the property, then it must be sold. The test is not what is reasonable. It is reasonable for the husband to want to go on living in the house, and reasonable for the wife to want her share of the trust property in cash. The true question is whether it is inequitable for the wife, once the matrimonial home has gone, to want to realise her investment. Nothing said in the cases which I have cited can be used to suggest that it is, and, in my judgment, it clearly is not. The conversion of the property into a form in which both parties can enjoy their rights equally is the prime object of the trust; the preservation of the house as a home for one of them singly is not an object at all. If the true object of the trust is made paramount, as it should be, there is only one order that can be made."

Before turning to the subsequent bankruptcy decisions, I should state that, with regard to the distinction made in *Jones v. Challenger* [1961] 1 Q.B. 176, I look on the secondary purpose behind the joint acquisition of Domenico and Mary Citro's home as having come to an end, whereas the secondary purpose behind the joint acquisition of Carmine and Josephine Citro's home still exists.

In *In re Solomon (A Bankrupt), Ex parte Trustee of the Property of the Bankrupt v. Solomon* [1967] Ch. 573 the husband's trustee in bankruptcy applied for an order for the sale of the matrimonial home under section 30. Although the marriage was still subsisting, the husband had deserted the wife more than 10 years earlier. Goff J., at pp. 588–589, gave four reasons for his conclusion that a sale of the property ought to be ordered. His first reason, in line with *Jones v. Challenger* [1961] 1 Q.B. 176 and *Rawlings v. Rawlings* [1964] P. 398, was that the marriage, though not legally at an end, was in fact virtually so. His fourth reason was:

> "because this is not a question between the husband and wife, but between the wife and the trustee in bankruptcy on behalf of the husband's creditors."

In *Boydell v. Gillespie* (1970) 216 E.G. 1505 the husband had executed a deed of arrangement, whereby he assigned to a trustee for his creditors a number of interests, including his half share of the beneficial interest in the matrimonial home where he and his wife were living. On the application of the trustee, Plowman J. ordered a sale of all the properties, including the matrimonial home. He distinguished an earlier decision, *In re Hardy's Trust*, The Times, 23 October 1970, where it had been the simple case of a dispute between husband and wife. The report continues (1970) 216 E.G. 1505, 1507:

> "Here it was not the husband who was trying to get the wife out of the matrimonial home; it was a husband and wife who were united in trying to prevent the trustee under the deed of arrangement from selling the house with vacant possession for the benefit of [the husband's] creditors. There was no dispute in the matter as between the defendants themselves. He (his Lordship) did not think that [the wife] was entitled to pray this doctrine in aid for the purpose of depriving [the husband's] creditors of their rights under the deed of arrangement."

In re Turner (A Bankrupt), Ex parte Trustee of the Property of the Bankrupt v. Turner (A Bankrupt) [1974] 1 W.L.R. 1556, another decision of Goff J., was also a case where a bankrupt husband was living with his wife in the matrimonial home. The husband's trustee in bankruptcy sought an order for sale. The trustee was represented by counsel, but the husband and wife appeared in person. In applying the guiding principle, Goff J. thought that the trustee's claim based on his statutory duty gave him the stronger claim and required his voice to be treated as the one which ought to prevail in equity. The judge found support in *Boydell v. Gillespie* (1970) 216 E.G. 1505, although he observed that it did not appear whether *Jones v. Challenger* [1961] 1 Q.B. 176 and *In re Solomon* [1967] Ch. 573 had been brought to Plowman J.'s attention. Having quoted from *Boydell's* case (1970) 216 E.G. 1505, Goff J. continued [1974] 1 W.L.R. 1556, 1559:

> "Plowman J. there rejected the claim of the wife to pray in aid the doctrine of *In re Hardy's Trust* and I think that I ought to follow his conclusion and say that, in the circumstances of this case, the wife is not entitled to pray in aid the *Jones v. Challenger* [1961] 1 Q.B. 176 line of cases and is not entitled to deprive the husband's creditors in the bankruptcy of their share in the matrimonial home."

In re Densham (A Bankrupt), Ex parte Trustee of the Property of the Bankrupt v. The Bankrupt [1975] 1 W.L.R. 1519, a third decision of Goff J., was yet another case where a bankrupt husband was living with his wife in the matrimonial home, although there the wife's beneficial interest in it was less than half. Goff J. made an order for sale, but his reasoning did not add anything of general value to the earlier authorities. However, for the first time in the bankruptcy cases, consideration was given to the effect of there being young children of the marriage. Counsel for the husband and the wife stressed the possible harmful effects on the children, but Goff J., following *Burke v. Burke* [1974] 1 W.L.R. 1063, thought that that had only an indirect bearing on the matter: see p. 1531G.

In *In re Bailey (A Bankrupt) (No. 25 of 1975)* [1977] 1 W.L.R. 278 the parties had been divorced in 1974 and the husband became bankrupt in 1975. On an application by the husband's trustee in bankruptcy, the wife contended that the order for sale should be postponed until the son of the marriage had completed his full-time education in the summer of 1978. The Divisional Court of Bankruptcy, on appeal from the county court, rejected that contention and ordered sale within a short period. Much of the judgments was taken up with a discussion as to how far the interests of children could be taken into account and both Sir Robert Megarry V.-C. and Walton J., also following *Burke v. Burke*, thought that their interests were only incidentally to be taken into consideration. Sir Robert Megarry V.-C. said, at p. 282, that the matrimonial property cases were not cases in which matters of commercial obligation arose, as in the case of bankruptcy, where the claims of the creditors as asserted through the trustee in bankruptcy must be considered. Walton J., having accepted that the children's welfare was a very big factor to be taken into account in the matrimonial cases, said, at p. 283:

"But when one has cases which are between the trustee in bankruptcy and a former spouse, or, indeed, an existing spouse (because it sometimes works out that way) of the bankrupt then the situation is vastly different ..."

I now come to *In re Holliday* [1981] Ch. 405 which, as I have said, is the only reported bankruptcy decision in which a sale within a short period has not been ordered. It is also the only previous case in which the bankruptcy decisions have been considered by this court. It must therefore be examined with some care. So far as material, the facts in *In re Holliday* were these. The parties were married in 1962 and had three children, born in 1965, 1968 and 1973. The matrimonial home was jointly acquired in 1970. In 1974 the husband left the wife and ceased to live in the matrimonial home. The wife petitioned for divorce and decree nisi was pronounced in 1975. On or shortly before 3 March 1976 the wife gave notice of her intention to bring on her application for ancillary relief, whereupon, on that same day, the husband filed his own bankruptcy petition, asking for immediate adjudication. A receiving order was then and there made against him and he was at once adjudicated bankrupt. In due course his trustee in bankruptcy applied to the court for an order for the sale of the matrimonial home. The wife responded by launching a motion to annul the adjudication. Foster J. dismissed the wife's application and later made an order for the sale of the matrimonial home within a short period.

The wife's appeals to this court came first before Buckley and Goff L.JJ. and Sir David Cairns. It was held that Foster J. had been correct in deciding that the husband could not pay his debts and that the bankruptcy petition had not been an abuse of the process of the court. That appeal was dismissed accordingly. The leading judgment was given by Goff L.J. who, in turning to the wife's appeal against the order for sale, dealt with the position where there has been no bankruptcy, at p. 415:

"Where the property in question is a matrimonial home, then the provision of a home for both parties is a secondary or collateral object of the trust for sale (see *per* Devlin L.J. in *Jones v. Challenger* [1961] 1 Q.B. 176, 181) and the court will not ordinarily order a sale if the marriage be still subsisting and no question of bankruptcy has supervened. Where, however, the marriage has come to an end by divorce or death of one of the parties or is dead in fact, though still subsisting at law, then apart from any question how far the secondary or collateral object can be said to be still subsisting if there are young or dependent children, though there remains a discretion it is one in which as I see it, some very special circumstances need to be shown to induce the court not to order a sale: see *Jones v. Challenger* ... and *Rawlings v. Rawlings* [1964] P. 398 ..."

Goff L.J. then considered how far the interests of children were to be taken into consideration where no bankruptcy had supervened. Again he preferred the view expressed by Buckley L.J. in *Burke v. Burke* [1974] 1 W.L.R. 1063, that is to say that the existence of young or dependent children did not prolong the secondary purpose, but was a factor incidentally to be taken into account so far as it affected the equities in the matter: see p. 417F. Next, at p. 418, he held that where the beneficial interest of one of the parties to a marriage was vested in a trustee in bankruptcy, the matter could be dealt with in the Chancery Division under section 30 of the Law of Property Act 1925, even though proceedings for ancillary relief were pending in the Family Division. Having then referred to the previous bankruptcy decisions, he concluded that the court had to exercise its discretion in accordance with the guiding principle (see above), for which purpose there ought to be an adjournment so that the parties could consider the position and file further evidence, if advised.

Sir David Cairns agreed with the judgment of Goff L.J. Buckley L.J. also agreed and added some short observations of his own. He said, at p. 421:

> "When considering whether in the existing circumstances a sale should be ordered or not, the conflicting legal and moral claims to be taken into account and weighed against each other are, as I am at present inclined to think those of the creditors asserted through the trustee in bankruptcy on the one hand (rather than any claim of the trustee in bankrutpcy) and those of the wife on the other, taking all relevant facts, including the existence of the children, into account."

The matter came back for further consideration on fresh evidence in May 1980. Goff L.J. having died in the meantime, the parties agreed that the matter should be disposed of by the other two members of the court. In the course of stating the facts, Buckley L.J. said, at p. 422, that the value of the equity of redemption in the matrimonial home might be taken to be of the order of £26,500. The only creditors who called for consideration in the husband's bankruptcy were his former solicitors, to whom he owed about £1,260 for costs, his bank, to whom he owed about £5,000, and his wife's mother, to whom he owed about £250 in respect of a loan. Those debts added up to about £6,500 and about £7,500 was needed in order fully to discharge the obligations and expenses under the bankruptcy. On the other side, the wife would have needed something between £20,000 and £25,000 to buy another house of comparable capacity in the neighbourhood, she was without capital and her present income was of the order of £87 per week. Buckley L.J., having said that the wife's situation was attributable to the husband's former conduct, which seemed to afford the wife strong and justifiable grounds for saying that it would be unfair to her to enforce the trust for sale at that juncture, continued, at p. 424:

> "Of course, the creditors are entitled to payment as soon as the debtor is in a position to pay them. They are entitled to payment forthwith: they have an unassailable right to be paid out of the assets of the debtor. But in my view, when one of those assets is an undivided share in land in respect of which the debtor's right to an immediate sale is not an absolute right, that is an asset in the bankruptcy which is liable to be affected by the interest of any other party interested in that land, and if there are reasons which seem to the court to be good reasons for saying that the trust for sale of the land should not be immediately enforced, then that is an asset of the bankruptcy which is not immediately available because it cannot be immediately realised for the benefit of the creditors."

He concluded that the house should not be sold, without the consent of the wife or pursuant to an order of the court, before 1 July 1985, some five years in the future.

Sir David Cairns agreed that in all the circumstances of the case the voice of the wife, on behalf of herself and the children, should prevail to the extent that the sale of the house should be deferred for a substantial period. He continued, at p. 425:

"I reach that view because I am satisfied that it would at present be very difficult, if not impossible, for the wife to secure another suitable home for the family in or near Thorpe Bay; because it would be upsetting for the children's education if they had to move far away from their present schools, even if it were practicable, having regard to the wife's means, to find an alternative home at some more distant place; because it is highly unlikely that postponement of the payment of the debts would cause any great hardship to any of the creditors; and because none of the creditors thought fit themselves to present a bankruptcy petition and it is quite impossible to know whether any one of them would have done so if the debtor had not himself presented such a petition."

In referring to the earlier cases, he said that the trustee had succeeded there because no sufficiently substantial case of hardship of defendants had been established.

Finally, there is *In re Lowrie (A Bankrupt)* [1981] 3 All E.R. 353, another case where the husband and wife were living in the matrimonial home. The husband having been adjudicated bankrupt in 1979, his trustee applied to the county court for an order for sale, which order was made but suspended for 30 months. The trustee appealed successfully to the Divisional Court in Bankruptcy, who ordered a sale within a short period. In giving the first judgment, Walton J. said, at p. 355:

"One must always look at the whole of the circumstances of the case, and in exceptional circumstances there is no doubt that the trustee's voice will not be allowed to prevail in equity and the sale will not be ordered. A brilliant example of just such a situation is to be found in *In re Holliday (A Bankrupt)* ... where the petition in bankruptcy had been presented by the husband himself as a tactical move, and quite clearly as a tactical move, to avoid a transfer of property order in favour of his wife, or ex-wife, at a time when no creditors whatsoever were pressing and he was in a position in the course of a year or so out of a very good income to discharge whatever debts he had. He had gone off leaving the wife in the matrimonial home, which was the subject matter of the application, with responsibility for all the children on her own. One can scarcely, I think, imagine a more exceptional set of facts and the court gave effect to those exceptional facts."

He then reviewed the facts in detail and concluded that there were no exceptional circumstances which justified a postponement of the order for sale. Although Goulding J. had more difficulty in coming to that conclusion, he agreed with Walton J. that the appeal must be allowed. He continued, at p. 358:

"In all cases where a home is the subject of co-ownership between a trustee in bankruptcy for the benefit of the bankrupt's creditors on the one hand and the wife of the bankrupt on the other, the court, in exercising its discretionary jurisdiction to order or not to order a sale pursuant to section 30 of the Law of Property Act 1925 has to effect a comparison of merits and hardship which in its nature is very difficult, because the position of creditors on the one hand and a family on the other are in themselves hard to compare."

In my view Walton J., in describing the circumstances in which the trustee's voice will not prevail as "exceptional," stated a correct test. Alternatively, he might have described them as "special," which to my mind means exactly the same thing.

The broad effect of these authorities can be summarised as follows. Where a spouse who has a beneficial interest in the matrimonial home has become bankrupt under debts which cannot be paid without the realisation of that interest, the voice of the creditors will usually prevail over the voice of the other spouse and a sale of the property ordered within a short period. The voice of the other spouse will only prevail in exceptional circumstances. No distinction is to be made between a case where the property is still being enjoyed as the matrimonial home and one where it is not.

What then are exceptional circumstances? As the cases show, it is not uncommon for a wife with young children to be faced with eviction in circumstances where the realisation of her beneficial interest will not produce enough to buy a comparable home in the same neighbourhood, or indeed elsewhere. And, if she has to move elsewhere, there may be problems over schooling and so forth. Such circumstances, while engendering a natural sympathy in all who hear of them, cannot be described as exceptional. They are the melancholy consequences of debt and improvidence with which every civilised society has been familiar. It was only in *In re Holliday* [1981] Ch. 405 that they helped the wife's voice to prevail, and then only, as I believe, because of one special feature of that case. One of the reasons for the decision given by Sir David Cairns was that it was highly unlikely that postponement of payment of the debts would cause any great hardship to any of the creditors, a matter of which Buckley L.J. no doubt took account as well. Although the arithmetic was not fully spelled out in the judgments, the net value of the husband's half share of the beneficial interest in the matrimonial home was about £13,250, against which had to be set debts of about £6,500 or £7,500 as the sum required to obtain a full discharge. Statutory interest at 4 per cent. on £6,500 for five years would have amounted to no more than £1,300 which, when added to the £7,500, would make a total of less than £9,000, well covered by the £13,250. Admittedly, it was detrimental to the creditors to be kept out of a commercial rate of interest and the use of the money during a further period of five years. But if the principal was safe, one can understand that that detriment was not treated as being decisive, even in inflationary times. It must indeed be exceptional for creditors in a bankruptcy to receive 100p. in the £ plus statutory interest in full and the passage of years before they do so does not make it less exceptional. On the other hand, without that special feature, I cannot myself see how the circumstances in *In re Holliday* could fairly have been treated as exceptional. I am confirmed in that view by the belief that it would be shared by Balcombe L.J., who in *Harman v. Glencross* [1986] Fam. 81, 95 said that the decision in *In re Holliday* was very much against the run of the recent authorities. I would not myself have regarded it as an exceptional circumstance that the husband had presented his own petition, even "as a tactical move." That was not something of the creditors' choosing and could not fairly have been held against them. I do not say that in other cases there might not be other exceptional circumstances. They must be identified if and when they arise.

If *In re Holliday* is put on one side, are the bankruptcy cases, all of which were decided at first instance or in the Divisional Court in Bankruptcy, consistent with the principles stated in *Jones v. Challenger* [1961] 1 Q.B. 176? I will take first the case where the property is no longer being enjoyed as the matrimonial home, either because the marriage has been dissolved or because the bankrupt spouse has gone to live elsewhere and the marriage is dead in fact if not in law. The decisions in this category are *In re Solomon* [1967] Ch. 573 and *In re Bailey* [1977] 1 W.L.R. 278. Here it is clear that there is no inconsistency because, even if he was not bankrupt, the husband would usually be entitled to demand a sale. His trustee in bankruptcy cannot be in any worse position than he himself.

The more interesting question is whether there is an inconsistency in the case where the property is still being enjoyed as the matrimonial home, as it was in *Boydell v. Gillespie* (1970) 216 E.G. 1505, *In re Turner* [1974] 1 W.L.R. 1556, *In re Densham* [1975] 1 W.L.R. 1519 and *In re Lowrie* [1981] 3 All E.R. 353. It would have been open to the wife in each of those cases to argue that the secondary purpose was still existing, that the husband's beneficial interest to which the trustee had succeeded was, in the words of Buckley L.J. in *In re Holliday* [1981] Ch. 405, 424C, "an asset in the bankruptcy which is liable to be affected by the interest of any other party interested in that land" and that the trustee had no greater right to demand a sale than the husband himself. That argument may have been advanced in *Boydell v. Gillespie* (1970) 216 E.G. 1505 and I think it likely that Goff J. had it in mind in *In re Turner* [1974] 1

W.L.R. 1556. Perhaps it was unfortunate that there the husband and wife represented themselves, because after that the point appears to have got lost. In none of the decisions is there to be found any overt consideration of the argument or any reasoned explanation of its rejection. They simply assume that there is no distinction between the two cases.

Here I should state that Mr Cameron, who appears for the bankrupts' wives, has not argued for any distinction between these two cases, notwithstanding that the secondary purpose behind the joint acquisition of Carmine and Josephine Citro's home still exists. Having been puzzled by the point myself and having thought it right to consider it, I have come to a clear conclusion that the assumption made in the earlier decisions is correct. Shortly stated, my reasoning is this. In the husband and wife cases exemplified by *Jones v. Challenger* [1961] 1 Q.B. 176 it is held that neither spouse has a right to demand a sale of the property while the purpose of its enjoyment as a matrimonial home still exists. In order to be so enjoyed it must be occupied by the spouses jointly. As a matter of property law, the basis of their joint occupation is their joint ownership of the beneficial interest in the home. Although the vesting of one of their interests in a trustee for creditors does not in itself destroy the secondary purpose of the trust, the basis for their joint occupation has gone. It must, I think, be implicit in the principle of *Jones v. Challenger* that the secondary purpose can only exist while the spouses are not only joint occupiers of the home but joint owners of it as well.

I am therefore of the opinion that the earlier authorities, as I have summarised them, correctly state the law applicable to the present case. Did Hoffmann J. correctly apply it to the facts which were before him? I respectfully think that he did not. First, for the reasons already stated, the personal circumstances of the two wives and their children, although distressing, are not by themselves exceptional. Secondly, I think that the judge erred in fashioning his orders by reference to those which might have been made in the Family Division in a case where bankruptcy had not supervened. That approach, which tends towards treating the home as a source of provision for the children, was effectively disapproved by the earlier and uncontroversial part of the decision of this court in *In re Holliday*. Thirdly, and perhaps most significantly, he did not ask himself the critical question whether a further postponement of payment of their debts would cause hardship to the creditors. It is only necessary to look at the substantial deficiencies referred to earlier in this judgment in order to see that it would. Since then a further 18 months' interest has accrued and the trustee has incurred the costs of these proceedings as well.

In all the circumstances, I think that these cases are clearly distinguishable from *In re Holliday* and ought to have been decided accordingly. Part at least of the reason why they were not was that the points with which we have been concerned were not as fully argued below as they have been here. In particular, a close examination of the figures in order to see whether a postponement would cause increasing hardship to the creditors was not undertaken. That is not to imply any criticism of counsel. It is a characteristic of our system that the higher court often seems partial towards thinking that the important point is the one which was not taken in the lower court.

Finally, I refer to section 336 of the Insolvency Act 1986 which, although it does not apply to either of these cases, will apply to such cases in the future. In subsection (5) of that section the court is required, in the circumstances there mentioned, to "assume, unless the circumstances of the case are exceptional, that the interests of the bankrupt's creditors outweigh all other considerations." I have no doubt that that section was intended to apply the same test as that which has been evolved in the previous bankruptcy decisions, and it is satisfactory to find that it has. I say that not least because section 336 only applies to the rights of occupation of those who are or have been married. The case law will continue to apply to unmarried couples, who nowadays set up house together in steadily increasing numbers. A difference in the basic tests applicable to the two classes of case would have been most undesirable.

I would allow both appeals by deleting the provisos for postponement from

Hoffmann J.'s orders and substituting short periods of suspension, the length of which can be discussed with counsel.

NOTES:

1. Bingham L.J. agreed with the judgment of Nourse L.J.; Sir George Waller dissented on the basis that he considered that the circumstances were "very special".

2. For comment, see [1991] C.L.J. 45; [1991] Conv. 302; (1991) 107 L.Q.R. 177; (1992) 55 M.L.R. 284. For comment on *Re Holliday (A Bankrupt)*, see [1981] Conv. 79; (1981) 97 L.Q.R. 200.

3. The *ratio decidendi* of *Re Citro*, and the purported reconciliation of the bankruptcy cases with *Jones v. Challenger*, was analysed by the Court of Appeal in *Abbey National plc v. Moss* (1993) 26 H.L.R. 249. The defendant had been persuaded to transfer her house into the joint names of herself and her daughter on the understanding that the house would not be sold during the lifetime of the defendant. The daughter subsequently applied to the plaintiffs for a loan secured by a joint mortgage of the house; and she forged the signature of the defendant on all the documentation. When the daughter moved out of the house and defaulted on the repayments, the plaintiffs applied under section 30 for an order for sale. According to Peter Gibson L.J. (with whom Ralph Gibson L.J. agreed), the *ratio* of *Re Citro* included the proposition that the collateral purpose (that the property be occupied as a matrimonial home) necessarily ended when the husband became bankrupt and his beneficial interest in the house vested in the trustee in bankruptcy *because the joint occupation of the home was based on the joint ownership of the beneficial interest*; and on that basis the bankruptcy cases could be explained as applications of the collateral purpose principle rather than as contradictions of the principle. However, where the collateral purpose was not based on joint ownership (in *Abbey National plc v. Moss* the Court of Appeal held that the collateral purpose was to provide a home *for the defendant* for the rest of her life), that purpose might continue even if one of the co-owners had disposed of or charged his beneficial interest: see *Jones (A.E.) v. Jones (F.W.)* [1977] 1 W.L.R. 438, 442 *per* Lord Denning M.R.; *Stott v. Radcliffe* (1982) 126 Sol.J. 319; *Harris v. Harris* (1995) 72 P. & C.R. 408, 412–413 *per* Waite L.J., 413 *per* Evans L.J. In such circumstances, it was for the person seeking an order for sale to persuade the court to make that order. According to Hirst L.J., dissenting, the *ratio* of *Re Citro* was the wider proposition that where an application under section 30 was made by the trustee in bankruptcy of one co-owner, there was a presumption (rebuttable only in exceptional circumstances) that a sale would be ordered. On the facts the Court of Appeal refused to order a sale.

Clarke [1994] Conv. 331 argued that the majority view reflected an appropriately more flexible approach where the section 30 application for a sale was made by creditors who did not have the *duty* imposed on a trustee in bankruptcy to realise the assets of the bankrupt. However, Hopkins (1995) 111 L.Q.R. 72 argued that it was inappropriate to distinguish between types of creditor; that in all such cases the courts should consider (i) whether there was a continuing collateral purpose and, if so, (ii) whether the vesting of a share of the ownership in the trustee in bankruptcy or the interest of the creditor was consistent with the continuance of that purpose; and that, where the second question received a negative answer, a sale should be ordered in the absence of exceptional circumstances.

4. In *Lloyds Bank plc v. Byrne and Byrne* (1991) 23 H.L.R. 472 the Court of Appeal held that the principles applicable to an application by a trustee in bankruptcy were equally applicable to an application by a chargee under a charging order obtained against the equitable interest of one co-owner. In *Barclays Bank plc v. Hendricks* [1996] 1 F.L.R. 258 Laddie J. expressly endorsed the approach in *Lloyds Bank plc v. Byrne and Byrne* but also noted that the application of the majority view in *Abbey National plc v. Moss* would have produced the same result. See *supra*, p. 316.

The jurisdiction of the court under section 14 of the Trusts of Land and Appointment of Trustees Act 1996 is now regulated by section 335A of the Insolvency Act 1986: Trusts of Land and Appointment of Trustees Act 1996, s.15(4). Sections 336 and 337 of the Insolvency Act 1986 make further provision in relation to the matrimonial home rights of a bankrupt's spouse and in relation to the occupation rights of a bankrupt who has children living with him.

Insolvency Act 1986, ss.335A-337

Rights under trusts of land

335A.—(1) Any application by a trustee of a bankrupt's estate under section 14 of the Trusts of Land and Appointment of Trustees Act 1996 (powers of court in relation to trusts of land) for an order under that section for the sale of land shall be made to the court having jurisdiction in relation to the bankruptcy.

(2) On such an application the court shall make such order as it thinks just and reasonable having regard to—
   (a) the interests of the bankrupt's creditors;
   (b) where the application is made in respect of land which includes a dwelling house which is or has been the home of the bankrupt or the bankrupt's spouse or former spouse—
      (i) the conduct of the spouse or former spouse, so far as contributing to the bankruptcy,
      (ii) the needs and financial resources of the spouse or former spouse, and
      (iii) the needs of any children; and
   (c) all the circumstances of the case other than the needs of the bankrupt.

(3) Where such an application is made after the end of the period of one year beginning with the first vesting under Chapter IV of this Part of the bankrupt's estate in a trustee, the court shall assume, unless the circumstances of the case are exceptional, that the interests of the bankrupt's creditors outweigh all other considerations.

(4) The powers conferred on the court by this section are exercisable on an application whether it is made before or after the commencement of this section.

Rights of occupation, etc. of bankrupt's spouse

336.—(1) Nothing occurring in the initial period of the bankruptcy (that is to say, the period beginning with the day of the presentation of the petition for the bankruptcy order and ending with the vesting of the bankrupt's estate in a trustee) is to be taken as having given rise to any matrimonial home rights under Part IV of the Family Law Act 1996 in relation to a dwelling house comprised in the bankrupt's estate.

(2) Where a spouse's matrimonial home rights under the Act of 1996 are a charge on the estate or interest of the other spouse, or of trustees for the other spouse, and the other spouse is adjudged bankrupt—

(a) the charge continues to subsist notwithstanding the bankruptcy and, subject to the provisions of that Act, binds the trustee of the bankrupt's estate and persons deriving title under that trustee, and

(b) any application for an order under section 33 of that Act shall be made to the court having jurisdiction in relation to the bankruptcy.

(4) On such an application as is mentioned in subsection (2) the court shall make such order under section 33 of the Act of 1996 as it thinks just and reasonable having regard to—

(a) the interests of the bankrupt's creditors,

(b) the conduct of the spouse or former spouse, so far as contributing to the bankruptcy,

(c) the needs and financial resources of the spouse or former spouse,

(d) the needs of any children, and

(e) all the circumstances of the case other than the needs of the bankrupt.

(5) Where such an application is made after the end of the period of one year beginning with the first vesting under Chapter IV of this Part of the bankrupt's estate in a trustee, the court shall assume, unless the circumstances of the case are exceptional, that the interests of the bankrupt's creditors outweigh all other considerations.

Rights of occupation of bankrupt

337.—(1) This section applies where—

(a) a person who is entitled to occupy a dwelling house by virtue of a beneficial estate or interest is adjudged bankrupt, and

(b) any persons under the age of 18 with whom that person had at some time occupied that dwelling house had their home with that person at the time when the bankruptcy petition was presented and at the commencement of the bankruptcy.

(2) Whether or not the bankrupt's spouse (if any) has matrimonial home rights under Part IV of the Family Law Act 1996 —

(a) the bankrupt has the following rights as against the trustee of his estate—

  (i) if in occupation, a right not to be evicted or excluded from the dwelling house or any part of it, except with the leave of the court,

  (ii) if not in occupation, a right with the leave of the court to enter into and occupy the dwelling house, and

(b) the bankrupt's rights are a charge, having the like priority as an equitable interest created immediately before the commencement of the bankruptcy, on so much of his estate or interest in the dwelling house as vests in the trustee.

(3) The Act of 1996 has effect, with the necessary modifications, as if—

(a) the rights conferred by paragraph (a) of subsection (2) were matrimonial home rights under that Act,

(b) any application for leave such as is mentioned in that paragraph were an application for an order under section 33 of that Act, and

(c) any charge under paragraph (b) of that subsection on the estate or interest of the trustee were a charge under that Act on the estate or interest of a spouse.

(4) Any application for leave such as is mentioned in subsection (2)(a) or otherwise

by virtue of this section for an order under section 33 of the Act of 1996 shall be made to the court having jurisdiction in relation to the bankruptcy.

(5) On such an application the court shall make such order under section 33 of the Act of 1996 as it thinks just and reasonable having regard to the interests of the creditors, to the bankrupt's financial resources, to the needs of the children and to all the circumstances of the case other than the needs of the bankrupt.

(6) Where such an application is made after the end of the period of one year beginning with the first vesting (under Chapter IV of this Part) of the bankrupt's estate in a trustee, the court shall assume, unless the circumstances of the case are exceptional, that the interests of the bankrupt's creditors outweigh all other considerations.

NOTES:

1. For analysis of the provisions, which are rather less favourable to the interests of the bankrupt's family than the original proposals of the Cork Committee (*Report of the Insolvency Law Review Committee* (1982, Cmnd. 8558)), see Miller [1986] Conv. 393; Cretney (1991) 107 L.Q.R. 177.

2. Where the bankrupt and his (former) spouse are both trustees of the matrimonial home, section 335A(1) requires any application under section 14 of the 1996 Act to be made in accordance with and subject to the new statutory guidelines. Section 336(2) affords protection to the bankrupt's spouse who is not a trustee but who has matrimonial home rights under the Family Law Act 1996: those rights (which were previously unenforceable against a trustee in bankruptcy) are now enforceable and can only be terminated by the bankruptcy court in accordance with the statutory guidelines. Contrary to the recommendation of the Cork Committee, section 336 does not extend to co-owners other than husband and wife. Section 337 affords protection to the bankrupt who has responsibility for children but who has no spouse or no spouse entitled or willing to occupy the family home: the section confers on the bankrupt himself rights of occupation, analogous to the matrimonial home rights under the Family Law Act 1996 and subject to a similar regulatory regime.

3. The disapplication of section 15 of the 1996 Act in the context of cases involving the trustee in bankruptcy removes the purposes for which the property is held from the list of matters relevant in determining the application. However, perhaps the most significant factor is the qualification contained in all three sections that after one year the interests of the bankrupt's creditors are assumed to outweigh all other considerations, unless the circumstances of the case are exceptional. In effect, therefore, the assumption provides at best a one-year breathing space during which the bankrupt and/or his family may arrange alternative accommodation. However, even that protection is unlikely to be significant since the year runs from the date of the bankruptcy order (and not the date of the determination of the application under section 14 of the Trusts of Land and Appointment of Trustees Act 1996 or, as the case may be, section 33 of the Family Law Act 1996).

4. The reference to "exceptional circumstances" in sections 335A(3), 336(5) and 337(6) has been interpreted as a reference to the existing case law: *Re*

Citro (A Bankrupt) [1991] Ch. 142, 159 *per* Nourse L.J., 160 *per* Bingham L.J.

6. Purchasers of co-owned land

The position of the purchaser of co-owned land has always been reasonably straightforward, at least in theory. There is a single title to be investigated (notwithstanding that the purchaser may have to deal with a maximum of four trustees); and, provided that the purchaser complies with the statutory requirements (essentially by paying the purchase money to two trustees or to a trust corporation), the conveyance or transfer overreaches the equitable interests of the beneficiaries and the purchaser acquires the land free from those interests: *City of London Building Society v. Flegg* [1988] A.C. 54, *ante*, p. 197. The purchaser is not concerned with the trusts affecting the proceeds of sale: Law of Property Act 1925, s.27(1); and the purchaser is not answerable for the loss or misapplication of the proceeds of sale: Trustee Act 1925, s.14(1). (Further provisions for the protection of purchasers, now contained in the Trusts of Land and Appointment of Trustees Act 1996, are considered *infra*.)

Where the legal estate is vested in at least two trustees, there should be no problem for the purchaser; he will necessarily deal with the vendors as trustees and the theory outlined above will operate in practice. Similarly, there should be no problem for the purchaser where, although the legal estate is vested in one person only, he knows that the land is subject to co-ownership and thus held in trust; for he can insist on the appointment of a second trustee.

The difficulties arise where the legal estate is vested in one person only and the purchaser does *not* know that that person is in fact the sole trustee for two or more beneficiaries. In these circumstances, the purchaser does not realise that there is a trust and that he must pay the purchase money to two trustees in order to ensure that the beneficial interests are overreached; and the position of the beneficiaries in such circumstances is no less problematic. Three questions arise for consideration: first, whether the conveyance or transfer by the sole trustee is effective to transfer the legal estate to the purchaser; secondly, whether the equitable interests of the beneficiaries (which *ex hypothesi* have not been overreached) are binding on the purchaser; and, thirdly, whether those interests, if binding, confer a right of occupation on the beneficiary so as to prevent the purchaser obtaining possession of the land.

These questions have been examined almost exclusively in the context of the family home and, more specifically, in the context of disputes between the beneficiary under the trust and a legal mortgagee/chargee of the land. Moreover, following the decision of the House of Lords in *Abbey National Building Society v. Cann* [1991] 1 A.C. 56, *ante*, p. 219, *post*, p. 886, the context for such disputes is further confined to post-acquisition mortgages. The litigation has arisen largely in this context because a mortgage by a sole trustee is a rather less visible transaction than a sale; but the same principles apply to both situations: see *Chhokar v. Chhokar* [1984] F.L.R. 313.

Moreover, the provisions of the Trusts of Land and Appointment of

Trustees Act 1996 on the protection of purchasers require separate consideration in relation to registered and unregistered land.

6.1 *Capacity of sole trustee to effect a valid conveyance/transfer or mortgage*

6.1.1 *Position in unregistered land*   Prior to the enactment of the Trusts of Land and Appointment of Trustees Act 1996 it had been argued that a single trustee for sale could not pass good title to a purchaser. He could not give a valid receipt for the proceeds of sale: Trustee Act 1925, s.14(2); and see *Bull v. Bull* [1955] 1 Q.B. 234, 238 *per* Denning L.J.; *Waller v. Waller* [1967] 1 W.L.R. 451, 453 *per* Goff J. Moreover, since the powers of trustees for sale were expressly modelled on the powers conferred by the Settled Land Act 1925, and since that Act conferred only limited mortgaging powers, it was further argued that trustees for sale, *a fortiori* a single trustee for sale, could not create a valid mortgage: see Clayton [1981] Conv. 19; but see Rudden (1963) 27 Conv. 51, 56.

The argument based on limited powers is no longer available since, as has been seen, the 1996 Act confers on trustees of land all the powers of an absolute owner.

In any event, notwithstanding the above arguments, the capacity of a single trustee for sale to effect a valid mortgage was assumed *sub silentio: Caunce v. Caunce* [1969] 1 W.L.R. 286, *ante,* p. 39; *Kingsnorth Finance Co. Ltd v. Tizard* [1986] 1 W.L.R. 783, *ante,* p. 42; and see Garner (1969) 33 Conv. 240.

6.1.2 *Position in registered land*   The effectiveness of the registration of a disposition of registered land to transfer the legal estate of a registered proprietor would seem to be clear: Land Registration Act 1925, ss.20(1), 69(1); but, on the basis of similar arguments to those outlined above, it was questioned whether a single trustee for sale had the capacity to effect a valid transfer or mortgage of registered land: see Clayton [1981] Conv. 19; Smith (1986) 49 M.L.R. 519, 523. Again, some of those arguments are no longer available; but, in this context also, provided that there was no restriction entered in the proprietorship register, the capacity to effect a valid mortgage was assumed *sub silentio* in *Williams & Glyn's Bank Ltd v. Boland* [1981] A.C. 487, *ante,* p. 193.

6.2 *Enforceability of equitable interests under trusts*

6.2.1 *Position in unregistered land*   The enforceability of equitable interests under trusts that have not been overreached is determined by the equitable doctrine of notice: see *Caunce v. Caunce* [1969] 1 W.L.R. 286, *ante,* p. 39; *Kingsnorth Finance Co. Ltd v. Tizard* [1986] 1 W.L.R. 783, *ante,* p. 42.

6.2.2 *Position in registered land*   It has been seen that, in the context of registered land, equitable interests under trusts are minor interests capable of protection by the entry of a restriction on the proprietorship register; and that such an entry is designed to ensure that a purchaser of the land complies with the overreaching requirements. However, it has also been seen that, where equitable interests under trusts have not been so protected, so that they have not been effectively overreached, they may nonetheless be enforceable against purchasers/mortgagees as overriding interests within section 70(1)(g) of the Land Registration Act 1925: see *ante*, pp. 193 *et seq.*

6.3 *Substance of the rights of the beneficiaries*

Where a purchaser/mortgagee discovers that he has acquired land or a mortgage over land which is subject to the interest of a beneficiary under a trust, questions arise (i) as to whether the beneficiary has a right of occupation enforceable as such against the purchaser/mortgagee and (ii) as to whether the purchaser/mortgagee can enforce a sale of the property in order to recover at least part of the purchase price or loan. Both these questions have been considered in the preceding section.

6.4 *Purchaser protection under the Trusts of Land and Appointment of Trustees Act 1996*

The 1996 Act re-enacts the former protection for purchasers in relation to consent requirements. Where the disposition creating the trust makes a sale of the land subject to the consent of two or more persons, the consent of any two of those persons is deemed sufficient in favour of the purchaser: section 10(1).

However, apart from that provision, unregistered and registered land are treated separately.

6.4.1 *Protection for purchasers of unregistered land*

Trusts of Land and Appointment of Trustees Act 1996, s.16

Protection of purchasers

16.—(1) A purchaser of land which is or has been subject to a trust need not be concerned to see that any requirement imposed on the trustees by section 6(5), 7(3) or 11(1) has been complied with.

(2) Where—

(a) trustees of land who convey land which (immediately before it is conveyed) is subject to the trust contravene section 6(6) or (8), but

(b) the purchaser of the land from the trustees has no actual notice of the contravention,

the contravention does not invalidate the conveyance.

(3) Where the powers of trustees of land are limited by virtue of section 8—

(a) the trustees shall take all reasonable steps to bring the limitation to the notice of any purchaser of the land from them, but

(b) the limitation does not invalidate any conveyance by the trustees to a purchaser who has no actual notice of the limitation.

(4) Where trustees of land convey land which (immediately before it is conveyed) is

subject to the trust to persons believed by them to be beneficiaries absolutely entitled to the land under the trust and of full age and capacity—

    (a) the trustees shall execute a deed declaring that they are discharged from the trust in relation to that land, and

    (b) if they fail to do so, the court may make an order requiring them to do so.

(5) A purchaser of land to which a deed under subsection (4) relates is entitled to assume that, as from the date of the deed, the land is not subject to the trust unless he has actual notice that the trustees were mistaken in their belief that the land was conveyed to beneficiaries absolutely entitled to the land under the trust and of full age and capacity.

(6) Subsections (2) and (3) do not apply to land held on charitable, ecclesiastical or public trusts.

(7) This section does not apply to registered land.

NOTES:

1. Section 6(5) requires the trustees to have regard to the rights of the beneficiaries; section 7(3) requires the trustees to obtain the consent of the beneficiaries to a partition of the land; and section 11(1) requires the trustees to consult with the beneficiaries: see *supra*, p. 314. It must be questioned whether a purchaser is protected under subsection (1) where he is a party to the breach of the relevant duty.

2. Ferris and Battersby [1998] Conv. 168, 176–178 argue (i) that "actual notice" in subsections (2) and (3) should be interpreted strictly as a reference to "knowledge of an objective state of affairs" but that such knowledge on the part of an agent should be imputed to the purchaser; and (ii) that actual notice can only invalidate the conveyance *in equity* so that the conveyance is ineffective to overreach the beneficial interests.

3. Subsections (4) and (5) are intended to deal with the situation where there may be uncertainty as to whether a trust has terminated. The trustees are required to execute a deed of discharge when they convey land on the termination of the trust; and a purchaser may rely on the deed provided that he does not have actual notice that the trustees were mistaken.

6.4.2 *Protection for purchasers of registered land*   Section 16 of the 1996 Act does not apply to registered land: section 16(7). It is arguable that the protection afforded by that section to a purchaser of unregistered land is both unnecessary and inappropriate for a purchaser of registered land. First, such protection may be rendered unnecessary by section 94 of the Land Registration Act 1925, as amended by the 1996 Act: subsection (1) provides that land subject to a trust of land shall be registered in the names of the trustees; subsection (4) provides that "there shall be entered on the register such restrictions as may be prescribed, or may be expedient, for the protection of the rights of the persons beneficially interested in the land"; and subsection (5) provides that the registrar is entitled to the protection of section 16(5) of the 1996 Act. Secondly, the provisions of section 16 may be inappropriate in the context of registered land: if there are no restrictions entered on the register, the purchaser is entitled to be registered as proprietor and, in accordance with principles of land registration, is unaffected by any contravention of the beneficiaries' rights on the part of the trustees.

However, these arguments seem to ignore the realities of the overriding interests of beneficiaries in actual occupation of the land. It is, of course, well established that such a beneficiary has an overriding interest where the purchaser deals with a single trustee and thus fails to overreach the interests under a trust of land: see *supra*, p. 333. However, it is also arguable that, even where the purchaser deals with two trustees, there may be no overreaching where the transfer is otherwise *ultra vires* by reason of a breach of duty on the part of the trustees: see Ferris and Battersby [1998] Conv. 168. On this basis, it is arguable that the 1996 Act has reversed the decision of the House of Lords in *City of London Building Society v. Flegg* [1988] A.C. 54, where the trustees failed to consult with the other beneficiaries.

The effect of the disapplication of section 16 of the 1996 Act in relation to registered land appears to be that it will be necessary for purchasers and, in particular, mortgagees to make enquiries of persons in actual occupation, even where they are dealing with two trustees; and they will have to enquire into compliance with consent and consultation requirements and into the potentially vitiating factors referred to in section 6 of the 1996 Act, *supra*, p. 298. If this is correct, it seems that the 1996 Act has had the effect of implementing a version of the Law Commission's recommendation for the protection of beneficiaries in occupation against overreaching: Law Com. No. 188, *Transfer of Land: Overreaching: Beneficiaries in Occupation* (1989), para. 4.3, *ante*, p. 205.

7. Termination of co-ownership

7.1 *Partition*

Joint tenancies and tenancies in common may be terminated by physical partition of the land, where each of the co-owners becomes sole owner at law and in equity of a separate and specific parcel of the formerly co-owned land. Partition thus destroys the unity of possession that characterises all forms of co-ownership. It may be effected by conveyance pursuant to the agreement of all the co-owners. Moreover, under section 7 of the Trusts of Land and Appointment of Trustees Act 1996, the trustees may effect a partition of the land provided that the beneficiaries are of full age and absolutely entitled to the land. The trustees must obtain the consent of all the beneficiaries or, if any beneficiary refuses to consent, obtain an order of the court under section 14 relieving them of the obligation to do so. In its terms the power only applies where the beneficiaries are tenants in common; but, where the beneficiaries consent to the partition, they can readily effect the severance of any equitable joint tenancy.

7.2 *Union in sole owner*

Joint tenancies and tenancies in common will be terminated where the land becomes vested in one of the co-owners.

In the case of joint tenancies, this is the effect of the doctrine of survivorship where one of two (remaining) joint tenants dies: see *supra*, p. 274. Where sole ownership results from the operation of the doctrine of survivorship, there is a potential practical difficulty. Notwithstanding the statutory declaration that a survivor of joint tenants, who is solely and beneficially interested, has the right to deal with the legal estate as if it were not held on trust for sale (Law of Property Act 1925, s.36(2)), a purchaser from the survivor cannot be certain that there has been no prior severance of the joint tenancy. In such circumstances, the purchaser can insist on the appointment of a second trustee, thereby ensuring that he can overreach any equitable interests. However, a more convenient solution is contained in the Law of Property (Joint Tenants) Act 1964. Section 1 provides that, for the purposes of section 36(2) of the Law of Property Act 1925, the survivor of two or more joint tenants (or his personal representatives) "shall, in favour of a purchaser of the legal estate, be deemed to be solely and beneficially interested if he conveys as beneficial owner or the conveyance includes a statement that he is so interested". The Act does not apply where a memorandum of severance has subsequently been indorsed on or annexed to the original conveyance to the joint tenants; nor where (a petition for) a bankruptcy order against one of the joint tenants has been registered under the Land Charges Act 1972. See Jackson (1964) 28 Conv. 329, (1966) 30 Conv. 27. The 1964 Act does not apply to registered land. This may have been explicable at the time of its enactment on the grounds (i) that the name of the deceased joint tenant would be deleted from the register and that, in the absence of some entry on the register, the surviving joint tenant would have sole power of disposition; and (ii) that the full scope of overriding interests under section 70(1)(g) of the Land Registration Act 1925 had not yet become apparent.

In the case of both joint tenancies and tenancies in common, sole ownership of the land may be effected by voluntary transfer of the land to one of the co-owners. A co-owner may convey his share to another co-owner: Law of Property Act 1925, s.72(4); but in the case of joint tenants any such conveyance takes effect as a release: *ibid.* s.36(2); and see *Re Schär* [1951] Ch. 280.

A conveyance of the land by all the co-owners to a sole third party purchaser will also terminate the co-ownership of the land and transfer the co-ownership to the proceeds of sale provided that the purchaser complies with the overreaching requirements.

5

LEASES

A. Introduction

The development of the leasehold interest has been outlined above; and it has been seen that the lease is one of only two ownership interests in land which are capable of existing as legal estates and which may be the subject-matter of substantive registration under the Land Registration Act 1925. The lease remains in theory inferior to the fee simple, since *ex hypothesi* a lease must be granted for a fixed maximum duration and therefore does not have the potential for perpetual duration. However, in practical commercial terms the lease has assumed very considerable importance and the rights of ownership and occupation conferred by a lease may be no less secure and no less valuable than those conferred by a fee simple.

Essentially a lease is a commercial transaction whereby the right of temporary and conditional use and occupation of land is granted for a price. (It is the *transaction* that is commercial: the land may be used for commercial, residential or other purposes). The right of use and occupation is temporary in the sense that, under the general law, that right is necessarily granted for a fixed maximum duration; the right is conditional in the sense that the grant is subject to express or implied terms as to the ancillary rights and obligations of the parties. Although the contractual nature of the transaction was in part responsible for the exclusion of leases from the feudal system of land holding, that same characteristic permitted a flexibility which in turn enabled the lease to be adapted in accordance with changing commercial needs; and, although the lease has a central role in the modern system of land ownership, its contractual foundations are periodically emphasised and exploited.

As a matter of terminology, the definition section of the Law of Property Act 1925 refers to a "term of years": see *infra*. However, in this chapter the more familiar terms "lease" and "tenancy" are used, more or less interchangeably.

B. Types of Leases

Law of Property Act 1925, s.205(1)

General definitions

(xxvii) "Term of years absolute" means a term of years (taking effect either in possession or in reversion whether or not at a rent) with or without impeachment for waste, subject or not to another legal estate, and either certain or liable to determination by notice, re-entry, operation of law, or by a provision for cesser on redemption, or in any other event (other than the dropping of a life, or the determination of a determinable life interest); but does not include any term of years determinable with life or lives or with the cesser of a determinable life interest, nor, if created after the commencement of this Act, a term of years which is not expressed to take effect in possession within twenty-one years after the creation thereof where required by this Act to take effect within that period; and in this definition the expression "term of years" includes a term for less than a year, or for a year or years and a fraction of a year or from year to year.

NOTES:

1. Although it is clear from the above definition that the lease covers a variety of arrangements in form and duration, it wholly fails to identify the essential characteristics of a lease. Those essential characteristics are considered in the next section; and, for present purposes, it is sufficient to note that a lease or tenancy involves the grant of *exclusive possession* for a *fixed maximum duration*.

2. The arrangements covered by the above definition can be classified as *fixed term leases* or *periodic tenancies*. Although the terminology of leases and tenancies is interchangeable, the term "lease" tends to be used for longer fixed term arrangements.

3. Certain other "tenancies" are identified below.

1. Fixed term leases

A fixed term lease involves the express grant of exclusive possession for any fixed period of time. The longer the term, the more the grant of a fixed term lease in practice resembles the grant of a fee simple estate. Thus it is usual for the lessee under a long fixed term lease to pay only nominal (ground) rent but in effect to purchase the lease in return for a lump sum payment ("premium"), which may be borrowed and its repayment secured by the grant of a mortgage. Unlike periodic tenancies, fixed term leases can only be created expressly: see *infra*, p. 386. Under the general law a fixed term lease automatically ends at the expiry of the fixed term; but see *infra*, p. 473.

2. Periodic tenancies

A periodic tenancy continues from period to period, with the usual reference periods being a week or a month or a year. A periodic tenancy can be created expressly or by implication.

Where a periodic tenancy is expressly created, the reference period of the tenancy will normally be made clear. However, where it is not made clear, the period is usually the period by reference to which the rent is calculated; and the frequency with which the rent is payable is irrelevant. Thus the grant of exclusive possession in return for a rent obligation of £5,200 per year payable weekly creates a yearly tenancy; a rent obligation of £100 per week creates a weekly tenancy: see *Ladies Hosiery & Underwear Ltd v. Parker* [1930] 1 Ch. 304, 328–329 *per* Maugham J.; and a rent obligation of £100 per week, which is payable quarterly, also creates a weekly tenancy: *E.O.N. Motors Ltd v. Secretary of State for the Environment* (1981) 258 E.G. 1300.

Periodic tenancies may arise by implication where the owner of land permits a person to take (exclusive) possession of land and there is payment and acceptance of rent; and again the reference period would usually be the period by reference to which the rent is calculated: *Javad v. Mohammed Aqil* [1991] 1 W.L.R. 1007, 1012 *per* Nicholls L.J. However, the courts have refused to find that a periodic tenancy has been created where such a finding is not justified by the surrounding circumstances.

Javad v. Mohammed Aqil [1991] 1 W.L.R. 1007

(CA, Mustill, Ralph Gibson and Nicholls L.JJ.)

The parties were negotiating for a 10-year lease of business premises. It was anticipated that an agreement would be concluded; and the landlord allowed the tenant into possession. The tenant paid £2,500, expressed in a receipt signed by the landlord to be "rent for three months in advance"; and on two further occasions the tenant paid rent on a quarterly basis. Negotiations eventually broke down and the landlord sought to recover possession of the premises. The trial judge and the Court of Appeal held that the tenant was a tenant at will (see *infra*, p. 343) and that the landlord was entitled to possession.

NICHOLLS L.J.:
Much of the argument before us was directed at the legal consequence which follows from proof of possession and payment of rent by reference to a quarterly period. For the tenant it was submitted that proof of those facts raises a presumption in favour of a periodic tenancy which can only be rebutted, and the occupant be held to be a tenant at will, by an express agreement to that effect. Alternatively, this presumption is not rebutted by the fact that the grant of a lease is under discussion, in a case where a substantial sum has been paid over as rent in advance. [Counsel for the tenant] relied on a brief passage in the judgment of Buckley J. in *D'Silva v. Lister House Development Ltd* [1971] Ch. 17, 31. For the landlord it was submitted that today there is no presumption in favour of an intention to create a periodic tenancy arising from possession with consent plus periodic payments of rent. At a later stage [counsel for the landlord] modified this submission so as to make it applicable only in cases

where negotiations for the sale or lease of property were taking place. He prayed in aid observations by Ormrod L.J. in *Longrigg, Burrough & Trounson v. Smith* (1979) 251 E.G. 847.

I cannot accept the tenant's submissions. They are contrary both to principle and to authority. I shall consider first the position in principle. A tenancy, or lease, is an interest in land. With exceptions immaterial for present purposes, a tenancy springs from a consensual arrangement between two parties: one person grants to another the right to possession of land for a lesser term than he, the grantor, has in the land. The extent of the right thus granted and accepted depends primarily upon the intention of the parties.

As with other consensually-based arrangements, parties frequently proceed with an arrangement whereby one person takes possession of another's land for payment without having agreed or directed their minds to one or more fundamental aspects of their transaction. In such cases the law, where appropriate, has to step in and fill the gaps in a way which is sensible and reasonable. The law will imply, from what was agreed and all the surrounding circumstances, the terms the parties are to be taken to have intended to apply. Thus if one party permits another to go into possession of his land on payment of a rent of so much per week or month, failing more the inference sensibly and reasonably to be drawn is that the parties intended that there should be a weekly or monthly tenancy. Likewise, if one party permits another to remain in possession after the expiration of his tenancy. But I emphasise the qualification "failing more." Frequently there will be more. Indeed, nowadays there normally will be other material surrounding circumstances. The simple situation is unlikely to arise often, not least because of the extent to which statute has intervened in landlord-tenant relationships. Where there is more than the simple situation, the inference sensibly and reasonably to be drawn will depend upon a fair consideration of all the circumstances, of which the payment of rent on a periodical basis is only one, albeit a very important one. This is so, however large or small may be the amount of the payment.

To this I add one observation, having in mind the facts of the present case. Where parties are negotiating the terms of a proposed lease, and the prospective tenant is let into possession or permitted to remain in possession in advance of, and in anticipation of, terms being agreed, the fact that the parties have not yet agreed terms will be a factor to be taken into account in ascertaining their intention. It will often be a weighty factor. Frequently in such cases a sum called "rent" is paid at once in accordance with the terms of the proposed lease: for example, quarterly in advance. But, depending on all the circumstances, parties are not to be supposed thereby to have agreed that the prospective tenant shall be a quarterly tenant. They cannot sensibly be taken to have agreed that he shall have a periodic tenancy, with all the consequences flowing from that, at a time when they are still not agreed about the terms on which the prospective tenant shall have possession under the proposed lease, and when he has been permitted to go into possession or remain in possession merely as an interim measure in the expectation that all will be regulated and regularised in due course when terms are agreed and a formal lease granted.

Of course, when one party permits another to enter or remain upon his land on payment of a sum of money, and that other has no statutory entitlement to be there, almost inevitably there will be some consensual relationship between them. It may be no more than a licence determinable at any time, or a tenancy at will. But when and so long as such parties are in the throes of negotiating larger terms, caution must be exercised before inferring or imputing to the parties an intention to give to the occupant more than a very limited interest, be it licence or tenancy. Otherwise the court would be in danger of inferring or imputing from conduct, such as payment of rent and the carrying out of repairs, whose explanation lies in the parties' expectation that they will be able to reach agreement on the larger terms, an intention to grant a lesser interest, such as a periodic tenancy, which the parties never had in contemplation at all.

I turn to the authorities . . .

The decision of the Court of Common Pleas in *Doe d. Lord v. Crago* (1848) 6 C.B. 90 is clear authority for the proposition that regard must be had to the particular circumstances, whatever they may be, in which the rent payments were made. So far as I can see from the authorities, that principle, expressed well over a century ago, has never been doubted. That decision is inconsistent with the tenant's submission in the present case. Of course, the circumstances in which the principle falls to be applied have much changed since those early Victorian days. But those changes have not invalidated the underlying principle. The shift in emphasis discernible in judicial observations in this field in recent cases is no more than a reflection of the same approach applied in the different circumstances which come before the court today. Because of the widespread intervention of statute in the landlord-tenant area, a typical case today invariably involves more than the simple facts of possession and an unexplained payment of rent.

NOTES:

1. For comment, see Bridge [1991] C.L.J. 232.

2. In *Dreamgate Properties Ltd v. Arnot* (1997) 76 P. & C.R. 25 the Court of Appeal expressly left open the question whether the court, in determining whether or not the parties agreed to create a periodic tenancy, should concentrate exclusively on objective evidence and should therefore disregard matters that went to the subjective attitudes of the parties.

3. For clear statements that the statutory protection of tenants has undermined the old common law presumption that possession and the payment and acceptance of rent give rise to a periodic tenancy, see also *Longrigg, Burrough & Trounson v. Smith* (1979) 251 E.G. 847, 849 *per* Ormrod L.J.; *Cardiothoracic Institute v. Shrewdcrest Ltd* [1986] 1 W.L.R. 368, 379 *per* Knox J.

Once created, in practice a periodic tenancy continues until either the landlord or the tenant determines it by giving appropriate notice; but in theory the continuation of the tenancy requires a positive decision not to determine. In *Hammersmith and Fulham LBC v. Monk* [1992] 1 A.C. 478 Lord Bridge stated (at 484, 490):

[F]rom the earliest times a [periodic] tenancy has been an estate which continued only so long as it was the will of both parties that it should continue, albeit that either party could only signify his unwillingness that the tenancy should continue beyond the end of any [period] by giving the appropriate advance notice to that effect. . . . The fact that the law regards a tenancy from year to year which has continued for a number of years, considered retrospectively, as a single term in no way affects the principle that continuation beyond the end of each year depends upon the will of the parties that it should continue or that, considered prospectively, the tenancy continues no further than the parties have already impliedly agreed upon by their omission to serve notice to quit.

The theoretical analysis of periodic tenancies assumes significance in the context of termination where there are joint landlords or joint tenants: see *infra*, p. 473.

3. Tenancies at will

A tenancy at will arises whenever a person occupies land *as a tenant* with the consent of the owner, but on terms that either party may determine the tenancy at any time: *Errington v. Errington and Woods* [1952] 1 K.B. 290, 296 *per* Denning L.J.; *Wheeler v. Mercer* [1957] A.C. 416, 427 *per* Viscount Simonds. A tenancy at will may be created expressly: see, *e.g. Hagee (London) Ltd v. A.B. Erikson and Larson* [1976] Q.B. 209. However, such tenancies normally arise by implication and only during a period of transition: *Heslop v. Burns* [1974] 1 W.L.R. 1241, 1253 *per* Scarman L.J. Thus a tenancy at will arises where a prospective tenant is allowed into possession of premises during negotiations for a lease: *Javad v. Mohammed Aqil* [1991] 1 W.L.R. 1007, *supra*, p. 341; or where an intended tenant is allowed into possession of premises pursuant to a (deemed) contract for a lease: see *infra*, p. 388; or where a tenant "holds over" with the consent of the landlord on the expiry of an existing lease: *Canterbury Cathedral v. Whitbread* (1995) 72 P. & C.R. 9.

As has been seen, a tenancy at will may be converted into a periodic tenancy by the payment and acceptance of rent; but there is no longer a presumption to that effect: *Javad v. Mohammed Aqil* [1991] 1 W.L.R. 1007, *supra*, p. 341.

4. Tenancies at sufferance

A tenancy at sufferance arises where a tenant "holds over" on the expiry of an existing lease without the consent or dissent of the landlord: *Remon v. City of London Real Property Co. Ltd* [1921] 1 K.B. 49, 58 *per* Scrutton L.J.; *Wheeler v. Mercer* [1957] A.C. 416, 427 *per* Viscount Simonds. If the landlord subsequently consents to the tenant holding over, the tenant becomes a tenant at will; but, if the landlord subsequently signals his objection to the tenant holding over, the tenant becomes a trespasser. A tenancy at sufferance cannot give rise to any obligation to pay rent in the strict sense; but the tenant is subject to a claim for "mesne profits" as compensation for the use and occupation of the land: *Bayley v. Bradley* (1848) 5 C.B. 396, 406 *per* Wilde C.J.; *Leigh v. Dickeson* (1884) 15 Q.B.D. 60, 68 *per* Lindley L.J.; *Vaughan-Armatrading v. Sarsah* (1995) 27 H.L.R. 631, 636 *per* Simon Brown L.J.

5. Tenancies by estoppel

In some circumstances a person may purport to grant a lease where he has neither the fee simple nor a superior leasehold estate. Although the purported tenant cannot thereby acquire a legal lease, in accordance with the estoppel principle the landlord is not permitted to deny the validity of the lease; and, equally, the tenant is not permitted to deny the landlord's title. If the landlord subsequently acquires title to the land, the acquisition of title is said to "feed the estoppel": the purported lease becomes fully effective and the tenant acquires a legal estate. The doctrine, which applies to purported grants of other legal estates and interests, was analysed in *First National Bank plc v. Thompson* [1996] Ch. 231, where Millett L.J. stated (at 236–240):

Confusingly, the expressions "title by estoppel" and "feeding the estoppel" have … come to be used to describe the consequences of two distinct doctrines of the common law. One of these is a particular species of estoppel by representation. It requires an express and unambiguous assertion or representation of title by the grantor, and usually takes the form of a recital in the grant. The other is more widely based. It is not a species of estoppel by representation and does not depend upon the presence of any recital or other express representation of title. It is the product of the fundamental principle of the common law which precludes a grantor from disputing the validity or effect of his own grant. Contrary to the submissions to us by counsel for Mr Thompson, it is exclusively the creation of the common law, not equity; and the companion doctrine of "feeding the estoppel," which applies in both kinds of case, operates automatically without further assurance. It appears to be merely the product of the relative character of title to land in English law.

In *Goodtitle v. Bailey* (1777) 2 Cowp. 597 the plaintiff, being entitled to land in remainder expectant on the death of a life tenant, purported to convey the land in fee to the defendant. The conveyance took the form of a deed of release, which was only available to the owner of a legal estate in possession. After the death of the life tenant the plaintiff brought an action for ejectment against the defendant, relying on his own want of the necessary title in possession at the date of the release. The deed of release contained no representation that the plaintiff was entitled to an estate in possession; on the contrary, it correctly recited that he was entitled in remainder only. Despite this the defendant successfully pleaded that the plaintiff was estopped by his own deed. Lord Mansfield C.J. said, at pp. 600–601:

"it shall never lie in [the grantor's] mouth to dispute the title of the party to whom he has so undertaken; no more than it shall be permitted to a mortgagor to dispute the title of his mortgagee. No man shall be allowed to dispute his own solemn deed."

. . .

The common rule that a mortgagor cannot dispute the title of his mortgagee was recognised in *Right d. Jefferys v. Bucknell* (1831) 2 B. & Ad. 278, and the similar rule that a lessor cannot dispute the title of his own lessee has an equally long history. Neither depends on what has sometimes been called "the technical doctrine of estoppel," that is to say, estoppel by representation, but on the refusal of the common law to permit the grantor of a legal estate to deny that he had the legal title.

In *Webb v. Austin* (1844) 7 Man. & G. 701 the freehold owner granted a lease for 89 years to a lessee who mortgaged the term by assignment subject to a proviso for reassignment on redemption and afterwards granted an underlease for 21 years. The question was whether the lessee could make title to the rents reserved by the underlease. The purchaser objected that at the date of the underlease the lessee had no legal estate in the land. The mortgagees were willing to execute any conveyance that might be necessary to make title to the purchaser. It was held that the lessee, with the concurrence of the mortgagees, could make a good title. Giving the judgment of the court, Tindal C.J. said, at p. 724, that, where a tenancy is granted by a lessor who has no title but who afterwards acquires title, the tenancy:

"first operates by way of estoppel, and finally, when the grantor obtains an ownership, it attaches on the seisin and creates an interest, or produces the relation of landlord and tenant; and there is a term commencing by estoppel, but for all purposes it becomes an estate or interest. It binds the estate of the lessor etc., and therefore continues in force against the lessor, his heirs, etc. It also binds the assigns of the lessor and of the lessee."

The question often arose where the original lessor had assigned the lease and the lessee sued the assignee on the covenants in the lease. There being no privity of contract, the lessee was compelled to rely on privity of estate, and was met by a denial of the assignee's title. In *Sturgeon v. Wingfield* (1846) 15 M. & W. 224 the lessor had no legal estate in the land at the date of the lease, since he had mortgaged it by an assignment subject to a proviso for reassignment on redemption, but had subsequently taken a fresh demise. Parke B. held that the lessee was entitled to recover from the assignee of the original lessor. The lease was at first good by way of estoppel only; but when the lessor took a fresh demise it "became a lease in interest" and the reversion on it (which also started life as a reversion by estoppel only) was afterwards assigned to the defendant.

In the leading case of *Cuthbertson v. Irving* (1859) 4 H. & N. 742 the estoppel had not been fed. This distinguished it from earlier authorities. Martin B., giving the judgment of the court, said, at pp. 754-755:

> "There are some points in the law relating to estoppels which seem clear. First, when a lessor without any legal estate or title demises to another, the parties themselves are estopped from disputing the validity of the lease on that ground; in other words a tenant cannot deny his landlord's title, nor can the lessor dispute the validity of the lease. Secondly, where a lessor by deed grants a lease without title and subsequently acquires one, the estoppel is said to be fed, and the lease and reversion then take effect in interest and not by estoppel . . ."

The terms of the lease are set out in full in the report; as usual, they did not include any recital of the lessor's title. Martin B. stated, at p. 757, that if any estate or interest (which was later held to mean any estate or interest at law) passed from the lessor, or if the real title was shown upon the face of the lease, there was no estoppel. The defendant appealed to a strong Court of Exchequer Chamber ((1860) 6 H. & N. 135) which included Willes and Blackburn JJ. and argued that an assignee of the original lessor or lessee by estoppel could be bound only if the estoppel had been fed; this argument was unanimously rejected.

In *Universal Permanent Building Society v. Cooke* [1952] Ch. 95 the defendant agreed to buy a freehold shop with a flat over. Before completion of the purchase she granted a weekly tenancy to her sister, who went into possession. The defendant subsequently completed the purchase and, by a separate transaction which took place on the day following completion, mortgaged the property to the plaintiff. There was, of course, no question of any recital or other express representation of title made by the defendant. Nevertheless the sister was held to have a tenancy by estoppel which became a tenancy in interest when the defendant acquired the legal estate and, since this preceded the grant of the mortgage, had priority over it. The case is noteworthy in that the grant which gave rise to the estoppel was not by deed (or even in writing); this was consistent with earlier authority.

The estoppel bound the grantor and all persons claiming under him whether for value or not (with one exception to be mentioned later). But the title of the grantee was precarious, for it could not of course prevail over the title of the true owner and the persons claiming under him. If, however, the grantor subsequently acquired the legal title from the true owner, the grantee's title became secure, for there was no longer anyone (the exceptional case apart) who was capable of challenging it. This is the most natural explanation of what would otherwise be a curious doctrine by which, in the words of Lord Moulton in *Rajapakse v. Fernando* [1920] A.C. 892, 897, "the benefit of [the grantor's] subsequent acquisition goes automatically to the earlier grantee, or, as it is usually expressed, 'feeds the estoppel.'"

The two kinds of estoppel operated in similar fashion, but their consequences were not identical. Where the technical doctrine of estoppel applied, that is to say, where the grant contained an express recital or other clear and unequivocal representation of the grantor's title, he was estopped from denying that he had the particular title which he had asserted; the estoppel was not excluded by his ownership of some other and lesser estate. Moreover, the estoppel bound the grantor and all persons claiming under him, whether for value or not and with or without notice; so that if the grantor afterwards acquired the legal estate which he had represented that he owned the grantee obtained a title which was good against the whole world. Equity, it seems, did not find it possible to intervene in order to protect the bona fide purchaser for value without notice in such a case.

Where, however, the grant contained no such recital or other representation, the grantor was estopped only from denying that he had a legal title. Had the estoppel been based on some implied representation by conduct, one would have expected the grantor to be estopped from denying that he had a title sufficient to support the grant. But this was not the case. No title by estoppel could arise if the grantor had *any* present legal estate in the property, even if it was insufficient to support the grant. In such a case the grantee obtained an estate in interest and not by estoppel but it could not exceed the estate of his grantor. There being no estoppel to be fed the grantor's subsequent acquisition of a larger title capable of supporting the estate which he had granted did not enure for the benefit of the grantee. The principle is so stated in all the classic cases and was so restated by this court in *Universal Permanent Building Society v. Cooke* [1952] Ch. 95. This is sufficient in itself to demonstrate that the doctrine did not rest on representation express or implied.

Moreover, the estoppel did not bind a bona fide purchaser for value from the grantor without notice of the earlier transaction: *Right d. Jefferys v. Bucknell* (1831) 2 B. & Ad. 278, 283; *General Finance, Mortgage, and Discount Co. v. Liberator Permanent Benefit Building Society* (1878) 10 Ch.D. 15. In such a case the purchaser took the legal estate free from the interest previously granted. This was the rule at law; there was no need for equity to intervene. Where, therefore, a grantor made two successive grants for value, the first when he had no title (which the first grantee should perhaps have discovered) and the second after he had acquired the title, the second grantee (if without notice of the first transaction) was bound by the earlier grant only where it contained a distinct and unequivocal averment of title.

NOTES:

1. Tenancies by estoppel may arise where the purported lease is granted otherwise than by deed, provided that the "grant" would have been sufficient to create a legal lease if the "grantor" had owned the legal estate: *E.H. Lewis & Son Ltd v. Morelli* [1948] 2 All E.R. 1021; *Universal Permanent Building Society v. Cooke* [1952] Ch. 95.

2. Tenancies by estoppel may arise where a mortgagor purports to grant a lease contrary to the terms of the mortgage: see *post*, p. 825.

3. As stated by Millett L.J., a tenancy by estoppel cannot arise where the purported landlord has any legal estate in the land in question: *Universal Permanent Building Society v. Cooke, supra*. Where he has a legal estate that is insufficient to support the purported lease (for example, where the owner of a 10-year lease purports to grant a 20-year lease), the purported lease operates as an assignment of the landlord's estate: *Beardman v. Wilson* (1868) L.R. 4 C.P. 57; *St Giles Hotel Ltd v. Microworld Technology Ltd* (1997) 75 P. & C.R. 380. See generally Martin [1978] Conv. 137.

4. In *Bruton v. London and Quadrant Housing Trust* [1998] Q.B. 834 the Court of Appeal held that there was no tenancy by estoppel where (because the "landlord" had no legal estate) both the "landlord" and the "tenant" proceeded on the basis that they were creating a licence rather than a tenancy; but the House of Lords ([1999] 3 W.L.R. 150) disagreed with this reasoning.

5. As between the parties to the purported lease, and their successors in title, a tenancy by estoppel operates in the same way as a true tenancy: *Webb v. Austin* (1844) 7 Man. & G. 701; *Cuthbertson v. Irving* (1859) 4 H. & N. 742. Thus, where a tenant is sued for breach of covenant, it is no defence for

the tenant to establish that the landlord does not have good title. Moreover, contrary to the earlier view apparently expressed in *Harrison v. Wells* [1967] 1 Q.B. 263, this rule applies even after the tenant has given up possession: *Industrial Properties (Barton Hill) Ltd v. Associated Electrical Industries Ltd* [1977] Q.B. 580. However, the rule does not apply where the tenant has been evicted by title paramount: *ibid.*; nor does it apply where the landlord's title has expired: *National Westminster Bank Ltd v. Hart* [1983] Q.B. 773.

6. In *First National Bank plc v. Thompson* the doctrine of "feeding the estoppel" was held to apply in the context of registered land where a person purported to create a registered charge over land to which he only subsequently acquired title.

7. For discussion of the doctrine of "feeding the estoppel" in the context of the acquisition of equitable ownership rights, see *Abbey National Building Society v. Cann* [1991] 1 A.C. 56, *post*, p. 886.

C. Essential Characteristics of a Lease

In *Street v. Mountford* [1985] A.C. 809 Lord Templeman stated (at 818) that "[t]o constitute a tenancy the occupier must be granted exclusive possession for a fixed or periodic term certain in consideration of a premium or periodical payments". This formulation, which was repeated at various points in Lord Templeman's speech, involves three substantive requirements: exclusive possession, certainty of duration and rent or other consideration. It also involves the formal requirement of a grant: see *infra*, p. 386.

1. Exclusive possession

The right to exclusive possession is the central characteristic of a lease. In *Street v. Mountford* Lord Templeman stated (at 816):

The traditional view that the grant of exclusive possession for a term at a rent creates a tenancy is consistent with the elevation of a tenancy into an estate in land. The tenant possessing exclusive possession is able to exercise the rights of an owner of land, which is in the real sense his land albeit temporarily and subject to certain restrictions. A tenant armed with exclusive possession can keep out strangers and keep out the landlord unless the landlord is exercising limited rights reserved to him by the tenancy agreement to enter and view and repair.

Exclusive possession thus connotes territorial control: see *Westminster City Council v. Clarke* [1992] 2 A.C. 288, 300–302 *per* Lord Templeman.

The legal concept of exclusive possession is to be distinguished from the fact of exclusive occupation. However, the significance of the distinction and its relevance to the distinction between leases and licences is discussed below: see *infra*, p. 361.

2. Certainty of duration

2.1 *Commencement*

The date of commencement of the term must be fixed before the lease takes effect. Normally the term commences on the date of the execution of the lease. However, a term may be expressed to commence from an earlier date; but in such a case the lease operates only from the date of execution. Thus a lease granted on 1 January 1995, expressed to be a seven-year lease commencing on 1 January 1994, takes effect as a six-year lease commencing on the later date: *Bradshaw v. Pawley* [1980] 1 W.L.R. 10, 14 *per* Megarry V.-C. In both the above cases the lease takes effect immediately and it is referred to as a *lease in possession*.

It is also possible to grant a *reversionary lease*, where the term commences at some future date. However, the postponement of the commencement of the term is subject to a statutory limit of 21 years; and a lease according to which the term is expressed to commence more than 21 years after the date of the grant is void: Law of Property Act 1925, s.149(3). That subsection also declares void a contract for the grant of a lease under which the commencement of the term is postponed for more than 21 years after the date of the grant. On the other hand, the subsection does not affect the validity of a contract to grant a lease more than 21 years in the future, provided that, when the lease is granted, the term will commence within 21 years of the date of the grant: *Re Strand and Savoy Properties Ltd* [1960] Ch. 528, noted at (1960) 76 L.Q.R. 352; *Weg Motors Ltd v. Hales* [1962] Ch. 49, 68 *per* Lord Evershed M.R., 78 *per* Donovan L.J. The rule is thus directed at the time lapse between the grant of the lease and the commencement of the term, not at the time lapse between the contract and the grant of the lease.

2.2 *Duration*

A lease may be granted for any length of time, however long or short: Law of Property Act 1925, s.205(1)(xxvii), *supra,* p. 340. The only requirement is that the maximum duration of the lease must be ascertainable at the commencement of the term. This strict principle has recently been reiterated by the House of Lords.

Prudential Assurance Co. Ltd v. London Residuary Body [1992] 2 A.C. 386

(HL, Lord Templeman, Lord Griffiths, Lord Goff, Lord Browne-Wilkinson, Lord Mustill)

[The facts are stated in the judgment of Lord Templeman.]

LORD TEMPLEMAN:

My Lords, this appeal arises out of a memorandum of agreement dated 19 December 1930 and said to have created a lease for a term which was not limited to expire by effluxion of time and cannot now be determined by the landlord.

By the agreement, the London County Council let to one Nathan a strip of land with a frontage of 36 feet to Walworth Road, a thoroughfare in Southwark, and a depth of 25 feet at a rent of £30 per annum from 19 December 1930 "until the tenancy shall be determined as hereinafter provided." The only relevant proviso for determination is contained in clause 6 which reads:

> "The tenancy shall continue until the said land is required by the council for the purposes of the widening of Walworth Road and the street paving works rendered necessary thereby and the council shall give two months' notice to the tenant at least prior to the day of determination when the said land is so required and thereupon the tenant shall give vacant possession to the council of the said land . . ."

By the agreement, the tenant was authorised to erect "temporary one storey shops or buildings of one storey and for the retention of such shops or buildings as temporary structures" until the land was required for road widening and he was then bound to remove the temporary structures and clear the land. The council agreed to pay all the costs of road making and paving works. The agreement was clearly intended to be of short duration and could have been secured by a lease for a fixed term, say five or ten years with power for the landlord to determine before the expiry of that period for the purposes of the road widening. Unfortunately the agreement was not so drafted. Over 60 years later Walworth Road has not been widened, the freehold is now vested in the appellant second to fourth defendants, who purchased the property from the first defendant, the London Residuary Body, after it had issued a notice to quit, the defendants have no road making powers and it does not appear that the road will ever be widened. The benefit of the agreement is now vested in the respondent plaintiffs, the Prudential Assurance Co. Ltd. The agreement purported to grant a term of uncertain duration which, if valid, now entitles the tenant to stay there for ever and a day at the 1930 rent of £30; valuers acting for both parties have agreed that the annual current commercial rent exceeds £10,000.

A demise for years is a contract for the exclusive possession and profit of land for some determinate period. Such an estate is called a "term". Thus *Co. Litt.*, 19th ed. (1832), vol. 1, para. 45b said that:

> "['Terminus'] in the understanding of the law does not only signify the limits and limitation of time, but also the estate and interest that passes for that time."

Blackstone's Commentaries on the Laws of England, 2nd ed. (1766), vol. II, said, at p. 143:

> "Every estate which must expire at a period certain and prefixed, by whatever words created, is an estate for years. And therefore this estate is frequently called a term, *terminus*, because its duration or continuance is bounded, limited and determined: for every such estate must have a certain beginning, and certain end."

In *Say v. Smith* (1563) Plowd. 269 a lease for a certain term purported to add a term which was uncertain; the lease was held valid only as to the certain term. Anthony Brown J. is reported to have said, at p. 272:

> "every contract sufficient to make a lease for years ought to have certainty in three limitations, viz. in the commencement of the term, in the continuance of it, and in the end of it; so that all these ought to be known at the commencement of the lease, and words in a lease, which don't make this appear, are but babble . . . And these three are in effect but one matter, showing the certainty of the time for which the lessee shall have the land, and if any of these fail, it is not a good lease, for then there wants certainty."

The Law of Property Act 1925, taking up the same theme provided, by section 1(1), that:

"The only estates in land which are capable of subsisting or of being conveyed or created at law are—(a) An estate in fee simple absolute in possession; (b) A term of years absolute."

Section 205(1)(xxvii) was in these terms:

" 'Term of years absolute' means a term of years ... either certain or liable to determination by notice, re-entry, operation of law, or by a provision for cesser on redemption, or in any other event (other than the dropping of a life, or the determination of a determinable life interest); ... and in this definition the expression 'term of years' includes a term for less than a year, or for a year or years and a fraction of a year or from year to year; . . ."

The term expressed to be granted by the agreement in the present case does not fall within this definition.

Ancient authority, recognised by the Act of 1925, was applied in *Lace v. Chantler* [1944] K.B. 368. A dwelling house was let at the rent of 16s. 5d. per week. Lord Greene M.R. (no less) said, at pp. 370–371:

"Normally there could be no question that this was an ordinary weekly tenancy, duly determinable by a week's notice, but the parties in the rent-book agreed to a term which appears there expressed by the words 'furnished for duration,' which must mean the duration of the war. The question immediately arises whether a tenancy for the duration of the war creates a good leasehold interest. In my opinion, it does not. A term created by a leasehold tenancy agreement must be expressed either with certainty and specifically or by reference to something which can, at the time when the lease takes effect, be looked to as a certain ascertainment of what the term is meant to be. In the present case, when this tenancy agreement took effect, the term was completely uncertain. It was impossible to say how long the tenancy would last. Mr Sturge in his argument has maintained that such a lease would be valid, and that, even if the term is uncertain at its beginning when the lease takes effect, the fact that at some future time it will be rendered certain is sufficient to make it a good lease. In my opinion, that argument is not to be sustained. I do not propose to go into the authorities on the matter, but in *Foa's Landlord and Tenant*, 6th ed. (1924), p. 115, the law is stated in this way, and, in my view, correctly: 'The habendum in a lease must point out the period during which the enjoyment of the premises is to be had; so that the duration, as well as the commencement of the term, must be stated. The certainty of a lease as to its continuance must be ascertainable either by the express limitation of the parties at the time the lease is made; or by reference to some collateral act which may, with equal certainty, measure the continuance of it, otherwise it is void.' "

The legislature concluded that it was inconvenient for leases for the duration of the war to be void and therefore by the Validation of Wartime Leases Act 1944 Parliament provided, by section 1(1), that any agreement entered into before or after the passing of the Act which purported to grant a tenancy for the duration of the war:

"shall have effect as if it granted or provided for the grant of a tenancy for a term of 10 years, subject to a right exercisable either by the landlord or the tenant to determine the tenancy, if the war ends before the expiration of that term, by at least one month's notice in writing given after the end of the war; . . ."

Parliament granted the fixed and certain term which the agreements between the parties lacked in the case of tenancies for the duration of the war and which the present agreement lacks.

When the agreement in the present case was made, it failed to grant an estate in the land. The tenant however entered into possession and paid the yearly rent of £30 reserved by the agreement. The tenant entering under a void lease became by virtue of possession and the payment of a yearly rent, a yearly tenant holding on the terms of the agreement so far as those terms were consistent with the yearly tenancy. A yearly tenancy is determinable by the landlord or the tenant at the end of the first or any subsequent year of the tenancy by six months' notice unless the agreement between the parties provides otherwise. Thus in *Doe d. Rigge v. Bell* (1793) 5 Durn. & E. 471 a parol agreement for a seven-year lease did not comply with the Statute of Frauds 1677 (29 Car. 2, c.3) but the tenant entered and paid a yearly rent and it was held that he was tenant from year to year on the terms of the agreement. Lord Kenyon C.J. said, at p. 472:

> "Though the agreement be void by the Statute of Frauds as to the duration of the lease, it must regulate the terms on which the tenancy subsists in other respects, as to the rent, the time of year when the tenant is to quit, etc. ... Now, in this case, it was agreed, that the defendant should quit at Candlemas; and though the agreement is void as to the number of years for which the defendant was to hold, if the lessor chooses to determine the tenancy before the expiration of the seven years, he can only put an end to it at Candlemas."

Now it is said that when in the present case the tenant entered pursuant to the agreement and paid a yearly rent he became a tenant from year to year on the terms of the agreement including clause 6 which prevents the landlord from giving notice to quit until the land is required for road widening. This submission would make a nonsense of the rule that a grant for an uncertain term does not create a lease and would make nonsense of the concept of a tenancy from year to year because it is of the essence of a tenancy from year to year that both the landlord and the tenant shall be entitled to give notice determining the tenancy.

In *Doe d. Warner v. Browne* (1807) 8 East 165 there was an agreement to lease at a rent of £40 per annum and it was agreed that the landlord, W. Warner, should not raise the rent nor turn out the tenant "so long as the rent is duly paid quarterly, and he does not expose to sale or sell any article that may be injurious to W. Warner in his business." The tenant duly paid his rent and did not commit any breach of covenant. The landlord gave six months' notice and it was held that the notice was good. These were the days when it was possible to have a lease for life. Lord Ellenborough C.J. asked, at p. 166:

> "what estate the defendant was contended to have? And whether he were not in this dilemma; that either his estate might enure for life, at his option; and then according to Lord Coke such an estate would, in legal contemplation, be an estate for life; which could not be created by parol: or if not for life, being for no assignable period, it must operate as a tenancy from year to year; in which case it would be inconsistent with, and repugnant to the nature of such an estate, that it should not be determinable at the pleasure of either party giving the regular notice."

Lawrence J. said, at p. 167:

> "If this interest be not determinable so long as the tenant complies with the terms of the agreement, it would operate as an estate for life; which can only be created by deed ... The notion of a tenancy from year to year, the lessor binding himself not to give notice to quit, which was once thrown out by Lord Mansfield, has been long exploded."

In *Cheshire Lines Committee v. Lewis & Co.* (1880) 50 L.J.Q.B. 121 an agreement for a weekly tenancy contained an undertaking by the landlord not to give notice to quit until the landlord required to pull down the demised buildings. Lush J., after citing *Doe d. Warner v. Browne* (1807) 8 East 165 said of that case (1880) 50 L.J.Q.B. 121, 124:

> "This reasoning applies with at least equal force to the present case. This is not a mere constructive tenancy as that was. It is as explicit as words can make it that the

defendants are to hold 'upon a weekly tenancy at a weekly rental, and that the tenancy is to be determined by either of the parties on giving a week's notice to the other.' There is this difference between the two cases, that in *Doe d. Warner v. Browne* the lessor engaged not to turn out the tenant so long as he observed the conditions, and in this case [the company's agent] engages that the tenant shall hold until the company require to pull down the buildings. But, as that is an event which may never happen, the distinction is merely between the contingency of the tenant breaking the conditions and the contingency of the company wanting the premises in order to pull them down. The restriction is as repugnant to the nature of the tenancy in the one case as in the other. It is therefore no legal answer to the ejectment to say that the contingency provided for has not happened."

These authorities indicate plainly enough that the agreement in the present case did not create a lease and that the tenancy from year to year enjoyed by the tenant as a result of entering into possession and paying a yearly rent can be determined by six months' notice by either landlord or tenant. The landlord has admittedly served such a notice. The Court of Appeal have however concluded that the notice was ineffective and that the landlord cannot give a valid notice until the land is required "for the purposes of the widening of Walworth Road" in conformity with clause 6 of the agreement.

The notion of a tenancy from year to year, the landlord binding himself not to give notice to quit, which was exploded long before 1807 according to Lawrence J. in *Doe d. Warner v. Browne* (1807) 8 East 165, 167, was however revived and applied by the Court of Appeal in *In re Midland Railway Co.'s Agreement* [1971] Ch. 725. In that case a lease for a period of six months from 10 June 1920 was expressed to continue from half year to half year until determined. The agreement provided for the determination of the agreement by three months' written notice given by either party to the other subject to a proviso that the landlords should not exercise that right unless they required the premises for their undertaking. The successors to the landlords served a six months' written notice to quit under section 25 of the Landlord and Tenant Act 1954 although they did not require the premises for their undertaking. The Court of Appeal, upholding Foster J., declared that the notice to quit was invalid and of no effect because the landlords did not require the premises for their undertaking. The Court of Appeal held that the decision in *Lace v. Chantler* [1944] K.B. 368 did not apply to a periodic tenancy and declined to follow *Doe d. Warner v. Browne* (1807) 8 East 165 or *Cheshire Lines Committee v. Lewis & Co.* (1880) 50 L.J.Q.B. 121. Russell L.J. delivering the judgment of the court held that the decision in *Lace v. Chantler* [1944] K.B. 368 did not apply to a tenancy from year to year and said [1971] Ch. 725, 733:

"we are persuaded that, there being no authority to prevent us, it is preferable as a matter of justice to hold parties to their clearly expressed bargain rather than to introduce for the first time in 1971 an extension of a doctrine of land law so as to deny the efficacy of that bargain."

My Lords, I consider that the principle in *Lace v. Chantler* [1944] K.B. 368 reaffirming 500 years of judicial acceptance of the requirement that a term must be certain applies to all leases and tenancy agreements. A tenancy from year to year is saved from being uncertain because each party has power by notice to determine at the end of any year. The term continues until determined as if both parties made a new agreement at the end of each year for a new term for the ensuing year. A power for nobody to determine or for one party only to be able to determine is inconsistent with the concept of a term from year to year: see *Doe d. Warner v. Browne* (1807) 8 East 165 and *Cheshire Lines Committee v. Lewis & Co.* (1880) 50 L.J.Q.B. 121. In *In re Midland Railway Co.'s Agreement* [1971] Ch. 725 there was no "clearly expressed bargain" that the term should continue until the crack of doom if the demised land was not required for the landlord's undertaking or if the undertaking ceased to exist. In the present case there was no "clearly expressed bargain" that the tenant shall be entitled to enjoy his "temporary structures" in perpetuity if Walworth Road is never widened. In any event principle and precedent dictate that it is beyond the power of the landlord and the tenant to create a term which is uncertain.

A lease can be made for five years subject to the tenant's right to determine if the war ends before the expiry of five years. A lease can be made from year to year subject to a fetter on the right of the landlord to determine the lease before the expiry of five years unless the war ends. Both leases are valid because they create a determinable certain term of five years. A lease might purport to be made for the duration of the war subject to the tenant's right to determine before the end of the war. A lease might be made from year to year subject to a fetter on the right of the landlord to determine the lease before the war ends. Both leases would be invalid because each purported to create an uncertain term. A term must either be certain or uncertain. It cannot be partly certain because the tenant can determine it at any time and partly uncertain because the landlord cannot determine it for an uncertain period. If the landlord does not grant and the tenant does not take a certain term the grant does not create a lease.

The decision of the Court of Appeal in *In re Midland Railway Co.'s Agreement* [1971] Ch. 725 was taken a little further in *Ashburn Anstalt v. Arnold* [1989] Ch. 1. That case, if it was correct, would make it unnecessary for a lease to be of certain duration. In an agreement for the sale of land the vendor reserved the right to remain at the property after completion as licensee and to trade therefrom without payment of rent

> "save that it can be required by Matlodge [the purchaser] to give possession on not less than one quarter's notice in writing upon Matlodge certifying that it is ready at the expiration of such notice forthwith to proceed with the development of the property and the neighbouring property involving, *inter alia*, the demolition of the property."

The Court of Appeal held that this reservation created a tenancy. The tenancy was not from year to year but for a term which would continue until Marlodge certified that it was ready to proceed with the development of the property. The Court of Appeal held that the term was not uncertain because the vendor could either give a quarter's notice or vacate the property without giving notice. But of course the same could be said of the situation in *Lace v. Chantler* [1944] K.B. 368. The cumulative result of the two Court of Appeal authorities *In re Midland Railway Co's Agreement* [1971] Ch. 725 and *Ashburn's* case [1989] Ch. 1 would therefore destroy the need for any term to be certain.

In the present case the Court of Appeal were bound by the decisions in *In re Midland Railway Co.'s Agreement* and *Ashburn's* case. In my opinion both these cases were wrongly decided. A grant for an uncertain term does not create a lease. A grant for an uncertain term which takes the form of a yearly tenancy which cannot be determined by the landlord does not create a lease. I would allow the appeal. The trial judge, Millett J., reached the conclusion that the six months' notice served by the London Residuary Body was a good notice. He was of course bound by the Court of Appeal decisions but managed to construe the memorandum of agreement so as to render clause 6 ineffective in fettering the right of the landlord to serve a notice to quit after the landlord had ceased to be a road widening authority. In the circumstances this question of construction need not be considered. For the reasons which I have given the order made by Millett J. must be restored.

NOTES:

1. There were two senses in which there could be said to be uncertainty on the facts of *Lace v. Chantler* [1944] 1 K.B. 368: first, that the termination event (the end of the war) was conceptually uncertain so that there could be genuine disagreement as to its meaning; secondly, and assuming no

disagreement on the first issue, that it was uncertain at the commencement of the lease when the war would end. It is clear that the Court of Appeal based its decision on the uncertainty in the second sense; and it held that the requirement of certain duration is not satisfied unless the maximum duration of the lease is certain at the commencement of the lease (what has been termed "prospective certainty"). However, in *Ashburn Anstalt v. Arnold* [1989] Ch. 1 the Court of Appeal seemed to distinguish *Lace v. Chantler, inter alia*, on the ground that that case (and the supposed mischief of the certainty requirement) involved uncertainty in the first sense; and, in those circumstances, the Court of Appeal apparently felt free to assert that the requirement of certain duration is satisfied provided only that there would be no doubt whether the determining event had occurred (what has been termed "retrospective certainty"). The House of Lords in *Prudential Assurance Co. Ltd v. London Residuary Body* has clearly ruled that "prospective certainty" is required.

2. The requirement of ascertainable maximum duration had been compromised in the context of periodic tenancies in *Re Midland Railway Co.'s Agreement* [1971] Ch. 725. Russell L.J. stated (at 732–734):

Now it appears to us that that [the decision in *Lace v. Chantler*] is confined to a case in which that which was purported to be done was simply to create a leasehold interest for a single and uncertain period. The applicability of this matter of certainty to a periodic tenancy was not under consideration. If *Lace v. Chantler* had been a case in which there was simply a periodic tenancy with a proviso that the landlord would not give notice during the continuance of the war, this court might not have concluded that such an agreement, which would of course have left the tenant free to determine on notice at any time, was inoperative to create a leasehold. There is nothing in the reasoning of the judgments to lead to the necessary conclusion that such must have been so.

If you have an ordinary case of a periodic tenancy (for example, a yearly tenancy), it is plain that in one sense at least it is uncertain at the outset what will be the maximum duration of the term created, which term grows year by year as a single term springing from the original grant. It cannot be predicated that in no circumstances will it exceed, for example, 50 years; there is no previously ascertained maximum duration for the term; its duration will depend upon the time that will elapse before either party gives notice of determination. The simple statement of the law that the maximum duration of a term must be certainly known in advance of its taking effect cannot therefore have direct reference to periodic tenancies. The question therefore is whether authority or principle should lead us to mould or enlarge that simple statement of the law so as to adapt and apply it to such a tenancy as this. It is argued that the principle of avoidance through uncertainty is only not applicable to an ordinary periodic tenancy because of the ability of either party at any time to define the maximum by giving notice of determination. This, it is suggested, provides the necessary degree of certainty: because of this power neither party is left in a state of unknowing what is his maximum commitment to the other. But where (it is said) one or other party is, by the terms of the document, deprived of that power until a future event or the fulfilment of a condition the date the occurrence of which (if at all) is uncertain, that person is in such a state of unknowing. Therefore it is said the term should be held void; and reference is made to the statement in *Hill and Redman's Law of Landlord and Tenant*, 15th ed. (1970), p. 3, which suggests that an ordinary periodic tenancy does not conflict with the ancient doctrine, because although the maximum duration of the term be originally indefinite, it can be made subject to a definite limit by either party giving notice to determine.

In the course of the argument we found this approach logically attractive. Here is one term growing period by period and there is no knowing (on one side) its maximum length, if (on that side) there is no power to determine save in an event the occurrence of which is in point of time uncertain. Why logically should that differ from a lease directly for a term of which the maximum duration is uncertain? But in the end we are persuaded that, there being no authority to prevent us, it is preferable as a matter of justice to hold parties to their clearly expressed bargain rather than to introduce for the first time in 1971 an extension of a doctrine of land law so as to deny the efficacy of that bargain.

We were referred to a number of decided cases, but in none of them was it held that a curb on the power to determine a periodic tenancy infringed the principle that an estate of leasehold to be effective must be certain in its maximum duration: rather they were cases in which the question in debate was whether the curb was repugnant to the nature of a periodic tenancy.

Accordingly we hold that in the present case the proviso in clause 2 is not such as to negative the tenancy on the ground of uncertainty of duration. Moreover, we do this on the broad ground, and not on the narrow ground that the particular proviso leaves it open to the defendants by adjustment of the requirements of their undertaking to assume the power to determine the leasehold interest.

There remains the question whether the proviso must in law be rejected as repugnant to the nature of the estate created—a half-yearly periodic tenancy.

Our instinct, as previously indicated, is to give effect if possible to the bargain made by the parties. It may well be that if in a periodic tenancy an attempt was made to prevent the lessor ever determining the tenancy, that would be so inconsistent with the stated bargain that either a greater estate must be found to have been constituted or the attempt must be rejected as repugnant. But short of that we see no reason why an express curb on the power to determine which the common law would confer upon the lessor should be rejected as repugnant to the nature of the leasehold interest granted. In *Breams Property Investment Co. Ltd v. Stroulger* [1948] 2 K.B. 1, a curb on the lessors for three years unless they required the premises for their own use was upheld in this court, notwithstanding the earlier cases of *Warner v. Browne* (1807) 8 East 165 and *Cheshire Lines Committee v. Lewis & Co.* (1880) 50 L.J.Q.B. 121. It follows that in a periodic tenancy a similar curb for 10, 20 or 50 years should not be rejected as repugnant to the concept of a periodic tenancy; and once the argument based on uncertainty is rejected we see no distinction in the present case.

In *Centaploy Ltd v. Matlodge Ltd* [1974] Ch. 1 a purported periodic tenancy under which the landlord had no right of termination and which was thus terminable by the tenant only was held to be void as "a complete contradiction in terms" and repugnant to the nature of a periodic tenancy.

3. The approach in *Re Midland Railway Co.'s Agreement* had been endorsed and, in conjunction with the approach to the question of uncertainty discussed in note 1 above, applied by the Court of Appeal in the context of a purported fixed term tenancy in *Ashburn Anstalt v. Arnold*. In *Prudential Assurance Co. Ltd v. London Residuary Body* the Court of Appeal was thus faced with the conflicting decisions in *Lace v. Chantler* and *Ashburn Anstalt v. Arnold*. Scott L.J. favoured the decision in *Lace v. Chantler*, distinguishing *Ashburn Anstalt v. Arnold* on the ground (which he did not pretend to find satisfactory) that in the latter case the uncertain duration of the term could be controlled by *both* parties: (1991) 63 P. & C.R. 386, 398. On the same basis, the decision in *Ashburn Anstalt v. Arnold* was applied by the Court of Appeal in *Canadian Imperial Bank of Commerce v. Bello* (1991) 64 P. & C.R. 48.

That decision, although not referred to in the House of Lords in *Prudential Assurance Co. Ltd v. London Residuary Body*, must be regarded as wrongly decided.

4. Leaving aside restrictions on the entitlement of the landlord to give notice to quit, it would still seem to be difficult to reconcile the substance of a periodic tenancy, which continues indefinitely until determined by appropriate notice, with the requirement that the maximum duration must be ascertainable *at the commencement of the lease*. Although it had been suggested that the strict requirement of certain duration was not applicable to periodic tenancies (see *Re Midland Railway Co.'s Agreement* [1971] Ch. 725, 732 *per* Russell L.J.) that approach clearly sidestepped the issue; and it has been rejected by the House of Lords. Instead, it has been argued that periodic tenancies do comply with the requirement, provided that each party has the power to define the maximum duration by giving notice of termination: see *Re Midland Railway Co.'s Agreement* [1971] Ch. 725, 733 *per* Russell L.J.; *Prudential Assurance Co. Ltd v. London Residuary Body* [1992] 2 A.C. 386, 394 *per* Lord Templeman; and see *Hammersmith and Fulham LBC v. Monk* [1992] 1 A.C. 478, where Lord Bridge stated (at 490):

[T]he fact that the law regards a tenancy from year to year which has continued for a number of years, considered retrospectively, as a single term in no way affects the principle that continuation beyond the end of each year depends upon the will of the parties that it should continue or that, considered prospectively, the tenancy continues no further than the parties have already impliedly agreed upon by their omission to serve notice to quit.

See Wilde (1993) 57 M.L.R. 117, *infra*, note 6.

5. Lord Browne-Wilkinson was clear in his condemnation of "an ancient and technical rule of law which requires the maximum duration of a term of years to be ascertainable from the outset". He stated (at 396–397):

No one has produced any satisfactory rationale for the genesis of this rule. No one has been able to point to any useful purpose that it serves at the present day. If, by overruling the existing authorities, this House were able to change the law for the future only I would have urged your Lordships to do so. But for this House to depart from a rule relating to land law which has been established for many centuries might upset long established titles. I must therefore confine myself to expressing the hope that the Law Commission might look at the subject to see whether there is in fact any good reason now for maintaining a rule which operates to defeat contractually agreed arrangements between the parties (of which all successors in title are aware) and which is capable of producing such an extraordinary result as that in the present case.

6. For discussion of *Prudential Assurance Co. Ltd v. London Residuary Body*, see Bridge [1993] C.L.J. 26; Smith [1993] Conv. 461; Sparkes (1993) 109 L.Q.R. 93; Bright (1993) 13 *Legal Studies* 38; Wilde (1993) 57 M.L.R. 117.

Wilde (1993) 57 M.L.R. 117 regards the reasoning of the House of Lords in relation to fixed term tenancies as unexceptional but argues that the reasoning in relation to periodic tenancies is logically flawed: that an ordinary (annual) periodic tenancy satisfies the requirement of certainty of duration because "the parties are regarded as only agreeing to a certain one year term at any single point of creation or continuation and ... each one year term within the tenancy is at its commencement of certain maximum possible duration"; and, moreover, that any stipulation that the landlord may not give notice unless the land is required for road widening must logically be seen as co-extensive with the current term only, so that the certain maximum duration is unaffected.

The decision seems to focus on the proprietary aspect of leases rather than their contractual aspect and, consequently, to reflect a preference for certainty over contractual sanctity. Sparkes (1993) 109 L.Q.R. 93 favours the reassertion of the preference for certainty, arguing that the law provides a number of escape routes from the consequences of the certainty rule; and Smith [1993] Conv. 461 and Bridge [1993] C.L.J. 26 are only marginally less enthusiastic. On the other hand, Bright (1993) 13 *Legal Studies* 38 challenges the sharpened focus on the proprietary aspect of leases with the consequent emphasis on strict certainty; she argues that contracts should be upheld, subject to modification where the passage of time and supervening (non-) developments have resulted in a contractual imbalance that ought in fairness to be corrected.

7. Provided that the term has a certain commencement and a certain duration, a lease need not be granted for a single continuous period: it may comprise the aggregate of a series of discontinuous periods. This possibility was established in *Smallwood v. Sheppards* [1895] 2 Q.B. 627; but it has been exploited in the context of timeshare arrangements: see *Cottage Holiday Associates Ltd v. Customs and Excise Commissioners* [1983] Q.B. 735; where Woolf J. held (at 739) that the grant of a lease for one week in each year for 80 years constituted a single term of 80 weeks.

8. A series of statutory provisions have sought to reconcile certain arrangements with the common law requirement that the maximum duration of the lease must be ascertainable at the commencement of the term.

Leases for life or until marriage, if granted at a rent or in consideration of a fine, are automatically converted into 90-year terms, determinable by written notice after the death or marriage of the relevant person: Law of Property Act 1925, s.149(6). Prior to 1997, where no rent or fine was payable, the grantee appeared to become a tenant for life under a strict settlement by virtue of section 1 of the Settled Land Act 1925: see *ante*, p. 269; but, where possible, the courts sought to avoid that conclusion where it would have been contrary to the clear intention of the parties: see *post*, pp. 520, 562. However, since the coming into force of the Trusts of Land and Appointment of Trustees Act 1996, no new strict settlements under the Settled Land Act 1925 may be created either expressly or otherwise. The trust for land that replaces the strict settlement does not involve the same consequences as the strict settlement and it may therefore be seen as a more acceptable means of giving effect to lifetime rent-free occupation of land.

Perpetually renewable leases are automatically converted into 2000-year terms, determinable only by the lessee: Law of Property Act 1922, s.145, Sched. 15; and see *Parkus v. Greenwood* [1950] Ch. 644; *Caerphilly Concrete*

Products Ltd v. Owen [1972] 1 W.L.R. 372; but for the judicial tendency to avoid construing a lease as perpetually renewable, see *Marjorie Burnett Ltd v. Barclay* (1981) 258 E.G. 642, 644 *per* Nourse J.

3. Rent or other consideration

Although most leases are in fact granted in return for the payment of rent or other consideration, contrary to the repeated statement of Lord Templeman in *Street v. Mountford* (and see the doubt expressed in *Scrimgeour v. Waller* (1980) 257 E.G. 61, 63 *per* Sir David Cairns), the payment of rent is not a requirement of a lease. Such a requirement would be inconsistent with the Law of Property Act 1925, s.205(1)(xxvii): see *Ashburn Anstalt v. Arnold* [1989] Ch. 1, 9–10 *per* Fox L.J.; *Prudential Assurance Co. Ltd v. London Residuary Body* (1991) 63 P. & C.R. 386, 397 *per* Scott L.J.; *Canadian Imperial Bank of Commerce v. Bello* (1991) 64 P. & C.R. 48, 55 *per* Ralph Gibson L.J.; *Skipton Building Society v. Clayton* (1993) 66 P. & C.R. 223, 230 *per* Slade L.J. On the other hand, as Scott L.J. noted in *Prudential Assurance Co. Ltd v. London Residuary Body*, "it is very difficult to conceive of a periodic tenancy without a reservation of rent". In practice the absence of rent may be a factor which suggests that the arrangement constitutes a licence: *Colchester BC v. Smith* [1991] Ch. 448, 485 *per* Ferris J.; but the reservation of rent is not conclusive of the existence of a tenancy: see, *e.g. Westminster City Council v. Basson* (1991) 62 P. & C.R. 57.

Rent is essentially periodical payments made during the continuance of the lease in return for the use of the land comprised in the lease. The consideration for the use of the land may also take the form of payments in kind or the performance of services: see *Pitcher v. Tovey* (1692) 4 Mod. 71; *Doe d. Edney v. Benham* (1845) 7 Q.B. 976; *Duke of Malborough v. Osborn* (1864) 5 B. & S. 67; but the operation of the statutory rent control machinery requires the consideration to be quantified in money terms: see *Barnes v. Barrett* [1970] 2 Q.B. 657, 667 *per* Sachs L.J.; *Bostock v. Bryant* (1990) 61 P. & C.R. 23, 26 *per* Stuart-Smith L.J.; and see Lee [1991] Conv. 270.

The amount of any rent must be certain, although the requirement is satisfied when the rent can be calculated with certainty at the time when payment is due: *Greater London Council v. Connolly* [1970] 2 Q.B. 100, 109 *per* Lord Denning M.R. Moreover, the courts have demonstrated considerable flexibility in determining whether or not the rent is certain, in order to avoid the consequences of uncertainty.

Corson v. Rhuddlan Borough Council (1989) 59 P. & C.R. 185

(CA, Balcombe, Ralph Gibson and Staughton L.JJ.)

In 1967 the predecessor in title of the defendant council granted to the plaintiffs a 21-year lease of a golf club at an annual rent of £1,150. The lease included an option to call for a further 21-year term "at a rental to be agreed (but such rental shall not in any event exceed the rental hereby reserved)".

When the plaintiffs claimed to exercise the option, the defendant contended that the option was void for uncertainty.

RALPH GIBSON L.J.:
It seems plain to me, therefore, that in the absence of authority requiring us to take a different course, it is proper to apply to this clause the principle applied by Lord Tomlin to the document in *Hillas & Co. v. Arcos* (1932) 147 L.T. 503, namely that the court should, if it can:

> "so balance matters that without violation of essential principle the dealings of men may as far as possible be treated as effective."

In *Brown v. Gould* [1972] Ch. 53, Megarry J. referred to the reluctance of the court to hold an instrument void for uncertainty as a basic principle. If we are free to do so, I would hold that in this case the contractual intention of the parties is clear that, upon proper notice being given, the council should be under an obligation to grant a new lease at a fair rent to be agreed between the parties, that fair rent not to be in excess of £1,150. It is just and necessary to imply the provision for the rent to be a fair rent.

There is said to be authority in the way of taking that course. In *King's Motors v. Lax* [1970] 1 W.L.R. 426 the option clause was contained in a seven-year lease of a petrol station and provided for a further term of seven years. As in this case, there was a requirement as to the giving of notice six months before the end of the term and of due performance of the covenants in the lease, but the rent was to be "as may be agreed between the parties." There was no statement as to the maximum rent. [Counsel for the defendant] submitted that that case had been approved in *Beer v. Bowden* [1981] 1 W.L.R. 522 by this court and that the reference in the option clause in this case to a maximum rent did not serve to distinguish this case from the grounds of decision in *Lax's* case. As was pointed out in the course of argument by Balcombe L.J., the correctness of the decision in *Lax's* case was not treated as a matter of decision for this court in *Beer v. Bowden*. The *Lax* case was concerned with an option clause, as contrasted with the rent revision clause before the court in *Beer v. Bowden*, and was thus regarded as distinguishable. It is, again, I think, not necessary for this court to decide whether the decision in the *Lax* case was correct because the provision for a maximum rent is, in my judgment, a material distinction. For my part, however, I incline to the view that it was, as [counsel for the plaintiffs] submitted, wrongly decided, and I would respectfully differ from the view of Goff L.J. that the option clause was in that case precluded from being a valid contract because the rent was not ascertainable. I see no reason why different principles should be applicable to the construction, so far as concerns voidness for uncertainty, of a rent revision clause in an existing lease as contrasted with an option for a new lease or further lease in an existing lease. *Foley v. Classique Coaches Ltd* [1934] 2 K.B. 1 established that the presence of the words "to be agreed by the parties" is not fatal to the existence of an enforceable contract if it is otherwise plain, upon the construction of the whole of the document in its context, including of course those words, that there was a clear contractual intention of the parties to be bound by the clause. A provision that the rent should be a fair rent could, I think, have been implied in the *Lax* case. I can see no risk of difficulty arising from such a conclusion. If parties intend an option clause to be no more than an indication that the landlord will be willing to consider a request for a new lease without obligation and on terms to be agreed, there is no difficulty in making that intention clear if there is thought to be any utility in including such a statement in the document.

NOTES:
1. *Brown v. Gould* [1972] Ch. 53 concerned an option to renew a lease at a rent "to be fixed having regard to the market value of the premises".

Notwithstanding the absence of provision of specified machinery for the working out of that formula, Megarry J. rejected the contention that the option was void for uncertainty; he stated (at 61):

The question is not, I think, whether the clause is proof against wilful misinterpretation, but whether someone genuinely seeking to discover its meaning is able to do so. To that question I would answer Yes.

2. Martin [1990] Conv. 290 suggests that, while the Court of Appeal assimilated rent revision clauses, options for new leases and options for further leases, all of which fall to be considered in the context of a subsisting lease, a stricter rule may apply where the parties to the disputed agreement have no subsisting contractual relationship.

D. THE DISTINCTION BETWEEN LEASES AND LICENCES

1. The significance of the lease/licence distinction

The right to occupy land in return for payment is consistent with the grant of a lease or a (contractual) licence: see *post*, p. 495. However, the consequences of the two alternatives are very different. Under the general law, a lease is an interest in land: indeed, it is one of only two interests in land which, after 1925, can exist as legal estates and which are capable of substantive registration under the Land Registration Act 1925. As such, a lease, and the right to exclusive possession under that lease, is assignable by the lessee; the lease is enforceable against the original lessor; and, if the lessor should transfer his interest in the land (whether the fee simple or a superior lease), the lease is capable of binding the transferee. By contrast, the corresponding characteristics of a licence are somewhat precarious. Although, the law has admitted some changes in recent years, a contractual licence is no more than a personal right conferred by the licensor/landowner; and, although in some circumstances the original licensor may be restrained from revoking such a licence, the licence cannot without more bind a transferee of the land from the original licensor: see *post*, pp. 512 *et seq*.

However, these differences, which are the consequences of general land law principles, are only part of the picture. For the distinction between leases and licences also determines the applicability of certain statutory regimes under the landlord and tenant legislation. Detailed consideration of such legislation is outside the scope of this book; but a very brief summary of its principal features will indicate the further significance of the lease/licence distinction. The Rent Act 1977 provides protection in the form of rent control and security of tenure for ("regulated") tenants but not licensees (save for a very limited form of protection afforded to licensees occupying under "restricted contracts"); and, although Rent Act protection only applies to tenancies created before 1989, a significant number of such tenancies continue in existence. The Housing Act 1988, which replaced the Rent Act in the private rental sector, continues to distinguish between ("assured") tenants and licensees, although the protection afforded to such tenants is at a much reduced level. Tenants of business premises and agricultural land are also afforded greater protection than licensees: see, respectively, Landlord and Tenant Act 1954, Part II; Agricultural Holdings Act 1986 (but contrast the minimal security of tenure afforded to farm business tenancies under the Agricultural Tenancies Act 1995). On the other hand, the Housing Act 1985 provides security of tenure in the public rental sector for "secured" tenants, a term which is defined to include both tenants and licensees. In addition to these forms of protection, residential tenants under long leases (leases for a term exceeding 21 years) may have the right to purchase the freehold of the property or the right to be granted a new lease. This right has existed since 1967 in the case of long leases of houses: Leasehold Reform Act 1967, ss.1–4; and it was subsequently extended to long leases of flats: Leasehold Reform, Housing and Urban Development Act 1993, Part I.

It is hardly surprising that these differences, both under the general law and under the various statutory landlord and tenant regimes, have led to disputes and litigation over the proper characterisation of rights to occupy land in return for payment. The resolution of such disputes has been no easy task. Observation of the physical realities rarely reveals any distinction between a lease and a licence; and perusal of any agreement is unlikely to assist even the intelligent non-(property) lawyer: for whether the agreement confers a lease or a licence, it will deal with the same essential matters such as the duration of the agreement, the level of payments and the rights and obligations of the parties.

In examining the approach of the courts to such disputes, it must be remembered that their decisions have been made against the background of various strictly non-legal considerations. First, the landlord and tenant legislation is a supreme example of social legislation, designed as a matter of government policy to deal with homelessness and the associated problems; but the legislation has been a shifting background. For different governments have adopted different attitudes in balancing the interests of residential occupiers against the interests of landlords; and those different attitudes have been reflected in the legislation. Secondly, since it is clear that statutory protection for tenants inevitably involves a corresponding restriction on the freedom of landlords to deal with their property, it is not surprising that landlords have sought to minimise those restrictions and that they have therefore endeavoured to devise arrangements that do not confer Rent Act protection. Thirdly, although the strict legal issue before the court may be the determination of whether an arrangement constitutes a lease or a licence, the court is inevitably aware of both the immediate consequences of its determination for the parties and the longer-term consequences of similar decisions for the wider homelessness issue. The finding that an occupier is a tenant, and therefore entitled to the protection of some statutory regime, may benefit the particular occupier in the short term; but the response of (prospective) landlords may be the withdrawal of their properties from the rental market and the exacerbation of the general problem of homelessness.

For possible reform in relation to the significance of the lease/licence distinction, see Law Com. No. 162, *Landlord and Tenant: Reform of the Law* (1987), paras 4.9–4.11.

2. The criteria for the lease/licence distinction

In fact, the courts had established a conclusive test to determine lease/licence disputes long before the enactment of landlord and tenant legislation. In *Lynes v. Snaith* [1899] 1 Q.B. 486, Lawrence J. stated (at 488):

[I]t is clear that the defendant was a tenant ... and not a licensee; for the admissions state that she was in exclusive possession, a fact which is wholly inconsistent with her having been a mere licensee.

Provided, therefore, that the other essential characteristics of a lease were present, the grant of exclusive possession determined conclusively that the occupier was a tenant. This test continued to be applied after the enactment of the landlord and tenant legislation, subject only to a limited range of exceptional cases. These exceptions were catalogued in *Facchini v. Bryson* [1952] 1 T.L.R. 1386, where Denning L.J. said (at 1389–1390):

In all the cases where an occupier has been held to be a licensee there has been something in the circumstances, such as a family arrangement, an act of friendship or generosity, or such like, to negative any intention to create a tenancy. In such circumstances it would be obviously unjust to saddle the owner with a tenancy, with all the momentous consequences that that entails nowadays, when there was no intention to create a tenancy at all. In the present case, however, there are no special circumstances. ... The occupation has all the features of a ... tenancy, and the parties cannot by the mere words of their contract turn it into something else. Their relationship is determined by the law and not by the label which they choose to put on it. ... It is not necessary to go so far as to find the document a sham. It is simply a matter of finding the true relationship of the parties. It is most important that we should adhere to this principle, or else we might find all landlords granting licences and not tenancies, and we should make a hole in the Rent Acts through which could be driven—I will not in these days say a coach and four—but an articulated vehicle.

Nonetheless, exclusive possession remained a necessary condition of a tenancy, and therefore of statutory protection for the tenant; and sometimes, even where there were no special circumstances, the courts would find that the occupier had not been granted exclusive possession and *for that reason* had not been granted a tenancy.

However, in the mid-1970s statutory protection was extended to the (hitherto unprotected) tenants of furnished premises; and also to certain contractual licensees, provided that they were entitled to "exclusive occupation" of the property. The response of many landlords (who did not withdraw their properties from the rental market) was to create what became known as "non-exclusive occupation agreements", according to which the occupiers expressly agreed to share the property with anyone whom the owner chose to instal. Such arrangements were clearly designed to circumvent all statutory protection; but the courts seemed prepared to sanction them. The approach of the Court of Appeal in *Somma v. Hazelhurst and Savelli* [1978] 1 W.L.R. 1014 is in marked contrast to that adopted in *Facchini v. Bryson*; Cumming-Bruce L.J. said (at 1024–1025):

Counsel for the [occupiers], basing himself on the judgment of Denning L.J. in *Facchini v. Bryson* [1952] 1 T.L.R. 1386, 1389 and the reasoning in *Marchant v. Charters* [1977] 1 W.L.R. 1181, 1185, submits that in a "Rent Act" situation any permission to occupy residential premises exclusively must be a tenancy and not a licence, unless it comes into the category of hotels, hostels, family arrangements or service occupancy or a similar undefined special category. We can see no reason why an ordinary landlord not in any of these special categories should not be able to grant a licence to occupy an ordinary house. If that is what both he and the licensee intended and if they can frame any written agreement in such a way as to demonstrate that it is not really an agreement for a lease masquerading as a licence, we can see no reason in law or justice why they should be prevented from achieving that object. Nor can we see why their common intentions should be categorised as bogus or unreal or as sham merely on the ground that the court disapproves of the bargain.

Against a background of legislative changes which shifted the balance of statutory protection back in favour of property owners, the courts continued to give effect to the supposed express intentions of the parties and thereby to countenance the highly artificial "non-exclusive occupation agreements". For comment, see Partington (1979) 42 M.L.R. 331.

However, in *Street v. Mountford* [1985] A.C. 809 the House of Lords favoured the reinstatement of substance over form; and exclusive possession once again became the central consideration. In that case, it was common ground that the occupier had been granted the right of exclusive possession and that the other characteristics of a tenancy were present. The question was whether in such circumstances it inevitably followed that a tenancy had been granted.

Street v. Mountford [1985] A.C. 809

(HL, Lord Scarman, Lord Keith, Lord Bridge, Lord Brightman, Lord Templeman)

[The facts are stated in the judgment of Lord Templeman.]

LORD TEMPLEMAN:
My Lords, by an agreement dated 7 March 1983, the respondent Mr Street granted the appellant Mrs Mountford the right to occupy the furnished rooms numbers 5 and 6 at 5, St Clements Gardens, Boscombe, from 7 March 1983 for £37 per week, subject to termination by 14 days' written notice and subject to the conditions set forth in the agreement. The question raised by this appeal is whether the agreement created a tenancy or a licence.

A tenancy is a term of years absolute. This expression, by section 205(1)(xxvii) of the Law of Property Act 1925, reproducing the common law, includes a term from week to week in possession at a rent and liable to determination by notice or re-entry. Originally a term of years was not an estate in land, the lessee having merely a personal action against his lessor. But a legal estate in leaseholds was created by the

Statute of Gloucester 1278 and the Act of 1529 21 Hen. VIII, c. 15. Now by section 1 of the Law of Property Act 1925 a term of years absolute is an estate in land capable of subsisting as a legal estate. In the present case if the agreement dated 7 March 1983 created a tenancy, Mrs Mountford having entered into possession and made weekly payments acquired a legal estate in land. If the agreement is a tenancy, the occupation of Mrs Mountford is protected by the Rent Acts.

A licence in conjunction with land while entitling the licensee to use the land for the purposes authorised by the licence does not create an estate in the land. If the agreement dated 7 March 1983 created a licence for Mrs Mountford to occupy the premises, she did not acquire any estate in the land. If the agreement is a licence then Mrs Mountford's right of occupation is not protected by the Rent Acts. Hence the practical importance of distinguishing between a tenancy and a licence.

In the course of argument, nearly every clause of the agreement dated 7 March 1983 was relied upon by the appellant as indicating a lease and by the respondent as indicating a licence. The agreement, in full, was in these terms:

"I Mrs Wendy Mountford agree to take from the owner Roger Street the single furnished room number 5 and 6 at 5 St Clements Gardens, Boscombe, Bournemouth, commencing 7 March 1983 at a licence fee of £37 per week.

I understand that the right to occupy the above room is conditional on the strict observance of the following rules:

1. No paraffin stoves, or other than the supplied form of heating, is allowed in the room.

2. No one but the above-named person may occupy or sleep in the room without prior permission, and this personal licence is not assignable.

3. The owner (or his agent) has the right at all times to enter the room to inspect its condition, read and collect money from meters, carry out maintenance works, install or replace furniture or for any other reasonable purpose.

4. All rooms must be kept in a clean and tidy condition.

5. All damage and breakages must be paid for or replaced at once. An initial deposit equivalent to 2 weeks' licence fee will be refunded on termination of the licence subject to deduction for all damage or other breakages or arrears of licence fee, or retention towards the cost of any necessary possession proceedings.

6. No nuisance or annoyance to be caused to the other occupiers. In particular, all music played after midnight to be kept low so as not to disturb occupiers of other rooms.

7. No children or pets allowed under any circumstances whatsoever.

8. Prompt payment of the licence fee must be made every Monday in advance without fail.

9. If the licence fee or any part of it shall be seven days in arrear or if the occupier shall be in breach of any of the other terms of this agreement or if (except by arrangement) the room is left vacant or unoccupied, the owner may re-enter the room and this licence shall then immediately be terminated (without prejudice to all other rights and remedies of the owner).

10. This licence may be terminated by 14 days' written notice given to the occupier at any time by the owner or his agent, or by the same notice by the occupier to the owner or his agent.

Occupier's signature

Owner/agent's signature

Date 7 March 1983

I understand and accept that a licence in the above form does not and is not intended to give me a tenancy protected under the Rent Acts.

Occupier's signature."

On 12 August 1983 on Mrs Mountford's application a fair rent was registered. Mr Street then made application under section 51(a) of the County Courts Act 1959 for a declaration that Mrs Mountford's occupancy was a licence and not a tenancy. The recorder in the county court held that Mrs Mountford was a tenant entitled to the protection of the Rent Acts and made a declaration accordingly. The Court of Appeal held that Mrs Mountford was a licensee not entitled to the protection of the Rent Acts. Mrs Mountford appeals.

On behalf of Mrs Mountford her counsel, Mr Hicks Q.C., seeks to reaffirm and re-establish the traditional view that an occupier of land for a term at a rent is a tenant providing the occupier is granted exclusive possession. It is conceded on behalf of Mr Street that the agreement dated 7 March 1983 granted exclusive possession to Mrs Mountford. The traditional view that the grant of exclusive possession for a term at a rent creates a tenancy is consistent with the elevation of a tenancy into an estate in land. The tenant possessing exclusive possession is able to exercise the rights of an owner of land, which is in the real sense his land albeit temporarily and subject to certain restrictions. A tenant armed with exclusive possession can keep out strangers and keep out the landlord unless the landlord is exercising limited rights reserved to him by the tenancy agreement to enter and view and repair. A licensee lacking exclusive possession can in no sense call the land his own and cannot be said to own any estate in the land. The licence does not create an estate in the land to which it relates but only makes an act lawful which would otherwise be unlawful.

On behalf of Mr Street his counsel, Mr Goodhart Q.C., relies on recent authorities which, he submits, demonstrate that an occupier granted exclusive possession for a term at a rent may nevertheless be a licensee if, in the words of Slade L.J. in the present case [1985] 49 P. & C.R. 324, 332:

"there is manifested the clear intention of both parties that the rights granted are to be merely those of a personal right of occupation and not those of a tenant."

In the present case, it is submitted, the provisions of the agreement dated 7 March 1983 and in particular clauses 2, 4, 7 and 9 and the express declaration at the foot of the agreement manifest the clear intention of both parties that the rights granted are to be those of a personal nature and not those of a tenant.

My Lords, there is no doubt that the traditional distinction between a tenancy and a licence of land lay in the grant of land for a term at a rent with exclusive possession. In some cases it was not clear at first sight whether exclusive possession was in fact granted. For example, an owner of land could grant a licence to cut and remove standing timber. Alternatively the owner could grant a tenancy of the land with the right to cut and remove standing timber during the term of the tenancy. The grant of rights relating to standing timber therefore required careful consideration in order to decide whether the grant conferred exclusive possession of the land for a term at a rent and was therefore a tenancy or whether it merely conferred a bare licence to remove the timber.

In *Glenwood Lumber Co. Ltd v. Phillips* [1904] A.C. 405, the Crown in exercise of statutory powers "licensed" the respondents to hold an area of land for the purpose of cutting and removing timber for the term of 21 years at an annual rent. Delivering the advice of the Judicial Committee of the Privy Council, Lord Davey said, at pp. 408–409:

"The appellants contended that this instrument conferred only a licence to cut timber and carry it away, and did not give the respondent any right of occupation or interest in the land itself. Having regard to the provisions of the Act under the powers of which it was executed and to the language of the document itself, their Lordships cannot adopt this view of the construction or effect of it. In the so-called licence itself it is called indifferently a licence and a demise, but in the Act it is spoken of as a lease, and the holder of it is described as the lessee. It is not, however, a question of words but of substance. If the effect of the instrument is to give the holder an exclusive right of occupation of the land, though subject to certain reservations or to a restriction of the purposes for which it may be used, it is in law a demise of the land itself. By [the Act] it is enacted that the lease shall vest in the lessee the right to take and keep exclusive possession of the lands described therein subject to the conditions in the Act provided or referred to, and the lessee is empowered (amongst other things) to bring any actions or suits against any party unlawfully in possession of any land so leased, and to prosecute all trespassers thereon. The operative part and habendum in the licence is framed in apt language to carry out the intention so expressed in the Act. And their Lordships have no doubt that the effect of the so-called licence was to confer a title to the land itself on the respondent."

This was a case in which the court after careful consideration of the purposes of the grant, the terms of the grant and the surrounding circumstances, came to the conclusion that the grant conferred exclusive possession and was therefore a tenancy.

A contrary conclusion was reached in *Taylor v. Caldwell* (1863) 3 B. & S. 826 in which the defendant agreed to let the plaintiff have the use of the Surrey Gardens and Music Hall on four specified days giving a series of four concerts and day and night fetes at the gardens and hall on those days, and the plaintiff agreed to take the gardens and the hall and to pay £100 for each day. Blackburn J. said, at p. 832:

"The parties inaccurately call this a 'letting,' and the money to be paid a 'rent', but the whole agreement is such as to show that the defendants were to retain the possession of the hall and gardens so that there was to be no demise of them, and that the contract was merely to give the plaintiffs the use of them on those days."

That was a case where the court after considering the purpose of the grant, the terms of the grant and the surrounding circumstances came to the conclusion that the grantee was not entitled to exclusive possession but only to use the land for limited purposes and was therefore a licensee.

In the case of residential accommodation there is no difficulty in deciding whether the grant confers exclusive possession. An occupier of residential accommodation at a rent for a term is either a lodger or a tenant. The occupier is a lodger if the landlord provides attendance or services which require the landlord or his servants to exercise unrestricted access to and use of the premises. A lodger is entitled to live in the premises but cannot call the place his own. In *Allan v. Liverpool Overseers* (1874) L.R. 9 Q.B. 180, 191–192 Blackburn J. said:

"A lodger in a house, although he has the exclusive use of rooms in the house, in the sense that nobody else is to be there, and though his goods are stowed there, yet he is not in exclusive occupation in that sense, because the landlord is there for the purpose of being able, as landlords commonly do in the case of lodgings, to have his own servants to look after the house and the furniture, and has retained to himself the occupation, though he has agreed to give the exclusive enjoyment of the occupation to the lodger."

If on the other hand residential accommodation is granted for a term at a rent with exclusive possession, the landlord providing neither attendance nor services, the grant is a tenancy; any express reservation to the landlord of limited rights to enter and view the state of the premises and to repair and maintain the premises only serves to emphasise the fact that the grantee is entitled to exclusive possession and is a tenant. In the present case it is conceded that Mrs Mountford is entitled to exclusive possession and is not a lodger. Mr Street provided neither attendance nor services and only reserved the limited rights of inspection and maintenance and the like set forth in clause 3 of the agreement. On the traditional view of the matter, Mrs Mountford not being a lodger must be a tenant.

There can be no tenancy unless the occupier enjoys exclusive possession; but an occupier who enjoys exclusive possession is not necessarily a tenant. He may be owner in fee simple, a trespasser, a mortgagee in possession, an object of charity or a service occupier. To constitute a tenancy the occupier must be granted exclusive possession for a fixed or periodic term certain in consideration of a premium or periodical payments. The grant may be express, or may be inferred where the owner accepts weekly or other periodical payments from the occupier.

Occupation by service occupier may be eliminated. A service occupier is a servant who occupies his master's premises in order to perform his duties as a servant. In those circumstances the possession and occupation of the servant is treated as the possession and occupation of the master and the relationship of landlord and tenant is not created; see *Mayhew v. Suttle* (1854) 4 El. & Bl. 347. The test is whether the servant requires the premises he occupies in order the better to perform his duties as a servant:

"Where the occupation is necessary for the performance of services, and the occupier is required to reside in the house in order to perform those services, the occupation being strictly ancillary to the performance of the duties which the occupier has to perform, the occupation is that of a servant; *per* Mellor J. in *Smith v. Seghill Overseers* (1875) L.R. 10 Q.B. 422, 428."

The cases on which Mr Goodhart relies begin with *Booker v. Palmer* [1942] 2 All E.R. 674. The owner of a cottage agreed to allow a friend to install an evacuee in the cottage rent free for the duration of the war. The Court of Appeal held that there was no intention on the part of the owner to enter into legal relationships with the evacuee. Lord Greene M.R. said, at p. 677:

"To suggest there is an intention there to create a relationship of landlord and tenant appears to me to be quite impossible. There is one golden rule which is of very general application, namely, that the law does not impute intention to enter into legal relationships where the circumstances and the conduct of the parties negative any intention of the kind. It seems to me that this is a clear example of the application of that rule."

The observations of Lord Greene M.R. were not directed to the distinction between a contractual tenancy and a contractual licence. The conduct of the parties (not their professed intentions) indicated that they did not intend to contract at all.

In the present case, the agreement dated 7 March 1983 professed an intention by both parties to create a licence and their belief that they had in fact created a licence. It was submitted on behalf of Mr Street that the court cannot in these circumstances decide that the agreement created a tenancy without interfering with the freedom of contract enjoyed by both parties. My Lords, Mr Street enjoyed freedom to offer Mrs Mountford the right to occupy the rooms comprised in the agreement on such lawful terms as Mr Street pleased. Mrs Mountford enjoyed freedom to negotiate with Mr Street to obtain different terms. Both parties enjoyed freedom to contract or not to contract and both parties exercised that freedom by contracting on the terms set forth in the written agreement and on no other terms. But the consequences in law of the agreement, once concluded, can only be determined by consideration of the effect of the agreement. If the agreement satisfied all the requirements of a tenancy, then the agreement produced a tenancy and the parties cannot alter the effect of the agreement by insisting that they only created a licence. The manufacture of a five-pronged implement for manual digging results in a fork even if the manufacturer, unfamiliar with the English language, insists that he intended to make and has made a spade.

It was also submitted that in deciding whether the agreement created a tenancy or a licence, the court should ignore the Rent Acts. If Mr Street has succeeded, where owners have failed these past 70 years, in driving a coach and horses through the Rent Acts, he must be left to enjoy the benefit of his ingenuity unless and until Parliament intervenes. I accept that the Rent Acts are irrelevant to the problem of determining the legal effect of the rights granted by the agreement. Like the professed intention of the parties, the Rent Acts cannot alter the effect of the agreement.

In *Marcroft Wagons Ltd v. Smith* [1951] 2 K.B. 496 the daughter of a deceased tenant who lived with her mother claimed to be a statutory tenant by succession and the landlords asserted that the daughter had no rights under the Rent Acts and was a trespasser. The landlords expressly refused to accept the daughter's claim but accepted rent from her while they were considering the position. If the landlords had decided not to apply to the court for possession but to accept the daughter as a tenant, the moneys paid by the daughter would have been treated as rent. If the landlords decided, as they did decide, to apply for possession and to prove, as they did prove, that the daughter was not a statutory tenant, the moneys paid by the daughter were treated as mesne profits. The Court of Appeal held with some hesitation that the landlords never accepted the daughter as tenant and never intended to contract with her although the landlords delayed for some six months before applying to the court for possession. Roxburgh J. said, at p. 507;

> "Generally speaking, when a person, having a sufficient estate in land, lets another into exclusive possession, a tenancy results, and there is no question of a licence. But the inference of a tenancy is not necessarily to be drawn where a person succeeds on a death to occupation of rent-controlled premises and a landlord accepts some rent while he or the occupant, or both of them, is or are considering his or their position. If this is all that happened in this case, then no tenancy would result."

In that case, as in *Booker v. Palmer* the court deduced from the conduct of the parties that they did not intend to contract at all.

Errington v. Errington and Woods [1952] 1 K.B. 290 concerned a contract by a father to allow his son to buy the father's house on payment of the instalments of the father's building society loan. Denning L.J. referred, at p. 297, to the judgment of Lord Greene M.R. in *Booker v. Palmer* [1942] 2 All E.R. 674, 677 where, however, the circumstances and the conduct of the parties negatived any intention to enter into legal relationships. Denning L.J. continued, at pp. 297–298:

> "We have had many instances lately of occupiers in exclusive possession who have been held to be not tenants, but only licensees. When a requisitioning authority allowed people into possession at a weekly rent: ... when a landlord told a tenant on his retirement that he could live in a cottage rent free for the rest of his days: ... when a landlord, on the death of the widow of a statutory tenant, allowed her daughter to remain in possession, paying rent for six months: *Marcroft Wagons Ltd v. Smith* [1951] 2 K.B. 496; when the owner of a shop allowed the manager to live in a flat above the shop, but did not require him to do so, and the value of the flat was taken into account at £1 a week in fixing his wages: ... in each of those cases the occupier was held to be a licensee and not a tenant. ... The result of all these cases is that, although a person who is let into exclusive possession is prima facie to be considered a tenant, nevertheless he will not be held to be so if the circumstances negative any intention to create a tenancy. Words alone may not suffice. Parties cannot turn a tenancy into a licence merely by calling it one. But if the circumstances and the conduct of the parties show that all that was intended was that the occupier should be granted a personal privilege, with no interest in the land, he will be held to be a licensee only."

In *Errington v. Errington and Woods* [1952] 1 K.B. 290 and in the cases cited by Denning L.J. at p. 297 there were exceptional circumstances which negatived the prima facie intention to create a tenancy, notwithstanding that the occupier enjoyed exclusive occupation. The intention to create a tenancy was negatived if the parties did not intend to enter into legal relationships at all, or where the relationship between the parties was that of vendor and purchaser, master and service occupier, or where the owner, a requisitioning authority, had no power to grant a tenancy. These exceptional circumstances are not to be found in the present case where there has been the lawful, independent and voluntary grant of exclusive possession for a term at a rent.

If the observations of Denning L.J. are applied to the facts of the present case it may fairly be said that the circumstances negative any intention to create a mere licence.

Words alone do not suffice. Parties cannot turn a tenancy into a licence merely by calling it one. The circumstances and the conduct of the parties show that what was intended was that the occupier should be granted exclusive possession at a rent for a term with a corresponding interest in the land which created a tenancy.

In *Cobb v. Lane* [1952] 1 T.L.R. 1037, an owner allowed her brother to occupy a house rent free. The country court judge, who was upheld by the Court of Appeal, held that there was no intention to create any legal relationship and that a tenancy at will was not to be implied. This is another example of conduct which negatives any intention of entering into a contract, and does not assist in distinguishing a contractual tenancy from a contractual licence.

In *Facchini v. Bryson* [1952] 1 T.L.R. 1386, an employer and his assistant entered into an agreement which, inter alia, allowed the assistant to occupy a house for a weekly payment on terms which conferred exclusive possession. The assistant did not occupy the house for the better performance of his duty and was not therefore a service occupier. The agreement stipulated that "nothing in this agreement shall be construed to create a tenancy between the employer and the assistant." Somervell L.J. said, at p. 1389:

> "If, looking at the operative clauses in the agreement, one comes to the conclusion that the rights of the occupier, to use a neutral word, are those of a lessee, the parties cannot turn it into a licence by saying at the end 'this is deemed to be a licence;' nor can they, if the operative paragraphs show that it is merely a licence, say that it should be deemed to be a lease."

Denning L.J. referred to several cases including *Errington v. Errington and Woods* and *Cobb v. Lane* and said, at pp. 1389–1390:

> "In all the cases where an occupier has been held to be a licensee there has been something in the circumstances, such as a family arrangement, an act of friendship or generosity, or such like, to negative any intention to create a tenancy. ... In the present case, however, there are no special circumstances. It is a simple case where the employer let a man into occupation of a house in consequence of his employment at a weekly sum payable by him. The occupation has all the features of a service tenancy, and the parties cannot by the mere words of their contract turn it into something else. Their relationship is determined by the law and not by the label which they choose to put on it: ..."

The decision, which was thereafter binding on the Court of Appeal and on all lower courts, referred to the special circumstances which are capable of negativing an intention to create a tenancy and reaffirm the principle that the professed intentions of the parties are irrelevant. The decision also indicated that in a simple case a grant of exclusive possession of residential accommodation for a weekly sum creates a tenancy.

In *Murray Bull & Co. Ltd v. Murray* [1953] 1 Q.B. 211 a contractual tenant held over, paying rent quarterly, McNair J. found, at p. 217:

> "both parties intended that the relationship should be that of licensee and no more ... The primary consideration on both sides was that the defendant, as occupant of the flat, should not be a controlled tenant."

In my opinion this case was wrongly decided. McNair J. citing the observations of Denning L.J. in *Errington v. Errington and Woods* [1952] 1 K.B. 290, 297 and *Marcroft Wagons Ltd v. Smith* [1951] 2 K.B. 496 failed to distinguish between first, conduct which negatives an intention to create legal relationships, secondly, special circumstances which prevent exclusive occupation from creating a tenancy and thirdly, the professed intention of the parties. In *Murray Bull & Co. Ltd v. Murray* the conduct of the parties showed an intention to contract and there were no relevant special circumstances. The tenant holding over continued by agreement to enjoy exclusive possession and to pay a rent for a term certain. In those circumstances he continued to be a tenant notwithstanding the professed intention of the parties to create a licence and their desire to avoid a controlled tenancy.

In *Addiscombe Garden Estates Ltd v. Crabbe* [1958] 1 Q.B. 513 the Court of Appeal considered an agreement relating to a tennis club carried on in the grounds of a hotel. The agreement was:

"described by the parties as a licence ... the draftsman has studiously and successfully avoided the use either of the word 'landlord' or the word 'tenant' throughout the document *per* Jenkins L.J. at p. 522."

On analysis of the whole of the agreement the Court of Appeal came to the conclusion that the agreement conferred exclusive possession and thus created a tenancy. Jenkins L.J. said, at p. 522:

"The whole of the document must be looked at; and if, after it has been examined, the right conclusion appears to be that, whatever label may have been attached to it, it in fact conferred and imposed on the grantee in substance the rights and obligations of a tenant, and on the grantor in substance the rights and obligations of a landlord, then it must be given the appropriate effect, that is to say, it must be treated as a tenancy agreement as distinct from a mere licence."

In the agreement in the *Addiscombe* case it was by no means clear until the whole of the document had been narrowly examined that exclusive possession was granted by the agreement. In the present case it is clear that exclusive possession was granted and so much is conceded. In these circumstances it is unnecessary to analyse minutely the detailed rights and obligations contained in the agreement.

In the *Addiscombe* case Jenkins L.J. referred, at p. 528, to the observations of Denning L.J. in *Errington v. Errington and Woods* to the effect that "The test of exclusive possession is by no means decisive." Jenkins L.J. continued:

"I think that wide statement must be treated as qualified by his observations in *Facchini v. Bryson* [1952] 1 T.L.R. 1386, 1389; and it seems to me that, save in exceptional cases of the kind mentioned by Denning L.J. in that case, the law remains that the fact of exclusive possession, if not decisive against the view that there is a mere licence, as distinct from a tenancy, is at all events a consideration of the first importance."

Exclusive possession is of first importance in considering whether an occupier is a tenant; exclusive possession is not decisive because an occupier who enjoys exclusive possession is not necessarily a tenant. The occupier may be a lodger or service occupier or fall within the other exceptional categories mentioned by Denning L.J. in *Errington v. Errington and Woods* [1952] 1 K.B. 290.

In *Isaac v. Hotel de Paris Ltd* [1960] 1 W.L.R. 239 an employee who managed a night bar in a hotel for his employer company which held a lease of the hotel negotiated "subject to contract" to complete the purchase of shares in the company and to be allowed to run the nightclub for his own benefit if he paid the head rent payable by the company for the hotel. In the expectation that the negotiations "subject to contract" would ripen into a binding agreement, the employee was allowed to run the nightclub and he paid the company's rent. When negotiations broke down the employee claimed unsuccessfully to be a tenant of the hotel company. The circumstances in which the employee was allowed to occupy the premises showed that the hotel company never intended to accept him as a tenant and that he was fully aware of that fact. This was a case, consistent with the authorities cited by Lord Denning in giving the advice of the Judicial Committee of the Privy Council, in which the parties did not intend to enter into contractual relationships unless and until the negotiations "subject to contract" were replaced by a binding contract.

In *Abbeyfield (Harpenden) Society Ltd v. Woods* [1968] 1 W.L.R. 374 the occupier of a room in an old people's home was held to be a licensee and not a tenant. Lord Denning M.R. said, at p. 376:

"The modern cases show that a man may be a licensee even though he has exclusive possession, even though the word 'rent' is used, and even though the word 'tenancy' is used. The court must look at the agreement as a whole and see whether a tenancy really was intended. In this case there is, besides the one room, the provision of services, meals, a resident housekeeper, and such like. The whole arrangement was so personal in nature that the proper inference is that he was a licensee."

As I understand the decision in the *Abbeyfield* case the court came to the conclusion that the occupier was a lodger and was therefore a licensee, not a tenant.

In *Shell-Mex and B.P. Ltd v. Manchester Garages Ltd* [1971] 1 W.L.R. 612 the Court of Appeal after carefully examining an agreement whereby the defendant was allowed to use a petrol company's filling station for the purposes of selling petrol, came to the conclusion that the agreement did not grant exclusive possession to the defendant who was therefore a licensee. At p. 615 Lord Denning M.R. in considering whether the transaction was a licence or a tenancy said:

"Broadly speaking, we have to see whether it is a personal privilege given to a person (in which case it is a licence), or whether it grants an interest in land (in which case it is a tenancy). At one time it used to be thought that exclusive possession was a decisive factor. But that is not so. It depends on broader considerations altogether. Primarily on whether it is personal in its nature or not: see *Errington v. Errington and Woods* [1952] 1 K.B. 290."

In my opinion the agreement was only "personal in its nature" and created "a personal privilege" if the agreement did not confer the right to exclusive possession of the filling station. No other test for distinguishing between a contractual tenancy and a contractual licence appears to be understandable or workable.

Heslop v. Burns [1974] 1 W.L.R. 1241 was another case in which the owner of a cottage allowed a family to live in the cottage rent free and it was held that no tenancy at will had been created on the ground that the parties did not intend any legal relationship. Scarman L.J. cited with approval, at p. 1252, the statement by Denning L.J. in *Facchini v. Bryson* [1952] 1 T.L.R. 1386, 1389:

"In all the cases where an occupier has been held to be a licensee there has been something in the circumstances, such as a family arrangement, an act of friendship or generosity, or such like, to negative any intention to create a tenancy."

In *Marchant v. Charters* [1977] 1 W.L.R. 1181 a bedsitting room was occupied on terms that the landlord cleaned the rooms daily and provided clean linen each week. It was held by the Court of Appeal that the occupier was a licensee and not a tenant. The decision in the case is sustainable on the grounds that the occupier was a lodger and did not enjoy exclusive possession. But Lord Denning M.R. said, at p. 1185:

"What is the test to see whether the occupier of one room in a house is a tenant or a licensee? It does not depend on whether he or she has exclusive possession or not. It does not depend on whether the room is furnished or not. It does not depend on whether the occupation is permanent or temporary. It does not depend on the label which the parties put upon it. All these are factors which may influence the decision but none of them is conclusive. All the circumstances have to be worked out. Eventually the answer depends on the nature and quality of the occupancy. Was it intended that the occupier should have a stake in the room or did he have only permission for himself personally to occupy the room, whether under a contract or not? In which case he is a licensee."

But in my opinion in order to ascertain the nature and quality of the occupancy and to see whether the occupier has or has not a stake in the room or only permission for himself personally to occupy, the court must decide whether upon its true construction the agreement confers on the occupier exclusive possession. If exclusive possession at a rent for a term does not constitute a tenancy then the distinction between a contractual tenancy and a contractual licence of land becomes wholly unidentifiable.

In *Somma v. Hazelhurst* [1978] 1 W.L.R. 1014, a young unmarried couple H. and S. occupied a double bedsitting room for which they paid a weekly rent. The landlord did not provide services or attendance and the couple were not lodgers but tenants enjoying exclusive possession. But the Court of Appeal did not ask themselves whether H. and S. were lodgers or tenants and did not draw the correct conclusion from the fact that H. and S. enjoyed exclusive possession. The Court of Appeal were diverted from the correct inquiries by the fact that the landlord obliged H. and S. to enter into separate agreements and reserved power to determine each agreement separately. The landlord also insisted that the room should not in form be let to either H. or S. or to both H. and S. but that each should sign an agreement to share the room in common with such other persons as the landlord might from time to time nominate. The sham nature of this obligation would have been only slightly more obvious if H. and S. had been married or if the room had been furnished with a double bed instead of two single beds. If the landlord had served notice on H. to leave and had required S. to share the room with a strange man, the notice would only have been a disguised notice to quit on both H. and S. The room was let and taken as residential accommodation with exclusive possession in order that H. and S. might live together in undisturbed quasi-connubial bliss making weekly payments. The agreements signed by H. and S. constituted the grant to H. and S. jointly of exclusive possession at a rent for a term for the purposes for which the room was taken and the agreement therefore created a tenancy. Although the Rent Acts must not be allowed to alter or influence the construction of an agreement, the court should, in my opinion, be astute to detect and frustrate sham devices and artificial transactions whose only object is to disguise the grant of a tenancy and to evade the Rent Acts. I would disapprove of the decision in this case that H. and S. were only licensees and for the same reason would disapprove of the decision in *Aldrington Garages Ltd v. Fielder* (1978) 37 P. & C.R. 461 and *Sturolson & Co. v. Weniz* (1984) 272 E.G. 326.

In the present case the Court of Appeal (1984) 49 P. & C.R. 324 held that the agreement dated 7 March 1983 only created a licence. Slade L.J., at p. 329, accepted that the agreement and in particular clause 3 of the agreement "shows that the right to occupy the premises conferred on the defendant was intended as an exclusive right of occupation, in that it was thought necessary to give a special and express power to the plaintiff to enter. ..." Before your Lordships it was conceded that the agreement conferred the right of exclusive possession on Mrs Mountford. Even without clause 3 the result would have been the same. By the agreement Mrs Mountford was granted the right to occupy residential accommodation. The landlord did not provide any services or attendance. It was plain that Mrs Mountford was not a lodger. Slade L.J. proceeded to analyse all the provisions of the agreement, not for the purpose of deciding whether his finding of exclusive possession was correct, but for the purpose of assigning some of the provisions of the agreement to the category of terms which he thought are usually to be found in a tenancy agreement and of assigning other provisions to the category of terms which he thought are usually to be found in a licence. Slade L.J. may or may not have been right that in a letting of a furnished room it was "most unusual to find a provision in a tenancy agreement obliging the tenant to keep his rooms in a 'tidy condition' " (p. 329). If Slade L.J. was right about this and other provisions there is still no logical method of evaluating the results of his survey. Slade L.J. reached the conclusion that "the agreement bears all the hallmarks of a licence rather than a tenancy save for the one important feature of exclusive occupation": p. 329. But in addition to the hallmark of exclusive occupation of residential accommodation there were the hallmarks of weekly payments for a periodical term. Unless these three hallmarks are decisive, it really becomes impossible to distinguish a contractual tenancy from a contractual licence save by reference to the professed intention of the parties or by the judge awarding marks for drafting. Slade L.J. was finally impressed by the statement at the foot of the agreement by Mrs Mountford "I understand and accept that a licence in the above form does not and is not intended to give me a tenancy protected under the Rent Acts." Slade L.J. said, at p. 330:

> "it seems to me that, if the defendant is to displace the express statement of intention embodied in the declaration, she must show that the declaration was either a deliberate sham or at least an inaccurate statement of what was the true substance of the real transaction agreed between the parties; . . ."

My Lords, the only intention which is relevant is the intention demonstrated by the agreement to grant exclusive possession for a term at a rent. Sometimes it may be difficult to discover whether, on the true construction of an agreement, exclusive possession is conferred. Sometimes it may appear from the surrounding circumstances that there was no intention to create legal relationships. Sometimes it may appear from the surrounding circumstances that the right to exclusive possession is referable to a legal relationship other than a tenancy. Legal relationships to which the grant of exclusive possession might be referable and which would or might negative the grant of an estate or interest in the land include occupancy under a contract for the sale of the land, occupancy pursuant to a contract of employment or occupancy referable to the holding of an office. But where as in the present case the only circumstances are that residential accommodation is offered and accepted with exclusive possession for a term at a rent, the result is a tenancy.

The position was well summarised by Windeyer J. sitting in the High Court of Australia in *Radaich v. Smith* (1959) 101 C.L.R. 209, 222, where he said:

> "What then is the fundamental right which a tenant has that distinguishes his position from that of a licensee? It is an interest in land as distinct from a personal permission to enter the land and use it for some stipulated purpose or purposes. And how is it to be ascertained whether such an interest in land has been given? By seeing whether the grantee was given a legal right of exclusive possession of the land for a term or from year to year or for a life or lives. If he was, he is a tenant. And he cannot be other than a tenant, because a legal right of exclusive possession is a tenancy and the creation of such a right is a demise. To say that a man who has, by agreement with a landlord, a right of exclusive possession of land for a term is not a tenant is simply to contradict the first proposition by the second. A right of exclusive possession is secured by the right of a lessee to maintain ejectment and, after his entry, trespass. A reservation to the landlord, either by contract or statute, of a limited right of entry, as for example to view or repair, is, of course, not inconsistent with the grant of exclusive possession. Subject to such reservations, a tenant for a term or from year to year or for a life or lives can exclude his landlord as well as strangers from the demised premises. All this is long established law: see *Cole on Ejectment* (1857) pp. 72, 73, 287, 458."

My Lords, I gratefully adopt the logic and the language of Windeyer J. Henceforth the courts which deal with these problems will, save in exceptional circumstances, only be concerned to inquire whether as a result of an agreement relating to residential accommodation the occupier is a lodger or a tenant. In the present case I am satisfied that Mrs Mountford is a tenant, that the appeal should be allowed, that the order of the Court of Appeal should be set aside and that the respondent should be ordered to pay the costs of the appellant here and below.

NOTES:

1. For comment, see Clarke [1985] All E.R.Rev. 190; Tromans [1985] C.L.J. 351; Street (as in *Street v. Mountford*) [1985] Conv. 328; Anderson (1985) 48 M.L.R. 712; Clarke [1986] Conv. 39; Bridge [1986] Conv. 344.

2. For a judicial analysis of the speech of Lord Templeman, see *Hadjiloucas v. Crean* [1988] 1 W.L.R. 1006, 1020–1022 *per* Mustill L.J.:

> I now return to those aspects of *Street v. Mountford* which gave rise to particular debate on the argument of the present appeal. The first stems from the reliance placed by counsel on the following passages from the speech of Lord Templeman, at pp. 817, 827:
>
>> "In the case of residential accommodation there is no difficulty in deciding whether the grant confers exclusive possession. An occupier of residential accommodation for a rent is either a lodger or a tenant. ...
>> Henceforth the courts which deal with these problems will, save in exceptional circumstances, only be concerned to inquire whether as a result of an agreement relating to residential accommodation the occupier is a lodger or a tenant."
>
> If these passages are plucked from their context, they can well be understood as conveying that the only issues which the judge is required to consider where the application of the Rent Acts is in question are whether the occupier is a lodger and whether he or she falls into one of the special categories identified by Lord Templeman, such as an owner in fee simple, a trespasser, a mortgagee in possession, a service occupier, and so on. In my judgment, however, it becomes quite plain, once the speech is read as a whole, that this is not what the two passages are intended to convey. Since, however, the hard-pressed judge or recorder in a busy county court will not always have the opportunity for careful perusal of that speech, it may be useful to suggest a way in which it may be analysed.
>
> Lord Templeman began by contrasting the two views of the law which had been advanced in argument. The traditional view, for which the occupier contended, was that the distinction between a tenancy and a licence of land lay in the grant of land at a rent with exclusive possession. A licensee lacking exclusive possession could not be said to own any estate in the land. As I read it, the whole of the speech between pp. 816 and 818, in the midst of which we find the first of the passages under review, was an exposition of this traditional view, which Lord Templeman plainly regarded as still being good law, followed by an application of it to the facts of the instant case. That led inevitably to the conclusion that Mrs Mountford was a tenant, since it was never suggested that she fell into one of the special categories, and it was expressly conceded in the House of Lords (see pp. 816B, 818D, 823B and 826D) that the effect of the agreement was to give her exclusive possession.
>
> Lord Templeman then proceeded to deal in chronological order with the authorities cited in favour of the argument for the landlords, which was essentially that the intention of the parties should be predominant and that a person with exclusive possession and not in one of the special categories could still be a licensee if it could be seen that this was what the parties had desired. Some of the authorities discussed by Lord Templeman were treated as instances where it could be seen that the parties had not set out to create a legal relationship: see *Booker v. Palmer* [1942] 2 All E.R. 674; *Marcroft Wagons Ltd v. Smith* [1951] 2 K.B. 496; *Cobb v. Lane* [1952] 1 T.L.R. 1037; *Isaac v. Hotel de Paris Ltd* [1960] 1 W.L.R. 239. These need not be explored here. It is, however, instructive to look briefly at the way in which the others were explained.
>
> First, there was *Errington v. Errington and Woods* [1952] 1 K.B. 290 which Lord Templeman treated as falling within the special categories. He went on to say [1985] A.C. 809, 821:
>
>> "These exceptional circumstances are not to be found in the present case where there has been the lawful, independent and voluntary grant of exclusive possession for a term at a rent."
>
> Next, in the context of a discussion of *Facchini v. Bryson* [1952] 1 T.L.R. 1386, Lord Templeman said, at p. 822, "The decision also indicated that in a simple case a grant

of exclusive possession of residential accommodation for a weekly sum creates a tenancy". *Murray Bull & Co. Ltd v. Murray* [1953] 1 Q.B. 211 was regarded, at p. 822, as having been wrongly decided through a failure to distinguish between conduct which negatives an intention to create a legal relationship, special circumstances which prevent exclusive occupation from creating a tenancy, and the professed intention of the parties. *Addiscombe Garden Estates Ltd v. Crabbe* [1958] 1 Q.B. 513 was a case where, when the document had been narrowly examined, it could be seen that it granted exclusive possession. Lord Templeman added, at p. 823:

> "Exclusive possession is of first importance in considering whether an occupier is a tenant; exclusive possession is not decisive because an occupier who enjoys exclusive possession is not necessarily a tenant."

Then, in the context of a dictum of Lord Denning M.R. in *Shell-Mex and B.P. Ltd v. Manchester Garages Ltd* [1971] 1 W.L.R. 612 Lord Templeman went on to say, at p. 824:

> "In my opinion the agreement was only 'personal in its nature' and created 'a personal privilege' if the agreement did not confer the right to exclusive possession of the filling station. No other test for distinguishing between a contractual tenancy and a contractual licence appears to be ... workable."

Finally, after quoting from another dictum of Lord Denning M.R., this time in *Marchant v. Charters* [1977] 1 W.L.R. 1181, 1185, Lord Templeman said, at p. 825:

> "But in my opinion in order to ascertain the nature and quality of the occupancy and to see whether the occupier has or has not a stake in the room or only permission for himself personally to occupy, the court must decide whether upon its true construction the agreement confers on the occupier exclusive possession. If exclusive possession at a rent for a term does not constitute a tenancy then the distinction between a contractual tenancy and a contractual licence of land become wholly unidentifiable."

With the exception of a discussion of three cases on shared occupancy, to which I will return at a later stage, this concluded Lord Templeman's review of the English authorities. He then proceeded to deal with the instant case, stating, at pp. 826–827, his disagreement with the view expressed by Slade L.J. (1984) 49 P. & C.R. 324, 329, on the ground that:

> "the only intention which is relevant is the intention demonstrated by the agreement to grant exclusive possession for a term at a rent. Sometimes it may be difficult to discover whether, on the true construction of an agreement, exclusive possession is conferred. Sometimes it may appear from the surrounding circumstances that there was no intention to create legal relationships. Sometimes it may appear from the surrounding circumstances that the right to exclusive possession is referable to a legal relationship other than a tenancy ... But where as in the present case the only circumstances are that residential accommodation is offered and accepted with exclusive possession for a term at a rent, the result is a tenancy."

It is at the very end of this extended discussion of the cases that one finds the second of the passages which were relied on in the present case, and which I have already quoted.

Now it seems to me quite plain on a reading of the speech as a whole that when Lord Templeman referred to the "occupier" in the two passages under review, the word was implicitly qualified by "exclusive", just as "occupier" and "possession" had been similarly qualified on more than 50 occasions in the course of the speech. Otherwise, there would be a conflict with the theme of the discussion, which was to the effect that (a) an occupier cannot be a tenant unless his occupation is exclusive; and (b) an occupier for a fixed term at a rent will be a tenant unless he falls into one of the special categories. Nor can Lord Templeman have intended to convey, in the first of the passages under discussion, that for the purpose of deciding a case of the present kind the judge has merely to rule out the possibility that the occupier is a lodger to find that the occupation is exclusive, for such reasoning would treat exclusive occupation as the consequence of a tenancy, whereas elsewhere it is made clear that it is a prerequisite. The core of the decision is, as it seems to me, the passage at p. 826 from which I have already quoted.

Since an intention to confer exclusive possession was conceded in *Street v. Mountford* [1985] A.C. 809 the decision has nothing directly to say about the manner in which the existence of such an intention should be ascertained. Sometimes the task will be straightforward (see p. 817H) and sometimes it will be difficult (see p. 826H). The terms of the agreement will always be of prime importance, though not always decisive. Sometimes a meticulous perusal of the document will be required, as in *Addiscombe Garden Estates Ltd v. Crabbe* [1958] 1 Q.B. 513 and *Shell-Mex and B.P. Ltd v. Manchester Garages Ltd* [1971] 1 W.L.R. 612; on other occasions it will not. The surrounding circumstances will always be material on this point as well as on the questions of sham and intention to create legal relations. *Street v. Mountford* does not itself explain how the exercise is to be performed, but I do not read Lord Templeman's speech as suggesting that special techniques are to be applied any different from those of the ordinary law of contract: and there is, of course, nothing inconsistent in this with the principle, now well established, that the court must be careful not to allow any camouflage to prevent the transaction from being seen for what is really is.

3. Analysis of the issues is somewhat confused by the inconsistent use of the terms "exclusive possession" and "exclusive occupation" and by the failure to distinguish between these concepts as statements of fact and statements of legal entitlement. It is suggested that the term "exclusive occupation" should be used to denote the fact that the occupier(s) enjoy sole occupation; and that the term "exclusive possession" should be reserved for those situations where the occupier(s) have the legal right to exclude all other persons (including the landlord) from the property. Adopting this terminology, it seems that the speech of Lord Templeman may be analysed as follows:

   (i) Exclusive occupation without more is insufficient to create a tenancy: exclusive possession is required.

   (ii) There is no exclusive possession and thus no tenancy where the owner of the property and the exclusive occupier do not intend to create a legal relationship or where the circumstances negative the intention that the exclusive occupier is to have exclusive possession and thus the legal entitlement to exclude the owner. One or both of these two factors (which seem not to be mutually exclusive) may explain the pre-*Street v. Mountford* decisions where occupiers who had apparently been granted exclusive possession were held not to be tenants. The latter factor would seem to provide the explanation for the denial of tenant status to occupiers of serviced accommodation and, in particular, the tenant/lodger distinction.

   (iii) In the absence of any such negative factor, the exclusive occupier would probably be held to have exclusive possession.

   (iv) An occupier who is found to have been granted exclusive possession (for a certain term at a rent) would be presumed to be a tenant.

   (v) Even where the exclusive occupier has exclusive possession and thus the legal right to exclude all other persons from the property, that right may be attributable to a legal relationship other than a tenancy such as fee simple ownership.

4. As noted by Mustill L.J. in *Hadjiloucas v. Crean*, the House of Lords was not required to consider whether exclusive possession had been granted: it was conceded that it had. However, Lord Templeman did purport to expound the overriding principle for the determination of that question. Provided that the parties intended to create *a* legal relationship, the subjective intention of the parties is of no relevance: the "nature and quality" of the occupation, in particular whether the occupier has been granted exclusive possession, depends upon the effect of the agreement between the parties: [1985] A.C. 809, 819, 825. First, the legal characterisation and consequences of the transaction resulting from the agreement cannot be determined by the label attached by the parties nor can it be overriden by express agreement between the parties: *Street v. Mountford, supra; Duke v. Wynne* [1990] 1 W.L.R. 766. Secondly, in determining the effect of the agreement "the court should be astute to detect and frustrate sham devices and artificial transactions whose only object is to disguise the grant of a tenancy and to evade the Rent Acts": *Street v. Mountford, supra*, 825. In construing an agreement the courts are prepared to ignore particular provisions, which would prima facie preclude a tenancy, if the surrounding circumstances reveal that such provisions could not have been intended to form part of the substance of the agreement: see, *e.g. Markou v. Da Silvaesa* (1986) 52 P. & C.R. 204; *Aslan v. Murphy (No. 1)* [1990] 1 W.L.R. 766, where the court struck out a provision which purported to exclude the occupier from the premises between 10.30 a.m. and 12 noon each day; and see *Antoniades v. Villiers* [1990] 1 A.C. 417, *infra*, p. 380. Thirdly, in the context of shared occupation, where the owner has required the occupiers to sign separate agreements, the courts may insist on reading the agreements together, and treating them as one transaction, if the surrounding circumstances indicate that they are in fact interdependent: see *A.G. Securities v. Vaughan; Antoniades v. Villiers, infra*, p. 380.

5. In *Burrows v. Brent LBC* (1996) 29 H.L.R. 167 the former landlord had obtained a possession order against the former tenant for non-payment of rent; but it agreed temporarily not to execute the order and to permit the former tenant to remain in occupation on condition that she continued to pay a sum equivalent to the rent and a sum off the arrears. The House of Lords held that, pending any revival of the former tenancy, the parties did not intend to create any legal relationship and that the former tenant was a "tolerated trespasser". See also *Westminster City Council v. Basson* (1990) 62 P. & C.R. 57.

6. Recognition of the nature and significance of the tenant/lodger distinction is important. First, in *Markou v. Da Silvaesa, supra*, it was stated that the distinction arises not from the provision of attendance or services *per se* but from the fact that such provision requires the landlord to exercise unrestricted access to, and use of, the premises: *ibid*. 211 *per* Ralph Gibson L.J. However, the courts have adopted different views as to whether the relevant consideration is the access that would be required to provide the services to which the occupier is entitled under the terms of the agreement: see *Marchant v. Charters* [1977] 1 W.L.R. 1181, 1186 *per* Lord Denning M.R.; *Markou v. Da Silvaesa, supra*, 211 *per* Ralph Gibson L.J.; *Huwyler v. Ruddy* (1995) 28 H.L.R. 550, 555–556 *per* Peter Gibson L.J.; or whether the courts should

consider the services actually provided and thus the extent to which the landlord actually exercises his right of access: see *Aslan v. Murphy (No. 1)* [1990] 1 W.L.R. 766, 773 *per* Lord Donaldson M.R. Secondly, since the distinction turns on the right of unrestricted access, it is therefore just one of a number of factors which may negative exclusive possession; it does not follow that an exclusive occupier must be either a lodger or a tenant: *Brooker Settled Estates Ltd v. Ayers* (1987) 54 P. & C.R. 165.

7. The decision in *Street v. Mountford* has generated a significant amount of litigation in the context of the provision of accommodation by local authorities, pursuant to their duties in relation to the homeless under the Housing Act 1985 (now Part VII of the Housing Act 1996). In *Ogwr BC v. Dykes* [1989] 1 W.L.R. 295, noted at [1989] Conv. 192, the Court of Appeal held that, notwithstanding that the occupiers had been granted exclusive possession, the fact that the local authority provided the accommodation pursuant to its statutory duties towards the homeless negatived any intention to create a tenancy. In *Family Housing Association v. Jones* [1990] 1 W.L.R. 779, noted at [1990] Conv. 397, the accommodation was arranged by a housing association on referral from the local authority; but the Court of Appeal held that, where exclusive possession had been granted, the homelessness "background" did not negative the consequences of that grant (and see *infra*). Moreover, in *Westminster City Council v. Clarke* [1992] 2 A.C. 288, noted at [1992] Conv. 113, 285, the House of Lords emphasised the duties and responsibilities of the local authority but those factors were held to negative the grant of exclusive possession; and again in *Camden LBC v. Shortlife Community Housing Ltd* (1992) 90 L.G.R. 358 the homelessness "background" was held to negative the grant of exclusive possession rather than the consequences of such a grant. The approach of the courts in the later cases seems to place greater emphasis on the question of exclusive possession and to narrow the potential scope of the factors negativing the creation of a tenancy despite an apparent grant of exclusive possession: see [1993] Conv. 157.

A further dimension to this issue was considered in *Bruton v. London and Quadrant Housing Trust*. The housing trust was granted a licence by the local authority to arrange temporary accommodation in property owned by the local authority. The agreement between the housing trust and the occupier stated that the housing trust had no legal title to the property and the parties proceeded on the basis that they were creating a licence rather than a tenancy. In those circumstances the Court of Appeal [1998] Q.B. 834, noted at (1998) 114 L.Q.R. 345, held that the absence of legal title precluded the housing trust from granting a tenancy. (The court noted that a tenancy was held to have been granted in very similar circumstances in *Family Housing Association v. Jones, supra*, but that the Court of Appeal in that case appeared to have overlooked the fact that the housing association had no title to the property in question.) However, on appeal, the House of Lords ([1999] 3 W.L.R. 150) applied the decision in *Family Housing Association v. Jones* and held that the absence of legal title was irrelevant.

The significance of the lease/licence distinction in this context has been reduced by the removal of secure tenancy status from tenancies granted pursuant to the statutory duties: Housing Act 1996, s.216(3), Sched. 17, para. 3.

8. In *Gray v. Taylor* [1998] 1 W.L.R. 1093 the Court of Appeal held that a right of exclusive possession in an almshouse did not create a tenancy: the right to exclusive possession was referable to the relationship of trustee and beneficiary; it was only by reason of that relationship that the trustees had the power to grant the right; and the grant of a tenancy might obstruct the duties of the trustees.

9. Although *Street v. Mountford* involved residential occupation, and certain aspects of the decision (notably the tenant/lodger dichotomy) are inapplicable in the context of non-residential occupation, the renewed emphasis on the primacy of exclusive possession has been acknowledged in the context of commercial occupation: see, *e.g. London & Associated Investment Trust Ltd v. Calow* (1986) 53 P. & C.R. 340, 352 *per* Judge Paul Baker Q.C.; *Dellneed Ltd v. Chin* (1987) 53 P. & C.R. 172, 187 *per* Millett J.; *Smith v. Northside Developments Ltd* (1988) 55 P. & C.R. 164, 166–167 *per* Sir John Arnold, noted at [1989] Conv. 55; *Hunts Refuse Disposals Ltd v. Norfolk Environmental Waste Services Ltd* [1997] 1 E.G.L.R. 16, 18 *per* Hutchison L.J.; but see the more ambivalent approach in *Dresden Estates Ltd v. Collinson* (1988) 55 P. & C.R. 47, 51–52 *per* Glidewell L.J., noted at [1987] Conv. 220; (1987) 50 M.L.R. 655.

10. *Street v. Mountford* was a case of single occupation: multiple occupation introduces further complicating factors.

A.G. Securities v. Vaughan; Antoniades v. Villiers [1990] 1 A.C. 417

(HL, Lord Bridge, Lord Templeman, Lord Ackner, Lord Oliver, Lord Jauncey)

[The facts are stated in the judgment of Lord Oliver.]

LORD OLIVER:
My Lords, since lettings of residential property of an appropriate rateable value attract the consequences of controlled rent and security of tenure provided by the Rent Acts, it is not, perhaps, altogether surprising that those who derive their income from residential property are constantly seeking to attain the not always reconcilable objectives on the one hand of keeping their property gainfully occupied and, on the other, of framing their contractual arrangements with the occupants in such a way as to avoid, if they can, the application of the Acts. Since it is only a letting which attracts the operation of the Acts, such endeavours normally take the form of entering into contractual arrangements designed, on their face, to ensure that no estate is created in the occupant for the time being and that his occupation of the land derives merely from a personal and revocable permission granted by way of licence. The critical question, however, in every case is not simply how the arrangement is presented to the outside world in the relevant documentation, but what is the true nature of the arrangement. The decision of this House in *Street v. Mountford* [1985] A.C. 809 established quite clearly that if the true legal effect of the arrangement entered into is that the occupier of residential property has exclusive possession of the property for an ascertainable period in return for periodical money payments, a tenancy is created, whatever the label the parties may have chosen to attach to it. Where, as in that case,

the circumstances show that the occupant is the only occupier realistically contemplated and the premises are inherently suitable only for single occupation, there is, generally, very little difficulty. Such an occupier normally has exclusive possession, as indeed she did in *Street v. Mountford*, where such possession was conceded, unless the owner retains control and unrestricted access for the purpose of providing attendance and services. As my noble and learned friend, Lord Templeman, observed in that case, the occupier in those circumstances is either a lodger or a tenant. Where, however, the premises are such as, by their nature, to lend themselves to multiple occupation and they are in fact occupied in common by a number of persons under different individual agreements with the owner, more difficult problems arise. These two appeals, at different ends of the scale, are illustrations of such problems.

The relevant facts have been fully set out in the speech of my noble and learned friend, Lord Templeman, which I have had the advantage of reading in draft, and I reiterate them only to the extent necessary to emphasise the points which appear to me to be of critical importance.

Antoniades v. Villiers and another

The appellants in this appeal are a young couple who at all material times were living together as man and wife. In about November 1984 they learned from a letting agency that a flat was available in a house at 6, Whiteley Road, London S.E. 19, owned by the respondent, Mr Antoniades. They inspected the flat together and were told that the rent would be £174 per month. They were given the choice of having the bedroom furnished with a double bed or two single beds and they chose a double bed. So, right from the inception, there was never any question but that the appellants were seeking to establish a joint home and they have, at all material times, been the sole occupants of the flat.

There is equally no question but that the premises are not suitable for occupation by more than one couple, save on a very temporary basis. The small living-room contains a sofa capable of being converted into a double bed and also a bed-table capable of being opened out to form a narrow single bed. The appellants did in fact have a friend to stay with them for a time in what the trial judge found to be cramped conditions, but the size of the accommodation and the facilities available clearly do not make the flat suitable for multiple occupation. When it came to drawing up the contractual arrangements under which the appellants were to be let into possession, each was asked to and did sign a separate licence agreement in the terms set out in the speech of my noble and learned friend, Lord Templeman, under which each assumed an individual, but not a joint, responsibility for payment of one half of the sum of £174 previously quoted as the rent.

There is an air of total unreality about these documents read as separate and individual licences in the light of the circumstance that the appellants were together seeking a flat as a quasi-matrimonial home. A separate licensee does not realistically assume responsibility for all repairs and all outgoings. Nor in the circumstances can any realistic significance be given to clauses 16 and 17 of the document. It cannot realistically have been contemplated that the respondent would either himself use or occupy any part of the flat or put some other person in to share accommodation specifically adapted for the occupation by a couple living together. These clauses cannot be considered as seriously intended to have any practical operation or to serve any purpose apart from the purely technical one of seeking to avoid the ordinary legal consequences attendant upon letting the appellants into possession at a monthly rent. The unreality is enhanced by the reservation of the right of eviction without court order, which cannot seriously have been thought to be effective, and by the accompanying agreement not to get married, which can only have been designed to prevent a situation arising in which it would be quite impossible to argue that the "licensees" were enjoying separate rights of occupation.

The conclusion seems to me irresistible that these two so-called licences, executed contemporaneously and entered into in the circumstances already outlined, have to be read together as constituting in reality one single transaction under which the appellants became joint occupiers. That of course does not conclude the case because the question still remains, what is the effect?

The document is clearly based upon the form of document which was upheld by the Court of Appeal as an effective licence in *Somma v. Hazelhurst* [1978] 1 W.L.R. 1014. That case, which rested on what was said to be the impossibility of the two licensees having between them exclusive possession, was overruled in *Street v. Mountford* [1985] A.C. 809. It was, however, a case which related to a single room and it is suggested that a similar agreement relating to premises containing space which could, albeit uncomfortably, accommodate another person is not necessarily governed by the same principle. On the other hand, the trial judge found that apart from the few visits by the respondent (who, on all but one occasion, sought admission by knocking on the door) no one shared with the appellants and that they had exclusive possession. He held that the licences were "artificial transactions designed to evade the Rent Acts," that a tenancy was created and that the appellants occupied as joint tenants.

His decision was reversed by the Court of Appeal, *ante*, p. 438E, on, broadly, the grounds that he had erred in treating the subsequent conduct of the parties as admissible as an aid to construction of the agreements and that in so far as the holding above referred to constituted a finding that the licences were a sham, that was unsupported by the evidence inasmuch as the appellants' intention that they should enjoy exclusive possession was not shared by the respondent. The licences could not, therefore, be said to mask the real intention of the parties and fell to be construed by reference to what they said in terms.

If the documents fall to be taken seriously at their face value and to be construed according to their terms, I see, for my part, no escape from the conclusion at which the Court of Appeal arrived. If it is once accepted that the respondent enjoyed the right—whether he exercised it or not—to share the accommodation with the appellants, either himself or by introducing one or more other persons to use the flat with them, it is, as it seems to me, incontestable that the appellants cannot claim to have had exclusive possession. The appellants' case therefore rests, as Mr Colyer frankly admits, upon upholding the judge's approach that the true transaction contemplated was that the appellants should jointly enjoy exclusive possession and that the licences were mere sham or window-dressing to indicate legal incidents which were never seriously intended in fact, but which would be inconsistent with the application to that transaction of the Rent Acts. Now to begin with, I do not, for my part, read the notes of the judge's judgment as showing that he construed the agreement in the light of what the parties subsequently did. I agree entirely with the Court of Appeal that if he did that he was in error. But though subsequent conduct is irrelevant as an aid to construction, it is certainly admissible as evidence on the question of whether the documents were or were not genuine documents giving effect to the parties' true intentions. Broadly what is said by Mr Colyer is that nobody acquainted with the circumstances in which the parties had come together and with the physical lay-out and size of the premises could seriously have imagined that the clauses in the licence which, on the face of them, contemplate the respondent and an apparently limitless number of other persons moving in to share the whole of the available accommodation, including the bedroom, with what, to all intents and purposes, was a married couple committed to paying £174 a month in advance, were anything other than a smoke-screen; and the fact that the respondent, who might be assumed to want to make the maximum profit out of the premises, never sought to introduce anyone else is at least some indication that that is exactly what it was. Adopting the definition of a sham formulated by Purchase L.J. in *Hadjiloucas v. Crean* [1988] 1 W.L.R. 1006, 1013, Mr Colyer submits that the licences clearly incorporate clauses by which neither party intended to be bound and which were obviously a smoke-screen to cover the real intentions of both contracting parties. In the Court of Appeal, *ante*, pp. 446H–447A,

Bingham L.J. tested the matter by asking two questions, viz: (1) on what grounds, if one party had left the premises, could the remaining party have been made liable for anything more than the £87 which he or she had agreed to pay, and (2) on what ground could they have resisted a demand by the respondent to introduce a further person into the premises? For my part, however, I do not see how this helps. The assumed negative answers prove nothing, for they rest upon the assumption that the licences are not sham documents, which is the very question in issue.

If the real transaction was, as the judge found, one under which the appellants became joint tenants with exclusive possession, on the footing that the two agreements are to be construed together, then it would follow that they were together jointly and severally responsible for the whole rent. It would equally follow that they could effectively exclude the respondent and his nominees.

Although the facts are not precisely on all fours with *Somma v. Hazelhurst* [1978] 1 W.L.R. 1014, they are strikingly similar and the judge was, in my judgment, entitled to conclude that the appellants had exclusive possession of the premises. I read his finding that, "the licences are artificial transactions designed to evade the Rent Acts" as a finding that they were sham documents designed to conceal the true nature of the transaction. There was, in my judgment, material on which he could properly reach this conclusion and I, too, would allow the appeal.

A. G. Securities v. Vaughan and others

The facts in this appeal are startlingly different from those in the case of *Antoniades*. To begin with the appeal concerns a substantial flat in a mansion block consisting of four bedrooms, a lounge, a sitting-room and usual offices. The trial judge found, as a fact, that the premises could without difficulty provide residential accommodation for four persons. There is no question but that the agreements with which the appeal is concerned reflect the true bargain between the parties. It is the purpose and intention of both parties to each agreement that it should confer an individual right on the licensee named, that he should be liable only for the payment which he had undertaken, and that his agreement should be capable of termination without reference to the agreements with other persons occupying the flat. The judge found that the agreements were not shams and that each of the four occupants had arrived independently of one another and not as a group. His finding was that there was never a group of persons coming to the flat all together. That has been challenged because, it is said, the evidence established that initially in 1977 and 1978 there was one occupant who was joined by three others who, although they came independently and not as a trio, moved in at about the same time. Central heating was then installed, so that the weekly payments fell to be increased and new agreements were signed by the four occupants contemporaneously. Speaking for myself, I cannot see how this can make any difference to the terms upon which the individuals were in occupation. If they were in as licensees in the first instance, the mere replacement of their agreements by new agreements in similar form cannot convert them into tenants, and the case has, in my judgment, to be approached on the footing that agreements with the occupiers were entered into separately and individually. The only questions are those of the effect of each agreement *vis-à-vis* the individual licensee and whether the agreements collectively had the effect of creating a joint tenancy among the occupants of the premises for the time being by virtue of their having between them exclusive possession of the premises.

Taking first, by way of example, the position of the first occupier to be let into the premises on the terms of one of these agreements, it is, in my judgment, quite unarguable, once any question of sham is out of the way, that he has an estate in the premises which entitles him to exclusive possession. His right, which is, by definition, a right to share use and occupation with such other persons not exceeding three in number as the licensor shall introduce from time to time, is clearly inconsistent with any exclusive possession in him alone even though he may be the only person in physical occupation at a particular time. He has no legal title which will permit him to exclude other persons to whom the licensor may choose to grant the privilege of entry. That must equally apply to the additional licensees who join him. None of them has individually nor have they collectively the right or power lawfully to exclude a further nominee of the licensor within the prescribed maximum.

I pause to note that it has never been contended that any individual occupier has a tenancy of a particular room in the flat with a right to use the remainder of the flat in common with the tenants of other rooms. I can envisage that as a possibility in cases of arrangements of this kind if the facts support the marking out with the landlord's concurrence of a particular room as the exclusive domain of a particular individual. But to support that there would, I think, have to be proved the grant of an identifiable part of the flat and that simply does not fit with the system described in the evidence of the instant case.

The real question—and it is this upon which the respondents rely—is what is the position when the flat is occupied concurrently by all four licensees? What is said then is that since the licensor has now exhausted, for the time being, his right of nomination, the four occupants collectively have exclusive possession of the premises because they can collectively exclude the licensor himself. Because, it is argued, (1) they have thus exclusive possession, and (2) there is an ascertainable term during which all have the right to use and occupy, and (3) they are occupying in consideration of the payment of periodic sums of money, *Street v. Mountford* [1985] A.C. 809 shows that they are collectively tenants of the premises. They are not lodgers. Therefore they must be tenants. And because each is not individually a tenant, they must together be joint tenants.

My Lords, there appear to me to be a number of fallacies here. In the first place, the assertion of an exclusive possession rests, as it seems to me, upon assuming what it is sought to prove. If, of course, each licence agreement creates a tenancy, each tenant will be sharing with other persons whose rights to be there rest upon their own estates which, once they have been granted, they enjoy in their own right independently of the landlord. Collectively they have the right to exclude everyone other than those who have concurrent estates. But if the licence agreement is what it purports to be, that is to say, merely an agreement for permissive enjoyment as the invitee of the landlord, then each shares the use of the premises with other invitees of the same landlord. The landlord is not excluded for he continues to enjoy the premises through his invitees, even though he may for the time being have precluded himself by contract with each from withdrawing the invitation. Secondly, the fact that under each agreement an individual has the privilege of user and occupation for a term which overlaps the term of user and occupation of other persons in the premises, does not create a single indivisible term of occupation for all four consisting of an amalgam of the individual overlapping periods. Thirdly, there is no single sum of money payable in respect of use and occupation. Each person is individually liable for the amount which he has agreed, which may differ in practice from the amounts paid by all or some of the others.

The respondents are compelled to support their claims by a strange and unnatural theory that, as each occupant terminates his agreement, there is an implied surrender by the other three and an implied grant of a new joint tenancy to them together with the new incumbent when he enters under his individual agreement. With great respect to the majority in the Court of Appeal, this appears to me to be entirely unreal. For my part, I agree with the dissenting judgment of Sir George Waller in finding no unity of interest, no unity of title, certainly no unity of time and, as I think, no unity of possession. I find it impossible to say that the agreements entered into with the respondents created either individually or collectively a single tenancy either of the entire flat or of any part of it. I agree that the appeal should be allowed.

NOTES:

1. For comment, see Clarke [1989] All E.R.Rev. 171; Harpum [1989] C.L.J. 19; Smith [1989] Conv. 128; Baker (1989) 105 L.Q.R. 165; Hill (1989) 52 M.L.R. 408.

2. In the context of multiple or shared occupation, legal characterisation of the arrangements is not a simple choice between licence and tenancy: the occupiers may be licensees; they may be joint tenants of the whole property; or they may be "parallel" tenants, each occupier having a tenancy of a separate part of the property. In *A.G. Securities v. Vaughan*, all three characterisations were possible but only the first two were argued; in *Antoniades v. Villiers* only the first two characterisations were possible on the facts.

3. In *Mikeover Ltd v. Brady* [1989] 3 All E.R. 618 the Court of Appeal held that two identical agreements which conferred on the occupiers the joint right of exclusive occupation did not create a (joint) tenancy because the obligation of each licensee to pay part only of the rent was genuinely intended to be entirely independent of the obligation of the other licensee. *Antoniades v. Villiers* was distinguished apparently on the ground that the agreements in that case, which included similar obligations in relation to rent, were held to be interdependent and were therefore to be "read together".

4. *A.G. Securities v. Vaughan* was applied in *Stribling v. Wickham* [1989] 2 E.G.L.R. 35, noted at [1989] Conv. 192.

5. The different views of the courts in *Facchini v. Bryson* [1952] I T.L.R. 1386 and *Somma v. Hazelhurst and Savelli* [1978] I W.L.R. 1014 as to the relevance of Rent Act protection in determining lease/licence disputes has been noted. In *Street v. Mountford* Lord Templeman made two references to the Rent Acts (at 819, 825), which together seem to allude to the notoriously elusive distinction between avoidance and evasion of statutory regimes. It is permissible to create an arrangement for residential occupation that falls outside the Rent Acts; but it is not permissible to create an arrangement that objectively falls within the Rent Acts and then to seek to disguise it as an arrangement outside the Rent Acts. In *Stribling v. Wickham* [1989] 2 E.G.L.R. 35 Buckley L.J. (at 38) urged an even-handed approach to the consideration of the question whether the transaction is, or contains, a pretence and whether that pretence is designed to evade the Rent Acts. However, in *A.G. Securities v. Vaughan; Antoniades v. Villiers* Lord Templeman seems to have adopted a much more tenant-oriented stance. He stated (at 458–459):

Parties to an agreement cannot contract out of the Rent Acts; if they were able to do so the Acts would be a dead letter because in a state of housing shortage a person seeking residential accommodation may agree to anything to obtain shelter. The Rent Acts protect a tenant but they do not protect a licensee. Since parties to an agreement cannot contract out of the Rent Acts, a document which expresses the intention, genuine or bogus, of both parties or of one party to create a licence will nevertheless create a tenancy if the rights and obligations enjoyed and imposed satisfy the legal requirements of a tenancy. A person seeking residential accommodation may concur in any expression of intention in order to obtain shelter. Since parties to an agreement cannot contract out of the Rent Acts, a document expressed in the language of a licence must nevertheless be examined and construed by the court in order to decide whether the rights and obligations enjoyed and imposed create a licence or a tenancy. A person seeking residential accommodation may sign a document couched in any language in order to obtain shelter. Since parties to an agreement cannot contract out of the Rent Acts, the grant of a tenancy to two persons jointly cannot be concealed, accidentally or by design, by the creation of two documents in the form of licences. Two persons seeking residential accommodation may sign any number of documents in order to obtain joint shelter. In considering one or more documents for the purpose of deciding whether a tenancy has been created, the court must consider the surrounding circumstances including any relationship between the prospective occupiers, the course of negotiations and the nature and extent of the accommodation and the intended and actual mode of occupation of the accommodation. If the owner of a one-bedroomed flat granted a licence to a husband to occupy the flat provided he shared the flat with his wife and nobody else and granted a similar licence to the wife provided she shared the flat with the husband and nobody else, the court would be bound to consider the effect of both documents together. If the licence to the husband required him to pay a licence fee of £50 per month and the licence to the wife required her to pay a further licence fee of £50 per month, the two documents read together in the light of the property to be occupied and the obvious intended mode of occupation would confer exclusive occupation on the husband and wife jointly and a tenancy at the rent of £100.

Landlords dislike the Rent Acts and wish to enjoy the benefits of letting property without the burden of the restrictions imposed by the Acts. Landlords believe that the Rent Acts unfairly interfere with freedom of contract and exacerbate the housing shortage. Tenants on the other hand believe that the Acts are a necessary protection against the exploitation of people who do not own the freehold or long leases of their homes. The court lacks the knowledge and the power to form any judgment on these arguments which fall to be considered and determined by Parliament. The duty of the court is to enforce the Acts and in so doing to observe one principle which is inherent in the Acts and has been long recognised, the principle that parties cannot contract out of the Acts.

E. Formalities for the Creation of Leases

The landlord and tenant relationship may be created *at law* by a lease, using that term in its technical sense of the document creating the relationship; or *in equity* by a contract for a lease. Provided that the lease complies with the formalities required by law, it creates the legal relationship of landlord and tenant and confers on the tenant a legal term of years which, like all legal estates and interests, is universally enforceable. By contrast, a contract for a lease (including a purported lease which fails to comply with the formalities required by law) does not create the relationship of landlord and tenant at law. On the other hand, if the contract is valid and enforceable, the relationship of landlord and tenant will be created in equity; but the equitable interest thereby created has certain potential disadvantages as compared to a legal lease: in particular, it will be unenforceable against a purchaser from the landlord unless it is protected by the appropriate form of registration or, in the case of registered land, unless it is enforceable as an overriding interest. It follows that the preference will normally be for the legal relationship of landlord and tenant, which requires compliance with certain formalities under the Law of Property Act 1925.

1. Formal requirements for the creation of a legal lease

Law of Property Act 1925, ss.52, 54

Conveyances to be by deed

52.—(1) All conveyances of land or of any interest therein are void for the purpose of conveying or creating a legal estate unless made by deed.

(2) This section does not apply to—

. . .

(d) leases or tenancies or other assurances not required by law to be made in writing;

. . .

Creation of interests in land by parol

54.—(1) All interests in land created by parol and not put in writing and signed by the persons so creating the same, or by their agents thereunto lawfully authorised in writing, have, notwithstanding any consideration having been given for the same, the force and effect of interests at will only.

(2) Nothing in the foregoing provisions of this Part of this Act shall affect the creation by parol of leases taking effect in possession for a term not exceeding three years (whether or not the lessee is given power to extend the term) at the best rent which can be reasonably obtained without taking a fine.

NOTES:

1. For the requirements of a deed, see the Law of Property (Miscellaneous Provisions) Act 1989, s.1, *ante*, p. 64.

2. For the purposes of section 54(2) the term of a lease exceeds three years only if it is initially granted for a fixed period exceeding three years. Thus the category of leases exempted from the formal requirements of section 52(1) includes leases granted for a period not exceeding three years even though they contain an option for renewal which, if exercised, will extend the total period of the exclusive possession of the tenant beyond three years: *Hand v. Hall* (1877) 2 Ex.D. 355, 358 *per* Lord Cairns C.; and it also includes periodic tenancies (assuming that the reference period does not exceed three years): *Re Knight, ex parte Voisey* (1882) 21 ChD. 442, 456 *per* Sir George Jessel M.R., 458 *per* Brett L.J.; *Hammond v. Farrow* [1904] 2 K.B. 332, 335 *per* Wills J. However, the exempted category does not include leases granted for a period exceeding three years merely because they are determinable within three years: *Kushner v. Law Society* [1952] 1 K.B. 264, 272–274 *per* Lord Goddard L.C.J. See Sparkes [1992] Conv. 252, 337.

3. For the purposes of section 54(2) the lease must "[take] effect in possession" so that a reversionary lease, that creates a term to commence at a future date, is not within the exception: *Long v. Tower Hamlets LBC* [1998] Ch. 197, noted at (1997) 113 L.Q.R. 394; [1998] Conv. 229.

4. The exemption applies only to the *creation* of leases within section 54(2). A subsequent *express assignment* of any legal lease must be effected by deed: *Crago v. Julian* [1992] 1 W.L.R. 372. However, where an *assignment* occurs

by operation of law (because the assignor-lessee has purported to grant a sub-lease of the whole of the remainder of the term), the assignment is effective to convey the legal lease to the assignee, notwithstanding the absence of a deed or other writing: *Milmo v. Carreras* [1946] 1 K.B. 306; and see *Parc (Battersea) Ltd v. Hutchinson* (1999), *The Times*, April 9, 1999.

2. Effect of non-compliance with the formal requirements

The effect of non-compliance with the formal requirements for a legal lease must be considered both at law and in equity. The following discussion assumes a purported but informal or defective seven-year lease.

2.1 *Effect at law*
At law, despite the failure to create the intended seven-year legal lease, a legal tenancy may still arise independently of the defective lease. If the intended tenant enters into possession of the property with the consent of the intended landlord, he becomes a tenant at will: see Law of Property Act 1925, s.54(1); and see *supra*, p. 343. Moreover, subject to the qualifications already discussed, the tenancy at will may be converted into a periodic tenancy by the payment and acceptance of rent: *Javad v. Mohammed Aqil* [1991] 1 W.L.R. 1007, *supra*, p. 341; *Long v. Tower Hamlets LBC* [1998] Ch. 197. Such a tenancy will be a legal tenancy since, as has been seen, a periodic tenancy is within the scope of section 54(2) and there are no formal requirements for its creation. Moreover, the tenancy will be deemed to incorporate all the intended terms of the defective lease in so far as they are consistent with the periodic tenancy: *Martin v. Smith* (1874) L.R. 9 Ex. 50, 52 *per* Kelly C.B.

2.2 *Effect in equity*
Independently of the legal periodic tenancy, the defective lease may also be accorded some effect in equity. In *Browne v. Warner* (1808) 14 Ves. Jun. 156, 409, a purported legal lease that was void for lack of formalities had nonetheless been recognised in equity as an agreement for a lease. In *Parker v. Taswell* (1858) 2 De G. & J. 559 it was argued that that decision had not survived the enactment of the Real Property Act 1845 and the formal requirements for legal leases contained in section 3 of the Act (the predecessor of section 52(1) of the Law of Property Act 1925). Lord Chelmsford said (at 570–571):

The legislature appears to have been very cautious and guarded in language, for it uses the expression "shall be void at law"—that is as a lease. If the legislature had intended to deprive such a document of all efficacy, it would have said that the instrument should be "void to all intents and purposes." There are no such words in the Act. I think it would be too strong to say that because it is void at law as a lease, it cannot be used as an agreement enforceable in equity, the intention of the parties having been that there should be a lease, and the aid of equity being only invoked to carry that intention into effect.

The result is that equity deems the defective lease to be a contract for the intended lease; and, as a contract for the creation/transfer of an interest in land, which *ex hypothesi* the landlord has failed to execute, equity would normally grant a decree of specific performance in respect of it.

2.2.1 *The doctrine in* Walsh v. Lonsdale   If the intended lease were then properly executed, pursuant to the decree of specific performance, the parties would be in the same position as if there had been initial compliance with the formal requirements for a legal lease. However, under what is normally referred to as the doctrine in *Walsh v. Lonsdale* (1882) 21 ChD. 9, the intended tenant does not actually have to obtain or even seek a decree of specific performance of the deemed contract. Provided that it is clear that a decree *would* be granted, equity applies the doctrine of conversion and "looks on that as done which ought to be done". The intended tenant does not have a legal lease: that must await the formal execution of the intended lease. However, the tenant is regarded in equity as having a lease on terms identical to those contained in the defective lease: *Swain v. Ayers* (1888) 21 Q.B.D. 289, 293 *per* Lord Esher M.R. The doctrine applies equally to a defective lease which is deemed to be a contract for a lease under the principle in *Parker v. Taswell* and to an actual agreement for a lease which is unexecuted: *Zimbler v. Abrahams* [1903] 1 K.B. 577, 581 *per* Vaughan Williams L.J. Moreover, the doctrine is not confined to (deemed) contracts for *leases*: it applies to (deemed) contracts for the creation or conveyance of *any* legal estate or interest in land.

The (hypothetical) availability of specific performance, which is the basis of the doctrine in *Walsh v. Lonsdale*, depends upon three factors.

2.2.1.1 *Valid (deemed) contract*   Specific performance may be decreed only in respect of (deemed) contracts which are formally valid; and formal validity depends upon compliance with section 2 of the Law of Property (Miscellaneous Provisions) Act 1989.

Law of Property (Miscellaneous Provisions) Act 1989, s.2

Contracts for sale etc. of land to be made by signed writing

2.—(1) A contract for the sale or other disposition of an interest in land can only be made in writing and only by incorporating all the terms which the parties have expressly agreed in one document or, where contracts are exchanged, in each.

(2) The terms may be incorporated in a document either by being set out in it or by reference to some other document.

(3) The document incorporating the terms or, where contracts are exchanged, one of the documents incorporating them (but not necessarily the same one) must be signed by or on behalf of each party to the contract.

(4) Where a contract for the sale or other disposition of an interest in land satisfies the conditions of this section by reason only of the rectification of one or more documents in pursuance of an order of a court, the contract shall come into being, or be deemed to have come into being, at such time as may be specified in the order.

(5) This section does not apply in relation to—

(a) a contract to grant such a lease as is mentioned in section 54(2) of the Law of Property Act 1925 (short leases);

(b) a contract made in the course of a public auction; or

(c) a contract regulated under the Financial Services Act 1986;

and nothing in this section affects the creation or operation of resulting, implied or constructive trusts.

(6) In this section—

"disposition" has the same meaning as in the Law of Property Act 1925;

"interest in land" means any estate, interest or charge in or over land.

(7) Nothing in this section shall apply in relation to contracts made before this section comes into force.

(8) Section 40 of the Law of Property Act 1925 (which is superseded by this section) shall cease to have effect.

NOTES:

1. The section applies to relevant contracts entered into on or after 27 September 1989. Under section 40 of the Law of Property Act 1925, which continues to apply to contracts entered into before that date, the question was one of enforceability rather than formal validity. A person seeking to establish that a (deemed) contract for a lease was enforceable, and that it created the relationship of landlord and tenant in equity, had to be able to point either (a) to some written evidence of the principal terms of the contract, signed by the person against whom enforcement was sought: *Tiverton Estates Ltd v. Wearwell Ltd* [1975] Ch. 146; or (b) to some act of "part performance", that is some act which pointed to the existence of a contract between the parties, by the person seeking to enforce the contract: *Steadman v. Steadman* [1976] A.C. 536. Under the 1989 Act the question is one of validity; and a valid contract is prima facie enforceable: see *infra*.

2. Howells [1990] Conv. 441 argues that section 2 requires a "contractual instrument": see Law Com. No. 164, *Transfer of Land: Formalities for Contracts for Sale etc. of Land* (1987), para. 4.5; and that that requirement precludes the necessary step in the operation of the doctrine in *Walsh v. Lonsdale* whereby a defective lease is deemed to constitute a contract. There is no such difficulty in the case of an actual (unexecuted) contract.

3. On section 2 generally, see *ante*, p. 61.

2.2.1.2 *Consideration*   Equity would normally require that the (deemed) contract is for valuable consideration.

2.2.1.3 *Discretion of the court*   Like all equitable remedies, specific performance is not available as of right: it lies in the discretion of the court. Thus, even if the plaintiff can establish that the contract is valid so that he is prima facie entitled to specific performance, there may be some factor which would lead the court, in the exercise of its discretion, to refuse the remedy. The remedy has been refused where the intended tenant was in breach of his obligations under the terms of the intended lease: *Coatsworth v. Johnson* (1886) 55 L.J.Q.B. 220; *Swain v. Ayers* (1888) 21 Q.B.D. 289; where the intended tenant had failed to fulfil a condition precedent to the grant of the lease: *Cornish v. Brook Green Laundry Ltd* [1959] 1 Q.B. 394; where the decree of specific performance would have required the intended landlord to execute a sub-lease in breach of his own head-lease: *Warmington v. Miller* [1973] Q.B. 877; and where the intended lease related to property outside the jurisdictional limits of the (county) court: *Foster v. Reeves* [1892] 2 Q.B. 255 (and see now the County Courts Act 1984, s.23(d)).

2.2.2 *The decision in* Walsh v. Lonsdale   It would now appear that in certain circumstances the intended tenant under the defective seven-year lease has two leases/tenancies: first, the legal periodic tenancy which arises from the entry into possession and the payment and acceptance of rent; and, secondly, the equitable seven-year lease which arises under the doctrine in *Walsh v. Lonsdale*. Although both tenancies are deemed to be on terms identical to those contained in the defective lease, that principle is subject to consistency with the periodic tenancy and the equitable lease respectively; and it is not impossible that a conflict may arise.

Walsh v. Lonsdale (1882) 21 ChD. 9

(CA, Jessel M.R., Cotton and Lindley L.JJ.)

In 1879, by agreement in writing, Lonsdale agreed to grant to Walsh a seven-year lease of a mill. One of the terms of the lease was that the lessor could demand the payment of one year's rent in advance. No formal lease was executed but Walsh took possession of the mill and paid rent quarterly in arrears. In 1882 Lonsdale demanded a year's rent in advance and, when Walsh refused to pay, he levied distress for it (by seizing goods belonging to Walsh). Walsh claimed damages for wrongful distress, an injunction to prevent the sale of the goods pursuant to the distress and for specific performance of the agreement for the lease. Walsh argued that distress was a common law remedy; that, in the absence of formal execution of the seven-year lease, at law he was a tenant from year to year; that an obligation to pay rent a year in advance was inconsistent with such a tenancy; and that Lonsdale therefore had no entitlement to levy distress.

JESSEL M.R.:
It is not necessary on the present occasion to decide finally what the rights of the parties are. If the Court sees that there is a fair question to be decided it will take security so that the party who ultimately succeeds may be in the right position. The question is one of some nicety. There is an agreement for a lease under which possession has been given. Now since the Judicature Act the possession is held under the agreement. There are not two estates as there were formerly, one estate at common law by reason of the payment of the rent from year to year, and an estate in equity under the agreement. There is only one Court and the equity rules prevail in it. The tenant holds under an agreement for a lease. He holds, therefore, under the same terms in equity as if a lease had been granted, it being a case in which both parties admit that relief is capable of being given by specific performance. That being so, he cannot complain of the exercise by the landlord of the same rights as the landlord would have had if a lease had been granted. On the other hand, he is protected in the same way as if a lease had been granted; he cannot be turned out by six months' notice as a tenant from year to year. He has a right to say, "I have a lease in equity, and you can only re-

enter if I have committed such a breach of covenant as would if a lease had been granted have entitled you to re-enter according to the terms of a proper proviso for re-entry." That being so, it appears to me that being a lessee in equity he cannot complain of the exercise of the right of distress merely because the actual parchment has not been signed and sealed.

NOTES:

1. For comment, see Sparkes (1988) 8 O.J.L.S. 350.

2. The doctrine in *Walsh v. Lonsdale* has been held to operate on a defective lease where the title of the landlord itself depended upon the operation of the doctrine. In *Industrial Properties (Barton Hill) Ltd v. Associated Electrical Industries Ltd* [1977] Q.B. 580 the plaintiff company agreed to purchase certain business premises from the vendors, who were the directors and shareholders of the plaintiff company; the purchase price was paid but no formal conveyance was executed. The plaintiffs purported to grant to the defendant company a 21-year lease, determinable after seven years and subject to a covenant to repair. The defendants terminated the lease after seven years and gave up possession. When the plaintiffs sued for breach of the covenant, the defendants argued that the plaintiffs had had no entitlement to grant the lease and therefore had no entitlement to sue on the covenant. Roskill L.J. said (at 608–610):

But the plaintiff company argued that that "lease" took effect in equity as an agreement for a lease and that since the plaintiff company were in a position to obtain the legal estate from the trustees and could without difficulty have done so had A.E.I. so required, and since equity assumes that to be done which ought to be done, the parties were to be treated as being in the same position as if a lease had been granted. Reliance was naturally placed by the respondents upon the well known doctrine enunciated by Jessel M.R. in *Walsh v. Lonsdale* (1882) 21 Ch.D. 9. Judge Fay accepted this argument. The defendants challenged this conclusion of the judge. Mr Nourse invited us to say that the judge was wrong in holding that the *Walsh v. Lonsdale* doctrine applied at all. In that case, he said, as was the fact, the defendant landlord was possessed of the legal estate and the plaintiff tenant was in direct contractual relationship with him. Thus, as Jessel M.R. held at pp. 14 and 15 of the report, the defendant held under the same terms in equity (since he held under an agreement for a lease) as if a lease had been granted, it being, he added, "a case in which both parties admit that relief is capable of being given by specific performance".

Does it make any difference that A.E.I. as lessees had no contractual relationship with the persons in whom the legal estate was vested? Mr Nourse says that it does. He relied strongly upon the judgment of Farwell J. in *Manchester Brewery Co. v. Coombs* [1901] 2 Ch. 608, 617, as showing that the *Walsh v. Lonsdale* doctrine had no application to a case where the alleged lessor had never had the legal estate, and also upon the judgment of the Divisional Court in *Schalit v. Joseph Nadler Ltd* [1933] 2 K.B. 79, 82.

It appears to be the case that no decision has in terms yet so extended the *Walsh v. Lonsdale* doctrine. But facts such as those giving rise to the present dispute must be rare in the extreme and I find the argument based solely on lack of precedent unconvincing if, authority apart, principle appears to require the application of the doctrine so as to achieve an inherently just and to prevent an obviously unjust result.

Mr Nourse relied strongly upon the peril in which he claimed A.E.I. to be and against which, he said, they would obtain no protection if his argument were wrong. This was, he said, unregistered land. Registration under the Land Charges Act would be in personam and not in rem against the property. This agreement for a lease, if such it were, could only have been registered against the plaintiff company and not against the trustees in whom the freehold was vested. If therefore the trustees sought to sell the freehold the purchaser from them would not upon a search have discovered or been put on notice of the existence of this agreement for a lease and indeed would, since this was unregistered land, have bought free of A.E.I.'s interest even had the purchaser known of the existence of that interest. Mr Nourse accepted that since the 1959 contract had been registered, a purchaser would have been on notice of the plaintiff company's interest under that contract but that, he said, would not have served to protect A.E.I. in respect of their interest. He placed reliance in this connection upon *Megarry and Wade*, 4th ed., pp. 1040–1041, 1045 and 1048–1049. Such a purchaser could therefore have evicted A.E.I. as trespassers.

It is not in my view necessary in this appeal to consider whether as canvassed in argument that statement as to the effect of registration and non-registration on p. 1049 is correct, or whether in such cases the courts would be powerless because this was unregistered land to protect A.E.I. against eviction by a purchaser with actual notice otherwise than by registration of their interest.

If I may say so, I found Mr Nourse's argument most ingenious, but in truth quite unreal. The 1959 contract was, as I have just said, registered. That being so, any purchaser must have become aware of its existence and in reality would buy subject to A.E.I.'s lease. Assuming the law to be as contended for by Mr Nourse, so far as I can see, the risk upon the existence of which he laid so much stress in argument, could only materialise in the event of a deliberate and well planned fraud designed to injure A.E.I., to which both the plaintiff company and the trustees would have to be parties if the fraud were to have any prospect of success. I cannot therefore think that this part of his submission is well founded. A.E.I. were at all times during the currency of the "lease" in possession. They could always have sued for trespass and, as already stated, the risk of eviction by title paramount could only arise, if at all, in the event of fraud by both the trustees and the plaintiff company.

Mr Bernstein in reply to this part of Mr Nourse's argument relied upon *Parker v. Taswell* (1858) 2 De G. & J. 559 in support of his argument that this "lease" took effect as an agreement for a lease. In that case the instrument in question offended against section 3 of the statute of 1845 (8 & 9 Vict. c. 106). It was therefore "void at law" and thus ineffective to pass the legal estate. But Lord Chelmsford L.C. held at pp. 570–571 that though "void at law" the instrument was nevertheless effective as an agreement enforceable in equity "the intention of the parties having been that there should be a lease and the aid of equity being only invoked to carry that intention into effect."

It seems to me that in the present case if at any time during the currency of the "lease" the true facts had emerged and either A.E.I. or the plaintiff company had sought execution of a lease effective to pass the legal estate to A.E.I., the court would without doubt have granted specific performance. Suppose A.E.I. had wished to dispose of their lease but on the true facts emerging on an inquiry as to title, their intended purchasers had required such a title to be shown? Could the plaintiff company have refused to execute such a document? Conversely, suppose the plaintiff company had wished to sell the reversion and their purchasers had queried the efficacy of the "lease". Could A.E.I. have refused to execute such a document? In either case the court would, I apprehend, have readily granted specific performance. Nor would the innocent misrepresentation by the plaintiff company's solicitors to which I have referred earlier in this judgment have afforded A.E.I. a ready escape since, as already pointed out, that misrepresentation never in any way induced A.E.I. to act otherwise than they would have done had that misrepresentation never been made.

I therefore see no obstacle to treating this "lease" as an agreement for a lease and to applying to it the *Walsh v. Lonsdale* doctrine. Even if I had been of the opposite opinion on the estoppel question, I would have unhesitatingly have held this "lease" effective as an agreement for a lease.

The Court of Appeal also held that the defendants were estopped from denying the title of the landlords: see *supra*, p. 348.

2.2.3 *Leases and agreements for leases compared*   It has been said that the result of the doctrine in *Walsh v. Lonsdale* is that "there is no distinction ... between a lease and an agreement for a lease": see *Re Maughan* (1885) 14 Q.B.D. 956, 958 *per* Field J. However, there remain significant differences:

   (i) It is generally asserted that the operation of the doctrine in *Walsh v. Lonsdale* is dependent upon the availability of specific performance (but for a detailed critique of this orthodoxy, see Gardner (1987) 7 O.J.L.S. 60); if specific performance is not available, the tenant may still have the legal periodic tenancy.

  (ii) The agreement for a lease/equitable lease remains an *equitable* interest in land, which is liable to be defeated by a purchaser of the legal estate unless protected by the appropriate form of registration: in the case of unregistered land as a class C(iv) land charge under the Land Charges Act 1972; in the case of registered land as a minor interest unless the tenant is in actual occupation so that the interest is enforceable against a purchaser, as an overriding interest under section 70(1)(g) of the Land Registration Act 1925. If the tenant is dependent upon a periodic tenancy, that will be enforceable against a purchaser as a *legal* interest; but it will also be subject to early termination by the appropriate notice to quit.

 (iii) Covenants in an equitable lease may become unenforceable when the original parties assign their interests: see *infra*, pp. 435, 440.

 (iv) In the absence of a formal legal lease or conveyance, the tenant will not acquire the benefit of easements and similar rights under section 62 of the Law of Property Act 1925: *Borman v. Griffith* [1930] 1 Ch. 493; and see *post*, p. 649.

F. Rights and Obligations of the Parties

The relationship of landlord and tenant is such that it is necessary to define the rights and obligations of the parties beyond the basic terms relating to the parties, the property, the commencement and duration of the term and the rent. For example, it is important that both parties should know their obligations in relation to the repair and maintenance of the property. Moreover, it is also important to know whether these and other obligations will be enforceable if either the landlord or the tenant transfers his interest to a third party. These matters are considered in this and the following two sections. This section considers the substance of the rights and obligations of the parties. The following section considers the enforceability of those rights and obligations, in particular by and against successors in title of the original parties. The final section considers the remedies available for enforcement.

The rights and obligations of the landlord and tenant are determined by the terms of the lease, including terms implied by the common law and by statute. In most cases the rights and obligations of the parties will be defined in the lease itself by express covenants. However, certain rights and obligations are regarded as necessary incidents of the landlord and tenant relationship so that covenants dealing with those rights and obligations are automatically implied into every lease; and it will be convenient to consider such covenants first. Secondly, certain common express covenants will be considered. Thirdly, the concept of "usual covenants" will be examined.

Although the term "covenant" technically means an undertaking contained in a deed, the term is used to denote the terms of any lease or agreement for a lease.

1. Implied covenants

In the absence of corresponding express covenants, certain covenants are implied into the relationship of landlord and tenant.

1.1 *Covenants by the landlord*

1.1.1 *Quiet enjoyment*   A covenant by the landlord to permit the tenant quiet enjoyment of the property is regarded as essential to the landlord and tenant relationship: *Budd-Scott v. Daniell* [1902] 2 K.B. 351; *Markham v. Paget* [1908] 1 Ch. 697; *Kenny v. Preen* [1963] 1 Q.B. 499.

Kenny v. Preen [1963] 1 Q.B. 499

(CA, Pearson, Ormerod and Donovan L.JJ.)

The plaintiff was the tenant of a flat owned by the defendant. The defendant purported to serve notice to quit, but the plaintiff's solicitor wrote to the defendant and disputed the validity of the notice. Over the next two years the defendant wrote a number of letters to the plaintiff, threatening physically to remove her and her possessions from the flat. In addition, he repeatedly knocked on the door of the flat and shouted similar threats to her. The plaintiff claimed that the defendant was in breach of the implied covenant for quiet enjoyment; and the county court judge awarded her damages and an injunction restraining further breaches. The defendant appealed on the ground that there had been no substantial physical interference with the possession of the property.

PEARSON L.J.:
Mr Lester has contended on behalf of the landlord that the evidence does not reveal any breach of the covenant, because the landlord only made communications to the tenant and did nothing amounting to physical interference with the tenant's possession and enjoyment of the premises. He relied on passages in the judgment in *Owen v. Gadd* [1956] 2 Q.B. 99 and in judgments in previous cases there cited, as showing that some direct physical interference is necessary to constitute a breach of the covenant.

Mr Sheridan has contended on behalf of the tenant, first, that a mere challenge by the landlord to the tenant's title, a denial by him of her title, would be sufficient to constitute a breach of the covenant; secondly, that in this case there was in fact some physical interference with the tenant's possession and enjoyment of the premises; and thirdly, more generally, that on the facts of this case, taken as a whole, there was a breach of the covenant. He cited *Edge v. Boileau* (1885) 16 Q.B.D. 117 as showing that physical interference is not necessarily required to constitute a breach of the covenant. That was a case in which the landlord was held to have committed a breach of the covenant by telling the subtenants to pay their rent to him instead of to the tenant. It is easy to see that that was an interference by the landlord with the tenant's enjoyment of his rights as tenant.

The judge accepted Mr Sheridan's first contention that a mere challenge by the landlord to the tenant's title, a denial by him of her title, would be sufficient to constitute a breach of the covenant. I am not able to adopt the judge's view on that point. We are not concerned in this case with a denial of the tenant's initial title by virtue of the letting, and I am not considering whether or not that could be a breach of the covenant. In this case the landlord was asserting that the tenant's title, her right to possession of the premises, although initially valid, had been wholly determined by a notice to quit. In my judgment, a landlord by merely making that assertion, however wrong he may be, does not commit a breach of covenant. He is entitled to make that assertion, at any rate if he believes it to be true, frequently, emphatically and even rudely. He is entitled also to threaten proceedings in the courts for possession and damages.

In the present case, however, there was much more than that. The landlord evaded answering the solicitors' letters raising the tenant's defences to his claim. He concentrated his attention on the tenant herself and tried, by a series of threatening communications, to drive her out of her possession of the premises. The threats were not merely of legal proceedings: there were threats of physical eviction of the tenant and removal of her belongings. Moreover, there was an element of direct physical interference by repeatedly knocking on the door and shouting the threats to her. That element of direct physical interference was not trivial but substantial in this case, because it was persisted in and because it has to be seen against the background of the threatening letters.

The implied covenant for quiet enjoyment is not an absolute covenant protecting a tenant against eviction or interference by anybody, but is a qualified covenant protecting the tenant against interference with the tenant's quiet and peaceful possession and enjoyment of the premises by the landlord or persons claiming through or under the landlord. The basis of it is that the landlord, by letting the premises, confers on the tenant the right of possession during the term and impliedly promises not to interfere with the tenant's exercise and use of the right of possession during the term. I think the word "enjoy" used in this connection is a translation of the Latin word "fruor" and refers to the exercise and use of the right and having the full benefit of it, rather than to deriving pleasure from it.

The nature of the implied covenant was explained in *Budd-Scott v. Daniell* [1902] 2 K.B. 351 in judgments of a Divisional Court. Lord Alverstone C.J. said (at pp. 355–356): "Apart from authority it would certainly seem, on principle and in common sense, that when one person agrees to give possession of his house for a time to another, that ought to carry with it an agreement that he, the landlord, and those claiming through him, will not dispossess the tenant during that time. Therefore, unless there is some special meaning attached to the word 'demise,' the good sense of the thing would seem to be that, upon an agreement to let, a covenant or contract was to be implied that the landlord and those claiming under him would not disturb the possession of the tenant. Unless driven to do so by authority, I should hesitate a long time before drawing any distinction in that respect between the words 'agree to let' and 'demise'."

The Lord Chief Justice said that, because reference had been made to a previous case—*Baynes & Co. v. Lloyd & Sons* [1895] 2 Q.B. 610—in which Kay L.J. had said that the implied covenant was only to be implied if the word "demised" was used, and could not be implied if some other word was used.

Also in the same case, *Budd-Scott v. Daniell,* Channell J. said (at p. 361): "I must say that, speaking for myself, until I read this judgment of the Court of Appeal in *Baynes & Co. v. Lloyd & Sons* [1895] 2 Q.B. 610, I always had thought that from the mere fact of letting there was some agreement implied by the landlord that the tenant should not be disturbed, though there might be a question as to what that agreement was. As to this question also, however, I should have thought that it had been now settled that the agreement was only against disturbance by the lessor and those claiming under him, and was limited to the duration of the lessor's interest. If the undertaking is limited in that way, it would seem, as was pointed out by Cockburn C.J. in *Hall v. City of London Brewery Co.* (1862) 2 B. & S. 737, to be nothing more than that which the act of letting into possession for a fixed period would itself in common sense import. If a man lets a house for a year, he most undoubtedly does undertake that he will not himself interfere with the possession of his tenant during that time, and it is only reasonable that his undertaking should be held to extend to those claiming under him."

Reference may also be made to *Markham v. Paget* [1908] 1 Ch. 697. Swinfen Eady J. (at p. 718) read an extract from *Platt on Covenants,* and the concluding words of the extract are these: " 'for, as against the party himself, the court will not consider the word *lawful,* nor drive the covenantee to an action of trespass, when, by the generally implied covenant in law, the vendor had engaged not to annul his own deed, either by a rightful or an illegal entry.' " That is surely the same principle emerging there, that the landlord is not allowed to "annul his own deed" by interfering with the possession which he himself has conferred on the tenant.

I would decide on two grounds in favour of the tenant's contention that there was, in this case, a breach of the covenant for quiet enjoyment. First, there was a deliberate and persistent attempt by the landlord to drive the tenant out of her possession of the premises by persecution and intimidation, and intimidation included threats of physical eviction of the tenant and removal of her belongings. In my view that course of conduct by the landlord seriously interfered with the tenant's proper freedom of action in exercising her right of possession, and tended to deprive her of the full benefit of it, and was an invasion of her rights as tenant to remain in possession undisturbed, and so would in itself constitute a breach of covenant, even if there were no direct physical interference with the tenant's possession and enjoyment. No case of this kind has ever been considered by the courts before, and I do not think the dicta in the previous cases should be read as excluding a case of this kind where a landlord seeks, by a course of intimidation, to "annul his own deed", to contradict his own demise, by ousting the tenant from the possession which the landlord has conferred upon her.

Secondly, if direct physical interference is a necessary element in the breach of covenant that element can be found in this case to a substantial extent, as I have already stated.

NOTES:

1. The substance of the covenant for quiet enjoyment is that the tenant should be able to enjoy the property free from disturbance by adverse claimants to the property: *Hudson v. Cripps* [1896] 1 Ch. 265, 268 *per* North J.

2. Examples of breaches of the covenant for quiet enjoyment include the removal of doors and windows: *Lavender v. Betts* [1942] 2 All E.R. 72; and the disconnection of gas and electricity supplies: *Perera v. Vandiyar* [1953] 1 W.L.R. 672. There is some disagreement in the cases on the issue whether there must be *physical interference.* For the view that physical interference is

necessary, see *Browne v. Flower* [1911] 1 Ch. 219, 228 *per* Parker J., *infra;* *Owen v. Gadd* [1956] 2 Q.B. 99, 107 *per* Lord Evershed M.R., 107–108 *per* Romer L.J.; *Kenny v. Preen* [1963] 1 Q.B. 499, 515 *per* Donovan L.J.; for the contrary view, see *ibid*. 513 *per* Pearson L.J., 514 *per* Ormerod L.J.; *McCall v. Abelesz* [1976] Q.B. 585, 594 *per* Lord Denning M.R. For a review of the case law, see Russell (1977) 40 M.L.R. 651.

3. To the extent that a landlord may be in breach of a covenant for quiet enjoyment on the basis of interference with the enjoyment of land he may also be liable in the tort of nuisance: *Sampson v. Hodson-Pressinger* [1981] 3 All E.R. 710. However, the Court of Appeal has recently held that the covenant for quiet enjoyment does not require the landlord of older property to alter or improve the property by carrying out a programme of effective sound-proofing against the noise generated by the ordinary use of neighbouring property occupied by another tenant of the landlord: *Southwark LBC v. Mills* [1999] 2 W.L.R. 409; nor is the landlord liable in nuisance in such circumstances: *Baxter v. Camden LBC* [1999] 1 All E.R. 237.

4. The covenant extends to any acts of the landlord and to the *lawful* acts of persons claiming under the landlord: *Sanderson v. Berwick-upon-Tweed Corp.* (1884) 13 Q.B.D. 547; but it does not extend to the unlawful acts of such persons: *ibid.*; nor to interference by persons claiming under a superior title: *Jones v. Lavington* [1903] 1 K.B. 253; nor to interference by persons claiming under a predecessor in title of the landlord: *Celsteel Ltd v. Alton House Holdings Ltd (No. 2)* [1987] 1 W.L.R. 291.

5. In *Branchett v. Beaney* [1992] 3 All E.R. 910 the Court of Appeal held that damages for injured feelings and mental distress are not recoverable in an action for breach of covenant for quiet enjoyment. However, where the conduct constituting the breach of covenant also constitutes a tort such as trespass or nuisance, damages may include an element of compensation for injured feelings and mental distress: *Drane v. Evangelou* [1978] 1 W.L.R. 455; *Guppy's (Bridport) Ltd v. Brookling* (1983) 14 H.L.R. 1.

6. Breach of the covenant for quiet enjoyment may also give rise to civil liability under sections 27 and 28 of the Housing Act 1988 (unlawful eviction) or the Protection from Harassment Act 1997 (unreasonable harassment); and it may also constitute a criminal offence under section 1 of the Protection from Eviction Act 1977 (unlawful eviction and harassment), section 6 of the Criminal Law Act 1977 (violence for the purposes of securing entry) or the Protection from Harassment Act 1997 (unreasonable harassment).

7. The implied covenant will be displaced by an express covenant for quiet enjoyment, even if the scope of the express covenant is more restricted: *Line v. Stephenson* (1838) Bing. N.C. 678; but in appropriate circumstances the tenant may still be able to rely on the covenant against derogation from grant (*infra*): *Grosvenor Hotel Co. v. Hamilton* [1894] 2 Q.B. 836, 840 *per* Lindley L.J. In any event, the same circumstances may give rise to breaches of both covenants: *Lawson v. Hartley-Brown* (1995) 71 P. & C.R. 242, noted at [1997] Conv. 304.

1.1.2 *Non-derogation from grant*

Browne v. Flower [1911] 1 Ch. 219

(Ch D., Parker J.)

The lessors had granted leases of two flats in a building which was mortgaged to the first defendant. The first flat was situated on the ground, first and second floors of the building; the second flat, which was leased to the plaintiffs, together with the benefit of an express covenant for quiet enjoyment, was situated on the ground floor. Each flat had windows overlooking a garden owned by the lessors. Each lease included a stipulation that the tenants would not create any nuisance to the lessors or the occupiers of adjoining premises. With the permission of the first defendant, the first flat was subsequently divided to create two smaller flats; and in order to provide access to the upper floors, an iron staircase was erected in the garden, between the windows of two bedrooms in the plaintiffs' flat. The flat on the upper floors was leased to the second defendant. The plaintiffs sought an order for the removal of the staircase on the ground that it constituted an interference with the enjoyment of their flat.

PARKER J.:
The plaintiffs next relied on the maxim that no one can be allowed to derogate from his own grant. This maxim is generally quoted as explaining certain implications which may arise from the fact that, or the circumstances under which, an owner of land grants or demises part of it, retaining the remainder in his own hands. The real difficulty is in each case to ascertain how far such implications extend. It is well settled that such a grant or demise will (unless there be something in the terms of the grant or demise or in the circumstances of the particular case rebutting the implication) impliedly confer on the grantee or lessee, as appurtenant to the land granted or demised to him, easements over the land retained corresponding to the continuous or apparent quasi-easements enjoyed at the time of the grant or demise by the property granted or demised over the property retained. For example, if the owner of a house with windows overlooking vacant land of the same owner grant or demise the house, the grant or demise will in general by implication confer on the grantee or lessee easements of light and support over or by the vacant land. The terms of the grant or demise or the special circumstances of the case may, however, rebut the implication. Further, the circumstances of the case may be such that though at the time of the grant or demise there be no continuous or apparent quasi-easements enjoyed by the property granted or demised over the property retained, yet easements over the property retained may be impliedly created and become appurtenant to the property granted or demised. Thus, if the grant or demise be for the purpose of erecting a building with defined windows overlooking other land of the grantor or lessor, an easement of light to such windows over such other land will be created, and similarly there will be created an easement of support by the land retained for the building to be built. But again these implications may be rebutted by the special circumstances of the case. Inasmuch as our law does not recognise any easement of prospect or privacy, and (as I have already held) the plaintiffs' lights are not interfered with, it is difficult to find any easement which can have been interfered with by the erection of the staircase in question.

But the implications usually explained by the maxim that no one can derogate from his own grant do not stop short with easements. Under certain circumstances there will be implied on the part of the grantor or lessor obligations which restrict the user of the land retained by him further than can be explained by the implication of any easement known to the law. Thus, if the grant or demise be made for a particular purpose, the grantor or lessor comes under an obligation not to use the land retained by him in such a way as to render the land granted or demised unfit or materially less fit for the particular purpose for which the grant or demise was made. In *Aldin v. Latimer Clark, Muirhead & Co.* [1894] 2 Ch. 437 land having been demised for the purpose of carrying on the business of a timber merchant, the lessor came under an obligation not to build on land retained by him so as to interrupt the access of air to sheds on the demised property used for drying timber, although the law does not recognise any easement of air unless it comes through or to some defined passage or aperture. Similarly in the case of *Grosvenor Hotel Co. v. Hamilton* [1894] 2 Q.B. 836 the lessee was held entitled to prevent the lessor from using property retained by him in such a way as to cause on the demised property vibrations which did not amount to a legal nuisance, though there is no such easement known to the law as an easement of freedom from vibration any more than there is an easement of freedom from noise. Once again, though possibly there may not be known to the law any easement of light for special purposes, still the lease of a building to be used for a special purpose requiring an extraordinary amount of light might well be held to preclude the grantor from diminishing the light passing to the grantee's windows, even in cases where the diminution would not be such as to create a nuisance within the meaning of the recent decisions: see *Herz v. Union Bank of London* (1859) 2 Giff. 686. In none of these cases would any easement be created, but the obligation implied on the part of the lessor or grantor would be analogous to that which arises from a restrictive covenant. It is to be observed that in the several cases to which I have referred the lessor had done or proposed to do something which rendered or would render the demised premises unfit or materially less fit to be used for the particular purpose for which the demise was made. I can find no case which extends the implied obligations of a grantor or lessor beyond this. Indeed, if the implied obligations of a grantor or lessor with regard to land retained by him were extended beyond this, it is difficult to see how they could be limited at all. A landowner may sell a piece of land for the purpose of building a house which when built may derive a great part of its value from advantages of prospect or privacy. It would, I think, be impossible to hold that because of this the vendor was precluded from laying out the land retained by him as a building estate, though in so doing he might destroy the views from the purchaser's house, interfere with his privacy, render the premises noisy, and to a great extent interfere with the comfortable enjoyment and diminish the value of the property sold by him. It is quite reasonable for a purchaser to assume that a vendor who sells land for a particular purpose will not do anything to prevent its being used for that purpose, but it would be utterly unreasonable to assume that the vendor was undertaking restrictive obligations which would prevent his using land retained by him for any lawful purpose whatsoever merely because his so doing might affect the amenities of the property he had sold. After all, a purchaser can always bargain for those rights which he deems indispensable to his comfort.

Under these circumstances the question is whether the existence of this staircase renders the plaintiffs' premises unfit or materially less fit to be used for the purposes for which they were demised, that is, for the purposes of a residential flat. In my opinion it does not. The two rooms in question can be and are still in fact used for the same purpose for which they were used prior to the erection of the staircase. It is only the comfort of the persons so using the rooms that is interfered with by what has been done. Either they have less privacy, or if they secure their privacy by curtains they have less light. Much as I sympathise with the plaintiffs, it would, in my opinion, be extending the implications based on the maxim that no one can derogate from his own grant to an unreasonable extent if it were held that what has been done in this case was a breach of an implied obligation.

Lastly it was suggested that what has been done constituted a breach of the covenant for quiet enjoyment contained in the plaintiffs' agreement. I do not think this point was really pressed, and indeed it could hardly be pressed after the recent decisions on the nature of such a covenant. It appears to me that to constitute a breach of such a covenant there must be some physical interference with the enjoyment of the demised premises, and that a mere interference with the comfort of persons using the demised premises by the creation of a personal annoyance such as might arise from noise, invasion of privacy, or otherwise is not enough. In my opinion, therefore, this action fails.

NOTES:

1. The principle in *Browne v. Flower* was applied in *Harmer v. Jumbil (Nigeria) Tin Areas Ltd* [1921] 1 Ch. 200. The plaintiff was granted a 21-year lease of land, together with the benefit of a covenant for quiet enjoyment, for the express purpose of the storage of explosives. He obtained the necessary licence, which was granted subject to the condition that it would be withdrawn if specified distances were not maintained between the stores and buildings on adjoining land. The lessor knew that the grant of the licence involved restrictions on the use of adjoining land. Subsequently, the successor in title of the lessor granted a lease of some adjoining land to the defendants for the purpose of mining. The defendants agreed that they would not interfere with the activities of the plaintiff; but they erected some buildings within the distances specified in the plaintiff's licence. The plaintiff claimed that the acts of the defendants (who were admitted to be in the same position as the original lessor) constituted a derogation from grant. Eve J. dismissed the claim on the ground that the original lessor could not be held to have agreed to such restrictions on the use of his land; but the Court of Appeal allowed the plaintiff's appeal. Younger L.J. elaborated on the doctrine of non-derogation from grant. He said (at 225–227):

Now if these questions are to be answered in a sense favourable to the lessee, it must be on the principle that a grantor shall not derogate from his grant, a principle which merely embodies in a legal maxim a rule of common honesty. "A grantor having given a thing with one hand," as Bowen L.J. put it in *Birmingham, Dudley and District Banking Co. v. Ross* (1888) 38 Ch.D. 295, 313 "is not to take away the means of enjoying it with the other." "If A. lets a plot of land to B.," as Lord Loreburn phrases it in *Lyttelton Times Co. v. Warners* [1907] A.C. 476, 481 "he may not act so as to frustrate the purpose for which in the contemplation of both parties the land was hired". The rule is clear but the difficulty is, as always, in its application. For the obligation laid upon the grantor is not unqualified. If it were, that which was imposed in the interest of fair dealing might, in unscrupulous hands, become a justification for oppression, or an instrument of extortion. The obligation therefore must in every case be construed fairly, even strictly, if not narrowly. It must be such as, in view of the surrounding circumstances, was within the reasonable contemplation of the parties at the time when the transaction was entered into, and was at that time within the grantor's power to fulfil. But so limited, the obligation imposed may, I think, be infinitely varied in kind, regard being had to the paramount purpose to serve which it is imposed. If, for instance, the purpose of a grant would in a particular case be frustrated by some act of the lessor on his own land which, while involving no physical interference with the enjoyment of the demised property, would yet be completely effective to stop or render unlawful its continued user for the purpose for which alone it was let, I can see no reason at all in principle why "ut res magis valeat quam pereat" that act should not be prohibited, just as clearly as an act which, though less completely effective in its result, achieved it by some physical interference. There can, in my judgment, be no valid principle in the contention which was addressed to us in this case by Mr Courthope Wilson, that, while the lease of 1911 carried with it the obligation of doing or permitting nothing on the adjoining land which would make the explosives magazine less fit for use as a magazine, that is to say, more likely to blow up, it did leave the lessor perfectly free to use his land for his own convenience in any way he chose, even although the result of his doing so would ipso facto make the continued user of a powder magazine as such a statutory offence. If that contention were to be accepted it would enable this grantor, if so minded, in pure caprice, to defeat the whole purpose of the grant and completely sterilise the property in his tenant's hands, he himself remaining entitled to the rent reserved for the whole term.

In my judgment the principle here applicable is far too great to be in effect destroyed, in the case of such a property as this, by introducing this distinction which, so far as I can see, has no sound foundation on which to rest.

2. For recent applications of the principle, see *Johnson & Sons Ltd v. Holland* [1988] 1 E.G.L.R. 264, where the landlord erected a large hoarding, thereby obscuring advertisements on the wall of the tenant's premises; *Lawson v. Hartley-Brown* (1995) 71 P. & C.R. 242, where the landlord built two further floors on top of the single-storey property leased to the tenant; and *Chartered Trust plc v. Davies* (1997) 76 P. & C.R. 396, where the landlord leased a unit in a retail development and failed to take action to prevent the tenants of other units from committing a nuisance by obstructing access.

3. There is no derogation from grant where the landlord leases a unit in a business development and then leases another unit to another tenant whose business may compete with that of the first tenant: *Port v. Griffith* [1936] 1 All E.R. 295; *Romulus Trading Co. Ltd v. Comet Properties Ltd* [1996] 2 E.G.L.R. 70.

4. For the application of the principle in the context of easements, see *post*, p. 635.

5. See generally Elliott (1964) 80 L.Q.R. 244; Peel (1965) 81 L.Q.R. 28.

1.1.3 *Repair and maintenance*   There is no generally applicable implied undertaking by the landlord as to the state of repair of the property or its fitness for the purpose for which it is intended to be used; nor any implied covenant that the landlord will carry out repairs. However, certain covenants have progressively been implied in the context of residential leases.

1.1.3.1 *Covenants implied by common law*   At common law, there is an implied undertaking by the landlord that *furnished* premises are fit for human habitation at the commencement of the tenancy: *Smith v. Marrable* (1843) 11 M. & W. 5. More recently, the House of Lords has held that covenants for repair and maintenance may be implied in order to give business efficacy to the lease. Thus, where a tenant has expressly covenanted to carry out interior maintenance, the landlord may be held impliedly to have covenanted to maintain the exterior of the premises: *Barrett v. Lounova (1982) Ltd* [1990] 1 Q.B. 348; in the context of a tenancy of a flat in a tower block of flats the landlord was held to have an implied duty to take reasonable care to keep the common parts and services in a state of reasonable repair and usability: *Liverpool City Council v. Irwin* [1977] A.C. 239; and a landlord was held to have an implied duty to maintain a path providing the only wheelchair access for the tenant: *King v. South Northamptonshire DC* (1992) 24 H.L.R. 284; but contrast *Duke of Westminster v. Guild* [1985] Q.B. 688; and see *post*, p. 622

In addition, the potential liability in negligence of a landlord who designed and built the property may provide a remedy for the tenant: *Rimmer v. Liverpool City Council* [1985] Q.B. 1; *Targett v. Torfaen BC* [1992] 3 All E.R. 27; but this duty of the landlord to ensure that the property is reasonably safe when let does not take effect as an implied covenant.

1.1.3.2 *Covenants implied by statute* Certain covenants imposing obligations on the landlord in relation to repair and maintenance are implied by statute. In the case of a house let for human habitation at a low rent (not exceeding £80 per year in London, £52 elsewhere), there is an implied condition that the house is fit for human habitation at the commencement of the tenancy and an implied undertaking that the landlord will keep the house fit for human habitation during the tenancy: Landlord and Tenant Act 1985, ss.8, 10.

In theory at least section 11 of the Landlord and Tenant Act 1985 applies more widely. In any lease or agreement for a lease of a dwelling house granted after 23 October 1961 where the term is less than seven years there is an implied covenant by the landlord (i) to keep in repair the structure and exterior of the house and (ii) to keep in repair and proper working order the installations in the house for the supply of water, gas and electricity, for sanitation and for space- and water-heating. Moreover, in the case of leases of dwelling houses forming part only of a building and granted after January 14, 1989 the obligation applies to any part of the building in which the landlord has an estate or interest and to any installations which serve the premises and which form part of any part of the building in which he has an estate or interest or which are owned or controlled by the landlord. The obligation of the landlord cannot normally be excluded or limited or transferred to the tenant: Landlord and Tenant Act 1985, ss.11(4), 12. However, the obligation does not extend to repairs for which the tenant is liable under his duty to use the premises in a tenant-like manner: *ibid.* s.11(2)(a); and see *infra*, p. 410.

The obligation under section 11 (and section 8) does not extend to defects on the premises comprised in the lease unless and until the landlord has notice of them: *O'Brien v. Robinson* [1973] A.C. 912; although notice need not be acquired from the tenant: *Dinefwr BC v. Jones* [1987] 2 E.G.L.R. 58. However, the principle in *O'Brien v. Robinson* has been stated to be the exception to the general rule that, where the defect is on land *not* comprised in the lease, the obligation of the landlord arises irrespective of notice: *British Telecommunications plc v. Sun Life Assurance Society plc* [1996] Ch. 69, 78–79 *per* Nourse L.J.; and see [1997] Conv. 59. It is suggested that the rule should be no different in respect of covenants "to repair" (as opposed to "keep in repair"): see *Passley v. Wandsworth LBC* (1996) 30 H.L.R. 165, noted at [1997] Conv. 59; and see Law Com. No. 238, *Landlord and Tenant: Responsibility for State and Condition of Property* (1996), para. 2.12.

In practice, the courts have tended to construe the obligation to repair restrictively: see Law Commission Consultation Paper No. 123, *Landlord and Tenant: Responsibility for State and Condition of Property* (1992), *infra*.

A landlord who lets property on terms that he has an obligation (or right) to repair or maintain the property owes a duty to all persons who might reasonably be expected to be affected by defects in the property to take reasonable care to see that those persons are reasonably safe from personal injury or damage to their property: Defective Premises Act 1972, s.4. The duty had been construed as being owed also to the tenant: *Smith v. Bradford Metropolitan Council* (1982) 44 P. & C.R. 171; but this duty of the landlord does not take effect as an implied covenant.

Finally, there is considerable statutory regulation intended to ensure that residential property is fit for human habitation, to eliminate insanitary conditions and to engender the improvement of individual properties and whole neighbourhoods. Again, these provisions are not directly concerned with the agreement between landlord and tenant, although leases frequently contain an *express* covenant, normally by the tenant, to comply with all statutory requirements: see Law Commission Consultation Paper No. 123, *Landlord and Tenant: Responsibility for State and Condition of Property* (1992), paras 2.50–2.62.

1.1.3.3 *Assessment of the current approach to covenants relating to repair and maintenance*

Law Commission Consultation Paper No. 123, Landlord and Tenant: Responsibility for State and Condition of Property (1992), paras 3.3–3.16

CONDITION OF PREMISES

Repair

3.3 Until now, most obligations, both contractual and statutory, have been obligations "to repair". It is clear that "disrepair" is related to the physical condition of whatever had to be repaired, and not to the questions of lack of amenity or inefficiency. Accordingly, there may be no obligation to ensure that the building let is fit for use for its intended purpose. This is graphically made by the facts of a recent case concerning a terraced house in Wales let by the local council [*Quick v. Taff Ely BC* [1986] Q.B. 809, 815 *per* Dillon L.J.]: "The evidence shows that there was considerable condensation on the walls, windows and metal surfaces in all rooms of the house. Water had frequently to be wiped off the walls; paper peeled off walls and ceilings, woodwork rotted, particularly inside and behind the fitted cupboards in the kitchen. Fungus or mould growth appeared in places and particularly in the two back bedrooms there was a persistent and offensive smell of damp. Among the places where there was mould growth were the wooden sills and surrounds of the windows in the bedrooms, and some of these have become rotten. Additionally, in the bedrooms condensation caused the nails used for fixing the ceiling plasterboard to sweat and ... there was some perishing of the plaster due to excessive moisture."

3.4 As the law stands, the tenants had only limited recourse against the landlord. Much of the condition of the premises resulted from condensation which was not caused by any deterioration of the exterior or structure of the house, for which the landlord was responsible, and therefore there was no repair which it was liable to carry out. Lawton and Neill L.JJ. reached that conclusion with regret. In another case [*Post Office v. Aquarius Properties Ltd* [1987] 1 All E.R. 1055], Ralph Gibson L.J. said [at p. 1063]: "I found it at first to be a startling proposition that, when an almost new building lets ground water into the basement so that water is ankle deep for some years, that state of affairs is consistent with there being no condition of disrepair under a repairing covenant in standard form whether given by landlord or tenant."

3.5 The nature and extent of the work which falls within the term repair can best be explained by examining a number of the issues which the courts have had to determine in this context.

Improvement

3.6 A sharp distinction has been drawn between "repair" and improvement work; the latter does not come within the duty to repair. This is justifiable on the grounds that, in the absence of a special bargain, a lease entitles the tenant to enjoy the property in the state in which it was let to him, without the landlord being obliged to improve it, and obliges the tenant to hand the property back to the landlord at the end of the lease, in a specified state of repair but without improvement. The transaction is, therefore, essentially the hiring of a property in its existing state for an agreed fee, but without any obligation on either party to make any further capital investment in it.

3.7 The different treatment of improvement may be much more difficult to justify in practice. As Sir John Megaw said in a recent judgment [*McDougall v. Easington DC* [1989] 1 E.G.L.R. 93, 96], "Assume facts such as exist in the present case [an unsatisfactory system-built house requiring extensive remedial work, involving removing the front and rear elevations, the roof structure and the rain dispersal system]: that is, serious defects in the structure which can be properly remedied (I must, of course, avoid the word 'repaired') only by works which fall outside the meaning of 'repairs', or defects which it is sensible should be remedied by such works rather than by repeated temporary or ephemeral repairs. ... On those assumptions, the landlord, under the law as it has been interpreted, cannot be compelled by the tenant to remedy the defects. ... All this arises because of the distinction which the law has drawn between 'repairs' and works of remedy of serious defects which fall outside the meaning of 'repairs'." However, it may be, as he went on to suggest, that the difficulties are in practice too rare to justify legislation which might result in more problems than it solved.

...

Inherent Defects

3.9 Despite the dismissal of earlier suggestions that rectifying inherent defects in premises let could never fall within the definition of repair, similar questions have been raised by a recent case concerning the position of a building part of which was never suitable for its purpose [*Post Office v. Aquarius Properties Ltd* [1987] 1 All E.R. 1055]. A recently built office building in the City of London was let in 1969. For some years, when the water table rose, the basement was ankle deep in water because of the form of construction. In fact, this does not appear to have caused inconvenience because the basement was not used. The case was disposed of on the basis that it is not repair to change a state of affairs which has always existed [*ibid.* 1065 *per* Slade L.J.], although this view does not find universal favour [see *Stent v. Monmouth DC* (1987) 54 P. & C.R. 193, 209 *per* Stocker L.J.]. If repair, as it is now understood, were not the test, the conclusion might not be the same. Judged on the basis of intended use, the decision might turn on whether there was evidence of intention to use the basement for a purpose for which the flooding would have made it unsuitable. If there was such evidence, it is hard to see why there should not be a duty to do the remedial work, although there would be the further question of who should pay for it.

3.10 As Ralph Gibson L.J. pointed out [in commenting on *Quick v. Taff Ely BC* [1986] Q.B. 809], "the reasoning ... is equally applicable whether the original defect resulted from error in design, or in workmanship, or from deliberate parsimony or any other cause" [*Post Office v. Aquarius Properties Ltd* [1987] 1 All E.R. 1055, 1063].

3.11 Clearly, there will be cases in which a satisfactory repair—in the general sense of works carried out to remedy a deficiency which renders property unusable—will involve changing a state of affairs which existed before the lease was granted, and possibly since the property was built. The present distinction, between defects in a building as originally built and faults which develop later, will produce anomalies. Whether or not a party has to cure a particular physical defect may depend on whether it was built into the property or it developed later, even though the prejudicial effect of the defect is the same whatever and whenever its origin.

3.12 Liability for curing inherent defects can be linked to the more general question of responsibility for remedying matters which existed before the lease was granted, which will necessarily include inherent defects. To the extent that the defective state of the property is apparent at the date of the letting, the parties can assess their position, although this may involve taking expensive professional advice. There may, however, be a lack of equality. Defects may be known to the landlord which are not apparent, or which would save the tenant a great deal of investigation if the information were volunteered. At present, the landlord has no obligation to tell the tenant what he knows.

. . .

Date of Letting

3.14 The standard to which a property is to be repaired normally depends on its age and nature at the date when it is let [*Lurcott v. Wakely & Wheeler* [1911] 1 K.B. 905; *Brew Bros Ltd v. Snax (Ross) Ltd* [1970] 1 Q.B. 612; Landlord and Tenant Act 1985, s.11(3)]. There is apparent fairness in this, when balancing the economic interests of the parties: if the tenant is to repair, it is reasonable that he should give back at the end of the lease a property which is neither better nor worse than he received at the start. However, the appropriateness of the principle may be more apparent than real.

3.15 First, it is never possible to do more than "have regard" to the age and nature of the property: there is no hard and fast rule. If, when the lease starts, the property is dilapidated, that does not necessarily render any repairing obligation nugatory. On the other hand, if the lease is lengthy some natural deterioration is allowable, so one does not look exclusively at the condition of the property when the lease was granted. Secondly, no account is taken of changes in the meantime to the surrounding neighbourhood [*Anstruther-Gough-Calthorpe v. McOscar* [1924] 1 K.B. 716], which may make the earlier standard of repair wholly inappropriate. Thirdly, this construction of repairing covenants can lead to misunderstanding and inconvenience when property is sub-let. The head lease and sub-lease may contain identical repairing covenants, which would appear to be appropriate when the mesne landlord wants to pass on to the sub-tenant the duties imposed on him by the head lease. However, the two covenants may be interpreted differently merely because of the different dates on which the lease and the sub-lease were granted, so that the mesne landlord is unintentionally left with some duty to repair. Fourthly, and more fundamentally, if the property is let for a specified period so that it may be used throughout for a particular purpose, the state at the date of the letting may be seen as less relevant than whether it allows the objective to be achieved. Fifthly, the requirements of a reasonably minded class of tenant likely to take the property are also to be judged as at the commencement of the lease [*Proudfoot v. Hart* (1890) 25 Q.B.D. 42; *Trustees of the*

Dame Margaret Hungerford Charity v Beazeley [1993] 29 E.G. 100, noted at [1994] Conv. 145]. ...

Modernisation

3.16 A duty to repair does not normally carry a duty to modernise the premises. If the only way to do satisfactory remedial work is by adopting a better, more modern form of construction or design, the work is likely to be one of improvement. However, that presupposes these facts: remedial work to the building is needed and it is possible using new techniques. It is open to question whether neglecting the work, which may mean that the building falls into disuse, can be justified merely because of changes in building methods.

1.1.3.4 *Proposals for reform* Following the review of the current law relating to repairing obligations, the Law Commission provisionally proposed (Law Commission Consultation Paper No. 123, *Landlord and Tenant: Responsibility for State and Condition of Property* (1992), para. 5.7) that the primary responsibility should be placed on the landlord, who should be under a "duty to maintain". That duty was formulated as follows:

To put and keep the demised property, and all parts of it, in such state and condition that it may safely, hygienically and satisfactorily be used, and continue in the immediate future to be used, for its intended purpose with an appropriate degree of convenience and comfort for the occupants.

The duty would have included making good all defects whether original or developed later (and including the impact of legal requirements), by repair, replacement, improvement or renewal, as appropriate; and the standard required would have been such as was appropriate in putting those premises to that use. For the case against such radical reform, see Smith [1994] Conv. 186.

The final Report (Law Com. No. 238, *Landlord and Tenant: Responsibility for State and Condition of Property* (1996)) is rather less radical in its recommendations. First, the Report has abandoned the provisional recommendation that residential and commercial leases should be treated in the same way: it recommends the continuation of the current application of section 11 of the Landlord and Tenant Act 1985 to residential leases; and it accepts that the parties to commercial leases should be free to make their own agreements but it recommends an implied default covenant where the parties do not make express provision for repairs. Secondly, the Report has abandoned the provisional recommendation to replace the concept of "repair" with a "duty to maintain": instead it recommends the retention of the concept of "repair" as interpreted for the purposes of section 11 of the Landlord and Tenant Act 1985. Thirdly, the Report recommends the modification of the concept of "fitness for human habitation" and the extension of its application. Finally, the Report recommends that the court should have power to decree specific performance of repairing obligations in leases and tenancies: see *infra*, p. 466.

Law Commission Report No. 238, Landlord and Tenant: Responsibility for State and Condition of Property (1996)

Summary of recommendations

Part VII Implied Terms

11.3 We recommend that there should be implied into every lease, other than—
  (a) a lease of a dwelling-house for a term of less than seven years within the provisions of sections 11 to 15 of the Landlord and Tenant Act 1985;
  (b) a lease of an agricultural holding;
  (c) a farm business tenancy; or
  (d) an oral lease;
  a covenant that the landlord shall keep the premises in repair.

11.4 The standard of repair should be that which is appropriate having regard to the age, character and prospective life of the premises and to their locality.
  ...

11.10 [The] covenant should not apply where—
  (i) there was an express repairing obligation in relation to all of the relevant premises either in the lease itself or in an agreement by the parties; or
  (ii) the parties had made an express agreement that excluded its operation; or
  (iii) a repairing obligation was either imposed on one of the parties by any other statute, or would have been if it had not been effectively excluded.
  For these purposes, a "repairing obligation" would mean an obligation both to repair the premises or to keep them in repair, and to make and to keep them fit for human habitation.

11.11 The parties would be free to modify [the] covenant by express agreement.
  ...

11.13 We make the following subsidiary recommendations—
  (a) To avoid the possible trap that parties may not appreciate the significance of an implied covenant to *keep in repair*, we recommend that its meaning should be defined so as to make it clear that the obligation is both to *put* the premises in repair at the commencement of the term and to *keep* it in repair for the duration of the lease.
  (b) Where the covenant to keep in repair is implied, the landlord should have a right to enter the premises on giving 24 hours' notice in writing to the occupier, to enable him or his authorised agent to inspect the condition and the state of repair of the premises.
  (c) By way of exception to the implied repairing covenant, the landlord should not be required to undertake any of the following matters:
    (i) any work of repairs that the tenant is obliged to carry out under his implied covenant to take proper care of the premises;
    (ii) the rebuilding or reinstatement of the premises in whole or in part if they are destroyed by inevitable accident; and
    (iii) the repair of any tenant's fixtures.

Part VIII Fitness for Human Habitation

11.16 Subject to certain exceptions ... we recommend that there should be implied into a lease of a dwelling-house which is for a term of less than seven years a covenant by the lessor—
  (a) that the dwelling-house is fit for human habitation at the commencement of the lease; and

(b) that the lessor will keep it fit for human habitation during the lease.

11.17 We recommend that the implied obligation of fitness should not require the lessor—
   (a) to carry out any works or repairs for which the tenant is liable by virtue either of the implied obligation to take proper care of the premises (explained in paragraph 11.41) or under some express covenant having the same effect;
   (b) to rebuild or reinstate the house if it is destroyed by inevitable accident; and
   (c) to keep in repair or maintain any tenants' fixtures.

11.18 We also recommend that the landlord should not be liable on the implied covenant in two circumstances—
   (a) where the principal cause of the unfitness is some breach of covenant by the lessee; or
   (b) where the unfitness was caused by disrepair for which the landlord was not responsible because of the exclusion or modification of his liability under section 11 of the Landlord and Tenant Act 1985 to repair.

11.19 We recommend that a landlord should not be liable under the implied covenant if the property cannot be made fit for human habitation at reasonable expense.

11.20 We recommend that it should no longer be possible to exclude the obligation of fitness by granting a tenant a lease for three years or more on the terms that he makes the property fit.

11.21 We recommend that the implied obligation should apply to any lease under which a dwelling-house is let wholly or mainly for human habitation...

11.22 We recommend that the implied obligation should apply to a lease of such premises for a term of less than seven years...
   . . .

11.24 We recommend that the implied fitness obligation should not apply to—
   (a) a lease which is tenancy of an agricultural holding or a farm business tenancy;
   (b) leases to those bodies listed in section 14(4) and 14(5) of the Landlord and Tenant Act 1985;
   (c) a lease of a dwelling-house if that house—
      (i) is on land which at the time of the grant of that lease is either held or has been acquired (whether compulsorily or by agreement) for development by an authority which possesses powers of compulsory acquisition;
      (ii) is being used by that authority to provide temporary housing accommodation pending development of the land; and
      (iii) is of a standard that is adequate for the time being.
   . . .

11.27 We recommend that in any lease to which the proposed implied covenant of fitness applies, the landlord should have the right to enter and view the state and condition of the premises at reasonable times of the day, on giving to the occupier 24 hours' notice in writing.

11.28 We recommend that in determining whether a dwelling-house is fit for human habitation for the purposes of the implied obligation of fitness, the criteria should be the same as those applied in section 604 of the Housing Act 1985 (as amended).

NOTES:

1. For comment, see Bridge [1996] Conv. 342.

2. The Report recommends a complementary implied default repairing covenant in respect of the common parts of the building where the leased premises are situated and other parts of the premises under the control of the landlord.

3. The default covenant would only apply to leases granted after the new regime came into force.

4. The Law Commission views the default covenant as a means of encouraging the parties to make express provision; and it would be excluded by any express provision in relation to repairs.

5. The default covenant would have no application to leases of dwelling-houses granted for a term of less than seven years which are subject to the regime of sections 11–15 of the Landlord and Tenant Act 1985. The recommendations in the Report would result in a comprehensive code for such leases, comprising the 1985 Act, the implied covenant on fitness for human habitation and an implied covenant by the tenant to take proper care of the property (see *infra*, p. 412).

6. In the light of the recommended retention of section 11 of the Landlord and Tenant Act 1985 and its concept of "repair", the modification of the concept of "fitness for habitation" and the extended application of the implied covenant on fitness for habitation is seen as the solution to the potential problems of inherent defects (see, *e.g. Quick v. Taff Ely BC* [1986] Q.B. 809; *Post Office v. Aquarius Properties Ltd* [1987] 1 All E.R. 1055).

7. The modified criteria for determining fitness for habitation are set out in clause 7 of the draft Bill:

7(1) A dwelling-house is fit for human habitation for the purposes of section 5 unless—
    (a) it fails to meet one or more of the requirements set out in subsection (2); and
    (b) by reason of that failure, it is not reasonably suitable for occupation.
(2) Those requirements are—
    (a) the dwelling-house is structurally stable;
    (b) it is free from serious disrepair;
    (c) it is free from dampness prejudicial to the health of the occupants (if any);
    (d) it has adequate provision for lighting, heating and ventilation;
    (e) it has an adequate piped supply of wholesome water;
    (f) there are satisfactory and suitably located facilities for the preparation and cooking of food by the occupants (if any), including a sink with a satisfactory supply of hot and cold water;
    (g) there is a suitably located water-closet for the use of the occupants (if any);
    (h) there is a suitably located fixed bath or shower and wash-basin for the use of the occupants (if any), each of which is provided with a satisfactory supply of hot and cold water; and
    (i) the dwelling-house has an effective system for the draining of foul, waste and surface water.

1.2 Covenants by the tenant

1.2.1 Obligation not to commit waste   The common law recognises two kinds of "waste": voluntary waste involves positive action having an adverse effect on the reversionary interest of the landlord; permissive waste involves the failure to do what ought to be done to prevent the property from falling into disrepair. All tenants are liable for voluntary waste. Tenants under fixed term leases are liable for permissive waste: *Yellowly v. Gower* (1855) 11 Ex.D. 274; *Mancetter Developments Ltd v. Garmanston Ltd* [1986] Q.B.

1212; and there is some authority for the view that yearly tenants may also be liable for permissive waste to the extent that they fail to keep the premises in wind- and water-tight condition: *Wedd v. Porter* [1916] 2 K.B. 91, 100 *per* Swinfen-Eady L.J. In any event periodic tenants are subject to an implied covenant to use the premises in a tenant-like manner, which involves an obligation not to damage the premises wilfully or negligently, to take proper care of the premises and to carry out those repairs that a reasonable tenant would carry out.

Warren v. Keen [1954] 1 Q.B. 15

(CA, Somervell, Denning and Romer L.JJ.)

DENNING L.J.:

Apart from express contract, a tenant owes no duty to the landlord to keep the premises in repair. The only duty of the tenant is to use the premises in a husbandlike, or what is the same thing, a tenantlike manner. That is how it was put by Sir Vicary Gibbs C.J. in *Horsefall v. Mather* (1815) Holt N.P. 7 and by Scrutton L.J. and Atkin L.J. in *Marsden v. Edward Heyes Ltd* [1927] 2 K.B. 1, 7–8. But what does "to use the premises in a tenantlike manner" mean? It can, I think, best be shown by some illustrations. The tenant must take proper care of the place. He must, if he is going away for the winter, turn off the water and empty the boiler. He must clean the chimneys, when necessary, and also the windows. He must mend the electric light when it fuses. He must unstop the sink when it is blocked by his waste. In short, he must do the little jobs about the place which a reasonable tenant would do. In addition, he must, of course, not damage the house, wilfully or negligently; and he must see that his family and guests do not damage it and if they do, he must repair it. But apart from such things, if the house falls into disrepair through fair wear and tear or lapse of time, or for any reason not caused by him, then the tenant is not liable to repair it.

The landlord sought to put upon the tenant a higher obligation. She said that the duty of the tenant was to keep the premises wind and water tight and to make fair and tenantable repairs thereto. That seems to be based on *Hill and Redman on Landlord and Tenant*, 11th ed., p. 186. I do not think that is a correct statement of the obligation.

Take the first branch, "to keep the premises wind and water tight". Lord Tenterden, in one or two cases at Nisi Prius, used that expression and it was followed by the Court of Appeal in *Wedd v. Porter* [1916] 2 K.B. 91, 100, but it is very difficult to know what "wind and water tight" means. I asked counsel whether there was any case to be found in the books where a tenant had been held liable for breach of that obligation. I wanted to see what sort of thing it had been held to cover. But there was no such case to be found. In the absence of it, I think that the expression "wind and water tight" is of doubtful value and should be avoided. It is better to keep to the simple obligation "to use the premises in a tenantlike manner."

Take the second branch, "to make fair and tenantable repairs." Lord Kenyon used the expression in *Ferguson v. Anon* (1798) 2 Esp. 590, which is only reported by Espinasse, who was notoriously defective. It is said that he only heard half of what went on and reported the other half. If you read the whole sentence used by Lord Kenyon, however, it is clear that he was only referring to cases where a tenant does damage himself, such as breaking the windows or the doors. Then, of course, he must repair them. The sentence, used by Lord Kenyon, was explained by Bankes L.J. in *Marsden v. Heyes* by saying that if a tenant commits waste—that is, if he commits voluntary waste by doing damage himself—he must do such repairs to the premises as will enable them to exclude wind and water. So explained, it does not support the proposition stated in *Redman*.

It was suggested by [counsel for the landlord] that an action lies against a weekly tenant for permissive waste. I do not think that that is so. It has been held not to lie against a tenant at will, see the *Countess of Shrewsbury's* case (1600) 5 Co.Rep. 13b, and in my opinion it does not lie against a weekly tenant. In my judgment, the only obligation on a weekly tenant is to use the premises in a tenantlike manner. That does not cover the dampness and other defects alleged in the particulars of claim. The appeal should be allowed accordingly.

NOTES:

1. For comment, see (1954) 70 L.Q.R. 9; [1954] C.L.J. 71.

2. For discussion of the obligation to use the premises in a tenant-like manner, see *Wycombe Health Authority v. Barnett* (1982) 264 E.G. 619.

3. There is much uncertainty surrounding the law of waste and the implied obligation of tenant-like user as they apply to tenancies and licences. For recommendations for reform, see Law Com. No. 238, *Landlord and Tenant: Responsibility for State and Condition of Property* (1996).

Law Commission Report No. 238, Landlord and Tenant: Responsibility for State and Condition of Property (1996)

Summary of recommendations

Part X Waste

11.39 We recommend that the law of waste should no longer apply to—
  (a) a tenant holding under a lease;
  (b) a tenant at will;
  (c) a tenant at sufferance; or
  (d) a licensee of land.

11.40 Our recommendations do not affect the application of the tort of waste as it applies to any other relationship and in particular to any person who occupies any property as a beneficiary under the terms of any will or trust.

11.41 To replace both the law of waste and the implied covenant of tenant-like user, we recommend the creation of an implied statutory covenant or duty by which any tenant or licensee would undertake—
  (a) to take proper care of the premises which had been let to him or of which he was in occupation or possession;
  (b) to make good any damage wilfully done or caused to the premises by him, or by any other person lawfully in occupation or possession of or visiting the premises; and
  (c) not to carry out any alterations or other works the actual or probable result of which is to destroy or alter the character of the premises or any part of the premises to the detriment of the interest of the landlord or licensor.
  The covenant of tenant-like user that is presently implied at common law should be abolished.

11.43 We recommend that the parties should be free to exclude or modify the implied covenant or duty by express agreement...

11.44 We recommend that in relation to tenancies at will or sufferance and bare licences, the tenant or licensee shall, for the purposes of assessing damages for breach of the implied statutory duty, be deemed to have entered into a covenant with the licensor or landlord for valuable consideration, in the terms of the duty in question.

NOTE:

1. Consistent with the general approach in the Report, the implied covenant would be a default covenant subject to express modification or exclusion; but it would not be impliedly excluded by an undertaking by the occupier to repair and/or maintain the property.

1.2.2 *Access*   Where the landlord is under an obligation to carry out repairs, there is an implied covenant by the tenant to permit the landlord to enter the premises for that purpose: *Saner v. Bilton* (1878) 7 Ch D. 815; and see Law Com. No. 238, *Landlord and Tenant: Responsibility for State and Condition of Property* (1996), para. 11.13(b), *supra*, p. 408.

2. Express covenants

There is virtually no limit to the range of express covenants that may be included in a lease; three of the more important covenants are referred to in the following paragraphs. Since leases are almost invariably drafted by the landlord or his legal advisers, it is no surprise that, for the most part, these covenants tend to impose obligations on the tenant.

2.1 *Rent*

It has been seen that the payment of rent is not an essential element of the landlord and tenant relationship: *Ashburn Anstalt v. Arnold* [1989] Ch. 1, *supra*, p. 359. However, it is very unusual for a landlord not to require the payment of rent and the obligation to pay rent will normally be the subject matter of an express covenant. Moreover, in the case of longer leases the landlord will normally include a rent review clause, providing for the periodic review of the rent payable under the lease. Rent review clauses have generated a substantial volume of litigation but they are outside the scope of this book.

2.2 *Repair*

A lease may contain express covenants relating to the obligations of the tenant (and the landlord) to repair the property. In the case of leases of dwelling houses for less than seven years it has been seen that certain obligations are imposed on the landlord by the Landlord and Tenant Act 1985: *supra*; and those obligations cannot normally be excluded by the parties. Otherwise covenants relating to repair are a matter for negotiation between the parties, although there is a tendency for the tenant to assume more responsibility in the case of longer leases. However, since such covenants almost invariably use the terminology of "repair", such covenants tend to be construed along the same lines as implied covenants and to give rise to the same difficulties: see, *e.g. Post Office v. Aquarius Properties Ltd* [1987] 1 All E.R. 1055; and see Law Commission Consultation Paper No. 123, *Landlord and Tenant: Responsibility for State and Condition of Property* (1992), *supra*, p. 404. For an express covenant by a *landlord*, imposing obligations beyond mere "repair", see *Credit Suisse v. Beegas Nominees Ltd* [1994] 4 All E.R. 803.

Express covenants for repair by tenants commonly contain an exception of "fair wear and tear". It is now established that the exception covers only the remedying of things that wear out in the course of normal and reasonable use: *Haskell v. Marlow* [1928] 2 K.B. 45. However, where such wear and tear results in further damage, the tenant is not exempt from repairing that damage; and such repair may necessarily involve the repair of the original wear and tear: *ibid.; Regis Property Co. Ltd v. Dudley* [1959] A.C. 370.

For recommendations for reform, see Law Com. No. 238, *Landlord and Tenant: Responsibility for State and Condition of Property* (1996), *supra*, p. 407.

2.3 Assignment, sub-letting and parting with possession

Prima facie a tenant is entitled to assign the lease or to create a sub-lease. However, covenants against assignment, sub-letting and otherwise parting with possession are common, particularly in the context of shorter leases. Such covenants may be *absolute*; or they may be *qualified* in that the covenant only applies to assignment, sub-letting and parting with possession *without the licence or consent of the landlord*. Qualified covenants are controlled by statute. First, the landlord must not unreasonably withhold consent: Landlord and Tenant Act 1927, s.19(1). Secondly, where the application for consent is made in writing, the landlord must respond within a reasonable time and he must give his consent unless it is reasonable not to do so; and, if he withholds consent, he must give reasons and show that consent is being reasonably withheld: Landlord and Tenant Act 1988, s.1.

Since the legislation contains no definition of reasonableness, it is necessary to determine that question by reference to the common law principles. In *International Drilling Fluids Ltd v. Louisville Investments (Uxbridge) Ltd* [1986] Ch. 513 Balcombe L.J. expounded the following propositions (at 586–587):

(1) The purpose of a covenant against assignment without the consent of the landlord, such consent not to be unreasonably withheld, is to protect the lessor from having his premises used or occupied in an undesirable way, or by an undesirable tenant or assignee: *per* A.L. Smith L.J. in *Bates v. Donaldson* [1896] 2 Q.B. 241, 247, approved by all the members of the Court of Appeal in *Houlder Brothers & Co. Ltd v. Gibbs* [1925] Ch. 575.

(2) As a corollary to the first proposition, a landlord is not entitled to refuse his consent to an assignment on grounds which have nothing whatever to do with the relationship of landlord and tenant in regard to the subject matter of the lease: see *Houlder Brothers & Co. Ltd v. Gibbs*, a decision which (despite some criticism) is binding on this court: *Bickel v. Duke of Westminster* [1977] Q.B. 517. A recent example of a case where the landlord's consent was unreasonably withheld because the refusal was designed to achieve a collateral purpose unconnected with the terms of the lease is *Bromley Park Garden Estates Ltd v. Moss* [1982] 1 W.L.R. 1019.

. . .

(4) It is not necessary for the landlord to prove that the conclusions which led him to refuse consent were justified, if they were conclusions which might be reached by a reasonable man in the circumstances: *Pimms Ltd v. Tallow Chandlers Co.* [1964] 2 Q.B. 547, 564.

(5) It may be reasonable for the landlord to refuse his consent to an assignment on the ground of the purpose for which the proposed assignee intends to use the premises,

even though that purpose is not forbidden by the lease: see *Bates v. Donaldson* [1896] 2 Q.B. 241, 244.

(6) There is a divergence of authority on the question, in considering whether the landlord's refusal of consent is reasonable, whether it is permissible to have regard to the consequences to the tenant if consent to the proposed assignment is withheld. In an early case at first instance, *Sheppard v. Hong Kong and Shanghai Banking Corporation* (1872) 20 W.R. 459, 460, Malins V.-C. said that by withholding their consent the lessors threw a very heavy burden on the lessees and they therefore ought to show good grounds for refusing it. In *Houlder Brothers & Co. Ltd v. Gibbs* [1925] Ch. 575, 584, Warrington L.J. said:

"An act must be regarded as reasonable or unreasonable in reference to the circumstances under which it is committed, and when the question arises on the construction of a contract the outstanding circumstances to be considered are the nature of the contract to be construed, and the relations between the parties resulting from it."

In a recent decision of this court, *Leeward Securities Ltd v. Lilyheath Properties Ltd* (1983) 271 E.G. 279 concerning a sub-letting which would attract the protection of the Rent Act, both Oliver L.J. and O'Connor L.J. made it clear in their judgments that they could envisage circumstances in which it might be unreasonable to refuse consent to an underletting, if the result would be that there was no way in which the tenant (the sub-landlord) could reasonably exploit the premises except by creating a tenancy to which the Rent Act protection would apply, and which inevitably would affect the value of the landlord's reversion. O'Connor L.J. said, at p. 283:

"It must not be thought that, because the introduction of a Rent Act tenant inevitably has an adverse effect upon the value of the reversion, that that is a sufficient ground for the landlords to say that they can withhold consent and that the court will hold that that is reasonable."

To the opposite effect are the dicta, *obiter* but nevertheless weighty, of Viscount Dunedin and Lord Phillimore in *Viscount Tredegar v. Harwood* [1929] A.C. 72, 78, 82. There are numerous other dicta to the effect that a landlord need consider only his own interests: see, e.g., *West Layton Ltd v. Ford* [1979] Q.B. 593, 605, and *Bromley Park Garden Estates Ltd v. Moss* [1982] 1 W.L.R. 1019, 1027. Those dicta must be qualified, since a landlord's interests, collateral to the purposes of the lease, are in any event ineligible for consideration: see proposition (2) above. But in my judgment a proper reconciliation of those two streams of authority can be achieved by saying that while a landlord need usually only consider his own relevant interests, there may be cases where there is such a disproportion between the benefit to the landlord and the detriment to the tenant if the landlord withholds his consent to an assignment that it is unreasonable for the landlord to refuse consent.

(7) Subject to the propositions set out above, it is in each case a question of fact, depending upon all the circumstances, whether the landlord's consent to an assignment is being unreasonably withheld: see *Bickel v. Duke of Westminster* [1977] Q.B. 517, 524, and *West Layton Ltd v. Ford* [1979] Q.B. 593, 604, 606–607.

NOTES:

1. It has been held that, where a court is considering a tenant's application for a declaration that the landlord is unreasonably withholding consent, the landlord cannot rely on the absence of information that he did not request: *Norwich Union Life Insurance Society v. Shopmoor Ltd* [1999] 1 W.L.R. 531; nor can the landlord rely on reasons that he did not specify or articulate: *Footwear Corp. Ltd v. Amplight Properties Ltd* [1999] 1 W.L.R. 551.

2. Pursuant to proposition (2), the landlord cannot withhold consent to a

proposed under-lease on the ground that the proposed rent might have a deflationary effect on the achievable rents in respect of the landlord's other properties in the vicinity: *Norwich Union Life Insurance Society v. Shopmoor Ltd* [1999] 1 W.L.R. 531; but a landlord may withhold consent to a proposed change of use on an assignment so as to protect himself from commercial competition: *Sportoffer Ltd v. Erewash BC* (1999, unreported).

3. Proposition (3) related to the burden of proof, which was on the tenant but is now on the landlord: Landlord and Tenant Act 1988, s.1(6).

4. Section 22 of the Landlord and Tenant (Covenants) Act 1995 amends section 19 of the Landlord and Tenant Act 1927 by making special provision in relation to non-residential leases granted after 1995. The parties may include in such a lease a clause specifying the circumstances in which the landlord may withhold his consent to an assignment or the conditions on which he may grant such consent. One such condition is likely to be that the tenant enters into an "authorised guarantee agreement", guaranteeing performance of the covenants in the lease by the assignee: see *infra*, p. 437. Where such a clause is included, the landlord may withhold consent in the specified circumstances or impose the specified conditions and he will not be regarded as unreasonably withholding his consent or imposing unreasonable conditions: Landlord and Tenant Act 1927, s.19(1A).

3. Usual covenants

Where the grant of a lease is preceded by a contract, which makes no reference to the rights and obligations of the parties, it is an implied term of that contract that the lease will contain the "usual covenants" and that, if the lease does not include such covenants, it will be rectified accordingly. In fact there are two categories of usual covenants. The first category comprises those covenants which are set out in *Hampshire v. Wickens* (1878) 7 Ch D. 555 and which will be implied in every lease that is deemed to be subject to the usual covenants: covenants by the *tenant* to pay rent (subject to the right of the landlord to re-enter in the event of non-payment); to pay rates and other taxes on the premises except those for which the landlord is liable; to keep and leave the premises in repair; where the landlord has covenanted to repair, to permit the landlord to enter and view the state of the premises; and a covenant by the *landlord* to permit the tenant quiet enjoyment of the premises. The second category of usual covenants will vary according to the circumstances of the particular case and depends upon such matters as the nature of the property, its location, the purpose for which it is leased and any relevant trade usage: *Flexman v. Corbett* [1930] 1 Ch. 672; *Chester v. Buckingham Travel Ltd* [1981] 1 W.L.R. 96.

Chester v. Buckingham Travel Ltd [1981] 1 W.L.R. 96

(Ch.D., Foster J.)

The parties entered into an agreement for a 14-year lease (extendable by statute) of business premises. The property was located in a residential area and formed part of a complex comprising also a garage, a yard and four residential flats. The tenant had obtained specific performance of the agreement; but the court was called upon to determine what covenants should be included in the lease.

FOSTER J.:

It is well settled that in the technical sense, the term "usual covenant" is limited to those which are set out clearly in the judgment of Sir George Jessel M.R. in *Hampshire v. Wickens* (1878) 7 Ch.D. 555. He said, at pp. 561–562:

> "Usual covenants may vary in different generations. The law declares what are usual covenants according to the then knowledge of mankind. Lord Eldon L.C., in *Church v. Brown* (1808) 15 Ves.Jur. 258, 264, puts it thus: 'Before the case of *Henderson v. Hay* (1792) 3 Bro.C.C. 632, therefore, upon an agreement to grant a lease with nothing more than proper covenants, I should have said they were to be such covenants as were just as well known in such leases as the usual covenants under an agreement to convey an estate.' Now what is well known at one time may not be well known at another time, so that you cannot say that usual covenants never change. I have therefore looked at the last edition of *Davidson's Precedents in Conveyancing*, to see whether the usage is said to have changed. He says, [2nd ed.] vol. V, pp. 48, 49: 'The result of the authorities appears to be that in a case where the agreement is silent as to the particular covenants to be inserted in the lease, and provides merely for the lease containing "usual covenants", or, which is the same thing, in an open agreement without any reference to the covenants, and there are no special circumstances justifying the introduction of other covenants, the following are the only ones which either party can insist upon, namely, covenants by the lessee 1. to pay rent, 2. to pay taxes, except such [as] are expressly payable by the landlord, 3. to keep and deliver up the premises in repair, and 4. to allow the lessor to enter and view the state of repair. And the usual qualified covenant by the lessor for quiet enjoyment by the lessee.'
>
> When he refers to 'special circumstances' he means peculiar to a particular trade, as for example, in leases of public houses, where the brewers have their own forms of leases, the 'usual covenants' would mean the covenants always inserted in the leases of certain brewers.
>
> There is no mention of any other 'usual covenants,' and as nothing in this case has been lost for want of industry on the part of the counsel who have argued it, I am justified in saying that there is nothing in any text-book or book of precedents to show that a covenant not to assign is a usual covenant.
>
> I am therefore of opinion that it is not a usual covenant, and I dismiss the action with costs."

I reiterate that in this case also there has been nothing which has been lost for want of industry on the part of the counsel who have argued it.

In *Flexman v. Corbett* [1930] 1 Ch. 672, Maugham J. said, at pp. 680–681:

> "I will add only that my view that the question is one of fact is supported by the authority of *Bennett v. Womack* (1828) 7 B.C. 627 and *Hampshire v. Wickens* (1878) 7 Ch.D. 555, 561 and ... *Allen v. Smith* [1924] 2 Ch. 308. I might also add the case of *Brookes v. Drysdale* (1877) 3 C.P.D. 52, in which it was held that a condition that assignments or under-leases shall be registered by the lessor's solicitor and the fee paid to him, was not a usual covenant."

Of the four cases there cited, the first and fourth were assignment cases and the second and third were open contract cases. In my judgment, there is no distinction between the two and the test as to what is or what is not a usual clause is the same in both.

Meaning of usual covenants

If, in the agreement, these are not defined or not even mentioned, the court inserts them and the usual covenants in the technical sense are always included. For the defendants, it was submitted that "usual" means occurring in ordinary use: see Maugham J. in *Flexman v. Corbett* [1930] 1 Ch. 672, 678. For the plaintiff, it was submitted that for a covenant to be usual it must pass the test of what the court will imply into an agreement. He put his submission in this way: "In an open contract for the grant of a lease there is an implied term that the lease should contain usual and proper covenants—that is the usual covenants in the strict sense, together with such other covenants that on the particular facts of the case the parties must have impliedly intended the lease to contain". He referred me to three cases. (a) *The Moorcock* (1889) 14 P.D. 64 (the business efficacy test). (b) *Shirlaw v. Southern Foundries (1926) Ltd* [1939] 2 K.B. 206 (the officious bystander test) and (c) *Liverpool City Council v. Irwin* [1977] A.C. 239, 251 (the necessary implication test). In my judgment, these cases deal with quite another subject, namely, what the court will imply into a formal document. But when the court has to decide what is a usual covenant it is not implying anything into a document but merely deciding, in an assignment case, whether the existing lease includes an unusual covenant which should have been disclosed and in an open contract case, what covenants should be inserted. In my judgment, the cases where the court implies something are irrelevant and I reject the plaintiff's submission. I only have to decide what covenants which are usual should be included in the lease.

Usual covenants in 1971

In coming to a conclusion on this question, in my judgment, it is a question of fact to be determined by the court, not necessarily on the view of conveyancing counsel but by looking at the nature of the premises, their situation, the purpose for which they are being let, the length of the term, the evidence of conveyancers and the books of precedents. In *Flexman v. Corbett* [1930] 1 Ch. 672 Maugham J. said, at p. 678:

> "I think it right to express my opinion, after having heard and considered all the numerous authorities which have been cited to me, that the question whether particular covenants are usual covenants is a question of fact, and that the decision of the court on that point must depend upon the admissible evidence given before the court in relation to that question. I think that it is proper to take the evidence of conveyancers and others familiar with the practice in reference to leases and that it is also permissible to examine books of precedents. It is permissible to obtain evidence with regard to the practice in the particular district in which the premises in question are situated. I would add that in my view it is a complete mistake to suppose that the usual covenants in regard to a lease, for instance, of a country house are necessarily usual covenants in regard to the lease of a London residence, and I would add that it seems to me that it may very well be that what is usual in Mayfair or Bayswater is not usual at all in some other part of London such, for instance, as Whitechapel. Further, in my opinion, 'usual' in this sense means no more than 'occurring in ordinary use,' and I think that it is an error to suppose that the court is entitled to hold that a particular covenant is not usual because it may be established that there are some few cases in which that covenant is not used. If it is established that (to put a strong case) in nine cases out of ten the covenant would be found in a lease of premises of that nature for that purpose and in that district, I think that the court is bound to hold that the covenant is usual. The court must bear in mind here the ultimate question which is being decided, which is whether the form of the covenant is such as to constitute a defect in the subject-matter of the contract: and if it were established that the lease is in the form in which it would be anticipated as being in the great majority of cases, having regard to the nature of the property and

to the place where it is situated and to the purposes for which the premises are to be used, it does not seem to me reasonable to say that there is a defect in the subject-matter of the contract."

In this case, the premises are situated in Chelsea, in a predominantly residential area and the premises are part of a complex of properties consisting of (1) the plaintiff's premises (2) a garage (3) a yard and (4) four residential flats. The term is under 14 years but, of course, as these are business premises, a new lease may be granted by statute. I was quoted three precedents and I had before me an affidavit filed on behalf of the defendants by Mr M.J. Woodrow, a solicitor since 1959, who is second senior partner out of nine in the property department of Norton Rose, Botterell and Roche and who has, during the last 15 or 20 years, had considerable experience of commercial leases in London, acting for both landlords and tenants.

NOTES:

1. Foster J. held that, in addition to the *Hampshire v. Wickens* covenants, four further covenants should be included in the lease (primarily on the basis of affidavit evidence that such covenants were (very) usual in modern commercial leases and that they were appropriate and/or reasonable in the particular circumstances): (i) a fully qualified covenant restricting alterations to the property; (ii) a covenant not to permit the acquisition of easements by third parties; (iii) a fully qualified covenant restricting use of the property otherwise than as a garage/workshop; (iv) a covenant not to permit any nuisance, annoyance or disturbance. Foster J. also held (on the basis of existing precedents) that a proviso for re-entry in the event of breach of *any* covenant was usual and should be included in the lease. Foster J. rejected arguments for the inclusion of a number of other covenants (again primarily on the basis of affidavit evidence which established that, while such covenants were not uncommon, they were not usual): (i) a covenant not to hold auctions on the property; (ii) covenants against assignment, sub-letting and parting with possession; (iii) a covenant to pay the costs of the landlord incurred in connection with procedures preliminary to forfeiture proceedings.

2. For analysis, and criticism of the approach based on frequent use rather than the contractual principle that the lease should include only those covenants that are "necessary incidents" of the landlord and tenant relationship, see Crabb [1992] Conv. 18.

G. ENFORCEABILITY OF LEASEHOLD COVENANTS

As between the original parties, leasehold covenants are enforceable as a matter of contract. However, it is not uncommon for the lease and/or the freehold reversion to be assigned. In those circumstances, the question arises as to the continuing enforceability of the covenants. The law has been changed by the Landlord and Tenant (Covenants) Act 1995 but only in respect of "new tenancies", that is, tenancies granted after 1995 (other than tenancies granted pursuant to a pre-1996 agreement, option or court order: *ibid.* s.1). The result is that there are now two regimes for the enforceability of leasehold covenants; and the regime applicable to "old tenancies" will remain relevant for some considerable time. For discussion of the two regimes, see Bridge [1996] C.L.J. 313.

1. The law applicable to "old tenancies"

1.1 *Basic principles*

In *City of London Corp. v. Fell* [1993] Q.B. 589, Nourse L.J. stated (at 603–604):

A lease of land, because it originates in contract, gives rise to obligations enforceable between the original landlord and the original tenant in contract. But because it also gives the tenant an estate in the land, assignable, like the reversion, to others, the obligations, so far as they touch and concern the land, assume a wider influence, becoming, as it were, imprinted on the term or the reversion as the case may be, enforceable between the owners thereof for the time being as conditions of the enjoyment of their respective estates. Thus landlord and tenant stand together in one or other of two distinct legal relationships. In the first it is said that there is privity of contract between them, in the second privity of estate.

1.1.1 *Privity of contract and privity of estate*   It has been seen that, as between the original landlord and the original tenant, a lease may be analysed both as a contract and as a grant of an interest in land: as between the original parties there is both a contractual relationship ("privity of contract") and the relationship of landlord and tenant ("privity of estate"); but the two relationships are independent.

The contractual relationship is similar to any other contract between the parties: it imposes obligations which normally continue for the entire duration of the contract. Thus, even where the original parties transfer their respective interests, their contractual relationship, and more specifically their liability to perform the obligations of that relationship, continues. As a corollary, if the original landlord transfers his interest, there is no privity of contract between the transferee and the original tenant; similarly, if the original tenant transfers his interest, there is no privity of contract between the transferee and the original landlord; and, if both the original parties transfer their respective interests, there is no privity of contract between the respective transferees. In other words, privity of contract is exclusive to the original parties to the contract. (In fact, it has been common practice for landlords to require, as a condition of granting consent to an assignment of the lease, that the assignee covenants directly with the landlord to observe all the original tenant's covenants for the duration of the lease. However, such a covenant creates a new privity of contract between the landlord and the assignee.)

By contrast, the landlord and tenant relationship and privity of estate depends upon the holding of the relevant interests in the land: thus privity of estate as between the original parties continues only so long as neither party transfers his interest. However, unlike privity of contract, privity of estate is not restricted to the original parties but exists between those persons who currently hold the interests of the original landlord and tenant. Thus, if the original landlord transfers his interest, privity of estate exists between the transferee and the original tenant; similarly, if the original tenant transfers his interest, privity of estate exists between the transferee and the original landlord; and, if both the original parties transfer their respective interests, privity of estate exists between the respective transferees. On the other hand, if the original tenant or any subsequent transferee of the lease creates a sub-lease, there is no privity of estate between the original landlord (or any transferee of the leasehold reversion) and the subtenant. Unlike a transfer of the original interest, a sub-lease creates a new (lesser) interest. Thus privity of estate in respect of the original lease will continue between the holders of the original interests under that lease; and new relationships of both privity of contract and privity of estate will be created between the parties to the sub-lease.

The existence of privity of contract and/or privity of estate is central to the question of the enforceability of covenants contained in "old tenancies". First, where there is privity of contract between the person seeking to enforce such covenants and the person against whom enforcement is sought, all such covenants are prima facie enforceable as a matter of contract law. Secondly, where there is privity of estate between the person seeking to enforce such covenants and the person against whom enforcement is sought, only those covenants that "touch and concern" the land are enforceable: see *infra*. Thirdly, where there is neither privity of contract nor privity of estate between the person seeking to enforce such covenants and the person against whom enforcement is sought, such covenants are only enforceable where the benefit has been expressly assigned or where the principles governing covenants relating to freehold land apply: see *post*, Chapter 8.

1.1.2 *Covenants that "touch and concern" the land*   In the absence of privity of contract between the person seeking to enforce a leasehold covenant and the person against whom enforcement is sought, enforceability of the covenant may depend upon whether the covenant "touches and concerns" the land or, to use the terminology of the Law of Property Act 1925, "has reference to the subject-matter of the lease"; the two formulations have been held to be synonymous: *Hua Chiao Commercial Bank Ltd v. Chiaphua Industries Ltd* [1987] A.C. 99, 106–107 *per* Lord Oliver; *Caerns Motor Services v. Texaco Ltd* [1994] 1 W.L.R. 1249, 1259 *per* Judge Paul Baker Q.C. Such covenants are to be distinguished from covenants that impose personal or collateral obligations.

The meaning of "touch and concern" has been considered in two recent decisions of the Privy Council and the House of Lords; in both cases the leading judgment was delivered by Lord Oliver.

Hua Chiao Commercial Bank Ltd v. Chiaphua Industries Ltd [1987] A.C. 99

(PC, Lord Bridge, Lord Brandon, Lord Oliver, Lord Goff, Sir Ivor Richardson)

In 1979 the landlord granted to the respondents a five-year lease of premises in Hong Kong. The lease provided that on or before the execution of the lease the tenant should pay a security deposit, which would be returned at the end of the lease provided that the tenant had not breached any of the terms of the lease. The landlord assigned its interest to the appellant bank by way of mortgage; the landlord defaulted on the repayments to the appellant bank and subsequently went into liquidation. In 1984 the lease expired; and since the tenant had committed no breach of its terms it claimed the return of the security deposit. The question arose as to whether the obligation to return the deposit was a covenant that "touched and concerned" the land so as to be enforceable against the appellant bank.

LORD OLIVER:

There is a considerable measure of common ground between the parties. It is not in dispute that the bank constitutes, by assignment, "the landlord" for the purposes of the lease. Equally it is not in dispute that the test of whether the original landlord's covenant to return the amount of the deposit is enforceable against a successor in title is the same as it would be if the lease had been a lease of land in England, that is to say, whether the covenant is one "entered into by a lessor with reference to the subject matter of the lease" or, to use the common law terminology, whether it is a covenant which "touches and concerns the land". Nor is there any disagreement about the formulation of the test for determining whether any given covenant touches or concerns the land. Their Lordships have been referred to and are content to adopt the following passage from *Cheshire and Burn's Modern Law of Real Property*, 13th ed. (1982), pp. 430–431:

> "If the covenant has direct reference to the land, if it lays down something which is to be done or is not to be done upon the land, or, and perhaps this is the clearest way of describing the test, if it affects the landlord in his normal capacity as landlord or the tenant in his normal capacity as tenant, it may be said to touch and concern the land. Lord Russell C.J. [in *Horsey Estate Ltd v. Steiger* [1899] 2 Q.B. 79, 89] said: 'The true principle is that no covenant or condition which affects merely the person, and which does not affect the nature, quality, or value of the thing demised or the mode of using or enjoying the thing demised, runs with the land;' and Bayley J. at an earlier date asserted the same principle [in *Congleton Corp. v. Pattison* (1808) 10 East 130, 138]: 'In order to bind the assignee, the covenant must either affect the land itself during the term, such as those which regard the mode of occupation, or it must be such as per se, and not merely from collateral circumstances, affects the value of the land at the end of the term.'
>
> If a simple test is desired for ascertaining into which category a covenant falls, it is suggested that the proper inquiry should be whether the covenant affects either the landlord qua landlord or the tenant qua tenant. A covenant may very well have reference to the land, but, unless it is reasonably incidental to the relation of landlord and tenant, it cannot be said to touch and concern the land so as to be capable of running therewith or with the reversion."

. . .

The tenant argues, however, that inasmuch as the tenant's obligation to pay over the deposit on the execution of the lease was an obligation to secure the performance of covenants which touched and concerned the land, it was an obligation inextricably associated with covenants whose benefit and burden would pass with the reversion in the lease respectively. The landlord's obligation to repay if those covenants are observed is, it is argued, inseparable from that associated obligation and must therefore possess the same characteristics as the covenants whose performance is secured by the associated obligation. To put it another way the obligation to deposit is an obligation of the tenant assumed by him qua tenant and it follows that the correlative obligation of the landlord is an obligation assumed by him qua landlord. This argument is reflected in the judgment of McMullin V.-P. in the Court of Appeal, who observed:

> "The plain fact is that the provisions of clause 4(h) are so clearly intended to encourage compliance with the very many covenants enjoining the lessee to make proper use of the land and not to cause a diminution in its value that it would be wholly unrealistic to regard it as being otherwise than inextricably bound up with those undertakings generally."

That the original tenant's obligation to make the deposit is "bound up" with his obligation to perform the tenant's covenants in the lease is undeniable, but the former is, of course, a once-for-all contractual obligation between the original parties as regards which no question of transfer with the term or with the reversion can arise. The sum deposited is to be paid on or before the execution of the lease. What this appeal is concerned with, however, is only the landlord's obligation to repay once the lease has expired without breach of covenant, there being neither any obligation on the original landlord to pay over the amount of the deposit to an assignee of the reversion nor any obligation on the original tenant to assign to an assignee of the term his contractual right to receive back the amount of the deposit when and if the condition for its repayment is fulfilled. It is bound up with the tenant's covenant only, as it were, at one remove, as being an obligation correlative to a contractual obligation which is itself connected with the performance of covenants touching and concerning the land. The expression "inextricably bound" appears to derive from the speech of Lord Atkin in *Moss' Empires Ltd v. Olympia (Liverpool) Ltd* [1939] A.C. 544, a case strongly relied upon by the tenant. The question in that case arose out of a lease which contained a series of repairing and decorating covenants on the part of the tenant numbered (iv) to (viii) inclusive. The covenant numbered (vii) obliged the tenant in each year of the term to expend at least £500 upon the performance of the covenants to repair and decorate for which receipts were to be produced to the lessor, any shortfall in any year in the amount expended to be paid to the lessor and any excess in expenditure over the amount of £500 in any year to be treated pro tanto as a satisfaction of the liability for future years. An assignee of the lease having failed to expend the full sum of £500 in certain years, the question arose whether the obligation was one which bound the assignee as one touching and concerning the land or whether it was merely a collateral covenant binding only as between the original parties. Lord Atkin observed, at p. 551:

> "this is not a bare obligation to pay money which does not touch the thing demised. On the contrary, the performance of the repairing covenants and the obligations under clause (vii) are so inextricably bound together that it would be impossible to sever clause (vii), and treat it as a collateral promise to pay money. The relevant clauses read as a whole provide a scheme whereby if things work smoothly the obligation of the tenant over the term is limited to £500 a year, less than one-sixth of the total rent, while the lessor is provided with sums which, if he chooses, he may apply towards meeting the obligation which he has assumed of performing structural repairs. In my opinion the clause in question closely touches the thing demised, and runs with the land."

Similarly Lord Porter said, at p. 560:

> "This is not a bare or mere covenant to pay £500 or even to pay the difference between the sum spent and proved and £500. It is part of a number of covenants whereby the mutual obligations of landlord and tenant in repairing and redecorating the premises are fulfilled and is inextricably bound up with them."

On the facts of that case the decision is scarcely a surprising one, for the obligation was to expend not less than the stipulated sum upon the preservation of the estate in the proper performance of the repairing covenants in the lease, an obligation clearly affecting the value of the lessor's estate and so directly touching and concerning the thing demised. That was, however, a very different case from the present and their Lordships are not persuaded that it is, or was ever intended to be, authority for the proposition that every covenant which is related, however obliquely, to some other obligation which touches and concerns the land necessarily takes on from that very relationship, the same character as regards transmissibility to or against successors in title. To say that the obligation to "return" the amount of the deposit is "inextricably bound up with" covenants which touch and concern the land in the sense in which the expression was used by McMullin V.-P. in the instant case—i.e. that, in order to determine whether or not the obligation to pay could have arisen against anyone, it would be necessary to survey the other covenants—does not, in their Lordships' view, answer the critical question of whether it itself touches and concerns the land. It certainly does not per se affect the nature quality or value of the land either during or at the end of the term. It does not per se affect the mode of using or enjoying that which is demised. And to ask whether it affects the landlord qua landlord or the tenant qua tenant is an exercise which begs the question. It does so only if it runs with the reversion or with the land respectively. There is not, on any conceivable construction of the clause, anything which either divests the original tenant of his contractual right to receive back after assignment the deposit which he has paid or which entitles an assignee from him to claim the benefit of the sum to the exclusion of his assignor; and, plainly, the money cannot be repaid more than once. Equally, there is not on any conceivable construction anything in the clause which entitles the assignee of the reversion to take over from his assignor the benefit of the sum deposited or which obliges the assignee, in enforcing the covenants against the tenant for the time being, to give credit for money which he himself has never received and to which he has no claim. Whilst it is true that the deposit is paid to the original payee because it is security for the performance of contractual obligations assumed throughout the term by the payer and because the payee is the party with whom the contract is entered into, it is, in their Lordships' view, more realistic to regard the obligation as one entered into with the landlord qua payee rather than qua landlord. By demanding and receiving this security, he assumes the obligation of any mortgagee to repay on the stipulated condition and that obligation remains, as between himself and the original payer, throughout the period of the lease, even though neither party may, when the condition is fulfilled, have any further interest in the land demised. The nature of the obligation is simply that of an obligation to repay money which has been received and it is neither necessary nor logical, simply because the conditions of repayment relate to the performance of covenants in a lease, that the transfer of the reversion should create in the transferee an additional and co-extensive obligation to pay money which he has never received and in which he never had any interest or that the assignment of the term should vest in the assignee the right to receive a sum which he has never paid.

NOTES:

1. For comment, see [1987] Conv. 288.

2. The passage cited from *Cheshire and Burn* has stood the test of time: the final paragraph was approved in *Breams Property Investment Co. Ltd v. Stroulger* [1948] 2 K.B. 1, 7 *per* Scott L.J. See now 15th ed. (1994) p. 446.

3. Covenants by the *tenant* that have been held to touch and concern the land include covenants to pay rent, to repair the property, to insure the property against fire, not to use the property otherwise than as a dwelling house and not to assign without the landlord's consent; covenants by the

landlord that have been held to touch and concern the land include covenants for quiet enjoyment, to supply the property with water, not to build on certain parts of the adjoining land and not to determine a periodic tenancy during its first three years.

4. Options granted by the landlord to the tenant deserve special mention. An option to purchase the freehold (or right of pre-emption over the freehold) does not touch and concern the land: *Woodall v. Clifton* [1905] 2 Ch. 257; it follows (i) that the benefit of such options must be expressly assigned to an assignee of the lease: *Griffith v. Pelton* [1958] Ch. 205; and (ii) that the option must be protected by the appropriate form of registration (unless, in the case of registered land, the option constitutes an overriding interest). On the other hand, an option to renew the lease does touch and concern the land: *Phillips v. Mobil Oil Co. Ltd* [1989] 1 W.L.R. 888; but, although that should be sufficient to pass the benefit and the burden to assignees of the tenant and landlord respectively, it has been held that the option will be unenforceable against an assignee of the landlord unless protected by the appropriate form of registration: *ibid.*; and see *Markfaith Investment Ltd v. Chiap Hua Flashlights Ltd* [1991] 2 A.C. 43, 59 *per* Lord Templeman.

P. & A. Swift Investments v. Combined English Stores Group plc [1989] A.C. 632

(HL, Lord Keith, Lord Roskill, Lord Templeman, Lord Ackner, Lord Oliver)

A sub-lease was granted to a subsidiary of the defendant; and the defendant joined in the sub-lease as surety, guaranteeing that the sub-tenant would pay the rent and observe the other covenants. The head-lease was subsequently assigned to the plaintiff; but there was no express assignment of the benefit of the surety's covenant. The sub-tenant defaulted on the rent and the question arose whether the plaintiff could enforce the defendant's covenant.

[There was no privity of contract or privity of estate between the plaintiff and the surety; and, as noted, there had been no express assignment of the benefit of the covenant. The claim of the plaintiff to enforce the covenant therefore rested on the common law rule under which the benefit would run with the land if, but only if, the assignee [of the reversion] had the legal estate in the land and the covenant was one which touched and concerned the land. The plaintiff clearly had the legal estate; and it was held that the leasehold reversion was "land" for the purposes of the common law rule. The question remained whether the covenant of a surety to pay a sum of money was a covenant that touched and concerned the land. The trial judge held that the covenant did touch and concern the land and gave judgment for the plaintiff. Since the point had been decided in the same way by the Court of Appeal in *Kumar v. Dunning* [1989] Q.B. 193, the defendant appealed to the House of Lords under section 12 of the Administration of Justice Act 1969 (the "leapfrog procedure").]

LORD TEMPLEMAN:

The surety denies liability, pleading that the surety's covenant does not touch and concern the land and does not run with the reversion so as to be enforceable by the respondent landlord. The respondent landlord replies that a covenant by a surety, in whatever form or expression the surety covenant may take, is a covenant that the tenant's covenants shall be performed and observed. A covenant by a surety that a tenant's covenant which touches and concerns the land shall be performed and observed must itself be a covenant which touches and concerns the land; the benefit of that surety's covenant will run with the reversion, and the covenant is therefore enforceable without express assignment. I agree. A surety for a tenant is a quasi tenant who volunteers to be a substitute or twelfth man for the tenant's team and is subject to the same rules and regulations as the player he replaces. A covenant which runs with the reversion against the tenant runs with the reversion against the surety. For these reasons and for the reasons to be given by my noble and learned friend, Lord Oliver of Aylmerton, I would dismiss the appeal.

LORD OLIVER:

In my opinion the question of whether a surety's covenant in a lease touches and concerns the land falls to be determined by the same test as that applicable to the tenant's covenant. That test was formulated by Bayley J. in *Congleton Corporation v. Pattison* (1808) 10 East 130 and adopted by Farwell J. in *Rogers v. Hosegood* [1900] 2 Ch. 388, 395:

> "the covenant must either affect the land as regards mode of occupation, or it must be such as per se, and not merely from collateral circumstances, affects the value of the land."

The meaning of those words "per se, and not merely from collateral circumstances" has been the subject matter of a certain amount of judicial consideration and the judgment of Sir Nicolas Browne-Wilkinson V.-C. in *Kumar v. Dunning* [1989] Q.B. 193 (where the problem was identical to that in the instant case save that the covenant was given on an assignment and not on the grant of the lease), contains a careful and helpful review of the authorities. No useful purpose would be served by repeating this here and I am both grateful for and content to accept both his analysis and his conclusion that the correct principle was that pronounced by Best J. in *Vyvyan v. Arthur* (1823) 1 B. & C. 410, 417, and approved by this House in *Dyson v. Forster* [1909] A.C. 98:

> "The general principle is, that if the performance of the covenant be beneficial to the reversioner, in respect of the lessor's demand, and to no other person, his assignee may sue upon it; but if it be beneficial to the lessor, without regard to his continuing owner of the estate, it is a mere collateral covenant, upon which the assignee cannot sue."

The Vice-Chancellor stated his conclusion, at p. 204:

> "From these authorities I collect two things. First, that the acid test whether or not a benefit is collateral is that laid down by Best J., namely, is the covenant beneficial to the owner for the time being of the covenantee's land, and to no one else? Secondly, a covenant simply to pay a sum of money, whether by way of insurance premium, compensation or damages, is a covenant capable of touching and concerning the land provided that the existence of the covenant, and the right to payment thereunder, affects the value of the land in whomsoever it is vested for the time being."

It is objected that this states the matter too broadly because, for example, it is said that it would involve the conclusion that a simple covenant to pay an annuity of £x per annum to the owner for the time being of Blackacre would then be treated as a covenant touching and concerning the land because it would enhance the value of the land. This is, I think, to read the Vice-Chancellor's words too literally, for it is, as it seems to me, implicit in them that he is referring to a monetary obligation related to something which issues out of or is to be done on or to the land. His approach to the problem, (which, again, I respectfully adopt) emerges from the following passage from his judgment, at pp. 200–201:

"The surety covenant is given as a support or buttress to covenants given by a tenant to a landlord. The covenants by the tenant relate not only to the payment of rent, but also to repair, insurance and user of the premises. All such covenants by a tenant in favour of the landlord touch and concern the land, i.e., the reversion of the landlord. The performance of some covenants by tenants relates to things done on the land itself (e.g. repair and user covenants). Other tenants' covenants (e.g. payment of rent and insurance) require nothing to be done on the land itself. They are mere covenants for the payment of money. The covenant to pay rent is the major cause of the landlord's reversion having any value during the continuance of the term. Where there is privity of estate, the tenants' covenant to pay rent touches and concerns the land: *Parker v. Webb* (1822) 3 Salk. 4. As it seems to me, in principle a covenant by a third party guaranteeing the performance by the tenant of his obligations should touch and concern the reversion as much as do the tenants' covenants themselves. This view accords with what, to my mind, is the commercial common sense and justice of the case. When, as in the present case, the lease has been assigned on the terms that the sureties will guarantee performance by the assignee of the lease, justice and common sense ought to require the sureties, not the original tenant, to be primarily liable in the event of default by the assignee. So long as the reversion is not assigned, that will be the position. Why should the position between the original tenant and the sureties be rendered completely different just because the reversion has been assigned, a transaction wholly outside the control of the original tenant and the sureties?"

I entirely agree and would add only this. It has been said that the surety's obligation is simply that of paying money and, of course, in a sense that is true if one looks only at the remedy which the landlord has against him in the event of default by the tenant. But for my part I do not think that this is a complete analysis. The tenant covenants that he will do or refrain from doing certain things which undoubtedly touch and concern the land. A surety covenants that those things shall be done or not done as the case may be. Now it is true that the remedy for breach will sound in damages only, but the primary obligation is the same, namely that which is covenanted to be done will be done. Take for instance the tenant's covenant to repair. There is nothing here requiring personal performance by the tenant. The effect of the covenant is that the tenant must procure the premises to be kept in repair. Equally, a guarantee by the surety of the repairing covenant is no more than a covenant or warranty that the guarantor will procure that the tenant, in turn, procures the premises to be kept in repair. The content of the primary obligation is, as it seems to me, exactly the same and if that of the tenant touches and concerns the land that of the surety must, as it seems to me, equally do so.

Formulations of definitive tests are always dangerous, but it seems to me that, without claiming to expound an exhaustive guide, the following provides a satisfactory working test for whether, in any given case, a covenant touches and concerns the land: (1) the covenant benefits only the reversioner for time being, and if separated from the reversion ceases to be of benefit to the covenantee; (2) the covenant affects the nature, quality, mode of user or value of the land of the reversioner; (3) the covenant is not expressed to be personal (that is to say neither being given only to a specific reversioner nor in respect of the obligations only of a specific tenant); (4) the fact that a covenant is to pay a sum of money will not prevent it from touching and concerning the land so long as the three foregoing conditions are satisfied and the covenant is connected with something to be done on, to or in relation to the land.

For my part, I am entirely satisfied that the decision of the Court of Appeal in *Kumar v. Dunning* [1989] Q.B. 193 was correct and was reached for the correct reasons. The instant case is indistinguishable in any material respect. Nothing I think turns upon the precise terms of the covenant in either case. It follows that I would dismiss this appeal.

NOTES:

1. It is not clear whether the decisions in *Hua Chiao Commercial Bank Ltd v. Chiaphua Industries Ltd* and in *P. & A. Swift Investments v. Combined English Stores Group plc* can be reconciled. The earlier decision was cited in argument in the later case but it was not referred to in the judgments. In *Kumar v. Dunning* [1989] Q.B. 193 Browne-Wilkinson V.-C. said (at 206):

Lord Oliver [in *Hua Chiao Commercial Bank Ltd v. Chiaphua Industries Ltd*] plainly rejected any general rule that every covenant which is related, however obliquely, to some other obligation which touches and concerns the land itself necessarily touches and concerns the land: see p. 107C. But he did not rule out the possibility that a covenant closely connected and bound up with a covenant which does touch and concern the land can itself touch and concern the land. The ratio of the decision, in my judgment, is to be found at p. 112F–H. Lord Oliver points out that the assignee of the reversion was not entitled to receive the deposit from the original lessor on the assignment of the reversion: nor was an assignee of the term entitled to recover it at the end of the term. The liability to repay the deposit at the end of the term remained throughout on the original landlord and was an obligation to repay to the original tenant. So viewed, the decision is entirely consistent with the test laid down by Best J. The benefit of the covenant to repay could not touch and concern the land because someone other than the owner for the time being of the term could take the benefit of it.

For comment, see [1987] Conv. 290; [1988] C.L.J. 180.

2. *P. & A. Swift Investments v. Combined English Stores Group plc* was applied in *Coronation Street Industrial Properties Ltd v. Ignall Industries plc* [1989] 1 W.L.R. 304.

3. Harpum [1988] C.L.J. 180 concludes that *Kumar v. Dunning* (and *P. & A. Swift Investments v. Combined English Stores Group plc*) has (i) provided for the first time a coherent test for determining whether a covenant touches and concerns the land and (ii) assimilated the tests for both leasehold and freehold covenants.

4. In *Caerns Motor Services Ltd v. Texaco Ltd* [1994] 1 W.L.R. 1249 Judge Paul Baker Q.C. expressed the view that the question whether a covenant touches and concerns the land should be approached differently according to whether or not there is privity of estate between the parties. See also *System Floors Ltd v. Ruralpride Ltd* [1995] 1 E.G.L.R. 48.

1.2 *Operation of the basic principles*

City of London Corp. v. Fell [1994] 1 A.C. 458

(HL, Lord Templeman, Lord Goff, Lord Jauncey, Lord Browne-Wilkinson, Lord Mustill)

LORD TEMPLEMAN:

At common law, after an assignment, the benefit of a covenant by the original landlord which touches and concerns the land runs with the term granted by the lease. The burden of a covenant by the original tenant which touches and concerns the land also runs with the term: see *Spencer's Case* (1583) 5 Co.Rep. 16a.

By statute, the benefit of a covenant by the original tenant which touches and concerns the land runs with the reversion. Section 141 of the Law of Property Act 1925 replacing section 1 of the Grantees of Reversions Act 1540 (32 Hen. 8, c. 34), section 10 of the Conveyancing Act 1881 (44 & 45 Vict. c. 41) and section 2 of the Conveyancing Act 1911 provides:

"Rent reserved by a lease, and the benefit of every covenant or provision therein contained, having reference to the subject matter thereof, and on the lessee's part to be observed or performed, and every condition of re-entry and other condition therein contained, shall be annexed and incident to and shall go with the reversionary estate in the land ... immediately expectant on the term granted by the lease ..."

By statute, the burden of a covenant by the original landlord which touches and concerns the land also runs with the reversion. Section 142 of the Act of 1925 reproducing section 2 of the Act of 1540 and section 11 of the Conveyancing Act 1881 provides:

"(1) The obligation under a condition or of a covenant entered into by a lessor with reference to the subject matter of the lease shall, if and so far as the lessor has power to bind the reversionary estate immediately expectant on the term granted by the lease, be annexed and incident to and shall go with that reversionary estate ... and may be taken advantage of and enforced by the person in whom the term is from time to time vested ... and ... the obligation aforesaid may be taken advantage of and enforced against any person so entitled."

The principle that the benefit and burden of covenants in a lease which touch and concern the land run with the term and with the reversion is necessary for the effective operation of the law of landlord and tenant. Common law, and statute following the common law, recognise two forms of legal estate in land, a fee simple absolute in possession and a term of years absolute: see section 1 of the Act of 1925. Common law, and statute following the common law, were faced with the problem of rendering effective the obligations under a lease which might endure for a period of 999 years or more beyond the control of any covenantor. The solution was to annex to the term and the reversion the benefit and burden of covenants which touch and concern the land. The covenants having been annexed, every legal owner of the term granted by the lease and every legal owner of the reversion from time to time holds his estate with the benefit of and subject to the covenants which touch and concern the land. The system of leasehold tenure requires that the obligations in the lease shall be enforceable throughout the term, whether those obligations are affirmative or negative. The owner of a reversion must be able to enforce the positive covenants to pay rent and keep in repair against an assignee who in turn must be able to enforce any positive covenants entered into by the original landlord. Common law retained the ancient rule that the burden of a covenant does not run with the land of the covenantor except in the case of a lease, but even that rule was radically modified by equity so far as negative covenants were concerned: see *Tulk v. Moxhay* (1848) 2 Ph. 774.

The effect of common law and statute on a lease is to create rights and obligations which are independent of the parallel rights and obligations of the original human covenantor who and whose heirs may fail or the parallel rights and obligations of a corporate covenantor which may be dissolved. Common law and statute achieve that effect by annexing those rights and obligations so far as they touch and concern the land to the term and to the reversion. Nourse L.J. neatly summarised the position when he said in an impeccable judgment [1993] Q.B. 589, 604:

"The contractual obligations which touch and concern the land having become imprinted on the estate, the tenancy is capable of existence as a species of property independently of the contract."

The common law did not release the original tenant from liability for breaches of covenant committed after an assignment because of the sacred character of covenant in English law. I understand that Scots law releases the original tenant once he has been replaced by a permitted or accepted assignee. This only means that the fortunate English landlord has two remedies after an assignment, namely his remedy against the assignee and his remedy against the original tenant. It does not follow that if the liability of the original tenant is released or otherwise disappears then the term granted by the lease will disappear or that the assignee will cease to be liable on the covenants.

As between landlord and assignee the landlord cannot enforce a covenant against the assignee because the assignee does not covenant. The landlord enforces against the assignee the provisions of a covenant entered into by the original tenant, being provisions which touch and concern the land, because those provisions are annexed by the lease to the term demised by the lease. The assignee is not liable for a breach of covenant committed after the assignee has himself in turn assigned the lease because once he has assigned over he has ceased to be the owner of the term to which the covenants are annexed.

Covenants are introduced on the creation of a lease but are not necessary to sustain a lease. Upon an assignment of a lease, the provisions of the covenants by the original tenant continue to attach to the term because those provisions touch and concern the land and not because there continues to exist an original tenant who has ceased to own any interest in the demised land but remains liable in contract to fulfil the promises he made under covenant.

NOTE:

1. The systematic application of the basic principles is outlined below.

1.2.1 *The rights of the original landlord*

1.2.1.1 *The rights of the original landlord against the original tenant*

(1) The privity of contract that exists between the original parties means that any covenants contained in the lease are mutually enforceable as a matter of contract law. Moreover, because enforceability depends upon privity of contract, there is no requirement that the covenants should touch and concern the land.

(2) Since covenants in leases are deemed to be made on behalf of the covenantor and his successors in title unless a contrary intention is expressed (Law of Property Act 1925, s.79), privity of contract means that the original tenant remains subject to primary liability to perform his covenants throughout the entire duration of the lease, notwithstanding that he has assigned his interest: *Warnford Investments Ltd v. Duckworth* [1979] Ch. 127, 137 *per* Megarry V.-C.

(3) Prima facie the liability of the original tenant continues for as long as the lease continues *in accordance with the contract between the original parties*; and thus it continues during any extension pursuant to an option in the original lease: *Baker v. Merckel* [1960] 1 Q.B. 657. However, where a business tenancy is assigned during the contractual term, it has been held that liability does not continue during any *statutory* extension or continuation of

the tenancy: *City of London Corp. v. Fell* [1994] 1 A.C. 458, noted at [1994] C.L.J. 28; [1994] Conv. 247; and it may be presumed that the same principle applies to other statutory extensions. Although the prima facie position may be modified by the terms of the lease, the normal inequality of bargaining power between the original parties means that the exclusion of continuing liability during the contractual term is less likely than the extension of continuing liability during any *statutory* extension or continuation of the lease: see *Herbert Duncan Ltd v. Cluttons* [1993] Q.B. 589. However, continuing liability is excluded by statute where the court orders the transfer of a tenancy of the matrimonial home from one spouse to the other by way of financial provision following divorce: Family Law Act 1996, Sched. 7, para. 7 (2); it is also excluded where a perpetually renewable lease is assigned: Law of Property Act 1922, Sched. 15, para. 5.

(4) The continuing liability applies even though the original tenant has no control over the assignee: *Thames Manufacturing Co. Ltd v. Perrots (Nichol & Peyton) Ltd* (1984) 50 P. & C.R. 1; *Allied London Investments Ltd v. Hambro Life Assurance Ltd* (1985) 50 P. & C.R. 207; *Weaver v. Mogford* [1988] 2 E.G.L.R. 48. Moreover, in a series of cases it was held that the extent of the continuing liability could increase as a result of a variation of the terms of the lease agreed between the assignee of the lease and the original landlord: see, e.g. *Centrovincial Estates plc v. Bulk Storage Ltd* (1983) 46 P. & C.R. 393; *Selous Street Properties Ltd v. Oronel Fabrics Ltd* [1984] 1 E.G.L.R. 50, noted at [1984] Conv. 443; *Gus Property Management Ltd v. Texas Homecare Ltd* [1993] 2 E.G.L.R. 62. However, the Court of Appeal has subsequently held that those cases could be justified only on the basis that the original tenant covenanted to pay the increased rent as agreed between the assignee of the lease and the original landlord. In the absence of such a covenant, it was held that the liability of the original tenant was limited to the rent payable under the original terms of the lease: *Friends' Provident Life Office v. British Railways Board* [1996] 1 All E.R. 336; *Beegas Nominees Ltd v. BHP Petroleum Ltd* (1998) 77 P. & C.R. 14. Section 18 of the Landlord and Tenant (Covenants) Act 1995, which applies to "old tenancies" as well as "new tenancies", provides that the liability of the original tenant (or his guarantor) cannot be increased by any post-assignment variation in the terms of the lease which the landlord has an absolute right to refuse; but that provision has almost certainly been rendered redundant by *Friends' Provident Life Office v. British Railways Board.*

(5) The landlord will normally first seek redress against an assignee of the lease in respect of breaches of covenants that touch and concern the land: see *infra.* However, there is no requirement that he should do so; and the continuing liability of the original tenant provides potential insurance against the insolvency of the assignee: see *R.A. Securities Ltd v. Mercantile Credit Co. Ltd* [1995] 3 All E.R. 581; *Mytre Investments Ltd v. Reynolds* [1995] 3 All E.R. 588; *Hindcastle Ltd v. Barbara Attenborough Associates Ltd* [1997] A.C. 70; and see *infra*, p. 485.

(6) If the landlord proposes to enforce covenants for the payment of fixed charges such as rent and service charges against the original tenant (or his

guarantor), he must serve notice on the tenant within six months of the date of the payments becoming due: Landlord and Tenant (Covenants) Act 1995, s.17. Moreover, where the landlord enforces the original tenant's contractual liability, the original tenant has the right to apply for an "overriding lease", which is interposed between the interest of the landlord and that of the current tenant: *ibid.* s.19. Although an overriding lease may give the original tenant more effective remedies against the current (defaulting) tenant, it is deemed to be an "old tenancy" for the purposes of the 1995 Act, so that the contractual liability under the overriding lease will survive any assignment of that lease.

(7) In certain circumstances, the original tenant may have rights of indemnity against the defaulting assignee in respect of any payments made pursuant to his continuing liability. Where the relevant covenant touches and concerns the land, indemnity may be available directly from the current assignee: *Moule v. Garrett* (1872) L.R. 7 Ex. 107; otherwise the availability of indemnity depends upon an unbroken chain of express or implied covenants: Law of Property Act 1925, s.77(1)(C); Land Registration Act 1925, s.24(1)(b); and see *Johnsey Estates Ltd v. Lewis & Manley (Engineering) Ltd* [1987] 2 E.G.L.R. 69. In reality these rights of indemnity are largely theoretical. Since the assignee will be directly liable to the landlord in respect of most covenants (see *infra*), the landlord will normally only rely on the continuing liability of the original tenant where the assignee is insolvent: see, *e.g. Weaver v. Mogford* [1988] 2 E.G.L.R. 48; *R.P.H. Ltd v. Mirror Group Newspapers and Mirror Group Holdings* (1992) 65 P. & C.R. 252.

(8) Where the original landlord has assigned the reversion, he ceases to be entitled to sue in respect of breaches of covenants that "have reference to the subject-matter of the lease", including those breaches that occurred before the assignment: see *infra*.

1.2.1.2 *The rights of the original landlord against a surety for the original tenant*   Where a surety has guaranteed the performance of the original tenant's covenants, the landlord can enforce the surety's covenant as a matter of contract.

1.2.1.3 *The rights of the original landlord against an assignee of the lease*

(1) The burden of the original tenant's covenants that touch and concern the land passes with the lease, so that the assignee of the lease is directly liable to the original landlord for breach of such covenants: *Spencer's Case* (1583) 5 Co.Rep. 16a.

(2) Liability is confined to breaches occurring while the lease is vested in the assignee. It does not extend to breaches occurring before the lease was assigned: *Grescot v. Green* (1700) 1 Salk 199; *Granada Theatres Ltd v. Freehold Investments (Leytonstone) Ltd* [1959] Ch. 592, 606 *per* Jenkins L.J.; nor to breaches occurring after the assignee himself assigns the lease: *Onslow v. Currie* (1817) 2 Madd. 330; *Paul v. Nurse* (1828) 8 B. & C. 486; but, even where the assignee subsequently assigns the lease, he remains liable to the

landlord for breaches committed while he was the tenant: *Harley v. King* (1835) 2 Cr.M. & R. 18.

(3) As already noted, the liability of an assignee may extend beyond these principles where, most commonly as a condition of the landlord's consent to the assignment, the assignee covenants directly with the landlord to observe and perform *all* the original tenant's covenants. In such a case, because there is privity of contract between the landlord and the assignee, the liability of the assignee will extend to covenants that do not touch and concern the land and it will continue for the remainder of the lease: *J. Lyons & Co. Ltd v. Knowles* [1943] K.B. 366; *Estates Gazette Ltd v. Benjamin Restaurants Ltd* [1994] 1 W.L.R. 1528.

1.2.2 *The rights of an assignee of the reversion*

1.2.2.1 *The rights of an assignee of the reversion against the original tenant* The benefit of the original tenant's covenants that "have reference to the subject-matter of the lease" passes with the reversion by virtue of section 141(1) of the Law of Property Act 1925, so that the assignee of the reversion may enforce those covenants against the tenant. The entitlement of the assignee is exclusive. Moreover, it extends to breaches that occurred before the assignment: *Re King* [1963] Ch. 459, 489 *per* Upjohn L.J., 497 *per* Diplock L.J.; *London & County (A. & D.) Ltd v. Wilfred Sportsman Ltd* [1971] Ch. 764, 784 *per* Russell L.J.; and the rule applies even where the defaulting original tenant assigned his lease before the reversion was assigned: *Arlesford Trading Co. Ltd v. Servansingh* [1971] 1 W.L.R. 1080, 1082 *per* Russell L.J., thereby imposing liability where there had never been either privity of contract or privity of estate between the parties.

1.2.2.2 *The rights of an assignee of the reversion against a surety for the original tenant* An assignee of the reversion may acquire the benefit of the surety's covenant under the common law rules: *P. & A. Swift Investments v. Combined English Stores Group plc* [1989] A.C. 632, *supra*, p. 425.

1.2.2.3 *The rights of an assignee of the reversion against an assignee of the lease* An assignee of the reversion is in the same position as the original landlord: see 1.2.1.3, *supra*.

1.2.3 *The rights of the original tenant*

1.2.3.1 *The rights of the original tenant against the original landlord* In theory privity of contract means that, subject to any modification by the terms of the lease, continuing liability in respect of *all* covenants applies to the original landlord no less than to the original tenant, so that the original landlord remains liable to the original tenant after he has assigned the leasehold reversion: *Stuart v. Joy* [1904] 1 K.B. 362, 367–368 *per* Cozens-Hardy L.J. In practice, since the landlord tends to undertake many fewer obligations than the tenant, the incidence of continuing liability on the part of the original landlord is limited: but see *Hua Chiao Commercial Bank Ltd v. Chiaphua Industries Ltd* [1987] A.C. 99, *supra*, p. 421.

1.2.3.2 *The rights of the original tenant against an assignee of the reversion* The burden of the original landlord's covenants that "have reference to the subject-matter of the lease" passes with the reversion by virtue of section 142(1) of the Law of Property Act 1925, so that the assignee of the reversion is directly liable to the tenant for breach of such covenants. However, liability is confined to breaches occurring while the reversion is vested in the assignee: *Duncliffe v. Caerfelin Properties Ltd* [1989] 2 E.G.L.R. 38, 39–40 *per* Garland J.

1.2.4 *The rights of an assignee of the lease*

1.2.4.1 *The rights of an assignee of the lease against the original landlord*
(1) The benefit of the original landlord's covenants that touch and concern the land also passes with the lease, so that an assignee of the lease may enforce those covenants against the original landlord: *Spencer's Case* (1583) 5 Co.Rep. 16a.
(2) It has been suggested that, by virtue of section 142(1) of the Law of Property Act 1925, the liability of the original landlord to an assignee of the lease in respect of covenants that touch and concern the land may continue even after the original landlord has assigned the reversion: see *Celsteel Ltd v. Alton House Holdings Ltd (No. 2)* [1986] 1 W.L.R. 666, 672 *per* Scott J., [1987] 1 W.L.R. 291, 296 *per* Fox L.J.

1.2.4.2 *The rights of an assignee of the lease against an assignee of the reversion*
(1) The enforceability of covenants between assignees of the lease and assignees of the reversion depends upon *Spencer's Case* (1583) 5 Co.Rep. 16a.
(2) It has been held that where an assignee of a lease assigns the lease, he remains entitled to sue the assignee of the reversion for breaches committed by the latter while the former was the tenant: *City and Metropolitan Properties Ltd v. Greycroft Ltd* [1987] 1 W.L.R. 1085. The principle would seem to be equally applicable to the original tenant as against the original landlord: 1.2.3.1 *supra*; or as against an assignee of the reversion: 1.2.3.2 *supra*.

2.2.5 *Sub-leases* Where the tenant or an assignee of the lease creates a sub-lease, a new landlord and tenant relationship is created between the tenant and the sub-tenant; and the above principles apply to that relationship.

However, the present concern is with the enforceability of the covenants contained in the original (head-) lease. There is no privity of contract or privity of estate between the original landlord (or an assignee of the reversion) and the sub-tenant; and there is no scope for the operation of the common law rules. However, it may be possible for the landlord to enforce any negative covenants against the sub-tenant by way of injunction under the doctrine in *Tulk v. Moxhay* (1848) 2 Ph. 774, *post*, p. 728. Moreover, all covenants in the head-lease may be indirectly enforceable against a sub-tenant through forfeiture proceedings: see *infra*, p. 440; but see *Hemingway Securities Ltd v. Dunraven Ltd* (1994) 71 P. & C.R. 30, noted at [1995] Conv. 416, *infra*, p. 457.

2.2.6 *Equitable leases and equitable assignments of legal leases*   Many of the principles outlined above apply equally where the lease is equitable or where, although the lease is legal, the assignments of the lease and/or reversion are equitable. Privity of contract and the continuing liability of the original parties is not affected: *John Betts & Sons Ltd v. Price* (1924) 40 T.L.R. 589, 590 *per* Branson J. Moreover, sections 141 and 142 of the Law of Property Act 1925 have been held to apply to equitable leases and assignments: see, respectively, *Rickett v. Green* [1910] 1 K.B. 253, 259 *per* Darling J.; *Weg Motors Ltd v. Hales* [1962] Ch. 49, 73 *per* Lord Evershed M.R.

However, the assimilation of legal and equitable leases is not complete. The rules in *Spencer's Case* have been held not to apply to equitable leases and equitable assignments of legal leases because those rules are based exclusively on privity of estate, which has traditionally been regarded as a *legal* relationship: see, respectively, *Purchase v. Lichfield Brewery Co.* [1915] 1 K.B. 184, 187–188 *per* Horridge J.; *Friary Holroyd and Healey's Breweries Ltd v. Singleton* [1899] 1 Ch. 86, 90 *per* Romer J. In practice, the difficulty centres on the unenforceability of the original tenant's covenants against the equitable assignee of the lease. Various means of surmounting the difficulty have been proposed: see Smith [1978] C.L.J. 98, who favours the typically no-nonsense approach of Denning L.J. in *Boyer v. Warbey* [1953] 1 Q.B. 234, where he stated (at 245–246):

I know that before the Judicature Act 1873 it was said that the doctrine of covenants running with the land only applied to covenants under seal and not to agreements under hand. ... But since the fusion of law and equity, the position is different. The distinction between agreements under hand and covenants under seal has been largely obliterated. There is no valid reason nowadays why the doctrine of covenants running with the land—or with the reversion—should not apply equally to agreements under hand as to covenants under seal; and I think we should so hold, not only in the case of agreements for more than three years which need the intervention of equity to perfect them, but also in the case of agreements for three years or less which do not.

2. The law applicable to "new tenancies"

It was the privity of contract principle, and the consequences of the continuing liability of the original tenant, that prompted a thorough examination by the Law Commission of the law on the enforceability of leasehold covenants: Law Commission Working Paper No. 95, *Privity of Contract and Estate: Duration of Liability of Parties to Leases* (1986); Law Com. No. 174, *Landlord and Tenant: Privity of Contract and Estate* (1988). The problem was summarised in *Hindcastle Ltd v. Barbara Attenborough Associates Ltd* [1997] A.C. 70, where Lord Nicholls stated (at 83):

Sometimes, in post-assignment cases, the landlord's protection may be achieved at an unreasonably high price to others. The insolvency may occur many years after the lease was granted, long after the original tenant parted with his interest in the lease. He paid the rent until he left, and then took on the responsibility of other premises. A person of modest means is understandably shocked when out of the blue he receives a rent demand from the landlord of the property he once leased. Unlike the landlord, he has no control over the identity of the assignees down the line. He has no opportunity to reject them as financially unsound. He is even more horrified when he discovers that the rent demanded exceeds the current rental value of the property.

As a result of pressure from representatives of landlords, whose interests stood to be severely affected by the original proposal to abolish the privity of contract principle for all existing and future leases, the proposals and successive draft legislation became progressively less radical. As a consequence the Landlord and Tenant (Covenants) Act 1995 contains three significant concessions to landlords: first, the 1995 Act applies only to "new tenancies"; secondly, landlords are given the means of securing release from liability following assignment of the reversion; and, thirdly, landlords are given power to make their consent to assignment conditional on the tenant agreeing to guarantee the assignee's performance of the covenants.

2.1 *Release of covenants on assignment*

Landlord and Tenant (Covenants) Act 1995, s.5

Tenant released from covenants on assignment of tenancy
    5.—(1) This section applies where a tenant assigns premises demised to him under a tenancy.
    (2) If the tenant assigns the whole of the premises demised to him, he—
    (a) is released from the tenant covenants of the tenancy, and
    (b) ceases to be entitled to the benefit of the landlord covenants of the tenancy,
as from the assignment.
    (3) If the tenant assigns part only of the premises demised to him, then as from the assignment he—
    (a) is released from the tenant covenants of the tenancy, and
    (b) ceases to be entitled to the benefit of the landlord covenants of the tenancy,
only to the extent that those covenants fall to be complied with in relation to that part of the demised premises.
    (4) This section applies as mentioned in subsection (1) whether or not the tenant is tenant of the whole of the premises comprised in the tenancy.

NOTES:
    1. Section 5 provides for release from liability on an *assignment*: it does not in its terms operate where the tenant *sub-lets* the property comprised in the lease.
    2. The release from liability for breach of the tenant covenants is complemented by the abolition of the indemnity covenants implied by the Law

of Property Act 1925, s.77(1)(C),(D) and the Land Registration Act 1925, s.24(1)(b),(2): Landlord and Tenant (Covenants) Act 1995, s.14.

3. The release from liability does not affect the tenant's liability arising from a breach of a tenant covenant occurring before the assignment nor does it affect the tenant's right of action in respect of breaches of landlord covenants occurring before the assignment: *ibid*. s.24(1),(4).

4. The release from liability also releases to the same extent the liability of any guarantor of the tenant's liability: *ibid*. s.24(2).

5. In so far as section 5 removes the continuing liability of the original tenant pursuant to the privity of contract principle, it may be regarded as the central provision of the legislation. However, as already noted, the removal of such liability is qualified. Section 16 of the 1995 Act provides for the original tenant who has been released from liability by virtue of section 5 to enter into an "authorised guarantee agreement", whereby he guarantees performance of the tenant covenants by the assignee until there is a subsequent assignment or until such other time as the assignee is released from his liability under the Act. An authorised guarantee agreement may also require the original tenant to enter into a new tenancy of the premises comprised in the assignment, where the lease is disclaimed by the liquidator or trustee in bankruptcy of the assignee. On the other hand, it seems to have been intended that the landlord should be able to require the original tenant to enter into such an agreement only where it was reasonable to do so. Consequently, an authorised guarantee agreement can only be required where (i) the tenancy includes a covenant against assignment without the consent of the landlord, (ii) the consent is made subject to a condition (lawfully imposed) that the tenant enters into such an agreement and (iii) the agreement is entered into in pursuance of that condition: *ibid*. s.16(3). However, in the case of *commercial* leases, landlords may now stipulate in advance the circumstances in which and the conditions on which they are willing to consent to an assignment of a tenancy; and a refusal of consent where those conditions are not met cannot be regarded as unreasonable: Landlord and Tenant Act 1927, s.19 (as amended by section 22 of the 1995 Act). It is probable that one condition that will frequently be stipulated will be that the original tenant enters into an authorised guarantee agreement.

Sections 17–19 of the 1995 Act apply to a tenant who has entered into an authorised guarantee agreement. If the landlord proposes to enforce covenants for the payment of fixed charges, he must serve notice on the tenant within six months of the date of the payments becoming due: *ibid*. s.17; the liability cannot be increased by any post-assignment variation in the terms of the lease which the landlord has an absolute right to refuse: *ibid*. s.18; and, where the landlord enforces the agreement, the tenant has the right to apply for an "overriding lease": *ibid*. s.19.

6. In contrast with the automatic release of the tenant under section 5, where the landlord assigns the reversion, he must apply to the tenant to be released from the landlord covenants. If the tenant objects to the release, the landlord is entitled to apply to the county court for release: *ibid*. s.8. Where the landlord is released from the landlord covenants, he ceases to be bound by those covenants and ceases to be entitled to the benefit of the tenant covenants

as from the assignment of the reversion: *ibid.* s.6; but the release from liability does not affect the landlord's liability arising from a breach of landlord covenants occurring before the assignment nor does it affect the landlord's right of action in respect of breaches of tenant covenants occurring before the assignment: *ibid.* s.24(1),(4). Section 7 makes corresponding provision for former landlords who were not released from the landlord covenants on the former assignment of the reversion.

7. Where the assignment of the lease or the reversion is in breach of covenant or takes effect by operation of law ("excluded assignments"), sections 5–7 do not operate on that assignment: section 11 defers the release (or, in the case of the landlord, the opportunity to apply for release) until the next assignment that is not an excluded assignment.

2.2 *Transmission of covenants*

Landlord and Tenant (Covenants) Act 1995, ss.3, 4

Transmission of benefit and burden of covenants

3.—(1) The benefit and burden of all landlord and tenant covenants of a tenancy—
- (a) shall be annexed and incident to the whole, and to each and every part, of the premises demised by the tenancy and of the reversion in them, and
- (b) shall in accordance with this section pass on an assignment of the whole or any part of those premises or of the reversion in them.

(2) Where the assignment is by the tenant under the tenancy, then as from the assignment the assignee—
- (a) becomes bound by the tenant covenants of the tenancy except to the extent that—
  - (i) immediately before the assignment they did not bind the assignor, or
  - (ii) they fall to be complied with in relation to any demised premises not comprised in the assignment; and
- (b) becomes entitled to the benefit of the landlord covenants of the tenancy except to the extent that they fall to be complied with in relation to any such premises.

(3) Where the assignment is by the landlord under the tenancy, then as from the assignment the assignee—
- (a) becomes bound by the landlord covenants of the tenancy except to the extent that—
  - (i) immediately before the assignment they did not bind the assignor, or
  - (ii) they fall to be complied with in relation to any demised premises not comprised in the assignment; and
- (b) becomes entitled to the benefit of the tenant covenants of the tenancy except to the extent that they fall to be complied with in relation to any such premises.

(4) In determining for the purposes of subsection (2) or (3) whether any covenant bound the assignor immediately before the assignment, any waiver or release of the covenant which (in whatever terms) is expressed to be personal to the assignor shall be disregarded.

(5) Any landlord or tenant covenant of a tenancy which is restrictive of the user of land shall, as well as being capable of enforcement against an assignee, be capable of being enforced against any other person who is the owner or occupier of any demised premises to which the covenant relates, even though there is no express provision in the tenancy to that effect.

(6) Nothing in this section shall operate—

(a) in the case of a covenant which (in whatever terms) is expressed to be personal to any person, to make the covenant enforceable by or (as the case may be) against any other person; or

(b) to make a covenant enforceable against any person if, apart from this section, it would not be enforceable against him by reason of its not having been registered under the Land Registration Act 1925 or the Land Charges Act 1972.

(7) To the extent that there remains in force any rule of law by virtue of which the burden of a covenant whose subject matter is not in existence at the time when it is made does not run with the land affected unless the covenantor covenants on behalf of himself and his assigns, that rule of law is hereby abolished in relation to tenancies.

Transmission of rights of re-entry

4. The benefit of a landlord's right of re-entry under a tenancy—

(a) shall be annexed and incident to the whole, and to each and every part, of the reversion in the premises demised by the tenancy, and

(b) shall pass on an assignment of the whole or any part of the reversion in those premises.

NOTES:

1. Sections 3 and 4 provide a statutory framework for the enforceability of covenants between the assignees of the original parties to the lease. First, the requirement that only covenants that "touch and concern" the land are transmissible has been abandoned: under the new regime, the benefit and burden of all landlord and tenant covenants are transmissible unless the covenant is expressed to be personal: s.3(6)(a). Secondly, the former common law rules and statutory rules (sections 141 and 142 of the Law of Property Act 1925) for the passing of the benefit and burden by virtue of privity of estate are replaced by much clearer and more comprehensive statutory provisions.

2. The benefit and burden of all landlord and tenant covenants are annexed to the whole, and to each and every part, of the leased premises and the reversion: s.3(1). Where the tenant assigns the lease, from the date of the assignment the assignee becomes bound by the tenant covenants and entitled to the benefit of the landlord covenants: s.3(2); but the assignee is not bound by any tenant covenant nor entitled to the benefit of any landlord covenant in relation to any time before the assignment: s.23(1). Where the landlord assigns the reversion, from the date of the assignment the assignee becomes bound by the landlord covenants and entitled to the benefit of the tenant covenants: s.3(3); but the assignee is not bound by any landlord covenant nor entitled to the benefit of any tenant covenant in relation to any time before the assignment: s.23(1). However, sections 3(2) and (3) do not operate to transmit the benefit and burden of covenants where those covenants were not binding on the assignor immediately before the assignment; nor do they operate to transmit the benefit and burden of covenants where the covenants apply, in their terms or in their practical application, in relation to premises not included in the assignment: s.28(1),(2). The benefit of a landlord's right of re-entry is also annexed to the reversion and passes on an assignment of the whole or any part

of the reversion: s.4; but the assignee may re-enter the leased premises on the ground of a breach of covenant occurring prior to the assignment: section 23(3).

2.3 Sub-leases
The position of sub-leases is not affected by the 1995 Act except to the extent that the enforcement of covenants restrictive of user may have been extended by section 3(5).

2.4 Equitable leases and equitable assignments of legal leases
The position in relation to equitable leases and equitable assignments of legal leases is assimilated to that of legal leases and legal assignments since the definition of "tenancy" includes an agreement for a tenancy and the definition of "assignment" includes an equitable assignment: s.28(1).

H. REMEDIES FOR BREACH OF COVENANT

In principle, the usual common law and equitable remedies for breach of contract are available to both landlord and tenant to remedy breaches of leasehold covenants. Thus common law damages are recoverable in respect of loss caused by breaches of covenant; and the equitable remedies of injunction and specific performance may be available to enforce covenants. However, contractual remedies are by no means the only, nor indeed necessarily the most appropriate, remedies either for the landlord or for the tenant.

1. Remedies available to the landlord

1.1 Forfeiture
The most comprehensive remedy potentially available to the landlord is the remedy of forfeiture. Although such action may result in the termination of the lease before the agreed term has expired, the procedure is clearly designed "to give tenants who have hitherto lacked the will or the means to comply with their obligations one last chance to summon up that will or find the necessary means before the landlord re-enters": *Expert Clothing Service & Sales Ltd v. Hillgate House Ltd* [1986] Ch. 340, 358 *per* Slade L.J.

The proprietary nature of forfeiture was demonstrated in *Kataria v. Safeland plc* (1997) *The Times*, December 3, 1997, where the Court of Appeal held that an assignee of the landlord who had assigned the personal right to recover arrears of rent to his predecessor in title remained entitled to exercise a peaceable right to re-enter the premises and forfeit the lease on the grounds of non-payment of rent.

1.1.1 Availability of forfeiture
Where a tenant is in breach of a term of the lease, the landlord may wish to have the right to terminate the lease before the agreed term has expired. The entitlement to terminate (or "forfeit") the lease depends on whether the relevant term takes the form of a condition

or a covenant. Where the term is formulated as a condition on which the continuance of the lease depends, non-compliance with the condition entitles the landlord to re-enter the property and forfeit the lease: *Doe d. Lockwood v. Clarke* (1807) 8 East 185. On the other hand, where the relevant term is formulated as a covenant, subject to one exception, breach of the covenant does not entitle the landlord to re-enter and forfeit unless the lease includes a forfeiture clause, conferring a right to that effect: *Doe d. Willson v. Phillips* (1824) 2 Bing. 13. The exception to the requirement of an express forfeiture clause relates to agreements for leases because a forfeiture clause is implied into such an agreement as a "usual covenant": see *supra*, p. 416. Otherwise, in the absence of an express forfeiture clause, damages provide the only remedy for breach of covenant. In practice, the obligations of the tenant normally take the form of covenants and the lease normally includes a forfeiture clause.

Even if a lease contains the necessary forfeiture clause and there has been a breach of covenant which entitles the landlord to forfeit, the breach does not automatically terminate the lease; rather it renders the lease voidable at the option of the landlord. If he wishes to forfeit the lease, he must "re-enter" the property. Re-entry is normally effected by commencing an action for possession; but it may also be effected by peaceable physical re-entry of the property itself. However, where there is a residential occupier residing in any part of the property, re-entry otherwise than by court proceedings will almost certainly give rise to criminal and/or tortious liability on the part of the landlord: see Protection from Eviction Act 1977, ss.1–4; Housing Act 1988, s.27; Protection from Harassment Act 1997; and in any event the landlord who elects to forfeit by actual re-entry may be criminally liable for any actual or threatened violence: see Criminal Law Act 1977, s.6. More generally, the courts now seem to regard even lawful peaceable re-entry as undesirable and a procedure which is not to be encouraged: see, *e.g. Billson v. Residential Apartments Ltd* [1992] 1 A.C. 494, 536 *per* Lord Templeman; *W.G. Clark (Properties) Ltd v. Dupre Properties Ltd* [1992] Ch. 297, 307 *per* Thomas Morison Q.C.; but, for a contrary view, see Clarke (1992) 45 C.L.P. 81, 94 *et seq.*; and see *infra*, p. 461.

The landlord is not obliged to exercise his option to forfeit the lease; he may elect to waive the breach and to treat the lease as continuing: *Billson v. Residential Apartments Ltd* [1992] 1 A.C. 494, 534 *per* Lord Templeman. See *infra*, p. 459.

Even where a breach of covenant gives grounds for forfeiture and the landlord elects not to waive the breach, proceedings for possession will not inevitably result in judgment for the landlord and the termination of the lease. The tenant and/or persons with derivative interests may be granted relief against forfeiture: see *infra*, pp. 452, 457.

Under the present law of forfeiture there are two almost wholly separate regimes: sections 210–212 of the Common Law Procedure Act 1852, as supplemented by section 38 of the Supreme Court Act 1981 and sections 138–140 of the County Courts Act 1984, deal with forfeiture for non-payment of rent; and section 146 of the Law of Property Act 1925 deals with forfeiture for breaches of other covenants.

1.1.2 *Formal procedural requirements*

1.1.2.1 *Non-payment of rent*   The landlord must make a formal demand for rent due and unpaid unless (i) the lease expressly exempts the landlord from making a formal demand (as is usually the case); or (ii) half a year's rent is in arrear and the value of goods on the premises available for distress is insufficient to satisfy the arrears: Common Law Procedure Act 1852, s.210; County Courts Act 1984, ss.138(1), 139(1).

When the landlord commences an action for possession, the tenant may effectively stop the proceedings by paying all the arrears of rent and costs before the date of judgment. However, somewhat paradoxically, in the High Court this opportunity is only available to the tenant where at least half a year's rent is in arrear: Common Law Procedure Act 1852, s.212, as construed in *Standard Pattern Co. Ltd v. Ivey* [1962] Ch. 432, 438 *per* Wilberforce J. No such limitation appears to apply in the county court, although payment must be made not less than five days before the date of the trial: County Courts Act 1984, s.138(2).

1.1.2.2 *Breaches of other covenants*   Forfeiture for breach of covenant other than non-payment of rent is largely governed by section 146 of the Law of Property Act 1925.

Law of Property Act 1925, s.146(1)

Restrictions on and relief against forfeiture of leases and underleases

   146.—(1) A right of re-entry or forfeiture under any proviso or stipulation in a lease for a breach of any covenant or condition in the lease shall not be enforceable, by action or otherwise, unless and until the lessor serves on the lessee a notice—
   (a) specifying the particular breach complained of; and
   (b) if the breach is capable of remedy, requiring the lessee to remedy the breach; and
   (c) in any case, requiring the lessee to make compensation in money for the breach;
and the lessee fails, within a reasonable time thereafter, to remedy the breach, if it is capable of remedy, and to make reasonable compensation in money, to the satisfaction of the lessor, for the breach.

NOTES:
   1. The preliminary procedures required by the subsection apply where the landlord wishes to forfeit the lease "by action or otherwise", that is whether the landlord seeks to forfeit by an action for possession or by peaceable re-entry.
   2. Where the lease has been assigned (even in breach of covenant), the notice must be served on the current lessee/assignee: *Old Grovebury Manor Farm Ltd v. W. Seymour Plant Sales & Hire Ltd* [1979] 1 W.L.R. 1397,

1399–1400 *per* Lord Russell; *Fuller v. Judy Properties Ltd* (1991) 64 P. & C.R. 176, 180–181 *per* Stocker L.J.

3. A section 146 notice will be void if it does not comply with the requirements of the subsection: *Glass v. Kencakes* [1966] 1 Q.B. 611, 622 *per* Paull J.; and any purported forfeiture based on the notice will similarly be void: *Re Riggs, ex parte Lovell* [1901] 2 K.B. 16, 20 *per* Wright J. First, the notice must specify the particular breach complained of; but, provided that it gives the tenant adequate notice of what is required of him in order to remedy the breach, it need not give detailed particulars of every constituent element of the breach: *Fox v. Jolly* [1916] 1 A.C. 1; *Adagio Properties Ltd v. Ansari* [1998] 2 E.G.L.R. 69. Secondly, it has been held that the notice need require the tenant to remedy the breach only if the breach is "capable of remedy"; but since it may be unclear whether a breach is capable of remedy (see *infra*), landlords should normally expressly require any breach to be remedied "if it is capable of being remedied": *Glass v. Kencakes* [1966] 1 Q.B. 611, 629 *per* Paull J. Thirdly, it has also been held that the landlord need not require the tenant to provide financial compensation if he does not want it: *Lock v. Pearce* [1893] 2 Ch. 271, 276 *per* Lord Esher M.R., 279 *per* Lindley L.J. See also *Rugby School (Governors) v. Tannahill* [1935] 1 K.B. 87, 91 *per* Greer L.J.: the relevant breach involved the use of premises for the purposes of prostitution and the landlords were concerned that any compensation would be paid from the proceeds of such activities.

4. The landlord may only proceed to forfeit the lease if the tenant fails to remedy the (remediable) breach and to make reasonable compensation within a reasonable time after the service of the section 146 notice. If the tenant does comply with the notice, the landlord no longer has any ground for forfeiture; but, if the tenant does not comply with the notice, or cannot do so because the breach is irremediable, the landlord may proceed with the forfeiture, subject to claims for relief against forfeiture by the tenant or by persons with derivative interests. Whether the tenant has been given a reasonable time to comply with the notice must depend on the facts of each case: *Hick v. Raymond & Reid* [1893] A.C. 22, 29 *per* Lord Herschell L.C.; and, where the tenant has not been given a reasonable time, a purported forfeiture by actual re-entry is void: *Cardigan Properties Ltd v. Consolidated Property Investments Ltd* [1991] 1 E.G.L.R. 64.

5. It is clear that the question whether a breach is capable of remedy is central to the operation of section 146. The question, which has been construed as turning on "whether the harm that has been done to the landlord by the relevant breach is for practical purposes capable of being retrieved" was considered at some length in *Expert Clothing Services & Sales Ltd v. Hillgate House Ltd* [1986] Ch. 340, *infra*, p. 444.

6. There are special provisions where the breach relates to a covenant to "keep or put in repair". Under section 18(2) of the Landlord and Tenant Act 1927 a right of re-entry or forfeiture cannot be enforced unless the landlord can prove that the tenant knew of the service of the section 146 notice. Under section 1 of the Leasehold Property (Repairs) Act 1938, which applies to leases granted for seven years or more with at least three years of the term

unexpired at the commencement of the action, the section 146 notice must include a statement as to the entitlement of the tenant to serve a counter-notice; and, where the tenant does serve a counter-notice, the landlord is then precluded from taking any further proceedings for the enforcement of any right of re-entry or forfeiture unless he first obtains the leave of the court, which may be granted on certain specified grounds (essentially that immediate repairs are necessary): *ibid.* s.1(5); and see *Associated British Ports v. C.H. Bailey plc* [1990] 2 A.C. 703. For special provisions where the breach relates to internal decorative repairs, see Law of Property Act 1925, s.147.

7. Section 146(8)–(10) specify certain exceptional cases where the section 146 procedure has no (or limited) application (although relief against forfeiture for underlessees under section 146(4) is still available: see *infra*, p. 457).

8. It is uncertain whether the section 146 procedure applies to forfeiture for denial of title: see *Warner v. Sampson* [1958] 1 Q.B. 404; *W.G. Clark (Properties) Ltd v. Dupre Properties Ltd* [1992] Ch. 297, noted at [1993] Conv. 299.

Expert Clothing Service & Sales Ltd v. Hillgate House Ltd [1986] Ch. 340

(CA, O'Connor and Slade L.JJ., Bristow J.)

In 1978 the plaintiffs granted to the defendants a 25-year lease of premises, which the defendants convenanted to convert into a gymnasium and health club. Following proceedings for possession that were settled, the defendants convenanted that the conversion of the premises would be substantially completed (and the premises ready for occupation) by 28 September 1982 and fully completed as soon as reasonably possible thereafter. However, no work had been undertaken by 28 September 1982. Moreover, contrary to a term of the lease, the defendants had charged the premises to their bank without giving notice to the plaintiffs. The plaintiffs refused to accept the rent due on 29 September 1982. They served a section 146 notice on the defendants, alleging that they were in breach of covenant (both as to the conversion work and as to the charge) and that the breaches were incapable of remedy; and they subsequently brought an action for possession. The question for the court was whether the notice (which did not require the tenant to remedy the breach) was valid.

SLADE L.J.:
In a case where the breach is "capable of remedy" within the meaning of the section, the principal object of the notice procedure provided for by section 146(1), as I read it, is to afford the lessee two opportunities before the lessor actually proceeds to enforce his right of re-entry, namely (1) the opportunity to remedy the breach within a reasonable time after service of the notice, and (2) the opportunity to apply to the court for relief from forfeiture. In a case where the breach is not "capable of remedy", there is clearly no point in affording the first of these two opportunities; the object of the notice procedure is thus simply to give the lessee the opportunity to apply for relief.

Unfortunately the authorities give only limited guidance as to what breaches are "capable of remedy" within the meaning of the section. As Harman J. pointed out in *Hoffmann v. Fineberg* [1949] Ch. 245, 253:

> "In one sense, no breach can ever be remedied, because there must always, *ex concessis*, be a time in which there has not been compliance with the covenant, but the section clearly involves the view that some breaches are remediable, and therefore it cannot mean that."

MacKinnon J. in *Rugby School (Governors) v. Tannabill* [1934] 1 K.B. 695 drew an important distinction in this context between positive and negative covenants. He said, at p. 701:

> "A promise to do a thing, if broken, can be remedied by the thing being done. But breach of a promise not to do a thing cannot in any true sense be remedied; that which was done cannot be undone. There cannot truly be a remedy; there can only be abstention, perhaps accompanied with apology."

From this MacKinnon J. concluded that the breach of a negative covenant of this sort was not one "capable of remedy" within the section, though the lessee was not necessarily left at the lessor's mercy, since the power to grant relief remained.

The relevant breach in the *Rugby School* case consisted of the breach of a covenant not to use premises for illegal or immoral purposes. On appeal ([1935] 1 K.B. 87), the Court of Appeal, while affirming the decision of MacKinnon J. that the particular breach was not capable of remedy, did not accept without qualification the broader test suggested by him for distinguishing remediable and irremediable breaches. Greer L.J. said, at pp. 90–91:

> "I think perhaps he went further than was really necessary for the decision of this case in holding that a breach of any negative covenant—the doing of that which is forbidden—can never be capable of remedy. It is unnecessary to decide the point on this appeal; but in some cases [with] the immediate ceasing of that which is complained of, together with an undertaking against any further breach, it might be said that the breach was capable of remedy. This particular breach, however—conducting the premises, or permitting them to be conducted, as a house of ill-fame—is one which in my judgment was not remedied by merely stopping this user. I cannot conceive how a breach of this kind can be remedied. The result of committing the breach would be known all over the neighbourhood and seriously affect the value of the premises. Even a money payment together with the cessation of the improper use of the house could not be a remedy."

Maugham L.J., having referred to certain authorities, said, at p. 93:

> "A reasonable construction has thus been put upon the section, the object being to allow the lessee to remedy the breach or to make compensation before action is brought against him. From that two things seem to me to follow: first, the remedy which is spoken of in the section must be a complete remedy. A partial remedy is not within the section, the concluding words of subsection (1) being: 'and the lessee fails, within a reasonable time thereafter, to remedy the breach, if it is capable of remedy, and to make reasonable compensation in money, to the satisfaction of the lessor, for the breach.' The second thing to be gathered from the section is that the breach must be capable of remedy within a reasonable time. The lessor is not to be kept out of his right of action for an unreasonable time. If, for example, the breach is of such a character that many months or perhaps years must elapse before the breach can be remedied, to the satisfaction of the lessor, such a case would not be as regards remedy within the section at all."

In the present case the judge accepted that the second breach relied on by the plaintiffs was capable of remedy. As he put it:

"Not much argument has been devoted to the second breach, that is to say failure to give notice of the charge, quite rightly in my judgment. Although it is a covenant to give notice within one month, the rule is not, as I understand it, that once the stated period in the lease has gone by the covenant thereafter becomes incapable of remedy. That in itself is not sufficient to render a breach incapable of remedy, and in this case it is quite clear no damage was done to the landlord by the giving of late notice or failing to give it and the landlord finding out by other means. Accordingly, if that were the only matter on the notice then I would be quite clearly of the opinion that the breach was capable of remedy and the notice would be defective."

The plaintiffs have not sought by a respondent's notice or in argument to challenge this part of the judge's decision. However, he regarded the other breach relied on by the plaintiffs, relating to the failure to reconstruct the premises, as being of a different order. Having cited part of the passage from the judgment of Maugham L.J. in *Rugby School (Governors) v. Tannahill* [1935] 1 K.B. 87, 93, cited above, he concluded:

"That I take as guidance to the proper approach in this case, and it seems to me—and I have no real hesitation about this—that this is not such a breach, having regard to the facts as I have outlined them, as to be capable of remedy within a reasonable time. It is going to take, according to the evidence, at the very least nine months to do the necessary works. Also there is the point that was taken—and I think it is valid—that the rent review provisions are linked to the reconstructed premises and there is no ready way in which the landlord can be reinstated in that position so that at 1982 he was obtaining a rent or assenting to a rent from reconstructed premises. It seems to me that this breach lies in the area of breaches which are incapable of remedy within a reasonable time."

The nine-month period thus referred to was, I understand, the period requested by the defendants in their application for relief, so as to enable them to do the necessary works.

In supporting the judge's conclusion that the breach relating to reconstruction of the premises was irremediable, Mr Collins, on behalf of the plaintiffs, has submitted to us three principal arguments. First, he pointed out that (as is common ground) the first defendant's failure to build by 28 September 1982 was a "once and for all" breach of the relevant covenant, and not a continuing breach: see, for example, *Stephens v. Junior Army and Navy Stores Ltd* [1914] 2 Ch. 516, 523 *per* Lord Cozens-Hardy M.R. He submitted that the breach of a covenant such as this, which can only be broken once, is ex hypothesi in no case capable of remedy.

Some superficial support for this conclusion is perhaps to be found in the judgments in *Scala House & District Property Co. Ltd v. Forbes* [1974] Q.B. 575, in which the Court of Appeal held that the breach of a covenant not to assign, underlet or part with possession was not a breach capable of remedy within the meaning of section 146(1). In the course of his judgment, Russell L.J., having referred to the relevant breach, said, at p. 585:

"If it is capable of remedy, and is remedied in reasonable time, the lessor is unable to prove that a condition precedent to his ability to seek to forfeit by action or otherwise has been fulfilled. Here at once is a problem. An unlawful subletting is a breach once and for all. The subterm has been created."

Russell L.J. then turned to the authorities, including the *Rugby School* case [1935] 1 K.B. 87, as to which he made these comments, at p. 585:

"this court expressed the view that breach of negative covenants might be capable of remedy, but not this one, on the ground that the stigma attaching to the premises would not be removed by mere cesser of the immoral user. I observe that it does not appear to have been considered whether the breach in that case was incapable of remedy on another ground, viz.: that the wrongful user had ceased before the section 146 notice."

After his review of the authorities, Russell L.J. continued, at p. 588:

"In summary upon the cases we have therefore a number of cases of user of premises in breach of covenant in which the decision that the breach is not capable of remedy has gone upon the 'stigma' point, without considering whether a short answer might be—if the user had ceased before the section 146 notice—that it was ex hypothesi incapable of remedy, leaving the lessee only with the ability to seek relief from forfeiture and the writ unchallengeable as such. If a user in breach has ceased before the section 146 notice (quite apart from the stigma cases) then either it is incapable of remedy and after notice there is nothing in the way of a writ; or the cesser of user has somehow deprived the lessor of his ability to seek to forfeit though he has done nothing to waive the breach, a situation in law which I find extremely difficult to spell out of section 146."

But whatever might be the position in user breach cases, Russell L.J. concluded that a breach by an unlawful subletting is not capable of remedy at all. As he put it, at p. 588:

"the introduction of such breaches into the relevant section for the first time by section 146 of the Act of 1925 operates only to confer a statutory ability to relieve the lessee from forfeiture on that ground. The subterm has been effectively created subject only to risks of forfeiture: it is a complete breach once for all: it is not in any sense a continuing breach. If the law were otherwise a lessee, when a subtenancy is current at the time of the section 146 notice, would have a chance of remedying the situation without having to apply for relief. But if the unlawful subletting had determined before the notice, the lessee could only seek relief from forfeiture."

It might well be regarded as anomalous if the once and for all breach of a negative covenant not to sublet were to be regarded as "capable of remedy" within section 146, provided that the unlawful subtenancy was still current at the date of the section 146 notice, but (as Russell L.J. considered) were not to be regarded as "capable of remedy" if the unlawful subtenancy had been determined at that date. Russell L.J. and James L.J. who agreed with his reasoning (see particularly at p. 591C–D), were clearly much influenced by this anomaly in reaching the conclusion that the remedy of a covenant against underletting is never capable of remedy.

However, in the *Scala House* case [1974] Q.B. 575 this court was addressing its mind solely to the once and for all breach of a negative covenant. No corresponding anomaly arises if the once and for all breach of a positive covenant is treated as capable of remedy. While the *Scala House* decision is, of course, authority binding on this court for the proposition that the breach of a negative covenant not to assign, underlet or part with possession is never "capable of remedy", it is not, in my judgment, authority for the proposition that the once and for all breach of a positive covenant is never capable of remedy.

Mr Neuberger, on behalf of the defendants, did not feel able to go so far as to support the view of MacKinnon J. that the breach of a positive covenant is *always* capable of remedy. He accepted, for example, that the breach of a covenant to insure might be incapable of remedy at a time when the premises had already been burnt down. Another example might be the breach of a positive covenant which in the event would be only capable of being fully performed, if at all, after the expiration of the relevant term.

Nevertheless, I would, for my part, accept Mr Neuberger's submission that the breach of a positive covenant (whether it be a continuing breach or a once and for all breach) will ordinarily be capable of remedy. As Bristow J. pointed out in the course of argument, the concept of capability of remedy for the purpose of section 146 must surely be directed to the question whether the harm that has been done to the landlord by the relevant breach is for practicable purposes capable of being retrieved. In the ordinary case, the breach of a promise to do something by a certain time can for practical purposes be remedied by the thing being done, even out of time. For these reasons I reject the plaintiffs' argument that the breach of the covenant to reconstruct by 28 September 1982 was not capable of remedy *merely* because it was not a continuing breach.

I would add this point. If this breach was, on these grounds alone, not capable of remedy, the very same grounds would appear to render the breach of the first defendant's covenant to give notice of the charge in favour of Lloyds Bank likewise incapable of remedy. But Mr Collins has not attempted to maintain the latter proposition, which would have been very difficult to sustain having regard to what one may suppose was the intention of the legislature in enacting section 146(1).

As his second main line of argument in this context, he submitted that the breach of the covenant to reconstruct was not capable of remedy because of the operation of the new rent review provisions incorporated in the lease by the schedule to the order of 29 June 1981. He pointed out that under these provisions the plaintiffs, on a rent review, would have an option, which they would clearly wish to exercise, to review the rent on the basis of the premises as reconstructed. He submitted that there was no ready way in which the plaintiffs could be effectively restored to the same position under the rent review clause as that in which they would have found themselves if the premises had been reconstructed by the due date.

Respectfully differing from the judge on this point, I do not think that this submission is well founded. When the rent review clause comes to be applied, the first defendant cannot rely on its own wrong (consisting of the failure to reconstruct) to reduce the rent which would otherwise have been payable as from the review date. The proper approach must be to assume for the purpose of the assessment that the required reconstruction has taken place. As Mr Neuberger pointed out, surveyors are quite accustomed to this kind of artificial assumption in rent review valuations. With the appropriate expert advice there would be little difficulty in ascertaining the rent to which the plaintiffs would have been entitled on the first rent review, and indeed on any subsequent rent review, if the defendants had complied with their building obligations in due time. While Mr Collins pointed out that, if this had been done, the premises might have been sublet by the rent review date and this would itself have facilitated the ascertainment of a fair rack market annual rental value, there is no certainty whatever that any such subletting would have taken place. In the context of the rent review clause, any damage resulting from the relevant breach of covenant was, in my opinion, capable of being remedied simply by the payment by the defendants of an appropriate sum of money.

I therefore turn to the third, and far the most important point, relied on by Mr Collins in support of the decision of the court below. His submissions in this context were to the following effect. The judgment of Maugham L.J. in the *Rugby School* case [1935] 1 K.B. 87, 93 and other judicial dicta indicate that if a breach is to be "capable of remedy" at all within the meaning of section 146, it must be capable of remedy *within a "reasonable time."* As was observed by Lord Herschell L.C. in *Hick v. Raymond & Reid* [1893] A.C. 22, 29: "there is of course no such thing as a reasonable time in the abstract. It must always depend upon circumstances". In the present case, it was submitted, what was a reasonable time was a question of fact. In deciding that the breach of the covenant to reconstruct was not capable of remedy within a reasonable time, the judge expressed himself as "having regard to the facts as I have found them".

Mr Collins drew attention to some of his particular earlier findings of fact. The plaintiffs and the second defendant had first come into contact in early 1976. The second defendant had obtained his planning permission in August 1976. The first defendant had obtained possession of the premises in anticipation of the contemplated lease in the summer of 1977. The lease had been granted in January 1978. However, by the autumn of 1978 the defendants had abandoned their health club project and in

March 1979 they so informed the plaintiffs. After that date nothing of practical value had been effected towards the conversion of the premises. The defendants, in their application for relief, had asked the judge for nine months to enable them to do the work. Having regard to this history of default on their part there was, in Mr Collin's submission, ample material on which the court below could properly find that, at the date of service of the section 146 notice, nine months was not a reasonable time and that accordingly the relevant breach was not capable of remedy within a reasonable time. Furthermore, he suggested, the defendants had neither the financial resources nor the will to do the work.

Though the judge did not spell them out in this manner, I infer that these were essentially the points which led him to conclude that the relevant breach was not capable of remedy within a reasonable time. With great respect to him, I have reached a different conclusion on this point for reasons which I will now attempt to explain.

While the words "within a reasonable time" do not appear in subparagraph (b) of section 146(1), I accept that a section 146 notice need not require the tenant to remedy the breach if it is not capable of remedy within a reasonable time after service of the notice: see, for example, the *Rugby School* case [1935] 1 K.B. 87, 93, and *Egerton v. Esplanade Hotels, London Ltd* [1947] 2 All E.R. 88, 91 *per* Morris J. This appears to be the proper inference from the concluding words of section 146(1) which leave the lessor at liberty to enforce his right of re-entry if "the lessee fails, within a reasonable time thereafter, to remedy the breach, ..." A requirement to remedy within a reasonable time is pointless in a case where remedy within a reasonable time from the service of the notice is impossible.

However, in my opinion, in considering whether or not remedy within a reasonable time is possible, a crucial distinction (which I infer from the judgment did not feature prominently in argument before the judge) falls to be drawn between breaches of negative user covenants, such as those under consideration in the *Rugby School* and the *Esplanade Hotels* cases, and breaches of positive covenants. In the two last-mentioned cases, where the relevant breaches consisted of allowing premises to be used as a brothel, even full compliance with the covenant within a reasonable time and for a reasonable time would not have remedied the breach. As Maugham L.J. pointed out in the *Rugby School* case, at p. 94:

> "merely ceasing for a reasonable time, perhaps a few weeks or a month, to use the premises for an immoral purpose would be no remedy for the breach of covenant which had been committed over a long period."

On the facts of cases such as those, mere cesser by the tenant of the offending use within a reasonable period and for a reasonable period of time could not have remedied the breaches because it could not have removed the stigma which they had caused to attach to the premises. The harm had been irretrievably done. In such cases, as Harman J. pointed out in *Hoffmann v. Fineberg* [1949] Ch. 245, 257, mere cesser will not enable the tenant to "make his record clean, as he could by complying, though out of time, with a failure to lay on the prescribed number of coats of paint."

In contrast with breaches of negative user covenants, the breach of a positive covenant to do something (such as to decorate or build) can ordinarily, for practical purposes, be remedied by the thing being actually done if a reasonable time for its performance (running from the service of the section 146 notice) is duly allowed by the landlord following such service and the tenant duly does it within such time.

In the present case there is no question of the breach of the covenant to reconstruct having given rise to any "stigma" against the lessors or the premises. Significantly, the lease in 1982 still had 20 years to run. Mr Collins has, I think, been able to suggest no convincing reasons why the plaintiffs would still have suffered irremediable damage if (i) the section 146 notice had required the lessee to remedy the breach, and (ii) the lessors had then allowed a reasonable time to elapse sufficient to enable the lessee to comply with the relevant covenant, and (iii) the lessee had complied with the covenant in such reasonable time and had paid any appropriate monetary compensation. Though he has submitted that a requirement directed to the defendants to remedy the breach would have been purposeless, on the grounds that they had neither the financial means nor the will to do the necessary work, these are matters which, in my opinion, a landlord is not entitled to prejudge in drafting his notice. An important purpose of the section 146 procedure is to give even tenants who have hitherto lacked the will or the means to comply with their obligations one last chance to summon up that will or find the necessary means before the landlord re-enters. In considering what "reasonable time" to allow the defendants, the plaintiffs, in serving their section 146 notice, would, in my opinion, have been entitled to take into account the fact that the defendants already had enjoyed 15 months in which to fulfil their contractual obligations to reconstruct and to subject the defendants to a correspondingly tight timetable running from the date of service of the notice, though, at the same time, always bearing in mind that the contractual obligation to reconstruct did not even arise until 29 June 1981, and that as at 8 October 1982 the defendants had been in actual breach of it for only some 10 days. However, I think they were not entitled to say, in effect: "We are not going to allow you any time at all to remedy the breach, because you have had so long to do the work already."

In my judgment, on the remediability issue, the ultimate question for the court was this: if the section 146 notice had required the lessee to remedy the breach and the lessors had then allowed a reasonable time to elapse to enable the lessee fully to comply with the relevant covenant, would such compliance, coupled with the payment of any appropriate monetary compensation, have effectively remedied the harm which the lessors had suffered or were likely to suffer from the breach? If, but only if, the answer to this question was "No," would the failure of the section 146 notice to require remedy of the breach have been justifiable. In *Rugby School (Governors) v. Tannahill* [1935] 1 K.B. 87; *Egerton v. Esplanade Hotels, London Ltd* [1947] 2 All E.R. 88 and *Hoffmann v. Fineberg* [1949] Ch. 245 the answer to this question plainly would have been "No." In the present case, however, for the reasons already stated, I think the answer to it must have been "Yes."

My conclusion, therefore, is that the breach of the covenant to reconstruct, no less than the breach of the covenant to give notice of charges, was "capable of remedy." In reaching this conclusion, I find it reassuring that no reported case has been brought to our attention in which the breach of a positive covenant has been held incapable of remedy, though I do not suggest that cases of this nature, albeit perhaps rarely, could not arise.

NOTES:

1. The assertion that a once and for all breach of a negative covenant is incapable of remedy is no longer accepted without qualification: see, *e.g. Bass Holdings Ltd v. Morton Music Ltd* [1988] Ch. 493, 541 *per* Bingham L.J.; *Hagee (London) Ltd v. Co-operative Insurance Society Ltd* (1991) 63 P. & C.R. 362, 371–372 *per* Harman J.; *Billson v. Residential Apartments Ltd* [1992] 1 A.C. 494, 508 *per* Browne-Wilkinson V.-C.; *Van Haarlam v. Kasner* (1992) 64 P. & C.R. 214, 223 *per* Harman J.

In *Savva v. Hussein* (1996) 73 P. & C.R. 150 the landlord served a section 146 notice in respect of alleged breaches of covenants (i) not to display unauthorised signs on the leased premises; and (ii) not to alter the leased premises without the consent of the landlord. The notice did not require the tenant to remedy the breaches. Staughton L.J. stated (at 153–154):

In this case the question is whether the breaches, if there were breaches, were capable of remedy. They amount to doing things without the consent of the landlord. That is what the covenant did not allow. In the case of *Billson v. Residential Apartments Ltd*

(1990) 60 P. & C.R. 392 Mummery J. touched on the question whether such a breach could ever be capable of remedy. He said, at p. 406:

"I reject the defendant's arguments on the ground that the breach of covenant committed by making the alterations in the property without the plaintiffs' consent 'first had and obtained' was not capable of remedy by the defendants. It was a breach of the covenant for the defendants to embark on alterations to the property without first applying for and seeking to obtain the plaintiffs' consent. Now that the alterations have been made without consent it is impossible for the defendants to comply with the covenant which required them first to apply for consent so that they could either obtain it or, if they did not obtain it, be in a position to contend that they were entitled to make improvements because the plaintiffs had unreasonably withheld consent.

In those circumstances I hold that the breach was not capable of remedy."

When that case reached the Court of Appeal, the Vice-Chancellor said ([1992] 1 A.C. 494, 507–508):

"The judge held, first, that since the alterations had been started without *prior* consent of the plaintiffs the breach was irremediable. Second, he held that even if he was wrong on the first point, remedying the breach would consist, not in doing the works of reinstatement, but in stopping the works, submitting the necessary plans and specifications and then awaiting the giving or unreasonable withholding of consent.

I prefer to express no view on the judge's first ground of decision, beyond expressing some doubt as to whether he was right in holding that the breach was irremediable."

It is established law in this court that the breach of a covenant not to assign without consent cannot be remedied. That was decided in *Scala House & District Property Co. Ltd v. Forbes* [1974] Q.B. 575. Even then relief from forfeiture was granted, so that may not be of any great consequence.

In my judgment, except in a case of breach of a covenant not to assign without consent, the question is: whether the remedy referred to is the process of restoring the situation to what it would have been if the covenant had never been broken, or whether it is sufficient that the mischief resulting from a breach of the covenant can be removed. When something has been done without consent, it is not possible to restore the matter wholly to the situation which it was in before the breach. The moving finger writes and cannot be recalled. That is not to my mind what is meant by a remedy, it is a remedy if the mischief caused by the breach can be removed. In the case of a covenant not to make alterations without consent or not to display signs without consent, if there is a breach of that, the mischief can be removed by removing the signs or restoring the property to the state it was in before the alterations.

I would hold that all the breaches complained of in this case were capable of remedy. It follows that the notice under section 146 should have required them to be remedied.

Aldous L.J. stated (at 156–157):

I agree with the judgment of Staughton L.J. In particular, I believe that the breaches of the covenant relied on by the plaintiff in this court were capable of being remedied. It follows that the section 146 notice was inappropriate. It also follows that the statement of law of Mummery J. referred to by my Lord in *Billson v. Residential Apartments Ltd* cannot be supported.

In one sense a breach can never be remedied because there must have been non-compliance with the covenant for there to be a breach. That cannot be the solution. Thus, the fact there has been a breach does not determine whether it can be remedied in the way contemplated by the Law of Property Act 1925, s.146. That was decided in

Expert Clothing Service & Sales Ltd v. Hillgate House Ltd [1986] 1 Ch. 340, 357 *per* Slade L.J.:

> "Breach of a positive covenant to do something ... can ordinarily, for practical purposes, be remedied by the thing being actually done."

I can see no reason why similar reasoning should not apply to some negative covenants. An important purpose of section 146 is to give tenants, who have not complied with their obligations, one last chance to do so before the landlord re-enters. Slade L.J. in *Expert Clothing*, proposed this test, at p. 358:

> "If the section 146 notice had required the lessee to remedy the breach and the lessors had then allowed a reasonable time to elapse to enable the lessee fully to comply with the relevant covenant, would such compliance, coupled with the payment of any appropriate monetary compensation, have effectively remedied the harm which the lessors had suffered or were likely to suffer from the breach?"

It is only if the answer to that question is "no" can it be said that the breach is not capable of being remedied.

What was proposed as the question to ask by Slade L.J., albeit in relation to a case of dispute about a positive covenant, is relevant to consideration as to whether a negative covenant can be remedied. There is in my view nothing in the statute, nor in logic, which requires different considerations between a positive and negative covenant, although it may be right to differentiate between particular covenants. The test is one of effect. If a breach has been remedied then it must have been capable of being remedied.

2. Where a tenant has sub-let the whole or part of the premises, and the landlord is seeking to forfeit the lease on the ground that the conduct of the sub-tenant constitutes the breach, the courts have sometimes suggested (i) that the breach may be remediable where the tenant takes immediate action to terminate the conduct of the sub-tenant as soon as he discovers it: see *Glass v. Kencakes* [1966] 1 Q.B. 611, 629 *per* Paull J.; but (ii) that the breach may be regarded as irremediable when the tenant is aware of the conduct of the sub-tenant but takes no action: see *British Petroleum Pension Trust Ltd v. Behrendt* (1985) 276 E.G. 199, 202 *per* Purchas L.J. It is suggested that such considerations are more relevant to the question of relief against forfeiture than to the issue of remediability.

1.1.3 *Relief against forfeiture for tenants*

1.1.3.1 *Non-payment of rent*   Since equity regarded the remedy of forfeiture as merely security for the payment of rent, equity would grant relief against forfeiture and reinstate the lease, provided that the tenant paid all arrears of rent and costs and provided that it was just and equitable to grant relief: *Howard v. Fanshawe* [1895] 2 Ch. 581, 588–589 *per* Stirling J.; *Ladup Ltd v. Williams & Glyn's Bank plc* [1985] 1 W.L.R. 851, 860 *per* Warner J. Although relief against forfeiture has long been largely regulated by statute, the equitable jurisdiction retains a residual role.

In the High Court, where the tenant fails to pay the arrears and costs before trial, and the landlord obtains judgment for possession, the tenant may claim relief against forfeiture under the Common Law Procedure Act 1852, s.210, provided that the claim is made within six months of execution of the judgment. The statute seems to apply only where half a year's rent is in arrear: *Billson v. Residential Apartments Ltd* [1992] 1 A.C. 494, 529 *per* Nicholls L.J. However, the residual equitable jurisdiction seems to be exercised along similar lines where the statute does not apply: *Howard v. Fanshawe* [1895] 2 Ch. 581, 588–589 *per* Stirling J.; *Lovelock v. Margo* [1963] 2 Q.B. 786, 788 *per* Lord Denning M.R.; but there is some flexibility over the six months limitation: see *Thatcher v. C.H. Pearce & Sons (Contractors) Ltd* [1968] 1 W.L.R. 748, 755–756 *per* Sir Jocelyn Simon P. In *Gill v. Lewis* [1956] 2 Q.B. 1 Jenkins L.J. stated (at 13):

> As to the conclusion of the whole matter, in my view, save in exceptional circumstances, the function of the court in exercising this equitable jurisdiction is to grant relief when all that is due for rent and costs has been paid up, and (in general) to disregard any other causes of complaint that the landlord may have against the tenant. The question is whether, provided all is paid up, the landlord will not have been fully compensated; and the view taken by the court is that if he gets the whole of his rent and costs, then he has got all he is entitled to so far as rent is concerned, and extraneous matters of breach of covenant, and so forth, are, generally speaking, irrelevant.

Exceptional circumstances are likely to exist and relief is likely to be refused where the landlord has not unreasonably altered his position and/or where a third party has acquired an interest in the property: see, *e.g. Stanhope v. Haworth* (1886) 3 T.L.R. 34; *Silverman v. A.F.C.O. (U.K.) Ltd* (1988) 56 P. & C.R. 185. However, where the property has been re-let to a third party, relief has been granted in the form of a reversionary lease: see *Fuller v. Judy Properties Ltd* (1992) 64 P. & C.R. 176, noted at [1992] Conv. 343; *Bank of Ireland Home Mortgages v. South Lodge Developments* [1996] 1 E.G.L.R. 91.

In the county court, the tenant may prevent the execution of any order for possession by paying the arrears of rent and costs within a period (not less than four weeks and extendable) specified by the court: County Courts Act 1984, s.138. Moreover, even where the landlord has recovered possession pursuant to the possession order, the tenant may apply for relief against forfeiture at any time within six months from the date of recovery, in which case the court has a discretion to make such order as it thinks fit: *ibid.* For the limits of the jurisdiction to grant relief against forfeiture for non-payment of rent, see *United Dominions Trust Ltd v. Shellpoint Trustees Ltd* [1993] 4 All E.R. 310, noted at (1994) 110 L.Q.R. 15.

Where the landlord forfeits a lease for non-payment of rent by peaceable re-entry, in the High Court the tenant must rely on the residual equitable jurisdiction: *Howard v. Fanshawe* [1895] 2 Ch. 581, 588–589 *per* Stirling J.; *Lovelock v. Margo* [1963] 2 Q.B. 786, 788 *per* Lord Denning M.R.; *Thatcher v. C.H. Pearce & Sons (Contractors) Ltd* [1968] 1 W.L.R. 748, 754–756 *per* Sir Jocelyn Simon P.; *Ladup Ltd v. Williams & Glyn's Bank plc* [1985] 1 W.L.R. 851, 860 *per* Warner J.; *Billson v. Residential Apartments Ltd* [1992] 1 A.C. 494, 512 *per* Browne-Wilkinson V.-C., 529 *per* Nicholls L.J. However, the county court has statutory jurisdiction to grant relief in cases of peaceable re-entry, provided that the tenant applies within six months of the re-entry: County Courts Act 1984, s.139(2).

1.1.3.2 *Breach of other covenants*

Law of Property Act 1925, s.146(2)

(2) Where a lessor is proceeding, by action or otherwise, to enforce such a right of re-entry or forfeiture, the lessee may, in the lessor's action, if any, or in any action brought by himself, apply to the court for relief; and the court may grant or refuse relief, as the court, having regard to the proceedings and conduct of the parties under the foregoing provisions of this section, and to all the other circumstances, thinks fit; and in case of relief may grant it on such terms, if any, as to costs, expenses, damages, compensation, penalty, or otherwise, including the granting of an injunction to restrain any like breach in the future, as the court, in the circumstances of each case, thinks fit.

NOTES:

1. It is clear that, where the landlord is enforcing his right of forfeiture by court proceedings, the right of the tenant to apply for relief against forfeiture *under section 146(2)* expires when the landlord has recovered judgment and entered into possession.

2. In *Billson v. Residential Apartments Ltd* [1992] 1 A.C. 494 the question arose as to whether the court had jurisdiction to grant relief *under section 146(2)* where the landlords had already made a peaceable re-entry (although the tenants had almost immediately regained possession). Lord Templeman, having analysed the subsection and reviewed the authorities, concluded (at 540):

A tenant may apply for appropriate declarations and relief from forfeiture under section 146(2) after the issue of a section 146 notice but he is not prejudiced if he does not do so. A tenant cannot apply for relief after a landlord has forfeited a lease by issuing and serving a writ, has recovered judgment and has entered into possession pursuant to that judgment. If the judgment is set aside or successfully appealed the tenant will be able to apply for relief in the landlord's action but the court in deciding whether to grant relief will take into account any consequences of the original order and repossession and the delay of the tenant. A tenant may apply for relief after a landlord has forfeited by re-entry without first obtaining a court order for that purpose but the court in deciding whether to grant relief will take into account all the circumstances, including delay, on the part of the tenant. Any past judicial observations which might suggest that the tenant is barred from obtaining relief after the landlord has re-entered without first obtaining a court order for that purpose are not to be so construed.

Lord Templeman (at 537–540) and Lord Oliver (at 544–546) distinguished or reinterpreted "past judicial observations" to the contrary in *Quilter v. Mapleson* (1882) 9 Q.B.D. 672, 675 *per* Jessel M.R., 676 *per* Lindley L.J., 677 *per* Bowen L.J.; *Rogers v. Rice* [1892] 2 Ch. 170, 172 *per* Lord Coleridge C.J.; *Pakwood Transport Ltd v. 15 Beauchamp Place Ltd* (1977) 36 P. & C.R. 112, 117 *per* Orr L.J. As suggested above, their Lordships were concerned to demonstrate that a landlord who elects to forfeit by actual re-entry is not treated more favourably than a landlord who elects to forfeit by court proceedings: see *Billson v. Residential Apartments Ltd* [1992] 1 A.C. 494, 524 *per* Nicholls L.J., 536 *per* Lord Templeman. For comment, see Bridge [1992] C.L.J. 216; Smith [1992] Conv. 273.

3. It is uncertain whether section 146(2) has extinguished the inherent equitable jurisdiction to grant relief in cases of forfeiture other than for non-payment of rent: for the view that it has, see *Official Custodian for Charities v. Parway Estates Developments Ltd* [1985] Ch. 151, 165 *per* Dillon L.J.; *Billson v. Residential Apartments Ltd* [1992] 1 A.C. 494, 516 *per* Browne-Wilkinson V.-C., 522 *per* Parker L.J.; but for the contrary view, see *ibid.* 528–529 *per* Nicholls L.J. For comment, see Bridge [1991] C.L.J. 401; Goulding [1991] Conv. 380; Smith [1992] Conv. 32. The question was not addressed by the House of Lords.

4. The approach of the courts to the exercise of the discretion under section 146(2) is probably not markedly different from the approach to the inherent equitable jurisdiction: see *Khar v. Delmounty Ltd* (1996) 75 P. & C.R. 232, 237–239 *per* Lord Woolf M.R. As to the latter jurisdiction, see *Shiloh Spinners Ltd v. Harding* [1973] A.C. 691, where Lord Wilberforce stated (at 723–724):

[I]t remains true today that equity expects men to carry out their bargains and will not let them buy their way out by uncovenanted payment. But it is consistent with these principles that we should reaffirm the right of courts of equity in appropriate and limited cases to relieve against forfeiture for breach of covenant or condition where the primary object of the bargain is to secure a stated result which can effectively be attained when the matter comes before the court, and where the forfeiture provision is added by way of security for the production of that result. The word "appropriate" involves consideration of the conduct of the applicant for relief, in particular whether his default was wilful, of the gravity of the breaches, and of the disparity between the value of the property of which forfeiture is claimed as compared with the damage caused by the breach.

By contrast with the position under the inherent equitable jurisdiction, relief is available under section 146(2) even where the breach is "wilful": *Billson v. Residential Apartments Ltd* [1992] 1 A.C. 494, 510–512 *per* Browne-Wilkinson V.-C.; *W.G. Clark (Properties) Ltd v. Dupre Properties Ltd* [1992] Ch. 297, 309 *per* Thomas Morison Q.C.

Consistent with these principles, relief will normally be granted to a tenant "who makes good the breach of covenant and is able and willing to fulfil his obligations in the future": *Earl Bathurst v. Fine* [1974] 1 W.L.R. 905, 908 *per* Lord Denning M.R. Relief was in fact refused in that case because the tenant (an American who had committed a criminal offence in France and had been barred from re-entering the United Kingdom) was held not to be a fit tenant, having regard to the unique nature and value of the property.

5. Where a lease contains a provision that a service or maintenance charge is to be treated as or deemed to be rent or additional rent, the tenant may seek relief against forfeiture for non-payment of such a charge in accordance with the rules applicable to non-payment of rent: *Escalus Properties Ltd v. Robinson* [1996] Q.B. 231. Where there is no such provision in the lease, the

rules relating to forfeiture for breach of other covenants apply; but it has been held that the court should exercise its discretion under section 146(2) in a manner which recognises the substantive similarity between a covenant to pay rent and a covenant to pay a service or maintenance charge: *Khar v. Delmounty Ltd* (1996) 75 P. & C.R. 232.

6. Although the court has jurisdiction to grant relief even where the breach is not capable of remedy, in such cases the discretion is rarely exercised in favour of the tenant because the factors that render the breach incapable of remedy may also provide good grounds for refusing relief. In particular, save in very exceptional circumstances, it has been the established practice of the courts not to grant relief where the breach of covenant involves illegal or immoral activities: *Hoffmann v. Fineberg* [1949] Ch. 245; *Borthwick-Norton v. Romney Warwick Estates Ltd* [1950] 1 All E.R. 798; *G.M.S. Syndicate Ltd v. Gary Elliott Ltd* [1982] Ch. 1. For exceptions to the practice, see *Central Estates (Belgravia) Ltd v. Woolgar (No. 2)* [1972] 1 W.L.R. 1048, where the breach had not affected the value of the premises, the lease was valuable and the tenant was elderly and in poor health; *Ropemaker Properties Ltd v. Noonhaven Ltd* [1989] 2 E.G.L.R. 50, where the immoral use had ceased and was unlikely to be renewed, any stigma attaching to the premises was likely to be short-lived, the lease was of very substantial value and the financial loss to the lessees would have been out of all proportion to their offence or to any conceivable damage to the landlords; and see *Van Haarlam v. Kasner* (1992) 64 P. & C.R. 214, 226–227 *per* Harman J.

7. In *G.M.S. Syndicate Ltd v. Gary Elliott Ltd* [1982] Ch. 1, where part of the premises had been sub-let and used for immoral purposes, relief was granted in respect of the part that had not been sub-let. Nourse J. referred to *Dumpor's Case* (1603) 4 Co.Rep. 119b and stated (at 12):

I emphasize that I do not intend to go beyond the circumstances of the present case, where the two parts of the demised property are physically separated one from the other and are capable of being distinctly let and enjoyed, and where the breaches complained of were committed on one part of the property and on that part alone. I have not considered what would have happened if the circumstances had been different.

Pursuant to the broad policy of the Landlord and Tenant (Covenants) Act 1995 to achieve a "clean break" on the assignment of leased premises (*supra*, p. 435), it is now provided (in relation to "new tenancies" (*ibid.* s.1)) that where a tenant has assigned or sub-let part of the leased premises the landlord's right to forfeit is limited to that part of the premises demised to the defaulting (sub-)tenant: *ibid.* s.21(1).

8. If relief is granted, it normally takes the form of reinstatement of the lease, together with all derivative interests: *Dendy v. Evans* [1910] 1 K.B. 263; *Official Custodian for Charities v. Mackey* [1985] Ch. 168. As noted above, relief is likely to be refused where the landlord has not unreasonably altered his position and/or where a third pary has acquired an interest in the property.

1.1.4 *Relief against forfeiture for persons with derivative interests* Under the general law, if a lease is forfeited, any sub-lease or other derivative interest created out of that lease is automatically extinguished: see, *e.g. Great Western Railway Co. v. Smith* (1876) 2 Ch D. 235, 253 *per* Mellish L.J.; *G.M.S. Syndicate Ltd v. Gary Elliott Ltd* [1982] Ch. 1, 8 *per* Nourse J.; but there is an exception where the lease and sub-lease are protected tenancies under the Rent Act: Rent Act 1977, s.137. However, under section 146(4), sub-lessees have a right independently of the lessee to apply for relief against forfeiture.

Law of Property Act 1925, s.146(4)

(4) Where a lessor is proceeding by action or otherwise to enforce a right of re-entry or forfeiture under any covenant, proviso, or stipulation in a lease, or for non-payment of rent, the court may, on application by any person claiming as under-lessee any estate or interest in the property comprised in the lease or any part thereof, either in the lessor's action (if any) or in any action brought by such person for that purpose, make an order vesting, for the whole term of the lease or any less term, the property comprised in the lease or any part thereof in any person entitled as under-lessee to any estate or interest in such property upon such conditions as to execution of any deed or other document, payment of rent, costs, expenses, damages, compensation, giving security, or otherwise, as the court in the circumstances of each case may think fit, but in no case shall any such under-lessee be entitled to require a lease to be granted to him for any longer term that he had under his original sub-lease.

NOTES:
1. The subsection applies to all cases of forfeiture, whether for non-payment of rent or for breach of other covenants.

2. In relation to forfeiture for non-payment of rent, sub-lessees may also seek relief in accordance with same principles which apply to lessees: *Doe d. Wyatt v. Byron* (1845) 1 C.B. 623 (applying the Common Law Procedure Act 1852, s.212); *Belgravia Insurance Co. Ltd v. Meah* [1964] 1 Q.B. 436 (applying the Common Law Procedure Act 1852, s.210, and the residual equitable jurisdiction); *Escalus Properties v. Robinson* [1996] Q.B. 231 (applying the County Courts Act 1984, ss.138–139). Moreover, in relation to forfeiture for breach of other covenants, the Court of Appeal has held that, by virtue of the definition of "lessee" in section 146(5) of the Law of Property Act 1925, a sub-lessee and an equitable assignee of an under-lease may seek relief against forfeiture under section 146(2): see, respectively, *Escalus Properties Ltd v. Dennis* [1996] Q.B. 231; *High Street Investments Ltd v. Bellshore Property Investments Ltd* (1996) 73 P. & C.R. 143. The significance of this extended availability of section 146(2) is that relief is retrospective and takes the form of the reinstatement of the lease as if it had never been forfeited: see *supra*, p. 456; by contrast, relief under section 146(4) takes effect from the date when relief is granted: see *infra*, p. 458.

However, this consolidation of the position of sub-lessees may have been potentially compromised by the decision in *Hemingway Securities Ltd v. Dunraven Ltd* (1994) 71 P. & C.R. 30. In that case, contrary to a covenant in the lease, the tenant sub-let the premises without the consent of the landlord. The court granted a mandatory injunction requiring the surrender of the sub-lease — (a) against the lessee for breach of the covenant; and (b) against the sub-lessee on the grounds (i) that the sub-lessee had induced a breach of the covenant and (ii) that the covenant was enforceable against him under the doctrine in *Tulk v. Moxhay* (1848) 2 Ph. 774, *post*, p. 728. Forfeiture and the section 146 procedure were not discussed. For comment, see [1995] Conv. 416.

3. It is suggested that sub-lessees may apply for relief under section 146(4) after a landlord has forfeited by actual re-entry and without first obtaining a court order for that purpose. Although the issue was not specifically addressed in *Billson v. Residential Apartments Ltd* [1992] 1 A.C. 494, it would seem consistent with the approach of the House of Lords to section 146(2): see *supra*, p. 454.

4. The right to claim relief conferred on sub-lessees extends to mortgagees of the demised property since a mortgage of a leasehold interest is effected by sub-lease or by charge expressed to be by way of legal mortgage (which confers the rights of a sub-lessee on the chargee: Law of Property Act 1925, s.87(1)): see *Grand Junction Co. Ltd v. Bates* [1954] 2 Q.B. 160, *post*, p. 813. However, a mortgagee is more likely than a sub-lessee in occupation to be unaware of breaches of covenant and forfeiture proceedings (although there are now procedures intended to ensure that mortgagees receive notice of any forfeiture proceedings). As a result a mortgagee may find himself unable to rely on the statutory jurisdiction for relief, especially in respect of forfeiture by court proceedings for breaches other than non-payment of rent; for section 146(4) is no longer available where the landlord has obtained possession under a court order and has re-entered the property: *Rogers v. Rice* [1892] 2 Ch. 170; *Abbey National Building Society v. Maybeech Ltd* [1985] Ch. 190. In this context, the courts have asserted a residual equitable jurisdiction to grant relief: *Abbey National Building Society v. Maybeech Ltd, supra*, 204 *per* Nicholls J.; but, for the denial of such jurisdiction, see *Official Custodian for Charities v. Parway Estates Developments Ltd* [1985] Ch. 151, 165 *per* Dillon L.J.; *Smith v. Metropolitan City Properties Ltd* [1986] 1 E.G.L.R. 52, 53 *per* Walton J., both relying on dicta in *Shiloh Spinners Ltd v. Harding* [1973] A.C. 691, 725 *per* Lord Wilberforce. As noted above, there are different judicial opinions on the survival of the inherent equitable jurisdiction in the context of forfeiture for breaches other than non-payment of rent.

5. Relief against forfeiture is not available to a squatter who has acquired a title by adverse possession against the tenant: *Tickner v. Buzzacott* [1965] Ch. 426.

6. Relief granted to a mortgagee normally takes the form of a grant similar to the original lease, subject to remedying any past breaches and to future compliance with the terms of the lease: see, *e.g. Belgravia Insurance Co. Ltd v. Meah* [1964] 1 Q.B. 436. As noted above, the new lease takes effect from the date of the order: *Cadogan v. Dimovic* [1984] 1 W.L.R. 609, 613 *per* Fox L.J., 616 *per* Robert Goff L.J.

7. Relief granted to a sub-lessee (other than a mortgagee) may be more complex, especially where the sub-lease related to part only of the property comprised in the head-lease. However, relief may involve the grant of a new

lease of the whole or part of the subject matter of the head-lease, although the maximum term of the new lease is limited to the term of the original sub-lease (including any potential extension pursuant to any relevant statutory regime): *Cadogan v. Dominic* [1984] I W.L.R. 609. There are no clear guidelines for determining the terms of the relief, either as to past breaches or as to future liabilities: see Tromans [1986] Conv. 187.

8. Contrary to the position where relief is granted to the tenant (see *Dendy v. Evans* [1910] 1 K.B. 263), interests deriving from the original sub-lease are not automatically reinstated: *Hammersmith and Fulham LBC v. Top Shop Centres Ltd* [1990] Ch. 237.

1.1.5 *Waiver*   As noted above, when a tenant commits a breach of covenant and the lease contains a forfeiture clause, the landlord may either determine the lease or waive the breach. However, once the landlord had elected either to determine the lease or to waive the breach, he cannot retract his election: *Billson v. Residential Apartments Ltd* [1992] 1 A.C. 494, 534 *per* Lord Templeman, citing *Jones v. Carter* (1846) 15 M. & W. 718, 726 *per* Parke B. and *Canas Property Co. Ltd v. K.L. Television Services Ltd* [1970] 2 Q.B. 433, 440 *per* Lord Denning M.R.; *Expert Clothing Service & Sales Ltd v. Hillgate House Ltd* [1986] Ch. 340, 359 *per* Slade L.J., citing *Scarf v. Jardine* (1882) 7 App.Cas. 345, 360 *per* Lord Blackburn; *G.S. Fashions Ltd v. B & Q plc* [1995] 1 W.L.R. 1088, noted at [1995] Conv. 161.

The essential nature of waiver was explained in *Matthews v. Smallwood* [1910] 1 Ch. 777.

Matthews v. Smallwood [1910] 1 Ch. 777

(Ch D., Parker J.)

I think that the law on the subject of waiver is reasonably clear. The right to re-enter is a legal right which, apart from release or abandonment or waiver, will exist, and can be exercised, at any time within the period fixed by the Statutes of Limitation; and if a defendant in an action of ejectment based upon that right of re-entry alleges a release or abandonment or waiver, logically speaking the onus ought to lie on him to shew the release or the abandonment or the waiver. Waiver of a right of re-entry can only occur where the lessor, with knowledge of the facts upon which his right to re-enter arises, does some unequivocal act recognising the continued existence of the lease. It is not enough that he should do the act which recognises, or appears to recognise, the continued existence of the lease, unless, at the time when the act is done, he has knowledge of the facts under which, or from which, his right of entry arose. Therefore we get the principle that, though an act of waiver operates with regard to all known breaches, it does not operate with regard to breaches which were unknown to the lessor at the time when the act took place. It is also, I think, reasonably clear upon the cases that whether the act, coupled with the knowledge, constitutes a waiver is a question which the law decides, and therefore it is not open to a lessor who has knowledge of the breach to say "I will treat the tenancy as existing, and I will receive the rent, or I will take advantage of my power as landlord to distrain; but I tell you that all I shall do will be without prejudice to my right to re-enter, which I intend to reserve". That is a position which he is not entitled to take up. If, knowing of the breach, he does distrain, or does receive the rent, then by law he waives the breach, and nothing which he can say by way of protest against the law will avail him anything. Logically, therefore, a person who relies upon waiver ought to shew, first, an act unequivocally recognising the subsistence of the lease, and, secondly, knowledge of the circumstances from which the right of re-entry arises at the time when that act is performed.

NOTES:

1. The above statement was cited with approval in *Fuller's Theatre and Vaudeville Co. Ltd v. Rofe* [1923] A.C. 435, 443 *per* Lord Atkinson, and in *Kammins Ballrooms Co. v. Zenith Investments* [1971] A.C. 850, 878–879 *per* Lord Pearson.

2. In *Cornillie v. Saha* (1996) 72 P. & C.R. 147 Aldous L.J. cited the above statement and continued (at 155–157):

To that statement of the law I would only add that which is implicit, namely, that there must be communication to the tenant of the recognition of the existence of the lease. In my view none of the other authorities to which we were referred added to that statement of the law.

...

Following the law as stated by Parker J. in *Matthews v. Smallwood*, it is necessary to identify the alleged act of waiver and then answer these three questions:
1. Does the alleged act of waiver unequivocally recognise the subsistence of the lease?
2. Did the [landlord] have knowledge of the breach of covenant from which the right of re-entry arose at the time of the alleged act of waiver?
3. Was the act of recognition communicated to the [tenant]?

3. The requirement as to knowledge is that the landlord must know of the facts which give rise to the right to forfeit; he need not know that as a matter of law he is entitled to forfeit the lease: *David Blackstone Ltd v. Burnetts (West End) Ltd* [1973] 1 W.L.R. 1487, 1501 *per* Swanwick J. The requirement is satisfied where the agent or employee of the landlord has knowledge of the relevant facts: *Metropolitan Properties Co. Ltd v. Cordery* (1979) 39 P. & C.R. 10. It may also be satisfied where the facts have been the subject of widespread media coverage: *Van Haarlam v. Kasner* (1992) 64 P. & C.R. 214; contrast *Official Custodian for Charities v. Parway Estates Developments Ltd* [1985] Ch. 151, where the facts appeared in the *London Gazette*.

4. The most common example of the required "unequivocal act recognising the continued existence of the lease" is the demand for or acceptance of rent which becomes due after the breach: *Segal Securities Ltd v. Thoseby* [1963] 1 Q.B. 887 and *David Blackstone Ltd v. Burnetts (West End) Ltd* [1973] 1 W.L.R. 1487 (demand); *Oak Property Co. Ltd v. Chapman* [1947] K.B. 886 and *Central Estates (Belgravia) Ltd v. Woolgar (No. 2)* [1972] 1 W.L.R. 1048 (acceptance). It is irrelevant that the rent is demanded or accepted "without prejudice": *Segal Securities Ltd v. Thoseby, supra,* 897–899 *per* Sachs J.; *Central Estates (Belgravia) Ltd v. Woolgar (No. 2), supra,* 1054 *per* Buckley L.J.; *Expert Clothing Service & Sales Ltd v. Hillgate House Ltd* [1986] Ch. 340, 359 *per* Slade L.J. However, it has been held that there is no waiver where the landlord merely demands or accepts rent which accrued due *before* the ground for forfeiture arose, since this recognises only that the tenancy

subsisted at a date prior to that on which the ground arose: *Re A Debtor* [1995] 1 W.L.R. 1127. The act of waiver may be that of the agent or employee of the landlord: *Central Estates (Belgravia) Ltd v. Woolgar (No. 2), supra,* 1052 *per* Lord Denning M.R., 1055 *per* Buckley L.J. Moreover, the legal effect of the act relied on as constituting the waiver must be considered objectively, without regard to the motive or intention of the landlord or the actual understanding or belief of the tenant: *Expert Clothing Service & Sales Ltd v. Hillgate House Ltd, supra,* 359 *per* Slade L.J., citing *Central Estates (Belgravia) Ltd v Woolgar (No. 2), supra,* 1054 *per* Buckley L.J.

5. Where no demand for or acceptance of rent is involved, the court is "free to look at *all* the circumstances of the case to consider whether the act of the [landlord] relied on ... was so unequivocal that, when considered objectively, it could only be regarded as having been done consistently with the continued existence of the tenancy": *Expert Clothing Service & Sales Ltd v. Hillgate House Ltd* [1986] Ch. 340, 359 *per* Slade L.J. Negotiations for variations to the lease may not, without more, constitute waiver: *ibid.* 359–362 *per* Slade L.J.; *Re National Jazz Centre* [1988] 2 E.G.L.R. 57, 58 *per* Peter Gibson J. However, in *Cornillie v. Saha* (1996) 72 P. & C.R. 147 the landlord was held to have waived a breach of a covenant against sub-letting the premises where, with knowledge of the fact of sub-letting, he commenced proceedings for access to the premises in order to investigate and remedy any disrepairs.

6. Waiver of a breach of covenant precludes forfeiture based on the particular breach only: Law of Property Act 1925, s.148(1); it does not constitute waiver of similar breaches in the future: *Billson v. Residential Apartments Ltd* [1992] 1 A.C. 494, 506–507 *per* Browne-Wilkinson V.-C. The same principle applies to a continuing breach: even where the landlord has waived the breach in the past, that waiver can be withdrawn for the future: *Cooper v. Henderson* (1982) 263 E.G. 592; *Greenwich LBC v. Discreet Selling Estates Ltd* (1990) 61 P. & C.R. 405; but it seems that the withdrawal may not operate during any period for which rent has been demanded or accepted and during which the landlord knows that the breach will definitely continue: *Segal Securities Ltd v. Thoseby* [1963] 1 Q.B. 887, 901–902 *per* Sachs J. Where a continuing breach has been waived after the service of a section 146 notice, but the waiver is then withdrawn, the landlord may forfeit the lease without the need to serve a new notice: *Penton v. Barnett* [1898] 1 Q.B. 276, 281–282 *per* Collins L.J.; *Greenwich LBC v. Discreet Selling Estates Ltd, supra,* 412–413 *per* Staughton L.J.

7. Waiver of a breach only precludes the right to forfeit the lease: the landlord is not precluded from claiming arrears of rent or from claiming damages for other breaches of covenant: *Stephens v. Junior Army and Navy Stores Ltd* [1914] 2 Ch. 516.

1.1.6 *Reform*   In 1985 the Law Commission recommended wholesale reform of the law relating to forfeiture: Law Com. No. 142, *Codification of the Law of Landlord and Tenant: Forfeiture of Tenancies* (1985). For discussion, see [1986] Conv. 165. In 1994 a draft bill was produced to implement those recommendations (with certain amendments): Law Com. No. 221, *Landlord and Tenant Law: Termination of Tenancies Bill* (1994). For discussion, see [1994] Conv. 177. The recommendations have been subject to further amendment and consultation: Law Commission, *Landlord and Tenant Law: Termination of Tenancies by Physical Re-entry* (1998), in particular, whereas the original Report recommended that a tenancy should be subject to termination for breach of covenant only by court order or consent, the Law Commission has now recommended that there should also be a statutory right of physical re-entry: In the following summary, references to paragraphs are to paragraphs in Law Com. No. 142, except where otherwise stated.

(1) The Law Commission has recommended that, subject to one principal exception (see paragraph (9) *infra*), the present law of forfeiture should be replaced by a "termination order scheme", under which court proceedings would be necessary to terminate a tenancy and the tenancy would continue in full force until the court ordered its termination. There would be no distinction between termination for non-payment of rent and termination for other reasons: the scheme would incorporate a uniform regime.

(2) The landlord would base his application for a "termination order" on "termination order events":
   (i) breaches of covenant (including all obligations owed by the tenant to the landlord, whether expressly undertaken or implied at common law or by statute), irrespective of whether the lease contains a "forfeiture clause";
  (ii) disguised breaches of covenant (including all obligations imposed on the tenant otherwise than by covenant, breach of which makes the tenancy terminable);
 (iii) insolvency events (events concerned with the actual or threatened bankruptcy or insolvency of the tenant, the happening of which makes the tenancy terminable).

[paras 5.1.–5.20]

(3) A termination order event would be regarded as waived if the conduct of the landlord, after he has knowledge of the event, is such that it would lead a reasonable tenant to believe, and does in fact lead the actual tenant to believe, that the landlord will not seek a termination order on the ground of that event. Where the event is a continuing breach of covenant, it should be a question of fact whether and how far the landlord has led the tenant reasonably to believe that he has waived it for the future as well as for the past.

[paras 6.8–6.9]

(4) A termination order event should generally remain available as a ground for a termination order despite the fact that its consequences may have been remedied.

[paras 7.1–7.13]

(5) The right of the landlord to commence termination order proceedings should exist for only six months after he has actual knowledge of the facts constituting the termination order event on which his application is based, unless the landlord extends that period through the optional notice procedure.

[paras 8.1–8.19]

(6) There should be no general requirement for the landlord to give notice to the tenant before commencing termination order proceedings; but in certain cases involving want of repair, a preliminary notice would be compulsory and, if the tenant served a counter-notice, the landlord would not be permitted to commence termination order proceedings without the leave of the court.

[paras 8.21–8.60]

(7) On an application for a termination order, the court would be able to make an absolute order, a remedial order or no order.

(i) an *absolute order*, which would terminate the tenancy on the date specified in the order, would reflect the view of the court that the tenancy should end without any further chances being given to the tenant. Such an order should be made if, and only if:

(a) the court is satisfied, by reason of the serious character of any termination order events occurring during the tenure of the present tenant and/or by reason of their frequency that the tenant is so unsatisfactory a tenant that he ought not in all the circumstances to remain tenant of the property;

(b) the court is satisfied that an assignment of the tenancy has been made in order to forestall the making of an absolute order under the foregoing paragraph, that there is a substantial risk of the continuance or recurrence of the state of affairs giving rise to a termination order event on which the proceedings are based, and that the new tenant ought not in all the circumstances to remain a tenant of the property;

(c) where the termination order event on which the proceedings are based is a wrongful assignment, or an insolvency event, the court is satisfied that no remedial action which the court could order would be adequate and satisfactory to the landlord;

(d) the court, though it would wish to make a remedial order is not satisfied that the tenant is willing, and is likely to be able, to carry out the remedial action which would be required of him.

(ii) a *remedial order* would have the effect of ending the tenancy if, but only if, the tenant failed to take specified remedial action within a specified time. If the court does not make an absolute order, it should make a remedial order *unless* one of the following situations exists, in which case it should decline to make any termination order:

(a) remedial action has already been taken;

(b) remedial action is impossible or unnecessary;

(c) remedial action ought not in all the circumstances to be required.

[paras 9.15–9.51]

(8) In accordance with the general law a termination order would have the effect of terminating all derivative interests (subtenancies and mortgages). Under the termination order scheme, the landlord would be able to preserve all such interests or, in certain circumstances, a complete branch of such interests affecting part only of the property. In respect of derivative interests not preserved by the landlord, the court should not normally allow a

termination order to terminate a tenancy unless and until it is satisfied that all owners of such interests have had an opportunity to apply for relief. On any such application the court would have power to preserve such interests, to grant new tenancies and, where the derivative interest is a mortgage, to direct the provision of appropriate security.

[paras 10.6–10.45, 10.53; Law Com. No. 221, paras 2.21–2.23]

(9) The exception to the proposed "termination order scheme" would be a statutory right of physical re-entry, although the framework for the right would be closely integrated with the termination order scheme and to that extent the right would be an alternative remedy to court proceedings for a termination order. Subject to notice requirements and certain other safeguards, the landlord's right of physical re-entry would arise on the happening of a termination order event. However, the landlord would be required to serve a notice on the tenant requiring the breach to be remedied within a reasonable time and, if the tenant failed to remedy the breach, the landlord could re-enter. Even then, physical re-entry would not terminate the tenancy immediately but would signal an election by the landlord that the tenancy should terminate at the end of a given period, normally three months, although the period might be extended. If the tenant challenged the landlord's right or sought relief, the dispute would be dealt with by the court in accordance with the termination order scheme and the tenancy would terminate if and when the court so ordered. The tenant would remain liable to pay rent and to observe and perform the tenant's covenants until the termination of the tenancy. The landlord would also be required to give notice, in advance of actual re-entry, to the owners of any derivative interests known to the landlord, who would be entitled to claim relief.

Safeguards that currently apply to the common law right of physical re-entry would be applied to the statutory right: re-entry would have to be peaceable; the right would generally not be available in the context of residential property; and the right would not be available in relation to repairing covenants. Finally, the right would not be available to terminate tenancies having a significant capital value.

Law Com. No. 142 included proposals for a complementary termination order scheme for tenants; but, given the preceived priority for reform of the existing law of forfeiture, the draft Bill did not seek to implement those proposals. However, for termination of a tenancy on the ground of the landlord's repudiatory breach of covenant, see *infra*, p. 481.

1.2 *Distress for rent*
The traditional remedy by which the landlord recovered arrears of rent was the right to levy distress: see, *e.g. Walsh v. Lonsdale* (1882) 21 Ch D. 9, *supra*, p. 391. In principle, the right arises as soon as any rent is in arrear; and it entitles the landlord, without any preliminary legal procedure, to enter the demised property, to seize any goods found there, to sell those goods and to use the proceeds in satisfaction of the arrears and expenses. However, there are numerous restrictions relating to the time and method of

entry: see *Khazanchi v. Faircharm Investments Ltd* [1998] 2 All E.R. 901; certain goods are immune from seizure; and there are rules as to the conduct of the sale. The remedy has been described as "riddled with inconsistencies, uncertainties, anomalies and archaisms". Law Commission Working Paper No. 97, *Landlord and Tenant: Distress for Rent* (1986), para. 5.1; and its abolition has been recommended: Law Com. No. 194, *Landlord and Tenant: Distress for Rent* (1991). However, it is accepted thats its abolition must await speedier court procedures for the recovery of rent arrears.

As an alternative to distress, a judicial form of execution against the goods of the tenant is available through the issue of a warrant of execution in the county court or through a writ of fieri facias in the High Court: see *McLeod v. Butterwick* [1998] 2 All E.R. 901; and see Hill-Smith [1983] Conv. 444.

Moreover, a landlord may bring an ordinary action for the recovery of a maximum of six years' arrears of rent: Limitation Act 1980, s.19.

1.3 *Damages for breach of covenants*
As indicated above, where a tenant is in breach of a covenant or condition in the lease, the landlord may, instead of commencing forfeiture proceedings, bring an action for damages, which would be assessed on the usual contractual basis.

However, there are special provisions in respect of breaches of covenant to "keep or put in repair". First, the provisions of the Leasehold Property (Repairs) Act 1938 apply in this context as they apply in the context of proceedings for the enforcement of a right of re-entry or forfeiture. In the case of leases granted for seven years or more with at least three years of the term unexpired at the commencement of the action, the landlord must serve a notice pursuant to section 146 of the Law of Property Act 1925, which must include a statement as to the entitlement of the tenant to serve a counter-notice; and, where the tenant does serve a counter-notice, the landlord is then precluded from taking any further proceedings for damages for breach of the repairing covenant unless he first obtains the leave of the court: see Smith [1986] Conv. 85. Secondly, section 18(1) of the Landlord and Tenant Act 1927 provides that damages for breach of covenant to keep premises in repair are limited to the amount by which the value of the reversion in the premises has been diminished by the breach: see Smith [1990] Conv. 335, 342–345.

These provisions have given rise to some difficulties: see Law Com. No. 142, *Codification of the Law of Landlord and Tenant: Forfeiture of Tenancies* (1988), paras 8.33–8.46. First, in *SEDAC Investments Ltd v. Tanner* [1982] 1 W.L.R. 1342 the landlord had carried out repairs himself without first calling on the tenant to do so; and it was held that he could not claim damages because the provisions of the 1938 Act presupposed that the section 146 notice would be served prior to the landlord carrying out any repairs. Secondly, in *Swallow Securities Ltd v. Brand* (1981) 45 P. & C.R. 328 it had been held that, even where the landlord carried out the repairs himself pursuant to the terms of a "self-help clause", the claim for reimbursement was in reality a claim for damages for breach of the repairing covenant and the claim was therefore subject to the procedural requirements of the 1938 Act (and, it would seem to follow, the limitation on damages contained in section 18(1) of the Landlord and Tenant Act 1927). However, in a number of subsequent cases involving similar facts, the courts declined to follow the decision.

The Court of Appeal has now formally overruled *Swallow Securities Ltd v. Brand* and has apparently limited *SEDAC Investments Ltd v. Tanner* to cases where there is no "self-help clause" or where the landlord fails to comply with any requirement in the "self-help clause" that he should first call upon the tenant to carry out repairs. In *Jervis v. Harris* [1996] 1 All E.R. 303, noted at [1997] Conv. 299, it was held (i) that, where the landlord carries out repairs himself pursuant to and in accordance with the terms of a "self-help clause", he does so by virtue of his contractual right under the terms of the lease and the procedural requirements of the Leasehold Property (Repairs) Act 1938 do not apply: *ibid.* 308 *per* Millett L.J.; and (ii) that the landlord's claim for the reimbursement of his expenditure is a claim in debt (and not a claim for damages for breach of covenant) so that again the procedural requirements of the 1938 Act do not apply: *ibid.* 306–310 *per* Millett L.J. Moreover, although the issue was not discussed in the case, it would seem to follow that the limitation on damages imposed by section 18(1) of the Landlord and Tenant Act 1927 does not apply in such cases.

However, even where section 18(1) of the 1927 Act does apply, the House of Lords has recently held that a landlord can recover as damages the cost of rectifying the breach provided that it was reasonable for him to do so: *Ruxley Electronics and Constructions Ltd v. Forsyth* [1996] A.C. 344.

1.4 *Specific performance*

The orthodox view was always that a landlord could not compel a tenant to perform his (repairing) covenants by means of a decree of specific performance: *Hill v. Barclay* (1810) 16 Ves. 402. However, in so far as the reasoning was based on lack of mutuality, it is no longer compelling, since a tenant may obtain specific relief to compel a landlord to perform his repairing covenants: see *infra*, p. 472; and the orthodoxy was abandoned in *Rainbow Estates Ltd v. Tokenhold Ltd* [1999] Ch. 64.

Rainbow Estates Ltd v. Tokenhold Ltd [1999] Ch. 64

(Ch D., Lawrence Collins Q.C.)

LAWRENCE COLLINS Q.C.:

Specific performance of landlord's repairing covenant

  Until relatively recently it was generally accepted that repairing covenants could not be specifically enforced, whether they were landlord's covenants or tenant's covenants. The decision on which that view rested was the decision of Lord Eldon L.C. in *Hill v. Barclay* (1810) 16 Ves. 402. In refusing a tenant relief against forfeiture for breach of a repairing covenant, Lord Eldon L.C. said, at p. 405, that the landlord "may bring an ejectment upon non-payment of rent: but he may also compel the tenant to pay the rent. He cannot have that specific relief with regard to repairs. He may bring an action for damages: but there is a wide distinction between damages and the actual expenditure upon repairs, specifically done. Even after damages recovered the landlord cannot compel the tenant to repair: but may bring another action. The tenant therefore ... may keep the premises until the last year of the term; and ... the most beneficial course for the landlord would be, that the tenant, refraining from doing the repairs until the last year of the term, should then be compelled to do them."

But, said Lord Eldon L.C.: "The difficulty upon this doctrine of a court of equity is, that there is no mutuality in it. The tenant cannot be compelled to repair."

The view that the landlord's covenant could not be specifically enforced came to be based on the theory that there was no mutuality because the tenant's covenant could not be specifically enforced, or because the works could not be adequately defined, or because effective compliance could not be obtained without the constant supervision of the court: cf. *Fry on Specific Performance.*, 6th ed. (1921), pp. 42–50, 222–223.

But today there is little or no life in these reasons. First, as regards the requirement of mutuality, it is now clear that it does not follow from the fact that specific performance is not available to one party that it is not available to the other: want of mutuality is a discretionary, and not an absolute, bar to specific performance. The court will grant specific performance if it can be done without injustice or unfairness to the defendant: *Price v. Strange*, [1978] Ch. 337, 357 *per* Goff L.J. Second, as regards the need for precision in the terms of the order, it is

"a question of degree and the courts have shown themselves willing to cope with a certain degree of imprecision in cases of orders requiring the achievement of a result in which the plaintiffs' merits appeared strong ... it is, taken alone, merely a discretionary matter to be taken into account ... It is, however, a very important one:" *per* Lord Hoffmann in *Co-op Insurance Society Ltd v. Argyll Stores (Holdings) Ltd* [1998] A.C. 1, 14.

So also, the objection to an order for specific performance based on the need for the court's constant supervision is designed to avoid repeated applications for committal which are likely to be expensive in terms of cost to the parties and the resources of the judicial system, but as regards orders to achieve a result, Lord Hoffmann said, at p. 13:

"Even if the achievement of the result is a complicated matter which will take some time, the court, if called upon to rule, only has to examine the finished work and say whether it complies with the order ... This distinction between orders to carry on activities and to achieve results explains why the courts have in appropriate circumstances ordered specific performance of building contracts and repairing covenants"

and he cited *Wolverhampton Corp v. Emmons* [1901] 1 K.B. 515 (building contract) and *Jeune v. Queens Cross Properties Ltd* [1973] 3 All E.R. 97, [1974] Ch. 97 (repairing covenant).

In particular, it became settled that the court will order specific performance of an agreement to build if (a) the building work is sufficiently defined; (b) damages would not compensate the plaintiff for the defendant's failure to build; and (it seems) (c) the defendant is in possession of the land so that the plaintiff cannot employ another person to build without committing a trespass: *Snell's Equity*, 29th ed, (1990), p. 595. The analogy with agreements to build was relied on by Sir John Pennycuick V.-C. in *Jeune v. Queens Cross Properties Ltd* in deciding that the court could specifically enforce a lessor's repairing covenant. In that case tenants complained of a failure by the landlord to reinstate properly a stone balcony at the front of a house in

Westbourne Terrace, London W.2, comprising four flats. The tenants sought an order that the landlord should reinstate the balcony in the form in which it existed prior to its partial collapse. Sir John Pennycuick V.-C. acknowledged that common sense and justice required the grant of the relief. But he acknowledged the view in some textbooks that "specific performance will never be ordered of repairing covenants in a lease," and said, at p. 99:

"So far as the general law is concerned, apart from a repairing covenant in a lease, it appears perfectly clear that in an appropriate case the court will decree specific performance of an agreement to build if certain conditions are satisfied."

The conditions were that the work was sufficiently defined by the contract; damages would not be an adequate remedy; and the defendant was in possession, and so the plaintiff could not have the work done without committing a trespass. These conditions were fulfilled, and after referring to the statement of Lord Upjohn in *Redland Bricks Ltd v. Morris* [1970] A.C. 652, 666 that the court must be careful to ensure that the defendant knows exactly what he has to do so that in carrying out an order he can give contractors the proper instructions, Sir John Pennycuick V.-C. said there was no difficulty about that, but a difficulty arose from the decision of Lord Eldon L.C. in *Hill v. Barclay* (1810) 16 Ves. 402. In holding that there was no reason in principle why an order should not be made against a landlord to do some specific work, he said [1974] Ch. 97, 100 (obiter) of *Hill v. Barclay*: "Now that decision is, I think, an authority laying down the principle that a landlord cannot obtain against his tenant an order for specific performance of a covenant to repair." In concluding that the landlord's covenant could be the subject of an order for specific performance, he said, at p. 101:

"Obviously, it is a jurisdiction which should be carefully exercised. But in a case … where there has been a plain breach of a covenant to repair and there is no doubt at all what is required to be done to remedy the breach, I cannot see why an order for specific performance should not be made."

More recently orders have been made against a landlord to enforce a covenant to employ a resident porter; what had to be done was capable of definition, and enforcing compliance would not involve superintendence by the court to an unacceptable degree: *Posner v. Scott-Lewis* [1987] Ch. 25, 33–37; and against a landlord requiring removal of dry rot, on the basis that, notwithstanding the difficulty of working out the appropriate order, damages would not be an adequate remedy; in particular, the condition of the premises was continually deteriorating: *Gordon v. Selico Ltd* (1986) 18 H.L.R. 219. See also *Peninsular Maritime Ltd v. Padseal Ltd* [1981] 2 E.G.L.R 43 (interlocutory mandatory injunction to use best endeavours to put a lift into working order) and *Tustian v. Johnston* [1983] 2 All E.R. 673, 681.

These decisions show that there is no longer any life in the proposition that the court will not grant specific performance against a landlord of a covenant to repair either because of lack of mutuality or because of the supposed need for constant supervision; and in the case of dwellings, there is now a statutory jurisdiction to order specific performance of a landlord's repairing covenant. Section 17 of the Landlord and Tenant Act 1985 (replacing the Housing Act 1974, s.125) provides:

"(1) In proceedings in which a tenant of a dwelling alleges a breach on the part of his landlord of a repairing covenant relating to any part of the premises in which the dwelling is comprised, the court may order specific performance of the covenant whether or not the breach relates to a part of the premises let to the tenant and notwithstanding any equitable rule restricting the scope of the remedy, whether on the basis of a lack of mutuality or otherwise."

Specific performance of tenant's repairing covenant

Is there any reason in principle why an order for specific performance should not be made against a tenant in appropriate circumstances? It would not be profitable to consider whether the statements in the older authorities that tenant's repairing covenants were not specifically enforceable were ratio or dicta: in *Rayner v. Stone* (1762) 2 Ed 128 the basis of the decision was that the work could not be sufficiently defined; in *Hill v. Barclay* (1810) 16 Ves. 402 the actual decision was that the tenant could not obtain relief against forfeiture for breach of the repairing covenant, and one reason (of several, alternative reasons) was lack of mutuality, in the sense that, if there were relief from forfeiture, the landlord would have to bring successive actions for damages since "the landlord cannot compel the tenant to repair ... there is no mutuality in it. The tenant cannot be compelled to repair" and otherwise the tenant would "have the option, against the will of the landlord, of keeping the lease upon those terms; from time to time breaking the covenant, which he cannot be compelled to perform:" per Lord Eldon L.C., at p. 405. See also *City of London v. Nash* (1747) 3 Atk. 511 and *Mosely v. Virgin* (1796) 3 Ves. 184 (dicta suggesting tenant's repairing covenants could not be specifically enforced).

The statement in *Jeune v. Queens Cross Properties Ltd.* [1974] Ch. 97, 100 that "a landlord cannot obtain against his tenant an order for specific performance of a covenant to repair" was obiter, as was the remark by Oliver J. in *Regional Properties Ltd v. City of London Real Property Co. Ltd* [1981] 1 E.G.L.R. 33, 34 that there was "grave doubt whether ... a tenant's covenant is capable of specific performance," although he went on to acknowledge that *Hill v. Barclay* (1810) 16 Ves. 402 may logically be much weakened as an authority, if indeed it ever was more than a mere dictum" by the decision of Sir John Pennycuick V.-C. in *Jeune v. Queens Cross Properties Ltd* [1974] Ch. 97.

According to *Halsbury's Laws of England,* 4th ed. reissue, Vol. 27(1)(1994), para. 368 "specific performance of a tenant's repairing covenant will not ordinarily be granted," citing *Hill v Barclay* (1810) 16 Ves. 402, but the editors go on, at footnote 4:

> "This has long been stated by textbook writers to be the law but the jurisdiction to grant specific performance of contracts to do building works has developed and there seems no reason in principle why such an order should not be made if the works are sufficiently defined ... and the order is not being sought as a means of circumventing the statutory restrictions on the recovery of damages ... It may be that the remedy will often be inappropriate because damages will be a sufficient remedy; but this may not be so where the landlord has no right of entry and the property is deteriorating rapidly ..."

Dowding and Reynolds, Dilapidations: The Modern Law and Practice (1995), pp. 555–559 suggest that there is no reason in principle why specific performance should not be granted: first, there is no logical reason for distinguishing between covenants to repair and other contractual obligations; second, if specific performance can be granted of a landlord's covenant there is no reason for a different rule for a tenant's covenant; third, there is no reason to distinguish between building obligations (for which specific performance can be granted) and repairing obligations; fourth, even if the older cases do decide that specific performance of a tenant's obligation can never be granted, the law relating to specific performance has developed significantly. See also *Woodfall, Landlord and Tenant,* (1994) para. 13.099, *Jones and Goodhart, Specific Performance,* 2nd ed. (1996), p. 189 and *Spry, Equitable Remedies,* 4th ed. (1990), p. 116.

Like the editors of *Halsbury's Laws* and of *Woodfall, Dowding and Reynolds* suggests, at p. 561, that the court will not allow the remedy of specific performance to circumvent the protection which the Leasehold Property (Repairs) Act 1938 was intended to confer on tenants: although the Act of 1938 does not apply to a claim for specific performance, the editors suggest that the court would be reluctant to make an order where an action for damages or forfeiture would be subject to the restrictions imposed by the 1938 Act and where the circumstances are such that leave would not be granted. The effect of the Act of 1938 is that, in the case of a tenancy of not less than seven years with three years or more unexpired, forfeiture or claims for damages for breach of repairing covenants are not available until certain conditions have been fulfilled. The court will only grant leave if the landlord can prove that one of the conditions specified in s.1(5) of the Act of 1938 has been fulfilled, and if the court is satisfied in the exercise of its discretion that leave ought to be granted. The conditions are (in summary): (a) that the immediate remedying of the breach is required for preventing substantial diminution in the value; (b) that the immediate remedying of the breach is required to give effect to any enactment, or court order; (c) where the lessee is not in occupation, that the immediate remedying of the breach is required in the interests of the occupier; (d) that the breach can be immediately remedied at an expense that is relatively small in comparison with the much greater expense that would probably be occasioned by postponement of the necessary work; or (e) that there are special circumstances which, in the opinion of the court, render it just and equitable that leave should be given.

In my judgment, a modern law of remedies requires specific performance of a tenant's repairing covenant to be available in appropriate circumstances, and there are no constraints of principle or binding authority against the availability of the remedy. First, even if want of mutuality were any longer a decisive factor (which it is not) the availability of the remedy against the tenant would restore mutuality as against the landlord. Second, the problems of defining the work and the need for supervision can be overcome by ensuring that there is sufficient definition of what has to be done in order to comply with the order of the court. Third, the court should not be constrained by the supposed rule that the court will not enforce the defendant's obligation in part; this is a problem raised by the Law Commission Report, Landlord and Tenant: Responsibility for State and Condition of Property, paras. 9.10 and 9.13, but it is not raised elsewhere as an objection; it is by no means clear that there is such a principle, and in any event if there is such a principle, it applies where the contract is in part unenforceable (*Jones and Goodhart, Specific Performance*, pp. 57–61); it does not mean that the court cannot in an appropriate case enforce compliance with a particular obligation such as a repairing covenant.

Subject to the overriding need to avoid injustice or oppression, the remedy should be available when damages are not an adequate remedy or, in the more modern formulation, when specific performance is the appropriate remedy. This will be particularly important if there is substantial difficulty in the way of the landlord effecting repairs: the landlord may not have a right of access to the property to effect necessary repairs, since (in the absence of contrary agreement) a landlord has no right to enter the premises, and the condition of the premises may be deteriorating.

In all cases the court must be astute to prevent oppression, even if tenants are no longer (as they were said to be in *Rayner v. Stone* (1762) 2 Ed. 128, 130) for the most part of "mean and low circumstances". The leading texts suggest that the remedy should not be available to circumvent the restrictions on the recovery of damages or forfeiture under the Act of 1938. The Act of 1938, however, does not apply to decrees of specific performance, and it would not be right to treat the legislation as covering the remedy when it does not in terms apply. That would be an impermissible extension of a statute to cover a case where it is not applicable. What the court should do is to prevent specific performance from being used to effectuate or encourage the mischief which the Act of 1938 was intended to remedy. The object of the Act of 1938 was to remedy the mischief of speculators or unscrupulous landlords buying the reversion of a lease which had little value, and then harassing the tenant with schedules of dilapidations, not with a view to ensuring that the property was kept in proper repair for the protection of the reversion, but to put pressure on the tenant: see authorities cited in *Jervis v. Harris* [1996] Ch. 195, 204–205. Although the court should not use the provisions of Section 1(5) of the Act of 1938 as if they were applicable, it should be astute to ensure that the landlord is not seeking the decree simply in order to harass the tenant; in so doing, the court may take into account considerations similar to those it must take into account under the Act of 1938.

It follows that not only is there a need for great caution in granting the remedy against a tenant, but also that it will be a rare case in which the remedy of specific performance will be the appropriate one: in the case of commercial leases, the landlord will normally have the right to forfeit or to enter and do the repairs at the expense of the tenant; in residential leases, the landlord will normally have the right to forfeit in appropriate cases.

NOTES:

1. For comment, see [1998] Conv. 495.

2. The Law Commission has recommended that specific performance should be available as a means of enforcing repairing covenants in all leases and tenancies; and that the remedy should be available to both landlords and tenants: Law Com. No. 238, *Landlord and Tenant: Responsibility for State and Condition of Property* (1996).

Law Commission Report No. 238, Landlord and Tenant: Responsibility for State and Condition of Property (1996)

Summary of recommendations

Part IX Specific Performance of Repairing Covenants

11.33 We recommend that:
   (a) a court should have power to decree specific performance of a repairing obligation in any lease or tenancy (including statutory tenancies);
   (b) the remedy should be available—
      (i) to a landlord, a tenant or any other party to the lease in respect of a breach of a repairing obligation by another party;
      (ii) notwithstanding any equitable rule restricting the scope of the remedy, such as the rule against partial performance; and
   (c) the remedy should not be granted as of right, but in the court's discretion whenever the court thinks fit, and subject of course to the usual equitable defences.
11.34 For these purposes, a repairing obligation would be widely defined (in the same terms as it is at present in section 17(2) of the Landlord and Tenant Act 1985) as a covenant to repair, maintain, renew, construct or replace any property.

NOTES:

1. The Report states (at para. 9.31):

As an equitable remedy, it would not be the only or even necessarily the usual method of enforcing repairing obligations, but should be decreed when a court, in the exercise of its discretion, considered it to be the most appropriate remedy to secure the required result ... The present contraints on the availability of the remedy, such as objections on the ground of mutuality, the need for the court's supervision or partial performance, would not apply to the statutory remedy. However, because specific performance would be decreed only if it was appropriate, a court would refuse it if, for example, the landlord sought the remedy towards the end of the term but intended to demolish the premises on the termination of the lease.

2. For comment, see Bridge [1996] Conv. 342.

2. Remedies available to the tenant

2.1 *Forfeiture*
As noted above, the Law Commission originally proposed that the termination order scheme, which would replace forfeiture, should include a complementary scheme available to tenants; but that part of the proposed scheme is not currently being pursued. However, as also noted, a tenant may be able to terminate a lease on the ground of the landlord's repudiatory breach of covenant: see *infra*, p. 481.

2.2 *Damages/reimbursement of expenditure*
A tenant may claim damages in respect of loss caused by the landlord's breach of covenant. Such restrictions that apply to landlords in respect of repairing covenants do not apply to tenants: there are no procedural requirements and damages are assessed as the difference between the value of the premises to the tenant in their condition of disrepair and what their value would have been if the covenants had been fulfilled: *Calabar Properties Ltd v. Stitcher* [1984] 1 W.L.R. 287. Moreover, where a landlord is in breach of his repairing covenants, the tenant is entitled to carry out the necessary work and claim reimbursement. Alternatively, provided that the tenant gave the landlord notice of the need of repair, he may deduct from future rent so much of the expenditure as is reasonable and proper: *Lee-Parker v. Izzet* [1971] 1 W.L.R. 1688; or the tenant may have an equitable right of set-off against a claim by the landlord in respect of non-payment of rent: *Melville v. Grapelodge Developments Ltd* (1978) 39 P. & C.R. 179; *British Anzani (Felixstowe) Ltd v. International Marine Management (U.K.) Ltd* [1980] Q.B. 137; and see *Eller v. Grovecrest Investments Ltd* [1995] Q.B. 272.

2.3 *Specific performance*
More recently it has been accepted that a tenant may obtain specific performance of the landlord's repairing covenants both under the court's inherent jurisdiction and under section 17 of the Landlord and Tenant Act 1985: see *Rainbow Estates Ltd v. Tokenhold Ltd* [1999] Ch. 64, *supra*, p. 466. Moreover, the Law Commission has recommended that such jurisdiction be afforded a new statutory basis: see *supra*, p. 471; and that it should also be available to a tenant in respect of the landlord's extended obligations in relation to fitness for human habitation: see *supra*, p. 408.

2.4 *Public law remedies*
Despite the expanding range of private law remedies potentially available, tenants will sometimes prefer to avoid the inherent direct confrontation with

the landlord. Instead, they will rely on the local authority to enforce corresponding statutory obligations relating to disrepair, fitness for human habitation and public health: see Law Commission Consultation Paper No. 123, *Landlord and Tenant: Responsibility for State and Condition of Property* (1992), paras 2.50–2.62.

J. DETERMINATION OF LEASES

1. Expiry

A fixed term lease terminates automatically on the expiry of the agreed term; and, in the absence of a contrary provision in the lease, there is no requirement that either party should serve notice on the other. However, where a fixed term lease contains a break clause, permitting the landlord and/ or tenant to terminate the lease before the expiry of the agreed term, notice is necessary to activate the break clause: see, *e.g. Industrial Properties (Barton Hill) Ltd v. Associated Electrical Industries Ltd* [1977] Q.B. 580.

The expiry of the agreed term does not necessarily terminate the rights of the tenant. Under the Rent Act 1977 and the Housing Acts 1985 and 1988 some fixed term residential tenancies are converted into periodic tenancies; and under Part II of the Landlord and Tenant Act 1954 some business tenants have a statutory right to a new lease.

2. Notice to quit

Notice to quit constitutes the normal method of termination in the case of periodic tenancies. Indeed, as has been seen, it is the essence of a periodic tenancy, and a necessary condition of the certain duration of such a tenancy, that both parties should have an unrestricted right to determine the tenancy by notice to quit: see *Prudential Assurance Co. Ltd v. London Residuary Body* [1992] 2 A.C. 386, *supra*, p. 349.

As with fixed term leases, the determination of a periodic tenancy by notice to quit does not necessarily terminate the rights of the tenant under the landlord and tenant legislation.

The length of notice required to terminate a periodic tenancy depends upon the reference period of the tenancy; but in all cases the notice must expire at the end of a reference period. At common law, a yearly tenancy may be determined by half a year's notice; otherwise the required period of notice is the reference period of the tenancy. However, by virtue of section 5 of the Protection from Eviction Act 1977, in the case of residential tenancies the landlord is required to give the tenant no less than four weeks' notice in writing and the notice must include prescribed information assuring the tenant that he cannot be evicted without court proceedings.

Problems have arisen in the context of termination where there are joint landlords and/or joint tenants, in particular the question whether a periodic tenancy may be determined at common law by notice given unilaterally by one only of two or more joint tenants or joint landlords.

Hammersmith and Fulham LBC v. Monk [1992] 1 A.C. 478

(HL, Lord Bridge, Lord Brandon, Lord Ackner, Lord Jauncey, Lord Browne-Wilkinson)

LORD BRIDGE:

As a matter of principle I see no reason why this question should receive any different answer in the context of the contractual relationship of landlord and tenant than that which it would receive in any other contractual context. If A and B contract with C on terms which are to continue in operation for one year in the first place and thereafter from year to year unless determined by notice at the end of the first or any subsequent year, neither A nor B has bound himself contractually for longer than one year. To hold that A could not determine the contract at the end of any year without the concurrence of B and vice versa would presuppose that each had assumed a potentially irrevocable contractual obligation for the duration of their joint lives, which, whatever the nature of the contractual obligations undertaken, would be such an improbable intention to impute to the parties that nothing less than the clearest express contractual language would suffice to manifest it. Hence, in any ordinary agreement for an initial term which is to continue for successive terms unless determined by notice, the obvious inference is that the agreement is intended to continue beyond the initial term only if and so long as all parties to the agreement are willing that it should do so. In a common law situation, where parties are free to contract as they wish and are bound only so far as they have agreed to be bound, this leads to the only sensible result.

Thus the application of ordinary contractual principles leads me to expect that a periodic tenancy granted to two or more joint tenants must be terminable at common law by an appropriate notice to quit given by any one of them whether or not the others are prepared to concur. But I turn now to the authorities to see whether there is any principle of the English law of real property and peculiar to the contractual relationship of landlord and tenant which refutes that expectation or whether the authorities confirm it. A useful starting point is the passage from *Blackstone's Commentaries*, Book II (1766), ch. 9, pp. 145–147, which explains clearly how the law developed the concept of a yearly tenancy from the earlier concept of a tenancy at will which gave the tenant no security of tenure ...

From the earliest times a yearly tenancy has been an estate which continued only so long as it was the will of both parties that it should continue, albeit that either party could only signify his unwillingness that the tenancy should continue beyond the end of any year by giving the appropriate advance notice to that effect. Applying this principle to the case of a yearly tenancy where either the lessor's or the lessee's interest is held jointly by two or more parties, logic seems to me to dictate the conclusion that the will of all the joint parties is necessary to the continuance of the interest.

In *Doe d. Aslin v. Summersett* (1830) 1 B. & Ad. 135, the freehold interest in land let on a yearly tenancy was vested jointly in four executors of a will to whom the land had been jointly devised. Three only of the executors gave notice to the tenant to quit. It was held by the Court of King's Bench that the notice was effective to determine the tenancy. Delivering the judgment, Lord Tenterden C.J. said, at pp. 140–141:

"Upon a joint demise by joint tenants upon a tenancy from year to year, the true character of the tenancy is this, not that the tenant holds of each the share of each so long as he and each shall please, but that he holds the *whole of all* so long as he *and all* shall please; and so soon as any one of the joint tenants gives a notice to quit, he effectually puts an end to *that* tenancy; the tenant has a right upon such a notice to give up *the whole*, and unless he comes to a new arrangement with the other joint tenants as to their shares, he is compellable so to do. The hardship upon the tenant, if he were not entitled to treat a notice from one as putting an end to the tenancy as to the whole, is obvious; for however willing a man might be to be sole tenant of an estate, it is not very likely he should be willing to hold undivided shares of it; and if upon such a notice the tenant is entitled to treat it as putting an end to the tenancy as to the whole, the other joint tenants must have the same right. It cannot be optional on one side, and on one side only."

Now it was rightly pointed out in argument that part of the reasoning in this passage was dictated by considerations derived from the incidents of joint land tenure at law which were swept away by the reforming legislation of 1925. But this can in no way detract from the validity of the proposition emphasised in the judgment that the yearly tenant of a property let to him by joint freeholders "holds the *whole* of *all* so long and he *and all* shall please". This by itself is a sufficient and independent ground for the conclusion of the court that notice to quit by any one joint freeholder was effective to determine the tenancy. Precisely the same reasoning would apply to the operation of a notice to quit by one of two or more joint yearly tenants.

Summersett's case was followed in *Doe d. Kindersley v. Hughes* (1840) 7 M. & W. 139 and *Alford v. Vickery* (1842) Car. & M. 280 ...

In this century the English cases directly in point are *Howson v. Buxton* (1928) 97 L.J.K.B. 749, *Leek and Moorlands Building Society v. Clark* [1952] 2 Q.B. 788 and *Greenwich London Borough Council v. McGrady* (1982) 81 L.G.R. 288. I will defer consideration of *Howson v. Buxton* until later. In *Leek and Moorlands Building Society v. Clark* the point directly in issue was whether one of two joint lessees could validly surrender the lease before the full period of the lease had run without the concurrence of the other joint lessee. Delivering the reserved judgment of the court in favour of the defendant lessees Somervell L.J. said [1952] 2 Q.B. 788, 792–793:

"Counsel for the plaintiffs sought to rely on *Doe d. Aslin v. Summersett* as supporting a submission that Mr Ellison, by what he did, had brought the joint tenancy to an end. That case was dealing with a lessee from year to year of land which he held from two joint lessors. A notice to quit was served signed by one only of the joint lessors. It was argued that the other lessor had adopted the notice, but Lord Tenterden, who delivered the judgment of the Court of King's Bench, held that without any such adoption a notice to quit by one of the joint lessors, who were joint tenants, put an end to the tenancy as to both.

The ratio of the decision is, we think, to be found in the following sentence, 1 B & Ad. 135, 140: 'Upon a joint demise by joint tenants'— that is, the lessors in that case—'upon a tenancy from year to year, the true character of the tenancy is this, not that the tenant holds of each the share of each so long as he and each shall please, but that he holds the whole of all so long as he and all shall please, and as soon as any one of the joint tenants'—that is, the lessors in that case—'gives a notice to quit, he effectively puts an end to that tenancy.' It is to be noted that Lord Tenterden was dealing with a notice to quit in respect of a periodic tenancy. He was not dealing with a right to determine a lease for say 21 years at the end, say, of the seventh or fourteenth year. Nor was he dealing with surrender.

There is, we think, force in the submission made on behalf of the plaintiffs, that in the case of a periodic tenancy Lord Tenterden's principle would apply when there were joint lessees. A periodic tenancy continues from period to period unless the notice agreed or implied by law is given. But if one of two joint lessees who 'hold the whole' wishes it not to continue beyond the end of a period, it might well be held that it did not continue into a new period. That would happen only if all, that is, the joint lessees, shall please.

If one considers a lease to joint lessees for a term certain with a right of renewal, it would be obvious, we think, that both must join in requiring a renewal. A periodic tenancy renews itself unless either side brings it to an end. But if one of two or more joint lessees does not desire it to continue, we would have thought that it was in accordance with Lord Tenterden's principle, and with common sense, that he should be able to make that effective."

The judgment added, at pp. 794–795:

"Even if we are wrong in what we have said with regard to a right to determine within the period of the lease as distinct from a right to terminate a periodic tenancy, we would have thought it plain that one of two joint lessees cannot, in the absence of express words or authority, surrender the rights held jointly. If property or rights are held jointly, prima facie a transfer must be by or under the authority of all interested. The answer suggested to this is the principle laid down in *Doe d. Aslin v. Summersett.* That case, for reasons which we have given, is not in our view an exception to the rule we have just stated. It is an illustration, in a highly technical field, of the general principle that if a joint enterprise is due to terminate on a particular day, all concerned must agree if it is to be renewed or continued beyond that day. To use Lord Tenterden's phrase, it will only be continued if 'all shall please.' "

In *McGrady's* case the point at issue was precisely the same as in the present appeal. After citing the judgment of the court in *Leek and Moorlands Building Society v. Clark* [1952] 2 Q.B. 788, Sir John Donaldson M.R. said (1982) 81 L.G.R. 288, 290–291:

"In my judgment it is clear law that if there is to be a surrender of a joint tenancy, that is, a surrender before its natural termination, then all must agree to the surrender. If there is to be a renewal, which is the position at the end of each period of a periodic tenancy, then again all must concur. In this case Mrs McGrady made it quite clear by her notice to quit that she was not content to renew the joint tenancy on and after 15 June 1981. That left Mr McGrady, the defendant, without any tenancy at all, although it was faintly argued by Mr Osman that upon, as he put it, the severance of a joint tenancy the joint tenant who did not concur was left with a sole tenancy. That cannot be the law, and no authority has been cited in support of it. ..."

In the instant case it has not been suggested ... that the notice to quit given by Mrs Powell could have had the effect of "severing" the joint tenancy and leaving the appellant in possession as sole tenant ...

These then are the principles and the authorities which the appellant seeks to controvert. In the light of the careful analysis in the judgment of Slade L.J. (1990) 89 L.G.R. 357, 366–369, of *Howson v. Buxton* (1928) 97 L.J.K.B. 749, which I gratefully adopt and need not repeat, it is now rightly accepted that the case affords no greater support for the appellant than can be derived from the obiter dictum of Scrutton L.J. who said with reference to a notice to determine a yearly tenancy, at p. 752:

"I personally take the view that one joint tenant cannot give a notice to terminate the tenancy unless he does so with the authority of the other joint tenant ..."

Despite the eminence of the author of this observation, I do not feel able to give any weight to it in the absence of any indication of the reasoning on which it is based.

There are three principal strands in the argument advanced for the appellant. First, reliance is placed on the judgment in *Gandy v. Jubber* (1865) 9 B. & S. 15, for the proposition that a tenancy from year to year, however long it continues, is a single term, not a series of separate lettings. ... The fact that the law regards a tenancy from year to year which has continued for a number of years, considered retrospectively, as a single term in no way affects the principle that continuation beyond the end of each year depends on the will of the parties that it should continue or that, considered prospectively, the tenancy continues no further than the parties have already impliedly agreed upon by their omission to serve notice to quit.

The second submission for the appellant is that, whatever the law may have been before the enactment of the Law of Property Act 1925, the effect of that statute, whereby a legal estate in land vested in joint tenants is held on trust for sale for the parties beneficially entitled, coupled with the principle that trustees must act unanimously in dealing with trust property, is to reverse the decision in *Summersett's* case (1830) 1 B. & Ad. 135 and to prevent one of two joint tenants determining a periodic tenancy without the concurrence of the other. It is unnecessary to consider the position where the parties beneficially entitled are different from those who hold the legal interest. But where, as here, two joint tenants of a periodic tenancy hold both the legal and the beneficial interest, the existence of a trust for sale can make no difference to the principles applicable to the termination of the tenancy. At any given moment the extent of the interest to which the trust relates extends no further than the end of the period of the tenancy which will next expire on a date for which it is still possible to give notice to quit. If before 1925 the implied consent of both joint tenants, signified by the omission to give notice to quit, was necessary to extend the tenancy from one period to the next, precisely the same applies since 1925 to the extension by the joint trustee beneficiaries of the periodic tenancy which is the subject of the trust.

Finally, it is said that all positive dealings with a joint tenancy require the concurrence of all joint tenants if they are to be effective. Thus, a single joint tenant cannot exercise a break clause in a lease, surrender the term, make a disclaimer, exercise an option to renew the term or apply for relief from forfeiture. All these positive acts which joint tenants must concur in performing are said to afford analogies with the service of notice to determine a periodic tenancy which is likewise a positive act. But this is to confuse the form with the substance. The action of giving notice to determine a periodic tenancy is in form positive; but both on authority and on the principle so aptly summed up in the pithy Scottish phrase "tacit relocation" the substance of the matter is that it is by his omission to give notice of termination that each party signifies the necessary positive assent to the extension of the term for a further period.

For all these reasons I agree with the Court of Appeal that, unless the terms of the tenancy agreement otherwise provide, notice to quit given by one joint tenant without the concurrence of any other joint tenant is effective to determine a periodic tenancy.

LORD BROWNE-WILKINSON:

My Lords, there are two instinctive reactions to this case which lead to diametrically opposite conclusions. The first is that the flat in question was the joint home of the appellant and Mrs Powell: it therefore cannot be right that one of them unilaterally can join the landlords to put an end to the other's rights in the home. The second is that the appellant and Mrs Powell undertook joint liabilities as tenants for the purpose of providing themselves with a joint home and that, once the desire to live together has ended, it is impossible to require that the one who quits the home should continue indefinitely to be liable for the discharge of the obligations to the landlord under the tenancy agreement.

These two instinctive reactions are mirrored in the legal analysis of the position. In certain cases a contract between two persons can, by itself, give rise to a property interest in one of them. The contract between a landlord and a tenant is a classic example. The contract of tenancy confers on the tenant a legal estate in the land: such legal estate gives rise to rights and duties incapable of being founded in contract alone. The revulsion against Mrs Powell being able unilaterally to terminate the appellant's rights in his home is property based: the appellant's property rights in the home cannot be destroyed without his consent. The other reaction is contract based: Mrs Powell cannot be held to a tenancy contract which is dependent for its continuance on the will of the tenant.

The speech of my noble and learned friend, Lord Bridge of Harwich, traces the development of the periodic tenancy from a tenancy at will. He demonstrates that a periodic tenancy is founded on the continuing will of both landlord and tenant that the tenancy shall persist. Once either the landlord or the tenant indicates, by appropriate notice, that he no longer wishes to continue, the tenancy comes to an end. The problem is to determine who is "the landlord" or "the tenant" when there are joint lessors or joint lessees.

In property law, a transfer of land to two or more persons jointly operates so as to make them, *vis-à-vis* the outside world, one single owner. "Although as between themselves joint tenants have separate rights, as against everyone else they are in the position of a single owner:" *Megarry and Wade, The Law of Real Property* 5th ed. (1984), p. 417. The law would have developed consistently with this principle if it had been held that where a periodic tenancy has been granted by or to a number of persons jointly, the relevant "will" to discontinue the tenancy has to be the will of all the joint lessors or joint lessees who together constitute *the* owner of the reversion or the term as the case may be.

At one stage the law seems to have flirted with adopting this approach. Thus in *Doe d. Whayman v. Chaplin* (1810) 3 Taunt. 120 there was a periodic tenancy and four persons were the joint lessors. Three only of the joint lessors gave notice to quit against the wishes of the fourth. It is reported, at p. 122, that at one stage the court inclined to the view that in order to determine the tenancy all four lessors had to agree. However, after further argument, it was held that each of the three who had given notice to quit was entitled to put an end to the tenancy of his share and the three who had given notice to quit were therefore entitled to recover three parts of the land. As a result, the defendant apparently was entitled to stay on the land in right of his tenancy of one part as tenant in common with the three lessors who had given notice. Although the decision is difficult for a modern lawyer to understand fully, one thing is clear: the giving of notice to quit by three out of the four joint lessors was not sufficient to determine the tenancy of the whole land.

Despite this flirtation, the law was in my judgment determined in the opposite sense by *Doe d. Aslin v. Summersett* (1830) 1 B. & Ad. 135. The contractual, as opposed to the property, approach was adopted. Where there were joint lessors of a periodic tenancy, the continuing "will" had to be the will of all the lessors individually, not the conjoint will of all the lessors collectively. This decision created an exception to the principles of the law of joint ownership: see *Megarry and Wade*, 5th ed., pp. 421–422.

It was submitted that this House should overrule *Summersett's* case. But, as my noble and learned friend, Lord Bridge of Harwich, has demonstrated, the decision was treated throughout the 19th century as laying down the law in relation to the rights of joint lessors. It is not suggested that the position of joint lessees can be different. Since 1925 the law as determined in *Summersett's* case has been applied to notices to quit given by one of several joint lessees. In my judgment no sufficient reason has been shown for changing the basic law which has been established for 160 years unless, as was suggested, the 1925 legislation has altered the position.

Before 1925 property belonging to two or more persons concurrently could be held by them in undivided or divided shares at law. The Law of Property Act 1925 changed this and requires that, even in the case of joint tenants, they hold the legal estate as joint tenants on trust for themselves as joint tenants in equity: section 36(1). It was suggested that the interposition of this statutory trust for sale has altered the position: since the appellant and Mrs Powell held the legal estate in the periodic tenancy as trustees and trustees must act unanimously, neither of them individually could give a valid notice to quit.

In my view this submission fails. The trust property in question was a periodic tenancy. As between the lessor and the lessees the nature of the contract of tenancy cannot have been altered by the fact that the lessees were trustees. The tenancy came to an end when one of the lessees gave notice to quit. It may be that, as between the lessees, the giving of the notice to quit was a breach of trust, theoretically giving rise to a claim by the appellant against Mrs Powell for breach of trust. Even this seems to me very dubious since the overreaching statutory trusts for sale imposed by the Law of Property Act 1925 do not normally alter the beneficial rights inter se of the concurrent owners: see *In re Warren* [1932] 1 Ch. 42, 47 *per* Maugham J.; and *Bull v. Bull* [1955] 1 Q.B. 234. But even if, contrary to my view, the giving of the notice to quit by Mrs Powell was a breach of trust by her, the notice to quit was not a nullity. It was effective as between the lessor and the lessees to terminate the tenancy. The fact that a trustee acts in breach of trust does not mean that he has no capacity to do the act he wrongly did. The breach of trust as between Mrs Powell and the appellant could not affect the lessors unless some case could be mounted that the lessors were parties to the breach, a case which Mr Reid, for the appellant, did not seek to advance. Therefore in my judgment the 1925 legislation does not affect this case.

NOTES:

1. For discussion, see [1992] C.L.J. 218; [1992] Conv. 279; (1992) 108 L.Q.R. 375; [1983] Conv. 194.

2. The decision was applied by the House of Lords in *Harrow LBC v. Johnstone* [1997] 1 W.L.R. 459, noted at [1997] Conv. 288; and it made no difference that the joint tenant serving the notice to quit was subject to an injunction prohibiting her from excluding or attempting to exclude the other joint tenant from the property. The decision was also applied by the Court of Appeal in *Newham LBC v. Hill* (1998) 76 P. & C.R. D24.

3. The decision clearly turns on the theoretical analysis, rather than the practical reality, of the periodic tenancy, in combination with a contractual bias in the approach to the implications of that analysis. If the analysis followed the practical reality, and the tenancy continued until terminated by notice to quit, the service of such notice could be seen as analgous to the exercise of a break clause in a fixed term lease and it would thus require the consent of both joint tenants to be effective: see Webb [1983] Conv. 194, 207–210. However, according to Lord Bridge, the true theoretical analysis is that a periodic tenancy continues for another period only because the joint tenants consent, such consent being inferred from the omission to serve notice to quit. On that analysis, the omission to serve notice to quit is more analogous to the exercise of an option to renew; and it is thus the omission to serve notice *and not the service of notice* which constitutes the positive dealing requiring the consent of all joint tenants.

4. Tee [1992] C.L.J. 218 and Dewar (1992) 108 L.Q.R. 375 question whether the property and contract based approaches are diametrically opposed as Lord Browne-Wilkinson asserts; they suggest that notice to quit by one joint tenant could be treated as a form of surrender or release of his interest which accrues to the other joint tenant(s) by analogy to the doctrine of survivorship; see also Webb [1983] Conv. 194, 206–207. There is some support for that solution: see *Re Schär* [1951] Ch. 280; but it had been dismissed in *Greenwich LBC v. McGrady* (1982) 46 P. & C.R. 223, 224 *per* Sir John Donaldson M.R. and it was not argued in *Hammersmith and Fulham LBC v. Monk*.

5. Webb [1983] Conv. 194, in a critical analysis of *Greenwich LBC v. McGrady* (1982) 46 P. & C.R. 223, questions the perceived view of the decision in *Doe d. Aslin v. Summersett* (1830) 1 B. & Ad. 135 that notice to

quit by one of two joint landlords is sufficient to determine a periodic tenancy. He argues that the case in fact decided that notice to quit by one of two joint landlords, save where that landlord was acting as agent for both, terminated the tenancy *of that landlord's share only* and thus the right of the tenant to exclude that landlord; but that the tenant or the other landlord was entitled to treat the tenancy as terminated *as to all shares* because the tenant originally took the tenancy on the basis that he would have an exclusive right against all the landlords. He further argues that the underlying notion of separate or severable leases, even if tenable under pre-1926 law, could not survive the changes in the law affecting concurrent interests in the Law of Property Act 1925. However, the argument that, because joint tenants or landlords are trustees for sale, one cannot act unilaterally so as to bind the other was rejected in *Hammersmith and Fulham LBC v. Monk*. For earlier rejection of the argument, see *Parsons v. Parsons* [1983] 1 W.L.R. 1390, 1399 *per* Donald Rattee Q.C.

6. In *Crawley BC v. Ure* [1996] Q.B. 13, noted at [1995] Conv. 424, the Court of Appeal considered the suggestion, doubted by Lord Browne-Wilkinson, that a joint tenant who unilaterally served notice to quit might be in breach of trust. It was argued that a joint tenant who failed to consult the other joint tenant(s) before serving notice to quit was in breach of the duty imposed by section 26(3) of the Law of Property Act 1925 (now section II of the Trusts of Land and Appointment of Trustees Act 1996). The court held that, although the duty of consultation imposed by section 26(3) was not limited to the execution of the trust for sale (see *Re Jones* [1931] 1 Ch. 375, 377–378 *per* Bennett J.), it only applied to what Lord Bridge in *Hammersmith and Fulham LBC v. Monk* had termed "positive" acts of the trustees. Since the serving of notice to quit had been analysed as constituting a "negative" act, it followed that there was no breach of section 26(3).

7. In *Hounslow LBC v. Pilling* [1993] 1 W.L.R. 1242 the Court of Appeal held a purported notice to quit given by one of two joint tenants to be ineffective: since the tenancy agreement required four weeks' notice "or such lesser period as the [landlord] may accept" and the landlord had accepted only three days' notice, the court held that the notice in fact constituted the attempted exercise of a break clause; and a break clause cannot be exercised unilaterally by one joint tenant: *Hammersmith and Fulham LBC v. Monk* [1992] 1 A.C. 478, 490 *per* Lord Bridge. For comment, see Tee [1994] C.L.J. 227.

8. The "(re)contractualisation" of leases by the courts is evident also in the recent acceptance of the applicability of the doctrines of frustration, repudiation, misrepresentation and unconscionability: see *infra*, p. 481; but the decision of the House of Lords in *Prudential Assurance Co. Ltd v. London Residuary Body* [1992] 2 A.C. 386, *supra*, p. 349, on the requirement of certain duration demonstrates that the doctrinal movement is not uniform. There is arguably a similar diversity of approach in the current landlord and tenant legislation: thus, while many of the rights of tenants are conferred by statute and cannot be excluded by agreement, there is an assumption that the

terms of private sector assured tenancies are determined by genuine agreement between the parties.

3. Surrender

Surrender takes place where the tenant surrenders his lease to his immediate landlord. The lease merges with the title of the landlord (whether the freehold title or a superior leasehold interest) and is extinguished, although third party rights affecting the lease continue to bind the landlord: *E.S. Schwab & Co. Ltd v. McCarthy* (1975) 31 P. & C.R. 196.

Express surrender must be effected by deed: Law of Property Act 1925, s.52(1). However, there will be a surrender by operation of law where the tenant does some act which is inconsistent with the continuance of the lease.

4. Merger

Merger takes place where the tenant acquires the freehold title or superior leasehold interest of the landlord (or where a third party acquires the interests of both landlord and tenant) with the result that the interests merge and the lease is extinguished.

5. Frustration

It has long been established that the contractual doctrine of frustration may operate to discharge or suspend individual terms in a lease: *Cricklewood Property and Investment Trust Ltd v. Leighton's Investment Trust Ltd* [1945] A.C. 221. However, it has only recently been accepted by a majority of the House of Lords that the doctrine may apply to discharge the whole lease: *National Carriers Ltd v. Panalpina (Northern) Ltd* [1981] A.C. 675. Their Lordships made it clear that the doctrine will apply only in exceptional cases, a view which was underlined by the finding that there was no frustration in the circumstances of the instant case: the tenants had been granted a 10-year lease of a warehouse and, when the only access road was closed, they were effectively unable to use the warehouse for 20 months.

6. Repudiation

Hussein v. Mehlman [1992] 2 E.G.L.R. 87

(County Court, Stephen Sedley Q.C.)

The defendant landlord granted to the plaintiffs a three-year tenancy of a house. By virtue of the Landlord and Tenant Act 1985, s.11, the tenancy was subject to a covenant by the defendant to keep in repair the structure of the property and the installations for the supply of utilities and for space and water heating. Largely as a result of defects existing at the time of the grant of the tenancy, parts of the property became uninhabitable, other parts were affected by leaking water or damp and there was no heating. When the defendant made it clear that he would not effect repairs, the plaintiffs vacated the property, returned the keys and brought an action for breach of contract. Stephen Sedley Q.C. held that, in principle, the breach of the covenant by the defendant, combined with the clear intention no longer to be bound by it, constituted a repudiatory breach, which the plaintiffs had accepted. The most important question was whether the doctrine of repudiatory breach was applicable to leases.

STEPHEN SEDLEY Q.C.:

Although a contract of letting, whether for a term of years certain or for a periodic "springing" term, differs from other contracts in creating an estate in land, it is nevertheless a contract: see *United Scientific Holdings Ltd v. Burnley Borough Council* [1978] A.C. 904, approving *C.H. Bailey Ltd v. Memorial Enterprises Ltd* [1974] 1 W.L.R. 728; and, most recently, *Hammersmith and Fulham L.B.C. v. Monk* [1992] 1 A.C. 478. Since, in the ordinary way, any contract may be brought to an end by one party's repudiatory conduct, the question to be answered is whether a contract of letting is an exception to the rule.

[His Lordship referred to *Total Oil Great Britain Ltd v. Thompson Garages (Biggin Hill) Ltd* [1972] 1 Q.B. 318, where Lord Denning M.R. said, at p. 324:

"A lease is a demise. It conveys an interest in land. It does not come to an end like an ordinary contract on repudiation and acceptance. There is no authority on the point, but there is one case that points that way. It is *Cricklewood Property and Investment Trust Ltd v. Leighton's Investment Trust Ltd* [1945] A.C. 221. Lord Russell of Killowen and Lord Goddard, at pp. 234 and 244, were both of opinion that frustration does not bring a lease to an end. Nor, I think, does repudiation and acceptance."

The *Total Oil* decision, at its fullest, is therefore to be found in the judgment of Lord Denning. If it stood by itself it would, at this level, be binding authority for the proposition that because of the special character of a demise of land a lease is not terminable by frustration nor, therefore, by repudiation and acceptance.

However, since the *Total Oil* case was decided in 1971, both the major and the minor premises upon which Lord Denning's second holding was based appear to have been destroyed by decisions of the House of Lords. As I have already indicated, the major premise that a lease of land is in its essence different from other contracts has been overset, in particular by the decision of the House of Lords in *United Scientific Holdings Ltd v. Burnley Borough Council*. The minor premise that a lease cannot be determined by frustration has been overset by the decision of the House of Lords in *National Carriers Ltd v. Panalpina (Northern) Ltd* [1981] A.C. 675, in which a demised warehouse became unusable because of a street closure, and the tenants withheld rent, claiming that the lease had been frustrated. The House of Lords (Lord Russell of Killowen dissenting) held that the doctrine of frustration was in principle applicable to leases but that it did not operate on the facts of the instant case. Their Lordships declined to follow the *dicta* in the *Cricklewood* case. The *Total Oil* case was cited but was not referred to in the speeches. Lord Hailsham, at p. 690D, said:

"I conclude that the matter is not decided by authority and that the question is open to your Lordships to decide on principle. In my view your Lordships ought now so to decide it. Is there anything in principle which ought to prevent a lease from ever being frustated? I think there is not. In favour of the opposite opinion, the difference in principle between real and chattel property was strongly urged. But I find it difficult to accept this, once it has been decided, as has long been the case, that time and demise charters even of the largest ships and of considerable duration can in principle be frustrated."

Lord Wilberforce, at p. 694E, said:

"It was pointed out, however, by Atkin L.J. in *Matthey v. Curling* [1992] 2 A.C. 180, 200, in a passage later approved by Viscount Simon [1945] A.C. 221, 230, that as a lease can be determined, according to its terms, upon the happening of certain specified events, there is nothing illogical in implying a term that it should be determined on the happening of other events—namely, those which in an ordinary contract work a frustration...

A man may desire possession and use of land or buildings for, and only for, some purpose in view and mutually contemplated. Why is it an answer, when he claims that this purpose is "frustrated", to say that he has an estate if that estate is unusable and unsaleable? In such a case the lease, or the conferring of an estate, is a subsidiary means to an end, not an aim or end of itself."

He concluded, at p. 696G:

"It was not until the *Cricklewood* case that the argument was put on principle and fully explored. The governing decision (of the Court of Appeal) was summary, unargued, and based upon previous cases which will not bear the weight of a generalisation. I think that the movement of the law of contract is away from a rigid theory of autonomy towards the discovery—or I do not hesitate to say imposition— by the courts of just solutions, which can be ascribed to reasonable men in the position of the parties.

This reasoning, it seems to me, not only takes away the minor premise of the *Total Oil* judgment but has fundamental implications for its major premise: it continues the process, to which I have referred, of assimilating leases to other contracts. It follows, in my judgment, that unless some special exception can be established for acts of repudiation, not only has *Total Oil* ceased to be authority for the proposition that a lease cannot be repudiated: the decisions which have rendered it obsolete point powerfully in the direction of repudiation being a legitimate ground for termination of a lease. I bear in mind, however, that the House of Lords was extremely cautious about the range of situations in which it would allow the doctrine of frustration to operate on a lease and that Lord Hailsham posed the choice, in the language of *HMS Pinafore*, as lying only between "never" and "hardly ever", coming down in favour of the latter.

Very recently the Court of Appeal has held, apparently without argument to the contrary and without any citation of authority, that a tenancy agreement which one party is induced to enter into by the fraud of the other can be rescinded at the innocent party's election: *Killick v. Roberts* [1991] 1 W.L.R. 1146, 1149. This seems another step down the same road.

It is perhaps a relief that the *Total Oil* case is no longer good law, because it appears to have silently overruled an important line of cases (not cited in argument) in which, throughout the 19th century, the courts took it as axiomatic that a contract of letting could be terminated by the innocent party without notice if the other party failed to fulfil a fundamental term of the contract.

[His Lordship referred to *Edwards v. Etherington* (1825) Ry. & M. 268; *Collins v. Barrow* (1831) 1 M. & Rob. 112; *Izon v. Gorton* (1839) 5 Bing. N.C. 501; *Arden v. Pullen* (1842) 10 M. & W. 321; *Smith v. Marrable* (1843) 11 M. & W. 5. He continued:]

Although the vocabulary of repudiation is not consistently used in these cases—the earliest, for example, speaks of "exempting" the defendant from the demand for rent and others speak of the tenant being allowed to "throw up" the letting or "to withdraw", by 1842 Lord Abinger is using the phrase "the contract of letting" and

Alderson B. is speaking about the tenant "avoiding" the lease for the landlord's default. When in 1877 the Exchequer Division decided *Wilson v. Finch-Hatton* (1877) 2 Ex.D. 336 and followed *Smith v. Marrable*, all three barons used the language of repudiation and Pollock B. sought to cut away furnished lettings from the doctrine that rent issues out of the realty and to hold instead that this was simply "a sum paid for the accommodation afforded by the use of the house." (The divergent path which Parke B. charted in relation to demises of real property in *Hart v. Windsor* (1843) 12 M. & W. 68, shortly after he decided *Smith v. Marrable*, has now, it appears, all but converged again with the path of contract, at least since the decision in *C.H. Bailey Ltd v. Memorial Enterprises Ltd*.)

It follows, if the foregoing is right, that the passage at present to be found in chapter 17 of *Woodfall's Law of Landlord and Tenant*, para. 1–1836, which says, in terms, that a lease or tenancy does not come to an end by repudiation, citing the *Total Oil* case, is wrong. So is the final sentence of para. 420 of vol. 27 of *Halsbury's Laws of England* (4th ed.), which advances the same proposition in relation to leases, citing not only *Total Oil* but *Panalpina* in the footnote, but treating the latter, apparently, as confined to the doctrine of frustration.

I recognise that the proposition that a contract of tenancy can be repudiated like any other contract has a number of important implications, which it is not appropriate to explore on the facts of this case. For example, if the obligation to pay rent is as fundamental as the obligation to keep the house habitable, it will follow that a default in rent payments is a repudiatory act on the tenant's part. That this may follow is not, however, a reason for going back on what appears to me to be the inexorable effect of binding authority. It will, however, have effect subject not only to all the statutory provisions which now hedge the right to recover possession but also, I would think, to the provisions contained in the contract of letting itself in relation to forfeiture (where there is a term certain): in other words, the right to terminate by acceptance of repudiatory conduct may itself be modified by further contractual provisions which lay down conditions, supported by statute, for the exercise of the right.

NOTES:

1. For comment, see [1993] C.L.J. 212; [1993] Conv. 71; [1995] Conv. 379.

2. For comment on *Killick v. Roberts* [1991] 1 W.L.R. 1146, see [1992] C.L.J. 21; [1992] Conv. 269.

3. In *Chartered Trust plc v. Davies* (1997) 76 P. & C.R. 396, *supra*, p. 402, the Court of Appeal held that a breach of the landlord's covenant for non-derogation from grant constituted a repudiation of the lease. In *Nynehead Developments Ltd v. RH Fibreboard Containers Ltd* [1999] 2 E.G. 139 H. H. Judge Weeks Q.C., sitting as a High Court judge, held (applying the principles in *Hong Kong Fir Shipping Co. Ltd v. Kawasaki Kisen Kaisha Ltd* [1962] 2 Q.B. 26, 69 *per* Diplock L.J.) that the covenant for non-derogation from grant constituted neither a condition nor a warranty; and therefore that the breach of such a covenant could only constitute a repudiation of the lease where the breach deprived the tenant of substantially the whole of the intended benefit under the lease. For comment, see [1999] Conv. 150.

4. For the setting aside of a lease of grounds of unconscionability, see *Boustany v. Pigott* (1993) 69 P. & C.R. 298, noted at [1996] Conv. 454; and see *post*, pp. 856 *et seq*.

7. Disclaimer

Under section 178 of the Insolvency Act 1986, the liquidator of an insolvent company may disclaim a lease owned by the company if that lease constitutes onerous property, that is, property "which is unsaleable or not readily saleable, or is such that it may give rise to a liability to pay money or perform any other onerous act". Section 178(4) provides that the disclaimer "(a) operates so as to determine, as from the date of the disclaimer, the rights, interests and liabilities of the company in or in respect of the property disclaimed; but (b) does not, except so far as is necessary for the purpose of releasing the company from any liability, affect the rights or liabilities of any other person". Section 315 contains similar provisions in relation to disclaimer by the trustee in bankruptcy of a tenant. The effect of these provisions in the context of pre-1996 "old tenancies" was recently clarified by the House of Lords in *Hindcastle Ltd v. Barbara Attenborough Associates Ltd* [1997] A.C. 70, noted at [1997] Conv. 24.

Where the only parties involved are the landlord and the insolvent tenant, the disclaimer determines the tenant's rights and obligations and, as a necessary corollary, the landlord's obligations and rights. In those circumstances the disclaimer also terminates the lease. On the other hand, where the landlord has the benefit of covenants entered into by third parties, notwithstanding that the disclaimer determines the insolvent tenant's rights and obligations, the disclaimer "does not, except so far as is necessary for the purpose of releasing the company from any liability, affect the rights or liabilities of any other person". Thus, where there has been no assignment of the lease, the liability of any guarantor of the original tenant remains unaffected by the disclaimer; and, where the insolvent tenant is not the original tenant but an assignee, the liabilities of the original tenant, of any intermediate assignee who has covenanted directly with the landlord and of any guarantor remain unaffected by the disclaimer; and the lease is deemed to continue for the purpose of preserving those liabilities until such time as the landlord recovers possession of the leased property or a vesting order is made in favour of any person interested in the property. Thirdly, where a third party has acquired a sub-lease under the lease prior to the disclaimer, the sub-lease continues subject to the same rights and obligations as would be applicable if the insolvent tenant's interest had continued.

Although the Landlord and Tenant (Covenants) Act 1995 does not directly amend the law relating to disclaimer, the effect of disclaimer in the context of post-1995 "new tenancies" may be affected indirectly by the provisions of the 1995 Act. It has been seen (*supra*, p. 436) that the assignment of a tenancy releases the former tenant from continuing liability under the lease, although in many cases the former tenant will be required to enter into an authorised guarantee agreement so that he remains potentially liable until the next assignment of the tenancy. The release of the former tenant also releases any guarantor of the former tenant and it is not certain whether the guarantor can be required to enter into an authorised guarantee agreement: see [1996] Conv. 161.

8. Effect on sub-leases

At common law, it has long been established that the termination of a lease by expiry or by a landlord's notice to quit automatically and simultaneously terminates any sub-leases derived out of the lease; but that sub-leases survive the termination of a lease by surrender or merger. Only recently has the Court of Appeal held that a tenant's notice to quit also terminates any sub-leases: *Pennell v. Payne* [1995] Q.B. 192; but the suggestion in that case that a tenant's exercise of a break clause in a fixed term lease has the same effect has been questioned: see [1995] Conv. 263.

6

LICENCES AND PROPRIETARY ESTOPPEL

A. INTRODUCTION

1. The scope of licences

In English law there is no general right to enter on land in the possession of another person; and entry without the permission of that other person constitutes a trespass which may be actionable as a tort and which may render the trespasser liable in damages. Permission to enter upon land or do some other act in relation to land in the possession of another person may be conferred by licence. By reason of the permission, the licensee is not a trespasser; but, according to the orthodoxy, he is not thereby granted any proprietary interest in the land. In the much-repeated words of Vaughan C.J. in *Thomas v. Sorrell* (1673) Vaughan. 330 (at 351):

A dispensation or license properly passeth no interest, nor alters or transfers property in anything, but only makes an action lawful, which without it had been unlawful.

More recently Lord Templeman stated in *Street v. Mountford* [1985] A.C. 809 (at 814):

A licence in connection with land while entitling the licensee to use the land for the purposes authorised by the licence does not create an estate in the land.

It is this negative characteristic which distinguishes licences from interests in or over land that are similar in their substantive content. Thus, as has been seen, the entitlement to occupy residential property may result from a licence or from a lease (or from a number of other interests in land); and, as will be seen, the entitlement to use a footpath across land belonging to another person may result from a licence or from an easement.

However, the range of factual circumstances covered by the concept of licences is extremely wide; and licences fulfil many purposes and assume many forms. On the one hand, a licence may be a lease-substitute, which entitles the licensee to the long-term occupation of residential or business premises, or an easement-substitute, which entitles the licensee to exercise some right over the land of the licensor. On the other hand, a licence may provide the lawful basis for the postman and the milkman to make doorstep deliveries and for the theatregoer to view a theatrical performance. Thus, although in some circumstances a licence may "shadow" a recognised interest in land, in other circumstances a licence may have a substantive content which has no equivalent among the recognised interests in land.

These various arrangements are traditionally classified into four main categories of licence (although it cannot be said that this classification is definitive or that the categories are mutual exclusive: Dawson & Pearce, *Licences Relating to the Occupation and Use of Land* (1979), identify nine categories of licence). The four traditional categories are: (i) bare licences, (ii) licences coupled with an interest, (iii) contractual licences and (iv) what may be termed estoppel licences, where the licence forms part of a set of circumstances that give rise to a claim to proprietary estoppel.

This chapter considers each of the four categories in turn; and, in respect of each category, examines (a) the nature of the licence, (b) the method(s) of creation, (c) the question of revocability by the licensor and (d) the question of the effect of the licence on successors in title to the original licensor.

2. The licence as an interest in land: overture

The proposition that a licence confers no proprietary interest on the licensee has traditionally determined the answer at common law to the two central issues relating to licences (the third and fourth issues identified in the preceding paragraph). First, a licence may be revoked by the licensor at any time, although a licensee who has provided consideration for the licence may have a contractual remedy in damages; and, secondly, a licence is personal to the original parties and cannot affect successors in title to the original licensor. However, the law relating to licences has developed significantly in recent years; and the proposition that a licence confers no proprietary interest, and the related questions of the enforceability of licences and their role in modern land law, require re-examination in the light of those developments. Although it still may not be possible to argue that a licence constitutes a conventional proprietary interest, it has been suggested that the potential enforceability of the right of occupation or enjoyment contemplated by a licence may justify the conclusion that in certain circumstances a licence constitutes "quasi-property": see *infra*, p. 608.

Moreover, although unrelated to the principal issues of revocability and effect on successors in title, the Court of Appeal has recently confirmed that a licensee may have certain "quasi-proprietary" rights against a trespasser. In *Dutton v. Manchester Airport plc* [1999] 2 All E.R. 675 it was held that a licensee may obtain an order for the possession of land against a trespasser where such a remedy is necessary to vindicate and give effect to the right of occupation conferred on the licensee by his contract with the licensor. More specifically, it was held that the remedy is available not only to a licensee who is in de facto possession of the land but also to a licensee who is not in occupation of the land. Laws L.J. stated (at 689):

In my judgment the true principle is that a licensee not in occupation may claim possession against a trespasser if that is a necessary remedy to vindicate and give effect to such rights of occupation as by contract with his licensor he enjoys. This is the same principle as allows a licensee who is in de facto possession to evict a trespasser. There is no respectable distinction, in law or logic, between the two situations. An estate owner may seek an order whether he is in possession or not. So, in my judgment, may a licensee, if other things are equal. In both cases, the plaintiff's remedy is strictly limited to what is required to make good his legal right. The principle applies although the licensee has no right to exclude the licensor himself. Elementarily he cannot exclude any occupier who, by contract or estate, has a claim to possession equal or superior to his own. Obviously, however, that will not avail a bare trespasser.

In this whole debate, as regards the law of remedies in the end I see no significance as a matter of principle in any distinction drawn between a plaintiff whose right to occupy the land in question arises from title and one whose right arises only from contract. In every case the question must be, what is the reach of the right, and whether it is shown that the defendant's acts violate its enjoyment. If they do, and (as here) an order for possession is the only practical remedy, the remedy should be granted. Otherwise the law is powerless to correct a proved or admitted wrongdoing; and that would be unjust and disreputable. The underlying principle is in the Latin maxim (for which I make no apology) *"ubi ius, ibi sit remedium"*.

B. BARE LICENCES

1. Nature

The first traditional category of licence is the bare licence. This is the simplest form of licence. It is a permission to enter upon land for which no consideration is provided by the licensee. Bare licences may be granted expressly, for example an invitation to a dinner party at the house of another person or the frequently-cited (but probably rather less frequently encountered in fact these days) permission for the child to retrieve his or her ball from the garden of a neighbour. Bare licences may also be granted by implication from the circumstances; and many such implied licences are granted pursuant to the principle approved in *Robson v. Hallett* [1967] 2 Q.B. 939, 951 *per* Lord Parker C.J., 953–954 *per* Diplock L.J., that, subject to express exclusion, the occupier of any dwelling-house gives an implied licence to any member of the public to enter upon his land and to inquire whether he may conduct his lawful business. This principle provides the juridical basis for the lawful entry of such persons as the postman and the milkman: *Holden v. White* [1982] Q.B. 679, 687 *per* Ormrod L.J.

2. Creation

It will be apparent from the above examples that no formalities are required for the creation of a bare licence. The question whether a licence has been granted is, therefore, a question of fact to be determined in the circumstances of each case.

3. Revocability

A bare licence is revocable at any time and without prior notice, irrespective of any initial indication given by the licensor as to the duration of the licence; and the licensee has no legal redress for revocation. Again, it is a question of fact whether a licence has been revoked but any words or conduct will suffice, provided that they make it clear that the permission to be on the land has been withdrawn: see *Robson v. Hallett* [1967] 2 Q.B. 939; *Gilham v. Breidenbach* [1982] R.T.R. 328. However, the licensee must be given a reasonable time to leave the land of the licensor (and what constitutes a reasonable time will depend on the nature and purpose of the licence and all other circumstances); and only after the expiry of that time does the licensee become a trespasser.

4. Effect on successors in title

Since a bare licence can be revoked at will by the licensor, *a fortiori* it would seem to follow that a successor in title to the land of the licensor cannot be bound by it.

C. LICENCES COUPLED WITH AN INTEREST

1. Nature

The second traditional category of licence is the licence coupled with (the grant of) an interest. However, such terminology does tend to misplace the emphasis and thus potentially to mislead as to the status of such a licence. A licence within this second category usually provides the necessary permission to enter upon land specifically to exploit a distinct interest in the land, where, for example, the landowner has granted to the licensee the right to cut growing timber or crops (a profit à prendre); or to exploit a distinct interest in other property located on the land, where, for example the landowner has sold to the licensee cut timber. Thus the licence to enter upon the land is ancillary to the property interest; and its rationale is exclusively to enable the interest to be exploited. This category of licence was explained in *Wood v. Leadbitter* (1845) 13 M. & W. 838. Alderson B. stated (at 844–845):

We cannot do better than refer to Lord C.J. Vaughan's elaborate judgment in the case of *Thomas v. Sorrell* (1673) Vaughan 330 ...

In the course of his judgment the Chief Justice says (at p. 351), "A dispensation or license properly passeth no interest, nor alters or transfers property in anything, but only makes an action lawful, which without it had been unlawful. As a license to go beyond the seas, to hunt in a man's park, to come into his house, are only actions which, without license, had been unlawful. But a license to hunt in a man's park, and carry away the deer killed to his own use; to cut down a tree in a man's ground, and to carry it away the next day after to his own use, are licenses as to the acts of hunting and cutting down the tree, but as to the carrying away of the deer killed and tree cut down, they are grants. So, to license a man to eat my meat, or to fire the wood in my chimney to warm him by, as to the actions of *eating*, firing my wood, and warming him, they are licenses; but it is consequent necessarily to those actions that my property may be destroyed in the meat eaten, and in the wood burnt. So as in some cases, by consequent and not directly, and as its effect, a dispensation or license may destroy and alter property."

Now, attending to this passage, in conjunction with the title "License" in Brooke's Abridgment, from which, and particularly from paragraph 15, it appears that a license is in its nature revocable, we have before us the whole principle of the law on this subject. A mere license is revocable: but that which is called a license is often something more than a license; it often comprises or is connected with a grant, and then the party who has given it cannot in general revoke it, so as to defeat his grant, to which it was incident.

It may further be observed, that a license under seal (provided it be a mere license) is as revocable as a license by parol; and, on the other hand, a license by parol, coupled with a grant, is as irrevocable as a license by deed, provided only that the grant is of a nature capable of being made by parol. But where there is a license by parol, coupled with a parol grant, or pretended grant, of something which is incapable of being granted otherwise than by deed, there the license is a mere license; it is not an incident to a *valid* grant, and it is therefore revocable. Thus, a license by A. to hunt in his park, whether given by deed or by parol, is revocable; it merely renders the act of hunting lawful, which, without the license, would have been unlawful. If the license be, as put by Chief Justice Vaughan, a license not only to hunt, but also to take away the deer when killed to his own use, this is in truth a grant of the deer, with a license annexed to come on the land: and supposing the grant of the deer to be good, then the license would be irrevocable by the party who had given it; he would be estopped from defeating his own grant, or act in the nature of a grant. But suppose the case of a parol license to come on my lands, and there to make a watercourse, to flow on the land of the licensee. In such a case there is no valid grant of the watercourse, and the license remains a mere license, and therefore capable of being revoked. On the other hand, if such a license were granted by deed, then the question would be on the construction of the deed, whether it amounted to a grant of the watercourse; and if it did, then the license would be irrevocable.

The wider, post-Judicature Act and post-*Walsh v. Lonsdale*, scope of this category of licence is exemplified by *James Jones & Sons Ltd v. Earl of Tankerville* [1909] 2 Ch. 440.

James Jones & Sons Ltd v. Earl of Tankerville [1909] 2 Ch. 440

(Ch D., Parker J.)

The plaintiff company entered into two contracts with the defendant to purchase timber growing on his land. The contracts provided for various operations on the land of the defendant which would enable the plaintiff to cut, saw and remove the timber. The defendant subsequently removed the plaintiff and damaged machinery erected on the land pursuant to the contracts. The plaintiff sought an injunction and damages.

PARKER J.:
The plaintiffs ask for injunctions restraining the defendant from preventing the due execution of the contracts, as well as for damages. It was argued that this is a claim for specific performance, and that the contracts are such that the Court cannot or, at

any rate, will not grant specific performance, but will leave the plaintiffs to their remedy by way of damages only. It is said that in contracts of this sort there is a want of mutuality which precludes the remedy by way of specific performance. A contract for the sale of specific timber growing on the vendor's property, on the terms that such timber is cut and carried away by the purchaser, certainly confers on the purchaser a licence to enter and cut the timber sold, and, at any rate as soon as the purchaser has severed the timber, the legal property in the severed trees vests in him. A licence to enter a man's property is prima facie revocable, but is irrevocable even at law if coupled with or granted in aid of a legal interest conferred on the purchaser, and the interest so conferred may be a purely chattel interest or an interest in realty. If A. sells to B. felled timber lying on A.'s land on the terms that B. may enter and carry it away, the licence conferred is an irrevocable licence because it is coupled with and granted in aid of the legal property in the timber which the contract for sale confers on B.: *Wood v. Manley* (1839) 11 Ad. & E. 34. On the other hand, if A. by instrument not under seal for good consideration agrees that B. shall have the right of shooting and carrying away game on A.'s estate for a term of years, the licence conferred is at law a revocable licence, because the nature of the interest intended to be conferred is a profit à prendre, and cannot at law be created otherwise than by deed. The agreement, however, confers on B. a good interest in equity, and the licence is in equity an irrevocable licence, and a Court of Equity would accordingly restrain its revocation, and it would make no difference that B. had agreed to keep down the rabbits, though this term could hardly be specifically enforced by any Court: see *Frogley v. Earl of Lovelace* (1859) John. 333; *Lowe v. Adams* [1901] 2 Ch. 598. Even, therefore, if no interest at law passes by a contract for the sale of specific growing timber to be cut by the purchaser, it is difficult to see why on principle equity should not restrain the vendor from revoking the licence conferred by such a contract, though it might be unable to compel the purchaser to cut the timber if he refused to do so. When once the purchaser has cut any part of the timber, the legal property in the timber so cut is certainly in the purchaser, and the licence so far as that timber is concerned is irrevocable even at law, and a Court of Equity in granting an injunction would only be restraining the violation of a legal right. An injunction restraining the revocation of the licence, when it is revocable at law, may in a sense be called relief by way of specific performance, but it is not specific performance in the sense of compelling the vendor to do anything. It merely prevents him from breaking his contract, and protects a right in equity which but for the absence of a seal would be a right at law, and since the Judicature Act it may well be doubted whether the absence of a seal in such a case can be relied on in any Court: *Walsh v. Lonsdale* (1882) 21 Ch. D. 9. I do not think, therefore, that there is any substance in the objection that a timber contract of the kind I am considering cannot be specifically enforced by injunction because of a want of mutuality, and though there is no direct authority on the point, it seems clear from the judgments in *Buxton v. Lister* (1746) 3 Atk. 383 and *Gervais v. Edwards* (1848) 2 D. & War. 80 that neither Lord Hardwicke nor Lord St Leonards can have thought any such objection could be entertained. It is clear in both these cases that what was contemplated was specific performance in the sense of compelling the execution of an instrument under seal which would turn into legal rights what were under the contract rights in equity only, and I see no reason why the legal rights of entry which would be conferred by the execution of such an instrument would be rights which a Court of Equity would refuse to protect by injunction because the instrument might contain provisions which the Court could not specifically enforce.

I am, however, not at all clear that a contract for the sale of timber to be cut by the purchaser does not confer an interest at law of such a nature as to make the licence to enter and cut ab initio an irrevocable licence. Baron Alderson in his well-known judgment in *Wood v. Leadbitter* (1845) 13 M. & W. 838, commenting upon the case of *Webb v. Paternoster* (1619) Pal. 71, says that even if the licence in that case had been a mere parol licence, that is, a licence not under seal, yet the strong probability was that Webb had purchased the hay as a growing crop with liberty to stack it on the land, and then the licence might be good as coupled with an interest. Inasmuch as he says elsewhere that a licence to enter on the land of the licensor and make a watercourse to flow on the land of the licensor would be revocable unless under seal, because an easement of this nature would lie in grant only, and that a valuable consideration for such a licence would make no difference, he must have been of opinion that the mere purchase of a growing crop of hay would or might confer an interest at law. Growing hay is not an emblement, and therefore what he says cannot be explained on the hypothesis that he was thinking of the sale of a mere chattel. Further, in *Marshall v. Green* (1875) 1 C.P.D. 35 the plaintiff sued for trespass and trover in that the defendant had entered and cut down trees on the plaintiff's land. The land was in lease, but the trees were reserved. Amongst other things the defendant pleaded leave and licence, and an agreement under which the plaintiff had sold the trees to him with liberty to cut down and remove them. It appeared that this agreement was verbal only, and that after the defendant had cut six of the trees the plaintiff repudiated the bargain and withdrew the licence. The defendant nevertheless cut down and carried away the remainder of the trees. A verdict was entered for the plaintiff, leave being reserved to the defendant to move for a verdict in his favour on the ground that the facts disclosed a right on the defendant's part to cut down and remove the trees. The defendant moved accordingly, and obtained a rule nisi which was subsequently made absolute. The actual points decided were (1) that the case was not within s.4 but was within s.17 of the Statute of Frauds, and (2) that the fact of the purchaser having cut six trees before the sale was repudiated was an acceptance and receipt of part of the goods sold within the meaning of s.17. But it seems clear that, unless the agreement conferred an irrevocable licence, the plaintiff was entitled to succeed both in trespass and trover, though the defendant might have had a counter-claim for damages for breach of contract, and if the licence were irrevocable it could, on the principles laid down in *Wood v. Leadbitter*, only have been because the contract conferred on the defendant an interest at law in the timber comprised in it.

Lastly, in determining the effect of such a contract at law the effect of the Sale of Goods Act 1893 has now to be considered. Goods are there defined in such a manner as to include growing timber which is to be severed under the contract of sale, whether by the vendor or the purchaser, and s.52 of the Act seems to confer on the Court a statutory power of enforcing at the instance of a purchaser specific performance of a contract for the sale of ascertained goods, whether or not the property has passed by the contract.

I come to the conclusion, therefore, that the Court has ample jurisdiction to grant the injunctions asked for, though, of course, it is in its discretion, if it so thinks fit, to award damages in lieu of relief by way of injunction. Under the circumstances of this case, however, there is, in my opinion, every reason for not exercising this discretion.

With regard to the timber already cut which is the plaintiffs' property; with regard to their tenancy of the cattle boxes; with regard to their sawmills, machinery, and other property on the defendant's land, their rights at law under the contract have not only been infringed, but have been deliberately and wantonly disregarded with every circumstance of indignity and violence, and even if I thought that damages would be an adequate remedy for what they have suffered, I should feel it incumbent on me, if I could, to assert the authority of the law by refusing to allow the defendant to retain the benefits he has attempted to gain by his high-handed and illegal action. I propose, therefore, to grant relief by way of injunction, not by way of damages only.

NOTE:

1. The scope of what qualifies as an "interest" in this context was discussed in *Hounslow LBC v. Twickenham Garden Developments Ltd* [1971] Ch. 233. The case concerned the right of building contractors to be on land in order to carry out a building contract on that land. Megarry J. stated (at 243–245, 254):

In *Hurst v. Picture Theatres Ltd* [1915] 1 K.B. 1 [*infra*, p. 498], the majority in the Court of Appeal held that a ticket-holder in a cinema who was forcibly evicted before the conclusion of the performance was entitled to damages for assault, on the basis that the right to see the performance amounted to a grant or interest. The decision has been criticised, and one of the grounds of criticism has been that for the purpose of deciding whether there is a licence coupled with an interest or grant, the right to see a performance cannot fairly be described as an interest or be the subject-matter of a grant. No authoritative definition of what suffices as an interest for this purpose ever seems to have been given. The examples usually put forward are proprietary in nature, such as the rights that I have mentioned to enter and sever growing timber or crops, to take away timber or crops already severed, and so on.

Vaughan v. Hampson (1875) 33 L.T. 15, however, carries the idea further. There, a solicitor acting under a proxy from a creditor attended a general meeting of creditors convened by the debtor at his solicitor's office. During the course of the meeting the debtor's solicitor asked the creditor's solicitor to leave and, upon his refusing to do so, mollitur manus imposuit, etc. The ejected solicitor thereupon sued the debtor's solicitor for assault, and succeeded on demurrer. The case was so plain to the Court of Exchequer that despite the argument of Herschell Q.C., relying inter alia on *Wood v. Leadbitter* (1845) 13 H. & W. 838 [*infra*, p. 496], counsel for the plaintiff was not called upon. Cleasby B. said, at p. 16:

> "The question is whether or not the plaintiff was a trespasser on the occasion in question. We are of opinion that he was not. He was, on the contrary, one of a number of persons who went to the defendant's office by invitation to attend a meeting of creditors, in order to discuss what steps should be taken in the matter of the liquidation proceedings against the bankrupt, for some of whose creditors the plaintiff was acting as the solicitor and duly appointed proxy on the occasion. The defendant had given the plaintiff leave and licence to be present, and the latter therefore had a right, coupled with an interest, entitling him to be on the defendant's premises."

Pollock B. entirely agreed, saying: "In the present case there was, as my brother Cleasby has said, a right coupled with an interest in the plaintiff to be where he was." Amphlett B. concurred, adding: "If we could come to any other conclusion I think it would be a great scandal to the law." The plaintiff there plainly had no shred of proprietary interest in the defendant's land or any chattels on it: yet he was held to have a right coupled with an interest which prevented him from being a trespasser, despite the revocation of any licence to be on the premises. No question of any packing-up period could very well arise on those facts.

This unanimous decision of the Court of Exchequer appears to have been somewhat neglected by the courts and by the books. It might well have provided support for the majority in *Hurst v. Picture Theatres Ltd* had it been cited. In *Cowell v. Rosehill Racecourse Co. Ltd* (1937) 56 C.L.R. 605, 608 it was cited in argument as being "not expressly put on equitable grounds," on the erroneous basis that it was the first case decided after the Judicature Act 1873, whereas in fact it was decided over nine months before that Act came into force; and the judgments ignore it. In the *Winter Garden* case it was not even suggested that the licence was coupled with a grant: see *per* Lord Greene M.R. in the Court of Appeal [1946] 1 All E.R. 678, 685, and the argument of counsel for the respondents in the House of Lords [1948] A.C. 173, 182 (apparently assuming that only an interest in land sufficed).

If for this purpose "interest" is not confined to an interest in land or in chattels on the land, what does it extend to? If a right to attend a creditor's meeting or to see a cinema performance suffices to constitute an interest, can it be said that the right and duty to do works on land fall short of being an interest? I cannot see why it should. Yet if this be so, it is not easy to see any fair stopping place in what amounts to an interest, short of any legitimate reason for being on the land.

. . .

I feel great doubt whether the word "interest" means anything more than an interest in property, though it matters not whether that property is real or personal, or legal or equitable. Today, with contractual licences recognised as being capable of being made irrevocable in their own right, there is no need to torture the word "interest" into embracing miscellaneous collections of rights. I do not have to decide whether *Vaughan v. Hampson* (1875) 33 L.T. 15 is good law today, and I do not do so. [Counsel for the plaintiff licensor] described it as "a curiosity"; and I do not dissent. I merely say that I should hesitate long before holding that a licence was coupled with an interest unless that interest was an interest in property, and that I doubt very much whether in this case the contractor's licence is coupled with any interest.

See further, *infra*, p. 501.

2. Creation, revocability and effect on successors in title

As the above extracts indicate, licences in this category are purely ancillary to a distinct property interest. It follows that the requirements as to creation and the questions of revocability and effect on successors in title of the original licensor depend upon the nature of the interest to which the licence is ancillary. Thus, provided that the qualifying interest has been validly created (and the interest may be a defective legal interest that is recognised in equity under the doctrine in *Walsh v. Lonsdale*), the grantee automatically acquires the necessary licence to exploit that interest; the licence continues (and cannot be revoked by the grantor/licensor) during the subsistence of that interest; and, in so far as the interest binds a successor in title of the grantor/licensor, the licence also binds that successor in title.

D. CONTRACTUAL LICENCES

The third traditional category of licence is the contractual licence. A contractual licence is a permission to enter upon land which has its origin in some contract and which is thus distinguished from a bare licence in that it is granted to the licensee in return for consideration. It is in the context of contractual licences that most of the developments of recent years referred to above have taken place; and it is in this context that the issues of revocability and, in particular, effect on successors in title have given rise to controversy. More specifically, it has been argued that the status of the contractual licence has been undergoing the same process of evolution from contract to property which in the nineteenth century led to the recognition of estate contracts and restrictive covenants as equitable proprietary interests in land. However, the most recent decision of the Court of Appeal in *Ashburn Anstalt v. Arnold* [1989] Ch. 1 marks a reverse in that evolutionary process: see *infra*, p. 522.

1. Nature

The uncertainty that has surrounded contractual licences is due in part to the fact that the term "contractual licence" has been applied to an extremely wide range of very different circumstances. Thus the contractual licence has provided the juridical basis for the theatregoer to view a theatrical performance: *Hurst v. Picture Theatres Ltd* [1915] 1 K.B. 1, *infra*, p. 498; or for the motorist to park his car in a commercial car park: *Ashby v. Tolhurst* [1937] 2 K.B. 242. The contractual licence has also provided the juridical basis for the "front of house rights" in a theatre or cinema: *Clore v. Theatrical Properties Ltd and Westby & Co. Ltd* [1936] 3 All E.R. 483; and for the right of the building contractor working on the development of a site belonging to another person to enter the site: *Hounslow LBC v. Twickenham Garden Developments Ltd* [1971] Ch. 233, *infra*, p. 502. The latter case also demonstrates that it is immaterial whether the right to enter the land is the primary purpose of the contract or merely secondary. Finally, the contractual licence has provided the juridical basis for the long-term occupation of residential (or even commercial) premises. Such occupation may be consequent upon largely informal arrangements: see *Tanner v. Tanner* [1975] 1 W.L.R. 1346; *Chandler v. Kerley* [1978] 1 W.L.R. 693; *Hardwick v. Johnson* [1978] 1 W.L.R. 683; and see *infra*, p. 509. Alternatively, such occupation may be consequent upon more formal lease-substitutes. The high point of the residential contractual licence as a lease-substitute was *Somma v. Hazelhurst and Savelli* [1978] 1 W.L.R. 1014; and, although that decision was overruled by the House of Lords in *Street v. Mountford* [1985] A.C. 809, it has been seen that the lease-substitute is in no sense defunct: see *ante*, p. 361. These different circumstances, all covered by the term "contractual licence" give rise to different problems; and it is hardly surprising that principles developed in the context of the shorter-term (commercial) arrangements should prove to be less than wholly appropriate in the context of longer-term (residential) arrangements.

2. Creation

Since contractual licences have their origin in contract, their creation depends upon whether there is a valid contract. Most such contracts are express contracts; but in some circumstances the courts have been prepared to imply a contractual licence: see *infra*, p. 509.

3. Revocability

3.1 *Position at common law*

At common law, a contractual licence was treated as no different in principle from a bare licence. Consequently, it could be revoked by the licensor at any time, notwithstanding that the revocation constituted a breach of contract.

Wood v. Leadbitter (1845) 13 M. & W. 838

(Court of Exchequer, Alderson B.)

The plaintiff had purchased a four-day ticket for admission to the grandstand and inclosure during a horse-racing meeting at Doncaster racecourse. He was subsequently requested to leave (it was assumed without good reason) and, when he refused, he was removed (without any unnecessary violence) by the defendant. The plaintiff brought an action for assault and false imprisonment on the ground that he had an irrevocable licence to enter and remain in the inclosure during the period of the race meeting.

Following the passage cited above (*supra*, p. 490), Alderson B. concluded that nothing in the subsequent case law affected the clear dichotomy of mere licences (which were revocable) and licences coupled with interests (which were irrevocable). He continued (at 855):

It was suggested that, in the present case, a distinction might exist, by reason of the plaintiff's having paid a valuable consideration for the privilege of going on the stand. But this fact makes no difference: whether it may give the plaintiff a right of action against those from whom he purchased the ticket, or those who authorised its being issued and sold to him, is a point not necessary to be discussed; any such action would be founded on a breach of contract, and would not be the result of his having acquired by the ticket a right of going upon the stand, in spite of the owner of the soil; and it is sufficient, on this point, to say that in several of the cases we have cited ... the alleged licence had been granted for a valuable consideration, but that was not held to make any difference.

NOTES:

1. *Wood v. Leadbitter* was relied upon by Goddard L.J. in *Thompson v. Park* [1944] 1 K.B. 408; see the discussion of that case in *Hounslow LBC v. Twickenham Garden Developments Ltd* [1971] Ch. 233, *infra*, p. 502.

2. The revocation of a licence pursuant to the principle stated in *Wood v. Leadbitter* did not deprive the evicted licensee of his claim in damages for breach of contract: see *Kerrison v. Smith* [1897] 2 Q.B. 445.

3.2 Position in equity
Two related developments significantly improved the position of the contractual licensee. First, where a contractual licence purported to confer a right to enter and remain on land for a particular purpose or for a specified period of time, the courts demonstrated a willingness to imply a negative contractual term, according to which the licensor undertook not to revoke the licence before the purpose or period for which it had been granted had been completed. Secondly, the courts demonstrated a willingness to use the equitable remedies to restrain the licensor from revoking a contractual licence contrary to the terms of the contract, *including any implied term as to non-revocation*. Thus, where it is still practicable to restrain the licensor from revoking the licence, the courts may grant the equitable remedy of an injunction; and in appropriate circumstances an injunction may even be reinforced by a decree of specific performance to ensure that the contract is actually carried out: see *Verrall v. Great Yarmouth BC* [1981] Q.B. 202. Where the licence has been irreversibly revoked, the hypothetical availability of the equitable remedies may provide a basis for an action for assault; and, in any event, damages remain available as a remedy for breach of a contractual licence: see *Tanner v. Tanner* [1975] 1 W.L.R. 1346, *infra*, p. 509. The seeds of these developments were first seen in *Hurst v. Picture Theatres*

Ltd [1915] 1 K.B. 1, although only as an alternative and secondary ground for the decision.

Hurst v. Picture Theatres Ltd [1915] 1 K.B. 1

(CA, Buckley, Kennedy and Phillimore L.JJ.)

The plaintiff had purchased a ticket for admission to a film performance in the defendant's theatre. During the course of the performance, the plaintiff was requested to leave and, when he refused, he was removed (without any unnecessary violence) by an employee of the defendant. The plaintiff brought an action for assault and false imprisonment on the ground that he had an irrevocable licence to enter and remain in the theatre for the duration of the film performance.

A majority of the Court of Appeal (Phillimore L.J. dissenting) affirmed the decision of Channell J. that the defendant was liable in damages for assault.

BUCKLEY L.J.:
Let me at the outset say what *Wood v. Leadbitter* (1845) 13 M. & W. 838 seems to me to have decided. It affirmed that a mere licence, whether or not it be under seal, by which I mean a licence not coupled with an interest or a grant whether it be under seal or not, is revocable. It affirmed also that if there be a licence coupled with an interest or coupled with a grant, it is not, or at any rate in general is not, revocable. For those two propositions, I read these two sentences from the case of *Wood v. Leadbitter*: "A mere licence is revocable; but that which is called a licence is often something more than a licence; it often comprises or is connected with a grant, and then the party who has given it cannot in general revoke it, so as to defeat his grant, to which it was incident. It may further be observed, that a licence under seal (provided it be a mere licence) is as revocable as a licence by parol; and, on the other hand, a licence by parol, coupled with a grant, is as irrevocable as a licence by deed, provided only that the grant is of a nature capable of being made by parol." Those are propositions with which, as it seems to me, no one quarrels or can quarrel. *Wood v. Leadbitter* rested, I think, upon one of two grounds—I will indicate them both—but I think it was the second of those which I am going to mention. The first ground is that the man who bought his ticket for the race meeting had not obtained any grant of the right to come during the currency of the meeting to see any particular spectacle from its commencement to its termination. If that were the ground, it would, I think, be erroneous. I conceive he had the right to see what was to be seen during the days covered by his ticket. But I do not think that was the ground on which the Court decided it. They decided it upon the ground, which will be found at p. 842 and onwards, that no incorporeal inheritance affecting land can be created or transferred otherwise than by deed, a proposition which was discussed with some elaboration in the course of the judgment. What Alderson B. was saying there was: this man has got no deed; he has got nothing under seal; he has therefore not got a grant; he cannot in this Court be heard to say he is a grantee, and because he is not a grantee he is a mere licensee, and being a mere licensee (whether it is under seal or not under seal does not make any difference) the licence is revocable.

Let me for a moment discuss this present case upon the footing that *Wood v. Leadbitter* stands as good law at this date. I am going to say presently that to my mind it does not, but suppose it does stand as good law at this date. What is the grant in this case? The plaintiff in the present action paid his money to enjoy the sight of a particular spectacle. He was anxious to go into a picture theatre to see a series of views or pictures during, I suppose, an hour or a couple of hours. That which was granted to him was the right to enjoy looking at a spectacle, to attend a performance from its beginning to its end. That which was called the licence, the right to go upon the premises, was only something granted to him for the purpose of enabling him to have that which had been granted him, namely, the right to see. He could not see the performance unless he went into the building. His right to go into the building was something given to him in order to enable him to have the benefit of that which had been granted to him, namely, the right to hear the opera, or see the theatrical performance, or see the moving pictures as was the case here. So that here there was a licence coupled with a grant. If so, *Wood v. Leadbitter* does not stand in the way at all. A licence coupled with a grant is not revocable; *Wood v. Leadbitter* affirmed as much.

So far I have been treating it as if *Wood v. Leadbitter* were law as now administered in every Court. Let us see how that matter stands. *Wood v. Leadbitter* was a case decided in a Court of law before the Judicature Act; it was a case to be decided, therefore, simply upon the principles which are applicable in a Court of law as distinguished from a Court of Equity. What was the principle which would have been administered in a Court of Equity in the year 1845, the date of *Wood v. Leadbitter*, or subsequently? For that I look at the decision of Wood V.-C. in *Frogley v. Earl of Lovelace* (1859) John. 333. Other cases have been cited to us; I select this one because it seems to me to be the most pertinent, and to state the proposition in the most plain manner. The facts in *Frogley v. Earl of Lovelace* were these: the defendant was lessor to the plaintiff of certain lands for twenty-one years; he had executed a lease to him, but previously to the execution of the lease this memorandum was indorsed, but was not under seal: "It is hereby agreed that [the lessee] shall have the exclusive right of sporting over, and killing the game upon, the lands included in the within-written lease, and also upon the lands adjacent thereto belonging to the said Earl" (describing such adjacent lands) "during the continuance of the said term, if the said Ralph Frogley shall so long live; he undertaking to keep and leave a fair stock of game thereupon, and not to keep such an excessive quantity of hares and rabbits as to do damage to the said Earl or his under-tenants in the neighbourhood." On February 9, 1859, the lessor served the lessee with a notice that after that date he revoked, rescinded, and put an end to that agreement. The question was whether he could do so or not. The suit was brought in a Court of Equity for specific performance, for the execution of a proper instrument under seal giving effect to the document which was not under seal. The plaintiff moved for an injunction as prayed by his bill, namely, an injunction to give effect to his rights until that deed had been executed, and that was the matter which came before the Vice-Chancellor. At p. 339 the Vice-Chancellor says this: "The memorandum is a mere writing not under seal and the case of *Wood v. Leadbitter* has decided that, in order to acquire a right such as that which is here claimed by the plaintiff, an instrument under seal is necessary; and that, at law, an instrument purporting to grant such a right, though given for a valuable consideration, is revocable at any time, and without paying back the money. At law, therefore, the plaintiff has no remedy until the defendant shall have executed a deed containing a proper and legal grant of the exclusive right of sporting in accordance with the terms of the agreement." Finding, therefore, that the plaintiff's interest was incapable of being supported at law upon the footing of *Wood v. Leadbitter*, he gave him relief in equity, and in so doing he says: "It appears to me that the plaintiff is clearly entitled to an injunction in the interval until the defendant shall have executed a proper legal grant of the right claimed by the plaintiff". What could be plainer? According to *Wood v. Leadbitter* the plaintiff would have been dismissed from a Court of Law; he would have had no case. He comes into a Court of Equity, and he obtains relief in equity because he would have no remedy at law, and his remedy is given until he has been clothed with such rights under a proper instrument as that he has a remedy at law, and then he is left to his legal rights. I will read a few words from the judgment of Kay J. in *McManus v. Cooke* (1887) 35 Ch.D. 681. Kay J. says: "*Hewlins v. Shippam* (1826)

5 B. & C. 221, *Wood v. Leadbitter*, and other authorities at common law were cited, and it was argued that the right claimed could only be granted by deed, and that therefore the licence was revocable; but this common law doctrine was not allowed to prevail in equity." As I have shown, in *Frogley v. Earl of Lovelace* it was not allowed to prevail in equity.

The position of matters now is that the Court is bound under the Judicature Act to give effect to equitable doctrines. The question we have to consider is whether, having regard to equitable considerations, *Wood v. Leadbitter* is now law, meaning that *Wood v. Leadbitter* is a decision which can be applied in its integrity in a Court which is bound to give effect to equitable considerations. In my opinion, it is not. Cozens-Hardy J., as he then was, the present Master of the Rolls, in the case of *Lowe v. Adams* [1901] 2 Ch. 598 said this, at p. 600: "Whether *Wood v. Leadbitter* is still good law having regard to *Walsh v. Lonsdale* (1882) 21 Ch.D. 9"—which is a decision of the Court of Appeal—"is very doubtful". The present Lord Parker, then Parker J., in the case of *Jones v. Earl of Tankerville* [1909] 2 Ch. 440 says this, at p. 443: "An injunction restraining the revocation of the licence, when it is revocable at law, may in a sense be called relief by way of specific performance, but it is not specific performance in the sense of compelling the vendor to do anything. It merely prevents him from breaking his contract, and protects a right in equity which but for the absence of a seal would be a right at law, and since the Judicature Act it may well be doubted whether the absence of a seal in such a case can be relied on in any Court." What was relied on in *Wood v. Leadbitter*, and rightly relied on at that date, was that there was not an instrument under seal, and therefore there was not a grant, and therefore the licensee could not say that he was not a mere licensee, but a licensee with a grant. That is now swept away. It cannot be said as against the plaintiff that he is a licensee with no grant merely because there is not an instrument under seal which gives him a right at law.

His Lordship then considered the "new approach" outlined above:

There is another way in which the matter may be put. If there be a licence with an agreement not to revoke the licence, that, if given for value, is an enforceable right. If the facts here are, as I think they are, that the licence was a licence to enter the building and see the spectacle from its commencement until its termination, then there was included in that contract a contract not to revoke the licence until the play had run to its termination. It was then a breach of contract to revoke the obligation not to revoke the licence, and for that the decision in *Kerrison v. Smith* [1897] 2 Q.B. 445 is an authority.

   ...

   The defendants had, I think, for value contracted that the plaintiff should see a certain spectacle from its commencement to its termination. They broke that contract and it was a tort on their part to remove him. They committed an assault upon him in law. It was not of a violent kind, because, like a wise man, the plaintiff gave way to superior force and left the theatre. They sought to justify the assault by saying that they were entitled to remove him because he had not paid. He had paid, the jury have so found. Failing on that question of fact, they say that they were entitled to remove him because his licence was revocable. In my opinion, it was not. There was, I think, no justification for the assault here committed. Under the circumstances it was for the jury to give him such a sum as was right for the assault which was committed upon him, and for the serious indignity to a gentleman of being seized and treated in this way in a place of public resort. The jury have found that he was originally in the theatre as a spectator, that the assault was committed upon him, and that it was a wrongful act.

   I think that the appeal which has been brought before us, and which is founded simply upon the question of law which I have discussed at the beginning of this judgment, fails and must be dismissed with costs.

NOTES:

1. Kennedy L.J. delivered a concurring judgment. Phillimore L.J. dissented, arguing that the Judicature Acts 1873–1875 and the decision in *Walsh v. Lonsdale* (1882) 21 Ch D. 9 could not assist the contractual licensee *unless he had obtained specific performance of the contract.*

2. For a contemporary and largely critical discussion of the decision, see (1915) 31 L.Q.R. 217.

3. The finding that there was a licence coupled with a grant of an interest (the first ground for the decision) has been criticised on the ground that the case involved no recognised interest. The interest identified by Buckley L.J. (the right to see a film performance) was rejected by the Australian High Court in *Cowell v. Rosehill Racecourse Co. Ltd* (1937) 56 C.L.R. 605, where Latham C.J. observed (at 616) that "the right to see a spectacle cannot, in the ordinary sense of legal language, be regarded as a proprietary interest. Fifty thousand people who pay to see a football match do not obtain fifty thousand interests in the football ground"; and see the discussion in *Hounslow LBC v. Twickenham Garden Developments Ltd* [1971] Ch. 233, 243–245, 254 *per* Megarry J., *supra*, p. 493. *Cowell v. Rosehill Racecourse Co. Ltd* was an appeal from the Supreme Court of New South Wales, where the Judicature Act had not been adopted. The High Court of Australia declined to follow the decision in *Hurst v. Picture Theatres Ltd*, thus departing from the usual acceptance of decisions of the English Court of Appeal under the proviso that some "manifest error [was] apparent in the decision": see (1937) 53 L.Q.R. 318; and see the comments of Megarry J. in *Hounslow LBC v. Twickenham Garden Developments Ltd*, *supra* at 250 (*infra*, p. 507).

4. The implication of a negative contractual term according to which the licensor undertakes not to revoke the licence (the second ground for the decision) is readily understandable in the case of short-term licences, such as licences to view a theatre performance; and doubtless in such cases there is a strong presumption that a non-revocation term should be implied. The presumption may be rather less strong in the case of longer-term licences and it remains a question of fact whether a contractual licence is properly construed as including a non-revocation term. Where a contractual licence is not granted, expressly or by implication, for a specific purpose or a specific period, but is construed as being revocable in principle rather than perpetual, the licensee must be given reasonable (in the circumstances) notice of revocation: see *Winter Garden Theatre (London) Ltd v. Millennium Productions Ltd* [1948] A.C. 173.

5. This general approach to contractual licences was confirmed by the Court of Appeal and by the House of Lords in *Winter Garden Theatre (London) Ltd v. Millennium Productions Ltd* [1946] 1 All E.R. 678; [1948] A.C. 173. That case was included in a full discussion of contractual licences in *Hounslow LBC v. Twickenham Garden Developments Ltd* [1971] Ch. 233.

Hounslow LBC v. Twickenham Garden Developments Ltd [1971] Ch. 233

(Ch D., Megarry J.)

The plaintiff council purported to terminate its building contract with the defendant building contractor pursuant to the terms of the contract. The defendant refused to accept the termination and continued to work on the building site. Having failed to recover possession of the site, the plaintiff council issued a writ claiming damages for trespass and an injunction to restrain further trespass.

Megarry J.:
First, then, there is the question whether the borough is entitled, irrespective of the validity of the notices, to evict the contractor and resume possession of the site. Mr Harman [counsel for the plaintiff] says that all that the contractor had was a bare licence to occupy the land. It was not a licence coupled with an interest, for the contractor had no interest. Nor was it a contractual licence, for although the licence arose under the contract, the contractor was not paying for any right to go on the land: instead, he was being paid by the borough to work on the borough's land. A licence, he contended, amounted to a contractual licence only if the right to go on the land was the primary purpose of the contract, and here the contractor's occupation of the land was merely a secondary or ancillary purpose. The argument placed heavy reliance on the decision in *Thompson v. Park* [1944] K.B. 408, which, although cited in argument in *Winter Garden Theatre (London) Ltd v. Millennium Productions Ltd* [1948] A.C. 173, was not mentioned in any of the speeches. The emphasis was on the decision of the Court of Appeal in the former case in contrast with dicta in the House of Lords in the latter. Further, it was said that the contract was not specifically enforceable, and so the court should not hesitate to evict the contractor, even though that would prevent him from performing his contract.
  Mr Neill [counsel for the defendant], on the other hand, urged that the contractor had a licence coupled with a variety of interests. In any case, he said, the licence was a contractual licence, and since the *Winter Garden* case the court would protect a contractual licensee against premature eviction. The distinction between primary purposes and secondary or ancillary purposes was unreal and wrong, for it was a fundamental of the contract that the contractor was to execute the works on this particular site. Whether or not the contract was specifically enforceable was irrelevant: in fact, it was specifically enforceable, but even if it were not the court would not grant an injunction at the behest of a party to the contract who was seeking to break his contract.
  The threefold classification of licences is well known. There are licences coupled with an interest, contractual licences, and bare licences. A licence to go on land to sever and remove trees or hay, or to remove timber or hay that have already been severed, are accepted examples of a licence coupled with an interest: see, e.g., *Wood v. Manley* (1839) 11 Ad. & El. 34. Such a licence is irrevocable. The other two forms of licence, however, have been held to be revocable. *Wood v. Leadbitter* (1845) 13 M. & W. 838, the Doncaster racecourse case, is the foundation for the doctrine that the licensor may effectually revoke such a licence even if it is a breach of contract to do so. The licensee may sue the licensor in contract for that breach, but apart from that cannot complain if, refusing to leave, he is forcibly evicted. That doctrine was emphatically reaffirmed by the Court of Appeal in *Thompson v. Park* [1944] K.B. 408.
  [Megarry J. discussed the meaning of "interest" for the purposes of the category of licences coupled with an interest: see *supra*, p. 493. He continued:]
  If for this purpose "interest" is not confined to an interest in land or in chattels on the land, what does it extend to? If a right to attend a creditor's meeting or to see a

cinema performance suffices to constitute an interest, can it be said that the right and duty to do works on land fall short of being an interest? I cannot see why it should. Yet if this be so, it is not easy to see any fair stopping place in what amounts to an interest, short of any legitimate reason for being on the land. In the present case, Mr Neill deployed before me a whole network of rights under the contract capable, he said, of constituting an interest, both individually and collectively. They included possession of the site under condition 21(1) (when read with conditions 9, 10 and 16), an insurable interest in executed works, goods and materials under condition 20(1), (2), and a number of other rights. At least Mr Neill could assert that the contractor had rights on the land that were no less weighty than the right to see films or watch horse-racing.

There is, however, an alternative route to irrevocability, namely, by means of a contract. Let it be assumed that there is no "interest" which can be coupled with a licence, but merely a contract. This, per se, may preclude revocation. In *Hurst v. Picture Theatres Ltd* [1915] 1 K.B. 1, 10, Buckley L.J. put the point shortly:

> "There is another way in which the matter may be put. If there be a licence with an agreement not to revoke the licence, that, if given for value, is an enforceable right. If the facts here are, as I think they are, that the licence was a licence to enter the building and see the spectacle from its commencement until its termination, then there was included in that contract a contract not to revoke the licence till the play had run to its termination. It was then a breach of contract to revoke the obligation not to revoke the licence, and for that the decision in *Kerrison v. Smith* [1897] 2 Q.B. 445 is an authority."

This point was developed further in the *Winter Garden* case in the Court of Appeal [1946] 1 All E.R. 678. In that case, there had been a grant of a licence to use a theatre for plays and so on in return for certain payments, with an option for the licensees to extend the licence, and this had been duly exercised. The licensors later purported to determine the licence, and there were cross claims for declarations as to the effectiveness of this revocation. The House of Lords reversed the decision of the Court of Appeal in favour of the licensees, the difference between the two decisions being essentially one of construction. The Court of Appeal held that the licensors had no power to revoke the licence, whereas the House of Lords held that they had that power. Nothing that I can see in the speeches in the House of Lords suggests that the Court of Appeal was wrong in the law which that court applied to an irrevocable licence. Indeed, Lord Uthwatt confessed that he found Lord Greene M.R.'s propositions of law unanswerable: see [1948] A.C. 173, 202.

Lord Greene M.R., at p. 680, first disposed of any concept that a contractual licence was an entity distinct from the contract:

> "Counsel for the respondents put in the forefront of his argument a proposition of this nature. There is a thing called a licence, which is something which, so to speak, has a separate existence, distinct from the contract which creates it; and there is a rule of law governing that particular thing which says that a licence is determinable at will. That seems to me to be putting the matter on the wrong footing. A licence created by a contract is not an interest. It creates a contractual right to do certain things which otherwise would be a trespass. It seems to me that, in considering the nature of such a licence and the mutual rights and obligations which arise under it, the first thing to do is to construe the contract according to ordinary principles. There is the question whether or not the particular licence is revocable at all and, if so, whether by both parties or by only one. There is the question whether it is revocable immediately or only after the giving of some notice. Those are questions of construction of the contract. It seems to me quite inadmissible to say that the question whether a licence is revocable at all can be, so to speak, segregated and treated by itself, leaving only the other questions to be

decided by reference to the true construction of the contract. As I understand the law, rightly or wrongly, the answers to all these questions must depend on the terms of the contract when properly construed in the light of any relevant and admissible circumstances."

Whereas in equity, at all events, a contract for a grant or conveyance may be regarded as bringing into being some estate or interest in the land, separate from the contract that creates it, a licence is no separate entity but merely one of the manifestations of the contract. I think that the speech of Lord Simon in the House of Lords is at least consistent with this view: see [1948] A.C. 173, 189, 191.

Secondly, Lord Greene M.R. said, at p. 684;

"The respondents have purported to determine the licence. If I have correctly construed the contract their doing so was a breach of contract. It may well be that, in the old days, that would only have given rise to a right to sue for damages. The licence would have stood revoked, but after the expiration of what was the appropriate period of grace the licensees would have been trespassers and could have been expelled, and their right would have been to sue for damages for breach of contract, as was said in *Kerrison v. Smith* [1897] 2 Q.B. 445. But the matter requires to be considered further, because the power of equity to grant an injunction to restrain a breach of contract is, of course, a power exercisable in any court. The general rule is that, before equity will grant such an injunction, there must be, on the construction of the contract, a negative clause express or implied. In the present case it seems to me that the grant of an option which, if I am right, is an irrevocable option, must imply a negative undertaking by the licensor not to revoke it. That being so, in my opinion, such a contract could be enforced in equity by an injunction. Then the question would arise, at what time can equity interfere? If the licensor were threatening to revoke, equity, I apprehend, would grant an injunction to restrain him from carrying out that threat. But supposing he has in fact purported to revoke, is equity then to say: 'We are now powerless. We cannot stop you from doing anything to carry into effect your wrongful revocation'? I apprehend not. I apprehend equity would say: 'You have revoked and the licensee had no opportunity of stopping you doing so by an injunction; but what the court of equity can do is to prevent you from carrying that revocation into effect and restrain you from doing anything under it.' In the present case, nothing has been done. The appellants are still there. I can see no reason at all why, on general principles, equity should not interfere to restrain the licensors from acting upon the purported revocation, that revocation being, as I consider, a breach of contract. Looking at it in that rather simple way, one is not concerned with the difficulties which are suggested to arise from the decision of this court in *Hurst v. Picture Theatres Ltd* [1915] 1 K.B. 1."

James Jones & Sons Ltd v. Earl of Tankerville [1909] 2 Ch. 440 does not appear to have been cited, but the views of Parker J. at p. 443 seem to have been similar.

Quite apart, then, from the question whether the contractor has a licence coupled with an interest, there is the question whether the contractor has a contractual licence which either expressly or by implication is subject to a negative obligation by the borough not to revoke it. If this is so, then, on the law laid down by the Court of Appeal, equity would interfere to prevent the borough from revoking the licence or, if it had been revoked, from acting on the revocation. A fortiori, equity would refuse to grant the borough an injunction to enforce the revocation.

Now in this case the contract is one for the execution of specified works on the site during a specified period which is still running. The contract confers on each party specified rights on specified events to determine the employment of the contractor under the contract. In those circumstances, I think that there must be at least an implied negative obligation of the borough not to revoke any licence (otherwise than in accordance with the contract) while the period is still running, just as in *Hurst v. Picture Theatres Ltd* [1915] 1 K.B. 1 there was an implied negative obligation not to revoke the licence until the performance had concluded: see at pp. 10, 13 *per* Buckley and Kennedy L.JJ.

Again, in the *Winter Garden* case [1946] 1 All E.R. 678, 685, Lord Greene, on the view that the contract conferred an irrevocable licence (a view which the House of Lords held to be wrong), said that the grant of such a licence "must imply a negative undertaking by the licensor not to revoke it." In the House of Lords [1948] A.C. 173, 189, Lord Simon said of *Hurst v. Picture Theatres Ltd* that the licence in such a case is

> "granted under contractual conditions, one of which is that a well-behaved licensee shall not be treated as a trespasser until the event which he has paid to see is over, and until he has reasonable time thereafter to depart."

Lord Porter, too, at p. 194 accepted the view that the contractual licence for the purpose of doing an act or a series of acts was not revocable once the performance of a particular act had begun. Lord Uthwatt said, at p. 202:

> "The settled practice of the courts of equity is to do what they can by an injunction to preserve the sanctity of a bargain. To my mind, as at present advised, a licensee who has refused to accept the wrongful repudiation of the bargain which is involved in an unauthorised revocation of the licence is as much entitled to the protection of an injunction as a licensee who has not received any notice of revocation."

The case of building operations is really a fortiori a cinema performance, because it must be obvious to all from the outset that far more is involved in the building contractor moving his equipment on to a site, hiring his labour, making his sub-contracts and so on, and then in putting a stop to all operations, than is involved in a member of a cinema audience going in, sitting down and then getting up and leaving. The views expressed by Farwell J. in *Foster & Dicksee v. Hastings Corporation* (1903) 87 L.T. 736, 739, a case on a building or engineering contract, also seem to support this conclusion; and I have heard nothing in argument which appears to me to oust the implication of a negative obligation.

There is a further consideration of some importance. This is not a case in which the issue is merely one of damages, as in *Wood v. Leadbitter, Hurst v. Picture Theatres Ltd* or *Cowell v. Rosehill Racecourse Co. Ltd.* The borough is seeking equitable relief, namely, an injunction to expel what on one view may be a trespasser and on another view may be someone with a contractual right to remain; and on the latter view the borough is asking the court to assist it in breaking its contract. I do not think that the court will do this. As Farwell J. said of a plaintiff in one case,

> "The relief which he seeks he can obtain only in the court of equity and that court will not extend relief to one who is putting forward a claim to equitable assistance merely to enable him thereby to escape from his contractual obligations":

In re Buchanan-Wollaston's Conveyance [1939] Ch. 217, 223, affirmed [1939] Ch. 738. That was a very different type of case, but I think the principle must be general. Equity will not assist a man to break his contract. Here, the borough is in effect saying to the court, "You should grant an injunction to evict the contractor even if in so doing you would be helping me to break my contract." I do not think that equity is any more ready to help an applicant who says that it does not matter whether or not he is breaking his contract than one who is avowedly doing so.

Accordingly, if the borough has not validly determined the employment of the contractor under condition 25, the contractor has two grounds upon which to resist an injunction to leave the site: first, that the contractor has a licence coupled with an interest; and second, that the borough is seeking to evict the contractor in breach of contract. That brings me to *Thompson v. Park* [1944] K.B. 408, more fully reported in [1944] 2 All E.R. 477 and 170 L.T. 207, and most fully, I think, in 113 L.J.K.B. 561. There, a schoolmaster who held the school premises under a lease had entered into an arrangement to allow another schoolmaster (whom I shall call "the licensee") to carry on his school on the same premises, the two schools to be united for some purposes and separate for others. The licensee later gave the lessee notice to determine the arrangement, and the lessee accepted this. Subsequently it was disputed whether or not that notice had been merely provisional; and for the purposes of the interlocutory proceedings the Court of Appeal assumed that the agreement had not been terminated. The lessee then removed the licensee's furniture and equipment from the school and stored it in out-buildings; and the licensee subsequently forcibly and riotously reinstated himself in the school. The lessee then sought an interlocutory injunction to restrain the licensee from trespassing; and although Asquith J. refused to grant it, the Court of Appeal, consisting of Goddard and du Parcq L.JJ., reversed his decision. In essence, what the Court of Appeal decided was that a landowner was entitled to an injunction to exclude a licensee even though the licence was unrevoked: and this proposition is very much in point in the case before me.

The judgment of Goddard L.J., with which du Parcq L.J. agreed, referred to *Wood v. Leadbitter, Kerrison v. Smith* [1897] 2 Q.B. 445, and a passage from *Salmond on Torts* 9th ed. (1936). I can see no trace of any argument that the licensee had a licence coupled with an interest. It was plainly argued that the licensee had a contractual right to be there, but this argument was rejected. The basis of the decision appears to have been the old distinction, set out in *Salmond* at p. 258, between the licensor's power to revoke the licence effectively and his right or liberty to do it lawfully. He had the power: he did it: if he did it wrongfully he may have to pay damages: but still he did it. The passage cited from *Salmond* simply sets out in broad terms the doctrine of *Wood v. Leadbitter*; and on this the court relied. Yet the very next sentence in *Salmond* is:

> "Since the fusion of law and equity by the Judicature Act, however, the rule in *Wood v. Leadbitter* has apparently to a very large extent, even if not wholly, ceased to be in force."

No mention of this sentence, or of what follows afterwards, appears in the judgment. *Salmond* continues:

> "The reason given for this change is that a licence granted for a fixed period is in all ordinary cases specifically enforceable—an injunction being obtainable to prevent an act based upon its premature revocation. A licensee, therefore, cannot be now treated as a trespasser because of doing an act which the licensor may be compelled by a decree of specific performance to allow him to do."

There is then a discussion of *Hurst v. Picture Theatres Ltd* [1915] 1 K.B. 1.

I confess to feeling great difficulty about the grounds given for the decision in *Thompson v. Park* [1944] K.B. 408. The court there relied upon a case which the Court of Appeal had previously held to be no longer law, without mentioning that decision of the Court of Appeal, even though it was binding on it. The court also cited and approved a passage in a textbook which, in a passage not mentioned, that book said was no longer in force. The judgment of Goddard L.J. is understandably pungent, and it might be suspected that the case was decided quasi in furore: the licensee's high-handed and riotous behaviour was such as to make any court ready to condemn his conduct.

A judge of first instance is placed in a position of some difficulty when he is faced, as I am, with decisions of the Court of Appeal and dicta in the House of Lords which it seems impossible to reconcile. But while preserving to the full the respect due to superior courts, I think it is my duty to do the best I can to resolve the conflict so far as that is necessary for the purposes of this case. I would only utter the traditional prayer that on what I say (I hope with due humility) about these and other decisions of higher courts, the most favourable construction will be placed. It seems to me that the actual result in *Thompson v. Park* could be amply supported merely by saying that if a person forcibly and riotously breaks into a building in the occupation of the landowner, the court will grant to that landowner an interlocutory injunction expelling the intruder, even though the intruder has acted under a disputed claim to a subsisting licence to share the occupation of the building with the landowner. As Goddard L.J. pointed out, the status quo to be preserved was not that which existed after the intruder's illegal and criminal acts, but that which existed before they were committed: see 113 L.J.K.B. 564, 565. If *Thompson v. Park* is read in that somewhat restricted sense, much of the difficulty disappears. Further, the fact that the only licence claimed was a licence to share, and not a licence for exclusive occupation, seems to me to be of importance. As Goddard L.J. said [1944] K.B. 408, 409: "The court cannot specifically enforce an agreement for two people to live peaceably under the same roof." If the courts sought to enforce a licence to share, a multitude of practical problems would arise which would be absent if the licence was for exclusive occupation. I may also mention that in *Errington v. Errington and Woods* [1952] 1 K.B. 290, 298, 299 Denning L.J. plainly regarded *Thompson v. Park* as having lost its force as regards revocation of the licence.

I have said little about *Cowell v. Rosehill Racecourse Co. Ltd* (1937) 56 C.L.R. 605, where the High Court of Australia, with Evatt J. dissenting, followed *Wood v. Leadbitter* in preference to *Hurst v. Picture Theatres Ltd*. The case concerned the eviction from a racecourse of a racegoer who had bought a ticket which entitled him to be there; and his claim for damages for assault was dismissed. I, of course, am concerned not with the law of Australia but with the law of England, and it is only in that respect that I say anything about the case. One sentence in the dissenting judgment of Evatt J. seems to me of high significance. He said, at p. 652:

"I think the fallacy in the criticism of *Hurst's* case lies in the continuous insistence upon discovering a proprietary right as a condition of equitable intervention."

He might, perhaps, with justice have added that the judgments in *Hurst's* case did much to attract this criticism, though the alternative basis of contractual rights was by no means undiscoverable. But with all the advantage that the *Winter Garden* case gives me I would respectfully say that the law in England is that to be found not in *Cowell's* case, but in *Hurst's* case when viewed in the light of the *Winter Garden* case. If I may add to the melancholy list of cases on this branch of the law that were not cited, *Cowell's* case does not appear to have been cited in any of the three stages of the *Winter Garden* case: 115 L.J.Ch. 185; [1946] 1 All E.R. 678; [1948] A.C. 173.

There was considerable argument on the question whether or not the contract in the case before me is specifically enforceable. If it is, then of course this greatly strengthens the contractor's claim to retain possession of the site: an injunction to evict the contractor could scarcely be granted if the contractor is entitled to a decree of specific performance to compel performance of the contract. If the contract is not specifically enforceable, then the contractor must resist the injunction on some other basis. In *Hurst v. Picture Theatres Ltd* [1915] 1 K.B. 1, 8, 9, Buckley L.J. seems to have attached considerable importance to specific performance. On the view that I take, in the present case it does not matter whether the contract is or is not specifically enforceable: the court will not assist the borough in a breach of contract. But I was referred to *Wolverhampton Corporation v. Emmons* [1901] 1 Q.B. 515, and *Carpenters Estates Ltd v. Davies* [1940] Ch. 160, and I must say that I cannot at present see why this contract should not be held to be specifically enforceable by the borough against the contractor. The work to be done is sufficiently defined, I do not think damages would be adequate compensation, and the contractors obtained possession of the land under the contract: see also *Fry on Specific Performance*, 6th ed. (1921), pp. 47–50. No doubt the doctrine of mutuality is subject to many exceptions, but if in the present case the contract is specifically enforceable by the borough, it is not easy to see why it should not also be specifically enforceable by the contractor. I accept that there might well be difficulties in relation to matters such as the due provision of architect's certificates and so on, but I do not think that those difficulties would prove insuperable. However, as I have indicated, I do not consider that this point has to be decided, and I do not do so.

. . .

Even when I discard those matters which do not seem to me to arise for decision, I cannot say that I find the subject an easy one: but doing the best I can, I would broadly summarise the position relating to contractual licences as follows:

(1) A licence to enter land is a contractual licence if it is conferred by a contract; it is immaterial whether the right to enter the land is the primary purpose of the contract or is merely secondary. (2) A contractual licence is not an entity distinct from the contract which brings it into being, but merely one of the provisions of that contract. (3) The willingness of the court to grant equitable remedies in order to enforce or support a contractual licence depends on whether or not the licence is specifically enforceable. (4) But even if a contractual licence is not specifically enforceable, the court will not grant equitable remedies in order to procure or aid a breach of the licence.

To that summary I must add four points. First, as regards a licence coupled with an interest, I feel great doubt whether the word "interest" means anything more than an interest in property, though it matters not whether that property is real or personal, or legal or equitable. Today, with contractual licences recognised as being capable of being made irrevocable in their own right, there is no need to torture the word "interest" into embracing miscellaneous collections of rights. I do not have to decide whether *Vaughan v. Hampson* (1875) 33 L.T. 15 is good law today, and I do not do so. Mr Harman described it as "a curiosity"; and I do not dissent. I merely say that I should hesitate long before holding that a licence was coupled with an interest unless that interest was an interest in property, and that I doubt very much whether in this case the contractor's licence is coupled with any interest.

Second, I have said nothing about an ejected licensee's right to claim damages for assault, for such issues do not arise in this case. All that I need say, in order to avoid possible misunderstanding, is that in the light of the *Winter Garden* case I find it difficult to see how a contractual licensee can be treated as a trespasser so long as his contract entitles him to be on the land; and this is so whether or not his contract is specifically enforceable. I do not think that the licence can be detached from the contract, as it were, and separately revoked; the licensee is on the land by contractual right, and not as a trespasser. I may add that I say nothing about the rights of licensees against third parties.

Third, there may be another road to the irrevocability of a licence, namely, the doctrine of a licence acted upon. This was not a topic that was discussed before me, and I do not rely upon it for my decision. But in *Feltham v. Cartwright* (1839) 5 Bing.N.C. 569, a case which seems to have dropped rather out of sight, it was plainly laid down that the licence there in question, "having been acted on, was not revocable" to use the words of Vaughan J. at p. 572. There, a landlord distrained on the premises demised. The tenant then signed a document undertaking to give the landlord possession of the premises within a week, in consideration of the landlord giving her the furniture distrained for rent. This agreement was treated as conferring on the landlord a licence to enter the premises at the end of the week; but when he did this, the tenant sued him in trespass. The Court of Common Pleas held that the landlord was no trespasser. "This agreement was acted on," said Tindal C.J. (at p. 572), "for the plaintiff sold some of the furniture on her own account, and knew that a person sent by her landlord was working in the garden:" and he, Vaughan J. and Coltman J. all in terms said that the licence could not be revoked after it had been acted upon. I do not propose to say more about this case than that the apparent omission to consider it in *Wood v. Leadbitter* cannot add to the stature of that case. It was not cited in the *Winter Garden* case [1948] A.C. 173 either; but I observe that Lord Porter said, at p. 194:

> "If the contention that licences given for a consideration are not revocable were confined to a limited licence to do a particular act or series of acts, I do not think I should disagree provided the performance of a particular act had been actually begun."

Plainly the doctrine of a licence acted upon is not confined to cases such as *Armstrong v. Sheppard & Short Ltd* [1959] 2 Q.B. 384, 399 where the act authorised by the licence has been completed.

...

NOTES:

1. For comment, see (1970) 34 Conv. 421; (1971) 87 L.Q.R. 309; (1971) 34 M.L.R. 199.

2. For contemporary discussions of the developments in relation to revocability prior to and immediately following the decision in *Winter Garden Theatre (London) Ltd v. Millenium Productions Ltd* [1948] A.C. 173, see Walford (1947) 12 Conv. 121; Wade (1948) 64 L.Q.R. 57; Cheshire (1953) 16 M.L.R. 1; Evershed (1954) 70 L.Q.R. 326.

3. For further discussion of the doctrine of "licence acted upon", see Cullity (1965) 29 Conv. 19. For comment on the related but distinct principle in *Armstrong v. Sheppard & Short Ltd* [1959] 2 Q.B. 384, see (1958) 22 M.L.R. 692; (1959) 23 Conv. 393; [1960] C.L.J. 42.

Although, contractual licences are usually created expressly, the principle of the irrevocability of contractual licences provided a potentially effective means of protecting informal residential occupation arrangements. As a result, in some circumstances the courts have been prepared to provide that protection by the *inference* (or even *imposition*: see *Tanner v. Tanner* [1975] 1 W.L.R. 1346, 1350 *per* Lord Denning M.R.) of a contractual licence containing a (necessarily) implied non-revocation term.

Tanner v. Tanner [1975] 1 W.L.R. 1346

(CA, Lord Denning M.R., Browne L.J., Brightman J.)

The plaintiff, who was married, and the defendant formed a relationship and they decided to purchase a house to provide accommodation for the defendant and the children of the relationship. The house was purchased in the sole name of the plaintiff. The defendant thereupon moved out of her flat and occupied the house, for which she bought furniture and furnishings. The relationship terminated soon afterwards and the plaintiff, having offered the defendant £4,000 to vacate the house (which the defendant refused), obtained an order for possession. The defendant was rehoused by the local authority but she appealed against the possession order.

LORD DENNING M.R.:
It seems to me plain on the evidence that the house was acquired in the contemplation and expectation that it would provide a home for the defendant and the twin

daughters. The babies were only eight months old at the time. She gave up her flat in Steels Road (where she was protected by the Rent Acts) to move into this house. It was obviously provided for her as a house for herself and the twins for the foreseeable future.

It is said that they were only licensees—bare licensees—under a licence revocable at will: and that the plaintiff was entitled in law to turn her and the twins out on a moment's notice. I cannot believe that this is the law. This man had a moral duty to provide for the babies of whom he was the father. I would go further. I think he had a legal duty towards them. Not only towards the babies. But also towards their mother. She was looking after them and bringing them up. In order to fulfil his duty towards the babies, he was under a duty to provide for the mother too. She had given up her flat where she was protected by the Rent Acts—at least in regard to rent and it may be in regard also to security of tenure. She had given it up at his instance so as to be able the better to bring up the children. It is impossible to suppose that in that situation she and the babies were bare licensees whom he could turn out at a moment's notice. The plaintiff recognised this when he offered to pay the defendant £4,000 to get her out. What was then their legal position? She herself said in evidence: "The house was supposed to be ours until the children left school." It seems to me that enables an inference to be drawn, namely, that in all the circumstances it is to be implied that she had a licence—a contractual licence—to have accommodation in the house for herself and the children so long as they were of school age and the accommodation was reasonably required for her and the children. There was, it is true, no express contract to that effect, but the circumstances are such that the court should imply a contract by the plaintiff—or, if need be, impose the equivalent of a contract by him—whereby they were entitled to have the use of the house as their home until the girls had finished school. It may be that if circumstances changed—so that the accommodation was not reasonably required—the licence might be determinable. But it was not determinable in the circumstances in which he sought to determine it, namely, to turn the defendant out with the children and to bring in his new wife with her family. It was a contractual licence of the kind which is specifically enforceable on her behalf: and which the plaintiff can be restrained from breaking; and he could not sell the house over her head so as to get her out in that way. That appears from *Binions v. Evans* [1972] Ch. 359, 367–368.

If therefore the defendant had sought an injunction restraining the plaintiff from determining the licence, it should have been granted. The order for possession ought not to have been made.

It was said that this point (of an implied contract) was not pleaded. But to my mind it arose on the claim itself. The plaintiff pleaded a licence which had been determined. So the question was, what was the licence and what were the terms of it? Points about estoppel were raised too. Those are all ways of stating the legal effect of the facts. The facts were sufficiently pleaded, it seems to me, for the court to deal with it on the basis of an implied contract.

But what is to be done? The judge ordered possession in six weeks. Thereupon the local housing authority (as they usually do when an order for possession is made) provided accommodation for the defendant and the children. She moved out in pursuance of the order and does not ask to be put back now. Seeing that the order ought not to have been made and we reverse it, what is to be done? It seems to me that this court has ample power, when it reverses an order of the court below, to do what is just and equitable to restore the position as fairly as it can in the circumstances. The plaintiff has obtained an unjust benefit and should make restitution. In the circumstances the court can and should assess compensation to be payable by him. He has not been paying any maintenance for these children for years—ever since the defendant went into the house. It seems to me a reasonable sum for loss of this licence (which the defendant ought not to have lost) would be £2,000. So I would allow the appeal and say that the order for possession shall be set aside, and as compensation to her for being wrongly turned out, the sum of £2,000 to be payable by the plaintiff. I would allow the appeal accordingly.

NOTES:

1. The Court of Appeal inferred a licence in *Hardwick v. Johnson* [1978] 1 W.L.R. 683. The plaintiff purchased a house in her own name to provide accommodation for the defendants, who were her son and daughter-in-law. It was informally agreed that the defendants would pay the plaintiff £7 per week but, whatever the basis of this payment, very little money was actually paid and the plaintiff soon stopped asking for it. The defendants' marriage broke down and the son moved out, leaving the wife and their daughter in the house. The court dismissed the plaintiff's action for possession and held that, subject to unspecified changes in circumstances that might justify the revocation of the licence, the wife could remain in the house as long as she paid £7 per week. Lord Denning M.R. expressly referred to the licence as an *equitable* licence rather than a *contractual* licence; but Roskill L.J. and Browne L.J. expressly preferred the latter label.

2. The Court of Appeal also inferred a contractual licence in *Chandler v. Kerley* [1978] 1 W.L.R. 693. The plaintiff and the defendant, who was married but separated from her husband, formed a relationship. The plaintiff later purchased the matrimonial home of the defendant and her husband in the expectation that he would move in with the defendant and her two children. However, the plaintiff ended the relationship and sought possession of the house. The Court of Appeal held that the defendant had a contractual licence terminable by reasonable notice, which in the circumstances was interpreted as 12 months.

3. The above cases should be contrasted with *Horrocks v. Forray* [1976] 1 W.L.R. 230. The deceased, who was married, and the defendant had formed a relationship. The defendant and the child of the relationship had been generously maintained by the deceased for 17 years; and, less than a year before his death, the deceased purchased in his own name a house for the defendant and the child. When the plaintiffs, the executors of the deceased, brought an action for possession, the defendant, relying on the authority of *Tanner v. Tanner* [1975] 1 W.L.R. 1346, argued that she had a contractual licence to remain in the house (although she offered three possible alternatives as to the duration of her entitlement). The Court of Appeal held that there was no justification for inferring a contractual licence. Scarman L.J. stated (at 239):

Mr Goldblatt, for the defendant, has sought to persuade the court that a contract is to be inferred from a course of conduct, from the development of the relationship between the parties and its course over a period of years. This submission is, as a matter of law, open to him. That has been clearly decided, as I understand it, in two cases in the Court of Appeal to which he has referred us, *Ward v. Byham* [1956] 1 W.L.R. 496 and *Tanner v. Tanner* [1975] 1 W.L.R. 1346. In each of those cases, however, the relationship of man and mistress was either broken or on the point of collapse. The parties to the relationship, the man and the woman, had to consider what best should be done for the innocent product of their relationship, the illegitimate children. In a very real sense, both in *Ward v. Byham* and in *Tanner v. Tanner*, the man and the woman were making arrangements for the future at arm's-length. The woman was concerned for herself and her children, the man was concerned to limit and define his financial responsibilities towards the woman and the children. Here is a fertile area for the growth of an inference of a legally binding contract; and for myself I do not find it surprising, when I look at the facts in *Ward v. Byham* or *Tanner v. Tanner*, that the court came to the conclusion that a contract was to be inferred from the conduct of the parties. But how different is this case. Right up to the death of the man there was a continuing, warm relationship of man and mistress. He was maintaining his mistress in luxurious, even, so the judge thought, extravagant style, and, we now know, in a style beyond his means: his estate is now at risk of being insolvent.

Mr Goldblatt has tried to tempt us to draw an inference of contract by dangling in front of our eyes various contracts that might be inferred. If one looks at that sort of fishing exercise with a dispassionate lawyer's eye, one begins to wonder whether he is not in difficulty in finding in the relationship any one, certain, contract. Since he is saying that three or four possibilities arise …, one wonders whether these parties, in fact, entered into a legally binding agreement or intended to create legal relations upon the basis of terms sufficiently formulated to be clear and certain. But his real difficulty is that, whatever relationship did exist between these two, it could as well be referable to the continuance of natural love and affection as to an intention to enter into an agreement which they intended to have legal effect. In the other two cases, that relationship had ended and it was necessary to tie up the bits. In the present case the relationship was continuing until the unhappy and unexpected death of the man. Therefore Mr Goldblatt is in difficulty with the facts of the case.

Fortunately for this court, the facts have been subjected to a most careful and detailed analysis by the trial judge, who, as Megaw L.J. has already commented, directed himself absolutely correctly on the question of law, that is to say, the effect and scope of *Tanner v. Tanner* [1975] 1 W.L.R. 1346.

. . .

Here was a generous provision made for a woman who was still the mistress and for the child of that relationship. It was generous beyond what one would reasonably expect the man to accept a legally binding obligation to provide. It was generous, not because he was bound or was binding himself to be generous, but because he chose to be generous to the woman for whom there was a big place in his heart. Once one reaches that situation, one can see how the judge inferred that this was a case where there was no contract and where really it was unreasonable to infer a contract.

Tanner v. Tanner was also distinguished in *Coombes v. Smith* [1986] 1 W.L.R. 808: in the latter case the licensee had provided no sufficient consideration.

4. For comment on the above cases, see (1976) 40 Conv. 236; 351 (especially 361–364); (1976) 92 L.Q.R. 168; [1978] Conv. 459; 461; [1979] Conv. 184 (especially 190–193); (1979) 95 L.Q.R. 11; (1979) 42 M.L.R. 203; (1980) 96 L.Q.R. 248 (especially 255–258).

4. Effect on successors in title

Notwithstanding the strengthening of the position of the contractual licensee *as against the original licensor*, consistent with contractual principles, the orthodox view is that a contractual licence cannot bind a successor in title of the licensor; and the authorities traditionally cited for that view are the decision of the House of Lords in *King v. David Allen and Sons (Billposting) Ltd* [1916] 2 A.C. 54 and the decision of the Court of Appeal in *Clore v. Theatrical Properties Ltd* [1936] 3 All E.R. 483. Both cases are discussed in *Ashburn Anstalt v. Arnold* [1989] Ch. 1, *infra*, p. 522.

However, this orthodoxy was strenuously challenged, and not without considerable success, by Lord Denning, who for more than 20 years persisted in his endeavours to elevate the contractual licence to the status of an equitable interest in land.

Errington v. Errington and Woods [1952] 1 K.B. 290

(CA, Somervell, Denning and Hodson L.JJ.)

A father, wishing to provide a home for his son who had recently married, bought a house with the help of a building society mortgage. He paid a lump sum towards the purchase price, the remainder of which was provided by the building society's loan. The loan was repayable by instalments. He retained the conveyance in his own name and paid the rates, but he promised that if the son and daughter-in-law continued in occupation and duly paid all the instalments, he would then transfer the property to them. The father died and by his will left the house to his widow. Up to that time the son and his wife had lived in the house and paid the instalments. The son then separated from his wife and left the house. The daughter-in-law continued to pay the mortgage instalments. The widow then sought possession of the house from the daughter-in-law. The country court judge dismissed the action. He held that the daughter-in-law was a tenant at will but that the claim against her was statute-barred. That reasoning was rejected by the Court of Appeal, though the actual decision of the judge was upheld.

DENNING L.J.:
It seems to me that, although the couple had exclusive possession of the house, there was clearly no relationship of landlord and tenant. They were not tenants at will but licensees. They had a mere personal privilege to remain there, with no right to assign or sub-let. They were, however, not bare licensees. They were licensees with a contractual right to remain. As such they have no right at law to remain, but only in equity, and equitable rights now prevail. I confess, however, that it has taken the courts some time to reach this position. At common law a licence was always revocable at will, notwithstanding a contract to the contrary: *Wood v. Leadbitter* (1845) 13 M. & W. 838. The remedy for a breach of the contract was only in damages. That was the view generally held until a few years ago: see, for instance, what was said in *Booker v. Palmer* [1942] 2 All E.R. 674, 677 and *Thompson v. Park* [1944] K.B. 408, 410. The rule has, however, been altered owing to the interposition of equity. Law and equity have been fused for nearly 80 years, and since 1948 it has been clear that, as a result of the fusion, a licensor will not be permitted to eject a licensee in breach of a contract to allow him to remain: see *Winter Garden Theatre (London) Ltd v. Millennium Productions Ltd* [1946] 1 All E.R. 678, 680 *per* Lord Greene, and in the House of Lords *per* Lord Simon; nor in breach of a promise on which the licensee has acted, even though he gave no value for it: see *Foster v. Robinson* [1951] 1 K.B. 149, 156, where Sir Raymond Evershed M.R. said that as a result of the oral arrangement to let the man stay, he was entitled as licensee to occupy the premises without any payment of rent for the rest of his days. This infusion of equity means that contractual licences now have a force and validity of their own and cannot be revoked in breach of the contract. Neither the licensor nor anyone who claims through him can disregard the contract except a purchaser for value without notice.

NOTES:

1. The Court of Appeal held that the son and daughter-in-law were not tenants at will since such a tenancy is *ex hypothesi* determinable on demand by either party: in the instant case the father could not eject the couple as long as they continued to pay the mortgage instalments. Nor were the couple tenants at a rent equivalent to the mortgage instalments since they were not bound to pay the instalments.

2. The case is usually treated as deciding that a contractual licence creates an equitable interest capable of binding a successor in title of the original licensor; and that was the view of Denning L.J.: see *Binions v. Evans* [1972] Ch. 359, 367. However, the court did not expressly address the question whether the widow brought the action in her capacity as successor in title or in her capacity as personal representative (in which case the effect of the contract on a successor in title was not in issue): see *National Provincial Bank v. Ainsworth* [1965] A.C. 1175, 1252 *per* Lord Wilberforce.

3. Wade (1952) 68 L.Q.R. 337 concluded that the usual interpretation of the decision could not stand with the earlier authorities of *King v. David Allen and Sons (Billposting) Ltd* [1916] 2 A.C. 54 and *Clore v. Theatrical Properties Ltd* [1936] 3 All E.R. 483 (neither of which was cited to the court); and that, more broadly, the court should not have invented a new equitable proprietary interest. However, Wade also argued that the result could have been achieved without the unsettling and undesirable invention of a new proprietary interest. On the facts the couple had the benefit of an estate contract, which, although not registered, would be binding on the widow, since she could not claim to be a purchaser for money or money's worth.

4. Hargreaves (1953) 69 L.Q.R. 466 argued that the reasoning of the Court of Appeal was fundamentally flawed: "the inconsistencies and incongruities are so manifest, the reasoning so demonstrably unsatisfactory, the number of cases overlooked or misunderstood so great". However, he argued that the decision was readily supportable: the transaction should have been considered either as a conditional gift of the house, enforceable in equity through the principle of proprietary estoppel, or as an enforceable contract for a determinable life interest, with an ultimate limitation in fee simple on full payment of the mortgage instalments.

5. Cheshire (1953) 16 M.L.R. 1 defended the reasoning on its own terms. He dismissed the supposed incompatibility with *King v. David Allen and Sons (Billposting) Ltd* [1916] 2 A.C. 54 and *Clore v. Theatrical Properties Ltd* [1936] 3 All E.R. 483 and regarded the recognition of the contractual licence as a new equitable interest in land as the "normal evolution" of the equitable principle, which has long been applied to the estate contract, that a contractual and specific claim to specific land is enforceable against third parties. However, his argument did not distinguish between contractual licences and estoppel licences; and it relied heavily on the proprietary estoppel cases. See also Moriarty (1984) 100 L.Q.R. 376, 394–397.

6. It is arguable that the decision in *Errington v. Errington and Woods* was a response to a multi-faceted problem of residential security: see Crane (1952) 16 Conv. 323; Pollock (1952) 16 Conv. 436; Sheridan (1953) 17 Conv. 440;

Hanbury [1954] C.L.J. 201; [1955] C.L.J. 47; Moriartry (1984) 100 L.Q.R. 376, 394–397.

7. In particular, the decision provided a temporary solution to the problem of residential security for the deserted wife who could claim no legal or beneficial ownership in the matrimonial home. In a series of cases the Court of Appeal developed the doctrine of the "deserted wife's equity", according to which the deserted wife was treated as having an "equity", a species of contractual licence, which conferred on her a right to occupy the matrimonial home vested in her husband; and in accordance with the decision in *Errington v. Errington and Woods* that the "equity" was binding not only on the husband/licensor but also on any successor in title of the husband who had notice of it: see *Bendall v. McWhirter* [1952] 2 Q.B. 466; *Ferris v. Weaven* [1952] 2 All E.R. 233; *Lee v. Lee* [1952] 2 Q.B. 489; *Street v. Denham* [1954] 1 W.L.R. 624; *Jess B. Woodcock & Sons Ltd v. Hobbs* [1955] 1 W.L.R. 152; *Westminster Bank Ltd v. Lee* [1956] Ch. 7; *National Provincial Bank Ltd v. Hastings Car Mart Ltd* [1964] Ch. 665; and see Megarry (1952) 68 L.Q.R. 379; Crane (1955) 19 Conv. 343; Crane (1965) 29 Conv. 254, 464. In *National Provincial Bank Ltd v. Ainsworth* [1965] A.C. 1175 the House of Lords rejected (i) the doctrine of the "deserted wife's equity", (ii) the categorisation of the wife as a licensee of her husband and (iii) the notion that the right of the wife to occupy the matrimonial home was anything other than a personal right enforceable against the husband: see [1965] C.L.J. 216; Crane (1965) 29 Conv. 254, 464; (1965) 81 L.Q.R. 353; (1966) 29 M.L.R. 74. However, the decision of the House of Lords in *National Provincial Bank Ltd v. Ainsworth* prompted the enactment of the Matrimonial Homes Act 1967 (now consolidated in Part IV of the Family Law Act 1996). As has been seen (*ante*, p. 152), that Act gives a spouse (husband or wife) who is not on the legal title "matrimonial home rights", which constitute a charge on the interest of the other spouse and which, if protected by registration, are enforceable against a successor in title of the other spouse.

8. The reasoning of the Court of Appeal in *Errington v. Errington and Woods* was severely criticised by Russell L.J. (dissenting) in the Court of Appeal in *National Provincial Bank Ltd v. Hastings Car Mart Ltd* [1964] Ch. 665; and by the House of Lords on appeal in *National Provincial Bank Ltd v. Ainsworth* [1965] A.C. 1175. For discussion of those cases, see *Ashburn Anstalt v. Arnold* [1989] Ch. 1, *infra*, p. 522.

9. Crane (1967) 31 Conv. 332 and Todd [1981] Conv. 347 saw the decision of the House of Lords in *National Provincial Bank Ltd v. Ainsworth* [1965] A.C. 1175 as the end of the contractual licence as a (quasi-) interest in land, after which the Court of Appeal concentrated on developing the licence protected by estoppel. However, Lord Denning was not that easily discouraged.

Binions v. Evans [1972] Ch. 359

(CA, Lord Denning M.R., Stephenson and Megaw L.JJ.)

The defendant and her husband, who was an employee of the Tredegar Estate, lived rent free in a cottage owned by the estate. After the husband died the trustees of the estate entered into an agreement with the defendant, who was then 73 years old, whereby "in order to provide a temporary home" for the defendant "but not otherwise" they agreed to permit the defendant "to reside in and occupy" the cottage and garden "as tenant at will of them free of rent for the remainder of her life" (or until earlier determination by the defendant). The defendant undertook to keep the cottage and the garden in good repair and condition, personally to occupy the cottage as a private residence, not to assign or sub-let and, on ceasing to live there, to give vacant possession forthwith to the trustees. The trustees subsequently sold the cottage to the plaintiffs. The contract provided that the property was sold "subject to the tenancy" of the cottage in favour of the defendant; and in consequence the plaintiffs paid a reduced price. The plaintiffs then gave the defendant notice to quit and sought possession on the ground that the defendant was a trespasser, her tenancy at will having been terminated. The county court judge decided that the plaintiffs held the cottage "on trust to permit the defendant to reside there during her life or as long as she desires"; and he refused the order for possession. The plaintiffs appealed.

LORD DENNING M.R.:

Seeing that the defendant has no legal estate or interest in the land, the question is what right has she? At any rate, she has a contractual right to reside in the house for the remainder of her life or as long as she pleases to stay. I know that in the agreement it is described as a tenancy: but that does not matter. The question is: What is it in reality? To my mind it is a licence, and no tenancy. It is a privilege which is personal to her. On all the modern cases, which are legion, it ranks as a contractual licence, and not a tenancy: see *Shell-Mex and B.P. Ltd v. Manchester Garages Ltd* [1971] 1 W.L.R. 612.

What is the status of such a licence as this? There are a number of cases in the books in which a similar right has been given. They show that a right to occupy for life, arising by contract, gives to the occupier an equitable interest in the land: just as it does when it arises under a settlement: see *In re Carne's Settled Estates* [1899] 1 Ch. 324 and *In re Boyer's Settled Estates* [1916] 2 Ch. 404. The courts of equity will not allow the landlord to turn the occupier out in breach of the contract: see *Foster v. Robinson* [1951] 1 K.B. 149, 156; nor will they allow a purchaser to turn her out if he bought with knowledge of her right—*Errington v. Errington and Woods* [1952] 1 K.B. 290, 299.

It is instructive to go back to the cases before the Supreme Court of Judicature Act 1873. They show that, if a landlord, by a memorandum in writing, let a house to someone, let us say to a widow, at a rent, for her life or as long as she pleased to stay, the courts of equity would not allow the landlord to turn her out in breach of his contract. If the landlord were to go to the courts of law and obtain an order in ejectment against her, as in *Doe d. Warner v. Browne* (1807) 8 East 165, the courts of equity would grant an injunction to restrain the landlord from enforcing his rights at law, as in *Browne v. Warner* (1808) 14 Ves. 409. The courts of equity would give the agreement a construction, which Lord Eldon L.C. called an "equitable construction," and construe it as if it were an agreement to execute a deed granting her a lease of the house for life—*Browne v. Warner* (1807) 14 Ves. 156, 158. They would order the landlord specifically to perform the contract, so construed, by executing such a deed. This court did so in *Zimbler v. Abrahams* [1903] 1 K.B. 577. This means that she had an equitable interest in the land. So much so that if a purchaser wished to buy her interest from her, he had to pay her its full value as such. Malins V.-C. so held in *In re King's Leasehold Estates* (1873) L.R. 16 Eq. 521, 527, where he described it as an "equitable interest." It follows that, if the owner sold his reversion to another, who took with notice of the widow's interest, his successor could not turn her out any more than he could. She would have, I should have thought, at least as strong a case as the occupier in *Webb v. Paternoster* (1619) Poph. 151, which received the blessing of Lord Upjohn in *National Provincial Bank Ltd v. Hastings Car Mart Ltd* [1965] A.C. 1175, 1239.

Suppose, however, that the defendant did not have an equitable interest at the outset, nevertheless it is quite plain that she obtained one afterwards when the Tredegar Estate sold the cottage. They stipulated with the plaintiffs that they were to take the house "subject to" the defendant's rights under the agreement. They supplied the plaintiffs with a copy of the contract: and the plaintiffs paid less because of her right to stay there. In these circumstances, this court will impose on the plaintiffs a constructive trust for her benefit: for the simple reason that it would be utterly inequitable for the plaintiffs to turn the defendant out contrary to the stipulation subject to which they took the premises. That seems to me clear from the important decision of *Bannister v. Bannister* [1948] 2 All E.R. 133, which was applied by the judge, and which I gladly follow.

This imposing of a constructive trust is entirely in accord with the precepts of equity. As Cardozo J. once put it: "A constructive trust is the formula through which the conscience of equity finds expression", see *Beatty v. Guggenheim Exploration Co.* (1919) 225 N.Y. 380, 386: or, as Lord Diplock put it quite recently in *Gissing v. Gissing* [1971] A.C. 886, 905, a constructive trust is created "whenever the trustee has so conducted himself that it would be inequitable to allow him to deny to the *cestui que trust* a beneficial interest in the land acquired".

I know that there are some who have doubted whether a contractual licensee has any protection against a purchaser, even one who takes with full notice. We were referred in this connection to Professor Wade's article, Licences and Third Parties, in (1952) 68 L.Q.R. 337, and to the judgment of Goff J. in *In re Solomon, A Bankrupt, Ex parte Trustee of the Property of the Bankrupt v. Solomon* [1967] Ch. 573. None of these doubts can prevail, however, when the situation gives rise to a constructive trust. Whenever the owner sells the land to a purchaser, and at the same time stipulates that he shall take it "subject to" a contractual licence, I think it plain that a court of equity will impose on the purchaser a constructive trust in favour of the beneficiary. It is true that the stipulation (that the purchaser shall take it subject to the rights of the licensee) is a stipulation for the benefit of one who is not a party to the contract of sale; but, as Lord Upjohn said in *Beswick v. Beswick* [1968] A.C. 58, 98, that is just the very case in which equity will "come to the aid of the common law". It does so by imposing a constructive trust on the purchaser. It would be utterly inequitable that the purchaser should be able to turn out the beneficiary. It is to be noted that in the two cases which are said to give rise to difficulty, *King v. David Allen and Sons (Billposting) Ltd* [1916] 2 A.C. 54 and *Clore v. Theatrical Properties Ltd and Westby & Co. Ltd* [1936] 3 All E.R. 483, there was no trace of a stipulation, express or implied, that the purchaser should take the property subject to the right of the contractual licensee. In the first case, if Mr King had protected himself by stipulating that the company should take the lease "subject to the rights of David Allen", I cannot think that he would have been held liable in damages. In the second case the documents were exceedingly complicated, but if Mr Clore had acquired the theatre "subject to the rights of the licensees", I cannot suppose that this court would have allowed him to disregard those rights.

In many of these cases the purchaser takes *expressly* "subject to" the rights of the licensee. Obviously the purchaser then holds the land on an imputed trust for the licensee. But, even if he does not take expressly "subject to" the rights of the licensee, he may do so *impliedly*. At any rate when the licensee is in actual occupation of the land, so that the purchaser must know he is there, and of the rights which he has: see *Hodgson v. Marks* [1971] Ch. 892. Whenever the purchaser takes the land impliedly subject to the rights of the contractual licensee, a court of equity will impose a constructive trust for the beneficiary. So I still adhere to the proposition I stated in *Errington v. Errington and Woods* [1952] 1 K.B. 290, 299; and elaborated in *National Provincial Bank Ltd v. Hastings Car Mart Ltd* [1964] Ch. 665, 686–689, namely, that, when the licensee is in actual occupation, neither the licensor nor anyone who claims through him can disregard the contract except a purchaser for value without notice.

In my opinion the defendant, by virtue of the agreement, had an equitable interest in the cottage which the court would protect by granting an injunction against the landlords restraining them from turning her out. When the landlords sold the cottage to a purchaser "subject to" her rights under the agreement, the purchaser took the cottage on a constructive trust to permit the defendant to reside there during her life, or as long as she might desire. The courts, will not allow the purchaser to go back on that trust. I entirely agree with the judgment of Judge Bulger. I would dismiss this appeal.

MEGAW L.J.:

What was the effect in law of [the] agreement, as between the trustees and the defendant? In my view, Judge Bulger was right in holding that the effect was the same as the effect of the agreement considered by this court in *Bannister v. Bannister* [1948] 2 All E.R. 133. In that case the defendant had orally agreed to sell two cottages to her brother-in-law, the plaintiff, in reliance on this statement: "I do not want to take any rent, but will let you stay" in one of the cottages "as long as you like rent free". Troubles arose between the parties a few years later and the plaintiff sought to turn the defendant out, claiming that she was a mere tenant at will. The court (Scott L.J., Asquith L.J. and Jenkins J.) held, at p. 137:

"... the plaintiff holds no. 30 in trust during the life of the defendant to permit the defendant to occupy the same for so long as she may desire to do so and subject thereto in trust for the plaintiff. A trust in this form has the effect of making the beneficiary a tenant for life within the meaning of the Settled Land Act 1925, and, consequently, there is a very little practical difference between such a trust and a trust for life simpliciter."

As was said by the court, at p. 136:

"Similar words in deeds and wills have frequently been held to create a life interest determinable (apart from the special considerations introduced by the Settled Land Act 1925) on the beneficiary ceasing to occupy the premises: ..."

I confess that I have had difficulty in seeing precisely how the Settled Land Act of 1925 was applicable. But the court in *Bannister v. Bannister* [1948] 2 All E.R. 133 so held, and I am certainly content, and we are probably bound, to follow that authority. I see no relevant distinction. The fact that the transaction—the creation of the trust—was there effected orally, whereas here there is an agreement in writing, surely cannot be a ground for saying that the principle is not here applicable. The fact that there is here express provision for determination by the beneficiary cannot provide a relevant distinction. The defendant in *Bannister v. Bannister* [1948] 2 All E.R. 133 was free to give up occupation whenever she wished. The fact and nature of the obligations imposed upon the defendant by the agreement in the present case must tend in favour of, rather than adversely to, the creation of an interest in land, as compared with *Bannister's* case.

I realise that the application of the Settled Land Act 1925 may produce some odd consequences; but no odder than those which were inherent in the decision in *Bannister v. Bannister* [1948] 2 All E.R. 133. I do not find anything in the possible, theoretical, consequences to lead me to the conclusion that *Bannister's* case should not be followed.

The plaintiffs took with express notice of the agreement which constitutes, or gives rise to, the trust. They cannot turn the defendant out of the house against her will; for that would be a breach of the trust which binds them.

If for some reason *Bannister v. Bannister* [1948] 2 All E.R. 133 did not apply, so that there would then be no trust and the defendant would possibly have no "interest in land" within the technical meaning of those words, there would none the less be a continuing contractual obligation as between the trustees and the defendant. It would then be what is sometimes called an irrevocable licence. It would be irrevocable—that is not determinable by the licensors, the trustees, without the consent of the licensee, the defendant—because it is founded on a contract. The agreement was based on consideration—the provisions made by the defendant as her side of the agreement. That irrevocable licence, that contractual right to continue in occupation, remained binding upon the trustees. They could not, and did not, free themselves from it unilaterally by selling the land to the plaintiffs. As the plaintiffs took with express notice of, and indeed expressly subject to, the agreement between the trustees and the defendant, the plaintiffs would, on ordinary principles, be guilty of the tort of interference with existing contractual rights if they were to evict the defendant. For that would be knowingly to interfere with her continuing contractual rights with a third party, the trustees. In the ordinary way, the court would intervene to prevent the plaintiffs from interfering with those rights. I should have thought that ordinary principles of equity would have operated in the same way. However, it may be that there are special technical considerations in the law relating to land which would require to be reviewed before one could confidently assert that the ordinary principles as to the protection of known contractual rights would apply. There are, for example, passages in the speech of Lord Upjohn in *National Provincial Bank Ltd v. Hastings Car Mart Ltd* [1965] A.C. 1175, 1239, which indicate doubts and difficulties in this sphere. Since, in my opinion, this case is governed by *Bannister v. Bannister* [1948] 2 All E.R. 133 I do not think it necessary to pursue that topic further.

I would dismiss the appeal.

STEPHENSON L.J.:

The words "tenant for life" are not used, but that in one sense is what the landlords are agreeing that this widow should become. If, however, these words were in the agreement they would be used like "tenant at will" in the context of the whole agreement as conferring a life interest, whatever called or however described, which was determinable by the so-called tenant for life on four weeks' notice or by ceasing permanently to live in the cottage.

Apart from authority, I would not have thought that such an interest could be understood to amount to a tenancy for life within the meaning of the Settled Land Act 1925, and I would have thought that the other terms of her tenancy (as I think it ought properly to be called) are inconsistent with a power to ask for the legal estate to be settled on her or to sell the cottage. But *Bannister v. Bannister* [1948] 2 All E.R. 133 is a clear decision of this court that such words as have been used in this agreement (excepting, I must concede, the words "as tenant at will of them") create a life interest determinable (apart from the special considerations introduced by the Settled Land Act 1925) on the beneficiary ceasing to occupy the premises and the landlords hold the cottage on trust to permit her to occupy it "during her life or as long as she lives", as Judge Bulger held, and subject thereto in trust for them.

I therefore find it unnecessary to consider or decide the vexed questions (1) whether this agreement is or creates an irrevocable contractual licence to occupy, and (2) whether such a licence has been elevated to a status equivalent to an estate or interest in land by decisions of this court such as *Errington v. Errington and Woods* [1952] 1 K.B. 290 or *Foster v. Robinson* [1951] 1 K.B. 149 or still awaits legislation before it can so achieve transmissibility to subsequent purchasers with notice: see the rival views set out by Goff J. in *In re Solomon, A Bankrupt, Ex parte Trustee of the Property of the Bankrupt v. Solomon* [1967] Ch. 573, 582–586.

On the whole of the document the defendant appears to me to agree to assume the rights and obligations of a tenant and the plaintiffs' predecessors those of a landlord, not those of a licensee and licensor: see *Addiscombe Garden Estates Ltd v. Crabbe* [1958] 1 Q.B. 513. Accordingly, I prefer to regard the defendant as a tenant for life and not a licensee.

NOTES:

1. Lord Denning M.R. rejected the argument that the defendant had (i) a tenancy at will, on the ground that such a conclusion was inconsistent with the principal term of the written agreement; or (ii) a 90-year lease, determinable after her death, pursuant to section 149(6) of the Law of Property Act 1925, on the ground that no rent was payable as required by that subsection; or (iii) any other leasehold interest, on the ground that the maximum duration of the term was not fixed.

2. Lord Denning M.R. considered and rejected the argument that the defendant was a tenant for life under a strict settlement, on the grounds (a) that the consequences of such a conclusion were contrary to the intentions of the parties and (b) that a strict settlement requires an *express* limitation in trust. The first ground is hardly compelling since, if the arrangement came within the statutory definition, the statutory consequences should follow: see Baker (1972) 88 L.Q.R. 336; Hayton (1972) 36 Conv. 277. The second ground was more convincing to Baker (1972) 88 L.Q.R. 336; but it was criticised by Oakley (1972) 35 M.L.R. 551; Martin (1972) 36 Conv. 266; Hayton (1972) 36 Conv. 277. The views of Lord Denning M.R. on the inapplicability of the Settled Land Act 1925 to the facts of *Binions v. Evans* were approved in *Ivory v. Palmer* [1975] I.C.R. 340; but they were regarded as unconvincing in *Griffiths v. Williams* (1977) 248 E.G. 947, *infra*, p. 569, and were rejected in *Ungurian v. Lesnoff* [1990] Ch. 206, noted at [1990] C.L.J. 25; [1990] Conv. 223; and see *Costello v. Costello* (1994) 70 P. & C.R. 297, noted at [1994] Conv. 391.

3. Hornby (1977) 93 L.Q.R. 561 argues that where a person is given a personal right of occupation, *and there is no grant of an estate in land nor any factor which otherwise indicates a strict settlement*, there is no strict settlement; and that it was therefore wrong for the Court of Appeal in *Bannister v. Bannister* [1948] 2 All E.R. 133 and for the majority of the Court of Appeal in *Binions v. Evans* to invoke the strict settlement machinery. This view was endorsed in *Dent v. Dent* [1996] 1 All E.R. 659. David Young Q.C. held that the court should consider the context in which an exclusive right to occupy property for life was granted or agreed to before determining whether it created a strict settlement or some other property interest or some form of licence. In particular, the court should consider whether the grant or

agreement constituted the creation or restructuring of property rights or merely an undertaking as to personal rights of occupation.

4. Even if the creation of a strict settlement is a defensible interpretation of the arrangement, most commentators accept that it is an inconvenient interpretation (for the reasons outlined by Lord Denning M.R.), which should be avoided if alternative remedies exist.

5. On Megaw L.J.'s preferred remedy of an injunction to restrain the purchasers from committing the tort of interference with contractual relations, see Baker (1972) 88 L.Q.R. 336; Smith (1977) 41 Conv. 318 (especially 322–326); Thompson [1985] C.L.J. 280, 293 *et seq.*; Thompson [1988] Conv. 201, 206.

6. Oakley (1972) 35 M.L.R. 551 argues that the appropriate remedy for the defendant would have been the granting of an injunction to prevent her eviction; and that there was no justification for conferring an interest in land under a constructive trust. However, Lord Denning M.R. does not appear to suggest that the substance of the equitable interest that the defendant obtained was anything more than protection against eviction; and the imposition of the constructive trust may be nothing more than a convenient generic label indicating the continuing availability of equitable assistance to provide that protection: see Hayton (1972) 36 Conv. 277; see also *Ashburn Anstalt v. Arnold* [1989] Ch. 1, *infra*, p. 522.

7. Martin (1972) 36 Conv. 266 suggests that the intentions of the parties could have been effected (i) by the grant of a short periodic tenancy at a nominal rent (or rent free) with an absolute covenant against assignment or sub-letting or parting with possession; or (ii) by the grant of a fixed term lease at a nominal rent, with an absolute covenant against assignment or sub-letting or parting with possession, determinable by the service of a notice after the death of the tenant: see *Griffiths v. Williams* (1977) 248 E.G. 947, *infra*, p. 569.

8. Thompson [1994] Conv. 391 argues for legislative reform enabling the creation of a trust-based life interest in property which cannot be sold during the relevant lifetime without the consent of all interested parties.

9. Moriarty (1984) 100 L.Q.R. 376, 394–397, seeks to distinguish two types of contractual licence. In *King v. David Allen and Sons (Billposting) Ltd* [1916] 2 A.C. 54 and *Clore v. Theatrical Properties Ltd* [1936] 3 All E.R. 483 the parties intended to set up commercial arrangements which could not give rise to recognised proprietary rights enforceable against successors in title; by contrast the residential licence cases involved informal attempts to confer (enforceable) rights in land. He argues that there are good policy reasons for refusing to hold that arrangements of the first type can bind successors in title; and that there are equally good policy reasons for holding that arrangements of the second type can bind successors in title.

10. For more comprehensive attempts at the rationalisation of contractual licences following *Binions v. Evans*, see Smith [1973] C.L.J. 123; Bandali (1973) 37 Conv. 402.

11. Notwithstanding that the judgment of Lord Denning M.R. constituted the minority view, his reasoning has frequently been taken as the *ratio*

decidendi of the case. It was applied in *D.H.N. Food Distributors Ltd v. Tower Hamlets LBC* [1976] 1 W.L.R. 852, noted at [1977] C.L.J. 12; in *Lyus v. Prowsa Developments Ltd* [1982] 1 W.L.R. 1044; and, albeit somewhat reluctantly, in *Re Sharpe* [1980] 1 W.L.R. 219; and a flexible role for the constructive trust was given qualified support in *Ashburn Anstalt v. Arnold* [1989] Ch. 1, *infra. See also Midland Bank Ltd v. Farmpride Hatcheries Ltd* (1980) 260 E.G. 493, noted at [1982] Conv. 67, where the Court of Appeal accepted that a contractual licence was capable of binding a successor in title of the licensor, and *Pennine Raceway Ltd v. Kirklees Metropolitan BC* [1983] Q.B. 382, noted at [1983] Conv. 317, where a contractual licence was held to confer an interest in land on the licensee for the purposes of compensation for the withdrawal of planning permission.

The authorities on contractual licences were the subject of lengthy analysis in *Ashburn Anstalt v. Arnold* [1989] Ch. 1.

Ashburn Anstalt v. Arnold [1989] Ch. 1

(CA, Fox, Neill and Bingham L.JJ.)

The defendant company had sold its sub-lease of shop premises. Under the terms of the agreement the defendant was permitted to remain in occupation of the premises rent free until it received notice that the purchaser was ready to redevelop the site together with other adjoining land, at which time it would give up possession and in due course be granted a lease of shop premises on the redeveloped site. Both the sub-lease and the head-lease subsequently merged with the freehold, title to which was registered. The plaintiff purchased the freehold of the whole site "subject to" the agreement with the defendant. The plaintiff then sought possession without serving the notice provided for in the agreement. The defendant argued that it was a lessee or, in the alternative, a contractual licensee and that, in either case, its interest, although not protected on the register, was binding on the plaintiff as an overriding interest under section 70(1)(g) of the Land Registration Act 1925. At first instance, the defendant succeeded on the basis that it was a contractual licensee. The Court of Appeal held that the defendant was in fact a lessee (but see *Prudential Assurance Co. Ltd v. London Residuary Body* [1992] 2 A.C. 386, *ante*, p. 349); and that the lease was binding on the plaintiff. However, the Court of Appeal proceeded to consider also whether the defendant would have succeeded as a contractual licensee.

FOX L.J.:
If, as we have concluded, Arnold & Co. is a tenant, it follows that the plaintiff holds the land subject to the tenancy. That is sufficient to dispose of the claim, as the action is for possession. Since, however, we have heard full argument on the case, we will consider the position on the basis that we are wrong, and no tenancy was created.

It is Arnold & Co.'s case that even if the 1973 agreement created no tenancy after 28 February 1973, so that its occupancy thereafter is that of a contractual licensee only, its rights are nevertheless binding upon a purchaser for value with notice of the licence. Lord Templeman in *Street v. Mountford* [1985] A.C. 809, 814 said:

"A licence in connection with land while entitling the licensee to use the land for the purposes authorised by the licence does not create an estate in the land."

That was not challenged on behalf of Arnold & Co., but it was said that a contractual licence does give rise to an interest (as opposed to an estate) in the land; we must assume for this purpose that the rights are of sufficiently certain duration to be capable of subsisting as an interest in land. If they are not, the point does not arise. The question then is whether Arnold & Co.'s proposition is correct in law. Until comparatively recently it would, we think, have been rejected. As long ago as 1674, in *Thomas v. Sorrell* (1674) Vaug. 330, 351, Vaughan C.J. said:

"A dispensation or licence properly passeth no interest, nor alters or transfers property in any thing, but only makes an action lawful, which without it had been unlawful."

A number of cases in this century support that view.

Daly v. Edwardes (1900) 83 L.T. 548 was concerned with "front of house" rights in a theatre. In 1894 Edwardes granted to Daly a licence of two theatres for a term of years. The lease contained a covenant by the lessee not, inter alia, to part with any estate or interest in the premises. Daly granted to Warr:

"the free and exclusive licence or right to the use of the refreshment rooms and bars in the theatre together with the free right of access thereto."

The lessor claimed that this was a breach of the covenant against disposing of any estate or interest in the premises. That claim failed. Rigby L.J. said, at p. 551:

"On the whole, I think that the proper conclusion is that Frank Warr and Co. took no estate or interest in land, but that they were entitled for all reasonable purposes, to consider themselves as having an exclusive licence to provide refreshments and all that follows from that privilege, and nothing else."

Vaughan Williams L.J. said, at p. 551, that the agreement was "really a grant of a privilege and licence merely masquerading as a lease". The case went to the House of Lords as *Edwardes v. Barrington* (1901) 85 L.T. 650, and the decision of the Court of Appeal was affirmed.

In *Frank Warr & Co. Ltd v. London County Council* [1904] 1 K.B. 713, the London County Council compulsorily acquired the Globe Theatre. At the time of the acquisition Warr had front of house rights at the theatre under a subsisting agreement with the lessee. Compensation was only payable to persons having an interest in the land acquired. The claim failed. Collins M.R. said, at p. 722:

"Do those parts of the agreement amount merely to a licence properly so called, or to a grant of an interest in, or something arising out of, the land? To my mind it is clear that they create nothing more than a licence properly so called."

These cases, it seems to us, clearly proceed on the basis that a contractual licence creates no interest in land.

The next case is *King v. David Allen and Sons (Billposting) Ltd* [1916] 2 A.C. 54. King owned premises in Dublin. David Allen had for many years under an agreement between the predecessors of King and David Allen, enjoyed the right to exhibit posters on the wall of the premises. King wished to let the premises to a third party. David Allen had no objection provided its rights were preserved. In July 1913 King and David Allen agreed that David Allen should have exclusive permission to fix posters to the flank wall of a cinema which it was proposed to build on the site. In August 1913 King agreed with F., a trustee for a company to be formed, that a lease should be granted to the company. King was to assign to F., as a trustee for the company, his interest in the 1913 agreement, and F. agreed that the company would accept the lease and ratify the 1913 agreement. The company, when formed, duly did so. The cinema was built. The July agreement was not referred to in the lease and King did not assign his interest under that agreement to the company. David Allen attempted to post advertisements on the flank wall but the company, despite opposition from King (a director), prevented it. David Allen then sued King alleging that he was in breach of the July agreement by putting it out of his power to perform it. The claim succeeded. The company was not a party to the action but the effect of the licence vis-à-vis the company was in issue because King would not have been liable to David Allen in damages had the licence which he agreed to grant been binding on the company, which had notice of it. The House of Lords regarded the contract as creating nothing but a personal obligation. Earl Loreburn said, at p. 62:

> "Well, if the agreement of 1 July, which purports to be on the face of it a licence, was equivalent to creating an incorporeal hereditament or a sufficient interest in land, Mr King did not break his contract in making the lease, and would not be responsible for any trespasses that were committed by his licensees. But we must look at the document itself, and it seems to me that it does not create any interest in the land at all; it merely amounts to a promise on the part of Mr King that he would allow the other party to the contract to use the wall for advertising purposes, and there was an implied undertaking that he would not disable himself from carrying out his contract."

Lord Buckmaster L.C. said, at pp. 59–60:

> "There are two circumstances to which attention has been quite properly called by the appellant's counsel, which are no doubt important in considering what the agreement effected. The first is the fact of the rent reserved, and the next that there is a term of years granted and that arrangements are introduced into the agreement to prevent other people having competing rights with Messrs David Allen and Sons upon this wall. Those considerations do not, in my opinion, necessarily conflict with the view that this is nothing but a licence—a licence for a fixed term of years, but a licence which creates no estate or interest in the land ..."

We are unable to reconcile the approach of the House of Lords in *King v. David Allen* with the submission, on behalf of Arnold & Co., that a mere contractual licence is an interest in land binding on a purchaser with notice. The two front of house rights cases to which we have referred are to the same effect.

The next case of consequence is *Clore v. Theatrical Properties Ltd* [1936] 3 All E.R. 483, which was again concerned with front of house rights. The agreement provided:

> "the lessor does hereby demise and grant unto the lessee the free and exclusive use of all the refreshment rooms ... of the theatre ... for the purpose only of the supply to and accommodation of the visitors to the theatre and for no other purpose ..."

The definition clause provided that the terms "lessor" and "lessee" should include their executors, administrators and assigns. The assignee of the lessor sought to prevent an assignee of the lessee from exercising any of the rights under the agreement. It was held that the agreement was not a lease but a licence, and was not binding upon a third party. The court, as we read the judgments, regarded the case as falling within the examples of *Daly v. Edwardes* (1900) 83 L.T. 548 and *Frank Warr & Co. Ltd v. London County Council* [1904] 1 K.B. 713. The licensee had sought to rely upon *De Mattos v. Gibson* (1859) 4 De G. & J. 276 and *Lord Strathcona Steamship Co. Ltd v. Dominion Coal Co. Ltd* [1926] A.C. 108. That was not accepted, Lord Wright M.R. regarded these authorities as confined to charterparties and said, at p. 491: "I do not think that a personal covenant as in the present case can be binding on a third party with notice ..."

Down to this point we do not think that there is any serious doubt as to the law. A mere contractual licence to occupy land is not binding on a purchaser of the land even though he has notice of the licence.

We come now to a case which is of central importance on the present issue. That is *Errington v. Errington and Woods* [1952] 1 K.B. 290. A father, wishing to provide a home for his son who had recently married, bought a house with the help of a building society mortgage. He paid a lump sum towards the purchase price, the remainder of which was provided by the building society's loan. The loan was repayable by instalments. He retained the conveyance in his own name and paid the rates, but he promised that if the son and daughter-in-law continued in occupation and duly paid all the instalments, he would then transfer the property to them. The father died and by his will left the house to his widow. Up to that time the son and his wife had lived in the house and paid the instalments. The son then separated from his wife and left the house. The daughter-in-law continued to pay the mortgage instalments. The widow then sought possession of the house from the daughter-in-law. The county court judge dismissed the action. He held that the daughter-in-law was a tenant at will and that the claim against her was statute-barred. That reasoning was rejected by the Court of Appeal, though the actual decision of the judge was upheld. Denning L.J., whose reasons for dismissing the appeal were concurred in by Somervell L.J., said, at pp. 298–299:

"it seems to me that, although the couple had exclusive possession of the house, there was clearly no relationship of landlord and tenant. They were not tenants at will but licensees. They had a mere personal privilege to remain there, with no right to assign or sub-let. They were, however, not bare licensees. They were licensees with a contractual right to remain. As such they have no right at law to remain, but only in equity, and equitable rights now prevail. I confess, however, that it has taken the courts some time to reach this position. At common law a licence was always revocable at will, notwithstanding a contract to the contrary: *Wood v. Leadbitter* (1845) 13 M. & W. 838. The remedy for a breach of the contract was only in damages. That was the view generally held until a few years ago: see, for instance, what was said in *Booker v. Palmer* [1942] 2 All E.R. 674, 677 and *Thompson v. Park* [1944] K.B. 408, 410. The rule has, however, been altered owing to the interposition of equity. Law and equity have been fused for nearly 80 years, and since 1948 it has been clear that, as a result of the fusion, a licensor will not be permitted to eject a licensee in breach of a contract to allow him to remain: see *Winter Garden Theatre (London) Ltd v. Millennium Productions Ltd* [1946] 1 All E.R. 678, 680 *per* Lord Greene, and in the House of Lords *per* Lord Simon; nor in breach of a promise on which the licensee has acted, even though he gave no value for it: see *Foster v. Robinson* [1951] 1 K.B. 149, 156, where Sir Raymond Evershed M.R. said that as a result of the oral arrangement to let the man stay, he was entitled as licensee to occupy the premises without any payment of rent for the rest of his days. This infusion of equity means that contractual licences now have a force and validity of their own and cannot be revoked in breach of the contract. Neither the licensor nor anyone who claims through him can disregard the contract except a purchaser for value without notice."

It is not in doubt that the actual decision was correct. It could be justified on one of three grounds. (i) There was a contract to convey the house on completion of the payments giving rise to an equitable interest in the form of an estate contract which would be binding on the widow: see *Megarry & Wade, The Law of Real Property* 5th ed. (1984), p. 806. The widow was not a purchaser for value. (ii) The daughter-in-law had changed her position in reliance upon a representation binding on the widow as a privy of the representor: see *Spencer Bower and Turner, Estoppel by Representation* 3rd ed. (1977), p. 123. (iii) The payment of the instalments by the son or the daughter-in-law gave rise to direct proprietary interests by way of constructive trust, although it is true that, until *Gissing v. Gissing* [1971] A.C. 886, the law relating to constructive trusts in this field was not much considered.

Accordingly, it does not appear to have been necessary, in order to produce a just result, to have accepted the broad principle stated, at p. 299, in the passage which we have quoted, that "Neither the licensor nor anyone who claims through him can disregard the contract except a purchaser for value without notice". That statement itself is not supported by any citation of authority, and indeed we do not think it could have been supported on the authorities. None of the cases prior to *Errington v. Errington and Woods* to which we have referred, except *Thomas v. Sorrell* (1674), Vaugh. 330, is mentioned in the judgments and it does not appear that any was cited.

The decision of the House of Lords in *Winter Garden Theatre (London) Ltd v. Millennium Productions Ltd* [1948] A.C. 173 does not advance the matter. It was the first occasion on which a licensee was held entitled to an injunction restraining the licensor from revoking a licence in breach of contract. The case was concerned with contract only. In our view it is not an authority for the proposition that a contractual licence creates an interest in land capable of binding third parties.

National Provincial Bank Ltd v. Hastings Car Mart Ltd [1965] A.C. 1175 was the case in which the House of Lords, reversing the majority decision of the Court of Appeal [1964] Ch. 665, rejected the deserted wife's equity. Russell L.J., who dissented in the Court of Appeal, stated, at pp. 696–697:

"It is therefore necessary to consider what is the law in connection with title to unregistered land relating to rights such as those now in question. For this purpose, I consider that the deserted wife's right cannot be greater than that of a person in occupation under a contractual licence from the owner to occupy, which licence is by its terms not revocable for a period, and breach of which would be restrained by injunction against the licensor. What is the position of such a licensee in the case of unregistered land? Has he a right capable of enforcement not only against the licensor but also against a purchaser or mortgagee from the licensor?

On authority it seems to me that the answer is that he has not such a right against a purchaser for value even with actual notice of the licence. I do not propose to discuss the question exhaustively. I am content to refer generally to the article on this question on Licences and Third Parties by Professor H.W.R. Wade (68 L.Q.R. 337), and the cases there discussed of *King v. David Allen and Sons (Billposting) Ltd* [1916] 2 A.C. 54 in the House of Lords, and *Clore v. Theatrical Properties Ltd* [1936] 3 All E.R. 483 in the Court of Appeal, and to add some comments.

I am regretfully aware that this view runs counter to much that has been said, particularly by the present Master of the Rolls, especially in *Bendall v. McWhirter* [1952] 2 Q.B. 466 and is in conflict with an instructive article on Licences to Live in Houses by Mr L.A. Sheridan ((1953) 17 Conveyancer and Property Lawyer 440). But the decision of the House of Lords in *King's* case necessarily involved a decision that a contractual licence to post advertisements on a wall for a period of years was not binding upon a purchaser from the licensor with actual notice of the licence, because it created a mere personal obligation on the licensor and not an estate or interest in the land. I cannot accept that that decision depends for its validity on the fact that the licence had not yet been acted upon. In this connection, I venture to repeat that the actual occupation is not the right; it is a form of notice of a right; the right must be sought elsewhere. Since in *King's* case there was actual notice of the licence which conferred the right, the question of occupation would not seem to affect the matter. The licence rights would (or would not) affect the purchaser with actual notice of them whether or not they had been partly exercised. The *Clore* case seems plainly a case in which this court held that a personal licence to occupy, which had been acted upon for many years, was not enforceable against a purchaser with actual notice, expressly for the same reason that it created no interest in the land. I do not think that its binding authority can be properly undermined by saying that this court mistakenly assumed that as between the contracting parties revocation in breach of contract would not be restrained by injunction in accordance with what Lord Uthwatt in *Winter Garden Theatre (London) Ltd v. Millennium Productions Ltd* [1948] A.C. 173, 202 described as 'the settled practice of the courts of Equity ... to do what they can by an injunction to preserve the "sanctity of a bargain."' I do not, with respect, think that the *Clore* case can be described as one in which the licensee was not in actual occupation. The grant was of the free and exclusive use of substantial and defined parts of the premises for the purpose of exercising front of the house rights. Surely the licensee was in actual occupation of, for example, the wine cellars. And the judgment appealed from in terms declared that the defendant had 'no right to the use and occupation' of those parts referred to in the licence.

In *In re Webb's Lease* [1951] Ch. 808, in this court, the question whether the lessee could refuse to recognise the licence by the lessor to fix advertisements was not in issue for determination; counsel for the lessee conceded that he could not; but the lessee did not want to; he simply wanted as against the lessor to be entitled to receive the licence payments from the licensee. In that context the remarks of Lord Evershed M.R. [1951] Ch. 808, 821 and of Jenkins L.J. [1951] Ch. 808, 830, 831 cannot be taken as binding authority.

I desire to add on *Errington v. Errington and Woods* [1952] 1 K.B. 290, in this court, nothing to the comments in Professor Wade's article, save that I find it not easy to see, on authority, how that which has a purely contractual basis between A and B is, though on all hands it is agreed that it is not to be regarded as conferring any estate or interest in property on B, nevertheless to be treated as producing the equivalent result against a purchaser C, simply because an injunction would be granted to restrain A from breaking his contract while he is still in a position to carry it out."

When the case reached the House of Lords the observations of Russell L.J. were not expressly accepted, but nor were they rejected. Lord Hodson said, at pp. 1223–1224:

"To describe a wife as a licensee, unless that overworked word is merely used to describe a person lawfully on land and not a trespasser, is not only uncomplimentary but inaccurate. She is not a person who needs any licence from her husband to be where she has a right to be as a wife. *Thomas v. Sorrell* (1674) Vaugh. 330, 351 contains the classic definition of a licence propounded by Vaughan C.J.: 'A dispensation or licence properly passeth no interest, nor alters or transfers property in any thing, but only makes an action lawful, which without it had been unlawful.' This shows the fallacy of the analogy for the wife would not be a trespasser in her husband's house in the absence of a licence from her husband."

Lord Upjohn also considered the position of a licence, at p. 1239:

"Your Lordships heard much interesting discussion as to the rights of contractual licensees to remain in occupation as against third parties. As I emphatically decline to equate the deserted wife with a contractual licensee or to draw any analogy between the two I shall be very brief on this subject. The cases of *Foster v. Robinson* [1951] 1 K.B. 149 and *Errington v. Errington and Woods* [1952] 1 K.B. 290 were much canvassed before your Lordships. In the latter case the licensees were in exclusive occupation upon the terms of paying off the mortgage instalments and after the matrimonial rupture the wife continued to do so. This, I would have thought, would have given the spouses an interest in the land, in accordance with a well-known line of authority starting with *Webb v. Paternoster* (1619) Pop. 151, valid against all except a purchaser for value without notice.
The more interesting and really text-book case is *Foster v. Robinson*. Whether the right (undoubted contractually against the owner of the property) of Robinson the retired servant to remain in exclusive occupation of his cottage rent-free for the rest of his life will by judicial decision one day be held to create an equitable estate or interest binding all except purchasers for value without notice, or whether, as Russell L.J. thinks, statutory legislation is required to bring about that result is a matter

upon which I propose to express no opinion. On the other hand, Roxburgh J. in *Thompson v. Earthy* [1951] 2 K.B. 596, 599, may have taken the view that an exclusive licensee may thereby have an interest in the land, and Professor Cheshire supports this view in a very interesting article on this matter in (1953) 16 Modern Law Review 1. He does, I think, in that article, underestimate the difficulties created by *King v. David Allen and Sons (Billposting) Ltd* and *Clore v. Theatrical Properties Ltd.* But if it is later decided that a licensee having an irrevocable licence to remain in occupation of the land for a defined period creates an interest in land and is valid against subsequent purchasers with notice that would not affect my view that the purely personal, evanescent and changeable rights exerciseable against her husband by the deserted wife cannot affect a purchaser from the husband."

Lastly, we refer to the observations of Lord Wilberforce, at pp. 1250–1251;

"1. *The licence theory.* One main line of argument, for conferring upon the deserted wife an interest binding her husband's successors in title, has been to this effect: the wife is a licensee in the house under, so it is sometimes said, an irrevocable licence, or at least a licence which is only revocable by the court: some licences which are irrevocable are binding on purchasers with notice: ergo the wife's rights are binding on purchasers with notice. I hope that I do justice to the argument by this brief summary. I confess that I find it far from helpful. In the first place, I doubt the utility of describing the wife as a licensee. If all that is done by this is to place some descriptive label on the capacity in which the wife remains in the house, I suppose that the word 'licensee' is as good as any other, though I would think that most wives would consider this description a strange one. But what is achieved by the description? After she has been so described, the incidents of the description have to be ascertained, and the only correct process is surely to analyse what the nature of the wife's rights are, the answer being that they are rights of co-habitation and support and the right to resist dispossession by her husband if that would interfere with marital rights. What is not surely legitimate is to start by describing the wife as a licensee, and then to ascribe to her rights which are defined by reference to other kinds of licences: that is an argument per saltum. The second comment which must be made on the argument is that even if one accepts the leap from the wife as licensee to other (e.g., contractual) licensees, one has not reached a solution, for the legal position of contractual licensees, as regards 'purchasers', is very far from clear. The Court of Appeal has attempted to reach a generalisation by which licences, or at least licences coupled with occupation, are binding upon 'purchasers' but I note that the members of that court are not wholly agreed as to this doctrine. No doubt the time will come when this whole subject will have to be reviewed; this is not the occasion for it and I think that it would be undesirable now to say anything which might impede the development of this branch of the law. Neither contractual licences nor those licences where money has been expended by the licensee in my view afford any useful analogy or basis upon which to determine the character of the wife's rights.

I would only add, with reference to the authorities (1) that I must not be taken as accepting the arguments placed before the Court of Appeal whereby such cases as *King v. David Allen and Sons (Billposting) Ltd* and *Clore v. Theatrical Properties Ltd* are put on one side as not, or no longer, relevant authorities; (2) that, while accepting the actual decision I do not find that the case of *Errington v. Errington and Woods,* even if reconcilable with the two cases I have mentioned, is of assistance as to the transmissibility of contractual licences. The Court of Appeal in that case seem to have treated it simply as one of contract and not to have focused their argument on the precise legal position of the plaintiff, i.e. whether she was the legal personal representative or the successor in title of the licensor."

These cases were the subject of consideration by Goff J. in *In re Solomon, A Bankrupt, Ex parte Trustee of the Property of the Bankrupt v. Solomon* [1967] Ch. 573. Goff J. concluded that the wife in that case was not a contractual licensee, and accordingly he did not have to decide which authority he should follow. But he expressed a preference for the reasoning of Russell L.J. in the *Hastings Car Mart* case [1964] Ch. 665 and was hesitant to recognise the existence of a new species of equitable right.

It is convenient to pause at this point because, although there are later cases in what may be regarded as this series, there is none in which a contractual licence is held to bind a third party in the absence of a finding that the third party took the land as a constructive trustee. It is therefore appropriate to review how the law stands, or ought to stand, in the absence of such a finding.

Young v. Bristol Aeroplane Co. Ltd [1944] K.B. 718 establishes the familiar rule that this court is bound to follow its own decisions save that (relevantly to this case) it is entitled and bound to decide which of two conflicting decisions of its own it will follow, and it is bound to refuse to follow a decision of its own which, though not expressly overruled, cannot in its opinion stand with a decision of the House of Lords.

It must, we think, be very doubtful whether this court's decision in *Errington v. Errington and Woods* [1952] 1 K.B. 290 is consistent with its earlier decisions in *Daly v. Edwardes* (1900) 83 L.T. 548; *Frank Warr & Co. Ltd v. London County Council* [1904] 1 K.B. 713 and *Clore v. Theatrical Properties Ltd* [1936] 3 All E.R. 483. That decision cannot be said to be in conflict with any later decision of the House of Lords, because the House expressly left the effect of a contractual licence open in the *Hastings Car Mart* case. But there must be very real doubts whether *Errington* can be reconciled with the earlier decisions of the House of Lords in *Edwardes v. Barrington* (1901) 85 L.T. 650 and *King v. David Allen and Sons (Billposting) Ltd* [1916] 2 A.C. 54. It would seem that we must follow those cases or choose between the two lines of authority. It is not, however, necessary to consider those alternative courses in detail, since in our judgment the House of Lords cases, whether or not as a matter of strict precedent they conclude this question, state the correct principle which we should follow.

Our reasons for reaching this conclusion are based upon essentially the same reasons as those given by Russell L.J. in the *Hastings Car Mart* case [1964] Ch. 665, 697 and by Professor Wade in the article, "Licences and Third Parties" (1952) 68 L.Q.R. 337, to which Russell L.J. refers. Before *Errington* the law appears to have been clear and well understood. It rested on an important and intelligible distinction between contractual obligations which gave rise to no estate or interest in the land and proprietary rights which, by definition, did. The far-reaching statement of principle in *Errington* was not supported by authority, not necessary for the decision of the case and per incuriam in the sense that it was made without reference to authorities which, if they would not have compelled, would surely have persuaded the court to adopt a different ratio. Of course, the law must be free to develop. But as a response to problems which had arisen, the *Errington* rule (without more) was neither practically necessary nor theoretically convincing. By contrast, the finding on appropriate facts of a constructive trust may well be regarded as a beneficial adaptation of old rules to new situations.

The constructive trust principle, to which we now turn, has been long established and has proved to be highly flexible in practice. It covers a wide variety of cases from that of a trustee who makes a profit out of his trust or a stranger who knowingly deals with trust properties, to the many cases where the courts have held that a person who directly or indirectly contributes to the acquisition of a dwelling house purchased in the name of and conveyed to another has some beneficial interest in the property. The test, for the present purposes, is whether the owner of the property has so conducted himself that it would be inequitable to allow him to deny the claimant an interest in the property: see *Gissing v. Gissing* [1971] A.C. 886, 905 *per* Lord Diplock.

In *Bannister v. Bannister* [1948] 2 All E.R. 133, on the plaintiff's oral undertaking that the defendant continue to live in a cottage rent free for as long as she wished, the defendant agreed to sell to him that and an adjacent cottage. The conveyance contained no reference to the undertaking. The plaintiff thereafter occupied the whole cottage save for one room which was occupied by the defendant. The plaintiff after a time sought to expel the defendant. The Court of Appeal (Scott and Asquith L.JJ. and Jenkins J.) held that he was not entitled to. Scott L.J., giving the judgment of the court, said, at p. 136:

"It is, we think, clearly a mistake to suppose that the equitable principle on which a constructive trust is raised against a person who insists on the absolute character of a conveyance to himself for the purpose of defeating a beneficial interest, which, according to the true bargain, was to belong to another, is confined to cases in which the conveyance itself was fraudulently obtained. The fraud which brings the principle into play arises as soon as the absolute character of the conveyance is set up for the purpose of defeating the beneficial interest. ... Nor is it, in our opinion, necessary that the bargain on which the absolute conveyance is made should include any express stipulation that the grantee is in so many words to hold as trustee. It is enough that the bargain should have included a stipulation under which some sufficiently defined beneficial interest in the property was to be taken by another."

In *In re Schebsman, decd.* [1944] Ch. 83, 89, Lord Greene M.R. said:

"It is not legitimate to import into the contract the idea of a trust when the parties have given no indication that such was their intention."

Du Parcq L.J. said, at p. 104, that "the court ought not to be astute to discover indications of such an intention". We do not, however, regard either of these observations as differing from what Scott L.J. said in *Bannister v. Bannister*. It is, we think, in every case a question of what is the reasonable inference from the known facts.

We come then to four cases in which the application of the principle to particular facts has been considered.

In *Binions v. Evans* [1972] Ch. 359, the defendant's husband was employed by an estate and lived rent free in a cottage owned by the estate. The husband died when the defendant was 73. The trustees of the estate then entered into an agreement with the defendant that she could continue to live in the cottage during her lifetime as tenant at will rent free; she undertook to keep the cottage in good condition and repair. Subsequently the estate sold the cottage to the plaintiffs. The contract provided that the property was sold subject to the tenancy. In consequence of that provision the plaintiffs paid a reduced price for the cottage. The plaintiffs sought to eject the defendant, claiming that she was tenant at will. That claim failed. In the Court of Appeal Megaw and Stephenson L.JJ. decided the case on the ground that the defendant was a tenant for life under the Settled Land Act 1925. Lord Denning M.R. did not agree with that. He held that the plaintiffs took the property subject to a constructive trust for the defendant's benefit. In our view that is a legitimate application of the doctrine of constructive trusts. The estate would certainly have allowed the defendant to live in the house during her life in accordance with their agreement with her. They provided the plaintiffs with a copy of the agreement they made. The agreement for sale was subject to the agreement, and they accepted a lower purchase price in consequence. In the circumstances it was a proper inference that on the sale to the plaintiffs, the intention of the estate and the plaintiffs was that the plaintiffs should give effect to the tenancy agreement. If they had failed to do so, the estate would have been liable in damages to the defendant.

In *D.H.N. Food Distributors Ltd v. Tower Hamlets Borough Council* [1976] 1 W.L.R. 852, premises were owned by Bronze Investments Ltd but occupied by an associated company (D.H.N.) under an informal agreement between them—they were part of a group. The premises were subsequently purchased by the council and the issue was compensation for disturbance. It was said that Bronze was not disturbed and that D.H.N. had no interest in the property. The Court of Appeal held that D.H.N. had an irrevocable licence to occupy the land. Lord Denning M.R. said, at p. 859:

"It was equivalent to a contract between the two companies whereby Bronze granted an irrevocable licence to DHN to carry on their business on the premises. In this situation Mr Dobry cited to us *Binions v. Evans* [1972] Ch. 359 to which I would add *Bannister v. Bannister* [1948] 2 All E.R. 133 and *Siew Soon Wah v. Young Tong Hong* [1973] A.C. 836. Those cases show that a contractual licence (under which a person has a right to occupy premises indefinitely) gives rise to a constructive trust, under which the legal owner is not allowed to turn out the licensee. So, here. This irrevocable licence gave to DHN a sufficient interest in the land to qualify them for compensation for disturbance."

Goff L.J. made this a ground for his decision also.

On that authority, Browne-Wilkinson J. in *In re Sharpe (A Bankrupt), Ex parte Trustee of the Bankrupt's Property v. The Bankrupt* [1980] 1 W.L.R. 219 felt bound to conclude that, without more, an irrevocable licence to occupy gave rise to a property interest. He evidently did so with hesitation. For the reasons which we have already indicated, we prefer the line of authorities which determine that a contractual licence does not create a property interest. We do not think that the argument is assisted by the bare assertion that the interest arises under a constructive trust.

In *Lyus v. Prowsa Developments Ltd* [1982] 1 W.L.R. 1044, the plaintiffs contracted to buy a plot of registered land which was part of an estate being developed by the vendor company. A house was to be built which would then be occupied by the plaintiffs. The plaintiffs paid a deposit to the company, which afterwards became insolvent before the house was built. The company's bank held a legal charge, granted before the plaintiffs' contract, over the whole estate. The bank was under no liability to complete the plaintiffs' contract. The bank, as mortgagee, sold the land to the first defendant. By the contract of sale it was provided that the land was sold subject to and with the benefit of the plaintiffs' contract. Subsequently, the first defendant contracted to sell the plot to the second defendant. The contract provided that the land was sold subject to the plaintiffs' contract so far, if at all, as it might be enforceable against the first defendant. The contract was duly completed. In the action the plaintiffs sought a declaration that their contract was binding on the defendants and an order for specific performance. The action succeeded. This again seems to us to be a case where a constructive trust could justifiably be imposed. The bank were selling as mortgagees under a charge prior in date to the contract. They were therefore not bound by the contract and on any view could give a title which was free from it. There was, therefore, no point in making the conveyance subject to the contract unless the parties intended the purchaser to give effect to the contract. Further, on the sale by the bank a letter had been written to the bank's agents, Messrs Strutt & Parker, by the first defendant's solicitors, giving an assurance that their client would take reasonable steps to make sure the interests of contractual purchasers were dealt with quickly and to their satisfaction. How far any constructive trust so arising was on the facts of that case enforceable by the plaintiffs against owners for the time being of the land we do not need to consider.

In re Sharpe [1980] 1 W.L.R. 219 seems to us a much more difficult case in which to imply a constructive trust against the trustee in bankruptcy and his successors, and we do not think it could be done. Browne-Wilkinson J. did not, in fact, do so. He felt (understandably, we think) bound by authority to hold that an irrevocable licence to occupy was a property interest. In *In re Sharpe* although the aunt provided money for the purchase of the house, she did not thereby acquire any property interest in the ordinary sense, since the judge held that it was advanced by way of a loan, though, no doubt, she may have had some rights of occupation as against the debtor. And when the trustee in bankruptcy, before entering into the contract of sale, wrote to the aunt to find out what rights, if any, she claimed in consequence of the provision of funds by her, she did not reply. The trustee in bankruptcy then sold with vacant possession. These facts do not suggest a need in equity to impose constructive trust obligations on the trustee or his successors.

We come to the present case. It is said that when a person sells land and stipulates that the sale should be "subject to" a contractual licence, the court will impose a constructive trust upon the purchaser to give effect to the licence: see *Binions v. Evans* [1972] Ch. 359, 368 *per* Lord Denning M.R. We do not feel able to accept that as a general proposition. We agree with the observations of Dillon J. in *Lyus v. Prowsa Developments Ltd* [1982] 1 W.L.R. 1044, 1051:

> "By contrast, there are many cases in which land is expressly conveyed subject to possible incumbrances when there is no thought at all of conferring any fresh rights on third parties who may be entitled to the benefit of the incumbrances. The land is expressed to be sold subject to incumbrances to satisfy the vendor's duty to disclose all possible incumbrances known to him, and to protect the vendor against any possible claim by the purchaser. ... So, for instance, land may be contracted to be sold and may be expressed to be conveyed subject to the restrictive covenants contained in a conveyance some 60 to 90 years old. No one would suggest that by accepting such a form of contract or conveyance a purchaser is assuming a new liability in favour of third parties to observe the covenants if there was for any reason before the contract or conveyance no one who could make out a title as against the purchaser to the benefit of the covenants."

The court will not impose a constructive trust unless it is satisfied that the conscience of the estate owner is affected. The mere fact that that land is expressed to be conveyed "subject to" a contract does not necessarily imply that the grantee is to be under an obligation, not otherwise existing, to give effect to the provisions of the contract. The fact that the conveyance is expressed to be subject to the contract may often, for the reasons indicated by Dillon J., be at least as consistent with an intention merely to protect the grantor against claims by the grantee as an intention to impose an obligation on the grantee. The words "subject to" will, of course, impose notice. But notice is not enough to impose on somebody an obligation to give effect to a contract into which he did not enter. Thus, mere notice of a restrictive covenant is not enough to impose upon the estate owner an obligation or equity to give effect to it: *London County Council v. Allen* [1914] 3 K.B. 642.

NOTES:

1. The Court of Appeal concluded that the facts did not justify the imposition of a constructive trust. In particular, the plaintiffs did not appear to have paid a lower price for the site to reflect any interest or claim of the defendant; and the terms of the sale to the plaintiffs were insufficient to indicate that the plaintiffs were assuming an obligation to give effect to the defendant's agreement.

2. There was general welcome for the disapproval of dicta to the effect that a contractual licence is an equitable interest in land or can without more bind a successor in title of the licensor: Oakley [1988] C.L.J. 353; Thompson [1988] Conv. 201; Sparkes (1988) 104 L.Q.R. 175; Hill (1988) 51 M.L.R. 226.

3. Thompson [1988] Conv. 201 argues that the imposition of a constructive trust is not the appropriate solution to the problem: it runs directly counter to the doctrine of privity and creates uncertainty as to the ambit of the trust.

4. For earlier academic reviews of the constructive trust cases leading to *Re Sharpe* [1980] 1 W.L.R. 219, see Martin [1980] Conv. 207; Woodman (1980) 96 L.Q.R. 336. They express the views (i) that the cases provide dubious authority for the proposition that contractual licences give rise to equitable

interests under constructive trusts; and (ii) that *Re Sharpe* could and should have been seen as an estoppel licence. On the basis of these cases Everton [1982] Conv. 118 (at 125–132, 183–184) argues for the recognition of a new concept of "quasi-property". For earlier proposals on both contractual licences and licences protected by proprietary estoppel, see Everton (1976) 40 Conv. 209, 416.

5. On *D.H.N. Food Distributors Ltd v. Tower Hamlets LBC* [1976] 1 W.L.R. 852, see [1977] C.L.J. 12; (1977) 93 L.Q.R. 170, 172–173.

6. For subsequent judicial affirmation of the repudiation of the "heretical view that a contractual licence creates an interest in land capable of binding third parties", see *Camden LBC v. Shortlife Community Housing* (1992) 90 L.G.R. 358, 373 *per* Millett J.; and see *Canadian Imperial Bank of Commerce v. Bello* (1992) 64 P. & C.R. 48, 51 *per* Dillon L.J.; *Nationwide Anglia Building Society v. Ahmed* (1995) 70 P. & C.R. 381, 387–389 *per* Aldous L.J.

7. Hill (1988) 51 M.L.R. 226 argues that the clarification as to the effect of contractual licences on third parties only serves to highlight the general assumption that estoppel licences are capable of binding third parties. He expresses the view that the potential effect on successors in title should be similar unless the two types of licence can be clearly and defensibly distinguished. See *infra*, p. 605.

8. For discussion of the decision of the Court of Appeal that the defendant was a lessee, see *ante*, p. 349.

5. Contractual licences and interests in land

It is arguable that the controversy surrounding the effect of contractual licences on successors in title of the original licensor has been unnecessarily exacerbated by the terminology of proprietary interests in land and by an insistence on an exhaustive dichotomy of proprietary interests, which are enforceable against successors in title, and personal rights affecting land, which are not enforceable against successors in title. This approach is exemplified by Russell L.J., who, in his judgment in *National Provincial Bank Ltd v. Hastings Car Mart Ltd* [1964] Ch. 665, stated (at 669) that contractual licences cannot bind third parties because they are not property rights. However, it has been argued that such an approach is self-fulfilling because it begins with the conclusion: (i) a licence is not a proprietary interest; (ii) the capacity to bind third parties is a characteristic exclusive to proprietary interests; (iii) therefore a licence cannot bind third parties. It has therefore been suggested that a more appropriate approach, which better reflects the practical issue raised by the factual and legal circumstances of contractual licences, would be simply to pose the question whether a contractual licence is enforceable against successors in title of the original licensor. Such an approach would not only concentrate on the practical issue; it would also avoid the unnecessary obscuring of that issue by the consideration of other attributes of established proprietary interests, such as assignability, which are not normally in issue in the context of contractual licences.

Although the Court of Appeal in *Ashburn Anstalt v. Arnold* has purported to settle the status of contractual licences and the question of their enforceability against successors in title, the decision is not wholly free from uncertainty. Moreover, the subsequent case law has continued to use the terminology of proprietary interests: see, *e.g. Camden LBC v. Shortlife Community Housing* (1992) 90 L.G.R. 358, 373 *per* Millett J.; *Canadian Imperial Bank of Commerce v. Bello* (1992) 64 P. & C.R. 48, 51 *per* Dillon L.J. Further consideration by the House of Lords may produce authoritative clarification; but it is arguable that such clarification may be better achieved if the real issue of enforceability is addressed directly.

E. PROPRIETARY ESTOPPEL

1. Development of the doctrine

The doctrine of proprietary estoppel is a form of equitable estoppel which creates or affects property rights. Within the particular context of licences, it may operate to confer an interest in land on a licensee or at least to restrict the owner of the land in question from exercising his strict legal rights and revoking a licence. However, the operation of the doctrine extends beyond the context of licences and the doctrine has been invoked generally to prevent the unconscionable assertion of strict legal property rights. The essence of the doctrine is that where A gives some assurance to B, or otherwise encourages some belief in B, that B has or will acquire some interest in A's property, and A intends that assurance or belief to be relied upon (or knows that it will be relied upon or that it is being relied upon), then if B does rely on that assurance or belief and acts to his detriment, A will not be permitted to act inconsistently with the assurance or belief where it would be unconscionable for him to do so, unless B has in some way disqualified himself from seeking the assistance of equity. Where, to use the traditional formulation, "an equity has thus been raised in favour of B", it is for the court to determine the appropriate remedy to "satisfy that equity". As will be seen, proprietary estoppel can give rise to rights in B that are enforceable not only against A but also against successors in title of A.

The formulation of the requirements for the operation of the doctrine has proceeded through various stages. The classic earlier authorities are the cases of *Ramsden v. Dyson* (1866) L.R. 1 H.L. 129 (*per* Lord Cranworth L.C. at 140–141; *per* Lord Kingsdown at 170) and *Willmott v. Barber* (1880) 15 Ch D. 96 (*per* Fry J. at 105–106). These and other more recent authorities are discussed in an exhaustive analysis by Oliver J. in *Taylors Fashions Ltd v. Liverpool Victoria Trustees Co. Ltd* [1982] Q.B. 133.

Taylors Fashions Ltd v. Liverpool Victoria Trustees Co. Ltd; Old & Campbell Ltd v. Liverpool Victoria Trustees Co. Ltd [1982] Q.B. 133

(QBD, Oliver J.)

The second plaintiffs were the freehold owners of adjoining commercial premises (Nos 21 and 22), titles to which were unregistered. In 1948 (i) they granted to the predecessors in title of the first plaintiffs a 28-year lease of No. 22, with an option to renew the lease for a further 14 years provided that the tenants installed a lift in the premises; but the option was not registered as a class C(iv) land charge under the Land Charges Act 1925; (ii) they sold the freehold of Nos 21 and 22 to the defendants, who also owned the freehold of No. 20; and (iii) they themselves were granted a 42-year lease of No. 21, subject to termination after 28 years if the tenants of No. 22 did not exercise the option to renew. In 1958 the lease of No. 22 was assigned to the first plaintiffs, who, with the acquiescence of the defendants, installed a lift in the premises. In 1962, the defendants granted to the second plaintiffs a 14-year lease of No. 20, with an option to renew the lease for a further 14 years if the tenants of No. 22 exercised their option to renew. The second plaintiffs carried out extensive work on Nos 20 and 21. In 1976 the first plaintiffs served notice on the defendants, purporting to exercise the option to renew the lease of No. 22. The defendants argued that, since the option had not been registered when they purchased the freehold of No. 22 in 1948, the option was void as against them; and they served notice to quit on the first and second plaintiffs. Both plaintiffs sought, *inter alia*, a declaration that the defendants were estopped from asserting their strict legal rights.

OLIVER J.:

The points which arise for decision, therefore, are these. (1) Is Taylors' option, as the defendants claim and as the plaintiffs contest, void against the defendants for want of registration? (2) If it is, are the defendants estopped as against Taylors from relying upon this ground of invalidity having regard to the expenditure by Taylors made with the defendants' concurrence in 1959 and 1960? (3) If the option is indeed unenforceable against the defendants, has it nevertheless been "exercised" for the purposes of the break and renewal clauses in the lease to Olds? (4) If it has not, are the defendants estopped as against Olds from relying upon the invalidity of an option which their own grants assert to be subsisting?

The first of these questions has been the subject matter of previous decisions to which I shall have to refer, but Mr Scott, for Taylors, submits that I am not bound by them and presents an argument which, so far as I know, has not been presented, at any rate in this form, in any of the previous cases. He puts the case thus. The Land Charges Act 1925 (which was the statute in force at the material time) was concerned with the registration of interests in land or equitable burdens on land and was designed to substitute registration as a land charge for the equitable doctrine of notice in those cases where, prior to 1925, the binding effect of the interest on a subsequent purchaser depended upon notice. The Act of course, also applies to certain statutory or legal interests (for instance, a puisne mortgage) but the important point for Mr Scott is that it applies to interests in land, not to merely contractual rights, or, in those cases where it does apply to merely contractual burdens, it applies only to those which, prior to 1925, depended for their enforceability against subsequent purchasers on the doctrine of notice (e.g. restrictive covenants). The Act provides, in section 10, that interests or obligations of this sort may be registered as land charges of the appropriate class and class C defines estate contracts as including "a valid option to purchase, a right of pre-emption or any other like right". Section 13(2) provides that a land charge of this type

> "shall be void as against a purchaser of the land charged therewith, or of any interest in such land, unless the land charge is registered in the appropriate register before the completion of the purchase."

That means, Mr Scott submits, that it is void as a land charge, that is, as an interest in or incumbrance on the land, even if the purchaser has notice of the interest, and one sees this reflected in sections 198 and 199 of the Law of Property Act 1925 which provide respectively that registration shall constitute actual notice and that a purchaser shall not be prejudicially affected by notice of a registrable charge if it is not registered. But, Mr Scott submits, none of this touches contractual obligations which, by statute and quite independently of any equitable doctrine of notice, bind a purchaser as an integral part of the land purchased. The obligation resting on a reversioner under an option to renew in a lease is one of the obligations which, ever since the statute 32 Hen. 8 c. 34 [Grantees of Reversions Act 1540], has run with the land and remained binding at law quite regardless of any question of notice. It binds the reversioner not because it is an interest in land, although it may incidentally create one, but because it is a contractual obligation statutorily annexed to the land to which the Land Charges Act 1925 has no application. Indeed it is expressly provided in section 6 of the Law of Property Act 1925 that nothing in Part I of the Act (and this must I think be referring particularly to the provisions of section 1(3)) affects prejudicially the right to enforce (inter alia) lessor's covenants the burden of which runs with the reversion.

There is, I think, a logic in Mr Scott's submissions, which accord with the view of the original authors of *Wolstenholme and Cherry's Conveyancing Statutes*, with what Harman J. thought was the policy of the legislation in *Hollington Brothers Ltd v. Rhodes* [1951] 2 All E.R. 578 and with the practice of the legal profession up to 1960. This view of the matter moreover derives some support from the analysis of the anomalous nature of covenants running with the land contained in the judgment of Farwell J. in *Muller v. Trafford* [1901] 1 Ch. 54, 61. They are not executory in nature but bind the land from their inception and "pass with it in much the same way as title deeds". But whatever might have been my view of the matter if it were still res integra, it is not so in fact and the judgment of Buckley J. in *Beesly v. Hallwood Estates Ltd* [1960] 1 W.L.R. 549 is direct authority for the proposition that an unregistered option for renewal in a lease is void and unenforceable against a purchaser for money or money's worth of the reversion. That case is no less an authority because the actual decision in favour of the plaintiff was based on an entirely different point and was affirmed by the Court of Appeal [1961] Ch. 105 on that ground. It has been adopted as correct, although apparently without argument, by the Court of Appeal in *Greene v. Church Commissioners for England* [1974] Ch. 467 and *Kitney v. MEPC Ltd* [1977] 1 W.L.R. 981, although in neither case was Mr Scott's point argued. Nor indeed is it clear that the case before Buckley J. was argued in this way. Mr Scott submits that I am not bound by *Beesly's* case, and that, on the authority of *National Enterprises Ltd v. Racal Communications Ltd* [1975] Ch. 397 the existence of two Court of Appeal decisions where the specific point was not argued does not preclude me from declining to follow it. That may be so, but nevertheless *Beesly's* case was a considered judgment on a difficult point of statutory interpretation and it has been followed and acted upon for the past 18 years. Quite apart from judicial comity and from the respect that I would feel for any decision from that source, I am mindful of the remarks of Maugham J. in *In re Smith* [1930] 1 Ch. 88, 90, remarks, I should add, which were also made in the context of the 1925 property legislation. He said:

> "I take this opportunity of repeating what I have said on previous occasions, that where a learned judge, after consideration, has come to a definite decision on a

matter arising out of this exceedingly complicated and difficult legislation, it is very desirable that the court should follow that decision, and accordingly I should be strongly inclined, whatever my own view was, to follow what I take to be the positive decision of Tomlin J."

In my judgment, *Beesly's* case [1961] Ch. 105 must be taken as representing the law and I would not feel at liberty, at this level, to depart from it now, even where I so minded to do.

I approach the case, therefore, on the footing that, whatever the parties may have thought, the option was in fact void as against the defendants (although of course still contractually binding as between the original parties) from the moment when they completed their purchase. This brings me to the second and fourth questions which I have postulated above. As regards the general principles applicable I can treat the two questions together, although there are certain circumstances peculiar to Olds and some additional arguments of law in their case to which I shall have to refer later on. The starting point of both Mr Scott's and Mr Essayan's arguments on estoppel is the same and was expressed by Mr Essayan in the following proposition: if A under an expectation created or encouraged by B that A shall have a certain interest in land, thereafter, on the faith of such expectation and with the knowledge of B and without objection by him, acts to his detriment in connection with such land, a Court of Equity will compel B to give effect to such expectation. This is a formulation which Mr Millett [counsel for the defendants] accepts but subject to one important qualification, namely that at the time when he created and encouraged the expectation and (I think that he would also say) at the time when he permitted the detriment to be incurred (if those two points of time are different) B not only knows of A's expectation but must be aware of his true rights and that he was under no existing obligation to grant the interest.

This is the principal point upon which the parties divide. Mr Scott and Mr Essayan contend that what the court has to look at in relation to the party alleged to be estopped is only his conduct and its result, and not— or, at any rate, not necessarily— his state of mind. It then has to ask whether what that party is now seeking to do is unconscionable. Mr Millett contends that it is an essential feature of this particular equitable doctrine that the party alleged to be estopped must, before the assertion of his strict rights can be considered unconscionable, be aware both of what his strict rights were and of the fact that the other party is acting in the belief that they will not be enforced against him.

The point is a critical one in the instant case and it is one upon which the authorities appear at first sight to be divided. The starting point is *Ramsden v. Dyson* (1866) L.R. 1 H.L. 129 where a tenant under a tenancy at will had built upon the land in the belief that he would be entitled to demand a long lease. The majority in the House of Lords held that he would not, but Lord Kingsdown dissented on the facts. There was no—or certainly no overt—disagreement between their Lordships as to the applicable principle, but it was stated differently by Lord Cranworth L.C. and Lord Kingsdown and the real question is how far Lord Cranworth was purporting to make an exhaustive exposition of principle and how far what he stated as the appropriate conditions for its application are to be treated, as it were, as being subsumed sub silentio in the speech of Lord Kingsdown. Lord Cranworth expressed it thus, at pp. 140–141:

"If a stranger begins to build on my land supposing it to be his own, and I, perceiving his mistake, abstain from setting him right, and leave him to persevere in his error, a court of equity will not allow me afterwards to assert my title to the land on which he had expended money on the supposition that the land was his own. It considers that, when I saw the mistake into which he had fallen, it was my duty to be active and to state my adverse title; and that it would be dishonest in me to remain wilfully passive on such an occasion, in order afterwards to profit by the mistake which I might have prevented. But it will be observed that to raise such an equity two things are required, first, that the person expending the money supposes himself to be building on his own land; and, secondly, that the real owner at the time of the expenditure knows that the land belongs to him and not to the person expending the money in the belief that he is the owner. For if a stranger builds on my land knowing it to be mine, there is no principle of equity which would prevent my claiming the land with the benefit of all the expenditure made on it. There would be nothing in my conduct, active or passive, making it inequitable in me to assert my legal rights."

So here, clearly stated, is the criterion upon which Mr Millett relies. Lord Kingsdown stated the matter differently and rather more broadly although in the narrower context of landlord and tenant. He says, at p. 170:

"The rule of law applicable to the case appears to me to be this: If a man, under a verbal agreement with a landlord for a certain interest in land, or, what amounts to the same thing, under an expectation, created or encouraged by the landlord, that he shall have a certain interest, takes possession of such land, with the consent of the landlord, and upon the faith of such promise or expectation, with the knowledge of the landlord, and without objection by him, lays out money upon the land, a court of equity will compel the landlord to give effect to such promise or expectation. This was the principle of the decision in *Gregory v. Mighell* (1811) Ves.Jun. 328 and, as I conceive, is open to no doubt."

So here, there is no specific requirement, at any rate in terms, that the landlord should know or intend that the expectation which he has created or encouraged is one to which he is under no obligation to give effect.

Mr Millett does not—nor could he in the light of the authorities—dispute the principle. What he contends is that even if (which he contests) this is a case where the defendants could be said to have encouraged the plaintiffs' expectations—and that it is not necessarily the same as having encouraged or acquiesced in the expenditure—the principle has no application to a case where, at the time when the expectation was encouraged, both parties were acting under a mistake of law as to their rights.

There is, he submits, a clear distinction between cases of proprietary estoppel or estoppel by acquiescence on the one hand and promissory estoppel or estoppel by representation (whether express or by conduct) on the other. In the latter case, the court looks at the knowledge of the party who has acted and the effect upon him of his having acted. The state of mind of the promisor or representor (except to the extent of knowing, either actually or inferentially, that his promise or representation is likely to be acted upon) is largely irrelevant. In the former case, however, it is essential, Mr Millett submits, to show that the party alleged to have encouraged or acquiesced in the other party's belief himself knew the true position, for if he did not there can be nothing unconscionable in his subsequently seeking to rely upon it. Mr Millett concedes that there may be cases which straddle this convenient dichotomy—cases which can be put either as cases of encouragement or proprietary estoppel on Lord Kingsdown's principle or as estoppel by representation, express or implied. But, he submits, the party alleging the estoppel must, whichever way he elects to put his case or even if he runs them as alternatives, demonstrate the presence of all the essential ingredients of whatever type of estoppel he relies on. He cannot manufacture a third and new hybrid type of estoppel by an eclectic application of some of the ingredients of each. So, if he wishes to put his case as one of estoppel by representation, he must, for instance, show an unequivocal representation of existing fact. Equally, if he wants to rely upon the circumstances of the case as raising a proprietary estoppel arising from acquiescence in his having acted upon an erroneous supposition of his legal rights, then he must accept the burden of showing that the error was known to the other party.

So far as proprietary estoppel or estoppel by acquiescence is concerned, he supports his submission by reference to the frequently cited judgment of Fry J. in *Willmott v. Barber* (1880) 15 Ch.D. 96 which contains what are described as the five "probanda".

The actual case was one where what was alleged was a waiver by acquiescence. A lease contained a covenant against assigning subletting or parting with possession without the lessor's consent and the lessee had let a sublessee into possession of part of the land under an agreement with him which entitled him to occupy that part for the whole term and conferred an option to purchase the remaining land for the balance of the term outstanding when the option was exercised. The sublessee built on the land and the head landlord was aware that he was in possession and was expending money. It was, however, proved that he did not then know that his consent was required to a sub-letting or assignment. The question arose between the sublessee and the head landlord when the sublessee tried to exercise his option over the remaining land and found himself met with the response that the head landlord refused consent to the assignment. The case was, on Fry J.'s finding of fact, one simply of acquiescence by standing by and what was being argued was that the landlord was estopped by his knowledge of the plaintiff's expenditure on the part of the land of which the plaintiff *was* in possession from withholding his consent to an assignment of that part of which he was not. It having been found as a fact that the landlord did not, at the time of the plaintiff's expenditure, know about the covenant against assignment and that there was nothing in what had passed between them to suggest either that the landlord was aware that the plaintiff was labouring under the belief that no consent was necessary or to encourage that belief, Fry J. dismissed the plaintiff's claim. It has to be borne in mind, however, in reading the judgment, that this was a pure acquiescence case where what was relied on was a waiver of the landlord's rights by standing by without protest. It was a case of mere silence where what had to be established by the plaintiff was some duty in the landlord to speak. The passage from the judgment in *Willmott v. Barber* (1880) 15 Ch.D. 96 most frequently cited is where Fry J. says, at pp. 105–106:

"A man is not to be deprived of his legal rights unless he has acted in such a way as would make it fraudulent for him to set up those rights. What, then, are the elements or requisites necessary to constitute fraud of that description? In the first place the plaintiff must have made a mistake as to his legal rights. Secondly, the plaintiff must have expended some money or must have done some act (not necessarily upon the defendant's land) on the faith of his mistaken belief. Thirdly, the defendant, the possessor of the legal right, must know of the existence of his own right which is inconsistent with the right claimed by the plaintiff. If he does not know of it he is in the same position as the plaintiff, and the doctrine of acquiescence is founded upon conduct with a knowledge of your legal rights. Fourthly, the defendant, the possessor of the legal right, must know of the plaintiff's mistaken belief of his rights. If he does not, there is nothing which calls upon him to assert his own rights. Lastly, the defendant, the possessor of the legal right, must have encouraged the plaintiff in his expenditure of money or in the other acts which he has done, either directly or by abstaining from asserting his legal right. Where all these elements exist, there is fraud of such a nature as will entitle the court to restrain the possessor of the legal right from exercising it, but, in my judgment, nothing short of this will do."

Mr Millett's submission is that when one applies these five probanda to the facts of the instant case it will readily be seen that they are not all complied with. In particular, Mr Millett submits, the fourth probandum involves two essential elements, viz., (i) knowledge by the possessor of the legal right of the other party's belief; and (ii) knowledge that that belief is mistaken. In the instant case the defendants were not aware of their inconsistent right to treat the option as void and equally they could not, thus, have been aware that the plaintiff's belief in the validity of the option was a mistaken belief. The alternative approach via estoppel by representation is not, he submits, open to the plaintiffs in this case because so far as Taylors were concerned the defendants made no representation to them at all and so far as Olds were concerned the representation of the continuing validity of the option, if there was one at all, was a representation of law.

Now, convenient and attractive as I find Mr Millett's submissions as a matter of argument, I am not at all sure that so orderly and tidy a theory is really deducible from the authorities—certainly from the more recent authorities, which seem to me to support a much wider equitable jurisdiction to interfere in cases where the assertion of strict legal rights is found by the court to be unconscionable. It may well be (although I think that this must now be considered open to doubt) that the strict *Willmott v. Barber* (1880) 15 Ch.D. 96 probanda are applicable as necessary requirements in those cases where all that has happened is that the party alleged to be estopped has stood by without protest while his rights have been infringed. It is suggested in *Spencer Bower and Turner, Estoppel by Representation*, 3rd ed. (1977), para. 290 that acquiescence, in its strict sense, is merely an instance of estoppel by representation and this derives some support from the judgment of the Court of Appeal in *De Bussche v. Alt* (1878) 8 Ch.D. 286, 314. If that is a correct analysis then, in a case of mere passivity, it is readily intelligible that there must be shown a duty to speak, protest or interfere which cannot normally arise in the absence of knowledge or at least a suspicion of the true position. Thus for a landowner to stand by while a neighbour lays drains in land which the landowner does not believe that he owns (*Armstrong v. Sheppard & Short Ltd* [1959] 2 Q.B. 348) or for a remainderman not to protest at a lease by a tenant for life which he believes he has no right to challenge (*Svenson v. Payne* (1945) 71 C.L.R. 531) does not create an estoppel. Again, where what is relied on is a waiver by acquiescence, as in *Willmott v. Barber* itself, the five probanda are no doubt appropriate. There is, however, no doubt that there are judicial pronouncements of high authority which appear to support as essential the application of all the five probanda over the broader field covering all cases generally classified as estoppel by "encouragement" or "acquiescence": see, for instance, the speech of Lord Diplock in *Kammins Ballrooms Co. Ltd v. Zenith Investments (Torquay) Ltd* [1971] A.C. 850, 884.

Mr Scott submits, however, that it is historically wrong to treat these probanda as holy writ and to restrict equitable interference only to those cases which can be confined within the strait-jacket of some fixed rule governing the circumstances in which, and in which alone, the court will find that a party is behaving unconscionably. Whilst accepting that the five probanda may form an appropriate test in cases of silent acquiescence, he submits that the authorities do not support the absolute necessity for compliance with all five probanda, and, in particular, the requirement of knowledge on the part of the party estopped that the other party's belief is a mistaken belief, in cases where the conduct relied on has gone beyond mere silence and amounts to active encouragement. In Lord Kingsdown's example in *Ramsden v. Dyson* (1866) L.R. 1 H.L. 129, for instance, there is no room for the literal application of the probanda, for the circumstances there postulated do not presuppose a "mistake" on anybody's part, but merely the fostering of an expectation in the minds of *both* parties at the time but from which, once it has been acted upon, it would be unconscionable to permit the landlord to depart. As Scarman L.J. pointed out in *Crabb v. Arun District Council* [1976] Ch. 179, the "fraud" in these cases is not to be found in the transaction itself but in the subsequent attempt to go back upon the basic assumptions which underlay it.

Certainly it is not clear from the early cases that the courts considered it in all cases an essential element of the estoppel that the party estopped, although he must have known of the other party's belief, necessarily knew that that belief was mistaken.

[Oliver J. referred to *Stiles v. Cowper* (1748) 3 Atk. 692, *Jackson v. Cator* (1800) 5 Ves.Jun. 688, *Gregory v. Mighell* (1811) 18 Ves.Jun. 328, *Plimmer v. Mayor of Wellington* (1884) 9 App.Cas. 699, *Sarat Chunder Dey v. Gopal Chunder Laha* (1892) 19 L.R. Ind.App. 203, *Craine v. Colonial Mutual Fire Insurance Co. Ltd* (1920) 28 C.L.R. 305, *In re Eaves* [1940] Ch. 109. He continued:]

Mr Millett's dichotomy does, it is fair to say, derive some small support from the judgment of Evershed M.R. in *Hopgood v. Brown* [1955] 1 W.L.R. 213, 223 where he refers to Fry J.'s formulation of the requisites of estoppel in *Willmott v. Barber* (1880)

15 Ch.D. 96 as addressed and limited to cases of estoppel by acquiescence and as not intended as a comprehensive formulation of the necessary requisites of estoppel by representation. That, however, does not necessarily imply his acceptance of the proposition that all the probanda are applicable to every case of estoppel by acquiescence and it seems clear from his earlier pronouncement in *Electrolux Ltd v. Electrix Ltd* (1953) 71 R.P.C. 23, 33 that that was not, indeed, his view.

Furthermore the more recent cases indicate, in my judgment, that the application of the *Ramsden v. Dyson* (1866) L.R. 1 H.L. 129 principle—whether you call it proprietary estoppel, estoppel by acquiescence or estoppel by encouragement is really immaterial—requires a very much broader approach which is directed rather at ascertaining whether, in particular individual circumstances, it would be unconscionable for a party to be permitted to deny that which, knowingly, or unknowingly, he has allowed or encouraged another to assume to his detriment than to inquiring whether the circumstances can be fitted within the confines of some preconceived formula serving as a universal yardstick for every form of unconscionable behaviour.

So regarded, knowledge of the true position by the party alleged to be estopped, becomes merely one of the relevant factors—it may even be a determining factor in certain cases—in the overall inquiry. This approach, so it seems to me, appears very clearly from the authorities to which I am about to refer. In *Inwards v. Baker* [1965] 2 Q.B. 29 there was no mistaken belief on either side. Each knew the state of the title, but the defendant had been led to expect that he would get an interest in the land on which he had built and, indeed, the overwhelming probability is that that was indeed the father's intention at the time. But it was not mere promissory estoppel, which could merely be used as a defence, for, as Lord Denning M.R. said, at p. 37, "it is for the court to say in what way the equity can be satisfied". The principle was expressed very broadly both by Lord Denning M.R. and by Danckwerts L.J. Lord Denning said at p. 37:

"But it seems to me, from *Plimmer's* case (1884) 9 App.Cas. 699, 713–714 in particular, that the equity arising from the expenditure on land need not fail 'merely on the ground that the interest to be secured has not been expressly indicated ... the court must look at the circumstances in each case to decide in what way the equity can be satisfied.' "

And a little further down he said:

"All that is necessary is that the licensee should, at the request or with the encouragement of the landlord, have spent the money in the expectation of being allowed to stay there. If so, the court will not allow that expectation to be defeated where it would be inequitable so to do. "

And Danckwerts L.J. said, at p. 38:

"It seems to me that this is one of the cases of an equity created by estoppel, or equitable estoppel, as it is sometimes called, by which the person who has made the expenditure is induced by the expectation of obtaining protection, and equity protects him so that an injustice may not be perpetrated."

An even more striking example is *E.R. Ives Investment Ltd v. High* [1967] 2 Q.B. 379. Here again, there does not appear to have been any question of the persons who had acquiesced in the defendant's expenditure having known that his belief that he had an enforceable right of way was mistaken. Indeed, at the stage when the expenditure took place, both sides seem to have shared the belief that the agreement between them created effective rights. Nevertheless the successor in title to the acquiescing party was held to be estopped. Lord Denning M.R. said, at pp. 394–395:

"The right arises out of the expense incurred by Mr High in building his garage, as it is now, with access only over the yard: and the Wrights standing by and acquiescing in it, knowing that he believed he had a right of way over the yard. By so doing the Wrights created in Mr High's mind a reasonable expectation that his access over the yard would not be disturbed. That gives rise to an 'equity arising out of acquiescence.' It is available not only against the Wrights but also their successors in title. The court will not allow that expectation to be defeated when it would be inequitable so to do. It is for the court in each case to decide in what way the equity can be satisfied ..."

It should be mentioned that the Wrights themselves clearly also believed that Mr High had a right of way, because when they came to sell, they sold expressly subject to it. So, once again, there is an example of the doctrine of estoppel by acquiescence being applied without regard to the question of whether the acquiescing party knew that the belief of the other party in his supposed rights was erroneous.

Mr Scott and Mr Essayan have also drawn my attention to the Privy Council decision in *Bank Negara Indonesia v. Hoalim* [1973] M.L.J. 3, where again it seems that the misconception of the legal position which gave rise to the assurance creating the estoppel seems to have been shared by both parties. This is, however, rather a case of promissory estoppel than of the application of the *Ramsden v. Dyson* principle. More nearly in point is *Crabb v. Arun District Council* [1976] Ch. 179 where the plaintiff had altered his legal position in the expectation, encouraged by the defendants, that he would have a certain access to a road. Now there was no mistake here. Each party knew that the road was vested in the defendants and each knew that no formal grant had been made. Indeed I cannot see why in considering whether the defendants were behaving unconscionably, it should have made the slightest difference to the result if, at the time when the plaintiff was encouraged to open his access to the road, the defendants had thought that they were bound to grant it. The fact was that he had been encouraged to alter his position irrevocably to his detriment on the faith of a belief, which was known to and encouraged by the defendants, that he was going to be given a particular right of access—a belief which, for all that appears, the defendants probably shared at that time.

The particularly interesting features of the case in the context of the present dispute are, first, the virtual equation of promissory estoppel and proprietary estoppel or estoppel by acquiescence as mere facets of the same principle and secondly the very broad approach of both Lord Denning M.R. and Scarman L.J., both of whom emphasised the flexibility of the equitable doctrine. It is, however, worth noting that Scarman L.J. adopted and applied the five probanda in *Willmott v. Barber* (1880) 15 Ch.D. 96 which he described as "a valuable guide". He considered that those probanda were satisfied and it is particularly relevant here to note again the fourth one—namely that the defendant, the possessor of the legal right, must know of the plaintiff's mistaken belief. If Scarman L.J. had interpreted this as meaning—as Mr Millett submits that it does mean—that the defendant must know not only of the plaintiff's belief but also that it was mistaken, then he could not, I think, have come to the conclusion that this probandum was satisfied, for it seems clear from Lord Denning's recital of the facts that, up to the critical moment when the plaintiff acted, *both* parties thought that there *was* a firm assurance of access. The defendants had, indeed, even erected a gate at their own expense to give effect to it. What gave rise to the necessity for the court to intervene was the defendants' attempt to go back on this subsequently when they fell out with the plaintiff. I infer therefore that Scarman L.J. must have construed this probandum in the sense which Mr Scott and Mr Essayan urge upon me, namely that the defendant must know merely of the plaintiff's belief which, in the event, turns out to be mistaken.

Finally, there ought to be mentioned the most recent reference to the five probanda which is to be found in *Shaw v. Applegate* [1977] 1 W.L.R. 970. That was a case where the plea of estoppel by acquiescence failed on appeal, but it is significant that two members of the court expressed serious doubt whether it was necessary in every case of acquiescence to satisfy the five probanda. Buckley L.J. said, at pp. 977–978:

"As I understand that passage" and there he is referring to the passage from the judgment of Fry J. in *Willmott v. Barber* to which I have already referred, "what the judge is there saying is that where a man has got a legal right—as the plaintiffs have in the present case, being legal assignees of the benefit of the covenant binding the defendant—acquiescence on their part will not deprive them of that legal right unless it is of such a nature and in such circumstances that it would really be dishonest or unconscionable of the plaintiffs to set up that right after what has occurred. Whether in order to reach that stage of affairs it is really necessary to comply strictly with all five tests there set out by Fry J. may, I think, still be open to doubt, although no doubt if all those five tests were satisfied there would be shown to be a state of affairs in which it would be dishonest or unconscionable for the owner of the right to insist upon it. In *Electrolux Ltd v. Electrix Ltd* (1953) 71 R.P.C. 23 Sir Raymond Evershed M.R. said, at p. 33: 'I confess that I have found some difficulty—or should find some difficulty if it were necessary to make up my mind and express a view whether all five requisites which Fry J. stated in *Willmott v. Barber* (1880) 15 Ch.D. 96 must be present in every case in which it is said that the plaintiff will be deprived of his right to succeed in an action on the ground of acquiescence. All cases (and this is a trite but useful observation to repeat) must be read in the light of the facts of the particular case.' So I do not, as at present advised, think it is clear that it is essential to find all the five tests set out by Fry J. literally applicable and satisfied in any particular case. The real test, I think, must be whether upon the facts of the particular case the situation has become such that it would be dishonest or unconscionable for the plaintiff, or the person having the right sought to be enforced, to continue to seek to enforce it."

And Goff L.J. referred again to the judgment in *Willmott v. Barber* (1880) 15 Ch.D. 96 and said, at p. 980:

"But for my part, I share the doubt entertained by Sir Raymond Evershed M.R. in the *Electrolux* case, whether it is necessary in all cases to establish the five tests which are laid down by Fry J., and I agree that the test is whether, in the circumstances, it has become unconscionable for the plaintiff to rely upon his legal right."

So here, once again, is the Court of Appeal asserting the broad test of whether in the circumstances the conduct complained of is unconscionable without the necessity of forcing those incumbrances into a Procrustean bed constructed from some unalterable criteria.

The matter was expressed by Lord Denning M.R. in *Moorgate Mercantile Co. Ltd v. Twitchings* [1976] Q.B. 225, 241 as follows:

"Estoppel is not a rule of evidence. It is not a cause of action. It is a principle of justice and of equity. It comes to this: when a man, by his words or conduct, has led another to believe in a particular state of affairs, he will not be allowed to go back on it when it would be unjust or inequitable for him to do so. Dixon J. put it in these words: 'The principle upon which estoppel in pais is founded is that the law should not permit an unjust departure by a party from an assumption of fact which he has caused another party to adopt or accept for the purpose of their legal relations.' Sir Owen said so in 1937 in *Grundt v. Great Boulder Proprietary Gold Mines Ltd* (1937) 59 C.L.R. 641, 674. In 1947 after the *High Trees case* (*Central London Property Trust Ltd v. High Trees House Ltd* [1947] K.B. 130), I had some correspondence with Sir Owen about it: and I think I may say that he would not limit the principle to an assumption of fact, but would extend it, as I would, to include an assumption of fact or law, present or future. At any rate, it applies to an assumption of ownership or absence of ownership. This gives rise to what may be called proprietary estoppel. There are many cases where the true owner of goods or of land had led another to believe that he is not the owner, or, at any rate, is not claiming an interest therein, or that there is no objection to what the other is doing. In such cases it has been held repeatedly that the owner is not to be allowed to go back on what he has led the other to believe. So much so that his own title to the property, be it land or goods, has been held to be limited or extinguished, and new rights and interests have been created therein. And this operates by reason of his conduct—what he has led the other to believe—even though he never intended it."

The inquiry which I have to make therefore, as it seems to me, is simply whether, in all the circumstances of this case, it was unconscionable for the defendants to seek to take advantage of the mistake which, at the material time, everybody shared, and, in approaching that, I must consider the cases of the two plaintiffs separately because it may be that quite different considerations apply to each.

The first plaintiffs failed to establish that the defendants had created or encouraged their belief that they had a valid option; and they failed to establish that they would not have installed the lift in any event. However, the defendants were estopped from asserting the invalidity of the option as against the second plaintiffs; the terms of the leases in 1948 and in 1962, and the subsequent encouragement to incur expenditure on the premises, constituted representations that the option in relation to No. 22 was valid.

NOTES:

1. The seeds of this broad formulation of the doctrine of (proprietary) estoppel had already been sown: see *Inwards v. Baker* [1965] 2 Q.B. 29, 37 *per* Lord Denning M.R., 38 *per* Danckwerts L.J.; *Ward v. Kirkland* [1967] Ch. 194, 235 *per* Ungoed-Thomas J.; and especially *Crabb v. Arun DC* [1976] Ch. 179, 187–188 *per* Lord Denning M.R., 195 *per* Scarman L.J. The broad formulation was expressly adopted and applied by Robert Goff J. in *Amalgamated Investment and Property Co. Ltd v. Texas Commerce International Bank Ltd* [1982] Q.B. 84, 103–107; in the Court of Appeal it was also approved by Lord Denning M.R. but Eveleigh L.J. and Brandon L.J. based their judgments specifically on estoppel by convention. The broad formulation was unanimously approved by the Court of Appeal in *Habib Bank Ltd v. Habib Bank AG Zurich* [1981] 1 W.L.R. 1265, noted at (1981) 97 L.Q.R. 513; [1982] Conv. 450; *John v. George* (1995) 71 P. & C.R. 375; *Lloyds Bank plc v. Carrick* [1996] 4 All E.R. 630, noted at [1996] Conv. 295; *Jones v. Stones* (1999), *The Times*, June 3, 1999.

2. In *Swallow Securities Ltd v. Isenberg* [1985] 1 E.G.L.R. 132, 134, Cumming-Bruce L.J. acknowledged that the broad formulation of Oliver J. represented a concise statement of the doctrine of proprietary estoppel but added that the *Willmott v. Barber* probanda "will probably prove to be the necessary and essential guidelines to assist the court to decide the question whether it is unconscionable for the plaintiffs to assert their legal rights ..." However, to the extent that the defendants' claim in *Swallow Securities Ltd v. Isenberg* was based on the passive acquiescence of the plaintiff, it could be argued that the continued reliance on the *Willmott v. Barber* probanda is consistent with the statement of Oliver J. that they may remain relevant in such cases: see *Taylors Fashions Ltd v. Liverpool Victoria Trustees Co. Ltd* [1982] Q.B. 133, 147. On the other hand, the *Willmott v. Barber* probanda

have occasionally been applied in cases involving more than mere passive acquiescence. In *Coombes v. Smith* [1986] 1 W.L.R. 808, *Taylors Fashions Ltd v. Liverpool Victoria Trustees Co. Ltd* was neither referred to in the judgment of Jonathan Parker Q.C. nor cited in argument. The claim based on proprietary estoppel was rejected following a (strict) application of the *Willmott v. Barber* probanda. Similarly, in *Matharu v. Matharu* (1994) 68 P. & C.R. 93 Roch L.J., who delivered the majority judgment of the Court of Appeal, made no mention of *Taylors Fashions Ltd v. Liverpool Victoria Trustees Co. Ltd*. He held that the landowner was estopped from asserting his strict legal rights; but the conduct of the landowner was assessed by reference to (a liberal interpretation of) the *Willmott v. Barber* probanda: see [1995] Conv. 61; (1995) 58 M.L.R. 412.

3. Thompson [1983] C.L.J. 257 and Lunney [1992] Conv. 239 discussed and advocated the development of a flexible unified estoppel; but Evans [1988] Conv. 346 argued that the flexible approach is largely and properly confined to proprietary estoppel.

2. Requirements of the doctrine

Although *Taylors Fashions Ltd v. Liverpool Victoria Trustees Co. Ltd* indicates a broad approach to proprietary estoppel, there remain certain essential elements of the doctrine that must be established as preconditions of a successful claim. There must have been a representation made or an expectation created by the landowner as to the present or future rights of the claimant in the land; the claimant must have acted to his detriment; and he must have done so in reliance on the representation or expectation. If those three elements are established, it will usually follow that it would be unconscionable for the landowner to deny the representation or expectation and to insist on his own strict legal rights. However, there may be cases where it will be necessary to consider unconscionability as a separate question, in order to ensure that the doctrine is applied in accordance with its underlying rationale.

2.1 *Representation or expectation*
The representation or expectation must relate to a present or future interest or right in or over the land of the person making the representation or creating the expectation: *Western Fish Products Ltd v. Penwith DC* [1981] 2 All E.R. 204, 217 *per* Megaw L.J. Successful claims have been brought in respect of *personal* property but only where the claim related to the entire property of the person making the representation or creating the expectation and where that property also included land: *Re Basham* [1986] 1 W.L.R. 1498. On the other hand, it has frequently been stated that there is no requirement that the representation should be formulated in terms of a specific recognised proprietary interest and that, where necessary, the court will look to all the circumstances to "rationalise" the expectations of the claimant and the terms of the remedy: see, for example, *Ramsden v. Dyson* (1866) L.R. 1 H.L. 129, 171 *per* Lord Kingsdown; *Plimmer v. Mayor of Wellington* (1884) 9 App.Cas.

699, 713–714 *per* Sir Arthur Hobhouse; *Inwards v. Baker* [1965] 2 Q.B. 29, 37 *per* Lord Denning M.R.

However, the courts have sometimes rejected proprietary estoppel claims on grounds related to the lack of precision in the alleged representation. First, the representation may be no more than part of incomplete negotiations for some family or commercial transaction or arrangement: in such circumstances the claimant will normally not be permitted unilaterally by his own acts to rely on the representation alone in order to impose any obligation on the landowner: see *Coombes v. Smith* [1986] 1 W.L.R. 808; *Attorney-General of Hong Kong v. Humphreys Estate (Queen's Gardens) Ltd* [1987] A.C. 114; *Pridean Ltd v. Forest Taverns Ltd* (1996) 75 P. & C.R. 447. Secondly, in a more specific application of *Attorney-General of Hong Kong v. Humphreys Estate (Queen's Gardens) Ltd* and what may be termed the "incomplete transaction" principle, it has recently been held that, where there is a representation involving a promise that the claimant will acquire property under the will of the landowner, the claimant must establish words or conduct by the landowner which go beyond mere statements of intention and which, in all the circumstances, the claimant can reasonably claim to be an irrevocable promise as to the disposal of the landowner's property: *Taylor v. Dickens* [1998] 1 F.L.R. 806; *Gillett v. Holt* [1998] 3 All E.R. 917. Thirdly, the Court of Appeal recently held that, in the context of a representation that a tenancy would be granted, the absence of detailed terms of a sufficiently "concrete character" constituted an "insuperable difficulty" in establishing a proprietary estoppel claim: *Orgee v. Orgee* [1997] E.G.C.S. 152, noted at (1998) 114 L.Q.R. 351; *Willis v. Hoare* (1998) 77 P. & C.R. D42.

The representation may be active: *Plimmer v. Mayor of Wellington (1884);* *Inwards v. Baker,* (1884) 9 App.Cas. 699; [1965] 2 Q.B. 29; Pascoe v. Turner [1979] 1 W.L.R. 431; or it may be passive, where the landowner simply acquiesced in the expectation or assumption of the claimant. However, in either case it must be established that the landowner intended the claimant to rely on it: *Crabb v. Arun DC* [1976] Ch. 179, 188 *per* Lord Denning M.R.; *J.T. Developments Ltd v. Quinn* (1990) 62 P. & C.R. 33, 46 *per* Ralph Gibson L.J.; or that the landowner knew that claimant would rely on it: *Crabb v. Arun DC* [1976] Ch. 179, 188 *per* Lord Denning M.R.; or that the landowner knew that the claimant was relying on it: *Gillett v. Holt* [1998] 3 All E.R. 917, 928–929 *per* Carnwath J.; *Barclays Bank plc v. Zaroovabli* [1997] Ch. 321, 330–331 *per* Sir Richard Scott V.-C. It now seems to be accepted that, except in cases of passive acquiescence, it is not strictly necessary that the landowner should have known of his own legal rights nor that the claimant was mistaken as to his rights; but such knowledge may be a factor in considering whether or not the landowner was acting unconscionably in seeking to deny his representation: see *Taylors Fashions Ltd v. Liverpool Victoria Trustees Co. Ltd* [1982] Q.B. 133; *Matharu v. Matharu* (1994) 68 P. & C.R. 93.

The representation must normally have been given (or the expectation created) by the landowner himself or his employee or agent: *Ivory v. Palmer* [1975] I.C.R. 340; *Swallow Securities Ltd v. Isenberg* [1985] 1 E.G.L.R. 132; *Matharu v. Matharu* (1994) 68 P.C.R. 93. (The rights of the fee simple owner cannot be restricted in consequence of a representation given (or expectation created) by the tenant of the fee simple owner: *Ward v. Kirkland* [1967] Ch. 194, 241 *per* Ungoed-Thomas J.) However, the doctrine may operate where the person sought to be estopped has not himself made any representation to the claimant, provided that both parties have acted in relation to each other upon a joint assumption: *John v. George* (1995) 71 P. & C.R. 375.

2.2 Detriment

The most obvious (and probably the most common) form of detriment will be the expenditure of money, although the expenditure of money may not constitute a detriment to the claimant if it can be seen as beneficial to the claimant, for example, where the claimant moves into rent-free accommodation, contributes to the household expenditure and carries out work on the house: see *Coombes v. Smith* [1986] 1 W.L.R. 808. However, the doctrine does not seem to be restricted to cases where the claimant has incurred financial expenditure or even to cases where the claimant has suffered a (precisely) quantifiable financial loss.

In some circumstances, the detriment may be retrospective in the sense that the action of the claimant, which is taken in reliance upon the representation or expectation, and which would almost certainly be beneficial if the representation or expectation were honoured, would however result in detriment to the claimant if the landowner were permitted to renege on that representation or expectation: *Appleby v. Cowley* (1982) *The Times*, April 14, 1982 *per* Megarry V.-C.; *Watts v. Story* (1983) 134 N.L.J. 631 *per* Dunn L.J. This approach provides a clear reflection of unconscionability as the underlying principle of proprietary estoppel: see *Crabb v. Arun DC* [1976] Ch. 179, 195 *per* Scarman L.J.; *Taylors Fashions Ltd v. Liverpool Victoria Trustees Co. Ltd* [1982] Q.B. 133, 155 *per* Oliver J.; *Amalgamated Investment and Property Co. Ltd v. Texas Commerce International Bank Ltd* [1982] Q.B. 84, 104–105 *per* Goff J., 122 *per* Lord Denning M.R.

By way of examples, the requirement of detriment has been held to be satisfied where the claimant has made or financed permanent or substantial improvements to the land in question: *Inwards v. Baker* [1965] 2 Q.B. 29; *Griffiths v. Williams* (1977) 248 E.G. 947; *Pascoe v. Turner* [1979] 1 W.L.R. 431; where the claimant has provided unpaid services in the home of the landowner: *Greasley v. Cooke* [1980] 1 W.L.R. 1306; *Re Basham* [1986] 1 W.L.R. 1498; where the claimant has given up existing accommodation and employment in order to live nearer the landowner: *Jones (A.E.) v. Jones (F.W.)* [1977] 1 W.L.R. 438; and where the claimant has refrained from taking action that would be unnecessary provided that the representation were honoured: *Crabb v. Arun D.C., supra.*

There is a further link between the requirement of detriment and the requirement of unconscionability on the part of the landowner. Where there is significant detriment (in reliance upon the representation of the landowner), a court will readily conclude that it would be unconscionable for the landowner to deny the representation. Equally, where there is no detriment (or no potential detriment if the landowner were to deny the representation), it would be difficult for a court to conclude that it would be unconscionable for the landowner to deny the representation: *Watts v. Story* (1983) 134 N.L.J. 631 *per* Dunn L.J. Between those extremes, a court may seek to balance the detriment suffered and any benefit received and conclude that no equity arises or that any such equity has been satisfied: *Appleby v. Cowley* (1982) *The Times*, April 14, 1982; *supra*; *Watts v. Story* (1983, unreported); *Coombes v. Smith* [1986] 1 W.L.R. 808; *Sledmore v. Dalby* (1996) 72 P. & C.R. 196.

2.3 Reliance

It must be established that the claimant relied on the representation in the sense that he was induced by it to act to his detriment: see *Dodsworth v. Dodsworth* (1973) 228 E.G. 1115, 1117 *per* Russell L.J.; *Amalgamated Investment and Property Co. Ltd v. Texas Commerce International Bank Ltd* [1982] Q.B. 84, 105 *per* Goff J. In *Taylors Fashions Ltd v. Liverpool Victoria Trustees Co. Ltd* [1982] Q.B. 133 Oliver J. drew a distinction (at 156) between detrimental acts performed "on the faith of" a belief that the option was valid (which would constitute detrimental reliance) and detrimental acts performed merely "in" that belief (which would not be sufficient to constitute detrimental reliance). What is required is that the claimant should have "altered his position": *Re Basham* [1986] 1 W.L.R. 1498, 1504 *per* Edward Nugee Q.C.; and that he should have done so on the faith of a belief either than he owned a sufficient interest in the property to justify the expenditure or other detriment or that he would obtain such an interest: *Brinnand v. Ewens* [1987] 2 E.G.L.R. 67, 68 *per* Nourse L.J. On the other hand, it is not necessary to establish that the claimant altered his position *exclusively* in reliance on the representation. It is sufficient that the representation constituted an effective inducement: *Amalgamated Investment and Property Co. Ltd v. Texas Commerce International Bank Ltd* [1982] Q.B. 84, 104–105 *per* Goff J.; *Wayling v. Jones* (1993) 69 P. & C.R. 170, 173 *per* Balcombe L.J.

In *Wayling v. Jones* (1993) 69 P. & C.R. 170 the Court of Appeal adopted an approach to the question of reliance that in one respect may be seen as more generous to the claimant than the orthodox approach. The evidence established (i) that the claimant would have acted as he did (to his detriment) even if the deceased had not promised that he would leave his property to the claimant; but (ii) that the deceased *had* made such a promise; and (iii) that the claimant would *not* have acted as he did (to his detriment) if the deceased had reneged on his promise. On that basis, the court held that reliance was established.

More generally, it is now well established that, where a representation has been made and the claimant has acted to his detriment in circumstances that give rise to the inference that he acted in reliance on the representation, such reliance is presumed and the burden of proof shifts to the landowner to establish that there was no such reliance: *Greasley v. Cooke* [1980] 1 W.L.R. 1306, noted at [1981] Conv. 154; (1981) 44 M.L.R. 461; *Habib Bank Ltd v. Habib Bank AG Zurich* [1981] 1 W.L.R. 1265; *Watts v. Story* (1983) 134 N.L.J. 631; *Coombes v. Smith* [1986] 1 W.L.R. 808, noted at [1986] C.L.J.

394; *Wayling v. Jones* (1993) 69 P. & C.R. 170, noted at [1995] Conv. 409; (1995) 111 L.Q.R. 389.

2.4 *Unconscionability*

As has been seen, while unconscionability on the part of the landowner is an essential part of the rationale behind the doctrine of proprietary estoppel, it is inextricably linked with the other elements of the doctrine and it will usually be found to be established whenever those other elements are established. However, it is important to note that the courts seem increasingly to insist that all four elements be established. Thus, detrimental reliance on a representation will not be sufficient to bring the doctrine into operation unless the landowner is indeed acting unconscionably in seeking to enforce his strict legal rights: *Sledmore v. Dalby* (1996) 72 P. & C.R. 196, *per* Hobhouse L.J.; *Taylor v. Dickens* [1998] 1 F.L.R. 806, 820–822. Conversely, unconscionability alone, without detrimental reliance on a representation, is insufficient in itself to found a proprietary estoppel claim: *Taylor v. Dickens* [1998] 1 F.L.R. 806, 819–820 *per* Judge Weeks Q.C.

The influence of the broad overall approach in *Taylors Fashions Ltd v. Liverpool Victoria Trustees Co. Ltd* [1982] Q.B. 133 on these more specific requirements is well illustrated in the case of *Re Basham* [1986] 1 W.L.R. 1498.

Re Basham [1986] 1 W.L.R. 1498

(Ch D., Edward Nugee Q.C.)

The plaintiff's mother married the deceased in 1936, when the plaintiff was 15. For many years, on the understanding, based on repeated statements by the deceased, that he would leave all his property (including a house) to her, the plaintiff (and later the plaintiff's husband) subordinated her wishes to those of the deceased. She worked unpaid in his businesses; she worked in the house and garden; she provided meals; she sorted out a boundary dispute; and she refrained from moving away when her husband was offered employment with tied accommodation elsewhere. When the deceased died intestate, the plaintiff sought a declaration that she was entitled to all his property.

EDWARD NUGEE Q.C.:
The plaintiff relies on proprietary estoppel, the principle of which, in its broadest form, may be stated as follows: where one person, A, has acted to his detriment on the faith of a belief, which was known to and encouraged by another person, B, that he either has or is going to be given a right in or over B's property, B cannot insist on his strict legal rights if to do so would be inconsistent with A's belief. The principle is commonly known as proprietary estoppel, and since the effect of it is that B is prevented from asserting his strict legal rights it has something in common with estoppel. But in my judgment, at all events where the belief is that A is going to be given a right in the future, it is properly to be regarded as giving rise to a species of constructive trust, which is the concept employed by a court of equity to prevent a

person from relying on his legal rights where it would be unconscionable for him to do so. The rights to which proprietary estoppel gives rise, and the machinery by which effect is given to them, are similar in many respects to those involved in cases of secret trusts, mutual wills and other comparable cases in which property is vested in B on the faith of an understanding that it will be dealt with in a particular manner, of which Nourse J. said in *In re Cleaver, decd.* [1981] 1 W.L.R. 939, 947:

> "The principle of all these cases is that a court of equity will not permit a person to whom property is transferred by way of gift, but on the faith of an agreement or clear understanding that it is to be dealt with in a particular way for the benefit of a third person, to deal with that property inconsistently with that agreement or understanding. If he attempts to do so after having received the benefit of the gift equity will intervene by imposing a constructive trust on the property which is the subject matter of the agreement or understanding."

The factor which gives rise to the equitable obligation in the cases to which Nourse J. referred is B's receipt of the property on the faith of an understanding. In cases of proprietary estoppel the factor which gives rise to the equitable obligation is A's alteration of his position on the faith of a similar understanding. A third situation in which the court imposes a constructive trust is where A and B set up house together in a property which is in the name of B alone, and A establishes a common intention between A and B, acted on by A to his (or more usually her) detriment, that A should have a beneficial interest in the property: see the statements of principle by Nourse L.J. and Browne-Wilkinson V.-C. in *Grant v. Edwards* [1986] 3 W.L.R. 114. Here too, if the two elements of common understanding or intention and detrimental acts on the part of A are established, they give rise to an equitable obligation enforceable against B which is in the nature of a constructive trust. A common theme can be discerned in each of these classes of case; and although different situations may give rise to differences of detail in the manner in which the court will give effect to the equity which arises in favour of A, one would expect the general principles applicable in the different situations to be the same unless there is a sound reason to the contrary.

In the present case it is in my judgment clearly established by the evidence, first, that the plaintiff had a belief at all material times that she was going to receive both the cottage and the remainder of the deceased's property on his death, and secondly, that this belief was encouraged by the deceased. Mr Browne for the defendants submitted that the fact that the deceased made a number of gifts to the plaintiff's daughter, and had promised her a further quite substantial gift, and the fact that on his deathbed he indicated a wish to make a will leaving an unspecified sum of money to the plaintiff's son, and that the plaintiff made no objection to such gifts, was inconsistent with a belief on her part that the whole of his estate was going to come to her. I do not think these gifts or intended gifts detract from such a belief. As I have said, the plaintiff, her husband and her two children formed a close-knit family, and it is in my judgment quite consistent with the belief of the plaintiff, and of independent third parties such as neighbours, that the whole of the deceased's estate was to go to the plaintiff, that she should have raised no objection if, instead of it all going to her direct, some part of it was given to other members of her immediate family. As the plaintiff's daughter put it, her understanding was that the plaintiff was to inherit everything for the benefit of the family; and, as Mr Henderson for the plaintiff submitted, the position was similar to that which would have existed had the deceased left a will giving everything to the plaintiff hoping that she would do the right thing by the son and daughter. Under such a will there would have been no obligation on the plaintiff to pass on any part of the estate to her children, but she might well have been expected to do so. Moreover where a constructive trust affects the whole of the estate which the constructive trustee leaves at his death, as in *In re Cleaver, decd.* [1981] 1 W.L.R. 939, it is only gifts which are calculated to defeat the intention of the persons involved (A and B) that are objectionable: see *per* Nourse J., at p. 947. I bear in mind that all claims to the property of a deceased person must be scrutinised with very great care; but I am satisfied that the deceased encouraged the plaintiff in the belief that all the property he possessed at the date of his death would pass to her, and I do not consider that the fact that he made certain gifts during his lifetime, and indicated a wish to make others, including the gift of a legacy to the plaintiff's son, is inconsistent with such a belief. The gifts of which evidence was given were in favour of the plaintiff's children and in the circumstances did not in substance conflict, in my judgment, with his intention to benefit the plaintiff.

The third element that the plaintiff must prove in order to raise a constructive trust in a case of proprietary estoppel is that she acted to her detriment. Mr Browne accepted that the plaintiff did a very great deal for the deceased, and it is clear that she did not receive any commensurate reward for this during his lifetime. There is some evidence, though not very much, of occasions when the plaintiff or husband acted or refrained from acting in a way in which they might not have done but for their expectation of inheriting the deceased's property: I refer to the occasions when the husband refrained from selling his building land, and refrained from taking a job in Lincolnshire which would have made it impossible for the plaintiff to continue caring for her mother and the deceased, and the occasions when the plaintiff instructed solicitors at her own expense in connection with the boundary dispute between the deceased and Mr Kenworthy, and the expenditure of time and money on the house and garden and on carpeting the house, when the deceased had ample means of his own to pay for such matters. It may be that none of these incidents, taken by itself, would be very significant, but the cumulative effect of them supports the view that the plaintiff and her husband subordinated their own interests to the wishes of the deceased. Mr Browne submitted that all this could be attributed to the plaintiff's natural love and affection for her stepfather; but in my judgment the plaintiff's acts went well beyond what was called for by natural love and affection for someone to whom she had no blood relationship, and both she and her husband made it very clear in their evidence that there was no great love and affection between her husband and the deceased, and that he was only willing to pay for meals that the plaintiff provided for the deceased and to work as he did in the garden of the cottage because of the expectation that the deceased's estate would in due course pass to the plaintiff.

The fourth element that the plaintiff has to prove is that the acts done by her were done in reliance on or as a result of her belief that she would become entitled to the deceased's property on his death. On this I derive some assistance from observations of Lord Denning M.R. in *Greasley v. Cooke* [1980] 1 W.L.R. 1306. There, the defendant came as a maid in 1938 to live in the house of a widower. He died in 1948, and after his death the defendant stayed on in the house looking after his son and daughter until their deaths in 1975, receiving no payment for doing so. She and the son lived as husband and wife throughout this period, and she was treated as one of the family. The county court judge held that she believed, because of what was said to her by the son, that she would be allowed to live and remain in the house as long as she wished, though the judge said that she might have expected the son to make provision for her to this effect by his will. However he held that she failed to prove that the reason why she looked after the son and daughter without payment was because of her belief that she would be entitled to live in the house as long as she wished, and he dismissed her claim to be entitled to remain. The Court of Appeal reversed his decision. Lord Denning M.R. said, at pp. 1311–1312:

"The first point is on the burden of proof. Mr Weeks referred us to many cases, such as *Reynell v. Sprye* (1852) 1 De G.M. & G. 660, 708; *Smith v. Chadwick* (1882) 20 Ch.D. 27, 44 and *Brikom Investments Ltd v. Carr* [1979] Q.B. 467, 482–483 where I said that when a person makes a representation intending that another should act on it: 'It is no answer for the maker to say: "You would have gone on with the transaction anyway". That must be mere speculation. No one can be sure what he would, or would not, have done in a hypothetical state of affairs which never took place. ... Once it is shown that a representation was calculated to influence the judgment of a reasonable man, the presumption is that he was so influenced.' So here. These statements to Miss Cooke were calculated to influence her—so as to put her mind at rest—so that she should not worry about being turned out. No one can say what she would have done if Kenneth and Hedley had not made those statements. It is quite possible that she would have said to herself: 'I am not married to Kenneth. I am on my own. What will happen to me if anything happens to him? I had better look out for another job now: rather than stay here where I have no security.' So, instead of looking for another job, she stayed on in the house looking after Kenneth and Clarice. There is a presumption that she did so, relying on the assurances given to her by Kenneth and Hedley. The burden is not on her, but on them, to prove that she did not rely on their assurances. They did not prove it, nor did their representatives. So she is presumed to have relied on them. So on the burden of proof it seems to me that the judge was in error.

The second point is about the need for some expenditure of money—some detriment—before a person can acquire any interest in a house or any right to stay in it as long as he wishes. It so happens that in many of these cases of proprietary estoppel there has been expenditure of money. But that is not a necessary element. I see that in *Snell's Principles of Equity,* 27th ed. (1973), p. 565, it is said: 'A must have incurred expenditure or otherwise have prejudiced himself.' But I do not think that that is necessary. It is sufficient if the party, to whom the assurance is given, acts on the faith of it—in such circumstances that it would be unjust and inequitable for the party making the assurance to go back on it: see *Moorgate Mercantile Co. Ltd v. Twitchings* [1976] Q.B. 225 and *Crabb v. Arun District Council* [1976] Ch. 179, 188. Applying those principles here it can be seen that the assurances given by Kenneth and Hedley to Doris Cooke—leading her to believe that she would be allowed to stay in the house as long as she wished—raised an equity in her favour. There was no need for her to prove that she acted on the faith of those assurances. It is to be presumed that she did so. There is no need for her to prove that she acted to her detriment or to her prejudice. Suffice it that she stayed on in the house—looking after Kenneth and Clarice—when otherwise she might have left and got a job elsewhere. The equity having thus been raised in her favour, it is for the courts of equity to decide in what way that equity should be satisfied. In this case it should be by allowing her to stay on in the house as long as she wishes."

Waller and Dunn L.JJ. agreed, and Waller L.J., at p. 1313, quoted a passage from the judgment of Sir George Jessel M.R. in *Smith v. Chadwick* (1882) 20 Ch.D. 27, 44–45:

"Again, on the question of the materiality of the statement, if the court sees on the face of it that it is of such a nature as would induce a person to enter into the contract, or would tend to induce him to do so, or that it would be a part of the inducement, to enter into the contract, the inference is, if he entered into the contract, that he acted on the inducement so held out, and you want no evidence that he did so act. ... But unless it is shewn in one way or the other than he did not rely on the statement the inference follows."

On the evidence in the present case I am satisfied that one reason why the plaintiff did so much for the deceased was her belief that, although she was not a blood relative of his, he would leave his estate to her on his death; but, on the authority of *Greasley v. Cooke* [1980] 1 W.L.R. 1306, if the evidence was not sufficient to establish this positively, the plaintiff would still be entitled to succeed on the fourth element in the absence of proof that she did not rely on the deceased's statements.

The four elements in the broad statement of principle with which I began this consideration of the law are thus in my judgment made out. Mr Browne however, submitted that there are two reasons why the plaintiff is not entitled to rely on proprietary estoppel in the present case. His main submission was that the representation or belief on which a plaintiff, A in the foregoing statement of principle, relies must be related to an existing right; that is to say, unless there is a representation that A has a present right or interest, equity cannot intervene because there is nothing which equity can protect or make effective by the operation of an estoppel. What has to be shown, he submitted, is that A has been given an informal title, and equity will then prevent B, the owner of the property concerned, from taking it away from him. Linked to this submission, and deriving its main force from it, was his second submission, namely that proprietary estoppel must be related to a particular property and cannot extend to property as indefinite and fluctuating as the whole of a deceased's estate.

In a number of the leading cases the law is stated in a manner which is consistent with Mr Browne's submissions. Thus in *Ramsden v. Dyson* (1866) L.R. 1 H.L. 129, 170, Lord Kingsdown states it as follows:

"The rule of law applicable to the case appears to me to be this: If a man, under a verbal agreement with a landlord for a certain interest in land, or, what amounts to the same thing, under an expectation, created or encouraged by the landlord, that he shall have a certain interest, takes possession of such land, with the consent of the landlord, and upon the faith of such promise or expectation, with the knowledge of the landlord, and without objection by him, lays out money upon the land, a court of equity will compel the landlord to give effect to such promise or expectation."

Similarly, in *Inwards v. Baker* [1965] 2 Q.B. 29, 37, Lord Denning M.R. said:

"It is an equity well recognised in law. It arises from the expenditure of money by a person in actual occupation of land when he is led to believe that, as the result of that expenditure, he will be allowed to remain there."

I was also referred to *Moorgate Mercantile Co. Ltd v. Twitchings* [1976] Q.B. 225, 242, where Lord Denning M.R. drew a parallel between the facts of that case, in which H.P. Information Ltd had held out the vendor of a car as the owner of it free from any hire purchase agreement, and those cases in equity

"when the owner of land, by his conduct, leads another to believe that he is not the owner, or, at any rate, that the other can safely spend money on it. It is held that he cannot afterwards assert his ownership so as to deprive the other of the benefit of that expenditure: see *Ramsden v. Dyson* (1866) L.R. 1 H.L. 129. The Court of Equity will look to the circumstances to see in what way the equity can be satisfied: see *Inwards v. Baker* [1965] 2 Q.B. 29."

Mr Browne also relied on the five probanda set out in the judgment of Fry J. in *Willmott v. Barber* (1880) 15 Ch.D. 96, 105, and submitted, rightly, that they were not all satisfied in the present case, and further submitted that it was necessary that they should be satisfied in order that a claim based on proprietary estoppel should succeed.

In this, as in other branches of the law, it is not difficult to find statements of principle couched in terms which are broad enough to cover the facts of the particular case under consideration, but which subsequent cases show to have been narrower than is necessary to encapsulate the developed law. The law, in Lord Tennyson's words, slowly broadens down from precedent to precedent, and in few areas is this more clear than that with which I am concerned. The broadening process is brought out by Oliver J.'s consideration of the authorities in *Taylors Fashions Ltd v. Liverpool Victoria Trustees Co. Ltd (Note)* [1982] Q.B. 133, which is summed up, at pp. 151–152:

"the more recent cases indicate, in my judgment, that the application of the *Ramsden v. Dyson* (1866) L.R. 1 H.L. 129 principle—whether you call it proprietary estoppel, estoppel by acquiescence or estoppel by encouragement is really immaterial—requires a very much broader approach which is directed rather at ascertaining whether, in particular individual circumstances, it would be unconscionable for a party to be permitted to deny that which, knowingly, or unknowingly, he has allowed or encouraged another to assume to his detriment than to inquiring whether the circumstances can be fitted within the confines of some preconceived formula serving as a universal yardstick for every form of unconscionable behaviour."

No case was cited to me, and I know of no case, which affords support for Mr Browne's main submission, that the belief on which A relies must be related to an existing right. Mr Browne accepted that this suggested requirement would have been satisfied if the plaintiff had been living with the deceased at the cottage, but he contended that the fact that she lived a short distance down the road made all the difference. In my judgment the question whether it is unconscionable for the deceased's personal representatives to assert a legal title to his property cannot turn on a factor of this kind. Although statements of principle such as those of Lord Kingsdown in *Ramsden v. Dyson* (1866) L.R. 1 H.L. 129, 170 and Lord Denning M.R. which I have quoted, and which were worded in broad enough terms to cover the cases in which they were made, might suggest the contrary, it is in my judgment established that the expenditure of A's money on B's property is not the only kind of detriment that gives rise to a proprietary estoppel. *Greasley v. Cooke* [1980] 1 W.L.R. 1306 is an example of a case in which A was not shown to have incurred any such expenditure: see in particular the second point referred to by Lord Denning M.R. in the passage at p. 1311 which I have quoted from his judgment. Nor in my judgment is it necessary, notwithstanding the terms of such statements of principle, that A should have been in occupation of B's land, or even in enjoyment of some right over it. In *Crabb v. Arun District Council* [1976] Ch. 179, A acted to his detriment in parting with part of his land without having secured for himself a right of way to his remaining land, which was thereby rendered landlocked. But because he did so in the belief, encouraged by B, that he would be granted a right of way over B's adjoining land, the Court of Appeal held that an equity arose in his favour and that he was entitled to be granted such a right of way. It appears from the judgments that A had not spent any money on the access road over B's land, and that he had not even been using the access road himself prior to parting with the portion of his own land that would have given him direct access to the highway: the access road over which he was expecting to obtain a right of way was being used by B's lorries: see pp. 186B and 197A, but not by vehicles belonging to A; or at least if it was being used by A, this was a factor of so little importance in the minds of the members of the Court of Appeal that none of them thought it necessary to refer to it. The important factors were A's belief, B's encouragement of that belief and A's acts in reliance upon that belief.

Moreover if, as in my judgment is the case, the equity which arises in favour of A in cases of proprietary estoppel is in the nature of a constructive trust, and is similar to the equity which arises in cases of the kind referred to by Nourse J. in the passage which I have quoted from *In re Cleaver, decd.* [1981] 1 W.L.R. 939, 947, I can see no ground for making what would appear to be an arbitrary distinction between the two and holding that in cases of proprietary estoppel it is necessary for A to be in enjoyment of B's property, when such a requirement is clearly not present in those other cases. If proprietary estoppel were limited to cases in which A believed that he already had an interest in B's property, such a requirement might make more sense. *Willmott v. Barber* (1880) 15 Ch.D. 96 was a case of this kind; and the use of the word "estoppel" suggests such a limitation. But as Oliver J. indicated in the *Taylors Fashions* case [1982] Q.B. 133 equitable doctrines cannot be confined within a straitjacket by the labels which have become attached to them. It is clear that the doctrine which bears the label "proprietary estoppel" is not limited to cases like *Willmott v. Barber* (1880) 15 Ch.D. 96 where A believes that he already has the interest which he asks the court to confirm, but extends to cases in which A believes that he will obtain an interest in the future; and this being so, I see no justification for importing a requirement that he should in addition already be in enjoyment of some lesser interest.

Similar reasoning leads me to reject Mr Browne's second submission, that the belief must relate to some clearly identified piece of property, movable or immovable, and that a claim cannot be based on proprietary estoppel where the expectation is that A will inherit B's residuary estate. It is clear that in other cases of constructive trust, such as those arising from mutual wills, the trust can bind the whole of B's estate: see, for example, *In re Cleaver, decd.* [1981] 1 W.L.R. 939 and the leading Australian case of *Birmingham v. Renfrew* (1937) 57 C.L.R. 666, to which Nourse J. refers at length at pp. 945–947 of his judgment. If the belief that B will leave the whole of his estate to A is established by sufficiently cogent evidence, as in my judgment it is in the present case, I see no reason in principle or in authority why the doctrine of proprietary estoppel should not apply so as to raise an equity against B in favour of A extending to the whole of B's estate.

Accordingly I hold that the plaintiff succeeds in this action and is entitled to relief in relation to both the cottage and the remainder of the deceased's net estate.

The question then arises in what manner effect should be given to the equity which has arisen in the plaintiff's favour. The extent of the equity is to have made good, so far as may fairly be done between the parties, the expectations which the deceased encouraged: see *Griffiths v. Williams* (1978) 248 E.G. 947, 949 *per* Goff L.J. Prima facie, therefore, the plaintiff is entitled to a declaration that the defendants, as personal representatives of the deceased, hold the whole of his net estate on trust for the plaintiff.

NOTES:

1. Hayton [1987] C.L.J. 215 argued that the decision "extends equitable proprietary estoppel principles to the limit. ... Justice was achieved for [the claimant], but probably at too high a price". In particular, he doubted whether the behaviour of the deceased was sufficiently unconscionable to justify the conversion of a mere hope of property into an entitlement. Nonetheless, he endorsed the judgment in so far as it held that proprietary estoppel claims may be established in relation both existing *and future* property rights and in relation to both specific *and unspecific* property (although a similar claim to unspecific property had failed in *Layton v. Martin* [1986] 2 F.L.R. 227); and see Martin [1987] Conv. 211; Davis (1993) 13 O.J.L.S. 99.

2. In *Taylor v. Dickens* [1998] 1 F.L.R. 806 the landowner promised the claimant that he would make a will leaving his property to the claimant; and he did so. Thereafter, the claimant refused to accept any payment for work that he did on the land. When the landowner died, the claimant discovered that the will had been changed and that he had been left nothing. Judge Weeks Q.C., sitting as a High Court judge, held that a proprietary estoppel claim could not be based on a mere promise to make a will unless the claimant could further establish that the landowner had promised not to revoke the will. He regarded the statement of principle in *Re Basham* as too wide, stating (at 821–822):

First, it omits the requirement of unconscionability which nearly all the judgments in this field insist on ...

Secondly, it is not sufficient for A to believe that he is going to be given a right over B's property if he knows that B has reserved the right to change his mind. In that case,

A must also show that B created or encouraged a belief on A's part that B would not exercise that right.

This requirement is shown by the *Attorney-General of Hong Kong v. Humphreys Estates* [1987] A.C. 114. . .

In the present case Mr Taylor knew that wills were revocable and that Mrs Parker could change her mind. His wife gave evidence that on no less than three occasions she told him not to count his chickens before they were hatched. He was confident that Mrs Parker would not revoke her will, but he agrees that she never said she would not do so. He expected her not to and trusted that she would not do so.

I have, however, no credible evidence that Mrs Parker created or encouraged that belief, or that Mr Taylor relied on that belief. What he relied on was her statements in 1988 and 1991 that she was going to make a will in his favour, and her subsequent true statements that she had done so.

As appears from *Re Goodchild* [1997] 1 W.L.R. 1216 there is a difference between saying you will make a will and saying you will not revoke a will. *Re Basham* [1986] 1 W.L.R. 1498 and *Wayling v. Jones* (1993) 69 P. & C.R. 170 were both cases where a person said they would make a will and did not. This is a case where a person said she would make a will and did.

In my judgment, Mr Taylor's claim fails for the same reason as the . . . claim failed in *Humphreys Estate*.

For comment, see [1998] Conv. 210; (1998) 114 L.Q.R. 351.

3. In *Gillett v. Holt* [1998] 3 All E.R. 917 the facts were materially similar to those in *Taylor v. Dickens*, except that the claimant brought his action as soon as he discovered that the landowner had changed his will and before the landowner had died. The action was dismissed. Carnwath J. stated (at 926–930):

Re Basham [1986] 1 W.L.R. 1498 was cited with approval by the Court of Appeal in *Jones v. Watkins* [1987] CA Transcript 1200. In that case the plaintiff claimed to have helped the deceased on his farm over a long period, in reliance on promises that he would inherit it. The claim failed, principally because he did not establish that he had suffered substantial detriment in reliance on the promises. Slade L.J. referred to the statement of principle in *Re Basham*, and added:

"If in such a case it would be unconscionable to permit A to rely on his strict legal rights, the court will exercise its equitable jurisdiction and by its order make good to him, so far as fairly may be done between the parties, the expectation which A has encouraged."

His judgment also discusses two particular elements: the nature of the representation required, and the meaning of "detriment". As to the former, he noted—

"the equivocal nature of the promises (as found by the judge) which, by their nature, would not have been capable of giving rise to a legally binding contract even if supported by a mutual intent to create legal relations and consideration."

However (following cases such as *Inwards v. Baker* [1965] 2 Q.B. 29 and *Crabb v Arun D.C.* [1976] Ch. 179), he agreed with the judge that the equivocal nature of the promises did not prevent a proprietary estoppel arising, although it might affect the remedy:

"The equivocal nature of the promises found by the judge is clearly one relevant factor when considering whether or not it would be unconscionable to permit the administrators to rely on their strict legal title, having regard to any detriment suffered by the plaintiff in reliance on them."

...

Mr Nugee's formulation was also accepted as correct (without argument) by the Court of Appeal in *Wayling v. Jones* (1993) 69 P. & C.R. 170 at 172. In that case the plaintiff had lived with the deceased and helped him to run his businesses, and had been promised that he would inherit a particular hotel. Balcombe L.J. (at 173) added the following points:

"(1) There must be a sufficient link between the promises relied upon and the conduct which constitutes the detriment ... (2) The promises relied upon do not have to be the sole inducement for the conduct: it is sufficient if they are an inducement ... (3) Once it has been established that promises were made, and that there has been conduct by the plaintiff of such a nature that inducement may be inferred then the burden of proof shifts to the defendants to establish that he did not rely on the promises ..."

On the facts of that case the plaintiff succeeded.

More recently, in *Taylor v. Dickens* [1998] 1 F.L.R. 806 at 821 Judge Weeks Q.C., sitting as a judge of the High Court, criticised Mr Nugee's formulation:

"In my judgment, in two material respects it is stated too widely. First, it omits the requirement of unconscionability which nearly all the judgments in this field insist on ... Secondly, it is not sufficient for A to believe that he is going to be given a right over B's property if he knows that B has reserved the right to change his mind. In that case, A must also show that B created or encouraged a belief on A's part that B would not exercise that right."

The claim failed in that case. The deceased had told the plaintiff that she would make a will in his favour. She had done so, but she later revoked it; he was aware that wills could be revoked, and she had never told him that she would not exercise that right. The judge said (at 822):

"As appears from *Re Goodchild*, there is all the difference between saying you will make a will and saying you will not revoke a will. *Re Basham* and *Wayling v. Jones* were both cases where a person said they would make a will and did not. This is a case where a person said she would make a will and did."

I understand that *Taylor v. Dickens* may be going to the Court of Appeal; and so Judge Weeks' criticisms of *Re Basham* may be considered at a higher level.

As the authorities stand, Mr Martin [counsel for the landowner] accepted that I should treat *Re Basham* as correct, but he asked me to approach it with care. It appears to be the only case in which a proprietary estoppel has been established in relation to an entire residuary estate, as opposed to a specific property. Further, as Mr Martin said, if Mr Nugee's formulation is applied too literally "any intending testator who mentions his intention to leave assets by will runs the risk that the representee will (unknown to the testator) rely to his detriment on the representation and so turn something that was merely an expression of intention into a binding promise". He suggested that "the overriding principle" is that the testator should be held to his representation "only if it would be unconscionable for him to go back on it". I agree with Mr Martin that this is the overriding principle. That was made clear in *Jones v. Watkins*. In so far as it is not expressly stated in Mr Nugee's formulation, that may be a valid criticism; but it is clear from later parts of his judgment that he had well in mind that the underlying "concept" was to prevent a person from relying on his legal rights where it would be "unconscionable" for him to do so (see [1986] 1 W.L.R. 1498 at 1504).

Another problem, as Mr Martin says, is that, under Mr Nugee's formulation, it appears to be sufficient for the plaintiff to act to his detriment in reliance on the promise, even if the promisor does not know he is doing so. The formulation requires that the promisor should have encouraged the promisee's "belief", but not necessarily that he should have encouraged, or even been aware of, his course of action in reliance on that belief. Thus an equity may be created over the promisor's estate without his knowledge. Mr McDonnell [counsel for the claimant] supported that interpretation of *Re Basham*. He referred me to some words of Lord Denning M.R. in *Moorgate Mercantile Co. Ltd v. Twitchings* [1976] Q.B. 225 at 242 (cited by him also in *Crabb v. Arun D.C.* [1976] Ch. 179 at 187):

> "In such cases it has been held repeatedly that the owner is not to be allowed to go back on what he has led the other to believe. So much so that his own title to the property, be it land or goods, has been held to be limited or extinguished, and new rights and interests have been thereby created therein. And this operates by reason of his conduct—what he has led the other to believe—*even though he never intended it.*" (My emphasis.)

I do not accept Mr McDonnell's approach. As I read it, that dictum is saying no more than that the necessary ingredients for the estoppel may be found in the parties' conduct, without them having formed any actual intention to alter the property rights. In *Moorgate Mercantile* itself, the finance company was well aware how car dealers were relying on the information which was supplied to them. In *Crabb v. Arun D.C.* itself, Lord Denning M.R. ([1976] Ch. 179 at 188) spoke of the need for a promise, or the creation or encouragement of a belief, by one party "knowing or intending that the other will act on that belief". Similarly, in his classic statement of the principle in *Ramsden v. Dyson* (1866) L.R. 1 H.L. 129 at 142 (adopted by Scarman L.J. in *Crabb v. Arun D.C.* [1976] Ch. 179 at 193–194), Lord Kingsdown referred to the need for a "verbal agreement" or "an expectation, created or encouraged by the landlord", followed by action by the other party "upon the faith of such promise or expectation, *with the knowledge of the landlord*, and without objection by him" (my emphasis).

Again, I doubt that Mr Nugee intended that to be the effect of his judgment. He referred in the following passage for the need for an "understanding" analogous to that in the mutual wills cases. It is true that in the context of proprietary estoppel apparently, unlike that of mutual wills (cf. *Re Goodchild (decd)* [1997] 1 W.L.R. 1216), something less than a binding contract will suffice. However, by the word "understanding" I understand the judge to mean a mutual understanding—which may be express or inferred from conduct—between promisor and promisee, both as to the content of the promise and as to what the promisee is doing, or may be expected to do, in reliance on it. On the facts of *Re Basham*, there was plenty of evidence of such a mutual understanding. For example, in relation to the work done by the plaintiff and her husband:

> "The deceased never paid for any of this, but told them, 'You'll lose nothing for this, doing all these jobs', and promised them that what was his would be theirs." (see [1986] 1 W.L.R. 1498 at 1503.)

Normally it is the promisor's knowledge of the detriment being suffered in reliance on his promise which makes it "unconscionable" for him to go back on it.

More generally, I agree with Mr Martin that particular care is needed where considering proprietary estoppel in the context of an alleged promise to make a will. I am not convinced, with respect to Judge Weeks, that it is critical whether the will is made and revoked, or never made at all; nor that the plaintiff's subjective awareness or unawareness of the possibility of revocation can be the vital factor. It would be odd if the plaintiff's proprietary rights should be diminished merely because he was unfortunate enough to have a wife who (as in *Taylor v. Dickens*) regularly reminded him "not to count his chickens before they were hatched".

Rather, I think that homely expression is an apt statement of how, in normal circumstances, and in the absence of a specific promise, any reasonable person would regard—and should be expected by the law to regard—a representation by a living person as to his intentions for his will. Subject to specific statutory exceptions (such as for dependants), the right to decide, and change one's mind as to, the devolution of one's estate is a basic and well understood feature of English law. The law allows one to disappoint the expectations of those who have no more than a moral claim on one's affections, however strong. During the lifetime of the potential testator, that is a risk which anyone seeking to rely on such a representation necessarily faces.

This point did not arise in *Re Basham* and *Wayling v. Jones*, because the promisors' intentions, on which the plaintiff had relied, had remained unchanged until death, and there was no suggestion they had ever considered changing them. It is, however, supported and illustrated by *Re Goodchild.* ...

To summarise, the principle of proprietary estoppel, unlike that of mutual wills, does not depend on a binding contract in law. As *Crabb v. Arun D.C.* shows, it may be founded on an agreement in principle, or a mere "expectation, created or encouraged" by the party alleged to be bound, in reliance on which the other party has acted to his detriment. But the party to be bound must have been aware that he was so acting. Further, in the application of the principle to statements about the intended contents of a will, the facts must be looked at against the ordinary presumption that such intentions are subject to change. It may be easier to infer a fixed intent when the subject matter is a particular property, which the plaintiff has been allowed to enjoy in return for services, than in relation to a whole estate. In any event, the plaintiff needs to show words or conduct by the prospective testator which go beyond mere statements of intention, and which, having regard to all the circumstances, he can reasonably claim to have regarded as amounting to an irrevocable promise by the prospective testator as to how his estate would be disposed of.

For comment, see [1999] C.L.J. 25; [1999] Conv. 46.

4. For discussion of representations as to future rights generally, see Davis [1996] Conv. 193.

5. Davis (1993) 13 O.J.L.S 99 argues that the decision in *Re Basham* involved circular reasoning in that the court relied on constructive trust authorities to support the establishment of a proprietary estoppel claim and then concluded that the estoppel generated a constructive trust. For discussion of the relationship between proprietary estoppel and constructive trusts, see *infra*, p. 607.

3. Satisfying the equity

If the requirements of proprietary estoppel are established, so that an equity is raised in favour of the claimant, it is for the court to determine the appropriate remedy to "satisfy the equity". Consideration of the cases in this section should provide an indication of the range of remedies adopted and of the flexible approach of the courts. However, a number of preliminary observations should be made.

First, the origins of estoppel would suggest that the doctrine cannot provide the claimant with a cause of action; and that the doctrine is limited to providing the claimant with a defence to an action brought by the landowner in which he seeks to assert his strict legal rights - with the result that the landowner is simply prevented from enforcing those rights. This limitation, which is summarised in the maxim that estoppel acts as a shield rather than a sword, still applies to some manifestations of the doctrine, for example *promissory* estoppel. However, as the cases (and most of the cases in this section) demonstrate, *proprietary* estoppel not only provides the claimant with a defence; it may also provide a cause of action as a result of which the claimant may acquire a recognised proprietary interest or some other right in the land in question. This extension to the original function of estoppel, and the differentiation between proprietary and promissory estoppel (which are not always readily distinguishable in practice), is well established but cannot really be said to have been convincingly justified by the courts.

Secondly, there has been much discussion in recent years as to what the courts are, and should be, seeking to achieve when determining the nature of the remedy in proprietary estoppel cases: see, for example, Moriarty (1984) 100 L.Q.R. 376; Thompson [1986] Conv. 406; Dewar (1986) 49 M.L.R. 741; Evans [1988] Conv. 346; Davis (1993) 13 O.J.L.S. 99; Cooke (1997) 17 *Legal Studies* 258; Robertson (1998) 18 *Legal Studies* 360; Gardner (1999) 115 L.Q.R. 438. The discussion presents a dichotomy of expectation loss and reliance loss. According to the expectation loss approach, the courts should be granting a remedy that gives effect to the expectation of the claimant generated by the representation or otherwise; according to the reliance loss approach, the courts should be seeking to compensate the claimant for the detriment incurred in reliance on the representation or expectation. It is submitted that there may be less significance in the distinction than may be apparent at first sight. It can hardly be denied that the courts have generally granted a remedy that *in practice* gives effect to the expectation of the claimant even where the value of the remedy greatly exceeds the financial detriment suffered by the claimant. However, the proponents of the reliance loss approach argue that the reliance loss approach is not, and should not be, limited to the reimbursement of financial expenditure and that the fulfilment of the expectation reflects the wider detriment suffered by the claimant as a result of his reliance on the expectation; and, on that basis, it has even been argued that the remedy in *Pascoe v. Turner* [1979] 1 W.L.R. 431 (*infra*, p. 566) can be justified by reference to the reliance loss approach: see Robertson (1998) 18 *Legal Studies* 360. Proponents of the reliance loss approach also accept that, where the courts have not given full effect to the expectation, it would have been impossible or inappropriate to do so. However, in such circumstances, the courts have frequently granted some alternative right over the land in question: see, *e.g. Griffiths v. Williams* (1977) 248 E.G. 947 (*infra*, p. 569); or they have awarded compensation for the loss of expectation: see, *e.g. Wayling v. Jones* (1993) 69 P. & C.R. 170 (*infra*, p. 586). In fact, there appear to be very few cases where the courts have awarded the claimant compensation for financial expenditure only and in each case there has been some specific reason for so doing: see, *e.g. Dodsworth v. Dodsworth* (1973) 228 E.G. 1115 (*infra*, p. 581).

3.1 *Dismissal of action for possession by legal owner*

Inwards v. Baker [1965] 2 Q.B. 29

(CA, Lord Denning M.R., Danckwerts and Salmon L.JJ.)

In 1931 the defendant wished to purchase a plot of land and build a bungalow for himself but the land was too expensive. His father suggested that the defendant should instead build a larger bungalow on land belonging to the father. The defendant built the bungalow, largely through his own labour (the defendant and his father each spent about £150), and he was still living there when his father died in 1951. Under his father's will, made in 1922, the land in question was devised to trustees on trust for persons other than the defendant; and in 1963 the trustees obtained an order for possession. The defendant appealed to the Court of Appeal.

LORD DENNING M.R.:
The trustees say that at the most Jack Baker had a licence to be in the bungalow but that it had been revoked and he had no right to stay. The judge has held in their favour. He was referred to *Errington v. Errington and Woods* [1952] 1 K.B. 290, but the judge held that that decision only protected a contractual licensee. He thought that, in order to be protected, the licensee must have a contract or promise by which he is entitled to be there. The judge said: "I can find no promise made by the father to the son that he should remain in the property at all—no contractual arrangement between them. True the father said that the son could live in the property, expressly or impliedly, but there is no evidence that this was arrived at as the result of a contract or promise—merely an arrangement made casually because of the relationship which existed and knowledge that the son wished to erect a bungalow for residence". Thereupon, the judge, with much reluctance, thought the case was not within *Errington's* case [1952] 1 K.B. 290, and said the son must go.

The son appeals to this court. We have had the advantage of cases which were not cited to the country court judge—cases in the last century, notably *Dillwyn v. Llewelyn* (1862) 4 De G.F. & J. 517 and *Plimmer v. Wellington Corporation* (1884) 9 App.Cas. 699. This latter was a decision of the Privy Council which expressly affirmed and approved the statement of the law made by Lord Kingsdown in *Ramsden v. Dyson* (1866) L.R. 1 H.L. 129, 170. It is quite plain from those authorities that if the owner of land requests another, or indeed allows another, to expend money on the land under an expectation created or encouraged by the landlord that he will be able to remain there, that raises an equity in the licensee such as to entitle him to stay. He has a licence coupled with an equity. Mr Goodhart urged before us that the licensee could not stay indefinitely. The principle only applied, he said, when there was an expectation of some precise legal term. But it seems to me, from *Plimmer's* case in particular, that the equity arising from the expenditure on land need not fail "merely on the ground that the interest to be secured has not been expressly indicated ... the court must look at the circumstances in each case to decide in what way the equity can be satisfied" (1884) 9 App.Cas. 699, 713–714.

So in this case, even though there is no binding contract to grant any particular interest to the licensee, nevertheless the court can look at the circumstances and see whether there is an equity arising out of the expenditure of money. All that is necessary is that the licensee should, at the request or with the encouragement of the landlord, have spent the money in the expectation of being allowed to stay there. If so, the court will not allow that expectation to be defeated where it would be inequitable so to do. In this case it is quite plain that the father allowed an expectation to be created in the son's mind that this bungalow was to be his home. It was to be his home for his life or, at all events, his home as long as he wished it to remain his home. It seems to me, in the light of that equity, that the father could not in 1932 have turned to his son and said: "You are to go. It is my land and my house". Nor could he at any time thereafter so long as the son wanted it as his home.

Mr Goodhart put the case of a purchaser. He suggested that the father could sell the land to a purchaser who could get the son out. But I think that any purchaser who took with notice would clearly be bound by the equity. So here, too, the present plaintiffs, the successors in title of the father, are clearly themselves bound by this equity. It is an equity well recognised in law. It arises from the expenditure of money by a person in actual occupation of land when he is led to believe that, as the result of that expenditure, he will be allowed to remain there. It is for the court to say in what way the equity can be satisfied. I am quite clear in this case it can be satisfied by holding that the defendant can remain there as long as he desires to as his home.

NOTES:

1. For comment, see Crane (1965) 29 Conv. 222; (1965) 81 L.Q.R. 183.

2. In *Dodsworth v. Dodsworth* (1973) 228 E.G. 1115 (*infra*, p. 581), the Court of Appeal was of the view that, as a matter of law, the decision in *Inwards v. Baker* involved the creation of a strict settlement under the Settled Land Act 1925 and conferred on the defendant the status of tenant for life. Such a conclusion would have produced consequences (in particular, powers of disposition conferred on the tenant for life) that would have been inappropriate and undesirable. By way of response, the courts have expressly avoided those consequences by granting alternative remedies in similar cases: see, *e.g. Dodsworth v. Dodsworth, supra*; *Griffiths v. Williams* (1977) 248 E.G. 947, *infra*, p. 569; but they have sometimes felt bound to hold that a strict settlement had been created, albeit accidentally: see *Ungurian v. Lesnoff* [1990] Ch. 206, noted at [1990] C.L.J. 25; *Costello v. Costello* (1994) 70 P. & C.R. 297, noted at [1994] Conv. 391. However, in *Dent v. Dent* [1996] 1 All E.R. 659 it was held that the court should consider the context in which an exclusive right to occupy property for life was granted or agreed to before determining whether it created a strict settlement or some other property interest or some form of licence. In particular, the court should consider whether the grant or agreement constituted the creation or restructuring of property rights or merely an undertaking as to personal rights of occupation. Since the coming into force of the Trusts of Land and Appointment of Trustees Act 1996, no new strict settlements under the Settled Land Act 1925 may be created either expressly or otherwise. The trust for land that replaces the strict settlement does not involve the same consequences as the strict settlement and it may therefore be seen as a more acceptable means of satisfying the equity where the circumstances indicate that the claimant should be entitled to lifetime occupation of the property.

3. See also *Matharu v. Matharu* (1994) 68 P. & C.R. 93, noted at [1995] Conv. 61; (1995) 58 M.L.R. 412.

Jones (A.E.) v. Jones (F.W.) [1977] 1 W.L.R. 438

(CA, Lord Denning M.R., Roskill and Lawton L.JJ.)

In 1968, at the request of his father, the defendant had given up his job and moved to live near his father. The defendant and his family moved into a house which the father had purchased in his own name. The defendant gave his father sums amounting to 25 per cent of the purchase price but the father led the defendant to believe that the house was his. The father died in 1972 and his widow sought an order for possession. The judge found that the defendant had a 25 per cent share in the beneficial interest of the house and that it would be inequitable to make a possession order. The widow then brought a further action claiming rent or the sale of the property. The judge ordered a rent to be fixed and, in default of payment, the sale of the property. The defendant appealed to the Court of Appeal.

LORD DENNING M.R.:
First the claim for rent. It is quite plain that these two people were in equity tenants in common having a three-quarter and one-quarter share respectively. One was in occupation of the house. The other not. Now the common law said clearly that one tenant in common is not entitled to rent from another tenant in common, even though that other occupies the whole. That appears from *M'Mahon v. Burchell* (1846) 2 Ph. 127, 134–135 *per* Lord Cottenham L.C., and *Henderson v. Eason* (1851) 17 Q.B. 701, 720. Of course if one of the tenants let the premises at a rent to a stranger and received the rent, there would have to be an account, but the mere fact that one tenant was in possession and the other out of possession did not give the one that is out any claim for rent. It did not do so in the old days of legal tenants in common. Nor does it in modern times of equitable tenants in common. In *Bull v. Bull* [1955] 1 Q.B. 234, 239, I said:

> "... the son, although he is the legal owner of the house, has no right to turn his mother out. She has an equitable interest which entitles her to remain in the house as tenant in common with him until the house is sold."

As between tenants in common, they are both equally entitled to occupation and one cannot claim rent from the other. Of course, if there was an ouster, that would be another matter: or if there was a letting to a stranger for rent that would be different, but there can be no claim for rent by one tenant in common against the other whether at law or in equity.

Second, the order for sale. Here comes into play the doctrine of proprietary estoppel. It has been considered by this court in *Inwards v. Baker* [1965] 2 Q.B. 29 and *Crabb v. Arun District Council* [1976] Ch. 179. It is quite plain that the principles of those cases apply here.

Old Mr Jones' conduct was such as to lead his son Frederick reasonably to believe that he could stay there and regard Philmona as his home for the rest of his life. On the basis of that reasonable expectation, the son gave up his work at Kingston-upon-Thames and moved to Blundeston. He paid the £ 1,000 too in the same expectation. He did work on the house as well. It was all because he had been led to believe this his father would never turn him out of the house: it would be his family's home for the rest of his life. He and the rest of the family thought that the father would alter his will or make over the house to the son. The father did not do it, but nevertheless he led the son to believe that he could stay there for the rest of his life. On those two cases it is clear that old Mr Jones would be estopped from turning the son out. After his death, the plaintiff is equally estopped from turning the defendant out.

Similarly, the plaintiff is not entitled to an order for the property to be sold. Nor for any payment to be made by Frederick to her pending sale. Even though there is an implied trust for sale, nevertheless, the courts will not allow it to be used so as to defeat the purposes contemplated by the parties. That appears from *Bedson v. Bedson* [1965] 2 Q.B. 666: see what I said at p. 679, and *per* Russell L.J., at pp. 697 and 698. No order for the sale of this property should be made because that would defeat the very purpose of the acquisition, namely that the son Frederick would be able to be there for his life and remain in it as his home.

The two doctrines go hand in hand to show that no order should be made so as to disturb the son in his possession of the house: nor should he be made to pay anything for staying there.

The ultimate result of the case is that the son has a proprietary interest of a one-quarter share in the house. He is able to stay there for life by virtue of his interest in it, and the plaintiff is estopped from turning him out. Nor can it be sold without his consent. The appeal should be allowed and an order made accordingly.

ROSKILL L.J.:

Lord Denning M.R. has referred to the decision of this court, consisting of himself, Lawton L.J. and Scarman L.J., in *Crabb v. Arun District Council* [1976] Ch. 179. I would refer to the three questions, posed by Scarman L.J. at the beginning of his judgment, which the court has to ask in relation to the now well-settled law on estoppel, at p. 193: "First, is there an equity established?" The answer here is unquestionably Yes. "Secondly, what is the extent of the equity, if one is established?"—and the answer, shortly, is that the equity is of a possessory nature entitling the defendant to remain in this house, but it would not, in my judgment, extend to the defendant's wife. "And, thirdly, what is the relief appropriate to satisfy the equity?" All the members of the court in *Crabb v. Arun District Council* thought that in some circumstances a court might impose the making of payment of some form or another as a condition of giving effect to the equity, but in the present case it seems to me that it would be wrong to impose as a condition of protecting the equity that the defendant should pay rent to the plaintiff for the following reasons. First, the point of law which I have already mentioned [that a tenant in common in occupation of the co-owned land is not as a general rule liable to pay rent to the other tenant(s) in common]. Secondly, the representation made by the father to the defendant which seems to me to be just as binding upon the plaintiff, who was the administratrix of his will, as upon the deceased father. Thirdly, it is plain that the defendant moved into this house thinking that he was going to benefit. With all respect to Mr Sunnucks' able argument, I am unable to see why equity should fail to protect the defendant.

For those reasons I would allow this appeal and set aside the order for payment of rent, and I would also refuse an order for sale.

I would mention one thing. It was suggested by Mr Sunnucks that if we took the view which we do we ought to order a life interest to be created in favour of the defendant. In my judgment, at this stage it would be wrong so to do. This does not seem to have been the subject of argument below, and it seems to me that the defendant's real case was that he should not pay the rent, and not to seek the creation of a life interest.

I would allow the appeal accordingly.

NOTES:

1. For comment, see (1977) 41 Conv. 279; (1978) 41 M.L.R. 208.

2. On the position relating to rent obligations between co-owners, see *ante*, p. 318.

3.2 *Transfer of fee simple*

Dillwyn v. Llewelyn (1862) 4 De G.F. & J. 517

(Court of Appeal in Chancery, Lord Westbury L.C.)

The plaintiff's father signed a memorandum to the effect that he was giving part of his land to the plaintiff for the purpose of providing him with a site on which to build a house. The plaintiff proceeded to build a house, spending some £14,000, with the knowledge and approval of his father. The father died, having made no alteration to his will, which predated and was mentioned in the memorandum and which purported to settle his property in a manner inconsistent with the terms of the memorandum. The plaintiff sought an order requiring the fee simple to be conveyed to him.

LORD WESTBURY L.C.:
About the rules of the court there can be no controversy. A voluntary agreement will not be completed or assisted by a court of equity; in cases of mere gift, if anything be wanting to complete the title of the donee, a court of equity will not assist him in obtaining it, for a mere donee can have no right to claim more than he has received. But the subsequent acts of the donor may give the donee that right or ground of claim which he did not acquire from the original gift. Thus, if A. gives a house to B., but makes no formal conveyance, and the house is afterwards, on the marriage of B., included, with the knowledge of A., in the marriage-settlement of B., A. would be bound to complete the title of the parties claiming under that settlement. So if A. puts B. in possession of a piece of land, and tells him, "I give it you, that you may build a house on it"; and B., on the strength of that promise, with the knowledge of A., expends a large sum of money in building a house accordingly, I cannot doubt that the donee acquires a right from the subsequent transaction to call on the donor to perform that contract which arises from the contract, and to complete the imperfect donation which was made. The case is somewhat analogous to that of verbal agreement, not binding originally for want of the memorandum in writing signed by the party to be charged, but which becomes binding by virtue of the subsequent part performance. The early case of *Foxcraft v. Lister* (1701) 2 Vern. 456 is an example nearly approaching to the terms of the present case.
    Sir John Romilly M.R., however, seems to have thought that a question might still remain as to the extent of the estate taken by the donee; and that, in this particular case, the extent of the donee's interest depended on the terms of the memorandum. I am not of that opinion. The equity of the donee and the estate to be claimed by virtue of it depend on the transaction, that is, on the acts done, and not on the language of the memorandum, except as that shows the purpose and intent of the gift. The estate was given as the site of a dwelling-house to be erected by the son. The ownership of the dwelling-house and the ownership of the estate must be considered as intended to be co-extensive and co-equal. No one builds a house for his own life only, and it is absurd to suppose that it was intended by either party that the house, at the death of the son, should become the property of the father. If, therefore, I am right in the conclusion of law that the subsequent expenditure by the son, with the approbation of the father, supplied a valuable consideration originally wanting, the memorandum signed by the father and son must be thenceforth regarded as an agreement for the soil, extending to the fee-simple of the land. In a contract for sale of an estate, no words of limitation are necessary to exclude the fee-simple; but further, upon the construction of the memorandum itself, taken apart from the subsequent acts, I should be of opinion

that it was the plain intention of the testator to vest in the son the absolute ownership of the estate.

The only inquiry, therefore, is, whether the son's expenditure, on the faith of the memorandum, supplied a valuable consideration and created a binding obligation. On this I have no doubt, and it, therefore, follows that the intention to give the fee-simple must be performed, and that the decree ought to declare the son the absolute owner of the estate comprised in the memorandum. I propose, therefore, to reverse the decree of the Master of the Rolls, and to declare that, by virtue of the original gift made by the testator, and of the subsequent expenditure by the plaintiff, with the approbation of the testator, and of the right and obligation resulting therefrom, the plaintiff is entitled to have a conveyance from the trustees of the testator's will, and the other parties interested under the same, of all their estate and interest under the testator's will in the estate of Hendrefoilan, in the pleading mentioned; and, with this declaration, refer it to the judge in chambers to settle such conveyance accordingly.

Pascoe v. Turner [1979] 1 W.L.R. 431

(CA, Orr, Lawton and Cumming-Bruce L.JJ.)

The plaintiff and the defendant lived together in a house purchased by the plaintiff. The plaintiff ended the relationship after nine years and moved out of the house. On a number of occasions the plaintiff told the defendant that the house and its contents were hers but he never conveyed the property to her. Nonetheless, in reliance upon the plaintiff's representations and with the knowledge of the plaintiff, the defendant spent her own money and herself did work on redecoration, improvements and repairs; and she bought furniture and furnishings for the house. The plaintiff, having first purported to determine the defendant's "licence to occupy", subsequently sought an order for possession.

CUMMING-BRUCE L.J.:

The judge found that the plaintiff had made a gift to her of the contents of the house. I have no doubt that he was right about that. She was already in possession of them as a bailee when he declared the gift. Counsel for the plaintiff submitted that there was no gift because it was uncertain what he was giving her. He pointed to a safe and to the defendant's evidence that she had sent round an orange bedroom suite to the plaintiff so that he should have a bed to sleep on. The answer is that he gave her everything in the house, but later, recognising his need, she gave back some bits and pieces to him. So much for the contents.

Her rights in the realty are not quite so simply disposed of because of section 53 and section 54 of the Law of Property Act 1925. There was nothing in writing. The judge considered the plaintiff's declarations, and decided that they were not enough to found an express trust. We agree. But he went on to hold that the beneficial interest in the house had passed under a constructive trust inferred from words and conduct of the parties. He relied on the passage in *Snell's Principles of Equity*, 27th ed. (1973), p. 185, in which the editors suggest a possible definition of a constructive trust. But there are difficulties in the way. The long and short of events in 1973 is that the plaintiff made an imperfect gift of the house. There is nothing in the facts from which an inference of a constructive trust can be drawn. If it had not been for section 53 of the Law of Property Act 1925 the gift of the house would have been a perfect gift, just as the gift of the contents was a perfect gift. In the event it remained an imperfect gift and, as Turner L.J. said in *Milroy v. Lord* (1862) 4 De G.F. & J. 264, 274: "there is no equity in this court to perfect an imperfect gift". So matters stood in 1973, and if the facts had stopped there the defendant would have remained a licensee at will of the plaintiff.

But the facts did not stop there. On the judge's findings the defendant, having been told that the house was hers, set about improving it within and without. Outside she did not do much: a little work on the roof and an improvement which covered the way from the outside toilet to the rest of the house, putting in a new door there, and Snowcem to protect the toilet. Inside she did a good deal more. She installed gas in the kitchen with a cooker, improved the plumbing in the kitchen and put in a new sink. She got new gas fires, putting a gas fire in the lounge. She redecorated four rooms. The fitted carpets she put in the bedrooms, the stair carpeting, and the curtains and the furniture that she bought are not part of the realty, and it is not clear how much she spent on those items. But they are part of the whole circumstances. There she was, on her own after he left her in 1973. She had £1,000 left of her capital, and a pension of some kind. Having as she thought been given the house, she set about it as described. On the repairs and improvement to the realty and its fixtures she spent about £230. She had £300 of her capital left by the date of the trial, but she did not establish in evidence how much had been expended on refurbishing the house with carpets, curtains and furniture. We would describe the work done in and about the house as substantial in the sense that that adjective is used in the context of estoppel. All the while the plaintiff not only stood by and watched but encouraged and advised, without a word to suggest that she was putting her money and her personal labour into his house. What is the effect in equity?

The cases relied upon by the plaintiff are relevant for the purpose of showing that the judge fell into error in deciding that on the facts a constructive trust could be inferred. They are the cases which deal with the intention of the parties when a house is acquired. But of those cases only *Inwards v. Baker* [1965] 2 Q.B. 29 is in point here. For this is a case of estoppel arising from the encouragement and acquiescence of the plaintiff between 1973 and 1976 when, in reliance upon his declaration that he was giving and, later, that he had given the house to her, she spent a substantial part of her small capital upon repairs and improvements to the house. The relevant principle is expounded in *Snell's Principles of Equity,* 27th ed., p. 565 in the passage under the heading "Proprietary Estoppel", and is elaborated in *Spencer Bower and Turner, Estoppel by Representation,* 3rd ed. (1977), chapter 12 entitled "Encouragement and Acquiescence".

The cases in point illustrating that principle in relation to real property are *Dillwyn v. Llewelyn* (1862) 4 De G.F. & J. 517; *Ramsden v. Dyson* (1866) L.R. 1 H.L. 129 and *Plimmer v. Wellington Corporation* (1884) 9 App.Cas. 699. One distinction between this class of case and the doctrine which has come to be known as "promissory estoppel" is that where estoppel by encouragement or acquiescence is found on the facts, those facts give rise to a cause of action. They may be relied upon as a sword, not merely as a shield. In *Ramsden v. Dyson* the plaintiff failed on the facts, and the dissent of Lord Kingsdown was upon the inferences to be drawn from the facts. On the principle, however, the House was agreed, and it is stated by Lord Cranworth L.C. and by Lord Wensleydale as well as by Lord Kingsdown. Likewise in *Plimmer's* case the plaintiff was granted a declaration that he had a perpetual right of occupation.

The final question that arises is: to what relief is the defendant entitled upon her counterclaim?

[Cumming-Bruce L.J. referred to *Dillwyn v. Llewelyn* (1862) 4 De G.F. & J. 517, *supra,* p. 565; *Plimmer v. Mayor of Wellington* (1884) 9 App.Cas. 699, *infra,* p. 579; *Thomas v. Thomas* [1956] N.Z.L.R. 785; *Crabb v. Arun D.C.* [1976] Ch. 179, *infra,* p. 573. He continued:]

So the principle to be applied is that the court should consider all the circumstances, and the counterclaimant having at law no perfected gift or licence other than a licence revocable at will, the court must decide what is the minimum equity to do justice to her having regard to the way in which she changed her position for the worse by reason of the acquiescence and encouragement of the legal owner. The defendant submits that the only appropriate way in which the equity can here be satisfied is by perfecting the imperfect gift as was done in *Dillwyn v. Llewelyn.*

Counsel for the plaintiff on instructions has throughout submitted that the plaintiff is entitled to possession. The only concession that he made was that the period of notice given in the letter of April 9, 1976, was too short. He made no submission upon the way the equity, if there was an equity, should be satisfied save to submit that the court should not in any view grant a remedy more beneficial to the defendant than a licence to occupy the house for her lifetime.

We are satisfied that the problem of remedy on the facts resolves itself into a choice between two alternatives: should the equity be satisfied by a licence to the defendant to occupy the house for her lifetime, or should there be a transfer to her of the fee simple?

The main consideration pointing to a licence for her lifetime is that she did not by her case at the hearing seek to establish that she had spent more money or done more work on the house than she would have done had she believed that she had only a licence to live there for her lifetime. But the court must be cautious about drawing any inference from what she did not give in evidence as the hypothesis put is one that manifestly never occurred to her. Then it may reasonably be held that her expenditure and effort can hardly be regarded as comparable to the change of position of those who have constructed buildings on land over which they had no legal rights.

This court appreciates that the moneys laid out by the defendant were much less than in some of the cases in the books. But the court has to look at all the circumstances. When the plaintiff left her she was, we were told, a widow in her middle fifties. During the period that she lived with the plaintiff her capital was reduced from £4,500 to £1,000. Save for her invalidity pension that was all that she had in the world. In reliance upon the plaintiff's declaration of gift, encouragement and acquiescence she arranged her affairs on the basis that the house and contents belonged to her. So relying, she devoted a quarter of her remaining capital and her personal effort upon the house and its fixtures. In addition she bought carpets, curtains and furniture for it, with the result that by the date of the trial she had only £300 left. Compared to her, on the evidence the plaintiff is a rich man. He might not regard an expenditure of a few hundred pounds as a very grave loss. But the court has to regard her change of position over the years 1973 to 1976.

We take the view that the equity cannot here be satisfied without granting a remedy which assures to the defendant security of tenure, quiet enjoyment, and freedom of action in respect of repairs and improvements without interference from the plaintiff. The history of the conduct of the plaintiff since April 9, 1976, in relation to these proceedings leads to an irresistible inference that he is determined to pursue his purpose of evicting her from the house by any legal means at his disposal with a ruthless disregard of the obligations binding upon conscience. The court must grant a remedy effective to protect her against the future manifestations of his ruthlessness. It was conceded that if she is granted a licence, such a licence cannot be registered as a land charge, so that she may find herself ousted by a purchaser for value without notice. If she has in the future to do further and more expensive repairs she may only be able to finance them by a loan, but as a licensee she cannot charge the house. The plaintiff as legal owner may well find excuses for entry in order to do what he may plausibly represent as necessary works and so contrive to derogate from her enjoyment of the licence in ways that make it difficult or impossible for the court to give her effective protection.

Weighing such considerations this court concludes that the equity to which the facts in this case give rise can only be satisfied by compelling the plaintiff to give effect to his promise and her expectations. He has so acted that he must now perfect the gift.

NOTES:

1. For comment, see [1979] Conv. 379; (1979) 42 M.L.R. 574.

2. See also *Re Basham* [1986] 1 W.L.R. 1498, *supra*, p. 549; *Voyce v. Voyce* (1991) 62 P. & C.R. 290; *Lim Teng Huan v. Ang Swee Chuan* [1992] 1 W.L.R. 113, noted at [1993] Conv. 173; *Durant v. Heritage* [1994] E.G.C.S. 134.

3. In *Wayling v. Jones* (1993) 69 P. & C.R. 170 the claimant established an equity against the executors of the landowner but the executors had already sold the land in question. If the land had not been sold it seems clear that the Court of Appeal would have satisfied the equity by ordering the transfer of the fee simple to the claimant. In the circumstances, the court awarded the claimant the net proceeds of sale plus interest: see *infra*, p. 586.

3.3 *Grant of lease*

Griffiths v. Williams (1977) 248 E.G. 947

(CA, Megaw, Orr and Goff L.JJ.)

The defendant lived for most of her life in her mother's house and she looked after her there. She expended her own money on repairs and improvements both in the interests of her mother's comfort and because she believed that she would be entitled to live in the house for the rest of her own life. Indeed her mother had prepared a will leaving the defendant a life interest in the house; but a later will left the house absolutely to the plaintiff, the defendant's daughter. When the defendant's mother died and the plaintiff sought possession of the house, the defendant invoked the doctrine of proprietary estoppel.

GOFF L.J.:

[The] equity is said to arise because the grandmother had repeatedly assured Mrs Williams that she would be allowed to live in the house for the whole of her life, and because, on the faith of those assurances, Mrs Williams had expended money upon the property which otherwise she would not have done. It emerged at the trial that she had spent in all, out of her own moneys, a sum of £2,000. Part of that was spent upon improvements to the property which consisted of putting in a bathroom and an indoors toilet, rewiring for electricity, concreting the yard, and repairs to one of the walls; but part of it had been spent in paying outgoings. In so far as the expenditure was of the latter character, I doubt whether it would raise an equity in Mrs Williams' favour, because it could be regarded simply as current payment for the benefits which she was enjoying by being allowed to live in the house. But in so far as money was spent upon permanent improvements such as I have mentioned, it would be capable of creating what is known as a promissory [sic] estoppel. It seems that a grant in aid towards the improvements was obtained from the local authority; but, even so, as I read the evidence Mrs Williams did incur expenditure out of her own money on improvements. But the evidence does not show how the £2,000 should be broken down between expenditure of that character and expenditure on current repairs.

In these circumstances, in my judgment, we have to determine three questions, which were propounded by Scarman L.J. in his judgment in the case of *Crabb v. Arun District Council* [1976] Ch. 179 [*infra*, p. 573]...

If [the court] finds that there is an equity, then it must determine the nature of it, and then, guided by that nature and exercising discretion in all the circumstances, it has to determine what is the fair order to make between the parties for the protection of the claimant.

So I direct my mind to the first question: Was there here an equity? Mr McCarthy [counsel for the plaintiff] says that there was not, because the defendant failed to prove, and the learned judge did not find, that the grandmother at the time the improvements were effected knew that Mrs Williams was making a mistake as to her position. He relies on the passage in *Snell's Equity*, 27th ed. at p. 566/C, where it is said:

> "Knowledge of the mistake makes it dishonest for him to remain wilfully passive in order afterwards to profit by the mistake he might have prevented. The knowledge must accordingly be proved by 'strong and cogent evidence.' "

He also points to the learned judge's judgment, where he said:

> "It was clear that Mrs Williams—and I think this would apply to most sensitive people in her position—was reluctant to admit, even to herself, that in spending her own money on housekeeping and house improvement, she was thinking predominantly of her own inheritance rather than the care and comfort of her mother. What she did say, however, was that had it occurred to her that her enjoyment and benefit of these improvements, or rather of the house as improved (a house that she had always regarded as her home) would be limited to her mother's life span, she would have had to think whether she was not obliged to look more closely to her own future.... It was equally clear, however, that none of this occurred to her at the time, or perhaps even not until it was put to her in this court."

In so far as it is necessary to prove that Mrs Williams made a mistake, I think the mistake is to be found in her belief that she would be allowed to live in the house for the whole of her life. But I do not myself think that it really depends upon mistake. The equity is based upon the fact that where one has made a representation on the faith of which another party has expended his money, then the man who made the representation will not, to the prejudice of the other, be allowed to go back on it and assert his strict legal rights if to do so would be unconscionable.

[Goff L.J. cited the judgment of Lord Denning M.R. in *Inwards v. Baker* [1965] 2 Q.B. 29, 37, *supra*, p. 561. He continued:]

The facts in that case were different, but the principle appears to me to apply precisely to the facts of the present case. Mrs Williams' evidence, which the learned judge preferred to that of Mrs Griffiths, was as follows: "Whenever the question arose in any discussion Mrs Williams had always been assured that the house was her home for life. That was always what was said and she never expected more than a life interest". That does not read as if it was the lady giving evidence, but the notes of the evidence appear throughout in that form, and this was obviously a record which the learned judge was making of the evidence which had been given before him. Then Mr Hedley Williams, whose evidence the learned judge also accepted, said—or the effect of his evidence is recorded—as follows: "He had always understood that the house was his mother's for life, and this had been said to, or in front of, him over many years by both his grandmother and his mother"; and, again, "As to the improvements etc. there was no objection by the grandmother and he had never heard any mention (prior to his grandmother's death) of his mother leaving, or being asked to leave". So when the learned judge speaks of what Mrs Williams would have thought had it occurred to her, it is clear that it would have occurred to her but for the fact that Mrs Cole, the testatrix, was throughout repeatedly assuring Mrs Williams that she could live in the house for the rest of her life. It seems to me, on this evidence, clear that Mrs Williams expended her money on the faith of those repeated assurances, and it is, I think, an irresistible inference that Mrs Cole knew that Mrs Williams was relying on the assurances which she herself was repeatedly making to her daughter. In my judgment, therefore, there is no doubt at all in this case but that an equity is made out.

I therefore pass to the second question, and that is: What is the equity? That must be an equity to have made good, so far as may fairly be done between the parties, the representation that Mrs Williams should be entitled to live in the house rent-free for the rest of her life.

So I come to the third question, which is really the one which gives rise to such difficulties as there are in this case. In *Dodsworth v. Dodsworth* (1973) 228 E.G. 1115 [*infra*, p. 581] this court unanimously decided that if an equity of this nature were implemented by giving the claimant the right to occupy the house (as it was in that case) for his life, the result would be to create a tenancy for life within the meaning of the Settled Land Act, and so the party setting up the equity would get more than it was ever represented that he should have, because he would get all the statutory powers of a tenant for life under the Act: he could sell the property and take the income of the proceeds for his life, or he could grant a long lease. In that case the court does not seem to have considered what may in such cases be a difficult problem, namely, what is the "settlement"?. I think there are many authorities which establish that a right to occupy property for one's life is the equivalent of a tenancy for life under the Act. But the Act defines "settlement" in section 1 in these terms:

"Any deed, will, agreement for a settlement or other agreement, Act of Parliament, or other instrument, or any number of instruments, whether made or passed before or after, or partly before and partly after, the commencement of this Act, under or by virtue of which instrument or instruments any land, after the commencement of this Act, stands for the time being. . ."

and then follow the various limitations which make it settled land.

Where the interest arises under a contract or other agreement, of course, there is no difficulty, because that falls fairly and squarely within the words of subsection (1) of section 1. But where what is set up is an equity arising from acting upon a representation, it is not obvious how that can be brought within the terms of section 1(1). There are two other cases in which this type of problem was considered by this court, namely, *Binions v. Evans* [1972] 1 Ch. 359 and *Bannister v. Bannister* [1948] 2 All E.R. 133. In *Binions v. Evans* the Master of the Rolls thought that such an equity would not in any event create a settlement; but, with all respect, I think his reasoning leads to difficulties, because at p. 367 he reached the conclusion that it created an equitable interest, and once that is established then the ground on which he said (at p. 366) there was no settlement appears to me to be undermined. The other two Lord Justices who heard that case, Megaw L.J. and Stephenson L.J., felt that they were bound by the earlier decision in *Bannister v. Bannister* to hold that there was a settlement; but they did not direct themselves to any question under section 1; nor, I think, need they have done so, because in *Binions v. Evans* and the earlier case of *Bannister v. Bannister* there was actually an agreement. So that the difficulty which in my view arises, on the case of *Dodsworth v. Dodsworth* and upon the present case, of seeing whether there can be a settlement when you have an interest which appears to give you a tenancy for life but there does not obviously appear to be anything which is a "settlement" within the Act, did not arise in those two earlier cases. If it were necessary, we would have to decide what is, I think, a serious problem—whether *Dodsworth v. Dodsworth* is binding upon us or whether it was decided strictly *per incuriam* because the learned Lord Justices who heard it did not advert to section 1 of the Settled Land Act, and, if it be not binding upon us, whether in truth it be right, and if so, what is the answer to the conundrum posed by subsection (1) of section 1. It may be that in such a case there is a settlement, and it is the order of the court declaring the equity, which is an "instrument" and, therefore, the "settlement" within the meaning of that subsection.

Happily, by the good sense of the parties in accepting a solution of the problem which I propounded for their consideration, it is unnecessary for this court to resolve those problems. In *Dodsworth v. Dodsworth*, having decided that a right of occupation for the whole life of the claimant would be a wrong way of giving effect to the equity because it would create a settlement under the Settled Land Act and give the claimant too much, the court then adopted an alternative suggestion of compensation by recouping the claimant his expenditure (I think with interest) and giving him possession until payment. They recognised that that really went too far the other way; and certainly it would not be appropriate in this case–if for no other reason, because of the difficulty of quantification. But it seems to me that *Dodsworth v. Dodsworth* proceeded upon the basis which I have spelt out of *Crabb's* case—that the third problem is one of discretion: the court ought to see, having regard to all the circumstances, what is the best and fairest way to secure protection for the person who has been misled by the representations made to him and subsequently repudiated.

In the present case, it seemed to me, and I suggested to the parties, that the fairest way of dealing with the matter would be to direct the plaintiffs to grant Mrs Williams a long lease, determinable upon her death, at a nominal rent, since that would give her the right of occupation for her whole life and could not in any event give her the statutory powers under the Settled Land Act. The nominal rent would be an obligation not contemplated when the representations were made to her, but perfect equity is seldom possible.

There appeared to be only two objections to this course. One was that she might assign the lease; but that can be dealt with by including in the lease an absolute covenant not to assign, and by her giving an undertaking to this court, which I understand she is prepared to do, not to assign. The other difficulty was that, if she were to marry again, her husband might be able to claim a protected tenancy under the Rent Acts. I know that to Mrs Williams that appears a flight of fantasy; but we have to take precautions to see that what we propose is something which will not go wrong in an event which is not impossible and could happen. Counsel have made inquiries and they assure us that the husband would not be entitled to protection under the Rent Acts if the rent did not exceed two-thirds of the rateable value at the relevant date; and they have ascertained that that rateable value is £46 per annum. Therefore, if we direct the lease to be at a rent of £30 per annum we will have served the two ends of keeping it below two-thirds of the rateable value and making it nominal; and that is what I would propose. I took the precaution of making it clear to counsel, and they have made it clear to the parties, that, while we might order that as a term after deciding whether or not a life interest would be a "settlement" within the meaning of the Act, if we were to decide that it was not a settlement within the Act Mrs Williams would be entitled to claim a full life interest without reservation of any rent, and therefore we could only adopt this course of a long lease at this stage if the parties consented to it, otherwise we must first determine the problem which I have mentioned and then consider what it would be right to order in the light of that determination. Counsel, having withdrawn and consulted with their clients and taken instructions, say that they are content that we should adopt the solution proposed by me.

NOTES:

    1. For comment, see [1978] Conv. 250.

    2. See also *J.T. Development Ltd v. Quinn* (1991) 62 P. & C.R. 33.

    3. On the application of the Settled Land Act 1925, see *supra*, p. 562.

3.4 *Enforcement of option to renew lease*

See *Taylors Fashions Ltd v. Liverpool Victoria Trustees Co. Ltd* [1982] Q.B. 133, *supra*, p. 535.

3.5 *Grant of easement*

Crabb v. Arun DC [1976] Ch. 179

(CA, Lord Denning M.R., Lawton and Scarman L.JJ.)

The plaintiff owned a plot of land, which had access at point "A" onto a road owned by the defendant council; he also had a right of way along the road to the public highway. Intending to sell the land in two separate parts, he sought from the defendant an additional right of access to the land at point "B" and an additional right of way along the road. There was some dispute as to whether this was agreed by the defendant; but the defendant subsequently fenced the boundary between the plaintiff's land and the road and erected gates at both points of access. The plaintiff sold part of the land, with access at point "A", without reserving any rights in favour of the land retained. The defendant then blocked access point "B", leaving the retained land without access. The plaintiff claimed that the defendant was estopped from denying him that access.

SCARMAN L.J.:
The plaintiff and the defendants are adjoining landowners. The plaintiff asserts that he has a right of way over the defendants' land giving access from his land to the public highway. Without this access his land is in fact landlocked, but, for reasons which clearly appear from the narration of the facts already given by my Lords, the plaintiff cannot claim a right of way by necessity. The plaintiff has no grant. He has the benefit of no enforceable contract. He has no prescriptive right. His case has to be that the defendants are estopped by their conduct from denying him a right of access over their land to the public highway. If the plaintiff has any right, it is an equity arising out of the conduct and relationship of the parties. In such a case I think it is now well settled law that the court, having analysed and assessed the conduct and relationship of the parties has to answer three questions. First, is there an equity established? Secondly, what is the extent of the equity, if one is established? And, thirdly, what is the relief appropriate to satisfy the equity? See *Duke of Beaufort v. Patrick* (1853) 17 Beav. 60; *Plimmer v. Wellington Corporation* (1884) 9 App.Cas 699 and *Inwards v. Baker* [1965] 2 Q.B. 29, a decision of this court, and particularly the observations of Lord Denning M.R. at p. 37. Such therefore I believe to be the nature of the inquiry that the courts have to conduct in a case of this sort. In pursuit of that inquiry I do not find helpful the distinction between promissory and proprietary estoppel. This distinction may indeed be valuable to those who have to teach or expound the law; but I do not think that, in solving the particular problem raised by a particular case, putting the law into categories is of the slightest assistance.

Nor do I think it necessary in a case such as this to inquire minutely into the law of agency. These defendants could, of course, only act through agents; but, as I have already made clear, from the very nature of the case, there would be no question of grant, no question of legally enforceable contract. We are in the realm of equity; and within that realm we find that equity, to its eternal credit, has developed an immensely flexible, yet perfectly clear, doctrine: see *E.R. Ives Investment Ltd v. High* [1967] 2 Q.B. 379, *per* Danckwerts L.J. at p. 399. The approach of equity, when there is a question of agency in a field such as this, must I think be a very simple one. It will merely be that, within reasonable limits, those to whom a defendant entrusts the conduct of negotiations must be treated as having the authority, which, within the course of the negotiations, they purport to exercise. I put it in that way in the light of the comments of Lord Denning M.R. in *Moorgate Mercantile Co. Ltd v. Twitchings* [1976] Q.B. 225, 243–comments which were themselves made upon a judgment to the same effect in *Attorney-General to the Prince of Wales v. Collom* [1916] 2 K.B. 193, 203. I would add only one reservation to this broad proposition. The defendant, if he thinks that an agent has exceeded his instructions, can always so inform the plaintiff before the plaintiff acts to his detriment in reliance upon what the agent has said or done. If a defendant has done so, the plaintiff cannot then establish the equity: for the defendant will have intervened to prevent him acting to his detriment. Nothing of that sort happened in this case. After the meeting in July 1967, to which both my Lords have referred, the plaintiff was left to form his own conclusions as to the intentions of the defendants.

I come now to consider the first of the three questions which I think in a case such as this the court have to consider. What is needed to establish an equity? In the course of an interesting addition to his submissions this morning, Mr Lightman [counsel for the defendants] cited *Ramsden v. Dyson* (1866) L.R. 1 H.L. 129, 142, to support his proposition that in order to establish an equity by estoppel there must be a belief by the plaintiff in the existence of a right created or encouraged by the words or actions of the defendant. With respect, I do not think that that is today a correct statement of the law. I think the law has developed so that today it is to be considered as correctly stated by Lord Kingsdown in his dissenting speech in *Ramsden v. Dyson*. Like Lord Denning M.R., I think that the point of dissent in *Ramsden v. Dyson* was not on the law but on the facts. Lord Kingsdown's speech, in so far as it dealt with propositions of law, has been often considered, and recently followed by this court in *Inwards v. Baker* [1965] 2 Q.B. 29. So what is the effect of looking to Lord Kingsdown's speech for a statement of the law? Lord Kingsdown said (1866) L.R. 1 H.L. 129, 170:

> "The rule of law applicable to the case appears to me to be this: If a man, under a verbal agreement with a landlord for a certain interest in land, or, what amounts to the same thing, *under an expectation, created or encouraged by the landlord*",—my italics—"that he shall have a certain interest, takes possession of such land, with the consent of the landlord, and upon the faith of such promise or expectation, with the knowledge of the landlord, and without objection by him, lays out money upon the land, a court of equity will compel the landlord to give effect to such promise or expectation."

That statement of the law is put into the language of landlord and tenant because it was a landlord and tenant situation with which Lord Kingsdown was concerned; but it has been accepted as of general application. While *Ramsden v. Dyson* may properly be considered as the modern starting-point of the law of equitable estoppel, it was analysed and spelt out in a judgment of Fry J. in 1880 in *Willmott v. Barber* (1880) 15 Ch.D. 96, a decision to which Pennycuick V.-C. referred in his judgment. I agree with Pennycuick V.-C. in thinking that the passage from Fry J.'s judgment, from p. 105, is a valuable guide as to the matters of fact which have to be established in order that a plaintiff may establish this particular equity. Moreover, Mr Lightman for the defendants sought to make a submission in reliance upon the judgment. Fry J. said, at pp. 105–106:

> "It has been said that the acquiescence which will deprive a man of his legal rights must amount to fraud, and in my view that is an abbreviated statement of a very true proposition. A man is not to be deprived of his legal rights unless he has acted in such a way as would make it fraudulent for him to set up those rights. What, then, are the elements or requisites necessary to constitute fraud of that description? In the first place the plaintiff must have made a mistake as to his legal rights. Secondly, the plaintiff must have expended some money or must have done some act (not necessarily upon the defendant's land) on the faith of his mistaken belief. Thirdly, the defendant, the possessor of the legal right, must know of the existence of his own right which is inconsistent with the right claimed by the plaintiff. If he

does not know of it he is in the same position as the plaintiff, and the doctrine of acquiescence is founded upon conduct with a knowledge of your legal rights. Fourthly, the defendant, the possessor of the legal right, must know of the plaintiff's mistaken belief of his rights. If he does not, there is nothing which calls upon him to assert his own rights. Lastly",—if I may digress, this is the important element as far as this appeal is concerned—"the defendant, the possessor of the legal right, must have encouraged the plaintiff in his expenditure of money or in the other acts which he has done, either directly or by abstaining from asserting his legal right."

Mr Lightman, in the course of an interesting and vigorous submission, drew the attention of the court to the necessity of finding something akin to fraud before the equity sought by the plaintiff could be established. "Fraud" was a word often in the mouths of those robust judges who adorned the bench in the 19th century. It is less often in the mouths of the more wary judicial spirits today who sit upon the bench. But it is clear that whether one uses the word "fraud" or not, the plaintiff has to establish as a fact that the defendant, by setting up his right, is taking advantage of him in a way which is unconscionable, inequitable or unjust. It is to be observed from the passage that I have quoted from the judgment of Fry J., that the fraud or injustice alleged does not take place during the course of negotiation, but only when the defendant decides to refuse to allow the plaintiff to set up his claim against the defendant's undoubted right. The fraud, if it be such, arises after the event, when the defendant seeks by relying on his right to defeat the expectation which he by his conduct encouraged the plaintiff to have. There need not be anything fraudulent or unjust in the conduct of the actual negotiations—the conduct of the transaction by the defendants.

The court therefore cannot find an equity established unless it is prepared to go as far as to say that it would be unconscionable and unjust to allow the defendants to set up their undoubted rights against the claim being made by the plaintiff. In order to reach a conclusion upon that matter the court does have to consider the history of the negotiations under the five headings to which Fry J. referred. I need not at this stage weary anyone with an elaborate statement of the facts. I have no doubt upon the facts of this case that the first four elements referred to by Fry J. exist. The question before the judge and now in this court is whether the fifth element is present: have the defendants, as possessor of the legal right, encouraged the plaintiff in the expenditure of money or in the other acts which he has done, either directly or by abstaining from asserting their legal rights? The first matter to be considered is the meeting on site of July 26, 1967. Pennycuick V.-C. made a finding of fact about the meeting; and for myself I am not prepared to dissent from his finding. But the substance of the finding of fact has to be regarded; not its phrasing. One must not be misled by words or phrases into misconstruing the nature of the finding. Pennycuick V.-C. found there was no definite assurance given by the defendants' representative to the plaintiff and his architect. Like Lord Denning M.R., I do not really know what the phrase "definite assurance" means. If it means that no grant was there and then brought into existence, or that no binding contract was then entered into, I agree with Pennycuick V.-C. If it means anything else, it is so imprecise that I disregard it, and I look at the rest of the judgment to find what he did find. He accepted the evidence of Mr Alford, the plaintiff's architect; he summarised the effect of that evidence; and his summary is of importance because I think it contains the clue as to his substantial findings of fact. Pennycuick V.-C. quotes Mr Alford as having said in evidence:

"The precise position"—that is the position of the projected point of access, point B—"was determined in the light of what I envisaged as future development; the reason for the second entrance was because we were going to treat the green and red land as separate for user; this was made clear to Mr Stonier, and Mr Stonier"—*i.e.* Mr Queen—"had agreed the gate at B,"

and continues:

"and [Mr Alford] said that Mr Stonier said nothing to suggest that he had no authority. In cross-examination [Mr Alford] agreed that they were simply agreeing on the best position for an entrance and that the next step would be for their own solicitors to tie the matter up with the council; at the time he thought there were no problems, but basically they were agreeing the position, and he said: 'I thought we had got final agreement but that it would then be a matter for the solicitors,' and he foresaw further processes."

Then Pennycuick V.-C. says:

"I accept the evidence of Mr Alford, but I think that [the plaintiff] was rather over sanguine in his interpretation of what was said by the council's representative and did not appreciate the difference between acceptance in principle and a firm commitment."

That was a finding that there was acceptance in principle that there should be access and a right of way over the defendants' land at point B; and I am content to go no further and to base my judgment on what I believe to be that finding of Pennycuick V.-C. Clearly the plaintiff and Mr Alford came away from that meeting in the confident expectation that a right would in due course be accorded to the plaintiff. Mr Alford did foresee "further processes". Of course, there would be further processes. The nature of the legal right to be granted had to be determined. It might be given by way of licence. It might be granted by way of easement. Conditions might be imposed. Payment of a sum of money might be required. But those two men, the plaintiff and his architect, came away from the meeting in the confident expectation that such a right would be granted upon reasonable conditions. What happened? By August—a month or less, after the meeting—posts for a fence were already on the ground, though not erected. There was already an indication, at about that time, I think—if not then, certainly soon after—of the presence of a gap at point B, that being the point of access agreed in principle. During the later months of 1967 nothing relevant transpired in the conduct of the negotiations between the plaintiff and the defendants. I accept Mr Lightman's submission that relationship as well as conduct is relevant: but during this period their relationship did not develop at all. They remained adjoining landowners, one of whom had agreed in principle at a meeting upon the site that there should be a right of way from point B over his land to the public road. Yet, things were happening. In the later months of 1967 the defendants, who were the local authority, were busy developing on neighbouring land, which the plaintiff's predecessor in title had sold them, a council housing estate. Lorries were being used for carting building materials, removing debris and so forth; and these lorries were in fact going upon the land of the plaintiff. Unfortunately materials on the land, the property of the plaintiff, were being pilfered. And so there came a meeting in January 1968, the point of which was to draw the attention of the defendants' officers to the situation which was developing. By the time the meeting took place the fence, which the defendants were obliged under the conveyance of their estate to erect between their land and the plaintiff's land, was substantially in position with gaps at point A, the access to the northern land, and at point B, the access in dispute. Nobody on behalf of the defendants gave the slightest indication to the plaintiff and his representatives at that meeting that there was going to be any difficulty or was likely to be any difficulty about access at point B. The confident expectation with which the plaintiff and Mr Alford left the meeting in July remained remarkably undisturbed by the meeting of January 1968. Indeed it was reinforced because there on the ground, plain for all to see, was a fence with gaps which accorded exactly with the agreement in principle reached in the previous July. Ten days later the defendants ordered gates, and by March the gates were installed. I ask myself: as at March 1968 had these defendants encouraged the plaintiff to think that he had or was going to be given a right? To use the language of Fry J., had they done it directly or had they done it by abstaining from asserting a legal right? Their encouragement of the belief in the mind of the plaintiff and Mr Alford was both direct and indirect. It was direct because of what they had done on the ground. It was indirect because ever since the July meeting they had abstained from giving the plaintiff or his architect any indication that they were standing on their rights, or had it in mind to go back, as, of course, they were entitled at that stage to go back, upon the agreement in principle reached at that meeting. And so matters proceeded until September 1968. By now, be it observed, over a year had passed since that first meeting when there was agreement in principle. Nothing had been done to disabuse the minds of the plaintiff and Mr Alford of the expectation reasonably induced by what the defendants' engineer then said: and there had been the direct encouragement of the gates. In September 1968, without telling the defendants or giving them any notice, so far as I am aware, the plaintiff entered into a contract to sell the northern piece of land without reservation over that land of any right of way. This was the act which was detrimental to the interests of the plaintiff. He did it in the belief that he had or could enforce a right of way and access at point B in the southern land.

One of the points taken by Mr Lightman is that the defendants had no notice of the sale, and therefore no opportunity to correct what on his case was a false belief in the mind of the plaintiff. Mr Millett [counsel for the plaintiff] in the course of his submissions conceded that he had not found in the books any case in which the sort of estoppel which we are here considering had arisen when the fact known to the defendants was an intention and not the realisation of that intention. That is, of course, what differentiates this case from one such as *E.R. Ives Investment Ltd v. High* [1967] 2 Q.B. 379. There the party who was found to be estopped did have notice of what the other party was doing at the time he was doing it. Therefore I think Mr Lightman rightly invites us to face this question: Does the fact that the defendants had no notice of the sale of the northern land before it was completed destroy the equity? Mr Lightman will concede, as I understand this part of his argument, no more than this: that the plaintiff might have been able to establish an equity if he had referred to the defendants before binding himself to the purchaser of the northern land: for that would have given the defendants an opportunity of disabusing the mind of the plaintiff before he acted to his detriment. The point is worthy of careful consideration. I reject it because, in my judgment, in this sort of proceedings, the court must be careful to avoid generalisation. I can conceive of cases in which it would be absolutely appropriate for a defendant to say: "But you should not have acted to your detriment until you had had a word with me and I could have put you right". But there are cases in which it is far too late for a defendant to get himself out of his pickle by putting upon the plaintiff that sort of duty; and this, in my judgment, is one of those cases. If immediately following the July meeting the clerk to the defendant authority had written saying: "I have had a report of the meeting with the assistant engineer and I must inform you that whether or not there is to be an easement or a licence is a matter which can only be decided by the council", the plaintiff would not now establish his equity: in selling the northern land without reservation of a right of way, he would have acted at his own risk. But one has to look at the whole conduct of the parties and the developing relationship between them. By September 1968, $13^{1}/_{2}$ months after the initial meeting, the plaintiff must really and reasonably have been attaching importance to the abstention of the defendants from declaring to him in correspondence, or by telephone to his agent, their true position, namely, that there would be no acceptance in principle of a right until the matter had been considered by the authority itself. By that time there had been, as well, the laying out of the fence and the installing of the gates. It is for those reasons—the passage of time, the abstention and the gates—that I think the defendants cannot rely upon the fact that the plaintiff acted, without referring to the defendants, on his intention—an intention of which they had had notice ever since their agent was informed of it at the meeting in July 1967. I think therefore an equity is established.

I turn now to the other two questions—the extent of the equity and the relief needed to satisfy it. There being no grant, no enforceable contract, no licence, I would analyse the minimum equity to do justice to the plaintiff as a right either to an easement or to a licence upon terms to be agreed. I do not think it is necessary to go further than that. Of course, going that far would support the equitable remedy of injunction which is sought in this action. If there is no agreement as to terms, if agreement fails to be obtained, the court can, in my judgment, and must, determine in these proceedings upon what terms the plaintiff should be put to enable him to have the benefit of the equitable right which he is held to have. It is interesting that there has been some doubt amongst distinguished lawyers in the past as to whether the court can so proceed. Lord Kingsdown refers in fact to those doubts in a passage, which I need not quote, in *Ramsden v. Dyson* (1866) L.R. 1 H.L. 129, 171. Lord Thurlow clearly thought that the court did have this power. Other lawyers of that time did not. But there can be no doubt that since *Ramsden v. Dyson* the courts have acted upon the basis that they have to determine not only the extent of the equity, but also the conditions necessary to satisfy it, and they have done so in a great number and variety of cases. I need refer only to the interesting collection of cases enumerated in *Snell's Principles of Equity*, 27th ed. (1973), at pp. 567–568, para. 2(b).

In the present case the court does have to consider what is necessary now in order to satisfy the plaintiff's equity. Had matters taken a different turn, I would without hesitation have said that the plaintiff should be put upon terms to be agreed if possible with the defendants, and, if not agreed, settled by the court. But, as already mentioned by Lord Denning M.R. and Lawton L.J., there has been a history of delay, and indeed high-handedness, which it is impossible to disregard. In January 1969 the defendants, for reasons which no doubt they thought good at the time, without consulting the plaintiff, locked up his land. They removed not only the padlocks which he had put on the gates at point B, but the gates themselves. In their place they put a fence— rendering access impossible save by breaking down the fence. I am not disposed to consider whether or not the defendants are to be blamed in moral terms for what they did. I just do not know. But the effect of their action has been to sterilise the plaintiff's land; and for the reasons which I have endeavoured to give, such action was an infringement of an equitable right possessed by the plaintiff. It has involved him in loss, which has not been measured; but, since it amounted to sterilisation of an industrial estate for a very considerable period of time, it must surpass any sort of sum of money which the plaintiff ought reasonably, before it was done, to have paid the defendants in order to obtain an enforceable legal right. I think therefore that nothing should now be paid by the plaintiff and that he should receive at the hands of the court the belated protection of the equity that he has established. Reasonable terms, other than money payment, should be agreed: or, if not agreed, determined by the court.

NOTES:

1. For comment, see (1976) 40 Conv. 156.

2. Atiyah (1976) 92 L.Q.R. 174 argues that the plaintiff had a remedy based in contract; but see (1976) 92 L.Q.R. 342 for a riposte by Millett, who as counsel for the plaintiff had conceded the absence of any contract.

3. See *E.R. Ives Investment Ltd v. High* [1967] 2 Q.B. 379, *ante*, p. 142, discussed at (1967) 31 Conv. 332; (1967) 30 M.L.R. 580; [1968] C.L.J. 26. See also *Hopgood v. Brown* [1955] 1 W.L.R. 213, noted at (1955) 19 Conv. 221; *Ward v. Kirkland* [1967] Ch. 194, noted at (1966) 30 Conv. 233.

4. In *Western Fish Products v. Penwith DC* [1981] 2 All E.R. 204, noted at [1982] Conv. 450, the Court of Appeal held that an estoppel could not be raised to prevent a statutory body from exercising its statutory discretion or from performing its statutory duty. In that case the plaintiff, in reliance on an alleged representation by the planning officer that planning permission would be granted, had renovated an industrial site. The court held that there had

been no relevant representation; but it also held that the council alone had power to determine planning applications and, in the absence of clear evidence of delegation, it could not be bound by any representation on the part of its officers.

3.6 *Perpetual licence*

Plimmer v. Mayor etc. of Wellington (1884) 9 App.Cas. 699

(PC, Lord Watson, Sir Barnes Peacock, Sir Robert Collier, Sir Richard Couch, Sir Arthur Hobhouse)

With the permission of the Crown, the appellant had erected a wharf and later a jetty on the foreshore of Wellington (New Zealand) harbour. Part of the harbour, including the land occupied by the appellant, became vested by statute in the provincial government; but the appellant continued to use the jetty. Moreover, at the request of the provincial government, the appellant extended the jetty and built a warehouse. The land subsequently vested in the respondent corporation, which took possession of the jetty and warehouse. The appellant claimed statutory compensation on the ground that he had "an estate or interest in, to or out of the land".

[Sir Arthur Hobhouse referred to the judgments of Lord Kingsdown and Lord Cranworth in *Ramsden v. Dyson* (1866) L.R. 1 H.L. 129. He continued:]

In the present case, the equity is not claimed because the landowner has stood by in silence while his tenant has spent money on his land. This is a case in which the landowner has, for his own purposes, requested the tenant to make the improvements. The Government were engaged in the important work of introducing immigrants into the colony. For some reason, not now apparent, they were not prepared to make landing-places of their own, and in fact they did not do so until the year 1863. So they applied to John Plimmer to make his landing-place more commodious by a substantial extension of his jetty and the erection of a warehouse for baggage. Is it to be said that, when he had incurred the expense of doing the work asked for, the Government could turn round and revoke his licence at their will? Could they in July 1856 have deprived him summarily of the use of the jetty? It would be in a high degree unjust that they should do so, and that the parties should have intended such a result is, in the absence of evidence, incredible.

With respect to the occupant's belief in his own title and the knowledge of that belief on the part of the Government, it may be worth while to remark that the land in question was not like ordinary private property. It was the bed of the sea, useless till somebody converts it to use, and not unfrequently used by unauthorised persons to get profit by accommodating the public. It is difficult to suppose that a person who is so using the sea bed, and the Government who are its owners, can go on dealing with one another in the way stated in this case for a series of years, except with a sense in the minds of both that the occupant has something more than a merely precarious tenure. Their Lordships will not be the first to hold, and no authority has been cited to them to shew that after such a landowner has requested such a tenant to incur expense on his land for his benefit, he can without more and at his own will take away the property so improved. Their Lordships consider that this case falls within the principle stated by Lord Kingsdown as to expectations created or encouraged by the landlord, with the addition that in this case the landlord did more than encourage the expenditure, for he took the initiative in requesting it.

On this view it becomes quite intelligible why, before the Government interfered with Plimmer's jetty in executing their works of 1857–61, they should have obtained his permission, which on the other view was not necessary. And the subsequent transactions down to 1878, though they do not lend any strong support to the same view, are consistent with it, and are rather more favourable to it than to the opposite one. The Government used, paid for, and gave a legal status to the property which it is now said they might have taken to themselves.

The question still remains as to the extent of interest which Plimmer acquired by his expenditure in 1856. Referring again to the passage quoted from Lord Kingsdown's judgment, there is good authority for saying what appears to their Lordships to be quite sound in principle, that the equity arising from expenditure on land need not fail merely on the ground that the interest to be secured has not been expressly indicated.

In such a case as *Ramsden v. Dyson* (1866) Law Rep. 1 H.L. 129 the evidence (according to Lord Kingsdown's view) shewed that the tenant expected a particular kind of lease, which Vice-Chancellor Stuart decreed to him, though it does not appear what form of relief Lord Kingsdown himself would have given. In such a case as *Duke of Beaufort v. Patrick* (1853) 17 Beav. 60 nothing but perpetual retention of the land would satisfy the equity raised in favour of those who spent their money on it, and it was secured to them at a valuation. In such a case as *Dillwyn v. Llewelyn* (1862) 4 D.F. & J. 517 nothing but a grant of the fee simple would satisfy the equity which the Lord Chancellor held to have been raised by the son's expenditure on his father's land. In such a case as that of the *Unity Bank v. King* (1858) 25 Beav. 72 the Master of the Rolls, holding that the father did not intend to part with his land to his sons who built upon it, considered that their equity would be satisfied by recouping their expenditure to them. In fact, the Court must look at the circumstances in each case to decide in what way the equity can be satisfied.

In this case their Lordships feel no great difficulty. In their view, the licence given by the Government to John Plimmer, which was indefinite in point of duration but was revocable at will, became irrevocable by the transactions of 1856, because those transactions were sufficient to create in his mind a reasonable expectation that his occupation would not be disturbed; and because they and the subsequent dealings of the parties cannot be reasonably explained on any other supposition. Nothing was done to limit the use of the jetty in point of duration. The consequence is that Plimmer acquired an indefinite, that is practically a perpetual, right to the jetty for the purposes of the original licence, and if the ground was afterwards wanted for public purposes, it could only be taken from him by the legislature.

An analogy to this process may be found in such cases as *Winter v. Brockwell* (1807) 8 East 308 and *Liggins v. Inge* (1831) 7 Bing. 682. These cases shew that where a landowner permits his neighbour to execute works on his (the neighbour's land), and the licence is executed, it cannot be revoked at will by the licensor. If indefinite in duration, it becomes perpetual. Their Lordships think that the same consequence must follow where the licence is to execute works on the land of the licensor, and owing to some supervening equity the licence has become irrevocable.

There are perhaps purposes for which such a license would not be held to be an interest in land. But their Lordships are construing a statute which takes away private property for compensation, and in such statutes the expression "estate or interest in, to or out of land" should receive a wide meaning. Indeed the statute itself directs that, in ascertaining the title of anybody to compensation, the Court shall not be bound to regard strict legal rights only, but shall do what is reasonable and just. Their Lordships have no difficulty in deciding that the equitable right acquired by John Plimmer is an interest in land carrying compensation under the Acts of 1880 and 1882.

3.7 *Licence to occupy until expenditure reimbursed or loan repaid*

Dodsworth v. Dodsworth (1973) 228 E.G. 1115

(CA, Russell, Stamp and James L.JJ.)

[The facts are stated in the judgment of Russell L.J.]

RUSSELL L.J.:

In this case the plaintiff, aged over 70, owned in 1967 a bungalow near Boston, Lincolnshire, and lived there alone. Her younger brother and his wife—the two defendants—returned to England from Australia and were looking for a house to acquire as their home. The plaintiff persuaded them to join her in her bungalow. The judge held on the evidence that the defendants spent a sum of over £700 on improvements to the plaintiff's bungalow in the expectation, encouraged and induced by the plaintiff, that the defendants and the survivor of them would be able to remain in the bungalow as their home—sharing of course with the plaintiff while she lived—for as long as they wished to do so, in circumstances that raised an equity in favour of the defendants on the footing of principles exemplified in a passage from Lord Kingsdown's speech in *Ramsden v. Dyson* (1866) L.R. 1 H.L. 129 and in other cases since then. The judge, however, held on the evidence that the parties did not intend to create a legal relationship. Not many months after the defendants moved into the bungalow, the plaintiff repented of her invitation for reasons, or alleged reasons, which need not be rehearsed. She started proceedings for possession: the defendants counterclaimed to assert an equity. The plaintiff did not appear at the hearing, and her claim for possession was non-suited. The question on the counterclaim was whether the proper way in which the equity should be satisfied would be to make some order which would assure the defendants in their occupation of the bungalow as their home for as long as they wished, or on the other hand to declare in effect that possession could only be obtained against them by the plaintiff if they were repaid their outlay on improvements to the bungalow.

The judge decided upon the latter as the appropriate course. His main ground was this. The plaintiff was anxious to sell the bungalow and buy a smaller and less expensive one for herself. She could not do this, having no other capital asset, if the defendants were entitled to stay rent free. She would therefore have to continue sharing her home for the rest of her life with the defendants, with whom she was, or thought she was, at loggerheads. Against this the defendants would, on leaving, recover and have available towards another home the expenditure which they laid out in the expectation, albeit encouraged by the plaintiff, of ability to stay there as their home. We think that the judge in balancing these considerations was entitled, and right, to come to that decision. We do not accept that the judge was wrong on the ground submitted to us that where the extent of the expectations was defined, though without intention to create legal relationship, between the parties, compensation for outlay could not be an appropriate satisfaction of the equity. On the appeal, the plaintiff having died intestate after notice of appeal, leave was given to the respondents, who are her administrators under a grant of letters of administration, to be joined as parties to the appeal. They do not contend that there was not an equity. They support the view, in the changed circumstances, of the judge that it was proper to satisfy the defendants' equity by protecting their occupation unless and until their expenditure was reimbursed.

Now it is clear that the ground upon which the judge mainly decided upon the appropriate remedy has, by the plaintiff's death, disappeared. But what is the situation now? Apart from the equity, the situation is this. The estate vested in the legal personal representatives consists only of the bungalow. This is subject to a standing mortgage of some £200 to £300. Its value free of any occupation rights in the defendants might be £5,000. Under the Administration of Estates Act 1925 the administrators hold the bungalow on trust for sale and to pay out of the proceeds of sale debts, duties, if any, and administration expenses (which must include their costs of this appeal), and then to divide among ten stirpes of beneficiaries, the first defendant in fact being one stirps. The immediate problem seems to be this. If immediate and direct effect is given to the expectations of the defendants, to take effect in priority to the respondents' entitlement and statutory duties, we cannot see but that it will lead, by virtue of the provisions of the Settled Land Act, to a greater and more extensive interest than was ever contemplated by the plaintiff and the defendants. The defendants would necessarily become joint tenants for life. As such they could sell the property, or quit and let it. In the one case, they would be entitled to the income of the invested proceeds of sale for life and the life of the survivor: in the other, they would be entitled to the net rents. None of these possibilities could conceivably have been embodied in the expectations giving rise to the equity in question, and we do not think that it can be right to satisfy such an equity by conferring upon the defendants a greater interest in the property than was envisaged by the parties. This, we should say, is a point which appears to have been overlooked in *Inwards v. Baker* [1965] 2 Q.B. 29.

Is it possible in the present case to give effect to this expectation without falling foul of this impact of the Settled Land Act? It is suggested that in the first place an order should be made which maintains the existing immediate binding trust for sale by requiring its execution to be subject to the consents of the defendants while in occupation of the bungalow as their home. This, it was argued, would preserve a trust for sale and thus exclude the operation of the Settled Land Act, and so avoid conferring an excessive interest on the defendants. But this alone would not preserve the defendants in rent-free occupation. It would be necessary further to make some order depriving the administrators of ability, pending sale with such consent, from obtaining possession from the defendants in order to let the property at a rent. But as soon as that is done, what does it amount to but putting ahead of the statutory trust for sale, etc., the equivalent of an interest which brings in the Settled Land Act with its conferment of an interest greater than the expectation which led to the expenditure by the defendants on the property which is the root of their equity? ...

In short, therefore, we do not see how we can sensibly, and without awarding to the defendants a greater interest in law than was within their induced expectation, satisfy their equity save by securing their occupation until their expenditure has been reimbursed.

NOTES:

1. See also *Burrows and Burrows v. Sharp* (1991) 23 H.L.R. 82, noted at [1992] Conv. 54.

2. On the application of the Settled Land Act 1925, see *supra*, p. 562.

Re Sharpe (A Bankrupt) [1980] 1 W.L.R. 219

(Ch D., Browne-Wilkinson J.)

The first respondent purchased a leasehold property for £17,000, of which £12,000 was provided by his elderly aunt on the understanding that she would be able to stay there as long as she wished and that she would be looked after by the first respondent and his wife. The aunt also spent £2,000 on furnishings and paid off £9,000 of the first respondent's debts. The first respondent finally went bankrupt and the trustee in bankruptcy, before offering the property for sale, sought to establish whether the aunt claimed any interest. She failed to respond to two inquiries. Only after the trustee had contracted to sell the property with vacant possession did she claim a beneficial interest or, in the alternative, a right to remain in the property by virtue of an irrevocable licence or equitable right.

BROWNE-WILKINSON J.:

In my judgment, if, as in this case, moneys are advanced by way of loan there can be no question of the lender being entitled to an interest in the property under a resulting trust. If he were to take such an interest, he would get his money twice: once on repayment of the loan and once on taking his share of the proceeds of sale of the property.

I turn then to the alternative claim that Mrs Johnson is entitled to something less than an aliquot share of the equity in the premises, namely, the right to stay on the premises until the money she provided indirectly to acquire them has been repaid. This right is based upon the line of recent Court of Appeal decisions which has spelt out irrevocable licences from informal family arrangements, and in some cases characterised such licences as conferring some equity or equitable interest under a constructive trust. I do not think that the principles lying behind these decisions have yet been fully explored and on occasion it seems that such rights are found to exist simply on the ground that to hold otherwise would be a hardship to the plaintiff. It appears that the principle is one akin to or an extension of a proprietary estoppel stemming from Lord Kingsdown's well-known statement of the law in *Ramsden v. Dyson* (1866) L.R. 1 H.L. 129, 170. In a strict case of proprietary estoppel the plaintiff has expended his own money on the defendant's property in an expectation encouraged by or known to the defendant that the plaintiff either owns the property or is to have some interest conferred on him. Recent authorities have extended this doctrine and, in my judgment, it is now established that, if the parties have proceeded on a common assumption that the plaintiff is to enjoy a right to reside in a particular property and in reliance on that assumption the plaintiff has expended money or otherwise acted to his detriment, the defendant will not be allowed to go back on that common assumption and the court will imply an irrevocable licence or trust which will give effect to that common assumption. Thus in *Errington v. Errington and Woods* [1952] 1 K.B. 290, Denning L.J. held that the son, who had paid the instalments under the mortgage in the expectation that the property would eventually become his, had an equitable right to stay in occupation until the mortgage was paid off. In *Tanner v. Tanner* [1975] 1 W.L.R. 1346, the plaintiff was held entitled to a licence to occupy a house bought in contemplation of it being a home for herself and her children, there being no express contract to that effect. In *Hardwick v. Johnson* [1978] 1 W.L.R. 683, where the plaintiff's house had been occupied by the plaintiff's son and his first wife under an informal family arrangement, the Court of Appeal imputed an intention to grant an irrevocable licence to the wife on payment by her of a weekly sum.

Applying those principles to the present case, I have little doubt that as between the debtor on the one hand and Mrs Johnson on the other, the circumstances in which she provided the money by way of loan in order to enable the premises to be bought do give rise to some right in Mrs Johnson. It is clear that she only loaned the money as part of a wider scheme, an essential feature of which was that she was to make her home in the property to be acquired with the money loaned. Say that immediately after the property had been bought the debtor had tried to evict Mrs Johnson without repaying the loan; can it be supposed that the court would have made an order for possession against her? In my judgment, whether it be called a contractual licence or an equitable licence or an interest under a constructive trust, Mrs Johnson would be entitled as against the debtor to stay in the house. *Dodsworth v. Dodsworth* (1973) 228 E.G. 1115 shows that there are great practical difficulties in finding that she is entitled to a full life interest: but there is no reason why one should not imply an intention that she should have the right to live there until her loan is repaid, which was the result reached in *Dodsworth v. Dodsworth.*

Unfortunately, this case does not arise for decision simply between Mrs Johnson on the one hand and the debtor on the other. She has to show some right good against the trustee in bankruptcy and the purchaser from the trustee in bankruptcy. Due to an unfortunate procedural position, the purchaser is not a party to this application and nothing I can say can, or is intended to, bind him. As an antidote to the over-indulgence of sympathy which everyone must feel for Mrs Johnson, I put on record that the purchaser's plight is little better. He apparently had no reason to suspect that there was any flaw in the trustee's right to sell with vacant possession. As a result of the trustee's inability to complete the sale he cannot open the business he intended and he and his wife and two children are being forced to live in a small motorised caravan parked in various places on or near Hampstead Heath.

Is then Mrs Johnson's right against the debtor binding on the trustee in bankruptcy? This is an important and difficult point and, were it not for the urgency of the matter and the late stage of the term, I would like to have given it longer consideration. In general the trustee in bankruptcy steps into the shoes of the debtor and takes the debtor's property subject to all rights and equities affecting it: see *Halsbury's Laws of England* 4th ed., vol. 3 (1973), para. 594. However, the trustee in bankruptcy is free to break any merely contractual obligation of the debtor, leaving the other party to his remedy in damages, which damages will only give rise to a right to prove in the bankruptcy.

Are rights of the kind spelt out in the cases I have referred to merely contractual licences or do they fetter the property and create some right over it? On the authorities as they stand, I think I am bound to hold that the rights under such an irrevocable licence bind the property itself in the hands of the trustee in bankruptcy. Lord Denning M.R. has, on a number of occasions, said that these licences arise under a constructive trust and are binding on the third party's acquiring with notice. These statements are for the most part obiter dicta with which other members of the court have not associated themselves, preferring to rest their decision on there being a contractual licence. But in *Binions v. Evans* [1972] Ch. 359, a third party taking with notice of, and expressly subject to, such a licence was held bound by it. In that case the liability could not have depended merely on contract. Closer to the present case is a decision which was not referred to in argument and therefore my comments on it must be treated with some reserve. In *D.H.N Food Distributors Ltd v. Tower Hamlets London Borough Council* [1976] 1 W.L.R. 852 certain premises were legally owned by one company (Bronze) but occupied by an associated company (D.H.N) under an informal arrangement between them. The premises were compulsorily acquired and the question was whether any compensation for disturbance was payable, it being said that Bronze had not been disturbed. The Court of Appeal held that D.H.N. had an irrevocable licence to remain in the premises indefinitely and this gave D.H.N. a compensatable interest in the land. Lord Denning M.R. said, at p. 859:

> "It was equivalent to a contract between the two companies whereby Bronze granted an irrevocable licence to D.H.N. to carry on their business on the premises. In this situation Mr Dobry cited to us *Binions v. Evans* [1972] Ch. 359, to which I would add *Bannister v. Bannister* [1948] 2 All E.R. 133 and *Siew Soon Wah v. Young Tong Hong* [1973] A.C. 836. Those cases show that a contractual licence (under which a person has the right to occupy premises indefinitely) gives rise to a constructive trust, under which the legal owner is not allowed to turn out the licensee. So, here. This irrevocable licence gave to D.H.N. a sufficient interest in the land to qualify them for compensation for disturbance."

Goff L.J. also made this a ground for his decision: see pp. 860–861.

It seems to me that this is a decision that such contractual or equitable licence does confer some interest in the property under a constructive trust. Accordingly, in my judgment, it follows that the trustee in bankruptcy takes the property subject to Mrs Johnson's right to live there until she is repaid the moneys she provided to acquire it.

Mr Moss, for the trustee in bankruptcy, argued that this was the wrong approach. He said that the species of constructive trust which Lord Denning M.R. was considering in the cases was different from the traditional constructive trust known to equity lawyers. It is not, Mr Moss says, a substantive right but an equitable remedy: see *per* Lord Denning M.R. in *Hussey v. Palmer* [1972] 1 W.L.R. 1286, 1290 and in *Binions v. Evans* [1972] Ch. 359, 368. Then, says Mr Moss, the time to decide whether to grant such a remedy is when the matter comes before the court in the light of the then known circumstances. In the present case those circumstances are that the debtor is a bankrupt and Mrs Johnson has failed to put forward her claim until after the trustee has contracted to sell the property to an innocent third party, notwithstanding two inquiries as to whether she had a claim. Accordingly, he says, it would not be equitable to grant her an interest under a constructive trust at this time.

I cannot accept that argument in that form. Even if it be right to say that the courts can impose a constructive trust as a remedy in certain cases—which to my mind is a novel concept in English law—in order to provide a remedy the court must first find a right which has been infringed. So far as land is concerned an oral agreement to create any interest in it must be evidenced in writing: see section 40 of the Law of Property Act 1925. Therefore if these irrevocable licences create an interest in land, the rights cannot rest simply on an oral contract. The introduction of an interest under a constructive trust is an essential ingredient if the plaintiff has any right at all. Therefore in cases such as this, it cannot be that the interest in property arises for the first time when the court declares it to exist. The right must have arisen at the time of the transaction in order for the plaintiff to have any right the breach of which can be remedied. Again, I think the *D.H.N. Food Distributors Ltd* case [1976] 1 W.L.R. 852 shows that the equity predates any order of the court. The right to compensation in that case depended on substantive rights at the date of compulsory acquisition, not on what remedy the court subsequently chose to grant in the subsequent litigation.

Accordingly, if I am right in holding that as between the debtor and Mrs Johnson she had an irrevocable licence to remain in the property, authority compels me to hold that that gave her an interest in the property before the bankruptcy and the trustee takes the property subject to that interest. In my judgment the mere intervention of the bankruptcy by itself cannot alter Mrs Johnson's property interest. If she is to be deprived of her interest as against the trustee in bankruptcy, it must be because of some conduct of hers which precludes her from enforcing her rights, that is to say, the ordinary principles of acquiescence and laches which apply to all beneficiaries seeking to enforce their rights apply to this case.

I am in no way criticising the trustee in bankruptcy's conduct; he tried to find out if she made any claim relating to the £12,000 before he contracted to sell the property. But I do not think that on ordinary equitable principles Mrs Johnson should be prevented from asserting her rights even at this late stage. She is very old and in bad health. No one had ever advised her that she might have rights to live in the property. As soon as she appreciated that she was to be evicted she at once took legal advice and asserted her claim. This, in my judgment, is far removed from conduct which precludes enforcement by a beneficiary of his rights due to his acquiescence, the first requirement of acquiescence being that the beneficiary knows his or her rights and does not assert them.

Accordingly, I hold that Mrs Johnson is entitled as against the trustee in bankruptcy to remain in the property until she is repaid the sums she advanced. I reach this conclusion with some hesitation since I find the present state of the law very confused and difficult to fit in with established equitable principles. I express the hope that in the near future the whole question can receive full consideration in the Court of Appeal, so that, in order to do justice to the many thousands of people who never come into court at all but who wish to know with certainty what their proprietary rights are, the extent to which these irrevocable licences bind third parties may be defined with certainty.

Doing justice to the litigant who actually appears in the court by the invention of new principles of law ought not to involve injustice to the other persons who are not litigants before the court but whose rights are fundamentally affected by the new principles.

Finally, I must reiterate that I am in no way deciding what are the rights of the purchaser from the trustee as against Mrs Johnson. It may be that as a purchaser without express notice in an action for specific performance of the contract his rights will prevail over Mrs Johnson's. As to that, I have heard no argument and express no view. I do, however, express my sympathy for him in the predicament in which he finds himself.

I therefore dismiss the trustee's application for possession against Mrs Johnson.

NOTES:

1. For comment, see [1980] Conv. 207; (1980) 96 L.Q.R. 336.

2. For discussion of the relationship between proprietary estoppel and constructive trusts, see *infra*, p. 607.

3.8 *Compensation for loss of expectation*

Wayling v. Jones (1993) 69 P. & C.R. 170

(CA, Balcombe, Leggatt and Hoffmann L.JJ.)

The plaintiff, Wayling, and the deceased, Jones, started to live together in a homosexual relationship in 1971; and, with the exception of a period of about one year in 1975, they continued to do so until the death of the deceased in 1987. During that time the deceased owned a series of properties and businesses. The plaintiff acted as his companion and chauffeur and gave substantial assistance in running the businesses. In return the deceased provided the plaintiff with pocket money and most of his living and clothing expenses. The deceased frequently assured the plaintiff that he would leave him the property and business that he owned at the time; and in 1982 the deceased made a will in which he left the plaintiff the hotel that he then owned. He subsequently sold that hotel and purchased another; and, although he repeated his assurances in respect of the new hotel, he never altered his 1982 will. The plaintiff claimed to be entitled to the proceeds of sale of the hotel which the deceased owned at the time of his death but which had been sold by the executors. The High Court dismissed his claim and he appealed to the Court of Appeal.

BALCOMBE L.J.:

The judge took the principles of proprietary estoppel from the judgment of Mr Edward Nugee Q.C. sitting as a High Court judge in *Re Basham* [1986] 1 W.L.R. 1498, 1503:

"The plaintiff relies on proprietary estoppel, the principle of which in its broadest form may be stated as follows: where one person (A) has acted to his detriment on the faith of a belief which was known to and encouraged by another person (B) that he either has or is going to be given a right in or over B's property B cannot insist on his strict legal rights if to do so would be inconsistent with A's belief."

and before us this was accepted by both parties as a sufficiently accurate statement of the general principle.

The judge found that the plaintiff believed he would inherit [the hotel] and that that belief was encouraged by the deceased. ... He went on to find that the plaintiff suffered a detriment by not asking for, or receiving, higher wages and continuing to serve the deceased until his death. However, he held that the plaintiff's claim in proprietary estoppel failed because he was unable to prove that he suffered a detriment *in reliance upon* his belief. This holding was based upon certain answers given by the plaintiff in cross-examination, but before I turn to consider those answers it is necessary that I should first set out the relevant legal principles:

(1) There must be a sufficient link between the promises relied upon and the conduct which constitutes the detriment—see *Eves v. Eves* [1975] 1 W.L.R. 1338, 1345 *per* Brightman J.; *Grant v. Edwards* [1986] Ch. 638, 648–649 *per* Nourse L.J., 655–657 *per* Browne-Wilkinson V.-C., in particular the passage where he equates the principles applicable in cases of constructive trust to those of proprietary estoppel.

(2) The promises relied upon do not have to be the sole inducement for the conduct: it is sufficient if they are an inducement—*Amalgamated Investment and Property Co. Ltd v. Texas Commerce International Bank Ltd* [1982] Q.B. 84, 104–105.

(3) Once it has been established that promises were made, and that there has been conduct by the plaintiff of such a nature that inducement may be inferred, then the burden of proof shifts to the defendants to establish that he did not rely on the promises—*Greasley v. Cooke* [1986] 1 W.L.R. 1306; *Grant v. Edwards* [1986] Ch. 638, 657.

In the present case I am satisfied that the plaintiff's conduct in helping the deceased run [the deceased's businesses] for what was at best little more than pocket money ... was conduct from which his reliance on the deceased's clear promises could be inferred. The question is whether the defendants have established that the plaintiff did not rely on these promises.

In his affidavit evidence the plaintiff stated that he relied on the deceased's promises. In his oral evidence in chief he said:

Q. One question, Mr Wayling. Assuming you were in the Royal Hotel Bar, before Dan's death and Dan was there, if Dan had told you that he was not going to give the Royal Hotel to you but to somebody else after his death, what would you have done?

A. I would have left.

In cross-examination he agreed that he had lived with the deceased for some 10 years without any promises having been made to him—the first time he was promised an inheritance was about 1981. Later in cross-examination came the following questions and answers:

Q. If he had not made that promise to you, would you still have stayed with him?

A. Yes ...

Q. Just to continue on from that. So far as you are concerned, from that reply you gave, you would have remained with the deceased whether or not he made those promises?

A. Whatever business venture he would have had, yes.

Q. The promises were not the reason why you remained with the deceased?

A. No, we got on very well together. He always wanted to reward me.

Finally in re-examination he said:

Q. You told Mr Oughton when you were asked to look at what Evan Evans meant in his affidavit and your answer was: I believed he'd keep the promise—that is about Dan?

A. That's right.

Q. You were then asked this question: If he had not made the promise, you would still have stayed.
A. Yes.
Q. And you said you would?
A. Yes.
Q. What does that mean?
A. He needed me, he couldn't do without me, you know.
Q. What work would you have done in the business if you had stayed?
A. In a business?
Q. Yes.
A. Whatever Dan found, whatever business it would have been. I don't think he would have got anything else anyway.
Q. Would you have looked for another job?
A. No.
Q. Did you ever complain about your earnings in the Royal Hotel to Dan?
A. Yes.
Q. What was the answer?
A. He said: "You'll get everything after I'm gone, anyway, so."
Q. What did you do as a result of that?
A. Just carried on.

The judge evidently formed the immediate view that these answers were fatal to the plaintiff's case based on proprietary estoppel, as at the end of the plaintiff's re-examination he intervened:

"Mr Howells, in view of the answers of Mr Wayling now to the question, first of all, that he was asked to deal with at the end of Mr Oughton's cross-examination and in view of his answers now in re-examination, where does your case on proprietary estoppel stand?"

This view is reflected in his judgment. He quotes his note of the questions and answers I have recorded above and, after setting out the submissions of counsel, summarises his conclusion as follows:

"I have no doubt that the weight of his answers was to the effect that whether or not Mr Jones carried out his promise he would remain with Mr Jones because Mr Jones needed him ...
As I understand his evidence the promises did not influence him to remain in Mr Jones's service."

On this aspect of the case the judge concluded:

"In my judgment causation, 'reliance' in the terminology of proprietary estoppel, is not established by the evidence. If it were established I would have awarded Mr Wayling the net proceeds of sale of the hotel which are of the order of £70,000 as recompense to him for his detriment and to avoid his suffering injustice. The estate would have been well able to bear a payment of that kind. But as it is, under this cause of action Mr Wayling does not succeed."

Mr Hugh Bennett Q.C., who appeared for the plaintiff on the appeal, submitted that the judge misunderstood the effect of the questions and answers in cross-examination which I have set out above. He submitted:
(1) That the questions and answers related to the parties living together and not to the plaintiff working for the deceased in reliance of the promises.
(2) That in any event the questions were based on the hypothesis that no promises had ever been made. But they had been made, and the relevant question was: "What

would you, the plaintiff, have done if the deceased, having made his promises, told you that he did not propose to implement them?" That question was asked in chief, received a positive answer as set out above "I would have left", and this was never taken up in the cross-examination which was based on an entirely different, and irrelevant, hypothesis.

Mr Oughton for the defendants submitted that the answer "Whatever business he would have had, Yes" given by the plaintiff to the question "you would have remained with the deceased whether or not he made those promises?" indicates that the plaintiff was not considering only his personal relationship with the deceased and that Mr Bennett's first submission therefore fails. I am by no means clear that the plaintiff was thereby saying that he would have worked for pocket money even if there had been no promises, but in any event I am satisfied that his answers in cross-examination do not relate to the only question that mattered: "What would you have done if the deceased had told you that he was no longer prepared to implement his promises?" To that question the plaintiff had given his answer in chief as already mentioned.

On the application of the principles set out above to the facts of this case I am satisfied: (a) that the promises were made; (b) that the plaintiff's conduct was of such a nature that inducement may be inferred; (c) that the defendants have not discharged the burden upon them of establishing that the plaintiff did not rely on the promises. The judge fell into error in holding that the plaintiff did not rely on the promises to his detriment. On this issue I would allow the appeal.

The judge said that if reliance had been established he would have awarded the plaintiff the net proceeds of the sale of the hotel. I see no reason to differ from his conclusion which appears to me to accord with the justice of the case. We were told that the hotel was sold on July 15, 1988 and that the net proceeds of sale were £72,386.65. I would accordingly order that the first and second defendants (who are the executors of the deceased's last will, the other defendants being beneficiaries under that will) should pay to the plaintiff the sum of £72,386.65 with interest from July 15, 1988.

NOTES:

1. Cooke (1995) 111 L.Q.R. 389 expresses the view that the unorthodox approach to reliance was "unusually generous" but she suggests that it may be restricted to "family property" cases. She notes that it was not followed by the Court of Appeal in two subsequent "commercial" cases: *Meghraj Bank Ltd v. Arsiwalla* (1994, unreported); *Walton v. Walton* (1994, unreported).

2. Davis [1995] Conv. 409 argues that in another respect the judgment of Balcombe L.J. may be *more* restrictive in its approach to (detrimental) reliance. It may be seen to be suggesting that the courts may impose limits on the sufficiency of the link between the detrimental conduct and the promises relied upon; and to that extent it may be seen to be assimilating the requirements of proprietary estoppel and common intention constructive trusts.

3. Davis also notes that the case seems to be the first in which the claim has been brought against a landowner (or in this case his executors) who has disposed of the land. She argues that in such circumstances the decision might be justifiable on the basis that the claimant acquired an interest in the property at the time of reliance or on the death of the landowner and that he was tracing that interest into the proceeds of sale. However, the court did not adopt that reasoning but effectively awarded compensation for the loss of an interest in land that the court would have awarded if the landowner (or his

executors) had still owned the land. According to Davis, this extension of the doctrine of proprietary estoppel amounts to the creation of a new head of civil liability.

4. The award of compensation for loss of expectation is only marginally less uncommon. Davis identifies only two previous cases in which compensation has been awarded other than as the repayment of expenditure. In *Holiday Inns Inc. v. Broadhead* (1974) 232 E.G. 951 the claimant incurred considerable expenditure in obtaining planning permission for land in reliance on the expectation that the landowner would grant him a lease but, since a lease had been granted to a third party, he was awarded half the value of the freehold reversion; and in *Baker v. Baker* (1993) 25 H.L.R. 408 the claimant had made a substantial contribution to the purchase price of a house in reliance on the expectation that he would be able to live there for the remainder of his life and the Court of Appeal held that he should be compensated for the lost value of that expectation.

3.9 No remedy required

Appleby v. Cowley (1982), The Times, April 14, 1982

(Ch D., Megarry V.-C.)

The plaintiff was the current head of a set of barristers' chambers in Nottingham, acting on behalf of himself and the current members of chambers. The premises had been purchased in 1964 by a company controlled by the defendant, who was the head of chambers at the time. The premises were occupied under a licence; and the barristers effectively reimbursed the expenditure incurred by the company, an amount which represented about one-third of the market rent. This arrangement continued after the defendant took silk and moved to London. In 1972 the current members of chambers proposed to extend the premises at a cost of a further £7,500; they obtained the consent of the defendant and it was agreed (the agreement being recorded in a letter of May 1972) that they would receive a proportion of the proceeds of sale on any disposal of the premises. Soon afterwards they spent approximately £7,700 on repairs and renovations. In 1973 the defendant indicated his intention to dispose of the premises. The plaintiff claimed, *inter alia*, a right, based on proprietary estoppel, to occupy the premises indefinitely subject to indemnifying the defendant for any expenditure incurred in relation to the premises.

MEGARRY V.-C.:
As I have indicated, I think that the circumstances of the first two sets of expenditure on the building (namely, on moving in, and on the repairs and redecorations costing a little less than £7,000 in all over a nine-year period) give little support to any claim based on proprietary estoppel. In particular, Mr Cowley's knowledge that this £7,000 was being spent has not been sufficiently established.

The plaintiffs' real case rests on the £7,500 spent on an extension in 1972 and the £7,700 spent in repairing and renovating the roof and exterior walls in 1973. The basis of this claim is that members of chambers had a firm expectation of having an indefinite right to occupy the building, and that knowing this expectation, Mr Cowley allowed members of chambers to make these payments, being payments which it would be sensible for them to make only on the basis of their expectation. To make good this claim Mr Sparrow [counsel for the plaintiff] has to dispose of the letter of May 1972 that I have quoted, which records the agreement reached between Mr Cowley and Mr Appleby.

In the face of that agreement I cannot see how any case of proprietary estoppel can be established in relation to the extension. Mr Cowley and Mr Appleby were expressly agreeing the basis on which the extension could be erected, a basis which was designed to secure to Mr Appleby, and through him the other members of the chambers, the increase in value of the building resulting from the erection of the extension. However, Mr Sparrow contended that Mr Cowley could not rely on that agreement. His argument ran along the lines that the letter was framed in terms of tenancy, whereas Mr Cowley was contending that throughout Mr Appleby had no more than a revocable licence. Even if one accepts that to the full, I cannot see why that precludes Mr Cowley from relying on the agreement to meet a claim of proprietary estoppel. The parties have still agreed how the expenditure is to be recouped, and no intervention by equity is needed to bring about that result. Mr Sparrow also made submissions about misrepresentations which he said Mr Cowley had made. I propose to say nothing about this save that I reject the submissions.

That leaves the fourth head of expenditure, the repairs and renovations to the roof and exterior walls in 1973 at a cost of some £7,700. On behalf of Mr Cowley it was contended that this was covered by the agreement of May 1972, though not in terms; for this showed the basis of occupation. I did not find this submission persuasive. Indeed, with its use of the term "tenancy", the letter offered a greater encouragement to spend money on the premises than it would have done had the letter spoken of revocable licence. As the law has developed, it may be that in cases in which a claim based on proprietary estoppel is made, the real question comes down simply to whether or not the assertion of strict legal rights would be unconscionable, without any detailed conditions or criteria being specified: see *Taylors Fashions Ltd v. Liverpool Victoria Trustees Co. Ltd* [1982] Q.B. 133, 151–155 and *Amalgamated Investment and Property Co. Ltd v. Texas Commerce International Bank Ltd* [1982] Q.B. 84, 103–104. In the present case, would it be unconscionable for the company to take the benefit of these remedial works to its building?

I think that there are circumstances in which the answer would be Yes. If soon after the works had been done the company had evicted all the members of chambers, or had required them to make payments equal to the full rental value of the chambers, then the company might well be said to be reaping the fruits of the expenditure unfairly. However, that is not what has happened. When the work was being done the rental value of the premises for which some £1,500 a year had been paid for some 10 years was about £4,300; and as events have turned out, Mr Cowley is making no claim for use and occupation at a rate greater than £1,500 a year until 30th November 1976 onwards. In those circumstances I think Mr Cowley may echo the phrase of Lord Hardwicke L.C. in *Attorney-General v. Balliol College Oxford* (1744) 9 Mod. 407 at 412, when directing an inquiry in chambers, and say that the plaintiffs have had "sufficient satisfaction" for their expenditure. Certainly I do not think that Mr Cowley is acting unconscionably. It may be a nice academic point whether the result is that no case of proprietary estoppel has been established, or whether it is that such a case has been established but no remedy should be granted. I shall not debate that. All I need do is to say that the claim on proprietary estoppel fails. Certainly I can see nothing which comes within measurable distance of establishing any sort of a case that because of the expenditure the plaintiffs are beneficially entitled to the building, subject to indemnifying Mr Cowley.

Sledmore v. Dalby (1996) 72 P. & C.R. 196

(CA, Butler-Sloss, Roch and Hobhouse L.JJ.)

The appellant, Mrs Sledmore, and her husband were the freehold owners of a house ("No. 15A"). In 1965, their daughter married the respondent, Dalby, and they moved into the house as the tenants of the Sledmores. However, it was found that the Dalbys had stopped paying rent when the daughter became ill and the respondent became unemployed; and that tenancy had come to an end in 1976. However, the respondent continued to pay the outgoings on the house. Between 1976 and 1979 the Sledmores formed the intention of giving the house to the Dalbys and, to the knowledge of the appellant, Mr Sledmore told the Dalbys of that intention. During that period, with the encouragement of, and some financial contribution from, Mr Sledmore, the respondent carried out substantial work on the house, including the construction of a bathroom and an additional bedroom, the renovation of the kitchen and the installation of central heating. In 1979 Mr Sledmore conveyed his share of the house to the appellant, who altered her will to ensure that her daughter inherited the house to the exclusion of the respondent. Mr Sledmore died in 1980 and the daughter died in 1983. Although the respondent spent most of his time elsewhere with his partner, he spent a few nights each week in the house; and one of his grown-up daughters also lived there. The appellant was in financial difficulties; and her own house was too large for her and was in need of repair. She therefore sought possession of No. 15A. The county court judge dismissed the claim for possession and made a declaration that the respondent had a non-assignable, non-transmissible personal licence to occupy the house for so long as he wished. The appellant appealed.

ROCH L.J.:

The Recorder decided that the wills of 1979 and subsequent deaths of Mr Sledmore and Jacqueline Dalby did not alter what had happened between 1976 and 1979. Prior to the making of the 1979 wills representations had been made and work had been carried out and money spent by the respondent. No work or expenditure of any consequence had been made by the respondent after the 1979 wills. On September 12, 1979, when the undivided share of Mr Sledmore was conveyed to the appellant, the appellant was not a purchaser for value nor was she a purchaser without notice of the respondent's equity. Consequently the conveyance of September 12, 1979, had no effect on the respondent's equity and the freehold acquired by the appellant was subject to it. The judge found that the appellant was aware of and approved of what was being said in 1976 by her husband. The judge then directed himself as to the law and during that part of his judgment he cited this extract from the judgment of Lord Denning in *Inwards v. Baker* [1965] 2 Q.B. 29 at 37:

"So in this case, even though there is no binding contract to grant any particular interest to the licensee, nevertheless the court can look at the circumstances and see whether there is an equity arising out of the expenditure of money. All that is necessary is that the licensee should, at the request or with the encouragement of the landlord, have spent the money in the expectation of being allowed to stay there. If so, the court will not allow that expectation to be defeated where it would be inequitable so to do."

The Recorder's essential finding comes at page 27E of his judgment:

"There was plainly knowledge and, to say the least, acquiesence, if not outright encouragement by Mr and Mrs Sledmore that they (referring to the Dalbys) should improve that house. As far as Mr Dalby was concerned, having been told in 1976, at the time of his wife's breast illness, that the house would be theirs, he set about to improve it and of course motives were to improve it for the benefit of his family. ... At all events I am satisfied that the circumstances which give rise to the equity are all met in this case. Mr Dalby did act to his detriment, he did incur expenditure in the way I have said. He did so in the expectation that he would obtain an interest. I do not find that he ever thought at the relevant time that he actually had already acquired an interest. I find that his expectation was and ought to have been that he would acquire an interest sufficient to justify the expenditure. I find that this was encouraged by Mr Sledmore particularly with the participation of Mrs Sledmore and the knowledge of this belief was there at the time when the expenditure was incurred. He (referring to Mr Sledmore) must have known that the property was his and that his property was being improved and he was entitled to interfere ... It was all done by Mr Dalby with the object of assisting his family, of course, but in the knowledge fostered by Mr and Mrs Sledmore that it would be theirs in due course."

The Recorder then went on to consider how to give effect to the equity and reminded himself that cases such as *Crabb v. Arun District Council* [1976] Ch. 179 and *Pascoe v. Turner* [1979] 1 W.L.R. 431 had laid down that a court must search for "the minimum equity to do justice" to the person "who is entitled to the equity, and shaping it to the facts of the case". The Recorder then went on to ask what it was that Mr Dalby was entitled to expect. The Recorder found that he was bound to look at the parties, circumstances at the present time. At page 30B of his judgment he said:

"But, as I say, one has to look at the parties and try to find what is a legitimate and minimum equity that can give effect to the equity that has arisen. I have concluded that the way in which this equity can be properly, and should be properly, put into effect in this case is not by giving Mr Dalby a beneficial interest in the property in the sense of acquiring any of the equity, either the whole estate or any smaller part thereof....; I take the view that in the first place, and the simplest thing I can do, is simply to dismiss the claim for possession."

The Recorder then went on to make the declaration that the respondent was entitled to a non-assignable personal licence as I have already set out.

A cross-notice of appeal was served on behalf of the respondent in this case claiming that the respondent should have had the property transferred to him absolutely as owner in fee simple. Mr Lakin did not pursue that claim before us.

Mr Scott on behalf of the appellant distilled the grounds of appeal in the notice of appeal and in his skeleton argument down to three points ... The first point urged by Mr Scott was that at its highest the evidence in this case disclosed no more than statements by Mr Sledmore of his testamentary intention, and that such statements should not be permitted to form the basis of an equity arising by way of proprietary estoppel because that would place a fetter on testamentary freedom. Nothing that was said by Mr Sledmore could have raised in Mr Dalby an expectation or belief that Mr Dalby alone was to have any interest in the property. It was clear at all times that Mr and Mrs Sledmore intended the respondent to have an interest in the property only as long as he was the husband of their daughter and living with her at the property. By 1979 Mr and Mrs Sledmore clearly intended to exclude the respondent from having any proprietary interest in the property. ...

The second ground relied on by Mr Scott is that if the events between 1976 and 1979 did create an equity, that equity was satisfied by the appellant's will made in 1979. If the respondent had not received the benefit he expected or believed he would receive, that was due to the forces of destiny in the shape of his wife's death and not to any attempt by the appellant to enforce her strict legal rights.

The third ground is put in two ways. First that the judge was wrong in his conclusion as to the extent of the equity. Alternatively the judge should have found that it was no longer inequitable to allow the respondent's expectation to be defeated.

Mr Lakin at the outset of his argument stated that he relied on this being a case of proprietary estoppel and not merely promissory estoppel. Mr Lakin made that point because of the difference between the effect of promissory estoppel which may be only temporary whereas the effect of proprietary estoppel is permanent in that it will last as long as the interest created by the proprietary estoppel endures. For that reason, the court's function in determining the extent of the equity created by a proprietary estoppel is especially important, and it is in relation to this area that I regard the Recorder's decision as being deficient. Because of the view that I have formed concerning the third broad ground advanced by Mr Scott on behalf of the appellant, I do not consider it necessary to examine in detail either of the first two broad grounds.

In relation to those two grounds I will simply content myself with saying that the representation made by Mr Sledmore with the appellant's knowledge and consent in 1976 that one day this house would become the property of Jacqueline Dalby and the respondent and the encouragement given by Mr Sledmore to the respondent to carry out the works of improvement to the property between 1976 and 1979 contained by necessary implication a representation that Mr and Mrs Dalby and their children should be allowed to remain in the house, if that was their desire, until such time that the house was willed to them. The appellant's will in 1979 was not, in my view, a satisfaction of that expectation.

The respondent's expectation, in my opinion, would have been that he would remain in the house certainly as long as his wife was alive and he was living with her and, probably, whilst his daughters were still living with their parents or, following his wife's death with him, if only because the prime reason for the improvement in the house was that the elder daughter had by 1977 reached the age where she needed a bedroom of her own.

The task for a court in determining the extent of an equity created by proprietary estoppel is set out in the 29th edition of *Snell's Equity* (at p. 576):

> "The extent of the equity is to have made good, so far as may fairly be done between the parties, the expectations of A which O has encouraged. A's expectation or belief is the maximum extent of the equity, so that if, for example, A's expectation is that he could stay in a house for the rest of his life, this will not be given effect to in such a way as to confer on him the rights of a tenant for life under the Settled Land Act 1925, for that, with its concomitant right of sale, would give him a greater interest than he was entitled to expect. Accordingly A may have to be content with something less than his expectations, *e.g.* some form of lease at a rent. In other cases a full life interest operating under the Settled Land Act 1925 may be given. Further, the position of O has to be considered. Thus the courts are reluctant to compel two persons to live together when they have fallen out, and even after O has died, the due administration of his estate and the rights of those taking under it are factors to be considered."

I would respectfully adopt that passage as an accurate statement of the decided cases and the law. In the present case the respondent clearly has assumed that he will be allowed to stay in this house for the rest of his life rent free. In my judgment this is a case where the respondent has to be content with something less than his expectations. The Recorder should have considered the position of the appellant and her needs and balanced those against the present use of the premises made by the respondent and his present need for them.

Although the Recorder acknowledged the existence of the principles stated in the passage from *Snell* which I have cited ... nowhere does the Recorder make any assessment of the respondent's present use of and need for the house on the one hand or of the appellant's situation and need for the house on the other. Nor does the Recorder at any point ask himself the question whether it was still inequitable to allow the respondent's expectation to be defeated by permitting the appellant to enforce her legal rights, as owner of the property.

...

The conclusion that I have reached is that it is no longer inequitable to allow the expectation created in the respondent's mind by Mr Sledmore's oral statements and by his encouragement of the respondent to carry out the improvements to the house which were carried out between 1976 and 1979 to be defeated. The respondent has lived rent free in this accommodation for over 18 years. During that time the insurance of the property has been paid for by the Sledmore family and the property has been rerooted at their expense. The use made by the respondent of the house at the time of the trial was minimal and it is clear that there was accommodation for him elsewhere. He is a man in employment and therefore capable of paying for his accommodation. Whilst the respondent has lived in this house his elder daughter has married and left home and his younger daughter has reached the age of 27 and is able to maintain herself.

On the other hand, the evidence indicates that the appellant is vulnerable in that she is liable to lose her present accommodation and that she has a pressing need for this house which is her property. ...

I would allow this appeal and make an order for possession in the appellant's favour on the basis that the minimum equity to do justice to the respondent on the facts of this case was an equity which has now expired.

HOBHOUSE L.J.:

I agree that this appeal should be allowed as proposed in the judgment of Roch L.J. and I agree with his reasons for so doing.

However, I would go further than Roch L.J.; I consider that the judgment appealed from is open to more fundamental criticism. The decision of the County Court judge in the present case was said to be an application of the principles of equitable estoppel, yet his conclusion produces a clear injustice. The doctrine of estoppel exists for the purpose of enabling courts to do justice, modifying what otherwise might be the strict legal rights of the parties. If the supposed application of such a doctrine produces injustice not justice, then something has gone wrong.

...

The judge decided that there was an equitable proprietary estoppel and that Mrs Sledmore was not entitled to the possession of number 15A and that the defendant should have the right to occupy it for the remainder of his life apparently free of any payment.

The disproportion of this result is obvious as, in my judgment, is its injustice. The defendant by virtue of carrying out very limited improvements to number 15A between 1976 and 1978 and incurring an expenditure which was likewise limited, has been held to have acquired a right to occupy number 15A for the remainder of his natural life rent free to the exclusion of Mrs Sledmore, although his tenancy has been lawfully terminated and he has no right to an extension of that tenancy. Further, he has, since 1976, had the benefit of the occupation of number 15A, together with such members of the family as were living there from time to time, without paying any rent for such occupation. The primary case which he has been presenting to the courts, right up to the time that he abandoned it before this Court, was that his expenditure in 1976 to 1978 entitled him without more to have transferred to him the freehold title.

The doctrine of proprietary estoppel can be traced back further than other types of equitable and common law estoppel *in pais*. It has many similar features to promissory estoppel and to estoppel by representation and by conduct. Because of its historical origins there has been a tendency to analyse proprietary estoppel differently and, indeed, to characterise it in a different way. But in proprietary estoppel there has to be some conduct on the part of the party affected, either encouraging or acquiescing in the other party's acting to his detriment. The party asserting the estoppel must be able to show that his own conduct was attributable to an expectation or a mistake contributed to by the conduct (including inaction) of the affected party. There are therefore elements of assumption on the part of the party asserting the estoppel which the party affected is not permitted, in equity, to disregard. In the equitable doctrine of proprietary estoppel, it is also necessary to consider the extent of the equity so created and what is, in the circumstances, the equitable way in which to give effect to it.

In other types of estoppel the same elements can be identified: conduct/ representation/promise; reliance; detriment; just outcome. However, the emphasis and consequences may vary. In estoppel by representation or promise, a representation or promise must be clear and unequivocal; provided that there is reliance, the detriment element may be limited. In proprietary estoppel the emphasis is the other way round: the detriment must be distinct and substantial; the conduct of the affected party may be no more than acquiescence. It is said that the effect of proprietary estoppel is permanent, whereas estoppel by representation is merely temporary. However, in so far as such terms are valid as a source of distinction, the differences probably reflect no more than the difference of subject matter. The same applies to the oft-quoted but misleading statement (see *per* Brandon L.J. in *Amalgamated Investment and Property Co. Ltd v. Texas Commerce International Bank Ltd* [1982] 1 Q.B. 84 131) that common law estoppel may only be used as a shield whereas equitable proprietary estoppel may be used to found a cause of action. One element which is often present in proprietary estoppel in contrast to common law estoppel is restitution. In many of its applications the equitable doctrine of proprietary estoppel bears a close relationship to restitutionary principles where one party has acquiesced in or encouraged another in conduct whereby that other at his own expense would have, if no remedy were granted, unjustly enriched the former (*Ramsden v. Dyson* (1866) L.R. 1 H.L. 129).

These general considerations have been discussed (with a review of the leading English authorities) by the High Court of Australia in *Commonwealth of Australia v. Verwayen* (1990) 95 A.L.R. 321 which understandably was not cited to us by counsel. The judgment of Mason C.J. contains a discussion of the law of estoppel which is of particular value. I will cite three passages (at pp. 331–333) which are relevant to what I have said and to the correct approach to the present case:

> "In conformity with the fundamental purpose of all estoppels to afford protection against the detriment which would flow from a party's change of position if the assumption that led to it were deserted, these developments have brought a greater underlying unity to the various categories of estoppel. Indeed, the consistent trend in the modern decisions points inexorably towards the emergence of one overarching doctrine of estoppel rather than a series of independent rules. The element which both attracts the jurisdiction of a Court of Equity and shapes the remedy to be given is unconscionable conduct on the part of the person bound by the equity, and the remedy required to satisfy an equity varies according to the circumstances of the case. As Robert Goff J. said in *Amalgamated Investment and Property Co. Ltd v. Texas Commerce International Bank Ltd* [1982] Q.B. 84 at 103: 'Of all doctrines, equitable estoppel is surely one of the most flexible' ... However, in moulding its decree, the court, as a court of conscience, goes no further than is necessary to prevent unconscionable conduct.
>
> ... it should be accepted that there is but one doctrine of estoppel, which provides that a court of Common Law or Equity may do what is required, but not more, to prevent a person who has relied upon an assumption as to a present, past or future state of affairs (including a legal state of affairs), which assumption the party estopped has induced him to hold, from suffering detriment in reliance upon the

assumption as a result of the denial of its correctness. A central element of that doctrine is that there must be a proportionality between the remedy and the detriment which is its purpose to avoid. It would be wholly inequitable and unjust to insist upon a disproportionate making good of the relevant assumption."

There are similarly illuminating passages in the judgment of Deane J. at pp. 346 *et seq.*

It is thus always necessary to ask what is the assumption made by the party asserting the estoppel for which the party affected is to be treated as responsible. In the present case it was no more than the assumption that the mother, Mrs Sledmore, would leave number 15A to her daughter Jacqueline Dalby. That was the assumption which the defendant recognised was capable of encompassing and fulfilling his legitimate expectation. That assumption was never falsified. The disappointment of the defendant was that his wife sadly died and did so before his mother-in-law: further, 20 years later, his mother-in-law is still alive. Therefore there is no assumption in the relevant sense which was ever falsified. The assumption upon which the defendant was entitled to say that he incurred the expenditure was in fact fulfilled.

The other aspect clearly illustrated by the quotations which I have made from Mason C.J. is the need for proportionality. This is to say little more than that the end result must be a just one having regard to the assumption made by the party asserting the estoppel and the detriment which he has experienced. Here it is unreal to suggest that the conclusion of the County Court judge is proportionate to what happened over 15 years earlier. Similarly, it is unreal to say that the defendant has suffered any injustice. He expended money in 1976 to 1978 upon his then family home and he and his family fully enjoyed the benefits of such expenditure. He has also enjoyed within the same framework over a period of over 15 years the rent-free occupation of the property. By the same token it cannot be properly said that there was anything unconscionable in Mrs Sledmore seeking the possession of number 15A in 1990.

In my judgment there is no estoppel operating against the plaintiff. Her claim in this action falsifies no legitimate assumption or expectation. The effect of any equity that may at any earlier time have existed has long since been exhausted and no injustice has been done to the defendant. The plaintiff is entitled to an order for possession and the defendant's counter-claim must be dismissed. This appeal should be allowed accordingly.

BUTLER-SLOSS L.J.:
I agree with the judgment of Roch L.J. and that the appeal is allowed.

NOTES:

1. For comment, see [1997] C.L.J. 34; [1997] Conv. 458; (1997) 113 L.Q.R. 232.

2. Milne [1997] C.L.J. 34 identifies two different approaches to proprietary estoppel claims. According to the first, adopted by Roch and Butler-Sloss L.JJ., the equity arises as soon as there is detrimental reliance by the claimant. The presence or absence of unconscionability determines the availability and extent of any remedy, with the result that a potentially remediable equity may become exhausted or spent. This approach involves what Adams [1997] Conv. 458 refers to as "'floating' equity reasoning", and potential uncertainty, because the availability and extent of any remedy may depend upon the precise time when the estoppel claim is determined by the court and changes in circumstances since the time of the events relevant to the creation of the estoppel. According to the second approach, arguably adopted by Hobhouse L.J., no equity can arise unless and until the current landowner acts unconscionably (by seeking to enforce his strict legal rights). Milne prefers the

second approach, not least because it permits a more transparent and coherent approach to the enforcement of estoppel claims against third party transferees from the original landowner: see also Milne [1997] Web J.C.L.I.

3. More generally, Pawlowski (1997) 113 L.Q.R. 232 questions whether it is legitimate for the courts to take into consideration the respective personal circumstances and housing needs of the claimant and legal owner and to deny the claimant a remedy because the circumstances of the legal owner have changed for the worse by the date of the hearing.

4. Effect of misconduct

It will be apparent from the cases extracted above that, in determining whether the claimant has established an equity and/or in determining what remedy is appropriate to satisfy that equity, the courts have taken into consideration the (mis)conduct of the parties. Thus in *Crabb v. Arun DC* [1976] Ch. 179 the Court of Appeal, in deciding that the claimant should not be required (as originally envisaged by the parties) to pay for the right of access, expressly referred to the procrastination by the representor: *ibid.* 189–190 *per* Lord Denning M.R., 199 *per* Scarman L.J. In *Pascoe v. Turner* [1977] 1 W.L.R. 431 the Court of Appeal was quite clearly influenced by the behaviour of the representor in ordering a transfer of the fee simple rather than granting a licence for life: *ibid.* 438–439 *per* Cumming-Bruce L.J. Moreover, in *J. Willis & Son v. Willis* [1986] 1 E.G.L.R. 62 the Court of Appeal refused all relief to a claimant who had put forward fictitious and fraudulent evidence in support of his alleged alteration of position. For discussion of the effect of misconduct, see Thompson [1986] Conv. 406.

The effect of subsequent misconduct by an existing estoppel licensee was considered in *Williams v. Staite* [1979] 1 Ch. 291.

Williams v. Staite [1979] 1 Ch. 291

(CA, Lord Denning M.R., Goff and Cumming-Bruce L.JJ.)

The defendants occupied a cottage which was owned by the first defendant's mother. The mother had told the defendants that the cottage was a wedding present and that they could live there as long as they wished; and, in reliance upon that representation, the defendants had given up the opportunity of acquiring another property. The cottage was never transferred to them but they both carried out and financed improvements to it. When the mother died, her executors sold the cottage to a builder. He sought to evict the defendants but the court, following the approach in *Inwards v. Baker* [1965] 2 Q.B. 29, held that the defendants had an equitable licence which entitled them to remain in the cottage as long as they wished. The cottage was then sold to the present plaintiff. As a result of a protracted dispute over the defendants' use of a paddock the plaintiff sought possession of the cottage, claiming that by their conduct the defendants had forfeited their entitlement to the equitable licence.

LORD DENNING M.R.:

The action eventually came before Judge Hopkin Morgan in September 1976. Mr Williams claimed that the licence had been determined. The judge accepted, of course, Judge Bulger's findings that the Staites had an equitable licence to be in the cottage for life. But he found that their conduct had been such that the licence could be revoked. He held that Mr and Mrs Staite had lost any right to be there because of their conduct. So he ordered them out. I will read the judge's findings. They raise quite an interesting point of law. He asked this question: "Can the equitable licence for life pronounced by Judge Bulger be revoked by virtue of the subsequent conduct of the defendants?" He held that it could. He said:

"This conduct, as I have found, consisted in (a) bringing improper and unjustifiable pressure to bear on the plaintiff in an attempt to persuade him, quite deliberately falsely, that they, the defendants, were entitled to do whatever they wished as regards no. 2, its garden and the paddock without reference to or permission of the owner whereas in fact their licence was only to occupy the cottage and its garden and no more; (b) in acting in deliberate, even though minor, breach of their solemn promises to [the judge] on August 16, 1974; and (c) in giving false evidence in an attempt to deceive the court as to the extent of their licence."

Those findings show that the judge took a very poor view of Mr and Mrs Staite. He did not believe them: and he thought they had wrongly laid claim to the paddock. His finding about the paddock is not challenged in this court. The judge held that, because of their conduct, Mr and Mrs Staite had forfeited any right even to live in no. 2.

We have had much discussion as to the circumstances in which the court can revoke a licence of this kind. It is considered in *Megarry and Wade, The Law of Real Property*, 4th ed. (1975), in a section headed "Licence protected by estoppel or in equity". The distinguished authors say, at p. 778:

"The principle of estoppel may operate to prevent revocation of a right which one party has led the other to suppose was permanent. ... The revocation of a licence may also be restrained by injunction on equitable grounds."

I start with this: following Judge Bulger's decision, Mr and Mrs Staite had an equitable licence under which they were entitled to live in no. 2 Brook Cottages for their lives or for as long as they wished it to be their home. It may in some circumstances be revoked, but I do not think it can be revoked in such circumstances as are found in the present case. I know that the judge took a poor view of the conduct of the Staites—and I am not sure he was altogether fair to them—in their using the paddock as they did, and the other matters he mentioned, but to my mind their conduct, however reprehensible, was not such as to justify revocation of their licence to occupy the cottage as their home.

This suggestion was put to us: "Suppose they had made Mr Williams' life in no. 1 intolerable, could not the licence be revoked then?" That may be. In an extreme case, it might be so. But in the ordinary way I should have thought that bad conduct by Mr and Mrs Staite would not be a ground for revocation. The remedy of Mr Williams would be to bring an action for nuisance, trespass, or an injunction, and so forth. He should resort to those remedies before revoking the licence. Their conduct would have to be bad in the extreme before they could be turned out of their own home. They have nowhere else to go. It seems to me none of the judge's three items, (a), (b) or (c), would be sufficient to justify the revocation of the licence.

It seems to me that there was no justification for the revocation of this licence. The appeal should be allowed. The Staites should be allowed to remain.

GOFF L.J.:

I agree that this appeal succeeds. The case, in my judgment, is a novel one. In all the previous cases the person who sought to set up an equity against the other party's claim at law had done nothing wrong save that he had acted without securing his legal position. There was no impropriety on his part. The question, therefore, was whether the relationship and conduct of the parties made it unconscionable for the legal owner to assert his legal rights.

As Scarman L.J. said in *Crabb v. Arun District Council* [1976] Ch. 179, 192–193:

"... the court ... has to answer three questions. First, is there an equity established? Secondly, what is the extent of the equity, if one is established? And, thirdly, what is the relief appropriate to satisfy the equity?"

In the normal type of case to which I have been referring, whether there is an equity and its extent will depend, I think, simply upon the initial conduct said to give rise to the equity, although the court may have to decide how, having regard to supervening circumstances, the equity can best be satisfied. Thus, in *Crabb v. Arun District Council*, where the court directed that the person setting up the equity should have an easement, the court felt that had the matter been dealt with soon after the conduct which gave rise to the equity it would have ordered that the party setting up the equity should make compensation for the grant of the easement; but, as time had elapsed during which by the conduct of the party against whom the equity was raised the other party's land had been sterile for a number of years, the court in fact ordered that there should be no compensation. Similarly, in *Dodsworth v. Dodsworth* (1973) 228 E.G. 1115, to which our attention has been referred, the court took into account in determining how the equity should be satisfied the fact that in the meantime the lady who had offered to share her house had died.

The present case, in my judgment, is different because on the judge's findings, despite Mr Francis' noble efforts to defend his clients' conduct, I take the view that the Staites had been guilty of very grave misconduct towards the plaintiff in relation to the adjoining property. As Mr Francis pointed out, seven specific matters are complained of, all of which are trifling in themselves, and in respect of some of which no relief was claimed at all, and all of which, so far as necessary, had been covered by injunction mandatory or negative granted by the judge. But the real complaint made against the Staites of their conduct is that, as soon as they learned that the plaintiff had purchased the property, they went to see him and said he was in for "bloody trouble" and then proceeded to carry that threat into effect forthwith and, when he came to take occupation of the house which he had purchased, he found that the Staites had blocked the entrance to the paddock so that the furniture could not be brought in through the only, or only practicable, way.

So the novel point is argued. It is said that the court has to determine when the matter is brought before it whether there is any equity to restrain the legal owner from exercising his legal right and, therefore, where there has been conduct of the kind I have been describing, impropriety in relation to the property by the party setting up the equity, the court has to consider whether he comes with clean hands so as to be entitled to equitable relief. If that be right in law and on the facts, it is a complete answer, and the party seeking to set up the equity is left with no right at all and the legal owner is at liberty to exercise his legal right.

If it were necessary to decide that novel point, I am inclined to think that it is right in principle and, when a party raises an equity of this character and it is alleged against him that his own behaviour has been wrong, the court has to decide on the facts whether a sufficient answer to his equity has been made out. Also, although the seven specific points were in themselves trivial, I think it would be for serious consideration whether the threat and its implementation were not such as to afford an answer to the alleged equity.

However, in my judgment, it is not necessary to determine either of those points. There appear to me to be two complete answers to the case raised by the plaintiff. The first is that that was not the case pleaded below, and it was not the basis on which the trial proceeded or upon which the judge decided it. The case was that the defendants had a right under a licence but that it had been forfeited. The second point is that the matter came earlier before Judge Bulger who, although he only refused an order for possession, did, as it seems to me, determine at that stage that there was an equity and what it was. Thus, he said:

"The Staites clearly had a licence to live at no. 2 until the date [Mr Carver] purported to revoke the licence, but have they got an equity to stay there after that date? I think they have."

Then again, later in his judgment, he was considering whether the defendants had an equity to stay on.

Therefore, it seems to me, for those two reasons the case which Mr Baker has so ably presented on behalf of the plaintiff is not maintainable in this court. The only thing that is left, therefore, is the case sought to be made below that in some way the equity which the defendants have been held to have, by decision binding on the plaintiff as a successor in title, has been forfeited or determined. In my judgment, however, it cannot stand in that way either. Excessive user or bad behaviour towards the legal owner cannot bring the equity to an end or forfeit it. It may give rise to an action for damages for trespass or nuisance or to injunctions to restrain such behaviour, but I see no ground on which the equity, once established, can be forfeited. Of course, the court might have held, and might hold in any proper case, that the equity is in its nature for a limited period only or determinable upon a condition certain. In such a case the court must then see whether, in the events which have happened, it has determined or it has expired or been determined by the happening of that condition. No such case was ever raised before us, and there is no suggestion in the judgment of Judge Bulger that the equity was so limited or determined.

For those reasons, in my judgment, the judge below reached a wrong conclusion, and this appeal should be allowed.

CUMMING-BRUCE L.J.:
I agree, and agree for the reasons stated by Goff L.J.

NOTES:
1. For comment, see [1978] Conv. 386; (1979) 95 L.Q.R. 11; (1979) 42 M.L.R. 203.

2. Thompson [1986] Conv. 406 seeks to reconcile the apparent difference of opinion between Lord Denning M.R., who expressed the view that in extreme cases rights granted in satisfaction of an equity could be lost, and Goff L.J., who expressed the view that such rights could never be forfeited. He suggests that, where the court has made a final resolution of the dispute by requiring the grant of a recognised interest in land (as in *Pascoe v. Turner* and *Griffiths v. Williams*), such an interest cannot be lost by subsequent misconduct. On the other hand, where the court has made an order which is not intended to be final, which confers interim rights pending future developments and which requires the continuing protection of equity, in such circumstances it is suggested that that protection can be forfeited as a result of misconduct.

3. In *J. Willis & Son v. Willis* [1986] 1 E.G.L.R. 62 Parker L.J. ventured the opinion (at 63):

When the question is whether the equitable licence is established at all, it will normally be the case that the degree of misconduct required [to bar the claim] is less than would be required if it were sought to cancel a pre-existing equitable licence, if indeed—and there is some ground for saying that it cannot—such an equitable licence, once established, can be destroyed by such misconduct.

4. Moriarty (1984) 100 L.Q.R. 376 argues that courts do not have discretion as to the *nature* of the remedy; and that the function of the doctrine of proprietary estoppel and thus the only available remedy is the perfection of an imperfect gift. According to this view, the court has a discretion to the limited extent of being able to deny all remedy where the (mis)conduct justifies that response. Thompson [1986] Conv. 406 argues that this view is inconsistent both with statements of principle to be found in the case law and, more specifically, with articulated discussions as to the suitability and merits of what are clearly perceived to be *alternative* remedies in particular cases: see, *e.g. Dodsworth v. Dodsworth* (1973) 228 E.G. 1115; *Griffiths v. Williams* (1977) 248 E.G. 947; *Pascoe v. Turner* [1979] 1 W.L.R. 431.

5. Proprietary estoppel and interests in land

Certain questions remain unresolved in connection with the precise status of the rights of the claimant during the course of the development, recognition and satisfaction of his claim. Where the claimant establishes his claim in litigation and the court grants a remedy in the form of a recognised proprietary interest, the rights of the claimant and the effect of those rights on successors in title of the original licensor will be defined by the normal incidents and characteristics of that particular proprietary interest. Where appropriate, the interest can be protected by entry on the relevant register: see Battersby (1995) 58 M.L.R. 637, 640–643. So much is uncontroversial. The questions for consideration here are, first, the effect on successors in title of a remedy in the form of the dismissal of an action by the legal owner to assert his legal rights; and secondly, the nature and status of the rights of the claimant before the court has recognised the claim and granted a particular remedy.

As to the first question, there is an apparent absence of modern direct authority and the law is in need of clarification: see Smith [1973] C.L.J. 123, 125–129; Todd [1981] Conv. 347. Battersby [1991] Conv. 36 argues that, if the court is minded to confer a right capable of binding third parties, the court must select from those proprietary rights recognised by the general law; that the court has no jurisdiction to create new proprietary rights; and, following *Ashburn Anstalt v. Arnold* [1989] Ch. 1, that the court has no jurisdiction to declare than an occupational licence has proprietary effect. For a similar argument, based on an analysis of the earlier authorities, see Baughen (1994) 14 *Legal Studies* 147. Such a solution would, of course, remove the problem under consideration but it could also restrict the flexibility of the equitable jurisdiction.

The second question is rather more difficult. Suppose that objectively all the requirements of proprietary estoppel can be established; but that, before any claim is litigated and recognised by the court, the landowner transfers the land to a successor in title. What rights can the claimant enforce against the successor in title? It is important to appreciate that *ex hypothesi* the question does not concern the enforcement of rights which the court may ultimately grant in satisfaction of that claim. It is concerned with the status of the unlitigated claim, a claim which may fail or which, if successful, may be remedied by the grant of any of a wide range of proprietary interests that could affect the land in question. Until the court recognises the claim and satisfies the equity by granting a specific remedy, it is impossible to assert that the claimant has any right over the land at all, much less that he has a particular interest. For that reason it has been argued that as a matter of principle the unrecognised claim or "inchoate equity" cannot constitute an interest in land, largely because of the difficulties of categorisation within the framework of interests recognised by the 1925 property legislation, and that it is incapable of binding a successor in title to the land: see Bailey [1983] Conv. 99; Hayton [1990] Conv. 370, especially at 380–384. On the other hand, it has been argued that the inchoate equity should be capable of binding a successor in title: Battersby [1991] Conv. 36, 45; Baughen (1994) 14 *Legal Studies* 147, 154; Battersby (1995) 58 M.L.R. 637, 642.

In fact, there appear to be an increasing number of dicta in recent cases to the effect that the inchoate equity arises as soon as the conscience of the landowner is affected by the dealings between the parties; and that from that moment the claimant has some right over the land which is capable of binding a successor in title to the land. For example, in *Re Sharpe* [1980] 1 W.L.R. 219 Browne-Wilkinson J. stated (at 225) that "it cannot be that the interest in property arises for the first time when the court declares it to exist"; see also *Sen v. Headley* [1991] Ch. 425, 440 *per* Nourse L.J.; *Voyce v. Voyce* (1991) 62 P. & C.R. 290, 294 *per* Dillon L.J.

In the case of unregistered land, the inchoate equity is not included in any of the categories of land charge under the Land Charges Act 1972 nor is it apparently capable of being overreached under section 2(1) of the Law of Property Act 1925. However, the equity has been held to be enforceable against a donee of the land: *Voyce v. Voyce, supra,* 294 *per* Dillon L.J., 296 *per* Nicholls L.J.; *E.R. Ives Investment Ltd v. High* [1967] 2 Q.B. 379 provides some authority for the proposition that the equity will bind a purchaser of a legal estate (*a fortiori* an equitable interest) in the land who has *actual* notice of the circumstances giving rise to the claim: *ibid.* 393 *per* Lord Denning M.R., 400 *per* Danckwerts L.J., 405 *per* Winn L.J.; and see also *Lloyds Bank plc v. Carrick* [1996] 4 All E.R. 630, 642 *per* Morritt L.J. It is less clear whether the equity will bind a purchaser who has only *constructive* notice of the circumstances giving rise to the claim. In *Bristol & West Building Society v. Henning* [1985] 1 W.L.R. 778 Browne-Wilkinson L.J. suggests (at 781) that constructive notice may be sufficient; but in *Re Sharpe* [1980] 1 W.L.R. 219 the judgment of Browne-Wilkinson J. contains (at 226) dicta to the contrary. See Maudsley (1956) 20 Conv. 281, 291; Crane (1967) 31 Conv. 332, 339; Thompson [1983] Conv. 50, 56; Battersby (1995) 58 M.L.R. 637, 640–643. However, some doubt may have been created by comments in *United Bank of Kuwait plc v. Sahib* [1997] Ch. 107. In a very brief consideration of the issue, Peter Gibson L.J. seems to suggest that a purchaser will not be bound by a claim based in proprietary estoppel unless he himself would be acting unconscionably by denying the claim: *ibid.* 142. If a proprietary estoppel claim has already been commenced and the claim is for an established property right, the claimant could register a pending land action under section 5 of the Land Charges Act 1972: see *Haslemere Estates Ltd v. Baker* [1982] 1 W.L.R. 1109, 1119–1120 *per* Megarry V.-C.

In the case of registered land, it is the practice of the Land Registry to permit an inchoate equity to be protected as a minor interest by the entry of a notice or caution (under the Land Registration Act 1925, s.49(1)(f)): see Law Com. No. 254, *Land Registration for the Twenty-First Century* (1998), para. 3.35; and, if the claimant is in actual occupation of the land in question, there is some judicial support for the view that the equity constitutes an overriding interest within section 70(1)(g) of the Land Registration Act 1925: see *Lee-Parker v. Izzet (No. 2)* [1972] 1 W.L.R. 775, 780; but see *Canadian Imperial Bank of Commerce v. Bello* (1992) 64 P. & C.R. 48, 52, where the Court of Appeal endorsed the view that the equity does not constitute a qualifying interest under paragraph (g), and *Habermann v. Koehler* (1996) 73 P. & C.R. 515, where the Court of Appeal remitted the matter for determination. For discussion, see Battersby (1995) 58 M.L.R. 637, 640–643. Consistent with the position in relation to unregistered land, if a proprietary estoppel claim has already been commenced and the claim is for an established property right, it would seem that the claimant could register a pending land action under section 59 of the Land Registration Act 1925.

Given the wide range of estoppel claims, it has been argued that an all-or-nothing response to the question whether inchoate equities are capable of enforcement against purchasers is inappropriate in that it fails to differentiate sufficiently between those cases where the position of the claimant merits protection against a purchaser and those cases where it does not. The difficulty, of course, is the formulation of a solution that achieves that balance. Critchley [1998] Conv. 502 argues that the comments of Peter Gibson L.J. in *United Bank of Kuwait plc v. Sahib* [1997] Ch. 107, *supra*, p.603, may be interpreted as advancing a solution based on the approach to contractual licences endorsed in *Ashburn Anstalt v. Arnold* [1989] Ch. 1. Such a solution could be seen as having the advantage of assimilating the position of estoppel licences and contractual licences in relation to purchasers; but it may not be regarded as ideal because exclusive reliance on the constructive trust reasoning may fail to produce the desired result in the more varied range of estoppel claims. Milne [1997] Web J.C.L.I. argues that the constructive trust reasoning is in fact inappropriate in the context of estoppel-based claims because such reasoning presupposes (i) potential liability on the part of the vendor if the purchaser is free to ignore the claimant's equity and/ or (ii) an agreement between the vendor and the purchaser that the sale is subject to the claimant's equity. He argues instead that the claimant's equity should only be enforceable against a purchaser from the original landowner where it operates *directly* against the purchaser by reason of his own unconscionable reliance on his strict legal rights; and the comments of Peter Gibson L.J. in *United Bank of Kuwait plc v. Sahib* could be interpreted consistently with that approach.

The Law Commission has provisionally recommended, in the context of its blueprint for land registration in the next century, that an equity arising by estoppel or acquiescence in relation to registered land should be regarded as an interest from the time at which it arises (although the Law Commission acknowledges that that moment will not always be easy to define). As a consequence, it will be clear that such an inchoate equity would be capable of binding a purchaser either as a protected minor interest or as an overriding interest: Law Com. No. 254, *Land Registration for the Twenty-First Century* (1998), paras 3.33–3.36. It is clearly arguable that such a recommendation should be extended to unregistered land while it continues to exist and that inchoate equities arising by estoppel should be capable of registration under the Land Charges Act 1972.

F. Multiple Characterisation

1. Contractual licences and licences protected by proprietary estoppel

In response to a judicial plea for (judicial) clarification and rationalisation of the rights of licensees (see *Re Sharpe* [1980] 1 W.L.R. 219, 226 *per* Browne-Wilkinson J.), a vigorous academic debate developed on the relationship between contractual licences and licences protected by proprietary estoppel.

There are two distinct but related issues. The first relates to the overlap between the two types of licence and the extent to which both analyses can be applied to the same factual circumstances. The second issue relates to the capacity of the two types of licence to bind a purchaser from the original licensor. The issues are related because it is difficult to justify the current position on the second issue (which differentiates between the two types of licence) if there is a substantial degree of overlap in their applicability.

There is surprisingly little judicial comment on the first issue. In *Ashburn Anstalt v. Arnold* [1989] Ch. 1, which appears to be the only case directly in point, the Court of Appeal suggested that *Errington v. Errington* [1952] 1 K.B. 290, although decided as a contractual licence case, could be explained as an estoppel case. Otherwise, judicial comment relates to the overlap between contract and estoppel generally and is inconsistent. In *E.R. Ives Investment Ltd v. High* [1967] 2 Q.B. 379 the Court of Appeal applied estoppel principles where a (contractual) easement was void by reason of non-registration. However, in *Lloyds Bank plc v. Carrick* [1996] 4 All E.R. 630 the Court of Appeal expressly declined to apply the doctrine of proprietary estoppel where an estate contract was void by reason of non-registration.

In relation to the second issue, the current position on the enforceability of contractual licences and licences protected by estoppel respectively has been discussed above; but it may be that the absence of judicial comment on the differential treatment of the two types of licences is simply a reflection of the view that they are quite distinct.

Academic commentators have tended to treat the two issues together. The early contributors asserted that contractual licences and licences protected by estoppel were fundamentally different and that that difference should be reflected in the capacity of the two types of licence to affect successors in title of the licensor. According to Todd [1981] Conv. 347, contractual terms are "reasonably precisely defined" whereas a representation inferred from conduct is "a much vaguer notion". However, Moriarty (1984) 100 L.Q.R. 376 argues that the case law does not bear out this theory: see, *e.g. Williams v. Staite* [1979] Ch. 291; *Tanner v. Tanner* [1975] 1 W.L.R. 1346; *Chandler v. Kerley* [1978] 1 W.L.R. 693; and Battersby [1991] Conv. 36 points out that it is somewhat paradoxical that (vague) estoppels can apparently bind successors in title whereas (precise) contractual arrangements cannot. Similar criticisms have been made of the thesis of Briggs [1981] Conv. 212 that contractual licences and licences protected by proprietary estoppel are mutually exclusive, being based on promises and representations respectively: see Thompson [1983] Conv. 50; but Briggs repeated the thesis at [1983] Conv. 285 in what Battersby describes as a "somewhat petulant" reply to the criticisms of Thompson.

Moriarty (1984) 100 L.Q.R. 376 argues that the distinguishing feature is the element of *request* which converts detrimental reliance into consideration and thus provides the essential characteristic of contractual arrangements; but he argues that this distinction is insufficient justification for any difference in capacity to affect successors in title.

Thompson [1983] Conv. 50, [1985] C.L.J. 280, 295–299, argues that the two types of licence are not mutually exclusive but that they can co-exist on the same set of facts and that their capacity to affect successors in title should be the same. It is suggested that the argument is not wholly compelling: what Thompson establishes is that an initial contractual arrangement may be overtaken by events which activate the doctrine of proprietary estoppel. In any event, Thompson argues that contractual licences and licences protected by proprietary estoppel should only bind a successor in title where (i) the successor in title is not a purchaser for value; or (ii) the successor in title has express notice of the licence; or (iii) the licensee is in exclusive occupation of the land in question.

Smith *Property Law* (1998), at 462–463, concentrates on the discretionary nature of the remedies in an attempt to explain the differential treatment of the two types of licence. He argues that if contractual licences were held to be enforceable against purchasers, the parties to the contract could effectively create new forms of property interests that would automatically bind purchasers; and that for various reasons that has traditionally been seen as undesirable. By contrast, even where a claimant establishes the requirements of proprietary estoppel, the court retains some discretion as to the availability and choice of remedy; and in that way the court can exercise some control over the creation of novel enforceable property rights. However, Smith accepts that the potential enforceability of estoppel licences may still create difficulties for purchasers in respect of certainty and discoverability.

The conclusions of the Court of Appeal in *Ashburn Anstalt v. Arnold* [1989] Ch. 1 on the capacity of contractual licences to bind successors in title has undermined the views of Moriarty and Thompson; but, as Hill (1988) 51

M.L.R. 226 points out (at 233), that case has heightened the need for a similar ruling on licences protected by proprietary estoppel or, alternatively, a compelling justification for the difference in the capacity of the two types of licence to affect successors in title. Such limited judicial comment as there has been since *Ashburn Anstalt v. Arnold* suggests support for the former approach: see *Canadian Imperial Bank of Commerce v. Bello* (1992) 64 P. & C.R. 48, 52 *per* Dillon L.J.; *United Bank of Kuwait plc v. Sahib* [1997] Ch. 107, 142 *per* Peter Gibson L.J.

2. Contractual licences and constructive trusts

See *Binions v. Evans* [1972] Ch. 359, *supra*, p. 516; *Ashburn Anstalt v. Arnold* [1989] Ch. 1, *supra*, p. 522.

3. Licences protected by proprietary estoppel and constructive trusts

It is clear from some of the cases extracted above that there is a close relationship between the doctrine of proprietary estoppel and certain manifestations of the (remedial) constructive trust. Both concepts operate as remedial devices to prevent a person from insisting upon his strict legal rights as against another person where such insistence would be inequitable or unconscionable in the light of the dealings between those persons. Indeed in some cases courts have used the terminology of constructive trusts as a generic label for the remedy granted to satisfy an equity generated by proprietary estoppel: see, *e.g. Re Sharpe (A Bankrupt)* [1980] 1 W.L.R. 219, 225 *per* Browne-Wilkinson J. *supra*, p. 582; *Re Basham* [1986] 1 W.L.R. 1498, 1503–1504 *per* Edward Nugee Q.C., *supra*, p. 549.

In the context of the acquisition of equitable ownership rights in the family home (see *ante*, p. 65), there is no lack of recent judicial dicta to the effect that the so-called "common intention constructive trust" and proprietary estoppel have become indistinguishable: see *Grant v. Edwards* [1986] Ch. 638, 656 *per* Browne-Wilkinson V.-C.; *Lloyd's Bank plc v. Rosset* [1991] 1 A.C. 107, 132 *per* Lord Bridge; but for an express assertion that the two concepts have not yet been assimilated, see *Stokes v. Anderson* [1991] 1 F.L.R. 391, 399 *per* Nourse L.J. Formal recognition and acknowledgment of the "illusory distinction" between the two concepts in the context of the family home has been urged by Hayton [1990] Conv. 370, (1993) 109 L.Q.R. 485; but caution has been urged by Ferguson (1993) 109 L.Q.R. 114; Welstead [1995] Conv. 61; Lawson (1996) 16 *Legal Studies* 218. For a comprehensive "re-think" of family property, see Gardner (1993) 109 L.Q.R. 263.

However, as the cases extracted in this chapter demonstrate, the range of remedies available to satisfy equities generated by proprietary estoppel is far wider than the granting of a share in the equitable ownership of property.

G. FUNCTION OF LICENCES

Moriarty (1984) 100 L.Q.R. 376 argues that it is misleading to view licences simply as permissions negativing trespasses; and that it should be recognised that both contractual licences and licences protected by proprietary estoppel are mechanisms through which the law sanctions the informal creation of proprietary rights in land. Such recognition would remove the obscurity surrounding the selection of particular remedies; it would spotlight the absurdity of denying that contractual licences are capable of binding third parties; and, perhaps most importantly, it would provide a firm basis for the sensible discussion of the more harmonious accommodation of licences within the structure of English land law. Contemporary criticism of this thesis has been noted: see Thompson [1986] Conv. 406. Moreover, as Battersby [1991] Conv. 36 notes (at 37–38), subsequently developments (the enactment of section 2 of the Law of Property (Miscellaneous Provisions) Act 1989 and the conclusion of the Court of Appeal in *Ashburn Anstalt v. Arnold* [1989] Ch. 1 on the capacity of contractual licences to bind third parties) have rendered much of the argument relating to *contractual* licences no longer tenable. On the other hand, there are distinct echoes of Moriarty in the conclusion of Battersby that "proprietary estoppel is a mechanism whereby, informally, proprietary interests of an orthodox kind can be created". See also Baughen (1994) 14 *Legal Studies* 147.

Dewar (1986) 49 M.L.R. 741 asserts that the debate over licences relating to land has taken place within a framework characterised by what he terms "conceptual formalism", according to which only arguments of a conceptual nature are regarded as valid. He argues that in so far as conceptual formalism purports to explain or evaluate the licence, it falls short significantly in two respects. First, it ignores or obscures an important and controversial aspect of the judicial deployment of the licence as a mechanism of dispute-settlement: why did the Court of Appeal in *Tanner v. Tanner* [1975] 1 W.L.R. 683 or in *Errington v. Errington and Woods* [1952] 1 K.B. 290 decide the case in terms of (inferred) contractual licences rather than proprietary estoppel? Secondly, it offers an evaluation of the licence that is demonstrably false in a significant range of cases: how can it be argued that the courts conferred conventional proprietary interests in cases such as *Inwards v. Baker* [1965] 2 Q.B. 29 or *Dodsworth v. Dodsworth* (1973) 228 E.G. 1115? He concludes that "the licence represents a *form* of property right that is markedly different from those conventionally encountered in land law, in that it cannot be assigned and relates specifically to the use or occupation of land". This idea may be compared with Everton's "quasi-property", which is defined as "a right which, by direct or indirect means, is specifically enforceable by the court, and ... without bestowing any beneficial ownership, confers a right of enjoyment of property": see [1982] Conv. 118, 177 (at 184).

7

EASEMENTS

A. Introduction

Land can rarely be regarded in isolation, sufficient in itself. Almost inevitably, its enjoyment will be affected by its relationship with neighbouring land. This reality is recognised in the concept of natural rights which exist automatically as an incident of land ownership. For example, a landowner has a natural right to have his undeveloped land supported by the land of his neighbour: see *Dalton v. Angus* (1881) 6 App.Cas., 740, 791, *per* Lord Selborne L.C. However, such natural rights may be insufficient to ensure full enjoyment of the land. The landowner may wish to acquire a right of support for a building constructed on his land; he may wish to acquire a right of access to his land across the land of his neighbour; indeed, he may wish to acquire a range of other rights over the land of his neighbour that increase the enjoyment and convenience of his own ownership. Since such rights are outside the category of natural rights, they must be acquired either by agreement between the landowners concerned or by implication of law. This chapter is concerned with these rights as *easements*, although the substantive content of many easements may instead be acquired, according to the circumstances, by licence, by restrictive covenant or by simple contract. This chapter does not discuss the related topic of profits à prendre.

The classic example of an easement is the right of way exercised by the principal landowner over the land of another person. Further common examples include the right of the principal landowner to instal pipes under neighbouring land so as to permit the passing of water or sewerage through the pipes and the right of the principal landowner to fix a signboard on a neighbouring building so as to advertise the business conducted on the principal land. In such cases the right involves the principal landowner doing something on the neighbouring land or, perhaps more accurately, the right involves the neighbouring landowner permitting the principal landowner to do something on his land. Such easements are known as *positive* easements. There are also *negative* easements, although they are fewer in number; and the substantive content of negative easements must usually be acquired through restrictive covenants: *Phipps v. Pears* [1965] 1 Q.B. 76, 82–83 *per* Denning L.J., *infra*, p. 629. Such negative easements are characterised by the fact that, for the benefit of the principal landowner, the neighbouring landowner refrains from doing something that he would otherwise be permitted to do on his own land. For example, the easement of light, the right to receive light to a building on the principal land, involves the neighbouring landowner refraining from obstructing the passage of light to the principal land by building or otherwise; and the easement of support for buildings involves the neighbouring landowner refraining from removing the soil or demolishing a building on his own land without providing alternative means of support for buildings on the principal land.

What characterises every easement is that both the burden and the benefit of the substantive right are necessarily attached to land. It is clear that an easement involves a burden on land, the burden of permitting something to be done on that land or of refraining from doing something on that land. However, it is also necessary that the benefit of the easement is attached to other land. As it is sometimes expressed, an easement cannot exist "in gross": see *infra*, p. 617. Thus, an easement is a right attached to one piece of land, referred to as the "dominant tenement" or "dominant land", and exerciseable over another piece of land, referred to as the "servient tenement" or "servient land". This essential characteristic of easements is further demonstrated by the fact that when the dominant land is transferred into different ownership the benefit of any existing easements is automatically transferred as part of the land; and, similarly, when the servient land is transferred into different ownership the burden of any existing easements is in most cases automatically transferred as part of the land: see *infra*, p. 631.

B. Nature of Easements

No satisfactory definition of an easement has been formulated. Where it is alleged that an easement has been acquired, the question whether the alleged right is capable of constituting an easement is addressed by reference to what are termed the "essential characteristics" of easements. *Re Ellenborough Park* [1956] Ch. 131 provides the authority for the four recognised essential characteristics. In addition to these positive requirements, there are a number of largely negative requirements which must be satisfied before the alleged right is admitted to the category of easements. For a general survey, see Peel (1964) 28 Conv. 450.

1. Essential characteristics

Re Ellenborough Park [1956] Ch. 131

(CA, Evershed M.R., Birkett and Romer L.JJ.)

Ellenborough Park was an open piece of land in Weston-super-Mare. In 1855 the owners of the park and the surrounding land laid out the surrounding land in plots forming two rows. The question raised was whether the purchasers (and their successors in title) of plots of land on Ellenborough Crescent which fronted on the park (and of the further row of plots separated from the park only by the plots on Ellenborough Crescent) enjoyed easements over the park. It was agreed that the conveyance of one plot in 1864 was typical of all the relevant conveyances. That plot had been conveyed "together with all ways paths passages easements rights and appurtenances to the said plot of land ... and also the full enjoyment at all times hereafter in common with the other persons to whom such easements may be granted of the pleasure ground set out and made in the centre of the square called Ellenborough Park ... subject to the payment of a fair and just proportion of the costs charges and expenses of keeping in good order and condition the said pleasure ground". Moreover, each conveyance contained a covenant by the vendors to maintain the park as an ornamental garden or pleasure park. Danckwerts J. held that the purchasers of the plots and their successors in title enjoyed (legal) easements over the park. The owners of the park appealed to the Court of Appeal.

EVERSHED M.R.:

The substantial question in the case ... is one of considerable interest and importance. ... [I]f the house owners are now entitled to an enforceable right in respect of the use and enjoyment of Ellenborough Park, that right must have the character and quality of an easement as understood by, and known to, our law. It has, therefore, been necessary for us to consider carefully the qualities and characteristics of easements, and, for such purpose, to look back into the history of that category of incorporeal rights in the development of English real property law.

...

For the purposes of the argument before us Mr Cross [counsel for the appellants] and Mr Goff [counsel for the respondents] were content to adopt, as correct, the four characteristics formulated in Dr Cheshire's Modern Real Property, 7th ed., pp. 456 et seq. They are (1) there must be a dominant and a servient tenement: (2) an easement must "accommodate" the dominant tenement: (3) dominant and servient owners must be different persons, and (4) a right over land cannot amount to an easement, unless it is capable of forming the subject-matter of a grant.

Two of the four may be disregarded for present purposes, namely, the first and the third. If the garden or park is, as it is alleged to be, the servient tenement in the present case, then it is undoubtedly distinct from the alleged dominant tenements, namely, the freeholds of the several houses whose owners claim to exercise the rights. It is equally clear that if these lands respectively constitute the servient and dominant tenements then they are owned by different persons. The argument in the case is found accordingly, to turn upon the meaning and application to the circumstances of the present case of the second and fourth conditions; that is, first, whether the alleged easement can be said in truth to "accommodate" the dominant tenement—in other words, whether there exists the required "connexion" between the one and the other: and, secondly, whether the right alleged is "capable of forming the subject-matter of a grant". The exact significance of this fourth and last condition is, at first sight perhaps, not entirely clear. As between the original parties to the "grant", it is not in doubt that rights of this kind would be capable of taking effect by way of contract or licence. But for the purposes of the present case, as the arguments made clear, the cognate questions involved under this condition are: whether the rights purported to be given are expressed in terms of too wide and vague a character; whether, if and so far as effective, such rights would amount to rights of joint occupation or would substantially deprive the park owners of proprietorship or legal possession; whether, if and so far as effective, such rights constitute mere rights of recreation, possessing no quality of utility or benefit; and on such grounds cannot qualify as easements.

. . .

[I]t is clear from the deed ... that the original common vendors were engaged upon a scheme of development ... designed to produce a result of common experience; namely, a row of uniform houses facing inwards upon a park or garden which was intended to form, and formed in fact, an essential characteristic belonging, and properly speaking "appurtenant", to all and each of them. In substance, instead of each house being confined to its own small or moderate garden, each was to enjoy in common, but in common exclusively with the other houses in the Crescent, a single large "private" garden. In our judgment the substance of the matter is not in this respect affected by the fact that some few houses in the immediate proximity of, but not actually fronting upon, the park were also entitled to share the privilege. This extension of the privilege may no doubt be unusual and (at first sight at any rate) out of line with the conception of the square and its surrounding houses as a symmetrical unit. It has therefore a bearing upon the question of the "connexion" between the right enjoyed and the premises of the relevant house owners; and must be discussed under the head of Dr Cheshire's second condition. But, in our judgment, the language of the deed of 1864 is clearly to the effect that the right of enjoyment of the garden was intended to be annexed to the premises sold, rather than given as a privilege personal to their purchaser. The enjoyment was not exclusive to those premises alone; it was to be held in common with the like rights annexed to the other houses in (and in some few cases in close proximity to) the square or crescent. But it was not contemplated that like rights should be otherwise extended so as to belong in any sense to premises not forming part of (or at least closely connected with) the square or their owners. The position of the grant in the deed and its language show that, in the respects we have mentioned, the right granted was intended and treated as in pari materia with the rights of way and drainage similarly conferred. The relevant part of the deed opens with the general formula "Together with all ways ... easements rights and appurtenances to the said plot of land ... apertaining". The rights of way (admittedly easements properly so called) follow immediately the general formula, being linked to it by the words "and particularly". The next two words are "And also", which, in turn, introduce the garden rights now in question in language which repeats the phrase used in relation to the rights of way—"in common with the other persons to whom such easements may be granted".

In our judgment, if the construction of this part of the deed does not tend to the conclusion that the garden rights, like the rights of way, were particular examples of the general grant of easements and rights appurtenant to the plot conveyed, it is at least made clear that the garden rights were (so far, of course, as they properly could be) of the same character, quoad the land conveyed, as the rights of way and drainage. It was conceded that the rights, if effectual and enforceable, were conditional; that is, upon the house owners making their appropriate contributions to the cost of upkeep. In this respect, again, they were analogous, by the terms of the deed, to the rights of way over Crescent and Walliscote Roads. As a complement to the rights of enjoyment of the garden, subject to the condition of contribution, was the covenant by the vendors against building on the park and to the effect that the park should at all times remain as an ornamental garden. Mr Cross did not seriously challenge Mr Goff's contention that, in their context, the words of the covenant to which we have last referred could fairly be construed as implying a negative covenant on the vendors' part against any user by them of the park otherwise than as a garden. There is clear authority that, if such be the substantial effect of the covenant, its benefit and burden will run with the land. The last consideration appreciably reinforces the view which we take of the meaning and intention of the deed, to attach the garden rights in all respects like the rights of way and drainage to the land conveyed.

It remains to interpret the actual terms of the grant itself—"the full enjoyment of the pleasure ground set out and made", etc. Mr Cross fastened upon the presence of the word "full", and the absence of any indication of the way in which the pleasure ground was to be used—or of any limitations upon its use—and contended that the right or privilege given was a jus spatiandi in its strict sense, that is, a right to go or wander upon the park and every part of it and enjoy its amenities (and even its produce) without stint. We do not so construe the words in their context. Although we are now anticipating to some extent the question which arises under the fourth of Dr Cheshire's conditions, it seems to us, as a matter of construction, that the use contemplated and granted was the use of the park as a garden, the proprietorship of which (and of the produce of which) remained vested in the vendors and their successors. The enjoyment contemplated was the enjoyment of the vendors' ornamental garden in its physical state as such—the right, that is to say, of walking on or over those parts provided for such purpose, that is, pathways and (subject to restrictions in the ordinary course in the interest of the grass) the lawns; to rest in or upon the seats or other places provided; and, if certain parts were set apart for particular recreations such as tennis or bowls, to use those parts for those purposes, subject again, in the ordinary course, to the provisions made for their regulation; but not to trample at will all over the park, to cut or pluck the flowers or shrubs, or to interfere in the laying out or upkeep of the park. Such use or enjoyment is, we think, a common and clearly understood conception, analogous to the use and enjoyment conferred upon members of the public, when they are open to the public, of parks or gardens such as St. James's Park, Kew Gardens or the Gardens of Lincoln's Inn Fields. In our judgment, the use of the word "full" does not import some wider, less well understood or less definable privilege. The adjective does not in fact again appear when the enjoyment of the garden is later referred to. It means no more than that to each plot was annexed the right of enjoyment of the park as a whole—notwithstanding that it was divided by Walliscote Road. Nor does any difficulty arise out of the condition as to contribution, and Mr Cross did not, indeed, so suggest. The obligation being a condition of the enjoyment, each house would be bound to contribute its due (that is, proportionate) share of the reasonable cost of upkeep.

. . .

We pass, accordingly, to a consideration of the [second] of Dr Cheshire's conditions—that of the accommodation of the alleged dominant tenements by the rights as we have interpreted them. For it was one of the main submissions by Mr Cross on behalf of the appellant that the right of full enjoyment of the park, granted to the purchaser by the conveyance of 1864 was insufficiently connected with the enjoyment of the property conveyed, in that it did not subserve some use which was to be made of that property; and that such a right accordingly could not exist in law as an easement. In this part of his argument Mr Cross was invoking a principle which is, in our judgment, of unchallengeable authority, expounded, in somewhat varying language, in many judicial utterances, of which the judgments in *Ackroyd v. Smith* (1850) 10 C.B. 164 are, perhaps, most commonly cited. We think it unnecessary to review the authorities in which the principle has been applied; for the effect of the decisions is stated with accuracy in Dr Cheshire's Modern Real Property, 7th ed., at p. 457. After pointing out that "one of the fundamental principles concerning easements is that they must be not only appurtenant to a dominant tenement, but also connected with the normal enjoyment of the dominant tenement" and referring to certain citations in support of that proposition the author proceeded: "We may expand the statement of the principle thus: a right enjoyed by one over the land of another does not possess the status of an easement unless it accommodates and serves the dominant tenement, and is reasonably necessary for the better enjoyment of that tenement, for if it has no necessary connexion therewith, although it confers an advantage upon the owner and renders his ownership of the land more valuable, it is not an easement at all, but a mere contractual right personal to and only enforceable between the two contracting parties".

. . .

Can it be said, then, of the right of full enjoyment of the park in question, which was granted by the conveyance of 1864 and which, for reasons already given, was in our view, intended to be annexed to the property conveyed, that it accommodated and served that property? It is clear that the right did, in some degree, enhance the value of the property, and this consideration cannot be dismissed as wholly irrelevant. It is, of course, a point to be noted; but we agree with Mr Cross's submission that it is in no way decisive of the problem; it is not sufficient to show that the right increased the value of the property conveyed, unless it is also shown that it was connected with the normal enjoyment of that property. It appears to us that the question whether or not this connexion exists is primarily one of fact, and depends largely on the nature of the alleged dominant tenement and the nature of the right granted. As to the former, it was in the contemplation of the parties to the conveyance of 1864 that the property conveyed should be used for residential and not commercial purposes. That appears from the conveyance itself, and the covenant by the purchaser, that the dwelling-house, etc., which he bound himself to build should not "be occupied or used as an open or exposed shop or for any purpose of trade or commerce other than a lodging-house or private school or seminary" without the vendor's written consent. Since it has been conceded that all the conveyances of plots for building purposes fronting or near Ellenborough Park were as regards (inter alia) user substantially the same as the conveyance of 1864, the inevitable inference is that the houses, which were to be built upon the plots, were to constitute a residential estate. As appears from the map, the houses, which were built upon the plots around and near to Ellenborough Park, varied in size, some being large detached houses and others smaller and either semi-detached or in a row. We have already stated that the purchasers of all the plots, which actually abutted on the park, were granted the right to enjoy the use of it, as were also the purchasers of some of the plots which, although not fronting upon the park, were only a short distance away from it. As to the nature of the right granted, the conveyance of 1864 shows that the park was to be kept and maintained as a pleasure ground or ornamental garden, and that it was contemplated that it should at all times be kept in good order and condition and well stocked with plants and shrubs; and the vendors covenanted that they would not at any time thereafter erect or permit to be erected any dwelling-house or other building (except a grotto, bower, summer-house, flower-stand, fountain, music-stand or other ornamental erection) within or on any part of the pleasure ground. On these facts Mr Cross submitted that the requisite connexion between the right to use the park and the normal enjoyment of the houses which were built around it or near it had not been established. He likened the position to a right granted to the purchaser of a house to use the Zoological Gardens free of charge or to attend Lord's Cricket Ground without payment. Such a right would undoubtedly, he said, increase the value of the property conveyed but could not run with it at law as an easement, because there was no sufficient nexus between the enjoyment of the right and the use of the house. It is probably true, we think, that in neither of Mr Cross's illustrations would the supposed right constitute an easement, for it would be wholly extraneous to, and independent of, the use of a house as a house, namely, as a place in which the householder and his family live and make their home; and it is for this reason that the analogy which Mr Cross sought to establish between his illustrations and the present case cannot, in our opinion, be supported. A much closer analogy, as it seems to us, is the case of a man selling the freehold of part of his house and granting to the purchaser, his heirs and assigns, the right, appurtenant to such part, to use the garden in common with the vendor and his assigns. In such a case, the test of connexion, or accommodation, would be amply satisfied; for just as the use of a garden undoubtedly enhances, and is connected with, the normal enjoyment of the house to which it belongs, so also would the right granted, in the case supposed, be closely connected with the use and enjoyment of the part of the premises sold. Such, we think, is in substance the position in the present case. The park became a communal garden for the benefit and enjoyment of those whose houses adjoined it or were in its close proximity. Its flower beds, lawns and walks were calculated to afford all the amenities which it is the purpose of the garden of a house to provide; and, apart from the fact that these amenities extended to a number of householders, instead of being confined to one (which on this aspect of the case is immaterial), we can see no difference in principle between Ellenborough Park and a garden in the ordinary signification of that word. It is the collective garden of the neighbouring houses, to whose use it was dedicated by the owners of the estate and as such amply satisfied, in our judgment, the requirement of connexion with the dominant tenements to which it is appurtenant. The result is not affected by the circumstance that the right to the park is in this case enjoyed by some few houses which are not immediately fronting on the park. The test for present purposes, no doubt, is that the park should constitute in a real and intelligible sense the garden (albeit the communal garden) of the houses to which its enjoyment is annexed. But we think that the test is satisfied as regards these few neighbouring, though not adjacent, houses. We think that the extension of the right of enjoyment to these few houses does not negative the presence of the necessary "nexus" between the subject-matter enjoyed and the premises to which the enjoyment is expressed to belong.

...

For the reasons which we have stated, we are unable to accept the contention that the right to the full enjoyment of Ellenborough Park fails in limine to qualify as a legal easement for want of the necessary connexion between its enjoyment and the use of the properties comprised in the conveyance of 1864, and in the other relevant conveyances.

We turn next to Dr Cheshire's fourth condition for an easement—that the right must be capable of forming the subject-matter of a grant. As we have earlier stated, satisfaction of the condition in the present case depends on a consideration of the questions whether the right conferred is too wide and vague, whether it is inconsistent with the proprietorship or possession of the alleged servient owners, and whether it is a mere right of recreation without utility or benefit.

To the first of these questions the interpretation which we have given to the typical deed provides, in our judgment, the answer; for we have construed the right conferred as being both well defined and commonly understood. In these essential respects the right may be said to be distinct from the indefinite and unregulated privilege which, we think, would ordinarily be understood by the Latin term "jus spatiandi", a privilege of wandering at will over all and every part of another's field or park, and which, though easily intelligible as the subject-matter of a personal licence, is something substantially different from the subject-matter of the grant in question, namely, the provision for a limited number of houses in a uniform crescent of one single large but private garden.

Our interpretation of the deed also provides, we think, the answer to the second question; for the right conferred no more amounts to a joint occupation of the park with its owners, no more excludes the proprietorship or possession of the latter, than a right of way granted through a passage, or than the use by the public of the gardens of Lincoln's Inn Fields (to take one of our former examples) amount to joint occupation of that garden with the London County Council, or involve an inconsistency with the possession or proprietorship of the council as lessees. ... We see nothing repugnant to a man's proprietorship or possession of a piece of land that he should decide to make it and maintain it as an ornamental garden, and should grant rights to a limited number of other persons to come into it for the enjoyment of its amenities.

...

The third of the questions embraced in Dr Cheshire's fourth condition rests primarily on a proposition stated in Theobald's *The Law of Land*, 2nd ed. (1929), at p. 263, where it is said that an easement "must be a right of utility and benefit and not one of mere recreation and amusement".

[Having concluded that the authorities cited (*Mounsey v. Ismay* (1865) 3 H. & C. 486; *Solomon v. Vintners Co.* (1859) 4 H. & N. 585; *Dyce v. Lady James Hay* (1852) 1 Macq. 305; *Dempster v. Cleghorn* (1813) 2 Dow 40) provided no real support for the proposition, Evershed M.R. continued:]

In any case, if the proposition be well-founded, we do not think that the right to use a garden of the character with which we are concerned in this case can be called one of mere recreation and amusement. No doubt a garden is a pleasure—on high authority, it is the purest of pleasures— but, in our judgment, it is not a right having no quality either of utility or benefit as those words should be understood. The right here in suit is, for reasons already given, one appurtenant to the surrounding houses as such, and constitutes a beneficial attribute of residence in a house as ordinarily understood. Its use for the purposes, not only of exercise and rest but also for such domestic purposes as were suggested in argument— for example, for taking out small children in perambulators or otherwise—is not fairly to be described as one of mere recreation or amusement, and is clearly beneficial to the premises to which it is attached. ...

As appears from what has been stated earlier, the right to the full enjoyment of Ellenborough Park, which was granted by the 1864 and other relevant conveyances, was, in substance, no more than a right to use the park as a garden in the way in which gardens are commonly used. In a sense, no doubt, such a right includes something of a jus spatiandi, inasmuch as it involves the principle of wandering at will round each part of the garden, except of course, such parts as comprise flower beds, or are laid out for some other purpose, which renders walking impossible or unsuitable. We doubt, nevertheless, whether the right to use and enjoy a garden in this manner can with accuracy be said to constitute a mere jus spatiandi. Wandering at large is of the essence of such a right and constitutes the main purpose for which it exists. A private garden, on the other hand, is an attribute of the ordinary enjoyment of the residence to which it is attached, and the right of wandering in it is but one method of enjoying it. On the assumption, however, that the right now in question does constitute a jus spatiandi, or that it is analogous thereto, it becomes neccessary to consider whether the right, which is in question in these proceedings, is, for that reason, incapable of ranking in law as an easement.

Farwell J. twice indicated that in his opinion the jus spatiandi is an interest which is not known to our law; and we think it is true to say that this principle has been widely accepted in the profession without sufficient regard being had, perhaps, to the exact language in which Farwell J. expressed himself or the circumstances in which his view of the matter was propounded.

[Having referred to *International Tea Stores Co. v. Hobbs* [1903] 2 Ch. 165; *Attorney-General v. Antrobus* [1905] 2 Ch. 188, Evershed M.R. continued:]

It will be noted that in both of these cases the judge said that a jus spatiandi is "not known to our law" and the question arises as to what precisely he meant by using that phrase. If, however, one attributes to the phrase "not known to the law" its ordinary signification, namely, that it was a right which our law had refused to recognize, it is clear, we think, that he would at least have expressed himself in less general terms had his attention been drawn to *Duncan v. Louch* (1845) 6 Q.B. 904. That case was not, however, cited to him in either the *International Tea Stores* case or in *Attorney-General v. Antrobus* for the sufficient reason that it was not relevant to any issue that was before the judge upon the questions which arose for decision. There is no doubt, in our judgment, but that *Attorney-General v. Antrobus* was rightly decided; for no right can be granted (otherwise than by Statute) to the public at large to wander at will over an undefined open space, nor can the public acquire such a right by prescription. We doubt very much whether Farwell J. had in mind, notwithstanding the apparent generality of his language, a so-called jus spatiandi granted as properly appurtenant to an estate; for the whole of his judgment was devoted to a consideration of public rights; and, although this cannot be said of his observations as to the gardens and park in the *International Tea Stores* case, the view which he there expressed was entirely obiter upon a point which was irrelevant to the case and had not been argued. Inasmuch, therefore, as this observation is unsupported by any principle or any authority that are binding upon us, and is in conflict with the decision in *Duncan v. Louch*, we are unable to accept its accuracy as an exhaustive statement of the law and, in reference, at least, to a case such as that now before the court, it cannot, in our judgment, be regarded hereafter as authoritative.

Duncan v. Louch, on the other hand, decided more than 100 years ago but not, as we have observed, quoted to Farwell J. in either of the two cases which we have cited, is authoritative in favour of the recognition by our law as an easement of a right closely comparable to that now in question which, if it involves in some sense a *jus spatiandi*, is nevertheless properly annexed and appurtenant to a defined hereditament.

Duncan v. Louch was an action brought by the plaintiff on account of obstruction by the defendant of what the plaintiff had in fact proved under his documents of title was a right to use Terrace Walk for the purposes of pleasure, that is, to pass and repass over every part of the close. ... Lord Denman C.J., in his judgment said (at p. 913) "there is no doubt in this case. Taking the right, as Mr Peacock suggests, to be like the right of the inhabitants of a square to walk in the square for their pleasure I cannot doubt that, if a stranger were to put a padlock on the gate and exclude one of the inhabitants, he might complain of the obstruction". Similarly, Patteson J. (*ibid.*): "I do not understand the distinction that has been contended for between a right to walk, pass and repass forwards and backwards over every part of a close, and a right of way from one part of the close to another. What is a right of way but a right to go forwards and backwards from one place to another?" And Coleridge J., in his judgment, described the right proved as an "easement".

The reasoning of the decision and the circumstances of the case, no less than the language used, particularly by Lord Denman C.J., involve acceptance as an easement of a right such as that with which, according to our interpretation of the effect of the relevant deeds, we are here concerned.

...

We agree with Danckwerts J. in regarding *Duncan v. Louch* as being a direct authority in the defendants' favour. It has never, so far as we are aware, been since questioned, and we think it should, in the present case, be followed.

For the reasons which we have stated, Danckwerts J. came, in our judgment, to a right conclusion in this case and, accordingly, the appeal must be dismissed.

NOTES:

1. For comment, see [1955] C.L.J. 154; [1956] C.L.J. 24; (1955) 19 Conv. 220; (1956) 20 Conv. 61; (1955) 71 L.Q.R. 324; (1956) 72 L.Q.R. 16; (1955) 18 M.L.R. 599.

2. The four essential characteristics are considered further below.

1.1 *There must be a dominant and a servient tenement*

(1) It has already been noted that, according to the orthodox view, an easement is a right exercisable over one piece of land *and attached to another piece of land*; and that an easement cannot exist "in gross": see *Ackroyd v. Smith* (1850) 10 C.B. 164, 187–188 *per* Cresswell J.; *Rangeley v. Midland Railway Co.* (1868) 3 Ch.App. 306, 310–311 *per* Cairns L.J.; *Hawkins v. Rutter* [1892] 1 Q.B. 668, 671–672 *per* Lord Coleridge C.J.; *Attorney-General v. Copeland* [1901] 2 K.B. 101, 106 *per* Lord Alverstone C.J.; *Todrick v. Western National Omnibus Co.* [1934] Ch. 561, 591 *per* Maugham L.J.; *Re Ellenborough Park* [1956] Ch. 131, 163 *per* Evershed M.R.; *Alfred F. Beckett Ltd v. Lyons* [1967] Ch. 449, 483 *per* Winn J. It follows that a right to walk across land, conferred as a *personal* right and unconnected with the enjoyment or occupation of land of the grantee, cannot constitute an easement; rather it will constitute a licence. However, Sturley (1980) 96 L.Q.R. 557 argues that the rule precluding easements in gross "exists on the weakest of authority for reasons that are no longer compelling" (excessive burden on the servient land and unjustified incumbrance on the title of the servient land); and that the rule

precludes potentially useful easements in gross; see also Gardner (1982) 98
L.Q.R. 279, 305–307; Rudden, "Economic Theory versus Property Law: The
Numerus Clausus Problem" in *Oxford Essays in Jurisprudence* (Eekelaar and
Bell eds, 1987), pp. 257 *et seq*. The requirement of dominant land may have
been justified at the time when the law of easements was developing, as a
reflection of an appropriately cautious approach to the creation of binding
property interests. On the other hand, there are many statutory exceptions to
the requirement, notably in the context of the public services and utilities; and
the requirement of dominant land has been discarded generally in some
jurisdictions.

(2) It follows from the principle that an easement cannot exist in gross that
there can be no easement where the grantee does not own an estate in the
dominant land *at the time of the purported grant of the easement*. Thus, it is
not permissible to include, as part of the dominant land, land that the grantee
may acquire in the future and thus to create an adverse interest of uncertain
extent that would be enforceable against successors in title of the servient
land: *London & Blenheim Estates Ltd v. Ladbroke Retail Parks Ltd* [1994] 1
W.L.R. 31, 35–38 *per* Peter Gibson L.J., noted at [1994] C.L.J. 229; *Voice v.
Bell* (1993) 68 P. & C.R. 441.

(3) Although the dominant land can usually be identified without difficulty,
extrinsic evidence may be admitted where the identity is not clear from the
deed: *Johnstone v. Holdway* [1963] 1 Q.B. 601, 612 *per* Upjohn J.; *The
Shannon Ltd v. Venner Ltd* [1965] Ch. 682, 693 *per* Danckwerts L.J.; *Land
Reclamation Co. Ltd v. Basildon DC* [1979] 1 W.L.R. 106, 110 *per*
Brightman J.

(4) It is equally clear that there can be no easement without (ascertainable)
servient land: *Woodman v. Pwllbach Colliery Co. Ltd* (1914) 111 L.T. 169,
172 *per* Cozens-Hardy M.R., 174 *per* Swinfen Eady L.J.

1.2 *An easement must accommodate the dominant tenement*
There are a number of aspects to the second essential characteristic.

(1) The easement must create a clear relationship of dominance and
servience between the two pieces of land; and the easement must have a
necessary and substantial connection with the enjoyment of the dominant
land, in the sense of being reasonably necessary for the better enjoyment of
that land. It is not sufficient that the right merely benefits a landowner as an
individual. In *Ackroyd v. Smith* (1850) 10 C.B. 164 the owners and
occupiers of premises were granted a right "of passing and repassing, for all
purposes, in, over, along, and through a certain road". Cresswell J. stated (at
187–188):

[T]he privilege or right in question does not inhere in the land, does not concern the
premises conveyed, or the mode of occupying them; it is not appurtenant to them. A
covenant, therefore, that such a right should be enjoyed, would not run with the land.
Upon the same principle, it appears to us that such a right, unconnected with the
enjoyment or occupation of land, cannot be annexed as an incident to it: nor can a
way appendant to a house or land be granted away or made in gross ... If a way be
granted in gross, it is personal only, and cannot be assigned. ... It is not in the power

of a vendor to create any rights not connected with the use or enjoyment of land, and annex them to it: nor can the owner of land render it subject to a new species of burden, so as to bind it in the hands of an assignee. ...

This principle is sufficient to dispose of the present case. It would be a novel incident annexed to land, that the owner and occupier should, for purposes unconnected with that land, and merely because he is owner and occupier, have a right of road over other land. And it seems to us that a grant of such a privilege or easement can no more be annexed, so as to pass with the land, than a covenant for any collateral purpose.

The problem in *Ackroyd v. Smith* was that the court construed the conveyance as purporting to grant the right of way for all purposes, *including purposes unconnected with the (dominant) land of the grantees*: such an unlimited right could not exist as an easement. Contrast the more limited (and validating) construction in *Thorpe v. Brumfitt* (1873) 8 Ch.App. 650. Both cases are discussed in *Todrick v. Western National Omnibus Co. Ltd* [1934] Ch. 561, 581–585 *per* Romer L.J. Contrast also *Moody v. Steggles* (1879) 12 Ch D. 261, where the right to fix a signboard for a public house on neighbouring property was held to constitute an easement, with *Clapman v. Edwards* [1938] 2 All E.R. 507, where a right to display advertisements on the servient land was held *not* to constitute an easement because the right was not limited to advertising for the benefit of the business carried on on the dominant land.

(2) The classic decision where a right over land was found to be a benefit to the grantee rather than a benefit to the land was *Hill v. Tupper* (1863) 2 H. & C. 121. A canal company leased some land on the bank of the canal to the plaintiff and purported to grant to him the sole and exclusive right or liberty to put or use boats on the canal. When the defendant, who owned premises abutting on the canal, also put pleasure boats on the canal, the plaintiff claimed damages for interference with his alleged easement. Pollock C.B. stated (at 127):

I do not think it necessary to assign any other reason for our decision than that the case of *Ackroyd v. Smith* expressly decided that it is not competent to create rights unconnected with the use and enjoyment of land, and annex them to it so as to constitute a property in the grantee. This grant merely operates as a licence or covenant on the part of the grantors, and is binding on them as between themselves and the grantee, but gives him no right of action in his own name for any infringement of the supposed exclusive right.

In *Re Ellenborough Park* [1956] Ch. 131 Evershed M.R. commented (at 175) that in *Hill v. Tupper* it was "clear that what the plaintiff was trying to do was to set up, under the guise of an easement, a monopoly which had no normal connection with the ordinary use of his land, but which was merely an independent business enterprise. So far from the right claimed sub-serving or accommodating the land, the land was but a convenient incident to the exercise of the right". For comment, see [1956] C.L.J. 24.

(3) The condition appears to be satisfied where the right benefits a commercial activity being conducted on the dominant land. In *Moody v. Steggles* (1879) 12 Ch D. 261 Fry J. stated (at 266):

It is said that the easement in question [easement to hang a signboard for a public house on the neighbouring house] relates, not to the tenement, but to the business of the occupant of the tenement, and that therefore I cannot tie the easement to the house. It appears to me that that argument is of too refined a nature to prevail, and for this reason, that the house can only be used by an occupant, and that the occupant only uses the house for the business which he pursues, and therefore in some manner (direct or indirect) an easement is more or less connected with the mode in which the occupant of the house uses it.

See also *Copeland v. Greenhalf* [1952] Ch. 488 (claimed easement to park cars awaiting repair on neighbouring land); *Wong v. Beaumont Property Trust Ltd* [1965] 1 Q.B. 173 (easement for ventilation duct to restaurant); *Woodhouse & Co. Ltd v. Kirkland (Derby) Ltd* [1970] 1 W.L.R. 1185 (easement of access to business premises for employees, suppliers and customers of the business).

(4) The condition has been held to be satisfied where an easement (right of way) granted for the benefit of land is exercised for the purpose of constructing works on part of that land but where the works are intended to benefit other land: *Britel Developments (Thatcham) Ltd v. Nightfreight (Great Britain) Ltd* [1998] 4 All E.R. 432.

(5) There is no requirement that the dominant land and the servient land should be adjoining, provided that they are sufficiently close that the dominant land receives a benefit from the right: *Bailey v. Stephens* (1862) 12 C.B. (N.S.) 91, 115 *per* Byles J.; *Birmingham, Dudley and District Banking Co. v. Ross* (1888) 38 Ch D. 295, 314 *per* Bowen L.J.; *Todrick v. Western National Omnibus Co. Ltd* [1934] Ch. 561, 572–573 *per* Lord Hanworth M.R., 580 *per* Romer L.J., 589 *per* Maugham L.J.; *Re Ellenborough Park* [1956] Ch. 131, 175 *per* Evershed L.J.; *Pugh v. Savage* [1970] 2 Q.B. 373, 381–382 *per* Cross L.J.

(6) There is no requirement that the easement be exclusive to a single dominant plot of land: *Re Ellenborough Park* [1956] Ch. 131, 172 *per* Evershed M.R.

(7) It is no objection to the validity of the easement acquired by express grant that the owner of the dominant land is required to contribute towards the maintenance of the servient land: *Re Ellenborough Park* [1956] Ch. 131, 169 *per* Evershed M.R. However, payments may negative a claim that an easement has been acquired by prescription: see *infra*, p. 670.

1.3 *The dominant and servient owners must be different persons*

(1) The third essential characteristic, that the dominant and servient owners must be different persons, would seem to follow inevitably from the nature of easements. First, an easement is *ex hypothesi* a right exercised over the land of *another* person; and, secondly, it would seem obvious that a landowner cannot have an easement over his own land since he already *prima facie* enjoys the substantive content of easements by virtue of his ownership rights over the land: *Bolton v. Bolton* (1879) 11 Ch D. 968, 970–971 *per* Fry J.; *Roe v. Siddons* (1889) 22 Q.B.D. 224, 236 *per* Fry L.J.; *Metropolitan Railway Co. v. Fowler* [1892] 1 Q.B. 165, 171 *per* Lord Esher M.R. Rights in the

nature of easements exercised by a landowner over his own land are sometimes referred to as "quasi-easements" in anticipation of a sale of the benefited part and the conversion of those rights into full easements: see *infra*, p. 640.

(2) However, the requirement operates only to preclude a person from having an easement over land to which he has a present right to actual possession. There is no difficulty in a tenant acquiring (by grant but not by prescription: see *infra*, p. 672) an easement for the duration of the lease over land in the possession of his landlord: *Borman v. Griffith* [1930] 1 Ch. 493. Moreover, although there appears to be no authority directly in point, there is no reason in principle for precluding the acquisition by a landlord of an easement over land currently in the possession of his tenant or the acquisition by a tenant of an easement over land currently in the possession of another tenant of the same landlord: for in each case the possession and enjoyment of the two plots are in the exclusive control of different persons for the duration of the lease: see *Beddington v. Atlee* (1887) 35 Ch D. 317; *Richardson v. Graham* [1908] 1 K.B. 39. Thus the third characteristic is perhaps better formulated by the proposition that the dominant land and the servient land must not be owned *and occupied* by the same person.

(3) It may also be possible for the trustee of one plot of land to acquire an easement over another plot of land of which he is the beneficial owner: see *Ecclesiastical Commissioners for England v. Kino* (1880) 14 Ch D. 213, 222 *per* Brett L.J.

1.4 *A right over land cannot amount to an easement unless it is capable of forming the subject-matter of a grant*

(1) Although many easements arise by implication of law (whether or not this involves the fiction that the easement was granted by deed), the fourth essential characteristic states that no right can constitute an easement unless that right is *capable* of being granted by deed. The characteristic covers two technical requirements and one more substantive requirement.

(2) The first technical requirement is that the grantor must be legally competent to grant an easement. This requirement would not be satisfied by certain statutory bodies: see, *e.g. Mulliner v. Midland Railway* (1879) 11 Ch D. 611, 623 *per* Jessel M.R.; nor by a tenant who has no power to bind the reversion: *Derry v. Sanders* [1919] 1 K.B. 223, 231 *per* Bankes L.J.; nor by a licensee of the servient land: *Quicke v. Chapman* [1903] 1 Ch. 659, 668 *per* Collins M.R. The second technical requirement is that the grantee must be legally competent to receive the grant of an easement. Again this requirement would not be satisfied by certain statutory bodies: *National Guaranteed Manure Co. Ltd v. Donald* (1859) 4 H. & N. 8; nor by a fluctuating body of persons, the usual example being "the inhabitants for the time being of the village of X". However, such a body of persons may have corresponding *customary rights*: see, *e.g. Brocklebank v. Thompson* [1903] 2 Ch. 344 (right of access to parish church); *Mercer v. Denne* [1905] 2 Ch. 538 (right to dry fishing nets on certain land); *New Windsor Corp. v. Mellor* [1975] Ch. 380 (right to use land for lawful sports and pastimes).

(3) The substantive requirement is that the right must be sufficiently definite. Thus, the following purported grants have been held to be incapable of creating easements: (i) a right to privacy: *Browne v. Flower* [1911] 1 Ch. 219, 225 *per* Parker J.; (ii) a right to a view: *William Aldred's Case* (1610) 9 Co.Rep. 57b, 58b *per* Wray C.J.; but views may be protected by an appropriately worded restrictive covenant: see *Wakeham v. Wood* (1981) 43 P. & C.R. 40; *Gilbert v. Spoor* [1983] Ch. 27; and see Polden [1984] Conv. 429; (iii) a general right to air: *Webb v. Bird* (1862) 13 C.B. (N.S.) 841, 843 *per* Wightman J.; *Bryant v. Lefever* (1879) 4 C.P.D. 172, 176–177 *per* Bramwell L.J., 180 *per* Cotton L.J.; *Harris v. Da Pinna* (1886) 33 Ch D. 238, 262 *per* Bowen L.J.; *Chastey v. Ackland* [1895] 2 Ch. 389, 396–397 *per* Lopes L.J.; but contrast a right to the passage of air through a defined channel: *Bass v. Gregory* (1890) 25 Q.B.D. 481, 482–483 *per* Pollock B.; or to a defined aperture: *Cable v. Bryant* [1908] 1 Ch. 259, 263–264 *per* Neville J.; (iv) a general right to light; but contrast a right to light to defined windows and skylights: *Easton v. Isted* [1903] 1 Ch. 405, 408–409 *per* Joyce J.; *Levet v. Gas Light & Coke Co.* [1919] 1 Ch. 24, 27 *per* Peterson J.; (v) a right to receive radio and television signals: *Hunter v. Canary Wharf Ltd* [1997] A.C. 655, 709 *per* Lord Hoffmann, 726–727 *per* Lord Hope. For analysis of the courts' approach to these purported easements, see Dawson and Dunn (1998) 18 *Legal Studies* 510.

(4) It was in this context that the Court of Appeal in *Re Ellenborough Park* [1956] Ch. 131 discussed the widely held view that a *"ius spatiandi"* or "privilege of wandering at will over all and every part of another's park or field" cannot constitute an easement: see *supra*, pp. 615 *et seq.*

2. Supplementary requirements

In addition to the above four essential characteristics of easements, there are a number of supplementary negative requirements which must be satisfied. Although the textbooks generally discuss these matters under the fourth characteristic above, they do not fit neatly into any of the four principal characteristics enumerated in *Re Ellenborough Park* [1956] Ch. 131.

2.1 No positive action can be required of the servient owner

It has been stated that an easement involves the servient owner either permitting something to be done on the servient land or refraining from doing something on the servient land. This exhaustive statement reflects the general rule that an easement should not normally involve the owner of the servient land in any positive action, in particular the expenditure of money.

The rule applies where the positive action is itself the content of the purported easement: *Regis Property Co. Ltd v. Redman* [1956] 2 Q.B. 612, 627–628 *per* Jenkins L.J., 632 *per* Lord Evershed M.R. (provision of hot water and central heating); *Rance v. Elvin* (1985) 49 P. & C.R. 65, (1985) 50 P. & C.R. 9 (provision of metered water supply); *Duffy v. Lamb* (1997) 75 P. & C.R. 364 (provision of metered electricity supply). On the other hand, where the supply already exists and there is an easement for the passage of water or electricity through pipes or cables from the servient land to the dominant land, the servient owner is under an obligation not to take any positive step to prevent the supply of water or electricity to the servient land and its subsequent passage to the dominant land: *ibid.*

The rule also applies to repairing obligations that are merely incidental to the easement: *Pomfret v. Ricroft* (1669) 1 Wms.Saund. 321; *Jones v. Pritchard* [1908] 1 Ch. 630, 637 *per* Parker J.; *Bond v. Nottingham Corp.* [1940] Ch. 429, 438–439 *per* Greene M.R.; *Stokes v. Mixconcrete (Holdings) Ltd* (1979) 38 P. & C.R. 488, 494–495 *per* Buckley L.J., 499–500 *per* Goff L.J.; *Holden v. White* [1982] Q.B. 679, 683–684 *per* Oliver L.J.; *Duke of Westminster v. Guild* [1985] Q.B. 688, 700 *per* Slade L.J. Waite [1985] C.L.J. 458 argues that the second limb of the rule is a relatively recent development in English law and is contrary to earlier authority upholding incidental repair obliations.

However, there is an established exception to the first limb of the rule. It has been held that a right to require a neighbouring landowner to keep in repair a boundary fence or wall may exist as an easement. In *Lawrence v. Jenkins* (1873) L.R. 8 Q.B. 274 Archibald J. (at 279) quoted *Gale on Easements* (4th ed., 1868), p. 460, where the obligation was described as "in the nature of a spurious easement affecting the land of the party who is bound to maintain the fence"; and in *Jones v. Price* [1965] 2 Q.B. 618 Willmer J. (at 631–633) referred to the right as "not a true easement" and as a "quasi-easement"; but in *Crow v. Wood* [1971] 1 Q.B. 77 Lord Denning M.R. (at 84–85) expressed the view that, if the point was not already established, the court should declare the right to be "in the nature of an easement", although Edmund Davies L.J. (at 86) expressed the view that a final decision as to the exact legal nature of the right was unnecessary. See also *Egerton v. Harding* [1975] Q.B. 62, noted at [1975] C.L.J. 34, for a discussion of the relationship between the easement of fencing and a similar right arising by custom.

Moreover, there are exceptions to the second limb of the rule, that easements must not involve incidental repair obligations.

(1) In the context of the landlord and tenant relationship, easements have been held to involve repairing obligations on the servient owner where the nature and circumstances of the agreement between the parties demand such obligations as a matter of necessity.

Liverpool City Council v. Irwin [1977] A.C. 239

(HL, Lord Wilberforce, Lord Cross, Lord Salmon, Lord Edmund-Davies and Lord Fraser)

The defendants were tenants of a maisonette on the ninth and tenth floors of a tower block owned by the plaintiffs. Access to the maisonette was provided by a staircase and two lifts; and there was an internal chute into which the tenants could discharge rubbish for collection at ground level. All these facilities frequently fell into disrepair: the lifts failed; the staircase became dangerous; and the rubbish chutes were blocked. However, the only document relating to the tenancy (signed by the defendants but not the plaintiffs) made no reference to maintenance. Eventually, the defendants and other tenants stopped paying rent and the plaintiffs started proceedings for possession.

LORD WILBERFORCE:

We have then a contract which is partly, but not wholly, stated in writing. In order to complete it, in particular to give it a bilateral character, it is necessary to take account of the actions of the parties and the circumstances. As actions of the parties, we must note the granting of possession by the landlords and reservation by them of the "common parts"—stairs, lifts, chutes, etc. As circumstances we must include the nature of the premises, viz., a maisonette for family use on the ninth floor of a high block, one which is occupied by a large number of other tenants, all using the common parts and dependent upon them, none of them having any expressed obligation to maintain or repair them.

. . .

What then should this contract be held to be? There must first be implied a letting, that is, a grant of the right of exclusive possession to the tenants. With this there must, I would suppose, be implied a covenant for quiet enjoyment, as a necessary incident of the letting. The difficulty begins when we consider the common parts. We start with the fact that the demise is useless unless access is obtained by the staircase; we can add that, having regard to the height of the block, and the family nature of the dwellings, the demise would be useless without a lift service; we can continue that, there being rubbish chutes built into the structures and no other means of disposing of light rubbish, there must be a right to use the chutes. The question to be answered—and it is the only question in this case—is what is to be the legal relationship between landlord and tenant as regards these matters.

There can be no doubt that there must be implied (i) an easement for the tenants and their licensees to use the stairs, (ii) a right in the nature of an easement to use the lifts, (iii) an easement to use the rubbish chutes.

But are these easements to be accompanied by any obligation upon the landlord, and what obligation? There seem to be two alternatives. The first, for which the council contends, is for an easement coupled with no legal obligation, except such as may arise under the Occupiers' Liability Act 1957 as regards the safety of those using the facilities, and possibly such other liability as might exist under the ordinary law of tort. The alternative is for easements coupled with some obligation on the part of the landlords as regards the maintenance of the subject of them, so that they are available for use.

My Lords, in order to be able to choose between these, it is necessary to define what test is to be applied, and I do not find this difficult. In my opinion such obligation should be read into the contract as the nature of the contract itself implicitly requires, no more, no less: a test, in other words, of necessity. The relationship accepted by the corporation is that of landlord and tenant: the tenant accepts obligations accordingly, in relation inter alia to the stairs, the lifts and the chutes. All these are not just facilities, or conveniences provided at discretion: they are essentials of the tenancy without which life in the dwellings, as a tenant, is not possible. To leave the landlord free of contractual obligation as regards these matters, and subject only to administrative or political pressure, is, in my opinion, inconsistent totally with the nature of this relationship. The subject matter of the lease (high rise blocks) and the relationship created by the tenancy demand, of their nature, some contractual obligation on the landlord.

. . .

I accept, of course, the argument that a mere grant of an easement does not carry with it any obligation on the part of the servient owner to maintain the subject matter. The dominant owner must spend the necessary money, for example in repairing a drive leading to his house. And the same principle may apply when a landlord lets an upper floor with access by a staircase: responsibility for maintenance may well rest on the tenant. But there is a difference between that case and the case where there is an essential means of access, retained in the landlord's occupation, to units in a building of multi-occupation, for unless the obligation to maintain is, in a defined manner, placed upon the tenants, individually or collectively, the nature of the contract, and the circumstances, require that it be placed on the landlord.

It remains to define the standard. My Lords, if, as I think, the test of the existence of the term is necessity the standard must surely not exceed what is necessary having regard to the circumstances. To imply an absolute obligation to repair would go beyond what is a necessary legal incident and would indeed be unreasonable. An obligation to take reasonable care to keep in reasonable repair and usability is what fits the requirements of the case. Such a definition involves—and I think rightly—recognition that the tenants themselves have their responsibilities. What it is reasonable to expect of a landlord has a clear relation to what a reasonable set of tenants should do for themselves.

NOTES:

1. The House of Lords held that the defendants had not established that the plaintiffs had failed to fulfil their obligations in relation to the maintenance of the common facilities.

2. *Liverpool City Council v. Irwin* was followed in *King v. South Northamptonshire DC* (1992) 24 H.L.R. 284, where the Court of Appeal held that a landlord had an implied duty to maintain a path which provided the only wheelchair access for the tenant.

3. However, in *Duke of Westminster v. Guild* [1985] Q.B. 688, noted at [1985] Conv. 66, the Court of Appeal declined to impose on the landlord a repairing obligation incidental to the implied easement of drainage under the landlord's property. *Liverpool City Council v. Irwin* was distinguished on the grounds that in the later case (i) there was a formal lease apparently representing the complete bargain between the parties and (ii) there were no special considerations of the kind present in the earlier case that made it appropriate to imply any term as a legal incident of the contract: [1985] Q.B. 688, 700 *per* Slade L.J.

(2) In relation to the easement of support for buildings, the orthodox position was stated in *Bond v. Nottingham Corp.* [1940] Ch. 429, 438–439 *per* Greene M.R.:

The owner of the servient land is under no obligation to repair that part of his building which provides support for his neighbour. He can let it fall into decay. If it does so, and support is removed, the owner of the dominant land has no cause for complaint. On the other hand, the owner of the dominant land is not bound to sit by and watch the gradual deterioration of the support constituted by his neighbour's building. He is entitled to enter and take the necessary steps to ensure that the support continues by effecting repairs, and so forth, to the part of the building which gives the support. But what the owner of the servient land is not entitled to do is, by an act of his own, to remove the support without providing an equivalent.

However, this principle has been effectively sidestepped by the recognition of tortious liability in negligence and/or nuisance on the part of the servient owner: see *Bradburn v. Lindsay* [1983] 2 All E.R. 408. The reliance on tortious liability as a means of sidestepping established rules of property law was questioned by Jackson [1984] Conv. 54; but see Waite [1987] Conv. 47.

(3) In *Holden v. White* [1982] Q.B. 679 the Court of Appeal rejected the argument that the servient owner could be liable under the Occupiers' Liability Act 1957 where the dominant owner or his visitors were injured as a result of the defective condition of a footpath over the servient land: see (1982) 98 L.Q.R. 541; [1983] Conv. 58. However, the decision has in effect been reversed by the Occupiers' Liability Act 1984.

2.2 An easement cannot amount to a claim to exclusive or joint possession
The limited nature of the rights inherent in an easement has been held to mean that a right cannot be an easement if it is in effect a claim to exclusive or joint possession of the purported servient land. However, some of the cases are difficult to reconcile and it has been suggested that this negative requirement represents "an intuitive rather than a reasoned response to the validity of certain claims of easement": Gray, *Elements of Land Law* (2nd ed., 1993), p. 1076.

Copeland v. Greenhalf [1952] Ch. 488

(Ch D., Upjohn J.)

The plaintiff owned an orchard and a strip of land about 150 feet long and 15 feet wide which provided access from the road to the orchard. The defendant carried on business as a wheelwright on premises on the opposite side of the road to the strip of land. The defendant claimed that for 50 years, with the knowledge of the plaintiff and her predecessors in title, he had stored vehicles awaiting repair and collection on one side of the strip of land; and that he had thereby acquired by prescription an easement over the strip.

UPJOHN J.:
I think that the right claimed goes wholly outside any normal idea of an easement, that is, the right of the owner or the occupier of a dominant tenement over a servient tenement. This claim (to which no closely related authority has been referred to me) really amounts to a claim to a joint user of the land by the defendant. Practically, the defendant is claiming the whole beneficial user of the strip of land on the south-east side of the track there; he can leave as many or as few lorries there as he likes for as long as he likes; he may enter on it by himself, his servants and agents to do repair work thereon. In my judgment, that is not a claim which can be established as an easement. It is virtually a claim to possession of the servient tenement, if necessary to the exclusion of the owner; or, at any rate, to a joint user, and no authority has been cited to me which would justify the conclusion that a right of this wide and undefined nature can be the proper subject-matter of an easement. It seems to me that to succeed, this claim must amount to a successful claim of possession by reason of long adverse possession. I say nothing, of course, as to the creation of such rights by deeds or by covenant; I am dealing solely with the question of a right arising by prescription.

NOTES:
1. Upjohn J. expressly restricted his remarks to easements acquired by prescription; and it is possible that the claimed easement could have been the

subject-matter of an appropriately worded grant. However, that distinction is not sufficient to reconcile the decision with all the cases referred to below.

2. In *Attorney-General of Southern Nigeria v. John Holt (Liverpool) Ltd* [1915] A.C. 599 Lord Shaw, delivering the judgment of the Privy Council, had expressed the view *obiter* (at 617) that the right to store trade goods on the servient land could constitute an easement; and in *Wright v. Macadam* [1949] 2 K.B. 744 the Court of Appeal held that the right of the tenant to store domestic coal in a shed on the landlord's land constituted an easement. *Wright v. Macadam* was not cited in *Copeland v. Greenhalf*. On that basis the latter decision has been questioned as having been decided *per incuriam*: see [1973] C.L.J. 30; but in *London & Blenheim Estates Ltd v. Ladbroke Retail Parks Ltd* [1992] 1 W.L.R. 1278 Judge Paul Baker Q.C. expressed the view that it would probably not have made any difference. He said (at 1286):

The matter must be one of degree. A small coal shed in a large property is one thing. The exclusive use of a large part of the alleged servient tenement is another. Hence I do not accept the submission that *Copeland v. Greenhalf* was wrongly decided.

3. *Copeland v. Greenhalf* was distinguished in *Miller v. Emcer Products Ltd* [1956] Ch. 304. Romer L.J. held (at 316) that the right of the tenant of the dominant land to use the lavatories situated on the servient land constituted an easement; and that, although the owner of the servient land would be excluded while the right was being exercised, that was in greater or lesser degree a common feature of many easements: see (1956) 72 L.Q.R. 172. *Copeland v. Greenhalf* was also distinguished in *Ward v. Kirkland* [1967] Ch. 194. Ungoed-Thomas J. held (at 222–223) that a right of access over the servient land to effect external repairs and maintenance to a cottage on the dominant land did not substantially interfere with the use of the servient land. See now the Access to Neighbouring Land Act 1992.

4. In *Grigsby v. Melville* [1972] 1 W.L.R. 1355 the defendant claimed, *inter alia*, an easement of storage in the cellar under the house on the adjoining land. The Court of Appeal upheld the decision of Brightman J. that in the particular circumstances no such right had been created; but Brightman J. also considered whether such an easement was in principle capable of existing. He quoted the above passage from the judgment of Upjohn J. in *Copeland v. Greenhalf* and continued (at 1364–1365):

[Counsel for the defendant] countered by observing that *Copeland v. Greenhalf* was inconsistent with *Wright v. Macadam* [1949] 2 K.B. 744, an earlier decision of the Court of Appeal in which it was held that the right of a tenant to store domestic coal in a shed on the landlord's land could exist as an easement for the benefit of the demised premises. I am not convinced that there is any real inconsistency between the two cases. The point of the decision in *Copeland v. Greenhalf* [1952] Ch. 488 was that the right asserted amounted in effect to a claim to the whole beneficial user of the servient tenement and for that reason could not exist as a mere easement. The precise facts in *Wright v. Macadam* [1949] 2 K.B. 744 in this respect are not wholly clear from the report and it is a little difficult to know whether the tenant had exclusive use of the coal shed or of any defined portion of it. To some extent a problem of this sort may be one of degree.

In the case before me, it is, I think, clear that the defendant's claim to an easement would give, to all practical intents and purposes, an exclusive right of user over the whole of the confined space representing the servient tenement. I think I would be at liberty, if necessary, to follow *Copeland v. Greenhalf* [1952] Ch. 488. I doubt, however, whether I need express any concluded view on this aspect of the case.

The comments of Brightman J. have been criticised, in particular, because he failed to refer to the fact that in *Copeland v. Greenhalf* Upjohn J. expressly limited his decision to easements acquired by prescription: see [1973] C.L.J. 30; (1973) 37 Conv. 60.

5. The negative requirement that an easement cannot amount to exclusive or joint possession of the purported servient land has also been considered in relation to car-parking. In *Sweet & Maxwell v. Michael-Michaels (Advertising) Ltd* [1965] C.L.Y. 2192, noted at (1966) 30 Conv. 3, a right to use one space in a car-park was held to constitute an easement; in *Bilkus v. Redbridge LBC* (1968) 207 E.G. 803 Buckley J. held that "unrestricted car-parking facilities" were capable of existing as an easement; and in *Newman v. Jones* (1982, unreported, but cited in *London & Blenheim Estates Ltd v. Ladbroke Retail Parks Ltd* [1992] 1 W.L.R. 1278) Megarry V.-C. stated that "in view of *Wright v. Macadam* ... I feel no hesitation in holding that a right for a landowner to park a car anywhere in a defined area nearby is capable of existing as an easement ..." Thus in *London & Blenheim Estates Ltd v. Ladbroke Retail Parks Ltd, supra,* noted at [1994] C.L.J. 229, Judge Paul Baker Q.C. concluded (at 1284–1288) that there was clear authority that in some circumstances the right to park cars can amount to an easement. He stated (at 1288):

The essential question is one of degree. If the right granted in relation to the area over which it is to be exercisable is such that it would leave the servient owner without any reasonable use of his land, whether for parking or anything else, it could not be an easement, though it might be some larger or different grant.

6. Luther (1996) 16 *Legal Studies* 51 argues that an analysis of the earlier case law demonstrates that the real issue in *Copeland v. Greenhalf* was whether the right claimed as an easement was sufficiently certain; that the references to exclusive possession in the judgment of Upjohn J. were misleading and have been misunderstood in subsequent cases; and that judges and commentators have developed the "degree of exclusion" and "substantial interference" tests in an attempt to justify and reconcile the decisions in the above cases.

2.3 *Recognition of new easements*

Subject to compliance with the positive and negative requirements discussed, the list of possible easements is not closed: "The category of servitudes and easements must alter and expand with the changes that take place in the circumstances of mankind": *Dyce v. Lady James Hay* (1852) 1 Macq. 305, 312–313 *per* Lord St Leonards L.C. On the other hand, there are limits: "It must not therefore be supposed that incidents of a novel kind can be devised, and attached to property, at the fancy or caprice of any owner": *Keppell v. Bailey* (1834) 2 My. & K. 517, 535 *per* Lord Brougham L.C.

"New" *positive* easements have included the right to go on land to open sluice gates: *Simpson v. Mayor of Godmanchester* [1897] A.C. 696; the right to store trade goods on neighbouring land: *Attorney-General of Southern Nigeria v. John Holt (Liverpool) Ltd* [1915] A.C. 599, 617 *per* Lord Shaw; the right to use communal gardens: *Re Ellenborough Park* [1956] Ch. 131; the right to use a lavatory on neighbouring land: *Miller v. Emcer Products Ltd* [1956] Ch. 304; the right to use neighbouring land for aircraft movements: *Dowty Boulton Paul Ltd v. Wolverhampton Corp. (No. 2)* [1976] Ch. 13; and the right to park cars anywhere within a defined area: *London & Blenheim Estates Ltd v. Ladbroke Retail Parks Ltd* [1992] 1 W.L.R. 1278, 1284–1288 *per* Judge Paul Baker Q.C.

However, the attitude of the courts to the recognition of "new" *negative* easements has been much stricter since such rights are regarded as more appropriately created and protected as restrictive covenants.

Phipps v. Pears [1965] 1 Q.B. 76

(CA, Lord Denning M.R., Pearson and Salmon L.JJ.)

The owner of two adjacent houses (Nos 14 and 16) demolished and rebuilt No. 16. The flank wall of the new house was built flat up against the exposed wall of No. 14 so that the two walls were touching but were not bonded together. The defendants, the subsequent owners of No. 14, demolished No. 14 pursuant to a demolition order made by the local authority. As a result, the flank wall of No. 16 was exposed and, because of the method of construction, was not weatherproof. The plaintiff, the subsequent owner of No. 16, sought damages for the resulting damage to his property.

LORD DENNING M.R.:

Then the plaintiff said that at any rate his house No. 16 was entitled to protection from the weather. So long as No. 14 was there, it afforded excellent protection for No. 16 from rain and frost. By pulling down No. 14, the defendant, he said, had infringed his right of protection from the weather. This right, he said, was analogous to the right of support. It is settled law, of course, that a man who has his house next to another for many years, so that it is dependent on it for support, is entitled to have that support maintained. His neighbour is not entitled to pull down his house without providing substitute support in the form of buttresses or something of the kind, see *Dalton v. Angus* (1881) 6 App.Cas. 740. Similarly, it was said, with a right to protection from the weather. If the man next door pulls down his own house and exposes his neighbour's wall naked to the weather whereby damage is done to him, he is, it is said, liable in damages.

The case, so put, raises the question whether there is a right known to the law to be protected—by your neighbour's house—from the weather. Is there an easement of protection?

There are two kinds of easements known to the law: positive easements, such as a right of way, which give the owner of land *a right himself to do something* on or to his neighbour's land: and negative easements, such as a right of light, which gives him *a right to stop his neighbour doing something* on his (the neighbour's) own land. The right of support does not fall neatly into either category. It seems in some way to partake of the nature of a positive easement rather than a negative easement. The one building, by its weight, exerts a thrust, not only downwards, but also sideways on to the adjoining building or the adjoining land, and is thus doing something to the neighbour's land, exerting a thrust on it, see *Dalton v. Angus* (at p. 793) *per* Lord Selborne L.C. But a right to protection from the weather (if it exists) is entirely negative. It is a right to stop your neighbour pulling down his own house. Seeing that it is a negative easement, it must be looked at with caution. Because the law has been very chary of creating any new negative easements.

Take this simple instance: Suppose you have a fine view from your house. You have enjoyed the view for many years. It adds greatly to the value of your house. But if your neighbour chooses to despoil it, by building up and blocking it, you have no redress. There is no such right known to the law as a right to a prospect or view, see *Bland v. Moseley* (1587), cited in 9 Co.Rep. 58a, cited by Lord Coke in *Aldred's* case (1610) 9 Co.Rep. 57b. The only way in which you can keep the view from your house is to get your neighbour to make a covenant with you that he will not build so as to block your view. Such a covenant is binding on him by virtue of the contract. It is also binding in equity on anyone who buys the land from him with notice of the covenant. But it is not binding on a purchaser who has no notice of it, see *Leech v. Schweder* (1874) 9 Ch.App. 463.

Take next this instance from the last century. A man built a windmill. The winds blew freely on the sails for thirty years working the mill. Then his neighbour built a schoolhouse only 25 yards away which cut off the winds. It was held that the miller had no remedy: for the right to wind and air, coming in an undefined channel, is not a right known to the law, see *Webb v. Bird* (1861) 10 C.B.N.S. 268; (1862) 13 C.B.N.S. 841. The only way in which the miller could protect himself was by getting his neighbour to enter into a covenant.

The reason underlying these instances is that if such an easement were to be permitted, it would unduly restrict your neighbour in his enjoyment of his own land. It would hamper legitimate development see *Dalton v. Angus* (at p. 824) *per* Lord Blackburn. Likewise here, if we were to stop a man pulling down his house, we would put a brake on desirable improvement. Every man is entitled to pull down his house if he likes. If it exposes your house to the weather, that is your misfortune. It is no wrong on his part. Likewise every man is entitled to cut down his trees if he likes, even if it leaves you without shelter from the wind or shade from the sun; see the decision of the Master of the Rolls in Ireland in *Cochrane v. Verner* (1895) 29 I.L.T. 571. There is no such easement known to the law as an easement to be protected from the weather. The only way for an owner to protect himself is by getting a covenant from his neighbour that he will not pull down his house or cut down his trees. Such a covenant would be binding on him in contract: and it would be enforceable on any successor who took with notice of it. But it would not be binding on one who took without notice.

NOTES:

1. For generally critical comment, see (1964) 80 L.Q.R. 318; (1964) 27 M.L.R. 614; (1965) 28 M.L.R. 264; but see (1964) 27 M.L.R. 768.

2. In *Sedgwick Forbes Bland Payne Group Ltd v. Regional Properties Ltd* (1979) 257 E.G. 64 Oliver J. expressed the view (at 70) that the reasoning in *Phipps v. Pears* may have been formulated too widely; and he refused to dismiss as unarguable the suggestion that, where a building is divided *horizontally*, the owner of the lower part may have an easement requiring the owner of the upper part to maintain the roof of the building and to that extent to provide weatherproofing for the lower part.

3. For an historical analysis of the courts' approach to negative easements, and a consequent proposal for their assimilation with restrictive covenants, see Dawson and Dunn (1998) 18 *Legal Studies* 510.

C. Legal and Equitable Easements

Easements may exist as legal or equitable interests in land. An easement can exist as a legal interest only if two requirements are satisfied: first, the easement must be granted for a period equivalent to a fee simple absolute in possession or a term of years absolute: Law of Property Act 1925, s.1(2)(a); secondly, the easement must be created by statute, by deed or by prescription: see *infra*. If either of these two requirements is not satisfied, the easement can exist only as an equitable easement.

In accordance with the general principles considered earlier, the significance of the legal/equitable dichotomy becomes apparent in the context of the enforceability of easements between persons other than the original dominant and servient owners. Enforceability requires the person seeking to enforce the easement to demonstrate that the benefit of the easement is attached to his land and that the burden of the easement is attached to the land of the person against who enforcement is sought. In fact the first issue rarely creates any difficulty. The characteristic of easements that they must accommodate the dominant land means that, on any transfer of the dominant land, the benefit of a validly created easement, irrespective of its legal or equitable status, will pass automatically as an integral part of the dominant land: see Law of Property Act 1925, ss.62, 187. The benefit of the easement attaches to the land (and not to a particular interest in the land), so that any current owner or tenant of the dominant land is entitled to the benefit of the easement: see respectively *Leech v. Schweder* (1874) 9 Ch.App. 463; *Thorpe v. Brumfitt* (1873) 8 Ch.App. 650; and prima facie the benefit attaches to each and every part of the dominant land: *Newcomen v. Coulson* (1877) 5 Ch D. 133, 141 *per* Jessel M.R.; and see *Callard v. Beeney* [1930] 1 K.B. 353, 355–356 *per* Talbot J.

The issue of enforceability therefore centres on the question whether the burden is attached to the servient land so as to be enforceable against the current servient owner.

In the context of unregistered land, legal easements are enforceable against any successor in title to the servient land, in accordance with the principle of universal enforceability applicable to all legal estates and interests in land. The enforceability of equitable easements created before 1926 depends upon the doctrine of notice. Equitable easements created after 1925 are in principle registrable as Class D(iii) land charges under section 2(5)(iii) of the Land Charges Act 1972: see *ante*, p. 142.

In the context of registered land, legal easements are included in the category of overriding interests: Land Registration Act 1925, s.70(1)(a), and are therefore enforceable against any successor in title to the servient land. According to the view that equitable easements do not constitute overriding interests, they are minor interests and their enforceability depends upon the entry of a notice or caution (as appropriate) on the register. However, it has been held that certain equitable easements are included in the formulation of section 70(1)(a) of the Land Registration Act 1925: see *Celsteel Ltd v. Alton House Holdings Ltd* [1985] 1 W.L.R. 204; *Thatcher v. Douglas* (1995) 146 N.L.J. 282; see *ante*, p. 182.

For detailed discussion of the continuing uncertainty as to the meaning and scope of equitable easements, see Barnsley (1999) 115 L.Q.R. 89.

D. Creation and Acquisition of Easements

The principal methods of the creation/acquisition of easements are (i) express or implied grant and reservation and (ii) prescription through long user. Easements have also been acquired by (iii) proprietary estoppel and (iv) statute.

1. Grant and reservation

The creation and acquisition of easements most frequently occurs by grant and/or reservation when a landowner disposes of part only of his land (although a landowner may also grant an easement to a neighbouring landowner without disposing of any part of his land). In this context a grant occurs where the transferor disposes of part of his land to the transferee on terms that the transferee acquires an easement over the land retained by the transferor; the land transferred to the transferee becomes the dominant land and the land retained by the transferor becomes the servient land. A reservation occurs where the transferor disposes of part of his land to the transferee on terms that the transferor acquires an easement over the land transferred to the transferee; the land retained by the transferor becomes the dominant land and the land transferred to the transferee becomes the servient land.

Although easements will generally be granted by express words in the conveyance or transfer of the land in question, in certain circumstances the grant and reservation of easements may be implied even in the absence of such express words.

1.1 *Express grant and reservation*

1.1.1 *Express grant* In order to create a *legal* easement, the grant must be contained in a deed: Law of Property Act 1925, s.52(1); Law of Property (Miscellaneous Provisions) Act 1989, s.1; and the easement must be granted for a period equivalent to a fee simple absolute in possession or a term of years absolute: Law of Property Act 1925, s.1(2)(a). In the absence of words of limitation or some indication of a contrary intention, a grant has the potential to take effect as a grant for a period equivalent to a fee simple, even if it is made in connection with the creation of a lease: *Graham v. Philcox*

[1984] Q.B. 747, 754–755 *per* May L.J., 761 *per* Purchas L.J., *infra*, p. 661. No special form of words is required: *Russell v. Watts* (1885) 10 App.Cas. 590, 611 *per* Lord Blackburn; *Dowty Boulton Paul Ltd v. Wolverhampton Corp. (No. 2)* [1976] Ch. 13, 23–24 *per* Russell L.J. Moreover, uncertainty as to the identity of the dominant land may be resolved by extrinsic evidence: see *supra*, p. 618.

If the formal requirements for the creation of a legal easement are not complied with, the effect at common law is the creation of a mere licence: *Wood v. Leadbitter* (1845) 13 M. & W. 838. However, the transaction may give rise to an equitable easement pursuant to the doctrine in *Walsh v. Lonsdale* (1882) 21 Ch D. 9; but the potential scope for that doctrine has been significantly reduced since section 2 of the Law of Property (Miscellaneous Provisions) Act 1989 introduced the stricter writing requirements for (deemed) contracts for the sale or disposition of land: see *ante*, p. 391. For the creation of equitable easements under the former, less strict requirements of section 40 of the Law of Property Act 1925, see *McManus v. Cooke* (1887) 35 Ch D. 681; *May v. Belleville* [1905] 2 Ch. 605.

See also section 62 of the Law of Property Act 1925, *infra*, p. 649.

1.1.2 *Express reservation*   If a landowner wishes to reserve an easement over land that he is selling for the benefit of land that he is retaining, he may do so by appropriate words in the conveyance or transfer of the land in question. Again, no special form of words is required; and a conveyance made "subject to a right of way" has been held to be sufficient to reserve an easement for the benefit of the land retained: *Pitt v. Buxton* (1970) 21 P. & C.R. 127; *Pallister v. Clark* (1975) 30 P. & C.R. 84; *Wiles v. Banks* (1983) 50 P. & C.R. 80.

Before 1926, in order to effect the reservation of an easement, it had been necessary for the purchaser also to execute the conveyance so as to re-grant the easement to the vendor: *Durham and Sunderland Railway v. Walker* (1842) 2 Q.B. 940, 967 *per* Tindal C.J.; and failure to comply with this requirement resulted in the reservation of an equitable easement only: *May v. Belleville* [1905] 2 Ch. 605. Between 1881 and 1925 it was also possible for the vendor to reserve an easement by making the entitlement of the purchaser subject to a use in favour of the vendor. These formal requirements were removed by section 65 of the Law of Property Act 1925; but it seems that the reservation of an easement technically still constitutes a re-grant, with the result that, where the words of reservation, construed in the light of the surrounding circumstances, are not free from ambiguity, they are construed against the purchaser and in favour of the vendor: *Bulstrode v. Lambert* [1953] 1 W.L.R. 1064, 1068 *per* Upjohn J.; *Mason v. Clarke* [1954] 1 Q.B. 460, 467 *per* Denning L.J.; [1955] A.C. 778, 786 *per* Lord Simonds; *Johnstone v. Holdway* [1963] 1 Q.B. 601, 612 *per* Upjohn L.J.; *St Edmundsbury and Ipswich Diocesan Board of Finance v. Clark (No. 2)* [1975] 1 W.L.R. 468, 477–480 *per* Sir John Pennycuick; but see the contrary view in *Cordell v. Second Clanfield Properties Ltd* [1969] 2 Ch. 9, 14–16 *per* Megarry J. See *infra*, p. 681.

1.2 *Implied grant and reservation*

Where a parcel of land is divided and a part is conveyed or transferred into separate ownership or occupation, in certain circumstances, easements may be created in favour of the transferee by implied grant or in favour of the transferor by implied reservation, even in the absence of express words. However, it should be noted that, even though there is no actual grant or reservation, implied easements are nonetheless recognised as *legal* easements with all the consequences that follow from that status.

Wheeldon v. Burrows (1879) 12 Ch D. 31

(CA, Thesiger, James and Baggallay L.JJ.)

Tetley owned a workshop and an adjacent plot of land. The workshop had windows overlooking, and receiving light from, the adjacent plot. The plot of land was sold to the plaintiff's husband and was later devised to the plaintiff; but there was no express reservation of an easement of light in favour of the workshop. The workshop was later sold to the defendant. When the plaintiff erected hoardings on her land, thereby blocking the light to the workshop, the defendant removed them. In an action for trespass by the plaintiff, the defendant asserted that he had an easement of light over the plot of land.

THESIGER L.J.:

We have had a considerable number of cases cited to us, and out of them I think that two propositions may be stated as what I may call the general rules governing cases of this kind. The first of these rules is, that on the grant by the owner of a tenement of part of that tenement as it is then used and enjoyed, there will pass to the grantee all those continuous and apparent easements (by which, of course I mean *quasi* easements), or, in other words, all those easements which are necessary to the reasonable enjoyment of the property granted, and which have been and are at the time of the grant used by the owners of the entirety for the benefit of the part granted. The second proposition is that, if the grantor intends to reserve any right over the tenement granted, it is his duty to reserve it expressly in the grant. Those are the general rules governing cases of this kind, but the second of those rules is subject to certain exceptions. One of those exceptions is the well-known exception which attaches to cases of what are called ways of necessity; and I do not dispute for a moment that there may be, and probably are, certain other exceptions, to which I shall refer before I close my observations upon this case.

  Both of the general rules which I have mentioned are founded upon a maxim which is as well established by authority as it is consonant to reason and common sense, viz., that a grantor shall not derogate from his grant. It has been argued before us that there is no distinction between what has been called an implied grant and what is attempted to be established under the name of an implied reservation; and that such a distinction between the implied grant and the implied reservation is a mere modern invention, and one which runs contrary, not only to the general practice upon which land has been bought and sold for a considerable time, but also to authorities which are said to be clear and distinct upon the matter. So far, however, from that distinction being one which was laid down for the first time by and which is to be attributed to Lord Westbury in *Suffield v. Brown* (1864) 4 D.J. & S. 185, it appears to me that it has existed almost as far back as we can trace the law upon the subject.

NOTES:

1. The Court of Appeal held that there was no implied reservation of an easement of light.

2. *Wheeldon v. Burrows* itself involved a claim of implied *reservation*; but, by way of providing a contrast, the judgment indicates one situation (the first general rule stated by Thesiger L.J., whereby a quasi-easement is converted into a full easement) where easements may be acquired by implied *grant* but not by implied *reservation*. Indeed the so-called "rule in *Wheeldon v. Burrows*" is usually taken to refer to the implied *grant* of an easement in that situation; but there are other circumstances in which easements are acquired by implied grant: see *infra*.

3. The two propositions in *Wheeldon v. Burrows* are illustrations of the more general principle that a transferor of land cannot derogate from his grant. The principle was expounded in *Browne v. Flower* [1911] 1 Ch. 219, 224–227 *per* Parker J. and has already been considered: see *ante*, p. 399. For applications of the principle in the present context, see *Bayley v. Great Western Railway Co.* (1884) 26 Ch D. 434; *Cable v. Bryant* [1908] 1 Ch. 259; *Ward v. Kirkland* [1967] Ch. 194, *infra*, p. 641, *Woodhouse & Co. Ltd v. Kirkland (Derby) Ltd* [1970] 1 W.L.R. 1185; *Lyme Valley Squash Club Ltd v. Newcastle under Lyme BC* [1985] 2 All E.R. 405. For discussion of the principle, see Elliott (1964) 80 L.Q.R. 244; Peel (1965) 81 L.Q.R. 28.

4. The analysis of the rule in *Wheeldon v. Burrows* as an application of the principle of non-derogation from grant renders the rule inoperative in the context of compulsory purchase. In *Sovmots Investments Ltd v. Secretary of State for the Environment* [1979] A.C. 144 Lord Wilberforce stated (at 168–169):

The rule [in *Wheeldon v. Burrows*] is a rule of intention, based on the proposition that a man may not derogate from his grant. He cannot grant or agree to grant land and at the same time deny to his grantee what is at the time of the grant obviously necessary to its reasonable enjoyment. To apply this to a case where a public authority is taking from an owner his land without his will is to stand the rule on its head: it means substituting for the intention of a reasonable voluntary grantor the unilateral, opposed, intention of the acquirer.

See also Lord Edmund-Davies, *ibid.* at 175. And see *infra*, p. 660.

1.2.1 *Implied grant*

1.2.1.1 *Easements of necessity*　　In the strict sense easements of necessity are implied only where the easement is one without which the property transferred cannot be used at all, and not where the easement is merely necessary to the reasonable enjoyment of that property: *Union Lighterage Co. v. London Graving Dock Co.* [1902] 2 Ch. 557, 573 *per* Stirling L.J. Necessity in this sense is illustrated most graphically where the land transferred is landlocked by surrounding land retained by the transferor; and in such circumstances, there will be an implied grant of a right of way over the land retained to provide the necessary access to the land transferred:

Pinnington v. Galland (1853) 9 Exch. 1, 12–13 *per* Martin B. However, there will be no implied grant of an easement of necessity where there is alternative access, provided that the use of that access is of right: *Barry v. Hasseldine* [1952] Ch. 835, 839 *per* Danckwerts J.; and provided that it is not unlawful: *Hansford v. Jago* [1921] 1 Ch. 322, 342–343 *per* Russell J. Moreover, it is irrelevant that the alternative means of access may be difficult and inconvenient: *Titchmarsh v. Royston Water Co. Ltd* (1899) 81 L.T. 673 (expensive construction work required); *MRA Engineering Ltd v. Trimster Co. Ltd* (1987) 56 P. & C.R. 1 (public footpath only); *Manjang v. Drammeh* (1990) 61 P. & C.R. 194 (access by water only).

The route of the right of way is determined by the servient owner: *Brown v. Alabaster* (1887) 37 Ch D. 490, 500 *per* Kay J., although it has been held that a servient owner has no right to alter the route of an easement of way once it has been fixed, unless such a right is an express or implied term of the grant of the easement or such a right is subsequently conferred on him: *Greenwich Healthcare NHS Trust v. London and Quadrant Housing Trust* [1998] 1 W.L.R. 1749, 1754 *per* Lightman J.; and the nature and extent of its permissible use are limited by reference to the purposes for which the dominant land was used at the time of the transfer: *Corp. of London v. Riggs* (1880) 12 Ch D. 798, 806–807 *per* Jessel M.R., *infra*, p. 689.

It has been suggested that easements of necessity are implied pursuant to a rule of public policy that land should not be rendered unusable by being landlocked: *Nickerson v. Barraclough* [1980] Ch. 325, 334 *per* Megarry V.-C.; and see Bodkin (1973) 89 L.Q.R. 87. That view was expressly rejected by the Court of Appeal. Brightman L.J. stated that the doctrine of easements of necessity is based upon an implication from the circumstances; but at the same time he acknowledged that public policy may require the court to frustrate the apparent intention of the parties where their agreement is contrary to public policy: [1981] Ch. 426, 438–441; see Crabb [1981] Conv. 442; Jackson (1981) 34 C.L.P. 113; (1982) 98 L.Q.R. 11.

1.2.1.2 *Easements of common intention*

Stafford v. Lee (1992) 65 P. & C.R. 172

(CA, Nourse and Purchas L.JJ.)

In 1955 the predecessor in title of the defendants conveyed an area of woodland to the predecessor in title of the plaintiffs. The land was described as having a frontage to Marley Drive, a private roadway; but, although that roadway provided the only practicable means of access to the land, the conveyance contained no express grant of a right of way. The land remained undeveloped until 1989, when the plaintiffs obtained planning permission for the erection of a dwelling-house. When the defendants asserted that the plaintiffs had no right of way along the roadway, the plaintiffs sought and obtained a declaration that they had a right of way for construction traffic and, subsequently, for all purposes connected with the use of the land as a dwelling-house. The defendants' appeal was dismissed.

NOURSE L.J.:

The plaintiffs put their case on three different grounds. First, they claimed an easement of necessity. Secondly, they relied on the rule in *Wheeldon v. Burrows* (1879) 21 Ch.D. 31. Thirdly, they sought to invoke the principle of *Pwllbach Colliery Company Limited v. Woodman* [1915] A.C. 634. The judge had no difficulty in holding that the plaintiffs could not establish an entitlement to the easement they claimed on either of the first two of those grounds. But he held that they could do so on the third. The defendants now appeal to this court. The plaintiffs have put in a respondents' notice seeking, if necessary, to have the judge's decision affirmed on one or other of the first two grounds.

Lord Parker's statement of the relevant principles in *Pwllbach Colliery Company Limited v. Woodman* [1915] A.C. 634, at p. 646, starts with his saying that apart from implied grants of ways of necessity, or of what are called continuous and apparent easements (*i.e.* those passing under the rule in *Wheeldon v. Burrows*), the cases in which an easement can be granted by implication may be classified under two heads. Having dealt with the first class, where the implication arises because the right in question is necessary for the enjoyment of some other right expressly granted, he continues, *ibid.*:

"The second class of cases in which easements may impliedly be created depends not upon the terms of the grant itself, but upon the circumstances under which the grant was made. The law will readily imply the grant or reservation of such easements as may be necessary to give effect to the common intention of the parties to a grant of real property, with reference to the manner or purposes in and for which the land granted or some land retained by the grantor is to be used. See *Jones v. Pritchard* [1908] 1 Ch. 630 and *Lyttelton Times Co. v. Warners* [1907] A.C. 476. But it is essential for this purpose that the parties should intend that the subject of the grant or the land retained by the grantor should be used in some definite and particular manner. It is not enough that the subject of the grant or the land retained should be intended to be used in a manner which may or may not involve this definite and particular use."

Intended easements, like all other implied easements, are subject to the general rule that they are implied more readily in favour of a grantee than a grantor. But even there, as Lord Parker points out, the parties must intend that the subject of the grant shall be used in some definite and particular manner. If the grantee can establish the requisite intention, the law will then imply the grant of such easements as may be necessary to give effect to it.

There are therefore two hurdles which the grantee must surmount. He must establish a common intention as to some definite and particular user. Then he must show that the easements he claims are necessary to give effect to it. Notwithstanding the submissions of Miss Baker, for the defendants, to the contrary, I think that the second hurdle is no great obstacle to the plaintiffs in this case. The real question is whether they can surmount the first.

It is axiomatic that in construing any conveyance you must take into account the facts in reference to which it was made. But here, no extrinsic evidence having been adduced on either side, we can refer only to the 1955 deed. At one point it seemed possible that some assistance might be gained from the terms of one of the restrictions in the 1949 conveyance, subject to which the 1955 deed was expressed to have effect. However, for reasons which need not be gone into, I agree with Miss Baker that that did not prove to be the case.

The defendants admitted in their defence that the 1955 deed did pass to Mrs Walker a right to use Marley Drive and that that right had passed to the plaintiffs. But they have at all times contended that the right was limited to use for all purposes necessary for the reasonable enjoyment of the land as woodland, being the manner of its enjoyment in 1955. Such a right is manifestly inadequate for the plaintiffs' purposes.

The first point to be made about the defendants' contention is that, although it may sometimes come to the same thing, the material question in a case of an intended easement is not how was the land enjoyed in 1955, but did the parties to the 1955 deed intend that it should be used in some definite and particular manner and, if so, what? As to that question, Miss Baker has submitted that in our present state of knowledge, or rather the lack of it, we cannot point to any definite or particular manner of intended use. She says that Mrs Walker may already have had a home in the neighbourhood and that the intention may have been that she would use the land for a paddock, a vegetable or a flower garden of her own, for a market garden, an apiary or for some other horticultural or agricultural use.

In my view Miss Baker's submissions are unrealistic. The requirement that the parties should have intended a definite and particular use for the land does not require that the intention be proved as a certainty. As always, it is enough that it is proved on the balance of probabilities. What help do we get from the 1955 deed in this regard? First, it is to be observed that Mrs Walker's address, far from being in the neighbourhood, is stated to be in distant Sussex. Secondly, and far more significantly, there is the plan.

Miss Baker, while accepting that a conveyance plan which is expressed to be for the purpose of identification only may yet be relied on in order to solve problems left undecided by the parcels—she referred us to *Wigginton & Milner Ltd v. Winster Engineering Ltd* [1978] 1 W.L.R. 1462 and *Scott v. Martin* [1978] 1 W.L.R. 841—has submitted that such a plan cannot be relied on for the purpose of establishing the parties' intention as to the use to which the land should be put. I cannot see why that should be so. The plan is part of the material agreed on by the parties. There is no reason why their common intention, if it is not expressed, should not be implied from that as much as from any other part of the agreed material. There is every reason why, if it can be, it should be so implied.

The significant, indeed the eye-catching, feature of the plan here is that it delineates, as the land conveyed, a plot adjoining and of comparable area to two other enclosures, each adjoining the other, which, from the legends they bear, are seen to be plots of land on which dwellings have already been constructed. In these circumstances and given, as the defendants accept, that some appurtenant right of way was intended over and along Marley Drive, what are the probabilities as to the intended use of the land? In my judgment, on the balance of probabilities, the parties can only have intended that it should be used for the construction of another dwelling to be used thereafter for residential purposes. I cannot see what other intention could reasonably be imputed to them. Having got to that point, I am satisfied that the easements claimed by the plaintiffs and declared in their favour by the judge are necessary, and are no more than are necessary, to give effect to the intention so established.

On that footing it is unnecessary to deal with the alternative grounds on which the plaintiffs would have relied in order to support the judge's decision. As at present advised, I think that the judge was plainly right to reject them. But since we have not called on Mr Rossdale to answer the appeal, it is inappropriate to express a concluded view to that effect.

NOTES:

1. *Stafford v. Lee* is consistent with a line of authorities which regard easements of common intention as being a category of implied easements independent of easements of necessity: see also *Lyttelton Times Co. Ltd v. Warners Ltd* [1907] A.C. 476, 481–482 *per* Lord Loreburn L.C.; *Jones v. Pritchard* [1908] 1 Ch. 630, 635–636 *per* Parker J.; *Pwllbach Colliery Co. Ltd*

v. Woodman [1915] A.C. 634, 646–648 *per* Lord Parker; *Cory v. Davies* [1923] 2 Ch. 95, 108–110 *per* Lawrence J.; *Re Webb's Lease* [1951] 1 Ch. 808, 828–830 *per* Jenkins L.J.

2. However, in *Wong v. Beaumont Property Trust Ltd* [1965] 1 Q.B. 173 the Court of Appeal purported to apply the principle in *Pwllbach Colliery Co. Ltd v. Woodman* while using the terminology of easements of necessity.

Wong v. Beaumont Property Trust Ltd [1965] 1 Q.B. 173

(CA, Lord Denning M.R., Pearson and Salmon L.JJ.)

The plaintiff was the assignee of a lease of three cellars. The lease contained covenants by the lessee to use the cellars as a restaurant, to eliminate all smells and to comply with health regulations. Although it was not realised when the lease was granted, compliance with these covenants was impossible without the construction of a ventilation duct on the outside wall of the adjoining property owned by the lessor. The plaintiff sought a declaration that he was entitled to enter the adjoining property, now owned by the defendants, in order to construct the ventilation duct.

LORD DENNING M.R.:

The question is: Has the plaintiff a right to put up this duct without the landlords' consent? If he is to have any right at all, it must be by way of easement and not merely by way of implied contract. He is not the original lessee, nor are the defendants the original lessors. Each is a successor in title. As between them, a right of this kind, if it exists at all, must be by way of an easement. In particular, an easement of necessity. The law on the matter was stated by Lord Parker of Waddington in *Pwllbach Colliery Co. Ltd v. Woodman* [1915] A.C. 634, where he said (at pp. 646–647), omitting immaterial words, "The law will readily imply the grant or reservation of such easements as may be necessary to give effect to the common intention of the parties to a grant of real property, with reference to the manner or purposes in and for which the land granted ... is to be used. But it is essential for this purpose that the parties should intend that the subject of the grant ... should be used in some definite and particular manner. It is not enough that the subject of the grant ... should be intended to be used in a manner which may or may not involve this definite and particular use". That is the principle which underlies all easements of necessity. If you go back to Rolle's Abridgment you will find it stated in this way: "If I have a field inclosed by my own land on all sides, and I alien this close to another, he shall have a way to this close over my land, as incident to the grant; for otherwise he cannot have any benefit by the grant".

I would apply those principles here. Here was the grant of a lease to the lessee for the very purpose of carrying on a restaurant business. It was to be a popular restaurant, and it was to be developed and extended. There was a covenant not to cause any nuisance; and to control and eliminate all smells; and to comply with the Food Hygiene Regulations. That was "a definite and particular manner" in which the business had to be conducted. It could not be carried on in that manner at all unless a ventilation system was installed by a duct of this kind. In these circumstances it seems to me that, if the business is to be carried on at all—if, in the words of Rolle's Abridgment (2 Rol.Abr. 60, pl. 17, 18) the lessee is to "have any benefit by the grant" at all—he must of necessity be able to put a ventilation duct up the wall. It may be that in Blackaby's time it would not have needed such a large duct as is now needed in the plaintiff's time. But nevertheless a duct of some kind would have had to be put up the wall. The plaintiff may need a bigger one. But that does not matter. A man who has a right to an easement can use it in any proper way, so long as he does not substantially increase the burden on the servient tenement. In this case a bigger duct will not substantially increase the burden.

There is one point in which this case goes further than the earlier cases which have been cited. It is this. It was not realised by the parties, at the time of the lease, that this duct would be necessary. But it was in fact necessary from the very beginning. That seems to me sufficient to bring the principle into play. In order to use this place as a restaurant, there must be implied an easement, by the necessity of the case, to carry a duct up this wall. The county court judge so held. He granted a declaration. I agree with him.

NOTES:

1. Pearson L.J. stated (at 183):

There is, therefore, this choice for the court: either to say the provisions of the lease cannot be carried out and must remain inoperative or to imply an easement of necessity into the lease. The court should read this lease in such a way that *res magis valeat quam pereat*, and therefore the right course is to imply an easement of necessity in this case.

Salmon L.J. stated (at 184):

It seems to me plain on the authorities that if a lease is granted which imposes a particular use on the tenant and it is impossible for the tenant so to use the premises unless an easement is granted, the law does imply such an easement as of necessity.

2. For comment, see (1964) 80 L.Q.R. 322.

3. The view that there is no essential difference between easements of necessity and easements of common intention is based on the arguments (i) that a common intention to grant a particular easement will normally be found only in cases of necessity: see *Nickerson v. Barraclough* [1980] Ch. 325, 336 *per* Megarry V.-C.; and (ii) that easements of necessity depend upon the actual or presumed intention of the parties: see *Nickerson v. Barraclough* [1981] Ch. 426, 440–441 *per* Brightman L.J. However, such a view does not assume the strict approach to easements of necessity discussed above.

1.2.1.3 *The rule in* Wheeldon v. Burrows   Easements of necessity and easements of common intention may be impliedly granted to the transferee; and they may also be impliedly reserved to the transferor: see *infra*, p. 646. The so-called "rule in *Wheeldon v. Burrows*" operates only to imply easements in favour of the transferee.

It has been seen that a landowner cannot have an easement over land which he both owns and occupies. However, he may use his land in such a way that one part derives benefit from another part so that, if the two parts were in separate ownership or occupation, the use would be in the nature of an easement. In such circumstances, the subsequent division of the land is anticipated by referring to such use as the exercise of a "quasi-easement". If and when the division eventually takes place and the quasi-dominant land is transferred, under the rule in *Wheeldon v. Burrows* the quasi-easement may be transformed into an easement *stricto sensu* by an implied grant in favour of the transferee. For example, where prior to the transfer the transferor had been using a road across the part (to be) retained in order to gain access to the part (to be) transferred, a corresponding easement may be implied in favour of the land transferred to the transferee over the land retained by the transferor: see *Borman v. Griffith* [1930] 1 Ch. 493.

The requirements for the operation of the rule were considered by Ungoed-Thomas J. in *Ward v. Kirkland* [1967] Ch. 194.

Ward v. Kirkland [1967] Ch. 194

(Ch D., Ungoed-Thomas J.)

In 1928 the predecessor in title of the plaintiff purchased a plot of land, including a cottage built on the boundary of the land and abutting a farmyard (the land and the farm having previously been in common ownership). The conveyance granted to the purchaser the right to use the farmyard for unloading coal and the right to use the existing water supply. In 1954 the plaintiff acquired the land on the same terms. In 1942 the defendant's husband became tenant of the adjoining farm; and in 1958 the defendant purchased the freehold of the farm, the conveyance being subject to the rights of the plaintiff. The position of the cottage meant that the only practicable way of maintaining the cottage wall on the boundary of the land, and cleaning the gutters and windows, involved entering the farmyard. From 1954 to 1958 the plaintiff went into the farmyard to effect maintenance work, although he never sought permission to do so; but in 1958 the defendant refused to allow him to enter. The plaintiff sought a declaration that he had an easement to enter the farmyard for the purposes of maintaining his property.

UNGOED-THOMAS J.:

Assuming that this right is capable of being an easement, how was the easement claimed created? An easement, of course, in its strict sense, excludes quasi-easements enjoyed by a dominant tenement over a servient tenement, or, I should say, a quasi-dominant over a quasi-servient tenement, whilst those tenements are in common ownership; so that an easement strictly so called could only in this case be created by [the] conveyance in 1928 or by user since 1928. The easement could not exist before 1928, because the two lands were in common ownership, and such a right could then only exist as a quasi-easement. The conveyance to the plaintiff in 1954 cannot have created the easement, though, of course, it may have transmitted it. For the plaintiff it is submitted that the easement arises (1) by implication of law; (2) by the application of the doctrine of derogation from grant; (3) by general words under section 62, Law of Property Act 1925, and (4) by prescription.

First, then, implication of law. Did the right to maintain the wall pass as an easement on the occasion of the conveyance in 1928 by the rector as common owner of the farm and the cottage? The source of the law on this subject is *Wheeldon v. Burrows* (1879) 12 Ch.D. 31, and the passage which bears on this most directly is where Thesiger L.J., delivering a judgment in which James L.J. and Baggallay L.J. concurred, said (at p. 49):

"We have had a considerable number of cases cited to us, and out of them I think that two propositions may be stated as what I may call the general rules governing cases of this kind. The first of these rules is, that on the grant by the owner of a tenement of part of that tenement as it is then used and enjoyed, there will pass to the grantee all those continuous and apparent easements (by which, of course, I mean quasi-easements), or, in other words, all those easements which are necessary to the reasonable enjoyment of the property granted, and which have been and are at the time of the grant used by the owners of the entirety for the benefit of the part granted."

There, it might appear that the words "in other words" in that passage would indicate that the requirement, "which are necessary to the reasonable enjoyment of the property granted", and the earlier words, "continuous and apparent easements", refer to the same easements. But Thesiger L.J. states (at pp. 58–59):

"... in the case of a grant you may imply a grant of such continuous and apparent easements or such easements as are necessary to the reasonable enjoyment of the property conveyed, and have in fact been enjoyed during the unity of ownership."

Reading that passage on its own, on first impression, it would appear that the "easements which are necessary to the reasonable enjoyment of the property conveyed" might be a separate class from "continuous and apparent easements". It has been recognised that there is some difficulty in these descriptions, to which I have referred, of the easements which come within the ambit of the doctrine of *Wheeldon v. Burrows*. It has been suggested that perhaps the "easements necessary to the reasonable enjoyment of the property conveyed" might refer to negative easements, whereas what we are concerned with here is positive easements. However that may be, I understand that there is no case in which positive easements which are not "continuous and apparent" have been held to come within the doctrine of *Wheeldon v. Burrows*. Here, there has certainly been continuous user, in the sense that the right has been in fact used whenever the need arose. But the words "continuous and apparent" seem to be directed to there being on the servient tenement a feature which would be seen on inspection and which is neither transitory nor intermittent; for example, drains, paths, as contrasted with the bowsprits of ships overhanging a piece of land.

Here, it is conceded that it was only possible or practicable for the occupiers of the cottage to maintain the boundary wall by going onto the defendant's property as claimed in this case. That would be obvious on an inspection of the properties. But here there was no feature on the defendant's property designed or appropriate for such maintenance. The question is whether that requirement is necessary. If it is not necessary, then there are no clearly defined limits to the area of user; and if the easement extends to maintain the whole wall, as it must, then there could be no interference with that easement and therefore no building in the yard along that wall.

Professor Cheshire, in his book on Real Property, says that:

"The two words 'continuous' and 'apparent' must be read together and understood as pointing to an easement which is accompanied by some obvious and permanent mark on the land itself, or at least by some mark which will be disclosed by a careful inspection of the premises."

Then he gives instances, and says:

"A right of way is not necessarily such a quasi-easement as will pass under the rule in *Wheeldon v. Burrows*. To do so it must be apparent. There is no difficulty where there is a definite made road over the quasi-servient tenement to and for the apparent use of the quasi-dominant tenement. Such will clearly pass upon a severance of the common tenement. But the existence of a formed road is not essential, and if there are other indicia which show that the road was being used at the time of the grant for the benefit of the quasi-dominant tenement and that it is necessary for the reasonable enjoyment of that tenement, it will pass to a purchaser of the latter."

It seems to me that in the absence of a continuous and apparent feature designed or appropriate for the exercise of the easement on the servient tenement, there is not a continuous and apparent easement within the requirements of *Wheeldon v. Burrows* in the case of alleged positive easements. I, therefore, come to the conclusion that the easement claimed was not created by implication of law.

Then it is claimed alternatively under the doctrine of derogation from grant. This may no longer be a very important consideration in view of the operation nowadays of general words, and I, for my part, would prefer to rest my conclusion upon the operation of general words rather than upon this doctrine of derogation from grant, which is not free from difficulty in this case. I will, however, refer to it briefly.

The principle is stated in *Birmingham, Dudley and District Banking Co. v. Ross* (1887) 38 Ch. D. 295, where Bowen L.J. said (at p. 313) that

"a grantor having given a thing with one hand is not to take away the means of enjoying it with the other."

This principle is not limited to easements or quasi-easements. In *Browne v. Flower* [1911] 1 Ch. 219., Parker J. said (at p. 224):

"The plaintiffs next relied on the maxim that no one can be allowed to derogate from his own grant. This maxim is generally quoted as explaining certain implications which may arise from the fact that, or the circumstances under which, an owner of land grants or demises part of it, retaining the remainder in his own hands." Then later (at p. 225): "Further, the circumstances of the case may be such that though at the time of the grant or demise there be no continuous or apparent quasi-easements enjoyed by the property granted or demised over the property retained, yet easements over the property retained may be impliedly created and become appurtenant to the property granted or demised. Thus, if the grant or demise be for the purpose of erecting a building with defined windows overlooking other land of the grantor or lessor, an easement of light to such windows over such other land will be created, and similarly there will be created an easement of support by the land retained for the building to be built."

Here, the house was clearly sold as a dwelling-house, and it cannot be properly or reasonably enjoyed as a dwelling-house without means of maintaining it as such. And it is common ground, as indeed it is quite obvious, that the only possible or practicable means of maintaining the cottage wall next to the defendant's farmyard is by going onto the yard for that purpose. The difficulty which I have felt about this submission is this: that derogation from the grant seems to indicate doing something which defeats in substantial measure the purpose of the grant. It generally arises, of course, in cases where the grantor does something on his own property which defeats the enjoyment of the property granted as it existed and was contemplated at the time of the grant; whereas, here, what is claimed is a right in the plaintiff to go onto the defendant's property for the purposes of doing certain works for the advantage of the plaintiff's cottage. There is clearly a distinction between those two categories; but it seems to me that the underlying principle of the doctrine of derogation from the grant applies to both categories. It is with hesitation and with an appreciation of the difficulties that I have come to this conclusion, and it is for that reason that I for my part would prefer to rely upon the operation of general words rather than upon the doctrine of derogation from grant.

NOTES:

1. The claim to an easement based on the operation of section 62 of the Law of Property Act 1925 on the 1928 conveyance succeeded: [1967] Ch.

194, 227–231; see *infra*, p. 649. The claim based on prescriptive acquisition for 20 years immediately preceding the plaintiff's claim failed because for a significant part of that period the plaintiff entered the servient land with the permission of the servient owner: [1967] Ch. 194, 232–234; see *infra*, p. 670.

2. The plaintiff also succeeded in a proprietary estoppel claim to rights of drainage for a bathroom and toilet: see *ante*, p. 573.

3. The requirement that the quasi-easement should be "continuous and apparent" was imported from the French law of prescription by Gale (*Gale on Easements* (1st ed., 1839), pp. 16–17): see *Suffield v. Brown* (1864) 4 De G.J. & S. 185, 195 *per* Lord Westbury; *Dalton v. Angus & Co.* (1881) 6 App.Cas. 740, 821 *per* Lord Blackburn; and see Simpson (1967) 83 L.Q.R. 240.

In French law "continuous" is used to describe a servitude (easement) that is capable of continuous enjoyment without human activity, for example a right of drainage. In English law, it has come to mean "permanent" in the sense of a permanent physical alteration of the land. It thus includes a right of way over a made road: *Brown v. Alabaster* (1887) 37 Ch D. 490; or over a worn track: *Hansford v. Jago* [1921] 1 Ch. 322; *Borman v. Griffith* [1930] 1 Ch. 493. In *Borman v. Griffith* Maugham J. stated (at 499):

> It is true that the easement, or, rather, quasi-easement, is not continuous. But the authorities are sufficient to show that a grantor of property, in circumstances where an obvious, that is, visible and made road is necessary for the reasonable enjoyment of the property by the grantee, must be taken prima facie to have intended to grant a right to use it.

In the case of positive easements the permanent physical alteration is usually to the servient land: *Ward v. Kirkland, supra,* 225 *per* Ungoed-Thomas J.; in the case of negative easements it is usually to the dominant land, for example a building receiving support or windows receiving light: *Philips v. Low* [1892] 1 Ch. 47, 52–53 *per* Chitty J.

"Apparent" has retained its meaning in French law. It denotes that the easement must be evidenced by some sign on the dominant land (*Schwann v. Cotton* [1916] 2 Ch. 120, 141 *per* Astbury J.) or on the servient land (*Ward v. Kirkland, supra,* 225 *per* Ungoed-Thomas J.), discoverable on "a careful inspection by a person ordinarily conversant with the subject": *Pyer v. Carter* (1857) 1 H. & N. 916, 922 *per* Watson B. It was failure to satisfy this requirement that prevented the operation of the rule in *Wheeldon v. Burrows* to the right of access for maintenance in *Ward v. Kirkland*: see 225–226 *per* Ungoed-Thomas J.; and see also *Polden v. Bastard* (1865) L.R. 1 Q.B. 156; *Suffield v. Brown* (1864) 4 De G.J. & S. 185.

In summary, "the two words 'continuous' and 'apparent' must be read together and understood as pointing to an easement which is accompanied by some obvious and permanent mark on the land itself, or at least some mark which will be disclosed by a careful inspection of the premises": *Cheshire & Burn* (see now 15th ed., 1994, p. 541), citing *Pyer v Carter* (1857) 1 H. & N. 916, and cited with approval in *Ward v. Kirkland, supra,* 225 *per* Ungoed-Thomas J.

4. The requirement that the easement should be "necessary to the reasonable enjoyment" of the dominant land has not been precisely defined. It does not involve compliance with the strict conditions for the implication of easements of necessity: see *supra*, p.635. On the other hand, it seems that it is no longer sufficient merely to establish that the claimed easement would make enjoyment of the property more convenient and comfortable (a test approved in *Schwann v. Cotton* [1916] 2 Ch. 459, 469 *per* Lord Cozens-Hardy M.R.). Thus, in *Millman v. Ellis* (1995) 71 P. & C.R. 158, noted at [1995] Conv. 346, the Court of Appeal held that the requirement was satisfied expressly on the ground that the claimed easement was necessary to avert what would otherwise be a dangerous means of access to the dominant land. The absence of a precise definition of the requirement is reflected in the cases on rights of way where there was an alternative means of access to the dominant land. In some cases the requirement has been held to be satisfied despite an alternative means of access: see *Borman v. Griffith* [1930] 1 Ch. 493; *Castagliola v. English* (1969) 210 E.G. 1425, 1431 *per* Megarry J.; *Horn v. Hiscock* (1972) 223 E.G. 1437, 1441 *per* Goulding J. In other cases, an alternative means of access has been held to be sufficient in itself to negative the requirement: see *Wheeler v. J.J. Saunders Ltd* [1996] Ch. 19, 25 *per* Staughton L.J, 36 *per* Sir John May, noted at [1995] Conv. 239. It is arguable that these cases may be reconciled by reference to the suitability of the alternative means of access in the particular circumstances.

5. There is some uncertainty, prompted by the ambiguous formulation in *Wheeldon v. Burrows* itself, as to whether the requirements of "continuous and apparent" and "necessary to the reasonable enjoyment" of the dominant land are synonymous, alternative or cumulative: see, *e.g. Ward v. Kirkland* [1967] Ch. 194, 224–225 *per* Ungoed-Thomas J.; *Squarey v. Harris-Smith* (1981) 42 P. & C.R. 118, 124 *per* Oliver L.J.; *Wheeler v. J.J. Saunders Ltd* [1996] Ch. 19, 31 *per* Peter Gibson L.J.; and see Simpson (1967) 83 L.Q.R. 240, 245–247. More recently, the balance of judicial opinion seems to have placed greater emphasis on the requirement that the easement should be "necessary to the reasonable enjoyment" of the dominant land: see, *e.g. Wheeler v. J.J. Saunders Ltd, supra.* It may be argued that this approach properly reflects the view that the rule in *Wheeldon v. Burrows* is based on the principle of non-derogation from grant: see *Sovmots Investments Ltd v. Secretary of State for the Environment* [1979] A.C. 144, *supra*, p. 635. On the other hand, the absence of discussion of the "continuous and apparent" requirement may simply reflect the absence of dispute as to whether that requirement was satisfied; where there was such a dispute the requirement was discussed as a discrete and cumulative requirement: see *Millman v. Ellis* (1995) 71 P. & C.R. 158, 162 *per* Sir Thomas Bingham M.R. Harpum (1977) 41 Conv. 415, 421–422, argues that the two requirements are cumulative, the first being a rule of conveyancing convenience, facilitating the discovery of incumbrances, while the second reflects the doctrine of non-derogation from grant.

6. The requirement that the quasi-easement should have been in use at the time of the conveyance has not been construed unduly strictly: *Castagliola v. English* (1969) 210 E.G. 1425, 1429 *per* Megarry J.

7. The rule in *Wheeldon v. Burrows* operates not only where the transferee acquires a legal estate but also where he acquires an equitable interest pursuant to a defective conveyance or a contract for a conveyance: *Borman v. Griffith* [1930] 1 Ch. 493, 499 *per* Maugham J.; *Horn v. Hiscock* (1972) 223 E.G. 1437, 1441 *per* Goulding J.

8. The rule operates in the same way where the transferor transfers the quasi-dominant land and the quasi-servient land to separate transferees by simultaneous conveyances or transfers. The transferee of the quasi-dominant land acquires as easements those quasi-easements over the servient land that he would have acquired had the servient land been retained by the transferor: *Swansborough v. Coventry* (1832) 2 Moo. & Sc. 362; *Barnes v. Loach* (1879) 4 Q.B.D. 494; *Allen v. Taylor* (1880) 16 Ch D. 355; *Schwann v. Cotton* [1916] 2 Ch. 120, 459; *Hansford v. Jago* [1921] 1 Ch. 322.

9. The operation of rule in *Wheeldon v. Burrows* may be excluded where there is evidence of a contrary intention. The evidence may be found in the conveyance or in the contract: see *Squarey v. Harris-Smith* (1981) 42 P. & C.R. 118, 128–130 *per* Oliver L.J.; but see *Lyme Valley Squash Club Ltd v. Newcastle under Lyme BC* [1985] 2 All E.R. 405, 411–413 *per* Judge Blackett-Ord V.-C., noted at [1985] Conv. 243. The contrary intention may exclude the operation of the rule in its entirety (*Borman v. Griffith* [1930] 1 Ch. 493, 499 *per* Maugham J.) or in respect of particular easements (*Squarey v. Harris-Smith* (1981) 42 P. & C.R. 118, 127–129 *per* Oliver L.J.). Moreover, the exclusion may be express (*ibid.*) or implied from some other term in the conveyance or contract (*Wheeler v. J.J. Saunders Ltd* [1996] Ch. 19). However, an express grant of an easement does not necessarily exclude the rule, which may operate to enlarge the express grant: *Millman v. Ellis* (1995) 71 P. & C.R. 158, 164–166 *per* Sir Thomas Bingham M.R., noted at [1995] Conv. 346.

1.2.2 *Implied reservation*   Where the owner of land sells part of his land, he is usually in a position to stipulate for the reservation of easements. Consequently, if he fails to include in the conveyance or transfer an *express* reservation, the courts will not readily *imply* the reservation of easements in his favour. However, the judgment of Thesiger L.J. in *Wheeldon v. Burrows* (1879) 12 Ch D. 31 recognised two exceptions (easements of necessity and reciprocal and mutual easements); and a third category (easements of common intention) seems to be acknowledged in the subsequent case law.

1.2.2.1 *Easements of necessity*   The principles relating to the implied *grant* of easements of necessity apply: indeed, some of the cases referred to above involved the implied *reservation* of easements of necessity.

1.2.2.2 *Reciprocal and mutual easements*   Where an easement is impliedly *granted* to the purchaser, the courts may be prepared to imply in favour of the grantor the reservation of any easement which is in its nature reciprocal. Thus the reservation of easements has been implied where, prior to the division, the land transferred and the land retained enjoyed reciprocal rights of support:

Richards v. Rose (1853) 9 Exch. 218; and the reservation of reciprocal rights of drainage in *Pyer v. Carter* (1857) 1 H.&N. 916 was explained by reference to the same principle: see *Wheeldon v. Burrows* (1879) 12 Ch D. 31, 59 *per* Thesiger L.J. The implied reservation of such easements was stated by Thesiger L.J. to be "very reasonable" and "consistent with reason and common sense"; but it is not clear whether such statements provide the juridical basis of implication. For the suggestion that such easements are properly categorised as easements of necessity, see *Williams v. Usherwood* (1981) 45 P. & C.R. 235, 254 *per* Cumming-Bruce L.J.

1.2.2.3 *Easements of common intention*   If a strict construction is applied to the above two categories of easements, identified by Thesiger L.J. as the exceptional easements that may be acquired by implied reservation, there is a third category of exceptional easements that may be implied in order to give effect to the common intention of the parties. However, the transferor who claims the implied reservation of such intended easements carries a heavy burden of proof and must establish that the parties intended that the land retained be used in some definite and particular manner: see *Lyttelton Times Co. Ltd v. Warners Ltd* [1907] A.C. 476, 481–482 *per* Lord Loreburn L.C.; *Jones v. Pritchard* [1908] 1 Ch. 630, 635–636 *per* Parker J.; *Pwllbach Colliery Co. Ltd v. Woodman* [1915] A.C. 634, 646–648 *per* Lord Parker; *Cory v. Davies* [1923] 2 Ch. 95, 108–110 *per* Lawrence J.; *Re Webb's Lease* [1951] 1 Ch. 808, 828–830 *per* Jenkins L.J., *infra*.

Re Webb's Lease [1951] 1 Ch. 808

(CA, Evershed M.R., Jenkins and Morris L.JJ.)

The defendant was the head-lessee of a three storey building of which he occupied the ground floor for his business purposes. For 10 years from 1939 the plaintiff occupied the upper floors under a tenancy agreement; but in 1949 the defendant granted the plaintiff a 21-year lease. In 1950 the plaintiff questioned the entitlement of the defendant to maintain two advertisements which covered a substantial part of the exterior walls of the upper floors of the building. The defendant had maintained the advertisements since 1939 without objection from the plaintiff; but neither the tenancy agreement nor the subsequent lease purported to reserve any such right to the defendant.

JENKINS L.J.:

As to the law applicable to the case, it is not disputed that as a general rule a grantor, whether by way of conveyance or lease, of part of a hereditament in his ownership, cannot claim any easement over the part granted for the benefit of the part retained, unless it is expressly reserved out of the grant. See (for instance) *Suffield v. Brown* (1864) 4 De G. J. & S. 185; *Crossley & Sons Ltd v. Lightowler* (1867) L. R. 2 Ch. 478.; *Wheeldon v. Burrows* (1879) 12 Ch. D. 31.

   There are, however, certain exceptions to the general rule. Two well-established exceptions relate to easements of necessity and mutual easements such as rights of support between adjacent buildings. But it is recognised in the authorities that these two specific exceptions do not exhaust the list, which is indeed incapable of exhaustive statement, as the circumstances of any particular case may be such as to raise a necessary inference that the common intention of the parties must have been to reserve some easement to the grantor, or such as to preclude the grantee from denying the right consistently with good faith, and there appears to be no doubt that where circumstances such as these are clearly established the court will imply the appropriate reservation.

. . .

The most comprehensive statement of the area of potential exceptions is probably that contained in the speech of Lord Parker in *Pwllbach Colliery Co. Ltd v. Woodman* [1915] A.C. 634, 646, where his Lordship, after referring to the exception with respect to easements of necessity, said this: "The second class of cases in which easements may impliedly be created depends not upon the terms of the grant itself, but upon the circumstances under which the grant was made. The law will readily imply the grant or reservation of such easements as may be necessary to give effect to the common intention of the parties to a grant of real property, with reference to the manner or purposes in and for which the land granted or some land retained by the grantor is to be used. See *Jones v. Pritchard* [1908] 1 Ch. 630, and *Lyttelton Times Co. Ltd v. Warners Ltd* [1907] A.C. 476. But it is essential for this purpose that the parties should intend that the subject of the grant or the land retained by the grantor should be used in some definite and particular manner. It is not enough that the subject of the grant or the land retained should be intended to be used in a manner which may or may not involve this definite and particular use."

The illustrations given by Lord Parker in support of this general proposition seem however to show that it is of less comprehensive import than would at first sight appear. He refers to *Jones v. Pritchard*, which was in effect a case of mutual easements, to *Lyttelton Times Co. Ltd v. Warners Ltd*, where both parties contemplated at the time of the grant that the grantor should carry on his printing works on the part of the premises retained, and it was held that the grantee could not in those circumstances complain of a nuisance to the premises granted due to noise and vibration unavoidably occasioned by the carrying on as contemplated of printing operations on the grantor's part of the premises, and to two other cases which appear to have proceeded on similar principles.

. . .

The question is whether the circumstances of the case as proved in evidence are such as to raise a necessary inference that the common intention of the parties was to reserve to the landlord during the twenty-one years' term some, and if so what, rights in regard to the display of advertisements over the outer walls of the demised premises, or such as to preclude the tenant from denying the implied reservation to the landlord of some such rights consistently with good faith.

That question must be approached with the following principles in mind: (i) If the landlord intended to reserve any such rights over the demised premises it was his duty to reserve them expressly in the lease of August 11, 1949 (*Wheeldon v. Burrows*); (ii) The landlord having failed in this duty, the onus was upon him to establish the facts to prove, and prove clearly, that his case was an exception to the rule (*Aldridge v. Wright* [1929] 2 K.B. 117); (iii) The mere fact that the tenant knew at the date of the lease of August 11, 1949, that the landlord was using the outer walls of the demised premises for the display of the advertisements in question did not suffice to absolve the landlord from his duty of expressly reserving any rights in respect of them he intended to claim, or to take the case out of the general rule: see *Suffield v. Brown; Crossley & Sons Ltd v. Lightowler*.

Applying these principles to the present case, I ask myself whether the landlord has on the meagre facts proved discharged the onus which lies upon him of proving it an exception to the general rule. He can, so far as I can see, derive no assistance from the passage quoted above from Lord Parker's speech in the *Pwllbach Colliery* case. It might, I suppose, be said to have been in the contemplation of the parties that the landlord would continue to use the ground floor of the premises for the purposes of his business as a butcher and provision merchant, but it cannot in my view be contended that the maintenance during the term of the lease of his advertisement over the door was a necessary incident of the user so contemplated. This applies a fortiori to the "Brymay" advertisement, the display of which on the outer wall of the demised premises by the Borough Billposting Company as licensees of the landlord was so far as I can see not related in any way to the use or occupation of the ground floor for the existing or any other purpose. The transaction with the Borough Billposting Company was simply a hiring out for reward of part of an outer wall of the demised premises for use as an advertising or billposting site or station.

The mere fact that the tenant knew of the presence of the advertisements at the date when the lease of August 11, 1949, was granted being, as stated above, beside the point, nothing is left beyond the bare circumstance that the advertisements were not only present at the date of the grant but had been continuously present without objection by the tenant since the commencement of his original tenancy in 1939. Does this circumstance suffice to raise a necessary inference of an intention common to both parties at the date of the lease that the landlord should have reserved to him the right to maintain these advertisements throughout the twenty-one years' term thereby granted? I cannot see that it does. The most that can be said is that the facts are consistent with such a common intention. But that will not do. The landlord must surely show at least that the facts are not reasonably consistent with any other explanation. Here he manifestly fails. It may be that neither party ever applied his mind at all to the question whether the outer walls were included in or excluded from the original tenancy or the lease ultimately granted, or what their respective rights as to the use of such walls for any purpose might be. It may be that the tenant, so far as he applied his mind to the matter at all, merely refrained from objecting to the presence of the advertisements because, whether the landlord was within his rights in maintaining them or not, he, the tenant, did not for the time being think it worth his while to object. As to the landlord, he may have been under the erroneous impression that notwithstanding the tenancy and subsequently notwithstanding the lease, he was entitled to use the outer walls for advertising purposes. If so, his own mistake will not avail him, at all events in the absence of evidence that the tenant was aware of it. On the other hand, the landlord may have thought, when he came to grant the lease, that, since the tenant had never objected to the advertisements during all the ten years of his previous tenancy, it could be assumed that the tenant would not object in the future, and have preferred accordingly to let the matter rest at that rather than raise the question by claiming a reservation.

In short, I can hold nothing more established by the facts proved than permissive user of the outer walls by the landlord for the display of the advertisements during the original tenancy and thereafter from the granting of the lease until the tenant's objection in January, 1950; with nothing approaching grounds for inferring, as a matter of necessary inference, an intention common to both parties that such permissive user should be converted by the lease into a reservation to the landlord of equivalent rights throughout the twenty-one years' term thereby granted.

NOTE:

1. For recent applications of the test in *Re Webb's Lease*, see *Chaffe v. Kingsley* (1997) 77 P. & C.R. 281; *Peckham v. Ellison* (1998), *The Times*, December 4, 1998.

1.3 *Section 62 of the Law of Property Act 1925*

1.3.1 *The operation of section 62*   A further means of acquisition of easements is provided by section 62 of the Law of Property Act 1925, which reads words into a conveyance of land.

Law of Property Act 1925, s.62(1), (2)

General words implied in conveyances

62.—(1) A conveyance of land shall be deemed to include and shall by virtue of this Act operate to convey, with the land, all buildings, erections, fixtures, commons, hedges, ditches, fences, ways, waters, watercourses, liberties, privileges, easements, rights, and advantages whatsoever, appertaining or reputed to appertain to the land, or any part thereof, or, at the time of conveyance, demised, occupied, or enjoyed with, or reputed or known as part or parcel of or appurtenant to the land or any part thereof.

(2) A conveyance of land, having houses or other buildings thereon, shall be deemed to include and shall by virtue of this Act operate to convey, with the land, houses, or other buildings, all outhouses, erections, fixtures, cellars, areas, courts, courtyards, cisterns, sewers, gutters, drains, ways, passages, lights, watercourses, liberties, privileges, easements, rights, and advantages whatsoever, appertaining or reputed to appertain to the land, houses, or other buildings conveyed, or any of them, or any part thereof, or, at the time of conveyance, demised, occupied, or enjoyed with, or reputed or known as part or parcel of or appurtenant to, the land, houses, or other buildings conveyed, or any of them, or any part thereof.

NOTES:

1. For the application of section 62 to dispositions of registered land, see Land Registration Act 1925, ss.19(3), 22(3).

2. The operation of the section may be excluded by express contrary intention: section 62(4); but the contrary intention must be expressed in clear and unequivocal terms: see *Squarey v. Harris-Smith* (1981) 42 P. & C.R. 119, 129–130 *per* Oliver L.J.; *William Hill (Southern) Ltd v. Cabras Ltd* (1987) 54 P. & C.R. 42, 46 *per* Nourse L.J.; *Pretoria Warehousing Co. Ltd v. Shelton* [1993] E.G.C.S. 120; and see [1994] Conv. 238.

3. The section operates only on a "conveyance" of a legal estate as defined by section 205(1)(ii) of the Law of Property Act 1925. It therefore operates on a conveyance of the fee simple: *International Tea Stores Co. v. Hobbs* [1903] 2 Ch. 165; or on the creation or assignment of a lease: *Wright v. Macadam* [1949] 2 K.B. 744, *infra*, p. 652; *Goldberg v. Edwards* [1950] Ch. 247, *infra*, p. 655; but it does not operate where a contract for the conveyance of a legal estate results in the creation of an equitable interest only: *Borman v. Griffith* [1930] 1 Ch. 493, 497–499 *per* Maugham J.

4. There is House of Lords authority for the view that the section only operates where, prior to the conveyance in question, the alleged dominant land and servient land have been in separate ownership or occupation: *Sovmots Investments Ltd v. Secretary of State for the Environment* [1979] A.C. 144, *infra*, p. 660. However, there is some suggestion that the requirement of prior diversity of ownership or occupation need not be satisfied where the right claimed is continuous and apparent: *Long v. Gowlett* [1923] 2 Ch. 177, 203 *per* Sargant J., *infra* p. 657; and see Harpum (1977) 41 Conv. 415; [1979] Conv. 113; Thompson [1995] Conv. 239; [1997] Conv. 453. For criticism of both requirements, see Smith [1978] Conv. 449; [1979] Conv. 311.

5. In its terms the section would appear to operate to transfer automatically

the benefit of any existing easements enjoyed with the land conveyed or transferred: see, *e.g. Graham v. Philcox* [1984] Q.B. 747, *infra*, p. 661. However, the section has been construed more widely (and perhaps unexpectedly) so as to operate *to convert into legal easements* mere licences to use the land conveyed or transferred: *International Tea Stores Co. v. Hobbs* [1903] 2 Ch. 165; *Wright v. Macadam* [1949] 2 K.B. 744, *infra*, p. 652; *Goldberg v. Edwards* [1950] Ch. 247, *infra*, p. 655.

However, the right thus claimed as an easement must satisfy all the essential characteristics and other requirements of easements discussed above. On this ground, section 62 has been held not to create easements where the right claimed was in its nature incapable of existing as an easement: *Wright v. Macadam, supra*, 749–751 *per* Jenkins L.J.; *Phipps v. Pears* [1965] 1 Q.B. 76, 84 *per* Lord Denning M.R.; and where the person conveying the land was not a capable grantor: *Quicke v. Chapman* [1903] 1 Ch. 659, 668 *per* Collins M.R., 671 *per* Romer L.J. (purported grant by licensee); *MRA Engineering Ltd v. Trimster Co. Ltd* (1987) 56 P. & C.R. 1, 7 *per* Nourse L.J. (purported grant after transfer of property). Moreover, the courts have tended to exclude the operation of the section where the right claimed is of a purely temporary nature: *Green v. Ashco Horticulturist Ltd* [1966] 2 All E.R. 232, 239 *per* Cross J.; see also *Wright v. Macadam, supra*, 751–752 *per* Jenkins L.J.; *Goldberg v. Edwards, supra*, 255 *per* Evershed M.R.

The justice of this "metamorphic" effect of section 62 (see Tee [1998] Conv. 115) has been questioned: *Wright v. Macadam, supra*, 754–755 *per* Tucker L.J.; *Green v Ashco Horticulturist Ltd* [1966] 1 W.L.R. 889, 897 *per* Cross J.; *Dewsbury v Davies* (1992, unreported but cited in Tee [1998] Conv. 115, 119–120) *per* Fox L.J.; but there is no doubt as to the current law. In 1971 the Law Commission recommended that section 62 should be amended and that it should operate to confer on the purchaser only those rights which in all the circumstances it is reasonable to contemplate that the parties intended to be conferred: Law Commission Working Paper No. 36, *Transfer of Land: Appurtenant Rights* (1971), paras 87–95. Tee urges judicial reform: either that "rights" passed under the section should retain their essential nature (so that a revocable licence would continue to be revocable notwithstanding the intervening conveyance or transfer); or that, when construing the statutory general words, the courts should give appropriate weight to the intention of the parties, thereby reverting to the approach adopted in relation to non-statutory general words.

6. Although the point has little practical significance, views differ as to whether the operation of section 62 results in the acquisition of easements through express grant or implied grant. For judicial assertion that the section operates as an implied grant, see *MRA Engineering Ltd v. Trimster Co. Ltd* (1987) 56 P. & C.R. 1, 7 *per* Nourse L.J.; for judicial assertion that the section operates as an express grant, see *Broomfield v. Williams* [1897] 1 Ch. 602, 610 *per* Lindley L.J., 161 *per* Rigby L.J.; *Goldberg v. Edwards* [1950] Ch. 247, 255 *per* Evershed M.R. There is no apparent agreement among textbook authors: *Megarry & Wade* (5th ed., 1984) and *Gray* (2nd ed., 1993) include discussion of the section in the context of implied grant; *Megarry's*

Manual (7th ed., 1993) and *Cheshire & Burn* (15th ed., 1994) include discussion in the context of express grant.

Wright v. Macadam [1949] 2 K.B. 744

(CA, Tucker, Singleton and Jenkins L.JJ.)

In 1940 the defendant let a flat to the plaintiff for one week; but at the expiration of the week the plaintiff continued in occupation, pursuant to her rights under the Rent Restriction Acts. In 1941 the defendant gave the plaintiff permission to use a garden shed for the storage of coal. In 1943 the defendant granted a new tenancy to the plaintiff and her daughter for one year. Although the tenancy made no reference to the garden shed, the plaintiff continued to use it until 1947, when the defendant sought to charge extra rental for its use. The plaintiff claimed that she had acquired an easement under section 62.

JENKINS L.J.:

The question in the present case, therefore, is whether the right to use the coal shed was at the date of the letting of August 28, 1943, a liberty, privilege, easement, right or advantage appertaining or reputed to appertain, to the land, or any part thereof, or, at the time of the conveyance, demised, occupied, or enjoyed with the land—that is the flat—or any part thereof. It is enough for the plaintiffs' purposes if they can bring the right claimed within the widest part of the sub-section—that is to say, if they can show that the right was at the time of the material letting demised, occupied or enjoyed with the flat or any part thereof.

The predecessor of s.62 of the Act of 1925, in the shape of s.6 of the Act of 1881, has been the subject of a good deal of judicial discussion, and I think the effect of the cases can be thus summarised. First, the section is not confined to rights which, as a matter of law, were so annexed or appurtenant to the property conveyed at the time of the conveyance as to make them actual legally enforceable rights. Thus, on the severance of a piece of land in common ownership, the quasi-easements de facto enjoyed in respect of it by one part of the land over another will pass although, of course, as a matter of law, no man can have a right appendant or appurtenant to one part of his property exercisable by him over the other part of his property. Secondly, the right, in order to pass, need not be one to which the owner or occupier for the time being of the land has had what may be described as a permanent title. A right enjoyed merely by permission is enough. The leading authority for that proposition is the case of *International Tea Stores Co. v. Hobbs* [1903] 2 Ch. 165. That was a decision of Sir George Farwell as a judge of first instance. It was a case in which the defendant, who owned two houses, let one of them for business purposes and there had been a practice of giving permission to the successive managers of the property let to pass and re-pass with their servants and so forth across a yard which was part of the property and remained in the defendant's occupation. The part of the property which had been let was later sold to the tenants, nothing being said in the conveyance about the right of way. The purchasers claimed to exercise the right of way by virtue of s.6 of the Act of 1881. That claim was disputed, and the point was taken that it could not be a right which would pass under the implied general words inasmuch as it was only precariously enjoyed. The learned judge held that the fact that the way was permissive only was irrelevant for this purpose, and that by virtue of s.6 of the Act of 1881 the grant included a corresponding right of way in fee simple. Dealing with the question of licence or permission, the learned judge said this (at p. 171). "Unless I am prepared to say that in no case can a tenant obtain under the Conveyancing Act 1881 a right of way unless he has enjoyed it as of right, I must hold in this case that the fact of licence makes no difference. In all these cases the right of way must be either licensed or unlicensed. If it is unlicensed it would be at least as cogent an argument to say, 'True you went there, but it was precarious, because I could have sent a man to stop you or stopped you myself any day.' If it is by licence, it is precarious, of course, in the sense that the licence, being ex hypothesi revocable, might be revoked at any time; but if there be degrees of precariousness, the latter is less precarious than the former. But, in my opinion, precariousness has nothing to do with this sort of case, where a privilege which is by its nature known to the law—namely, a right of way— has been in fact enjoyed. Lord Coleridge's argument was founded upon a misconception of a judgment of mine in *Burrows v. Lang* [1901] 2 Ch. 502, where I was using the argument of precariousness to show that the right which was desired to be enjoyed there was one which was unknown to the law—namely, to take water if and whenever the defendant chose to put water into a particular pond; such a right does not exist at law; but a right of way is well known to the law".

That case has been followed or cited with approval in subsequent cases, in particular in *Lewis v. Meredith* [1913] 1 Ch. 571, where Neville J. referred to it, saying: "I come to the conclusion that at the date of the grant the water was being, and had for a long time been, used for the tan pit and the mason's yard. Easement or right in the strict sense there could not be, for the common ownership precluded the acquisition of any right or easement by the occupiers, but *International Tea Stores Company v. Hobbs* shows that 'a right' permissive at the date of the grant may become a legal right upon the grant by the force of the general words in s.6 of the Conveyancing Act 1881. From this point of view the circumstances under which the quasi right was enjoyed become immaterial so long as it was actually enjoyed and was of a nature which could be granted, that is to say, a right known to the law: see *Burrows v. Lang*".

Again in *White v. Williams* [1922] 1 K.B. 727, Younger L.J. (as he then was) cited with apparent approval *International Tea Stores Co. v. Hobbs*. The relevant passage in his judgment, is this (at p. 740): "I doubt whether we can enter upon this question in view of the finding of the county court judge; but even if no more than an intermittent and temporary user had been exercised, the right would nevertheless in my opinion be included within these words in s.6, because it is a right known to the law and, that being so, it matters not, so far as s.6 of the Conveyancing Act is concerned, whether the user is continuous and permanent or permissive and precarious: *International Tea Stores Co. v. Hobbs*".

There is, therefore, ample authority for the proposition that a right in fact enjoyed with property will pass on a conveyance of the property by virtue of the grant to be read into it under s. 62, even although down to the date of the conveyance the right was exercised by permission only, and therefore was in that sense precarious.

The next proposition deducible from the cases is the one laid down in *Burrows v. Land*, which has been referred to in some of the passages I have already read. It is that the right in question must be a right known to the law. In *Burrows v. Lang* it was held that a so-called right to take, for the purposes of watering cattle, so much water, if any, as might happen to be left in an artificial watercourse after the owner of the watercourse had taken what he required for his own purposes, was not such a right. A certain amount of confusion has been introduced into the decision on this aspect of the case by the circumstance that some of the learned judges have used the word "precarious" in describing rights of a kind unknown to the law, and in particular the expression was so used by Farwell J. in the case of *Burrows v. Lang*; but in this context the precariousness enters into the character of the right as distinct from the title to the right. The right is precarious in the sense that, to take the example of the surplus water, there may be no water at all, and that the right is in itself liable to be defeated in that way. It is necessary to keep clearly in mind the distinction between "precariousness" in the sense in which it is used in relation to quasi rights of that description, and precariousness of title as used in relation to a permissively exercised right. For the purposes of s.62, it is only necessary that the right should be one capable of being granted at law, or, in other words, a right known to the law. If it is a right of that description it matters not, as the *International Tea Stores* case shows, that it has been in fact enjoyed by permission only. The reason for that is clear, for, on the assumption that the right is included or imported into the parcels of the conveyance by virtue of s.62, the grant under the conveyance supplies what one may call the defect in title, and substitutes a new title based on the grant.

There is one other point to be mentioned. A further exception has been recognised in cases in which there could in the circumstances of the case have been no expectation that the enjoyment of the right could be other than temporary. That exception was recognised by Cotton L.J. in *Birmingham, Dudley & District Banking Company v. Ross* (1889) 38 Ch.D. 295. The learned Lord Justice was dealing with a situation of this kind. There had been a building scheme under which an area of land was to be developed and built up. Somebody took a lease of one of the houses at a time when an adjoining plot only had built upon it old buildings of less height than those contemplated by the scheme; but it was well known to everybody that the intention was, and the building scheme demanded, that this plot should be built upon to a greater height. The question for the court was whether the lessor of the houses would be committing a derogation from grant in building on the adjoining plot inasmuch as the effect of that would be to obscure to some extent the light enjoyed by the lessee of the building already erected next door. It was held in those circumstances, as one might expect, that there was no derogation from grant and there was no such enjoyment of the light over the vacant plot as would bring s.6 of the Act of 1881 into operation. The learned Lord Justice said this (at p. 307): "Therefore, I think it could not be said that the light coming over the low building to these windows could be considered as enjoyed with it within the meaning of this section. The light did in fact at the time come over that building; but it came over it under such circumstances as to show that there could be no expectation of its continuance. It had not been enjoyed in fact for any long period; and in my opinion it was enjoyed under such circumstances, known to both parties, as could not make it light enjoyed within the meaning of that section". The learned Lord Justice, I think, meant no more than this, that it was knowledge common to both parties that the existing low building was going to be replaced by a higher one and, that being so, the fortuitous access of extra light to the lessee's building while the scheme was being carried to completion could not be regarded as an enjoyment of light which would pass to the lessee a right to have it continued in the same degree.

I think those are all the cases to which I can usefully refer, and applying the principles deducible from them to the present case one finds, I think, this. First of all, on the evidence the coal shed was used by Mrs Wright by the permission of Mr Macadam, but *International Tea Stores Co. v. Hobbs* shows that that does not prevent s.62 from applying, because permissive as the right may have been it was in fact enjoyed.

Next, the right was, as I understand it, a right to use the coal shed in question for the purpose of storing such coal as might be required for the domestic purposes of the flat. In my judgment that is a right or easement which the law will clearly recognise, and it is a right or easement of a kind which could readily be included in a lease or conveyance by the insertion of appropriate words in the parcels. This, therefore, is not a case in which a title to a right unknown to the law is claimed by virtue of s.62. Nor is it a case in which it can be said to have been in the contemplation of the parties that the enjoyment of the right should be purely temporary. No limit was set as to the time during which the coal shed could continue to be used. Mr Macadam simply gave his permission; that permission was acted on; and the use of the coal shed in fact went on down to August 28, 1943, and thereafter down to 1947. Therefore, applying to the facts of the present case the principles which seem to be deducible from the authorities, the conclusion to which I have come is that the right to use the coal shed was at the date of the letting of August 28, 1943, a right enjoyed with the top floor flat, within the meaning of s.62 of the Law of Property Act 1925, with the result that (as no contrary intention was expressed in the document) the right in question must be regarded as having passed by virtue of that letting, just as it would have passed if it had been mentioned in express terms in cl. 1, which sets out the subject-matter of the lease.

NOTES:

1. For comment, see (1950) 66 L.Q.R. 302.
2. For discussion of easements of storage, see *supra*, p. 627.

Goldberg v. Edwards [1950] 1 Ch. 247

(CA, Evershed M.R., Cohen and Asquith L.JJ.)

The first defendant was the fee simple owner of a house and an annexe. Access to the annexe was either by an outside passage or by a passage through the house. In January 1947 the first defendant agreed to lease the annexe to the plaintiffs and to allow them a right of access through the house. The plaintiffs went into possession of the annexe; but it was not until July 1947 that a formal lease was executed granting to the plaintiffs a two-year term (with an option to renew for a further two years) from January 1947. In January 1949 the first defendant leased the house to the second defendant, who barred the plaintiffs' access through the house. The plaintiffs sought an injunction to prevent the defendants from interfering with their access, which they claimed as an easement under section 62.

EVERSHED M.R.:

The various rights here claimed are these: first, a right for the plaintiffs personally to pass through the front door and along the passage of the house. Secondly, a right to maintain a signboard and an electric bell; thirdly, as a necessary corollary to that, a right for the plaintiffs' customers to use the front door and passage; and, fourthly, a right to use it for the passage of goods. As regards the signboard and the bell, it is to be observed that there is no indication of that matter in the pleadings or in the form of injunction. I need not pursue it, because the finding of the Vice-Chancellor shows quite clearly, to my mind, that everything except the plaintiffs' right to come and go via this route was expressly limited to such time as the landlord should occupy the house herself. In other words, it was a privilege which she herself allowed so long as she was there, because it did not interfere with her own affairs and business. It was clear that she was not making that privilege any part of the bargain between herself and the tenants of the annexe. It is plain, in my view, that these rights, other than the plaintiffs' personal right of passage, were not within the language of s.62 so as to be covered by the demise to them.

That leaves only the personal right. As I have indicated, my main difficulty has been in deciding whether that was similarly limited or limited in some other way so as not properly to be capable of being annexed to the subject-matter of the demise. Having regard to his judgment, I think that I am bound to regard the view of the judge as having been that, in contra-distinction to the other rights, it was intended to be something which the plaintiffs should enjoy qua lessees during the term of the demise, though it should not be enjoyed by their servants, workmen or any other persons with their authority. Therefore, I think, to quote Jenkins L.J. in the recent case of *Wright v. Macadam* [1949] 2 K.B. 744, 752: "It is a right or easement of a kind which could be readily included in a lease or conveyance by the insertion of appropriate words in the parcels". What those would be I will state later, because, in the view which I take, it is necessary to see that the injunction or declaration to which the plaintiffs may be entitled is properly formulated.

Wright v. Macadam was decided after the Vice-Chancellor gave judgment in this case. That is of some importance, because he considered *Birmingham, Dudley & District Banking Co. v. Ross* (1888) 38 Ch. D. 295, and *International Tea Stores Co. v. Hobbs* [1903] 2 Ch. 165. He was of opinion that *Birmingham, Dudley & District Banking Co. v. Ross* was nearer to the present case than *International Tea Stores Co. v. Hobbs*. But I think that it is the language of Farwell J. in the latter case, expressly approved by this court in *Wright v. Macadam*, which, on a proper analysis, is the more applicable here. On the hypothesis of fact which I am making, the privilege granted here was not temporary, like, for instance, a temporary right of light when it is obvious that buildings shortly to be erected will obscure it. The present privilege is in some ways indeed not dissimilar to that which in *Wright v. Macadam* was held to be covered by s.62, namely, a privilege for the tenant to use a shed for storing her coal. I therefore think that, if the right which I have defined was one which was being enjoyed at the time of the conveyance, it is covered by s.62.

That therefore leaves the final point: what is the "time of conveyance" within the meaning of s.62, sub-ss.1 and 2? The arrangement about this use of the passage appears to have been made at various dates, the last of which was January 13, 1947. The plaintiffs went into occupation of the annexe on January 18, 1947. The fitting of the bell and signboard took place after that. Several months passed (why, I know not, and it is quite immaterial) before the lease was executed on July 10, 1947, though the term was expressed to run from January 18. It is plain that before July 10 there was no written instrument whatever. Possession may no doubt have been attributable to an oral agreement of which, having regard to the position, specific performance might have been granted; but I fail to find any instrument in writing within the meaning of s.62 before the lease of July 10. It seems to me, therefore, that the phrase "at the time of conveyance" must mean in this case July 10. I am unable to accept the view that one should construe that as meaning at the time when the term granted by the lease is stated to have begun. On July 10, 1947, under the privilege granted, this right to ingress and egress was being enjoyed in fact. As I have held, though it is limited to the lessees themselves and does not extend to other persons, it would be capable of formulation and incorporation as a term of the lease, and it is, in my judgment, covered by s.62. To that extent, therefore, but to that limited extent only, the plaintiffs are entitled to succeed.

On that point alone I have come to a different conclusion from the Vice-Chancellor, who had not the assistance of *Wright v. Macadam*, which may perhaps have given a more general ambit to s.62 than it had before. I am anxious to guard myself from saying that rights, which were purely personal in the strict sense of that word, would necessarily in every case be covered by s.62. I base myself on the view that the right here given, though limited to the lessees, was given to them qua lessees; and, as such, it seems to me, it is covered by the principle of *Wright v. Macadam* and by s.62. The Vice-Chancellor was of the opinion that the right date to consider was January 18. With all respect to him, I have come to a different conclusion: I think that the words "at the time of conveyance" apply to no other date than July 10. I do not find that result startling or surprising, where a landlord chooses to let his tenant in six months before the grant of a lease and allows him to exercise certain privileges. He can always protect himself, if he wants to, by the terms of the lease. Further, it has to be assumed that the terms of the bargain are intended to be in accordance with the rights or privileges which the tenant is allowed to enjoy in fact. Therefore, I do not feel that there is any difficulty in the way of the my construction. On the other hand, there might be considerable difficulty in the way of the opposite view where, as sometimes happens, especially in the case of building agreements, a tenant may be let into possession long before the relevant lease, on the understanding that he does a great deal of work himself.

In my judgment the right of the plaintiffs, and it is the only right which they have established, is a right in themselves alone as lessees, and not in their servants or workmen or persons authorised by them, to pass through the defined passage to and from their works. That right, I think, should be exercised only during reasonable business hours. It is convenient that that should be stated by way of recital, and I would prefer, in the circumstances, not to go further into the question of what precise hours were intended to be covered by the privilege. That being the right, there should be a declaration to that effect. I do not believe that there is any necessity for an injunction. It may be added that the tenancy will expire in fact in about thirteen months' time, so that it is all less important than it might otherwise have been; but, if there is an assignment to a limited company, the result would appear to be that nobody could then exercise the right at all. I am hopeful, from the attitude adopted on behalf of the defendants, that there is here no lack of neighbourly spirit, so that matters will not be found difficult in practice. For the reasons and to the extent stated, the plaintiffs are entitled to the right which I have defined.

NOTE:

1. An alternative claim to the easement of way based on implied grant under the rule in *Wheeldon v. Burrows* failed on the ground that access through the house was not "necessary for the reasonable enjoyment" (*Borman v. Griffith* [1930] 1 Ch. 493, 499 *per* Maugham J.) or "necessary for the reasonable and convenient enjoyment" (*Gale on Easements* (11th ed.), p. 165) of the annexe. Previous tenants of the annexe had "apparently enjoyed [the annexe] both reasonably and conveniently" although they had been restricted to the outside access.

Long v. Gowlett [1923] 2 Ch. 177

(Ch D., Sargant J.)

In 1909 the owner of land adjoining the River Granta in Cambridgeshire divided the land into two plots and conveyed them by contemporaneous sales: the first lot to the defendant; and the second lot to the predecessor in title of the plaintiff. While in common ownership, the owner had been accustomed to go on to the second lot and to carry out work on the river bank so as to ensure the free flow of water to the mill on the first plot. The defendant claimed an easement (by virtue of section 6 of the Conveyancing Act 1881, the predecessor of section 62) to enter the second lot for that same purpose but the plaintiff sought an injunction and damages for trespass.

SARGANT J.:
The argument is not based in any way on the existence of any continuous and apparent easement existing over Lot 2 in favour of Lot 1; indeed, any such claim would be incompatible with the evidence, which clearly establishes that there was no defined way at all along the south bank. The claim is founded upon there having been a statutory introduction into the conveyance to the defendant of words equivalent to or identical with those either expressly contained or statutorily introduced in the corresponding conveyances in such cases as *James v. Plant* (1836) 4 Ad. & E. 749; *Watts v. Kelson* (1871) L.R. 6 Ch. 166; *Bayley v. Great Western Ry. Co.* (1884) 26 Ch. D. 434; and *White v. Williams* [1922] 1 K.B. 727.

It is, therefore, necessary for the purpose of dealing with the matter on this footing to consider whether, during the common ownership and occupation of Lot 1 and Lot 2 by Mr Nichols and his widow, and therefore at the date of the conveyance, there was a "privilege, easement, right or advantage" of the kind now claimed, which can properly be said to have been "demised, occupied or enjoyed" with Lot 1 over Lot 2. It is very difficult to see how this can have been the case. No doubt the common owner and occupier did in fact repair the bank of Lot 2, and cut the weeds there; and no doubt also this repair and cutting would enure not solely for the benefit of Lot 2 (which comprised, amongst other things, a lawn tennis court), so as to prevent its being flooded, but also and very likely to a greater extent for the benefit of Lot 1. But there is nothing to indicate that the acts done on Lot 2 were done otherwise than in the course of the ownership and occupation of Lot 2, or that they were by way of using a "privilege, easement or advantage" over Lot 2 in connection with Lot 1. The common owner and occupier of Whiteacre and Blackacre may in fact use Blackacre as an alternative and more convenient method of communication between Whiteacre and a neighbouring village. But it has never been held, and would I think be contrary to principle to hold, that (in default of there being a made road over Blackacre forming a continuous and apparent means of communication) a sale and conveyance of Whiteacre alone would carry a right to pass over Blackacre in the same way in which the common owner had been accustomed to pass. As it seems to me, in order that there may be a "privilege, easement or advantage" enjoyed with Whiteacre over Blackacre so as to pass under the statute, there must be something done on Blackacre not due to or comprehended within the general rights of an occupying owner of Blackacre, but of such a nature that it is attributable to a privilege, easement, right or advantage, however precarious, which arises out of the ownership or occupation of Whiteacre, altogether apart from the ownership or occupation of Blackacre. And it is difficult to see how, when there is a common ownership of both Whiteacre and Blackacre, there can be any such relationship between the two closes as (apart from the case of continuous and apparent easements or that of a way of necessity) would be necessary to create a "privilege, easement, right or advantage" within the words of s.6, subs. 2, of the statute. For this purpose it would seem that there must be some diversity of ownership or occupation of the two closes sufficient to refer the act or acts relied on not to mere occupying ownership, but to some advantage or privilege (however far short of a legal right) attaching to the owner or occupier of Whiteacre as such and de facto exercised over Blackacre. Let me illustrate my meaning from the latest case on the subject—namely, *White v. Williams.* Assume that the facts there had been that the grantor of Tydden Mawr had been the absolute owner in possession both of that upland farm and of the 772 acres of the adjoining mountain which were called Craig Goch, and that he had been accustomed for many years past, and as a regular practice, to remove his sheep from Tydden Mawr and to depasture them on Craig Goch during certain months of the year; it seems to me indisputable that, on a sale and conveyance of Tydden Mawr alone, the purchaser would not have obtained from the words of the statute the right to take his sheep from Tydden Mawr and graze them on Craig Goch during the months in question. And I understood Mr Greene not to contend otherwise. The vendor would have been enjoying in fact at the date of the conveyance the advantage of taking his sheep from Tydden Mawr and grazing them on Craig Goch; but that advantage would have been one that he possessed and enjoyed as the owner and occupier of Craig Goch, and not as an advantage enjoyed with or as an incident of his ownership and possession of Tydden Mawr.

Mr Greene for the defendant was challenged to produce from the very many cases in which, on a conveyance of Whiteacre, an easement over Blackacre has been held to pass under the statutory words or their equivalent, a single case in which both the closes in question had been in common ownership and occupation, or in which there had not been an actual enjoyment over Blackacre on the part of an owner or occupier of Whiteacre who was not the owner and occupier of Blackacre. And neither from among the cases cited to me, nor from any other case in the books, was he able (with one solitary exception) to produce such a case as required. The exception, however, is one of high authority—namely, that of *Broomfield v. Williams* [1897] 1 Ch. 602—and it is necessary to examine it with some attention.

In that case the common owner of a house and of adjoining land over which light had in fact been received through the windows of the house, sold and conveyed the house by a conveyance after the date of the Conveyancing Act 1881, but retained the adjoining land. It was held by the Court of Appeal that, although the retained land was marked on the plan on the conveyance as "building land", the vendor was not at liberty subsequently to build on the retained land so as to interfere substantially with the access of light to the windows of the house. A. L. Smith L.J., it is true, based his judgment solely on the principle that the grantor was not entitled to derogate from his grant; and this was quite sufficient to support the actual decision. But the other two members of the Court relied mainly, if not exclusively, on the express words of s.6, subs. 2, of the Act; and the decision is, therefore, undoubtedly binding on me with regard to the access of light, and also with regard to any other "privilege, easement, right or advantage" that is on the same footing as "light".

But such an easement or advantage as is now claimed is, in my judgment, very different from light, or a right to light. The access of light to a window over adjoining land is a physical fact plainly visible to any one buying a house. It is extremely similar to a continuous and apparent easement. It is mentioned in the subsection in the midst of a number of physical features ending with the word "watercourses"; and the special position of light to an existing window as compared with other easements is fully recognised in the Prescription Act 1832, which makes the acquisition of an easement of light depend on the enjoyment of the light simpliciter, and not, as in the case of other easements, on enjoyment as of right. The fact, therefore, that the inclusion of light in the subject matter of conveyance in s.6, subs. 2, has been held to entitle the grantee to the light coming to an existing window, does not necessarily involve the further inclusion of imperceptible rights or advantages, corresponding with intermittent practice or user as between two tenements of the common owner and occupier of both. Such an intermittent and non-apparent user or practice stands, in my judgment, on a completely different footing from the visible access of light to an existing window.

The importance of such a distinction is specially obvious in a case like the present, where there is a contemporaneous sale by a common owner to two separate purchasers of adjoining lots completely divided by a physical boundary. If the contention of the defendant is correct, it would be necessary in any such case for the purchaser to inquire how the common owner and occupier had been accustomed to make use of each close in connection with the other. Would the plaintiff, for instance, in this case be entitled, as against the defendant, to an alternative way over Lot 1 to reach Lot 2, because while both lots were in common ownership and occupation, it was the practice of Mr and Mrs Nichols by way of Lot 1 to repair the south bank of Lot 2? Any number of similar puzzles would arise, if the law were as the defendant would have it. The fact that the common owner and occupier sells two adjoining closes separately is, in my mind, a negation of the intention to preserve access between them: compare such a case as *Midland Ry. Co. v. Gribble* [1895] 2 Ch. 827.

The only two exceptions to this rule appear to be those of ways of necessity and of continuous and apparent easements. Had the general words of s.6, subs. 2, any such effect as is suggested by the defendant—and it must be remembered that these words were not new, but represented conveyancing practice for many years previously—it is difficult, if not impossible, to understand how there have not been numerous cases in which, on a severance of two closes, a subsisting practice by the common owner and occupier of both has not been given effect to by way of legal easement as a result of general words of this kind.

NOTES:

1. *Long v. Gowlett* was analysed by Ungoed-Thomas J. in *Ward v. Kirkland* [1967] Ch. 194, 227–230. He interpreted the case as turning on the

distinction between (i) the enjoyment of an advantage exclusively for the purposes of the alleged dominant land, which could be transferred or created by section 62, and (ii) the enjoyment of an advantage which might be attributable to the possession and ownership of the alleged servient land, which could not be transferred or created by section 62. If that is correct, it would seem that diversity of ownership or occupation would be *sufficient but not necessary* to establish that the advantage was distinct from the enjoyment of the alleged servient land and thus potentially to activate section 62. See also *Wright v. Macadam* [1949] 2 K.B. 744, 748 *per* Jenkins L.J.

2. The requirement of diversity of ownership or occupation was approved in *Sovmots Investments Ltd v. Secretary of State for the Environment* [1979] A.C. 144. The appellants were the developers and lessees of Centre Point, a complex of offices, retail shops and maisonettes in central London. The maisonettes remained unoccupied for five years until 1972, when Camden LBC made a compulsory purchase order. Although the order made no mention of various ancillary rights (including rights of passage for water, electricity and gas), the question arose whether those rights were acquired as easements, *inter alia*, by virtue of section 62. Lord Wilberforce stated (at 169):

[S]ection 62 does not fit this case. The reason is that when land is under one ownership one cannot speak in any intelligible sense of rights, or privileges, or easements being exercised over one part for the benefit of another. Whatever the owner does, he does as owner and, until a separation occurs, of ownership or at least of occupation, the condition for the existence of rights, etc., does not exist: see *Bolton v. Bolton* (1879) 11 Ch. D. 968, 970 *per* Fry J. and *Long v. Gowlett* [1923] 2 Ch. 177, 189, 198 *per* Sargant J., in my opinion a correct decision.

A separation of ownership, in a case like the present, will arise on the conveyance of one of the parts (*e.g.* the maisonettes), but this separation cannot be projected back to the stage of the compulsory purchase order so as by anticipation to bring into existence rights not existing in fact.

Lord Wilberforce did not refer to the possible exception to the requirement of diversity of ownership or occupation, namely where the right is continuous and apparent, referred to in *Long v. Gowlett* [1923] 2 Ch. 177, 203 *per* Sargant J.

3. No requirement of diversity of ownership or occupation was imposed in *Broomfield v. Williams* [1897] 1 Ch. 602; but that decision was distinguished in *Long v. Gowlett* [1923] 2 Ch. 177, 202–203 *per* Sargant J., in *Sovmots Investments Ltd v. Secretary of State for the Environment* [1979] A.C. 144, 176 *per* Lord Edmund-Davies, and in *Payne v. Inwood* (1996) 74 P. & C.R. 42, 48–51 *per* Roch L.J., on the ground that easements of light are *sui generis*. But Thompson [1997] Conv. 453 argues that the rationale for the exception of easements of light would encompass all continuous and apparent easements.

4. For criticism of the requirement of diversity of ownership or occupation prior to the decision in *Sovmots Investments Ltd v. Secretary of State for the Environment*, see Jackson (1966) 30 Conv. 340. For discussion of the requirements of section 62 in the light of the decision, see Harpum (1977) 41

Conv. 415, [1979] Conv. 113, who argues that, even where there is prior diversity of occupation, section 62 should only operate where the right claimed as an easement is apparent; Smith [1978] Conv. 449, [1979] Conv. 311, who argues that section 62 "should operate to transform all rights 'of the nature of easements' into easements on the sale of part, provided they are properly appurtenant to that part. The only questions then to be considered would be whether the right claimed is capable of being an easement and whether it was enjoyed with the land conveyed at the time of the conveyance".

Graham v. Philcox [1984] Q.B. 747

(CA, May and Purchas L.JJ.)

Maples owned a plot of land comprising a large house with a garden and a coach house. In 1960 he leased the first floor of the coach house, together with a right of way for all purposes across the land, to Braithwaite for five years; in 1963 the lease was assigned to Devaney. In 1975 Wilcox acquired the freehold of the coach house, subject to Devaney's continuing statutory tenancy of the first floor. In 1977, by which time the large house had been converted into semi-detached houses, Maples' executors conveyed the freehold of one of the houses to the defendants, subject to the right of way granted to the tenant of the first floor of the coach house. Later in 1977 the freehold of the coach house was acquired by the plaintiffs, subject to Devaney's tenancy. The plaintiffs subsequently persuaded Devaney to give up his flat, since when they occupied the coach house as a single dwelling. The defendants refused to permit the plaintiffs to use the right of way. The plaintiffs claimed that they had acquired an easement under section 62.

MAY L.J.:
The plaintiffs' case is that the right of way in dispute was an easement enjoyed and used by Devaney at the time of the conveyance of the coach house to Wilcox. By virtue of section 62(2) that conveyance operated to convey that right of way to Wilcox, who conveyed it to the plaintiffs' predecessors in title, who in turn conveyed it to the plaintiffs. Counsel submitted that this result flowed from the operation of the clear meaning of the subsection and it was what the judge described at any rate at first sight as a logical and simple approach. However, in the result, he rejected the argument. In relation to the conveyance by Maples' executors to Wilcox he said:

"The land was sold by personal representatives. The right of way was not enjoyed by them and it was not part of the property that they were enjoying. The right of way was totally a subject matter of the lease. So far as the purchaser was concerned he also was not enjoying the right of way and he had no right over the right of way as long as the lease continued. Neither the transferor nor the transferee were actually enjoying the easement."

A little later in his judgment he summarised his view in this way:

"On the general proposition I have come to the conclusion that so far as the right of way is concerned this was granted by the lease and came to an end upon Devaney's departure. Thereafter the right of way did not subsist independently of the lease or dependently on section 62 of the Law of Property Act."

It was on these grounds that the judge dismissed the plaintiffs' claim in the action.

In this court, Mr Reid on the plaintiffs' behalf again relied on what he submitted was the clear meaning of section 62(2). He contended that as the result of that statutory provision the conveyance operated to pass to Wilcox and thus to his successors in title the easement over 6A, Hungershall Park which I have described. Counsel submitted that the judge's approach started from a consideration of the user of the way *by the vendor*, which was incorrect, and thus he reached the wrong conclusion at the end. What the judge ought to have considered under section 62(2) was the use of the relevant way *with the land*.

In support of his submission, Mr Reid referred us to a number of authorities, among them *International Tea Stores Co. v. Hobbs* [1903] 2 Ch. 165, where Farwell J. said, at p. 172:

> "The real truth is that you do not consider the question of title to use, but the question of fact of user; you have to inquire whether the way has in fact been used, not under what title has it been used, although you must of course take into consideration all the circumstances of the case. ..."

In addition, in *Lewis v. Meredith* [1913] 1 Ch. 571, 579, Neville J. was considering the predecessor of section 62(2), namely section 6 of the Conveyancing Act 1881, and said:

> "Easement or right in the strict sense there could not be, for the common ownership precluded the acquisition of any right or easement by the occupiers, but *International Tea Stores Co. v. Hobbs* shows that 'a right' permissive at the date of the grant may become a legal right upon the grant by force of the general words in section 6 of the Conveyancing Act 1881. From this point of view the circumstances under which the quasi right was enjoyed became immaterial so long as it was actually enjoyed and was of a nature which could be granted, that is to say, a right known to the law: ..."

Both these cases were cited with approval in the judgments in this court in the later case of *Wright v. Macadam* [1949] 2 K.B. 744. In relation to the instant appeal, the facts of that case are of some interest. The defendant landlord let a flat comprising two rooms and the usual offices to Mrs Wright, one of the plaintiffs, for one week. She remained in occupation thereafter under the provisions of the Rent Restriction Acts and some two or three months later the landlord gave her permission to use a garden shed at the premises to store her coal. This state of affairs continued for about two and a half years and then the landlord granted a new tenancy for one year of the flat with an additional room to Mrs Wright and her daughter. The agreement creating the tenancy, which was under hand only, made no reference to the coal shed, but Mrs Wright and her daughter continued to use it for another four years until the defendant asked them to pay a small extra amount for its use. It seems from the report that Mrs Wright herself would have been prepared to do so, but her daughter was strenuously opposed to any such arrangement. When the defendant in consequence tried to stop Mrs Wright and her daughter from using the coal shed they brought the proceedings which ultimately came before the Court of Appeal. On the particular question which is material in the present case, this court there held that Mrs Wright and her daughter were entitled to continue to use the coal shed because when the new tenancy was granted, which was a "conveyance" for the purposes of section 62(2), the use of the coal shed was then being enjoyed with the original flat, which was part of the three rooms the subject of the fresh demise. Consequently section 62(2) applied so that the new tenancy operated to pass to the tenant not only the three rooms but also the right to use the coal shed.

Mr Godfrey on behalf of the defendants sought to support the judge's judgment principally on a basis which for my part I do not think was argued below; at least it finds little or no reference in the judgment. At the outset of the hearing of this appeal Mr Godfrey sought leave to file a respondent's notice out of time, which we granted.

His principal submission was that as the dominant tenement for the benefit of which the way is now claimed, namely the coach house, is not the same as and is indeed greater than the dominant tenement for the benefit of which the way was originally granted, namely only the upper flat in the coach house, therefore the plaintiffs cannot use that way now when the coach house is now one dwelling and the original two flats which it comprised have been combined into one. He referred us to the quotation from the judgment of Romer L.J. in *Harris v. Flower and Sons* (1904) 74 L.J.Ch. 127, 132, which is quoted in *Gale on Easements*, 14th ed. (1972), at p. 282:

"If a right of way be granted for the enjoyment of close A, the grantee, because he owns or acquires close B, cannot use the way in substance for passing over close A to close B."

There are similar passages in the judgments of Vaughan Williams and Cozens-Hardy L.JJ. in the same case. Mr Godfrey also relied on the decisions of Warrington J. in *Ankerson v. Connelly* [1906] 2 Ch. 644 and Kekewich J. in *Milner's Safe Co. Ltd v. Great Northern and City Railway Co.* [1907] 1 Ch. 208. Mr Godfrey submitted further that if one substantially alters a dominant tenement, an easement theretofore enjoyed with it can no longer be used, because by the alterations one has increased the burden of the use on the servient tenement. The easement is consequently lost, or at least suspended temporarily: thus in the present case the plaintiffs must accept that they cannot enforce their use of the disputed right of way for so long as the coach house remains one dwelling. Mr Godfrey also referred us to *Allan v. Gomme* (1840) 11 A. & E. 759 and submitted that alterations which in truth destroy the identity of the original dominant tenement, or which so affect its character as to make it no longer a tenement of the nature for the purpose of which the original easement was granted, create a situation in which the continued user of the way is either excessive in quantity or excessive as an activity not covered by the terms of the original grant, and the result is thus the extinguishment or at least the suspension of the easement.

However, I doubt whether any excessive user, at least of a discontinuous easement, in whatever respect the user may be excessive, will ever of itself bring to an end or indeed suspend such an easement: see *Gale on Easements*, 14th ed., pp. 346, 347. The owner of the servient tenement upon which, ex hypothesi, the excessive burden is placed is entitled to have that excessive user restrained. The fact that a court may grant an appropriate injunction or make a declaration to this end does not in my judgment either extinguish or suspend the easement. Provided that the owner of the dominant tenement subsequently reverts to lawful use of the easement, his prior excessive use of it is then irrelevant.

In my opinion the statement of Romer L.J. in *Harris v. Flower and Sons* (1904) 74 L.J.Ch. 127, 132, of the relevant principle of law which I have quoted must be considered in the context of the facts of that particular case. Having stated the proposition, Romer L.J. then went on to say: "The question is whether what the defendant does or claims the right to do comes within the proposition I have stated". He then went on to discuss the intended new user of the way in that case and concluded, at p. 133:

"That would substantially enlarge the grant of the right of way. The servient tenement is not obliged to submit to the carrying of building materials for the purpose I have indicated; and other instances might easily be given which would result in using the right of way for purposes of the land coloured white, and not for the true and proper enjoyment of the land to which the way was appurtenant."

In none of the judgments in any of the cases to which Mr Godfrey referred us is there suggestion that a mere alteration of a dominant tenement to which a right of way may be appurtenant is sufficient to extinguish it, or indeed to affect the entitlement to its use unless as the result of that alteration the extent of the user is thereby increased.

In my opinion, therefore, the mere alteration of the coach house into one dwelling cannot have had any effect upon the existence of the right of way. It should be borne in mind that there was no evidence whatever before the judge that the actual or anticipated user by the plaintiffs of the way was in any way excessive, either in quantity or quality.

Further, I do not think that on this issue any real distinction can be drawn between the instant case on the one hand and *Wright v. Macadam* [1949] 2 K.B. 744 on the other. In the latter case also the right for which the plaintiffs contended had, at the date of the conveyance relied on for the purposes of section 62(2), been enjoyed by the occupier of only part of the whole premises in respect of which the continued enjoyment of the right was claimed in the action.

Mr Godfrey then pointed to and compared some parts of some of the conveyancing documents to which I have referred in an attempt to support an argument based upon section 62(4) of the Act, that an intention appeared, either expressly or by necessary implication, in the conveyance to Wilcox of 5 November 1975 that section 62(2) should not apply to it. I intend no disrespect to Mr Godfrey when I say that I am satisfied that this point is really unarguable on the facts and documents in this case and I do not propose to deal with it in any further detail.

Finally, Mr Godfrey submitted that if, contrary to his primary submission, the right of way still subsisted, then it did so only for the benefit of the first floor of the coach house. For the reasons I have already given and in the light again of the decision in *Wright v. Macadam*, I disagree.

In my judgment the judge was, with respect, wrong in law in the approach that he adopted. The fundamental issue in this case was whether the right of way in dispute "was enjoyed with" at least part of the land and buildings conveyed to Wilcox in 1975. Where a transferor of land is the same person as the owner of an adjoining servient tenement, over which part of the land transferred enjoys a right of way at the time of the transfer, then in my opinion the effect of section 62(2) is indeed to enlarge the right in the sense that it thereafter enures for the benefit of the whole of the land transferred. If one makes appropriate substitutions for some of the words in section 62(2) and omits immaterial parts for the purposes of the present case the subsection can be rewritten in this way: "The conveyance (dated 5 November 1975) of the coach house operated to convey with the coach house the way over no. 6, Hungershall Park (still the property of the transferors in the conveyance) then enjoyed with the upper of the two flats (being part of the land and house—the coach house—transferred by the conveyance)".

For these reasons I think that on the principal issue in this case this appeal must be allowed.

NOTE:

1. For comment, see [1985] C.L.J. 15; [1985] Conv. 60.

1.3.2 *Section 62 and the rule in* Wheeldon v. Burrows *compared*   It will be apparent that section 62 and the rule in *Wheeldon v. Burrows* may produce broadly similar effects. However, there are certain differences, although these should not be asserted too dogmatically. First, whereas a right claimed pursuant to the rule in *Wheeldon v. Burrows* must satisfy one or more of the conditions that it is continuous and apparent or necessary for the reasonable enjoyment of the dominant land, section 62 seems to impose no such requirement but to apply to all rights appertaining or reputed to appertain to the dominant land: *Ward v. Kirkland* [1967] Ch. 194, 229 *per* Ungoed-Thomas J.; but see Harpum (1977) 41 Conv. 415. Secondly, whereas section 62 only operates on a conveyance of a legal estate, the rule in

Wheeldon v. Burrows is also activated by a contract to convey a legal estate: *Borman v. Griffith* [1930] 1 Ch. 493. Thirdly, whereas section 62 requires diversity of ownership or occupation of the dominant land and the servient land prior to the relevant conveyance (subject to the possible exception where the right claimed is continuous and apparent), the nature of the rule in *Wheeldon v. Burrows* is such that it operates where the dominant land and the servient land have previously been in single ownership and occupation. Fourthly, whereas the rule in *Wheeldon v. Burrows* requires that the quasi-easement should have been exercised at the time of the division and transfer of the land, and whereas there are dicta indicating a similar requirement in relation to section 62 (see *Broomfield v. Williams* [1897] 1 Ch. 602, 615 *per* Rigby L.J.; *Lewis v. Meredith* [1913] 1 Ch. 571, 579 *per* Neville J.; *Goldberg v. Edwards* [1950] Ch. 247, 256 *per* Evershed M.R.), it has been asserted that the operation of section 62 does not require proof of actual user at the date of the conveyance: *Re Yateley Common* [1977] 1 W.L.R. 840, 850–851 *per* Foster J.

2. Prescription

Prescription has been defined as the acquisition of rights by use or enjoyment during the time and in the manner fixed by law: see *Gale on Easements*, 16th ed., 1997, p. 169. However, the rights so acquired were founded "not on the ground that possession over a given period gave an indefeasible right, but on the assumption, where possession or enjoyment had been carried back as far as living memory would go, that a grant had once existed which had since been lost": *Bryant v. Foot* (1867) L.R. 2 Q.B. 161, 179 *per* Cockburn C.J. In this way, the law "clothes fact with right": see *Moody v. Steggles* (1879) 12 Ch D. 261, 265 *per* Fry J.; *Clippens Oil Co. Ltd v. Edinburgh and District Water Trustees* [1904] A.C. 64, 69–70 *per* Lord Halsbury L.C.

2.1 *Required period of enjoyment*
The presumption of a lawful grant may be made under one of three heads: (i) at common law; (ii) by lost modern grant; or (iii) under the Prescription Act 1832. It is usual to claim in the alternative under all three heads: see, *e.g. Tehidy Minerals Ltd v. Norman* [1971] 2 Q.B. 528, 543 *per* Buckley L.J.; *Mills v. Silver* [1991] Ch. 271, 278 *per* Dillon L.J.

2.1.1 *Prescription at common law*   At common law a grant of an easement is presumed only where appropriate user has existed from time immemorial and, for this purpose, the year 1189 came to be fixed as the limit of legal memory. Since actual proof of user from 1189 is normally impossible, the courts have been prepared to presume such user on the basis of evidence of long user: *Bryant v. Foot* (1867) L.R. 2 Q.B. 161, 180–181 *per* Cockburn C.J.; but that presumption can be rebutted by establishing that at some time since 1189 the right claimed has not existed or could not have existed: *Hubert*

v. Dale [1909] 2 Ch. 570, 577 *per* Joyce J. As a result, prescription at common law is in practice of little significance: *Mills v. Silver* [1991] Ch. 271, 278 *per* Dillon L.J.

2.1.2 *Lost modern grant*   Since the presumption that formed the basis of prescription at common law could readily be rebutted, the courts developed the fiction of a lost modern grant. Under the fiction (described as "revolting" in *Angus & Co. v. Dalton* (1877) 3 Q.B.D. 85, 94 *per* Lush J. but as "convenient and workable" in *Simmons v. Dobson* [1991] 1 W.L.R. 720, 723 *per* Fox L.J.), it is presumed from 20 years' appropriate user that an easement was granted after 1189 but before the user commenced and that the deed of grant has been lost: *Dalton v. Angus & Co.* (1881) 6 App.Cas. 740. The development of the fiction, which is only applicable where common law prescription does not operate, was explained by Cockburn C.J. in *Bryant v. Foot* (1867) L.R. 2 Q.B. 161 (at 181):

Juries were first told that from user, during living memory, or even during twenty years, they might presume a lost grant or deed; next they were recommended to make such presumption; and lastly, as the final consummation of judicial legislation, it was held that a jury should be told, not only that they might, but also that they were bound to presume the existence of such a lost grant, although neither judge nor jury, nor any one else, had the shadow of belief that any such instrument had ever really existed.

It is now settled that the presumption cannot be rebutted even by direct evidence that no grant was in fact made: *Tehidy Minerals Ltd v. Norman* [1971] 2 Q.B. 528, 552 *per* Buckley L.J. (following a review of the conflicting views in the litigation that culminated in *Dalton v. Angus & Co.* (1881) 6 App.Cas. 740). However, where another explanation for the user is at least equally possible, it has been held that no grant should be presumed: *Bridle v. Ruby* [1989] Q.B. 169, 177–178 *per* Parker L.J. Moreover, the presumption may be rebutted by establishing that no lawful grant *could* have been made at any relevant time: *Neaverson v. Peterborough RDC* [1902] 1 Ch. 557; *Hanning v. Top Deck Travel Group Ltd* (1993) 68 P. & C.R. 14.

By contast with the position under the Prescription Act 1832 (see *infra*), for the purposes of lost modern grant there is no requirement that the period of user should immediately precede the action in which the easement is asserted. Once the 20-year period has run, the easement is acquired and it is not lost by subsequent interruption or discontinuance of user: *Mills v. Silver* [1991] Ch. 271, 278 *per* Dillon L.J.

2.1.3 *Prescription Act 1832*   The Prescription Act 1832 did not supersede the first two methods of acquiring easements by prescription but sought to supplement them by providing an alternative method that did not involve the unreality of those methods. However, as with all methods of prescriptive acquisition of easements, the statute does not permit the acquisition as easements of rights that cannot in their nature be acquired under the common law principles of prescription. The Act was described as a "strange and perplexing statute": *Angus & Co. v. Dalton* (1877) 3 Q.B.D. 85, 118 *per*

Cockburn C.J.; and it has "long been criticised as one of the worst drafted Acts on the Statute Book": Law Reform Committee, *Fourteenth Report: Acquisition of Easements and Profits by Prescription* (1966), para. 40.

Section 2 of the Act provides that no claim to an easement (other than an easement of light: see *infra*) based on user enjoyed as of right and without interruption for 20 years can be defeated by reason only of proof that user began after 1189; and it further provides that a claim to an easement based on user enjoyed as of right and without interruption for 40 years is "deemed absolute and indefeasible" unless enjoyed by written consent or agreement. Section 4 provides that the relevant period of enjoyment must be "the period next before some suit or action" in which the claim is brought into question; and that no interruption in the period of enjoyment takes place unless it has been submitted to or acquiesced in for one year after the claimant had notice of the interruption and of the person making or authorising it.

User "as of right" (a requirement imposed by section 5) has been held to mean that the acquisition of easements under the Act requires the same nature of user as under the common law: *Gardner v. Hodgson's Kingston Brewery Co. Ltd* [1903] A.C. 229, 236 *per* Lord MacNaghten. See *infra*, p. 668.

The claimant must establish uninterrupted enjoyment for the required period immediately preceding the action in which the claim is asserted: *Reilly v. Orange* [1955] 2 Q.B. 112. Thus, in contrast to the position under lost modern grant, 20 years' user that ended five years before any claim to an easement is asserted by action does not confer any easement on the claimant: *Tehidy Minerals Ltd v. Norman* [1971] 2 Q.B. 528; see also *Hyman v. Van den Bergh* [1907] 2 Ch. 516, [1908] 1 Ch. 167. An interruption involves some overt act of obstruction by the servient owner (or a stranger); but an interruption is disregarded unless the dominant owner has submitted to it or acquiesced in it for one year after he had notice of it and the person responsible for it. Whether there has been submission or acquiescence for one year on the part of the dominant owner is a question of fact: *Davies v. Du Paver* [1953] 1 Q.B. 184, 203 *per* Birkett L.J., 206 *per* Morris L.J. The dominant owner must communicate his opposition to the interruption to the servient owner; and, although silence thereafter cannot be treated as conclusive evidence of submission or acquiescence by the dominant owner, where there has been interruption in fact for more than a year, the burden is on the dominant owner to establish that he did not submit or acquiesce: *Dance v. Triplow* (1992) 64 P. & C.R. 1, 3 *per* Glidewell L.J., noted at [1992] Conv. 197. In *Newnham v. Willison* (1987) 56 P. & C.R. 8 the Court of Appeal appears to have confused the (real) issue of interruption with the (irrelevant) issue of user as of right: see [1989] Conv. 357.

The Act makes special provision for easements of light. Section 3 provides that a claim to an easement of light based on user enjoyed for 20 years without interruption is "deemed absolute and indefeasible" unless enjoyed by written consent or agreement. Claimants to easements of light are not required to establish user "as of right": *Colls v. Home and Colonial Stores Ltd* [1904] A.C. 179, 205 *per* Lord Lindley. Section 4 applies to easements of light; but, although interruption may be effected by physical obstruction, the Rights of

Light Act 1959 provides for notional obstruction by the registration of a notice as a local land charge.

2.2 *Nature of user for acquisition of easements by prescription*

Under all three methods outlined above (with the exception of easements of light under the Prescription Act 1832), the acquisition of easements by prescription depends in theory on the acquiescence of the owner of the servient land in the open assertion of the right by the person claiming the right as an easement. A classic statement of the basis of the doctrine of prescriptive acquisition is contained in the judgment of Fry J. in *Dalton v. Angus & Co.* (1881) 6 App.Cas. 740. He stated (at 773–775):

[I]n my opinion, the whole law of prescription and the whole law which governs the presumption or inference of a grant or covenant rest upon acquiescence. The courts and the judges have had recourse to various expedients for quieting the possession of persons in the exercise of rights which have not been resisted by the persons against whom they are exercised, but in all cases it appears to me that acquiescence and nothing else is the principle upon which the expedients rest. It becomes then of the highest importance to consider of what ingredients acquiescence consists. In many cases, as, for instance, in the case of that acquiescence which creates a right of way, it will be found to involve, first, the doing of some act by one man upon the land of another; secondly, the absence of right to do that act in the person doing it; thirdly, the knowledge of the person affected by it that the act is done; fourthly, the power of the person affected by the act to prevent such act either by act on his part or by action in the courts; and lastly, the abstinence by him from any such interference for such a length of time as renders it reasonable for the courts to say that he shall not afterwards interfere to stop the acts being done. In some other cases, as, for example, in the case of lights, some of these ingredients are wanting; but I cannot imagine any case of acquiescence in which there is not shown to be in the servient owner: (i) a knowledge of the acts done; (ii) a power in him to stop the acts or to sue in respect of them; and (iii) an abstinence on his part from the exercise of such power. That such is the nature of acquiescence and that such is the ground upon which presumptions or inferences of grant or covenant may be made appears to me to be plain, both [sic] from reason, from maxim, and from the cases.

As regards the reason of the case, it is plain good sense to hold that a man who can stop an asserted right, or a continued user, and does not do so for a long time, may be told that he has lost his right by his delay and his negligence, and every presumption should therefore be made to quiet a possession thus acquired and enjoyed by the tacit consent of the sufferer. But there is no sense in binding a man by an enjoyment he cannot prevent, or quieting a possession which he could never disturb.

Qui non prohibet quod prohibere potest, assentire videtur (Co. Inst. 2nd part, vol.i, p. 305); *per* Parke B. in *Morgan v. Thomas* (1853) 8 Ex. 304: *Contra non valentem agere, nulla currit praescriptio* (Pothier, Traité de Obligations, Part iii., chap. viii, art. 2, §2; Broom's Maxims, 5th ed., 903), are two maxims which show that prescription and assent are only raised where there is a power of prohibition.

And again, the cases of *Chasemore v. Richards* (1859) 7 H.L.Cas. 349, *Webb v. Bird* (1861) 10 C.B.N.S. 268, (1862) 13 C.B.N.S. 841, *Sturges v. Bridgman* (1878) 11 Ch.D. 852, have established a principle which was stated by Willes J. in *Webb v. Bird* (1861) 10 C.B.N.S. 268, 285, in these terms. After alluding to the law relating to lights as exceptional, he proceeded. "In general a man cannot establish a right by lapse of time and acquiescence against his neighbour, unless he shows that the party against whom the right is acquired might have brought an action or done some act to put a stop to the claim without an unreasonable waste of labour and expense". "Consent or acquiescence", said Thesiger L.J. in delivering the judgment of the Court of Appeal in

Sturges v. Bridgman (1879) 11 Ch.D. 852, 863, "of the owner of the servient tenement lies at the root of prescription and of the fiction of a lost grant, and hence the acts or user, which go to the root of either the one or the other, must be, in the language of the civil law, *nec vi, nec clam, nec precario,* for a man cannot, as a general rule, be said to consent or to acquiesce in the acquisition by his neighbour of an easement through an enjoyment of which he has no knowledge, actual or constructive, or which he contests and endeavours to interrupt, or which he temporarily licences. It is a mere extension of the same notion, or rather it is a principle into which by strict analysis it may be resolved, to hold that an enjoyment which a man cannot prevent raises no presumption of consent or acquiescence".

NOTES:

1. The passage cited from the judgment of Thesiger L.J. in *Sturges v. Bridgman* has been much quoted: it was recently expressly approved in *Mills v. Silver* [1991] Ch. 271, 280 *per* Dillon L.J., 287–288 *per* Parker L.J.

2. Many of the requirements of the user relied upon by the claimant are included in the proposition that there must have been user "as of right".

2.2.1 *User* nec vi, nec clam, nec precario   The user must be *nec vi, nec clam, nec precario,* that is, without force, without secrecy and without permission.

2.2.1.1 *Forcible user*   Forcible user includes not only the use of physical force in order to exercise the claimed right but also continued exercise of the claimed right in the face of clear protests from the servient owner; and such protests may take the form of physical or legal action indicating that the servient owner is objecting to the claimed right: *Eaton v. Swansea Waterworks Co.* (1851) 17 Q.B.D. 267, 274 *per* Lord Campbell C.J., 275 *per* Coleridge J.; *Dalton v. Angus & Co.* (1881) 6 App.Cas. 740, 786 *per* Bowen J.; and see *Newnham v. Willison* (1987) 56 P. & C.R. 8.

2.2.1.2 *Secret user*   Secret user may result from the physical nature of the user: *Union Lighterage Co. v. London Graving Dock Co.* [1902] 2 Ch. 557 (fixing of dock to adjacent wharf by underground rods); or from the manner in which the dominant owner exercises the claimed right: *Liverpool Corp. v. H. Coghill and Son Ltd* [1918] 1 Ch. 307 (intermittent discharge of waste through sewers at night); *Scott-Whitehead v. National Coal Board* (1987) 53 P. & C.R. 263 (discharge of effluent into river). The courts have rejected the argument that easements of support for buildings are *inherently* secret; and they have demonstrated a readiness to hold that a reasonable person in the position of the servient owner would have discovered that his buildings were providing support for those of his neighbour: *Dalton v. Angus & Co., supra.; Lloyd's Bank v. Dalton* [1942] Ch. 466. The latter case illustrates the wider principle that there can be no acquiescence by the servient owner unless he has knowledge of the user, although means of knowledge (constructive knowledge) suffices: *Union Lighterage Co. v. London Graving Dock Co.* [1902] 2 Ch. 557, 568–569 *per* Vaughan Williams L.J., 571 *per* Romer L.J.,

574 *per* Stirling L.J. The question of the requirement of knowledge on the part of the servient owner arises where the servient land has been leased: see *infra*, p. 672.

2.2.1.3 *Permitted user*   Permitted user (falling short of a grant) will negative a claim to an easement by prescription: *Hyman v. Van den Bergh* [1907] 2 Ch. 516, 530 *per* Parker J.; for permission is incompatible with the requirement that user should be enjoyed "as of right". Permission may be expressly given or it may be inferred, for example, from periodic payments: *Gardner v. Hodgson's Kingston Brewery Co. Ltd* [1903] A.C. 229, 239 *per* Lord Lindley; *Bridle v. Ruby* [1989] Q.B. 169, 177 *per* Parker L.J.; *Mills v. Silver* [1991] Ch. 271, 292 *per* Stocker L.J. On the other hand, it has always been accepted that *unsolicited* permission would not negative a claim to an easement by prescription: see, *e.g. Tickle v. Brown* (1836) 4 Ad. & E. 369, 382 *per* Lord Denman C.J.; *Mills v. Colchester Corp.* (1867) L.R. 2 C.P. 476, 486 *per* Willis J.; but see *Rafique v. Trustees of the Walton Estate* (1993) 65 P. & C.R. 356, discussed at [1994] Conv. 196, 207–210. Even where the user was originally enjoyed by permission, that permission may lapse, either through expiry where the permission was given for a limited period only or through a change in the circumstances from which it can be inferred that the permission no longer covers the claimed user; and in such circumstances any continued user may be user as of right: *Healey v. Hawkins* [1968] 1 W.L.R. 1967, 1973 *per* Goff J. The practical effect of permission appears to be as follows: oral permission given during the prescriptive period relied upon will negative any claim to any easement by prescription (with the exception of an easement of light): *Gardner v. Hodgson's Kingston Brewery Co. Ltd, supra*; oral permission given before the prescriptive period but continuing throughout that period will negative any claim to any easement by prescription other than an easement of light or a claim based on 40 years' enjoyment; written permission given during the prescriptive period relied upon or before the prescriptive period but continuing throughout that period will negative any claim to any easement by prescription.

2.2.2 *Permission and acquiescence*   It is important to distinguish between permission given by the servient owner, which will negative user as of right, from the consent or acquiescence of the servient owner which is essential to a claim to an easement by prescription. The distinction had become blurred by dicta which appeared to suggest a principle of law that toleration of user without objection was insufficient to constitute the necessary acquiescence: see *Gardner v. Hodgson's Kingston Brewery Co. Ltd* [1903] A.C. 229, 231 *per* Earl of Halsbury L.C., 239 *per* Lord Lindley; *Alfred F. Beckett Ltd v. Lyons Ltd* [1967] Ch. 449, 474 *per* Harman L.J., 475 *per* Russell L.J.; *Ironside v. Cook* (1980) 41 P. & C.R. 326, 337 *per* Goff L.J.; *Patel v. W.H. Smith (Eziot) Ltd* [1987] 1 W.L.R. 853, 860 *per* Balcombe L.J. In *Mills v. Silver* [1991] Ch. 271, 279–282, Dillon L.J. rejected that suggestion as:

fundamentally inconsistent with the whole notion of acquisition of rights by prescription. It is difficult to see how, if there is such a principle, there could ever be a prescriptive right of way. It follows that the various passages in the judgments in question cannot be taken on their own out of context. If each case is looked at on its own and regarded as a whole, none lays down any such far reaching principle ... It is to be noted that a prescriptive right arises where there has been user as of right in which the servient owner has, with the requisite degree of knowledge ... acquiesced. Therefore mere acquiescence in or toleration of the user by the servient owner cannot prevent the user being user as of right for the purposes of prescription. Equally, where Lord Lindley says [*Gardner v. Hodgson's Kingston Brewery Co. Ltd* [1903] A.C. 229, 239] that the enjoyment must be inconsistent with any other reasonable inference than that it has been as of right ... he cannot be regarding user with the acquiescence or tolerance of the servient owner as an alternative reasonable inference which would preclude enjoyment as of right from being established. A priori, user in which the servient owner has acquiesced or which he has tolerated is not inconsistent with the concept of user as of right. To put it another way, user is not "precario" for the purposes of prescription just because until twenty years have run, the servient owner could stop it at any time by issuing his writ and asking for an injunction.

See also Parker L.J., *ibid.* at 287–288.

2.2.3 *Unlawful user*   The requirement of user as of right precludes the acquisition of an easement through unlawful activity: *Neaverson v. Peterborough RDC* [1902] 1 Ch. 557; *Cargill v. Gotts* [1981] 1 W.L.R. 441; *Hanning v. Top Deck Travel Group Ltd* (1993) 68 P. & C.R. 14.

2.2.4 *Mistake*   It appears to be no objection that the claimant has been exercising the right in the mistaken belief that an easement had in fact been expressly granted to him: *Bridle v. Ruby* [1989] Q.B. 169, 174–177 *per* Parker L.J., following *Earl De La Warr v. Miles* (1881) 17 Ch D. 535; Ralph Gibson L.J. expressed the view (at 178) that no significance should be attached to subjective mistakes which are not shown to have affected the conduct of the claimant or the understanding of that conduct by the servient owner. Both authority and principle seem to require that the user is exercised *as an easement*; and there was held to be no user as of right where the claimant mistakenly believed that he owned or was in adverse possession of the servient land: *Attorney-General of Southern Nigeria v. John Holt & Co. (Liverpool) Ltd* [1915] A.C. 599, 617–618 *per* Lord Shaw. The position where both the dominant and servient owners mistakenly believe that the claimant is entitled to exercise the user is less clear: in *Chamber Colliery Co. v. Hopwood* (1886) 32 Ch D. 549 a common mistake was held to preclude a prescriptive claim but the perceived entitlement was of limited duration. See Kodilinye [1989] Conv. 261.

2.2.5 *Continuous user*   The user must be continuous but this requirement has been interpreted reasonably and depends largely upon the nature of the user in question: "the crucial matter for consideration is whether for the necessary period the user is such as to bring home to the mind of a reasonable person that a continuous right of enjoyment is being asserted": *Mills v. Silver* [1991] Ch. 271, 288 *per* Parker L.J., citing *Sturges v. Bridgman* (1879) 11

Ch D. 852, 863 *per* Thesiger L.J.; *Hollins v. Verney* (1884) 13 Q.B.D. 304, 315 *per* Lindley L.J. Continuity is not broken where the user is varied by agreement: *Davis v. Whitby* [1974] Ch. 186, 192 *per* Lord Denning M.R.

2.2.6 *Ability to prevent user*   There can be no acquisition by prescription where the servient owner is unable to prevent the user. In *Sturges v. Bridgman* (1879) 11 Ch D. 852, the defendant carried on business as a confectioner; and for more than 20 years he (and his father) had used mortars and pestles to pound ingredients. The consequent noise and vibration caused no nuisance to the plaintiff, the adjoining owner and a physician, until he established a consulting room on his premises. When the plaintiff then sought to restrain the alleged nuisance, the defendant claimed that he had acquired an easement by prescription. It was held that there could be no prescriptive easement based on user that could be neither physically interrupted nor restrained by legal action.

2.2.7 *Fee simple user*   Subject to an exception in relation to easements of light under the Prescription Act 1832, it is generally asserted that the user must be by or on behalf of a fee simple owner and against a fee simple owner; but for an argument to the contrary, see Delany (1958) 74 L.Q.R. 82. In practical terms this means, first, that a tenant of the dominant land cannot acquire an easement by prescription for himself *as tenant*, although he can acquire an easement by prescription for his landlord, which he can exercise while the tenancy continues and which the landlord can grant to a subsequent tenant: *Pugh v. Savage* [1970] 2 Q.B. 373, 380 *per* Cross L.J. Secondly, a tenant cannot acquire an easement on behalf of his landlord against other land owned by the same person: *Wheaton v. Maple & Co.* [1893] 3 Ch. 48; *Kilgour v. Gaddes* [1904] 1 K.B. 457; *Simmons v. Dobson* [1991] 1 W.L.R. 720, noted at [1992] C.L.J. 220; [1992] Conv. 167. However, it has been held that this principle does not apply where a lessee has a unilateral statutory right, exercisable at any time and without obtaining any consent, to enlarge his leasehold interest into a fee simple: *Bosomworth v. Faber* (1992) 69 P. & C. R. 288, 292–293 *per* Dillon L.J. Thirdly, the acquisition of an easement by prescription against a fee simple owner is unlikely where the servient land was subject to a tenancy at the beginning of the period of user. In such circumstances it may be unreasonable to imply a lost grant by the fee simple owner at the relevant time. Moreover, where the servient land is tenanted throughout the period of user, a claim to an easement by prescription may be negatived on the ground that the fee simple owner did not know of the user: *Davies v. Du Paver* [1953] 1 Q.B. 184; *Diment v. N.H. Foot Ltd* [1974] 1 W.L.R. 1427; or, irrespective of whether he knew of the user, on the ground that he was unable to prevent it: *Pugh v. Savage, supra*, 383 *per* Cross L.J.; *Diment v. N.H. Foot Ltd, supra*, 1435–1436 *per* Pennycuick V.-C. However, none of these objections would apply where the user began against the fee simple owner (with no evidence to negative knowledge on his part), even if he subsequently granted a tenancy of the servient land: *Pugh v. Savage, supra*, 383–384 *per* Cross L.J.

2.3 *Reform*

In 1966 the Law Reform Committee recommended (by a majority of eight to six) the total abolition of the concept of prescriptive acquisition of easements. The Report of the Committee stated (*Fourteenth Report: Acquisition of Easements and Profits by Prescription* (1966), para. 32):

The main considerations ... are briefly, that there is little, if any, moral justification for the acquisition of easements by prescription, a process which either involves an intention to get something for nothing or, where there is no intention to acquire any right, is purely accidental. Moreover, the user which eventually develops into a full-blown legal right, enjoyable not only by the dominant owner himself but also by his successors in title for ever, may well have originated in the servient owner's neighbourly wish to give a facility to some particular individual, or (perhaps even more commonly) to give a facility on the understanding, unfortunately unexpressed in words or at least unprovable, that it may be withdrawn if a major change of circumstances ever comes about.

The Committee proceeded to make further recommendations on the basis that some form of prescription would be preserved. Those recommendations would apply to all easements other than rights of support (for which a new code of rights and procedures would be introduced).

Law Reform Committee, Fourteenth Report: Acquisition of Easements and Profits by Prescription (1966), para. 99(6)

   (i) The prescriptive period should be 12 years;

  (ii) This period should be a period in gross, not one before action brought;

 (iii) Periods when servient land is occupied by an infant, a person of unsound mind, a married woman, or a tenant for life or for years should no longer be excluded from time counted for the purposes of prescription, nor should the time when an abated action was pending;

 (iv) Prescription should cease to be related to a presumed lost grant, but only rights capable of subsisting as easements should be capable of being acquired by prescription;

  (v) A prescriptive easement should be capable of being acquired against the owner of a limited interest in the servient land so as to subsist as long as that servient owner's interest subsists;

 (vi) Where the servient owner is a tenant for life or has the powers of a tenant for life of the servient land, an easement should be capable of being acquired against him by prescription to the full extent that he could grant one under the Settled Land Act 1925;

 (vii) Where a person is in occupation of the servient land in virtue of a beneficial interest under a trust for sale, his occupation should be regarded as that of the trustees;

(viii) The owner of a limited interest in the dominant tenement should continue, as at present, to be capable of obtaining a prescriptive title which will enure for the benefit of the freeholder;

 (ix) A tenant should be able to prescribe against his own landlord and *vice versa*;

  (x) No one for whom it would be *ultra vires* to acquire the easement by grant should be capable of acquiring such easement by prescription, but *de facto* enjoyment by such a person should be available to support a prescriptive claim by a successor in title;

 (xi) Incapacity to make a grant on the part of a servient owner should not bar a prescriptive claim;

(xii) Enjoyment by force should not count in favour of the dominant owner;

(xiii) Enjoyment by the dominant owner must have been actually known to the servient owner or such that he ought reasonably to have known of it;

(xiv) Enjoyment must also have been of such a kind and frequency as, apart from consent or agreement, would only be justified by the existence of an easement;

(xv) It must also conduce to the beneficial enjoyment of ascertainable land of the dominant owner;

(xvi) Enjoyment by consent or agreement, whether written or oral, should not count, and the effect of consent or agreement should be assimilated to that of interruption. A consent or agreement which is indefinite as to its intended duration should operate only for, say, one year;

(xvii) Notional interruption, on lines similar to those adopted in the Rights of Light Act 1959, should be made available in respect of all kinds of easements. This should be by registration against the dominant land in the local land charges register after notices given by registered post to the occupier of the dominant land and by advertisement;

(xviii) Interruption, whether actual or notional, should endure for 12 months if it is to be effective in stopping time running;

(xix) If a workable statutory formula can be found, an easement acquired by prescription should be of the like character, extent and degree as the use enjoyed throughout the prescriptive period by the dominant owner;

(xx) Where a dominant owner, having acquired an easement by prescription, thereafter for a sufficient period enjoys an easement of a more onerous character over the servient land, he should be prescriptively entitled to a new easement of the more burdensome character;

(xxi) Where a dominant owner, having acquired an easement by prescription, thereafter fails to make use of it to its full extent, this should not prejudice his right to the easement;

(xxii) Where a dominant owner, having acquired an easement by prescription, makes no use of it for a continuous period of 12 years, he should thereupon cease to be entitled to the easement.

More recently, the Law Commission has provisionally recommended that the acquisition of easements by prescription over *registered land* should only be possible under the Prescription Act 1832. It would cease to be possible to assert or claim an easement on the basis of common law prescription or lost modern grant, although rights already acquired would be unaffected. The Law Commission has stressed that the proposal is not an endorsement of the Prescription Act 1832: it is no more than an interim measure, pending a review of the law of prescription as a whole; but it is regarded as a necessary (or at least highly desirable) part of its blueprint for land registration in the next century in order to accommodate the changes that would result from the anticipated introduction of electronic conveyancing: see Law Com. No. 254, *Land Registration for the Twenty-First Century* (1998), paras 10.79–10.94. The Law Commission has also provisionally recommended that rights acquired or in the course of being acquired by prescription should be interests in registered land: *ibid.* paras 3.37–3.38. It is clearly arguable that both recommendations should be extended to unregistered land while it continues to exist.

3. Proprietary estoppel

The grant of an easement may be the appropriate remedy for satisfying a successful claim based on proprietary estoppel: *Ward v. Kirkland* [1967] Ch. 194; *E.R. Ives Investment Ltd v. High* [1967] 2 Q.B. 379, *ante*, p. 142; *Crabb v. Arun DC* [1976] Ch. 179, *ante*, p. 573.

4. Statute

Statute is the source of a variety of easements and analogous rights. For example, rights of way have been granted to provide access following the division and enclosure of common land by the Inclosure Acts: see *Adeane v. Mortlock* (1839) 5 Bing. N.C. 236; *Benn v. Hardinge* (1992) 66 P. & C.R. 246; and rights of support have been granted for canals constructed under private Acts of Parliament: see *London & North Western Railway v. Evans* [1893] 1 Ch. 16.

Moreover, statutory rights analogous to easements have been granted in favour of public utility undertakings (and their privatised successors) in respect of electricity cables and pipes for gas, water and sewerage. For a general survey of these statutory easements, see Garner (1956) 20 Conv. 208.

More recently, the Access to Neighbouring Land Act 1992 has conferred discretionary jurisdiction on the courts to make an "access order" authorising the applicant landowner temporarily to enter upon adjoining or adjacent land for the purpose of carrying out on his own land works that are reasonably necessary for the preservation of the whole or any part of that land and which cannot be carried out or would be substantially more difficult to carry out without such entry. An access order made under the Act does not constitute an easement; but the availability of such orders provides a solution to a particular problem that has traditionally been approached as an easements-related issue.

E. CONTENT OF EASEMENTS

The precise content and the extent of the rights conferred by any particular easement depends upon the method of acquisition. In *Williams v. James* (1867) L.R. 2 C.P. 577 Willes J. stated (at 581):

The distinction between a grant and prescription is obvious. In the case of proving a right by prescription the user of the right is the only evidence. In the case of a grant the language of the instrument can be referred to, and it is of course for the court to construe that language; and in the absence of any clear indication of the intention of the parties, the maxim that a grant must be construed most strongly against the grantor must be applied.

The discussion in this section will concentrate almost exclusively on the easement of right of way, which may be defined as the right to pass and repass along a way, together with appropriate ancillary rights: see *V.T.*

Engineering Ltd v. Richard Barland & Co. Ltd (1968) 19 P. & C.R. 890, 896 *per* Megarry J. However, similar principles apply, *mutatis mutandis*, to other easements.

1. Easements acquired by express grant or reservation

Where an easement of right of way has been acquired by express grant or reservation, the extent of the rights conferred depends, in accordance with the normal principles for the construction of instruments, upon the construction of the natural meaning of the words of the instrument, read in the light of the surrounding circumstances existing at the time of the execution of the instrument: *Cannon v. Villars* (1878) 8 Ch D. 415, 420 *per* Jessel M.R.; *St Edmundsbury and Ipswich Diocesan Board of Finance v. Clark (No. 2)* [1975] 1 W.L.R. 468, 476 *per* Sir John Pennycuick. In the context of easements, and in particular rights of way, the court will consider the physical nature of the dominant land and the servient land at the time of the grant or reservation: *Todrick v. Western National Omnibus Co. Ltd* [1934] Ch. 190; *St Edmundsbury and Ipswich Diocesan Board of Finance v. Clark (No. 2)* [1975] 1 W.L.R. 468. On the other hand, the wording of the grant or reservation may be "so unambiguous that no surrounding circumstances could affect their construction": *ibid.* 477 *per* Sir John Pennycuick; and see *Keefe v. Amor* [1965] 1 Q.B. 334. Moreover, where a right of way is granted or reserved in general and unrestricted terms, for example a right of way "at all times and for all purposes", and there is nothing in the surrounding circumstances to limit the extent of the easement, the right of way may be used for the purposes for which the dominant land is used from time to time, even though such purposes differ from the purposes for which the dominant land was used at the time of the grant: *White v. Grand Hotel, Eastbourne, Ltd* [1913] Ch. 113, 116 *per* Cozens-Hardy M.R. Irrespective of whether the right of way may be used for different purposes, it is no objection that the use of the right of way imposes an increased burden on the servient land provided that the increase does not extend "beyond anything which was contemplated at the time of the grant": *Jelbert v. Davis* [1968] 1 W.L.R. 589, 595 *per* Lord Denning M.R. Whether the increase becomes excessive in this sense is a matter of fact and degree.

These principles were affirmed by the Court of Appeal in *White v. Richards* (1993) 68 P. & C.R. 105.

White v. Richards (1993) 68 P. & C.R. 105

(CA, Nourse, Stuart-Smith and Mann L.JJ.)

In 1987 the predecessor in title of the plaintiffs purchased some agricultural land (Lot 1). The conveyance reserved to the vendor "the right for the vendor or his servants or licensees at all times hereafter to pass and repass on foot and with or without motor vehicles over and along the track coloured brown on the plan so far as the said right may be necessary for the use and enjoyment of the retained land". In 1988 the plaintiffs purchased lot 1, subject to the same reservation. Shortly afterwards, the defendant purchased the land for the benefit of which the right of way had been reserved (Lot 2). The plaintiffs claimed that the defendant's subsequent use of the right of way was unauthorised by reason of the dimensions and weight of some of the vehicles used and by reason of their number. The county court judge granted declarations and injunctions effectively restricting user of the right of way (i) to vehicles of specified dimensions and weight and (ii) so as not to interfere unreasonably with the right of other persons to use it. The defendant appealed.

NOURSE L.J.:

The main question
The defendant accepts that the nature and extent of the right of way reserved by the 1987 conveyance must be ascertained from the words of the reservation read in the light of the surrounding circumstances. This well established principle, which was first clearly enunciated in the judgment of Sir George Jessel M.R. in *Cannon v. Villars* (1878) 8 Ch D. 415, 420 was reaffirmed in *St Edmundsbury and Ipswich Diocesan Board of Finance v. Clark (No. 2)* [1975] 1 W.L.R. 468....

In the present case it is convenient to start by dividing the material part of the reservation into its four components:

"... to pass and repass (i) on foot and (ii) with or without motor vehicles (iii) over and along the track coloured brown on the plan (iv) so far as the said right may be necessary for the use and enjoyment of the retained land."

The main question is as to the nature and extent of the right of passage with motor vehicles, for which purpose component (i) can be disregarded. Moreover, since the defendant does not claim a right to use Lot 2 for any other than agricultural purposes, there is no difficulty over component (iv), it being obvious that there is no implied restriction against use for such purposes.

The main question therefore depends on the natural meaning of components (ii) and (iii) read in the light of the surrounding circumstances. The words "motor-vehicles" are unrestricted and in themselves apt to include any motorvehicle, whatever its dimensions or weight. But the right is for them to pass and repass "over and along the track coloured brown on the plan". Although no guidance as to the width of the way can be gathered from the brown colouring, the right of passage is expressed to be over and along "the track", a plain reference to something existing at the date of the conveyance. So the judge was entirely correct to start, as he did, by ascertaining the physical characteristics of the track in January 1987.

In conducting that inquiry, the judge reviewed the evidence at length. His principal findings were as follows. On the basis of the expert evidence and from his own observations on site, he was quite satisfied that the average width of the track in 1987 was 2.7 metres or 8 feet 10 inches. With regard to the surface in 1987, he was satisfied that the major portion of the track was of crushed stone embedded in the top soil and intermittently covered with what was by then a well worn bituminous layer. The remaining 60 or 70 metres, being the part of the track nearest to Lot 2, also had a layer of crushed stone, although no bituminous material had been spread over it. The judge did not think that there was much in the way of stone dressing in those 60 or 70 metres. He thought that the plaintiffs' description of that part of it as no more than a dirt track was a fairly accurate representation of its appearance in 1987. As the track entered Lot 2 it turned and widened to about 15 feet....

So the main question is reduced to this. Are the words "motorvehicles", when read in the light of those characteristics, seen to be restricted to certain types of motorvehicle, in particular to those of certain dimensions and of a certain weight?

In *Todrick v. Western National Omnibus Co. Ltd* [1934] Ch. 190, a right of way had been reserved in these terms:

> "A perpetual right of way ... at all times and for all purposes with or without vehicles and animals from and to the public highway ... over across and along the private road or way coloured yellow on the said plan...."

The defendant company used, or proposed to use, the private road, which Farwell J. described as a short country lane, for the passage of motor omnibuses seven feet six inches wide and of a weight of at least three tons. The lane was nine feet wide for the most part, but where it led into the public highway there was a gateway with stone pillars, the width of the opening when the gates were opened being seven feet nine inches. The lane was bounded by a retaining wall belonging to the plaintiff, which his expert witness thought would suffer badly if vehicles of such a weight as motor omnibuses were driven frequently up and down it.

Distinguishing the decision of this court in *White v. Grand Hotel, Eastbourne, Ltd* [1913] 1 Ch. 113 Farwell J. held (at p. 207):

> "... when I consider that this is a road to which the only entrance is 7 feet 9 inches, wide, that the width of an omnibus is 7 feet 6 inches, leaving only 1 1/2 inches clearance on each side, that the weight of an omnibus is at least three tons, that this is a road which is retained by a wall the strength of which is at least in doubt, when I take all those circumstances into consideration, I am unable to come to any conclusions but that a user of this roadway by motor omnibuses is not such a user as can be justified by the terms of the grant. It is not having regard to the circumstances of the case, the situation of the land and the situation of the parties at the time of the grant, such a user as could have been in the contemplation of either of the parties, and is not such a user as is proper in my judgment for a way of this kind."

The test applied in the second sentence of this passage was suggested by the judgment of James L.J. in *United Land Co. v. Great Eastern Railway Co.* (1875) 10 Ch.App. 586, at 590:

> "I am of opinion that there is nothing in the circumstances of the case, or in the situation of the parties, or in the situation of the land, to prevent the words from having their full operation."

There is no practical difference between that test and the test propounded in *Cannon v. Villars*, which does not appear to have been cited to Farwell J.

When *Todrick v. Western National Omnibus Co. Ltd* reached this court ([1934] Ch. 561) the argument was mainly directed to another point, on which Farwell J.'s decision was reversed. Counsel for the defendant company did not press for the appeal to be allowed on the ground that the judge's decision on user by omnibuses had been wrong. However, all three members of the court (Lord Hanworth M.R., Romer and Maugham L.JJ.) gave their express approval to that part of his decision. Its authority was again recognised by this court in *Robinson v. Bailey* [1948] 2 All E.R. 791, where it was distinguished, and in *Jelbert v. Davis* [1968] 1 W.L.R. 589, where it was applied. The complaint made in each of these cases was that there had been excessive use of the right of way by authorised vehicles rather than use of it by unauthorised vehicles, as was the case in *Todrick*.

Judge Edwards treated the present case as being primarily one of use by unauthorised vehicles. At p. 22 of the note of his judgment, having repeated his findings as to the width of the track and stated that the right did not extend to the verges beyond the visible track as it was in 1987, he turned to the permissible width of vehicles using it:

"In my view I am entitled to and must declare a restriction on the size of vehicle which may use the track having regard to my findings as to its width as indeed was done in the *Todrick* case. It is clear to me ... that no vehicle with a wheel base on the outer edges of its wheels in excess of 8 feet could possibly use this track without trespass. An overall vehicle width limit of 9 feet, 2 inches wider than the right of way, is also more than generous to the Defendant. It allows for marginal overhangs of the Plaintiffs' land, not merely by 2 inches, but by a foot or so according to the line of the vehicle on the track and the angle taken by it on bends."

The judge then dealt with the permissible weight of vehicles using the track:

"With regard to weight the fact is that this road was never intended to take juggernaut lorries and cannot be improved to carry them. It seems to me that in 1987 this would have been evident to the parties to the conveyance. I do not think they could have contemplated anything in excess of a 10 ton gross weight vehicle being used on this track. Most agricultural vehicles would be within that limit. ... Taking a broad view of the Deed and the surrounding circumstances, I am satisfied that it would have been plain to the parties in 1987 that there must be some practical limit to the weight of vehicle which could properly use a track like this— that weight limit might have been less than 10 tons but would not have exceeded it. Accordingly I am satisfied that I can and must declare that no vehicle over 10 tons laden weight may use the track."

Mr Ainger [counsel for the defendant] submitted that the judge's approach, depending as it did on a rigid adherence to the physical characteristics of the track in 1987, was incorrect. He emphasised that what was reserved was a right "over and along the track coloured brown", which meant a right over and along the general route of the track shown on the plan. He suggested that since the word "track" appears on the plan, an Ordnance Survey plan, it must, when used in the reservation, bear the Ordnance Survey meaning, *i.e.* a permanent unmetalled way used by vehicles. Such a track was capable of fluctuating in width depending on the season, the axle width of the vehicles that had most recently used it and the degree to which the driver kept his vehicle to the centre of the existing route. There was no physical limit on either side of the track apart from the northern boundary of Lot 1 and the ditch alongside part of it. There was no evidence that the right to use the track was confined to the worn way visible at any point of time and it should be presumed that the way included both the worn track and reasonable verges sufficient for all agricultural use. As for authority, Mr Ainger relied primarily on the decision of this court in *Keefe v. Amor* [1965] 1 Q.B. 334.

These submissions must be rejected. The judge was right to focus his attention on "the track". There was no other point from which he could start. Moreover, by his reliance on *Todrick v. Western National Omnibus Co. Ltd*, he gave himself an impeccable direction as to the test to be applied. *Keefe v. Amor* was a very different case, because it is clear that the land over which the right of way had been granted, as shown on the plan, was readily identifiable as a strip 20 feet wide on the ground. The words of the grant, having clearly identified the width of the way, prevailed over its physical characteristics. Here the words of the grant, to the extent that they are clear, identify nothing but the track, so that it is only from its physical characteristics [that] the width of the way can be ascertained.

Having correctly directed himself as to the test to be applied, the judge correctly applied it to the facts he had found and granted relief in a form with which I do not think that this court ought to interfere....

The subsidiary question

I turn to the subsidiary question of excessive use. The judge's decision on this question was not at the forefront of Mr Ainger's attack and it can therefore be dealt with more briefly.

In *Jelbert v. Davis* a conveyance to the plaintiff of part of an agricultural estate had included the grant of a right of way in these terms:

"the right of way at all times and for all purposes over the driveway retained by the vendor leading to the main road in common with all other persons having the like right ..."

The plaintiff subsequently obtained planning permission to use part of his land as a tourist caravan site from April to October 31, in each year, two of the conditions being that no caravan should remain on the site in any one year for more than three weeks and that the total number of caravans and/or tents stationed on the site should not at any one time exceed 200. The physical characteristics of the driveway were adequate for its use by caravans. The defendants, one of whom owned the soil of the driveway, having objected to the proposed use, the plaintiff took proceedings in the county court to assert his rights. On the strength of *White v. Grand Hotel, Eastbourne, Ltd* and *Robinson v. Bailey* the defendants accepted that use of the way by caravans would be a use by authorised vehicles, but they contended that use by up to 200 caravans would be excessive. That contention was accepted by this court. It was held that the right must not be used so as to cause an unreasonable interference with the rights of other users.

Here the judge found that in the four months between October 1989 and January 1990 there were on average 14 to 16 vehicles using the track in and out every day, mostly very heavy lorries of 38 ton laden weight carrying rubble and building materials, and excavators and other heavy machinery as well. At p. 15, he continued:

"The effect on the quality of life at the Plaintiffs' house can be imagined. The children aged 7 and 5 should not be allowed out to the front of the house, and it was barely safe to allow them out at all. Noise and vibrations made peace and quiet in the Plaintiffs' home impossible and the Plaintiffs quite evidently did not have the free run of their own access due to the manifestly excessive user of it by their neighbour. Had a claim for damages for nuisance been included in the particulars of claim, the evidence I have heard would have justified an award under that head alone of at least £1,000."

The judge expressed his conclusion on this question at p. 24. Having stated that counsel for the plaintiffs had relied on *Todrick* and *Jelbert v. Davis*, he continued:

"The essence of excessive user is that it is user to such an extent as to interfere with the reasonable right of other persons to use the like right and this must include use which damages the surface of the route itself making it less easy and comfortable to use. In my opinion the events of October 1989 to January 1990 were the plainest of cases of excessive user. Not only were very heavy lorries constantly using the track, some at excessive speeds, but the track itself and surroundings were being torn apart."

In a case such as this it is inevitable that there should be an overlap between use by unauthorised vehicles and excessive use by vehicles both authorised and unauthorised. On the judge's findings, this is primarily a case of excessive use by unauthorised vehicles. But it may be assumed that the track was also used by authorised vehicles, that is to say by vehicles whose dimensions and weight did not exceed those laid down by the judge, which would necessarily have contributed to the excessive use as a whole. In any event, having once again correctly applied the correct test, the judge had good grounds for making the additional declaration. He did not think that an injunction in support of that declaration was called for at present and the plaintiffs have not argued to the contrary in this court. For these reasons I would affirm the judge's decision of the subsidiary question and the relief that he granted in respect of it.

NOTES:

1. *St Edmundsbury and Ipswich Diocesan Board of Finance v. Clark (No. 2)* [1975] 1 W.L.R. 468 also concerned an express reservation of a right of way. Sir John Pennycuick, delivering the judgment of the Court of Appeal, considered two points of construction (at 477–480):

First, what is the proper approach upon the construction of a conveyance containing the reservation of a right of way? We feel no doubt that the proper approach is that upon which the court construes all documents; that is to say, one must construe the document according to the natural meaning of the words contained in the document as a whole, read in the light of surrounding circumstances. In *Cannon v. Villars* (1878) 8 Ch D. 415 this principle was applied by Sir George Jessel M.R. to rights of way in a passage which has often been quoted and never, so far as we are aware, questioned. He said, at p. 420:

"... the grant of a right of way per se and nothing else may be a right of footway, or it may be a general right of way, that is a right of way not only for people on foot but for people on horseback, for carts, carriages, and other vehicles. Which it is, is a question of construction of the grant, and that construction will of course depend on the circumstances surrounding, so to speak, the execution of the instrument. Now one of those circumstances, and a very material circumstance, is the nature of the locus in quo over which the right of way is granted."

Then, after certain illustrations, he goes on:

"Prima facie the grant of a right of way is the grant of a right of way having regard to the nature of the road over which it is granted and the purpose for which it is intended to be used; and both those circumstances may be legitimately called in aid in determining whether it is a general right of way, or a right of way restricted to foot-passengers, or restricted to foot-passengers and horsemen or cattle, which is generally called a drift way, or a general right of way for carts, horses, carriages, and everything else."

Mr Vinelott contended that the proper method of construction is first to construe the words of the instrument in isolation and then look at the surrounding circumstances in order to see whether they cut down the prima facie meaning of the words. It seems to us that this approach is contrary to well-established principle. It is no doubt true that in order to construe an instrument one looks first at the instrument and no doubt one may form a preliminary impression upon such inspection. But it is not until one has considered the instrument and the surrounding circumstances in conjunction that one concludes the process of construction. Of course, one may have words so unambiguous that no surrounding circumstances could affect their construction. But that is emphatically not the position here, where the reservation is in the loosest terms, i.e. simply "right of way". Indeed, those words call aloud for an examination of the surrounding circumstances and, with all respect, Mr Vinelott's contention, even if well founded, seems to us to lead nowhere in the present case. We do not think a few words quoted from the judgment of Lord Greene M.R. in *Robinson v. Bailey* [1948] 2 All E.R. 791, 795, when read in their context, lend support to this contention.

Second, is the maxim *"omnia praesumuntur contra proferentem"* applicable against the vendor or against the purchaser where there is a conveyance subject to the reservation of a new right of way? In view of the full discussion of this question by Megarry J., and of the fact that we do not agree with his conclusion, we think it right to deal fairly fully with it. But it is necessary to make clear that this presumption can only come into play if the court finds itself unable on the material before it to reach a sure conclusion on the construction of a reservation. The presumption is not itself a factor to be taken into account in reaching the conclusion. In the present case we have indeed reached a sure conclusion, and on this footing the presumption never comes into play, so that the view which we are about to express upon it is not necessary to the decision of the present case.

The point turns upon the true construction of section 65(1) of the Law of Property Act 1925, which enacts as follows:

> "A reservation of a legal estate shall operate at law without any execution of the conveyance by the grantee of the legal estate out of which the reservation is made, or any regrant by him, so as to create the legal estate reserved, and so as to vest the same in possession in the person (whether being the grantor or not) for whose benefit the reservation is made."

Formerly the law was that on a conveyance with words merely reserving an easement, the easement was held to be created, provided that the purchaser executed the conveyance, without the necessity for words of regrant. The law treated the language of reservation as having the same effect as would the language of regrant though there was not in terms a regrant, and in those circumstances regarded the purchaser as the proferens for present purposes. This was a relaxation of the strict requirements for the creation of an easement. (An easement could be created without execution by the purchaser of a conveyance by reference to the Statute of Uses, once section 62 of the Conveyancing Act 1881 removed the technical objection that that statute could not operate to create an easement. This method disappeared with the repeal of the Statute of Uses in the 1925 property legislation, and is not of direct relevance to the present problem: though it is part of the background to the abolition by section 65 of the Law of Property Act 1925 of the need for execution of the conveyance by the purchaser.)

Section 65 must be read in the light, therefore, of two aspects of the preceding law. First: that previously the law was sufficiently relaxed from its prima facie stringency to permit the language of mere reservation to have the effect of a regrant though it was not in truth a regrant by its language. Second: that for this purpose the purchaser must execute the conveyance if an easement was to be created; that is to say, although a regrant in terms was not required. Against that background, are the words in section 65 "without ... any regrant by" the purchaser to be regarded as altering the law so that the purchaser is no longer to be regarded as the relevant proferens? Or are they to be regarded as merely maintaining for the avoidance of doubt the situation that had been already reached by the development of the law, viz. that mere words of reservation could be regarded as having the same effect as would the language of regrant though without there being in terms any purported regrant by the purchaser? We would, apart from authority, construe the words in the latter sense, so that the only relevant change in the law is the absence of the requirement that the purchaser should execute the conveyance. We read the section as if it were in effect saying that whereas an easement could be created by mere words of reservation without any words of regrant by the purchaser, provided that the purchaser executes the conveyance, hereafter the easement can be created by mere words of reservation without any words of regrant by the purchaser even if he does not execute the conveyance: it is not to be said that in the latter event the previous relaxation of the strict law has disappeared, so that the language of the conveyance must be more than the mere language of reservation. It will be observed that that view keeps in line, on the relevant point, a post-1925 conveyance executed by the purchaser, which is apparently not touched by section 65, and one which is executed by him.

The above is our view apart from authority. What then of authority? We start with the fact that Sir Benjamin Cherry, architect of the 1925 property legislation, made no reference to this suggested change of principle in the law in the first edition of *Wolstenholme and Cherry's Conveyancing Statutes* after the 1925 property legislation. Further, in more than one case since 1925, judges of high authority took it for granted that the old principle still prevails: see *Bulstrode v. Lambert* [1953] 1 W.L.R. 1064 *per* Upjohn J. at p. 1068; *Mason v. Clarke* [1954] 1 Q.B. 460, in the Court of Appeal, *per* Denning L.J. at p. 467 and in the House of Lords *per* Lord Simonds [1955] A.C. 778,

786. In these cases the contrary was not argued and the judicial statements are not of binding authority. But in *Johnstone v. Holdway* [1963] 1 Q.B. 601, in the Court of Appeal, Upjohn L.J., giving the judgment of the court, not only in terms re-stated the old principle but made it part of the ratio decidendi of his judgment. He said, at p. 612:

> "that the exception and reservation of the mines and minerals was to the vendor, that is the legal owner, but the exception and reservation of the right of way was to the company, the equitable owner. If the reservation of a right of way operated strictly as a reservation, then, as the company only had an equitable title, it would seem that only an equitable easement could have been reserved. But it is clear that an exception and reservation of a right of way in fact operates by way of regrant by the purchaser to his vendor and the question, therefore, is whether as a matter of construction the purchaser granted to the company a legal easement or an equitable easement."

The opposing view was expressed by Megarry J. in *Cordell v. Second Clanfield Properties Ltd* [1969] 2 Ch. 9 (upon motion and without being referred to *Johnstone v. Holdway* [1963] 1 Q.B. 601) and in the present case (after a full review of the authorities, including *Johnstone v. Holdway*). He distinguishes *Johnstone v. Holdway* as a decision based on mistake and states his own conclusion in the following words, [1973] 1 W.L.R. 1572, 1591:

> "The fair and natural meaning of section 65(1) seems to me to be that if a vendor reserves an easement, the reservation is to be effective at law without any actual or notional regrant by the purchaser, and so without the consequences that flow from any regrant. At common law, the rule that a reservation of an easement was to be construed against the purchaser depended solely upon the notional regrant. Apart from that, the words of reservation, being the words of the vendor, would be construed against the vendor in accordance with the general principle stated in *Norton on Deeds*, 2nd ed. (1928), just as an exception or a reservation of a rent would; it was the fiction of a regrant which made reservations of easements stand out of line with exceptions and reservations in the strict sense. With the statutory abolition of the fictitious regrant, reservations of easements fall into line with the broad and sensible approach that it is for him who wishes to retain something for himself to see that there is an adequate statement of what it is that he seeks to retain; and if after considering all the circumstances of the case there remains any real doubt as to the ambit of the right reserved, then that doubt should be resolved against the vendor. Accordingly, in this case I hold that the words 'subject also to a right of way over the land coloured red on the said plan to and from St Botolphs Church' in the 1945 conveyance should, if their meaning is not otherwise resolved, be construed against the church authorities and so in favour of Mr Clark."

We see much force in this reasoning. But we find it impossible to accept Megarry J.'s analysis of the decision in *Johnstone v. Holdway*. We are not prepared to infer from the report that experienced and responsible counsel misrepresented the terms of section 65 to the court and that the judge based his decision on the terms of the section as so misrepresented. It follows that the decision in *Johnstone v. Holdway* is binding upon this court and that we ought to follow it.

The Court of Appeal held that a right of way (part of the access from a village to the village church) was limited to pedestrian access. The terms of the reservation were sufficiently ambiguous that it was held to be appropriate to consider the physical restrictions on the land at the time of the reservation.

2. By contrast, in *Keefe v. Amor* [1965] 1 Q.B. 334, physical restrictions were held *not* to affect the construction of the grant. Wheeler was the fee

simple owner of a pair of semi-detached houses. Access from the public highway to the houses was across a 20 feet wide strip of land (the brown strip), also owned by Wheeler. In 1930 Wheeler conveyed the fee simple of one of the houses to the parents of the plaintiff. The conveyance included an express grant of a right of way over the brown strip, subject to a liability to contribute to the repair of the strip and the boundary wall. At the time of the conveyance the access to the strip from the highway was four feet six inches wide. The successor in title of Wheeler, the defendant, widened the access to seven feet six inches, thereby enabling vehicular access; but she sought to limit the plaintiff to pedestrian access only. The plaintiff sought a declaration that he was entitled to vehicular access. Russell L.J. stated (at 344–346):

The defendant contends that the nature of the right of way is to be ascertained not merely by reading the words of the grant (which do not define its quality with precision) but also by reference to the circumstances and the condition of the property at the time of the grant. She says further that when you do so it is demonstrated that only a footway was intended, or at least, that only such user as permitted entry or exit through a gap four feet six inches wide was intended. It is accepted on her behalf that, taken by itself, the grant would have to be construed as a right of way for all purposes, including vehicles, without limitation of their width.

What were the circumstances and the condition of the property at the time of the grant? The inward end of the "brown strip" abutted on the boundary wall of the plaintiff's property, No. 1—presumably a wall belonging to No. 1—in which was a doorway about three feet wide. Down one side of the "brown strip" was the wall referred to in the transfer. Down the other side was a hedge, which, at the inward end, left a gap of some seven feet or so, which afforded access between the "brown strip" and No. 2. At the highway frontage of the "brown strip" was a wall between the ends of the hedge and the other wall, continuous except for the gap of about four feet six inches between two 14-inch-square brick pillars suitable for a gateway; and from this gateway to the inward end of the "brown strip" was a gravelled strip appreciably wider than the gateway, with some kind of edging of tiles, and on each side beyond that edging were garden beds and bushes, though apparently not much kept up. In appearance it looked like a footpath rather than a roadway. During the tenancy of the plaintiff's parents (which had lasted since 1903), there did not appear to have been any vehicular use of the "brown strip" by them.

Bearing all those matters in mind, do they lead to the conclusion that the grant was of a footway only, or alternatively, if the grant was of a vehicular way, then that it was one limited as to the dimensions of the vehicle in the manner I have indicated? For myself, I think not. It is argued that that view, which I have just expressed, means that the plaintiff's parents could, had they been so minded, immediately after the transfer have insisted on the four feet six inch wide gap being widened, by pulling down a post and a part of the wall, if the vendor refused to do so, so as to enable a motor car, if they so wished to come right up to their property, to enter and leave, and it is said that this surely would not have been a situation intended by the parties at the time of the grant. But there are several aspects of the transfer which I think lead to the conclusion that the greater right was intended.

First and foremost, the right of way was expressed to be over the strip whose whole 20-feet width was coloured brown. It would have been perfectly simple to define it more narrowly if that had been intended, or, of course, to define it as a footway, or as a right of way to and from the then existing gateway. Moreover, the fact that the whole 20-feet width was regarded as available if necessary for the exercise of the right is stressed by the reference to the wall marked with a "T" as being "on the west side of the said right of way", showing that the whole of the 20-feet strip was being referred to as the right of way. Why (I ask myself) should the whole width be regarded as being available, if necessary, for use as a right of way, if all that was intended was the restricted right suggested by the defendant?

I further observe that there was no obligation imposed to contribute to the upkeep of the frontage wall and, further, that an express grant of the footway alone would have been quite superfluous in the circumstances. I refer, of course, to the history of previous user; and, whether one speaks of it as a way of necessity or whether one speaks of it, as I think more correctly, as a grant which would have been implied having regard to the pre-existing user, in either event an express grant in 1930 was technically a superfluity.

Finally, I would add that an obligation to pay a fair proportion of the cost of keeping the way in good repair and condition is at least unusual if all that was envisaged was the impact of human feet.

3. In *White v. Grand Hotel, Eastbourne, Ltd* [1913] Ch. 113 the predecessor in title of the defendants was granted an unqualified right of way over the land of the plaintiffs. At the time of the grant the dominant land was used as a private dwelling-house. The defendants subsequently acquired the dominant land and converted the premises into a garage and drivers' lodge in conjunction with their hotel business; and they widened the gateway to facilitate access. The plaintiffs sought to restrain the use of the right of way for such trade purposes. Cozens Hardy M.R. stated (at 116):

The plaintiffs' main point is this: they said that the right of way ... was limited in its nature; that it was only a right of way for what I may call domestic purposes as distinct from trade purposes; and that it was only for such use as could reasonably be expected to be in the contemplation of the parties at the time when the defendants' house ... was a private residence, and ought not to be altered now that [it] is turned into a garage. We heard that point fully argued by counsel for the appellants and we have come to the conclusion that there is no ground for limiting the right of way in the manner suggested. It is not a right of way claimed by prescription. It is a right of way claimed under a grant, and, that being so, the only thing the court has to do is to construe the grant; and unless there is some limitation to be found in the grant, in the nature of the width of the road or something of that kind, full effect must be given to the grant, and we cannot consider the subsequent user as in any way sufficient to cut down the generality of the grant.

See also *Robinson v. Bailey* [1948] 2 All E.R. 791, 794–796 *per* Lord Greene M.R.

4. In *Todrick v. Western National Omnibus Co. Ltd* [1934] Ch. 190, [1934] Ch. 561, Farwell J. and the Court of Appeal held that, notwithstanding the express reservation of a right of way at all times and for all purposes, the physical dimensions of the way itself necessarily limited the size of vehicles entitled to use the right. Having referred to *White v. Grand Hotel, Eastbourne, Ltd*, Farwell J. continued (at 206–207):

But in my judgment that case is quite a different case from the present one. In considering whether a particular use of a right of this kind is a proper use or not, I am entitled to take into consideration the circumstances of the case, the situation of the parties and the situation of the land at the time when the grant was made: see *United Land Co. v. Great Eastern Ry. Co.* (1875) L.R. 10 Ch. 586, 590 *per* James L.J.; and in my judgment a grant for all purposes means for all purposes having regard to the considerations which I have already mentioned. It would be ridiculous to suppose that merely because the grant was expressed to be for all purposes it entitled the owner of the dominant tenement to attempt to use it for something for which obviously it could not be used. For instance, it seems to me that it would be impossible to suggest that the grantee of a right of way would be entitled to take down it, or attempt to take down it, vehicles which were so wide that they could not pass without breaking down the walls or otherwise destroying the plaintiff's property. It would obviously not have been in the contemplation of the parties when the grant was made that the way should be used for such a purpose, and therefore in my judgment a grant of this kind must be construed as a grant for all purposes within the reasonable contemplation of the parties at the time of the grant. No one has suggested, and I do not think it could be suggested, that either of the parties at the time when this easement was purported to be granted had it in mind that motor omnibuses might be driven up and down it. But that is not enough in itself. The mere fact that the parties had not envisaged such a possibility is not alone ground for saying that it is an improper user of the way: all the relevant facts must be considered. What I have to consider is this: Here one has a roadway which may be described as somewhat like a short country lane. It is bounded by a wall which is a retaining wall and belongs to the plaintiff. ... Whatever else may be said, it is quite clear that when the wall was built it was not built with the idea of retaining a road used for such a purpose as that, and when I consider that this is a road to which the only entrance is 7 feet 9 inches, that the width of an omnibus is 7 feet 6 inches, leaving only $1^1/_2$ inches clearance on each side, that the weight of an omnibus is at least three tons, that this is a road which is retained by a wall the strength of which is at least in doubt, when I take all those circumstances into consideration, I am unable to come to any conclusion but that a user of this roadway by motor omnibuses is not such a user as can be justified by the terms of the grant. It is not having regard to the circumstances of the case, the situation of the land and the situation of the parties at the time of the grant, such a user as could have been in the contemplation of either of the parties, and is not such a user as is proper in my judgment for a way of this kind.

5. In *Jelbert v. Davis* [1968] 1 W.L.R. 589 the Court of Appeal considered the question of authorised but excessive user. In 1961 land was conveyed to the plaintiff "together with the right of way at all times and for all purposes over the driveway retained by the vendor leading to the main road in common with all other persons having the like right" subject to the payment of a contribution to the repair and maintenance of the driveway. At the time of the grant the land was used for agricultural purposes; but in 1966 the plaintiff obtained planning permission to use the land as a caravan site. The defendants (two neighbouring landowners also entitled to the right of way) disputed the entitlement of the plaintiff to use the right of way in connection with the caravan site. Lord Denning M.R. stated (at 594–597):

The planning permission did not affect the legal rights of the owners of the soil. The planning authority could not, and did not, give Mr Jelbert any right to go along this lane for himself or for the campers. He had to rely on his conveyance for such a right.
    The issue has been exceptionally well argued before us by counsel on both sides. It turns eventually on the true construction of the grant contained in the conveyance of October 5, 1961. In particular, of the words "the right of way at all times and for all purposes over the driveway leading to the main road". What is the extent of that right when the land is changed from agricultural use to a caravan and camping site? The change will mean no doubt that a *different* kind of vehicle will be used for *different* purposes. But that change is, by itself, quite permissible. It is covered by the words of the grant "at all times and for all purposes". That is shown by *White v. Grand Hotel,*

Eastbourne, Ltd [1913] 1 Ch. 113. In that case a private dwelling-house was turned into a hotel. That meant a different user. But it was held to be within the grant. That case was applied in *Robinson v. Bailey* [1948] 2 All E.R. 791. In that case a plot of land, which was expected to be used as a dwelling-house, was turned into a place for storing building materials. The different user was held to be within the right of way. In view of those cases Mr Lyndon-Stanford (who appears for Mr Davis and Mr Osborne) conceded that he could not complain that the way was to be used for caravans instead of agricultural vehicles, such as carts or tractors. He could not object, for instance, to a user in connection with ten caravans. But he did object, he said, to excessive user.

In my opinion a grant in these terms does not authorise an unlimited use of the way. Although the right is granted "at all times and for all purposes", nevertheless it is not a sole right. It is a right "in common with all other persons having the like right". It must not be used so as to interfere unreasonably with the use by those other persons, that is, with their use of it as they do now, or as they may do lawfully in the future. The only way in which the rights of all can be reconciled is by holding that none of them must use the way excessively.

More generally, the true proposition is that no one of those entitled to the right of way must use it to an extent which is beyond anything which was contemplated at the time of the grant. The law on this subject was stated by Farwell J. in *Todrick v. Western National Omnibus Co.* [1934] 1 Ch. 190, which was later approved by the Court of Appeal [1934] 1 Ch. 561. ...

The question thus turns on the facts and circumstances of the particular case. Is the proposed user so extensive as to be outside the reasonable contemplation of the parties at the time the grant was made? This way is 180 yards long. As you enter from the road there are stone gateposts. They are only 10 feet apart. Once you are through the gateposts and come into the drive, there is a hard metalled way. It has guttering on its outer fringes which is really part of the metalled way. It widens out from 10 feet at the gateposts up to 14 feet 6 inches and 15 feet inside. The judge, by an error, put it at 16 or 17 feet, that is, a couple of feet wider than it was. It is bordered by trees for the whole of the 180 yards of its length. If 200 units, such as caravans, dormobiles or cars, used this caravan site, there would be 600 people there. All those people might go out in a car two or three times a day. In the morning to the beach. In the afternoon for an outing. And such like. All of them would be using this driveway.

It seems to me that user on that scale would interfere greatly with the rights of Mr Osborne and Mr Davis. Mr Osborne lives at the lodge at the end of the driveway. He has his grandchildren there in the summer. He farms land further up the lane. If Mr Osborne wishes to bring a combine harvester up the lane, or a cattle lorry, or any other vehicle, he would find it very difficult indeed when there are 600 people in the camp. His life in the lodge would be far from peaceful. Mr Davis has a cottage close to the lane and is interested in the hotel nearby. He has to go up and down the lane to get to his cottage. He could not fail to be much inconvenienced. I must say that, on the evidence, I think that if this caravan site is used to its full intensity for 200 units, there would be such congestion that it would interfere with the reasonable use by Mr Davis and Mr Osborne of their own right of way: and it would be a nuisance to them.

In my opinion, therefore, the proposed user for 200 units would be excessive. It would be far beyond anything contemplated at the time of the grant. ... We were asked to state what number is permissible. I am afraid we cannot give any guidance on this point. It is a matter of fact and degree depending on what happens. Beyond saying that 200 units are too much, I am afraid we must leave it to the parties themselves to work out what is a reasonable user.

6. In *Rosling v. Pinnegar* (1986) 54 P. & C.R. 124 the predecessor in title of the appellant purchased a Georgian mansion, part of a larger estate. He was granted an unrestricted right of way over the estate in common with the residents of the local village, including the respondents. When the appellant

acquired the mansion it was in a poor condition; but the appellant renovated it and opened it to the public. The respondents claimed that the consequent use by members of the public of the right of way over the estate constituted excessive user; and the trial judge granted various injunctions limiting user of the right of way. On appeal the Court of Appeal held that the nature of the user was within the terms of the grant but that the increase in user was excessive.

7. In *Graham v. Philcox* [1984] Q.B. 747 the extension by virtue of section 62 of the Law of Property Act 1925 of a right of way, initially granted to the lessee of the upper storey of a two-storey house, to the whole house was held not to involve an excessive increase in use: see *supra*, p. 661.

2. Easements acquired by implied grant or reservation

2.1 *Implied grant*

Where an easement of right of way has been acquired by implied grant, the extent of the right will be limited by reference to the established or contemplated use at the time of the conveyance or transfer that gave rise to the easement.

Milner's Safe Co. Ltd v. Great Northern and City Railway [1907] 1 Ch. 208

(Ch D., Kekewich J.)

Several adjoining properties, each comprising a dwelling-house and a warehouse, were linked by a passageway from the public highway to the rear of the properties. In 1832 the properties were devised by their common owner to various devisees but there was no mention of the passageway. The properties were used for various business purposes and the passageway was used for loading and unloading vans in connection with those businesses. However, when the defendants acquired two of the properties and built a railway station, the plaintiffs, who owned two of the properties near the public highway, sought to prevent the defendants from using the passageway as a means of access for their passengers. Having held that the original devisees (and the subsequent owners) of the properties had acquired rights of way over the passageway by implied grant, Kekewich J. continued:

The next question is what rights ought to be implied, and this presents considerable difficulty. The construction of an express grant of a right of way must be governed by the language of the grant, and the Court cannot stop short of or go beyond the proper legal meaning and effect of that language, but a different rule applies to the construction of an implied grant. There the user of the right is the only satisfactory guide. In *Williams v. James* (1867) L.R. 2 C.P. 577 this is distinctly laid down in the judgments of Bovill C.J. and Willes J., and in *New Windsor Corporation v. Stovell* (1884) 27 Ch. D. 665, 672 North J. states the rule neatly thus: "In the case of an easement by usage where you have to measure the extent of the easement, not by the terms of any deed, as the deed is ex hypothesi lost, but simply from what has been done, there is no way of ascertaining the extent of the easement except from what has been done".

...

The plaintiffs say that the passage cannot properly be used as it is now used by, or by the licence or invitation of, the defendants. ... They found their complaint on the principle that a right of way or other easement cannot be properly exercised by the dominant tenement so as to increase the burden originally cast on the servient tenement, and to the detriment of the latter. For this principle, which could only be applied in favour of owners of the soil, there is authority to be found in decided cases and text-books; but, passing that by, I prefer to take as my guide the language of James L.J. in *Wimbledon and Putney Commons Conservators v. Dixon* (1875) 1 Ch. D. 362. He says (at p. 368): "I am satisfied that the true principle is the principle laid down in these cases, that you cannot from evidence of user of a privilege connected with the enjoyment of property in its original state, infer a right to use it, into whatsoever form or for whatever purpose that property may be changed, that is to say, if a right of way to a field be proved by evidence of user, however general, for whatever purpose, qua field, the person who is the owner of that field cannot from that say, I have a right to turn that field into a manufactory, or into a town, and then use the way for the purposes of the manufactory or town so built". Assuming this to be a sound enunciation of the law, the question is whether the principle can properly be applied here for the protection of the plaintiffs. A similar question was mooted in *Bayley v. Great Western Ry. Co.* (1884) 26 Ch. D. 434, but did not call for decision. It is urged on behalf of the defendants that the site of the two houses is still being used for business purposes, and that as the implied grant extended to business purposes the present user is within it. The answer, to my mind, is that not only was the erection of a railway not contemplated by the grantor, but it could not possibly have been within his contemplation, and a railway station is not merely in its construction, but in its mode of occupation, something entirely different from any dwelling-house, warehouse, or even manufactory, which could have been erected on the land.

NOTE:

1. See also *Stafford v. Lee* (1992) 65 P. & C.R. 172, *supra*, p. 636.

2.2 Implied reservation

Where an easement of right of way has been acquired by implied reservation, the extent of the right will be strictly limited by the circumstances which gave rise to the implied reservation.

Corp. of London v. Riggs (1880) 13 Ch D. 798

(Ch D., Jessel M.R.)

When the defendant conveyed land to the plaintiff, he retained a plot of land wholly surrounded by the land conveyed but did not include in the conveyance any express reservation of a right of way. At the time of the conveyance the retained land was used exclusively for agricultural purposes and, when the defendant started to build tea rooms on the retained land for the use of the public, the plaintiff sought a declaration that the defendant was entitled to a way of necessity for the use of the retained land for agricultural purposes only.

JESSEL M.R.:

The real question I have to decide is this—whether, on a grant of land wholly surrounding a close, the implied grant, or re-grant, of a right of way by the grantee to the grantor to enable him to get to the reserved, or excepted, or inclosed close, is a grant of a general right of way for all purposes, or only a grant of a right of way for the purpose of the enjoyment of the reserved or excepted close in its then state.

There is, as I have said, no distinct authority on the question. It seems to me to have been laid down in very early times—and I have looked into a great number of cases, and among others several black-letter cases—that the right to a way of necessity is an exception to the ordinary rule that a man shall not derogate from his own grant, and that the man who grants the surrounding land is in very much the same position as regards the right of way to the reserved close as if he had granted the close, retaining the surrounding land. In both cases there is what is called a way of necessity; and the way of necessity, according to the old rules of pleading, must have been pleaded as a grant, or, where the close is reserved, as it is here, as a re-grant.

Now the question is, what is the re-grant? I fail to find any exact decision on the point, or anything coming near it, for it does not seem to have been discussed any where; and the only scintilla I can find going anywhere near the point is an observation of the Lord Chancellor Cairns in *Gayford v. Moffatt* (1868) Law Rep. 4 Ch. 133, 135 in which he says, reading from Mr Serjeant Williams' note to *Pomfret v. Ricroft* (1669) 1 Wms.Saund. Ed. 1871, pp. 571–574: "This principle seems to be the foundation of that species of way which is usually called a way of necessity:" and then he goes on to say, "Now, that is exactly the interpretation of the words used in this grant, 'with all ways to the premises appertaining;' it means, with such a way as the law would hold to be necessarily appertaining to premises such as these—that is, a way of necessity; therefore, immediately after this lease was granted, this tenant occupying the inner close became entitled to a way of necessity through the outer close, and that way must be a way suitable to the business to be carried on on the premises demised, namely, the business of a wine and spirit merchant".

It is therefore obvious to me that Lord Cairns thought a way of necessity meant a way suitable for the user of the premises at the time when the way of necessity was created; and that is all I can find in the shape of authority on the subject.

Well, now, if we try the case on principle—treating this right of way as an exception to the rule—ought it to be treated as a larger exception than the necessity of the case warrants? That of course brings us back to the question, What does the necessity of the case require? The object of implying the re-grant, as stated by the older Judges, was that if you did not give the owner of the reserved close some right of way or other, he could neither use nor occupy the reserved close, nor derive any benefit from it. But what is the extent of the benefit he is to have? Is he entitled to say, I have reserved to myself more than that which enables me to enjoy it as it is at the time of the grant? And if that is the true rule, that he is not to have more than necessity requires, as distinguished from what convenience may require, it appears to me that the right of way must be limited to that which is necessary at the time of the grant; that is, he is supposed to take a re-grant to himself of such a right of way as will enable him to enjoy the reserved thing as it is.

That appears to me to be the meaning of a right of way of necessity. If you imply more, you reserve to him not only that which enables him to enjoy the thing he has reserved as it is, but that which enables him to enjoy it in the same way and to the same extent as if he reserved a general right of way for all purposes: that is—as in the case I have before me—a man who reserves two acres of arable land in the middle of a large piece of land is to be entitled to cover the reserved land with houses, and call on his grantee to allow him to make a wide metalled road up to it. I do not think that is a fair meaning of a way of necessity: I think it must be limited by the necessity at the time of the grant; and that the man who does not take the pains to secure an actual grant of a right of way for all purposes is not entitled to be put in a better position than to be able to enjoy that which he had at the time the grant was made. I am not aware of any other principle on which this case can be decided.

I may be met by the objection that a way of necessity must mean something more than what I have stated, because, where the grant is of the inclosed piece, the grantee is entitled to use the land for all purposes, and should therefore be entitled to a right of way commensurate with his right of enjoyment. But there again the grantee has not taken from the grantor any express grant of a right of way: and all he can be entitled to ask is a right to enable him to enjoy the property granted to him as it was granted to him. It does not appear to me that the grant of the property gives any greater right. But even if it did, the principle applicable to the grantee is not quite the same as the principle applicable to the grantor: and it might be that the grantee obtains a larger way of necessity—though I do not think he does—than the grantor does under the implied re-grant.

I am afraid that I am laying down the law for the first time—that I am for the first time declaring the law; but it is a matter of necessity from which I cannot escape.

3. Easements acquired by prescription

Where an easement is acquired by prescription, the extent of the right is limited to use for the purposes for which it was used during the period when it was being acquired. In *United Land Co. v. Great Eastern Railway Co.* (1875) 10 Ch.App. 586 Mellish L.J. stated (at 590):

Where a right of way is claimed by user, then, no doubt, according to the authorities, the purpose for which the way may be used is limited by the user; for we must judge from the way in which it has been used what the purposes were for which the party claiming has gained the right.

Although the nature of the user is thus restricted, the cases indicate that quite significant increases in user for established purposes will be permitted. Whether mere increase in user can without more constitute excessive user is not entirely clear.

British Railways Board v. Glass [1965] Ch. 538

(CA, Lord Denning M.R., Harman and Davies L.JJ.)

In 1847 the predecessors in title of the plaintiffs purchased a strip of land from the predecessors in title of the defendant for the purpose of constructing a railway line. Since the railway line cut off part of the land of the vendors from the public highway, the vendors reserved a right of way across the railway line from that part of their land to the remaining part of their land and to the public highway beyond; and for that purpose the purchasers constructed a level crossing. From 1938 onwards part of the land retained by the vendors (the blue land) was used as a caravan site; in 1942 six permanent caravans were established on the site; and thereafter the number of caravans increased substantially. The plaintiffs became concerned by the increase in the use of the level crossing generated by the caravan site and sought to limit its user; and the defendant claimed to be entitled to an easement of way for the developed use (i) under the express reservation and/or (ii) by prescription.

Ungoed-Thomas J. and the Court of Appeal (Harman and Davies L.JJ., Lord Denning M.R. dissenting) held that the right of way under the express reservation was not restricted by the obligation of the purchasers to construct "accommodation works" in compliance with section 68 of the Railways Clauses Consolidation Act 1845; but that it was a general right of way, not limited to use for agricultural or domestic purposes in the contemplation of the parties in 1847. The court proceeded to consider the claim based on prescription.

HARMAN L.J.:

If he has no general right of way, the defendant has a quite different defence, namely, a claim to a prescriptive right. In paragraph 11 of the statement of claim it is alleged that the defendant has been using the blue land as a caravan site since 1946. This proved an understatement and in the reply it is admitted that the use of the blue land as a caravan site began in or about the year 1938. The reply goes on to say that until 1945 there were no more than three caravans on the site but that the user has much increased since the year 1946.

It appeared from the evidence that before the last war there were three caravans and a tent dwelling permanently situated upon the "blue land", and that this number increased after the war began, when the Admiralty moved some of its departments to Bath, to six permanent caravans and five more that came and went, and there was a further increase in the spring of 1942 after the first bombs fell on Bath, and that after the war there were further increases from time to time until shortly before the writ was issued the number of caravans had increased to 29 and it was of this burden that the plaintiffs not unnaturally complained. All the caravanners and those who visited them, and their suppliers, had no access to the blue land save over the level crossing.

This part of the case has become largely academic because the local planning authority has, by exercise of its statutory powers, ordered the gradual clearance of the site from caravans. At the date of the hearing in the court below the number had been reduced to 16 and will be reduced to none by the end of the year 1966 or thereabouts. Nevertheless the judge considered the state of things when the writ was issued, and rightly so, and he came to the conclusion that the plaintiffs could not complain of the state of things as it then existed. He reached this conclusion upon the admissions appearing upon the face of the pleadings. The plaintiffs admitted that the "blue land" was used "as a caravan site", that is to say, the whole of the "blue land" and not merely such portions of it as had in fact been the standings of caravans. I understand that in fact there were no such permanent standings, but that caravans coming and going occupied any part of the field they chose. The prescriptive claim was not made in the right of individual caravans, which would have been a claim by individual caravanners, but by the defendant as the owner of the whole of the "blue land" and on the footing that it constituted "the caravan site", ... If the plaintiffs had not admitted that the "blue land" constituted a "caravan site", the defendant might have been in great difficulty in defining the area of the site. He was relieved of that difficulty by the pleadings and his case was that, admitting the whole "blue land" to be "a caravan site", the mere increase from, say, 10 to 29 caravans did not constitute such an increase in the burden of the prescriptive right as was a legitimate subject of complaint by the plaintiffs. The leading case on this subject is *Williams v. James* (1867) L.R. 2 C.P. 577. The headnote reads: "The defendant, being entitled by immemorial user to a right of way over the plaintiff's land from field N, used the way for the purpose of carting from field N some hay stacked there, which had been grown partly there and partly on land adjoining. The jury found in effect that the defendant in so doing had used the way bona fide, and for the ordinary and reasonable use of field N as a field: *Held*, that the mere fact that some of the hay had not been grown on field N did not make the carrying of it over the plaintiff's land an excess in the user of the right of way". Bovill C.J. says this (at p. 580): "In all cases of this kind which depend upon user the right acquired must be measured by the extent of the enjoyment which is proved. When a right of way to a piece of land is proved, then that is, unless something appears to the contrary, a right of way for all purposes according to the ordinary and reasonable use to which that land might be applied at the time of the supposed grant. Such a right cannot be increased so as to affect the servient tenement by imposing upon it any additional burden. It is also clear, according to the authorities, that where a person has a right of way over one piece of land to another piece of land, he can only use such right in order to reach the latter place. He cannot use it for the purpose of going elsewhere". Willes J. says this (at p. 582): "I agree with the argument of Mr Jelf that in cases like this, where a way has to be proved by user, you cannot extend the purposes for which the way may be used, or for which it might be reasonably inferred that parties would have intended it to be used. The land in this case was a field in the country, and apparently only used for rustic purposes. To be a legitimate user of the right of way, it must be used for the enjoyment of the nine acre field, and not colourably for other closes. I quite agree also with the argument that the right of way can only be used for the field in its ordinary use as a field. The right could not be used for a manufactory built upon the field. The use must be the reasonable use for the purposes of the land in the condition in which it was while the user took place".

Applying that to the present case, you must do what the judge did, namely, base your conclusion on a consideration of what must have been the supposed contents of the lost grant on which the prescription rests. If this be supposed to be a grant of the right to use the "blue land" as "a caravan site", then it is clear that a mere increase in the numbers of the caravans using the site is not an excessive user of the right. A right to use a way for this purpose or that has never been to my knowledge limited to a right to use the way so many times a day or for such and such a number of vehicles so long as the dominant tenement does not change its identity. If there be a radical change in the character of the dominant tenement, then the prescriptive right will not extend to it in that condition. The obvious example is a change of a small dwelling-house to a large hotel, but there has been no change of that character according to the facts found in this case. The caravan site never became a highly organised town of caravans with fixed standings and roads and all the paraphernalia attendant on such a place and in my opinion the judge was right in holding that there had been no such increase in the burden of the easement as to justify the plaintiffs in seeking as they did by injunction to restrict the user to three caravans or six or to prevent its use as what in the statement of claim is called "a caravan camp or site".

DAVIES L.J.:

If any prescriptive right has been acquired, it has been acquired not by any one or more caravans but by the "blue land" as dominant tenement. And it is not easy to contemplate an express grant of a right of way in respect of a specified or limited number of caravans. The "blue land" is still being used as a caravan site. Its use as such has been intensified. But there has been no alteration in the nature of its use.

The question whether a mere increase without any alteration in the character of the use of a right of way can be prevented by the owner of a servient tenement is oddly free from authority. We were referred in this connection to *Wimbledon and Putney Commons Conservators v. Dixon* (1875) 1 Ch.D. 362. It must be observed that in that case the court came to the conclusion that there had been a substantial alteration in the nature of the use of the dominant tenement and so of the right of way; consequently any observations as to mere increase in the use were obiter. James L.J. said (at p. 368): "We have then to consider whether the character of the property can be so changed as substantially to increase or alter the burden upon the servient tenement". Mellish L.J., in stating the problem, used these words (at p. 370): "... does that entitle Mr Drax [the owner of the dominant tenement] to alter substantially and increase the burden on the servient tenement by building any number of houses he pleases upon the property and giving to the persons who inhabit these houses a right to use the way for all purposes connected with the houses". Baggallay J.A. said (at p. 374): "... you must neither increase the burden on the servient tenement, nor substantially change the

Easements

nature of the user". None of those judges was, as I think, considering a mere increase in the use of a right of way. An increase of burden in this context must, I think, be taken to mean a different or additional burden. If there is a right of way to and from a particular house, it does not seem that the owner of the servient tenement could successfully complain if the number of persons living in the house was greatly increased or if the occupier of the house chose to use the right of way very much more frequently than previously. Suppose, as was said in the argument, a golf club were entitled to a right of way over adjoining land: if such a club were to double its membership, the burden on the servient tenement would be greatly increased but it is impossible to think that the owner of the servient tenement could prevent such user.

So here, once it is admitted, as it has been admitted, that the "blue land" as "a caravan site" acquired by prescription a right of way, it does not seem to me that the plaintiffs can prevent a mere increase in the number of caravans upon the site and the consequent increase in the use of the right of way. An increase in the number of caravans on a site is quite a different thing from the erection of a number of new houses, though no doubt from the point of view of the servient tenement the effect is somewhat similar.

NOTES:

1. Lord Denning M.R. also dissented on the question of the prescriptive right. In contrast to Davies L.J., he interpreted the decision in *Wimbledon and Putney Commons Conservators v. Dixon* (1875) 1 Ch D. 362 as precluding an increase in use.

2. For comment, see (1965) 81 L.Q.R. 17.

3. In *Woodhouse & Co. Ltd v. Kirkland (Derby) Ltd* [1970] 1 W.L.R. 1185 the plaintiffs, who were plumbers' merchants, had acquired a prescriptive right of way to their business premises over the defendants' land. The question arose as to whether this right, established for the most part by the use of the plaintiffs and their suppliers, extended also to (significantly increased) use by their customers. Plowman J. held that the easement extended to the customers; and he continued (at 1190–1192):

If, then, the plaintiffs' customers are entitled to use the defendants' passage, is it an objection that the number of such users considerably increased after 1963? Is this "excessive" user, within the principle that the owner of the dominant tenement is not entitled to increase the burden on the servient tenement? ... [I]n my judgment, the answer is "No". Distinction has to be drawn between mere increase in user and a user of a different kind or for a different purpose. The former is not, in my judgment, within the principle, the latter is. The difference may be illustrated by *British Railways Board v. Glass* [1965] Ch. 538. ... In my judgment the plaintiffs in the present case have not been guilty of excessive user of their right of way. It is unnecessary to consider whether an increase in user, if very great, can ever of itself amount to excessive user because that case is not this case.

4. In *Giles v. County Building Contractors (Hertford) Ltd* (1971) 22 P. & C.R. 978 the defendants had acquired by prescription a right of way over a road and then a footpath to their land. They obtained planning permission to develop their land by demolishing the two existing houses, erecting eight dwelling units and garages and replacing the footpath with vehicular access for seven of the units. The plaintiff, who also had a right of way over the road, sought to restrain the increased use of the road. Brightman J. gave

judgment for the defendants. Having cited the final paragraph of the judgment of Harman L.J. in *British Railways Board v. Glass,* he stated (at 987):

The important expressions, to my mind, are "change of identity" and "radical change in character". In my view, the use of the convent site for the erection of seven modern dwelling units in place of the two existing houses, cannot properly be described as "changing the identity" or "radically changing the character" of the convent site. I think it is evolution rather than mutation.

4. General

In addition to the specific observations above, a number of generally applicable observations may be made. First, the grant of an easement includes such ancillary rights as are reasonably necessary for its exercise and enjoyment; thus, an easement of way which extends to commercial vehicles would normally include the right to stop for a reasonable time for the purpose of loading and unloading: *Bulstrode v. Lambert* [1953] 1 W.L.R. 1064, 1070–1071 *per* Upjohn J. In *Soames-Forsythe Properties Ltd v. Tesco Stores Ltd* [1991] E.G.C.S. 22, noted at [1992] Conv. 199, a lease of a supermarket included the right for customers to use a car park and a right of way "on foot only" along a walkway between the supermarket and the car park; and it was held that customers of the supermarket had the right to take supermarket trolleys along the walkway. Secondly, subject to a contrary intention, the extent of an easement of way will be permitted to develop in accordance with technological advances: *Lock v. Abercester Ltd* [1939] Ch. 861, 864 *per* Bennett J. Thirdly, unless the class of persons entitled to take advantage of the easement is limited by the terms or circumstances of the grant, it seems that an easement may be used by any person who is expressly or impliedly authorised by the person entitled to possession of the dominant land: *Woodhouse & Co. Ltd v. Kirkland (Derby) Ltd* [1970] 1 W.L.R. 1185. Fourthly, the grant of an easement of way does not in itself impose any obligation on the grantor to maintain the way in a state of repair: see *supra,* p. 622; but the grantor may incur such an obligation if he carries out work and then fails to maintain that work: *Saint v. Jenner* [1973] Ch. 275, *infra,* p. 698. Fifthly, an easement acquired in respect of the dominant land may be used for the benefit of the dominant land only and not for the benefit of other land. Thus a right of way to the dominant land cannot be used as a means of access to other adjoining land in respect of which the easement was not acquired, unless access to that additional land is ancillary to the enjoyment of the dominant land: *National Trust for Places of Historic Interest or Natural Beauty v. White* [1987] 1 W.L.R. 907, 913–914 *per* Warner J.; *Jobson v. Record* (1997) 75 P. & C.R. 375. However, there are cases where the courts have effectively sanctioned the non-ancillary extension of a right of way for the benefit of land adjoining the dominant land. In *Bracewell v. Appleby* [1975] Ch. 408 and in *Jaggard v. Sawyer* [1995] 1 W.L.R. 269 the courts declined to grant injunctions to restrain such unlawful extensions (awarding damages in lieu under section 50 of the Supreme Court Act 1981). See also *Graham v. Philcox* [1984] Q.B. 747, *supra,* p.661. Sixthly, an easement of way must not be exercised in such a manner as to cause avoidable damage to the servient land or to intrude unreasonably on the rights and property of the servient owner: *Todrick v. Western National Omnibus Co. Ltd* [1934] Ch. 561, 575–576 *per* Lord Hanworth M.R.; *Bulstrode v. Lambert* [1953] 1 W.L.R. 1064, 1070 *per* Upjohn J.; nor must it be exercised in such a manner as to interfere unreasonably with the rights of other persons entitled to use it: *Jelbert v. Davis* [1968] 1 W.L.R. 589, 595 *per* Lord Denning M.R.; *Rosling v. Pinnegar* (1986) 54 P. & C.R. 124, 132–134 *per* May L.J. Finally, it has been held that a servient owner has no right to alter the route of an easement of way once it has been fixed, unless such a right is an express or implied term of the grant of the easement or is subsequently conferred on him: *Greenwich Healthcare NHS Trust v. London and Quadrant Housing Trust* [1998] 1 W.L.R. 1749, 1754 *per* Lightman J.

5. Interference with easements

Any wrongful interference with an easement potentially constitutes a nuisance in respect of which the remedies of damages and injunction are available: *Saint v. Jenner* [1973] Ch. 275. However, not every interference is wrongful and actionable. The interference must be substantial, which is a question of fact and degree depending upon the nature of the right, the nature of the dominant land and the servient land and the particular circumstances of the case.

Celsteel Ltd v. Alton House Holdings Ltd [1985] 1 W.L.R. 204

(Ch D., Scott J.)

The first defendants (Alton House Holdings) were the registered freehold proprietors of a block of flats and garages and a petrol filling station. The third plaintiff was the tenant of one of the flats and a garage under a contract for a 120-year lease from the predecessor in title of the first defendants, the contract also providing for access from the public highway to the garage. The first defendants granted to the second defendants (Mobil) a lease of the petrol filling station and of part of the driveway that provided access to the garages. When the second defendants proposed the construction of an automatic car-wash that would significantly reduce the width of the driveway, the plaintiffs sought an injunction.

SCOTT J.:

It has been settled law for a long time that an interference with a private right of way is not, per se, an actionable interference. In *Clifford v. Hoare* (1874) L.R. 9 C.P. 362 a vehicular right of way had been granted over a roadway 40 feet wide. The defendant erected a building which encroached two feet into the roadway. It was held that this encroachment did not represent an actionable interference with the right of way. The issue was treated as depending basically on the construction of the grant. What quality of enjoyment of the right of way had been intended to be granted? Lord Coleridge C.J. answered this question by saying, at p. 370: "the intention was to grant the plaintiff an easement only, the reasonable use and enjoyment of an ascertained way". Since the encroachment did not interfere with the reasonable use and enjoyment of the way, it did not represent an actionable interference. *Clifford v. Hoare* was a case where the interference had resulted in a reduction of the width of the way by a trivial amount. In *Pettey v. Parsons* [1914] 2 Ch. 653 the issue was whether a gate across a right of way represented an actionable interference. In the view of the Court of Appeal the gate would not do so provided it were kept open during business hours. It is to be noted that the servient owner was contending for the right to maintain a closed gate across the way. Lord Cozens-Hardy M.R. said, at p. 662, that an interference "is not actionable unless it is substantial". Swinfen Eady L.J. said, at p. 665: "the grantor ... cannot substantially interfere with the easement as granted" and that the relevant question was "whether the easement has been substantially interfered with". He said, at pp. 666–667, that the gate, open during business hours, "would be no interference with the reasonable use by the grantee of the easement ..." In the event, the court concluded that a gate kept open during business hours would not interfere with the reasonable use of the right of way and would not represent a substantial interference, whereas a gate closed at all times would do so. And in *Keefe v. Amor* [1965] 1 Q.B. 334, 346, Russell L.J. described as actionable:

"such obstacles as impede the user of the strip for such exercise of the right granted as from time to time is reasonably required by the dominant tenant."

There emerge from the three cases I have cited two criteria relevant to the question whether a particular interference with a right of way is actionable. The interference will be actionable if it is substantial. And it will not be substantial if it does not interfere with the reasonable use of the right of way. I must apply these criteria to the present case.

I will take first the position of the third plaintiff as lessee of garage 52. Both he and his son expressed the preference of reversing into the garage and exiting forwards. They were cross-examined at some length by Mr Laurence who sought to establish that it was preferable to drive in forwards and reverse out. There are advantages and disadvantages attached to both of the alternatives. Some may prefer one, others may prefer the other. In my view, a lessee whose right of way permits him to adopt either alternative as he may from time to time choose, suffers actionable interference if one alternative is precluded and he is constrained always to adopt the other. To put the point another way, use of the rear driveway in order to reverse into garage 52 is a reasonable use. An obstruction which prevents that use is, accordingly, in my judgment actionable.

Mr Laurence submitted that driving in forwards and reversing out was a reasonable use of the rear driveway. I agree with him. He submitted further that the proposed car wash would not substantially interfere with this particular use, and thus would not prevent reasonable access by the third plaintiff to garage 52. He argued from these premises that the car wash would not, on authority, constitute an actionable interference. I do not accept that authority justifies this argued conclusion. In the present case the test is not, in my view, whether the means of access still possible is a reasonable means of access. The correct test is whether insistence by the third plaintiff on being able to continue to use the other means of access is reasonable. In my opinion, it is. I do not think it is open to the defendants to deprive the third plaintiff of his preferred means of entry to garage 52 and then to justify themselves by arguing that most other people would prefer some other still available means of entry. Such an argument might avail the defendants if the third plaintiff's preference were unreasonable or perverse. But, in my view, it is neither of these things.

In addition to use of the rear driveway for the purpose of access to and egress from garage 52, the lease of garage 52 entitles the third plaintiff to a right of passage along the rear driveway. This right of passage would be interfered with by the narrowing of the relevant part of the driveway from nine to 4.14 metres. Whether this narrowing of the driveway represents an actionable interference I shall consider in the context of the leases of the flats.

I turn to the position of the first and fourth plaintiffs as lessees of garage 50. As I have said, access to and egress from garage 50 will to some extent be interfered with by the proposed car wash. It is, however, still possible, albeit perhaps with a little relatively easy manoeuvring, for even a large car either to reverse into the garage and exit forwards or to enter forwards and reverse out. I do not regard the small degree of extra difficulty that the car wash may cause as representing a substantial interference.

There remains the narrowing of the driveway. The flat leases, the lease of car parking space 32 and the two garage leases entitle the respective grantees to a vehicular right of passage along the rear driveway. The width of the driveway over which the right is exercisable will for an appreciable distance, say 10 to 12 metres, be reduced by the car wash from nine metres down to 4.14 metres. Is this substantial? Would this interfere with the grantees' reasonable use of the driveway?

There are 56 flats at Cavendish House. The rear driveway may be used by all of them, their visitors and licensees. Vehicles using the rear driveway may range from small cars to large commercial vans. On occasion, lorries may require to use the driveway. The plaintiffs were granted rights of way over a driveway nine metres or thereabouts in width, but with the usable width capable of being reduced by about two metres in the event of cars being parked along the east side of the driveway. I am reluctant to accept that a grantor, having granted a right of way over a nine-metre driveway, can reduce the width of the way by more than a half over an appreciable distance and then require the grantees to accept the reduction on the ground that what is left is all that they reasonably need. It seems to me that the proposed reduction will materially and permanently detract from the quality of the rear driveway and of the plaintiffs' rights over it. The facts of *Clifford v. Hoare* (1874) L.R. 9 C.P. 362 bear no comparison. The encroachment in that case was on any view trivial. That is not the case here. It does not seem to me possible to say that the permanent narrowing of the rear driveway from nine to 4.14 metres over the length of the proposed car wash would leave the rear driveway as convenient for the reasonable use of the plaintiffs as it was before the reduction. The plaintiffs have been granted a right of way over a nine-metre driveway. The enjoyment thereof to which they are entitled under their respective grants cannot, in my judgment, be limited by requiring them to accept a 4.14 metre driveway. If the freeholders wanted the right to construct a car wash on the driveway and thereby to reduce its width to 4.14 metres it was, in my judgment, incumbent on them to reserve that right in the leases. Not having done so, they are not, in my view, entitled to remedy the omission by arguing that 4.14 metres is all the plaintiffs reasonably need. The plaintiffs are, in my judgment, entitled under their grants to the relative luxury, if that is what it is, of a nine-metre right of way. That, after all, is part of what they have paid for.

In my judgment, therefore, the construction of the proposed car wash would represent a substantial interference with the rights of way over the rear driveway granted by the leases.

NOTES:

1. The decision was upheld by the Court of Appeal [1986] 1 W.L.R. 512.

2. In *Saint v. Jenner* [1973] Ch. 275 the plaintiff had a right of way along a track on land owned by the defendant. The defendant subsequently metalled the track; but, in order to reduce the speed of vehicles using the track, he constructed ramps at intervals. However, potholes developed on each side of the ramps, effectively increasing the height of the ramps so as to constitute a substantial interference with the enjoyment of the right of way. Although the servient owner normally has no obligation to repair and maintain the servient land for the purposes of the easement, the Court of Appeal held that a

servient owner who elects to carry out work has an obligation to maintain that work so as not to cause substantial interference.

3. In *Greenwich Healthcare NHS Trust v. London and Quadrant Housing Trust* [1998] 1 W.L.R. 1749 Lightman J. declined to decide whether and in what circumstances the alteration of the route of an easement of way would constitute a substantial and actionable interference with the easement.

F. Extinguishment of Easements

Once easements have been acquired, subject to registration requirements in the case of equitable easements, they endure through successive ownerships of the dominant land and the servient land. However, there are circumstances in which easements may be extinguished.

1. Unity of ownership and occupation

It follows from the principle that a landowner cannot have rights over his own land that an easement will be extinguished if the freehold of the dominant land and the servient land come into common ownership and occupation: *R. v. Inhabitants of Hermitage* (1692) Carth. 239. In such circumstances, the easement will not revive automatically if the two plots of land are subsequently separated again. On the other hand, if the freehold owner of the dominant land acquires a lease of the servient land, any easement will be merely suspended and will revive when the lease terminates or is assigned: *Thomas v. Thomas* (1835) 2 Cr.M. & R. 34; *Simper v. Foley* (1862) 2 John. & H. 555.

2. Release

An easement may be released by the owner of the dominant land. At law such a release must be effected by deed: *Lovell v. Smith* (1857) 3 C.B.N.S. 120; but in equity an informal release is likely to be recognised where it would be inequitable to permit the owner of the dominant land to revive the easement: *Davies v. Marshall* (1861) 10 C.B.N.S. 697; *Waterlow v. Bacon* (1866) L.R. 2 Eq. 514.

3. Implied release or abandonment

Mere non-user of an easement does not constitute abandonment of that easement. Something more is required if the court is to conclude that an easement has been abandoned. In *Gotobed v. Pridmore* (1971) 217 E.G. 759 Buckley L.J. summarised the position as follows:

To establish abandonment of an easement the conduct of the dominant owner must ... have been such as to make it clear that he had at the relevant time a firm intention that neither he nor any successor in title of his should thereafter make use of the easement.... Abandonment is not ... to be lightly inferred. Owners of property do not normally wish to divest themselves of it unless it is to their advantage to do so, notwithstanding that they may have no present use for it.

That passage was expressly adopted by the Court of Appeal in *Williams v. Usherwood* (1981) 45 P. & C.R. 235, 256 *per* Cumming-Bruce L.J., *Benn v. Hardinge* (1992) 66 P. & C.R. 246, 257 *per* Dillon L.J., *Bosomworth v. Faber* (1992) 69 P. & C.R. 288, 295 *per* Dillon L.J. and *Snell & Prideaux Ltd v. Dutton Mirrors Ltd* [1995] 1 E.G.L.R. 259, 261–262 *per* Stuart-Smith L.J. See also *Tehidy Minerals Ltd v. Norman* [1971] 2 Q.B. 528, 533 *per* Buckley L.J.

The test was held to be satisfied in *Williams v. Usherwood, supra,* where an expressly reserved right of way was held to have been abandoned when the dominant owner acquiesced in the closure of the access; and in *Bosomworth v. Faber, supra,* where a prescriptive right to the passage of water was held to have been abandoned when the dominant owner obtained a licence to disconnect and demolish the old supply system and to construct a new system.

In *Benn v. Hardinge, supra,* the Court of Appeal rejected the previously widely held view that non-user for a long period (in that case 175 years) would raise a presumption that the easement had been abandoned. However, the Law Commission has recommended the reinstatement of such a presumption if an easement could not be shown to have been exercised within the previous 20 years. The presumption, which would only apply to easements taking effect as overriding interests (and not to easements protected by registration), would be rebuttable if the dominant owner could show some reason for the non-user (such as user of some alternative right or the absence of any occasion to exercise the right): see Law Com. No. 254, *Land Registration for the Twenty-First Century* (1998), paras 5.21–5.23. Although the recommendation is made in the context of registered land, it is clearly arguable that it should be extended to unregistered land while it continues to exist.

Davis [1995] Conv. 291 questions whether it should be sufficient to establish an intention to abandon on the part of the dominant owner. Since the abandonment (or implied release) of an easement constitutes an exception to the statutory formality requirements for the release of rights in land, it is argued that the exception should operate, as with other exceptions to formality requirements, only where it would be unconscionable for the dominant owner to deny that the easement had been abandoned. Although the cases are far from conclusive, it is argued that the servient owner should have acted in reliance on the alleged abandonment of the easement, thereby establishing an estoppel.

4. Change of circumstances

In exceptional circumstances the courts may be prepared to find that an easement has become obsolete, in which case it may be regarded as having been extinguished. In *Huckvale v. Aegean Hotels Ltd* (1989) 58 P. & C.R. 163 Slade L.J. stated (at 173–174):

I think that no authority has been cited to us which establishes that a once valid easement can be extinguished in a case where dominant and servient tenements both still exist.

For all that, I would for my part be prepared to accept in principle that, even in a case of that nature, circumstances might have changed so drastically since the date of the original grant of an easement (for example by supervening illegality) that it would offend common sense and reality for the court to hold that an easement still subsisted. Nevertheless, I think that the court could properly so hold only in a very clear case. The authorities cited by Nourse L.J. illustrate how slow is the court to infer the *abandonment* of an easement. *A fortiori*, in my judgment, in the absence of evidence or proof of abandonment, the court should be slow to hold that an easement has been extinguished by frustration, unless the evidence shows clearly that because of a change in circumstances since the date of the original grant there is no practical possibility of its ever again benefiting the dominant tenement in the manner contemplated by that grant. If there has been abandonment, and that abandonment is proved, of course a quite different situation in law will arise.

See also Nourse L.J., *ibid.* at 170; Butler-Sloss L.J., *ibid.* at 172. For comment, see [1990] Conv. 292.

G. Reform

Certain specific proposals for reform of the law relating to the prescriptive acquisition of easements have been referred to: see Law Reform Committee, *Fourteenth Report: Acquisition of Easements and Profits by Prescription* (1966), *supra*, p. 673; Law Com. No. 254, *Land Registration for the Twenty-First Century* (1998), *supra*, p. 674.

Reform of the law relating to easements generally has been linked with reform of the law relating to covenants affecting freehold land: see *post*, p. 804.

8

COVENANTS AFFECTING FREEHOLD LAND

A. INTRODUCTION

1. The role of covenants

The industrial revolution was characterised by a shift from agriculture to trade, commerce and industry, which was accompanied by the movement of people from rural to urban areas. Land, particularly urban land, became an increasingly valuable commodity both for commercial and residential purposes; and, particularly in the case of land acquired for residential purposes, there was a desire to protect its amenity by restricting its present and future use. There was no public planning control so that the restrictions on the use of land depended upon private control operating between individual landowners.

The common law proved inadequate to meeting these needs. The law of contract provided a means of enforcement between the original parties to any agreement but the common law doctrine of privity of contract prevented the enforcement of such agreements against successors in title of the original parties. The law relating to easements provided no solution since easements to protect character, value, amenity or views were not recognised: see *ante*, p. 622. It was the intervention of equity and the development of the restrictive covenant as an equitable interest in land that provided a partial solution. However, that solution has remained partial and imperfect; and, in consequence, reform has long been on the agenda: see *infra*, p. 804.

2. Restrictive covenants and planning control

The advent of generally applicable public law planning control has not superseded the private law controls provided by the law relating to covenants. First, the potential scope of private law control is wider than the control provided by public planning law: private law can be used to enforce restrictions on the use of land that cannot be the legitimate concern of planning control. Secondly, even where some matter relating to the use of land is within the scope of both public and private law controls, those controls are cumulative. Thus, even where the local planning authority, in the exercise of its public law powers, has authorised a particular use of land, as a matter of private law that permission cannot authorise that use if the landowner has covenanted that he will not so use the land. In other words, a landowner who has covenanted with his neighbour not to build on his land cannot escape that promise by obtaining planning permission from the planning authority.

Law Commission Report No. 127, Transfer of Land: The Law of Positive and Negative Covenants (1984), paras 2.5–2.7

2.5 Planning law may overlap to some extent with restrictive covenants, but we do not believe that it has removed the need for them. Perhaps especially in residential property developments, restrictive covenants commonly regulate many things for which planning law would not cater—and do so for the mutual benefit of the residents and with the aim of preserving the character and standard of the development as a whole. Nor does it seem to us that these things are confined, as the Royal Commission suggested they might be, to matters affecting privacy. Powerful support for this view is to be found in this extract from the preface to the sixth edition of *Preston & Newsom's Restrictive Covenants Affecting Freehold Land*:

> "One thing that is abundantly plain is that there is no prospect whatever that restrictive covenants will become unnecessary and that their place will be taken by the planning laws. For planning standards are still too often below the standards imposed by restrictive covenants. Thus in *Re Bass Ltd's Application* (1973) 26 P. & C.R. 156 the Lands Tribunal held that the suggested modification would inflict upon the persons entitled to the benefit of the restriction noise, fumes, vibrations, dirt and the risk of accidents: these proposals had received planning permission. Again, in the *Wrotham Park* case [1974] 1 W.L.R. 798 it was the local authority itself which, having bought the land for a very small sum, put it up for sale and received £90,000 on the basis that it was to be built upon, thereby destroying an open space which the owners of surrounding houses valued and which had been deliberately created by the original covenantee."

It is also true that certain changes of use and building operations to which an adjoining resident might reasonably and justifiably object do not require planning permission at all.

2.6 It might perhaps be argued that the answer lies not in preserving the power to impose private restrictions but in extending the ambit of planning law. We think it unrealistic, however, to expect planning authorities to concern themselves with all the detailed matters for which restrictive covenants now commonly make provision. Indeed a Past President of the Royal Town Planning Institute has expressed the view that: "It puts planning authorities under unreasonable pressure if they are expected to safeguard the interests of adjoining owners". It must also be remembered that restrictive covenants may be used to serve purposes which are private and individual and for which planning law would not cater however far it were extended.

2.7 It must also be remembered that planning restrictions, even if they are wholly adequate to the needs of adjoining owners, are enforceable only by the planning authorities. Most owners would wish to have the power of enforcement in their own hands.

NOTES:

1. For general discussion of the relationship between restrictive covenants and planning control, see Mellows (1964) 28 Conv. 190.

2. On the relationship between restrictive covenants and planning control in the context of the discharge or modification of covenants, see *infra*, p. 792.

3. Terminology of covenants

A covenant is properly defined as a promise contained in a deed; the promise is enforceable between the parties to the covenant because, irrespective of consideration, the common law regards the formalities involved in a deed as a substitute for consideration. However, in practice the term is used to denote any enforceable promise affecting the use of land. The person who makes the promise and thus undertakes the burden of the covenant is the *covenantor*; the person in whose favour the promise is made and thus for whom the benefit of the covenant is intended is the *covenantee*. Covenants may be *positive*, where the covenantor promises to do something for the benefit of the covenantee (for example, to build a boundary wall between his land and the land of the covenantee); or they may be *negative*, where, for the benefit of the covenantee, the covenantor promises to refrain from doing something (for example, where the covenantor promises not to use his land for business purposes). Such covenants are most commonly entered into on the sale (or other transfer) of part of the land of the transferor.

4. The question of enforceability

As between the covenantor and covenantee, a covenant is enforceable in the same way as any other contract. However, covenants are not normally intended for the benefit of the original covenantee only; rather they are intended to preserve the character and value of the land through changes in ownership. In *Osborne v. Bradley* [1903] 2 Ch. 446, Farwell J. identified (at 450) three general classes of covenant (entered into by a purchaser of land):

(i) where the covenant is entered into simply for the vendor's own benefit; (ii) where the covenant is for the benefit of the vendor in his capacity of owner of a particular property; and (iii) where the covenant is for the benefit of the vendor, in so far as he reserves unsold property, and also for the benefit of other purchasers, as part of what is called a building scheme.

The need for continuing enforceability is clear in the case of covenants in classes (ii) and (iii). In such circumstances, it was essential that, because of the doctrine of privity, the law developed some non-contractual means of ensuring that covenants continued to be enforceable even after the original parties to the covenant had parted with their land.

The question of the continued enforceability of covenants relating to freehold land forms the principal subject-matter of this chapter. Since continuing enforceability depends upon the capacity of the benefit and burden of covenants to survive through changes in ownership of land, it will be apparent that most problems relating to the enforcement of covenants can be reduced to two questions:

(1) Has the benefit of the covenant passed to the person seeking to enforce the covenant?

(2) Has the burden of the covenant passed to the person against whom enforcement is sought?

So formulated, those questions presuppose an existing dispute as to enforceability; but, in substance, the same questions should be addressed at the earlier stage of drafting covenants:

(1) Can the covenant be drafted in such a way that the benefit of the covenant will pass to all persons who may legitimately seek to enforce the covenant?
(2) Can the covenant be drafted in such a way that the burden of the covenant will pass to all persons against whom enforcement may legitimately be sought?

In providing answers to these questions, it must be noted that the common law and equity have developed different rules as to whether and in what circumstances the benefit and burden of covenants may pass to successors in title of the original parties; and these different rules must be examined separately. However, it may be useful at this stage to provide a brief summary. First, both the common law and equity permit the passing of the benefit of both positive and negative (restrictive) covenants. Secondly, the common law does not permit the passing of the burden of any covenant, whether positive or negative. Thirdly, equity permits the passing of the burden of negative (restrictive) covenants but not positive covenants.

In order to illustrate the law relating to the enforceability of covenants, reference will be made to the diagram opposite, representing a neighbourhood of three houses which are subsequently transferred to successors in title.

Redacre and Blackacre are in common ownership but the owner decides to sell Blackacre. Pursuant to the conditions of sale the purchaser of Blackacre enters into three covenants with the vendor:

(i)   not to use Blackacre for business purposes;
(ii)   to maintain the exterior of Blackacre in good repair;
(iii) not to play recordings of the music of a specified list of popular musicians.

The examination of the rules relating to the passing of the benefit and burden of covenants will seek to discuss all questions of enforceability raised by the circumstances outlined above:

(a) enforcement by the original covenantee against the original covenantor;
(b) enforcement by the original owner of Greenacre against the original covenantor;
(c) enforcement by a successor in title of the original covenantee, or by a successor in title of the original owner of Greenacre, against the original covenantor;
(d) enforcement by the original covenantee, or by the original owner of Greenacre, against a successor in title of the original covenantor;
(e) enforcement by a successor in title of the original covenantee, or by a successor in title of the original owner of Greenacre, against a successor in title of the original covenantor.

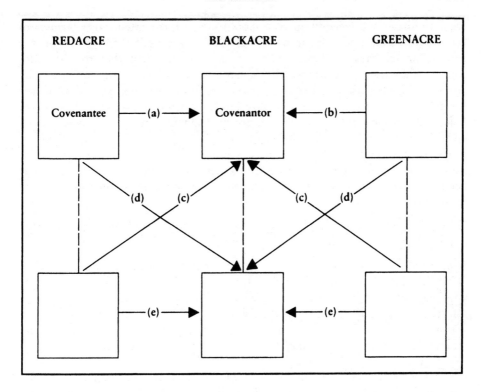

5. The notion of "touch and concern"

It will become apparent that there is one requirement for enforceability which is common to the rules of both common law and equity: that the covenant must "touch and concern" the land of the covenantee. It is therefore convenient to discuss that requirement at the outset. The requirement expresses the idea that, if a covenant is to be capable of enforcement by and/ or against persons other than the original parties, it must necessarily have been created for the benefit of the land of the original covenantee and not be merely personal to him: see the classification of covenants in *Osborne v. Bradley* [1903] 2 Ch. 446, *supra*, p. 705. As has been seen (*ante*, p. 421), the requirement originates in the law relating to leasehold covenants but it has been adapted to the context of covenants between freehold owners. Thus, whereas in the former context covenants relate to acts to be done or not to be done on the land of the *covenantee*, in the later context covenants relate to acts to be done or not to be done on the land of the *covenantor*. This point of difference renders inappropriate in the context of freehold covenants any requirement of *physical* "touching and concerning": see *Rogers v. Hosegood* [1900] 2 Ch. 388, 404 *per* Collins L.J. The requirement has been reformulated in terms of "benefiting" the land of the covenantee: see, *e.g. Newton Abbot Co-operative Society Ltd v. Williamson & Treadgold Ltd* [1952] Ch. 286 *per* Upjohn J.; *Marten v. Flight Refuelling Ltd* [1962] Ch. 115 *per* Wilberforce J.; alternatively, and by analogy with the law relating to easements, it has been argued that the requirement should be formulated in terms of "accommodation": see Hayton (1971) 87 L.Q.R. 539, 544–545. In the context of schemes of development, it may be sufficient that the covenant benefits the area covered by the scheme *as a whole* without necessarily benefiting directly the land of the person seeking to enforce the covenant: see *Lord Northbourne v. Johnston & Son* [1922] 2 Ch. 309, 319 *per* Sargant J.; *Gilbert v. Spoor* [1983] Ch. 27, 33 *per* Eveleigh L.J., noted at [1982] Conv. 452.

The substance of the requirement has been expressed in a variety of ways. Thus, adopting formulations from the context of leasehold covenants, it has been said that "the covenant must either affect the land as regards mode of occupation, or it must be such as *per se*, and not merely from collateral circumstances, affects the value of the land": *Rogers v. Hosegood* [1900] 2 Ch. 388, 395 *per* Farwell J., adopting the formulations of Lord Ellenborough C.J. and Bayley J. in *Congleton Corp. v. Pattison* (1808) 10 East 130, 135, 138; *Smith and Snipes Hall Farm Ltd v. River Douglas Catchment Board* [1949] 2 K.B. 500, 506 *per* Tucker L.J. Where the "effect on value" test is adopted, "the benefit of a covenant will pass if and in so far as it necessarily affects the value of the land, in this sense, that the owner of the land would get more for his land by reason of the covenant being attached to and annexed to it": *Forster v. Elvet Colliery Co. Ltd* [1908] 1 K.B. 629, 635 *per* Cozens-Hardy M.R. However, although the requirement may be satisfied where the pecuniary value of the land of the covenantee is enhanced by the covenant, it may also be satisfied where the covenant preserves the character or amenities of the land, even though the land of the covenantor *and the land of the covenantee* might be worth more if the burdened land were released from the covenant: *Kelly v. Barrett* [1924] 2 Ch. 379, 395–396 *per* Tomlin J.; *Marten v. Flight Refuelling Ltd* [1962] Ch. 115, 139 *per* Wilberforce J. More recent formulations, adopting the language of "benefit", require that the land of the covenantee "must be capable of deriving, and must derive, benefit from the covenant. A benefit for this purpose must be something affecting either the value of the land or the method of its occupation or enjoyment": *Re Gadd's Land Transfer* [1966] Ch. 56, 66 *per* Buckley J.

Strict compliance with the qualification that the benefit must not be attributable to collateral circumstances would probably exclude from the category of covenants that touch and concern the land covenants not to compete with a business conducted on the land of the covenantee. However, such covenants have been held to touch and concern the land of the covenantee: *Newton Abbot Co-operative Society Ltd v. Williamson & Treadgold Ltd* [1952] Ch. 286, *infra*, p. 769. This conclusion would follow from an extension of the analogy with easements and the adoption of the requirement that a covenant must "accommodate" the land of the covenantee; for that notion has been held to include benefit for a business conducted on the dominant land: see *ante*, p. 619.

Finally, in *Hemingway Securities Ltd v. Dunraven Ltd* (1994) 71 P. & C.R. 30 a covenant restricting the disposition of land was held to satisfy the "touch and concern" requirement, although it is difficult to see how such a covenant affects the mode of occupation or the value of the covenantee's land: see [1995] Conv. 416. Moreover, no reference was made to the contrary view expressed in *Shepherd Homes Ltd v. Sandham (No. 2)* [1971] 1 W.L.R. 1062, 1070 *per* Megarry J.

The notion of "touch and concern" and its proof are discussed further at various points in this chapter.

6. Procedural matters

There are a range of remedies and other procedures available to determine disputes relating to covenants.

First, a plaintiff covenantee who can establish (a) that the benefit of a covenant has passed to him, (b) that the burden of the covenant has passed to the defendant and (c) that the defendant has committed, or is threatening to commit, a breach of the covenant is potentially entitled to a range of remedies (or a combination of remedies) according to the circumstances: (i) a declaration as to (a), (b) or (c) above; (ii) an injunction, restraining a threatened breach of the covenant; (iii) a mandatory injunction, requiring the remedying of any action taken in breach of the covenant: see *Wakeham v. Wood* (1982) 43 P. & C.R. 40; (iv) common law damages by way of compensation for any past breach of the covenant; and (v) pursuant to section 50 of the Supreme Court Act 1981 (formerly section 2 of the Chancery Amendment Act 1858 (Lord Cairns' Act)), equitable damages by way of compensation for any past breach "in addition to" or "in substitution for" an injunction to restrain any future breach: see *Wrotham Park Estate Co. Ltd v. Parkside Homes Ltd* [1974] 1 W.L.R. 798; *Surrey CC v. Bredero Homes Ltd* [1993] 1 W.L.R. 1361, noted at [1992] Conv. 457; *Jaggard v. Sawyer* [1995] 1 W.L.R. 269, noted at [1995] Conv. 141; *Gafford v. Graham* (1998) 77 P. & C.R. 73, noted at (1998) 114 L.Q.R. 555. For an overview of the remedies for breach of restrictive covenant, see Martin [1996] Conv. 329.

Secondly, in any such enforcement action, the defendant covenantor, on the assumption that he has failed to negate any of matters (a), (b) or (c) above, may seek to establish that, notwithstanding the breach of covenant, it would be inappropriate in the circumstances for the court to grant any or all of the above remedies: see *infra*, p. 793.

Thirdly, a potential defendant in an enforcement action may seek to pre-empt any such action in one of two ways. First, pursuant to section 84(2) of the Law of Property Act 1925 any person interested in freehold land may apply to the court for a declaration (a) as to whether or not the land is, or would in any given event be, affected by a restriction; and (b) as to the nature and extent of any such restriction and its enforceability. This procedure may also be used by a vendor seeking to reassure a prospective purchaser of the land. Secondly, pursuant to section 84(1) any person interested in freehold land that is affected by a restriction as to its use, may apply to the Lands Tribunal for an order wholly or partially to discharge or modify that restriction: see *infra*, p. 791; and pursuant to section 84(9) a defendant in an action to enforce a restrictive covenant may request leave to apply to the Lands Tribunal for an order under section 84(1).

Finally, where a statutory body has been entrusted with functions to be discharged in the public interest and that body has been given power to acquire land for the purpose of discharging those functions, restrictive covenants affecting the land acquired cannot be enforced by injunction or damages, if the legislature has provided for an exclusive remedy by way of statutory compensation: *Brown v. Heathlands Mental Health NHS Trust* [1996] 1 All E.R. 133; *Greenwich Healthcare NHS Trust v. London and Quadrant Housing Trust* [1998] 1 W.L.R. 1749. For an examination of the issues, see Rutherford [1996] Conv. 260, [1998] Conv. 65.

B. Enforcement Between the Original Parties

1. Enforcement by the original covenantee against the original covenantor

The original covenantee can always enforce the covenant against the original covenantor: see issue (a) on the diagram. They are parties to a contract and the usual remedies of damages and/or injunction are in principle available. As a matter of contract, the contractual remedies continue to be available to the covenantee even after he has parted with his land (unless the covenant was so drafted as to apply only while the covenantee continued to own the land): *London CC v. Allen* [1914] 3 K.B. 642, 664 *per* Scrutton J. However, even where the covenant is not so limited, the covenantee who parts with the land before a breach of covenant is committed will be unable to obtain an injunction since he no longer has a legal interest to protect; and he will be able to obtain only nominal damages since he will have suffered no loss: *Formby v. Barker* [1903] 2 Ch. 539, 555 *per* Stirling L.J.; *London CC v. Allen, supra,* 661 *per* Buckley L.J. Similarly, by virtue of section 79(1) of the Law of Property Act 1925, the covenantor remains liable in contract in respect of breaches of covenant committed by his successors in title after he has parted with his land, again unless the covenant was so drafted as to apply only while the covenantee continued to own the land. Subject to those qualifications, all three covenants under consideration would be enforceable between the original parties.

2. Enforcement by the original owner of Greenacre against the original covenantor

There is a further dimension to the question of enforcement between the original parties to the covenant. Suppose that the purchaser of Blackacre (B) acts in breach of his covenant not to use Blackacre for business purposes. Irrespective of any enforcement action taken by the original owner of Redacre (R), the original owner of Greenacre (G) may argue that the observance of the covenant would benefit him (or rather that its non-observance would adversely affect him); and he may wish to enforce the covenant against B. The question is whether G, who it can be assumed would *in fact* benefit from the observance of the covenant, can take legal action to enforce it against B: see issue (b) on the diagram.

The doctrine of privity of contract would seem to indicate a negative answer. The fact that the performance of a contract would benefit a third party does not entitle that third party to take legal action in respect of a breach of the contract. On the other hand, the doctrine of privity creates no difficulties if the third party is named *as a covenantee* in the covenant: that person may sue on the covenant even if he is not named *as a party to the covenant*. Thus, if B covenanted "with R to confer a benefit on G", the doctrine of privity of contract would preclude G from suing B for breach of covenant; but, if B covenanted "with R *and with* G to confer a benefit on G", G would be named as a covenantee and would be able to sue B for a breach of the covenant even through G was not named as a *party* to the convenant. This avenue was widened by section 56(1) of the Law of Property Act 1925 so that it also applies where a person who is not a party to the covenant is included as a covenantee *by generic description*.

Section 56(1) provides:

A person may take an immediate or other interest in land or other property, or the benefit of any condition, right of entry, covenant or agreement over or respecting land or other property, although he may not be named as a party to the conveyance or other instrument.

Thus, if B covenanted "with R *and with the owners for the time being of Greenacre*", the covenant would be enforceable by G: *Re Ecclesiastical Commissioners for England's Conveyance* [1936] Ch. 430, *infra*, p. 713; *White v. Bijou Mansions Ltd* [1937] Ch. 610, 624–625 *per* Simonds J., *infra*, p. 713; and see *Lyus v. Prowsa Developments Ltd* [1982] 1 W.L.R. 1044, 1049 *per* Dillon J.; *Amsprop Trading Ltd v. Harris Distribution Ltd* [1997] 1 W.L.R. 1025, 1029–1033 *per* Neuberger J. The only limitation stems from the fact that the person relying on section 56(1) is treated as an original covenantee. It follows that he must be identifiable and in existence at the time of the covenant: *Kelsey v. Dodd* (1881) 52 L.J. Ch. 34, 39 *per* Jessel M.R.; *Forster v. Elvet Colliery Co. Ltd* [1908] 1 K.B. 629, 637 *per* Fletcher Moulton L.J.; *Grant v. Edmondson* [1931] 1 Ch. 1, 27 *per* Lawrence L.J. Thus, notwithstanding the terms of the generic description, successors in title of G would not be entitled to sue on the covenant *by virtue of section 56(1)*: their entitlement to sue would depend on the rules relating to the passing of the benefit from G: see *infra*.

Re Ecclesiastical Commissioners for England's Conveyance [1936] Ch. 430

(Ch D., Luxmoore J.)

In 1887 the Commissioners conveyed West Heath House to Gotto, who, on behalf of himself and his successors in title, covenanted with the

Commissioners and their successors to observe certain restrictive covenants. The conveyance also contained a separate covenant in similar terms, by which Gotto covenanted with the Commissioners' "assigns owners for the time being of the land adjoining or adjacent to the said land hereby conveyed". The applicants were the successors in title of Gotto and were seeking a declaration as to the enforceability of the second covenant. The respondents were successors in title to neighbouring land which had been sold by the Commissioners before the conveyance to Gotto.

LUXMOORE J.:

Having ascertained that restrictive covenants were imposed in respect of the West Heath House property and that the form of the covenants is such as to make the burden of them run with the land, it is necessary to consider whether they were imposed for the benefit of any and what other hereditaments. For it is well settled that apart from any building scheme, restrictive covenants may be enforced if they are expressed in the original deed to be for the benefit of a particular parcel or particular parcels of land, either expressly mentioned or clearly identified in the deed containing the original covenants. It was argued on behalf of the applicants that the right to enforce such covenants is limited to the original covenantees and their successors in title—the right in the case of the successors in title being limited to those whose land was the property of the original covenantees at the date when the covenants were imposed. It was also argued that the right to enforce the covenants did not extend to any owners of land who were neither express assignees of the benefit of the covenants, nor successors in title of the original covenantees in respect of land acquired by such successors from the Ecclesiastical Commissioners subsequent to the date of the deed by which the covenants were imposed. I think these arguments failed to give due consideration to the provisions of s.5 of the Real Property Act 1845, as repealed and re-enacted by s.56 of the Law of Property Act 1925. Sect.5 of the Act of 1845 provides that under an indenture, executed after October 1, 1845, the benefit of a condition or covenant respecting any tenements or hereditaments may be taken, although the taker thereof be not named as a party to the indenture. In the case of *Forster v. Elvet Colliery Co. Ltd* [1908] 1 K.B. 629, it was held that the condition or covenant referred to in the section must, in order to be enforceable by a person not a party to the deed, be one the benefit of which runs with the land of the person seeking to enforce it. The actual decision was upheld in the House of Lords under the name *Dyson v. Forster* [1909] A.C. 98, 102, but Lord Macnaghten expressed doubt whether the section ought to be so restricted. He refrained however from resolving the doubt, because he agreed with the view that the covenants in the particular case ran with the land and it was therefore unnecessary to do so.

The alteration which has been made in the verbiage of s.5 of the 1845 Act by s.56 of the 1925 Act has not in my opinion affected the position so as to limit the right of a person not a party to the deed to enforce covenants affecting land to those which run with the land. The material words are as follows: "A person may take ... the benefit of any condition, ... covenant or agreement ... respecting land or other property, although he may not be named as a party to the conveyance or other instrument." It seems to me that the effect of these words is to enlarge the scope of the earlier words, for it extends the rights of a person not a party to a deed to covenants affecting every kind of property personal as well as real. So far as every species of personal property other than lease-hold is concerned it is obvious that the covenants to be enforced cannot be restricted to those running with the property, for there are no such covenants. What it is necessary to consider is the true construction of the conveyance of 1887, in order to ascertain whether any persons, not parties thereto, are described therein as the covenantees, and whether such covenants are expressed to affect any and what hereditaments. To determine what is the true construction of that document it is necessary to consider the surrounding circumstances as they existed at the date when it was executed.

NOTES:

1. Luxmoore J. held that by virtue of section 56(1) the covenant had been enforceable *ab initio* by those persons who, at the date of the conveyance to Gotto, were owners of "adjoining or adjacent" land formerly owned by the Commissioners, notwithstanding that those persons had not been parties to the covenant. That finding was a prerequisite to the further and separate question whether the benefit of the covenant so conferred had passed to the respondents, the successors in title of those neighbouring landowners. The court assumed *sub silentio* that the benefit had passed.

2. For contemporary comment, see (1937) 1 Conv. 74.

White v. Bijou Mansions Ltd [1937] Ch. 610

(Ch D., Simonds J.)

In 1886 Fellows, the predecessor in title of the plaintiff, purchased part of an estate. He covenanted with the vendors to use the land for private residential purposes only; and the vendors covenanted that any subsequent conveyance of the estate would contain a similar covenant and that they would enforce any such covenant at the request of Fellows or his successors in title. In 1890 the vendors conveyed another part of the estate to Nicholson, a predecessor in title of the defendant, who duly covenanted to use the land for private residential purposes only; and the covenant purported to be made with "the vendors their heirs and assigns". The plaintiff brought an action to restrain the defendant from breaching that covenant.

SIMONDS J.:

Can the plaintiff here enforce that covenant? I turn to look at it once more. There are covenants entered into in the year 1890, the first with the Davidsons, the second with the Daws, and they are covenants which are not annexed to any particular parcel of land. They are covenants entered into four years after the plaintiff acquired the title to his land. They are covenants the benefit of which has not, expressly or by implication, or in any manner whatsoever, been assigned to the plaintiff, and it appears to me to be quite impossible, apart from any building scheme or from the special statutory provision to which I shall presently refer, that the plaintiff can avail himself of this covenant and enforce it. There is here no question of a building scheme. That question was not raised in the pleadings and although at a late stage, indeed in the course of his reply on the case, Mr Grant invited me to allow an amendment so that the issue of a building scheme might be raised, I did not think fit at that stage to allow such an amendment. There is therefore no question of a building scheme.

It remains to consider the only other ground on which, as it appears to me, Mr Grant can possibly rest his case. He claims that he is entitled to enforce this covenant, entered into on May 2, 1890, on the ground that either under s.5 of the Real Property Act 1845, or under s.56 of the Law of Property Act 1925, that right is conferred on him. In the view which I take of both these sections it is unnecessary for me to consider whether he is in any way entitled to call in aid s.56 of the Act of 1925, with regard to covenants or agreements contained in a deed executed in 1890. It is necessary for me to say something about the earlier section before I come to consider the later section.

Sect.5 of the Real Property Amendment Act 1845, which was, as its title suggests, an Act to amend the law of real property, was aimed at remedying certain mischiefs in the state of the common law as it then was. There was a highly technical and artificial rule that by an indenture, as distinguished from a deed poll, an immediate interest in land could not be granted in favour of a grantee unless that grantee was a party to the deed. That mischief this section was designed to remedy. Further, there was the defect, as it was supposed, in the common law, that a person could not take advantage of a covenant in a deed unless he was a party to the deed. Be it observed that the Act of 1845 dealt with real property. This section was confined to the case of an indenture, and of an immediate interest created by that indenture, for it was never the law that an estate in remainder could not be validly granted in favour of a grantee if he were not a party. Indeed the common form of settlement then for centuries in vogue had limited estates in remainder not only to persons not parties to the deed but to persons not yet in existence.

Accordingly, s.5 of the Act of 1845 provided that under an indenture executed after October 1, 1845, an immediate estate or interest in any tenements or hereditaments and the benefit of a condition or covenant in respect of any tenements or hereditaments may be taken although the taker thereof be not named a party to the same indenture. I think the important aspect of that section for my present purpose is this. It appears to me to be quite plain that the section was a limited operation. It is intended to confer a benefit only on those persons to whom the deed purports to grant an estate or interest or those persons with whom there purports to be a covenant or agreement. It is impossible, in my view, to regard this section as creating a benefit in favour of any persons who may like to avail themselves of it and say: "If we can take advantage of this it will be for our benefit." It seems to me clear that this section was intended merely to provide that A.B., the grantee under a deed, might take an immediate interest although he was not a party, and similarly that A.B., with whom the covenant was purported to be made by the deed, should be able to avail himself of it although he was not a party to the deed, and in the few cases which have arisen under this section since 1845—and there appear to be very few—it will be found in every case where it has been applied that it has been in favour of a person who although not a party to the deed was a person to or with whom a grant or covenant purported to be made. That was the position under the Act of 1845.

I now turn to consider s.56 of the Act of 1925, which, it is said, however inaptly, takes the place of the earlier section. Sect.56 of the Law of Property Act 1925 provides as follows: "(1) A person may take an immediate or other interest in land or other property, or the benefit of any condition, right of entry, covenant or agreement over or respecting land or other property, although he may not be named as a party to the conveyance or other instrument". I think many difficulties may well arise on that section which do not fall to me to-day to solve. It appears to one at once that, so far as any other than an immediate interest in land is concerned the section is superfluous, because a person always could take another interest in land though not a party. It is at least a question how far such a provision is necessary at all in the case of personalty. Without deciding it, I should be disposed to think that equitable estates even in land were not subject to the old artificial rule and it is very doubtful if an interest in personalty was ever so subject. However that may be, for the purposes of the present case I think I am only concerned with one aspect of this question. Just as under s.5 of the Act of 1845 only that person could call it in aid who, although not a party, yet was a grantee or covenantee, so under s.56 of this Act only that person can call it in aid who, although not named as a party to the conveyance or other instrument, is yet a person to whom that conveyance or other instrument purports to grant some thing or with which some agreement or covenant is purported to be made. To give it any other meaning appears to me to open the door to claims or assertion of rights which cannot have been contemplated by the Legislature, for if that be not the limitation which must be imposed on this section it appears to me that there is no limit and it will be open to anybody to come into Court and say: "Here is a covenant which if enforced will redound to my advantage, therefore I claim the benefit of the section. I claim that this covenant or condition is one which should be enforced in my favour because it is for my benefit, whether intended for my benefit or not intended for my benefit would not appear to matter." I cannot give to the section any such meaning as that. I interpret it as a section which can be called in aid only by a person in whose favour the grant purports to be made or with whom the covenant or agreement purports to be made. If that is so, whether the plaintiff's claim arises under the earlier or the later Act, he cannot sue on it in this Court because he is not a person who, under the deed of 1890, can point to any grant or any covenant purported to be made to or with him. That is the construction which I place on s.56, with the result that the plaintiff's claim must fail.

NOTES:

1. The decision of Simonds J. was upheld by the Court of Appeal [1938] Ch. 351. Sir Wilfred Green M.R. said (at 365):

It seems to me, reading [Nicholson's] covenant in the light of the circumstances of the case at the time, that the assigns of [the vendors] who are referred to are such persons as thereafter would take from [the vendors] any part or unsold portion of the estate which still remained vested in them, and it does not as a matter of construction cover the previous assigns of [the vendors].

Such a construction may seem at first sight difficult to reconcile with the view taken in *Re Ecclesiastical Commissioners for England's Conveyance*. But the distinction seems to be that in that case the covenant was made with the *present* owners of the land previously sold. It may also have been significant that the conveyance to Fellows expressly provided for enforcement of subsequent purchasers' convenants by the vendors and not by Fellows and his successors directly: see *Re Dolphin's Conveyance* [1970] Ch. 654, 662 *per* Stamp J.

2. For contemporary comment, see (1938) 2 Conv. 71, 260.

3. For an arguably less strict construction of section 56(1), see *Stromdale and Ball Ltd v. Burden* [1952] Ch. 223; *Drive Yourself Hire Co. (London) Ltd v. Strutt* [1954] 1 Q.B. 250.

4. Lord Denning M.R. asserted that section 56(1) effectively destroyed the doctrine of privity: see, in the context of real property, *Smith and Snipes Hall Farm Ltd v. River Douglas Catchment Board* [1949] 2 K.B. 500, 517, *infra*, p. 716, and, in the purely contractual context, *Beswick v. Beswick* [1966] Ch. 538, 556–557. The House of Lords in *Beswick v. Beswick* [1968] A.C. 58 unanimously rejected the assertion in the purely contractual context. However, in the context of real property, there was some support for the interpretation of section 56(1) outlined above and for the approach of Simonds J. in *White v. Bijou Mansions Ltd*: see, in particular, *Beswick v. Beswick, supra*, 105–106 *per* Lord Upjohn; and that approach has subsequently been endorsed in *Lyus v. Prowsa Developments Ltd* [1982] 1 W.L.R. 1044, 1049 *per* Dillon J., and in *Amsprop Trading Ltd v. Harris Distribution Ltd* [1997] 1 W.L.R. 1025, 1029–1033 *per* Neuberger J.

C. Passing the Benefit and Burden at Common Law

1. Enforcement by a successor in title of the original covenantee, or by a successor in title of the original owner of Greenacre, against the original covenantor: passing the benefit

It is now necessary to turn to the situation where the original covenantee (including any person treated as an original covenantee by virtue of section 56(1) of the Law of Property Act 1925) has transferred his land to a successor in title. The question is whether the successor in title of the original covenantee can enforce the covenant and, as has been seen, the answer to that question turns on whether the benefit of the covenant has passed to the successor in title. At this stage the passing of the burden is not an issue; the question under consideration is the enforcement of the covenant against the original covenantor: see issue (c) on the diagram.

At common law it has long been established that the benefit of a covenant can run with the land so that a successor in title of the original covenantee can enforce the covenant against the original covenantor: see *The Prior's Case* (1368) Y.B. 42 Edw. 3 pl. 14 fol. 3A. Enforcement at common law is possible irrespective of whether the covenant is positive or negative: *Forster v. Elvet Colliery Co. Ltd* [1908] 1 K.B. 629, affirmed on appeal *sub nom. Dyson v. Forster* [1909] A.C. 98; and irrespective of whether the covenantor owns land to which the burden of the covenant is attached: *Rogers v. Hosegood* [1900] 2 Ch. 388, 395 *per* Farwell J. The leading modern case on enforceability at common law is *Smith and Snipes Hall Farm Ltd v. River Douglas Catchment Board* [1949] 2 K.B. 500.

Smith and Snipes Hall Farm Ltd v. River Douglas Catchment Board [1949] 2 K.B. 500

(CA, Tucker, Somervell and Denning L.JJ.)

In 1938 the defendant drainage authority covenanted with the freehold owners of certain land which was subject to flooding that, in return for a contribution towards the costs, it would make good and thereafter maintain a series of flood prevention works. One of the original covenantees conveyed her land to the first plaintiff, together with the benefit of the covenant; and the second plaintiff, a company controlled by the first plaintiff, subsequently occupied the land under a yearly tenancy. In 1946 severe flooding caused damage to the plaintiffs' land and they claimed, *inter alia*, damages for breach of covenant. Morris J. and the Court of Appeal held that the defendant authority was in breach of covenant and that the breach caused the damage.

TUCKER L.J.:
It remains to consider whether, in these circumstances, the plaintiffs, or either of them, can sue in respect of this breach. It is said for the defendants that the benefit of the covenant does not run with the land so as to bind a stranger who has not and never

had an interest in the land to be benefited and there being no servient tenement to bear the burden. Further, it is contended that such a covenant must by the terms of the deed in which it is contained relate to some specific parcel of land, the precise extent and situation of which can be identified by reference to the deed alone. It is first necessary to ascertain from the deed that the covenant is one which "touches or concerns" the land, that is, it must either affect the land as regards mode of occupation, or it must be such as per se, and not merely from collateral circumstances, affects the value of the land, and it must then be shown that it was the intention of the parties that the benefit thereof should run with the land. In this case the deed shows that its object was to improve the drainage of land liable to flooding and prevent future flooding. The location of the land is described as situate between the Leeds and Liverpool Canal and the River Douglas and adjoining the Eller Brook. In return for lump sum payments the board covenants to do certain work to the banks of the Eller Brook, one of such banks being in fact situate upon and forming part of the plaintiffs' lands, and to maintain for all time the work when completed. In my view the language of the deed satisfies both tests. It affects the value of the land per se and converts it from flooded meadows to land suitable for agriculture, and shows an intention that the benefit of the obligation to maintain shall attach thereto into whosesoever hands the lands shall come.

With regard to the covenantor being a stranger the case of *The Prior* is referred to in *Spencer's* case (1368) 1 Sm. L.C. 10th ed. pp. 56, 73, 13th ed. 51, 65, 73, in these words: "In the case of a grandfather, father and two sons, the grandfather being seised of the manor of D, whereof a chapel was parcel: a prior, with the assent of his convent, by deed covenanted for him and his successors, with the grandfather and his heirs, that he and his convent would sing all the week in his chapel, parcel of the said manor, for the lords of the said manor and his servants, etc.; the grandfather did enfeoff one of the manor in fee, who gave it to the younger son and his wife in tail; and it was adjudged that the tenants in tail, as terre-tenants (for the elder brother was heir), should have an action of covenant against the prior, for the covenant is to do a thing which is annexed to the chapel, which is within the manor, and so annexed to the manor, as it is there said." The notes to *Spencer's* case state: "When such a covenant (namely, covenants running with the land made with the owner of the land to which they relate) is made it seems to be of no consequence whether the covenantor be the person who conveyed the land to the covenantee or be a mere stranger." In volume 4 of Bythewood & Jarman's Conveyancing, 4th ed., at p. 268, the following passage from the third report of the Real Property Commissioners is quoted with approval: "Expressions found in some books would lead to the opinion that, in considering this class of covenant with reference to the benefit of them, there is a distinction between those cases where the covenantor is a party by whom the estate is, or has been, conveyed, and those in which he is a stranger to the estate. We think the authority of Lord Coke on this point (which is express (Co. Litt 384b)) sufficient to warrant us in disregarding this distinction".

In *Rogers v. Hosegood* [1900] 2 Ch. 388, 395, Farwell J. in a passage where he refers, amongst others, to *The Prior's* case—and I quote from Farwell J.'s judgment because, although this case went to the Court of Appeal, his judgment was approved, and the Court of Appeal had to deal with a rather different point—after stating what are the requirements in order that the covenant may run with the land, proceeds: "It is not contended that the covenants in question in this case have not the first characteristic, but it is said that they fail in the second. I am of opinion that they posses both. Adopting the definition of Bayley J. in *Congleton Corporation v. Pattison* (1808) 10 East. 130, 135 the covenant must either affect the land as regards mode of occupation, or it must be such as *per se*, and not merely from collateral circumstances, affects the value of the land. It is to my mind obvious that the value of Sir J. Millais's land is directly increased by the covenants in question. If authority is needed, I would refer to *Mann v. Stephens* (1846) 15 Sim. 377, a case very similar to the present; *Vyvyan v. Arthur* (1823) 1 B. & C. 410; *The Prior's* case; *Fleetwood v. Hull* (1889) 23 Q.B.D. 35; *White v. Southend Hotel* Co. [1897] 1 Ch. 767. I see no difficulty in holding that the benefit of a covenant runs with the land of the covenantee, while the burden of the same covenant does not run with the land of the covenantor."

In this state of the authorities it seems clear, despite some dicta tending to the contrary view, that such a covenant if it runs with the land is binding on the covenantor though a mere stranger, and that this point will not avail the defendant board. As to the requirement that the deed containing the covenant must expressly identify the particular land to be benefited, no authority was cited to us and in the absence of such authority I can see no valid reason why the maxim "Id certum est quod certum reddi potest" should not apply, so as to make available extrinsic evidence to prove the extent and situation of the lands of the respective land owners adjoining the Eller Brook situate between the Leeds and Liverpool Canal and the River Douglas.

On this part of the case the learned judge said: "In my judgment the contractual obligations of the board are not to be regarded as covenants running with the land. They do not differ from obligations which by agreement a firm of contractors might agree to discharge in reference to some particular land. The catchment board do not own any land and there is no question of any obligation in relation to or connexion with any land of theirs. The circumstances are different from those in the case of *Shayler v. Woolf* [1946] Ch. 320. Section 78 of the Law of Property Act does not affect the question as to what are covenants relating to the land of a covenantee. Furthermore, much of the reasoning of Lindley L.J. in *Austerberry v. Corporation of Oldham* (1885) 29 Ch.D. 750, 780, 781, is applicable. Although work might have to be done on the land which formerly belonged to Mrs Ellen Smith, and now belongs to the first plaintiff, equally it might be that for the effectual preventing of flooding of low meadows work on the banks of Eller Brook at some place considerably higher up the brook might have to be undertaken". I do not find anything in the judgments in *Austerberry v. Corporation of Oldham* which conflicts with the law as I have endeavoured to set it out above, and I have accordingly arrived at the conclusion that the covenant is one which runs with the land referred to therein, which land is capable of identification, and that it is binding on the defendant board; and, further, that by virtue of s.78 of the Law of Property Act 1925 it can be enforced at the suit of the covenantee and her successors in title and the persons deriving title under her or them, so that both the plaintiff Smith and the plaintiff company can sue in respect of the damage resulting to their respective interests therein by reason of the defendants' breach of covenant.

NOTES:

1. Denning L.J. stated (at 516–517):

The law on this subject was fully expounded by Mr Smith in his note to *Spencer's* case which has always been regarded as authoritative. Such covenants are clearly intended, and usually expressed, to be for the benefit of whomsoever should be the owner of the land for the time being; and at common law each successive owner has a sufficient interest to sue because he holds the same estate as the original owner. The reason which Lord Coke gave for this rule is the reason which underlies the whole of the principle now under consideration. He said in his work upon Littleton that it was "to give damages to the party grieved". If a successor in title were not allowed to sue it would mean that the covenantor could break his contract with impunity, for it is clear that the original owner, after he has parted with the land, could recover no more than nominal damages for any breach that occurred thereafter. It was always held, however, at common law that, in order that a successor in title should be entitled to sue, he must be of the same estate as the original owner. That alone was a sufficient interest to entitle him to enforce the contract. The covenant was supposed to be made for the benefit of the owner and his successors in title, and not for the benefit of anyone else. This limitation, however, was, as is pointed out in Smith's Leading Cases, capable of being "productive of very serious and disagreeable consequences", and it has been removed by s.78 of the Law of Property Act 1925, which provides that a covenant relating to any land of the covenantee shall be deemed to be made with the covenantee and his successors in title, "and the persons deriving title under him or them" and shall have effect as if such successors "and other persons" were expressed.

The covenant of the catchment board in this case clearly relates to the land of the covenantees. It was a covenant to do work on the land for the benefit of the land. By the statute, therefore, it is to be deemed to be made, not only with the original owner, but also with the purchasers of the land and their tenants as if they were expressed. Now if they were expressed, it would be clear that the covenant was made for their benefit; and they clearly have sufficient interest to entitle them to enforce it because they have suffered the damage. The result is that the plaintiffs come within the principle whereby a person interested can sue on a contract expressly made for his benefit.

Denning L.J. also expressed the view (i) that the doctrine of privity of contract, restricted to its proper scope, did not preclude the plaintiffs suing on the original contract; and (ii) that the plaintiffs could rely on section 56(1) of the Law of Property Act 1925. However, since the plaintiffs were not identifiable at the time of the covenant, reliance on section 56(1) would be inconsistent with previous authority: see *supra*, p. 711.

2. For contemporary comment, see (1949) 12 M.L.R. 498.

3. The case is regarded as express or implicit authority that the following conditions must be satisfied for the passing of the benefit at common law:

(i) The covenant must touch and concern the land of the covenantee: see *supra*, p. 707

(ii) The benefit of the covenant must be intended to run with the land of the covenantee.

(iii) The land to be benefited must be identified in the document containing the covenant or identifiable by extrinsic evidence.

(iv) The covenantee must have a legal estate in the land to be benefited: see *Webb v. Russell* (1789) 3 T.R. 393, 402 *per* Lord Kenyon C.J.

(v) It has been asserted that the person seeking to enforce the covenant had to have the *same* legal estate as the original covenantee because the covenant was regarded as running with the estate and not with the land: *Westhoughton UDC v. Wigan Coal and Iron Co. Ltd* [1919] 1 Ch. 159, 171 *per* Swinfen Eady M.R.; but for the contrary view, see *ibid.*, 176 *per* Duke L.J. Moreover, no such requirement was imposed in *The Prior's Case*, where the original covenantee was tenant in fee simple but the successful plaintiff, his successor, was tenant in tail. In any event section 78(1) of the Law of Property Act 1925 has been interpreted as requiring only that the person seeking to enforce the covenant has some legal estate in the land.

4. *Smith and Snipes Hall Farm Ltd v. River Douglas Catchment Board* was followed in *Williams v. Unit Construction Co. Ltd* (1951), noted at (1955) 19 Conv. 262.

5. For the implications of *Federated Homes Ltd v. Mill Lodge Properties Ltd* [1980] 1 W.L.R. 594, see *infra*, p. 756.

6. It would seem that if the conditions for passing the benefit are satisfied then the benefit is permanently attached (or annexed) to the land; thus

subsequent successors in title can enforce the covenant provided that they have the required legal estate in the land.

7. The benefit of a covenant can be assigned as a chose in action in accordance with section 136 of the Law of Property Act 1925.

If these requirements are applied to the three covenants under consideration, the benefit of covenants (i) and (ii) would probably run with Redacre; in particular those two covenants would seem to touch and concern the land in so far as they are intended to preserve its character and value. By contrast, covenant (iii) would almost certainly be held not to touch and concern the land, but to be personal to the original covenantee, so that any benefit would be incapable of passing to a successor in title.

2. Enforcement by the original covenantee, or by the original owner of Greenacre, against a successor in title of the original covenantor: passing the burden

It is now necessary to turn to the situation where the original covenantee retains his land but where the original covenantor transfers his land to a successor in title. The question is whether the original covenantee can enforce the covenant against the successor in title of the original covenantor; and, as has been seen, the answer to that question turns on whether the burden of the covenant has passed to the successor in title: see issue (d) on the diagram.

2.1 *The rule in* Austerberry v. Oldham Corp.
Whereas the benefit of a covenant can run with the land of the covenantee, the common law has always maintained a clear rule that the burden of a covenant cannot run with the freehold land of the covenantor.

Austerberry v. Oldham Corp. (1885) 29 Ch D. 750

(CA, Cotton, Lindley and Fry L.JJ.)

The predecessor in title of the plaintiff had sold land to the predecessors in title of the defendant for use as a road. The purchasers "their heirs and assigns" covenanted with the vendor "his heirs and assigns" that they would construct the road, maintain it thereafter in good repair and, on payment of tolls, permit the public to use it. When the defendant corporation sought to recover part of the cost of recent repairs to the road, the plaintiff sought a declaration that the defendant was not entitled to do so. The plaintiff argued, *inter alia*, that the defendant corporation was bound by the covenant to repair the road without charge.

LINDLEY L.J.:
The Plaintiff says:—"You, the corporation, have bought or acquired this road under an Act of Parliament which places you in the position of, and in no better position than, those from whom you got it; you acquired it from certain trustees, and those trustees covenanted with my predecessors in title to keep this road open for the public, and to repair it: You are bound by that covenant to repair, and I am in a position to enforce against you that covenant". ... That gives rise to one or two questions of law.
   The first question which I will consider is whether that covenant runs with the land,

as it is called—whether the benefit of it runs with the land held by the Plaintiff, and whether the burden of it runs with the land held by the Defendants; because, if the covenant does run at law, then the Plaintiff, so far as I can see, would be right as to this portion of his claim. Now, as regards the benefit running with the Plaintiff's land, the covenant is, so far as the road goes, a covenant to repair the road; what I mean by that is, there is nothing in the deed which points particularly to that portion of the road which abuts upon or fronts the Plaintiff's land—it is a covenant to repair the whole of the road, no distinction being made between the portion of that road which joins or abuts upon his land and the rest of the road; in other words, it is a covenant simply to make and maintain this road as a public highway; there is no covenant to do anything whatever on the Plaintiff's land, and there is nothing pointing to the Plaintiff's land in particular. Now it appears to me to be going a long way to say that the benefit of that covenant runs with the Plaintiff's land. I do not overlook the fact that the Plaintiff as a frontager has certain rights of getting on to the road; and if this covenant had been so worded as to shew that there had been an intention to grant him some particular benefit in respect of that particular part of his land, possibly we might have said that the benefit of the covenant did run with this land; but when you look at the covenant it is a mere covenant with him, as with all adjoining owners, to make this road, a small portion of which only abuts on his land, and there is nothing specially relating to his land at all. I cannot see myself how any benefit of this covenant runs with his land.

But it strikes me, I confess, that there is a still more formidable objection as regards the burden. Does the burden of this covenant run with the land so as to bind the Defendants? The Defendants have acquired the road under the trustees, and they are bound by such covenant as runs with the land. Now we come to face the difficulty; does a covenant to repair all this road run with the land—that is, does the burden of it descend upon those to whom the road may be assigned in future? We are not dealing here with a case of landlord and tenant. The authorities which refer to that class of cases have little, if any, bearing upon the case which we have to consider, and I am not prepared to say that any covenant which imposes a burden upon land does run with the land, unless the covenant does, upon the true construction of the deed containing the covenant, amount to either a grant of an easement, or a rent-charge, or some estate or interest in the land. A mere covenant to repair, or to do something of this kind, does not seem to me, I confess, to run with the land in such a way as to bind those who may acquire it.

It is remarkable that the authorities upon this point, when they are examined, are very few, and it is also remarkable that in no case that I know of, except one which I shall refer to presently, is there anything like authority to say that a burden of this kind will run with the land. That point has often been discussed, and I rather think the conclusion at which the editors of the last edition of *Smith's* Leading Cases have come to is right, that no case has been decided which does establish that such a burden can run with the land in the sense in which I am now using that expression.

[Having referred to *Holmes v. Buckley* (1691) 1 Eq.C.Ab. 27, *Morland v. Cook* (1868) L.R. 6 Eq. 252, *Cooke v. Chilcott* (1876) 3 Ch.D. 694, *Western v. Macdermott* (1866) L.R. 1 Eq. 499, Lindley L.J. continued:]

I am not aware of any other case which either shews, or appears to shew, that a burden such as this can be annexed to land by a mere covenant, such as we have got here; and in the absence of authority it appears to me that we shall be perfectly warranted in saying that the burden of this covenant does not run with the land. After all it is a mere personal covenant. If the parties had intended to charge this land for ever, into whosesoever hands it came, with the burden of repairing the road, there are ways and means known to conveyancers by which it could be done with comparative ease; all that would have been necessary would have been to create a rent-charge and charge it on the tolls, and the thing would have been done. They have not done anything of the sort, and, therefore, it seems to me to shew that they did not intend to have a covenant which should run with the land. That disposes of the part of the case which is perhaps the most difficult.

The last point was this—that even if it did not run with the land at law, still, upon the authority of *Tulk v. Moxhay* (1848) 2 Ph. 774, the Defendants, having bought the land with notice of this covenant, take the land subject to it. Mr Collins very properly did not press that upon us, because after the two recent decisions in the Court of Appeal in *Haywood v. Brunswick Permanent Benefit Building Society* (1881) 8 Q.B.D. 403 and *London and South Western Railway Co v. Gomm* (1882) 20 Ch.D. 562 that argument is untenable. *Tulk v. Moxhay* cannot be extended to covenants of this description. It appears to me, therefore, that upon all points the Plaintiff has failed, and that the appeal ought to be dismissed with costs.

NOTES:

1. The common law rule in *Austerberry v. Oldham Corp.* has little practical importance in relation to *restrictive* covenants since the burden of such covenants can run in equity by virtue of the doctrine in *Tulk v. Moxhay* (1848) 2 Ph. 774, *infra*, p. 728.

2. Nonetheless, the common law rule is extremely inconvenient and it has been criticised in a series of official reports over the past 30 years: see *Report of the Committee on Positive Covenants Affecting Land* (1965), Cmnd. 2719; Law Com. No. 11, *Restrictive Covenants* (1967); Law Commission Working Paper No. 36, *Appurtenant Rights* (1971); Law Com. No. 127, *Positive and Restrictive Covenants* (1984); *Report of the Aldridge Working Party on Commonhold* (1987), Cm. 179; *Lord Chancellor's Consultation Paper on Commonhold* (1990), Cm. 1345. However, the rule has been consistently followed and it was recently confirmed by the House of Lords in *Rhone v. Stephens* [1994] 2 A.C. 310. Lord Templeman regarded it as inappropriate for the courts to overrule the *Austerberry* case, which had provided the basis for transactions relating to the rights and liabilities of landowners for over 100 years: on the contrary the potential problems of such judicial legislation, together with the experience in relation to the enforcement of positive covenants between landlord and tenant, pointed to the clear need for Parliamentary legislation to deal with the consequences. For comment, see [1994] C.L.J. 446; (1994) 110 L.Q.R. 346; and see *Thamesmead Town Ltd v. Allotey* (1998) 76 P. & C.R. D20.

3. In *Rhone v. Stephens* the House of Lords also rejected the argument that the rule in *Austerberry* had been reversed by section 79 of the Law of Property Act 1925, thereby reaffirming the views expressed by the House of Lords in *Tophams Ltd v. Earl of Sefton* [1967] 1 A.C. 50, 73 *per* Lord Upjohn, 81 *per* Lord Wilberforce: see [1994] 2 A.C. 310, 321–322 *per* Lord Templeman.

4. The *Austerberry* case clearly illustrates the principle that a covenant will not be enforceable unless it is established *both* that the benefit has passed to the person seeking enforcement *and* that the burden has passed to the person against whom enforcement is sought.

2.2 *Circumventing the rule in* Austerberry v. Oldham Corp.

Since the rule in *Austerberry v. Oldham Corp.* has never been successfully challenged directly, various indirect means of enforcing positive covenants have been adopted or suggested. For an overview of the well-rehearsed devices and a new proposal for a "mutual deed of covenant", see Prichard (1973) 37 Conv. 194.

2.2.1 *Doctrine of benefit and burden*   Where a conveyance confers certain

benefits on the purchaser and also imposes certain burdens in the form of positive covenants, in certain circumstances, neither the original purchaser nor his successors in title can take the benefits unless they also accept the burdens.

Halsall v. Brizell [1957] Ch. 169

(Ch D., Upjohn J.)

The developers of a building estate retained ownership of the roads when they sold the individual plots. By a deed of covenant, the developers declared themselves bound by a trust to keep the roads open and to permit the purchasers of individual plots to use them; and the purchasers covenanted to contribute to the cost of maintaining the roads. The question arose whether the defendants, the executors of a successor in title of one of the original purchasers, were liable to pay a contribution pursuant to the deed of covenant.

UPJOHN J.:

In so far as the deed of 1851 purports to make the successors of the original contracting parties liable to pay calls, is it valid and enforceable at all? I think that this much is plain: that the defendants could not be sued on the covenants contained in the deed for at least three reasons. First, a positive covenant in the terms of the seventh covenant does not run with the land. Secondly, these particular provisions with regard to the payment of calls plainly infringed the rule against perpetuities. Of course, these parties are not parties to the contract. Finally, it is conceded that the provision for distraining on failure to pay is not valid. A right to distrain can only be annexed to a rent-charge, which this certainly is not. But it is conceded that it is ancient law that a man cannot take benefit under a deed without subscribing to the obligations thereunder. If authority is required for that proposition, I need but refer to one sentence during the argument in *Elliston v. Reacher* [1908] 2 Ch. 665, where Lord Cozens-Hardy M.R. observed (at p. 669): "It is laid down in Co. Litt. 230b, that a man who takes the benefit of a deed is bound by a condition contained in it, though he does not execute it." If the defendants did not desire to take the benefit of this deed, for the reasons I have given, they could not be under any liability to pay the obligations thereunder. But, of course, they do desire to take the benefit of this deed. They have no right to use the sewers which are vested in the plaintiffs, and I cannot see that they have any right, apart from the deed, to use the roads of the park which lead to their particular house, No. 22, Salisbury Road. The defendants cannot rely on any way of necessity or on any right by prescription, for the simple reason that when the house was originally sold in 1931 to their predecessor in title he took the house on the terms of the deed of 1851 which contractually bound him to contribute a proper proportion of the expenses of maintaining the roads and sewers, and so forth, as a condition of being entitled to make use of those roads and sewers. Therefore, it seems to me that the defendants here cannot, if they desire to use this house, as they do, take advantage of the trusts concerning the user of the roads contained in the deed and the other benefits created by it without undertaking the obligations thereunder. Upon that principle it seems to me that they are bound by this deed, if they desire to take its benefits.

NOTES:

1. For comment, see [1957] C.L.J. 35; (1957) 73 L.Q.R. 154; (1957) 21 Conv. 160.

2. See also *Hopgood v. Brown* [1955] 1 W.L.R. 213, 226 *per* Evershed M.R.; *E.R. Ives Investment Ltd v. High* [1967] 2 Q.B. 379, 394 *per* Lord Denning M.R., 399–400 *per* Danckwerts L.J.; *Montague v. Long* (1972) 24 P. & C.R. 240, 247–248 *per* Graham J.

3. The doctrine was the subject of exhaustive analysis by Megarry V.-C. in *Tito v. Waddell (No. 2)* [1977] Ch. 106, 289–311. Under what Megarry V.-C. termed the "pure principle of benefit and burden", a benefit conferred by a transaction and a prima facie independent burden imposed by the same transaction may become linked, so that successors in title of the original parties who wish to enjoy the benefit are bound also to assume the linked burden, even where that burden involves a *positive* obligation. (It is the prima facie independence of the burden that distinguishes the pure principle from (i) the grant of rights whose enjoyment is, as a matter of construction, intrinsically conditional upon, or qualified by, the assumption of some burden; and (ii) the grant of property to which some burden is annexed.) Megarry V.-C. distilled the principle from the cases of *Halsall v. Brizell* [1957] Ch. 169 and *E.R. Ives Investment Ltd v. High* [1967] 2 Q.B. 379; but he acknowledged that the "full features of the principle" had not yet been worked out: see Crane (1977) 41 Conv. 432, Aughterson [1985] Conv. 12; Davis [1998] C.L.J. 522, 537–544.

4. The doctrine was discussed in *Rhone v. Stephens* [1994] 2 A.C. 310, *infra*.

Rhone v. Stephens [1994] 2 A.C. 310

(HL, Lord Templeman, Lord Oliver, Lord Woolf, Lord Lloyd, Lord Nolan)

In 1960 the freehold owner of a building conveyed one part of the building (the cottage) to a purchaser and retained the other part (the house). Clause 2 of the conveyance conferred, *inter alia*, mutual rights and obligations of support for the two parts of the building. By clause 3 the vendor covenanted for himself and his successors in title to maintain part of the roof of the building in wind- and watertight condition. The cottage and the house changed hands several times and were eventually acquired by the plaintiffs and the original defendant respectively (the current defendant being the executrix of the original defendant). Each conveyance of the house contained a covenant by the purchaser indemnifying the vendor against breaches of the covenant in clause 3; and each conveyance of the cottage contained an express assignment of the benefit of the covenant by the vendor to the purchaser. In 1984 the plaintiffs complained of severe leaks in the roof and consequent damage to their property; and, following inadequate repairs effected by the defendant, the plaintiffs commenced proceedings in the county court.

There was no doubt that the defendant was in breach of the terms of the covenant and that the benefit of the covenant had passed to the plaintiffs; the remaining and crucial question was whether the burden of the covenant had passed to the defendant. In answering that question both the Court of Appeal ((1993) 67 P. & C.R. 9, noted at [1993] Conv. 234) and the House of Lords confirmed (i) that the burden of covenants cannot run at common law: *Austerberry v. Oldham Corp., supra,* p. 720; and (ii) that the equitable doctrine in *Tulk v. Moxhay* (1848) 2 Ph. 774 is confined to the passing of the burden of *restrictive* covenants: see *infra,* p. 730. The final issue was the applicability of the doctrine of benefit and burden.

LORD TEMPLEMAN:
[Counsel for the plaintiffs] also sought to persuade your Lordships that the effect of the decision in the *Austerberry* case had been blunted by the "pure principle of benefit and burden" distilled by Sir Robert Megarry V.-C. from the authorities in *Tito v. Waddell (No. 2)* [1977] 1 Ch. 106, 301 et seq. I am not prepared to recognise the "pure principle" that any party deriving any benefit from a conveyance must accept any burden in the same conveyance. Sir Robert Megarry V.-C. relied on the decision of Upjohn J. in *Halsall v. Brizell* [1957] Ch. 169. In that case the defendant's predecessor in title had been granted the right to use the estate roads and sewers and had covenanted to pay a due proportion for the maintenance of these facilities. It was held that the defendant could not exercise the rights without paying his costs of ensuring that they could be exercised. Conditions can be attached to the exercise of a power in express terms or by implication. *Halsall v. Brizell* was just such a case and I have no difficulty in wholeheartedly agreeing with the decision. It does not follow that any condition can be rendered enforceable by attaching it to a right nor does it follow that every burden imposed by a conveyance may be enforced by depriving the covenantor's successor in title of every benefit which he enjoyed thereunder. The condition must be relevant to the exercise of the right. In *Halsall v. Brizell* there were reciprocal benefits and burdens enjoyed by the users of the roads and sewers. In the present case clause 2 of the 1960 conveyance imposes reciprocal benefits and burdens of support but clause 3 which imposed an obligation to repair the roof is an independent provision. In *Halsall v. Brizell* the defendant could, at least in theory, choose between enjoying the right and paying his proportion of the cost or alternatively giving up the right and saving his money. In the present case the owners of Walford House could not in theory or in practice be deprived of the benefit of the mutual rights of support if they failed to repair the roof.

NOTES:
1. On one interpretation of that passage, Lord Templeman treats *Halsall v. Brizell* as an example of the grant of a conditional or qualified right and refuses to recognise the so-called "pure principle of benefit and burden": although his formulation of the pure principle does not fairly represent the extensive discussion in *Tito v. Waddell (No. 2)*. Alternatively, he is simply reiterating the indisputable proposition that there must be limits to any pure principle. Ultimately, however, the categorisation and its terminology may not be important. Since his Lordship expresses his wholehearted agreement with the decision in *Halsall v. Brizell*, the crucial question centres on the limits of the principle expounded in that decision and its applicability *vel non* to the instant case. In determining that question, his Lordship fails clearly to distinguish statements of fact from propositions of law. However, he would seem to limit the application of the (pure) principle to cases (i) where the burden is "relevant" to the enjoyment of the benefit and (ii) where the

successor in title of the original covenantor has the opportunity to renounce the benefit of the transaction and thereby to escape the burden and where the successor in title can be deprived of the benefit if he fails to assume the linked burden; and, in respect of each limitation he distinguishes *Halsall v. Brizell* from the present case. As to the first condition, if the facts of *Halsall v. Brizell* exemplify the strictness of the requirement of relevance between benefit and burden, there can in practice be very limited scope for any pure principle distinct from the principle of conditional rights. As to the second condition, it is submitted that the supposed distinction between *Halsall v. Brizell* and the present case is unconvincing: for it is not clear how the successor in title in *Halsall v. Brizell* could renounce the right of access any more than the successors in title in the present case could renounce the right of support; and, as demonstrated in each case, there are appropriate legal means of remedying a failure to discharge the linked burden. Nonetheless, on the basis of these supposed limitations and/or points of distinction Lord Templeman concluded that, at least in the context of the present case, the rule in *Austerberry* had not been blunted by the principle of benefit and burden expounded in *Halsall v. Brizell* nor by any extension of that principle expounded in *Tito v. Waddell (No. 2)*. (For the wholesale rejection of the pure principle as "a mere maxim masquerading as a rule of law, false and misleading when read literally", see the decision of the Supreme Court of Victoria in *Government Insurance Office (NSW) v. K.A. Reed Services Pty Ltd* [1988] V.R. 829, 831–841 *per* Brooking J.) In the result, therefore, the covenant was held to be unenforceable against the defendant and the plaintiffs were left without a remedy. See [1994] C.L.J. 446; (1994) 110 L.Q.R. 346.

2. In the Court of Appeal (1993) 67 P. & C.R. 9 Nourse L.J. (at 15–16) appeared to accept the submission of the defendant, that three conditions must be satisfied before the burden can be enforced under the principle: (1) the benefit relied upon must (a) arise out of the same subject-matter as the burden or (b) be granted or reserved in exchange for, or in consideration of, the assumption of the burden (see *Four Oaks Estate Ltd v. Hadley* (1986) 83 L.S.Gaz. 2326); (2) the benefit must be specifically granted or reserved; and (3) the benefit must be real and substantial and not technical and minimal (see *Tito v. Waddell (No. 2)* [1977] Ch. 106, 305). These three conditions cannot be regarded as exhaustive since they do not seem to include the question whether or not successors in title of the original covenantor were *intended* to be able to take the benefit without also assuming the burden: although in the present case the wording of clause 3 would seem to put the answer to that question beyond doubt. Nourse L.J. concluded that the benefit of the easements conferred by clause 2 of the 1960 conveyance, which according to the plaintiffs constituted the linked benefit for the defendant and thus justified the enforcement of the burden imposed by clause 3, did not satisfy the third condition. In his view the easement of support, matched by a corresponding cross-easement, was both technical and minimal; and a further easement of eavesdrop (for the passage of rainwater over the defective section of the roof), if not technical, was certainly minimal.

3. For further confirmation of the limited scope of *Halsell v. Brizell*, see

Allied London Industrial Properties Ltd v. Castleguard Properties Ltd (1997) 74 P. & C.R. D43; *Thamesmead Town Ltd v. Allotey* (1998) 76 P. & C.R. D20.

4. For a detailed analysis of the doctrine of benefit and burden, see Davis [1998] C.L.J. 522.

2.2.2 *Chain of indemnity covenants*   If the original covenantor and each successive owner of the burdened land obtains an appropriately worded indemnity covenant from his purchaser, the continuing liability of the original covenantor can be indemnified by the person actually in breach: see *TRW Steering Systems Ltd v. North Cape Properties Ltd and Cornerstone Estates Ltd* (1993) 69 P. & C.R. 265. The plaintiffs in *Rhone v. Stephens* do not appear to have relied upon the chain of indemnity covenants in order to enforce the covenant; but that may be explained by the circumstances. The device is effective only so long as there is no break in the chain of indemnity covenants *and*, as the Law Commission observed (Law Commission Working Paper No. 36, *Transfer of Land: Appurtenant Rights* (1971), para. 27), "while the original covenantor is both traceable and worth powder and shot".

2.2.3 *Lease*   Where covenants are part of a conveyancing transaction, if the land is leased rather than sold to the covenantor, the rules as to the enforceability of leasehold covenants will apply: see *ante*, p. 419 *et seq. However, although reliance on leasehold covenants may facilitate the enforcement of positive covenants by the landlord, leasehold covenants will not be enforceable between neighbouring leaseholders (unless the freehold or intermediate leasehold interest is owned by a management company controlled by all the leaseholders): see Clarke (1995) 58 M.L.R. 486. For proposed reforms to provide a solution to this problem, see infra,* p. 804.

2.2.4 *Enlargement*   It has been suggested that use could be made of section 153 of the Law of Property Act 1925, which provides for certain long leases to be "enlarged" into freeholds "subject to all the same covenants as the term would have been subject to if it had not been so enlarged" (and a similar argument might be used in the context of leasehold enfranchisement under the Leasehold Reform Act 1967). The device was described by the Wilberforce Report as "untried and artificial": *Report of the Committee on Positive Covenants Affecting Land* (1965), Cmnd. 2719, para. 8(iv). For discussion, see Taylor (1958) 22 Conv. 101.

2.2.5 *Right of re-entry*   The covenantee may reserve a right of re-entry for breach of a positive covenant: see *Shiloh Spinners Ltd v. Harding* [1973] A.C. 691. The right can run with the land but only during the limited period permitted by the rule against perpetuities: see *Re Hollis' Hospital Trustees and Hague's Contract* [1899] 2 Ch. 540; and the exercise of the right is subject to the possibility of relief against forfeiture: see *ante*, p. 452. For discussion, see Tolson (1950) 14 Conv. 350.

2.2.6 *Estate   rentcharge*   The   Rentcharges   Act   1977   preserved   the possibility of creating estate rentcharges for the purpose of enforcing covenants or securing contributions towards the cost of maintaining or repairing property: see Rentcharges Act 1977, s.2(3)(c), (4), (5). For discussion, see Bright [1988] Conv. 99.

It should be apparent that, unless one of the above indirect devices were applicable,   all   three   covenants   under   consideration   would   become unenforceable at common law if B, the original covenantor, disposed of Blackacre. For the burden of the covenants would not pass to a successor in title of the original covenantor.

D. PASSING THE BENEFIT AND BURDEN IN EQUITY

1. Enforcement by the original covenantee, or by the original owner of Greenacre, against a successor in title of the original covenantor: passing the burden

It has been seen that as a general rule the burden of covenants cannot run at common law; and therefore that the covenants under consideration are unenforceable against a successor in title of the original covenantor. However, it remains to consider whether in such circumstances the covenants may be enforceable on the basis that the burden of the covenants has passed to the successor in title under the *equitable* rules: see issue (d) on the diagram.

1.1 *The doctrine in* Tulk v. Moxhay
It was almost inevitable that the inconvenience of the common law position would lead to the intervention of equity. However, in the case that gave its name to the modern equitable doctrine the court expressly rejected the proposition that the issue was whether the burden of a covenant could run with the land of the covenantor. In *Tulk v. Moxhay* (1848) 2 Ph. 774 Lord Cottenham based the decision very clearly on the doctrine of notice and on the principle that a purchaser who had notice of obligations undertaken by his vendor should be bound by those obligations.

Tulk v. Moxhay (1848) 2 Ph. 774

(Lord Cottenham L.C.)

In 1808 the plaintiff, who owned several houses and a piece of vacant land in Leicester Square, sold the piece of land to Elms. Elms covenanted, on behalf of himself, his heirs and assigns, with the plaintiff, his heirs and assigns, that he would "at all times thereafter at his own costs keep and maintain the piece of ground in sufficient and proper repair, in an open state, uncovered with any buildings, in neat and ornamental order". The piece of land eventually passed to the defendant. The conveyance contained no similar covenant but the defendant admitted that he had notice of the 1808 covenant. When the defendant indicated his intention to develop the land, the plaintiff sought an injunction to restrain what would have been a breach of the 1808 covenant.

LORD COTTENHAM L.C.:
That this Court has jurisdiction to enforce a contract between the owner of land and his neighbour purchasing a part of it, that the latter shall either use or abstain from using the land purchased in a particular way, is what I never knew disputed. Here there is no question about the contract: the owner of certain houses in the square sells the land adjoining, with a covenant from the purchaser not to use it for any other purpose than as a square garden. And it is now contended, not that the vendee could violate that contract, but that he might sell the piece of land, and that the purchaser from him may violate it without this Court having any power to interfere. If that were so, it would be impossible for an owner of land to sell part of it without incurring the risk of rendering what he retains worthless. It is said that, the covenant being one which does not run with the land, this Court cannot enforce it; but the question is, not whether the covenant runs with the land, but whether a party shall be permitted to use the land in a manner inconsistent with the contract entered into by his vendor, and with notice of which he purchased. Of course, the price would be affected by the covenant, and nothing could be more inequitable than that the original purchaser should be able to sell the property the next day for a greater price, in consideration of the assignee being allowed to escape from the liability which he had himself undertaken.

That the question does not depend upon whether the covenant runs with the land is evident from this, that if there was a mere agreement and no covenant, this Court would enforce it against a party purchasing with notice of it; for if an equity is attached to the property by the owner, no one purchasing with notice of that equity can stand in a different situation from the party from whom he purchased.

NOTES:
1. In so far as the decision has the effect of making a mere contractual obligation enforceable against a purchaser, it is open to the same criticism that was directed at the approach of Denning L.J. to contractual licences in *Errington v. Errington and Woods* [1952] 2 Q.B. 290, 299, *ante*, p. 513. The substance of that criticism had been accepted in *Keppell v. Bailey* (1834) 2 My. & K. 517, although the later cases of *Whatman v. Gibson* (1838) 9 Sim. 196 and *Mann v. Stephens* (1846) 15 Sim. 377 (as explained by Lord Cottenham in *Tulk v. Moxhay*) would appear to have anticipated the decision in *Tulk v. Moxhay*. See Bell [1981] Conv. 55.

2. This criticism was overlooked and in the early cases restrictions were held to bind purchasers even where the restrictions were personal to the covenantee rather than for the benefit of the land: see *Catt v. Tourle* (1869) L.R. 4 Ch.App. 654; *Luker v. Dennis* (1877) 7 Ch D. 227. The courts later rationalised the doctrine as "either an extension in equity of the doctrine of *Spencer's Case* (1583) 5 Co.Rep. 16a to another line of cases, or else an extension in equity of the doctrine of negative easements": *London and South Western Railway Co. v. Gomm* (1882) 20 Ch D. 562, 583 *per* Sir George Jessel M.R.; and analogies were also drawn with equitable charges upon land: *Re Nisbet and Potts' Contract* [1905] 1 Ch. 391, 397 *per* Farwell J. The analogy with negative easements is generally preferred: freehold covenants run with the land whereas

leasehold covenants run with the estate; and covenants must benefit "dominant land" whereas equitable charges can exist independently of any dominant or benefited land. Furthermore, the analogy with negative easements facilitated the acceptance of the new equitable proprietary interest and the recognition of the proper function of the doctrine of notice. For a survey of the development of the doctrine of *Tulk v. Moxhay*, see *London CC v. Allen* [1914] 3 K.B. 642, 664–673 *per* Scrutton J., *infra*, p. 735. See also Wade (1952) 68 L.Q.R. 337, 347–349; Hayton (1971) 87 L.Q.R. 539, 540–546.

3. For a comprehensive analysis of the doctrine in *Tulk v. Moxhay* and a comparison with the doctrine in *De Mattos v. Gibson* (1859) 4 De G. & J. 276, see Gardner (1982) 98 L.Q.R. 279.

1.2 *The developed doctrine in* Tulk v. Moxhay

In the cases that followed and built upon *Tulk v. Moxhay*, the courts developed a somewhat stricter set of conditions that must be satisfied if the burden of a covenant is to run with the land of the original covenantor so as to be enforceable in equity as against his successors in title. Those conditions are as follows:

(i) The covenant must be restrictive (negative) in substance.
(ii) The covenant must have been intended to benefit land retained by the convenantee.
(iii) The burden of the covenant must have been intended to run with the land of the covenantor.
(iv) The covenant must be protected by the appropriate form of registration.

1.2.1 *The covenant must be restrictive (negative) in substance*   Although the covenants in *Tulk v. Moxhay* appear to have included positive elements (the maintenance of the land in neat and ornamental order), and although clearly positive covenants were enforced in subsequent decisions (*Morland v. Cook*) (1868) L.R. 6 Eq. 252; *Cooke v. Chilcott* (1876) 3 Ch D. 694), it was established in *Haywood v. Brunswick Permanent Benefit Building Society* (1881) 8 Q.B.D. 403 that only restrictive (negative) covenants were within the doctrine; and that restriction was confirmed by the House of Lords in *Rhone v. Stephens* [1994] 2 A.C. 310.

Rhone v. Stephens [1994] 2 A.C. 310

(HL, Lord Templeman, Lord Oliver, Lord Woolf, Lord Lloyd, Lord Nolan)

[For the facts, see *supra*, p. 724.]

LORD TEMPLEMAN:

At common law a person cannot be made liable upon a contract unless he was a party to it. In *Cox v. Bishop* (1857) 8 De G.M. & G. 815 a lease was assigned to a man of straw and it was held that the covenants in the lease could not be enforced against an equitable assignee of the lease who had entered into possession. The covenants were not enforceable because there was no privity of contract or estate between the lessee and the assignee. The rigours of the common law which do not allow covenants to be enforced by and against successors in title were relaxed first by the doctrines laid down in *Spencer's Case* (1583) 5 Co. Rep. 16a and then by statutory extensions of those doctrines introduced by the Grantees of Reversions Act 1540 (32 Hen. 8, c. 34), the Conveyancing Act 1881 (44 & 45 Vict. c. 41) and the Conveyancing Act 1911, now repealed and reproduced in sections 141 and 142 of the Law of Property Act 1925. In the result, as between landlord and tenant both the burden and the benefit of a covenant which touches or concerns the land demised and is not merely collateral run with the reversion and the term at law whether the covenant be positive or restrictive. As between persons interested in land other than as landlord and tenant, the benefit of a covenant may run with the land at law but not the burden: see the *Austerberry* case.

Thus clause 3 of the 1960 conveyance, despite its express terms, did not confer on the owner for the time being of Walford Cottage the right at common law to compel the owner for the time being of Walford House to repair the roof or to obtain damages for breach of the covenant to repair. In this appeal, Mr Munby, on behalf of the plaintiffs, contends that equity will compel the owner of Walford House to comply with the covenant to repair the roof or to pay damages in lieu.

My Lords, equity supplements but does not contradict the common law. When freehold land is conveyed without restriction, the conveyance confers on the purchaser the right to do with the land as he pleases provided that he does not interfere with the rights of others or infringe statutory restrictions. The conveyance may however impose restrictions which, in favour of the covenantee, deprive the purchaser of some of the rights inherent in the ownership of unrestricted land. In *Tulk v. Moxhay* (1848) 2 Ph. 774, a purchaser of land covenanted that no buildings would be erected on Leicester Square. A subsequent purchaser of Leicester Square was restrained from building. The conveyance to the original purchaser deprived him and every subsequent purchaser taking with notice of the covenant of the right, otherwise part and parcel of the freehold, to develop the square by the construction of buildings. Equity does not contradict the common law by enforcing a restrictive covenant against a successor in title of the covenantor but prevents the successor from exercising a right which he never acquired. Equity did not allow the owner of Leicester Square to build because the owner never acquired the right to build without the consent of the persons (if any) from time to time entitled to the benefit of the covenant against building. In *Tulk v. Moxhay* the speech of Lord Cottenham L.C. contained the following passage, at pp. 777–778:

> "It is said that, the covenant being one which does not run with the land, this court cannot enforce it; but the question is, not whether the covenant runs with the land, but whether a party shall be permitted to use the land in a manner inconsistent with the contract entered into by his vendor, and with notice of which he purchased."

Equity can thus prevent or punish the breach of a negative covenant which restricts the user of land or the exercise of other rights in connection with land. Restrictive covenants deprive an owner of a right which he could otherwise exercise. Equity cannot compel an owner to comply with a positive covenant entered into by his predecessors in title without flatly contradicting the common law rule that a person cannot be made liable upon a contract unless he was a party to it. Enforcement of a positive covenant lies in a contract; a positive covenant compels an owner to exercise his rights. Enforcement of a negative covenant lies in property; a negative covenant deprives the owner of a right over property. As Lord Cottenham L.C. said in *Tulk v. Moxhay*, at p. 778: "if an equity is attached to the property by the owner, no one purchasing with notice of that equity can stand in a different situation from the party from whom he purchased."

Following *Tulk v. Moxhay* there was some suggestion that any covenant affecting land was enforceable in equity provided that the owner of the land had notice of the covenant prior to his purchase. In *Morland v. Cook* (1868) L.R. 6 Eq. 252 lands below sea level were partitioned by a deed containing a covenant that the expense of maintaining the sea wall should be borne by the owners of the lands and payable out of the lands by an acre-scot. Lord Romilly M.R. enforced the covenant against a subsequent purchaser of part of the lands on the grounds that he had purchased with notice of the covenant. In *Cooke v. Chilcott* (1876) 3 Ch.D. 694 a covenant by the purchaser of land with a well to erect a pump and reservoir and to supply water from the well to all houses built on the vendor's land was enforced against a subsequent purchaser of the land burdened with the covenant on the grounds that the covenant ran with the land but that in any event the defendant took with notice of the obligation. Malins V.-C. said, at p. 701:

"... I think that when a contract is entered into for the benefit of contiguous landowners, and one is bound by it, and the other entitled to the benefit of it, the covenant binds him for ever, and also runs with the land. But it is equally clear that he is bound by taking the land with notice of the covenant."

These last two cases did not survive the decision of the Court of Appeal in *Haywood v. Brunswick Permanent Benefit Building Society* (1881) 8 Q.B.D. 403. In that case land had been conveyed in consideration of a rent charge and a covenant to build and repair buildings; a mortgagee of the land was held not to be liable on the covenant either at law or in equity although the mortgagee had notice of the covenant. Brett L.J. said, at p. 408, that *Tulk v. Moxhay*:

"decided that an assignee taking land subject to a certain class of covenants is bound by such covenants if he has notice of them, and that the class of covenants comprehended within the rule is that covenants restricting the mode of using the land only will be enforced. It may be also, but it is not necessary to decide here, that all covenants also which impose such a burden on the land as can be enforced against the land would be enforced. ... it is said that if we decide for the defendants we shall have to overrule *Cooke v. Chilcott* (1876) 3 Ch.D. 694. If that case was decided on the equitable doctrine of notice, I think we ought to overrule it."

Cotton L.J. said, at p. 409:

"Let us consider the examples in which a court of equity has enforced covenants affecting land. We find that they have been invariably enforced if they have been restrictive, and that with the exception of the covenants in *Cooke v. Chilcott* (1876) 3 Ch.D. 694 only restrictive covenants have been enforced."

Cotton L.J. also said that *Tulk v. Moxhay*:

"lays down the real principle that an equity attaches to the owner of the land. ... The covenant to repair can only be enforced by making the owner put his hand into his pocket, and there is nothing which would justify us in going that length."

In *London and South Western Railway Co. v. Gomm* (1882) 20 Ch.D. 562 an option to purchase land on the happening of an uncertain event was held to be void for remoteness. It was argued that the covenant was enforceable in equity. Jessel M.R. said, at pp. 582–583:

"With regard to the argument founded on *Tulk v. Moxhay* (1848) 2 Ph. 774, that case was very much considered by the Court of Appeal at Westminster in *Haywood v. Brunswick Permanent Benefit Building Society* (1881) 8 Q.B.D. 403, and the court there decided that they would not extend the doctrine of *Tulk v. Moxhay* to affirmative covenants, compelling a man to lay out money or do any other act of what I may call an active character, but that it was to be confined to restrictive covenants. Of course that authority would be binding upon us if we did not agree to it, but I most cordially accede to it. I think that we ought not to extend the doctrine of *Tulk v. Moxhay* in the way suggested here. The doctrine of that case ... appears to me to be either an extension in equity of the doctrine of *Spencer's Case* (1583) 5 Co.Rep 16a to another line of cases, or else an extension in equity of the doctrine of negative easements; ... The covenant in *Tulk v. Moxhay* was affirmative in its terms," but was held by the court to imply a negative. Where there is a negative covenant expressed or implied ... the court interferes on one or other of the above grounds. This is an equitable doctrine, establishing an exception to the rules of common law which did not treat such a covenant as running with the land, and it does not matter whether it proceeds on analogy to a covenant running with the land or on analogy to an easement. The purchaser took the estate subject to the equitable burden, with the qualification that if he acquired the legal estate for value without notice he was freed from the burden."

Lindley L.J. said, at pp. 587–588, that because in *Haywood v. Brunswick Permanent Benefit Building Society* (1881) 8 Q.B.D. 403 it was sought to extend the doctrine of *Tulk v. Moxhay*:

"to a degree which was thought dangerous, considerable pains were taken by the court to point out the limits of that doctrine. ... The conclusion arrived at ... was that *Tulk v. Moxhay*, when properly understood, did not apply to any but restrictive covenants."

In the *Austerberry* case (1885) 29 Ch.D. 750 the owners of a site of a road covenanted that they and their successors in title would make the road and keep it in repair. The road was sold to the defendants and it was held that the repair covenant could not be enforced against them. Cotton L.J. said, at pp. 773–774:

"undoubtedly, where there is a restrictive covenant, the burden and benefit of which do not run at law, courts of equity restrain anyone who takes the property with notice of that covenant from using it in a way inconsistent with the covenant. But here the covenant which is attempted to be insisted upon on this appeal is a covenant to lay out money in doing certain work upon this land; and, that being so ... that is not a covenant which a court of equity will enforce: it will not enforce a covenant not running at law when it is sought to enforce that covenant in such a way as to require the successors in title of the covenantor to spend money, and in that way to undertake a burden upon themselves. The covenantor must not use the property for a purpose inconsistent with the use for which it was originally granted: but in my opinion a court of equity does not and ought not to enforce a covenant binding only in equity in such a way as to require the successors of the covenantor himself, they having entered into no covenant, to expend sums of money in accordance with what the original covenantor bound himself to do."

In *In re Nisbet and Potts' Contract* [1905] 1 Ch. 391 it was held that a title acquired by adverse possession was not paramount to, and did not destroy the equitable right of persons entitled to the benefit of prior restrictive covenants to enforce them against the land. Farwell J. said, at pp. 396–397:

"Covenants restricting the enjoyment of land, except of course as between the contracting parties and those privy to the contract, are not enforceable by anything in the nature of action or suit founded on contract. Such actions and suits alike depend on privity of contract, and no possession of the land coupled with notice of the covenants can avail to create such privity: *Cox v. Bishop* (1857) 8 De G. M. & G. 815. But if the covenant be negative, so as to restrict the mode of use and enjoyment of the land, then there is called into existence an equity attached to the property of such a nature that it is annexed to and runs with it in equity: *Tulk v. Moxhay* (1848) 2 Ph. 774. This equity, although created by covenant or contract, cannot be sued on as such, but stands on the same footing with and is completely analogous to an equitable charge on real estate created by some predecessor in title of the present owner of the land charged. ... effect is given to the negative covenant by means of the land itself. But the land cannot spend money on improving itself, and there is no personal liability on the owner of the land for the time being, because there is no contract on which he can be sued in contract."

For over 100 years it has been clear and accepted law that equity will enforce negative covenants against freehold land but has no power to enforce positive covenants against successors in title of the land. To enforce a positive covenant would be to enforce a personal obligation against a person who has not covenanted. To enforce negative covenants is only to treat the land as subject to a restriction.

NOTES:

1. It is important to note that the negative/positive distinction is one of substance rather than form. A covenant may be formulated in negative terms and yet be positive in substance, for example a covenant not to let buildings fall into disrepair. Similarly, a covenant may be formulated in positive terms and yet be negative in substance, for example a covenant to use land for residential purposes only. A convenient but not wholly conclusive test is whether the covenantor is required to incur expenditure in order to comply with the covenant: *Haywood v. Brunswick Permanent Benefit Building Society* (1881) 8 Q.B.D. 403, 409 *per* Cotton L.J.

2. The insistence that the doctrine is confined to restrictive covenants has been justified on different grounds. The more doctrinal grounds are referred to in the judgment of Lord Templeman; but see Gardner [1995] C.L.J. 60, 63–68. More practically, it is argued that such a limitation was consistent with the willingness of the courts to grant injunctions but their corresponding reluctance to order specific performance with its concomitant difficulties of supervision. Further, there are said to be policy reasons for the restriction based on the concern that a successor in title to the land of the covenantor may be rendered bankrupt through enforced compliance with an obligation that was automatically binding.

3. Bell [1981] Conv. 55 (and [1983] Conv. 327) argues that the reasoning in *Tulk v. Moxhay* was not confined to restrictive covenants; and that the subsequent restriction of the doctrine to restrictive covenants resulted from "the natural conservatism of the judiciary". Gardner (1982) 98 L.Q.R. 279, 293–298, argues that the restriction of the doctrine was not theoretically necessary but that it derives from the practicalities of the typical *Tulk v. Moxhay* fact situation and the willingness of the courts to grant appropriate remedies in that situation. Griffith [1983] Conv. 29 argues that *Tulk v. Moxhay* was implicitly confined to restrictive covenants; that, on closer analysis, the subsequent decisions which held positive covenants to be enforceable provided ambiguous authority at best; and that orthodoxy was restored in *Haywood v. Brunswick Permanent Benefit Building Society* (1881) 8 Q.B.D. 403.

1.2.2 The covenant must have been intended to benefit land retained by the covenantee   Notwithstanding early decisions to the contrary (see, *e.g.* Catt v. Tourle* (1869) L.R. 4 Ch.App. 654; *Luker v. Dennis* (1877) 7 Ch D. 227), consistent with the analogy subsequently drawn between restrictive covenants and negative easements, the courts determined that the doctrine in *Tulk v. Moxhay* required that the covenant must have been intended to benefit some "dominant land" retained by the covenantee. This condition in fact involves two requirements: first, that the covenantee (and any successors in title) must have retained an interest in land at the date of the covenant and at the time of enforcement: *London CC v. Allen* [1914] 3 K.B. 642, *infra*; and, secondly, that the covenant must touch and concern that land: see *supra*, p. 707.

London CC v. Allen [1914] 3 K.B. 642

(CA, Buckley and Kennedy L.JJ., Scrutton J.)

In 1907 Allen, the predecessor in title of the defendant, obtained permission from the plaintiff planning authority to develop certain land. The permission was subject to a condition that Allen entered into a covenant not to build on a particular part of the land. Allen subsequently entered into such a covenant on behalf of himself, his heirs and assigns and other persons claiming under him. When the defendant proceeded to build on the restricted part, the question arose whether the plaintiffs, who owned no land affected by the covenant, could enforce the covenant.

SCRUTTON J.:

The question then is whether it is essential to the doctrine of *Tulk v. Moxhay* that the covenantee should have at the time of the creation of the covenant, and afterwards, land for the benefit of which the covenant is created, in order that the burden of the covenant may bind assigns of the land to which it relates. It is clear that the covenantee may sue the covenantor himself, though the former has parted with the land to which the covenant relates: *Stokes v. Russell* (1790) 3 T.R. 678. To answer the question as to the assigns of the covenantor, and the land in their hands, requires the investigation of the historical growth of the doctrine of *Tulk v. Moxhay*. Though the covenantee in that case did hold adjacent land, there is no trace in the judgment of Lord Cottenham of the requirement that the covenantee should have and continue to hold land to be benefited by the covenant. I read Lord Cottenham's judgment as proceeding entirely on the question of notice of the covenant, and on the equitable ground that a man purchasing land with notice that there was a covenant not to use it in a particular way would not be allowed to violate the covenant he knew of when he bought the land. Lord Cottenham states the question, "Whether a party shall be permitted to use the land in a manner inconsistent with the contract entered into by his vendor and with notice of which he purchased", and answers it: "If there was a mere agreement and no covenant, this Court would enforce it against a party purchasing with notice of it; for if an equity is attached to the property by the owner, no one purchasing with notice of that equity can stand in a different situation from the party from whom he purchased".

Up to 1881, when counsel in *Haywood v. Brunswick Permanent Benefit Building Society* (1881) 8 Q.B.D. 403 stated (at p. 405) that *Tulk v. Moxhay* had been applied in fifteen cases, I cannot trace, nor could counsel before us discover, that *Tulk v. Moxhay* had been based on anything but notice of the covenant by the assignee. In the case cited, in which the Court of Appeal refused to extend the doctrine to an affirmative covenant to repair, Lindley L.J. said (at p. 410): "The result of these cases is that only such a covenant as can be complied with without expenditure of money will be enforced against the assignee on the ground of notice". Brett L.J. said (at p. 408): "That case" (*Tulk v. Moxhay*) "decided that an assignee taking land subject to a certain class of covenants is bound by such covenants if he has notice of them, and that the class of covenants comprehended within the rule is that covenants restricting the mode of using the land only will be enforced". Cotton L.J., after citing Lord

Cottenham that "No one purchasing with notice of that equity can stand in a different situation from the party from whom he purchased", said (at p. 409): "This lays down the real principle that an equity attaches to the owner of the land". Meanwhile in *De Mattos v. Gibson* (1859) 4 De G. & J. 276 Knight Bruce L.J. had put the principle as applying to all property thus (at p. 282): "Reason and justice seem to prescribe that, at least as a general rule, where a man, by gift or purchase, acquires property from another, with knowledge of a previous contract, lawfully and for valuable consideration made by him with a third person, to use and employ the property for a particular purpose in a specified manner, the acquirer shall not, to the material damage of the third person, in opposition to the contract and inconsistently with it, use and employ the property in a manner not allowable to the giver or seller", resting the matter on knowledge of the previous contract, that is notice. In *Catt v. Tourle* (1869) L.R. 4 Ch. 654, A., a brewer, had sold land to B. with a covenant that he should have the exclusive right to supply all ale consumed in any public-house erected on the land. C., with knowledge of the covenant, bought part of the land from B., erected a public-house on it, but did not take his beer from A. The Court of Appeal, citing *De Mattos v. Gibson*, restrained C., treating the covenant as negative, and resting the judgment on the ground that C. "clearly purchased with notice of the present covenant, and ... cannot be heard to say that he is now entitled to disregard its provisions". It is to be noted that A. is not stated to have owned any land, and as he might brew beer anywhere, the covenant could not relate to any particular land of his.

In *Luker v. Dennis* (1877) 7 Ch.D. 227 A., a brewer, granted a lease to B. of public-house X., with a covenant that B. should take from him all beer consumed not only in X., but also in public-house Y., which B. held of a different landlord. C. took public-house Y. from B. with notice of the covenant, and did not take his beer from A. It was argued before Fry J. that notice was not enough unless the covenantee had some interest in the land bound by the covenant, either as vendor or lessor. That learned judge refused to accede to this argument, and, citing *De Mattos v. Gibson* and *Catt v. Tourle*, granted the injunction, giving, as he said (at p. 236), "effect to the equitable doctrine of notice". I think up to this point the doctrine had been rested on notice, and did not depend on the covenantee having land in favour of which the covenant was created.

The first departure from this position occurs in the judgment of Jessel M.R. in *London and South Western Ry. Co. v. Gomm* (1882) 20 Ch.D. 562. The contract to be enforced was one to reconvey land on notice, and clearly therefore an affirmative covenant, and, as such, within the doctrine laid down in *Haywood's Case*, excluding such contracts from the doctrine of *Tulk v. Moxhay*. The Court also held that the sale was ultra vires the railway company, and void for remoteness. But Sir George Jessel, holding that the covenant did, but for its being ultra vires and void, create an interest in the land, discussed the nature of the right. He said: "The doctrine of that case",—*Tulk v. Moxhay*—"rightly considered, appears to me to be either an extension in equity of the doctrine of *Spencer's Case* to another line of cases, or else an extension in equity of the doctrine of negative easements; such, for instance, as a right to the access of light, which prevents the owner of the servient tenement from building so as to obstruct the light. The covenant in *Tulk v. Moxhay* was affirmative in its terms, but was held by the Court to imply a negative. Where there is a negative covenant expressed or implied, as, for instance, not to build so as to obstruct a view, or not to use a piece of land otherwise than as a garden, the Court interferes on one or other of the above grounds. This is an equitable doctrine, establishing an exception to the rules of common law which did not treat such a covenant as running with the land, and it does not matter whether it proceeds on analogy to a covenant running with the land or on analogy to an easement. The purchaser took the estate subject to the equitable burden, with the qualification that if he acquired the legal estate for value without notice he was freed from the burden. That qualification, however, did not affect the nature of the burden; the notice was required merely to avoid the effect of the legal estate, and did not create the right, and if the purchaser took only an equitable estate he took subject to the burden, whether he had notice or not". It will be noticed that the equitable estate or burden was held to arise independent of notice; which I respectfully think was contrary to the previous authorities; and that in Sir George Jessel's view it did not matter whether it was by analogy to covenants running with the land, or on analogy to an easement. Both, however, had this in common, that some land belonging to the covenantee was required, either for him to let, that the covenant might run with the land, or as a dominant tenement for the easement, an easement in gross being merely a personal right. Whether the "analogy" or "extension" spoken of by Sir George Jessel involved this condition as to land is not discussed. The other members of the Court did not discuss the foundation of *Tulk v. Moxhay*, though Lindley L.J. seems again to put it on notice. *Catt v. Tourle*—a decision of the Court of Appeal—and *Luker v. Dennis* were not cited to the Court.

In 1890, in *Clegg v. Hands* (1890) 44 Ch.D. 503 the doctrine of *Tulk v. Moxhay* was applied by the Court of Appeal to a case somewhat similar to *Catt v. Tourle*, without any discussion of Sir George Jessel's explanation of the doctrine, the case, however, being one of landlord and tenant. In *Rogers v. Hosegood* [1900] 2 Ch. 388, A., the mortgagor, and B., the mortgagee, of some land, conveyed plot X. to C., who entered into a restrictive covenant with the mortgagor only, who had not the legal estate in the land. This plot X, was purchased by D, with notice of the restrictive covenant. A. also conveyed some of his adjoining land, plot Y., to E., who had no notice of the restrictive covenant on plot X. D. then proceeded to erect buildings on plot X. said to contravene the restrictive covenant. E. then sued D. to enforce the covenant. Farwell J. (at p. 394) treated D. as obviously bound by the covenant. "He is obviously bound, by reason of notice, whether the covenant as regards him runs with the land or not". (This expression of the reason why he is bound does not harmonise with the later decisions, but does, I think, with all the earlier ones.) And he held that the benefit of the covenant passed to E. at law running with his land. There was an appeal. In the course of the argument of Mr Haldane, Q.C., that the covenant ran with the land in equity, Rigby L.J. said: "I do not think any covenant runs with the land in equity. The equitable doctrine is that a person who takes with notice of a covenant is bound by it"; a remark again which seems to me to harmonise with the earlier authorities. The Court held that the benefit of the covenant did not run with the land at law, as the covenantee, the mortgagor, had no legal interest in the land, but did run with the land in equity, as there was a clear intention to benefit that land, and equity would regard the mortgagor as the owner, and, citing Jessel M.R. in *London and South Western Ry. Co. v. Gomm*, continued, at p. 405: "These observations, which are just as applicable to the benefit reserved as to the burden imposed, shew that in equity, just as at law, the first point to be determined is whether the covenant or contract in its inception binds the land. If it does, it is then capable of passing with the land to subsequent assignees; if it does not, it is incapable of passing by mere assignment of the land. The benefit may be annexed to one plot and the burden to another, and when this has been once clearly done the benefit and the burden pass to the respective assignees, subject, in the case of the burden, to proof that the legal estate, if acquired, has been acquired with notice of the covenant". This makes land bound or benefited by the covenant essential to bind or benefit assigns. The judgment proceeds: "These authorities"—*Renals v. Cowlishaw* (1878) 9 Ch.D. 125 and *Child v. Douglas* (1854) Kay 560—"establish the proposition that, when the benefit has been once clearly annexed to one piece of land, it passes by assignment of that land, and may be said to run with it, in contemplation as well of equity as of law, without proof of special bargain or representation on the assignment. In such a case it runs, not because the conscience of either party is affected, but because the purchaser has bought something which inhered in or was annexed to the land bought. This is the reason why, in dealing with the burden, the purchaser's conscience is not affected by notice of covenants which were part of the original bargain on the first sale, but were merely personal and collateral, while it is affected by notice of those which touch and concern the land. The covenant must be one that is capable of running with the land before the question of the purchaser's conscience and the equity affecting it can come into discussion". This again appears to me to treat land as essential, on both sides of the covenant, to affect assigns whether of the benefit or burden.

This view seems to me to be adopted also by the Court of Appeal in *Formby v. Barker* [1903] 2 Ch. 539. A., the owner of land, conveyed all his land with a restrictive covenant against its being used in particular ways to B., who assigned it to C., who had notice of the covenant. A. died; C. began to use the land in a way forbidden by the covenant; the administratrix of A., who had no land, sued C. It was argued that the right to enforce such a covenant depended entirely on notice; members of the Court suggested in argument that the benefit of the covenant, if not pursued by the covenantee, must follow some land; and this was the argument put forward for the defendant, that without land the covenant was only one in gross. Romer L.J. asked (at p. 546), "Is there any case in which it has been held that such a covenant purporting to bind land for ever is valid except for the protection of an estate?" and counsel for the plaintiff did not refer him, as they might have done, to *Catt v. Tourle* and *Luker v. Dennis*, in neither of which cases had the plaintiff an estate, but only a trade. In the judgments, Vaughan Williams L.J. points out that A. conveyed his whole estate and had no contiguous estate which would be benefited by the covenant in question. I refer to, but do not read, the Lord Justice's judgment on pp. 550–552, but it seems to me, adopting the language of Collins L.J. in *Rogers v. Hosegood*, to negative the view that the doctrine of *Tulk v. Moxhay* depends on notice, and to make it depend, where there is no contractual privity, on a "relation of dominancy and serviency of lands" (p. 552), and to fail if the covenantee or his assign has no land to which the covenant relates. Romer L.J. thought that the assign of a covenantee could not sue unless the covenant related to or concerned some ascertainable property belonging to him or in which he was interested. Stirling L.J., while saying that different considerations would apply if the covenantee sued, a remark which leaves it doubtful whether he thought the covenantee could, though owning no land, have sued assigns of the land restricted, rested his judgment on the ground that damages, not injunction, would be the appropriate remedy.

The doctrine was again considered, and I think further developed, in *In re Nisbet and Potts' Contract* [1905] 1 Ch. 391. The owner of certain land had entered into restrictive covenants with the vendor, who owned an adjoining estate. A squatter, without notice of these covenants, acquired a title by adverse possession, and sold to A., who did not require a forty years' title, which would have disclosed the restrictive covenants. A. sold to B., who, having reason to believe there were restrictive covenants, declined to complete. B. took out a summons for a declaration that the title was not one which he ought to be compelled to accept. Farwell J. treated the nature of the right of action created under the doctrine of *Tulk v. Moxhay* as analogous to an equitable charge on real estate, not depending in any way on notice for its validity, but only defeated by a legal estate acquired for value and without notice. He held therefore that the squatter, though he had no notice and had the legal estate, was bound by the restrictive covenants, as apparently he only took the land subject to the equitable interest in it, and that as the purchaser from the squatter of the legal estate for value would, if he had required a forty years' title, have had notice of the covenants, he had constructive notice and was bound by the covenants. In the Court of Appeal [1906] 1 Ch. 386 the appellant argued that notice was part of the cause of action, the respondent that the doctrine rested on an interest in land, binding on the land itself, with a dominant and servient tenement. The Court of Appeal adopted the latter argument, and held that the restrictive covenant was an equitable interest in the land, whether the occupier of the land had notice of it or not, unless he had purchased the legal estate for value without notice. They do not expressly refer to the necessity of there being a dominant tenement to enforce the interest, but there was in fact such a dominant tenement in the case.

Lastly, in *Millbourn v. Lyons* [1914] 1 Ch. 34, where a person who had agreed to sell with a restrictive covenant died, and his personal representatives, having sold all their land, conveyed with a similar restrictive covenant, Neville J. enforced the title against a purchaser who knew of the restrictive covenant, and therefore objected to complete, on the ground that there was no restriction against him, as the vendors, at the date of the covenant, had no land to which the benefit of the covenant could be attached, and the Court of Appeal affirmed his judgment on similar grounds [1914] 2 Ch. 231.

I think the result of this long chain of authorities is that, whereas in my view, at the time of *Tulk v. Moxhay* and for at least twenty years afterwards, the plaintiffs in this case would have succeeded against an assign on the ground that the assign had notice of the covenant, since *Formby v. Barker, In re Nisbet and Potts' Contract* and *Millbourn v. Lyons*, three decisions of the Court of Appeal, the plaintiffs must fail on the ground that they have never had any land for the benefit of which this "equitable interest analogous to a negative easement" could be created, and therefore cannot sue a person who bought the land with knowledge that there was a restrictive covenant as to its use, which he proceeds to disregard, because he is not privy to the contract. I think the learned editors of Dart on Vendors and Purchasers, 7th ed., vol. ii, p. 769, are justified by the present state of the authorities in saying that the question of notice to the purchaser has nothing whatever to do with the question whether the covenant binds him, except in so far as the absence of notice may enable him to raise the plea of purchaser for valuable consideration without notice". If the covenant does not run with the land in law, its benefit can only be asserted against an assign of the land burdened, if the covenant was made for the benefit of certain land, all or some of which remains in the possession of the covenantee or his assign, suing to enforce the covenant. It may be, if the matter is considered by a higher tribunal, that tribunal may see its way to revert to what I think was the earlier doctrine of notice, or at any rate to treat it as co-existing with the later refinement of "an equitable interest analogous to a negative easement" binding on persons who are ignorant of it. The remarks of Lord Selborne in *Earl of Zetland v. Hislop* (1882) 7 App.Cas. 427, at pp. 446–447, are not favourable to the too rigid development or enforcement of the latter alternative; and the observations of Lord Macnaghten (p. 32), Lord Davey (p. 35), and Lord Lindley (p. 36) in *Noakes & Co. v. Rice* [1902] A.C. 24 seem to suggest that the doctrine of *Tulk v. Moxhay* may well be reconsidered and put on a proper footing. For I regard it as very regrettable that a public body should be prevented from enforcing a restriction on the use of property imposed for the public benefit against persons who bought the property knowing of the restriction, by the apparently immaterial circumstance that the public body does not own any land in the immediate neighbourhood. But, after a careful consideration of the authorities, I am forced to the view that the later decisions of this Court compel me so to hold.

NOTES:

1. The requirement of retained benefited land has been held to be satisfied where the covenantee retained only a road leading to the burdened land: *Re Gadd's Land Transfer* [1966] Ch. 56. The requirement has also been held to be satisfied by the existence of an interest in the servient land of the covenantor. Thus covenants have been held to be capable of enforcement under the doctrine in *Tulk v. Moxhay* in reliance on the leasehold reversion: *Hall v. Ewin* (1888) 37 Ch D. 74; and in reliance on the interest of a mortgagee of the burdened land: *Regent Oil Co. Ltd v. J.A. Gregory (Hatch End) Ltd* [1966] Ch. 402, 433 *per* Harman L.J., following *John Bros. Abergarw Brewery Co. v. Holmes* [1900] 1 Ch. 188.

2. Bell [1981] Conv. 55 points out that, although the plaintiff in *Tulk v. Moxhay* in fact retained land which benefited from the covenant, no *requirement* of benefited land was imposed by Lord Cottenham: see *London*

CC v. Allen [1914] 3 K.B. 642, 664 *per* Scrutton J. He argues that in subsequent cases the courts enforced covenants despite the absence of benefited land: *Catt v. Tourle* (1869) L.R. 4 Ch.App. 654; *Luker v. Dennis* (1877) 7 Ch D. 227; and that the restriction confirmed in *London CC v. Allen* had its origin in *London and South Western Railway Co. v. Gomm* (1882) 20 Ch D. 562, where Sir George Jessel M.R. was doubtless influenced by the generally conservative approach to the enforceability of covenants adopted a year earlier in *Haywood v. Brunswick Permanent Benefit Building Society* (1881) 8 Q.B.D. 403.

    3. Gardner (1982) 98 L.Q.R. 279, 299–310, argues that the requirement of retained benefited land was not theoretically necessary to the doctrine in *Tulk v. Moxhay* but that it was justified by the context in which the doctrine operates and its function within that context, namely the protection of amenity.

1.2.3 *The burden of the covenant must have been intended to run with the land of the covenantor*   Where the wording of the covenant clearly indicates that the covenant was intended to be personal to the original covenantor and binding on him alone, the burden of that covenant will not pass to his successors in title: *Re Royal Victoria Pavilion, Ramsgate* [1961] Ch. 581, 587–588 *per* Pennycuick J. Similarly, the wording of a covenant may clearly indicate that the burden is intended to run with the land of the covenantor, for example where the covenant is expressed to be made by the covenantor for himself, his heirs and assigns. The required intention that the burden should run with the land is now presumed by virtue of section 79(1) of the Law of Property Act 1925, subject to any indication of a contrary intention contained in the instrument creating the covenant: *Re Royal Victoria Pavilion, Ramsgate, supra*, 589 *per* Pennycuick J.

1.2.4 *The covenant must be protected by the appropriate form of registration*   Even where the first three requirements are satisfied, it must be remembered that the burden of restrictive covenants runs in equity only and that the resultant proprietary interest is therefore equitable only. It follows that to ensure universal enforceability such covenants should be protected by registration in the appropriate manner. Where title to the burdened land is not registered, the covenant constitutes a class D(ii) land charge and should be registered in the land charges register: Land Charges Act 1972, s.2(5)(ii); but in the case of restrictive covenants entered into *before* 1926, enforceability is dependent upon the doctrine of notice. Where title to the burdened land is registered, the covenant should be protected as a minor interest by the entry of a notice on the charges register or a caution on the proprietorship register as appropriate: Land Registration Act 1925, ss.40(3), 50, 53.

1.3 *Land subject to the burden*
The burden of a restrictive covenant is strictly limited to the burdened land identified in the covenant. Thus, it has been held that a covenant prohibiting the carrying on of a particular business on the burdened land does not prevent

the use of the burdened land to provide access to other land where the prohibited business is lawfully carried on: *Elliott v. Safeway Stores plc* [1995] 1 W.L.R. 1396; nor does such a covenant prevent the use of the burdened land to enhance the attractions of other land where the prohibited business is lawfully carried on: *Co-operative Retail Services Ltd v. Tesco Stores Ltd* (1998) 76 P. & C.R. 328.

1.4 *Persons subject to the burden*

A restrictive covenant that satisfies the above substantive and procedural requirements will bind a wide range of persons in addition to the fee simple owner of the burdened land. Lessees and sub-lessees are bound by covenants that bind the fee simple: *Wilson v. Hart* (1866) L.R. 1 Ch.App. 463; *Nicoll v. Fenning* (1881) 19 Ch D. 258; licensees of the burdened land are bound by any covenants affecting that land: *Mander v. Falcke* [1891] 2 Ch. 554; and see *Marten v. Flight Refuelling Ltd* [1962] Ch. 115, 122 *per* Wilberforce J.; and *a fortiori* adverse possessors will also be bound: *Re Nisbet and Potts' Contract* [1905] 1 Ch. 391, [1906] 1 Ch. 386.

If these principles are applied to issue (d) on the diagram, it can be seen that while covenant (i) is potentially enforceable against a successor in title of the original covenantor, covenant (ii) is positive and therefore outside the scope of the doctrine in *Tulk v. Moxhay*; as has already been seen, covenant (iii) does not touch and concern the land and therefore is also outside the scope of the doctrine in *Tulk v. Moxhay*.

2. Enforcement by a successor in title of the original covenantee, or by a successor in title of the original owner of Greenacre, against a successor in title of the original covenantor: passing the benefit and burden

It might appear that issue (e) on the diagram has already been covered by the principles discussed above: the benefit of a covenant can pass to a successor in title of the original covenantee (including any person treated as an original covenantee by virtue of section 56(1) of the Law of Property Act 1925) at common law; and the burden of a restrictive covenant can pass to a successor in title of the original covenantor under the doctrine in *Tulk v. Moxhay*. Thus, by combining those possibilities, the successors in title of the original covenantee can enforce a restrictive covenant against the successors in title of the original covenantor.

However, it is generally accepted that issue (e) cannot be answered in that manner, by combining common law rules (for the passing of the benefit of a covenant) and equitable rules (for the passing of the burden of a covenant). Where the original covenantor has disposed of his land so that the person seeking to enforce the covenant has to show that the burden has passed to the successor in title of the original covenantor under the *equitable* doctrine in *Tulk v. Moxhay*, it is generally accepted that, if the person seeking to enforce the covenant is a successor in title of the original covenantee, he must show that the benefit of the covenant has passed to him according to the *equitable* rules: *Re Union of London and Smith's Bank Ltd's Conveyance, Miles v.*

Easter [1933] Ch. 611, 630 *per* Romer L.J.; but support for this view is not unanimous: see Gray, *Elements of Land Law* (2nd ed., 1993), pp. 1149–1150, citing as authority *Rogers v. Hosegood* [1900] 2 Ch. 388, 395 *et seq. per* Farwell J. A successor in title of the original covenantee must also satisfy the equitable rules for passing the benefit where he acquires part only of the land of the original covenantee: *Miles v. Easter* [1933] Ch. 611, 630 *per* Romer L.J.; where he has only an equitable interest in the land: *Fairclough v. Marshall* (1878) 4 Ex.D. 37, 44 *per* Bramwell L.J.; *Earl of Leicester v. Wells-next-the-Sea UDC* [1973] Ch. 110, 117–118 *per* Plowman J.; and where he seeks enforcement in the context of a scheme of development: see *infra*, p. 774.

In order for the benefit of a covenant to pass in equity so as to enable the successor in title of the original covenantee to enforce the covenant, it must be established (i) that the covenant touches and concerns the land of the covenantee and his successors in title: see *supra*; and (ii) that the benefit has been transferred to the successor in title (a) by annexation, or (b) by assignment or (c) through the operation of a scheme of development.

Re Pinewood Estate, Farnborough [1958] Ch. 280

(Ch D., Wynn-Parry J.)

WYNN-PARRY J.:
It is not to be doubted that the applicants are bound by the terms of the deed, so far as the burden of the covenants therein contained is concerned. The question which I have to determine is whether the respondent, or, indeed, anybody else, is entitled to enforce those covenants.

. . .

I conclude that there is no building scheme, within the meaning of that phrase as used in *Elliston v. Reacher* [1908] 2 Ch. 374, in existence, and that, therefore, the respondent cannot assert with success that she can obtain the benefit of the restrictive stipulations by virtue of this document.

What, then, is her position? It is admitted by Mr Newsom that she could claim the benefit of the restrictive covenants if it could be shown either that the benefit had been annexed by proper words of annexation, or that there was a complete chain of assignments of the benefit of the covenants; but it is conceded on behalf of the respondent that there are no words of annexation, and it is conceded that the chain is not complete. In those circumstances, what the respondent says is that she is entitled to the benefit of the restrictive provisions because it is a deed which shows clearly by its language an intention that the parties should be mutually bound by the restrictions, and that that element of mutuality is enough to carry the benefit of the restrictive stipulations. That means that they are endeavouring to set up a further method by which the benefit of restrictive stipulations can be transferred. They rely on *Whatman v. Gibson* (1838) 9 Sim. 196; but upon examination it will be found that in that case there was a common vendor, and, indeed, I should have thought that that case was to be supported upon the basis that, notwithstanding the fact that it was decided so long ago, it really contains the essential elements which Parker J. required in *Elliston v. Reacher*. Therefore, I do not think that that case affords the respondent any support.

The real question is: Is there a fourth class at all? The first class is the *Elliston v. Reacher* type of case; the second consists of cases where there are proper words of annexation; the third consists of cases where there is a continuous chain of express assignments. But is there a fourth class? In *Osborne v. Bradley* [1903] 2 Ch. 446 Farwell J. said (at p. 450): "Negative covenants in conveyance in fee restricting the right of the purchaser to use the land purchased may for the purposes of a case like the present be considered as falling under three classes: (i) where the covenant is entered into simply for the vendor's own benefit [with that class I am not concerned in this case]; (ii) where the covenant is for the benefit of the vendor in his capacity of owner of a particular property; and (iii) where the covenant is for the benefit of the vendor, in so far as he reserves unsold property, and also for the benefit of other purchasers, as part of what is called a building scheme". That third class is obviously of the *Elliston v. Reacher* class.

Mr Newsom submitted, and I think he was right, that the second class stated by Farwell J. is really to be subdivided into two classes, namely, annexation and continuous chain of assignment. That, I think, emerges from *In re Union of London and Smith's Bank Ltd's Conveyance, Miles v. Easter* [1933] Ch. 611. The judgment of the Court of Appeal was delivered by Romer L.J. He said (at pp. 627–628). "That the plaintiff is bound by the covenants in question is not disputed, in view of the fact that he purchased his lands with notice of them. What is in dispute is the question whether the defendants are entitled to the benefit of such covenants. Now the defendants are not the original covenantees, and it therefore becomes necessary to ascertain what person other than the original covenantee is entitled to the benefit of a restrictive covenant affecting land. This question was put to himself by Hall V.-C. in *Renals v. Cowlishaw* (1878) 9 Ch.D. 125, and the answer was given in a judgment so well known that it is unnecessary to refer to it at length. It is a judgment that has received the approval both of this court and of the House of Lords, and has always been regarded as a correct statement of the law upon the subject. Stated shortly it laid down this: that, apart from what are usually referred to as building scheme cases (and this is not a case of that sort), a purchaser from the original covenantee of land retained by him when he executed the conveyance containing the covenant will be entitled to the benefit of the covenant if the conveyance shows that the covenant was intended to enure for the benefit of that particular land. It follows that, if what is being acquired by the purchaser was only part of the land shown by the conveyance as being intended to be benefited, it must also be shown that the benefit was intended to enure to each portion of that land. In such cases the benefit of the restrictive covenant will pass to the purchaser without being mentioned. It runs with the land. In all other cases the purchaser will not acquire the benefit of the covenant unless that benefit be expressly assigned to him—or, to use the words of the Vice-Chancellor, 'it must appear that the benefit of the covenant was part of the subject-matter of the purchase.' " In my view that passage establishes the other two classes.

But I can find no authority, certainly none was cited to me, which establishes the fourth class suggested. In my opinion, therefore, it is not open either to the respondent or to anybody else upon this line of reasoning to rely on these restrictive covenants.

NOTES:

1. For comment critical of the decision as involving an unduly strict approach to both express assignment and schemes of development, see [1957] C.L.J. 146; and see (1957) 21 Conv. 386; (1957) 20 M.L.R. 646.

2. For discussion of the subsequent tendency of the courts towards "a broad and reasonable view" in relation to the passing of the benefit of restrictive covenants (*Marten v. Flight Refuelling Ltd* [1962] Ch. 115, 131 *per* Wilberforce J.), see Wade [1972B] C.L.J. 157.

2.1 *Annexation*

Annexation is the equitable equivalent of the common law rules expounded in *Smith and Snipes Hall Farm Ltd v. River Douglas Catchment Board* [1949] 2 K.B. 500, *supra*, p. 716. It is the permanent fixing of the benefit of a covenant to the land of the covenantee *at the time of the covenant* so that from that time onwards the benefit of the covenant is effectively part of the land and passes automatically when the land is transferred. It is therefore irrelevant to the question of enforceability that a successor in title of the covenantee did not know of the existence of the covenant at the time of the transfer to him: *Rogers v. Hosegood* [1900] 2 Ch. 388, 408 *per* Collins L.J., *infra*.

It is asserted that there are three different types of annexation: express, implied and statutory. The first is well established; the second is of doubtful validity; and the third is of relatively recent origin and not wholly uncontroversial.

2.1.1 *Express annexation*   Express annexation occurs where the language of the covenant makes it sufficiently clear that the parties intend the benefit of the covenant to become a permanent part of the land of the covenantee rather than an advantage personal to the covenantee: *Chambers v. Randall* [1923] 1 Ch. 149, 155–156 *per* Sargant J. Whether this requirement is satisfied is inevitably a question of construction of the covenant and there is no need for the parties to use a particular form of words. However, the benefit of a covenant is likely to be held to have been annexed where the parties adopt a formulation stating that the covenant is made "for the benefit of Redacre" or "for the benefit of R in his capacity as owner of Readacre": *Osborne v. Bradley* [1903] 2 Ch. 446, 450 *per* Farwell J.; *Drake v. Gray* [1936] Ch. 451, 466 *per* Greene L.J. The requirement is usually illustrated by reference to two cases. In *Rogers v. Hosegood* [1900] 2 Ch. 388 it was held that the benefit of a number of covenants was annexed to the land of the covenantee where the covenant was expressed to be made "with the intent that the covenants might enure to the benefit of [the vendors] their heirs and assigns and others claiming under them to all or any of their lands adjoining". By contrast, in *Renals v. Cowlishaw* (1878) 9 Ch D. 125, (1879) 11 Ch D. 866, where the covenant was expressed to be made "with [the vendors], their heirs, executors, administrators, and assigns", and in *Reid v. Bickerstaff* [1909] 2 Ch. 305, where the covenant was expressed to be made "with [the vendors], their heirs and assigns", the absence of any clear indication that the covenant was for the benefit of the *land* led the court to hold that there was no annexation of the benefit of the covenant.

Rogers v. Hosegood [1900] 2 Ch. 388

(CA, Lord Alverstone M.R., Rigby and Collins L.JJ.)

In 1869 the Duke of Bedford purchased a plot of land and covenanted with the vendors not to build more than one dwelling-house on the plot. The covenant was expressed to be made "with intent that the covenants might so far as possible bind the premises thereby conveyed and every part thereof, into whosesoever hands the same might come, and might enure to the benefit of [the vendors] their heirs and assigns and others claiming under them to all or any of their lands adjoining". In 1872 another plot was sold by the vendors and in 1873 conveyed to Millais, who had no knowledge of the covenant. The trustees of Millais' will sought to restrain a successor in title of the original covenantor from building a block of flats in breach of the 1869 covenant.

COLLINS L.J.:

This case raises questions of some difficulty, but we are of opinion that the decision of Farwell J. is right and ought to be affirmed ... No difficulty arises in this case as to the burden of the covenants. The defendant is the assignee of the covenantor in respect of the two plots of land comprised in the conveyances of May 31 and July 31, 1869, and he took with notice of the covenants now sought to be enforced. Nor have we any hesitation in accepting the conclusion of Farwell J., that the buildings which the defendant proposes to erect will involve a breach of those covenants. The real and only difficulty arises on the question—whether the benefit of the covenants has passed to the assigns of Sir John Millais as owners of the plot purchased by him on March 25, 1873, there being no evidence that he knew of these covenants when he bought. Here, again, the difficulty is narrowed, because by express declaration on the face of the conveyances of 1869 the benefit of the two covenants in question was intended for all or any of the vendor's lands near to or adjoining the plot sold, and therefore for (among others) the plot of land acquired by Sir John Millais, and that they "touched and concerned" the land within the meaning of those words so as to run with the land at law we do not doubt. Therefore, but for a technical difficulty which was not raised before Farwell J., we should agree with him that the benefit of the covenants in question was annexed to and passed to Sir John Millais by the conveyance of the land which he bought in 1873. A difficulty, however, in giving effect to this view arises from the fact that the covenants in question in the deeds of May and July 1869 were made with the mortgagors only, and therefore in contemplation of law were made with strangers to the land: *Webb v. Russell* (1789) 3 T.R. 393, to which, therefore, the benefit did not become annexed. That a court of equity, however, would not regard such an objection as defeating the intention of the parties to the covenant is clear; and, therefore, when the covenant was clearly made for the benefit of certain land with a person who in the contemplation of such a court was the true owner of it, it would be regarded as annexed to and running with that land, just as it would have been at law but for the technical difficulty. We think this is the plain result of the observations of Hall V.-C. in the well-known passage in *Renals v. Cowlishaw* (1878) 9 Ch.D. 125, of Jessel M.R. in *London and South Western Ry. Co. v. Gomm* (1882) 20 Ch.D. 562, and of Wood V.-C. in *Child v. Douglas* (1854) Kay 560, which, we agree with Farwell J., are untouched on this point by anything decided in the subsequent proceedings in that case ... These observations, which are just as applicable to the benefit reserved as to the burden imposed, shew that in equity, just as at law, the first point to be determined is whether the covenant or contract in its inception binds the land. If it does, it is then capable of passing with the land to subsequent assignees; if it does not, it is incapable of passing by mere assignment of the land. The benefit may be annexed to one plot and the burden to another, and when this has been once clearly done the benefit and the burden pass to the respective assignees, subject, in the case of the burden, to proof that the legal estate, if acquired, has been acquired with notice of the covenant. The passage inclosed in a parenthesis in the report of the judgment of Hall V.-C. in *Renals v. Cowlishaw* supports the same view, nor are the general observations or the decision of the case itself inconsistent with it. There, in the original conveyance which imposed the restrictive covenant, there was no expression, as there is in the present case, that the restriction was intended for the benefit of any part of the estate retained, and it is in reference to such a case that the Vice-Chancellor said: "The plaintiffs ... rest their case upon their being 'assigns' of the Mill Hill Estate, and they say that, as the vendors to Shaw were the owners of that estate when they sold to Shaw a parcel of land adjoining it, the restrictive covenants entered into by the purchaser of that parcel of land must be taken to have been entered into with them for the purpose of protecting the Mill Hill Estate, which they retained; and, therefore, that the benefit of that restrictive covenant goes to the assign of that estate, irrespective of whether or not any representation that such a covenant had been entered into by a purchaser from the vendors was made to such assigns, and without any contract by the vendors that that purchaser should have the benefit of that covenant. The argument must, it would seem, go to this length—namely that in such a case a purchaser becomes entitled to" (the benefit of) "the covenant even although he did not know of the existence of the covenant, and that although he did not know of the existence of the covenant, and that although the purchaser is not (as the purchasers in the present case were not) purchaser of all the property retained by the vendor upon the occasion of the conveyance containing the covenants. It appears to me that the three cases to which I have referred shew that this is not the law of this Court; and that in order to enable a purchaser as an assign (such purchaser not being an assign of all that the vendor retained when he executed the conveyance containing the covenants, and that conveyance not shewing that the benefit of the covenant was intended to enure for the time being of each portion of the estate so retained or of the portion of the estate of which the plaintiff is assign) to claim the benefit of a restrictive covenant, this, at least, must appear, that the assign acquired his property with the benefit of the covenant, that is, it must appear that the benefit of the covenant was part of the subject-matter of the purchase". So in *Child v. Douglas* Wood V.-C. said: "Where part of the remaining property of the original vendor has been sold to another person, who must be considered to have bought the benefit of the former purchaser's covenant, and, more especially, when the subsequent purchaser has entered into a similar covenant on his own part, he must be considered to have done this in consideration of those benefits, and even whether he actually knew or was ignorant that this covenant was in fact inserted in the other purchase deeds, because he must be taken to have bought all the rights connected with his portion of the land". These authorities establish the proposition that, when the benefit has been once clearly annexed to one piece of land, it passes by assignment of that land, and may be said to run with it, in contemplation as well of equity as of law, without proof of special bargain or representation on the assignment. In such a case it runs, not because the conscience of either party is affected, but because the purchaser has bought something which inhered in or was annexed to the land bought. This is the reason why, in dealing with the burden, the purchaser's conscience is not affected by notice of covenants which were part of the original bargain on the first sale, but were merely personal and collateral, while it is affected by notice of those which touch and concern the land. The covenant must be one that is capable of running with the land before the question of the purchaser's conscience and the equity affecting it can come into discussion. When, as in *Renals v. Cowlishaw*, there is no indication in the original conveyance, or in the circumstances attending it, that the burden of the restrictive covenant is imposed for the benefit of the land reserved, or any particular part of it, then it becomes necessary to examine the circumstances under which any part of the land reserved is sold, in order to see whether a benefit, not originally annexed to it, has become annexed to it on the sale, so that the purchaser is deemed to have bought it with the land, and this can hardly be the case when the purchaser did not know of the existence of the restrictive covenant. But when, as here, it has been once annexed to the land reserved, then it is not necessary to spell an intention out of surrounding facts, such as the existence of a building scheme, statements at auctions, and such like circumstances, and the presumption must be that it passes on a sale of that land, unless there is something to rebut it, and the purchaser's ignorance of the existence of the covenant does not defeat the presumption. We can find nothing in the conveyance to Sir John Millais in any degree inconsistent with the intention to pass to him the benefit already annexed to the land sold to him. We are of opinion, therefore, that Sir John Millais's assigns are entitled to enforce the restrictive covenant against the defendant, and that his appeal must be dismissed.

NOTES:

1. The requisite intention that the benefit of the covenant should be annexed to land retained by the covenantee "must be manifested in the conveyance in which the covenant was contained when construed in the light of the surrounding circumstances, including any necessary implication in the conveyance from those surrounding circumstances"; the requisite intention cannot be inferred "from surrounding circumstances which fall short of those which would necessitate an implication in the conveyance itself": *J. Sainsbury plc v. Enfield LBC* [1989] 1 W.L.R. 590, 595–597 *per* Morritt J., citing *Reid v. Bickerstaff* [1909] 2 Ch. 305, 320 *per* Cozens-Hardy M.R.; *Miles v. Easter* [1933] Ch. 611, 628 *per* Romer L.J.; *Marquess of Zetland v. Driver* [1939] Ch. 1, 8 *per* Farwell J.; *Newton Abbot Co-operative Society Ltd v. Williamson & Treadgold Ltd* [1952] Ch. 286, 289 *per* Upjohn J.; *Shropshire CC v. Edwards* (1982) 46 P. & C.R. 270, 277–278 *per* Judge Rubin. It is open to debate whether this reasoning provides support for the notion of implied annexation: see *infra*, p. 750; or whether Morritt J. was merely defining the limits of express annexation. See [1991] Conv. 52.

2. It is also a requirement of express annexation that the land to be benefited must be identified with sufficient certainty in the instrument creating the covenant. There is authority that this requirement is quite strict: see *Renals v. Cowlishaw* (1879) 11 Ch D. 866, 868 *per* James L.J.; *Miles v. Easter* [1933] Ch. 611, 625 *per* Bennett J.; *Newton Abbot Co-operative Society Ltd v. Williamson & Treadgold Ltd* [1952] Ch. 286, 289–290 *per* Upjohn J. On the other hand, the identification of the land is in most circumstances inextricably linked with the issue of the intention to benefit. Consequently, it would be consistent with the approach to the question of intention that any uncertainty as to the identity of the land should be capable of being resolved by extrinsic evidence within the limits specified in *J. Sainsbury plc v. Enfield LBC* [1989] 1 W.L.R. 590; and *Shropshire CC v. Edwards* provides some authority for that view: (1982) 46 P. & C.R. 270, 277–278 *per* Judge Rubin.

3. Problems have arisen where the terms of a covenant purport expressly to annex the benefit of the covenant to a large area of land. These problems are illustrated by *Re Ballard's Conveyance* [1937] Ch. 473.

Re Ballard's Conveyance [1937] Ch. 473

(Ch D., Clauson J.)

In 1906 the applicant purchased some land and covenanted with "[the vendor] her heirs and assigns and successors in title owners from time to time of the Childwickbury Estate" not to build on the land except in accordance with specified conditions. The respondents were the current owners of the Childwickbury Estate and successors in title of the original covenantee. The applicant sought a declaration that the covenant was no longer enforceable. Clauson J. held that the terms of the covenant purported to annex the benefit of the covenant to the entire Childwickbury Estate, which extended to an area of about 1,700 acres. He continued (at 480-482):

That brings me to the remaining question, namely: Is the covenant one which, in the circumstances of the case, comes within the category of a covenant the benefit of which is capable of running with the land for the benefit of which it was taken? A necessary qualification in order that the covenant may come within that category is that it concerns or touches the land with which it is to run: see *per* Farwell J. in *Rogers v. Hosegood* [1900] 2 Ch. 388, 395. That land is an area of some 1700 acres. It appears to me quite obvious that while a breach of the stipulations might possibly affect a portion of that area in the vicinity of the applicant's land, far the largest part of this area of 1700 acres could not possibly be affected by any breach of any of the stipulations.

Counsel for the respondents asked for an adjournment in order to consider whether they would call evidence (as I was prepared to allow them to do) to prove that a breach of the stipulations or of some of them might affect the whole of this large area. However, ultimately no such evidence was called.

The result seems to me to be that I am bound to hold that, while the covenant may concern or touch some comparatively small portion of the land to which it has been sought to annex it, it fails to concern or touch far the largest part of the land. I asked in vain for any authority which would justify me in severing the covenant and treating it as annexed to or running with such part of the land as is touched by or concerned with it, though as regards the remainder of the land, namely, such part as is not touched by or concerned with the covenant, the covenant is not and cannot be annexed to it and accordingly does not and cannot run with it. Nor have I been able through my own researches to find anything in the books which seems to justify any such course. In *Rogers v. Hosegood* the benefit of the covenant was annexed to all or any of certain lands adjoining or near to the covenantor's land, and no such difficulty arose as faces me here; and there are many other reported cases in which, for similar reasons, no such difficulty arose. But the requirement that the covenant, in order that the benefit of it may run with certain lands, must concern or touch those lands, is categorically stated by Farwell J. in the passage I have cited, in terms which are unquestionably in accord with a long line of earlier authority.

I would observe that the construction of the document and the intention of the parties to be gathered therefrom is material on the question what is the area of land to which the covenantor and the covenantee intended to annex the benefit of the covenant, or, in technical language, what is the land with which the parties intended the covenant to run; but that on the question whether, in the circumstances of the case, this covenant is capable of being annexed to or of running with the land to which it is sought to annex it, it is necessary first to ascertain whether in fact the covenant touches or concerns that particular land. If on the facts it appears that the covenant does not touch or concern that particular land, the only question which remains is whether by the law in regard to annexation of a covenant to land as recognised in the *Prior's* case such annexation can take place unless it can be predicated of the covenant that it touches or concerns the land to which it is sought to annex it. That is a question of dry technical law on which it would not be right, at all events for a judge of first instance, to go beyond settled authority, or at all events beyond that which can logically be deduced from settled authority, though in the result the intention of the parties to the original covenant may be frustrated. As I have not been referred to and I cannot find any authority for the proposition that a covenant which it has been sought to annex to a particular area of land can be enforced by the person seised of that land, not being the original covenantee, in a case where it cannot truly be said that the covenant touches or concerns the land to which it was sought to annex it, I must hold that the attempted annexation has failed and that the covenant has not been effectually annexed to the land and does not run with it. The consequence is that I am bound to hold that the respondents cannot sue the applicant on the covenant.

As it is not suggested, nor does it appear, that the covenant in question is now enforceable by any one if the respondents are not in a position to enforce it, I shall declare that the property mentioned in the title to the summons is no longer affected by any of the restrictions contained in the conveyance of 1906.

NOTES:

1. The question whether the covenant is capable of benefiting the covenantee's land is to be determined on the facts of each case. Thus in *Marten v. Flight Refuelling Ltd* [1962] Ch. 115 a covenant not to use the burdened land for non-agricultural purposes was held to be capable of benefiting land of 7,500 acres; in *Earl of Leicester v. Wells-next-the-Sea UDC* [1973] Ch. 110 a covenant not to use the burdened land for any purpose other than smallholdings and allotments was held to be capable of benefiting land of 32,000 acres: see [1973] C.L.J. 28; and in *Wrotham Park Estate Co. Ltd v. Parkside Homes Ltd* [1974] 1 W.L.R. 798 a covenant not to build on the burdened land except in accordance with specified conditions was held to be capable of benefiting land of 4,000 acres.

2. Clauson J. seems to have assumed that, in the absence of evidence of benefit, the covenant in *Re Ballard's Conveyance* could not benefit the whole of the covenantee's land. However, more recent cases have tended to apply a contrary presumption: see *Wrotham Park Estate Co. Ltd v. Parkside Homes Ltd, supra*, 808 *per* Brightman J.:

There can be obvious cases where a restrictive covenant clearly is, or clearly is not, of benefit to an estate. Between these two extremes there is inevitably an area where the benefit to the estate is a matter of personal opinion, where responsible and reasonable persons can have divergent views sincerely and reasonably held. In my judgment, in such cases, it is not for the court to pronounce which is the correct view. I think that the court can only decide whether a particular view is one which can reasonably be held. If a restriction is bargained for at the time of sale with the intention of giving the vendor a protection which he desires for the land he retains, and the restriction is expressed to be imposed for the benefit of the estate so that both sides are apparently accepting that the restriction is of value to the retained land, I think that the validity of the restriction should be upheld so long as an estate owner may reasonably take the view that the restriction remains of value to his estate, and that the restriction should not be discarded merely because others may reasonably argue that the restriction is spent.

For comment, see (1974) 38 Conv. 289. See also *Marten v. Flight Refuelling Ltd* [1962] Ch. 115, 136 *per* Wilberforce J.; *Cryer v. Scott Bros. (Sunbury) Ltd* (1986) 55 P. & C.R. 183, 195–197 *per* Slade L.J.

3. *Miles v. Easter* [1933] Ch. 611, 628 *per* Romer L.J., and *Drake v. Gray* [1936] Ch. 451, 458 *per* Slesser L.J., provided earlier support for the proposition that annexation to the whole is not *ipso facto* annexation to all or any parts, although those cases were not cited in *Re Ballard's Conveyance*; and the proposition was endorsed in later cases: *Russell v. Archdale* [1964] Ch. 38, 46–47 *per* Buckley J., noted at (1962) 26 Conv. 306; (1962) 78 L.Q.R. 334, 482; *Re Jeff's Transfer (No. 2)* [1966] 1 W.L.R. 841, 846–850

per Stamp J., noted at (1966) 30 Conv. 236. In both cases the court refused to adopt the distinction made by Romer L.J. in *Drake v. Gray, supra,* 465, between a covenant made for the benefit "of Blackacre" (effecting annexation to the whole only) and a covenant made for the benefit of "lands retained by the vendor" (effecting annexation to each and every part): see Baker (1968) 84 L.Q.R. 22, 25–28; Hayton (1971) 87 L.Q.R. 539, 553. In *Re Selwyn's Conveyance* [1967] Ch. 674, noted at (1967) 31 Conv. 145, Goff J., while purporting to accept the views expressed in *Russell v. Archdale* and *Re Jeff's Transfer (No. 2),* held that the benefit of a covenant made with the intent that "this covenant shall enure for the protection of the adjoining or neighbouring land part of or lately part of [the vendor's land]" was annexed to every part of the land.

   4. A finding that the benefit of a covenant was annexed to the whole only of the covenantee's land, gave rise to two supposed difficulties. First, in the absence of a power to sever, a successor in title to part only of the original covenantee's land could not claim that the benefit of the covenant had passed to him: see *Russell v. Archdale, supra,* 46–47 *per* Buckley J.; and see Radcliffe (1941) 57 L.Q.R. 203, 210–211. Secondly, where a successor in title to the original covenantee disposed of part of the benefited land, he ceased to be entitled to enforce the covenant since he no longer owned the whole of the benefited land to which *ex hypothesi* the benefit of the covenant had been annexed: see *Stilwell v. Blackman* [1968] Ch. 508, 519 *per* Ungoed-Thomas J. The most absurd manifestation of the second of these problems was resolved in *Wrotham Park Estate Co. Ltd v. Parkside Homes Ltd* [1974] 1 W.L.R. 798, where Brightman J. held that the successor in title could continue to enforce the covenant provided that he retained "in substance" the benefited land: see [1974] C.L.J. 214. Both problems are completely resolved if the covenant is expressed to be made for the benefit of *the whole or any part or parts of* the covenantee's land: see *Marquess of Zetland v. Driver* [1939] Ch. 1, noted at (1938) 2 Conv. 71, 377; and see Radcliffe (1941) 57 L.Q.R. 203.

   5. In *Federated Homes Ltd v. Mill Lodge Properties Ltd* [1980] 1 W.L.R. 594 Brightman L.J. expressed the view (at 606) that "if the benefit of a covenant is, on a proper construction of a document, annexed to the land, prima facie it is annexed to every part thereof, unless the contrary clearly appears".

   6. It is not clear whether the *Marquess of Zetland v. Driver* formula or the principle asserted in *Federated Homes Ltd v. Mill Lodge Properties Ltd* means that, where a purported annexation of the benefit of a covenant to the whole of the land of the covenantee fails because the court finds that the covenant cannot benefit the whole of the land, the benefit of the covenant is nonetheless annexed to that part of the land which does in fact benefit.

2.1.2 *Implied annexation*   There is some support for the view that, even where there are no words in a covenant which provided for express annexation of the benefit of the covenant, it may be possible for the court to find the necessary intention permanently to fix the benefit of the covenant to the land of the covenantee and to identify that land from the circumstances of the case. This theory has been termed "implied annexation". The supposed authority for implied annexation is *Marten v. Flight Refuelling Ltd* [1962] Ch. 115.

Marten v. Flight Refuelling Ltd [1962] Ch. 115

(Ch D., Wilberforce J.)

The Crichel estate, which was held under a strict settlement, comprised about 7,500 acres of agricultural land, including Crook Farm, part of which had been requisitioned by the Air Ministry in 1942. In 1943, when the first plaintiff, as an infant, was the equitable owner in possession under the settlement, the special executors of the former tenant for life, the second plaintiffs, conveyed Crook Farm to the sitting tenant. He covenanted "with the vendor and its successors in title" not to use the land conveyed for non-agricultural purposes. In 1947 the Air Ministry permitted the defendants to occupy the requisitioned part of Crook Farm. In 1950 the first plaintiff attained her majority and she became absolute owner of the Crichel estate. In 1958 the Air Ministry purchased the requisitioned land, the conveyance being expressed to be subject to the restrictive covenant so far as it was valid, subsisting and capable of being enforced; but the defendants remained in occupation. The plaintiffs sought an injunction to restrain the defendants from continuing their non-agricultural activities.

WILBERFORCE J.:

First, are the plaintiffs, or is one of them, entitled to the benefit of the restrictive covenant? This involves several subsidiary questions, namely (a) whether the covenant was entered into for the benefit of any land of the covenantee; (b) whether that land is sufficiently defined or ascertainable by permissible inference or evidence; (c) whether that land is, or was, capable of being benefited by the covenant; (d) whether, since the first plaintiff is not the express assignee of the covenant, the action can be brought by the second plaintiff or by the two plaintiffs jointly.

(a) and (b). This would appear to be a simple point... However, an elaborate argument was addressed to me by the defendants to support a contention that the benefit of the covenant was not available to the plaintiffs. The conveyance, it was said, does not "annex" the benefit of the covenant to any land so that it would pass automatically on a conveyance of the land to a purchaser. Further, it does not indicate that it was made for the benefit of any land, and even supposing that it was so made, it does not identify or provide any material upon which to identify what that land is.

It is, however, well established by the authorities that the benefit of restrictive covenants can pass to persons other than the original covenantee, even in the absence of annexation, provided that certain conditions are fulfilled. There is, however, dispute as to the nature of these conditions.

The defendants' contentions are, first, that there must appear from the terms of the deed itself an intention to benefit some land, and, secondly, that the precise land to be benefited must also be stated in the deed, or at least must be capable of ascertainment from the terms of the deed by evidence which is admissible in accordance with the normal rules of interpretation of documents. They rely principally on *In re Union of London and Smith's Bank Ltd's Conveyance, Miles v. Easter* [1933] Ch. 611, and submit that the decision of Upjohn J. in *Newton Abbot Co-operative Society Ltd v.*

Williamson & Treadgold Ltd [1952] Ch. 286, which appears to admit parole evidence
for the purpose of identifying the land to be benefited, goes too far.

I proceed, therefore, first to examine *Miles v. Easter*. The facts in the case were
(briefly) that the defendant, who was the person seeking to enforce the covenant, was
the owner of the greater part of certain land coloured green which had previously been
owned by the Shoreham company. That company was possessed of certain lands of
considerable but undefined extent including some foreshore land and some land
coloured yellow. The conveyance of 1908 by which the covenant was imposed
contained other covenants expressed to be made "with the purchasers their heirs and
assigns or other the owner or owners for the time being of the land coloured pink or
any part or parts thereof", i.e., in language adapted and intended to annex the benefit
of these other covenants to particular land. The covenant which the defendant was
trying to enforce was not in this form at all; it used no language of annexation. In
these circumstances the Court of Appeal, affirming Bennett J., held that it had not been
shown that the covenant was taken for the benefit of the green land, and in doing so
relied particularly upon the existence of the other land which might, for all that
appeared from the document, have been intended to benefit from the restriction and
upon the contrast in the conveyancing language used.

In the judgment of the Court of Appeal the following passage occurs (at p. 631): "In the
first place, the 'other land' must be land that is capable of being benefited by the
covenant—otherwise it would be impossible to infer that the object of the covenant was to
enable the vendor to dispose of his land to greater advantage. In the next place, this land
must be 'ascertainable' or 'certain,' to use the words of Romer L.J. in *Formby v. Barker*
[1903] 2 Ch, 539, 554, and Scrutton L.J. in *London County Council v. Allen* [1914] 3
K.B. 642, 672, respectively. For, although the court will readily infer the intention to
benefit the other land of the vendor where the existence and situation of such land are
indicated in the conveyance or have been otherwise shown with reasonable certainty, it is
impossible to do so from vague references in the conveyance or in other documents laid
before the court as to the existence of other lands of the vendor, the extent and situation
of which are undefined". This passage is clearly and carefully expressed, and I resist the
invitation of the Attorney-General to interpret it in the light of certain expressions (to my
mind less clear) in the judgment of Bennett J. at first instance. It shows that the court's
opinion was that the existence and situation of the land to be benefited need not be
indicated in the conveyance, provided that it can be otherwise shown with reasonable
certainty, and the natural interpretation to place on these latter words is first that they
may be so shown by evidence dehors the deed, and secondly, that a broad and reasonable
view may be taken as to the proof of the identity of the lands. This general approach
would, I think, be consistent with the equitable origin and character of the enforcement of
restrictive covenants, which should not be constricted by technicalities derived from the
common law of landlord and tenant.

Against this approach the Attorney-General relies strongly on a passage in the same
judgment, where Romer L.J. said (at p. 634): "the first question that has to be
considered is whether or no an intention is shown in the deed of 1908, that the
restrictive covenants should enure for the benefit of any particular land of the
covenantees", and he argued that this showed that the court considered that only the
deed of conveyance should be looked at. With all respect, I do not think that this
consequence follows. In that particular case, reliance was placed on the deed and on
the deed alone: the fact that the court confined its consideration to the terms of the
deed does not, in the circumstances, carry any implication that no other evidence than
the deed itself could be considered.

Before passing to the *Newton Abbot* case, I should add that the rule as stated by the
Court of Appeal in *Miles v. Easter* seems to me to be clearly in line with other
statements of principle made by the courts. In *Rogers v. Hosegood* [1900] 2 Ch. 388—
a leading case on annexation—Collins L.J. said (at p. 407): "When, as in *Renals v.
Cowlishaw* (1879) 11 Ch.D. 866, there is no indication in the original conveyance, or
in the circumstances attending it, that the burden of the restrictive covenant is imposed

for the benefit of the land reserved, or any particular part of it, then it becomes necessary to examine the circumstances under which any part of the land reserved is sold, in order to see whether a benefit, not originally annexed to it, has become annexed to it on the sale, so that the purchaser is deemed to have bought it with the land, and this can hardly be the case where the purchaser did not know of the existence of the restrictive covenant".

This seems to support the view that an intention to benefit may be found from surrounding or attending circumstances, as indeed is frequently done in practice in the case, mentioned by Collins L.J. (at p. 408), of building schemes.

In *Formby v. Barker* [1903] 2 Ch. 539, which is one of the authorities which show that unless the covenantee retains some land intended to be benefited he cannot sue any person except the original covenantor, Vaughan Williams L.J. said (at p. 550): "I have not been able to find any case in which, after the sale of the whole of an estate in land, the benefit of a restrictive covenant has been enforced by injunction against an assignee of the purchaser at the instance of a plaintiff having no land retained by the vendor, although there are cases in which restrictive covenants seem to have been enforced at the instance of plaintiffs, other than the vendor, for the benefit of whose land it appears from the terms of the covenant, or can be inferred from surrounding circumstances, that the covenant was intended to operate". A reference to these passages was made by Upjohn J. in the *Newton Abbot* case, but I have thought it worth while to set them out here so that they can be compared with other citations.

I would add to these a reference to the facts in *Lord Northbourne v. Johnston & Son* [1922] 2 Ch. 309, where the covenant was expressed to be with the trustees of a settlement, their heirs and assigns, the deed containing no reference to any land at all. Sargant J. seems not to have doubted that it could be shown that the covenant was for the benefit of the unsold part of a particular building estate which in fact was vested in the trustees.

I pass now to the *Newton Abbot* case. The facts were that the original covenantee was the owner of a property called Devonia, in Fore Street, Bovey Tracey, on which she carried on business as an ironmonger. The original covenantor was the purchaser from her of other properties in Fore Street opposite Devonia, and the covenant was (briefly) against carrying on the business of an ironmonger. There was no reference in the conveyance by which the covenant was imposed to any land for whose benefit it was made, the only mention of Devonia being that the vendor was described as "of Devonia". The action was between assigns of the covenantee's son, who inherited her estate, and assigns of the covenantors.

Upjohn J. held that the benefit of the covenant was not annexed to Devonia, but held that, looking at the attendant circumstances, the land to be benefited was shown with reasonable certainty and that the land in question was Devonia.

This decision was attacked by the Attorney-General in a lively argument, and I was invited not to follow it. Of course, it relates to its own special facts, and no doubt I could leave it on one side. But I see nothing in it contrary to the principles which appear to be securely laid down. Here were two shops in common ownership facing each other in the same street, one of them, Devonia, an ironmonger's shop. The shops opposite are sold with a covenant against carrying on an ironmonger's business. What could be more obvious than that the covenant was intended for the protection or benefit of the vendor's property Devonia? To have rejected such a conclusion would, I venture to think, have involved not only an injustice but a departure from common sense. So far from declining the authority of this case, I welcome it as a useful guide. But it is only a guide, and I must ultimately reach my conclusion on the facts of the present case. These I now consider. They are not in dispute. I have the fact that the Crichel estate is, and for many years has been, not merely a conglomeration of separate farms and cottages, but a recognisable and recognised agricultural unit. Its identity in 1943 has been established by an agreed map: it has in fact hardly changed since 1928—the date of the vesting deed mentioned in the conveyance—or up to the present time. It has been managed as one for a number of years—thus, no doubt, acquiring its own character—is surrounded by its own ring-fence, has its mansion house, secondary residence, home farm, farm cottages, woodlands, ornamental water, all the indicia of an extremely valuable unit. Its character was entirely agricultural, with the single exception of the paper mill at Witchhampton, and it is surrounded by other similar or at least comparable estates in a district which is entirely agricultural—in the words of one witness "a rather unique area". The property sold in 1943, Crook Farm, was before the sale a part of the estate, the purchaser, Harding, being, as was his father before him, tenant of the farm from the estate: it was also a wholly agricultural property. The vendors of the farm were Hoare Trustees selling in the character of fiduciary owners of the Crichel estate as a whole: in taking any restrictive covenant they had, of course, no individual or personal interest, or any interest other than as owners of the estate as a whole.

On these facts I consider that I should come to the conclusion that the covenant was taken for the benefit of land of the vendors, that land being the Crichel estate. In doing so I do not, so it seems to me, go outside such surrounding or attendant circumstances as, in accordance with the authorities, it is legitimate for the court to take into account. A decision based on the mere wording of [the covenant] would, in my judgment, be unduly narrow and indeed technical, and would go far to undermine the usefulness of the rule which equity courts have evolved that the benefit of restrictive covenants may be capable of passing to assigns of the "dominant" land or of the covenant in cases other than those of annexation. I would add two observations: first, the rules in *Miles v. Easter* properly relate to cases where the covenant is sought to be enforced by an assign from the original covenantee. In this case, however, the second plaintiff is the original covenantee and the first plaintiff is the person for whose benefit in equity the covenant was taken. To that important extent the plaintiffs' case is stronger than that of the defendant in *Miles v. Easter*. Secondly, in holding that the covenant was for the benefit of the Crichel estate, I mean the Crichel estate as a whole, as a single agricultural estate which it was and is, and I express no opinion whether it enures for the benefit of each and every part, for example, if parts are separately sold off. That is not a question which arises in this case.

. . .

Question (c): Was the land capable of being benefited by the covenant? On this point, as on those last dealt with, the answer would appear to be simple. If an owner of land, on selling part of it, thinks fit to impose a restriction on user, and the restriction was imposed for the purpose of benefiting the land retained, the court would normally assume that it is capable of doing so. There might, of course, be exceptional cases where the covenant was on the face of it taken capriciously or not bona fide, but a covenant taken by the owner of an agricultural estate not to use a sold-off portion for other than agricultural purposes could hardly fall within either of these categories. As Sargant J. said in *Lord Northbourne v. Johnston & Son* (at p. 319): "Benefit or detriment is often a question of opinion on which there may be the greatest divergence of view, and the greatest difficulty in arriving at a clear conclusion". Why, indeed, should the court seek to substitute its own standard for those of the parties—and on what basis can it do so? However, much argument was devoted to this point, and evidence was called as to it.

. . .

Taken as a whole, the evidence comes to this, that a restriction of this character, in relation to such an estate as the Crichel estate, was at the relevant date and is at the present time, of value in that it preserves a measure of control over adjoining land. In relation to that part of the adjoining land which, in 1943, was already being used as an aerodrome, so far from the covenant being useless, it was of positive value, because the departure from agricultural use which had already taken place inevitably gave rise to uncertainty as to the future of the land and opened the door to possible further development: the covenant prevented the door from being opened further. [His Lordship analysed the evidence and continued:] It is on this general approach that, in my view, the benefit of the covenant is to be assessed, rather than in relation to particular effects which the benefit of it might produce.

. . .

Lastly, I should add that I reject a line of argument to the effect that development of the restricted land, by bringing with it development, or the possibility of development, of the Crichel estate, would actually raise land values rather than diminish them. The owners of the Crichel estate are surely entitled to set out values above those of this character of enrichment.

Question (d): Can the action be brought by the first plaintiff or by the two plaintiffs jointly?

I can deal with this point quite shortly. The second plaintiff is the original covenantee, and the first plaintiff is the person for whose benefit in equity the covenant was made. Taken together, the plaintiffs represent the whole legal and equitable interest in the covenant. The matter appears, therefore, to be completely covered by the judgment of Sargant J. in *Lord Northbourne v. Johnston & Son*, the reasoning of which I adopt. So much was not really contested by the Attorney-General, who, however, reserved the right to challenge that judgment should this case go to a higher court.

This brings me to a conclusion on the first main point, and I accordingly hold that the plaintiffs are entitled to the benefit of the restrictive covenant.

NOTES:

1. For comment, see (1961) 25 Conv. 430.

2. It has been argued that the instant case did not raise the question whether the benefit of the covenant had passed. The second plaintiffs were the original covenantees and the first plaintiff was the former beneficiary under the strict settlement for whom the second plaintiffs were in the position of trustees: see Baker (1968) 84 L.Q.R. 22, 30; Ryder (1972) 36 Conv. 20, 32. Wade [1972B] C.L.J. 157, 169 acknowledges this point but he argues that nonetheless Wilberforce J. "sets out on his analysis on the assumption that he is dealing with a claim by successors in title. ... It is submitted that it is his reasoning that matters, and that it is entirely convincing and correct". The announcement of the arrival of implied annexation is somewhat muted in Megarry and Wade, *The Law of Real Property* (5th ed., 1984), pp. 784–785.

3. More significantly, it is not clear on what basis it is asserted that the case provides authority or even support for the notion of implied annexation. As Ryder (1972) 36 Conv. 20 points out, the discussion on whether the plaintiffs had the benefit of the covenant passes quickly from express annexation to a consideration of *Miles v. Easter* [1933] Ch. 611 and *Newton Abbot Co-operative Society Ltd v. Williamson & Treadgold Ltd* [1952] Ch. 286, both cases on express assignment, and the proof of an intention to benefit the land of the covenantee. Within the context of assignment there is nothing controversial about adducing evidence from the surrounding circumstances: see Garner (1965) 29 Conv. 175; 176–178; and a similar relaxation has been noted in the context of express annexation: see *J. Sainsbury plc v. Enfield LBC* [1989] 1 W.L.R. 590, 595–597, *supra*, 747. The proposition that such evidence is sufficient *without more* to annex the benefit of the covenant to the land of the covenantee would have been a wholly different matter; but no such proposition appears in the judgment.

2.1.3 *Statutory annexation*   Many of the difficulties and uncertainties resulting from the central requirement of annexation, the establishment of an intention to benefit, may have been removed by the decision of the Court of Appeal in *Federated Homes Ltd v. Mill Lodge Properties Ltd* [1980] 1 W.L.R. 594, which appeared to recognise what has been termed "statutory annexation".

Federated Homes Ltd v. Mill Lodge Properties Ltd [1980] 1 W.L.R. 594

(CA, Brightman, Browne and Megaw L.JJ.)

In 1970 Mackenzie Hill, the owner of a development site which included three areas of land (the red land, the green land and the blue land), obtained outline planning permission to build 1,250 houses on the site. In 1971 Mackenzie Hill sold the blue land to the defendants, who covenanted "with the vendor that in carrying out the development of the blue land [they] shall not built at a greater density than a total of 300 dwellings so as not to reduce the number of units which the vendor might eventually erect on the retained land under the existing planning consent". The plaintiffs subsequently became owners of the green land and the red land by different routes. The green land passed to Brandt's and then to the plaintiffs, each conveyance containing an express assignment of the benefit of the defendants' covenant. The red land passed to Brandt's, then to BTA and finally to the plaintiffs; the first two conveyances each contained an express assignment of the benefit of the defendants' covenant; but the final conveyance to the plaintiffs did not. When the plaintiffs discovered that the defendants had obtained planning permission to erect more than 300 houses on the blue land, they sought to restrain the alleged breach of the 1971 covenant.

BRIGHTMAN L.J.:
Having reached the conclusion that the restrictive covenant was capable of assignment and is not spent, I turn to the question whether the benefit has safely reached the hands of the plaintiff. The green land has no problem, owing to the unbroken chain of assignments. I am disposed to think that that is sufficient to entitle the plaintiff to relief, and that the plaintiff's right to relief would be no greater at the present time if it were held that it also had the benefit of the covenant in its capacity as owner of the red land. However, the judge dealt with both areas of land and I propose to do the same.
    An express assignment of the benefit of a covenant is not necessary if the benefit of the covenant is annexed to the land. In that event, the benefit will pass automatically on a conveyance of the land, without express mention, because it is annexed to the land and runs with it. So the issue of annexation is logically the next to be considered.
    The judge said in his judgment:

"The next heading with which I must deal is 'annexation,' to which I will now come. It is a somewhat technical thing in the law of restrictive covenants. A good deal of argument was addressed to me on annexation by both sides. Submissions were made about express annexation, implied annexation, that is to say, annexation implied from surrounding circumstances, and annexation by assignment. In my judgment, there was in this case no 'annexation' of the benefit of the covenant to the retained land or any part of it. Section 78, in particular, of the Law of Property Act 1925 does not have the effect of annexing the benefit of the covenant to anything. It is simply a statutory shorthand for the shortening of conveyances, which it perhaps has done to some extent in this case. Annexation depends upon appropriate drafting, which is not here in this case, in spite of a recent process which can perhaps be called 'a widening of the law' in these matters. The attendant circumstances moreover, positively militate against annexation because, as Mr Price rightly pointed out to me (though he did so in the course of his argument on construction) the restriction in this particular case is of limited duration and plainly not applicable to ultimate purchasers of plots of the land intended to be benefited. 'Annexation,' in my judgment, is for the parties to the covenant itself to achieve if they wish to, and (though parties may no doubt provide for annexation at a later stage) I am not satisfied or prepared to hold that there is any such thing as 'delayed annexation by assignment' to which the covenantor is not party or privy."

The reference to "delayed annexation by assignment" is to a proposition that a covenant can, on a later assignment, thereby become annexed to the land by the act of the assignor and the assignee alone.

In my judgment the benefit of this covenant was annexed to the retained land, and I think that this is a consequence of section 78 of the Act of 1925, which reads:

"(1) A covenant relating to any land of the covenantee shall be deemed to be made with the covenantee and his successors in title and the persons deriving title under him or them, and shall have effect as if such successors and other persons were expressed. For the purposes of this subsection in connexion with covenants restrictive of the user of land 'successors in title' shall be deemed to include the owners and occupiers for the time being of the land of the covenantee intended to be benefited. (2) This section applies to covenants made after the commencement of this Act, but the repeal of section 58 of the Conveyancing Act 1881 does not affect the operation of covenants to which that section applied."

Mr Price [counsel for the defendants] submitted that there were three possible views about section 78. One view, which he described as "the orthodox view" hitherto held, is that it is merely a statutory shorthand for reducing the length of legal documents. A second view, which was the one that Mr Price was inclined to place in the forefront of his argument, is that the section only applies, or at any rate only achieves annexation, when the land intended to be benefited is signified in the document by express words or necessary implication as the intended beneficiary of the covenant. A third view is that the section applies if the covenant in fact touches and concerns the land of the covenantee, whether that be gleaned from the document itself or from evidence outside the document.

For myself, I reject the narrowest interpretation of section 78, the supposed orthodox view, which seems to me to fly in the face of the wording of the section. Before I express my reasons I will say that I do not find it necessary to choose between the second and third views because, in my opinion, this covenant relates to land of the covenantee on either interpretation of section 78. Clause 5 (iv) shows clearly that the covenant is for the protection of the retained land and that land is described in clause 2 as "any adjoining or adjacent property retained by the vendor". This formulation is sufficient for annexation purposes: see *Rogers v. Hosegood* [1900] 2 Ch. 388.

There is in my judgment no doubt that this covenant "related to the land of the covenantee", or, to use the old-fashioned expression, that it touched and concerned the land, even if Mr Price is correct in his submission that the document must show an intention to benefit identified land. The result of such application is that one must read clause 5 (iv) as if it were written: "The purchaser hereby covenants with the vendor and its successors in title and the persons deriving title under it or them, including the owners and occupiers for the time being of the retained land, that in carrying out the development of the blue land the purchaser shall not build at a greater density than a total 300 dwellings so as not to reduce, etc". I leave out of consideration section 79 as unnecessary to be considered in this context, since Mill Lodge is the original covenantor.

The first point to notice about section 78(1) is that the wording is significantly different from the wording of its predecessor section 58(1) of the Conveyancing Act 1881. The distinction is underlined by section 78(2), which applies section 78(1) only to covenants made after the commencement of the Act. Section 58(1) of the Act of 1881 did not include the covenantee's successors in title or persons deriving title under him or them, or the owner or occupiers for the time being of the land of the covenantee intended to be benefited. The section was confined, in relation to realty, to the covenantee, his heirs and assigns, words which suggest a more limited scope of operation than is found in section 78.

If, as the language of section 78 implies, a covenant relating to land which is restrictive of the user thereof is enforceable at the suit of (1) a successor in title of the covenantee, (2) a person deriving title under the covenantee or under his successors in title, and (3) the owner or occupier of the land intended to be benefited by the covenant, it must, in my view, follow that the covenant runs with the land, because ex hypothesi every successor in title to the land, every derivative proprietor of the land and every other owner and occupier has a right by statute to the covenant. In other words, if the condition precedent of section 78 is satisfied—that is to say, there exists a covenant which touches and concerns the land of the covenantee—that covenant runs with the land for the benefit of his successors in title, persons deriving title under him or them and other owners and occupiers.

This approach to section 78 has been advocated by distinguished textbook writers; see Dr Radcliffe's article "Some Problems of the Law Relating to Restrictive Covenants" (1941) 57 L.Q.R. 203, Professor Wade's article, "Covenants—A Broad and Reasonable View" and the apt cross-heading "What is wrong with section 78?" [1972B] C.L.J. 151, 171, and *Megarry and Wade, The Law of Real Property*, 4th ed. (1975), p. 764. Counsel pointed out to us that the fourth edition of *Megarry and Wade* indicates a change of mind on this topic since the third edition.

Although the section does not seem to have been extensively used in the course of argument in this type of case, the construction of section 78 which appeals to me appears to be consistent with at least two cases decided in this court. The first is *Smith and Snipes Hall Farm Ltd v. River Douglas Catchment Board* [1949] 2 K.B. 500. In that case an agreement was made in April 1938 between certain landowners and the catchment board under which the catchment board undertook to make good the banks of a certain brook and to maintain the same, and the landowners undertook to contribute towards the cost. In 1940 the first plaintiff took a conveyance from one of the landowners of a part of the land together with an express assignment of the benefit of the agreement. In 1944 the second plaintiff took a tenancy of that land without any express assignment of the benefit of the agreement. In 1946 the brook burst its banks and the land owned by the first plaintiff and tenanted by the second plaintiff was inundated. The two important points are that the agreement was not expressed to be for the benefit of the landowner's successors in title; and there was no assignment of the benefit of the agreement in favour of the second plaintiff, the tenant. In reliance, as I understand the case, upon section 78 of the Act of 1925, it was held that the second plaintiff was entitled to sue the catchment board for damages for breach of the agreement. It seems to me that that conclusion can only have been reached on the basis that section 78 had the effect of causing the benefit of the agreement to run with the land so as to be capable of being sued upon by the tenant.

The other case, *Williams v. Unit Construction Co. Ltd* (unreported in the usual series of law reports but fully set out in 19 Conveyancer 262), was decided by this court in 1951. There a company had acquired a building estate and had underleased four plots to Cubbin for 999 years. The underlessors arranged for the defendant company to build houses on the four plots. The defendant covenanted with Cubbin to keep the adjacent road in repair until adopted. Cubbin granted a weekly tenancy of one house to the plaintiff without any express assignment of the benefit of the covenant. The plaintiff was injured owing to the disrepair of the road. She was held entitled to recover damages from the defendant for breach of the covenant.

We were referred to observations in the speeches of Lord Upjohn and Lord Wilberforce in *Sefton v. Tophams Ltd* [1967] 1 A.C. 50, 73 and 81, to the effect that section 79 of the Act of 1925, relating to the burden of covenants, achieved no more than the introduction of statutory shorthand into the drafting of covenants. Section 79, in my view, involves quite different considerations and I do not think that it provides a helpful analogy.

It was suggested by Mr Price that, if this covenant ought to be read as enuring for the benefit of the retained land, it should be read as enuring only for the benefit of the retained land as a whole and not for the benefit of every part of it; with the apparent result that there is no annexation of the benefit to a part of the retained land when any severance takes place. He referred us to a passage in *In re Union of London and Smith's Bank Ltd's Conveyance* [1933] Ch. 611, 628, which I do not think it is necessary for me to read.

The problem is alluded to in *Megarry and Wade, The Law of Real Property*, 4th ed., p. 763.

"In drafting restrictive covenants it is therefore desirable to annex them to the covenantee's land 'or any part or parts thereof.' An additional reason for using this form of words is that, if there is no indication to the contrary, the benefit may be held to be annexed only to the whole of the covenantee's land, so that it will not pass with portions of it disposed of separately. But even without such words the court may find that the covenant is intended to benefit any part of the retained land; and small indications may suffice, since the rule that presumes annexation to the whole only is arbitrary and inconvenient. In principle it conflicts with the rule for assignments, which allows a benefit annexed to the whole to be assigned with part, and it also conflicts with the corresponding rule for easements."

I find the idea of the annexation of a covenant to the whole of the land but not to a part of it a difficult conception fully to grasp. I can understand that a covenantee may expressly or by necessary implication retain the benefit of a covenant wholly under his own control, so that the benefit will not pass unless the covenantee chooses to assign; but I would have thought, if the benefit of a covenant is, on a proper construction of a document, annexed to the land, prima facie it is annexed to every part thereof, unless the contrary clearly appears. It is difficult to see how this court can have reached its decision in *Williams v. Unit Construction Co. Ltd*, 19 Conveyancer 262, unless this is right. The covenant was, by inference, annexed to every part of the land and not merely to the whole, because it will be recalled that the plaintiff was a tenant of only one of the four houses which had the benefit of the covenant.

There is also this observation by Romer L.J. in *Drake v. Gray* [1936] Ch. 451, 465. He was dealing with the enuring of the benefit of a restrictive covenant and he said:

"... where one finds not 'the land coloured yellow' or 'the estate' or 'the field named so and so' or anything of that kind, but 'the lands retained by the vendor,' it appears to me that there is a sufficient indication that the benefit of the covenant enures to every one of the lands retained by the vendor, and if a plaintiff in a subsequent action to enforce a covenant can say: 'I am the owner of a piece of land that belonged to the vendor at the time of the conveyance,' he is entitled to enforce the covenant.

In the instant case the judge in the course of his judgment appears to have dismissed the notion that any individual plot-holder would be entitled, even by assignment, to have the benefit of the covenant that I have been considering. I express no view about that. I only say this, that I am not convinced that his conclusion on that point is correct. I say no more about it.

In the end, I come to the conclusion that section 78 of the Law of Property Act 1925 caused the benefit of the restrictive covenant in question to run with the red land and therefore to be annexed to it, with the result that the plaintiff is able to enforce the covenant against Mill Lodge, not only in its capacity as owner of the green land, but also in its capacity as owner of the red land.

NOTES:

1. On the question whether assignment constitutes delayed annexation, see *infra*, p. 765.

2. Although Brightman L.J. stated that he found it unnecessary to choose between the second and third views as to the effect of section 78(1), his summary (at 605) appears to support the third, most liberal view: "If ... there exists a covenant which touches and concerns the land of the covenantee, that covenant runs with the land". However, in *Bridges v. Harrow LBC* (1981) 260 E.G. 284, where only the second view was argued, Stuart-Smith J., having held that there was no indication in the relevant instrument of the land to be benefited, did not consider the third view. Webb [1982] Conv. 313 argues that, if section 78 has the effect of annexation, the third view is consistent with the recent more liberal approach to evidence of annexation generally.

3. It is difficult to see how Brightman L.J. was able to assert that his interpretation of section 78(1) was consistent with the decisions of the Court of Appeal in *Smith and Snipes Hall Farm Ltd v. River Douglas Catchment Board* [1949] 2 K.B. 500 and *Williams v. Unit Construction Co. Ltd* (1951), noted at (1955) 19 Conv. 262. In the former case, Tucker L.J. stated (at 506): "It is first necessary to ascertain from the deed that the covenant is one which 'touches or concerns' the land ... *and it must then be shown that it was the intention of the parties that the benefit thereof should run with the land*"; (italics added); in the latter case, Tucker L.J. referred to the argument of counsel that had emphasized the italicised words, analysed the wording of the covenant and concluded (at 265): "I think this covenant is one which clearly relates to the land of the covenantee within the meaning of section 78 of the Law of Property Act 1925 *and was intended to enure for the benefit of [the plaintiff]*" (italics added).

4. Newson (1981) 97 L.Q.R. 32, (1982) 98 L.Q.R. 202 argues that the parliamentary history of section 78(1) (the Conveyancing Act 1881, the Law of Property Act 1922, the Law of Property (Amendment) Act 1924 and the Law of Property Act 1925) demonstrates that the section did not alter the pre-1881 position that (i) annexation is a matter of intention and (ii) that the intention to annex must be found from something other than statutorily implied references to successors in title. On the other hand, Hurst (1982) 2 *Legal Studies* 53 argues that section 78(1) (and its precursor, section 58 of the Conveyancing Act 1881) should always have been interpreted as transmitting the benefit of covenants relating to land without any expression of intention. Radcliffe (1941) 57 L.Q.R. 203, 204–206, seems to have taken a similar view of section 78(1) (but not section 58), regarding that as "perhaps the most natural effect" of the section; and Bailey (1938) 6 C.L.J. 339, 354, observes that section 78(1) "has a more hopeful appearance than its predecessor".

Wade [1972B] C.L.J. 151, 171–175, expresses the view that, where a covenant relates to (touches and concerns) any land of the covenantee, section 78(1) (and section 58) should be interpreted as raising a presumption that his successors in title are intended to benefit; and he regards it as "extraordinary" that this interpretation of section 78(1) had previously been virtually ignored by judges, counsel and textbook writers. However, he does not appear to have regarded intention as irrelevant: "Whether a covenant is *capable* of touching and concerning land is an objective matter of law, independent of the intention of the parties. Whether, if so capable, it actually does relate to any given land"—and that is the precondition for the operation of section 78(1)— "is a matter of intention, to be collected from the deed and the surrounding circumstances". Todd [1985] Conv. 177 concludes that *Federated Homes Ltd v. Mill Lodge Properties Ltd* did not decide that section 78(1) has the effect of annexation independently of intention, arguing, *inter alia*, that Brightman L.J.'s reliance on Wade [1972B] C.L.J. 151 must have included acceptance of the element of intention in the operation of the section.

5. Todd [1985] Conv. 177 argues that the decision remains "fairly revolutionary", if of general application, and that it should be coined to the situation where enforcement is sought against the original covenantor. Moreover, in the light of the decision in *Federated Homes Ltd v. Mill Lodge Properties Ltd*, Todd argues that it may no longer be appropriate to draw a distinction between legal annexation and equitable annexation of the benefit *where enforcement is sought against the original covenantor*. On the other hand, where enforcement is sought against a successor in title of the original covenantor under the doctrine in *Tulk v. Moxhay*, so that legal annexation is not available, it may be defensible for equity to impose stricter requirements. Hayton (1980) 43 M.L.R. 445 argues that assignment must disappear since the benefit of a covenant that satisfies the requirements for assignment will be automatically annexed. See also [1980] Conv. 216.

6. Some commentators have asserted that the interpretation of section 78(1) was (strictly) obiter: the plaintiffs were clearly entitled to enforce the covenant as owners of the green land so that consideration of their entitlement to enforce the covenant as owners of the red land was unnecessary; and, on that basis, it is suggested that the decision in *Federated Homes Ltd v. Mill Lodge Properties Ltd* could be sidestepped. The assertion has been expressly rejected by the courts: see *Roake v. Chadha* [1984] 1 W.L.R. 40, 45 *per* Judge Paul Baker Q.C., *infra*, p. 762; and see *Allen v. Veranne Builders Ltd* [1988] E.G.C.S. 2. Moreover, since the issue was fully argued before the court, the suggestion is not wholly convincing.

7. For the effect of section 78(1) where the covenant purports to exclude the passing of the benefit except by express assignment, see *Roake v. Chadha* [1984] 1 W.L.R. 40, *infra*, p. 762.

8. The approach to section 78(1) in *Federated Homes Ltd v. Mill Lodge Properties Ltd* has been held to be inapplicable to its precursor, section 58 of the Conveyancing Act 1881: *J. Sainsbury plc v. Enfield LBC* [1989] 1 W.L.R. 590, 598–601 *per* Morritt J. Such a view was implicit in the observations of Brightman L.J. on the significantly different wording of the earlier section; but

Wade [1972B] C.L.J. 157, 173–175 and Hurst (1982) 2 *Legal Studies* 53, 63–72 argue that, properly interpreted, section 58 should also have been held to effect annexation.

9. The view that annexation to the whole of the land prima facie includes annexation to every part thereof is inconsistent with earlier authority (see *supra*, p. 653); and in *Bridges v. Harrow LBC* (1981) 260 E.G. 284 Stuart-Smith J. expressed the view (at 290) that annexation to every part of the land was a matter of intention and that it was necessary that some indication of that intention should be found in the covenant itself. However, the former view was supported in *Allen v. Veranne Builders Ltd* [1988] E.G.C.S. 2.

10. The case provides a clear indication of the relationship between the private law of covenants and public planning control. First, the court held that, although the defendants' covenant was made in response to the principle and the detail of the outline planning permission, the covenant survived the lapse of the permission after three years. Secondly, although the defendants obtained planning permission to build more than 300 houses on the blue land, that permission could not override the restriction in the covenant.

Roake v. Chadha [1984] 1 W.L.R. 40

(Ch D., Judge Paul Baker Q.C.)

In 1934 Lambert, the predecessor in title of the defendants, had purchased a plot on the Sudbury Court Estate. The vendors had laid out the estate in plots and intended to sell them off using a standard form of transfer. The instrument of transfer included a covenant by the purchaser not to build on the plot except in accordance with specified conditions; and it was expressed to be made "with the vendors but so that this covenant shall not enure for the benefit of any owner or subsequent purchaser of any part of the vendors' Sudbury Court Estate at Wembley unless the benefit of this covenant shall be expressly assigned". The plaintiffs were successors in title of a number of subsequent purchasers, who had not had the benefit of the covenant expressly assigned to them; but they sought a declaration that they were entitled to enforce the covenant against the defendants, who were proposing to build inconsistently with its terms.

JUDGE PAUL BAKER Q.C.:
The plaintiffs contend that the benefit of the covenant has become annexed to each of the plots respectively owned by them. Alternatively, it is contended that the benefit has passed under the general words of section 62 of the Law of Property Act 1925.

As to annexation, Mr Walter, appearing for the plaintiffs, conceded that the express terms of the covenant appeared to exclude annexation, and there was no suggestion that the case fell within the category known as building schemes. Mr Walter, however, in an interesting argument submitted that annexation had come about through the operation of section 78 of the Law of Property Act, as interpreted in *Federated Homes Ltd v. Mill Lodge Properties Ltd* [1980] 1 W.L.R. 594, a Court of Appeal decision. I can summarise his argument by the following four points.
(1) The covenant was a covenant relating to the land of the covenantee.

(2) Section 78(1) of the Law of Property Act 1925 provides, as regards such covenants relating to land that they are deemed:

"to be made with the covenantee and his successors in title and the persons deriving title under him or them, and shall have effect as if such successors and other persons were expressed. For the purposes of this subsection in connection with convenants restrictive of the user of land 'successors in title' shall be deemed to include the owners and occupiers for the time being of the land of the covenantee intended to be benefited."

(3) In the *Federated Homes* case it was held that by virtue of section 78(1) the benefit of a convenant relating to land retained by the convenantee ran with that land and was annexed to it and to every part of it. (4) The provisions of section 78, unlike those of section 79 relating to the burden of the covenant, cannot be excluded by the expression of a contrary intention.

. . .

I have no difficulty in accepting that the covenant in the standard form of the 1934 transfer is a covenant relating to the retained land of [the vendors] and that therefore section 78 comes into play. It is the third and fourth points which have given rise to the argument in this case.

I must begin, therefore, by examining the *Federated Homes* case [1980] 1 W.L.R. 594....

Mr Henty, for the defendant in the present case, has argued that ... the Court of Appeal's judgments in relation to the red land were obiter. I am unable to accept this view of the effect of the judgments. As it seems to me, the status of the covenant in relation to both pieces of land—the red and the green—was in issue in the case. If the defendant in subsequent proceedings had sought to challenge the validity of the covenant in relation to the red land, he could, as I would see it, be met by a plea of issue estoppel and consequently the principle underlying the court's conclusion cannot be regarded as obiter. That principle I take from the following passage in the judgment of Brightman L.J., at p. 605:

"If, as the language of section 78 implies, a convenant relating to land which is restrictive of the user thereof is enforceable at the suit of (1) a successor in title of the covenantee, (2) a person deriving title under the covenantee or under his successors in title, and (3) the owner or occupier of the land intended to be benefited by the covenant, it must, in my view, follow that the covenant runs with the land, because ex hypothesi every successor in title to the land, every derivative proprietor of the land and every other owner and occupier has a right by statute to the covenant. In other words, if the condition precedent of section 78 is satisfied—that is to say, there exists a covenant which touches and concerns the land of the covenantee—that covenant runs with the land for the benefit of his successors in title, persons deriving title under him or them and other owners and occupiers."

That seems to be the essential point of the decision. Mr Henty made a frontal attack on this use of section 78, which he reinforced by reference to an article by Mr G. H. Newsom Q.C. in (1981) 97 L.Q.R. 32 which is critical of the decision. The main lines of attack are (1) that the conclusion overlooks the legislative history of section 78 which it is said shows that it has a narrower purpose than is claimed and does not in itself bring about annexation; (2) this narrower purpose has been accepted in relation to the corresponding section 79 (relating to burden) by Lord Upjohn and Lord Wilberforce in *Sefton v. Tophams Ltd* [1967] 1 A.C. 50, 73, 81. Further, it is said by way of argument sub silentio that in a number of cases, notably *Marquess of Zetland v. Driver* [1939] Ch. 1 and *In re Jeff's Transfer (No. 2)* [1966] 1 W.L.R. 841, that the argument could have been used to good effect but was not deployed.

Now, all this is very interesting, and the views of Mr Newsom are entitled to very great respect seeing that until his recent retirement he was a practitioner of long experience who had made a special study of this branch of the law. He has written a valuable monograph on it. All the same, despite Mr Henty's blandishments, I am not going to succumb to the temptation of joining in any such discussion. Sitting here as a judge of the Chancery Division, I do not consider it to be my place either to criticise or to defend the decisions of the Court of Appeal. I conceive it my clear duty to accept the decision of the Court of Appeal as binding on me and apply it as best I can to the facts I find here.

Mr Walter's method of applying it is simplicity itself. The *Federated Homes* case [1980] 1 W.L.R. 594 shows that section 78 of the Act of 1925 brings about annexation, and that the operation of the section cannot be excluded by a contrary intention. As I have indicated, he supports this last point by reference to section 79, which is expressed to operate "unless a contrary intention is expressed", a qualification which, as we have already noticed, is absent from section 78. Mr Walter could not suggest any reason of policy why section 78 should be mandatory, unlike, for example, section 146 of the Act of 1925, which deals with restrictions on the right to forfeiture of leases and which, by an express provision "has effect notwithstanding any stipulation to the contrary".

I am thus far from satisfied that section 78 has the mandatory operation which Mr Walter claimed for it. But if one accepts that it is not subject to a contrary intention, I do not consider that it has the effect of annexing the benefit of the covenant in each and every case irrespective of the other express terms of the covenant. I notice that Brightman L.J. in the *Federated Homes* case did not go so far as that, for he said, at p. 606:

"I find the idea of the annexation of a covenant to the whole of the land but not to a part of it a difficult conception fully to grasp. I can understand that a covenantee may expressly or by necessary implication retain the benefit of a covenant wholly under his own control, so that the benefit will not pass unless the covenantee chooses to assign; but I would have thought, if the benefit of a covenant is, on a proper construction of a document, annexed to the land, prima facie it is annexed to every part thereof, unless the contrary clearly appears."

So at least in some circumstances Brightman L.J. is considering that despite section 78 the benefit may be retained and not pass or be annexed to and run with land. In this connection, I was also referred by Mr Henty to *Elphinstone's Covenants Affecting Land* (1946), p. 17, where it is said in a footnote:

"but it is thought that, as a covenant must be construed as a whole, the court would give due effect to words excluding or modifying the operation of the section..."

The true position as I see it is that even where a covenant is deemed to be made with successors in title as section 78 requires, one still has to construe the covenant as a whole to see whether the benefit of the covenant is annexed. Where one finds, as in the *Federated Homes* case, the covenant is not qualified in any way, annexation may be readily inferred; but where, as in the present case, it is expressly provided:

"this covenant shall not enure for the benefit of any owner or subsequent purchaser of any part of the vendor's Sudbury Court Estate at Wembley unless the benefit of this covenant shall be expressly assigned..."

one cannot just ignore these words. One may not be able to exclude the operation of the section in widening the range of the covenantees, but one has to consider the covenant as a whole to determine its true effect. When one does that, then it seems to me that the answer is plain and in my judgment the benefit was not annexed. That is giving full weight to both the statute in force and also what is already there in the covenant.

NOTES:

1. Unlike the situation in *Federated Homes Ltd v. Mill Lodge Properties Ltd* enforcement was sought against a successor in title of the original covenantor: so that the case would necessarily seem to involve the equitable rules for passing the benefit of the covenant.

2. For comment, see [1984] Conv. 68.

3. For the argument based on section 62 of the Law of Property Act 1925, see *infra*, p. 773.

2.2 *Assignment*

Where the benefit of a covenant has not been annexed to the land of the covenantee, a successor in title of the original covenantee may still be able to establish that the benefit of the covenant has passed to him through express assignment. However, in the light of the relaxation of the requirements for express annexation and the development of the concepts of implied annexation and statutory annexation, there may be very few occasions when it is necessary to rely on assignment: see Hayton (1980) 43 M.L.R. 445. It would seem to be possible for the benefit of a covenant to pass to a successor in title of the original covenantee by means of annexation *and* assignment. It has been argued that the two means are mutually exclusive: see Hayton (1971) 87 L.Q.R. 539, 564–568; but that argument is implicitly rejected in the reasoning of the Court of Appeal in *Federated Homes Ltd v. Mill Lodge Properties Ltd* [1980] 1 W.L.R. 594.

In the present context assignment means *equitable* assignment. Legal assignment of the benefit of covenant as a chose in action pursuant to section 136 of the Law of Property Act 1925 is only possible where the original covenantor retains his land and the person seeking to enforce the covenant is a successor in title to the *whole* of the land of the original covenantee. Where the original covenantor has disposed of his land and/or the person seeking to enforce the covenant is a successor in title to *part only* of the land of the original covenantee, he must comply with the equitable principles discussed in this section: *Miles v. Easter* [1933] 1 Ch. 611, 630 *per* Romer L.J.

2.2.1 *Annexation and assignment contrasted*   Certain differences between annexation and assignment may be identified.

First, whereas annexation necessarily takes effect at the date of the covenant, by contrast assignment is effected when the original covenantee transfers the benefited land to a successor in title.

Secondly, it has been seen that annexation permanently affixes the benefit of the covenant to the land of the original covenantee at the time of the covenant so that from that time onwards the benefit of the covenant is effectively part of the benefited land and passes automatically when the benefited land is transferred. By contrast, it is asserted that assignment simply transfers the benefit of the covenant to the assignee personally; and from that it would seem to follow that the benefit of the covenant must be assigned on every subsequent transfer of the benefited land. There are dicta in older cases which support the view that assignment of the benefit of a covenant to a successor in title effects what is termed "delayed annexation". Thus in *Rogers v. Hosegood* [1900] 2 Ch. 388 Collins L.J. said (at 408):

Where there is no indication in the original conveyance, or in the circumstances attending it, that the covenant is imposed for the benefit of the land reserved, or any particular part of it, then it becomes necessary to examine the circumstances under which any part of the land reserved is sold, in order to see whether a benefit, not originally annexed to it, *has become annexed to it on the sale*, so that the purchaser is deemed to have bought it with the land.

See also *Renals v. Cowlishaw* (1878) 9 Ch D. 125, 130–131 *per* Hall V.-C.; *Reid v. Bickerstaff* [1909] 2 Ch. 305, 320 *per* Cozens-Hardy M.R. Moreover, there is support from academic writers for the theory of delayed annexation: see Bailey [1938] 6 C.L.J. 339, 360–361; Wade [1957] C.L.J. 146; Bowles [1962] J.P.L. 234; Baker (1968) 84 L.Q.R. 22, 29–32; Wade [1972B] C.L.J. 157, 166; Hayton (1971) 87 L.Q.R. 539, 564–568. On the other hand, more recent cases seem to support the need for a complete chain of assignments linking the original covenantee and the successor in title seeking to enforce the covenant. In *Re Pinewood Estate, Farnborough* [1958] Ch. 280 the need for a chain of assignments was assumed, although the point appears to have been conceded and the three cases referred to above were not cited. The judgment of Ungoed-Thomas J. in *Stilwell v. Blackman* [1968] Ch. 508 contains dicta to support both views. However, in *Federated Homes Ltd v. Mill Lodge Properties Ltd* [1980] 1 W.L.R. 594 the "delayed annexation" argument was expressly rejected by the judge at first instance; and the reasoning of the Court of Appeal, in respect of both the green land and the red land, would seem implicitly to reject the argument. In finding that the benefit of the covenant had passed to the plaintiffs as owners of the green land, Brightman L.J. stressed the unbroken chain of assignments; by contrast, despite the express assignment of the benefit of the covenant on the first transfer of the red land from the original covenantee, it was the absence of an unbroken chain of assignments passing the benefit of the covenant to the plaintiffs as owners of the red land that necessitated consideration of annexation. The reasoning in both cases is inconsistent with the notion of "delayed annexation".

Thirdly, the difficulties encountered in the context of annexation, where a covenant benefited part only of a larger plot of land (see *Re Ballard's Conveyance* [1937] Ch. 473, *supra*, p. 747) have not occurred in the context of assignment. The courts have held that, irrespective of whether the benefit of a covenant had been annexed to the whole *only* of the covenantee's land, but subject to any term in the covenant to the contrary, the covenantee can expressly assign the benefit to successors in title of parts of the benefited land: *Russell v. Archdale* [1964] Ch. 38, 47–48 *per* Buckley J.; *Stilwell v. Blackman* [1968] Ch. 508, 528–529 *per* Ungoed-Thomas J., noted at (1968) 32 Conv. 60. For criticism of this arguably paradoxical situation, see Baker (1968) 84 L.Q.R. 22; Harris (1968) 31 M.L.R. 459; Hayton (1971) 87 L.Q.R. 539, 556–568.

For detailed discussion of the relationship between annexation and assignment, see Baker (1968) 84 L.Q.R. 226; Hayton (1971) 87 L.Q.R. 539.

2.2.2 *The requirements of assignment*   The leading cases on assignment are *Re Union of London and Smith's Bank Ltd's Conveyance, Miles v. Easter* [1933] Ch. 611, *infra*, and *Newton Abbot Co-operative Society Ltd v. Williamson & Treadgold Ltd* [1952] Ch. 286, *infra*, p. 769. The cases provide authority that the following conditions must be satisfied if assignment is to be effective:

(i)   The covenant must have been taken with the intention that it should benefit land retained by the covenantee and that land must have been capable of being benefited by the covenant; it seems that this requirement can be established by reference to the surrounding circumstances. Hayton (1971) 87 L.Q.R. 539, 554–559 argues that there is an additional implicit requirement: that the covenant must have been taken to enable the covenantee the better *either* (i) to dispose of his land as a whole *or* (ii) to dispose of the whole and each and every part.

(ii) The benefited land must have been certain or ascertainable; again it seems that this requirement can be established by reference to the surrounding circumstances.

(iii) The assignment of the benefit of the covenant must be contemporaneous with the transfer of the benefited land and will usually be effected by express words of assignment in the same document by which the covenantee (or, in the case of a subsequent assignment, his successor in title) transfers the benefited land to the transferee. The usual rationale for this requirement (and the necessary corollary that the benefit cannot be assigned subsequently) is that the covenant *ex hypothesi* benefits the covenantee's land and consequently renders it more saleable; and that, if the covenantee has succeeded in selling the land without assigning the benefit of the covenant, the benefit is somehow "spent" and ceases to be assignable. The benefit of a covenant that has not been annexed may also pass by operation of law on the death of the covenantee to the covenantee's executors, who hold it as a separate asset on bare trust for the devisee of the benefited land. The covenant can be enforced by the executors: *Ives v. Brown* [1919] 2 Ch. 314; or by the devisee: *Earl of Leicester v. Wells-next-the-Sea UDC* [1973] Ch. 110; and the devisee can effectively assign the benefit of the covenant on a subsequent transfer of the land.

Re Union of London and Smith's Banks Ltd's Conveyance, Miles v. Easter [1933] Ch. 611

(CA, Lord Hanworth M.R., Lawrence and Romer L.JJ.)

ROMER L.J.:
Now it may be conceded that the benefit of a covenant entered into with the covenantee or his assigns is assignable.... But it by no means follows that the assignee of a restrictive covenant affecting land of the covenantor is entitled to enforce it against an assign of that land. For the burden of the covenant did not run with the land at law, and is only enforceable against a purchaser with notice by reason of the equitable doctrine that is usually referred to as the rule in *Tulk v. Moxhay*. It was open,

therefore, to the Courts of Equity to prescribe the particular class of assignees of the covenant to whom they should concede the benefit of the rule. This they have done, and in doing so have included within the class persons to whom the benefit of the covenant could not have been assigned at law. For at law the benefit could not be assigned in pieces. It would have to be assigned as a whole or not at all. And yet in equity the right to enforce the covenant can in certain circumstances be assigned by the covenantee from time to time to one person after another. Who then are the assignees of the covenant that are entitled to enforce it?

[Romer L.J. referred to statements in *Formby v. Barker* [1903] 2 Ch. 539, 554 and in *London CC v. Allen* [1914] 3 K.B. 642, 672 and continued:]

It is plain from these and other cases, and notably that of *Renals v. Cowlishaw* (1878) 9 Ch.D. 125, that if the restrictive covenant be taken not merely for some personal purpose or object of the vendor, but for the benefit of some other land of his in the sense that it would enable him to dispose of that land to greater advantage, the covenant, though not annexed to such land so as to run with any part of it, may be enforced against an assignee of the covenantor taking with notice, both by the covenantee and by persons to whom the benefit of such covenant has been assigned, subject however to certain conditions. In the first place, the "other land" must be land that is capable of being benefited by the covenant—otherwise it would be impossible to infer that the object of the covenant was to enable the vendor to dispose of his land to greater advantage. In the next place, this land must be "ascertainable" or "certain", to use the words of Romer L.J. and Scrutton J. respectively. For, although the Court will readily infer the intention to benefit the other land of the vendor where the existence and situation of such land are indicated in the conveyance or have been otherwise shown with reasonable certainty, it is impossible to do so from vague references in the conveyance or in other documents laid before the Court as to the existence of other lands of the vendor, the extent and situation of which are undefined. In the third place, the covenant cannot be enforced by the covenantee against an assign of the purchaser after the covenantee has parted with the whole of his land.

This last point was decided, and in our opinion rightly decided, by Sargant J. in *Chambers v. Randall* [1923] 1 Ch. 149. As pointed out by that learned judge, the covenant having been entered into to enable the covenantee to dispose of his property to advantage, that result will in fact have been obtained when all that property has been disposed of. There is therefore no longer any reason why the Court should extend to him the benefit of the equitable doctrine of *Tulk v. Moxhay*. That is only done when it is sought to enforce the covenant in connection with the enjoyment of land that the covenant was intended to protect. But it was also held by Sargant J. in the same case, and in our opinion rightly held, that although on a sale of the whole or part of the property intended to be protected by the covenant the right to enforce the covenant may be expressly assigned to the purchaser, such an assignment will be ineffective if made at a later date when the covenantee has parted with the whole of his land. The covenantee must, indeed, be at liberty to include in any sale of the retained property the right to enforce the covenants. He might not otherwise be able to dispose of such property to the best advantage, and the intention with which he obtained the covenant would be defeated. But if he has been able to sell any particular part of his property without assigning to the purchaser the benefit of the covenant, there seems no reason why he should at a later date and as an independent transaction be at liberty to confer upon the purchaser such benefit. To hold that he could do so would be to treat the covenant as having been obtained, not only for the purpose of enabling the covenantee to dispose of his land to the best advantage, but also for the purpose of enabling him to dispose of the benefit of the covenant to the best advantage. Where, at the date of the assignment of the benefit of the covenant, the covenantee has disposed of the whole of his land, there is an additional reason why the assignee should be unable to enforce it. For at the date of the assignment the covenant had ceased to be enforceable at the instance of the covenantee himself, and he cannot confer any greater rights upon the assignee than he possessed himself.

NOTE:

1. For contemporary comment, see Holland (1933) 49 L.Q.R. 483.

Newton Abbot Co-operative Society Ltd v. Williamson & Treadgold Ltd
[1952] Ch. 286

(Ch D., Upjohn J.)

Mardon was the fee simple owner of "Devonia", where she carried on business as an ironmonger. In 1923 she conveyed the property opposite "Devonia" to purchasers, who covenanted "with the vendor that they the purchasers and persons deriving title under them will not carry on any business of such a nature which will in any way affect or be in competition with the business of a furnishing ironmonger". When Mardon died, her executors, in accordance with her will, assented in writing to the vesting of "Devonia" in her son; but there was no assent in respect of the benefit of the restrictive covenant. In 1948 the son leased "Devonia" to the Bovey Tracey Co-operative Society (which later became amalgamated with the plaintiffs) and purported to assign to them the goodwill of the ironmongery business and the benefit of the restrictive covenant. When the defendants, who had acquired the property opposite "Devonia" in 1947, started to sell ironmongery, the plaintiffs sought an injunction. Upjohn J. held that the benefited land was not identified sufficiently clearly in the 1923 conveyance to effect the annexation of the benefit of the covenant to "Devonia". He continued:

I turn then to [the] second submission, namely, that the plaintiffs are express assigns of the benefit of the restrictive covenant. Mr Bowles, on behalf of the defendants, contends that, even if it be assumed that his submission (with which I shall deal later) that the covenant was not taken for the benefit of Devonia, but of the business carried on thereat, is wrong, and the covenant was taken by Mrs Mardon for the benefit of Devonia to enable her to dispose of it to better advantage, yet there is here no complete chain of assignments vesting the benefit in the plaintiffs. He says that there was never any assignment of the benefit of the covenant by the executors of Mrs Mardon to Leonard Soper Mardon and therefore he was not in a position to assign the benefit of the covenant to the plaintiffs' predecessors in title. He relied on *Ives v. Brown* [1919] 2 Ch. 314 and *Lord Northbourne v. Johnston & Son* [1922] 2 Ch. 309.

In my judgment those authorities do not support his contention. The position as I see it was this: On the footing that the restrictive covenant was not annexed to the land so as to run with it, the benefit of the covenant is capable of passing by operation of law as well as by express assignment and formed part of Mrs Mardon's personal estate on her death: see *Ives v. Brown*.

It was not suggested that there was any implied assent to the assignment of the benefit of the covenant to the residuary legatee, but in my judgment, when her estate was duly wound up and administered, and this case has been argued before me on the footing that that happened many years ago, the benefit of the covenant was held by the executors as bare trustees for the residuary legatee, Leonard Soper Mardon, who was himself one of the executors. He therefore became entitled to the benefit of this restrictive covenant in equity and, in my judgment, he was entitled to assign the benefit in equity on an assignment of Devonia. No doubt had the covenant been assigned to him by the executors, he could also have assigned it at law. That this is the position is, in my judgment, made clear by the judgment of Sargant J. in *Lord Northbourne v. Johnston & Son*. . . .

The second main question was whether the defendants are liable to have the covenant enforced against them. This was Mr Bowles' main defence in this action and he says that the restrictive covenant was not taken for the benefit of Devonia, and he puts his case in this way: First, he says that in any event this was not taken for the benefit of any land, but was a covenant with Mrs Mardon personally, solely for the benefit of her business. Secondly, he says that in order that an express assign of the benefit may sue an assignee of the burden of the covenant there must be some reference in the conveyance creating that covenant to the land for the benefit of which it was taken. It will be convenient to deal with the first point first.

Mr Bowles strongly urged that the covenant was taken solely to protect the goodwill of the business carried on at Devonia, that it had no reference to the land itself, and that it was not taken for the benefit of that land; in brief, that it was a covenant in gross incapable of assignment. He urged that taking such a covenant would benefit the business in that an enhanced price could be obtained for the business, but no such enhanced price would be obtained for the land. He relied on the fact that the covenant did not mention the vendors' assigns and that it was a covenant against competition. Further, he pointed out that when Leonard Soper Mardon assigned to the Bovey Tracey Co-operative Society, the benefit of the covenant was assigned in the deed which assigned the business and not in the lease of Devonia. If that be the right view, then he said there could be no right to enforce the covenant against the defendants because the mere fact that the defendants took with notice is not sufficient to bind their consciences in equity, and he relied on the two cases of *Formby v. Barker* [1903] 2 Ch. 539 and *London County Council v. Allen* [1914] 3 K.B. 642. Those cases show, he submitted, and I agree with him, that in order to enforce a covenant such as this against an assign of the covenantor, you must show that the covenant created something analogous to an equitable easement, that is, you must find something in the nature of a dominant tenement for the benefit of which the covenant was taken and a servient tenement which was to be subject to that covenant. Here he says there was no dominant tenement; the covenant was taken not for the benefit of any land, but for the benefit of the business.

I do not accept this view of the transaction of 1923. In 1923 Mrs Mardon was carrying on the business of an ironmonger at Devonia. No doubt the covenant was taken for the benefit of that business and to prevent competition therewith, but I see no reason to think, and there is nothing in the conveyance of 1923 which leads me to believe, that that was the sole object of taking the covenant. Mrs Mardon may well have had it in mind that she might want ultimately to sell her land and the business and the benefit of the covenant in such manner as to annex the benefit of the covenant to Devonia for, by so doing, she would get an enhanced price for the totality of the assets which she was selling; a purchaser would surely pay more for a property which would enable him to sue in equity assigns of the defendants' premises taking with notice and to pass on that right, if he so desired, to his successors, than for a property which would only enable him to sue the original covenantor, for that is the result of the view urged on me by Mr Bowles.

Further, Mrs Mardon may well have thought that her own business might ultimately be closed down, or the goodwill thereof sold to someone who was going to carry it on on some other premises. She would then be left with Devonia, and Devonia could be sold at an enhanced price to someone intending to carry on the business of an ironmonger, because, if, as part of the sale transaction, he obtained the benefit of the covenant, he could prevent competition from the defendants' premises opposite in that trade.

In my judgment, it was always open to Mrs Mardon, when she desired to dispose either of the land or the business, to assign the benefit of the covenant with the one or the other or both as she chose. By taking this covenant, she was thereby enabled to sell her premises, or her business, to better advantage as she thought fit. In my judgment, Mrs Mardon was in the position of the vendor in the example given by Cozens-Hardy M.R. in *Reid v. Bickerstaff*, where he says [1909] 2 Ch. 305, 320: "For example, I sell a piece of land with a covenant that no public-house shall be erected thereon. I sell the adjoining lot to a purchaser who is ignorant of the existence of the covenant. I am at full liberty to release the covenant, or to assign the benefit of it to any particular purchaser, or to deal with the rest of my land as I think fit".

Accordingly, in my judgment, the defendants fail on this point.

Mr Bowles' second point was that, in order that the benefit of the covenant may be assignable, the land for which the benefit of the covenant is taken must in some way be referred to in the conveyance creating the covenant, and I was naturally pressed with the headnote in *In re Union of London and Smith's Bank Ltd's Conveyance* [1933] Ch. 611 which reads as follows: "Where on a sale otherwise than under a building scheme a restrictive covenant is taken, the benefit of which is not on the sale annexed to the land retained by the covenantee so as to run with it, an assign of the covenantee's retained land cannot enforce the covenant against an assign (taking with notice) of the covenantor unless he can show (i) that the covenant was taken for the benefit of ascertainable land of the covenantee capable of being benefited by the covenant, and (ii) that he (the covenantee's assign) is an express assign of the benefit of the covenant", and with the following passage in the judgment of Bennett J. (at p. 625): "In my judgment, in order that an express assignee of a covenant restricting the user of land may be able to enforce that covenant against the owner of the land burdened with the covenant, he must be able to satisfy the court of two things. The first is that it was a covenant entered into for the benefit or protection of land owned by the covenantee at the date of the covenant. Otherwise it is a covenant in gross, and unenforceable except as between the parties to the covenant: see *Formby v. Barker*. Secondly, the assignee must be able to satisfy the court that the deed containing the covenant defines or contains something to define the property for the benefit of which the covenant was entered into: see James L.J. in *Renals v. Cowlishaw* (1879) 11 Ch.D. 866".

With all respect to the statement of the judge, I am unable to agree that where a person is suing as an assign of the benefit of the covenant there must necessarily be something in the deed containing the covenant to define the land for the benefit of which the covenant was entered into. In the first place, the passage in the judgment of James L.J. in *Renals v. Cowlishaw*, on which the judge relied, does not in my judgment support the statement of the law for which it was cited. In *Renals v. Cowlishaw* there was no express assignment of the benefit of the restrictive covenant; and when James L.J. says that to enable an assign to take the benefit of restrictive covenants there must be something in the deed to define the property for the benefit of which they were entered into, he is, I think, dealing with the case where it is contended that the benefit of the covenant has been annexed to the land so as to run with the land. When he uses the word "assign" he is using the word as meaning an assign of the land and not an assign of the benefit of the covenant. Secondly, the views expressed by Bennett J. appear to me to be inconsistent with the views expressed in some of the earlier decisions. I do not propose to cite them, but I refer to the following observations on the law on this point, namely, the observations of Collins L.J., delivering the judgment of the Court of Appeal in *Rogers v. Hosegood* [1900] 2 Ch. 388, 407; those of Vaughan Williams L.J. in *Formby v. Barker* [1903] 2 Ch. 539, 551; and to the observations of Cozens-Hardy M.R. in *Reid v. Bickerstaff* [1909] 2 Ch. 305, 319, 325; and to the words of Buckley L.J. in the same case. Finally, in *In re Union of London and Smith's Bank Ltd's Conveyance* [1933] Ch. 611, Romer L.J., reading the judgment of the Court of Appeal, having considered the cases where the benefit of the covenant is annexed to land so as to run without express mention, says (at p. 628): "In all other cases the purchaser will not acquire the benefit of the covenant unless that benefit be expressly assigned to him—or, to use the words of the Vice-Chancellor, 'it must appear that the benefit of the covenant was part of the subject-matter of the purchase.' "

[Upjohn J. quoted a passage from the judgment of Romer L.J. in *Re Union of London and Smith's Bank Ltd's Conveyance, Miles v. Easter* [1933] Ch. 611, 631 (*supra*, p. 767), and continued:]

In my judgment, therefore, the problem which I have to consider is this: First, when Mrs Mardon took the covenant in 1923, did she retain other lands capable of being benefited by the covenant? The answer is plainly yes. Secondly, was such land "ascertainable" or "certain" in this sense that the existence and situation of the land must be indicated in the conveyance or otherwise shown with reasonable certainty?

Apart from the fact that Mrs Mardon is described as of Devonia, there is nothing in the conveyance of 1923 to define the land for the benefit of which the restrictive covenant was taken, and I do not think that carries one very far; but, for the reasons I have given, I am, in my judgment, entitled to look at the attendant circumstances to see if the land to be benefited is shown "otherwise" with reasonable certainty. That is a question of fact and, on the admitted facts, bearing in mind the close juxtaposition of Devonia and the defendants' premises, in my view the only reasonable inference to draw from the circumstances at the time of the conveyance of 1923 was that Mrs Mardon took the covenant restrictive of the user of the defendants' premises for the benefit of her own business of ironmonger and of her property Devonia where at all material times she was carrying on that business, which last-mentioned fact must have been apparent to the purchasers in 1923.

. . .

It follows, therefore, in my judgment, that Mrs Mardon could on any subsequent sale of her land Devonia, if she so chose, as part of the transaction of sale, assign the benefit of the covenant so as to enable the purchaser from her and his assignees of the land and covenant to enforce it against an owner of the defendants' premises taking with notice, and her legatee, Leonard Soper Mardon, was in no worse position. I do not regard the fact that he assigned the covenant in the deed containing the assignment of the business as affecting the matter. I say nothing as to the position when the plaintiffs' lease expires so that their estate in Devonia comes to an end, nor whether Leonard Soper Mardon, having apparently assigned away the entire benefit of the covenant, will then be in any position further to enforce it.

Mr Bowles took one further point. He submitted that a covenant restrictive of business could not be annexed to land, unless it was a covenant not to carry on a business so as to be a nuisance or annoyance to an adjoining occupier, but he cited no authority for that proposition and, in my judgment, it cannot be maintained: see *Nicoll v. Fenning* (1881) 19 Ch.D. 258.

Accordingly, in my judgment, the plaintiffs are entitled to succeed in this action and to an injunction as claimed under para. 1 of the statement of claim.

NOTE:

1. It must be arguable that, if the facts of *Newton Abbot Co-operative Society Ltd v. Williamson & Treadgold Ltd* were to recur, the court would find that the benefit of the covenant had been annexed: consider (i) the modern approach to express annexation and to the requirements of intention to benefit and identity of the benefited land propounded in *J. Sainsbury plc v. Enfield LBC* [1989] 1 W.L.R. 590; (ii) the development of the wider concept of implied annexation in *Marten v. Flight Refuelling Ltd* [1962] Ch. 115; and (iii) the development of statutory annexation in *Federated Homes Ltd v. Mill Lodge Properties Ltd* [1980] 1 W.L.R. 594. Contrast the contemporary restatement of the principles governing the assignment of the benefit of covenants affecting freehold land by Elphinstone (1952) 68 L.Q.R. 353, who

argued (i) that the covenant did not touch and concern "Devonia"; and (ii) that it was inadmissible to deduce the intention to benefit land and the identity of that land from the surrounding circumstances; and see Hayton (1971) 87 L.Q.R. 539, 568–570.

2.3 *Section 62 of the Law of Property Act 1925*

It has been argued that, on a transfer of the benefited land by the original covenantee, section 62 of the Law of Property Act 1925 operates to transfer the benefit of assignable covenants as "rights ... enjoyed with ... the land", unless a contrary intention is expressed in the deed of transfer: see Hayton (1971) 87 L.Q.R. 539, 570–573; Wade [1972B] C.L.J. 157, 175. An analogous argument was discussed but viewed with some doubt in *Rogers v. Hosegood* [1900] 2 Ch. 388. The question concerned the effect of a conveyance which was executed before the enactment of section 62 (and its precursor, section 6 of the Conveyancing Act 1881) but which contained a general words clause in similar terms. Farwell J. (at 398) doubted whether the benefit of the covenant could be said to "belong or be reputed to belong" to the benefited land; and since then the courts have tended to reiterate the early dicta, stressing the need for express assignment in the absence of annexation.

The argument was raised again in *Federated Homes Ltd v. Mill Lodge Properties Ltd* [1980] 1 W.L.R. 594, where it was accepted by the judge at first instance but not discussed in the judgments in the Court of Appeal. In *Shropshire CC v. Edwards* (1982) 46 P. & C.R. 270, 279, Judge Rubin expressly decided to follow the example of the Court of Appeal and "to remain silent on this highly debatable point". However, the argument was considered and rejected in *Roake v. Chadha* [1984] 1 W.L.R. 40 and in *Kumar v. Dunning* [1989] Q.B. 193.

In *Roake v. Chadha* [1984] 1 W.L.R. 40 Judge Paul Baker Q.C. said (at 46–47):

I must now turn to the alternative argument of the plaintiffs based on section 62 of the Law of Property Act 1925. This argument is directed to the conveyances or transfers conveying the alleged benefited land to the predecessors of the plaintiffs, and ultimately to the respective plaintiffs themselves. In each of these transfers, so I am prepared to assume, there is to be implied the general words of section 62 of the Act of 1925:

> "(1) A conveyance of land shall be deemed to include and shall by virtue of this Act operate to convey, with the land, all buildings, erections, fixtures, commons, hedges, ditches, fences, ways, waters, watercourses, liberties, privileges, easements, rights, and advantages whatsoever, appertaining or reputed to appertain to the land, or any part thereof, or, at the time of conveyance, demised, occupied, or enjoyed with, or reputed or known as part or parcel of or appurtenant to the land or any part thereof."

I do not think I need read subsection (2) which deals with the conveyance of land having houses and buildings and various corresponding rights in relation to buildings.

The argument is that the benefit of the covenant contained in the original transfer to the predecessor of the defendants, William Lambert, was carried by the words "rights and advantages whatsoever appertaining or reputed to appertain to the land, or any part thereof". It seems an argument on these lines was accepted by Mr John Mills Q.C., the deputy judge who gave the decision at first instance in the *Federated Homes* case

[1980] 1 W.L.R. 594, but I have not seen it, and so cannot comment on it. The proposition now contended for is not a new one. In *Rogers v. Hosegood* [1900] 2 Ch. 388, it was similarly put forward as an alternative argument to an argument based on annexation. In that case however it was decided that the benefit of the covenant was annexed so that the point on section 6 of the Conveyancing Act 1881, the forerunner of section 62 of the Law of Property Act 1925, did not have to be decided. Nevertheless, Farwell J. sitting in the Chancery Division, said, at p. 398:

> "It is not necessary for me to determine whether the benefit of the covenants would pass under the general words to which I have referred above, if such covenants did not run with the land. If they are not in fact annexed to the land, it may well be that the right to sue thereon cannot be said to belong, or be reputed to belong, thereto; but I express no final opinion on this point."

In the Court of Appeal the point was canvassed in argument but not referred to in the judgment of the court, which was given by Collins L.J.

In the present case, the covenant in terms precludes the benefit passing unless it is expressly assigned. That being so, as it seems to me, it is not a right "appertaining or reputed to appertain" to land within the meaning of section 62 of the Law of Property Act 1925. As to whether the benefit of a covenant not annexed can ever pass under section 62, I share the doubts of Farwell J. Mr Henty suggested—and there may well be something in this—that the rights referred to in section 62 are confined to legal rights rather than equitable rights which the benefit of restrictive covenants is. But again I place it on construction. It cannot be described as a right appertaining or reputed to appertain to land when the terms of the convenant itself would seem to indicate the opposite.

In *Kumar v. Dunning* [1989] Q.B. 193 Browne-Wilkinson V.-C. said (at 198):

The main intention of section 62 was to provide a form of statutory shorthand rendering it unnecessary to include such words expressly in every conveyance. It is a matter of debate whether, in the context of the section, the words "rights ... appertaining to the land" include rights arising under covenant as opposed to strict property rights. However, I will assume, without deciding, that rights under covenant are within the words of the section. Even on that assumption, it still has to be shown that the right "appertains to the land". In my judgment, a right under covenant cannot appertain to the land unless the benefit is in some way annexed to the land. If the benefit of a covenant passes under section 62 even if not annexed to the land, the whole modern law of restrictive covenants would have been established on an erroneous basis. Section 62(1) replaces section 6(1) of the Conveyancing Act 1881. If the general words "rights ... appertaining to land" operate to transfer the benefit of a negative restrictive covenant, whether or not such benefit was expressly assigned, it would make all the law developed since 1881 unnecessary. It is established that, in the absence of annexation to the land or the existence of a building scheme, the benefit of a restrictive covenant cannot pass except by way of *express* assignment. The law so established is inconsistent with the view that a covenant, the benefit of which is not annexed to the land, can pass under the general words in section 62.

2.4 *Schemes of development*

The terminological preference of Megarry J. is adopted here: in *Brunner v. Greenslade* [1971] Ch. 993 he said (at 999):

I prefer the more ample term "scheme of development" ... to the unduly narrow term "building scheme", which has acquired a considerable but undeserved measure of currency. "Scheme of development", I think, is the genus; "building scheme" a species.

A separate set of rules has been developed to regulate the enforcement of restrictive covenants in the context of schemes of development. The potential for a scheme of development exists where an area of land is to be divided up into a number of separately-owned but interdependent properties on the basis that there is a common intention to create a scheme of reciprocal rights and obligations among the owners of those properties, with the aim of "securing and preserving the amenities and values on a newly developed residential estate": *Brunner v. Greenslade* [1971] Ch. 993, 998 *per* Megarry J. A scheme of development can also be created where land has already been fully developed and leased, but where the fee simple owner later decides to sell the various plots as and when that becomes practicable: *Torbay Hotel Ltd v. Jenkins* [1927] 2 Ch. 225, 240–241 *per* Clauson J. In such circumstances, equity permits the operation of a "local law": *Reid v. Bickerstaff* [1909] 2 Ch. 305, 319 *per* Cozens-Hardy M.R.; *Re Dolphin's Conveyance* [1970] Ch. 654, 662 *per* Stamp J.; *Texaco Antilles Ltd v. Kernochan* [1973] A.C. 609, 624 *per* Lord Cross; or, alternatively, a "common law": *Baxter v. Four Oaks Properties Ltd* [1965] Ch. 816, 826 *per* Cross J.

According to Simonds J. in *Lawrence v. South County Freeholds Ltd* [1939] Ch. 656, 675 the "first hint" of the modern doctrine of schemes of development is found in the judgment of Lord Romilly M.R. in *Western v. Macdermott* (1865) L.R. 1 Eq. 499, although he acknowledges that the device of securing the same result by means of deeds of mutual covenants was described in 1838 as "perfectly familiar to the mind of every lawyer": see *Schreiber v. Creed* (1839) 10 Sim. 9, 33 *per* Shadwell V.-C.; and, according to Wynn-Parry J. in *Re Pinewood Estate, Farnborough* [1958] Ch. 280, 286–287, the essential elements of schemes of development are present in *Whatman v. Gibson* (1838) 9 Sim. 196.

The necessary mutual enforceability among all property owners within the scheme cannot be readily accommodated within the rules considered so far. There is no problem in respect of the passing of the burden of restrictive covenants made by the original purchasers of the properties within the scheme, provided that the rules of the doctrine in *Tulk v. Moxhay* are satisfied and provided that the developer ensures the running of the burden by the appropriate means of registration (although the developer would not be bound by the covenants himself unless he made similar covenants with each purchaser). The difficulty lies with the passing of the benefit. When the developer sells the first property in the scheme, the benefit of the purchaser's covenants can readily be annexed to the remaining properties which are retained by the developer and which constitute the benefited land. Similarly, when the developer sells the second property, the benefit of that purchaser's covenants can be annexed to the remaining properties retained by the developer; but the benefit cannot be annexed to the first property sold (except perhaps through reliance on section 56(1) of the Law of Property Act 1925). Moreover, on each subsequent sale there is a further reduction in the number of plots that constitute the benefited land.

Against that background equity developed the independent doctrine of schemes of development. Where such a scheme exists, the restrictive covenants can be enforced by and against all current owners of the properties comprised within the scheme, irrespective of when the original purchaser of each property entered into his covenants and irrespective of when the current owners acquired their properties.

For a theoretical analysis of the mutual enforceability of covenants under a scheme of development, see *Brunner v. Greenslade* [1971] Ch. 993, 1003 *et seq. per* Megarry J., *infra*, p. 787.

2.4.1 *The* Elliston v. Reacher *requirements for schemes of development*

Elliston v. Reacher [1908] 2 Ch. 374

(Ch D. Parker J.)

PARKER J.:

In my judgment, in order to bring the principles of *Renals v. Cowlishaw* (1878) 9 Ch.D. 125; (1879) 11 Ch.D. 866 and *Spicer v. Martin* (1888) 14 App.Cas. 12 into operation it must be proved (1) that both the plaintiffs and defendants derive title under a common vendor; (2) that previously to selling the lands to which the plaintiffs and defendants are respectively entitled the vendor laid out his estate, or a defined portion thereof (including the lands purchased by the plaintiffs and defendants respectively), for sale in lots subject to restrictions intended to be imposed on all the lots, and which, though varying in details as to particular lots, are consistent and consistent only with some general scheme of development; (3) that these restrictions were intended by the common vendor to be and were for the benefit of all the lots intended to be sold, whether or not they were also intended to be and were for the benefit of other land retained by the vendor; and (4) that both the plaintiffs and the defendants, or their predecessors in title, purchased their lots from the common vendor upon the footing that the restrictions subject to which the purchases were made were to enure for the benefit of the other lots included in the general scheme whether or not they were also to enure for the benefit of other lands retained by the vendors. If these four points are established, I think that the plaintiffs would in equity be entitled to enforce the restrictive covenants entered into by the defendants or their predecessors with the common vendor irrespective of the dates of the respective purchases. I may observe, with reference to the third point, that the vendor's object in imposing the restrictions must in general be gathered from all the circumstances of the case, including in particular the nature of the restrictions. If a general observance of the restrictions is in fact calculated to enhance the values of the several lots offered for sale, it is an easy inference that the vendor intended the restrictions to be for the benefit of all the lots, even though he might retain other land the value of which might be similarly enhanced, for a vendor may naturally be expected to aim at obtaining the highest possible price for his land. Further, if the first three points be established, the fourth point may readily be inferred, provided the purchasers have notice of the facts involved in the three first points; but if the purchaser purchases in ignorance of any material part of those facts, it would be difficult, if not impossible, to establish the fourth point. It is also observable that the equity arising out of the establishment of the four points I have mentioned has been sometimes explained by the implication of mutual contracts between the various purchasers, and sometimes by the implication of a contract between each purchaser and the common vendor, that each purchaser is to have the benefit of all the covenants by the other purchasers, so that each purchaser is in equity an assign of the benefit of these covenants. In my opinion the implication of mutual contract is not always a perfectly satisfactory explanation. It may be satisfactory where all the lots are sold by auction at the same time, but when, as in cases such as *Spicer v. Martin*, there is no sale by auction, but all the various sales are by private treaty and at various intervals of time, the circumstances may, at the date of one or more of the sales, be such as to preclude the possibility of any actual contract. For example, a prior purchaser may be dead or incapable of contracting at the time of a subsequent purchase, and in any event it is unlikely that the prior and subsequent purchasers are ever brought into personal relationship, and yet the equity may exist between them. It is, I think, enough to say, using Lord Macnaghten's words in *Spicer v. Martin*, that where the four points I have mentioned are established, the community of interest imports in equity the reciprocity of obligation which is in fact contemplated by each at the time of his own purchase.

NOTES:

1. The judgment of Parker J. was approved by the Court of Appeal [1908] 2 Ch. 665.

2. In *Reid v. Bickerstaff* [1909] 2 Ch. 305 Cozens-Hardy M.R. stated (at 319):

What are some of the essentials of a building scheme? In my opinion there must be a defined area within which the scheme is operative. Reciprocity is the foundation of the idea of a scheme. A purchaser of one parcel cannot be subject to an implied obligation to purchasers of an undefined and unknown area. He must know both the extent of his burden and the extent of his benefit. Not only must the area be defined, but the obligations to be imposed within that area must be defined. Those obligations need not be identical. For example, there may be houses of a certain value in one part and houses of a different value in another part. A building scheme is not created by the mere fact that the owner of an estate sells it in lots and takes varying covenants from various purchasers. There must be notice to the various purchasers of what I may venture to call the local law imposed by the vendors upon a definite area. *Keates v. Lyon* (1869) L.R. 4 Ch. 218, *Martin v. Spicer* (1888) 14 App.Cas. 12, *Osborne v. Bradley* [1903] 2 Ch. 446, and *Elliston v. Reacher* [1908] 2 Ch. 374, 665 seem to me to bear out what I have said.

And Buckley L.J. stated (at 322–323):

First as to the existence of a building scheme and the application of the doctrine of *Spicer v. Martin*. For the application of the principle of that case it is, I think, essential to establish as matter of fact the following state of things: that the vendor expressly or by implication contracted with the defendant in the action or his predecessor in title (whom I will call the purchaser) upon the footing that at the date of that contract the vendor told the purchaser that he was proposing to deal with a defined estate in a defined way, and that he offered to sell to the purchaser a plot forming a part of that defined estate on the terms that the purchaser should enter into such restrictive covenants relating to his plot as the scheme contemplated upon the footing that the purchaser should reciprocally have the benefit of such restrictive covenants relating to the other plots on the estate as were indicated by the scheme. There can be no building scheme unless two conditions are satisfied, namely, first, that defined lands constituting the estate to which the scheme relates shall be identified, and, secondly, that the nature and particulars of the scheme shall be sufficiently disclosed for the purchaser to have been informed that his restrictive covenants are imposed upon him for the benefit of other purchasers of plots within that defined estate with the reciprocal advantage that he shall as against such other purchasers be entitled to the benefit of such restrictive covenants as are in turn to be imposed upon them. Compliance with the first condition identifies the class of persons as between whom reciprocity of obligation is to exist.

Compliance with the second discloses the nature of the obligations which are to be mutually enforceable. There must be as between the several purchasers community of interest and reciprocity of obligation.

Some commentators have asserted that Cozens-Hardy M.R. added a further requirement to those enumerated in *Elliston v. Reacher*, that the area covered by the scheme of development must be defined: see Hayton (1971) 87 L.Q.R. 539, 548. However, it is not clear that his Lordship (who expressly approved the judgment of Parker J. in *Elliston v. Reacher* on appeal: [1908] 2 Ch. 665, 673) intended to add a further condition; nor is it clear that later courts have interpreted the case in that way. It seems that at most the courts have treated the comments as no more than an explanatory gloss on the second condition: see *Kelly v. Barrett* [1924] 2 Ch. 379, 401 *per* Pollock M.R.; *Re Wembley Park Estate Co. Ltd's Transfer* [1968] Ch. 491, 501 *per* Goff J.; *Emile Elias & Co. Ltd v. Pine Groves Ltd* [1993] 1 W.L.R. 305, 310 *per* Lord Browne-Wilkinson. More often the comments have been treated as simply confirming the requirements expounded in *Elliston v. Reacher*; and in *Eagling v. Gardner* [1970] 2 All E.R. 838 Ungoed-Thomas J. systematically considered the four requirements in *Elliston v. Reacher* and, although he referred to *Reid v. Bickerstaff*, he did not refer to the passage in the judgment of Cozens-Hardy M.R. It is even arguable that the judgment of Cozens-Hardy M.R. and, more particularly, that of Buckley L.J. signalled the recognition of the broader principle underlying schemes of development that was apparently forgotten during the first half of the twentieth century and not rediscovered until 1965: see *infra*, p. 779.

3. In *White v. Bijou Mansions Ltd* [1938] Ch. 351 Green M.R. stated (at 362):

The material thing I think is that every purchaser ... must know when he buys what are the regulations to which he is subjecting himself, and what are the regulations to which other purchasers on the estate will be called upon to subject themselves. Unless you have that, it is quite impossible in my judgment to draw the necessary inference, whether you refer to it as an agreement or as a community of interest importing reciprocity of obligation.

4. A scheme of development may exist even where the vendor retains a power to sell lots without taking covenants from the purchasers: *Elliston v. Reacher* [1908] 2 Ch. 374, 387–388 *per* Parker J., [1908] 2 Ch. 665, 672 *per* Cozens-Hardy M.R. It might be thought that it would be more difficult to establish that a scheme existed where the covenants were unenforceable in respect of a large proportion of the lots; but in *Texaco Antilles v. Kernochan* [1973] A.C. 609 a scheme of development was held to exist notwithstanding that 350 of the 500 lots were sold by a single conveyance without being subject to the covenants of the scheme.

5. There is no requirement that all covenants should be identical: *Elliston v. Reacher* [1908] 2 Ch. 374, 384 *per* Parker J.; *Reid v. Bickerstaff* [1909] 2 Ch. 305, 319 *per* Cozens-Hardy M.R. However, differences in matters of substance (for example, where only some of the plots in the alleged scheme are subject to user restrictions) militate against the finding of an intention to create a mutually enforceable local law based on reciprocity: *Emile Elias &*

Co. Ltd v. Pine Groves Ltd [1993] 1 W.L.R. 305, 311–312 *per* Lord Browne-Wilkinson.

6. A scheme of development comes into existence immediately the *first* property in the scheme is sold: *Brunner v. Greenslade* [1971] Ch. 993, 1003 *per* Megarry J.

2.4.2 Restatement of the requirements   The judgment of Parker J. in *Elliston v. Reacher* was generally regarded as laying down a definitive checklist of the requirements for the existence of a scheme of development and it has continued to be relied upon: see, *e.g. Re Pinewood Estate, Farnborough* [1958] Ch. 280, 284–286 *per* Wynn-Parry J.; *Page v. King's Parade Properties Ltd* (1967) 20 P. & C.R. 710, 715–716 *per* Goff J.; *Emile Elias & Co. Ltd v. Pine Groves Ltd* [1993] 1 W.L.R. 305, 309–310 *per* Lord Browne-Wilkinson. However, a series of cases have been decided by reference to a less prescriptive restatement of the equitable principle that forms the basis of schemes of development, namely the recognition and enforcement of the common intention of the parties that the various purchasers should be subject to a scheme of reciprocal rights and obligations. Whether that common intention exists is a question of fact, which can be established from the express terms of a mutual deed of covenant: *Baxter v. Four Oaks Properties Ltd* [1965] Ch. 816, *infra*; or from the terms of the conveyances to the individual purchasers: *Re Dolphin's Conveyance* [1970] Ch. 654, *infra*, p. 781; or, in the absence of such evidence, from the surrounding circumstances: *Elliston v. Reacher* [1908] 2 Ch. 374; *Texaco Antilles v. Kernochan* [1973] A.C. 609; *Lund v. Taylor* (1975) 31 P. & C.R. 167, *infra*, p. 785. It is perhaps not surprising that in the last situation the courts have adopted stricter requirements since the finding of a scheme of development sanctions the enforcement of restrictive covenants beyond what is possible under the rules already discussed. On the other hand, if the court is satisfied that the common intention exists, it would be inconsistent with the flexibility of equity to insist that each of the stated requirements must be established in every case. There is little doubt that schemes of development are much more likely to be found to exist on the basis of the modern approach than would be the case if the strict *Elliston v. Reacher* requirements were applied to the same facts. For comment on the relaxation of the strict requirements in *Elliston v. Reacher*, see Baker (1970) 86 L.Q.R. 445; [1971] C.L.J. 24; Hayton (1971) 87 L.Q.R. 539, 546–551.

Baxter v. Four Oaks Properties Ltd [1965] Ch. 816

(Ch D., Cross J.)

The owner of a large estate conveyed part of that estate to a purchaser. By an indenture, expressed to be made between the vendor, the purchaser and all other persons who might subsequently purchase land forming part of the estate, it was agreed that various covenants would be enforceable by and against the owners for the time being of parts of the estate. It appears that the original owner had not laid out the estate in lots before he began to sell it off but that he sold lots of the size required by the various purchasers. The question arose as to whether the covenants were enforceable under a scheme of development.

CROSS J.:

It is, of course, clear that a vendor who sells a piece of land to "A" and subsequently sells another piece of land to "B" cannot, as part of the later transaction, annex to "A's" land the benefit of a restrictive covenant entered into by "B" if it was not part of the bargain with "A" at the time of the sale to him that "A" should have the benefit of the covenant. On the other hand, for well over 100 years past where the owner of land deals with it on the footing of imposing restrictive obligations on the use of various parts of it as and when he sells them off for the common benefit of himself (in so far as he retains any land) and of the various purchasers inter se a court of equity has been prepared to give effect to this common intention notwithstanding any technical difficulties involved.

In the early days it was not unusual for the common vendor to have prepared a deed of mutual covenant to be executed by each purchaser. If the various sales all took place at the same time—as they would, for instance, if all the land in question was put up for sale by auction in lots—then the various purchasers would, no doubt, be brought into direct contractual relations with one another on signing the deed. But if the common vendor sold off different lots of land at intervals, it might well happen that by the time a later purchaser executed the deed, one of the earlier purchasers was dead. In such a case it would be difficult to found the right of the successors in title of the deceased earlier purchaser to enforce covenants against the later purchaser or his successors in title on any contract between the two original purchasers, even though each signed the deed.

The view taken by the courts has been rather that the common vendor imposed a common law on a defined area of land and that whenever he sold a piece of it to a purchaser who knew of the common law, that piece of land automatically became entitled to the benefit of, and subject to the burden of, the common law. With the passage in time it became apparent that there was no particular virtue in the execution of a deed of mutual covenant—save as evidence of the intention of the parties—and what came to be called "building schemes" were enforced by the courts if satisfied that it was the intention of the parties that the various purchasers should have rights inter se, even though no attempt was made to bring them into direct contractual relations.

A statement of the law on this point which is often quoted is contained in Parker J.'s judgment in *Elliston v. Reacher* [1908] 2 Ch. 374, 384...

The defendants naturally rely on Parker J.'s second requirement and argue that as [the vendor] did not lay out the estate in lots before he began to sell it off, there could be no enforceable building scheme here, even though [the vendor] and the purchasers from him may have thought that there was.

It is, however, to be observed that *Elliston v. Reacher* was not a case in which there was direct evidence afforded by the execution of the deed of mutual covenant that the parties in fact intended a building scheme. The question was whether one could properly infer that intention in all the circumstances. In such a case, no doubt the fact that the common vendor did not divide his estate into lots before beginning to sell it is an argument against there having been intention on his part and on the part of the various purchasers that there should be a building scheme, because it is, perhaps, prima facie unlikely that a purchaser of a plot intends to enter into obligations to an unknown number of subsequent purchasers. But I cannot believe that Parker J. was intending to lay down that the fact that the common vendor did not bind himself to sell off the defined area to which the common law was to apply in lots of any particular size but proposed to sell off parcels of various sizes according to the requirement of the various purchasers must, as a matter of law, preclude the court from giving effect to a clearly proved intention that the purchasers were to have rights inter se to enforce the provisions of the common law.

Re Dolphin's Conveyance [1970] Ch. 654

(Ch D., Stamp J.)

In 1871 the Dolphin sisters, owners of the Selly Hill Estate, sold four parcels of the estate to separate purchasers. Each purchaser covenanted to build on his property only in accordance with specified conditions; and the vendors covenanted to procure similar covenants from subsequent purchasers of any other part of the estate. In 1876 the remaining part of the estate was conveyed to Watts, the nephew of the sisters. He sold that remaining part in six parcels on terms identical to those of the 1871 conveyances (except that the last conveyance included no covenant by the vendor). In 1969 the plaintiffs purchased part of the estate, which the vendor, Coleman, had purchased in two lots, the first in 1871 from the sisters and the second in 1877 from Watts. The plaintiffs wished to develop the land in a manner inconsistent with the covenants; and they sought a declaration that the covenants were no longer enforceable by the current owners of the other parts of the estate.

STAMP J.:

I must make it clear that the defendants do not assert, nor could they, that the benefit of the covenants by the several purchasers from the Dolphins was in terms expressed to be attached to the vendors' land, and to each and every part of it, so as to pass without express assignment to a purchaser of the land to be benefited. Nor was there any express assignment of that benefit in the conveyances under which the defendants to this summons claim title. Nor is there any personal representative of any of the vendors in a position to enforce the covenants. But, to quote a passage in the judgment of Cross J. in *Baxter v. Four Oaks Properties Ltd* [1965] Ch. 816, 825:

> "...for well over 100 years past where the owner of land deals with it on the footing of imposing restrictive obligations on the use of various parts of it as and when he sells them off for the common benefit of himself (in so far as he retains any land) and of the various purchasers inter se a court of equity has been prepared to give effect to this common intention notwithstanding any technical difficulties involved."

It is the submission of the defendants that that was done by the vendors in the present case.

That it was the intention of the two Miss Dolphins, on the sale of the parcel comprised in Coleman's conveyance, that there should be imposed upon each and every part of the Selly Hill Estate the restrictions set out in the conveyance—precluding the erection of buildings other than dwelling houses having the characteristics specified in the restrictions—cannot be doubted. And each conveyance evidenced the same intention. Nor can it be doubted that each purchaser, when he executed his conveyance, was aware of that intention. The covenant by the vendor in each conveyance, to the effect that the same restrictions would be placed on all future purchasers and lessees, makes this clear. Furthermore, I would, unless constrained by authority to the contrary, conclude as a matter of construction of Coleman's conveyance, and of all the others, that the vendor was dealing with the Selly Hill Estate on the footing of imposing obligations for the common benefit, as well of himself, as of the several purchasers of that estate. It is trite law that if you find conveyances of the several parts of an estate all containing the same or similar restrictive covenants with the vendor, that is not enough to impute an intention on the part of that vendor that the restrictions should be for the common benefit of the vendor and of the several purchasers inter se: for it is at least as likely that he imposed them for the benefit of himself and of the unsold part of the estate alone. That is not this case. Here there is the covenant by the vendors that on a sale or lease of any other part of Selly Hill Estate

"it shall be sold or leased subject to the stipulations above mentioned numbered 1, 2, 3, 4, 5, 6, 7 and that the vendors their heirs or assigns will procure a covenant from each purchaser or lessee upon Selly Hill Estate to the effect of those seven stipulations."

What was the point of it? For what possible reason does a vendor of part of an estate who has extracted restrictive covenants from a purchaser, covenant with that purchaser that the other parts of the estate, when sold, shall contain the same restrictions, unless it be with the intention that the purchaser with whom he covenants, as well as he himself, shall have the benefits of the restrictions when imposed? In view of these covenants by the vendor in the several conveyances, I cannot do otherwise than find that the covenants were imposed, not only for the benefit of the vendors or of the unsold part of their estate, but as well for the benefit of the several purchasers. As a matter of construction of the conveyances, I find that what was intended, as well by the vendors as the several purchasers, was to lay down what has been referred to as a local law for the estate for the common benefit of all the several purchasers of it. The purpose of the covenant by the vendors was to enable each purchaser to have, as against the other purchasers, in one way or another, the benefit of the restrictions to which he had made himself subject.

Holding, as I do, that these covenants were imposed for the common benefits of the vendors and the several purchasers, and that they had a common interest in their enforcement. I must, in a moment, turn to consider what is, in my judgment, the separate and distinct question whether there is an equity in the owner of each parcel to enforce the covenants against the owners of the other parcels. But, before considering that question, I must advert to an argument advanced by Mr Grove on behalf of the plaintiffs on the effect of the covenants themselves. He points out that the covenants by the purchasers are not expressed, as they would have been in a deed of mutual covenant, to be with the other purchasers, and that there is no covenant by the vendor to enforce the covenants which he has agreed to extract from the other purchasers. No doubt this is so; but, in my judgment, it does not lead to a result which assists the plaintiffs. Had the vendors covenanted to the effect that they would enforce the restrictions, it would, no doubt, have emphasised the intention that all the purchasers should benefit, but would also have shown, on the authority of *White v. Bijou Mansions Ltd* [1938] Ch. 351, that the covenants were not intended to be enforceable by different action by one purchaser against another. Mr Grove urges that each purchaser was content to leave it to the vendors whether or not to enforce the obligations which they covenanted to impose on the other purchasers. I cannot accept this submission. If the vendors were to have no obligation to bring actions to enforce the restrictions—and I accept Mr Grove's submission that they had not—the covenant by the vendors to impose the conditions on the other purchasers was nothing more nor less than useless unless the purchaser himself was to have the right to do so. The absence of a covenant by the vendor to enforce the restrictions against the other purchasers leads to, and not away from, the conclusion that each purchaser was to have reciprocal rights and obligations vis-à-vis the others. How otherwise could effect be given to the intention?

As Cross J. pointed out in the course of the judgment in *Baxter v. Four Oaks Properties Ltd* [1965] Ch. 816, to which I have already referred, the intention that the several purchasers from a common vendor shall have the benefit of the restrictive covenants imposed on each of them, may be evidenced by the existence of a deed of mutual covenant to which all the several purchasers are to be parties. That common intention may also be evidenced by, or inferred from, the circumstances attending the sales: the existence of what has often been referred to in the authorities as a building scheme. I have been referred to a considerable number of authorities where the court has had to consider whether there were, or were not, present in the particular case those facts from which a building scheme—and, therefore, the common intention to lay down a local law involving reciprocal rights and obligations between the several purchasers—could properly be inferred. In *Elliston v. Reacher* [1908] 2 Ch. 374, 384, Parker J. laid down the necessary concomitants of such a scheme.

What has been argued before me is that here there is neither a deed of mutual covenant nor a building scheme. In the latter connection, it is pointed out that there was not a common vendor, for the parcels were sold off, first by the Dolphins and then by Watts. Nor, prior to the sales, had the vendors laid out the estate, or a defined portion of it, for sale in lots. Therefore, so it is urged, there were not present the factors which, on the authority of *Elliston v. Reacher* [1908] 2 Ch. 374, are necessary before one can find the existence of a building scheme.

In my judgment, these submissions are not well founded. To hold that only where you find the necessary concomitants of a building scheme or a deed of mutual covenant can you give effect to the common intention found in the conveyances themselves, would, in my judgment, be to ignore the wider principle on which the building scheme cases are founded and to fly in the face of other authority of which the clearest and most recent is *Baxter v. Four Oaks Properties Ltd* [1965] Ch. 816. The building scheme cases stem, as I understand the law, from the wider rule that if there be found the common intention and the common interest referred to by Cross J. at p. 825 in *Baxter v. Four Oaks Properties Ltd* the court will give effect to it, and are but an extension and example of that rule. Hall V.-C. remarked in his judgment in *Renals v. Cowlishaw* (1878) 9 Ch.D. 125, 129:

> "This right exists not only where the several parties execute a mutual deed of covenant, but wherever a mutual contract can be sufficiently established. A purchaser may also be entitled to the benefit of a restrictive covenant entered into with his vendor by another or others where his vendor has contracted with him that he shall be the assign of it, that is, have the benefit of the covenant. And such contract need not be express, but may be collected from the transaction of sale and purchase."

That passage was quoted, with approval, by Lord Macnaghten in *Spicer v. Martin* (1889) 14 App.Cas. 12, 24. (I ought perhaps to mention that the word "contract" in the last sentence I have quoted was substituted for the word "covenant" in the errata in the volume of the reports in which *Renals v. Cowlishaw* is reported.) Moreover, where deeds of mutual covenant have fallen to be considered, effect has been given not to the deed of mutual covenant itself as such but to the intention evidenced by its existence. *Baxter v. Four Oaks Properties Ltd* [1965] Ch. 816 is such a case. As Parker J. in *Elliston v. Reacher* [1908] 2 Ch. 374, 384, pointed out in a passage quoted by Cross J. in *Baxter v. Four Oaks Properties Ltd* [1965] Ch. 816, 826, the equity arising out of the establishment of the four points which he mentioned as the necessary concomitants of a building scheme has been sometimes explained by the implication of mutual contracts between the various purchasers and sometimes by the implication of a contract between each purchaser and the common vendor, that each purchaser is to have the benefit of all the covenants by the other purchasers, so that each purchaser is in equity an assign of the benefit of those covenants; but the implication of mutual contracts is not always a satisfactory explanation. Parker J., in *Elliston v. Reacher* [1908] 2 Ch. 374, 385, said:

> "It may be satisfactory where all the lots are sold by auction at the same time, but when, as in cases such as *Spicer v. Martin* (1889) 14 App.Cas. 12 there is no sale by

auction, but all the various sales are by private treaty and at various intervals of time, the circumstances may, at the date of one or more of the sales, be such as to preclude the possibility of any actual contract."

And he points out that a prior purchaser may be dead or incapable of contracting at the time of a subsequent purchase, and that in any event it is unlikely that the prior and subsequent purchasers are ever brought into personal relationship, and yet the equity may exist between them.

There is not, therefore, in my judgment, a dichotomy between the cases where effect has been given to the common intention inferred from the existence of the concomitants of a building scheme and those where effect has been given to the intention evidenced by the existence of a deed of covenant. Each class of case, in my judgment, depends upon a wider principle. Here the equity, in my judgment, arises not by the effect of an implication derived from the existence of the four points specified by Parker J. in *Elliston v. Reacher* [1908] 2 Ch. 374, 384, or by the implication derived from the existence of a deed of mutual covenant, but by the existence of the common interest and the common intention actually expressed in the conveyances themselves.

In *Nottingham Patent Brick and Tile Co. v. Butler* (1885) 15 Q.B.D. 261, 268, Wills J., in a passage which I find illuminating and which was referred to with approval in the Court of Appeal (1886) 16 Q.B.D. 778, put the matter thus:

"The principle which appears to me to be deducible from the cases is that where the same vendor selling to several persons plots of land, parts of a larger property, exacts from each of them covenants imposing restrictions on the use of the plots sold without putting himself under any corresponding obligation, it is a question of fact whether the restrictions were merely matters of agreement between the vendor himself and his vendees, imposed for his own benefit and protection, or are meant by him and understood by the buyers to be for the common advantage of the several purchasers. If the restrictive covenants are simply for the benefit of the vendor, purchasers of other plots of land from the vendor cannot claim to take advantage of them. If they are meant for the common advantage of a set of purchasers, such purchasers and their assigns may enforce them inter se for their own benefit. Where, for instance, the purchasers from the common vendor have not known of the existence of the covenants, that is a strong, if not a conclusive, circumstance to shew that there was no intention that they should enure to their benefit. Such was the case in *Keates v. Lyon* (1869) L.R. 4 Ch. 218; *Master v. Hansard* (1876) 4 Ch. D. 718; and *Renals v. Cowlishaw* (1879) 11 Ch. D. 866. But it is in all cases a question of intention at the time when the partition of the land took place, to be gathered, as every other question of fact, from any circumstances which can throw light upon what the intention was: *Renals v. Cowlishaw* (1879) 11 Ch. D. 866. One circumstance which has always been held to be cogent evidence of an intention that the covenants shall be for the common benefit of the purchasers is that the several lots have been laid out for sale as building lots, as in *Mann v. Stephens* (1846) 15 Sim. 377; *Western v. Macdermott* (1866) L.R. 2 Ch. 72; *Coles v. Sims* (1854) Kay 56; 5 D.M. & G. 1; or, as it has been sometimes said, that there has been 'a building scheme': *Renals v. Cowlishaw* (1879) 11 Ch. D. 866, 867."

I can approach the matter in another way. The conveyances of the several parts of the estate taking the form they do, and evidencing the same intention as is found in a deed of mutual covenant, I equate those conveyances with the deed of mutual covenant considered by Cross J. in *Baxter v. Four Oaks Properties Ltd* [1965] Ch. 816—the deed which he did not treat for the purposes of his judgment as itself bringing all the successive purchasers and persons claiming through them into contractual relations one with the other, but as showing the common intention. So equating them, I follow what I conceive to be the ratio decidendi of *Baxter v. Four Oaks Properties Ltd* [1965] Ch. 816 and give effect to that intention by holding that the restrictive covenants are enforceable by the successors in title of each of the original covenantors against any of them who purchased with notice of those restrictions.

NOTES:

1. For the modification of the covenants in this case, see *Re Farmiloe's Application* (1983) 48 P. & C.R. 317.

Lund v. Taylor (1975) 31 P. & C.R. 167

(CA, Russell and Stamp L.JJ., Sir John Pennycuick)

In 1932 Tellings became the fee simple owners of the Grange Estate, comprising a house and about six acres of land. Their architect prepared a plan of the estate, which showed a number of delineated plots. Between 1932 and 1938 most of the plots were sold. Each conveyance contained covenants by the purchaser with the vendors "so as to benefit and protect the lands and premises of the vendors' Grange Estate". The covenants of the various purchasers were similar in substance but there was some variation in the form of the covenants. There was no evidence that the purchasers saw the estate plan or that they were told that the vendor was proposing to procure similar covenants from the purchasers of other plots. Moreover, there was nothing in the individual conveyances to indicate that there was a scheme for mutually enforceable covenants over a defined area. The question arose as to whether a scheme of development existed so that the covenants were enforceable between successors in title of the original purchasers.

STAMP L.J.:

Because there was no extrinsic evidence, nor anything in his own conveyance to show a purchaser that there was a scheme relating to a defined area or that Tellings, if they did, intended that stipulations should be imposed in respect of each part of that area, he could not on the authority of *Reid v. Bickerstaff* be subject to an implied obligation to the other purchasers. On this ground alone the action must in our opinion fail. Whatever scheme involving reciprocal rights and obligations Tellings may have sought to establish, the necessary evidence that the several purchasers intended to be bound by a scheme or local law under which they were to have reciprocal rights and obligations is lacking...

Because it was submitted that in recent times the courts, in determining whether the necessary ingredients of a building scheme or local law are shown to have existed, have adopted what was called a more liberal approach than was formerly the case it is right that we should refer to the two cases relied upon in support of that submission. They are *Baxter v. Four Oaks Properties Ltd* [1965] Ch. 816 and *Re Dolphin's Conveyance* [1970] Ch. 654. In both those cases it had been submitted that in order to establish a building scheme the requirements laid down by Parker J. in *Elliston v. Reacher* [1908] 2 Ch. 374 must be satisfied. One of those requirements was, and we quote Parker J.'s judgment, that

"in order to bring the principles of *Renals v. Cowlishaw* and *Spicer v. Martin* into operation it must be proved ... (2) that previously to selling the lands to which the plaintiffs and defendants are respectively entitled the vendor laid out his estate or a defined portion thereof (including the land purchased by the plaintiffs and defendants respectively) for sale in lots subject to restrictions intended to be imposed on all the lots..."

In his judgment in *Baxter v. Four Oaks Properties Ltd* Cross J. rejected the condition that the defined estate should have been laid out for sale in lots. He pointed out that *Elliston v. Reacher* was not a case in which there was direct evidence afforded by the execution of a deed of mutual covenant that the parties intended a building scheme but *whether one could properly infer that intention in all the circumstances.* Cross J. took the view, also adopted in *Re Dolphin's Conveyance,* that Parker J. was not intending to lay down that the fact that the common vendor did not bind himself to sell off the defined area to which the local law was to apply in lots of any particular size but proposed to sell off parcels of various sizes according to the requirements of the various purchasers must, as a matter of law, preclude the court from giving effect to a clearly proved intention that the purchasers were to have rights *inter se* to enforce the provisions of the local law over the area.

In *Re Dolphin's Conveyance,* in which the *Baxter v. Four Oaks* case was followed, the area over which the scheme or local law was to extend was specified and the intention that the purchasers were to have rights *inter se* to enforce the stipulations of the local law was, so the judge thought, expressed clearly in every conveyance. The stipulations which each purchaser covenanted to observe in the several conveyances were identical and the first and every subsequent conveyance by the vendor contained a covenant by him, in effect, to obtain a covenant from every other purchaser to observe them; a useless series of covenants except upon the basis that all could enforce them. It would, no doubt, have been better if the draftsman of the conveyances in that case had added the words "to the intent that the covenants by the purchasers shall be mutually enforceable" and if a plan had been attached showing the area affected by the scheme; but the judge found a sufficient indication of that intention and a sufficient identification of that area.

No doubt the last mentioned two cases are authorities for the proposition that Parker J., in the well known passage of his judgment in *Elliston v. Reacher,* did not intend to lay down that the fact that the common vendor did not bind himself to sell off the defined area to which the local law was to apply in lots of any particular size was fatal to the creation of a local law over that area, but rather that if the vendor has done so you have one of the necessary ingredients from which the creation of the local law may be inferred. And where you find that all those concerned—the vendor and the several purchasers—have by the effect of the documents they have executed evidenced the intention to create such a local law over a defined area those cases are authority for saying that the court may give effect to that intention. But we find nothing in those cases indicating that the conditions from which a "building scheme" may be inferred from the facts are any different than was formerly the case.

In the instant case the creation of a building scheme cannot for the reasons we have given be inferred; and there is absent from the deeds themselves that clear evidence of intention to create reciprocal rights and obligations over a defined area which was found in *Baxter v. Four Oaks Properties Ltd* and in the *Dolphin's Conveyance* cases.

NOTES:

1. It is not permissible to infer a scheme of development from nothing more than the fact of a common vendor and the existence of common covenants in the instruments of transfer to the purchasers: *Re Wembley Park Estate Co. Ltd's Transfer* [1968] Ch. 491, 502–503 *per* Goff J.; *Jamaica Mutual Life Assurance Society v. Hillsborough Ltd* [1989] 1 W.L.R. 1101, 1108 *per* Lord Jauncey.

2. Law Com. No. 127, *Transfer of Land: The Law of Positive and Negative Covenants* (1984), para. 3.29 concludes:

As matters stand at present it seems that only two requirements are essential—namely, that the area of the scheme be defined; and that those who purchase from the creator of the scheme do so on the footing that all purchasers shall be mutually bound by, and mutually entitled to enforce, a defined set of restrictions (which may nonetheless vary to some extent as between lots).

3. The less prescriptive approach to schemes of development also permitted a rationalisation of the position in respect of sub-schemes and sub-plots. There is no difficulty in creating an independent sub-scheme among the purchasers of parts of a single plot in an existing scheme of development. However, in *Brunner v. Greenslade* [1971] Ch. 993 Megarry J. considered the enforceability, among such purchasers, of the covenants under the existing scheme of development.

Brunner v. Greenslade [1971] Ch. 993

(Ch D., Megarry J.)

In 1928 the owners of a plot of land, which constituted a single plot in an existing scheme of development, divided the land into five lots and sold them. Each conveyance was made subject to the restrictions that formed the substance of the existing scheme of development; but each purchaser covenanted with the vendors to observe the restrictions *by way of indemnity only*. The successor in title of one of the purchasers subsequently sold part of her plot to the defendant, who proposed to build a house contrary to the covenant under the existing scheme of development. The plaintiffs, the successors in title of another of the purchasers, sought a declaration that they were entitled to enforce the covenant.

MEGARRY J.:

In *Lawrence v. South County Freeholds Ltd* [1939] Ch. 656 Simonds J. held, in a reserved judgment, that on the facts before him no general scheme of development existed. It was accordingly not necessary to determine what rights as between the sub-purchasers there might have been if the main scheme had been held to exist. However, as the point had been fully argued, he expressed his views on it....

The substance of the views of Simonds J. was that where there is a head scheme, any sub-purchasers are bound inter se by the covenants of that head scheme even though they have entered into no covenants with the sub-vendor or with each other. What binds the sub-purchasers inter se is not any covenant of their own making (for there is none) but an equity independent of any contractual obligation entered into by them, and arising from the circumstances of the existence of the head scheme, the process of division into sub-lots and the disposal of those lots. If on the disposal the common intention was that the local law created by the head scheme should apply within the sub-area, then apply it would. It would be remarkable if the restrictions of the head scheme were to be reciprocally enforceable between the owners of a sub-lot and of a plot elsewhere on the estate, however distant, and yet be unenforceable as between neighbouring owners of sub-lots. I have ventured a somewhat free summary of the conclusions reached by Simonds J., but I think that it contains the kernel of his reasoning.

This conclusion is, of course, adverse to [the defendant's] contentions, and in particular his insistence on the importance of covenant. It is true that the law of restrictive covenants is founded in covenant, and that even the complexities of schemes of development may usually be explained in terms of covenant. Perhaps I may go back to first principles and try to summarise the matter in my own way. The most straightforward case is where A owns the entire estate and, having laid it out, himself sells individual lots to individual purchasers who enter into the covenants of the scheme. As soon as he sells a lot to the first purchaser, B, the scheme crystallises. Not only is B bound in respect of his lot to A, for the benefit of the remainder of the estate, but also A is bound, in respect of the remainder of the estate, to B, for the benefit of B's plot. It may be noted that while B is bound by the express covenants that he entered into, A may well have entered into no express covenants with B; and yet the concept of a scheme of development requires that A shall be treated as having impliedly bound himself by the provisions of the scheme. If A then sells another plot to C, C is taking part of the land that has already been subjected to the scheme in favour of B, and the covenants that he enters into are treated as being made for the benefit not only of A's remaining land but also of B's plot. If A continues to sell off one lot to each purchaser, and all the purchasers are different, in this way the whole concept of the enforceability of the covenants under a scheme of development, as between all within the area of the scheme, is readily explicable in terms of covenant, express or implied.

However, it is not always this simple case that occurs. Sometimes, as in the present case, one person purchases two or more lots or potential lots. There may then be the question whether C, as purchaser of one lot, can be bound as to that lot for the benefit of himself as the owner of another lot, and vice versa. If it is sought to explain the operation of a scheme of development in terms of covenant, the answer must be No; for C cannot effectually covenant with himself: see, for example, *Ridley v. Lee* [1935] Ch. 591 and *Rye v. Rye* [1962] A.C. 496. Yet if the answer is No, the consequence is that there are then haphazard islands of partial immunity within the area of the scheme, with C able to enforce the scheme against others, and others able to enforce it against C, but with C and his successors in title to any of his lots unable to enforce it inter se. Such immunities seem to me to be contrary to the whole basis of schemes of development, with their concept of a local law for the area of the scheme. If, then, the result of putting the basis of schemes of development upon a relentless application of the law governing covenants is to produce an unsatisfactory or unworkable result, some other basis must be sought.

Now it seems to me that such a basis has long existed, quite apart from the *Lawrence* case. In *Elliston v. Reacher* [1908] 2 Ch. 374, 385, after stating the familiar four requirements for a scheme of development, Parker J. said that it was

> "observable that the equity arising out of the establishment of the four points I have mentioned has been sometimes explained by the implication of mutual contracts between the various purchasers, and sometimes by the implication of a contract between each purchaser and the common vendor, that each purchaser is to have the benefit of all the covenants by the other purchasers, so that each purchaser is in equity an assign of the benefit of these covenants. In my opinion the implication of mutual contract is not always a perfectly satisfactory explanation. It may be satisfactory where all the lots are sold by auction at the same time, but when, as in cases such as *Spicer v. Martin*, there is no sale by auction, but all the various sales are by private treaty and at various intervals of time, the circumstances may, at the date of one or more of the sales, be such as to preclude the possibility of any actual contract. For example, a prior purchaser may be dead or incapable of contracting at the time of a subsequent purchase, and in any event it is unlikely that the prior and subsequent purchasers are ever brought into personal relationship, and yet the equity

may exist between them. It is, I think, enough to say, using Lord Macnaghten's words in *Spicer v. Martin*, that where the four points I have mentioned are established, the community of interest imports in equity the reciprocity of obligation which is in fact contemplated by each at the time of his own purchase."

That passage is, of course, primarily directed to deeds of mutual covenant. No doubt some of the difficulties where no mutual covenant is possible can be surmounted by other means, such as treating a purchaser's covenant as being made not merely with the vendor but also with previous purchasers of lots. Nevertheless, I think that the words of Parker J. show that he would have rested the mutual enforceability of the covenants of a scheme not merely on the principles of covenant but at least in part upon an equity born of the community of interest and reciprocity of obligation mentioned by Lord Macnaghten. This view is strongly supported by what Simonds J. said in the *Lawrence* case [1939] Ch. 656. After citing the latter part of the passage from the judgment of Parker J. that I have just read, he said, at p. 682:

"This, then, is the equity on which the plaintiffs must rely, an equity which is created by circumstances and is independent of contractual obligation."

The speech of Lord FitzGerald in *Spicer v. Martin* (1888) 14 App.Cas. 12, 18, 19, also seems to me to support this view, or at least to be fully consistent with it. For he based his opinion not on covenants entered into by the lessees of the sub-lots but on the covenants which the lessor of the sub-lots had entered into with the commissioners, who were the common vendors. Indeed, that case has some striking resemblances to the case now before me.

. . .

The major theoretical difficulties based on the law of covenant seem to me to disappear where instead there is an equity created by circumstances which is independent of contractual obligation. Further, whatever arguments there may be about unity of seisin destroying a covenant, by analogy to easements, I do not think that it precludes the application of a scheme of development as between purchasers of lots merely because they were initially in one hand.

I accordingly think that in this case I am fabricating no new equity, but merely emphasising an established equity. This view illustrates the way in which equity, in developing one of its doctrines, refuses to allow itself to be fettered by the concept upon which the doctrine is based if to do so would make the doctrine unfair or unworkable. After all, it is of the essence of a doctrine of equity that it should be equitable, and, I may add, that it should work: equity, like nature, does nothing in vain. In the field of schemes of development, equity readily gives effect to the common intention notwithstanding any technical difficulties involved: see *Baxter v. Four Oaks Properties Ltd* [1965] Ch. 816, 825, 826 *per* Cross J. It may be, indeed, that this is one of those branches of equity which work best when explained least.

Assuming that the requirements of a scheme exist, there is then the question of intention. Will the equity apply as between the purchasers of sub-lots only if a positive intention to this effect is established, as *Preston and Newsom's Restrictive Covenants Affecting Freehold Land Act* 4th ed. (1967), p. 42, seems to suggest, or will it apply unless a contrary intention appears? The true view is, I think, the latter. In the *Lawrence* case [1939] Ch. 656. 683, Simonds J. was plainly impressed by the improbability that the purchasers

"intended, while competent to enforce the covenants against the occupiers of the remotest houses on the estate and liable at their suit to have them enforced, yet to be powerless with regard to the conduct of their nearest neighbours."

No doubt purchasers may be infinitely various, but this sort of selective immunity and impotence is one for which few are likely to yearn: certainly I should be reluctant to presume any such yearning. An improbability such as this is likely to be present in every case in which a lot is divided. In any case where the requirements of a scheme are satisfied, and a purchaser of two or more actual or potential lots disposes of part of his land to others who have notice of the scheme, the position seems to me to be as follows. First, it will be presumed that each sub-purchaser will take the benefit and be subject to the burden of the equity arising from the scheme, and that the provisions of the scheme will accordingly be mutually enforceable as between all the sub-purchasers, even though they all claim through the same original purchaser from the common vendor. Such a presumption will be reinforced if the conveyances to the sub-purchasers are expressed to be made subject to the provisions of the scheme, or, a fortiori, if the sub-purchasers enter into covenants in terms of the scheme. Second, this presumption will be rebutted if the sub-purchasers enter into the new covenants of a sub-scheme which differ from those of the scheme: expressum facit cessare tacitum. In such a case, as between those within the sub-area, the new sub-scheme will supersede the main scheme for the estate, and there will be a new local law to replace the old: see *Knight v. Simmonds* [1896] 1 Ch. 653. Third, the presumption may be rebutted to the extent that the purchaser from the common vendor has disabled himself from enforcing the scheme against the sub-purchasers, for example, by reason of the rule that a man may not derogate from his grant: see *King v. Dickeson* (1889) 40 Ch.D. 596, as explained in the *Lawrence* case [1939] Ch. 656, 677, 680.

NOTES:

1. For comment, see [1971] C.L.J. 24.

2. The views expressed in *Brunner v. Greenslade* [1971] Ch. 993 in respect of sub-plots were approved by the Privy Council in *Texaco Antilles v. Kernochan* [1973] A.C. 609, 626 *per* Lord Cross.

E. EXTINGUISHMENT, DISCHARGE AND MODIFICATION

Where a restrictive covenant satisfies the necessary conditions for the passing of the benefit and burden, that covenant has the potential for indefinite duration and enforcement. However, a covenant will no longer be enforceable where the benefited land and the burdened land cease to be in separate ownership and occupation. Further, in some circumstances, although a covenant may remain technically enforceable, it may be deemed to be inappropriate to enforce it, either in its original form or at all.

1. Unity of ownership and occupation

Consistent with the principle applicable to easements, a restrictive covenant will cease to be enforceable where the benefited land and the burdened land cease to be in separate ownership and occupation: *Re Tiltwood, Sussex* [1978] Ch. 269, noted at [1978] Conv. 458; and, where the covenant relates simply to two properties, the covenant is extinguished: *ibid.* However, the effect may be different where such unity of ownership and occupation is (re)created from two or more properties which formed part of a scheme of development. In such circumstances, provided that the scheme continues in existence in relation to other properties, and subject to an indication to the contrary, the restrictive covenants are merely suspended and will revive if the unified properties are severed again: *Texaco Antilles Ltd v. Kernochan* [1973] A.C. 609, 624–626 *per* Lord Cross, discussed at (1973) 37 Conv. 280; (1977) 41 Conv. 107, 115–125.

2. Section 84 of the Law of Property Act 1925

Even where the benefit and burden of a restrictive covenant have passed, so that the covenant remains technically enforceable, enforcement may nonetheless be undesirable. In certain circumstances, therefore, the Lands Tribunal has power under section 84 of the Law of Property Act 1925 to discharge or modify the covenant, to order the payment of compensation to a person entitled to the benefit of a covenant and, when exercising its power to modify a covenant, to add further restrictions.

Law of Property Act 1925, s.84

Power to discharge or modify restrictive covenants affecting land

(1) The Lands Tribunal shall (without prejudice to any concurrent jurisdiction of the court) have power from time to time, on the application of any person interested in any freehold land affected by any restriction arising under covenant or otherwise as to the user thereof or the building thereon, by order wholly or partially to discharge or modify any such restriction on being satisfied—
   (a) that by reason of changes in the character of the property or the neighbourhood or other circumstances of the case which the Lands Tribunal may deem material, the restriction ought to be deemed obsolete; or
   (aa) that in a case falling within subsection (1A) below the continued existence thereof would impede some reasonable user of land for public or private purposes or, as the case may be, would unless modified so impede such user; or
   (b) that the persons of full age and capacity for the time being or from time to time entitled to the benefit of the restriction, whether in respect of estates in fee simple or any lesser estates or interests in the property to which the benefit of the restriction is annexed, have agreed, either expressly or by implication, by their acts or omissions, to the same being discharged or modified; or
   (c) that the proposed discharge or modification will not injure the persons entitled to the benefit of the restriction;
and an order discharging or modifying a restriction under this subsection may direct the applicant to pay to any person entitled to the benefit of the restriction such sum by way of consideration as the Tribunal may think it just to award under one, but not both, of the following heads, that is to say, either—
   (i) a sum to make up for any loss or disadvantage suffered by that person in consequence of the discharge or modification; or
   (ii) a sum to make up for any effect which the restriction had, at the time when it was imposed, in reducing the consideration then received for the land affected by it.
(1A) Subsection (1)(aa) above authorises the discharge or modification of a restriction by reference to its impeding some reasonable user of land in any case in which the Lands Tribunal is satisfied that the restriction, in impeding that user, either—

(a) does not secure to persons entitled to the benefit of it any practical benefits of substantial value or advantage to them; or

(b) is contrary to the public interest;

and that money will be an adequate compensation for the loss or disadvantage (if any) which any such person will suffer from the discharge or modification.

(1B) In determining whether a case is one falling within (1A) above, and in determining whether (in any such case or otherwise) a restriction ought to be discharged or modified, the Lands Tribunal shall take into account the development plan and any declared or ascertainable pattern for the grant or refusal of planning permissions in the relevant areas, as well as the period at which and context in which the restriction was created or imposed and any other material circumstances.

(1C) It is hereby declared that the power conferred by this section to modify a restriction includes power to add such further provisions restricting the user of or the building on the land affected as appear to the Lands Tribunal to be reasonable in view of the relaxation of the existing provisions, and as may be accepted by the applicant; and the Lands Tribunal may accordingly refuse to modify a restriction without some such addition.

NOTES:

1. Section 84 was amended by section 28 of the Law of Property Act 1969. For an analysis of section 84, see Polden (1986) 49 M.L.R. 195. For analysis of section 84 before its amendment in 1969, see Bodkin (1943) 7 Conv. 17; Newsom (1956) 20 Conv. 477, (1957) 21 Conv. 6; Mellows (1964) 28 Conv. 190.

2. On subsection (1)(a), see *Keith v. Texaco Ltd* (1977) 34 P. & C.R. 249; *Re Bradley Clare Estates Ltd's Application* (1987) 55 P. & C.R. 126; *Re Quaffers Ltd's Application* (1988) 56 P. & C.R. 142; *Re Cox's Application* [1985] J.P.L. 564. And see the recommendations for reform in Law Com. No. 201, *Transfer of Land: Obsolete Restrictive Covenants* (1991), *infra*, p. 806.

3. On subsection (1)(aa) generally, see *Re Bass Ltd's Application* (1973) 26 P. & C.R. 156 and the discussion by Wilkinson (1979) 129 N.L.J. 523; on subsection (1A)(a), see *Gilbert v. Spoor* [1983] Ch. 27, discussed by Polden [1982] Conv. 452, [1984] Conv. 429; and on subsections (1A)(b) and (1B), see *Re Martin's Application* (1988) 57 P. & C.R. 119.

4. Applications under subsection (1)(aa) raise the question of the relationship between restrictive covenants and planning control: see *supra*, p. 703. In particular, it has been argued by persons applying for the discharge or modification of a restrictive covenant that the grant of planning permission should be seen as establishing the ground under subsection (1)(aa) and subsection (1A)(b), in that the continued existence of the covenant "would impede some reasonable user of the land" and therefore "is contrary to the public interest". However, in *Re Bass Ltd's Application* (1973) 26 P. & C.R. 156, the Lands Tribunal ruled (i) that the existence of planning permission was "very persuasive", although not conclusive, in determining whether the applicants were proposing a reasonable user of the land (at 158); and (ii) that the existence of planning permission *per se* did not inevitably mean that the continued existence of the covenant was contrary to the public interest (at 159):

[A] planning permission only says, in effect, that a proposal will be allowed; it implies perhaps that such a proposal will not be a bad thing but it does not necessarily imply that it will be positively a good thing and in the public interest, and that failure of the proposal to materialise would be positively bad. Many planning permissions have got through by the skin of their teeth.

This approach has been approved by the Court of Appeal: see *Gilbert v. Spoor* [1983] Ch. 27, 34 *per* Eveleigh L.J. See also *Re Martin's Application* (1988) 57 P. & C.R. 119, where Fox L.J. stated (at 125):

In my view, the applicants' contention is wrong in so far as it suggests that the granting of planning permission ... necessarily involves the result that the Lands Tribunal must discharge the covenant. The granting of planning permission is, it seems to me, merely a circumstance which the Lands Tribunal can and should take into account when exercising its jurisdiction under section 84. To give the grant of planning permission a wider effect is, I think, destructive of the express statutory jurisdiction conferred by section 84. It is for the Tribunal to make up its own mind whether the requirements of section 84 are satisfied ... There is nothing in the Town and Country Planning Acts ... which suggests that these are intended to interfere in any way with the jurisdiction of the Lands Tribunal under section 84.

5. On subsection (1)(c), see *Re Forestmere Properties Ltd's Application* (1980) 41 P. & C.R. 390; *Re Bailey's Application* (1981) 42 P. & C.R. 108; *Re Livingstones' Application* (1982) 47 P. & C.R. 462.

6. For general observations on the jurisdiction of the Lands Tribunal under the various paragraphs of subsection (1), and on the burden of proof, see *Re University of Westminster* [1998] 3 All E.R. 1014.

3. Refusal to enforce restrictive covenants

Independently of the procedure under section 84 of the Law of Property Act 1925, the court may refuse to enforce a covenant where the plaintiff has acquiesced in the defendant's breach of the covenant. Alternatively, the conduct of the plaintiff and the circumstances of the breach may lead the court to refuse the remedy of an injunction but to award damages.

Gafford v. Graham (1998) 77 P. & C.R. 73

(CA, Nourse, Pill and Thorpe L.JJ.)

In 1976 the predecessor in title to the defendant purchased 12 acres of a 22 acre plot of land, including a bungalow, some stables and a yard (the "covenant land"). The purchaser covenanted (i) that, apart from the continued use of the bungalow as a residence, she would use the land only as a livery yard and for stabling (the "user restriction"); and (ii) that she would not build on the land without the approval of the vendors (the "building restriction"). The benefit of the covenants was annexed to each and every part of the land retained by the vendors; and it was not disputed that the burden of the covenants was imposed on the covenant land. In 1978 the plaintiff purchased part of the retained land, together with an express assignment of the benefit of the covenants. In 1980 the defendant purchased the remainder of the retained land; and in 1983 he purchased the covenant land. In 1986, the defendant converted the bungalow on the covenant land into a two-storey house without obtaining the approval of the plaintiff; and in 1989 he built an indoor riding school. The trial judge granted an injunction in relation to the breach of the user restriction and damages in substitution for an injunction in relation to the breach of the building restriction. The defendant appealed to the Court of Appeal.

NOURSE L.J.:

This appeal raises questions on (1) acquiescence and (2) the remedy of an injunction or damages in lieu in relation to breaches of restrictive covenants affecting freehold land.

. . .

Events between 1984 and 1989

In 1984 the defendant started to call the covenant land "the Hunter's Lodge Riding Centre". He put up a sign bearing that name. In his evidence the plaintiff thought that he first complained to his solicitors about the riding school in 1984, but their file disclosed that he did not contact them until 1987. On 27 March 1985 the plaintiff wrote to the defendant complaining of three matters, one of which was damage caused to his trees and the boundary fence by the defendant's horses. He made no complaint about a riding school as such.

In 1985 the defendant obtained planning permission for the conversion of the bungalow. The judge found that the plaintiff entered an objection to the application with the local planning authority but did not write to the defendant because, as the plaintiff claimed, he did not know where the defendant lived. The judge said he could have easily found that out. The defendant made no application for planning permission in respect of the extension to the barn. As to those two matters, the judge made the following further findings:

"The plaintiff was aware of the work beginning on the bungalow and although he raised it with his own solicitors he did not complain to Mr Graham. In 1986 extension works were carried out on the barn but Mr Gafford did nothing about it because he imagined the local authority would have it removed because no planning permission had been obtained for them. He telephoned the local authority offices about the matter and mentioned it to his own solicitors. The works were finished in a week but he did not get in touch with Mr Graham at all. The plaintiff told me that he would not have got anywhere. Mr Gafford has always had a copy of his title deeds and read them in 1987 to 1988. During the whole period he was aware of their terms and therefore was aware of the restrictive covenants. At all times he had the details of the covenants in his mind. Although he complained to his solicitors about these various matters no complaint was made to Mr Graham until the correspondence above-mentioned. The riding lessons were carried on for five years without challenge."

The correspondence referred to by the judge started with a letter of 7 March 1989. Before that, on 31 March 1988, the plaintiff had written to the local planning authority recording his objection to the granting of planning permission for the construction of the indoor riding school. He said:

"The proposed building would be an enormous structure, ugly and in full view from my property. I am surrounded on all sides by this poorly managed establishment and I suffer a constant assault by this dirt, noise, smell and animals and I am therefore opposed to any extension of this enterprise in any form. The application shows that an estimated 20 vehicles a day will be entering and leaving. The actual number is already about double that and the use of this building will certainly increase it further."

Notwithstanding the plaintiff's objection, planning permission was granted on 31 October 1988, after an appeal to the Secretary of State. The plaintiff said in evidence that in February 1989 he became aware that something was afoot, in that large quantities of concrete began arriving by lorry load, which he presumed was for the foundation work for the riding school. He wrote to the solicitors then acting for him on 22 February and on 7 March 1989 they wrote to the defendant at his home address in Chichester. Their letter alleged that the defendant was in breach of the covenants. . . .

The letter contained a request that the defendant should cease all building activities on the riding school forthwith and that he should make proposals on the matters complained of, including the conversion of the bungalow and the extension to the barn. It ended by saying that in the event that nothing had been heard from the defendant within seven days:

"we must formally put you on notice that our Client will consider himself at liberty to take whatever action seems to him necessary to preserve his position and that such action may include an injunction for damages and costs."

The judge recorded that a without prejudice reply was written by the defendant's solicitors on 15 March, two days after the work had started. On 10 April the plaintiff's solicitors wrote to the defendant's solicitors, stating their understanding that the defendant had not ceased building activities on his land. Having repeated the breaches alleged and the request that the defendant should cease all works and provide them with his proposals for rectification of the various breaches, they also repeated their threat to commence proceedings for an injunction.

On 11 April the defendant's solicitors replied asking for a precise statement of the damage suffered by the plaintiff and for a statement of the sort of consideration he would be seeking in exchange for giving his approval to the works. Meanwhile, without prejudice correspondence was being exchanged. On 28 April the plaintiff's solicitors wrote putting the defendant's solicitors on notice that:

"such correspondence or delay is not to be taken as any acquiescence on our Client's part and, further, any projects that your Client commences or continues on his land in breach of covenant are a matter for him and at his own risk."

The judge found that the construction of the riding school was completed by the end of April, at about the time that that letter would have been received.

On 12 May the plaintiff's solicitors wrote the defendant's solicitors a without prejudice letter which, with the agreement of both sides, was placed before the judge. In it they set out certain figures, on the basis of which they maintained that a reasonable amount to be paid to the plaintiff in settlement of the dispute was £100,800. The defendant's solicitors replied on 21 June stating that he had no intention of making any payment whatsoever. As I have said, the writ was issued on 29 August 1989. Notwithstanding his earlier threats, the plaintiff made no application for interlocutory relief.

The bungalow and the barn

I deal first with the conversion of the bungalow and the extension to the barn, the former having constituted a clear breach of both user and building restrictions and the latter a clear breach of the building restriction. The defendant claims that the plaintiff's rights to relief in respect of those breaches are barred by acquiescence. I have already read or referred to the judge's findings in respect of these two matters which, if taken in isolation, suggest that he thought that acquiescence had been made out. Although he did not make a clear distinction between the bungalow and the barn on the one hand and the other matters of complaint on the other, I think that the following further observations were directed, at least in part, to the bungalow and the barn:

"In view of the absence of complaint to Mr Graham over several years and the general inactivity in the matter, it was submitted on behalf of the defendants that by the date of the issue of the writ the plaintiff had lost any entitlement to claim equitable relief and if that is the case he has also lost his entitlement to seek damages in lieu. However, it seems to me that this argument overlooks the fact that the plaintiff also has the benefit of a legal assignment."

It appears that the judge's reference to a legal assignment was brought about by the citation to him in argument of the decision of this court in *Shaw v. Applegate* [1977] 1 W.L.R. 970, where, at p. 979H, Goff L.J., relying on the judgment of Farwell J. in *Osborne v. Bradley* [1903] 2 Ch. 446, 451, expressed the view that it is easier to establish a case of acquiescence where the right is equitable only. *Shaw v. Applegate* was a case where it was the original covenantor who was alleged to have been in breach, so that the right of the covenantee by assignment was indeed a legal right. Here [the trial judge] was evidently impressed by the express assignment to the plaintiff of the benefit of the covenant. That certainly gave the plaintiff a legal right as against [the predecessor in title to the defendant]. But he cannot now enforce the restrictions against her. He seeks to do so against one of her successors in title to the covenant land. His right against the defendant, being enforceable only because the burden of the covenant runs with the covenant land in equity, is equitable only. Accordingly, the judge was wrong to place weight on the assignment of the benefit of the covenant to the plaintiff.

For myself, I doubt whether a distinction ought any longer to be made between a legal and equitable right when considering a defence of acquiescence in a case of this kind. In *Shaw v. Applegate*, at p. 978D, Buckley L.J. said:

"The real test, I think, must be whether upon the facts of the particular case the situation has become such that it would be dishonest or unconscionable for the plaintiff, or the person having the rights sought to be enforced, to continue to seek to enforce it."

At p. 980C, Goff L.J. agreed that the test was whether, in the circumstances, it had become unconscionable for the plaintiff to rely on his legal right. If that is the correct test for a legal right, it could hardly be suggested, unconscionability being the soul of equity, that there should be some lower test for an equitable right. Moreover, in his admired judgment in *Taylors Fashions Ltd v. Liverpool Victoria Trustees Co. Ltd* [1982] Q.B. 133 (a case of common mistake as to the registrability of an option to renew a lease) Oliver J., after an extensive review of the earlier authorities on equitable estoppel, acquiescence and the like concluded, at p. 155C:

"The enquiry which I have to make therefore, as it seems to me, is simply whether, in all the circumstances of this case, it was unconscionable for the defendants to seek to take advantage of the mistake which, at the material time, everybody shared ..."

Thus here the enquiry must be whether, in all the circumstances, it would be unconscionable for the plaintiff to continue to seek to enforce the rights which he undoubtedly had in 1986 to complain of the conversion of the bungalow and the extension to the barn. On the facts found or referred to by the judge, I am unable to answer that question except in the affirmative. The plaintiff knew what his rights were. He never made any complaint or objection to the defendant at the time. His objection to the application for planning permission in respect of the bungalow and his complaints to his solicitors can avail him nothing. He made no complaint to the plaintiff until his solicitors wrote their letter of 7 March 1989, about three years after the acts complained of. He only complained of them then because of the much more serious threat presented by the proposed construction of the riding school. Before that he had effectively treated the conversion of the bungalow and the extension to the barn as incidents which were closed.

For these reasons, I would hold that the plaintiff acquiesced in the conversion of the bungalow and the extension to the barn, his acquiescence being a bar to all relief in respect of those matters. I would discharge the judge's awards of £20,000 and £750 damages accordingly. That makes it unnecessary to consider the quantum of those awards.

User between 1984 and 1989

I deal next with the question whether the defendant carried on a riding school business between 1984 and 1989 in breach of the user restriction. Again, had there been such a breach, it might have been material to the question of acquiescence in relation to later breaches. I have already stated my view that the carrying on of such a business, not simply as an incidental part of a livery business, would have constituted a breach... However, the judge made no finding as to the period between 1984 and 1989, except that the construction of the riding school followed a period when riding lessons were given outside, the lessons being carried on for five years without challenge.

I therefore conclude that there was no breach of the user restriction between 1984 and 1989 and that there was nothing in which the plaintiff could have acquiesced. On any footing the question of acquiescence during that period appears to be a sterile one. It is very difficult to see how acquiescence in the business of an outdoor riding school up to 1989 could amount to acquiescence in the much larger business of an indoor and outdoor riding school after that date.

The indoor riding school and the current business

I now come to the plaintiff's real and substantial complaints, which arise out of the construction of the indoor riding school and the carrying on of the much larger business to which it has led, the former having constituted a clear breach of the user and building restrictions and the latter a clear breach of the user restriction. Again, the defendant claims that the plaintiff's rights to relief in respect of those breaches are barred by acquiescence.

A helpful introduction to this part of the case is an observation of Fry L.J. in *Sayers v. Collyer* (1884) 28 Ch. D. 103, 110:

> "Acquiescence may either be an entire bar to all relief, or it may be a ground for inducing the Court to act under the powers of Lord Cairns' Act."

Here there can be no question of acquiescence being an entire bar to all relief in respect of the riding school and the current business. In contrast to his inaction over the conversion of the bungalow and the extension to the barn, the plaintiff acted promptly at the end of February 1989 when he first became aware that something was afoot, and his solicitors' letter of 7 March was received by the defendant before the construction works began. Further, their letter of 28 April demonstrated that the plaintiff would continue to assert whatever rights he had. The criticism which can be made of him is that he made no application for interlocutory relief. Had he carried out the threat made in the letter of 7 March, there could have been little doubt that he would have been granted an injunction restraining further execution of the works. There could have been no doubt as to the enforceability of the restrictions or their prohibitive effect and an interlocutory injunction would have followed almost as of course. Accordingly, the plaintiff's omission to apply for interlocutory relief was an important factor to be taken into account by the judge when considering whether he ought to grant a mandatory injunction at trial for the demolition of the building.

In refusing to grant such an injunction whilst holding the defendant to the terms of the user restriction, the judge said:

"By failing to issue a writ and motion for an interlocutory injunction at the outset, he or his advisers took the risk that the building would be completed before the trial of the action could take place. Moreover, it has been in existence for seven and a half years. It would not be right to compel its destruction now when it could be used, or adapted for use, in a way which would not violate the covenant. No reason has been advanced why it could not be used for stabling horses, which is an activity allowed by the stipulations."

Later, having referred to some observations of Sir Thomas Bingham M.R. in *Jaggard v. Sawyer* [1995] 1 W.L.R. 269, 283, and to the defendant's submission that the grant of any injunction would be oppressive and disproportionate, the judge said:

"As against that, it seems to me that Mr Graham, who was aware of the covenants and knew that use of his land was limited, disregarded the plaintiff's rights and, even after he was challenged, proceeded to complete the building work without stopping while the matter was investigated. He was determined to press ahead in the face of the complaint and saw the riding school as an opportunity for profit; hence the advertisement mentioned above. Knowing that the action had commenced he started up the business. This tells me much about his attitude and reflects little credit upon him. He has demonstrated that he does not care much about Mr Gafford or his rights and reasonable concerns. The decisions not to submit plans for approval were taken deliberately. In these circumstances it would not be oppressive to grant an injunction."

In regard to that reasoning, Mr Taylor, for the defendant, has contended that the adaptation of the riding school for the stabling of horses could only be achieved, if at all, at exorbitant expense. That may well be so, although it must at once be said that the evidence did not address that point. Mr Taylor submits that the injunctions granted by the judge, if they are allowed to stand, will sterilise the use of the building. On the other side, Mr Zelin has submitted that if the building cannot sensibly be adapted for any permissible use it is serving no useful purpose and should be demolished. He contrasts the facts here with those of *Wrotham Park Esate Co. Ltd v. Parkside Homes Ltd* [1974] 1 W.L.R. 798 where, at p.811B, Brightman J. evidently gave great weight to the unpardonable waste of much needed houses which would be the consequence of his directing that they should be pulled down.

The principles on which judges should act when deciding whether to grant injunctions or to award damages in lieu under Lord Cairns' Act were recently considered by this court in *Jaggard v. Sawyer*, where the earlier authorities are fully discussed. They need not be discussed again. While many of them might suggest that a judge's function in granting relief under that Act is more circumscribed than is the norm, it is important to emphasise that the principles, being principles of discretion, must always remain adaptable to the facts of individual cases. Such indeed was the view of Millett L.J. who, in a passage I entirely and gratefully adopt, said at p. 288A:

"Reported cases are merely illustrations of circumstances in which particular judges have exercised their discretion, in some cases by granting an injunction, and in others by awarding damages instead. Since they are all cases on the exercise of a discretion, none of them is a binding authority on how the discretion should be exercised. The most that any of them can demonstrate is that in similar circumstances it would not be wrong to exercise the discretion in the same way. But it does not follow that it would be wrong to exercise it differently."

In the present case I start from this position. Although the judge may have underestimated the cost and the practical difficulties of adapting the riding school for the stabling of horses, it would not be right for this court to interfere with his decision not to grant a mandatory injunction for its demolition. Without that part of his reasoning, a powerful case was still made out for the refusal of such a drastic order. As a general rule, someone who, with the knowledge that he has clearly enforceable rights and the ability to enforce them, stands by whilst a permanent and substantial structure is unlawfully erected, ought not to be granted an injunction to have it pulled down.

So what is to be done? There may be force in Mr Taylor's contention that the adaptation of the riding school would be a costly and impracticable exercise. Further, it may be realistic to suppose that the defendant would thus be left with far more stabling than would be needed for the purposes of a livery business. Equally, the court would be reluctant to force a building constructed for one purpose to be adapted to another unless no other solution was fair and reasonable.

It may well be that if those had been the only relevant considerations, the defendant would have shown insufficient grounds for the injunctions to be discharged, especially when account is taken of the judge's strictures on the conduct and attitude of the defendant, which amount to saying that he acted in blatant and calculated disregard of the plaintiff's rights. There is, however, a further factor which tips the balance in favour of an award of damages. By his solicitors' letter of 12 May 1989 the plaintiff made it clear that he would be prepared to accept a cash sum in settlement of the dispute. The suggested figure of £100,800 was obviously excessive and it would in any event have had to be reduced in order to leave the bungalow and the barn out of account. But the plaintiff's position was made clear. He would have been prepared to settle the dispute on payment of a cash sum. Why should he not be held to that position and granted damages in lieu of an injunction?

It is said that an insurmountable obstacle to such an award is presented by the observations of Lindley and A.L. Smith L.JJ. in *Shelfer v. City of London Electric Lighting Co. Ltd* [1895] 1 Ch. 287. At p. 315 Lindley L.J. said:

"But in exercising the jurisdiction thus given attention ought to be paid to well settled principles; and ever since Lord Cairns' Act was passed the Court of Chancery has repudiated the notion that the Legislature intended to turn that Court into a tribunal for legalising wrongful acts; or in other words the Court has always protested against the notion that it ought to allow a wrong to continue simply because the wrongdoer is able and willing to pay for the injury he may inflict."

At p. 322, A.L. Smith L.J. said:

"Many Judges have stated, and I emphatically agree with them, that a person by committing a wrongful act (whether it be a public company for public purposes or a private individual) is not thereby entitled to ask the Court to sanction his doing so by purchasing his neighbour's rights, by assessing damages in that behalf, leaving his neighbour with the nuisance, or his lights dimmed, as the case may be ...

In my opinion, it may be stated as a good working rule that-
(1) If the injury to the plaintiff's legal rights is small;
(2) And is one which is capable of being estimated in money,
(3) And is one which can be adequately compensated by a small money payment,
(4) And the case is one in which it would be oppressive to the defendant to grant an injunction-
then damages in substitution for an injunction may be given."

It is said that an award of sizeable damages in this case would disregard those observations, and in particular A.L. Smith L.J.'s good working rule.

In *Jaggard v. Sawyer* Sir Thomas Bingham M.R., having read those and an intervening passage from the judgment of A.L. Smith L.J., said at p. 278B:

"Many later cases have turned on the application of this good working rule to the particular facts of the case before the court. This case may be said to do the same."

At p. 286D Millett L.J., having read the observations of Lindley L.J. and A.L. Smith L.J.'s good working rule, said:

"Laid down just one hundred years ago, A.L. Smith L.J.'s check-list has stood the test of time; but it needs to be remembered that it is only a working rule and does not purport to be an exhaustive statement of the circumstances in which damages may be awarded instead of an injunction."

Then followed the passage I have already read. In the result, this court applied the good working rule and affirmed the judge's decision to make a small award of damages.

Both *Shelfer v. City of London Electric Lighting Co. Ltd* [1895] 1 Ch. 287 and *Jaggard v. Sawyer* [1995] 1 W.L.R. 269 were cases where the suggestion that the plaintiff's rights should be bought out for a cash sum was strongly resisted. Thus in *Jaggard v. Sawyer*, at p. 286G, Millett L.J. referred to Mrs Jaggard's understandable complaint that what the judge had in effect done was to grant Mr and Mrs Sawyer a right of way in perpetuity over her land for a once and for all payment. Here the plaintiff can make no such complaint. His willingness to settle the dispute on payment of a cash sum can properly be reflected by an award of damages. Nor, once that is established, can it be an objection that the amount of damages may be large. The injury to the plaintiff's legal rights must be adequately compensated. In such a case the first and third conditions of the good working rule do not apply.

I summarise the position as follows. The essential prerequisite of an award of damages is that it should be oppressive to the defendant to grant an injunction. Here that prerequisite is satisfied. It would be oppressive and therefore unfair to the defendant to allow the judge's injunctions to stand. The plaintiff should receive an award of damages instead. It would be unfair to him for them not adequately to compensate him for the injury to his legal rights. It is to the quantification of those damages that I finally turn.

Quantum of damages

Since the judge did not consider the quantum of damages in respect of the indoor riding school and the current business, either side could have asked for that question to be remitted to him. It was because they were both content that we should decide it ourselves that we gave counsel leave to put in further written submissions.

A welcome consequence of *Jaggard v. Sawyer* is that it has firmly established the *Wrotham Park* [1974] 1 W.L.R. 798 basis of assessing damages as the basis appropriate to cases such as this. There have been some differences of opinion as to the correct analysis of that decision, the difficulty being, as the plaintiffs there conceded, that the defendants' breaches of covenant had caused no diminution in the value of the land to which the benefit of the covenant was annexed: see [1974] 1 W.L.R. at p. 812F-G. No doubt it was for that reason that in *Surrey County Council v. Bredero Homes Ltd* [1993] 1 W.L.R. 1361, 1369, Steyn L.J. expressed the view that the *Wrotham Park* damages were defensible only on the basis that they were restitutionary in nature. However, that view was rejected in *Jaggard v. Sawyer* by both Sir Thomas Bingham M.R. and Millett L.J. who, agreeing with Megarry V.-C. in *Tito v. Waddell (No. 2)* [1977] Ch. 106 at p. 335, thought that Brightman J.'s approach had been compensatory, in that the damages awarded were intended to compensate the plaintiffs for not having obtained the price they would have been able to obtain for giving their consent, had they been asked to give it.

The compensatory analysis, if accompanied by a recognition that it was not a diminution in value of the dominant tenement that was compensated, is perfectly acceptable. Equally, in a case where there has been such a diminution, there seems to be no reason why it should not be taken into account in assessing the sum which might reasonably have been demanded as a quid pro quo for relaxing the covenant. Whatever the correct analysis may be, *Jaggard v Sawyer*, as both sides agree, is clear authority for the adoption of the *Wrotham Park* basis of assessing damages in this case. I therefore proceed to assess them by reference to the sum which the plaintiff might reasonably have demanded as a quid pro quo for relaxing the restrictions in perpetuity, so as to permit the construction of the indoor riding school and the carrying on of an indoor and outdoor riding school business.

This question was fully dealt with in evidence and argument before the judge on the footing that he would either grant a mandatory injunction for the demolition of the riding school or damages in lieu... The judge, having decided to grant a prohibitory injunction, did not consider the evidence pertaining to this head of damages and made no findings on it.

We have been supplied with transcripts of the evidence of all the witnesses and with copies of the trial bundles of documents. In agreeing that we should decide the question of damages ourselves, the parties have shown themselves to be content that we should do so without having had the advantage of seeing and hearing the witnesses give their evidence. We have, however, had the advantage of considering the detailed sequential written submissions of counsel, in which many references to the evidence have been made.

In the circumstances stated, it would not be profitable for the evidence to be examined and the submissions discussed. In the end, as with many questions of damages, it is a matter of judgment. Mr Zelin has submitted that the correct figure is £26,500, being the approximate mean between two valuations of the relaxation of the covenant..., the first based on the income assumed to have been generated by the business and the second on the marriage value between the land and the facility afforded by having the riding school. Mr Taylor has submitted that the correct figure is £5,000, being 5% of the approximate cost of constructing the riding school. I am in no doubt that [the former] valuations represent a far more realistic guide to the amount which the plaintiff might reasonably have demanded for a relaxation of the restrictions in the spring of 1989. I think that he might reasonably have demanded a round sum of £25,000 and I would award damages in that amount.

NOTES:

1. For comment, see (1998) 114 L.Q.R. 555.

2. For a discussion of the factors which may determine whether the plaintiff obtains injunctive relief or damages, and of the measure of damages, see Martin [1996] Conv. 329.

3. The question of acquiescence in a breach of covenant in respect of part only of the burdened land was considered in *Chatsworth Estates Co. v. Fewell* [1931] 1 Ch. 224. In 1897 the predecessors in title of the defendant purchased a property, Bella Vista, from the predecessors in title of the plaintiffs, the owners of Compton Place in Eastbourne. The conveyance included a covenant, expressly annexed to Compton Place, not to use Bella Vista otherwise than as a private residence, except with the consent of the owners of Compton Place. The same vendors had sold other properties in the neighbourhood on the same terms but they had subsequently consented to non-residential use. When the defendant, who purchased Bella Vista with notice of the covenant, started to use the property as a guest house, the plaintiffs sought an injunction. Farwell J. stated (at 229–231):

Although the area is no longer confined to single dwelling-houses, and the covenants have been somewhat relaxed in the sense that some boarding-houses or guest houses have been permitted, and some other houses have been put to uses not strictly within the covenants, still, on the whole, and taking it broadly, the area still retains its character of being a residential area.

That does not, however, determine the question before me, because although a block of flats does not necessarily render the area non-residential, its erection, or the conversion of a house into a block of flats, is undoubtedly a technical breach of the covenants. In those circumstances I have to consider whether it would be equitable for me to give the plaintiffs any relief by injuction or damages, or whether I must refuse all relief.

Nothing can be said against the defendant's conduct of his establishment except that it is a breach of covenant. That being so ought I to refuse the plaintiffs relief?

The defendant's first ground of defence is that there has been such a complete change in the character of the neighbourhood, apart from the plaintiffs' acts or omissions, that the covenants are now unenforceable. But to succeed on that ground the defendant must show that there has been so complete a change in the character of the neighbourhood that there is no longer any value left in the covenants at all. A man who has covenants for the protection of his property cannot be deprived of his rights thereunder merely by the acts or omissions of other persons unless those acts or omissions bring about such a state of affairs as to render the covenants valueless, so that an action to enforce them would be unmeritorious, not bona fide at all, and merely brought for some ulterior purposes. It is quite impossible here to say that there has been so complete a change in the character of this neighbourhood as to render the covenants valueless to the plaintiffs. Whether right or wrong the plaintiffs are bringing this action bona fide to protect their property, and it is hopeless to say that the change in the character of the neighbourhood is so complete that it would be useless for me to give them any relief.

The defendant really relied on the acts and omissions of the plaintiffs and their predecessors as a bar to equitable relief. Now the plaintiffs are not unduly insistent on the observance of these covenants in this sense, that they do not conduct inquisitorial examinations into their neighbours' lives, and do not make it their business to find out very carefully exactly what is being done, unless the matter is brought to their notice, either by complaints of other inhabitants, or by seeing some board or advertisement. I cannot think that plaintiffs lose their rights merely because they treat their neighbours with consideration. They are doing what they think sufficient to preserve the character of the neighbourhood. Whether they do enough is another matter, but I am quite satisfied that they are not intending, by their acts or omissions, to permit this area to be turned into anything other than a mainly residential area. There is no doubt however that they have permitted breaches of covenant in several cases where houses have been turned into flats, they have permitted at least four houses to be carried on as boarding-houses or hotels, and they have not prevented—in some cases because they did not know of them—some half a dozen other houses being used as boarding-houses or guest houses.

There are still however a very large number of private dwelling-houses in the area, and I am satisfied that while the use of Bella Vista as a guest house or boarding house may not at the moment cause any actual damage to Compton Place or its owners, there is a prospect of damage in the future if the defendant is allowed to continue to use Bella Vista in that way, because it might well lead to many other houses being so used which would undoubtedly damnify the owners of Compton Place, especially if they develop the park and grounds as intended. In that way it will certainly be detrimental to the plaintiffs to permit Bella Vista to be used as a guest house. But whether they are entitled to relief depends on the exact effect of their past acts and omissions.

Now, as stated in many authorities, the principle upon which this equitable doctrine rests is that the plaintiffs are not entitled to relief if it would be inequitable to the defendant to grant it. In some of the cases it is said that the plaintiffs by their acts and omissions have impliedly waived performance of the covenants. In other cases it is said that the plaintiffs, having acquiesced in past breaches, cannot now enforce the covenants. It is in all cases a question of degree. It is in many ways analogous to the doctrine of estoppel, and I think it is a fair test to treat it in that way and ask, "Have the plaintiffs by their acts and omissions represented to the defendant that the covenants are no longer enforceable and that he is therefore entitled to use his house as a guest house?"

Farwell J. concluded that in all the circumstances the plaintiffs had not represented that the covenants were no longer to be enforced. It may be noted that the plaintiffs had given the defendant an opportunity to make an application under section 84 of the Law of Property Act 1925 but the defendant had taken no action.

4. In *Attorney-General of Hong Kong v. Fairfax Ltd* [1997] 1 W.L.R. 149 a covenant was held to have been abandoned (so as to be no longer enforceable even in respect of new breaches) where over a long period of time the covenantor and its successors in title, with the actual or inferred knowledge of the covenantee, had made extensive use of the burdened land in a manner wholly inconsistent with the continuance of the covenant.

5. In *Shaw v. Applegate* [1977] 1 W.L.R. 970 the Court declined to hold that the successor in title to the covenantee had acquiesced in the breach of covenant. In 1967 the defendant purchased property and convenanted "with the vendor" not to use it as an amusement arcade. The following day the vendor sold various neighbouring properties to the plaintiffs and expressly assigned to them the benefit of the covenant, although notice of the assignment was not given to the defendant until 1973. From 1970 the defendant established and expanded an amusement arcade on his property but the plaintiffs took no action: it was established that they knew all the relevant facts but that they were unclear as to whether those facts amounted to a breach of the covenant. When they did commence proceedings in 1973 (soon after they themselves started an amusement arcade business), the defendant argued that they were not entitled to relief by reason of acquiescence and laches. Buckley L.J. stated (at 978–979):

The real test, I think, must be whether upon the facts of the particular case the situation has become such that it would be dishonest or unconscionable for the plaintiff, or the person having the right sought to be enforced, to continue to seek to enforce it.

In the present case, having regard to the doubtful state of mind of the parties during the period from the spring of 1971 to August 1973, I do not think that one could reach the conclusion that in this case the plaintiffs would be acting dishonestly or unconscionably in seeking to enforce their rights under the contract because of their failure to sue at an earlier date. After all, it should not, I think, be the policy of the courts to push people into litigation until they are really sure that they have got a genuine complaint and have got a case in which they are likely to be able to succeed, and acquiescence at a time when the parties are in doubt as to what their true rights are could, it seems to me, seldom satisfy the tests I have been discussing. Accordingly, in my judgment, there is not here sufficient acquiescence to bar the plaintiffs from all remedy in respect of this covenant, or to deprive them of any continuing cause of action.

But that is not the end of the matter for we then have to proceed to consider whether, in the circumstances of the case, it is a proper case for an injunction or whether we ought not, under the Chancery Amendment Act 1858 [Lord Cairns' Act], to award damages in lieu of an injunction. Undoubtedly the position is, I think, that the defendant was to some extent lulled into a false sense of security by the fact that the plaintiffs did not protest earlier than they did at the course of action he was pursuing; but, moreover, when the action was launched no application was made for interlocutory relief, and the defendant has continued to conduct his business on this land in the way indicated and has continued to build up the goodwill of that business, and it is clear that he has invested quite considerable sums of money in the installation of various kinds of amusement and gaming machines. It is now 1977, almost six years since he first began to operate this property as an amusement arcade and I think that it would be extremely hard after that length of time to restrain him by injunction from continuing to carry on this business, and if we were to grant the injunction sought it would involve his ceasing to use the lean-to for the purposes for which he has been using it, it would involve his dismantling a large number of fairly valuable machines and it is common ground that there is no other space, upon this property at any rate, where the defendant could make use of them. So it would, to a certain extent, operate in a mandatory fashion and probably subject the defendant to considerable loss.

In these circumstances, I think that the appropriate remedy in this case is not an injunction but damages. No attempt was made when the matter was before the judge to adduce evidence upon which any quantification of damages could be arrived at, and so, if my brethren agree with my view, the matter will have to go back to the Chancery Division for an inquiry as to damages, which will no doubt be conducted by a master.

For comment, see (1977) 41 Conv. 355.

F. Reform

Reform of the law relating to covenants affecting freehold land has been on the agenda since before *Tulk v. Moxhay* (1848) 2 Ph. 774. In 1832 the Real Property Commissioners considered recommending legislation to make the burden of such covenants run with the land in the same way as leasehold covenants; but they concluded that the matter should be left to be resolved by the courts of equity. The confidence of the Commissioners appeared to have been vindicated in *Tulk v. Moxhay*; but, as has been seen, the principle in that case was confined to restrictive covenants. However, it was not until 1965 that the Wilberforce Committee recommended that the law should provide for the running of positive covenants as well as negative covenants: *Committee on Positive Covenants Affecting Land* [1965], Cmnd. 2719.

Despite its terms of reference, the Wilberforce Committee indicated that certain of its principal recommendations should be applied also to restrictive covenants; and it became clear that it would be undesirable for the law relating to positive covenants to be reformed in isolation. The Law Commission was therefore asked to consider the law relating to restrictive covenants. Law Com. No. 11, *Transfer of Land: Report on Restrictive Covenants* (1967), summarised the principal defects as (i) the uncertainty as to the passing of the benefit of restrictive covenants and hence their enforceability and (ii) the inadequate procedure for the discharge or modification of outdated covenants: see (1967) 30 M.L.R. 681. The recommendations directed at the second defect were enacted by the Law of Property Act 1969: see *supra*, p. 791. However, the central recommendations were not implemented. The Law Commission had produced draft legislation, establishing a new interest in land (the "land obligation"), which was intended to take the place of both restrictive *and positive* covenants; but, in the face of criticism that the proposed "land obligation" could not be satisfactorily accommodated within the framework of the existing law, the legislation was never introduced.

In 1971 the Law Commission issued a working paper in which it recommended a comprehensive reform embracing not only positive and restrictive covenants but also easements and profits: Law Commission Working Paper No. 36, *Transfer of Land: Appurtenant Rights* (1971); but the scheme was seen as over-ambitious as a single-stage reform.

The Law Commission returned again to positive and restrictive covenants and in 1984 published Law Com. No. 127, *Transfer of Land: The Law of Positive and Restrictive Covenants* (1984), in which it recommended a revised version of its earlier proposal for a system of land obligations, replacing the present system of positive and restrictive covenants.

Under the proposed scheme the enforcement of land obligations would be based on the existing law of easements. Land obligations would normally subsist as *legal* interests in land and they would be enforceable by and against the current owners of the benefited land and the burdened land respectively. However, their enforceability against purchasers of the servient land would depend upon registration. The category of land obligations capable of existing as "neighbour obligations" between two plots of land would include restrictions on the use of the burdened land, obligations to carry out works on the benefited land or the burdened land, obligations to provide services and obligations to make payments in respect of other positive obligations. In each case it would be a requirement that the obligation should be for the benefit of the whole or any part of the benefited land. The Report envisaged that when the new system was introduced the present rules under which the benefit and burden of covenants run with the land would cease to apply. As a result covenants would be rendered unsuitable for creating indefinite obligations affecting land, since they would only constitute personal obligations between the original contracting parties. Accordingly, the assumption was that covenants would be superseded by land obligations. The Report also made proposals for resolving the difficulties of enforcing covenants in the context of multiple unit developments. It proposed the establishment of "development schemes" within which a developer could create mutually enforceable "development obligations", a special class of land obligations designed for use in property developments. However, in March 1998, the Government announced that it had decided not to implement Law Com. No. 127; but that the Law Commission would be asked to consider how future developments in property law might affect the recommendations in the Report: *Hansard* (HL), March 19, 1998, Written Answers 213.

In any event, the "development scheme" element of the proposals had largely been sidelined. In 1987 different proposals, based on overseas condominium laws, were put forward expressly to regulate separately owned properties within specified boundaries, each such development being called a "commonhold": *Commonhold: Freehold Flats and Freehold Ownership of Other Inter-dependent Buildings* (1987), Cm. 179; see [1986] Conv. 361; [1991] Conv 70; (1995) 58 M.L.R. 486. Under the proposals the registration at the Land Registry of a commonhold declaration would bring into being the commonhold and a commonhold association. The commonhold association (which would be controlled by the owners of the individual properties) would own the common parts of the development and would be responsible for maintenance and repairs. The rights and obligations of the individual owners (including the principal obligation to contribute to commonhold expenditure) would be enforceable by the individual owners or by the commonhold association. In order to avoid overlap, it was suggested that commonhold should take precedence over the development scheme (except where the scheme did not involve the appointment of a manager). The result would probably have been very limited scope for development schemes and development obligations. In 1990 the Lord Chancellor's Department issued a consultation paper, seeking views on certain aspects of draft legislation to implement the commonhold proposals and suggesting that the land obligations scheme (as modified) should constitute part of that legislation: *Commonhold— a Consultation Paper* (1990), Cm. 1345; see [1991] Conv. 170; (1995) 58 M.L.R. 486. A further draft bill was published in July 1996: *Commonhold Draft Bill, Commonhold Consultation Paper* (1996); but no legislation has been introduced: see [1997] Conv. 6, 169.

In 1991 the Law Commission published a report, which addressed the question of restrictive covenants that would be in existence when the land obligations scheme was introduced: Law Com. No. 201, *Transfer of Land: Obsolete Restrictive Covenants* (1991); see [1992] Conv 2. It was recommended (i) that all restrictive covenants should cease to have effect 80 years after their creation; and (ii) that, where it is established that a covenant is not obsolete, the covenant should be replaced with an equivalent land obligation. It was suggested that the recommendations should be included in the commonhold and land obligations legislation. However, although it was recognised that a similar obsolescence problem might arise in respect of land obligations, in the absence of further consultation, the Law Commission declined to propose the extension of the recommendations to land obligations (which may be both positive and negative).

9

MORTGAGES OF LAND

A. Introduction

1. Secured and unsecured loans

Where one person lends money to another, he may be content to rely on the personal obligation of the borrower to repay the loan. If the borrower fails to repay the loan in accordance with the agreement between the parties, the lender can sue the borrower to recover what is due; and, provided that the borrower remains solvent and has assets at least equal in value to the amount of the loan (and his other liabilities), this right to sue is sufficient protection for the lender. However, if the borrower cannot repay the loan because he is insolvent the lender will become one of the general creditors of the borrower and, along with them, will recover at best only a proportion of the original loan.

The potential consequences for the lender are obvious and, especially where the amount of the loan is substantial (for example, where the loan is made to finance the purchase of land or some major business venture), a lender will normally refuse to accept the risk of exclusive reliance on the personal obligation of the borrower. Instead he will require the borrower to provide some *security* for the repayment of the loan. Such security may be personal or real.

Personal security confers on the lender the right to sue a third party if the borrower fails to repay the loan. First, the third party may enter into a contract of *guarantee* with the lender, whereby he agrees to repay the lender if the borrower fails to do so. Secondly, the third party may enter into a contract of *indemnity*, whereby he agrees to make good any loss suffered by the lender as a result of entering into the loan transaction with the borrower. Thirdly, the third party may join in the loan transaction assuming primary liability jointly with the principal borrower. However, such personal security involves similar risks as the personal obligation of the borrower: it is only effective if the third party remains solvent.

These risks can be avoided by requiring the borrower to provide *real* security, where the borrower links the obligation to repay the loan to some specific property of his. The advantage of such real security is that, even if the

borrower becomes insolvent, the lender, as a *secured* creditor, will take
priority over the general *unsecured* creditors of the borrower and can demand
that the specific property be sold and that the loan be repaid from the
proceeds of sale.

Personal security is not considered further in this chapter.

2. Real security: mortgages and charges over land

Real security takes various forms but this chapter deals exclusively with
mortgages and charges; moreover, mortgages and charges can be created over
most types of property but this chapter deals almost exclusively with
mortgages and charges over land.

A mortgage of land may be defined as a conveyance or transfer of land
made to secure the future repayment of a loan or the discharge of some other
obligation. The legal machinery of a mortgage has never reflected the real
purpose of the transaction; the mortgage transaction was described by
Maitland as "one long suppressio veri and suggestio falsi": *Equity* (1936),
p. 182. It involves the transfer of an interest in land by the borrower to the
lender, but the transfer is made subject to a provision for redemption, that is,
a provision that, on repayment of the loan or discharge of the obligation, the
transfer becomes void or the interest is retransferred to the borrower. A
charge more closely reflects the nature and purpose of the transaction. It does
not involve the transfer of any property but merely identifies specific property
of the borrower and confers on the lender certain rights over that property in
order to secure repayment of the loan or discharge of the obligation: *London
County and Westminster Bank Ltd v. Tompkins* [1918] 1 K.B. 515, 528 *per*
Scrutton L.J.; *Weg Motors Ltd v. Hales* [1962] Ch. 49, 74 *per* Lord Evershed
M.R., 77 *per* Donovan L.J. In the present context a charge can be regarded,
for most practical purposes, as a type of mortgage; and unless a distinction is
expressly made, the following discussion applies to both mortgages and
charges.

3. Terminology

As a matter of terminology, the borrower is the mortgagor and the lender is
the mortgagee; and, contrary to common usage, it is the mortgagor who
grants the mortgage to the mortgagee: the mortgagor receives the mortgage
loan.

4. Development of the law relating to mortgages and charges

4.1 *Common law*

In order to understand some of the present concerns of the law relating to
mortgages of land, it is necessary to consider briefly the principles of the
earlier law. Prior to 1926, if the fee simple owner of land wished to mortgage
his land to another as security for the repayment of a loan, it was necessary to
convey the fee simple to the lender. The transaction was distinguished from a

conveyance on sale by including in the conveyance a provision for redemption, stipulating that on a certain date (the legal or contractual date for redemption) the mortgagor would repay the loan to the mortgagee and the mortgagee would reconvey the property to the mortgagor. Similarly, if the owner of a leasehold interest in land wished to mortgage his interest, it was originally necessary to assign the residue of the term to the mortgagee, subject to a provision for reassignment to the mortgagor on repayment of the loan.

Notwithstanding that this form and procedure did not accurately reflect the true nature of the transaction, the common law took its characteristically uncompromising attitude to the form of the mortgage transaction. First, since the mortgagee had acquired the fee simple in the property, he was entitled to enter into possession and to take the profits from the land in satisfaction of the interest due on the loan; and, even if the profits exceeded the interest payable, the mortgagee was under no obligation to account to the mortgagor for the surplus. Secondly, the common law regarded the date fixed for redemption as of the essence of the transaction: thus, the mortgagor was entitled to a reconveyance of the property if, *but only if*, the loan was repaid on that date. If the mortgagor failed to repay on the specified date, the common law regarded the right to redeem as extinguished; and, notwithstanding that the value of the property might far exceed the amount of the outstanding loan, the mortgagee was entitled to retain the property unencumbered by any interest of the mortgagor. Moreover, to compound the position of the borrower still further, the common law considered that the loan itself remained outstanding: *Kreglinger v. New Patagonia Meat and Cold Storage Co. Ltd* [1914] A.C. 25, 35 *per* Viscount Haldane L.C.

4.2 *Equity*

From the seventeenth century onwards, equity began to review the law relating to mortgages. Equity insisted on looking to the substance of the transaction rather than its form. Since the transaction was designed merely as a means of providing security for the repayment of a loan, it followed that the mortgagee should be afforded only those rights over the property that were necessary for the purpose of maintaining and protecting that security. Equity therefore intervened to modify the common law where it conferred additional rights on the mortgagee that were not necessary for that purpose. First, the right of the mortgagee to go into possession of the mortgaged property and to retain all the profits derived from the land clearly provided an advantage for the mortgagee unconnected with the purpose of the mortgage transaction. Equity therefore required the mortgagee who had taken possession to account to the mortgagor for the difference between the interest due on the loan and the full profits that could have been derived from the mortgaged property. As a consequence, it was usually no longer advantageous for the mortgagee to take possession of the mortgaged property; and, notwithstanding the entitlement of the mortgagee (see *infra*, pp. 824, 911 *et seq.*), it became the practice for the mortgagor to be permitted, formally or informally, to retain possession. Secondly, equity adopted the same approach to the right to redeem. It insisted that, even though the legal or contractual date for redemption had passed, the mortgagor should be permitted, on (late) repayment of the loan, to redeem the mortgage and to recover his property. Since the land was only conveyed to the mortgagee as security for repayment of the loan, provided that the loan was repaid (together with interest and costs), it would usually be unfair to deny redemption to the mortgagor. Thus equity conferred on the mortgagor an equitable right to redeem, which replaced the legal right after the contractual date for redemption, when the latter was lost.

Clearly some limit had to be imposed on the equitable right to redeem; otherwise the mortgage would not fulfil its purpose because the mortgagee would be unable to enforce the security and recover the loan. Equity therefore developed the decree of foreclosure, whereby the court declared that all the rights of the mortgagor, including the equitable right to redeem, were extinguished, leaving the mortgagee as absolute owner of the mortgaged land; but equity also developed certain safeguards against unfair applications for foreclosure. Foreclosure is considered *infra*, p. 891.

The equitable right to redeem should be distinguished from the so-called equity of redemption: *Kreglinger v. New Patagonia Meat and Cold Storage Co. Ltd* [1914] A.C. 25, 48 *per* Lord Parker. The equity of redemption denotes the totality of the equitable rights of the mortgagor in the mortgaged land; it is an equitable proprietory interest which comes into existence as soon as the mortgage is created: *Casborne v. Scarfe* (1738) 1 Atk. 603, 605 *per* Lord Hardwicke; *Re Sir Thomas Spencer Wells* [1933] Ch. 29, 52 *per* Lawrence L.J.

As a consequence of the intervention of equity the legal date for redemption no longer has any direct significance. It is normally fixed at six months after the creation of the mortgage but without any intention of either party that the loan should be repaid on that date. However, the date has indirect significance: that is when the powers of foreclosure and sale of the mortgagee arise: see *infra*, pp. 891, 894.

B. CREATION OF MORTGAGES

1. Legal and equitable mortgages and charges

Legal mortgages, which confer a legal interest on the mortgagee, may only be created where the property to be mortgaged is a legal interest, which in practice means a legal fee simple or a legal term of years. Equitable mortgages, which confer an equitable interest on the mortgagee, may be created where the property to be mortgaged is a legal interest; but the mortgage is necessarily equitable where the property to be mortgaged is an equitable interest.

2. Legal mortgages and charges

2.1 *Unregistered land*
It has been seen that prior to 1926 a legal mortgage of a fee simple was created by a conveyance of the fee simple subject to a provision for

redemption. A legal mortgage of a term of years could be created either by assignment of the complete term or by creating a sub-lease (normally for the term less a few days), the conveyance again being subject to a provision for redemption.

Consistent with the policy of the 1925 legislation, that the legal estate in land should remain in the person who effectively owns that land, the Law of Property Act 1925 provides that legal mortgages can no longer be created by a conveyance of the entire interest, but only by the grant of a derivative lease or the creation of a charge. An exhaustive statement of the post-1925 methods of creating legal mortgages and charges over unregistered land is provided in sections 85–87.

Law of Property Act 1925, ss.85–87

Mode of mortgaging freeholds

85.—(1) A mortgage of an estate in fee simple shall only be capable of being effected at law either by a demise for a term of years absolute, subject to a provision for cesser on redemption, or by a charge by deed expressed to be by way of legal mortgage:

Provided that the first mortgagee shall have the same right to the possession of documents as if his security included the fee simple.

(2) Any purported conveyance of an estate in fee simple by way of mortgage made after the commencement of this Act shall (to the extent of the estate of the mortgagor) operate as a demise of the land to the mortgagee for a term of years absolute, without impeachment for waste, but subject to cesser on redemption, in manner following, namely—

(a) A first or only mortgagee shall take a term of three thousand years from the date of the mortgage:

(b) A second or subsequent mortgagee shall take a term (commencing from the date of the mortgage) one day longer than the term vested in the first or other mortgagee whose security ranks immediately before that of such second or subsequent mortgagee:

and, in this subsection, any such purported conveyance as aforesaid includes an absolute conveyance with a deed of defeasance and any other assurance which, but for this subsection, would operate in effect to vest the fee simple in a mortgagee subject to redemption.

Mode of mortgaging leaseholds

86.—(1) A mortgage of a term of years absolute shall only be capable of being effected at law either by subdemise for a term of years absolute, less by one day at least than the term vested in the mortgagor, and subject to a provision for cesser on redemption, or by a charge by deed expressed to be by way of legal mortgage; and where a licence to subdemise by way of mortgage is required, such licence shall not be unreasonably refused:

Provided that a first mortgagee shall have the same right to the possession of documents as if his security had been effected by assignment.

(2) Any purported assignment of a term of years absolute by way of mortgage made after the commencement of this Act shall (to the extent of the estate of the mortgagor) operate as a subdemise of the leasehold land to the mortgagee for a term of years absolute but subject to cesser on redemption, in manner following, namely—

(a) The term to be taken by a first or only mortgagee shall be 10 days less than the term expressed to be assigned:

(b) The term to be taken by a second or subsequent mortgagee shall be one day longer than the term vested in the first or other mortgagee whose security ranks immediately before that of the second or subsequent mortgagee, if the length of the last mentioned term permits, and in any case for a term less by one day at least than the term expressed to be assigned:

and, in this subsection, any such purported assignment as aforesaid includes an absolute assignment with a deed of defeasance and any other assurance which, but for this subsection, would operate in effect to vest the term of the mortgagor in a mortgagee subject to redemption.

Charges by way of legal mortgage

87.—(1) Where a legal mortgage of land is created by a charge by deed expressed to be by way of legal mortgage, the mortgagee shall have the same protection, powers and remedies (including the right to take proceedings to obtain possession from the occupiers and the persons in receipt of rents and profits, or any of them) as if—

(a) where the mortgage is a mortgage of an estate in fee simple, a mortgage term for three thousand years without impeachment of waste had been thereby created in favour of the mortgagee; and

(b) where the mortgage is a mortgage of a term of years absolute, a sub-term less by one day than the term vested in the mortgagor had been thereby created in favour of the mortgagee.

NOTES:

1. Legal mortgages, whether mortgages by (sub-)demise or charges by way of legal mortgage, are within the definition of "conveyance": see Law of Property Act 1925, s.205(1)(ii); they must therefore be created by deed: *ibid.* s.52(1); Law of Property (Miscellaneous Provisions) Act 1989, s.1.

2. The overall effect of sections 85–87 is that any transaction that is in substance a mortgage takes effect in accordance with the stated policy. In *Grangeside Properties Ltd v. Collingwood Securities Ltd* [1964] 1 W.L.R. 139 the plaintiffs granted a 21-year lease to Eastern Trades Ltd, who assigned the entire term to the defendants to secure the repayment of a loan. When the plaintiffs subsequently sought to forfeit the lease, the defendants were held to be entitled to claim relief against forfeiture under section 146(4) of the Law of Property Act 1925. Although there had been a purported assignment of the entire term, the parties had intended that the transaction should provide security for the repayment of the loan. It followed that the transaction was in substance a mortgage; that it took effect as a sub-lease, pursuant to section 86(2); and that, when the lease was forfeited, the defendants as sub-lessees were entitled to claim relief under section 146(4). Harman L.J. stated (at 142–143):

Section 86(2) cannot have intended to alter the ancient law, which had always been, that Chancery would treat as a mortgage that which was intended to be a conveyance by way of security between A and B. Once a mortgage, always a mortgage and nothing but a mortgage, has been a principle for centuries. "By way of mortgage" must mean that which is in fact intended as a mortgage and it was that which the complainant in Chancery swore in his bill when he asked for an injunction to restrain the landlord from treating the proviso for redemption as exhausted at the end of the six months for which it was usually expressed to exist. It could not be that section 86(2) is intended to sweep away the view of the law which had always been that if you proved the thing was a mortgage, equity would allow you to have your equity of redemption to redeem on payment of the mortgage money, interest and costs. In my view this document did operate, although expressed as an absolute assignment, by way of sub-demise. I agree that the form of the document, the secrecy in which it was veiled, and various other matters, did entitle the landlords in the first instance to regard it with some suspicion, but having seen it and finding that there was a genuine loan and finding that there was a deposit of the title deeds, they had no right to continue their suspicions....

For comment, see (1964) 28 Conv. 178, 180.

3. *Mortgages by (sub-)demise*

(1) Since a mortgage by demise normally takes the form of a 3,000-year lease in favour of the mortgagee, leaving the mortgagor with the somewhat remote freehold reversion, it may be questioned whether this form of mortgage reflects the policy of the 1925 legislation. However, it must be remembered that the mortgagor owns the equity of redemption, which entitles him to repay the loan and thereby to terminate the lease of the mortgagee.

(2) The provision for cesser on redemption is strictly unnecessary since, on repayment of the loan, the term of years becomes a satisfied term and ceases automatically: Law of Property Act 1925, ss.5, 116. However, a memorandum of discharge and receipt for the repayment of the loan are normally endorsed on the mortgage deed: *ibid.*, s.115(1).

(3) Since the mortgagor retains the fee simple or the leasehold reversion in the mortgaged property, he is in a position to create further *legal* mortgages, by granting to each successive mortgagee a term of years one day longer than the term of the previous mortgage.

4. *Charges by deed expressed to be by way of legal mortgage*

(1) The charge has certain advantages over the mortgage by demise: (i) it is simpler in form: see Law of Property Act 1925, Sched. 5; (ii) it permits the mortgaging of freehold and leasehold interests in a unified transaction; (iii) in relation to mortgages of leasehold interests, it avoids the potential difficulty that an ordinary mortgage by way of sub-lease may constitute a breach of a covenant in the lease against sub-letting: *Grand Junction Co. Ltd v. Bates* [1954] 2 Q.B. 160, 168 *per* Upjohn J. For these reasons the legal charge has become the normal form of mortgage.

(2) The assimilation of the position of the legal chargee with that of the legal mortgagee is illustrated by *Grand Junction Co. Ltd v. Bates* [1954] 2 Q.B. 160. The second defendant assigned a lease to the first defendant, who created a charge by way of legal mortgage in favour of the second defendant in order to secure the repayment of a loan. When the plaintiff landlords subsequently sought to forfeit the lease, the second defendant was held to be entitled to claim relief against forfeiture under section 146(4) of the Law of Property Act 1925. Upjohn J. stated (at 166–169):

It is conceded that if the mortgage had been by way of sub-demise, the [second defendant] would have fallen fairly and squarely within the ambit of subsection (4).

But he is not a mortgagee by sub-demise; he is a mortgagee by way of legal charge. A mortgage by way of legal charge was a new method of mortgaging property, introduced by sections 85 and 86 of the Law of Property Act 1925....

[I]t was introduced as a conveyancing device ... with a view to simplifying conveyancing, and it would be a pity to introduce subtle differences between one way of creating a charge and another way of creating a charge unless the words of the Act so required....

Approaching section 87(1) in that spirit, I find that the mortgagee is to have the same "protection, powers and remedies" as though he had a sub-demise. A lessee by sub-demise undoubtedly has the right to protect his mortgage, where it is of a term of years, by applying for relief under section 146. That is a most important right possessed by a mortgagee by sub-demise, for it may be the only way of saving his security in the hands of some insolvent lessee. The effect of section 87 is, in my judgment, to give the mortgagee by way of legal charge this same right, because he has the same protection, as if he were an underlessee. I see no ground for confining section 87 to protection, powers and remedies merely as between the mortgagor and the mortgagee; it extends to protection, powers and remedies against all persons—indeed, it is plain that the section includes powers against occupiers and other persons in respect of rents and profits, and I think that the chargee by way of legal mortgage is entitled to say: "I am to be put in the same position as if I had a charge by way of sub-demise, and in that right, therefore, I can claim as an underlessee for the purposes of section 146." The [second defendant] is, in my judgment, therefore entitled to make a claim under section 146.

For comment see (1954) 18 Conv. 418. See also *Regent Oil Co. Ltd v. J.A. Gregory (Hatch End) Ltd* [1966] Ch. 402, noted at (1966) 30 Conv. 58; and see Miller (1966) 30 Conv. 30, 36 *et seq*.

5. As noted above, as a concept the charge is clearly a more accurate reflection of the security transaction; and the assimilation of the rights of a chargee to those of a mortgagee by demise can be seen as an interim compromise. The Law Commission has recommended that mortgages by demise should be abolished and that the rights of a chargee should be defined by statute and without reference to the rights of a lessee: Law Com. No. 204, *Transfer of Land: Land Mortgages* (1991), paras 2.14, 2.18.

2.2 Registered land

Registered land may be mortgaged in the same way as if it were unregistered land: Land Registration Act 1925, s.106(1); but such mortgages take effect only in equity as minor interests: *ibid.* s.106(2).

The only form of *legal* mortgage of registered land is a registered charge, which, unless created by (sub-)demise, takes effect as a charge by way of legal mortgage: *ibid.* s.27(1); and, subject to any entry on the register to the contrary, it confers on the registered chargee all the powers of a legal mortgagee: *ibid.* s.34(1). A registered charge must be created by deed: *ibid.* s.25; but the charge does not constitute a legal interest in the land until it is completed by entry in the charges register of the registered title of the land: *ibid.* ss.26(1), 106(2); see *Grace Rymer Investments Ltd v. Waite* [1958] Ch. 831; *E.S. Schwab and Co. Ltd v. McCarthy* (1976) 31 P. & C.R. 196, 201 *per* Oliver J., 212 *per* Sir John Pennycuick; and see *Barclays Bank plc v. Zaroovabli* [1997] Ch. 321, *ante*, p. 232, *infra*, p. 890. If the charge is not completed by entry on the register, the charge constitutes a minor interest which may be protected by notice or caution: Land Registration Act 1925, s.106(3).

Independently of its recommendations for the comprehensive reform of the law relating to mortgages, the Law Commission has provisionally recommended that it should no longer be possible to create a mortgage of registered land by (sub-)demise and that registered charges should always take effect as charges by way of legal mortgage: Law Com. No. 254, *Land Registration for the Twenty-First Century* (1998), paras 9.4–9.5.

3. Equitable mortgages and charges

3.1 *Equitable mortgages*
Equitable mortgages confer an equitable interest only on the mortgagee, either because the interest to be mortgaged is equitable, so that any mortgage of that interest is necessarily equitable; or because a purported legal mortgage is informal or defective, so that, although the transaction is ineffective to create a legal mortgage, it is effective to create an equitable mortgage.

3.1.1 *Mortgages of equitable interests*   The first type of equitable mortgage is self-explanatory and most commonly arises in the case of a mortgage of an interest under a trust. The method of creation of such a mortgage was unaffected by the 1925 legislation and continues to take the form of an assignment of the entire equitable interest, subject to a provision for reassignment on repayment of the loan. The assignment constitutes a disposition of a subsisting equitable interest in land and must therefore comply with the formal requirements of section 53(1)(c) of the Law of Property Act 1925.

3.1.2 *Informal or defective legal mortgages*   The second type of equitable mortgage could traditionally arise in a variety of circumstances; but in each case the position has been held to be affected by section 2 of the Law of Property (Miscellaneous Provisions) Act 1989: see *United Bank of Kuwait plc v. Sahib* [1997] Ch. 107.

First, an equitable mortgage can arise where there is a contract to create a legal mortgage or a purported but ineffective legal mortgage. Where the parties do not proceed beyond the contract stage or where they fail to comply with the necessary formalities for the creation of a legal mortgage, under the doctrine in *Walsh v. Lonsdale* the contract or the informal mortgage may be regarded by equity as creating an equitable mortgage. However, the contract or informal mortgage must satisfy the requirements of section 2 for a valid contract and there must be no obstacle to the grant of a decree of specific performance of the (deemed) contract: see *ante*, pp. 61, 389.

Secondly, an equitable mortgage can arise where the mortgagor purports to create a legal mortgage but he does not have a legal estate or he has no power to mortgage the legal estate. This is most likely to occur where one of two legal joint tenants purports to create a legal mortgage of the property by claiming to be solely entitled or by forging, or otherwise obtaining by improper means, the signature of the other joint tenant. In *Thames Guaranty Ltd v. Campbell* [1985] Q.B. 210 this principle, which was described by the Court of Appeal as the "doctrine of partial performance", was expressed in these terms (at 235):

It is a well established principle of equity that where, in the course of concluding a contract, a person has represented that he can grant a certain property, or is entitled to a certain interest in that property, and it later appears that there is a deficiency in his title or interest, the other party can obtain an order compelling him to grant what he has got. . . .

Thus the purported mortgage of the legal estate is analysed as a contract to mortgage the equitable interest of the mortgagor; and such a contract is subject to the requirements of section 2: *United Bank of Kuwait plc v. Sahib* [1997] Ch. 107, 121–123 *per* Chadwick J.

3.1.3 *Deposit of title deeds*   Perhaps most controversially, it appears that section 2 has removed the previously acknowledged method of creating an equitable mortgage by the deposit of the title deeds. In *United Bank of Kuwait plc v. Sahib, supra*, Chadwick J. stated (at 123–127):

A convenient statement of the rule is to be found in *Coote on Mortgages*, 9th ed., (1927), vol. 1, p. 86, in a passage cited by the Court of Appeal in *Thames Guaranty Ltd v. Campbell* [1985] Q.B. 210, 232–233:

"A deposit of title deeds by the owner of freeholds or leaseholds with his creditor for the purpose of securing either a debt antecedently due, or a sum of money advanced at the time of the deposit, operates as an equitable mortgage or charge, by virtue of which the depositee acquires, not merely the right of holding the deeds until the debt is paid, but also an equitable interest in the land itself. A mere delivery of the deeds will have this operation without any express agreement, whether in writing or oral, as to the conditions or purpose of the delivery, as the court would infer the intent and agreement to create a security from the relation of debtor and creditor subsisting between the parties, unless the contrary were shown; and the delivery would be sufficient part performance of such agreement to take the case out of [section 40 of the Law of Property Act 1925]."

It is, I think, important to keep in mind that (as is made clear in the passage just cited) it is not the mere deposit of title deeds which gave rise to an equitable mortgage or charge; it was necessary to establish that the deeds were deposited for the purpose of securing an obligation. In most cases there would be evidence of something said, written or done from which that purpose could be established and the obligation identified. But in some cases there would be no evidence other than that the depositor and the depositee were, or were about to become, debtor and creditor. In those cases the court could infer the purpose and identify the obligation from that fact alone. But the basis of the rule, as explained in *Coote on Mortgages*, was that the equitable charge arose because the court was satisfied from whatever evidence there was that the parties had made an agreement (expressly or by implication) that the debtor should grant security for an obligation which the court could identify, that the agreement was (or, but for the provisions of section 40 of the Law of Property Act 1925, would have been) specifically enforceable, and that the deposit of the title deeds was treated as an act of part performance sufficient to take the case out of section 40 and so enable the agreement to be enforced notwithstanding the absence of any memorandum in writing capable of satisfying subsection (1) of that section. In other words, the equitable charge which arose upon the deposit of title deeds was contract-based.

If this is a correct analysis of the basis of the rule that a deposit of title deeds for the purpose of securing a debt operated, without more, as an equitable mortgage or charge, then it is difficult to see how the rule can have survived section 2 of the Act of 1989. The conclusion that it did not survive is expressed by Professor Julian Farrand Q.C., the editor of *Emmet on Title*, 19th ed., para. 25.116. The contrary view, advanced arguendo, is that a charge created by the deposit of title deeds is more properly to be regarded as a sui generis equitable charge rather than an agreement to create a charge; so that its validity is unaffected by the Act of 1989. As Professor Farrand points out:

"The basis of the argument is that deposit of title documents has long been regarded as creating a security valid and enforceable *by the mortgagee*: this could not be the case if enforcement in the absence of writing satisfying section 40 of the Law of Property 1925 depended on the doctrine of part performance, because of the general principle that the person seeking to enforce an agreement must rely on *his own* part performance of it, not that of the other party."

Mr Pymont urged me to accept the view set out, arguendo, in that passage. He took me back to the decision of Lord Thurlow L.C. in *Russel v. Russel* (1783) 1 Bro.C.C. 269, from which the rule is said to have emerged. The reporter's note (which contains the only passage from which I can derive assistance) records, at p. 270:

"The same point has since been determined in the cases of *Featherstone v. Fenwick*, May 1784, and *Hurford v. Carpenter*, 17 and 18 April 1785, where Lord Thurlow held that the deposit of deeds entitled the holder to have a mortgage, and to have his lien effectuated; although there was no special agreement to assign; the deposit affords a presumption that such was the intent."

That note seems to reflect an understanding that the rule is contract-based; the deposit provides the evidence from which an agreement could be presumed or inferred.

A more explicit passage, in the judgment of Kenyon M.R. in *Edge v. Worthington* (1786) 1 Cox 211, 212 makes the position clear:

"It is to be lamented perhaps that the strict line of the statute of frauds and perjuries has been ever departed from, but it is now too late to alter the decisions in that respect. People have conducted themselves on the faith of the exceptions which have been made to the statute; and amongst others, that of depositing deeds is an excepted case. The cases have decided, that the court is to infer an agreement from the deposit of the deeds, and that the party so depositing ought to go on to execute such agreement; and that such a deposit constitutes a lien on the property.... The circumstance of the deeds being deposited leaves to the court to infer the agreement, or to admit parol evidence of the actual agreement. Here the parol evidence proves the actual agreement."

Kenyon M.R.'s view, as expressed in that passage, was that the deposit of the deeds was a fact which served two purposes: (i) it took the case out of the Statute of Frauds 1677 (29 Car. 2, c. 3) and (ii) it provided a basis from which (taken with such other evidence as there might be, including parol evidence) the existence of an agreement to create security could be inferred.

By 1803 Lord Eldon L.C., who had no enthusiasm for the rule, regarded it as settled that "the fact of the adverse possession of the deeds in the person claiming the lien, and out of the other, was a fact, that entitled the court to give an interest": see *Ex parte Coming* (1803), 9 Ves. 115, 117. The point came before Lord Eldon L.C. again in *Ex parte Langston* (1810) 17 Ves. 227. He said, at pp. 230–231:

"It has long been settled, that a mere deposit of title deeds upon an advance of money, without a word passing, gives an equitable lien (*Ex parte Mountfort* (1808) 14 Ves. 606, and the reference in the note, *Ex parte Coming* (1803), 9 Ves. 115, 117); and, as the court would infer from that deposit, that the money, then advanced, should be charged, as if there was a written agreement, there is no doubt, that, if it was made out by oath uncontradicted, additional advances would also be charged."

That passage suggests that Lord Eldon L.C. also treated the rule as contract-based: there was to be a charge as if there had been a written agreement which satisfied the Statute of Frauds 1677.

Some 40 years on, Kindersley V.-C. again treated the rule as contract-based when giving judgment in *Pryce v. Bury* (1853) 2 Drew. 41. He said, at pp. 42–43:

"The common rule of this court as to an equitable mortgage by deposit, is this: by the deposit, the mortgagor contracts that his interest shall be liable to the debt, and that he will make such conveyance or assurance as may be necessary to vest his interest in the mortgagee. He does not contract that he will make a perfect title, but he does bind himself to do all that is necessary to have the effect of vesting in the mortgagee such interest as he, the mortgagor, has."

Lord Selborne L.C. was also of the view that the rule was contract-based. In *Dixon v. Muckleston* (1872) L.R. 8 Ch.App. 115, 162 he said:

"the mere possession of deeds without evidence of the contract upon which the possession originated, or at least of the manner in which that possession originated, so that a contract may be inferred, will not be enough to create an equitable security."

Ten years later, in *Maddison v. Alderson* (1883) 8 App.Cas 467, in the course of an extensive examination of the law relating to part performance, Lord Selborne L.C. explained, at p. 480, that "the law of equitable mortgage by deposit of title deeds depends upon the same principles".

Much more recently, the rule was considered by Templeman J. in *In re Wallis & Simmonds (Builders) Ltd* [1974] 1 W.L.R. 391. He cited, with apparent approval, the passage from *Coote on Mortgages* which I have set out above, and a similar statement in *Halsbury's Laws of England*, 3rd ed., vol. 27 (1959), p. 168, and now 4th ed., vol. 32 (1980), para. 429. The statement in *Halsbury*, 4th ed.

"The deposit is a fact which admits evidence of an intention to create a charge which would otherwise be inadmissible, and raises a presumption of charge which throws upon the debtor the burden of rebutting it"

seems to me to restate the position in terms which are almost indistinguishable from those used by Kenyon M.R. in *Edge v. Worthington* (1786), 1 Cox 211 over 200 years ago. Templeman J. clearly thought that that was the correct approach. He said [1974] 1 W.L.R. 391, 399:

"If parties wish to do so, it is possible to make sure that a deposit of title deeds does not create a charge on the land. Of course, all things are possible, but having regard to the presumption which has prevailed since 30 years before Lord Eldon L.C.'s protest [in *Ex parte Whitbread* (1812) 19 Ves. 209], I begin looking at this case with a sceptical eye on the possibility being fulfilled."

It is presumption which, in the absence of other evidence, enables the court to infer the agreement upon which the equitable mortgage or charge is based.

Whether or not the enforcement of the agreement which is to be inferred or presumed from the deposit of title deeds was properly to be regarded as an example of the operation of the doctrine of part performance, as Lord Selborne L.C. suggested in

Maddison v. Alderson (1883), 8 App.Cas. 467, or as a sui generis exception to the Statute of Frauds 1677 which was outside the proper scope of that doctrine—in that the act of part performance relied upon was not the act of the mortgagee who was seeking to enforce the agreement—there can, in my view, be no doubt that the courts have, consistently, treated the rule that a deposit of title deeds for the purpose of securing a debt operates, without more, as an equitable mortgage or charge as contract-based, and have regarded the deposit as a fact which enabled the contract to be enforced notwithstanding the absence of evidence sufficient to satisfy the Statute of Frauds. It is impossible to distinguish those cases, of which *Ex parte Langston* (1810), 17 Ves. 227 is an example, in which the court, having inferred from the fact of the deposit an intention to create security, let in oral evidence to identify the scope of the obligation which was to be secured from cases in which there was no evidence beyond the fact of the deposit. In all those cases, the court was concerned to establish, by presumption, inference or evidence, what the parties intended, and then to enforce their common intention as an agreement.

It follows that I find no support in the decided cases for the view—put forward, arguendo, by Professor Farrand in *Emmet on Title* para. 25.116—that a charge created by deposit of title deeds is properly to be regarded as something distinct from an equitable charge arising from agreement. I think that the editor was correct when, immediately after the passage in which the basis for that view was set out (cited earlier in this judgment), he observed: "in the absence of direct authority in support of this argument, lenders cannot [now] safely assume that any security will be created by mere deposit of title deeds". That, in my view, is the effect of section 2 of the Act of 1989.

Given that the Act of 1989 was intended to give effect to the recommendations in the Law Commission Report (Law Com. No. 164) I do not find that conclusion altogether surprising. The recommendation that contracts relating to land should be incorporated in a signed document which contained all the terms was, clearly, intended to promote certainty. There is no reason why certainty should be any less desirable in relation to arrangements for security over land than in relation to any other arrangements in respect of land. The present case itself illustrates the need to be able to identify the obligation which is to be secured. I do not find it surprising that Parliament decided to enact legislation which would be likely to have the effect of avoiding disputes on oral evidence as to the obligation which the parties intended to secure.

NOTES:

1. Chadwick J. further held (at 127–129) (i) that an equitable charge could not be created unless there was an effective deposit of title deeds and there could be no effective deposit by one joint tenant without the consent of the other joint tenant; and (ii) that the creation of an equitable charge by a method that is not contract-based would have to satisfy the formal requirements of section 53(1)(c) of the Law of Property Act 1925.

2. For comment, see [1994] Conv. 465; [1995] C.L.J. 249.

3. The Court of Appeal expressly endorsed the reasoning of Chadwick J. and rejected a further series of arguments. Peter Gibson L.J. stated (at 137–141):

Mr Pymont made seven submissions as to why section 2 of the Act of 1989 did not apply to a deposit of title deeds.

(1) He submitted that there is nothing in the Act of 1989 which expressly or by necessary implication repeals the provisions of the Act of 1925 and later legislation recognising and extending the scope of a security by deposit of title deeds. He relied on four statutory provisions to the following effect: (a) section 13 of the Law of Property Act 1925, which provides that that Act is not to affect prejudicially the right or interest

of any person arising out of or consequent on the possession by him of any document relating to a legal estate in land; (b) section 97 of that Act relating to unregistered land which excepts from the operation of the section, governing the priority of legal and equitable mortgages, a mortgage protected by the deposit of documents relating to the legal estate affected; (c) section 66 of the Land Registration Act 1925, which allows the proprietor of any registered land to create a lien on the registered land by deposit of the land certificate, such lien to be equivalent to a lien created in the case of unregistered land by the deposit by a legal and beneficial owner of the registered estate of the documents of title; and (d) section 2(4) of the Land Charges Act 1972, which excepts from general equitable charges requiring registration under Class C(iii) any equitable charge secured by a deposit of documents relating to the legal estate affected.

Mr Pymont submitted that it was significant that none of those provisions was referred to in the Act of 1989 as having been repealed or otherwise affected by section 2. He drew attention to the fact that some commentators have concluded from this that section 2 was not intended to repeal the rule relating to the creation of security by deposit of title deeds: see *Snell's Equity*, 29th ed. (1990), p. 445, *Cheshire and Burn's Modern Law of Real Property*, 15th ed. (1994), p. 679 and Bently and Coughlan, "Informal dealings with land after section 2" (1990) 10 L.S. 325, 341.

I differ with reluctance from such distinguished property lawyers, but I am not persuaded that their views on this point are correct. The presence of section 13 in the Law of Property Act 1925, as Mr Munby for U.B.K. submitted, would appear to indicate that, without it, the Act, with its requirements of formalities for dispositions of interests in land, might have affected prejudicially the right or interest of a person with whom title deeds had been deposited. Significantly the Act of 1989, with its new and stricter requirements, contains no corresponding provision. Section 97 of the Act of 1925 relates not to the requirements governing the validity of a mortgage but to priorities between mortgagees. Section 66 of the Land Registration Act 1925 begs the question what lien is created by the deposit by a legal and beneficial owner of the documents of title to unregistered land. Section 2(4) of the Land Charges Act 1972 relates not to the validity of a charge, but to the way in which the deposit of the title deeds operates as a substitute for registration. In the scheme of the legislation, all mortgages must be registered unless protected by deposit of title deeds. In any event, earlier legislative references to rights or interests created by the deposit of title deeds must now be read in the light of the Act of 1989. The new formalities required by section 2 govern the validity of all dispositions of interests in land. I cannot see that the references relied on by Mr Pymont in the earlier legislation can displace what otherwise is the plain meaning and effect of section 2 on contracts in whatever form to mortgage land.

(2) Mr Pymont pointed to the fact that there is nothing in the Law Commission's report which initiated the reforms effected by the Act of 1989 to suggest that security by deposit of title deeds was intended to be affected or was even considered.

I accept that there is nothing in the report that expressly refers to the deposit of title deeds by way of security, or suggests that it created a problem that needed attention. But the intention of the Law Commission to include in its proposals contracts to grant mortgages was made plain (see paragraph 4.3 of the report), and, as a deposit of title deeds by way of security takes effect as an agreement to mortgage, in logic there is no reason why the creation of security by deposit of title deeds should have been excepted from the proposals. This is all the more likely when one considers the part played by the doctrine of part performance in the recognition by equity judges of the *Russel v. Russel* (1783) 1 Bro.C.C. 269 doctrine: see further (5) below. In any event, if the wording of section 2 is clear, as I think it is, the absence from the Law Commission's report of a reference to security by deposit of title deeds cannot alter the section's effect.

(3) Mr Pymont then reverted to section 2(4) of the Land Charges Act 1972 excepting equitable charges not secured by a deposit of documents from the requirement of registration. He said that, if a deposit of title deeds prima facie takes

effect as a contract to create a mortgage, such a security would be registrable as a Class C(iv) land charge, notwithstanding the exception from the requirement of registration as a Class C(iii) land charge, and that cannot be right.

The wording of section 2(4) of the Act of 1972 is to my mind a clear indication that, for the purposes of that Act, a deposit of title deeds gave rise to a general equitable charge which would have been registrable as a Class C(iii) land charge, but for being excepted. I accept that it was plainly not envisaged in that Act that it might also come within Class C(iv). As I have already said, it was part of the scheme of the legislation that all mortgages should be registered unless protected by deposit. It would be inconsistent with that scheme that a deposit of title deeds by way of security should be an estate contract registrable as a Class C(iv) land charge. It may be that, as Mr Munby submitted, the contract to grant a mortgage inherent in the deposit of title deeds by way of security was not considered to be a mere estate contract. But, whether or not that is right. I do not see that this statutory provision can affect the meaning of section 2 of the Act of 1989.

(4) Mr Pymont then said that the rule that a deposit of title deeds by way of security creates a mortgage is not dependent on any actual contract between the parties, though, if there is one, that contract will govern the parties' rights; if there is an actual contract, it must comply with section 2; but that does not affect the legal presumptions or inferences which arise when there is a mere deposit.

I accept that there need not be an express contract between the depositor of the title deeds and the person with whom they are deposited for an equitable mortgage to arise (subject to section 2). But I have already stated why it is clear from the authorities that the deposit is treated as rebuttable evidence of a contract to mortgage. Oral evidence is admissible to establish whether or not a deposit was intended to create a mortgage security, whether or not the original deposit was intended at the outset to be security for further advances, whether or not it was agreed subsequently that that deposit should be security for further advances and whether or not any memorandum of agreement accurately stated the terms of the contract or was complete. To allow inquiries of this sort after the Act of 1989 in order to determine whether an equitable mortgage has been created and on what terms seems to me to be wholly inconsistent with the philosophy of section 2, requiring as it does that the contract be made by a single document containing all the terms of the agreement if it is to be valid.

(5) Mr Pymont then submitted that it is well established that an act of part performance could only be relied upon if it were an act done by the person seeking to enforce the contract. He said that that requirement is not fulfilled if a plaintiff, with whom the title deeds are deposited, seeks to rely on the defendant's act of depositing the title deeds.

It is clear that the rule relating to the creation of an equitable mortgage by deposit proceeded on the footing that the act of deposit constituted a sufficient act of part performance of the presumed agreement to mortgage. I accept that that is contrary to the normal rule that an act of part performance can only be relied upon if done by the plaintiff and not the defendant. But in *Maddison v. Alderson* (1883) 8 App.Cas. 467, 480 Lord Selborne L.C. said that the law of equitable mortgage by deposit of title deeds depended upon the same principles as the cases of part performance to which he had been referring, and in each of which a valid contract was an essential feature. In *In re Beetham; Ex parte Broderick* (1886) 18 Q.B.D. 380 the Divisional Court considered whether certain facts were sufficient to establish an equitable mortgage by deposit of title deeds. Cave J., with whom Wills J. agreed, said, at pp. 382–383:

"The law on the subject ... forms a branch of the equitable doctrine of the specific performance of oral contracts relating to land based on part performance. It has been held that there is an inference from the mere deposit of title deeds that it was intended to give an interest in the land, and in that way there is something more than a mere oral contract, something in the nature of part performance, so as to take the case out of the Statute of Frauds."

Further as Smith J. pointed out in *Francis v. Francis* [1952] V.L.R. 321, 339–340, although Lord Eldon L.C. repeatedly criticised the way in which the doctrine of part performance had been applied in the case of mortgages created by deposits of title deeds, this criticism was based, not on the view that in such cases there is no act on the part of the mortgagee, but on the equivocal significance of the act of deposit. But even as early as Lord Eldon L.C.'s time the recognition by the courts of an equitable mortgage created by the mere deposit of title deeds was too settled to be challenged.

To the extent that part performance is an essential part of the rationale of the creation of an equitable mortgage by the deposit of title deeds, that too is inconsistent with the new philosophy of the Act of 1989. As the Law Commission said in its report, at paragraph 4.13:

> "Inherent in the recommendation that contracts should be made in writing is the consequence that part performance would no longer have a role to play in contracts concerning land."

(6) Mr Pymont then submitted that in other situations equity treats void dispositions, for example void leases and void mortgages, as agreements to dispose of what the disponor can dispose. He said that there was nothing in the Law Commission's report or in the problems there addressed to suggest that section 2 was intended to affect such agreements.

I have already referred to the express reference in the Law Commission's report to the intention to include in its proposals contracts to grant mortgages. In the same paragraph, paragraph 4.3, it was made clear that contracts to grant leases were also to be included. In my judgment, for the like reasons to those given in (2) above, the absence from the report of express mention of the effect of void dispositions as agreements to dispose cannot alter the effect of section 2.

(7) Mr Pymont submitted that, although equity will presume to infer an agreement from the deposit of title deeds, it does not follow that for all purposes the parties' rights are to be treated as if they lie in contract. He sought to derive support for this proposition from the remarks of Hoffmann J. in *Spiro v. Glencrown Properties Ltd.* [1991] Ch. 537, 544. There Hoffmann J. was considering how, for the purposes of the Act of 1989, an option to buy land should be characterised. He pointed out that an option was neither an offer nor a conditional contract, not having all the incidents of the standard form of either of those concepts, and said that each analogy is in the proper context a valid way of characterising the situation created by an option. He continued: "The question in this case is not whether one analogy is true and the other false, but which is appropriate to be used in the construction of section 2 ..." He concluded not that the option fell outside the scope of section 2 but that it came within it. In the present case, for the reasons already given, it seems to me clear that the deposit of title deeds takes effect as a contract to mortgage and as such falls within section 2.

For comment, see (1997) 113 L.Q.R. 533.

4. The Law Commission unequivocally stated its view that section 2 had removed this method of creating equitable mortgages, *in so far as the method was properly construed as part performance of a contract to create a mortgage*: Law Com. No. 204, *Transfer of Land: Land Mortgages* (1991), para. 2.9; but the point was not discussed in Law Com. No. 164, *Transfer of Land: Formalities for Contracts for Sale etc. of Land* (1987), which led to the 1989 Act.

5. On the other hand, it had been suggested that such arrangements should be regarded as a species of equitable charge no longer relying on a contractual analysis and thus unaffected by the 1989 Act; alternatively, that the concept of mortgages by deposit of title deeds was so well-established that, irrespective of

their true analysis, such mortgages should continue to be recognised as valid: see Howell [1990] Conv. 441; Hill [1990] 106 L.Q.R. 396; Bently and Coughlan (1990) 10 *Legal Studies* 325, 341–343; Adams [1991] Conv. 12; Baughen [1992] Conv. 330.

6. Under section 66 of the Land Registration Act 1925, provision is made for the creation of an equitable lien by deposit of the land certificate. Since this is the registered land equivalent of the creation of an equitable mortgage by the mere deposit of title deeds, which has become obsolete following the decision in *United Bank of Kuwait plc v. Sahib*, the Law Commission has provisionally recommended that section 66 should be repealed: Law Com. No. 254, *Land Registration in the Twenty-First Century* (1998), paras 9.8–9.11. The provisions in the Land Registration Rules 1925 for notice of such deposit to be given to the Land Registry have already been revoked.

3.2 *Equitable charges*

Equitable charges are the most informal form of equitable security. No formalities are necessary for their creation; all that is required is that the parties demonstrate an intention that certain property is to provide security for the repayment of a loan. In *Swiss Bank Corp. v. Lloyds Bank Ltd* [1982] A.C. 584 Buckley L.J. stated (at 595):

An equitable charge which is not an equitable mortgage is said to be created when property is expressly or constructively made liable, or specifically appropriated, to the discharge of a debt or some other obligation, and confers on the chargee a right of realisation by judicial process, that is to say, by the appointment of a receiver or an order for sale.

The practical distinction between equitable mortgages and equitable charges is found in the wider range of remedies available to the equitable mortgagee than to the equitable chargee: see *infra*, p. 952.

C. Rights and Duties of the Parties During the Continuance of the Mortgage

The rights and duties of the mortgagor and mortgagee during the continuance of the mortgage are outlined below, following the scheme of Law Com. No. 204, *Transfer of Land: Land Mortgages* (1991), paras 6.1 *et seq*. Some of the rights and duties mentioned are considered in greater detail in the later sections of this chapter on the protection of the mortgagor and the remedies of the mortgagee.

1. Documents of title

A first mortgagee of a legal estate in unregistered land is entitled to possession of the title deeds relating to the mortgaged land: Law of Property Act 1925, ss.85(1), 86(1), 87(1); but the mortgagor has the right to inspect the deeds and to make copies: *ibid.* s.96(1). When the mortgagor redeems the mortgage, he is entitled to recover the deeds, unless the mortgagee has notice of a subsequent mortgage, in which case the mortgagee must deliver the deeds to the mortgagee next in order of priority of whom the mortgagee has notice.

In the context of registered land, when a legal charge is registered, the land certificate must be deposited at the Land Registry; and it will be retained by the Land Registry until the charge is cancelled: Land Registration Act 1925, s.65. The chargee is issued with a charge certificate: *ibid.* s.63.

2. Insurance

The mortgagee is entitled to insure the mortgaged land and to charge the premiums to the mortgagor by adding them to the mortgage loan: Law of Property Act 1925, s.101(1)(ii). However, the statutory power is subject to various restrictions: *ibid.* s.108; and there is some uncertainty as to the application of any proceeds: see Law Commission Working Paper No. 99, *Transfer of Land: Land Mortgages* (1986), para. 3.28. Consequently, the statutory provisions are normally supplemented by extensive express provisions: see Law Com. No. 204, *Transfer of Land: Land Mortgages* (1991), para. 6.9.

3. Repairs

Since there are no statutory provisions relating to repairs, a mortgage deed normally includes express provisions dealing with the obligations of the mortgage in respect of the repair and condition of the mortgaged property: Law Com. No. 204, *Transfer of Land: Land Mortgages* (1991), para. 6.13.

4. Possession

One of the consequences of the machinery of legal mortgages is that the mortgagee is entitled to possession of the mortgaged land. However, since the right to possession is almost invariably exercised only as a (preliminary) remedy, it is discussed in the context of the remedies of the mortgagee: see *infra*, p. 911.

5. Leasing powers and powers to accept surrenders of leases

Statutory powers to lease the mortgaged land, and to accept surrenders of leases (but only in order to replace the surrendered lease with a new lease: *Barclays Bank Ltd v. Stasek* [1957] Ch. 28), are conferred on the mortgagor or mortgagee, whichever party is in possession of the mortgaged property: Law of Property Act 1925, ss.99, 100. Without these statutory powers, neither party would have (effective) power to grant leases binding on the other party: the mortgagor has no right to possession; and the right of the mortgagee to possession terminates on redemption of the mortgage with the result that any lease granted by the mortgagee would cease to bind the mortgagor: *Chapman v. Smith* [1907] 2 Ch. 97, 102 *per* Parker J.

In fact, the statutory power is normally excluded by express provision in the mortgage deed; but mortgagors in possession continue to grant leases. In such circumstances, it has been held that a Rent Act protected tenancy granted by a mortgagor after the creation of the mortgage will not bind the mortgagee: *Dudley and District Benefit Building Society v. Emerson* [1949] Ch. 707. The same principle was applied to a Rent Act statutory tenancy: *Britannia Building Society v. Earl* [1990] 1 W.L.R. 422, noted at [1990] Conv. 450; and see also *Quennell v. Maltby* [1979] 1 W.L.R. 318, 323 *per* Templeman L.J. However, in the context of registered land, a Rent Act protected/statutory tenancy has been held to be enforceable against a mortgagee as an overriding interest under section 70(1)(g) of the Land Registration Act 1925 where the tenancy was granted prior to the creation of the mortgage: *Woolwich Building Society v. Dickman* [1996] 3 All E.R. 204, *ante*, p. 224; and as an overriding interest under section 70(1)(k) where the tenancy was granted after the creation of the mortgage but before the mortgage had been registered: *Barclays Bank plc v. Zaroovabli* [1997] Ch. 321, *ante*, p. 232, *infra*, p. 890.

In any event, the mortgagee will be bound where he has consented to the grant; and in *Lever Finance Ltd v. Trustee of the Property of L.N. and H.M. Needleman* [1956] Ch. 375, the mortgagee was estopped from repudiating the lease: the mortgage deed required the mortgagees' consent to any lease but stated that the lessee was not concerned to see that that consent had been obtained. Similarly, the mortgagee will be bound where he subsequently adopts the lease: *Stroud Building Society v. Delamont* [1960] 1 W.L.R. 431; *Chatsworth Properties Ltd v. Effiom* [1971] 1 W.L.R. 144.

Any unauthorised lease which does not bind the mortgagee may nonetheless bind the mortgagor under the principle of estoppel: *Cuthbertson v. Irving* (1859) 4 H. & N. 742; but that principle has been limited to cases where the mortgage merely excludes the *statutory* power of leasing and does not contain a comprehensive covenant against leasing: *Iron Trades Employers Insurance Association Ltd v. Union Land and House Investors Ltd* [1937] Ch. 313.

6. Transfer of the mortgage

A mortgagee is not normally required to obtain the consent of the mortgagor to a transfer of the mortgage: Law of Property Act 1925, s.114; Land Registration Act 1925, s.33. However, there are certain statutory exceptions relating to building society mortgages and local authority mortgages: see, respectively, Building Societies Act 1986, ss.93, 94, 97; Local Government Act 1986, s.7.

7. Transfer of the interest of the mortgagor

Subject to any express restriction contained in the mortgage deed, the mortgagor is entitled to transfer the mortgaged land subject to the mortgage without the consent of the mortgagee. However, the original mortgagor remains liable on his personal covenant and the effectiveness of indemnity covenants depends upon the availability and solvency of successive transferees of the mortgaged land. The usual practice, therefore, is for a mortgagor to sell the property free of the mortgage by undertaking to discharge the mortgage out of the proceeds of sale; and for the purchaser to create a new mortgage in order to finance his purchase.

8. Regulation of interest rates

Rather surprisingly, the law currently provides only limited regulation of interest rates: see *infra*, p. 878.

9. Redemption

The right to redeem the mortgage and to recover the mortgaged land free from the mortgage is the fundamental right of the mortgagor: see *infra*, pp. 827 *et seq.*

10. Consolidation

Pursuant to the doctrine of consolidation, a mortgagee who holds two (or more) mortgages which have been created by the same mortgagor over different properties has an equitable right, where the mortgage money has become due on both mortgages, to refuse to permit one mortgage to be redeemed unless the other mortgage is also redeemed. Since 1881 the right has been excluded by statute, subject to a contrary intention expressed in at least one of the mortgage deeds: Law of Property Act 1925, s.93; but it is common practice for the right to be reserved in this way.

11. Discharge

A mortgage is usually discharged by the mortgagor paying all sums due under the mortgage. No formal document is required (see *supra*, p. 813) but a memorandum of discharge and receipt for the repayment of the loan are usually endorsed on the mortgage deed: Law of Property Act 1925, s.115(1). The receipt requires the payer to be named; but, if it appears that payment has been made by a person who is not entitled to the immediate equity of redemption, the receipt does not discharge the mortgage but transfers it to the payer: *ibid.* s.115(2); and see *Cumberland Court (Brighton) Ltd v. Taylor* [1964] Ch. 29.

Different methods of discharge apply in the case of registered land, where it is necessary to ensure the cancellation in the register of the registered charge: Land Registration Act 1925, s.35; Land Registration Rules, r.151 (Form 53).

There are additional requirements in the case of building society and other institutional mortgages: Building Societies Act 1986, Sched. 4, para. 2; Industrial and Provident Societies Act 1965, s.33; Friendly Societies Act 1974, s.57.

A mortgage may also be discharged by foreclosure and by a sale of the mortgaged property pursuant to the power of sale of the mortgagee: see *infra*, pp. 891, 894.

D. PROTECTION OF THE MORTGAGOR

Discussion of the protection of the mortgagor through the supervisory jurisdiction of equity is frequently prefaced by reference to the maxim "once a mortgage, always a mortgage" (*Seton v. Slade* (1802) 7 Ves. 265, 273 *per* Lord Eldon L.C.). This maxim has two aspects. The first has already been considered. In determining whether or not a particular transaction constituted a mortgage, equity looked to its substance rather than its form; and equity would not permit what was in fact a mortgage transaction to be disguised so as to deprive the mortgagor of his rights as mortgagor: see, *e.g. Barnhart v. Greenshields* (1853) 9 Moo.P.C. 18; *Waters v. Mynn* (1850) 15 L.T. (o.s.) 157. This precedence of substance over form can also be important for mortgagees: see *Grangeside Properties Ltd v. Collingwood Securities Ltd* [1964] 1 W.L.R. 139, *supra*, p. 812. The second aspect of the maxim has been alluded to but is discussed in more detail in this section: it centres on the right of the mortgagor to redeem the mortgage.

However, while the traditional protection is not without its significance, mortgagors may also seek the protection afforded by a wide range of more modern doctrines. For an analysis of the protection of mortgagors against the changing contextual and conceptual background, see Bamforth [1996] C.L.P. 207, 213–231.

1. The right of the mortgagor to redeem the mortgage

1.1 *Legal or contractual right to redeem*
The mortgagor is entitled to redeem the mortgage (and to recover the mortgaged property free from the mortgage) on the contractual date for redemption: *Crickmore v. Freestone* (1870) 40 L.J.Ch. 137; and, in the absence of agreement to the contrary, there is no right to redeem before that date: *Brown v. Cole* (1845) 14 Sim. 427.

1.2 *Equitable right to redeem*
It has been seen that equity gave the mortgagor the right to redeem the mortgaged land after the contractual date for redemption had passed and the legal right to redeem had been lost. However, there seems to be an established rule that a mortgagor who fails to redeem the mortgage on the contractual date for redemption and who is therefore dependent upon his equitable right to redeem is normally required to give six months' notice of his intention to redeem or to pay six months' interest in lieu; and if the mortgagor, having given six months' notice, fails to redeem on the date specified in the notice, he may be required to give a further six months' notice, in the absence of some reasonable explanation for the failure: *Smith v. Smith* [1891] 3 Ch. 550, 552–553 *per* Romer J.; *Cromwell Property Investment Co. Ltd v. Western and*

Toovey [1934] Ch. 322, 334–336 *per* Maugham J.; *Centrax Trustees Ltd v. Ross* [1979] 2 All E.R. 952, 955–956 *per* Goulding J. The rule is said to be based on the premise that the mortgagee is entitled to be given time to find a new investment for his money; but it has been criticised as inflexible since alternative investments can normally be arranged in less than six months.

A mortgagor can redeem without notice or interest in lieu where the mortgage is of a temporary nature: *Fitzgerald's Trustee v. Mellersh* [1892] 1 Ch. 385, 389–390 *per* Chitty J.; or where the mortgagee has demanded repayment or has otherwise taken some formal step to exercise his remedies for the enforcement of the security: *Re Alcock* (1883) 23 Ch D. 372, 376 *per* Cotton L.J.; *Smith v. Smith* [1891] 3 Ch. 550, 552 *per* Romer J.

1.3 *Protection of the right to redeem*

The conferment of the equitable right to redeem did not prevent lenders from seeking to take advantage of their stronger bargaining position in relation to borrowers; and mortgagees would sometimes endeavour to impose on their mortgagors terms which would effectively prevent or inhibit redemption even after the loan had been repaid. However, the courts have always been astute to protect fully the right to redeem. For, as Lord Macnaghten stated in *Noakes & Co. Ltd v. Rice* [1902] A.C. 24, 30, "[r]edemption is of the very nature and essence of a mortgage, as mortgages are regarded in equity. It is inherent in the thing itself". Thus the courts would strike down anything that threatened the integrity of the equity of redemption, anything that restricted the right of the mortgagor to redeem the mortgage and anything that adversely affected the mortgagor's enjoyment of the mortgaged property after he had fulfilled his obligations. The principle of protection was summarised in *Biggs v. Hoddinott* [1898] 2 Ch. 307, where Romer L.J. stated (at 314):

> There is a principle that … on a mortgage you cannot, between the mortgagor and mortgagee, clog, as it is termed, the equity of redemption so as to prevent the mortgagor from redeeming on payment of the principal, interest and costs.

This broad principle that there must be no clog or fetter on the equity of redemption embraces a number of more detailed rules and applications. As will become apparent, there is considerable uncertainty in some of these rules and some overlap between them.

However, before these rules are considered, a word of caution or explanation is appropriate. For many years there was a tendency to assume that a mortgage transaction inevitably involved a mortgagor in urgent need of funds, who would be compelled to accept any terms imposed by the mortgagee. This assumption was reflected in the statement of Lord Henley in *Vernon v. Bethell* (1762) 2 Eden 110, 113, that "necessitous men are not, truly speaking, free men, but, to answer a present exigency, will submit to any terms that the crafty may impose upon them". Although that statement was almost certainly a fair representation of the situation of mortgagors in the eighteenth century, that has generally not been the position for some time. First, in more recent times many mortgagors are commercial undertakings which enjoy equal bargaining power with the mortgagee; such mortgagors do not require the traditional protection of equity and, where protection is necessary, they are likely to rely on more commercially-oriented arguments, such as the restraint of trade doctrine. Secondly, the vast majority of non-commercial mortgagors borrow from institutional lenders (banks and building societies), which are subject to strict statutory control; again, the protection of equity that was doubtless necessary in the eighteenth century is no longer relevant to such mortgagors.

This change of context has had two consequences which should be noted. First, the equitable principles are less widely applicable in modern times, although the cases demonstrate that the principles remain relevant. Secondly, the principles can pose difficulties for the courts: they have tended to develop into rather rigid technical rules, which are less readily circumvented, notwithstanding their apparent inappropriateness in the particular context.

Against that background the principle that there must be no clog or fetter on the equity of redemption can be considered.

1.3.1 *Purported exclusion or postponement of the right to redeem*   The rule is that any provision in a mortgage transaction which directly or indirectly prevents the mortgagor from redeeming the mortgaged property when he has performed the obligation that the mortgage was intended to secure is repugnant to the essential nature of the transaction and is void. Thus it is clear that a mortgage cannot be made totally irredeemable: *Re Sir Thomas Spencer Wells* [1933] Ch. 29; nor can the right to redeem be made exercisable only within a limited period: *Salt v. Marquess of Northampton* [1892] A.C. 1; or only by certain persons: *Howard v. Harris* (1683) 1 Vern. 190; *Salt v. Marquess of Northampton, supra.* Moreover, equity has intervened to prohibit *potential* exclusion of the right to redeem, where the mortgage purports to extinguish the right to redeem on the occurrence of some specified event: *Toomes v. Conset* (1745) 3 Atk. 261; or where the mortgage purports to grant to the mortgagee an option to purchase all or part of the mortgaged property: *Samuel v. Jarrah Timber and Wood Paving Corp. Ltd* [1902] A.C. 323, *infra*, p. 830. On the other hand, there would probably be no objection to the grant of a right of pre-emption to the mortgagee, since the mortgagor could not be compelled to sell against his will. Further, equity has intervened to restrict the circumstances in which the right to redeem can be postponed: *Knightsbridge Estates Trust Ltd v. Byrne* [1939] Ch. 441, *infra*, p. 832.

1.3.1.1 *Options to purchase the mortgaged property*   A mortgagee is not permitted to obtain, as part of the mortgage transaction, an option to purchase the mortgaged property, since this could obviously prevent the mortgagor from recovering the mortgaged property and could thus change the whole nature of the transaction.

Samuel v. Jarrah Timber and Wood Paving Corp. Ltd [1902] A.C. 323

(HL, Earl Halsbury L.C., Lord MacNaghten, Lord Lindley)

The respondent company borrowed £5,000 from Samuel upon the security of a mortgage of debenture stock (valued at £30,000) in the company, subject to Samuel having the option to purchase the whole or any part of that stock within 12 months. When Samuel sought to exercise the option, the company sought to redeem the mortgage and claimed a declaration that the option was void in so far as it had the potential (realised in the circumstances) to preclude redemption. The House of Lords held that the option was void, affirming the judgment of Kekewich J. and of the Court of Appeal ([1903] 2 Ch. 1).

LORD LINDLEY:

The transaction was in my opinion a mortgage, plus, amongst other things, an option to purchase, which if exercised by the mortgagee would put an end to the mortgagor's right to redeem—i.e. would prevent him from getting back his mortgaged property. This was the view taken by Kekewich J. and by all the members of the Court of Appeal, and I am unable myself to view the transaction differently.

In *Lisle v. Reeve* [1902] 1 Ch. 53 Buckley J. suggested some instances in which he considered a mortgagee might validly stipulate for an option to buy the equity of redemption; but although his decision was affirmed first by the Court of Appeal and afterwards by this House (*Reeve v. Lisle* [1902] A.C. 461), the affirmance proceeded entirely on the fact that the agreement to buy the equity of redemption was no part of the original mortgage transaction, but was entered into subsequently, and was an entirely separate transaction to which no objection could be taken. It is plain that the decision would not have been affirmed if the agreement to buy the equity of redemption had been one of the terms of the original mortgage. The Irish case *Re Edward's Estate* (1861) 11 Ir.Ch.Rep. 367 is to the same effect.

I cannot help thinking that both parties intended that the two options to purchase the £30,000 debenture stock and to underwrite further capital or debenture stock if issued were to be exercisable even after payment off of the £5000. But the decisions of this House in *Noakes v. Rice* [1902] A.C. 24 and *Bradley v. Carritt* [1903] A.C. 253 conclusively shew that, whatever might have been intended, Samuel could not have been entitled to exercise either option after repayment of his loan. But these decisions and the previous decision of *Salt v. Northampton* [1892] A.C. 1 emphatically recognise the old doctrine, "Once a mortgage always a mortgage," which is too well settled to be open to controversy. Lord Hardwicke said in *Toomes v. Conset* (1745) 3 Atk. 261: "This Court will not suffer in a deed of mortgage any agreement in it to prevail that the estate become an absolute purchase in the mortgagee upon any event whatsoever". But the doctrine is not confined to deeds creating legal mortgages. It applies to all mortgage transactions. The doctrine "Once a mortgage always a mortgage" means that no contract between a mortgagor and a mortgagee made at the time of the mortgage and as part of the mortgage transaction, or, in other words, as one of the terms of the loan, can be valid if it prevents the mortgagor from getting back his property on paying off what is due on his security. Any bargain which has that effect is invalid, and is inconsistent with the transaction being a mortgage. This principle is fatal to the appellant's contention if the transaction under consideration is a mortgage transaction, as I am of opinion it clearly is.

NOTES:

1. All members of the House of Lords reluctantly agreed that the option must be declared void but they questioned the application of the equitable

principle to strike down a "perfectly fair bargain" between businessmen "without any trace or suspicion of oppression, surprise, or circumvention".

2. See the contemporary comment of Sir Frederick Pollock at (1903) 19 L.Q.R. 359:

The doctrine of "clogging" threatens to become an intolerable nuisance—an interference with the freedom of the subject. It was a useful enough doctrine in a primitive and more technical age when ignorant people were often entrapped into oppressive bargains, but today it is an anachronism and might with advantage be jettisoned. Instead the courts have taken to emphasising the doctrine in all its original crudity. It was open to them a few years since to have moulded the doctrine to meet the changing conditions of modern life, and to have confined redress to cases where there was something oppressive or unconscionable in the bargain, to make this the test, as it was the origin, of the doctrine; but the courts have preferred to adhere to technicality and an unprogressive judicial policy. ... Alas! for the cobwebs of technicality which lawyers are so fond of spinning, and which so often shut out the daylight of common sense.

3. In *Reeve v. Lisle* [1902] A.C. 461 a similarly constituted Appeal Committee of the House of Lords had construed a mortgage transaction and a related option agreement which was concluded 11 days later as independent transactions and held that the option agreement was binding on the mortgagor. It is arguable that the distinction between the two cases is more apparent than real. First, the mortgage transaction and the option agreement under consideration in *Reeve v. Lisle* had in essence been the subject-matter of an earlier *single* agreement between the parties. Secondly, although there was no suggestion of oppression or unconscionability in *Reeve v. Lisle*, the formulation of the distinction between that case and *Samuel v. Jarrah Timber and Wood Paving Corp. Ltd* assumes that once a mortgage has been executed the mortgagor is no longer under any potential pressure from the mortgagee. In *Lewis v. Frank Love Ltd* [1961] 1 W.L.R. 261 Plowman J. declined to exploit the *Reeve v. Lisle* exception in the context of a mortgage transaction and the grant of an option to the mortgagee to purchase part of the mortgaged property effected by separate documents on the same date. He declared himself (at 267) "quite satisfied that the loan ... and the grant of the option were part and parcel of the same transaction". For comment, see (1961) 25 Conv. 158; (1961) 77 L.Q.R. 165; (1961) 24 M.L.R. 385.

4. In *Kreglinger v. New Patagonia Meat and Cold Storage Co. Ltd* [1914] A.C. 25 Lord Parker questioned the scope of *Samuel v. Jarrah Timber and Wood Paving Corp. Ltd*; he said (at 52–53):

A agrees to give B an option for one year to purchase a property for £10,000. In consideration of such option B agrees to lend, and does lend, A £1,000 to be charged on the property without interest, and be repayable at the expiration or earlier exercise of the option. I cannot myself see that there is any inconsistency or repugnancy between the provisions of this perfectly simple and straightforward transaction. It would have been very different if A had conveyed the property to B with a proviso that on payment of the £1,000 there should be a reconveyance, and the deed had then provided for the year's option. Here the option would be inconsistent with, and would in fact have been destroyed by, the reconveyance.

5. In *Alec Lobb (Garages) Ltd v. Total Oil (Great Britain) Ltd* [1985] 1 W.L.R. 173 a subsequent transaction between a mortgagor and a mortgagee, involving (i) the lease and sub-lease back of the mortgaged property and (ii) a solus agreement for the duration of the sub-lease, was upheld. For comment, see [1983] Conv. 465, [1985] Conv. 141.

1.3.1.2 *Postponement of the right to redeem*   It has been seen that it is customary for the legal or contractual date for redemption to be fixed only a short time (usually six months) after the execution of the mortgage transaction; but that this has no direct practical significance since, as soon as the specified date passes, the legal right to redeem is replaced by the equitable right to redeem. However, in some circumstances the terms of the mortgage agreement may postpone the legal/contractual date for redemption. If the postponement renders the mortgage effectively irredeemable, or if the postponement is regarded as oppressive or unconscionable, the postponement will be void and the mortgagor will be permitted to redeem at an earlier date.

Knightsbridge Estates Trust Ltd v. Byrne [1939] Ch. 441

(CA, Greene M.R., Scott and Farwell L.JJ.)

The respondent company, Knightsbridge, had mortgaged a number of freehold properties to secure the repayment of a loan of £300,000, on which interest was payable at 6.5 per cent per annum. In 1931 Knightsbridge redeemed the mortgage by obtaining from the appellant a second loan on more favourable terms. The second loan, secured by a mortgage on the freehold properties, was to be repaid, with interest at a fixed rate of 5.25 per cent per annum, by 80 half-yearly instalments; and the mortgagees covenanted that they would not require repayment in any other manner, provided that the mortgagors complied with all the terms of the mortgage. When interest rates fell further, Knightsbridge wished to re-finance on still more favourable terms. They claimed to be entitled to redeem the mortgage, arguing that the provision for postponement was void. Luxmoore J. ([1938] Ch. 741) held that the provision was void; but his decision was reversed by the Court of Appeal.

GREENE M.R.:
We will deal first with the arguments originally presented on behalf of the respondents. The first argument was that the postponement of the contractual right to redeem for forty years was void in itself, in other words, that the making of such an agreement between mortgagor and mortgagee was prohibited by a rule of equity. It was not contended that a provision in a mortgage deed making the mortgage irredeemable for a period of years is necessarily void. The argument was that such a period must be a "reasonable" one, and it was said that the period in the present case was an unreasonable one by reason merely of its length. This argument was not the one accepted by the learned judge.

Now an argument such as this requires the closest scrutiny, for, if it is correct, it means that an agreement made between two competent parties, acting under expert advice and presumably knowing their own business best, is one which the law forbids them to make upon the ground that it is not "reasonable". If we were satisfied that the rule of equity was what it is said to be, we should be bound to give effect to it. But in the absence of compelling authority we are not prepared to say that such an agreement cannot lawfully be made. A decision to that effect would, in our view, involve an unjustified interference with the freedom of business men to enter into agreements best suited to their interests and would impose upon them a test of "reasonableness" laid down by the Courts without reference to the business realities of the case.

It is important to remember what those realities were. The respondents are a private company and do not enjoy the facilities for raising money by a public issue possessed by public companies. They were the owners of a large and valuable block of property, and so far as we know they had no other assets. The property was subject to a mortgage at a high rate of interest and this mortgage was liable to be called in at any time. In these circumstances the respondents were, when the negotiations began, desirous of obtaining for themselves two advantages: (1) a reduction in the rate of interest, (2) the right to repay the mortgage moneys by instalments spread over a long period of years. The desirability of obtaining these terms from a business point of view is manifest, and it is not to be assumed that these respondents were actuated by anything but pure considerations of business in seeking to obtain them. The sum involved was a very large one, and the length of the period over which the instalments were spread is to be considered with reference to this fact. In the circumstances it was the most natural thing in the world that the respondents should address themselves to a body desirous of obtaining a long term investment for its money. The resulting agreement was a commercial agreement between two important corporations experienced in such matters, and has none of the features of an oppressive bargain where the borrower is at the mercy of an unscrupulous lender. In transactions of this kind it is notorious that there is competition among the large insurance companies and other bodies having large funds to invest, and we are not prepared to view the agreement made as anything but a proper business transaction.

But it is said not only that the period of postponement must be a reasonable one, but that in judging the "reasonableness" of the period the considerations which we have mentioned cannot be regarded; that the Court is bound to judge "reasonableness" by a consideration of the terms of the mortgage deed itself and without regard to extraneous matters. In the absence of clear authority we emphatically decline to consider a question of "reasonableness" from a standpoint so unreal. To hold that the law is to tell business men what is reasonable in such circumstances and to refuse to take into account the business considerations involved, would bring the law into disrepute. Fortunately, we do not find ourselves forced to come to any such conclusion.

. . .

Assuming therefore, without in any way deciding, that the period during which the contractual right of redemption is postponed must be a "reasonable" one (a question which we will now proceed to examine), we are of opinion that the respondents have failed to establish (and the burden is on them) that there is anything unreasonable in the mere extension of the period for forty years in the circumstances of the present case.

But in our opinion the proposition that a postponement of the contractual right of redemption is only permissible for a "reasonable" time is not well-founded. Such a postponement is not properly described as a clog on the equity of redemption, since it is concerned with the contractual right to redeem. It is indisputable that any provision which hampers redemption after the contractual date for redemption has passed will not be permitted. Further, it is undoubtedly true to say that a right of redemption is a necessary element in a mortgage transaction, and consequently that, where the contractual right of redemption is illusory, equity will grant relief by allowing redemption. This was the point in the case of *Fairclough v. Swan Brewery Co.* [1912] A.C. 565. . . .

Moreover, equity may give relief against contractual terms in a mortgage transaction if they are oppressive or unconscionable, and in deciding whether or not a particular transaction falls within this category the length of time for which the contractual right to redeem is postponed may well be an important consideration. In the present case no question of this kind was or could have been raised.

But equity does not reform mortgage transactions because they are unreasonable. It is concerned to see two things—one that the essential requirements of a mortgage transaction are observed, and the other that oppressive or unconscionable terms are not enforced. Subject to this, it does not, in our opinion, interfere. The question therefore arises whether, in a case where the right of redemption is real and not illusory and there is nothing oppressive or unconscionable in the transaction, there is something in a postponement of the contractual right to redeem, such as we have in the present case, that is inconsistent with the essential requirements of a mortgage transaction? A part from authority the answer to this question would, in our opinion, be clearly in the negative. Any other answer would place an unfortunate restriction on the liberty of contract of competent parties who are at arm's length—in the present case it would have operated to prevent the respondents obtaining financial terms which for obvious reasons they themselves considered to be most desirable. It would, moreover, lead to highly inequitable results. The remedy sought by the respondents and the only remedy which is said to be open to them is the establishment of a right to redeem at any time on the ground that the postponement of the contractual right to redeem is void. They do not and could not suggest that the contract as a contract is affected, and the result would accordingly be that whereas the respondents would have had from the first the right to redeem at any time, the appellants would have had no right to require payment otherwise than by the specified instalments. Such an outcome to a bargain entered into by business people negotiating at arm's length would indeed be unfortunate, and we should require clear authority before coming to such a conclusion.

[Greene M.R. referred to the following authorities cited in argument: *Talbot v. Braddill* (1683) 1 Vern. 183; *Cowdry v. Day* (1859) 1 Giff. 316; *Teevan v. Smith* (1882) 20 Ch.D. 724; *Biggs v. Hoddinott* [1898] 2 Ch. 307; *Bradley v. Carritt* [1903] A.C. 253; *Williams v. Morgan* [1906] 1 Ch. 804; *Morgan v. Jeffreys* [1910] 1 Ch. 620; *Davis v. Symons* [1934] Ch. 442; he continued:]

In our opinion, if we are right in thinking that the postponement is by itself unobjectionable, it cannot be made objectionable by the presence in the mortgage deed of other provisions, unless the totality is sufficient to enable the Court to say that the contract is so oppressive or unconscionable that it ought not to be enforced in a Court of equity. If such other provisions are collateral advantages ... they will, of course, fall to be dealt with as such.

NOTES:

1. The decision of the Court of Appeal was affirmed by the House of Lords ([1940] A.C. 613) but on the ground that the mortgage was a debenture within the meaning of section 380 of the Companies Act 1929 so that, by virtue of section 74, postponement of redemption was permitted. See now the Companies Act 1985, s.193.

2. In *Biggs v. Hoddinott* [1898] 2 Ch. 307 Hoddinott, the fee simple owner of an hotel, mortgaged it to Biggs, a brewer. The mortgagor covenanted that during the continuance of the mortgage he would take his supplies (with certain exceptions) from the mortgagee; and the mortgage contained a proviso that the mortgagor would not redeem the mortgage, and the mortgagee would not call in the loan, for five years. Two years later the mortgagor sought to redeem the mortgage and the mortgagee sought to restrain the mortgagor from obtained supplies from elsewhere. On the validity of the proviso postponing the right to redeem, Romer J. stated (at 311-312):

Now, I am of opinion that it is obviously to the advantage of both the mortgagor and mortgagee that such a provision should be enforced. Of course, that does not prevent the Court in a proper case from preventing the application of the clause if it is too large, or there are circumstances connected with the proviso which render it, in the opinion of the Court, unreasonable or oppressive. In the present case I can find nothing unreasonable or oppressive in the proviso which prevents the mortgagors from redeeming for the five years. The term is not unreasonable, nor is there anything connected with the proviso which would render it unreasonable or oppressive in the eyes of the Court. It is said that it is not in itself bad, but that it is made so by reason of the covenant in the mortgage which compels the mortgagors during the continuance of the security to buy their beer from the mortgagee, who is a brewer. Well, that covenant is either in itself unreasonable, or not unreasonable. There is nothing before me to shew that as a covenant it is unreasonable, under the circumstances, there being a covenant almost corresponding by the mortgagee, the brewer, to supply. There is nothing oppressive in it itself. There is no evidence to shew me that it is unreasonable or oppressive. Whether, apart from being unreasonable or oppressive in fact, it ought to be void as infringing any principle of equity, I need not now decide, though I shall have to decide that hereafter. Either that covenant is void, or not void, on such a principle. If it be void, then I do not see why I should make the proviso precluding the redemption for five years bad, because there is also another void provision in the deed. And if it is not void, why should I disregard the proviso restricting the power to redeem for five years because of the existence of a covenant which the Court considers enforceable, and which is not unreasonable? It seems to me, therefore, that, looking at the mortgage as a whole, there is nothing here which in my opinion would prevent this proviso precluding the redemption for five years being enforced by the Court. I accordingly enforce it.

In *Knightsbridge Estates Trust Ltd v. Byrne* Greene M.R. expressed general approval of the decision of Romer J., but only on the understanding that a postponement of the right to redeem is not to be held unenforceable unless it is oppressive or unreasonable *in the sense that it renders the right to redeem illusory.*

3. In *Fairclough v. Swan Brewery Co. Ltd* [1912] A.C. 565 the mortgagor was the assignee of a lease of an hotel which had seventeen and a half years to run. The mortgagor borrowed £500 from the landlord brewery. He covenanted to repay the loan by instalments, with the final instalment payable only six weeks before the lease expired; and he further covenanted that during the continuance of the mortgage he would take all beer supplies from the mortgagee. When he later obtained supplies from elsewhere, and the mortgagee brought an action for breach of the covenant, the mortgagor claimed, *inter alia*, that the postponement of the right to redeem was void. Lord Macnaghten, delivering the judgment of the Privy Council, stated (at 570):

It is now firmly established by the House of Lords that the old rule still prevails and that equity will not permit any device or contrivance being part of the mortgage transaction or contemporaneous with it to prevent or impede redemption. The learned counsel on behalf of the [mortgagee] admitted, as he was bound to admit, that a mortgage cannot be made irredeemable. That is plainly forbidden. Is there any difference between forbidding redemption and permitting it, if the permission be a mere pretence? Here the provision for redemption is nugatory. The incumbrance on the lease the subject of the mortgage according to the letter of the bargain falls to be discharged before the lease terminates, but at a time when it is on the very point of expiring, when redemption can be of no advantage to the mortgagor even if he should be so fortunate as to get his deeds back before the actual termination of the lease. For all practical purposes this mortgage is irredeemable. It was obviously meant to be irredeemable. It was made irredeemable in and by the mortgage itself.

Notwithstanding the approval of the reasoning of the Privy Council expressed by Greene M.R. in *Knightsbridge Estates Trust Ltd v. Byrne*, it is suggested that the better approach to postponement is to be found in the assertion of Greene M.R. that (commercial) contracts should be upheld in the absence of oppression or unconscionability. It may be questioned how Greene M.R. would have decided *Knightsbridge Estates Trust Ltd v. Byrne* if the mortgagors had offered as security not the freehold properties but a 40-year lease: the arguments based on the sanctity of contract would have been no less applicable; and yet the postponement of the right to redeem until the end of the lease would seem to fall within the reasoning in *Fairclough v. Swan Brewery Co. Ltd*.

4. The decisions in *Biggs v. Hoddinott* and *Fairclough v. Swan Brewery Co. Ltd* can be explained and reconciled in economic terms. The postponement in the former case was an insignificant restriction on an appreciating asset (the fee simple), whereas the postponement in the latter case was an almost total restriction on a wasting asset (the last years of a lease). However, reconciliation on this basis was implicitly rejected as irrelevant by Lord Parker in *Kreglinger v. New Patagonia Meat and Cold Storage Co. Ltd* [1914] A.C. 25. He stated (at 53):

We will suppose that money is advanced to a company repayable at the expiration of fifteen years, not an unusual period, and that the company by way of security subdemises (as is often the case) to trustees for the lenders a number of leaseholds, some of which are held for terms less than fifteen years. It would, in my opinion, be a serious error to argue that this was an attempt to make an irredeemable mortgage. There would be the same error in objecting on the like ground to a mortgage of leaseholds to secure an annuity for a period exceeding the term of the lease. If the mortgage is irredeemable at all, this arises from the nature of the property mortgaged, and not from any penal or repugnant stipulation on the part of the mortgagee.

5. Neither the Privy Council in *Fairclough v. Swan Brewery Co. Ltd* nor the Court of Appeal in *Knightsbridge Estates Trust Ltd v. Byrne* referred to the decision of the Court of Appeal in *Santley v. Wilde* [1899] 2 Ch. 474, *infra*, p. 837.

6. Where a commercial agreement includes a mortgage which provides for the postponement of the right to redeem, then, if the commercial agreement is found to be in restraint of trade (see *infra*, p. 879) and if the postponement is referable to the period of restraint, the provision for postponement, even if not *per se* oppressive and unconscionable, may nonetheless be tainted by the restraint of trade and be held to be void.

7. Where a mortgage secures a regulated consumer credit agreement within the meaning of section 8 of the Consumer Credit Act 1974, the mortgagor is entitled to repay the loan at any time, notwithstanding that the mortgage contains a term postponing the right to redeem.

Santley v. Wilde [1899] 2 Ch. 474

(CA, Lindley M.R., Sir F.H. Jeune, Romer L.J.)

The mortgagor, Santley, owned the sub-lease of a theatre, which had 10 years to run. In order to finance the purchase of the head-lease, she borrowed £2,000 from Wilde and secured repayment by granting to him a mortgage of the sub-lease. The mortgagor covenanted to repay the loan over five years but further covenanted that throughout the remaining 10 years of the sub-lease, notwithstanding that the loan and interest had been repaid, she would pay to the mortgagee one-third of the net profits derived from the sub-lease. The mortgage provided for redemption of the mortgage only on payment of all moneys that the mortgagor had covenanted to pay. The mortgagor later claimed that she was entitled to redeem the mortgage on payment of principal and interest alone and that the provisions for the further payments and for the postponement of the right to redeem were void.

LINDLEY M.R.:
The question raised on this appeal is extremely important: I do not profess to be able to decide it on any principle which will be in harmony with all the cases; but it appears to me that the true principle running through them is not very difficult to discover, and I think that it can be applied so as to do justice in this case and in all other cases on the subject that may arise. The principle is this: a mortgage is a conveyance of land or an assignment of chattels as a security for the payment of a debt or the discharge of some other obligation for which it is given. This is the idea of a mortgage: and the security is redeemable on the payment or discharge of such debt or obligation, any provision to the contrary notwithstanding. That, in my opinion, is the law. Any provision inserted to prevent redemption on payment or performance of the debt or obligation for which the security was given is what is meant by a clog or fetter on the equity of redemption and is therefore void. It follows from this, that "once a mortgage always a mortgage"; but I do not understand that this principle involves the further proposition that the amount or nature of the further debt or obligation the payment or performance of which is to be secured is a clog or fetter within the rule....
A "clog" or "fetter" is something which is inconsistent with the idea of "security": a clog or fetter is in the nature of a repugnant condition. If I convey land in fee subject to a condition forbidding alienation, that is a repugnant condition. If I give a mortgage on a condition that I shall not redeem, that is a repugnant condition. The Courts of Equity have fought for years to maintain the doctrine that a security is redeemable. But when and under what circumstances? On the performance of the obligation for which it was given. If the obligation is the payment of a debt, the security is redeemable on the payment of that debt. That, in my opinion, is the true principle applicable to the cases, and that is what is meant when it is said there must not be any clog or fetter on the equity of redemption. If so, this mortgage has no clog or fetter at all. Of course, the debt or obligation may be impeachable for fraud, oppression, or over-reaching: there the obligation is tainted to that extent and is invalid. But, putting such cases out of the question, when you get a security for a debt or obligation, that security can be redeemed the moment the debt or obligation is paid or performed, but on no other terms.
 Now, let us see what the contract here is. It is not suggested that there has been fraud or undue influence or over-reaching or hard bargaining. Here is a lady who has a lease, of which there are ten years to run, subject to a rent and covenants. She wants to carry on a theatre, and she wants to borrow a sum of £2,000 for the purpose. What

is the security she offers? The security of the lease is probably absolutely insufficient. A security of that sort, unless it is kept up for the ten years, is very shaky. The lender took that view. He says, "I will lend you the money, and you may have five years in which to pay it; and you shall pay me a sum equal to one-third part of the net profit rents to be derived from any under-leases". What is the lender's position? It is obvious that his security depends not only on the solvency of the lady, but also on the success of the theatre. This is the kind of security proposed, and the lender says he will lend upon that. Accordingly the £2,000 is lent, and the mortgagor by her security covenants to repay the money by instalments; the deed then further goes on as follows: [His Lordship read the covenant by the mortgagor for payment of one-third of the net profit rents and also the proviso for redemption; and continued:—]

That means that this lease is granted or assigned by the mortgagor to the mortgagee as security not only for the payment of the £2,000 and interest, but also for the payment of the one-third of the net profit rents to the end of the term. If I am right in the principle which I have laid down, that does not clog the right of redemption upon the performance of the obligation for which the security was given. That is the nature of the transaction, and the good sense of it.

But it is said that is not good law. Those, however, who say so lose sight of the true principle underlying the expression that there must be no clog or fetter on the equity of redemption. The plaintiff says, "I will pay off the balance of the £2,000 and interest, and you will give me back the lease, and this is the end of my obligation". But the mortgagee says, "No; that is not the bargain: you cannot redeem on those terms. On the contrary, you may pay me the £2,000 and interest, but if you do, you must also pay the one-third profit rents". On principle that is right: it follows from what I have said. That is the bargain, and there has been no oppression, and there is no reasonable legal ground for relieving this lady.

SIR F. H. JEUNE:

I am of the same opinion. To my mind the case is covered by the decision in *Biggs v. Hoddinott* [1898] 2 Ch. 307. There is no doubt, in my judgment, what the bargain was, or that it was a reasonable bargain. There could not be anything more reasonable than that a person lending money on the security of a theatrical business should stipulate not only for the repayment of the sum lent and interest, but also for a share in such profits as might arise from the business, because if the business failed he would probably lose his money. This, then, was the bargain. Is is bad? It is not bad unless you hold that in a mortgage no collateral advantage can be obtained by reason of its being a mortgage. In *Biggs v. Hoddinott* the Court was brought face to face with the point that there was an additional or collateral advantage outside the mortgage. There the mortgagee of a public-house had stipulated for a collateral advantage to himself as regarded the sale of malt liquors, and it was felt necessary to press the case so far as to say that there could be no such bargain. That proposition, however, the Court rejected. It was rejected not only by the Master of the Rolls, but also by Chitty and Collins L.JJ., who laid down that it was not good law to say that there could be no collateral advantage to a mortgagee as part of his security. Another decision to the same effect is *Potter v. Edwards* (1857) 26 L.J. (Ch.) 468, which was referred to by Kay J. in *Mainland v. Upjohn* (1889) 41 Ch.D. 126 as being the first decision that broke in upon the series of cases that laid down the contrary principle. There the mortgagee lent £700, but stipulated that the mortgage should stand as a security for £1,000, and it was decided that the mortgagee might insist on the payment of the larger sum as a condition for redemption. Such a stipulation is not really a clog or fetter on the equity of redemption, because the equity of redemption only arises upon the performance of the whole of the stipulation. Therefore, we come back to this—what under the bargain is the event upon which the equity of redemption arises? Here it arises only when the money actually lent has been repaid, and when the share of profit rents has also been paid. So regarded, there is no fetter on the equity of redemption; and there is no hardship or oppression.

ROMER L.J.:
I agree, but will add a few words, as the case is important. Before *Biggs v. Hoddinott* there was, no doubt, considerable obscurity as to the extent of the equity rule with regard to contracts between mortgagors and their mortgagees. In that case it was pointed out that certain observations of the judges that had been more or less previously relied on, to the effect that a mortgagee could not stipulate for any collateral advantage, went too far and must be treated as not now representing the law....I take it that it is clearly established now, in the first place, that there is no such principle as is suggested, namely, that a mortgagee shall not stipulate for any collateral advantage for himself. He may so stipulate; and, if he does, he may obtain a collateral advantage; nothing can be said against it, and he can enforce it, always assuming that the bargain is not unconscionable or oppressive. In the second place, I take it also to be clear that there is now no such principle as is suggested, namely, that where a collateral advantage is stipulated for by the mortgagee as a condition of the loan, that advantage or contract is to be presumed to have been given or made under pressure. There is no such presumption, but each case must be decided according to its own circumstances. The Court will look into the circumstances of each case and see whether the bargain come to is unconscionable or oppressive.

These principles are now established by *Biggs v. Hoddinott*.

NOTE:
1. It is submitted that the decision is fair and that it is consistent with the principle that (commercial) contracts should be upheld in the absence of oppression or unconscionability. On the other hand, it is not clearly reconcilable with the cases discussed above. If the "further payments provision" is treated as part of the obligation of which performance is secured by the mortgage (the approach of Lindley M.R.), the necessary postponement of the right to redeem until the end of the sub-lease would seem to fall within the reasoning in *Fairclough v. Swan Brewery Co. Ltd*. If, however, the "further payments provision" is treated as a collateral advantage (the approach of Romer L.J.), the continuation of that obligation after repayment of principal and interest would seem to fall within the prohibition of collateral advantages: see *infra*. On the basis that this was the proper construction of the provision, the decision was criticised in *Noakes & Co. Ltd v. Rice* [1902] A.C. 24, 31–32 *per* Lord Macnaghten, 33–34 *per* Lord Davey; but those criticisms have themselves been treated as based on a misconception of the scope of the prohibition on collateral advantages: see *Kreglinger v. New Patagonia Meat and Cold Storage Co. Ltd* [1914] A.C. 25, 57–58 *per* Lord Parker.

1.3.2 *Collateral advantages*   A collateral advantage may be defined as a stipulation which purports to provide some benefit for the mortgagee in addition to the repayment of the loan and interest. Examples include mortgage loans made by breweries or oil companies where the loan is linked with a requirement on the part of the mortgagor to take his supplies of beer or petrol exclusively from the mortgagee (so-called "solus agreements").

At one time all collateral advantages were regarded as void because they were seen as a means of avoiding the restrictions imposed on interest rates by the old usury laws: *Jennings v. Ward* (1705) 2 Vern 520, 521. Even after the repeal of the usury laws in 1854, and thus the removal of the principal rationale for the prohibition of collateral advantages, the courts modified rather than abandoned the prohibition. Collateral advantages were permitted in so far as they were restricted to the continuance of the mortgage: *Biggs v. Hoddinott* [1898] 2 Ch. 307; but they were held to be invalid if they purported to continue *after* the redemption of the mortgage: *Noakes & Co. Ltd v. Rice* [1902] A.C. 24; *Bradley v. Carritt* [1903] A.C. 253. In *Kreglinger v. New Patagonia Meat and Cold Storage Co. Ltd* [1914] A.C. 25 the House of Lords endeavoured to "explain" those earlier decisions on a more principled basis in the course of a general reconsideration of collateral advantages.

Kreglinger v. New Patagonia Meat and Cold Storage Co. Ltd [1914] A.C. 25

(HL, Viscount Haldane L.C., Earl Halsbury, Lord Atkinson, Lord Mersey, Lord Parker)

Kreglinger, a firm of woolbrokers, agreed to lend £10,000 to the respondent company, a firm of meat packers. Repayment of the loan was secured by a floating charge on the respondent's undertaking and assets. Kreglinger agreed not to call in the loan for five years, provided that the interest was duly paid; but the respondent was entitled to repay the loan at any time. By the terms of the agreement, the respondent agreed that for a period of five years it would not sell any sheepskins to any person other than Kreglinger, provided that Kreglinger was willing to pay a price equal to the best price offered by any other person; and that the respondent would pay a commission to Kreglinger if it did sell any sheepskins to any other person. When the respondent repaid the loan after two and a half years and claimed to be free of the agreement in respect of the sheepskins, Kreglinger sought an injunction to prevent the respondent from acting in breach of that agreement. Swinfen Eady J. refused the injunction; and that decision was formally upheld by the Court of Appeal. The decision was reversed by the House of Lords.

VISCOUNT HALDANE L.C.:
What the respondents say is that the stipulation is one that restricts their freedom in conducting the undertaking or business which is the subject of the floating charge; that it was consequently of the nature of a clog on their right to redeem and invalid; and that, whether it clogged the right to redeem or was in the nature of a collateral advantage, it was not intended and could not be made to endure after redemption. The appellants, on the other hand, say that the stipulation in question was one of a kind usual in business, and that it was in the nature not of a clog but of a collateral bargain outside the actual loan, which they only agreed to make in order to obtain the option itself. They further say that even if the option could be regarded as within the doctrine of equity which forbids the clogging of the right to redeem, that doctrine does not in a case such as this extend to a floating charge.

My Lords, before I refer to the decisions of this House which the Courts below have considered to cover the case, I will state what I conceive to be the broad principles which must govern it.

It was not surprising that the Court of Chancery should at an early date have begun to exercise jurisdiction *in personam* over mortgagees. This jurisdiction was merely a special application of a more general power to relieve against penalties and to mould them into mere securities. The case of the common law mortgage of land was indeed a gross one. The land was conveyed to the creditor upon the condition that if the money he had advanced to the feoffor was repaid on a date and at a place named, the fee simple should revest in the latter, but that if the condition was not strictly and literally fulfilled he should lose the land for ever. What made the hardship on the debtor a glaring one was that the debt still remained unpaid and could be recovered from the feoffor notwithstanding that he had actually forfeited the land to his mortgagee. Equity, therefore, at an early date began to relieve against what was virtually a penalty by compelling the creditor to use his legal title as a mere security.

My Lords, this was the origin of the jurisdiction which we are now considering, and it is important to bear that origin in mind. For the end to accomplish which the jurisdiction has been evolved ought to govern and limit its exercise by equity judges. That end has always been to ascertain, by parol evidence if need be, the real nature and substance of the transaction, and if it turned out to be in truth one of mortgage simply, to place it on that footing. It was, in ordinary cases, only where there was conduct which the Court of Chancery regarded as unconscientious that it interfered with freedom of contract. The lending of money, on mortgage or otherwise, was looked on with suspicion, and the Court was on the alert to discover want of conscience in the terms imposed by lenders. But whatever else may have been the intention of those judges who laid the foundations of the modern doctrines with which we are concerned in this appeal, they certainly do not appear to have contemplated that their principle should develop consequences which would go far beyond the necessities of the case with which they were dealing and interfere with transactions which were not really of the nature of a mortgage, and which were free from objection on moral grounds.

The principle was thus in early days limited in its application to the accomplishment of the end which was held to justify interference of equity with freedom of contract. It did not go further. As established it was expressed in three ways. The most general of these was that if the transaction was once found to be a mortgage, it must be treated as always remaining a mortgage and nothing but a mortgage. That the substance of the transaction must be looked to in applying this doctrine and that it did not apply to cases which were only apparently or technically within it but were in reality something more than cases of mortgage, *Howard v. Harris* (1683) 1 Vern. 33; 2 Ch.Cas. 147 and other authorities shew. It was only a different application of the paramount doctrine to lay it down in the form of a second rule that a mortgagee should not stipulate for a collateral advantage which would make his remuneration for the loan exceed a proper rate of interest. The Legislature during a long period placed restrictions on the rate of interest which could legally be exacted. But equity went beyond the limits of the statutes which limited the interest, and was ready to interfere with any usurious stipulation in a mortgage. In so doing it was influenced by the public policy at the time. That policy has now changed, and the Acts which limited the rate of interest have been repealed. The result is that a collateral advantage may now be stipulated for by the mortgagee provided that he has not acted unfairly or oppressively, and provided that the bargain does not conflict with the third form of the principle. This is that a mortgage (subject to [an] apparent exception in the case of family arrangements...) cannot be made irredeemable, and that any stipulation which restricts or clogs the equity of redemption is void. It is obvious that the reason for the doctrine in this form is the same as that which gave rise to the other forms. It is simply an assertion in a different way of the principle that once a mortgage always a mortgage and nothing else.

My Lords, the rules I have stated have now been applied by Courts of Equity for nearly three centuries, and the books are full of illustrations of their application. But what I have pointed out shews that it is inconsistent with the objects for which they were established that these rules should crystallise into technical language so rigid that the letter can defeat the underlying spirit and purpose. Their application must correspond with the principal necessities of the time. The rule as to collateral advantages, for example, has been much modified by the repeal of the usury laws and by the recognition of modern varieties of commercial bargaining. In *Biggs v. Hoddinott* [1898] 2 Ch. 307 it was held that a brewer might stipulate in a mortgage made to him of an hotel that during the five years for which the loan was to continue the mortgagors would deal with him exclusively for malt liquor. In the seventeenth and eighteenth centuries a Court of Equity could hardly have so decided, and the judgment illustrates the elastic character of equity jurisdiction and the power of equity judges to mould the rules which they apply in accordance with the exigencies of the time. The decision proceeded on the ground that a mortgagee may stipulate for a collateral advantage at the time and as a term of the advance, provided, first, that no unfairness is shewn, and, secondly, that the right to redeem is not thereby clogged. It is no longer true that, as was said in *Jennings v. Ward* (1705) 2 Vern. 520, "a man shall not have interest for his money and a collateral advantage besides for the loan of it". Unless such a bargain is unconscionable it is now good. But none the less the other and wider principle remains unshaken, that it is the essence of a mortgage that in the eye of a Court of Equity it should be a mere security for money, and that no bargain can be validly made which will prevent the mortgagor from redeeming on payment of what is due, including principal, interest, and costs. He may stipulate that he will not pay off his debt, and so redeem the mortgage, for a fixed period. But whenever a right to redeem arises out of the doctrine of equity, he is precluded from fettering it. This principle has become an integral part of our system of jurisprudence and must be faithfully adhered to.

My Lords, the question in the present case is whether the right to redeem has been interfered with. And this must, for the reasons to which I have adverted in considering the history of the doctrine of equity, depend on the answer to a question which is primarily one of fact. What was the true character of the transaction? Did the appellants make a bargain such that the right to redeem was cut down, or did they simply stipulate for a collateral undertaking, outside and clear of the mortgage, which would give them an exclusive option of purchase of the sheepskins of the respondents? The question is in my opinion not whether the two contracts were made at the same moment and evidenced by the same instrument, but whether they were in substance a single and undivided contract or two distinct contracts. Putting aside for the moment considerations turning on the character of the floating charge, such an option no doubt affects the freedom of the respondents in carrying on their business even after the mortgage has been paid off. But so might other arrangements which would be plainly collateral, an agreement, for example, to take permanently into the firm a new partner as a condition of obtaining fresh capital in the form of a loan. The question is one not of form but of substance, and it can be answered in each case only by looking at all the circumstances, and not by mere reliance on some abstract principle, or upon the dicta which have fallen obiter from judges in other and different cases. Some, at least, of the authorities on the subject disclose an embarrassment which has, in my opinion, arisen from neglect to bear this in mind. In applying a principle the ambit and validity of which depend on confining it steadily to the end for which it was established, the analogies of previous instances where it has been applied are apt to be misleading. For each case forms a real precedent only in so far as it affirms a principle, the relevancy of which in other cases turns on the true character of the particular transaction, and to that extent on circumstances.

My Lords, if in the case before the House your Lordships arrive at the conclusion that the agreement for an option to purchase the respondents' sheepskins was not in substance a fetter on the exercise of their right to redeem, but was in the nature of a collateral bargain the entering into which was a preliminary and separable condition of the loan, the decided cases cease to present any great difficulty. In questions of this kind the binding force of previous decisions, unless the facts are indistinguishable, depends on whether they establish a principle. To follow previous authorities, so far as they lay down principles, is essential if the law is to be preserved from becoming unsettled and vague. In this respect the previous decisions of a Court of co-ordinate jurisdiction are more binding in a system of jurisprudence such as ours than in systems where the paramount authority is that of a code. But when a previous case has not laid down any new principle but has merely decided that a particular set of facts illustrates an existing rule, there are few more fertile sources of fallacy than to search in it for what is simply resemblance in circumstances, and to erect a previous decision into a governing precedent merely on this account. To look for anything except the principle established or recognised by previous decisions is really to weaken and not to strengthen the importance of precedent....

My Lords, it is not in my opinion necessary for your Lordships to form an opinion as to whether you would have given the same decisions as were recently given by this House in certain cases which were cited to us. These cases, which related to circumstances differing widely from those before us, have been disposed of finally, and we are not concerned with them excepting in so far as they may have thrown fresh light on questions of principle. What is vital in the appeal now under consideration is to classify accurately the transaction between the parties. What we have to do is to ascertain from scrutiny of the circumstances whether there has really been an attempt to effect a mortgage with a provision preventing redemption of what was pledged merely as security for payment of the amount of the debt and any charges besides that may legitimately be added. It is not, in my opinion, conclusive in favour of the appellants that the security assumed the form of a floating charge. A floating charge is not the less a pledge because of its floating character, and a contract which fetters the right to redeem on which equity insists as regards all contracts of loan and security ought on principle to be set aside as readily in the case of a floating security as in any other case. But it is material that such a floating charge, in the absence of bargain to the contrary effect, permits the assets to be dealt with freely by the mortgagor until the charge becomes enforceable. If it be said that the undertaking of the respondents which was charged extended to their entire business, including the right to dispose of the skins of which they might from time to time become possessed, the comment is that at least they were to be free, so long as the security remained a floating one, to make contracts in the ordinary course of business in regard to these skins. If there had been no mortgage such a contract as the one in question would have been an ordinary incident in such a business. We are considering the simple question of what is the effect on the right to redeem of having inserted into the formal instrument signed when the money was borrowed an ordinary commercial contract for the sale of skins extending over a period. It appears that it was the intention of the parties that the grant of the security should not affect the power to enter into such a contract, either with strangers or with the appellants, and if so I am unable to see how the equity of redemption is affected. No doubt it is the fact that on redemption the respondents will not get back their business as free from obligation as it was before the date of the security. But that may well be because outside the security and consistently with its terms there was a contemporaneous but collateral contract, contained in the same document as constituted the security, but in substance independent of it. If it was the intention of the parties, as I think it was, to enter into this contract as a condition of the respondents getting their advance, I know no reason either in morals or in equity which ought to prevent this intention from being left to have its effect. What was to be capable of redemption was an undertaking which was deliberately left to be freely changed in its details by ordinary business transactions with which the mortgage was not to interfere. Had the charge not been a floating one it might have been more difficult to give effect to this intention. In *Noakes & Co. v. Rice* [1902] A.C. 24 this difficulty is illustrated, for the House held that what had been inserted in the shape of a covenant by the mortgagor to buy the beer of the mortgagee after redemption of the public-house mortgaged was really a term of the mortgage and was inoperative as being, not merely a collateral agreement, but in truth a restriction on the right to get back the security free from the terms of the mortgage. That was the case of the mortgage of a specific property. The decision that the transaction was what it was held to be is at all events readily intelligible. In *Bradley v. Carritt* [1903] A.C. 253 it was decided that the mortgagor of shares in a tea company who had covenanted that he would use his best endeavours to secure that always thereafter the mortgagee should have the sale of the company's tea had permanently fettered himself in the free disposition and enjoyment of the shares. It was held that though the covenant did not operate in rem on the shares it amounted to a device or contrivance designed to impede redemption. The decision was a striking one. It was not unanimous, for Lord Lindley dissented from the conclusions of Lord Macnaghten and Lord Davey. It is binding on your Lordships in any case in which the transaction is really of the same kind, although it does not follow that all the dicta in the judgments of those of your Lordships' House who were in a majority must be taken as of binding authority. And it certainly cannot, in my opinion, be taken as authoritatively laying down that the mere circumstance that after redemption the property redeemed may not, as the result of some bargain made at the time of the mortgage, be in the same condition as it was before that time, is conclusive against the validity of that bargain. To render it invalid the bargain must, when its substance is examined, turn out to have formed part of the terms of the mortgage and to have really cut down a true right of redemption. I think that the tendency of recent decisions has been to lay undue stress on the letter of the principle which limits the jurisdiction of equity in setting aside contracts. The origin and reason of the principle ought, as I have already said, to be kept steadily in view in applying it to fresh cases. There appears to me to have grown up a tendency to look to the letter rather than to the spirit of the doctrine. The true view is, I think, that judges ought in this kind of jurisdiction to proceeed cautiously, and to bear in mind the real reasons which have led Courts of Equity to insist on the free right to redeem and the limits within which the purpose of the rule ought to confine its scope. I cannot but think that the validity of the bargain in such cases as *Bradley v. Carritt* and *Santley v. Wilde* [1899] 2 Ch. 474 might have been made free from serious question if the parties had chosen to seek what would have been substantially the same result in a different form. For form may be very important when the question is one of the construction of ambiguous words in which people have expressed their intentions. I will add that, if I am right in the view which I take of the authorities, there is no reason for thinking that they establish another rule suggested by the learned counsel for the respondents, that even a mere collateral advantage stipulated for in the same instrument as constitutes the mortgage cannot endure after redemption. The dicta on which he relied are really illustrations of the other principles to which I have referred.

There is a further remark which I wish to make about *Bradley v. Carritt*. It is impossible to read the report without seeing that there was a marked divergence of opinion among those members of your Lordships' House who took part in the decision as to the test by which the validity of contracts collateral to a mortgage is to be determined. Lord Davey observes that he cannot understand how, consistently with the doctrine of equity, a mortgagee can insist on retaining the benefit of a covenant in the mortgage contract materially affecting the enjoyment of the mortgaged property after redemption. Lord Lindley, on the other hand, doubts whether the covenant in question, a covenant that the mortgagor would use his influence as a shareholder to secure for the mortgagee in permanence the brokerage business of the company, ought to be looked on as really forming part of the terms of the security. He points out that when the usury laws were in force, and when every device for evading them had to be defeated by equity, the proposition that everything that was part of the mortgage transaction must cease with it, if it was not to infringe the doctrine that once a mortgage always a mortgage, was a convenient statement and as free from objection as most concise statements are, but that when the usury laws were abolished the language was too wide to be accurate.

My Lords, the views expressed by Lord Davey and Lord Lindley are not, so far as mere words go, contradictory. But I cannot shut my eyes to the fact that they represent divergent tendencies. Lord Davey seems to suggest that the doctrine about which, when expressed in general terms, there is little controversy had become finally crystallised in the particular expressions used in certain of the earlier authorities, and that, having become this rigid, it is to-day fatal to the freedom of mortgagor and mortgagee to make their own bargains, even in cases where the reason for applying the doctrine has ceased to exist. The tendency of Lord Lindley's language is, on the other hand, to treat the application of such a rule as a question in which the Courts must not lose sight of the dominating principle underlying the reasons which originally influenced the terms of the rule, reasons which have, in certain cases, become modified as public policy has changed. Speaking for myself, and notwithstanding the high authority of Lord Davey, I think that the tendency of Lord Lindley's conclusion is the one which is most consonant with principle, and I see no valid reason why this House should not act in accordance with it in the case now under consideration.

LORD PARKER:

My Lords, the defendants in this case are appealing to the equitable jurisdiction of the Court for relief from a contract which they admit to be fair and reasonable and of which they have already enjoyed the full advantage. Their title to relief is based on some equity which they say is inherent in all transactions in the nature of a mortgage. They can state no intelligible principle underlying this alleged equity, but contend that your Lordships are bound by authority. That the Court should be asked in the exercise of its equitable jurisdiction to assist in so inequitable a proceeding as the repudiation of a fair and reasonable bargain is somewhat startling, and makes it necessary to examine the point of view from which Courts of Equity have always regarded mortgage transactions. For this purpose I have referred to most, if not all, of the reported cases on the subject, and propose to state shortly the conclusion at which I have arrived.

My Lords, a legal mortgage has generally taken the form of a conveyance with a proviso for reconveyance on the payment of money by a specified date. But a conveyance in this form is by no means necessarily a mortgage. In order to determine whether it is or is not a mortgage, equity has always looked at the real intention of the parties, to be gathered not only from the terms of the particular instrument but from all the circumstances of the transaction, and has always admitted parol evidence in cases where the real intention was in doubt. Only if according to the real intention of the parties the property was to be held as a pledge or security for the payment of the money, and as such to be restored to the mortgagor when the money was paid, was the conveyance considered to be a mortgage. Further, the mortgage might be given to secure not only a single money payment but a series of money payments extending over many years, and again the money secured might or might not, according to the circumstances, constitute a debt due from mortgagor to mortgagee. There might also be mortgages by way of security for something other than a money payment or series of money payments, for example, mortgages by way of indemnity, but these may be disregarded for the purposes of this case.

Taking the simple case of a mortgage by way of conveyance with a proviso for reconveyance on payment of a sum of money upon a specified date, two events might happen. The mortgagor might pay the money on the specific date, in which case equity would specifically perform the contract for reconveyance. On the other hand, the mortgagor might fail to pay the money on the date specified for that purpose. In this case the property conveyed became at law an absolute interest in the mortgagee. Equity, however, did not treat time as of the essence of the transaction, and hence on failure to exercise what may be called the contractual right to redeem there arose an equity to redeem, notwithstanding the specified date had passed. Till this date had passed there was no equity to redeem, and a bill either to redeem or foreclose would have been demurrable. The equity to redeem, which arises on failure to exercise the contractual right of redemption, must be carefully distinguished from the equitable estate, which, from the first, remains in the mortgagor, and is sometimes referred to as an equity of redemption.

Now if, as was not infrequently the case, such a legal mortgage as above described contained a further stipulation that if default were made in payment of the money secured on the date specified the mortgagor should not exercise his equitable right to redeem, or should only exercise it as to part of the mortgaged property, or on payment of some additional sum or performance of some additional condition, such stipulation was always regarded in equity as a penal clause against which relief would be given. This is the principle underlying the rule against fetters or clogs on the equity of redemption. The rule may be stated thus: The equity which arises on failure to exercise the contractual right cannot be fettered or clogged by any stipulation contained in the mortgage or entered into as part of the mortgage transaction...

My Lords, there is another point which has some importance, namely, the terms upon which equity allowed redemption after the estate had become absolute at law. Except in the case of mortgages to secure moneys advanced by way of loan, to which I shall presently refer, equity only allowed redemption on the mortgagor giving effect so far as he could to the terms on which by the bargain between the parties he had a contractual right to redeem the property. Equity might, and most frequently did, impose further terms, e.g. payment of interest up to the date of redemption and proper mortgagees' costs. But except in the case of mortgages to secure moneys advanced by way of loan, I can find no trace in the authorities of any equitable right to redeem without giving effect as far as possible to the terms of the bargain. This is consistent with the principle underlying the rule as to clogging the equity. In relieving from penalties or forfeitures equity has always endeavoured to put the parties as far as possible into the position in which they would have been if no penalty or forfeiture had occurred. It is only in the case of mortgages to secure moneys advanced by way of loan that there was ever any equity to redeem on terms not involving performance of the bargain between the parties. The reason for this exception will appear presently.

There is another point of view from which a clog or fetter on the equitable right to redeem may be properly regarded. The nature of the equitable right is so well known that, upon a mortgage in the usual form to secure a money payment on a certain day, it must be taken to be a term of the real bargain between the parties that the property should remain redeemable in equity after failure to exercise the contractual right. Any fetter or clog imposed by the instrument of mortgage on this equitable right may be properly regarded as a repugnant condition and as such invalid. There are, however, repugnant conditions which cannot be regarded as mere penalties intended to deter the exercise of the equitable right which arises when the time for the exercise of the contractual right has gone by, but which are repugnant to the contractual right itself. A condition to the effect that if the contractual right is not exercised by the time specified the mortgagee shall have an option of purchasing the mortgaged property may properly be regarded as a penal clause. It is repugnant only to the equity and not to the contractual right. But a condition that the mortgagee is to have such an option for a period which begins before the time for the exercise of the equitable right has arrived, or which reserves to the mortgagee any interest in the property after the exercise of the contractual right, is inconsistent not only with the equity but with the contractual right itself, and might, I think, be held invalid for repugnancy even in a Court of law.

This consideration affords a possible and reasonable explanation of the rule referred to in some of the authorities, to the effect that a mortgagee cannot as a term of the mortgage enter into a contract to purchase, or stipulate for an option to purchase, any part of or interest in the mortgaged premises...

My Lords, I now come to the particular class of mortgages to which I have referred, that is to say, mortgages to secure borrowed money. For the whole period during which the Court of Chancery was formulating and laying down its equitable doctrines in relation to mortgages there existed statutes strictly limiting the rate of interest which could be legally charged for borrowed money. If a mortgagee stipulated for some advantage beyond repayment of his principal with interest, equity considered that he was acting contrary to the spirit of these statutes, and held the stipulation bad on this ground. There thus arose the rule so often referred to in the reported decisions, that in a mortgage to secure borrowed money the mortgagee could not contract for any such advantage. There was said to be an equity to redeem on payment of principal, interest, and costs, whatever might have been the bargain between the parties, and any stipulation by the mortgagee for a further or, as it was sometimes called, a collateral advantage came to be spoken of as a clog or fetter on this equity. It is of the greatest importance to observe that this equity is not the equity to redeem with which I have hitherto been dealing. It is an equity which arises ab initio, and not only on failure to exercise the contractual right to redeem. It can be asserted before as well as after such failure. It has nothing to do with time not being of the essence of a contract, or with relief from penalties or with repugnant conditions. It is not a right to redeem on the contractual terms, but a right to redeem notwithstanding the contractual terms, a right which depended on the exercise of the statutes against usury and the public policy thought to be involved in those statutes. Unfortunately, in some of the authorities this right is spoken of as a right incidental to mortgages generally, and not confined to mortgages to secure borrowed money. This is quite explicable when it is remembered that a loan is perhaps the most frequent occasion for a mortgage. But it is, I think, none the less erroneous. I can find no instance of the rule which precludes a mortgagee from stipulating for a collateral advantage having been applied to a mortgage other than a mortgage to secure borrowed money, and there is the authority of Lord Eldon in *Chambers v. Goldwin* (1804) 9 Ves. 254, at p. 271, for saying that this rule was based on the usury laws. The right (notwithstanding the terms of the bargain) to redeem on payment of principal, interest, and costs is a mere corollary to this rule, and falls with it. . . .

The last of the usury laws was repealed in 1854, and thenceforward there was, in my opinion, no intelligible reason why mortgages to secure loans should be on any different footing from other mortgages. In particular, there was no reason why the old rule against a mortgagee being able to stipulate for a collateral advantage should be maintained in any form or with any modification. Borrowers of money were fully protected from oppression by the pains always taken by the Court of Chancery to see that the bargain between borrower and lender was not unconscionable. Unfortunately, at the time when the last of the usury laws was repealed, the origin of the rule appears to have been more or less forgotten, and the cases decided since such repeal exhibit an extraordinary diversity of judicial opinion on the subject. It is little wonder that, with the existence in the authorities of so many contradictory theories, persons desiring to repudiate a fair and reasonable bargain have attempted to obtain the assistance of the Court in that behalf. My Lords, to one who, like myself, has always admired the way in which the Court of Chancery succeeded in supplementing our common law system in accordance with the exigencies of a growing civilisation, it is satisfactory to find, as I have found on analysing the cases in question, that no such attempt has yet been successful. In every case in which a stipulation by a mortgagee for a collateral advantage has, since the repeal of the usury laws, been held invalid, the stipulation has been open to objection, either (1) because it was unconscionable, or (2) because it was in the nature of a penal clause clogging the equity arising on failure to exercise a contractual right to redeem, or (3) because it was in the nature of a condition repugnant as well to the contractual as to the equitable right. It is true that in the case of *Santley v. Wilde* the attempt that was made to induce the Court in the exercise of its equitable jurisdiction to assist in repudiation of a fair and reasonable bargain ought, according to the opinion of other judges, to have been successful, but it is one thing to criticise a decision and quite another to take the responsibility of deciding a case.

My Lords, the present defendants rely chiefly on three cases which came up to your Lordships' House, and to which I must shortly refer. In the first of those cases, *Noakes*

& Co. v. Rice, the collateral advantage in question was a covenant tying the mortgaged premises, which consisted of a leasehold public-house, to the mortgagees' brewery. There was a proviso for reconveyance of the public-house to the mortgagor, upon payment on demand or without demand of all moneys thereby covenanted to be paid. There was, therefore, a contractual right to a reconveyance whenever the mortgagor thought fit to pay. The tie, however, was for the whole term of the lease, and was clearly inconsistent with and repugnant to this right. It was therefore bad. There is, I think nothing at variance with anything I have suggested to your Lordships either in the decision itself or in the speeches of any of the noble Lords who advised the House with the exception of the speech of Lord Davey.

It is with the greatest diffidence that I venture to criticise any opinion expressed by so great an authority, but I cannot wholly accept what Lord Davey lays down as to the equitable principle in relation to mortgages. It appears to me that he omits to notice that the doctrine as to clogs upon the equity of redemption is applicable to all mortgages, and not confined to mortgages to secure borrowed money, and, founding himself upon considerations which apply, if they apply at all, only to the latter class of mortgage, defines the equity to redeem in such a way that in many cases it could never fit the facts at all.

. . .

It appears to me that the noble Lord is reasserting in a modified form the doctrine which prevailed prior to the repeal of the usury laws, and was based on those laws. As long as it was impossible because of the usury laws for a mortgagee upon making a loan to stipulate for any collateral advantage, the equity was an equity to redeem on payment of principal of the loan with interest and costs, and any stipulation to the contrary might be considered a clog. A mortgagee may now stipulate for a collateral advantage, but Lord Davey assumes that the equity remains the same, and, if this be so, it follows that every collateral stipulation which cannot be considered in the nature of interest is still bad. In my opinion the equity cannot remain the same when the only reason for its existence is gone. Nor can I accept the proposition that upon the occasion of a loan the mortgagee cannot stipulate for any payment falling due after the principal is repaid. Such a rule would seriously interfere with business transactions and would be a hardship on mortgagees and mortgagors alike. . . .

My Lords, I come now to the second of the three cases to which I have referred, the case of *Bradley v. Carritt*. Here there was a mortgage of shares in a company expressed to be by way of security for borrowed money payable on or before a fixed date, with interest in the meantime. This involved an obligation to retransfer the shares if the money and interest was paid as agreed. On default there would be an equity to a reconveyance on payment of principal, interest, and costs. There was a clause enabling the mortgagee on default to take over the shares in satisfaction of the debt. This being in the nature of a penalty was a clog on the equity to redeem, and therefore bad. There was also a provision that the mortgagee should always thereafter, as shareholder, use his best endeavours to secure that the mortgagee or his firm should have the sale of the company's teas and in the event of such teas being sold otherwise than through the mortgagee or his firm the mortgagor was to pay the mortgagee a commission. It was as to this latter clause that the difficulty arose. Was it or was it not operative after redemption? The real question, in my opinion, was whether it was inconsistent with or repugnant to the contractual right of the mortgagee to have his property restored unfettered if he paid the money secured with interest as provided in the agreement, and the consequent equitable right to have the property so restored if he paid this money with interest and costs at any time. On this point there was room for difference of opinion, and accordingly we find Bingham J., A.L. Smith M.R., Sterling L.J., Vaughan Williams L.J., Lord Lindley, and Lord Shand taking one view, and Lords Macnaghten, Davey, and Robertson taking another. There is really no difficulty in the decision itself. It is merely to the effect that the case was within the principles of *Noakes & Co. v. Rice*. Lords Macnaghten, Davey, and Robertson all thought that if the stipulations in question were binding after redemption the mortgagor would not upon redemption get back his property intact; in other words, that the stipulation was repugnant both to the contractual right and the equity. But both Lord Macnaghten and Lord Davey also expressed opinions to the effect that all stipulations for collateral advantages must come to and end upon redemption. These expressions of opinion were not, I think, necessary to the decision, and though, of course, of the greatest weight, are not, I think, binding on your Lordships, more especially as Lord Lindley dissented from them. I think that Lord Lindley's conclusions on the point are more in accordance both with principle and authority.

My Lords, the last case to which it is necessary to refer is *Samuel v. Jarrah Timber and Wood Paving Corporation* [1904] A.C. 323. The mortgagee was to have an option to purchase the stock for twelve months. This option being inconsistent with both the contractual and equitable right of redemption was clearly invalid. To use Lord Macnaghten's language, it is an established rule that a mortgagee can never provide at the time of making the loan for any event in which the equity of redemption shall be discharged and the conveyance become absolute. As I have already said, I think the rule depends on the inconsistency or repugnancy involved in any such provision. If once you come to the conclusion that the parties intended that the property should be reconveyed on payment off of the moneys secured any provision which would prevent this must be rejected as inconsistent with and repugnant to the true intention. But, on the other hand, if you once come to the conclusion that this was not the real intention of the parties, then the transaction is not one of mortgage at all.

My Lords, after the most careful consideration of the authorities I think it is open to this House to hold, and I invite your Lordships to hold, that there is now no rule in equity which precludes a mortgagee, whether the mortgage be made upon the occasion of a loan or otherwise, from stipulating for any collateral advantage, provided such collateral advantage is not either (1) unfair and unconscionable, or (2) in the nature of a penalty clogging the equity of redemption, or (3) inconsistent with or repugnant to the contractual and equitable right to redeem.

In the present case it is clear from the evidence, if not from the agreement itself, that the nature of the transaction was as follows: The defendant company wanted to borrow £10,000, and the plaintiffs desired to obtain an option of purchase over any sheepskins the defendants might have for sale during a period of five years. The plaintiffs agreed to lend the money in consideration of obtaining this option, and the defendant company agreed to give the option in consideration of obtaining the loan.

I doubt whether, even before the repeal of the usury laws, this perfectly fair and businesslike transaction would have been considered a mortgage within any equitable rule or maxim relating to mortgages. The only possible way of deciding whether a transaction is a mortgage within any such rule or maxim is by reference to the intention of the parties. It never was intended by the parties that if the defendant company exercised their right to pay off the loan they should get rid of the option. The option was not in the nature of a penalty, nor was it nor could it ever become inconsistent with or repugnant to any other part of the real bargain within any such rule or maxim. The same is true of the commission payable on the sale of skins as to which the option was not exercised. Under these circumstances it seems to me that the bargain must stand and that the plaintiffs are entitled to the relief they claim.

NOTES:

1. In *Noakes & Co. Ltd v. Rice* [1902] A.C. 24 the purchaser of a lease of an hotel with 26 years to run mortgaged the lease to a brewery in order to finance the purchase. He covenanted that during the continuance of the lease, whether or not any part of the mortgage loan was outstanding, he would not sell any liquor that had not been purchased from the mortgagee.

2. In *Bradley v. Carritt* [1903] A.C. 253 the owner of shares in a tea company mortgaged the shares to a tea broker in order to secure the

repayment of a loan. The mortgagor agreed to use his best endeavours to ensure that the mortgagee would always thereafter be employed as broker for the sale of the company's teas; and he further agreed to pay commission to the mortgagee in respect of teas not sold through him.

3. The speech of Viscount Haldane was analysed by Ungoed-Thomas J. in *Re Petrol Filling Station, Vauxhall Bridge Road, London* (1968) 20 P. & C.R. 1. The plaintiffs, lessees of a petrol filling station, concluded a 20-year solus agreement with the defendant oil company. The defendants had indicated their willingness to make a secured loan to the plaintiffs to enable them to modernise the garage forecourt. Seven months later, following the renegotiation of the lease, the plaintiffs entered into a collateral agreement with the defendants in consideration of a loan by the defendants secured by a legal charge. The agreement provided, *inter alia*, for the *solus* agreement to remain in force during the continuance of the charge and to cease to operate on redemption. The plaintiffs later sought to challenge the *solus* agreement. Ungoed-Thomas J. gave judgment for the defendant. He stated (at 11–12):

The evidence does not, to my mind, establish in express terms that there was any binding agreement with regard to the loan before the sales agreement was executed, nor is it, in my view, justifiable to imply such an agreement. There doubtless was a moral obligation on the defendants to make a loan, and I would have come to my conclusion that it did not amount to a legal contract with the greater regret if the defendants had not in fact honoured such moral obligation and made a loan and if the plaintiffs had not deliberately chosen to rely on its affidavit evidence with eyes widely opened to the disadvantageous limitations of such a course.

If, in accordance with my view, the plaintiffs executed the sales agreement without there being any contract with regards to the loan, then it seems to me to follow that the sales agreement and the legal charge were what they appear on their face to be, namely, two separate contracts.

Secondly, even if there were, contrary to my view, a binding contract with regard to the loan and with regard to the sales agreement before or at the time of the sales agreement, the question would still remain whether they constituted one or two contracts. Having regard to authorities and the evidence, which I have already considered, including the commercial nature of the ties in the sales agreement, it seems to me that at its highest the defendant's agreement to lend "in return for the plaintiffs' agreeing to enter into a petrol sales agreement" as stated by Mr Pugh, was, in the words of Lord Haldane in the *Kreglinger* case, "in consideration of being given" a petrol sales agreement, which was "a collateral bargain the entering into which was a preliminary and separable condition of the loan".

Thirdly, even if there were one contract, as the plaintiffs contend, I, for my part, if I were driven to it, would conclude that that contract comprehending the sales agreement and the agreement to lend on the legal charge was not in its "real nature and substance", as a whole, a mortgage transaction, nor, to use Lord Haldane's words, "a mere mortgage", and so falls outside the doctrine of once a mortgage always a mortgage, of which the clog on the equity of redemption is an emanation. I again quote Lord Haldane, where he said:

"That the substance of the transaction must be looked to in applying this doctrine and that it did not apply to cases which were only apparently or technically within it but were in reality something more than cases of mortgage."

If there were the one contract, as the plaintiffs say, then it was "sometimes more than" a mortgage—it was a commercial transaction, of which the mortgage formed part, leaving at any rate the sales agreement part of the transaction with the sales agreement ties outside the ambit of the other part of the transaction, namely, the mortgage, altogether.

It is difficult to disagree with the view that the test of "severability" of collateral advantages "provides a convenient but indefinable rule for dealing with such cases on their merits": see *Megarry & Wade* (5th ed.), p. 971.

4. The speech of Lord Parker was analysed by Browne-Wilkinson J. in *Multiservice Bookbinding Ltd v. Marden* [1979] Ch. 84.

5. It seems clear that collateral advantages which are prima facie permissible, because they are not in the nature of a penalty clogging the equity of redemption and not inconsistent with or repugnant to the contractual and equitable right to redeem, like other mortgage terms, remain subject to (i) the equitable supervisory jurisdiction on the ground that they are unfair, unconscionable or oppressive and (ii) a number of more modern doctrines controlling both mortgage transactions and commercial agreements. These forms of control are considered below.

2. Unfair, unconscionable or oppressive terms

The courts have asserted a general jurisdiction to strike down any term in a mortgage transaction that is "unfair" or "unconscionable" or "oppressive": *Knightsbridge Estates Trust Ltd v. Byrne* [1939] Ch. 441, 457 *per* Greene M.R.; but the issue has tended to arise in relation to effective rates of interest payable on mortgage loans.

Multiservice Bookbinding Ltd v. Marden [1979] Ch. 84

(Ch D., Browne-Wilkinson J.)

In 1966 the plaintiff company borrowed £36,000 from the defendant in order to finance the purchaser of new premises; and the company mortgaged the premises to the defendant. The mortgagee was concerned to preserve the real value of the loan and, to that end, the mortgage provided (i) that the mortgage could not be redeemed for 10 years; (ii) that throughout the term of the mortgage, the mortgagor would pay interest at 2 per cent above the prevailing bank rate on the entire loan (notwithstanding that the mortgage provided for capital repayments); (iii) that arrears of interest would be capitalised after 21 days; and (iv) that payments of capital and interest would be index-linked to the Swiss franc. When the redemption statement was prepared in 1976, the value of sterling as against the Swiss franc had fallen by two-thirds; and the total cost of redeeming the mortgage would amount to £133,000. The effective rate of interest over the 10 years was 16 per cent or, if the index-linking of the capital repayments was treated as a charge on the loan, over 33 per cent. On the other hand, the plaintiff company had seen considerable capital growth over the 10 years and the book value of the mortgaged premises was £93,000.

Having held that the "Swiss franc uplift" provision in clause 6 of the mortgage was not contrary to public policy, Browne-Wilkinson J. continued:

I turn then to the question whether the mortgage is unconscionable or unreasonable. The plaintiffs' starting point on this aspect of the case is a submission that a lender on mortgage is only entitled to repayment of principal, interest and costs. If the lender additionally stipulates for a premium or other collateral advantage the court will not enforce such additional stipulation unless it is reasonable. Then it is submitted that clause 6, providing for the payment of the Swiss franc uplift in addition to the nominal amount of capital and interest, is a premium which in all the circumstances is unreasonable. Alternatively it is said that the terms of the mortgage taken together are unreasonable. In my judgment the argument so advanced is based on a false premise. Since the repeal of the usury laws there has been no general principle that collateral advantages in mortgages have to be "reasonable". The law is fully explained by the House of Lords in *G. and C. Kreglinger v. New Patagonia Meat and Cold Storage Co. Ltd* [1914] A.C. 25 and in particular in the speech of Lord Parker of Waddington. . . .

In his speech Lord Parker reviewed the whole of the law relating to clogs on the equity of redemption and collateral advantages. . . . He said. . ., at p. 60:

> "My Lords, after the most careful consideration of the authorities I think it is open to this House to hold, and I invite your Lordships to hold, that there is now no rule in equity which precludes a mortgagee, whether the mortgage be made upon the occasion of a loan or otherwise, from stipulating for any collateral advantage, provided such collateral advantage is not either (1) unfair and unconscionable, or (2) in the nature of a penalty clogging the equity of redemption, or (3) inconsistent with or repugnant to the contractual and equitable right to redeem."

It is not suggested in this case that any of the terms of the mortgage clog the equity of redemption or are inconsistent with the right to redeem. Therefore on Lord Parker's test, if the plaintiffs are to be excused from complying with any of the terms of the mortgage they must show that the term is, "unfair and unconscionable": the test is not one of reasonableness.

Lord Parker's reasoning is entirely consistent with that of Viscount Haldane L.C., [1914] A.C. 25 who stated, at p. 37, that since the repeal of the usury laws ". . . a collateral advantage may now be stipulated for by the mortgagee provided that he has not acted unfairly or oppressively. . .".

In the *Kreglinger* case the exact question whether the true test was "unconscionableness" or "unreasonableness" did not arise for decision because it was conceded that the bargain was a reasonable one in that case. But in my judgment the exact point was decided by the Court of Appeal in *Knightsbridge Estates Trust Ltd v. Byrne* [1939] Ch. 441. . . . Sir Wilfrid Greene M.R. having stated that a postponement of a right to redeem was not a clog on the equity of redemption, i.e, that the case did not fall within the second or third of Lord Parker's categories, said [1939] Ch. 441, 457:

> "Moreover, equity may give relief against contractual terms in a mortgage transaction if they are oppressive or unconscionable, and in deciding whether or not a particular transaction falls within this category the length of time for which the contractual right to redeem is postponed may well be an important consideration. In the present case no question of this kind was or could have been raised. But equity does not reform mortgage transactions because they are unreasonable. It is concerned to see two things—one that the essential requirements of a mortgage transaction are observed, and the other that oppressive or unconscionable terms are not enforced. Subject to this, it does not, in our opinion, interfere."

In commenting on the use of the word "reasonable" by Romer J. in *Biggs v. Hoddinott* [1898] 2 Ch. 307, Sir Wilfrid Greene M.R. said at p. 459:

"We do not think that the word 'unreasonable' should be interpreted as meaning that the court is to disregard the bargain made by the parties merely because it comes to the conclusion that it is an unreasonable one. A postponement of the right of redemption may be the badge of oppression, or it may be unreasonable in the sense that it renders the right of redemption illusory. We doubt whether Romer J. meant more than this."

Again in commenting on *Davis v. Symons* [1934] Ch. 442 in which Eve J. referred to the stipulation as being "extravagant and oppressive" but also used the word "reasonable", Sir Wilfried Green M.R. did not dissent from the former test but stated that if the word "reasonable" meant something less than oppressive it was not a correct test. Finally, the Court of Appeal overruled the decision of Luxmoore J. on this point, and said, at p. 463:

"In our opinion, if we are right in thinking that the postponement is by itself unobjectionable, it cannot be made objectionable by the presence in the mortgage deed of other provisions, unless the totality is sufficient to enable the court to say that the contract is so oppressive or unconscionable that it ought not to be enforced in a court of equity. If such other provisions are collateral advantages which are inadmissible upon the principles laid down by Lord Parker in the passage cited above, they will, of course, fall to be dealt with as such."

In my judgment the Court of Appeal in overruling the decision of Luxmoore J. based on the unreasonableness of the term made a decision, first that if a postponement of the right to redeem is not objectionable on the grounds that it is a clog on the right to redeem, it is enforceable like any other stipulation unless it falls into Lord Parker's first category as being oppressive or unconscionable; and secondly that mere unreasonableness does not make a term oppressive or unconscionable.

I have dealt with these authorities at some length because the sheet anchor of Mr Nugee's argument, that mere unreasonableness is sufficient to invalidate a stipulation, is the use of the word "unreasonable" by Goff J. in *Cityland and Property (Holdings) Ltd v. Dabrah* [1968] Ch. 166. In that case the plaintiff company was the freehold owner of a house of which the defendant had been the tenant for 11 years. His lease expired and the plaintiff company sold the freehold to him for £3,500, of which the defendant paid £600 in cash and the balance of £2,900 was left by the plaintiff company on mortgage. The mortgage was in unusual terms in that it contained simply a covenant to pay, by instalments, the sum of £4,553, that is to say, a premium of 57 per cent over the sum advanced. No explanation was given as to what this premium represented. The defendant defaulted in paying his instalments after only one year, and the plaintiff was seeking to enforce his security for the full sum of £4,553 less payments actually made. Not surprisingly Goff J. refused to permit this on the grounds that the excess over £2,900 was an unlawful premium. Bearing in mind the relative strength of lender and borrower, the size of the premium and the lack of any explanation or justification for it, the premium in that case was unconscionable and oppressive. The difficulty arises from a passage in the judgment, where after reviewing the authorities, including citations at length from Lord Parker's speech in the *Kreglinger* case [1914] A.C. 25, Goff J. quoted, at p. 180, this passage from *Halsbury's Laws of England*, 3rd ed., vol. 27 (1959), p. 238:

"... but a contract for payment to the mortgagee of a bonus in addition to the sum advanced is valid if the bonus is reasonable and the contract was freely entered into by the mortgagor."

Having quoted that passage Goff J. continued, at p. 180:

"It follows from those authorities that the defendant cannot succeed merely because this is a collateral advantage, but he can succeed if—and only if—on the evidence, the bonus in this case was, to use the language of Lord Parker, 'unfair and unconscionable,' or, to use the language used in *Halsbury's Laws of England*, 'unreasonable'; and I therefore have to determine whether it was or was not."

There are other passages in the judgment where Goff J. seems to treat the words "unreasonable" and "unconscionable" as being interchangeable. But in that case it was unnecessary for him to distinguish between the two concepts, since on either test the premium was unenforceable. I do not think that Goff J. intended to cut down the obvious effect of the *Kreglinger* case [1914] A.C. 25 in any way. Moreover, the decision of the Court of Appeal in *Knightsbridge Estates Trust Ltd v. Byrne* [1939] Ch. 441 was not cited to him.

I therefore approach the second point on the basis that, in order to be freed from the necessity to comply with all the terms of the mortgage, the plaintiffs must show that the bargain, or some of its terms, was unfair and unconscionable: it is not enough to show that, in the eyes of the court, it was unreasonable. In my judgment a bargain cannot be unfair and unconscionable unless one of the parties to it has imposed the objectionable terms in a morally reprehensible manner, that is to say, in a way which affects his conscience.

The classic example of an unconscionable bargain is where advantage has been taken of a young, inexperienced or ignorant person to introduce a term which no sensible well-advised person or party would have accepted. But I do not think the categories of unconscionable bargains are limited: the court can and should intervene where a bargain has been procured by unfair means.

Mr Nugee submitted that a borrower was, in the normal case, in an unequal bargaining position vis-à-vis the lender and that the care taken by the courts of equity to protect borrowers—to which Lord Parker referred in the passage I have quoted— was reflected in a general rule that, except in the case of two large equally powerful institutions, any unreasonable term would be "unconscionable" within Lord Parker's test. I cannot accept this. In my judgment there is no such special rule applicable to contracts of loan which requires one to treat a bargain as having been unfairly made even where it is demonstrated that no unfair advantage has been taken of the borrower. No decision illustrating Mr Nugee's principle was cited. However, if, as in the *Cityland* case [1968] Ch. 166, there is an unusual or unreasonable stipulation the reason for which is not explained, it may well be that in the absence of any explanation, the court will assume that unfair advantage has been taken of the borrower. In considering all the facts, it will often be the case that the borrower's need for the money was far more pressing than the lender's need to lend: if this proves to be the case, then circumstances exist in which an unfair advantage could have been taken. It does not necessarily follow that what could have been done has been done: whether or not an unfair advantage has in fact been taken depends on the facts of each case.

Applying those principles to this case, first I do not think it is right to treat the "Swiss franc uplift" element in the capital repayments as being in any sense a premium or collateral advantage. In my judgment a lender of money is entitled to insure that he is repaid the real value of his loan and if he introduces a term which so provides, he is not stipulating for anything beyond the repayment of principal. I do not think equity would have struck down clause 6 as a collateral advantage even before the repeal of the usury laws.

Secondly, considering the mortgage bargain as a whole, in my judgment there was no great inequality of bargaining power as between the plaintiffs and the defendant. The plaintiff company was a small but prosperous company in need of cash to enable it to expand: if it did not like the terms offered it could have refused them without being made insolvent or, as in the *Cityland* case [1968] Ch. 166, losing its home. The defendant had £40,000 to lend, but only, as he explained to the plaintiffs, if its real value was preserved. The defendant is not a professional moneylender and there is no evidence of any sharp practice of any kind by him. The borrowers were represented by independent solicitors of repute. Therefore the background does not give rise to any pre-supposition that the defendant took an unfair advantage of the plaintiffs.

Mr Nugee's main case is based on the terms of the mortgage itself. He points to the facts that (1) the defendant's principal and interest is fully inflation proofed (2) that interest is payable at two per cent above minimum lending rate and (3) that interest is payable on the whole £36,000 throughout the term of the loan. He says that although any one of these provisions by itself might not be objectionable, when all these are joined in one mortgage they are together "unfair and unconscionable". He adds further subsidiary points, amongst them that it is impossible to know the sum required for redemption when notice to redeem has to be given; that interest is payable in advance; that no days of grace were allowed for paying the instalments of capital and any expenses incurred by the lender are charged on the property and therefore under clause 6 subject to the Swiss franc uplift even though incurred long after 1966. He also contends that if there were capitalised arrears of interest, the Swiss franc uplift would be applied twice: once when the arrears are capitalised and again when the capitalised sum is paid: in my opinion this is not the true construction of the mortgage.

However, Mr Nugee's other points amount to a formidable list and if it were relevant I would be of the view that the terms were unreasonable judged by the standards which the court would adopt if it had to settle the terms of a mortgage. In particular I consider that it was unreasonable both for the debt to be inflation proofed by reference to the Swiss franc and at the same time to provide for a rate of interest two per cent above bank rate—a rate which reflects at least in part the unstable state of the pound sterling. On top of this interest on the whole sum advanced was to be paid throughout the term. The defendant made a hard bargain. But the test is not reasonableness. The parties made a bargain which the plaintiffs, who are businessmen, went into with their eyes open, with the benefit of independent advice, without any compelling necessity to accept a loan on these terms and without any sharp practice by the defendant. I cannot see that there was anything unfair or oppressive or morally reprehensible in such a bargain entered into in such circumstances.

NOTES:

1. For comment on *Multiservice Bookbinding Ltd v. Marden*, see Oakley [1978] C.L.J. 211; Crane [1978] Conv. 318; Wilkinson [1978] Conv. 346; Williams [1978] Conv. 432; Bishop and Hindley (1979) 42 M.L.R. 338. For comment on *Cityland and Property (Holdings) Ltd v. Dabrah* [1968] Ch. 166, see (1967) 31 Conv. 282. Bishop and Hindley (1979) 42 M.L.R. 338 suggest that the two decisions reflect the different judicial attitude to consumer and commercial mortgages and to low and high risk loans.

2. For the legality of index-linked payments in the context of building society mortgages, see the Building Societies Act 1986, s.10(10)(a) and see *Nationwide Building Society v. Registry of Friendly Societies* [1983] 1 W.L.R. 1226, 1231 *per* Peter Gibson J.

3. The Consumer Credit Act 1974 was not applicable because the mortgagor was not an individual: see *infra*, p. 877.

4. Equity regards as a penalty and thus unenforceable a provision whereby, in the event of default, the mortgagor is required to pay a higher rate of interest than is otherwise payable; on the other hand, no objection appears to have been taken to a provision that a discounted rate of interest is payable provided that the mortgagor complies with the mortgage terms: *Strode v. Parker* (1694) 2 Vern 316.

3. Undue influence and misrepresentation

The House of Lords has recently considered the equitable jurisdiction to set aside, or to decline to enforce, mortgage transactions procured by means of undue influence or misrepresentation.

Mortgage transactions may be set aside where the complainant establishes actual undue influence on the part of the lender or where undue influence can be presumed because the complainant establishes that the transaction constitutes "a manifest disadvantage to the party seeking to avoid it, explicable only on the basis that undue influence has been used to procure it": *Coldunell Ltd v. Gallon* [1986] Q.B. 1184, 1194 *per* Oliver L.J. See *National Westminster Bank plc v. Morgan* [1985] A.C. 686, as explained in *CICB Mortgages plc v. Pitt* [1994] A.C. 200, 207–209 *per* Lord Browne-Wilkinson. If actual undue influence is established, there is no need for the complainant to demonstrate that the transaction was manifestly disadvantageous: *ibid.*

The House of Lords also considered, in the context of husband and wife, the jurisdiction to set aside as against the lender a mortgage or surety transaction procured by undue influence, misrepresentation or some other vitiating conduct on the part of the principal borrower. In *Barclays Bank plc v. O'Brien* [1994] A.C. 180 and *CICB Mortgages plc v. Pitt* [1994] A.C. 200 it was held (i) that the transaction would be voidable if the principal borrower, in obtaining the consent, was acting as agent of the lender or if the lender had actual or constructive notice of the vitiating conduct; (ii) that the lender would be fixed with constructive notice if the transaction was not on its face to the financial advantage of the surety and the relationship between the principal borrower and the surety was one where there was a substantial risk that, in transactions of that kind, there had been undue influence, misrepresentation or some other vitiating conduct on the part of the principal borrower; but (iii) that the lender could avoid being fixed with constructive notice if he arranged a private meeting with the surety, informed him of the extent of his liability as surety and urged him to take independent legal advice.

Barclays Bank plc v. O'Brien [1994] A.C. 180

(HL, Lord Templeman, Lord Lowry, Lord Browne-Wilkinson, Lord Slynn, Lord Woolf)

The first and second defendants were husband and wife. They executed a second mortgage of the matrimonial home in order to secure overdraft facilities extended to the husband's company. Contrary to instructions, the relevant bank official failed to explain to the wife the effect of the mortgage (which had been misrepresented by the husband) and he failed to recommend that the wife should seek independent advice. When the bank subsequently brought proceedings for possession of the house, the wife successfully argued that the mortgage was unenforceable as against her.

LORD BROWNE-WILKINSON:

Undue influence

A person who has been induced to enter into a transaction by the undue influence of another ("the wrongdoer") is entitled to set that transaction aside as against the wrongdoer. Such undue influence is either actual or presumed. In *Bank of Credit and Commerce International SA v. Aboody* [1990] 1 Q.B. 923, 953, the Court of Appeal helpfully adopted the following classification.

Class 1: Actual undue influence

In these cases it is necessary for the claimant to prove affirmatively that the wrongdoer exerted undue influence on the complainant to enter into the particular transaction which is impugned.

Class 2: Presumed undue influence

In these cases the complainant only has to show, in the first instance, that there was a relationship of trust and confidence between the complainant and the wrongdoer of such a nature that it is fair to presume that the wrongdoer abused that relationship in procuring the complainant to enter into the impugned transaction. In Class 2 cases therefore there is no need to produce evidence that actual undue influence was exerted in relation to the particular transaction impugned: once a confidential relationship has been proved, the burden then shifts to the wrongdoer to prove that the complainant entered into the impugned transaction freely, for example by showing that the complainant had independent advice. Such a confidential relationship can be established in two ways.

Class 2(A)

Certain relationships (for example solicitor and client, medical advisor and patient) as a matter of law raise the presumption that undue influence has been exercised.

Class 2(B)

Even if there is no relationship falling within Class 2(A), if the complainant proves the de facto existence of a relationship under which the complainant generally reposed trust and confidence in the wrongdoer, the existence of such relationship raises the presumption of undue influence. In a Class 2(B) case therefore, in the absence of evidence disproving undue influence, the complainant will succeed in setting aside the impugned transaction merely by proof that the complainant reposed trust and confidence in the wrongdoer without having to prove that the wrongdoer exerted actual undue influence or otherwise abused such trust and confidence in relation to the particular transaction impugned.

As to dispositions by a wife in favour of her husband, the law for long remained in an unsettled state. In the 19th century some judges took the view that the relationship was such that it fell into Class 2(A), *i.e.* as a matter of law undue influence by the husband over the wife was presumed. It was not until the decisions in *Howes v. Bishop* [1909] 2 K.B. 390 and *Bank of Montreal v. Stuart* [1911] A.C. 120 that it was finally determined that the relationship of husband and wife did not as a matter of law raise a presumption of undue influence within Class 2(A). It is to be noted therefore that when the *Duval* case was decided in 1902 the question whether there was a Class 2(A) presumption of undue influence as between husband and wife was still unresolved.

An invalidating tendency?

Although there is no Class 2(A) presumption of undue influence as between husband and wife, it should be emphasised that in any particular case a wife may well be able to demonstrate that de facto she did leave decisions on financial affairs to her husband thereby bringing herself within Class 2(B), *i.e.* that the relationship between husband and wife in the particular case was such that the wife reposed confidence and trust in her husband in relation to their financial affairs and therefore undue influence is to be presumed. Thus, in those cases which still occur where the wife relies in all financial matters on her husband and simply does what he suggests, a presumption of undue influence within Class 2(B) can be established solely from the proof of such trust and confidence without proof of actual undue influence.

In the appeal in *C.I.B.C. Mortgages plc v. Pitt* (judgment in which is to be given immediately after that in the present appeal), *post*, p. 200, Mr Price for the wife argued that in the case of transactions between husband and wife, there was an "invalidating tendency", *i.e.* although there was no Class 2(A) presumption of undue influence, the courts were more ready to find that a husband had exercised undue influence over his wife than in other cases. Scott L.J. in the present case also referred to the law treating married women "more tenderly" than others. This approach is based on dicta in early authorities. In *Grigby v. Cox* (1750) 1 Ves.Sen. 517 Lord Hardwicke, whilst rejecting any presumption of undue influence, said that a court of equity "will have more jealousy" over dispositions by a wife to a husband. In *Yerkey v. Jones* (1939) 63 C.L.R. 649, 675, Dixon J. refers to this "invalidating tendency". He also refers to the court recognising "the opportunities which a wife's confidence in her husband gives him of unfairly or improperly procuring her to become surety": see p. 677.

In my judgment this special tenderness of treatment afforded to wives by the courts is properly attributable to two factors. First, many cases may well fall into the Class 2(B) category of undue influence because the wife demonstrates that she placed trust and confidence in her husband in relation to her financial affairs and therefore raises a presumption of undue influence. Second, the sexual and emotional ties between the parties provide a ready weapon for undue influence; a wife's true wishes can easily be overborne because of her fear of destroying or damaging the wider relationship between her and her husband if she opposes his wishes.

For myself, I accept that the risk of undue influence affecting a voluntary disposition by a wife in favour of a husband is greater than in the ordinary run of cases where no sexual or emotional ties affect the free exercise of the individual's will.

Undue influence, misrepresentation and third parties

Up to this point I have been considering the right of a claimant wife to set aside a transaction as against the wrongdoing husband when the transaction has been procured by his undue influence. But in surety cases the decisive question is whether the claimant wife can set aside the transaction, not against the wrongdoing husband, but against the creditor bank. Of course, if the wrongdoing husband is acting as agent for the creditor bank in obtaining the surety from the wife, the creditor will be fixed with the wrongdoing of its own agent and the surety contract can be set aside as against the creditor. Apart from this, if the creditor bank has notice, actual or constructive, of the undue influence exercised by the husband (and consequentially of the wife's equity to set aside the transaction) the creditor will take subject to that equity and the wife can set aside the transaction against the creditor (albeit a purchaser for value) as well as against the husband: see *Bainbrigge v. Browne* (1881) 18 Ch.D. 188 and *Bank of Credit and Commerce International SA v. Aboody* [1990] 1 Q.B. 923, 973. Similarly, in cases such as the present where the wife has been induced to enter into the transaction by the husband's misrepresentation, her equity to set aside the transaction will be enforceable against the creditor if either the husband was acting as the creditor's agent or the creditor had actual or constructive notice.

. . .

Although there may be cases where, without artificiality, it can properly be held that the husband was acting as the agent of the creditor in procuring the wife to stand as surety, such cases will be of very rare occurrence. The key to the problem is to identify the circumstances in which the creditor will be taken to have had notice of the wife's equity to set aside the transaction.

The doctrine of notice lies at the heart of equity. Given that there are two innocent parties, each enjoying rights, the earlier right prevails against the later right if the acquirer of the later right knows of the earlier right (actual notice) or would have discovered it had he taken proper steps (constructive notice). In particular, if the party asserting that he takes free of the earlier rights of another knows of certain facts which put him on inquiry as to the possible existence of the rights of that other and he fails to make such inquiry or take such other steps as are reasonable to verify whether such earlier right does or does not exist, he will have constructive notice of the earlier right and take subject to it. Therefore where a wife has agreed to stand surety for her husband's debts as a result of undue influence or misrepresentation, the creditor will take subject to the wife's equity to set aside the transaction if the circumstances are such as to put the creditor on inquiry as to the circumstances in which she agreed to stand surety.

It is at this stage that, in my view, the "invalidating tendency" or the law's "tender treatment" of married women, becomes relevant. As I have said above in dealing with undue influence, this tenderness of the law towards married women is due to the fact that, even today, many wives repose confidence and trust in their husbands in relation to their financial affairs. This tenderness of the law is reflected by the fact that voluntary dispositions by the wife in favour of her husband are more likely to be set aside than other dispositions by her: a wife is more likely to establish presumed undue influence of Class 2(B) by her husband than by others because, in practice, many wives do repose in their husbands trust and confidence in relation to their financial affairs. Moreover the informality of business dealings between spouses raises a substantial risk that the husband has not accurately stated to the wife the nature of the liability she is undertaking, *i.e.*, he has misrepresented the position, albeit negligently.

Therefore in my judgment a creditor is put on inquiry when a wife offers to stand surety for her husband's debts by the combination of two factors: (a) the transaction is on its face not to the financial advantage of the wife; and (b) there is a substantial risk in transactions of that kind that, in procuring the wife to act as surety, the husband has committed a legal or equitable wrong that entitles the wife to set aside the transaction.

It follows that unless the creditor who is put on inquiry takes reasonable steps to satisfy himself that the wife's agreement to stand surety has been properly obtained, the creditor will have constructive notice of the wife's rights.

What, then are the reasonable steps which the creditor should take to ensure that it does not have constructive notice of the wife's rights, if any? Normally the reasonable steps necessary to avoid being fixed with constructive notice consist of making inquiry of the person who may have the earlier right (*i.e.* the wife) to see whether such right is asserted. It is plainly impossible to require of banks and other financial institutions that they should inquire of one spouse whether he or she has been unduly influenced or misled by the other. But in my judgment the creditor, in order to avoid being fixed with constructive notice, can reasonably be expected to take steps to bring home to the wife the risk she is running by standing as surety and to advise her to take independent advice. As to past transactions, it will depend on the facts of each case whether the steps taken by the creditor satisfy this test. However for the future in my judgment a creditor will have satisfied these requirements if it insists that the wife attend a private meeting (in the absence of the husband) with a representative of the creditor at which she is told of the extent of her liability as surety, warned of the risk she is running and urged to take independent legal advice. If these steps are taken in my judgment the creditor will have taken such reasonable steps as are necessary to preclude a subsequent claim that it had constructive notice of the wife's rights. I should make it clear that I have been considering the ordinary case where the creditor knows only that the wife is to stand surety for her husband's debts. I would not exclude exceptional cases where a creditor has knowledge of further facts which render the presence of undue influence not only possible but probable. In such cases, the creditor to be safe will have to insist that the wife is separately advised.

I am conscious that in treating the creditor as having constructive notice because of the risk of Class 2(B) undue influence or misrepresentation by the husband I may be extending the law as stated by Fry J. in *Bainbrigge v. Browne* (1881) 18 Ch.D. 188, 197, and the Court of Appeal in the *Aboody* case [1990] 1 Q.B. 923, 973. Those cases suggest that for a third party to be affected by constructive notice of presumed undue influence the third party must actually know of the circumstances which give rise to a presumption of undue influence. In contrast, my view is that the risk of Class 2(B) undue influence or misrepresentation is sufficient to put the creditor on inquiry. But my statement accords with the principles of notice: if the known facts are such as to indicate the possibility of an adverse claim that is sufficient to put a third party on inquiry.

If the law is established as I have suggested, it will hold the balance fairly between on the one hand the vulnerability of the wife who relies implicitly on her husband and, on the other hand, the practical problems of financial institutions asked to accept a secured or unsecured surety obligation from the wife for her husband's debts. In the context of suretyship, the wife will not have any right to disown her obligations just because subsequently she proves that she did not fully understand the transaction: she will, as in all other areas of her affairs, be bound by her obligations unless her husband has, by misrepresentation, undue influence or other wrong, committed an actionable wrong against her. In the normal case, a financial institution will be able to lend with confidence in reliance on the wife's surety obligation provided that it warns her (in the absence of the husband) of the amount of her potential liability and of the risk of standing surety and advises her to take independent advice.

Notes:

1. In *CICB Mortgages plc v. Pitt* [1994] A.C. 200 a similar argument failed. Although the husband had exercised undue influence over the wife, the mortgage appeared to be a joint venture for their mutual benefit and there was nothing to put the mortgagee on inquiry. Lord Brown-Wilkinson stated (at 211):

Mr Price, for Mrs Pitt, argued that the invalidating tendency which reflects the risk of there being Class 2(B) undue influence was, in itself, sufficient to put the plaintiff on inquiry. I reject this submission without hesitation. It accords neither with justice nor with practical common sense. If third parties were to be fixed with constructive notice of undue influence in relation to every transaction between husband and wife, such transactions would become almost impossible. On every purchase of a home in the joint names, the building society or bank financing the purchase would have to insist on meeting the wife separately from her husband, advise her as to the nature of the transaction and recommend her to take legal advice separate from that of her husband. If that were not done, the financial institution would have to run the risk of a subsequent attempt by the wife to avoid her liabilities under the mortgage on the grounds of undue influence or misrepresentation. To establish the law in that sense would not benefit the average married couple and would discourage financial institutions from making the advance.

What distinguishes the case of the joint advance from the surety case is that, in the latter, there is not only the possibility of undue influence having been exercised but also the increased risk of it having in fact been exercised because, at least on its face, the guarantee by a wife of her husband's debts is not for her financial benefit. It is the combination of these two factors that puts the creditor on inquiry.

For comment on *Barclays Bank plc v. O'Brien* and *CICB Mortgages plc v. Pitt*, see [1994] C.L.J. 21; [1994] Conv. 140, 421; (1994) 110 L.Q.R. 167; (1994) 57 M.L.R. 467; [1994] *Restitution Law Review* 3; [1995] C.L.J. 280; [1995] Conv. 250; (1995) 15 *Legal Studies* 35; (1995) 15 O.J.L.S. 119.

2. *Barclays Bank plc v. O'Brien* has generated an enormous amount of litigation and theoretical discussion. The case law has been summarised by the Court of Appeal in *Royal Bank of Scotland plc v. Etridge (No.2)* [1998] 4 All E.R. 705.

Royal Bank of Scotland plc v. Etridge (No.2) [1998] 4 All E.R. 705

(CA, Stuart-Smith, Millett and Morritt L.JJ.)

STUART-SMITH L.J.
1. This is the judgment of the court, to which all members of the court have contributed, in eight conjoined appeals.

The law
2. In *Barclays Bank plc v. O'Brien* [1994] 1 A.C. 180 the House of Lords considered the question whether a bank is entitled to enforce its security against a wife where she has been induced by the undue influence or misrepresentation of her husband to charge the matrimonial home by way of collateral security for her husband's liability to the bank. The case was one of misrepresentation but the guidance which their Lordships gave was intended to be equally applicable to cases of undue influence. Lord Browne-Wilkinson, who delivered the only speech, was concerned to provide not only an analysis of the law, but a practical solution which would enable the matrimonial home to be available to creditors as security and at the same time provide the vulnerable wife with proper protection. Lord Browne-Wilkinson said ([1994] 1 A.C. 180 at 188):

"In a substantial proportion of marriages it is still the husband who has the business experience and the wife is willing to follow his advice without bringing a truly independent mind and will to bear on financial decisions. The number of recent cases in this field shows that in practice many wives are still subjected to, and yield to, undue influence by their husbands. Such wives can reasonably look to the law for some protection when their husbands have abused the trust and confidence reposed in them. On the other hand, it is important to keep a sense of balance in approaching these cases. It is easy to allow sympathy for the wife who is threatened with the loss of her home at the suit of a rich bank to obscure an important public interest, viz the need to ensure that the wealth currently tied up in the matrimonial home does not become economically sterile. If the rights secured to wives by the law renders vulnerable loans granted on the security of matrimonial homes, institutions will be unwilling to accept such security, thereby reducing the flow of loan capital to business enterprises. It is therefore essential that a law designed to protect the vulnerable does not render the matrimonial home unacceptable as security to financial institutions."

The solution which Lord Browne-Wilkinson proposed was that steps be taken to ensure that the risks which she was running were brought home to the wife and that she should be advised to take independent legal advice. Lord Browne-Wilkinson said ([1994] 1 A.C. 180 at 197):

"If the law is established as I have suggested, it will hold the balance fairly between on the one hand the vulnerability of the wife who relies implicitly on her husband and, on the other hand, the practical problems of financial institutions asked to accept a secured or unsecured surety obligation from the wife for her husband's debts. In the context of suretyship, the wife will not have any right to disown her obligations just because subsequently she proves that she did not fully understand the transaction: she will, as in all other areas of her affairs, be bound by her obligations unless her husband has, by misrepresentation, undue influence or other wrong, committed an actionable wrong against her. In the normal case, a financial institution will be able to lend with confidence in reliance on the wife's surety obligation provided that it warns her (in the absence of the husband) of the amount of her potential liability and of the risk of standing surety and advises her to take independent advice."

3. Unfortunately, as the number of cases which have come before the courts since *O'Brien's* case demonstrates, the protection which ought to be afforded to the wife by the provision of independent legal advice has in many cases proved illusory. The advice which the wife has received has often been perfunctory, limited to an explanation of the documents and yet inadequate to dispel her misunderstanding of the real extent of the liability which she was undertaking, and not directed to ensure that she was entering into the transaction of her own free will rather than as the result of illegitimate pressure from her husband or blind trust in him.

4. We shall deal first with the general law as it affects transactions between the wrongdoer and the complainant themselves (who need not be husband and wife or cohabitees) before turning to the particular problems which arise where the parties are husband and wife or cohabitees and the issue is between the complainant and a third party such as the bank. For convenience we shall assume that the complainant is the wife and the wrongdoer is the husband, although similar principles apply in other cases where there is an emotional relationship between cohabitees.

(1) THE POSITION AS BETWEEN WRONGDOER AND COMPLAINANT

Undue influence

5. Cases of undue influence are now classified in three categories. Class 1 consists of cases of actual (or express) undue influence. In these cases it is necessary for the complainant to prove affirmatively that she entered into the impugned transaction not of her own free will but as a result of actual undue influence exerted against her. Class 2 consists of cases of presumed undue influence. In these cases it is sufficient for the complainant to establish the existence of a relationship of trust and confidence between her and the wrongdoer of such a nature that it is fair to presume that the wrongdoer abused the relationship in procuring her to enter into the impugned transaction. Once such a relationship has been established, the burden shifts to the wrongdoer to prove that the complainant entered into the impugned transaction with her "full, free and informed thought" (*Zamet v. Hyman* [1961] 1 W.L.R. 1442 at 1444 per Lord Evershed M.R.).

6. The necessary relationship can be established in either of two ways. Class 2A consists of certain well-known relationships which are by presumption of law irrebuttably treated as relationships of trust and confidence. Class 2B consists of other cases where the complainant establishes by affirmative evidence that she was accustomed to repose trust and confidence in the wrongdoer.

7. The expressions "actual undue influence" and "presumed undue influence" might be taken to indicate that the difference between them lies merely in the means by which the exercise of undue influence is proved. But this is not the case. Presumed undue influence is concerned with the abuse of a relationship of trust and confidence. In *Tate v. Williamson* (1866) L.R. 2 Ch. App. 55 at 61 Lord Chelmsford L.C. spoke of the "influence which naturally grows out of [the] confidence" reposed by the person influenced in the person exercising the influence. Since the vice of the transaction lies in the abuse of a position of trust, the transaction must result in some unfair advantage to

the person in whom trust is reposed (or to another at his request) at the expense of the person who relies upon him; for even a dealing between a fiduciary and his principal will be upheld if it is affirmatively shown to be fair to the principal.

8. The equitable doctrine of undue influence, however, is not confined to cases of abuse of trust and confidence; it is also concerned to protect the vulnerable from exploitation. It is brought into play whenever one party has acted unconscionably in exploiting the power to direct the conduct of another which is derived from the relationship between them. This need not be a relationship of trust and confidence; it may be a relationship of ascendancy and dependence (*Allcard v. Skinner* (1887) 36 Ch.D. 145 (religious order and member of the order) is a classic case; for a more recent example, see *Re Craig (decd)* [1971] Ch. 95 (housekeeper and an elderly employer who had become dependent upon her)). In such cases actual undue influence has been said to involve—

> "some unfair and improper conduct, some coercion from outside, some overreaching, some form of cheating, and generally, though not always, some personal advantage obtained by a donee placed in some close and confidential relation to the donor" (see *Allcard v. Skinner* (1887) 36 Ch.D. 145 at 181 *per* Lindley L.J.)

This is often described in terms of the domination by the wrongdoer of the mind and will of the complainant so that "the mind of the latter became a mere channel through which the wishes of the former flowed" (see *Tufton v. Sperni* [1952] 2 T.L.R. 516 at 532 per Morris L.J.).

9. Importunity and pressure, if carried to the point at which the complainant can no longer exercise a will of her own, amounts to undue influence, but pressure is neither always necessary nor always sufficient. In *Bank of Montreal v. Stuart* [1911] A.C. 120 the wife succeeded in establishing that she was the victim of actual undue influence even though no pressure was exerted on her by her husband because none was needed:

> "She had no will of her own. Nor had she any means of forming an independent judgment even if she had desired to do so. She was ready to sign anything that her husband asked her to sign and do anything he told her to do. At the same time it is right to say that in her evidence in this action she repudiates the notion that any influence was exerted or any pressure put upon her ... She says she acted of her own free will ... Her declarations in the course of her cross-examination that she acted of her own free will and not under her husband's influence merely show how deeprooted and how lasting the influence of her husband was" (see [1911] A.C. 120 at 136–137 *per* Lord Macnaghten).

Today, perhaps, this would more readily be classified as a Class 2B case. It may be contrasted with the assessment of the circumstances in which Mrs O'Brien signed the charge in *Barclays Bank plc v. O'Brien* [1993] Q.B. 109 at 141–142 made by Scott L.J.:

> "Mr O'Brien was, Mrs O'Brien said, extremely insistent that she should sign. He made an emotional scene on the day she signed and told her that, if she did not sign, the company would be bankrupt and her son John would lose his home. These were heavy family pressures but not particularly unusual nor sufficient, in my opinion, to overset and bear down the will of Mrs O'Brien. She signed because she was persuaded that it was the right thing to do, not because her husband's pressure deprived her consent of reality."

10. Legitimate commercial pressure brought by a creditor, however strong, coupled with proper feelings of family loyalty and a laudable desire to help a husband or son in financial difficulty, may be difficult to resist. They may be sufficient to induce a reluctant wife or mother to agree to charge her home by way of collateral security, particularly if they are accompanied by family pressure or emotional scenes. But they are not enough to justify the setting aside of the transaction unless they go beyond what is permissible and lead the complainant to execute the charge not because,

however reluctantly, she is persuaded that it is the right thing to do, but because the wrongdoer's importunity has left her with no will of her own.

Manifest disadvantage

11. The requirement that the transaction should be manifestly disadvantageous to the complainant derives from *National Westminster Bank plc v. Morgan* [1985] A.C. 686. It has been widely criticised. In *CIBC Mortgages plc v. Pitt* [1994] 1 A.C. 200 Lord Browne-Wilkinson said that it may have to be reconsidered. There is no such requirement if actual undue influence is established: see *CIBC Mortgages plc v. Pitt*.

12. Whatever the true position in this regard, the presence of manifest disadvantage is obviously a powerful evidential factor. The more disadvantageous the transaction to the complainant the easier it is for her to establish that it has been procured by improper means, and the more difficult it is for the wrongdoer to rebut the inference. In *Allcard v. Skinner* (1887) 36 Ch.D. 145 at 185 Lindley L.J. spoke of a gift "so large as not to be reasonably accounted for on the ground of friendship, relationship, charity, or other ordinary motives on which ordinary men act ..."

13. In *Bank of Montreal v. Stuart* [1911] A.C. 120 at 137 the transaction was described as "immoderate and irrational"; and in *Wright v. Carter* [1903] 1 Ch. 27 at 55 as one "which no prudent person would for one moment have entertained". Similar expressions are to be found in all the classic cases where transactions have been set aside on the ground of presumed undue influence. But there is a great range of cases, from those where the transaction is merely such as to excite suspicion that it may have been procured by undue influence, but where it is not so disadvantageous that the suspicion may not readily be allayed, to those where the presumption that it has been procured by undue influence may be virtually impossible to rebut. At one extreme there are the cases where the most that can be said is that the transaction is "not on its face to the financial advantage of the complainant", to those such as the transactions in *Lancashire Loans Ltd v. Black* [1934] 1 K.B. 380 and *Credit Lyonnais Bank Nederland NV v Burch* [1997] 1 All E.R. 144 at 152 which " 'shocks' the conscience of the court". Cases of the kind last mentioned could equally well be regarded as cases of harsh and unconscionable bargains.

14. Just as the degree of unfairness in the transaction may vary widely, so may the nature of the relationship between the parties. The capacity of one person to influence the conduct of another varies with the degree of trust and confidence reposed by that other in him. In some relationships the capacity for influence may be slight; in others it may be overwhelming. It has, for example, been said to be "almost impossible" to uphold a substantial gift by a client to his solicitor: see *Wright v. Carter* [1903] 1 Ch. 27 at 57.

15. The fact that a transaction is manifestly disadvantageous to one of the parties has a dual significance: (i) it assists the complainant in establishing her claim against the wrongdoer in a case of presumed undue influence; and (ii) it is relevant to the way in which the transaction appears to a third party and thus assists her in establishing that the third party had constructive notice of the impropriety.

Rebutting the presumption

16. As between the complainant and the alleged wrongdoer, the presumption cannot be rebutted merely by evidence that the complainant understood what he or she was doing and intended to do it, but only by showing that she was either free from the influence of the alleged wrongdoer or had been placed by the receipt of independent legal advice in an equivalent position. As Hobhouse L.J. emphasised in the course of his dissenting judgment in *Banco Exterior Internacional v. Mann* [1995] 1 All E.R. 936 at 946, the problem is not lack of understanding but lack of independence: see *Zamet v. Hyman* [1961] 1 W.L.R. 1442 at 1450–1451 approving Lord Eldon L.C.'s celebrated dictum in *Huguenin v. Baseley* (1807) 14 Ves. 273 at 300, "The question is, not

whether she knew what she was doing, had done, or proposed to do, but how the intention was produced ..."

17. What needs to be shown to rebut the presumption is that—

"the gift was the spontaneous act of the donor acting under circumstances which enabled him to exercise an independent will and which justifies the Court in holding that the gift was the result of a free exercise of the donor's will" (see *Allcard v. Skinner* (1887) 36 Ch.D. 145 at 171 *per* Cotton L.J.)

The wrongdoer must prove that the complainant entered into the transaction as the result of the free exercise of her independent will. The most obvious, though not the only, way to prove this is by showing that the complainant entered into the transaction only after the nature and effect of the transaction were explained by some independent and qualified person fully informed of the material facts:

"so completely as to satisfy the Court that the [complainant] was acting independently of any influence from the [wrongdoer] and with the full appreciation of what [she] was doing ..." (see *Inche Noriah v. Shaik Allie Bin Omar* [1929] A.C. 127 at 135 *per* Lord Hailsham L.C.).

18. References to the complainant's freedom of action are references to her freedom from undue influence or illegitimate pressure. Where the impugned transaction is one of gift or other bounty, the donor must be shown to have acted voluntarily in the fullest sense of the word. Any sign of reluctance on her part may indicate that improper pressure is being brought to bear. Where the transaction is a commercial one, however, the case is different. As we have already pointed out, reluctance to enter into a contract of guarantee or collateral security is not necessarily indicative that any improper pressure is being brought to bear. If the reluctance of the proposed surety is overborne it may be because she has yielded to the external exigencies of the situation. Far from indicating the presence of improper pressure, such reluctance may show that she knew what she was doing and did it because she thought that it was the right thing to do.

Independent legal advice

19. A solicitor who is instructed to advise a person who may be subject to the undue influence of another must bear in mind that is not sufficient that she understands the nature and effect of the transaction if she is so affected by the influence of the other that she cannot make an independent decision of her own. It is not sufficient to explain the documentation and ensure that she understands the nature of the transaction and wishes to carry it out: see *Powell v. Powell* [1900] 1 Ch. 243 at 247, approved in *Wright v. Carter*. His duty is to satisfy himself that his client is free from improper influence, and the first step must be to ascertain whether it is one into which she could sensibly be advised to enter if free from such influence. If he is not so satisfied it is his duty to advise her not to enter into it, and to refuse to act further for her in the implementation of the transaction if she persists. In this event, while the contents of his advice must remain confidential, he should inform the other parties (including the bank) that he has seen his client and given her certain advice, and that as a result he has declined to act for her any further. He must in any event advise her that she is under no obligation to enter into the transaction at all and, if she still wishes to do so, that she is not bound to accept the terms of any document which has been put before her: see *Credit Lyonnais Bank Nederland NV v. Burch* [1997] 1 All E.R. 144.

20. Even the task of ensuring that she understands the full implications of the transaction may not be easy. As many of the cases before us demonstrate, where a wife is asked to stand surety or provide collateral security for her husband's indebtedness, there is an ever present danger that he may have misrepresented the position to her. Even without any actual misrepresentation by him, she is likely to misunderstand the full extent of the risk to which she is exposing herself. Her husband may truthfully

have explained that he has asked the bank to make a relatively small advance or to increase his overdraft by a relatively modest amount, that the bank has demanded a guarantee or charge in return, and that he expects to repay the advance or reduce the overdraft to within its previous limits within a short time. He may well satisfy his wife that the additional liability, and therefore her exposure, is both manageable and temporary. Where the bank is asking for a continuing all moneys unlimited guarantee or charge, the solicitor does not discharge his duty to the wife by telling her that the liability is "unlimited". That will not dispel the effect of what she has been told. He must bring home to her that she is being asked to undertake liability for the existing indebtedness (even though this was previously unsecured by her) as well as for future indebtedness to an unlimited extent, and not merely liability for the amount of the contemplated advance or increase in the overdraft. He should warn her that she will have no control over the extent of the liability which she is being asked to undertake, since the bank will be in a position to advance further credit at any time on the security of her guarantee or charge without reference to her. He should inform her of the alternatives which are open to her, which include giving a limited guarantee or charge, and if necessary he should offer to negotiate with the bank on her behalf. He should not assume that the bank's request is on a "take it or leave it" basis, or that it has an impregnable negotiating position. In fact its position vis-à-vis the wife is relatively weak, since (i) she is not obliged to give security, (ii) any security is better than none and (iii) the bank cannot afford the risk of taking a security which it knows the wife's solicitor has advised her she should not give.

21. These problems should be greatly eased for the future by the adoption by banks and building societies of the voluntary Code of Banking Practice published by the British Bankers' Association, the Building Societies Association and the Association for Payment Clearing Services. The current version of the code, which took effect from 1 July 1997, provides that an individual asked to give a guarantee or collateral security will be advised of the limit of his or her liability, and that an unlimited guarantee or security will not be taken. This is a very welcome step.

22. A solicitor who is asked to advise a client who may be subject to the undue influence of another "takes upon himself no light nor easy task": see *Wright v. Carter* [1903] 1 Ch. 27 at 57 per Stirling L.J. How far he should go in probing the matter in order to satisfy himself that his client is able to make a free and informed decision and is not merely agreeing to do what the wrongdoer wants is a matter of professional judgment: see *Massey v. Midland Bank plc* [1995] 1 All E.R. 929 at 934 per Steyn L.J. It must depend on all the circumstances of the case. Independent advice may be desirable but it is not always necessary. It depends on the nature of the proposed transaction and the relationship between the parties. Where there is a real conflict of interest, and certainly where there is a possibility that he may be called on to advise the wife not to enter into the proposed transaction, a solicitor should decline to act if he is also acting (otherwise than in a purely ministerial capacity) for another party to the transaction.

23. Where, however, a wife is asked to give a guarantee or collateral charge over the matrimonial home to support her husband's indebtedness, the transaction is not one which is necessarily to the wife's disadvantage or one into which she could not properly be advised to enter. If the marriage is secure and the indebtedness has been incurred by the business which provides the husband's livelihood and on which the prosperity of his wife and family depends, there may be no real conflict between the interests of the husband and the wife. In such a case it may not matter whether the business is carried on by the husband personally or through the medium of a small family company; or whether the wife holds 50% or indeed any of the shares in the company. It may be a very difficult question in any particular case whether it is worth putting the roof over their heads at risk in order to continue to carry on the business. But if it is, then the transaction may be as much in the interest of the wife as of the husband; and if it is not, it may be as much against his interest as against hers.

24. It is obviously unwise for the solicitor who is acting for the bank to advise the wife, unless the solicitor is instructed to act for the bank only in a ministerial capacity

at completion; for the bank's interests are necessarily in conflict with those of both husband and wife. But for the reasons we have mentioned there may be no conflict between the interests of the husband and those of the wife. A solicitor is therefore not necessarily disqualified from acting for the wife merely because he is also acting for the husband. In such a case it is a matter for his professional judgment whether he, or another solicitor in the same firm, can properly advise the wife, or whether he should advise her to go to another solicitor.

25. It is also a matter for the solicitor's professional judgment whether he should himself advise the wife on the wisdom of the transaction, or invite her to obtain other advice, for example from the accountant to the business. In order to enable him to exercise his judgment, however, it will usually be necessary for the solicitor to inform himself of the circumstances of the proposed transaction, the amount of the existing indebtedness and of the new advance, and of the reasons for the new advance or the bank's request for additional security. He may also need to probe the stability of the marriage. This would need to be done with sensitivity; but the wife should at least be warned that by entering into the transaction she could be putting at risk the one substantial asset on which she could rely should the marriage come to grief.

26. Even though the transaction may be one into which the wife can properly be advised to enter, and in which there is no real conflict of interest between her and her husband, the task of advising the wife carries a heavy responsibility. She is being asked to put at risk her largest, probably her only substantial, asset.

(2) THE POSITION AS BETWEEN THE COMPLAINANT AND THE THIRD PARTY

27. A transaction may be set aside for misrepresentation or undue influence whether it was procured by the misrepresentation or undue influence of the party seeking to uphold the transaction or that of a third party: see *Turnbull & Co v. Duval* [1902] A.C. 429, *Lancashire Loans Ltd v. Black* and *MacKenzie v. Royal Bank of Canada* [1934] A.C. 468. Until *O'Brien's* case the basis upon which a transaction could be set aside as against a third party who was not himself guilty of any impropriety was obscure. Two principal theories competed for supremacy. One was based on agency, the other on notice. If the husband could be treated as acting as agent for the bank when procuring his wife to become surety for the debt then the bank could not be in any better position than its agent the husband. But the theory is now almost totally discredited. As Lord Browne-Wilkinson ([1994] 1 A.C. 180 at 193–194) pointed out the supposed agency is highly artificial. In most cases the reality of the relationship is that the creditor stipulates for security, and in order to raise the necessary finance the principal debtor seeks to procure the support of the surety. In doing so he is acting on his own account and not as agent for the creditor.

28. Since *O'Brien's* case the doctrine of notice has gained the upper hand. Although there may be cases where, without artificiality, the husband can properly be treated as acting as the agent of the bank in procuring the wife to give security, such cases will be very rare. We doubt that it will ever be possible to treat him as the creditor's agent where he or his company is the principal debtor. But a person who has been induced to enter into a transaction by undue influence, misrepresentation or some other vitiating factor has an equity to have the transaction set aside, and the equity is enforceable against third parties, including third parties who have given value, with notice, actual constructive or imputed, of the equity: see *Bainbrigge v. Browne* (1881) 18 Ch.D. 188. That was a straightforward application of the ordinary priority rules, for the third party was a successor in title of the wrongdoer. But a similar rule applies whenever a party to a transaction has notice that the consent of the other party has been procured by the impropriety of a third party. There is no voidable transaction between husband and wife which is prior in time to the security which is impugned. The contract of guarantee or collateral charge is entered into by the wife directly with the bank; it is not entered into with the husband and later given by him to the bank.

Normally (for there are always exceptions: see *Dunbar Bank plc v. Nadeem* [1998] 3 All E.R. 876) there is only one transaction, not two in competition with one another; and there is no question of clearing the title, which is the function performed by the bona fide purchaser defence. But the transaction is liable to be set aside as against the bank if the bank had notice, actual constructive or imputed, that it was procured by improper means. This is not, we think, a true application of the bona fide purchaser defence, but the effect appears to be much the same, and the burden of proof is the same: see *Barclays Bank plc v. Boulter* [1997] 2 All E.R. 1002. It has been suggested that the true position is that the presence of constructive notice precludes the bank from relying on the change of position defence, but there are difficulties in this analysis, not least that there is no trace of it in *O'Brien's* case.

29. Actual notice speaks for itself. It is, however, desirable to say something about imputed and constructive notice.

Imputed notice

30. The notice of an agent is normally imputed to his principal. This, however, is subject to s.199(1)(ii)(b) of the Law of Property Act 1925, reproducing s.3 of the Conveyancing Act 1881. This provides:

> "A purchaser shall not be prejudicially affected by notice of ... (ii) any other instrument or matter or any fact or thing unless ... (b) in the same transaction with respect to which a question of notice to the purchaser arises, it has come to the knowledge of his counsel, as such, or of his solicitor or other agent, as such, or would have come to the knowledge of his solicitor or other agent, as such, if such inquiries and inspections had been made as ought reasonably to have been made by the solicitor or other agent"

"Purchaser" is defined as including a mortgagee whether legal or equitable.

31. The bank is not, therefore, affected by notice of anything which its solicitor has discovered unless he was acting as the bank's solicitor at the time when he discovered it: see *Halifax Mortgage Services Ltd (formerly BNP Mortgages Ltd) v. Stepsky* [1996] Ch. 207. This requirement has sometimes been overlooked. It appears, for example, to have been overlooked in *Lancashire Loans Ltd v. Black*, though there was more than enough in that case to justify setting aside the transaction as against the creditor without having to rely on notice imputed from the knowledge of its solicitor.

Constructive notice

32. Where there is a standard procedure for investigating title, a purchaser is fixed with constructive notice of everything which he would have discovered if he had followed the standard procedure. The doctrine of constructive notice is, however, wider than this. It also applies whenever a party is put on inquiry as the existence of another's rights. If he makes no inquiry he is fixed with constructive notice of whatever he would have discovered if he had made reasonable inquiry: see s.199(1)(ii)(a) of the 1925 Act.

33. If he does make inquiry, the question depends in the first instance on whether he has made reasonable inquiry. If he has, and the results of his inquiries are such as would reasonably allay suspicion, then he takes free from the other's rights. If he has taken reasonable steps to allay suspicion, the question is not whether he could reasonably have done more, but whether, in the light of all the information, including the results of his inquiries, at his disposal at the time when he gave value, any suspicions have reasonably been allayed.

In what circumstances is the bank put on inquiry?

34. The key question in *O'Brien's* case was to identify the circumstances in which a creditor is put on inquiry as to the existence of a surety's equity. Where the

relationship between the parties brings the case within Class 2(A) so as to raise a legal presumption of undue influence, notice of the relationship will automatically put the creditor on inquiry. Where the creditor has no notice of any such relationship, but knows that the surety is accustomed to place implicit trust in the debtor, the situation is the same: *Avon Finance Co. Ltd v. Bridger* (1979) [1985] 2 All E.R. 281 approved in *Barclays Bank plc v. O'Brien* [1994] 1 A.C. 180 at 198. Furthermore, where the transaction is so extravagantly improvident that it is difficult to explain in the absence of some impropriety, then the bank may likewise be put on inquiry: *Credit Lyonnais Bank Nederland NV v. Burch* was a case of this character.

35. It is now settled that the relationship of husband and wife does not bring the case within Class 2(A): see *Howes v. Bishop* [1909] 2 K.B. 390 and *Bank of Montreal v. Stuart.* Nor, it seems, does the relationship between cohabitees (though the relationship between an engaged couple apparently does). It cannot be said that every wife or cohabitee places implicit trust in her husband or partner, though many do. Furthermore, in the ordinary case, for the reasons we have already explained, the transaction by which a wife is asked to provide a guarantee or collateral security for the debts of the business from which the family derives its income cannot be said to be extravagantly or even necessarily improvident. Of course, the bank may know that it is because of its own knowledge of the account; but such cases apart, the transaction is normally not one into which the wife could not properly be advised to enter.

36. The effect of the landmark decision of the House of Lords in *O'Brien's* case is that, even so, the bank is put on inquiry by the combination of two factors: (a) the transaction is not on its face to the financial advantage of the wife; and (b) there is a substantial risk that, in procuring his wife to guarantee or provide collateral security for his debts, the husband has acted improperly. The risk which Lord Browne-Wilkinson identified is the risk that one party has exploited the emotional pressure and trust which derive from cohabitation whether inside or outside marriage. The result is that, where condition (a) is satisfied, the bank is put on inquiry if, but only if, the bank is aware that the parties are cohabiting or that the particular surety places implicit trust and confidence in the principal debtor in relation to her financial affairs.

37. Although Lord Browne-Wilkinson limited his observations to the case where the debtor and the proposed surety were married or cohabiting, it should not be overlooked that a transaction which a wife or cohabitee might well consider (and be advised) was in her interest may be virtually inexplicable in the case of anyone else in the absence of undue influence: see *Credit Lyonnais Bank Nederland NV v. Burch* [1997] 1 All E.R. 144 at 155.

What steps should the bank take if it is put on inquiry?

38. Lord Browne-Wilkinson indicated that the steps which the bank ought reasonably to take to avoid being fixed with constructive notice were to warn the wife, at a private meeting not attended by her husband, of the amount of the potential liability she was undertaking and of the risks involved and to advise the wife to take independent advice. This went beyond what was required by the then current Code of Banking Practice adopted by banks and building societies in March 1992, in that it called for the position to be explained by the bank to the wife in a personal interview before advising her to obtain independent legal advice. But Lord Browne-Wilkinson indicated that he regarded a personal interview with the bank as essential in order to avoid the risk of written warnings being unread or even intercepted by the husband.

39. This procedure was not adopted in any of the cases before us, though it is fair to say that they are all concerned with transactions which pre-dated *O'Brien's* case. We doubt, however, that the banks have been willing to adopt the procedure even after *O'Brien's* case. A personal interview with the wife is likely to expose the bank to far greater risks than those from which it wishes to be protected.

40. In the great majority of the cases which have come before the courts since *O'Brien's* case, but in which the transactions predated *O'Brien's* case, the banks have

contented themselves with following the Code of Banking Practice for the time being in force by requiring the wife to obtain independent legal advice and provide written confirmation that she has done so. This probably goes further than contemplated by *O'Brien's* case, since Lord Browne-Wilkinson considered that it would only be the exceptional case in which the bank should not only advise the wife to obtain independent legal advice but should insist that she do so. The efficacy of such steps has recently been considered in a number of cases in this court, which we consider below.

The effect of legal advice

41. It is now settled law that the question whether the bank can exercise its legal rights against the wife depends in the first instance on whether the wife has an equity to set aside the transaction and in the second on whether, at the time when it gave value, the bank had notice, actual imputed or constructive, of the wife's equity. In relation to the first question, the issue is whether the advice actually given was sufficient to rebut the presumption of undue influence. In relation to the second, the issue is different: it is whether, in the light of the facts known to the bank, including the availability of legal advice, any risk of the wife having an equity reasonably appeared to have been dispelled. The first question depends on what actually happened between the wife, her husband, and the solicitor. The second question depends on how the transaction appeared to the bank.

42. Although these issues raise questions of fact, the structure of the underlying transaction is so commonplace and the efficient funding of small businesses is so dependent on its validity, that the parties, and in particular the lending institutions, must be entitled to proceed in accordance with a settled practice which is effective to secure the validity of the transaction while at the same time affording the wife the protection of proper legal advice. It is highly undesirable that the validity of such transactions should depend on fine distinctions, particularly on distinctions in the wording of the instructions to the solicitors or the certificates they give.

43. There is now a consistent line of authority in this court which establishes the relevant principles. The leading authorities in order of decision are *Bank of Baroda v. Shah* [1988] 3 All E.R. 24; *Massey v. Midland Bank plc* [1995] 1 All E.R. 929; *Banco Exterior International v. Mann; Bank of Baroda v. Rayarel* (1995) 27 H.L.R. 387; *Midland Bank plc v. Serter* (1995) 71 P. & C.R. 264; *Bank Melli Iran v. Samadi-Rad* [1995] 2 F.L.R. 367; *Halifax Mortgage Services Ltd (formerly BNP Mortgages Ltd) v. Stepsky; Banco Exterior Internacional SA v. Thomas* [1997] 1 W.L.R. 221; *Barclays Bank plc v. Thomson* [1997] 4 All E.R. 816; and *National Westminster Bank plc v. Beaton* (1997) 30 H.L.R. 99.

44. These cases establish the following propositions:

(1) Where the wife deals with the bank through a solicitor, whether acting for her alone or for her and her husband, the bank is not ordinarily put on inquiry. The bank is entitled to assume that the solicitor has considered whether there is a sufficient conflict of interest to make it necessary for him to advise her to obtain independent legal advice. It is not necessary for the bank to ask the solicitor to carry out his professional obligation to give proper advice to the wife or to confirm that he has done so. The bank is ordinarily not required to take any steps at all: see *Rayarel's* case.

(2) Where the wife does not approach the bank through a solicitor, it is normally sufficient if the bank has urged her to obtain independent legal advice before entering into the transaction: see *Massey's* case and *Rayarel's* case. This is especially the case if the solicitor provides confirmation that he has explained the transaction to the wife and that she appears to understand it: see *Rayarel's* case.

(3) When giving advice to the wife the solicitor is acting exclusively as her solicitor: see *Serter's* case and *Thomson's* case. It makes no difference whether he is unconnected with the husband or the wife (see *Thomson's* case) or is also the husband's solicitor (see *Serter's* case, *Massey's* case and *Mann's* case) or that he has agreed to act in a ministerial capacity as the bank's agent at completion (see *Serter's* case and *Stepsky's*

case). Whoever introduces the solicitor to the wife and asks him to advise her, and whoever is responsible for his fees, the bank is entitled to expect the solicitor to regard himself as owing a duty to the wife alone when giving her advice (see *Thomson's* case). If the solicitor accepts the bank's instructions to advise the wife, he still acts as her solicitor and not the bank's solicitor when he interviews her (see *Thomson's* case).

(4) It follows that the bank is not fixed with imputed notice of what the solicitor learns in the course of advising the wife even if he is also the bank's solicitor. Such knowledge does not come to him in his capacity as the bank's solicitor: see *Stepsky's* case.

(5) The bank is entitled to rely on the fact that the solicitor undertook the task of explaining the transaction to the wife as showing that he considered himself to be sufficiently independent for this purpose: see *Mann's* case and *Rayarel's* case. The bank is not required to question the solicitor's independence, even if it knows that he is also the husband's solicitor: see *Massey's* case and *Rayarel's* case.

(6) The bank is not concerned to question the sufficiency of the advice, and is not put on further inquiry by the fact that the solicitor was asked only to explain the transaction to the wife and ensure that she understood it and not to see that she was sufficiently independent of her husband. Nor is the bank put on inquiry by the fact that the confirmation provided by the solicitor is similarly limited (*passim*).

45. Only one decision is inconsistent with these authorities, viz. the decision of Hobhouse and Mummery L.JJ. at an interlocutory stage of the proceedings in *Royal Bank of Scotland plc v. Etridge* [1997] 3 All E.R. 628. They held that, where a bank instructed a solicitor to act on its behalf for the purposes of ensuring that a wife received independent advice in respect of her liabilities under a proposed collateral charge to support her husband's indebtedness to the bank, it was arguable that the solicitor was acting as the bank's agent in carrying out his instructions, with the result that the bank would be fixed, presumably with imputed notice, if, notwithstanding his certificate to the contrary effect, he had not in fact carried them out.

46. We respectfully consider the decision to have been per incuriam. The court had the advantage of only a brief citation of authority. *Serter's* case was not cited; nor was *Thomson's* case (which had been decided but not yet reported). Each was authority binding on this court. In the later case of *National Westminster plc v. Beaton* this court followed *Thomson's* case in preference to *Etridge's* case. We consider that it was right to do so. In our judgment *Etridge's* case should not be regarded as good authority in future.

47. It follows from the need to avoid subtle distinctions that we attach no importance to the fact that the solicitor may not provide the bank with a full or adequate confirmation that he has followed his instructions. Where the bank has asked him to explain the transaction to the wife and confirm that she appeared to understand it, the bank is not in our opinion put on inquiry by the fact that the solicitor has confirmed that he has explained the transaction to her but not that she appeared to understand it. In any case we do not consider that such confirmation is an essential requirement. Where the bank has asked a solicitor to explain the transaction to the wife and he fails to confirm that he has done so, the bank is not entitled to assume that he has: see *Cooke v. National Westminster Bank plc* (1998) *The Times*, July 27, 1998. But at most this should put the bank on inquiry whether the solicitor has in fact advised the wife. If it fails to make further inquiry, then it takes the risk that he has not done so; but if he has and merely omitted to confirm the fact, then we think that the bank should not be affected by its failure to obtain confirmation before completing the transaction.

48. When advising the wife the solicitor obviously owes her a duty of care. We should, however, wish to guard against the notion that it follows from the fact that he is not also acting for the bank that he owes the bank no corresponding duty of care. Although in many respects the bank and the wife have conflicting interests, they share a common interest in ensuring that the wife should not enter into the transaction without her informed consent and free from the undue influence of her husband.

49. While the bank is normally entitled to assume that a solicitor who is asked to advise the wife will discharge his duties fully and competently, and that he will not have restricted himself to giving an explanation of the transaction and satisfying himself that she appears to understand it, it cannot make any such assumption if it knows or ought to know that it is false: *Burch's* case. If the bank is in possession of material information which is not available to the solicitor, or if the transaction is one into which no competent solicitor could properly advise the wife to enter, the availability of legal advice is insufficient to avoid the bank being fixed with constructive notice.

50. Ultimately the issue is whether, at the time when value is given, and in the light of all the information in the bank's possession, including its knowledge of the state of the account, the relationship of the parties, and the availability of legal advice for the wife, there is still a risk that the wife has entered into the transaction as a result of her husband's misrepresentation or undue influence.

NOTES:

1. For comment, see [1999] C.L.J. 28; [1999] Conv. 126; [1999] Conv. 176; (1999) 62 M.L.R. 609.

2. Lord Browne-Wilkinson expressed the view that the principles in *Barclays Bank plc v. O'Brien* are applicable to heterosexual and homosexual cohabitees. Subsequent cases have applied the principles to persons who, although not cohabiting, were in a stable sexual and emotional relationship: *Massey v. Midland Bank plc* [1995] 1 All E.R. 929; and even to persons in a relationship of employment: *Credit Lyonnais Bank Nederland NV v. Burch* [1997] 1 All E.R. 144; *Steeples v. Lea* [1998] 1 F.L.R. 138.

3. In seeking to establish that the lender is answerable to the surety for the undue influence on the part of the principal borrower, it seems that it is very difficult to establish that the principal borrower is the agent of the lender. It has been held that there must be agency "in a real sense": *CICB Mortgages plc v. Pitt* [1994] A.C. 200, 211 *per* Lord Browne-Wilkinson; and that condition is unlikely to be satisfied because in reality the principal borrower is acting in his own interests rather than those of the lender: see *Dunbar Bank plc v. Nadeem* [1997] 2 All E.R. 253, 270 *per* Robert Englehart Q.C.; *Royal Bank of Scotland plc v. Etridge (No. 2), supra,* para. 27

4. The alternative route to establishing that the lender is prima facie answerable to the surety is where the lender has notice of the undue influence (and consequently of the surety's equity to set aside the transaction). There has been much discussion as to the appropriateness of reliance on the doctrine of notice, especially in the context of registered land. Some commentators have expressed concern as to the application of the traditional doctrine: see Thompson [1994] Conv. 140; Sparkes [1995] Conv. 250; Mee [1995] C.L.J. 536. However, such concerns may be misplaced on the basis that in this context the courts are concerned with a broader concept of notice or knowledge: see Dixon and Harpum [1994] Conv. 421; Howell [1996] Conv. 34; or even on the basis that notice simply denotes the failure of the lender to take reasonable and appropriate steps in the circumstances to protect the surety: Battersby (1995) 15 *Legal Studies* 35. The judgment of the Court of Appeal in *Royal Bank of Scotland plc v. Etridge (No. 2)* seems to provide some support for this broader concept: see *supra,* paras 28, 32–33.

5. The cases appear to have established that the principles in *Barclays Bank plc v. O'Brien* do not apply in certain circumstances, although it is not clear whether this is because the transaction is not disadvantageous to the surety or because the lender is not deemed to have notice of undue influence on the part of the principal borrower. The principles have been held not to apply: (i) where the transaction *appears* to be for the joint benefit of the principal borrower and the surety: *CIBC Mortgages plc v. Pitt* [1994] A.C. 200; but the position would be different if the lender knew that the loan was in fact to be used for the sole benefit of the principal borrower: *Allied Irish Bank plc v. Byrne* [1995] 2 F.L.R. 325; or if the mortgage secured repayment of all existing and future debts of the principal borrower: *Midland Bank plc v. Greene* [1994] 2 F.L.R. 827; *Credit Lyonnais Bank Nederland NV v. Burch* [1997] 1 All E.R. 144; (ii) where the mortgage secures repayment of a loan to a business jointly owned by the surety and the principal borrower: *Britannia Building Society v. Pugh* (1996) 29 H.L.R. 423; but the position would be different if the surety had only a small share in the business (so that the burden of the mortgage liability substantially outweighed the benefit of the loan): *Bank of Scotland v. Bennett* [1997] 1 F.L.R. 801; or if, notwithstanding equal shares in the business, the principal borrower effectively controlled the business and the surety had no practical involvement: *Bank of Cyprus v. Markou* [1999] 2 All E.R. 707; (iii) where, notwithstanding the apparent purpose of the loan, the loan had in fact been applied for the benefit of the surety and the principal borrower: *Scotlife Home Loans (No. 2) Ltd v. Hedworth* (1995) 28 H.L.R. 771; (iv) where the terms of the mortgage appear to be manifestly disadvantageous to the surety but where the transaction actually intended by the mortgagee is not (manifestly) disadvantageous: *Dunbar Bank plc v. Nadeem* [1998] 3 All E.R. 876, noted at (1999) 115 L.Q.R. 213.

6. Notice of disadvantage and/or undue influence acquired by the solicitor in acting for the principal borrower is not imputed to the lender who instructs the same solicitor: *Halifax Mortgage Services Ltd v. Stepsky* [1996] Ch. 207.

7. The recent cases seem to demonstrate that the issues identified in *Barclays Bank plc v. O'Brien* are inextricably linked. This is particularly apparent in *Credit Lyonnais Bank Nederland NV v. Burch* [1997] 1 All E.R. 144. The relationship of employer and junior employee in that case was far removed from the paradigm relationship identified in *Barclays Bank plc v. O'Brien*. Nonetheless, in the context of such a relationship, the Court of Appeal held that the lender should have been all the more alert to the possibility of undue influence on the part of the principal borrower who stood to gain from a transaction that was manifestly disadvantageous to the surety. Millett L.J. stated (at 154):

In the present case, the only relationship between Mr Pelosi (and his company) on the one hand and Miss Burch on the other which has been proved (and of which the bank had any knowledge) was that of employer and junior employee. That is not a relationship within class 2A. At the same time, it is clearly one which is capable of developing into a relationship of trust and confidence with the attendant risk of abuse, particularly in the case of a small business where the parties are accustomed to work closely together.

Accordingly, it was for Miss Burch to prove that the relationship between her and Mr Pelosi had developed into a relationship of trust and confidence. Whether it had done so or not was a question of fact. While she had to prove this affirmatively, she did not have to prove it as a primary fact by direct evidence. It was sufficient for her to prove facts from which the existence of a relationship of trust and confidence could be inferred. In the present case, the excessively onerous nature of the transaction into which she was persuaded to enter, coupled with the fact that she did so at the request of, and after discussion with, Mr Pelosi, is in my judgment, quite enough to justify the inference, which is really irresistible, that the relationship of employer and employee had ripened into something more and that there had come into existence between them a relationship of trust and confidence which he improperly exploited for his own benefit.

It is arguable therefore that the fact that the transaction is manifestly disadvantageous to the surety will be sufficient to justify a prima facie conclusion that the lender has notice of undue influence on the part of the principal borrower: see *Royal Bank of Scotland plc v. Etridge (No. 2), supra*, paras 15, 37.

8. Any prima facie finding that the lending had notice of the undue influence must be based on the facts known to the lender at the relevant time: *Bank of Scotland v. Bennett* (1998) 77 P. & C.R. 447; and it is for the lender to rebut that finding: *Barclays Bank plc v. Boulter* [1997] 2 All E.R. 1002.

9. As Lord Browne-Wilkinson explained in *Barclays Bank plc v. O'Brien*, notice will normally be negatived if the lender insists that the surety attends a private meeting (in the absence of the principal borrower) with a representative of the lender at which the surety is told of the extent of his liability as surety, warned of the risk he is running and urged to take independent legal advice (although, where undue influence appears probable, the lender may have to *insist* on independent legal advice): [1994] A.C. 180 196–197. Lord Browne-Wilkinson recognised that these requirements applied to future transactions and should not be applied too rigidly to the pre-*Barclays Bank plc v. O'Brien* transactions that have been scrutinised in most of the recent cases. However, the courts in those cases have tended to apply a version of the requirements, subject to the overriding consideration that the guidance was intended to strike a fair balance between the need to protect sureties whose judgmental capacity was impaired and the need to avoid unnecessary impediments to the availability of security: see *Massey v. Midland Bank plc* [1995] 1 All E.R. 929, 934 *per* Steyn L.J.

10. Generally, the courts have been sympathetic to the position of lenders and have held that they have done sufficient to protect themselves, even where they have failed to satisfy all the requirements. In particular, it has been held that a certificate that legal advice has been given to the surety protects a lender, even where the lender has not had a private meeting with the surety or where the lender has failed to recommend that the surety should obtain independent legal advice: *Massey v. Midland Bank plc* [1995] 1 All E.R. 929, noted at [1995] Conv. 148, (1995) 111 L.Q.R. 51; *Banco Exterior Internacional v. Mann* [1995] 1 All E.R. 936, noted at [1995] Conv. 325; *Bank of Baroda v. Rayarel* (1995) 27 H.L.R. 387; *Midland Bank v. Serter*

(1995) 71 P. & C.R. 264. Moreover, the lender is entitled to assume (in the absence of clear indications to the contrary) that the solicitor who gave the advice was honest and competent so that the lender cannot be held responsible for defective advice: *Banco Exterior Internacional v. Mann* [1995] 1 All E.R. 936, 944 *per* Morritt L.J. However, the lender will not be able to rely on a solicitor's certificate where the lender has failed to reveal to the surety or the solicitor "facts relevant to the transaction, which are of a special and peculiar nature, and materially different in significantly disadvantageous respects from what someone in the surety's position might naturally expect": *Bank of Scotland v. Bennett* [1997] 1 F.L.R. 801, 839 *per* James Munby Q.C. Moreover, a certificate will not protect the lender where a change in the circumstances of the transaction requires that the surety obtain further legal advice: *Barclays Bank plc v. Caplan* [1998] 1 F.L.R. 532. The protection afforded by such a certificate has been held to apply even where the advice is given by the solicitor who is also acting for the principal borrower and the lender and where the lender has requested that the solicitor should advise the surety: *Barclays Bank plc v. Thomson* [1997] 2 All E.R. 816, noted at [1997] Conv. 216; *National Westminster Bank plc v. Beaton* (1997) 74 P. & C.R. D19; and the suggestion that the solicitor might be regarded as the appointed agent of the lender has been rejected: *Royal Bank of Scotland plc v. Etridge (No. 2), supra,* paras 44–46. For discussion of the potential tension between the provision of appropriate advice and the performance of the solicitor's duties to different parties, see Wong [1998] Conv. 457.

11. Protection for the lender was denied in *Credit Lyonnais Bank Nederland NV v. Burch* [1997] 1 All E.R. 144, where the lender had failed to explain the potential extent of the surety's liability and (as the circumstances almost certainly required) to *insist* that the surety obtain independent legal advice. However, Millett L.J. continued (at 155–157):

That is sufficient to dispose of this appeal, but I should not be taken to accept that it would necessarily have made any difference even if Miss Burch had entered into the transaction after taking independent legal advice. Such advice is neither always necessary nor always sufficient. It is not a panacea. The result does not depend mechanically on the presence or absence of legal advice. I think that there has been some misunderstanding of the role which the obtaining of independent legal advice plays in these cases.

It is first necessary to consider the position as between the complainant and the alleged wrongdoer.

. . .

It is next necessary to consider the position of the third party who has been put on enquiry of the possible existence of some impropriety and who wishes to avoid being fixed with constructive notice. One means of doing so is to ensure that the complainant obtains competent and independent legal advice before entering into the transaction. If she does so, and enters into the transaction nonetheless, the third party will usually escape the consequences of notice. This is because he is normally entitled to assume that the solicitor has discharged his duty and that the complainant has followed his advice. But he cannot make any such assumption if he knows or ought to know that it is false.

In the present case, the bank did not have actual notice of the exercise of undue influence, or even of the existence of a relationship of trust and confidence between Miss Burch and Mr Pelosi. It did not know for a fact that Miss Burch had no incentive to enter into the transaction. For all the bank knew, for example, the parties might be intending to set up home together and live off the profits of the company's business. It did not, therefore, know (as was the case) that no competent solicitor could possibly advise Miss Burch to guarantee the company's overdraft.

But it must have known that no competent solicitor could advise her to enter into a guarantee in the terms she did. He would be bound to inquire, of the bank if necessary, of the reason why it required additional security. Having discovered that it was to enable the limit of the company's overdraft to be increased from £250,000 to £270,000, he would be bound to advise Miss Burch that an unlimited guarantee was unnecessary and inappropriate for this purpose, and that, if she felt that she must accommodate Mr Pelosi's wishes, she should offer a limited guarantee with a limit of £20,000 or (better still) a guarantee of the company's liability in excess of £250,000 with a maximum of £270,000. The terms of Miss Burch's letters indicate that if she had been given appropriate advice of the alternatives which were legally available, she would have chosen one which was less onerous to her while still meeting the bank's ostensible requirements.

I do not, therefore, accept that a bank, in circumstances where it ought to appreciate the possibility that undue influence has been exercised, can escape the consequences by putting forward an unnecessarily onerous form of guarantee and relying on the failure of the guarantor's solicitor to advise her of the possibility of offering a guarantee on less onerous terms and more appropriate to the situation.

In the present case, the bank accepted an unlimited guarantee of her employer's indebtedness obtained by the employer from a junior employee with no incentive to give it; and who had, at the instance of her employer, declined to obtain legal advice, was known to be concerned at the unlimited nature of the obligation which she was undertaking, and was almost certainly unaware of the alternatives open to her. In my opinion, the transaction must be set aside...

See also *Steeples v. Lea* [1998] 1 F.L.R. 138. However, contrast the view expressed by Sir Richard Scott V.-C. in *Banco Exterior Internacional SA v. Thomas* [1997] 1 W.L.R. 221, 229 (emphasis added):

The case depends, of course, on the requisite undue influence being established. The judge dealt with this part of the case by asking himself, first, whether there was a presumption of undue influence. He found that there was. The bank has challenged this finding. There is, to my mind, some substance to their challenge. Mrs Dempsey [the surety] was advised by Mr Bishop [the leader's solicitor] as to the "nature and effect" of the transaction. Mr Bishop was satisfied that she understood it. After receiving Mr Bishop's advice, she continued with it. Later, she received very strong and positive advice from Mr Frere-Smith [the surety's solicitor] against the transaction. She rejected Mr Frere-Smith's advice and decided to continue with the transaction. She took no step, having received that advice, to have the transaction set aside. It is not alleged, and the evidence does not justify the conclusion, that Mrs Dempsey lacked the capacity to contract with the bank. Yet that is the conclusion towards which Mr Falconer's [counsel for the surety] submissions seem to me to tend. I would accept that the arrangement made between Mrs Dempsey and Mr Mulchay the [principal borrower] was one that any adviser would advise strongly against. *But the purpose of advisers is to advise. The recipient of the advice does not have to accept it. He or she can decide, fully informed by the advice that has been received, whether or not to proceed with the allegedly ill-advised and improvident transaction.* In the present case, Mrs Dempsey may well have been attracted by the offer of £500 per month (or £125 per week). She was of full age. She suffered from no mental infirmity. And she had had the nature and effect of the transaction with the bank explained to her by an independent solicitor.

See also *National Bank of Abu Dhabi v. Mohamed* (1997) 30 H.L.R. 383.

12. Where the lender is fixed with notice of the undue influence, the question arises as to whether the mortgage is wholly unenforceable against the lender so that it is to be set aside in its entirety or whether the mortgage is unenforceable and to be set aside only to the extent that the surety's consent is vitiated by the undue influence. The latter course might arguably be justified where the surety readily consented to assume limited liability but was misled into consenting to greater liability. In *TSB Bank plc v. Camfield* [1995] 1 W.L.R. 430, noted at [1995] Conv. 325, (1995) 111 L.Q.R. 555, the Court of Appeal held that the mortgage should be set aside in its entirety. That case was followed in *Castle Phillips Finance v. Piddington* (1994) 70 P. & C.R. 592, although the court used the doctrine of subrogation to permit the lender to enforce an earlier charge. However, in *Dunbar Bank plc v. Nadeem* [1998] 3 All E.R. 876 it was stated (obiter) that a surety is entitled to have the mortgage set aside only if he makes *restitutio in integrum* (or counter-restitution of his enrichment) to the mortgagee.

13. As indicated above, the *Barclays Bank plc v. O'Brien* principle has also generated a great deal of academic discussion. In particular, the decision of the Court of Appeal in *Credit Lyonnais Bank Nederland NV v. Burch* [1997] 1 All E.R. 144 has prompted calls for a rationalisation of the applicable principles. Chen-Wishart [1997] C.L.J. 60 argues for a jurisdiction based on substantive unfairness. Capper (1998) 114 L.Q.R. 479 argues for a jurisdiction based on unconscionability and see also (1997) 113 L.Q.R. 10; (1999) 115 L.Q.R. 81; but for a more cautionary view, see Hooley and O'Sullivan [1997] L.M.C.L.Q. 17. However, while the Court of Appeal in *Royal Bank of Scotland plc v. Etridge (No. 2)* recognised that cases such as *Burch* could equally well be regarded as cases of harsh and unconscionable bargains (para. 13), the extended statement of principle in the later case suggests that any jurisdictional rationalisation is unlikely to be effected by judicial development.

14. For earlier analysis of the underlying principles, see Birks and Chin, "On the Nature of Undue Influence" in Beatson and Friedmann (eds.), *Good Faith and Fault in Contract Law* (1995), p.57, who argue that undue influence and unconscionability are fundamentally distinct doctrines. And for discussion of undue influence within the framework of the law of restitution, see O'Dell [1997] C.L.J. 71; Birks (1998) 12 *Trusts Law International* 2.

4. Statutory consumer protection

By virtue of the jurisdiction under sections 137–139 of the Consumer Credit Act 1974 in relation to extortionate credit bargains, the courts have power to re-open certain mortgage agreements where the mortgagor is an individual. If the bargain is found to be "extortionate", in that it requires payments which are "grossly exorbitant" or it "otherwise grossly contravenes ordinary principles of fair dealing" (*ibid.* s.138(1)), the court may set aside or alter the terms of the agreement. There is some uncertainty as to the difference between an "extortionate" bargain and "unfair and unconscionable" terms considered above: see *Davies v. Directloans Ltd* [1986] 1 W.L.R. 823, 831 *per* Edward Nugee Q.C.

In practice, the courts have largely ignored the second limb of the definition of extortionate credit bargain: _Unfair Credit Transactions: Report by the Director General of Fair Trading_ (1991), para. 1.7. Moreover, in respect of the first limb, they have shown great reluctance to find that interest rates are grossly exorbitant unless the rate charged is very significantly higher than the rate prevailing at the time of the loan; and the courts have made it clear that the prevailing rate means the market rate _in the particular circumstances_: A. Ketley Ltd v. Scott [1981] I.C.R. 241; _Davies v. Directloans Ltd_ [1986] 1 W.L.R. 823. This produces a rather paradoxical result. The legislation was primarily intended to protect borrowers in the non-institutional mortgage market; loans to such borrowers tend to be high-risk so that lenders are justified in charging higher rates of interest; and thus the courts are less likely to (be able to) intervene. It has therefore been recommended that the concept of "extortionate credit bargain" should be replaced by "unjust credit transaction"; and that, in determining whether a transaction is unjust, the court should take into consideration (i) whether the transaction involved _excessive_ payments; (ii) whether the transaction involved business activity which is deceitful or oppressive or otherwise unfair or improper; and (iii) whether the lender exercised care and responsibility in making the loan: _Unfair Credit Transactions: Report by the Director General of Fair Trading_ (1991), para. 1.9. On the other hand, the Law Commission has recommended that the Consumer Credit Act 1974 should no longer apply to credit bargains secured by a land mortgage: Law Com. No. 204, _Transfer of Land: Land Mortgages_ (1991), para. 8.8.

For a review of the jurisdiction and for a wide range of suggested reforms, see Bently and Howells [1989] Conv. 164, 234. For discussion of the jurisdiction under section 129 to impose "time orders", rescheduling mortgage agreements, and under section 136 to amend mortgage agreements, see Dunn [1996] Conv. 209. For discussion of the wider application of the Consumer Credit Act 1974 to land mortgages, see Adams (1975) 39 Conv. 94.

The court has a similar jurisdiction under section 343 of the Insolvency Act 1986; and under section 244 where the mortgagor is a company and the mortgage is entered into within three years before the company goes into liquidation or an administration order is made.

A mortgager may also rely on the Unfair Terms in Consumer Contracts Regulations (S.I. 1994 No. 3159) to challenge the terms of a mortgage: see _Falco Finance Ltd v. Gough_ (1998, unreported), noted at (1999), 115 L.Q.R. 360.

5. Variable interest rates

For many years it has been accepted that the rate of interest payable by the mortgagor is variable unilaterally at any time by the mortgagee; and the vast majority of mortgages now purport to confer such a power to vary on the mortgagee. Although it is arguable that there may be some theoretical basis for questioning the validity of such a power, there appears to have been no successful challenge to the legality of variable interest rates. The equitable jurisdiction to set aside unfair and unconscionable terms would probably be of no assistance: it has been confined to cases where the relevant term has been imposed "in a morally reprehensible manner": *Multiservice Bookbinding Ltd v. Marden* [1979] Ch. 84, 110 *per* Browne-Wilkinson J.; and such a condition is unlikely to be established in the case of a power routinely included in most mortgages. Equally, as noted above, the provisions of the Consumer Credit Act 1974 dealing with extortionate credit bargains have been construed restrictively. For recommended reform, see *infra*, p. 964.

6. Anti-competitive restrictions

6.1 *Doctrine of restraint of trade*
Following the decision in *Biggs v. Hoddinott* [1898] 2 Ch. 307 it was assumed that it was permissible for a mortgagee to postpone the right to redeem for an acceptable period and to stipulate for a collateral advantage limited to the period of postponement, provided that the collateral advantage in the mortgage deed was not oppressive or unconscionable. However, even if the collateral advantage is thus not invalidated on any of the three grounds listed by Lord Parker in *Kreglinger v. New Patagonia Meat and Cold Storage Co. Ltd* [1914] A.C. 25, such an approach fails to take account of the doctrine of restraint of trade. That doctrine invalidates any contract that places an unreasonable restriction on the future freedom of a person to carry on his trade, business or profession; and the question of reasonableness embraces the public interest in addition to the interests of the contractual parties.

It had been assumed that the doctrine had no application in the context of mortgages; but that assumption was rejected in *Esso Petroleum Co. Ltd v. Harper's Garage (Stourport) Ltd* [1968] A.C. 269, 342 *per* Lord Wilberforce.

6.2 *European Community competition policy*
There is also some scope for challenging anti-competitive restrictions in mortgage transactions, on the ground that they infringe the European Community competition policy, if the restrictions affect trade between member states of the Community. Article 85 of the E.C. Treaty prohibits agreements and less formal arrangements that restrict competition between the parties to the arrangement or between one of those parties and a third party: see *Inntrepreneur Estates v. Mason* (1993) 68 P. & C.R. 53, *Inntrepreneur Estates (GL) Ltd v. Boyes* (1993) 68 P. & C.R. 77, noted at [1994] Conv. 150; and Article 86 prohibits the abuse of a dominant position in the market. Further discussion of these matters is outside the scope of this book.

E. PROTECTION OF THE MORTGAGEE

Like any purchaser, an intending mortgagee will investigate the title of the intending mortgagor to the intended mortgaged land. In addition a mortgagee will seek to ensure that his mortgage is enforceable, and, where appropriate, takes priority over any subsequent purchaser or mortgagee. For priorities, see *infra*, p. 953.

1. Investigation of title

The principal risk for a mortgagee would seem to be undocumented contribution-based ownership rights in the mortgaged land, that is the beneficial interest under a trust of an equitable co-owner who is not also a legal owner.

Where such an interest is discovered by the mortgagee, he will insist that the mortgage is executed, and a receipt for the mortgage loan is signed, by at least two trustees: in that way the mortgagee will not be concerned by the equitable interests under the trust, which will be overreached: Law of Property Act 1925, ss.2(1)(ii), 27(2); and see *City of London Building Society v. Flegg* [1988] A.C. 54, 73 *per* Lord Templeman, 90–91 *per* Lord Oliver. However, such interests have the potential to bind the mortgagee where the mortgagee has no actual knowledge of them and therefore does not comply with the requirements for overreaching. In the context of unregistered land, the interest may bind the mortgagee if he is deemed to have had constructive notice of the interest; see *Kingsnorth Finance Co. Ltd v. Tizard* [1986] 1 W.L.R. 783, *ante*, p. 42. In the context of registered land, the interest may bind the mortgagee as an overriding interest if the equitable owner is in actual occupation of the mortgaged land at the relevant time: Land Registration Act 1925, s.70(1)(g), *ante*, p. 187.

However, a series of case law developments, the principles of which are equally applicable to both registered and unregistered land, has ensured that in most circumstances, and in *all* cases of acquisition mortgages, the mortgage will take priority over any such interests in the mortgaged land.

1.1 *Consent to postponement*

Bristol and West Building Society v. Henning [1985] 1 W.L.R. 778

(CA, Donaldson M.R., Browne-Wilkinson and Lloyd L.JJ.)

In 1974 the first and second defendants started to live together. In 1975 they agreed that the first defendant would purchase a house in London with the assistance of a mortgage loan; and in 1978 they agreed that the first defendant would purchase the villa which was the subject of the litigation. The purchase of the villa, title to which was unregistered, was largely financed by a mortgage loan from the plaintiff building society; and the balance came from the proceeds of the house in London. Although the first defendant appeared to be the absolute owner of the villa, both defendants asserted that the second defendant had a one-half share in the beneficial interest. When the first defendant ceased to make the repayments due under the mortgage, the plaintiff started proceedings for possession of the villa.

BROWNE-WILKINSON L.J.:
The case came before Judge Clarke who dismissed the society's claim for possession. The defence put forward by Mrs Henning was, first, that she had a beneficial interest

both in the London house and in the villa. Alternatively, she argued that she had an irrevocable licence to remain in the villa. In either event, she argued that the society had notice of her rights which prevailed over those of the society. The society on the other hand argued that she had no beneficial interest in the villa. However, the society, by their counsel, accepted that as against Mr Henning, Mrs Henning had an irrevocable licence to stay in the villa. The society contended that such licence was not binding on the society, first, because it was purely contractual; second, (if it was a property interest) because it was not registered under the Land Charges Act 1972; third, because Mrs Henning was estopped from alleging a prior equity because she knew that the property was to be mortgaged; and, fourth, because the society was a purchaser for value without notice.

The judge, in his admirable judgment, rejected the claim that Mrs Henning had an equitable interest in the villa. However, he held that the irrevocable licence (which the society had conceded) conferred on her some property interest in the villa, applying the line of decisions exemplified by *In re Sharpe (A Bankrupt), Ex parte Trustee of the Bankrupt's Property v. The Bankrupt* [1980] 1 W.L.R. 219. He held that such interest was not registrable under the Land Charges Act 1972, that Mrs Henning was not estopped from setting up her equity and that the society had constructive notice of her rights. On those grounds he refused an order for possession. The society appeals against that decision and Mrs Henning cross-appeals against the decision that she had no beneficial interest in the equity.

There is a risk that the common sense answer in this case may get lost in the many different technicalities which can arise. The basic fact is that the mortgage was granted to the society with the full knowledge and approval of Mrs Henning. There was a joint project between her and Mr Henning to buy the villa with the assistance of such mortgage. Without it, the villa could never have been bought. Yet Mrs Henning is alleging that she has the right to stay in the villa in priority to the rights of the society which provided the bulk of the purchase money for it. Although she has unsuccessfully tried to find some way of paying the instalments under the mortgage, the logical result of her argument (if right) is that she is entitled to stay in possession indefinitely without making any payment. That would be a strange result which I would be reluctant to reach.

Mr Lindsay [counsel for the plaintiff] (who did not appear below) has in my judgment provided a short but complete solution to the technical problems raised by the case. I will assume (without deciding) that Mrs Henning was entitled either to a beneficial interest in the villa or to some lesser property right of the kind exemplified in *In re Sharpe* [1980] 1 W.L.R. 219. Since Mr and Mrs Henning did not declare any trust of the villa in writing or reach any express agreement between themselves as to the beneficial interests, the only way in which Mrs Henning can establish either right in the villa would be to show, inter alia, that as between her and Mr Henning there was an express or imputed intention or assumption that she should have such a right. The decision of the House of Lords in *Gissing v. Gissing* [1971] A.C. 886 establishes that, in the absence of express agreement or express trust, a right to a beneficial interest under a constructive trust can only be established by proving an express or imputed intention that a party other than the legal owner should have a beneficial interest in the property, which intention renders it inequitable for the legal owner to claim the sole beneficial interest: see especially *per* Lord Diplock at pp. 905–906. Similarly, in the absence of express agreement, such an intention or assumption must be proved in order to found the lesser property right of an irrevocable licence conferring a property interest: see *In re Sharpe* [1980] 1 W.L.R. 219. Therefore, in order to determine what, on the assumption made, is the nature of Mrs Henning's right in the villa, it is necessary first to determine from the parties' actions what were their express or imputed intentions as to her beneficial interest.

Once that is identified as the relevant question, in my judgment the answer becomes obvious. Mr and Mrs Henning did not contemporaneously express any intention as to the beneficial interests in the property. Therefore such intention if it exists has to be imputed to them from their actions. Mrs Henning knew of and supported the proposal to raise the purchase price of the villa on mortgage. In those circumstances, it is in my judgment impossible to impute to them any common intention other than that she authorised Mr Henning to raise the money by mortgage to the society. In more technical terms, it was the common intention that Mr Henning as trustee should have power to grant the mortgage to the society. Such power to mortgage must have extended to granting to the society a mortgage having priority to any beneficial interests in the property. I would not impute to the parties an intention to mislead the society by purporting to offer the unencumbered fee simple of the property as security when in fact there was to be an equitable interest which would take priority to the society. Indeed in evidence Mrs Henning said:

"I would have realised that the building society were expecting to be able to rely on the full value of the house as security of loan— but I never really thought about it— if somebody had explained it to me as you have now I would have appreciated it."

This evidence shows that, although she had no actual relevant intention at the time, it would be wrong to impute to the parties any intention other than that the society was to have a charge in priority to the parties' beneficial interests.

Mr Whitaker, for Mrs Henning, sought to avoid this conclusion by pointing out that such an intention left Mrs Henning at the mercy of Mr Henning and failed to provide the security which the house was designed to give her and her children. He points out that Mr Henning could at any time cease to pay the mortgage instalments and the society would then be able to take possession from Mrs Henning. That is true. But the fact that the arrangements made did not, because of the rights of a third party, provide full security cannot alter the only intention it is possible to impute to the parties. There was no way in which the villa could have been bought at all without the assistance of the mortgage to the society and the mortgage to the society could not be properly granted without giving the society a charge over the whole legal and equitable interest.

Since the nature of Mrs Henning's interest has to be found in the imputed intention of the parties and the imputed intention of the parties must have been that her interest was to be subject to that of the society, it is impossible for Mrs Henning to establish that she is entitled to some form of equitable interest which gives her rights in priority to the rights of the society. I would therefore hold that, even on the assumption that Mrs Henning has some equitable interest or right in the villa, such interest or right is subject to the society's charge and provides no defence to the society's claim for possession.

NOTES:

1. The principle in *Bristol and West Building Society v. Henning* was applied in the context of registered land in *Paddington Building Society v. Mendelsohn* (1985) 50 P. & C.R. 244.

2. The principle was endorsed by Lord Oliver in *Abbey National Building Society v. Cann* [1991] 1 A.C. 56. He stated (at 94):

The view that I have formed renders it strictly unnecessary to consider the ground upon which Mrs Cann's claim failed in the Court of Appeal. What was said was that, despite her initial evidence (in her affidavit) that she did not know of her son's intention to raise any of the money required for the purchase on mortgage, nevertheless her oral evidence before the judge disclosed that she was well aware that there was a shortfall which would have to be met from somewhere. Her own account of the matter was that his reason for selling was that he was in financial difficulties, so that she must have known that he was not going to be able to meet it out of his own resources. Dillon L.J. (with whom, on this point, the other two members of the court agreed) inferred that "she left it to George Cann to raise the balance" [1989] 2 F.L.R. 265,

276, from which he further inferred that George Cann had authority to raise that sum from the society. There was no finding to this effect by the judge, but I think, for my part, that it is a necessary conclusion once it is accepted, as it has to be, that she knew that there was a shortfall of some £4,000 apart from conveyancing costs, that George Cann was going to raise it, and that he was in financial difficulties. It is said that there was no evidence that he was going to raise it on the security of this property. There might, for instance, be other property available to him. He might obtain an unsecured loan. In the circumstances of his known lack of resources, however, this is fanciful and in my judgment the court was entitled to draw the inference that it did draw. If that is right, it follows that George Cann was permitted by her to raise money on the security of the property without any limitation on his authority being communicated to the society. She is not, therefore, in a position to complain, as against the lender, that too much was raised and even if, contrary to the view which I have formed, she had been able to establish an interest in the property which would otherwise prevail against the society, the circumstances to which I have alluded would preclude her from relying upon it as prevailing over the society's interest for the reasons given in the judgment of Dillon L.J. in the Court of Appeal.

3. The principle was extended in *Equity and Law Home Loans Ltd v. Prestidge* [1992] 1 W.L.R. 137. In that case a contribution-based equitable interest, which in accordance with the principle would have been postponed to the acquisition mortgage, was held to be postponed to a remortgage (to the extent of the loan secured by the acquisition mortgage), even though the equitable owner knew nothing of the remortgage. Mustill L.J. quoted from the judgment of Browne-Wilkinson L.J. in *Bristol and West Building Society v. Henning*; and he continued (at 143):

So it seems to me that one must ask this question: "What intention must one impute to the parties as regards the position which would exist if the mortgage which had been obtained in order to enable the purchase of the house, and which the parties intended to have priority over the second defendant's beneficial interest, should be replaced by another mortgage on no less favourable terms?" In my judgment, this question need only to be posed for it to be answered in favour of the plaintiffs. Any other answer would be absurd, for it would mean that if Mr Prestidge had in good faith and without the knowledge of the second defendant transferred the mortgage to another society in order, say, to obtain a more favourable rate of interest, she would suddenly receive a windfall in the shape of the removal of the encumbrance which she had intended should be created in consequence of a transaction which could not do her any harm and of which she was entirely ignorant.

If this answer is correct, it disposes of two objections to the judgment of the recorder, which were canvassed in argument. First, it is said that the second defendant's interest could not be encumbered by a mortgage of which she was unaware, especially in circumstances where there was ample on the documents to put the plaintiffs on notice of that interest. Well, this would have been right if the mortgage to the plaintiffs had been the first and only transaction. But it was not. The new mortgage was made against the background of a consent by the second defendant to the creation of an encumbrance, so that the transaction could proceed. This imputed consent must, in common sense, apply to the creation of a new encumbrance in replacement of the old, and whether the second defendant knew about it or not, provided that it did not change the second defendant's position for the worse.

The second objection receives the same answer. It presupposes that there was a scintilla temporis between the discharge of the first mortgage and the attachment of the second when the property was entirely unencumbered and the second defendant's interest therein was also unencumbered. It could be said that this interest could not effectively be re-encumbered by a transaction of which she was unaware. I doubt whether this argument is even technically correct, for it may very well be that if the position in law were closely examined (which very sensibly it was not in the argument before us) it would be found that the transactions were simultaneous. But apart from this, to give effect to such a technicality would go against the grain of the broad equity expounded in *Henning's* case. If it was just to enforce the first mortgage it must inevitably be just to enforce the second by virtue of an imputed consent which applied to the creation of both.

This leaves the fourth question: what is the position where the replacement mortgage creates a greater encumbrance than before? If the plaintiffs had sought to argue that they could enforce their charge in full the judgment in *Henning's* case would have provided a conclusive answer, for no intention to prefer a mortgage in any amount greater than £30,000 plus interest could properly be imputed to the second defendant. But the judge has not made any order to this effect, nor have the plaintiffs sought by cross-appeal to obtain one. The issue is therefore not whether the new mortgage has made the second defendant's position worse, but whether, as she contended, it has made it very much better. This would be a strange result if it were so, and I do not think that it is so. I repeat that the purchase could not have taken place at all without some encumbrance, and in my view it is a natural development of *Henning* to hold that in justice to both parties the original or substituted encumbrance should rank ahead of the beneficial interest as far as, but no further than, the consent which is to be imputed to the second defendant.

See also *Locabail (U.K.) Ltd v. Waldorf Investment Corp.* (1999), *The Times*, March 31, 1999.

4. The precise basis of the principle under consideration is uncertain. The judgments in *Bristol and West Building Society v. Henning, Paddington Building Society v. Mendelsohn* and *Equity and Law Home Loans Ltd v. Prestidge* used the language of imputed intention, which has been criticised since the *imputation* of intentions in this context has long been precluded: see *Gissing v. Gissing* [1971] A.C. 886, 904 *per* Lord Diplock; *Burns v. Burns* [1984] Ch. 317, 328–332 *per* Fox L.J.; *Lloyds Bank plc v. Rosset* [1991] 1 A.C. 107, 132–133 *per* Lord Bridge; and see Thompson [1986] Conv. 57; Thompson (1986) 49 M.L.R. 245; Dixon [1992] C.L.J. 223; Thompson [1992] Conv. 206; Smith (1992) 108 L.Q.R. 371. On the other hand, the facts of *Bristol and West Building Society v. Henning* and *Paddington Building Society v. Mendelsohn* arguably justify the conclusion that the equitable owner in fact agreed to the postponement; and, although the equitable owner in *Equity and Law Home Loans Ltd v. Prestidge* had no knowledge of the remortgage, it does not seem unreasonable to extend to the remortgage her (inferable) agreement in relation to the original mortgage. Alternative legal bases have been adopted. In *Abbey National Building Society v. Cann* Lord Oliver used the language of agency in holding that the contribution-based equitable interest was postponed to the full extent of an acquisition mortgage, even though the equitable owner was found to have authorised a limited mortgage loan, a finding based on constructive notice of the need for mortgage funding; for critical comment on the decision of the Court of Appeal, see Beaumont [1989] Conv. 158; Smith (1990) 106 L.Q.R. 32; and on the decision of the House of Lords, see Baughen [1991] Conv. 116; Thompson [1992] Conv. 206. In *Skipton Building Society v. Clayton* (1993) 66 P. & C.R.

223 Slade L.J. (at 228–229) used the language of estoppel, although on the facts there was held to be no postponement; see Crabb [1993] Conv. 478. Other possible legal bases have been suggested, dependent upon the particular circumstances, including subrogation: see Thompson [1992] Conv. 206; Smith (1992) 108 L.Q.R. 371; but a subrogation-based argument was held not to provide any basis for postponement to a remortgage in *City of London Building Society v. Flegg* [1986] Ch. 605, 613 *per* Dillon L.J.; and see Beaumont [1989] Conv. 158 for justification based on general notions of hardship.

5. There also remains some uncertainty as the relevance of the *extent* of the implied consent of the equitable owner. In *Bristol and West Building Society v. Henning* and *Paddington Building Society v. Mendelsohn* the equitable owner knew the amount of the mortgage loan and her contribution-based interest was postponed to the full extent of the loan; and in *Equity and Law Home Loans Ltd v. Prestidge* the equitable owner knew the amount of the original mortgage loan and her contribution-based interest was postponed to the remortgage to the extent of the original loan only. However, in *Abbey National Building Society v. Cann*, although the equitable owner was deemed to know that there was a shortfall of £4,000, her contribution-based interest was postponed to the full extent of the loan; see Baughan [1991] Conv. 116.

6. Although the principle was formulated in the context of acquisition mortgages (and remortgages), it would seem to be equally applicable to post-acquisition mortgages.

7. In fact, there should be no longer any need to have recourse to the principle in the context of acquisition mortgages in the light of the further aspect of *Abbey National Building Society v. Cann* discussed below.

8. For consideration of *express* consent to the postponement of rights, see *ante*, p. 224.

9. Where a mortgage is subject to a contribution-based equitable interest enforceable as an overriding interest, the mortgagee may be able to apply to the court for an order for the sale of the property under section 14 of the Trusts of Land and Appointment of Trustees Act 1996: see *ante*, p. 317.

1.2 *Acquisition mortgages and the* "scintilla temporis"

According to the orthodox view, where the purchase of land was financed at least in part by a mortgage loan, there was a *"scintilla temporis"* between the acquisition of the land by the purchaser and the granting of the mortgage to the mortgagee. During that time the purchaser held the fee simple or leasehold interest in the land unencumbered by the mortgage; and, during that time any contribution-based equitable interest crystallised and thus had the potential to bind and take priority over the mortgage. Assuming that the interest was not overreached by the mortgagee, it would be binding, in the context of unregistered land, where the mortgagee had notice at the time of the mortgage transaction and, in the context of registered land, where the claimant was in actual occupation of the land at the time that the mortgage was registered. As has been seen, in the context of registered land that potential was much reduced by the decision in *Abbey National Building Society v. Cann* that a contribution-based equitable interest would not bind a mortgagee as an overriding interest under section 70(1)(g) unless the claimant was in actual occupation of the land at the date of completion of the mortgage: see *ante*, p. 218.

However, the House of Lords proceeded to overrule the orthodoxy of the *"scintilla temporis"* and thus to eliminate the possibility that a contribution-based equitable interest can ever have priority over an acquisition mortgage, irrespective of whether title to the land is registered or unregistered.

Abbey National Building Society v. Cann [1991] 1 A.C. 56

(HL, Lord Bridge, Lord Griffiths, Lord Ackner, Lord Oliver, Lord Jauncey)

[For the facts, see *ante*, p. 219.]

LORD OLIVER:
If, then, the date at which it falls to be considered whether the claimant to an interest in the land is in actual occupation is the date of completion of the purchase, what has next to be determined is the nature, extent and effect of the interest claimed by him as an overriding interest. I defer for the moment the question whether the facts of the instant case disclose that Mrs Cann was in actual occupation at the relevant time. Up to the moment of completion she had, of course, a beneficial interest under the trust for sale affecting 30, Island Road in the hands of her son, George. He was, I will assume, also estopped by his promise to keep a roof over her head from denying her right as against him to terminate her occupation of the property without her consent, although that estoppel clearly could not have bound the Nationwide Building Society, whose charge had been effected by George with her consent. But it is difficult to see how she could, at that stage, have acquired any interest in 7, Hillview. She was not a party to the contract for the purchase of that property which was entered into by George alone. She assumed and, indeed, may have been led to believe that she would have an interest in and the right to occupy that property when George acquired it, but at the stage prior to its acquisition she had no more than a personal right against him. As against this, the society, which had no notice, either actual or constructive, of any rights which Mrs Cann might be minded to claim, had entered into an agreement to advance £25,000 on the security of the first legal charge on the property and that agreement had become binding and specifically enforceable against George on 6 August when the money was advanced at the request of his solicitors. In so far, therefore, as it is relevant to consider the priority of equities, the society, as an equitable chargee for money actually advanced, had an interest ranking in priority to what, at that stage, was merely Mrs Cann's expectation of an interest under a trust for sale to be created if and when the new property was acquired. One can, perhaps, test it in this way. If, prior to the acquisition of 7, Hillview, George Cann had been able to complete the sale of 30, Island Road, and had absconded with the proceeds, financing the purchase of 7, Hillview entirely by means of a mortgage advance, could his mother have claimed any interest in that property? I should have thought clearly not, save in so far as she might be entitled to a right of occupation by estoppel based on his promise to accommodate her and her having, in reliance on that promise, vacated 30, Island Road to enable that sale to be completed.

It is argued, however, that because the creation of a charge on property in favour of the society necessarily posits that the chargor has acquired an interest out of which the charge can be created, there must notionally be a point of time at which the estate vested in him free from the charge and in which the estoppel affecting him could be "fed" by the acquisition of the legal estate so as to become binding on and take priority over the interest of the chargee. This is a puzzling problem upon which it is not easy to reconcile the authorities.

The appellants rely upon the decision of the Court of Appeal in *Church of England Building Society v. Piskor* [1954] Ch. 553, a case concerned with unregistered conveyancing. The sequence of events in that case was that an agreement to purchase leasehold property was entered into in September 1946, the purchaser being let into possession in the following month on part payment of the price. He proceeded to grant a number of weekly tenancies under which the tenants took possession in November. At that stage the contract remained uncompleted and the tenancies were, therefore, necessarily equitable only. On 25 November 1946, completion took place and the property was assigned to the purchaser, being simultaneously charged by him in favour of the building society whose moneys had enabled the purchase to be completed. The charge contained the usual provision against leasing by the chargor. Default having been made in payment of principal and interest, the society sought possession against the tenants who argued that they had acquired tenancies by estoppel which was "fed" by the acquisition of the legal estate, thus converting their tenancies into legal tenancies binding on the society. The argument of the society was that the conveyance and the charge were in reality one single transaction with the result that the legal estate vested in the purchaser was, from the outset, subject to the society's charge and so could not be available to feed the estoppel free from it. This argument was rejected by the Court of Appeal. It was held that, despite the fact that the two documents were executed contemporaneously, the transaction necessarily involved conveyancing steps which, in contemplation of law, must be regarded as taking place in a defined order, so that there was a "scintilla temporis" between the purchaser's acquisition of the legal estate and the creation of the society's charge during which the estoppel could be fed. Reliance was also placed on a recital in the charge that the legal estate was "now vested in the mortgagors" which precluded the society from denying that the estate had not already vested at the time when the charge was granted. This was, however, only a subsidiary ground for the decision which rested squarely upon the acquisition of the estate out of which the charge was granted as an essential preliminary to the charge.

On the other side of the line are *In re Connolly Brothers Ltd (No. 2)* [1912] 2 Ch. 25 and *Security Trust Co. v. Royal Bank of Canada* [1976] A.C. 503. In the former, a company had granted debentures creating a first and floating charge on all the property present and future of the company and prohibiting the creation of any charges ranking in priority to or pari passu with the debentures. Subsequently, the company, being desirous of acquiring further freehold property, approached a Mrs O'Reilly, who agreed to advance the price but on terms that the loan be secured by a charge on the property. The company then agreed to buy the property. The contract was completed on 31 March 1904 and Mrs O'Reilly was present at completion. She drew a cheque in favour of the company, which was paid into its account, and, at the same time, it drew a cheque for the balance of the price in favour of the vendor, the same solicitor acting for all parties. The conveyance was executed but was retained, together with the other title deeds, by the solicitor on the vendor's behalf, and a few days later the company executed a memorandum of deposit in her favour. Warrington J. held that her charge had priority over the charge created by the debentures and his decision was upheld by the Court of Appeal, Sir Herbert Cozens-Hardy M.R. remarking, at p. 31:

> "we should be shutting our eyes to the real transaction if we were to hold that the unencumbered fee simple in the property was ever in the company so that it became subject to the charge of the debenture holders."

The reasoning, both of the Master of Rolls and of Buckley L.J., seems to have been that, since Mrs O'Reilly had a contractual right to the security at the time when she advanced the money, she necessarily had priority over the debentures. But that is, of course, always the case when a lender advances money on the understanding that he will get a security.

In re Connolly was cited in *Piskor's* case but was distinguished by Sir Raymond

Evershed M.R. on the ground that it involved a question of equitable priorities. So it did but I respectfully question whether this can be a valid ground of distinction. The debentures in *In re Connolly* were duly registered and Mrs O'Reilly clearly had constructive notice of their terms. The question was whether there was ever property upon which those terms could operate and the fact that both the charge in the debentures and Mrs O'Reilly's charge under her contract and the memorandum of deposit were equitable only was entirely immaterial. The question in issue was whether the company's legal estate, without the existence of which her charge could never have taken effect, existed at any point in time free from her charge so that the prior interest of the debenture holders could attach. No other analysis of the decision is possible save that the court considered the transaction consisting of the conveyance, the advance and the memorandum of deposit as a single transaction.

The more recent decision of the Privy Council in *Security Trust Co. v. Royal Bank of Canada* [1976] A.C. 503 is equally capable of analysis only on the "single transaction" basis. The facts were complicated but reduced to their simplest terms involved a contract for the purchase by a company of certain real estate on terms that a certain proportion of the price should be paid by a fixed date and that the balance should be secured by mortgage to the vendor. A conveyance and mortgage were executed and were held in escrow pending payment of the agreed proportion of the price. Default was made in payment by the fixed date but there was no rescission. The purchaser then created a debenture, creating a fixed charge on its existing property and a floating charge on future property. Under that debenture a receiver was appointed. Whether the sale agreement was then still on foot is open to doubt but the date for completion was extended in January 1971 by agreement with the receiver to 30 April of that year. On 30 April the contract was completed. The question which arose in the subsequent liquidation of the purchaser was whether the charge in the debenture took priority over the vendor's mortgage. In delivering the judgment of the Board, Lord Cross of Chelsea contrasted *Piskor's* case and *In re Connolly* observing, at pp. 519–520:

> "But the basic difference between the two lines of cases is that in cases such as *In re Connolly Brothers Ltd (No. 2)* and this case the charge under the debenture only bites on property which is already fettered by the agreement to give the other charge, whereas on the facts of *Church of England Building Society v. Piskor* the tenancy was created out of an interest which was then unfettered by any such agreement."

Again, I respectfully question whether this, although it records accurately what the Court of Appeal held in *Piskor's* case, really affords a valid ground for distinction. However one looks at it, the interests of the tenant in that case had to be legal interests in order to gain any priority and they could only be so by separating the conveyance and the charge and treating them as separate transactions. Although Romer L.J., in the course of his judgment, touched on the question of what the position would have been had there been evidence of some prior agreement to create the charge, this was never fully considered and the court never grasped the nettle that the transaction necessarily involved an enforceable agreement for the grant of a charge at the stage when the money was advanced in order to enable the conveyance to take place.

These three authorities were carefully reviewed by Mustill L.J. in the course of his judgment in *Lloyds Bank plc v. Rosset* [1989] Ch. 350, 388–393. He concluded that it was difficult to see how they could live together. I agree, I do not, for my part, consider that they can be reconciled. In neither *In re Connolly* nor the *Security Trust Co.* case could the charge which was given priority have been created unless and until the legal estate had been obtained by the chargor. In both cases the chargee had notice of the existence of the charge which failed to achieve priority. Both necessarily rest therefore upon the proposition that, at least where there is a prior agreement to grant the charge on the legal estate when obtained, the transactions of acquiring the legal estate and granting the charge are, in law as in reality, one indivisible transaction. It may be possible to justify the actual decision in *Piskor's* case on the subsidiary ground there advanced of an estoppel by deed, but I do not, for myself, see how it is possible to uphold the principal ground for the decision except by rejecting the ratio of *In re Connolly* and the *Security Trust Co.* case.

One is therefore presented with a stark choice between them. Of course, as a matter of legal theory, a person cannot charge a legal estate that he does not have, so that there is an attractive legal logic in the ratio in *Piskor's* case. Nevertheless, I cannot help feeling that it flies in the face of reality. The reality is that, in the vast majority of cases, the acquisition of the legal estate and the charge are not only precisely simultaneous but indissolubly bound together. The acquisition of the legal estate is entirely dependent upon the provision of funds which will have been provided before the conveyance can take effect and which are provided only against an agreement that the estate will be charged to secure them. Indeed, in many, if not most, cases of building society mortgages, there will have been, as there was in this case, a formal offer and acceptance of an advance which will ripen into a specifically enforceable agreement immediately the funds are advanced which will normally be a day or more before completion. In many, if not most, cases, the charge itself will have been executed before the execution, let alone the exchange, of the conveyance or transfer of the property. This is given particular point in the case of registered land where the vesting of the estate is made to depend upon registration, for it may well be that the transfer and the charge will be lodged for registration on different days so that the charge, when registered, may actually take effect from a date prior in time to the date from which the registration of the transfer takes effect: see section 27(3) of the Act of 1925 and the Land Registration Rules 1925, rule 83(2). Indeed, under rule 81 of the Rules of 1925, the registrar is entitled to register the charge even before registration of the transfer to the chargor if he is satisfied that both are entitled to be registered. The reality is that the purchaser of land who relies upon a building society or bank loan for the completion of his purchase never in fact acquires anything but an equity of redemption, for the land is, from the very inception, charged with the amount of the loan without which it could never have been transferred at all and it was never intended that it should be otherwise. The "scintilla temporis" is no more than a legal artifice and, for my part, I would adopt the reasoning of the Court of Appeal in *In re Connolly Brothers Ltd (No. 2)* [1912] 2 Ch. 25 and of Harman J. in *Coventry Permanent Economic Building Society v. Jones* [1951] 1 All E.R. 901 and hold that *Piskor's* case was wrongly decided. It follows, in my judgment, that Mrs Cann can derive no assistance from this line of argument.

NOTES:

1. Lord Jauncey stated (at 102):

[A] purchaser who can only complete a transaction by borrowing money for the security of which he is contractually bound to grant a mortgage to the lender eo instante with the execution of the conveyance in his favour cannot in reality ever be said to have acquired even for a scintilla temporis the unencumbered fee simple or leasehold interest in land whereby he could grant interests having priority over the mortgage ... Since no one can grant what he does not have, it follows that such a purchaser could never grant an interest which was not subject to the limitations on his own interest.

2. Smith (1990) 106 L.Q.R. 545 agrees that the *"scintilla temporis"* principle, though analytically difficult to fault, is artificial and in practice grossly unfair; but he asserts that the solution adopted in *Abbey National Building Society v. Cann*, at least to the extent that it accords priority to the full extent of the mortgage, is difficult to support in terms of legal logic or economic reality. Instead, he argues for equal priority between the sources of

finance, although he acknowledges that such an approach is contrary to the general preference for clear priority between competing proprietary interests.

3. Oakley [1990] C.L.J. 397 regrets the failure of the House of Lords to make clear precisely when a mortgage is indissolubly bound to a purchase; but he suggests that the priority accorded to an acquisition mortgage would attach to a remortgage where, as usually occurs, the subsequent mortgagee pays off the earlier mortgagee(s); see also Baughen [1991] Conv. 116. Such reasoning would justify the decision in *Equity and Law Home Loans Ltd v. Prestidge* [1992] 1 W.L.R. 137; and, although *Abbey National Building Society v. Cann* was not cited in that case, Mustill L.J. (at 144) expressly doubted whether there was a *"scintilla temporis"* between the discharge of the first mortgage and the creation of the second or, in any event, whether the court would permit such a technicality to defeat the broad equity of *Henning*: see Dixon [1992] C.L.J. 223; Smith (1992) 108 L.Q.R. 371.

2. Protection of mortgages

A mortgagee will wish to ensure continuing enforcement and/or gain priority for his mortgage against subsequent dealings in the mortgaged land. In the context of unregistered land, a first mortgagee (legal or equitable) is entitled to retain the title deeds (thereby effectively restraining dealings in the land that might endanger his security): Law of Property Act 1925, ss.85(1), 86(1), 87(1); and see *supra*, p. 823. A subsequent mortgagee may protect his mortgage by appropriate registration under the Land Charges Act 1972: a legal mortgage not protected by a deposit of title deeds is a "puisne mortgage" and registrable as a Class C(i) land charge; and an equitable mortgage not protected by a deposit of title deeds is a "general equitable charge" and registrable as a Class C(iii) land charge.

In the context of registered land which has been mortgaged, section 65 of the Land Registration Act 1925 requires the relevant land certificate to be deposited in the Land Registry throughout the continuance of the mortgage. In addition, every mortgage of registered land is capable of protection by the appropriate entry on the register. The importance of prompt registration is illustrated by *Barclays Bank plc v. Zaroovabli* [1997] Ch. 321, *ante*, p. 232. An unprotected mortgage lost priority to a lease granted by the registered proprietor after the creation of the mortgage but before its later registration because it is the date of registration that determines priority; see [1997] C.L.J. 496; (1997) 113 L.Q.R. 390.

F. Remedies of the Mortgagee

It has been seen that the whole purpose of a mortgage transaction is to provide security to the mortgagee for repayment of the loan. The various remedies available to a mortgagee to protect that security, and if necessary to enforce it, are therefore of crucial importance. In addition to the personal remedy against the mortgagor for breach of the personal covenant to repay the loan, the mortgagee has a number of remedies against the mortgaged land. Foreclosure and sale are directed primarily at the recovery of the loan and the termination of the mortgage transaction; the appointment of a receiver is directed primarily at the recovery of interest payable on the loan; and possession of the mortgaged property, although originally used as a means of securing the payment of interest and still in theory available for that purpose (see *Western Bank Ltd v. Schindler* [1977] Ch. 1), is now sought almost exclusively as a preliminary to the exercise of the power of sale so that the mortgagee may sell the property with vacant possession: see *Four-Maids Ltd v. Dudley Marshall (Properties) Ltd* [1957] Ch. 317, 320 *per* Harman J.

The remedies of the mortgagee are generally cumulative so that the mortgagee can exercise more than one remedy in order to recover his loan: *Rudge v. Richens* (1873) L.R. 8 C.P. 358; *Gordon Grant & Co. Ltd v. F.L. Boos* [1926] A.C. 781. However, following foreclosure, the mortgagee is permitted to sue on the personal covenant of the mortgagor only on condition that the foreclosure is re-opened: see *infra.* Underlying, and perhaps in addition to, the particular safeguards that have been imposed on the exercise of the individual remedies to protect the mortgagor, the Court of Appeal has recently asserted that a mortgagee who exercises his remedies owes a general duty to act fairly towards the mortgagor: *Palk v. Mortgage Services Funding plc* [1993] Ch. 330, 337–338 *per* Nicholls V.-C.

The following remedies are in principle available to legal mortgagees; the remedies available to equitable mortgagees and charges are considered at the end of this section.

1. Foreclosure

As noted above, the remedy of foreclosure, although now governed by statute, was the creation of equity and was seen as the necessary limitation on the otherwise unrestricted equitable right to redeem which equity had conferred on the mortgagor. As Jessel M.R. stated in *Carter v. Wake* (1877) 4 Ch D. 605, 606, "[t]he court simply removes the stop it has itself put on". It is the most drastic of the remedies available to the mortgagee since it amounts to the total and uncompensated extinction of the rights of the mortgagor. Its availability is therefore restricted by a number of procedural and substantive safeguards; and as a result it is uncommon for mortgagees to have recourse to it: see *Palk v. Mortgage Services Funding plc* [1993] Ch. 330, 336 *per* Nicholls V.-C.

The right of the mortgagee to foreclose cannot arise until the equitable right to redeem has arisen, either because the legal or contractual date for redemption has passed: *Williams v. Morgan* [1906] 1 Ch. 804; or because there has been a breach of a condition which has to be complied with to keep the legal right of redemption alive: *Twentieth Century Banking Corp. Ltd v. Wilkinson* [1977] Ch. 99, noted at (1976) 40 Conv. 442. At any time thereafter the mortgagee may request repayment of the loan and, if the mortgagor fails to make repayment, he may apply to the court for an order of *foreclosure nisi.* Such an order affords the mortgagor a final opportunity to repay the loan within a specified period (normally six months from the order nisi); and if repayment is still not made the court may make an order of *foreclosure absolute*. The effect of the order absolute is that the mortgagee becomes entitled to the mortgaged property, free from the rights of the mortgagor and of any subsequent mortgagees but subject to any prior incumbrances: Law of Property Act 1925, ss.88(2), 89(2). Where there are subsequent mortgagees, they must be made parties to the foreclosure action and must be given the opportunity to pay off any prior mortgage. In contrast to the position where the mortgagee enforces his security by sale (see *infra*, p. 910), the order for foreclosure absolute deprives the mortgagor of all interest in the mortgaged property, even if its value exceeds the amount of the outstanding loan(s).

The remedy is subject to three principal safeguards. First, under section 91(2) of the Law of Property Act 1925 the court may direct a sale of the mortgaged property in lieu of foreclosure: see *Twentieth Century Banking Corp. Ltd v. Wilkinson* [1977] Ch. 99. The availability of this alternative response is particularly appropriate where the value of the mortgaged property far exceeds the amount of the outstanding loan(s). However, this safeguard is not wholly effective: the subsection does not enable the court to direct a sale unless requested to do so by the mortgagor or any person interested either in the mortgage money or in the right of redemption; and such persons commonly do not attend the hearing. Secondly, where foreclosure is sought in the case of an instalment mortgage of a dwelling-house the court has power to adjourn the proceedings if it appears to the court that, in the event of its exercising that power, the mortgagor is likely to be able within a reasonable period to pay unpaid instalments as well as current instalments: Administration of Justice Act 1973, s.8(3). Thirdly, even after the court has made an order for foreclosure absolute, the court may "re-open the foreclosure" if equity justifies such action in the particular circumstances. In *Campbell v. Holyland* (1877) 7 Ch D. 166 Jessel M.R. stated (at 171–174):

The question in dispute is really whether a mortgagor can be allowed to redeem after an order of foreclosure absolute, and I think, on looking at the authorities, that no Chancellor or Vice-Chancellor has ever laid down that any special circumstances are essential to enable a mortgagor to redeem in such a case.

Now what is the principle? The principle in a Court of Equity has always been that, though a mortgage is in form an absolute conveyance when the condition is broken, in equity it is always security; and it must be remembered that the doctrine arose at the time when mortgages were made in the form of conditional conveyance, the condition being that if the money was not paid at the day, the estate should become the estate of the mortgagee; that was the contract between the parties; yet Courts of Equity interfered with actual contract to this extent, by saying there was a paramount intention that the estate should be security, and that the mortgage money should be debt; and they gave relief in the shape of redemption on that principle. Of course that would lead, and did lead, to this inconvenience, that even where the mortgagor was not willing to redeem, the mortgagee could not sell or deal with the estate as his own, and to remedy that inconvenience the practice of bringing a foreclosure suit was adopted, by which a mortgagee was entitled to call on the mortgagor to redeem within a certain time, under penalty of losing the right of redemption. In that foreclosure suit the Court made various orders—interim orders fixing a time for payment of the money—and at last there came the final order which was called foreclosure absolute, that is, in form, that the mortgagor should not be allowed to redeem at all; but it was form only, just as the original deed was form only; for the Courts of Equity soon decided that, notwithstanding the form of that order, they would after that order allow the mortgagor to redeem. That is, although the order of foreclosure absolute appeared to be a final order of the Court, it was not so, but the mortgagee still remained liable to be treated as mortgagee and the mortgagor still retained a claim to be treated as mortgagor, subject to the discretion of the Court. Therefore everybody who took an order for foreclosure absolute knew that there was still a discretion in the Court to allow the mortgagor to redeem.

Under what circumstances that discretion should be exercised is quite another matter. The mortgagee had a right to deal with an estate acquired under foreclosure absolute the day after he acquired it; but he knew perfectly well that there might be circumstances to entitle the mortgagor to redeem, and everybody buying the estate from a mortgagee who merely acquired a title under such an order was considered to have the same knowledge, namely, that the estate might be taken away from him by the exercise, not of a capricious discretion, but of a judicial discretion by the Court of Equity which had made the order.

That being so, on what terms is that judicial discretion to be exercised? It has been said by the highest authority that it is impossible to say *a priori* what are the terms. They must depend upon the circumstances of each case. For instance, in *Thornhill v. Manning* (1851) 1 Sim. (N.S.) 451, 454, Lord Cranworth said you cannot lay down a general rule. There are certain things laid down which are intelligible to everybody. In the first place the mortgagor must come, as it is said, promptly; that is, within a reasonable time. He is not to let the mortgagee deal with the estate as his own—if it is a landed estate, the mortgagee being in possession of it and using it—and then without any special reason come and say, "Now I will redeem". He cannot do that; he must come within a reasonable time. What is a reasonable time? You must have regard to the nature of the property. As has been stated in more than one of the cases, where the estate is an estate in land in possession—where the mortgagee takes it in possession and deals with it and alters the property, and so on—the mortgagor must come much more quickly than where it is an estate in reversion, as to which the mortgagee can do nothing except sell it. So that you must have regard to the nature of the estate in ascertaining what is to be considered reasonable time.

Then, again, was the mortgagor entitled to redeem, but by some accident unable to redeem? Did he expect to get the money from a quarter from which he might reasonably hope to obtain it, and was he disappointed at the last moment? Was it a very large sum, and did he require a considerable time to raise it elsewhere? All those things must be considered in determining what is a reasonable time.

Then an element for consideration has always been the nature of the property as regards value. For instance, if an estate were worth £50,000, and had been foreclosed for a mortgage debt of £5,000, the man who came to redeem that estate would have a longer time than where the estate was worth £5,100, and he was foreclosed for £5,000. But not only is there money value, but there may be other considerations. It may be an old family estate or a chattel, or picture, which possesses a special value for the mortgagor, but which possesses not the same value for other people; or it may be, as has happened in this instance, that the property, though a reversionary interest in the funds, is of special value to both the litigants: it may possess not merely a positive money value, but a peculiar value having regard to the nature of the title and other incidents, so that you cannot set an actual money value upon it. In fact, that is the real history of this contest, for the property does not appear to be of much more money value—though it is of some more—than the original amount of the mortgage. All this must be taken into consideration.

Then it is said you must not interfere against purchasers. As I have already explained, there are purchasers and purchasers. If the purchaser buys a freehold estate in possession after the lapse of a considerable time from the order of foreclosure absolute, with no notice of any extraneous circumstances which would induce the Court to interfere, I for one should decline to interfere with such a title as that; but if the purchaser bought the estate within twenty-four hours after the foreclosure absolute, and with notice of the fact that it was of much greater value than the amount of the mortgage debt, is it to be supposed that a Court of Equity would listen to the contention of such a purchaser that he ought not to be interfered with? He must be taken to know the general law that an order for foreclosure may be opened under proper circumstances and under a proper exercise of discretion by the Court; and if the mortgagor in that case came the week after, is it to be supposed a Court of Equity would so stultify itself as to say that a title so acquired would stand in the way? I am of opinion it would not.

See also *Kinnaird v. Trollope* (1888) 39 Ch D. 636, 642 *per* Stirling J.; *Ellis & Co.'s Trustee v. Dixon-Johnson* [1925] A.C. 489, 491 *per* Viscount Cave L.C.; *Gordon Grant & Co. Ltd v. Boos* [1926] A.C. 781, 784 *per* Lord *Phillimore; Lloyds and Scottish Trust Ltd v. Britten* (1982) 44 P. & C.R. 249, 256–257 *per* Judge Mervyn Davies Q.C.; *Cheah Theam Swee v. Equiticorp Finance Group Ltd* [1992] 1 A.C. 472, 476 *per* Lord Browne-Wilkinson.

The Law Commission has recommended that the remedy of foreclosure should be abolished: Law Com. No. 204; *Transfer of Land: Land Mortgages* (1991), paras 7.26–7.27.

2. Sale

The remedy of sale enables the mortgagee to realise the value of the mortgaged land and to recover the outstanding loan from the proceeds of sale.

2.1 *Power of sale*

The Law of Property Act 1925 distinguishes between the existence and the exercise of the power of sale. Where a mortgage is made by deed, subject to any contrary intention expressed in the mortgage deed, the mortgagee has a statutory power of sale which *arises* "when the mortgage money has become due": Law of Property Act 1925, s.101(1)(i), (4). It has been held that the mortgage money becomes due on the legal or contractual date for redemption or, in the case of an instalment mortgage, as soon as the first instalment of capital is due: *Payne v. Cardiff RDC* [1932] 1 K.B. 241; but in *Twentieth Century Banking Corp. Ltd v. Wilkinson* [1977] Ch. 99, the power of sale was held not to have arisen where interest was due and unpaid but capital repayments were not yet due.

However, the power of sale does not become *exercisable* unless and until one of three further conditions has been satisfied.

Law of Property Act 1925, s.103

Regulation of exercise of power of sale

103.—A mortgagee shall not exercise the power of sale conferred by this Act unless and until—

(i)   Notice requiring payment of the mortgage money has been served on the mortgagor or one of two or more mortgagors, and default has been made in payment of the mortgage money, or of part thereof, for three months after such service; or

(ii) Some interest under the mortgage is in arrear and unpaid for two months after becoming due; or

(iii) There has been a breach of some provision contained in the mortgage deed or in this Act, or in an enactment replaced by this Act, and on the part of the mortgagor, or of some person concurring in making the mortgage, to be observed or performed, other than and besides a covenant for payment of the mortgage money or interest thereon.

NOTES:

1. The mortgagee does not require the leave of the court before he can exercise the power of sale.

2. The distinction between the power of sale arising and becoming exercisable seems to have significance largely for the purchaser from the mortgagee—

(i)   Where the power of sale has arisen and has become exercisable, a purchaser from the mortgagee obtains good title to the mortgaged property free from the equity of redemption.

(ii) Where the power of sale has arisen but has not yet become exercisable, or where the power has been exercised irregularly or improperly, a purchaser from the mortgagee will still obtain good title to the mortgaged property free from the equity of redemption, unless he has actual (as opposed to merely constructive) knowledge that the power is not exercisable or has been exercised irregularly or improperly: Law of Property Act 1925, s.104(2); and see *Bailey v. Barnes* [1894] 1 Ch. 25, 30 *per* Stirling J.; *Lord Waring v. London & Manchester Assurance Co. Ltd* [1935] Ch. 310, 318 *per* Crossman J. It has been questioned whether the court should exercise a discretion in appropriate circumstances to overlook an irregularity of which the purchaser has notice: see [1988] Conv. 317. However, where the mortgagee sells the mortgaged property before the power of sale has become exercisable, he will be liable to the mortgagor in damages: Law of Property Act 1925, s.104(2).

(iii) Where the power of sale has not arisen, any purported sale by the mortgagee will operate as a transfer of the mortgage itself, vesting in the purchaser only the rights of the mortgagee.

In summary, therefore, it seems that the purchaser is concerned to see only that the power of sale has arisen, not that it has become exercisable: *Property and Bloodstock Ltd v. Emerton* [1968] Ch. 94, 114 *per* Danckwerts L.J. For discussion of the position of the purchaser, see Robinson [1989] Conv. 412.

3. Subject to note 2 above, a conveyance by a mortgagee pursuant to the statutory power of sale vests the legal estate in the mortgaged land in the purchaser: Law of Property Act 1925, ss.88(1), 89(1); and the purchaser takes the land subject to any prior mortgage but free from the rights of the vendor-

mortgagee, any subsequent mortgagees and the mortgagor: *ibid.* ss.2(1)(iii), 104(1). The similar result is achieved in the context of registered land under section 34(4) of the Land Registration Act 1925.

4. A contract for the sale of mortgaged land pursuant to the statutory power of sale extinguishes the equity of redemption. The mortgagee cannot be required to accept repayment and can only be restrained from completing the sale on the ground that he has not acted in good faith: *Lord Waring v. London & Manchester Assurance Co. Ltd* [1935] Ch. 310, 318 *per* Crossman J.; *Property and Bloodstock Ltd v. Emerton* [1968] Ch. 94, 114–115 *per* Danckwerts L.J.; *National and Provincial Building Society v. Ahmed* [1995] 2 E.G.L.R. 127, 128 *per* Millett L.J. Such a contract also prevails over an earlier contract of sale made by the mortgagor: *Duke v. Robson* [1973] 1 W.L.R. 267, noted at (1973) 37 Conv. 133.

5. Even where the statutory power of sale has become exercisable, the court has exercised its jurisdiction under section 91(2) to sanction a sale by the mortgagee and thereby to render it unimpeachable by the mortgagor. The circumstances were exceptional in that, notwithstanding that the prospects of impeaching the proposed sale were utterly remote, the mortgagor was likely to attempt to frustrate any sale pursuant to section 101(1): see *Arab Bank plc v. Merchantile Holdings Ltd* [1994] Ch. 71.

On the assumption that the power of sale has become exercisable, there are two principal issues relating to the duties of the mortgagee: the duties in relation to the sale and the duties in relation to the proceeds of sale.

2.2 Duties in relation to the sale

2.2.1 The substance of the duties of the mortgagee

Cuckmere Brick Co. Ltd v. Mutual Finance Ltd [1971] Ch. 949

(CA, Salmon, Cross and Cairns L.JJ.)

The plaintiffs owned certain land in respect of which there had been granted planning permission to erect 100 flats. They charged the land to the defendants by way of legal mortgage to secure the repayment of loans amounting to £50,000. The plaintiffs later obtained planning permission to erect 35 houses on the land. The mortgagees' statutory power of sale became exercisable and they instructed auctioneers to sell the land. The advertisements prepared by the auctioneers referred to the later planning permission only and the land was sold for £44,000. The plaintiffs, who had sought to have the sale postponed in order to re-advertise, claimed that the land with planning permission for flats was worth £75,000; and that if the auction had been attended by developers interested in erecting flats, the land would have sold for a figure in excess of £44,000.

SALMON L.J.:

It is well settled that a mortgagee is not a trustee of the power of sale for the mortgagor. Once the power has accrued, the mortgagee is entitled to exercise it for his own purposes whenever he chooses to do so. It matters not that the moment may be unpropitious and that by waiting a higher price could be obtained. He has the right to realise his security by turning it into money when he likes. Nor, in my view, is there anything to prevent a mortgagee from accepting the best bid he can get at an auction, even though the auction is badly attended and the bidding exceptionally low. Providing none of those adverse factors is due to any fault of the mortgagee, he can do as he likes. If the mortgagee's interests, as he sees them, conflict with those of the mortgagor, the mortgagee can give preference to his own interests, which of course he could not do were he a trustee of the power of sale for the mortgagor.

Mr Vinelott [counsel for the defendants] contends that the mortgagee's sole obligation to the mortgagor in relation to a sale is to act in good faith; there is no duty of care, and accordingly no question of negligence by the mortgagee in the conduct of the sale can arise. If this contention is correct it follows that, even on the facts found by the judge, the defendants should have succeeded.

It is impossible to pretend that the state of the authorities on this branch of the law is entirely satisfactory. There are some dicta which suggest that unless a mortgagee acts in bad faith he is safe. His only obligation to the mortgagor is not to cheat him. There are other dicta which suggest that in addition to the duty of acting in good faith, the mortgagee is under a duty to take reasonable care to obtain whatever is the true market value of the mortgaged property at the moment he chooses to sell it: compare, for example, *Kennedy v. De Trafford* [1896] 1 Ch. 762; [1897] A.C. 180 with *Tomlin v. Luce* (1889) 43 Ch.D. 191, 194.

The proposition that the mortgagee owes both duties, in my judgment, represents the true view of the law. Approaching the matter first of all on principle, it is to be observed that if the sale yields a surplus over the amount owed under the mortgage, the mortgagee holds this surplus in trust for the mortgagor. If the sale shows a deficiency, the mortgagor has to make it good out of his own pocket. The mortgagor is vitally affected by the result of the sale but its preparation and conduct is left entirely in the hands of the mortgagee. The proximity between them could scarcely be closer. Surely they are "neighbours". Given that the power of sale is for the benefit of the mortgagee and that he is entitled to choose the moment to sell which suits him, it would be strange indeed if he were under no legal obligation to take reasonable care to obtain what I call the true market value at the date of the sale. Some of the textbooks refer to the "proper price," others to the "best price". Vaisey J. in *Reliance Permanent Building Society v. Harwood-Stamper* [1944] Ch. 362, 364, 365, seems to have attached great importance to the difference between those two descriptions of "price". My difficulty is that I cannot see any real difference between them. "Proper price" is perhaps a little nebulous, and "the best price" may suggest an exceptionally high price. That is why I prefer to call it "the true market value".

In *Tomlin v. Luce* (1889) 41 Ch.D. 573; (1889) 43 Ch.D. 191, the first mortgagees by mistake misdescribed the property being offered for sale. It was knocked down for £20,000. When the buyers discovered the mistake they refused to complete unless they were allowed £895 off the purchase price. This allowance was made and the price accordingly reduced to £19,105. The second mortgagees, who can be treated as in the same position as mortgagors, brought an action against the first mortgagees claiming that those mortgagees were responsible for the mistake of their auctioneer, that as a result of this mistake £895 had been deducted from the purchase price, and that this deduction ought not to be allowed in taking the account between the first and second mortgagees. The trial judge found in favour of the plaintiff and disallowed the whole of the £895. This was obviously wrong because the first mortgagees could only be answerable for any loss occasioned by the misdescription. The question should have been: but for the misdescription, would the land have sold for anything and if so how much more than £19,105? The judge's order was accordingly varied in the Court of Appeal. Cotton L.J., after pointing out the judge's mistake, said at p. 194:

> "The defence seems really to have been ... directed to this, that the first mortgagees, selling under their power, employed a competent auctioneer, and were not answerable for any blunder which the auctioneer committed. There they were wrong, and that point was not, I think, argued before us. ... What we think is this,— that the first mortgagees are answerable for any loss which was occasioned by the blunder made by their auctioneer at the sale."

Bowen and Fry L.JJ. concurred. Although the point was not argued in the Court of Appeal, the passage in Cotton L.J.'s judgment which I have read must be treated with the greatest respect. He was a master in this branch of the law, and he and the other members of the court as well as counsel treated the point as too plain for argument. Indeed it had long been so regarded by the courts: see *Wolff v. Vanderzee* (1869) 20 L.T. 353 and *National Bank of Australasia v. United Hand-in-Hand and Band of Hope Co.* (1879) 4 App.Cas. 391 in which the Privy Council expressed the clear view that a mortgagee is chargeable with the full value of the mortgaged property sold if, from want of due care and diligence, it has been sold at an undervalue. It would seem, therefore, that many years before the modern development of the law of negligence, the courts of equity had laid down a doctrine in relation to mortgages which is entirely consonant with the general principles later evolved by the common law.

Then came *Kennedy v. De Trafford* [1896] 1 Ch. 762; [1897] A.C. 180 (with which I will presently deal) in which none of the authorities to which I have referred were cited. After that case came *McHugh v. Union Bank of Canada* [1913] A.C. 299, in which *Kennedy v. De Trafford* was not cited. In the *McHugh* case, Lord Moulton, in giving the opinion of an exceptionally strong Board, said, at p. 311:

> "It is well settled law that it is the duty of a mortgagee when realising the mortgaged property by sale to behave in conducting such realisation as a reasonable man would behave in the realisation of his own property, so that the mortgagor may receive credit for the fair value of the property sold."

In that case the plaintiffs recovered damages because of a depreciated price having been realised for mortgaged horses on account of the negligent manner in which the mortgagees had had them driven to market. Mr Vinelott argues that this case was concerned only with the duty of a mortgagee to take care to preserve the mortgaged property when he goes into possession so as not to preclude the equity of redemption and has nothing to do with the mortgagee's duty upon a sale. I am afraid that I cannot accept that the case is susceptible of being explained away in the manner which Mr Vinelott suggests.

I now come to *Kennedy v. De Trafford* [1896] 1 Ch. 762; [1897] A.C. 180 which is the linch-pin of the defendants' case on the law. Carswell and Dodson were tenants in common in fee simple of certain freehold property and in 1877 they mortgaged it to Sir Humphrey de Trafford for £60,000 with a provision for redemption and reconveyance to the mortgagors as tenants in common with the usual power of sale after six months notice. In 1886 Carswell was adjudicated bankrupt and Kennedy was appointed his trustee. Sir Humphrey de Trafford having died, his executors gave notice to pay off the mortgage. Kennedy having refused to redeem, the mortgagees gave him and Dodson notice of their intention to sell if they could obtain the principal interest and costs outstanding. Having advertised for tenders without results, the mortgagees in 1889 sold to Dodson for a sum equal to the principal interest and costs, £54,000 being left on mortgage and the residue paid off. Before the sale Kennedy was informed of all particulars except the name of the purchaser. In 1891 he discovered that the purchaser was Dodson. He did nothing until 1895, when he brought proceedings against the mortgagee, Dodson being joined as a defendant, to set aside the sale as invalid, alternatively for damages for negligence. Kennedy won at first instance but lost in the

Court of Appeal. From that decision he appealed to the House of Lords. The House did not take time for consideration but dismissed the appeal out of hand, Lord Herschell and Lord Macnaghten observing that it was as hopeless an appeal as they had ever heard. There was no allegation of bad faith against the mortgagees and the Court of Appeal and the House of Lords concluded that there was no evidence of negligence, nor that any better price could have been obtained than the price paid by Dodson. Mr Vinelott strongly relies, however, upon certain observations made in that case by Lindley L.J. in the Court of Appeal [1896] 1 Ch. 762, 772 and by Lord Herschell in the House of Lords [1897] A.C. 180, 183. The passage in Lindley L.J.'s judgment appears to me to be rather equivocal. In that passage he seems perhaps to be resiling from what he had said in *Farrar v. Farrars Ltd* (1888) 40 Ch.D. 395, 411, namely, that the duty of a mortgagee is to take reasonable precautions to obtain a proper price. I agree with Mr Vinelott that the word "recklessly" in the context of those passages connotes something akin to bad faith and more than gross carelessness. It means not caring whether or not the interests of the mortgagors are sacrified. I do not regard these passages, however, as overruling *Tomlin v. Luce* (1889) 43 Ch.D. 191 and the earlier authorities to which I have referred. Indeed they were never cited in *Kennedy v. De Trafford*. Lord Herschell, in the first part of the passage relied on by Mr Vinelott, certainly expresses grave doubt as to whether a mortgagee in exercising a power of sale is under any duty except to act in good faith. I think, however, that in the second part of that passage he expressly refrains from deciding whether or not in such circumstances a mortgagee owes a duty to take reasonable precautions as well as a duty to act in good faith. It was certainly unnecessary for him to decide that question for the purpose of the case he was considering because, as he points out, the mortgagees in that case had taken all reasonable precautions in exercising their powers of sale and no allegation of bad faith was made. In my view, therefore, *Kennedy v. De Trafford* does not weaken the effect of the other cases to which I have referred. I accordingly conclude, both on principle and authority, that a mortgagee in exercising his power of sale does owe a duty to take reasonable precautions to obtain the true market value of the mortgaged property at the date on which he decides to sell it. No doubt in deciding whether he has fallen short of that duty the facts must be looked at broadly, and he will not be adjudged to be in default unless he is plainly on the wrong side of the line.

CROSS L.J.:

A mortgagee exercising a power of sale is in an ambiguous position. He is not a trustee of the power for the mortgagor for it was given him for his own benefit to enable him to obtain repayment of his loan. On the other hand, he is not in the position of an absolute owner selling his own property but must undoubtedly pay some regard to the interests of the mortgagor when he comes to exercise the power.

Some points are clear. On the one hand, the mortgagee, when the power has arisen, can sell when he likes, even though the market is likely to improve if he holds his hand and the result of an immediate sale may be that instead of yielding a surplus for the mortgagor the purchase price is only sufficient to discharge the mortgage debt and the interest owing on it. On the other hand, the sale must be a genuine sale by the mortgagee to an independent purchaser at a price honestly arrived at.

Suppose, however, that the mortgagee acts in good faith but that through the negligence either of the mortgagee himself or of an agent employed by him a smaller purchase price is obtained that would otherwise have been the case? in 1869, in *Wolff v. Vanderzee* (1869) 20 L.T. 353, Stuart V.-C. held that a mortgagee was accountable to the mortgagor for the loss in purchase price occasioned by the negligence of the auctioneer employed by him in stating that the property was let at a rent lower than the rent in fact being paid by the tenant. It is to be observed that in deciding that case the Vice-Chancellor relied on *Marriott v. Anchor Reversionary Co. Ltd* (1861) 3 De G. F. & J. 177, where a mortgagee who had taken possession of a mortgaged ship with a view to its sale was held accountable for a loss incurred by the improvident working of the vessel in the period between the taking of possession and the sale.

In 1888 in *Farrar v. Farrars Ltd* (1888) 40 Ch.D. 395 (which was not a claim for damages for negligence but an unsuccessful attempt by the mortgagor to set aside the sale on the ground that one of the mortgagees was a shareholder in the company which was the purchaser) Lindley L.J. said, at p. 411, that if in the exercise of his power the mortgagee "acts bona fide and takes reasonable precautions to obtain a proper price" the mortgagor has no redress even though more might have been obtained if the sale had been postponed. That formulation of the mortgagee's duty is not on the face of it inconsistent with the decision of *Wolff v. Vanderzee* (1869) 20 L.T. 353.

In 1889, in *Tomlin v. Luce* (1889) 41 Ch.D. 573, Kekewich J., applying the same principle as that applied by Vice-Chancellor Stuart 20 years earlier, held that a mortgagee was liable to account to those interested in the equity of redemption for loss occasioned by a negligent misdescription of the property by their auctioneers. The Court of Appeal (Cotton, Bowen and Fry L.JJ. (1889) 43 Ch.D. 191) varied the order made below on the ground that the method of calculating the loss adopted by the judge was wrong. The mortgagees seem not to have argued in the Court of Appeal that they were not liable to account at all for an innocent mistake made by their auctioneers, and the Court of Appeal plainly thought that the judge was right on this point.

In 1896 came *Kennedy v. De Trafford* [1896] 1 Ch. 762; [1897] A.C. 180, which is the sheet anchor of the defendants' submissions of law and which, accordingly, it is necessary to consider in some detail. The mortgage there was by two tenants in common (one of whom subsequently became bankrupt) and the sale was by the mortgagee to the other tenant in common for a purchase price equal to what was owing under the mortgage, the greater part of the purchase price being left on a fresh mortgage. The trustee of the bankrupt mortgagor took proceedings against the mortgagee and the purchasing mortgagor, claiming to have the sale set aside or, alternatively, for damages against the mortgagee for negligence.

The judge of first instance held that the mortgagee acted in good faith and that the sale was not at such an undervalue as to be evidence of fraud; but he also held (a) that the mortgagee had not made reasonable efforts to get a better price before selling to the other mortgagor and (b) that the relationship between the purchasing mortgagor and the mortgagee on the one hand and the other mortgagor on the other was such as to put the purchasing mortgagor in the position of a trustee and to justify the setting aside of the sale.

The second ground was rejected both by the Court of Appeal and the House of Lords and need not be further considered here.

In deciding against the mortgagee on the first ground as well, the judge relied on the words used by Lindley L.J. in *Farrar's* case (1888) 40 Ch.D. 395, which I have cited above. In his judgment in *Kennedy v. De Trafford* [1896] 1 Ch. 762, as I read it, Lindley L.J. explained that when he had spoken of the mortgagee taking "reasonable precautions to obtain a proper price" he did not mean to imply that the mortgagee would be liable for mere negligence on his own part or on that of his agent, but simply that he must not "fraudulently or wilfully or recklessly" sacrifice the interests of the mortgagor. He was on, however, to say, at p. 773, that on the facts of the case before him the mortgagee had not failed to take any step which it was reasonable and proper for him to have taken.

In the House of Lords, Lords Herschell and Macnaghten both expressed the view that a mortgagee who acts in good faith is not liable for mere negligence in the exercise of his power of sale. But they both added (as had Lindley L.J.) that if the mortgagee as well as acting in good faith was under a duty to take reasonable precautions in the exercise of the power, the mortgagees in the case before them had taken reasonable precautions.

There are several points to be observed about this decision. The first concerns the use by Lindley L.J. and Lord Herschell of the word "recklessly". Plowman J., as I read his judgment in this case, thought that they meant by the word no more than "with gross negligence". With all respect to him, I cannot agree. They indicated that a man who acted "recklessly" in their sense of the word would not be acting in good faith. This shows, to my mind, that they were using the word in the sense of simply not caring whether what he did injured the mortgagor or not. Secondly, it is not, as I see it, possible to treat the views expressed by Lindley L.J. and Lords Herschell and Macnaghten to the effect that the only duty of the mortgagee is to act in good faith as limited to cases where the mortgagor is seeking to have the sale set aside and as not covering cases where he is simply asking that the mortgagee should be charged in his accounts with any loss attributable to his negligence. There was in fact an alternative claim for damages in *Kennedy v. De Trafford*, but in any case the language used is quite general. Whether the mortgagor can or cannot have the sale set aside will depend on whether the purchaser had notice of the breach of duty, but the standard of duty cannot vary with the nature of the remedy available for the breach of it. Thirdly, it is to be observed that though the view that the mortgagee's duty is simply to act in good faith is inconsistent with *Wolff v. Vanderzee* (1869) 20 L.T. 353 and *Tomlin v. Luce* (1889) 43 Ch.D. 191, those cases were not referred to either in the argument or the judgment. It is a curious fact that the textbooks do not comment on the inconsistency, but, while stating Lindley L.J.'s view of the law—namely, that the mortgage need only act in good faith—continue to refer to *Tomlin v. Luce* as an authority for making him liable for mere negligence.

The only other case to which it is necessary to refer is the Privy Council decision of *McHugh v. Union Bank of Canada* [1913] A.C. 299, where the mortgage security was a number of horses. The mortgagor did not allege that the mortgagee had been guilty of any breach of duty in connection with the actual sale of the horses. The points at issue were, first, whether he was liable in damages for the manner in which he had dealt with the horses between the time when he took possession of them and the date of the sale and, secondly, as to the amounts with which he was entitled to charge the mortgagor in respect of expenses. The opinion of the Board, delivered by Lord Moulton, does, however contain the following general statement which is inconsistent with the views expressed by Lindley L.J. and Lords Herschell and Macnaghten in *Kennedy v. De Trafford*. He said, at p. 311:

> "It is well settled law that it is the duty of a mortgagee when realising the mortgaged property by sale to behave in conducting such realisation as a reasonable man would behave in the realisation of his own property, so that the mortgagor may receive credit for the fair value of the property sold."

Lord Macnaghten was a member of the Board which heard the case but, as Cairns L.J. pointed out in the course of the argument in this case, he died on the very day (February 17, 1913) on which the opinion of the Board was delivered, and it would be wrong to assume that he gave his approval to the manner in which the mortgagee's duty is stated in the passage quoted above.

Mr Vinelott submitted—rightly, as I think—that even if Messrs. Geering & Colyer were guilty of professional negligence they did not act "recklessly" within the meaning of that word as used by Lindley L.J. and Lord Herschell in *Kennedy v. De Trafford* [1896] 1 Ch. 762; [1897] A.C. 180. They may have been hopelessly wrong, but they directed their minds to the question at issue and tried their best to answer it.

Mr Vinelott next submitted that we should accept the views expressed by Lindley L.J. and Lords Herschell and Macnaghten as an authoritative definition of the duty of a mortgagee exercising his power of sale and allow the appeal on that ground. I am not prepared to accede to this second submission. In the confused state of the authorities we are, I think, entitled—indeed, I think that we ought—to treat the views in question, though deserving of the greatest respect, as not essential to the decision in *Kennedy v. De Trafford* [1896] 1 Ch. 762; [1897] A.C. 180, and to consider for

Mortgages of Land

ourselves whether we prefer them to the views expressed in *Wolff v. Vanderzee* (1869) 20 L.T. 353 and *Tomlin v. Luce* (1889) 43 Ch.D. 191.

Approaching the problem in that way, I have no hesitation in saying that I prefer the latter. There is no doubt that a mortgagee who takes possession of the security with a view to selling it has to account to the mortgagor for any loss occurring through his negligence or the negligence of his agent in dealing with the property between the date of his taking possession of it and the date of the sale, including, as in the *McHugh* case [1913] A.C. 299, steps taken to bring the property to the place of sale. It seems quite illogical that the mortgagee's duty should suddenly change when one comes to the sale itself and that at that stage if only he acts in good faith he is under no liability, however negligent he or his agent may be.

Mr Vinelott further submitted that even if we should be of opinion that a mortgagee was liable to account to the mortgagor for loss occasioned by his own negligence in the exercise of his power of sale, it was not right that he should be liable for the negligence of any agent reasonably employed by him. It may well be that this point is not open to him in view of the way the argument proceeded below—but in any case I do not accept the submission. In support of it, counsel pointed out that a trustee is not liable for the default of an agent whom it is reasonable for him to employ. But the position of a mortgagee is quite different from that of a trustee. A trustee has not, *qua* trustee, any interest in the trust property, and if an agent employed by him is negligent his right of action against the agent is an asset of the trust. A mortgagee, on the other hand, is not a trustee and if he sues the agent for negligence any damages which he can recover belong to him. Of course, in many cases the mortgagee may suffer no damage himself by reason of the agent's negligence because the purchase price, though less than it should have been, exceeds what is owing to the mortgagee. In such circumstances it may be that nowadays the law would allow the mortgagor to recover damages directly from the agent although not in contractual relations with him; but that was certainly not so a hundred years ago when *Wolff v. Vanderzee* (1869) 20 L.T. 353 was decided. In those days the only way to achieve justice between the parties was to say that the mortgagee was liable to the mortgagor for any damage which the latter suffered by the agent's negligence and to leave the mortgagee to recover such damages, and also any damage which he had suffered himself, from the agent. I do not think that we can say that the mortgagee used to be liable to the mortgagor for the negligence of his agent but that that liability disappeared at some unspecified moment of time when the law had developed enough to allow the mortgagor to sue the agent himself.

In my judgment, therefore, if either the defendants or Messrs. Geering & Colyer were guilty of negligence in connection with the sale, the defendants are liable to compensate the plaintiffs for any damage which they have suffered by reason of that negligence.

NOTES:

1. The Court of Appeal held (Cross L.J. dissenting) that, in omitting to mention the earlier planning permission and refusing to postpone the sale in order to rectify that omission, the mortgagees had breached their duty to take reasonable care to obtain a proper price.

2. For comment see (1971) 35 Conv. 281; (1971) 87 L.Q.R. 303.

3. *Cuckmere Brick Co. Ltd v. Mutual Finance Ltd* has been followed in *Duke v. Robson* [1973] 1 W.L.R. 267; *Bank of Cyprus (London) Ltd v. Gill* [1980] 2 Lloyd's Rep. 51; *Standard Chartered Bank Ltd v. Walker* [1982] 1 W.L.R. 1410; *Tse Kwong Lam v. Wong Chit Sen* [1983] 1 W.L.R. 1349; *American Express International Banking Corp. v. Hurley* [1985] 3 All E.R. 564; *China and South Sea Bank Ltd v. Tan Soon Gin* [1990] 1 A.C. 536.

4. In *AIB Finance Ltd v. Debtors* [1998] 4 All E.R. 929, noted at [1998] Conv. 391, the question arose as to the duties of the mortgagee in relation to

the power of sale where the security included both combined business and residential premises and the goodwill of the business carried on there. The crucial fact in the present case was that before the mortgagees became entitled to possession, the mortgagors had closed down the business and had vacated the premises. In those circumstances, the Court of Appeal held that the mortgagee could not be held liable for the consequent reduction in the value of the security and the price obtained on sale. In particular, the mortgagee had no duty *before becoming entitled to possession and control* to take steps to preserve and safeguard the goodwill of the business so as to be able to sell the premises and the business as a going concern (although Nourse L.J. commented that it might be possible to conceive of circumstances in which the mortgagee could come under a duty of that kind). For the duties of a mortgagee in possession, see *infra*, p. 912.

5. The duty of the mortgagee to take reasonable care to obtain a proper price may be excluded by appropriate wording in the mortgage deed: *Bishop v. Bonham* [1988] 1 W.L.R. 742, 752 *per* Slade L.J.

6. Where the mortgagee's power of sale is exercised in respect of land mortgaged to a building society, the mortgagee has a duty "to take reasonable care to ensure that the price at which the land is sold is the best price that can reasonably be obtained": Building Societies Act 1986, Sched. 4, para. 1(1)(a); and see *Reliance Permanent Building Society v. Harwood-Stamper* [1944] Ch. 362.

2.2.2 *The juridical basis of the duties*   The "neighbour" approach adopted by the Court of Appeal in *Cuckmere Brick Co. Ltd v. Mutual Finance Ltd* was interpreted by the Court of Appeal in *Standard Chartered Bank Ltd v. Walker* [1982] 1 W.L.R. 1410 as signifying that the liability of the mortgagee is based in the tort of negligence.

Standard Chartered Bank Ltd v. Walker [1982] 1 W.L.R. 1410

(CA, Lord Denning M.R., Watkins and Fox L.JJ.)

A company secured its present and future indebtedness to the plaintiff bank by issuing a debenture giving the bank a charge over the assets of the company; and the defendants, directors of the company, guaranteed repayment by the company. The question arose as to whether a mortgagee and/or a receiver acting on the instructions of the mortgagee owed any duty to the guarantor in addition to that owed to the mortgagor.

LORD DENNING M.R.:
So far as mortgages are concerned the law is set out in *Cuckmere Brick Co. Ltd v. Mutual Finance Ltd* [1971] Ch. 949. If a mortgagee enters into possession and realises a mortgaged property, it is his duty to use reasonable care to obtain the best possible price which the circumstances of the case permit. He owes this duty not only to himself, to clear off as much of the debt as he can, but also to the mortgagor so as to reduce the balance owing as much as possible, and also to the guarantor so that he is made liable for as little as possible on the guarantee. This duty is only a particular

application of the general duty of care to your neighbour which was stated by Lord Atkin in *Donoghue v. Stevenson* [1932] A.C. 562 and applied in many cases since: see *Dorset Yacht Co. Ltd v. Home Office* [1970] A.C. 1004 and *Anns v. Merton London Borough Council* [1978] A.C. 728. The mortgagor and the guarantor are clearly in very close "proximity" to those who conduct the sale. The duty of care is owing to them—if not to the general body of creditors of the mortgagor. There are several dicta to the effect that the mortgagee can choose his own time for the sale, but I do not think this means that he can sell at the worst possible time. It is at least arguable that, in choosing the time, he must exercise a reasonable degree of care.

NOTES:

1. In *American Express International Banking Corp. v. Hurley* [1985] 3 All E.R. 564 Mann J. purported to follow *Cuckmere Brick Co. Ltd v. Mutual Finance Ltd* and its interpretation in *Standard Chartered Bank Ltd v. Walker*; and in discussing the liability of the mortgagee (and the receiver who had become the agent of the mortgagee) to the mortgagor (and the guarantor), he expressly based that liability in negligence.

2. The reinterpretation of the mortgagee's duty in terms of negligence was also reflected in the decision of the Court of Appeal in *Predeth v. Castle Phillips Finance Co. Ltd* [1986] 2 E.G.L.R. 144, where, contrary to the established principle that the mortgagee is free to choose the timing of any sale, the mortgagee was held liable in damages because he had failed to follow normal practice and to expose the property to the market for a reasonable time. For comment, see Thompson [1986] Conv. 442.

3. Davies and Palmer [1981] Conv. 329 favoured the reinterpretation of the mortgagee's obligations in terms of negligence.

4. The reinterpretation was disapproved by the Court of Appeal in *Parker-Tweedale v. Dunbar Bank plc* [1991] Ch. 12.

Parker-Tweedale v. Dunbar Bank plc [1991] Ch. 12

(CA, Purchas and Nourse L.JJ., Sir Michael Kerr)

The mortgagor was the sole legal owner of the mortgaged property but her husband, the plaintiff, owned the whole equitable interest. When the mortgagee sold the property in the exercise of its statutory power, the question arose as to whether a mortgagee owed any duty, in addition to that owed to the mortgagor, to a person with an equitable interest in the mortgaged property. The plaintiff relied on *Standard Chartered Bank Ltd v. Walker* and the interpretation in that case of the "neighbour" approach in *Cuckmere Brick Co. Ltd v. Mutual Finance Ltd.*

NOURSE L.J.:
This reference to "neighbours" has enabled the plaintiff to argue that the duty is owed to all those who are within the neighbourhood principle; i.e. to adapt the words of Lord Atkin, to all persons who are so closely and directly affected by the sale that the mortgagee ought reasonably to have them in contemplation as being so affected when he is directing his mind to the sale. Further support for the application of the neighbourhood principle in this context can be gained from the judgment of Lord

Denning M.R. in *Standard Chartered Bank Ltd v. Walker* [1982] 1 W.L.R. 1410, 1415, where it was held that the duty to take reasonable care to obtain a proper price was owed to a surety for the mortgage debt as well as to the mortgagor himself.

In my respectful opinion it is both unnecessary and confusing for the duties owed by a mortgagee to the mortgagor and the surety, if there is one, to be expressed in terms of the tort of negligence. The authorities which were considered in the careful judgments of this court in *Cuckmere Brick Co. Ltd v. Mutual Finance Ltd* [1971] Ch. 949 demonstrate that the duty owed by the mortgagee to the mortgagor was recognised by equity as arising out of the particular relationship between them. Thus Salmon L.J. himself said, at p. 967:

> "It would seem, therefore, that many years before the modern development of the law of negligence, the courts of equity had laid down a doctrine in relation to mortgages which is entirely consonant with the general principles later evolved by the common law."

The duty owed to the surety arises in the same way. In *China and South Sea Bank Ltd v. Tan Soon Gin* [1990] 1 A.C. 536, Lord Templeman, in delivering the judgment of the Privy Council, having pointed out that the surety in that case admitted that the moneys secured by the guarantee were due, continued at p. 543:

> "But the surety claims that the creditor owed the surety a duty to exercise the power of sale conferred by the mortgage and in that case the liability of the surety under the guarantee would either have been eliminated or very much reduced. The Court of Appeal [in Hong Kong] sought to find such a duty in the tort of negligence but the tort of negligence has not yet subsumed all torts and does not supplant the principles of equity or contradict contractual promises ... Equity intervenes to protect a surety."

Once it is recognised that the duty owed by the mortgagee to the mortgagor arises out of the particular relationship between them, it is readily apparent that there is no warrant for extending its scope so as to include a beneficiary or beneficiaries under a trust of which the mortgagor is the trustee. The correctness of that view was fully established in the clear and compelling argument of Mr Lloyd [counsel for the defendants], who drew particular attention to the rights and duties of the trustee to protect the trust property against dissipation or depreciation in value and the impracticabilities and potential rights of double recovery inherent in giving the beneficiary an additional right to sue the mortgagee, a right which is in any event unnecessary.

The only exception for which Mr Lloyd allowed was the special case where the trustee has unreasonably refused to sue on behalf of the trust or has committed some other breach of his duties to the beneficiaries, *e.g.* by consenting to an improvident sale, which disables or disqualifies him from acting on behalf of the trust. In such a case the beneficiary is permitted to sue on behalf of the trust. This exception is established by a series of authorities, some of which were recently considered by the Privy Council in *Hayim v. Citibank N.A.* [1987] A.C. 730. In delivering the judgment of their Lordships, Lord Templeman said, at p. 748:

> "These authorities demonstrate that a beneficiary has no cause of action against a third party save in special circumstances which embrace a failure, excusable or inexcusable, by the trustees in the performance of the duty owed by the trustees to the beneficiary to protect the trust estate or to protect the interests of the beneficiary in the trust estate."

It is important to emphasise that when a beneficiary sues under the exception he does so in right of the trust and in the room of the trustee. He does not enforce a right reciprocal to some duty owed directly to him by the third party.

NOTES:

1. For comment on the implications of *Parker-Tweedale v. Dunbar Bank plc* and the restoration of the orthodoxy that the equitable duty of the mortgagee arises because of the relationship of the parties, see Bently [1990] Conv. 431. In particular, it seems that the decisions in *Standard Chartered Bank Ltd v. Walker* and *Predeth v. Castle Phillips Finance Co. Ltd* will survive the removal of their negligence basis, certainly to the extent of duties owed by the mortgagee or receiver *to the mortgagor*: see *Re B. Johnson & Co.* [1955] Ch. 634; *Downsview Nominees Ltd v. First City Corp. Ltd* [1993] A.C. 295, 312–315 *per* Lord Templeman; *Medforth v. Blake* [1999] 3 All E.R. 97; and probably also to the extent of duties owed to a guarantor: see *Parker-Tweedale v. Dunbar Bank plc* [1991] Ch. 12, 18 *per* Nourse L.J.

2. The equitable duty is owed also to subsequent mortgagees: *Cuckmere Brick Co. Ltd v. Mutual Finance Ltd* [1971] Ch. 949, 966 *per* Salmon L.J.; *Downsview Nominees Ltd v. First City Corp. Ltd* [1993] A.C. 295, 311–312 *per* Lord Templeman.

3. In assessing the basis, and inevitably therefore the content, of the duty of the mortgagee, it should perhaps be remembered that the power of sale becomes exercisable *only where the mortgagor is in default*: thus, while it is not suggested that there should be no safeguards for the mortgagor, the mortgagor cannot be regarded as entitled to unqualified protection. It is arguable that the appropriate balance between the interests of the mortgagor and the mortgagee is struck by the substance of *Cuckmere Brick Co. Ltd v. Mutual Finance Ltd* against the background of the analysis in *Parker-Tweedale v. Dunbar Bank plc*.

2.2.3 *The timing of the sale*   The different bases of liability may also explain the different views expressed as to the selection of the time of the sale; and Davies and Palmer [1981] Conv. 329 noted that the reinterpretation of the mortgagee's duties in terms of negligence, with its concomitant notion of reasonableness, might have involved a more critical consideration of both "early" and "late" sales. However, the Privy Council has reasserted the proposition that the mortgagee is entitled to determine the timing of a sale: *China and South Sea Bank Ltd v. Tan Soon Gin* [1990] 1 A.C. 536, 545 *per* Lord Templeman; *Downsview Nominees Ltd v. First City Corp. Ltd* [1993] A.C. 295, 312–315 *per* Lord Templeman.

On the other hand, such statements have generally been made against a background of rising property values. Moreover, in such circumstances, disputes as to the timing of a sale have tended not unnaturally to involve the mortgagor challenging an early sale by the mortgagee. The collapse of the property market in the early 1990s produced a rather different background. The phenomenon of "negative equity", where the value of the mortgaged property is less than the amount of the outstanding mortgage debt, prompted a series of applications by mortgagors in which, in order to prevent further arrears, they sought an order of the court directing a sale, notwithstanding that the proceeds of sale would be insufficient to discharge the whole of the mortgage debt: see *infra*, p. 944.

2.2.4 *Sale to associated persons*   In *Farrar v. Farrars Ltd* (1888) 40 Ch D. 395 Lindley L.J. stated (at 409) that "a mortgagee cannot sell to himself, either alone or with others, nor to a trustee for himself, nor to anyone employed by him to conduct the sale. A sale by a person to himself is no sale at all". It is irrelevant that the mortgagee pays the full market value of the mortgaged property: *ibid.* However, the restriction does not apply where the court orders a sale pursuant to an application under section 91(2) of the Law of Property Act 1925: see *Palk v. Mortgage Services Funding plc* [1993] Ch. 330, 340 *per* Nicholls V.-C.

On the other hand, there is no absolute bar on a mortgagee selling to an associated person or company; but any such sale is subject to strict requirements.

Tse Kwong Lam v. Wong Chit Sen [1983] 1 W.L.R. 1349

(PC, Lord Fraser, Lord Brandon, Lord Brightman, Lord Templeman, Sir John Megaw)

The mortgagee arranged for the mortgaged property to be sold at public auction; and he advertised the auction in three newspapers, providing only a minimum description of the property. The particulars and conditions of sale contained only the bare legal requirements. At the auction there was only one bid, at the reserve price determined by the mortgagee without consultation and announced immediately before the auction began. The purchaser was the wife of the mortgagee, bidding on behalf of a company which was financed entirely by the mortgagee and whose directors and shareholders were the mortgagee and members of his family. The mortgagor claimed, *inter alia*, to have the sale set aside on the ground that it was improper and at an undervalue.

LORD TEMPLEMAN:
In *Warner v. Jacob* (1882) 20 Ch.D. 220, Kay J. after considering the authorities concluded, at p. 224:

> "a mortgagee is strictly speaking not a trustee of the power of sale. It is a power given to him for his own benefit, to enable him the better to realise his debt. If he exercises it bona fide for that purpose, without corruption or collusion with the purchaser, the court will not interfere even though the sale be very disadvantageous, unless indeed the price is so low as in itself to be evidence of fraud."

In *Martinson v. Clowes* (1882) 21 Ch.D. 857, North J. said, at p. 860:

> "It is quite clear that a mortgagee exercising his power of sale cannot purchase the property on his own account, and I think it clear also that the solicitor or agent of such mortgagee acting for him in the matter of the sale cannot do so either."

Mr Rattee, on behalf of the borrower, submitted that a mortgagee, his solicitor or agent cannot be allowed to purchase because they cannot resolve the conflict between their interest to buy for the lowest price with their duties to sell for the highest price. Therefore, he says, whenever there is such a conflict, the sale will not be upheld. In the present case there was clearly a conflict between the interest of the mortgagee in securing that the company secured the mortgaged property at the lowest price and the duty of the mortgagee to sell for the highest price. Mr Rattee admits that there can be no general rule that a company in which a mortgagee is interested cannot purchase the mortgaged property. He submits that the company can only do so where the sale is negotiated at arm's length and where it is clear that the mortgagee had no influence on the decision of the company to purchase or on the implementation of that decision.

In *Farrar v. Farrars Ltd* (1888) 40 Ch.D. 395 a solicitor who was one of three mortgagees and acted for the mortgagees negotiated a sale in principle and agreed a price at the time when he had no connection with the purchasers. He subsequently took shares in a company formed by the purchasers to carry the sale into effect. Lindley L.J. said, at p. 409–410:

"The plaintiffs on appeal did not question the view of the judge that there was no fraudulent sale at an undervalue, but they contended that fraud or no fraud, undervalue or no undervalue, the sale could not stand, inasmuch as it was in substance a sale by a mortgagee to himself and others under the guise of a sale to a limited company."

That submission was rejected. Lindley L.J. also said, at pp. 409–410:

"A sale by a person to a corporation of which he is a member is not, either in form or in substance, a sale by a person to himself... There is no authority for saying that such a sale is not warranted by an ordinary power of sale... But although this is true, it is obvious that a sale by a person to an incorporated company of which he is a member may be invalid upon various grounds, although it may not be reached by the rule which prevents a man from selling to himself or to a trustee for himself. Such a sale may, for example, be fraudulent and at an undervalue or it may be made under circumstances which throw upon the purchasing company the burden of proving the validity of the transaction, and the company may be unable to prove it."

And Lindley L.J. said, at p. 410:

"A mortgagee with a power of sale, though often called a trustee, is in a very different position from a trustee for sale. A mortgagee is under obligations to the mortgagor, but he has rights of his own which he is entitled to exercise adversely to the mortgagor. A trustee for sale has no business to place himself in such a position as to give rise to a conflict of interest and duty. But every mortgage confers upon the mortgagee the right to realise his security and to find a purchaser if he can, and if in exercise of his power he acts bona fide and takes reasonable precautions to obtain a proper price, the mortgagor has no redress, even although more might have been obtained for the property if the sale had been postponed: ..."

The Court of Appeal concluded, at p. 415:

"The sale here impeached having been made honestly and at a fair value, ought, in our opinion, to be allowed to stand, and there is no hard and fast rule which compels us to hold the contrary."

In the view of this Board on authority and on principle there is no hard and fast rule that a mortgagee may not sell to a company in which he is interested. The mortgagee and the company seeking to uphold the transaction must show that the sale was in good faith and that the mortgagee took reasonable precautions to obtain the best price reasonably obtainable at the time. The mortgagee is not however bound to postpone the sale in the hope of obtaining a better price or to adopt a piecemeal method of sale which could only be carried out over a substantial period or at some risk of loss...

In the present case in which the mortgagee held a large beneficial interest in the shares of the purchasing company, was a director of the company, and was entirely responsible for financing the company, the other shareholders being his wife and children, the sale must be closely examined and a heavy onus lies on the mortgagee to show that in all respects he acted fairly to the borrower and used his best endeavours to obtain the best price reasonably obtainable for the mortgaged property.

Sale by auction does not necessarily prove the validity of a transaction. In *Hodson v. Deans* [1903] 2 Ch. 647, at a sale by auction by a friendly society in exercise of their power of sale as mortgagees, the secretary of the committee which fixed the reserve and instructed the auctioneer bought the property for himself having "conceived the idea of buying ... and making a profit for himself out of the transaction" *per* Joyce J., at p. 651. Joyce J. found, at p. 653:

> "the property was sold at an undervalue, not of itself so great as to invalidate the sale, but still at an undervalue. The investment committee could not have sold privately to themselves either as representing the society or as individuals at a price fixed by themselves, nor could they, I think, have so sold to one or more of their number. It is said that any such objection is cured by the fact that the sale was by auction. I do not think so. At all events ... the onus is on the defendant to show that everything was done fairly and bona fide."

In *Kennedy v. De Trafford* [1897] A.C. 180 a mortgagee sold the mortgaged property to one of two mortgagors who were entitled to the equity of redemption as tenants in common for a sum equal to the mortgage debt. Lord Herschell, at p. 185, was

> "disposed to think that if a mortgagee in exercising his power of sale exercises it in good faith, without any intention of dealing unfairly by his mortgagor, it would be very difficult indeed, if not impossible, to establish that he had been guilty of any breach of duty towards the mortgagor."

But in that case he advised the House:

> "if you were to accept the definition ... for which the appellant contends, namely, that the mortgagee is bound to take reasonable precautions in the exercise of his power of sale, as well as to act in good faith, still in this case he did take reasonable precautions. Of course, all the circumstances of the case must be looked at."

The circumstances there were that the mortgagee had told each of the mortgagors that he wished to sell and was willing to take a sum sufficient to discharge the mortgage. No offer or objection was made by the mortgagor who subsequently sought to impugn the sale. In *McHugh v. Union Bank of Canada* [1913] A.C. 299, Lord Moulton in tendering the advice of the Privy Council said, at p. 311:

> "It is well settled law that it is the duty of a mortgagee when realising the mortgaged property by sale to behave in conducting such realisation as a reasonable man would behave in the realisation of his own property, so that the mortgagor may receive credit for the fair value of the property sold."

Finally in *Cuckmere Brick Co. Ltd v. Mutual Finance Ltd* [1971] Ch. 949, Salmon L.J. after considering all the relevant authorities including the views expressed in *Kennedy v. De Trafford* concluded, with the subsequent agreement of Cross and Cairns L.JJ., at p. 968:

> "both on principle and authority, that the mortgagee in exercising his power of sale does owe a duty to take reasonable precautions to obtain the true market value of the mortgaged property at the date on which he decides to sell it."

In the result their Lordships consider that in the present case the company was not debarred from purchasing the mortgaged property but, in view of the close relationship between the company and the mortgagee and in view in particular of the conflict of duty and interest to which the mortgagee was subject, the sale to the company can only be supported if the mortgagee proves that he took reasonable precautions to obtain the best price reasonably obtainable at the time of sale.

The Privy Council held that the mortgagee had not satisfied those requirements: he had failed to show that he had protected the interest of the mortgagor by taking expert advice as to the method of sale, as to the steps taken to make the sale a success and as to the amount of the reserve; but the Privy Council further held that, since the mortgagor had been guilty of inexcusable delay in pursuing his claim, he was not entitled to have the sale set aside (which would have been the normal remedy) but should be left to the alternative remedy in damages.

NOTE:

1. For comment, see Jackson [1984] Conv. 143. The Privy Council does not appear to have considered the relevance of section 104(2) of the Law of Property Act 1925.

2.3 *Duties in relation to the proceeds of sale*
Although the mortgagee is not trustee of the power of sale, he is trustee of the proceeds of sale.

Law of Property Act 1925, s.105

Application of proceeds of sale

105. The money which is received by the mortgagee, arising from the sale, after discharge of prior incumbrances to which the sale is not made subject, if any, or after payment into court under this Act of a sum to meet any prior incumbrance, shall be held by him in trust to be applied by him, first, in payment of all costs, charges, and expenses properly incurred by him as incident to the sale or any attempted sale, or otherwise; and secondly, in discharge of the mortgage money, interest, and costs, and other money, if any, due under the mortgage; and the residue of the money so received shall be paid to the person entitled to the mortgaged property, or authorised to give receipts for the proceeds of the sale thereof.

NOTES:

1. Suppose that a person grants three mortgages over his land to secure loans of £50,000, £30,000 and £10,000; and that, in the exercise of his power of sale, the second mortgagee sells the mortgaged land for £150,000. Under section 105, he is required to deal with the proceeds as follows: (i) to repay the loan of £50,000 to the first mortgagee; (ii) to reimburse his expenses in relation to the sale; (iii) to repay his own loan of £30,000; (iv) to pay the residue to the third mortgagee, who, having repaid his loan, must pay the final balance to the mortgagor.

2. Where a first mortgagee fails to pay the surplus to a second mortgagee, of whom he has notice, the first mortgagee will be liable to pay to the second mortgagee the sum secured by the second mortgage to the extent of the surplus: *West London Commercial Bank v. Reliance Permanent Building Society* (1885) 29 Ch D. 954.

3. In *Halifax Building Society v. Thomas* [1996] Ch. 217 a mortgage loan was obtained by fraud and the mortgagor defaulted on the repayments. When

the property was sold and the mortgagee repaid its loan from the proceeds, there was a surplus, which the mortgagee paid into a suspense account. Despite various arguments designed to prevent the unjust enrichment of the mortgagor, the Court of Appeal held that the surplus was held on trust for the mortgagor. However, it must be questioned whether the court would have reached the same conclusion if the mortgagor had not been convicted of conspiracy to obtain mortgage funds by deception and if the Crown Prosecution Service had not obtained confiscation and charging orders in respect of the mortgagor's interest in the surplus. For comment, see [1996] Conv. 387.

3. Appointment of receiver

Originally a receiver was appointed by the mortgagor at the request of the mortgagee in order to avoid the disadvantages of taking possession: see *infra*. Mortgagees later began to reserve to themselves the power to appoint a receiver; and this power is now conferred by statute: Law of Property Act 1925, s.101(1)(iii). The power arises and becomes exercisable in the same circumstances as the power of sale: *ibid.* ss.101(1)(iii), 109(1).

The receiver is empowered to receive the income from the property. He is required to apply it in the discharge of outgoings, interest on prior mortgages and his own commission before paying interest due to the appointing mortgagee; and any residue must be paid to the mortgagor unless the mortgagee directs it to be applied in the discharge of the principal money: *ibid.* s.109(8). Although appointed by the mortgagee, in order to enforce the security for the benefit of the mortgagee, the receiver is deemed to be the agent of the mortgagor; and the mortgagor is solely responsible for the acts and defaults of the receiver: *ibid.* s.109(2). However, the mortgagee may be liable (i) where the mortgage deed so provides: *ibid.*; and see *White v. Metcalf* [1903] 2 Ch. 567; or (ii) where the mortgagee directs or interferes with the activities of the receiver: *Standard Chartered Bank Ltd v. Walker* [1982] 1 W.L.R. 1410; *American Express International Banking Corp. v. Hurley* [1985] 3 All E.R. 564; or (iii) where the agency is terminated by the bankruptcy or liquidation of the mortgagor and the mortgagee treats the receiver as his own agent: *American Express International Banking Corp. v. Hurley, supra.*

For a statement of the duties of a receiver appointed by a mortgagee, see *Downsview Nominees Ltd v. First City Corp. Ltd* [1993] A.C. 295, 312–316 *per* Lord Templeman; *Medforth v. Blake* [1999] 3 All E.R. 97.

4. Possession

4.1 *The right of the mortgagee to possession of the mortgaged property*
In *Four-Maids Ltd v. Dudley Marshall (Properties) Ltd* [1957] Ch. 317 Harman J. stated (at 320):

[T]he right of the mortgagee to possession in the absence of some contract has nothing to do with default on the part of the mortgagor. The mortgagee may go into possession before the ink is dry on the mortgage unless there is something in the contract, express or by implication, whereby he has contracted himself out of that right. He has the right because he has a legal term of years in the property or its statutory equivalent.

In theory therefore the mortgagee has the right to take possession of the mortgaged property at any time and for any purpose: see *Western Bank Ltd v. Schindler* [1977] Ch. 1, 9–10 *per* Buckley L.J.

However, in practice, the right *qua* right has not commonly been exercised. Most mortgagees are institutional lenders; they do not want possession for their own purposes; and, even if they wish to secure the payment of interest, the appointment of a receiver provides a more effective and risk-free remedy: see *Refuge Assurance Co. Ltd v. Pearlberg* [1938] Ch. 687, 691–693 *per* Greene M.R. For those mortgagees who are tempted to exercise their right to possession, whether for its own sake or to secure the payment of interest, the intervention of equity and the imposition of a strict duty to account constitute a strong disincentive. Thus in *White v. City of London Brewery Co.* (1889) 42 Ch D. 237 the plaintiff mortgaged his 50-year lease of a public house to the defendant brewery to secure the repayment of a loan. The business failed; and the mortgagees exercised their right to take possession of the mortgaged property. They leased the property to a tenant, who covenanted to take his beer supplies from the mortgagees. When the public house was subsequently sold, the mortgagor sought an account of the rents and profits of the mortgaged property. The Court of Appeal held that the mortgagees had to account not for the rent which they actually received from the tenant but for the higher rent that they would have received if the public house had been leased free of the covenant. Moreover, the mortgagee in possession is also under a duty to take reasonable care in relation to the physical state of the property: *Palk v. Mortgages Services Funding plc* [1993] Ch. 330, 338 *per* Nicholls V.-C.

The result is that, although the theoretical right of the mortgagee to take possession of the mortgaged property remains, as indicated above, the taking of possession has for many years been treated by mortgagees almost exclusively as a preliminary remedy to the exercise of the power of sale so that the mortgagee may sell the property with vacant possession: *Four-Maids Ltd v. Dudley Marshall (Properties) Ltd* [1957] Ch. 317, 320 *per* Harman J.

This attitude was sometimes formally recognised by the inclusion in the mortgage deed of an attornment clause whereby the mortgagor was made tenant of the mortgagee, and thus entitled to possession; the incidence of such clauses is now rare but not unknown: see *Peckham Mutual Building Society v. Registe* (1980) 42 P. & C.R. 186; and see Miller (1966) 30 Conv. 30. Alternatively, the mortgage deed may include a simple undertaking by the mortgagee not to enforce the right to possession in the absence of default on the part of the mortgagor.

The courts and the legislature have manifested a corresponding tendency to view the taking of possession as more in the nature of a remedy and to restrict the exercise of that right/remedy accordingly.

4.2 *Common law restrictions on the mortgagee's right to possession*

The courts have assumed a limited inherent jurisdiction at common law to adjourn proceedings for possession to allow the mortgagor the opportunity to remedy his default. However, the courts have not always taken the same view as to the scope of this jurisdiction.

Mobil Oil Co. Ltd v. Rawlinson (1981) 43 P. & C.R. 221

(Ch D., Nourse J.)

NOURSE J.:

Contract and statute apart a legal mortgagee has, as an incident of his estate in the land, an unqualified right to possession of the mortgaged property. He may, as Harman J. put it in *Four-Maids Ltd v. Dudley Marshall (Properties) Ltd* (1957) Ch. 317, go into possession before the ink is dry on the mortgage and without default on the part of the mortgagor. If he does so, he is liable to account on the footing of wilful default and that will often deter him from taking possession himself. But during the present century it has become usual for mortgagees to seek an order for possession as a preliminary to realising the security by means of a sale with vacant possession out of court under the statutory power. In a normal case the court is not asked to grant any other relief.

Before 1936 a mortgagee who was only asking for possession had to commence his proceedings in the Queen's Bench Division. That was because possession alone could not be sought by summons in the Chancery Division. But in 1936, R.S.C., Ord. 55, r. 5A was amended so as to make that possible. The Chancery judges of the time issued a practice direction which said, amongst other things, that when possession was sought and the defendant was in arrear with any instalments due under the mortgage or charge and the master was of the opinion that the defendant ought to be given an opportunity to pay off the arrears, the master might adjourn the summons on such terms as he thought fit. That direction caused confusion. It led to a general view among the Chancery masters, no doubt assisted by the benevolent attitude which the legislature had by then assumed towards tenants faced with eviction by their landlords, that they had a discretion to adjourn a legal mortgagee's application for possession, at any rate in instalment cases, against the wishes of the mortgagee in order to enable the mortgagor to catch up on instalment arrears; and, inferentially, a right, if he did so, to continue to deny the mortgagee possession notwithstanding that on the default the whole of the mortgage money had become and thereafter remained repayable. By the end of the 1950s it had become necessary for the Chancery judges of a later generation to re-assert the legal mortgagee's right to possession. In the van of that movement was Harman J., although even he subscribed to the view that the practice direction had qualified the right in the case of an instalment mortgage: see *Four-Maids Ltd v. Dudley Marshall (Properties) Ltd.*

In 1961 the whole question was fully argued and considered in *Birmingham Citizens Permanent Building Society v. Caunt* [1962] Ch. 883, and it is on Russell J.'s judgment in that case that the foregoing summary of the earlier history is based. I well remember that decision and the general view of the profession that it had settled once and for all the limited extent of the court's power to adjourn a legal mortgagee's application for possession. The rule in regard to instalment mortgages, and a fortiori in regard to ordinary mortgages, was stated by Russell J. at the end of his judgment, in the following terms (at p. 912):

"Accordingly, in my judgment, where (as here) the legal mortgagee under an instalment mortgage under which by reason of default the whole money has become payable, is entitled to possession, the court has no jurisdiction to decline the order or to adjourn the hearing whether on terms of keeping up payments or paying arrears, if the mortgagee cannot be persuaded to agree to this course. To this the *sole exception* is that the application may be adjourned for a short time to afford to the mortgagor a chance of paying off the mortgagee in full or otherwise satisfying him; but this should not be done if there is no reasonable prospect of this occurring. When I say the sole exception, I do not, of course, intend to exclude adjournments which in the ordinary course of procedure may be desirable in circumstances such as temporary inability of a party to attend, and so forth."

The reason for the exception is that the court has never allowed a mortgagee to enforce his rights under the mortgage in the face of a concrete offer by the mortgagor to redeem.

Since then the court has twice been given additional powers of adjournment in cases where the mortgaged property consists of or includes a dwelling-house: see section 36 of the Administration of Justice Act 1970 and section 8 of the Administration of Justice Act 1973. But the general rule continues to apply to other types of property, for example commercial premises of the kind with which the present case is concerned. Moreover, in *Western Bank Ltd v. Schindler* [1977] Ch. 1 the Court of Appeal re-affirmed the prima facie unqualified right of a legal mortgagee to possession in unequivocal terms. And the judgment of Buckley L.J. demonstrates that there may well be occasions in the conditions of modern society when a mortgagee will be wise to go into possession in spite of his liability to account on the footing of wilful default.

NOTES:

1. Following the amendment to the Rules of the Supreme Court in 1936, the judges of the Chancery Division issued a Practice Direction, which provided:

When possession is sought and the defendant is in arrear with any instalments due under the mortgage or charge and the master is of the opinion that the defendant ought to be given an opportunity to pay off the arrears, the master may adjourn the summons on such terms as he thinks fit.

In *Redditch Benefit Building Society v. Roberts* [1940] Ch. 415, 420, Clauson L.J. stated that the amendment both to the rules of procedure and to the previous practice in the King's Bench Division were intended for the protection of the mortgagor; and a challenge to their legality was unsuccessful: *Hinkley and South Leicestershire Permanent Building Society v. Freeman* [1941] Ch. 32, 38–39 *per* Farwell J., approved by the Court of Appeal in *Re Yates Settlement Trust* [1954] 1 W.L.R. 564. However, in *Robertson v. Cilia* [1956] 1 W.L.R. 1502, 1508, Upjohn J. expressed the view that the power of the court to adjourn possession proceedings was restricted to those cases where the mortgagor was to be given an opportunity of trying to find the means of discharging the loan altogether; for comment, see (1957) 21 Conv. 68; (1957) 73 L.Q.R. 17. In *Four-Maids Ltd v. Dudley Marshall (Properties) Ltd* [1957] Ch. 317, 321, Harman J. confirmed the pre-1936 orthodoxy, limiting the application of the Practice Direction to those mortgages "whereby the principal as well as the interest is repaid by the mortgagor by commuted weekly or quarterly sums and whereby the mortgagee precludes himself, so long as those ... sums are paid, from going into possession"; for comment, see (1957) 21 Conv. 230; (1957) 73 L.Q.R. 300; but such a limited application of the Practice Direction was doubted in *Braithwaite v. Winwood* [1960] 1 W.L.R. 1257, 1264 *per* Cross J.; for comment, see [1961] C.L.J. 39; (1961) 25 Conv. 77. In *Birmingham Citizens Permanent Building Society v. Caunt*

[1962] Ch. 883, 895 Russell J. restored the pre-1936 approach and effectively rendered the Practice Direction a nullity; for comment, see (1962) 26 Conv. 150; (1962) 78 L.Q.R. 171. See generally Rudden (1961) 25 Conv. 278; and for an inside account of the approach adopted by the Chancery Masters, see Ball (1961) 77 L.Q.R. 331, 351–352.

2. n *Cheltenham and Gloucester Building Society v. Booker* (1996) 73 P. & C.R. 412 the Court of Appeal examined the circumstances in which the courts may exercise their inherent jurisdiction to permit a mortgagor to remain in possession of the mortgaged property pending a sale by the mortgagee. The court established the following pre-conditions: (i) that possession will not be required by the mortgagee pending completion of the sale but only by the purchasers on completion; (ii) that the presence of the mortgagor pending completion will enhance, or at least not depress, the sale price; (iii) that the mortgagor will co-operate in the sale of the property; and (iv) that the mortgagor will give vacant possession on completion. However, the court held that these pre-conditions are seldom likely to be satisfied; and, if they are satisfied, the court is likely to entrust the conduct of the sale to the mortgagor. For comment, see [1998] Conv. 223.

3. The mortgagee will be precluded from taking possession where the mortgaged property has been leased prior to the mortgage and the lease is binding on the mortgagee or where the property is subsequently leased with the consent of the mortgagee. However, where a lease is not binding on the mortgagee, the mortgagee is entitled to exercise his right to possession against the lessee: see *supra*, p. 824.

4. On contractual exclusion of the right to possession, see *Western Bank Ltd v. Schindler* [1977] Ch. 1, where Buckley L.J. stated (at 9–10):

A legal mortgagee's right to possession is a common law right which is an incident of his estate in the land. It should not, in my opinion, be lightly treated as abrogated or restricted. Although it is perhaps most commonly exercised as a preliminary step to an exercise of the mortgagee's power of sale, so that the sale may be made with vacant possession, this is not its only value to the mortgagee. The mortgagee may wish to protect his security: see *Ex parte Wickens* [1898] 1 Q.B. 543, 547, 549. If, for instance, the mortgagor were to vacate the property, the mortgagee might wish to take possession to protect the place from vandalism. He might wish to take possession for the purpose of carrying out repairs or to prevent waste. Where the contractual date for repayment is so unusually long delayed as it was in this case, a power of this nature to protect his security might well be regarded as of particular value to the mortgagee.

Mr Lightman has argued that a term excluding the right of a mortgagee to enter into possession should normally be implied if and for so long as the terms of the mortgage preclude the mortgagee from making immediate demand for payment or otherwise immediately enforcing his security. He drew our attention to *Esso Petroleum Co. Ltd v. Alstonbridge Properties Ltd* [1975] 1 W.L.R. 1474, and in particular to what Walton J. said at pp. 1483 and 1484. The judge there said that he accepted that the court would be ready to find such an implied term in an instalment mortgage, but that there must be something in the mortgage upon which to hang such a conclusion other than the mere fact that it is an instalment mortgage. In other words, he accepted that the fact that the mortgage was an instalment mortgage might make the inference easier to draw but would not in itself be a sufficient ground. With this I am disposed to agree. In my judgment, the proposition in the wide form in which Mr Lightman propounds it cannot be accepted. The conventional form of mortgage invariably fixes a contractual redemption date at some time in the future—very often six months after the date of the mortgage. An instalment mortgage ex hypothesi postpones payment of the instalments to dates after the date of the mortgage. If Mr Lightman were right in his submission, in none of these cases could the mortgagee be entitled to demand possession immediately after the execution of the mortgage, and yet by common consent that is his right at law, graphically described by Harman J. in *Four-Maids Ltd v. Dudley Marshall (Properties) Ltd* [1957] Ch. 317 as a right to go into possession before the ink is dry on the mortgage.

Taking possession may be tantamount to demanding payment in the context of the question whether the mortgagee can thereafter insist on notice to redeem, which was the question in *Bovill v. Endle* [1896] 1 Ch. 648. It would be an obvious inequity if the mortgagor could be turned out without an immediate right to resist this or to recover possession by redemption. By way of contrast, for reasons already indicated, a right to possession does not seem to me to be inconsistent with a postponed redemption date, particularly when that date is long postponed; and I see no equitable grounds for thinking that such a right would bear unfairly on the mortgagor if, as in this case, possession cannot be used as a mere stepping stone to a sale with vacant possession unless and until some event has occurred which makes the power of sale available to the mortgagee. Until such event occurs, the right to possession can only be exercised to protect the security, not as a means of enforcing it.

5. It has been held an express provision in a mortgage that the mortgagee is entitled to possession upon default by the mortgagor involves by necessary implication an exclusion of the right to possession on the part of the mortgagee until default: *Birmingham Citizens Permanent Building Society v. Caunt* [1962] Ch. 883, 890 *per* Russell J.

6. In the absence of some contractual or statutory provision to the contrary, the mortgagee's right to possession cannot be defeated by a cross-claim by a mortgagor, whether he is the principal debtor or merely the guarantor of the principal debt, even if the cross-claim is liquidated and admitted and in excess of the mortgage arrears, or by a cross-claim for unliquidated damages giving rise to a right of equitable set-off: *Mobil Oil Co. Ltd v. Rawlinson* (1981) 43 P. & C.R. 221, noted at [1982] Conv. 453; *National Westminster Bank plc v. Skelton* [1993] 1 W.L.R. 72; *Ashley Guarantee plc v. Zacaria* [1993] 1 W.L.R. 62, noted at [1993] Conv. 459; *Albany Home Loans Ltd v. Massey* [1997] 2 All E.R. 609, noted at [1998] Conv. 391.

4.3 *Equitable restrictions on the mortgagee's right to possession*
In *Quennell v. Maltby* [1979] 1 W.L.R. 318 the Court of Appeal asserted that equity had a wide discretion (hitherto unrecognised) to restrain the mortgagee from exercising the right to possession for purposes other than the protection or enforcement of his security.

Quennell v. Maltby [1979] 1 W.L.R. 318

(CA, Lord Denning M.R., Bridge and Templeman L.JJ.)

The plaintiff's husband owned a house which he mortgaged to secure the repayment of a bank loan. Although the mortgage included a prohibition against letting without the consent of the mortgagee, the mortgagor let the house, without obtaining such consent, to the defendants, who remained in the house as statutory tenants under the Rent Acts. The mortgagor wished to obtain vacant possession of the house and tried unsuccessfully to persuade the mortgagee to bring proceedings. The plaintiff therefore paid off the mortgagee; the mortgage was transferred to her; and, as successor to the mortgagee, she sought possession of the house. The judge made an order for possession and the defendants appealed.

LORD DENNING M.R.:

Now it has been held that, when the bank holds a charge and there is a clause in it whereby there are to be no tenancies granted or surrendered except with the consent of the bank in writing, then in those circumstances, if the mortgagor does thereafter grant tenancies without the consent of the bank, then those tenancies are not binding on the bank, and the tenants are not entitled to the protection of the Rent Acts. That was decided in *Dudley and District Benefit Building Society v. Emerson* [1949] Ch. 707. Mrs Quennell relies on that case. She says that, as transferee of the legal charge, she stands in the shoes of the bank and can obtain possession.

The judge accepted the submission. His decision, if right, opens the way to widespread evasion of the Rent Acts. If the owner of a house wishes to obtain vacant possession, all he has to do is charge it to the bank for a small sum. Then grant a new tenancy without telling the bank. Then get his wife to pay off the bank and take a transfer. Then get the wife to sue for possession.

That indeed was what happened here....

So the objective is plain. It was not to enforce the security or to obtain repayment or anything of that kind. It was in order to get possession of the house and to overcome the protection of the Rent Acts.

Is that permissible? It seems to me that this is one of those cases where equity steps in to mitigate the rigour of the law. Long years ago it did the same when it invented the equity of redemption. As is said in *Snell's Principles of Equity*, 27th ed. (1973), p. 376:

> "The courts of equity left the legal effect of the transaction unaltered but declared it to be unreasonable and against conscience that the mortgagee should retain as owner for his own benefit what was intended as a mere security."

So here in modern times equity can step in so as to prevent a mortgagee, or a transferee from him, from getting possession of a house contrary to the justice of the case. A mortgagee will be restrained from getting possession except when it is sought bona fide and reasonably for the purpose of enforcing the security and then only subject to such conditions as the court thinks fit to impose. When the bank itself or a building society lends the money, then it may well be right to allow the mortgagee to obtain possession when the borrower is in default. But so long as the interest is paid and there is nothing outstanding, equity has ample power to restrain any unjust use of the right to possession.

It is plain that in this transaction Mr and Mrs Quennell had an ulterior motive. It was not done to enforce the security or due payment of the principal or interest. It was done for the purpose of getting possession of the house in order to resell it at a profit. It was done so as to avoid the protection which the Rent Acts afford to tenants in their occupation. If Mr Quennell himself had sought to evict the tenants, he would not be allowed to do so. He could not say the tenancies were void. He would be estopped from saying so. They certainly would be protected against him. Are they protected against his wife now that she is the transferee of the charge? In my opinion they are protected. For this simple reason, she is not seeking possession for the purpose of enforcing the loan or the interest or anything of that kind. She is doing it simply for an ulterior purpose of getting possession of the house, contrary to the intention of Parliament as expressed in the Rent Acts.

On that simple ground it seems to me that this action fails and it should be dismissed. The legal right to possession is not to be enforced when it is sought for an ulterior motive. I would on this account allow the appeal and dismiss the action for possession.

BRIDGE L.J.:

I entirely agree. The situation arising in this case is one, it seems to me, in which the court is not only entitled but bound to look behind the formal legal relationship between the parties to see what is the true substance of the matter. Once one does that, on the facts of this case it is as plain as a pikestaff that the purpose of the bringing of these proceedings via Mrs Quennell is not for her own benefit to protect or enforce the security which she holds as the transferee of the legal charge but for the benefit of her husband as mortgagor to enable him to sell the property with the benefit of vacant possession. In substance she is suing as his agent. That being so, it seems to me inevitably to follow that she can be in no better position in these proceedings than her husband would be if they had been brought in his name. If they had been brought in his name, it is clear that the defendants would have had an unanswerable defence under the Rent Acts.

I agree that the appeal should be allowed.

TEMPLEMAN L.J.:

I agree that the appeal should be allowed....

The authorities establish that as a matter of law a lease made in breach of covenant by a mortgagor is void against the mortgagee and, I assume (but without deciding) for present purposes, against the transferee unless the lease is adopted by the mortgagee. Neither the bank nor the wife adopted the tenancy.

The estate, rights and powers of a mortgagee, however, are only vested in a mortgagee to protect his position as a mortgagee and to enable him to obtain payment. Subject to this, the property belongs in equity to the mortgagor. In the present case it is clear from the facts and the evidence that the mortgagee, Mrs Quennell, is not bona fide exercising her rights and powers for her own purposes as mortgagee but for the purpose of enabling the landlord mortgagor (her own husband) to repudiate his contractual obligations and defeat the statutory tenancy of the tenant which is binding on the landlord. Mrs Quennell does not even pretend to be acting in her own interests as mortgagee. She brings this action to oblige her husband. In my judgment the court must therefore treat this action, although in form brought by a mortgagee, as an action brought for and on behalf of the landlord mortgagor. The court should deal with it as though the mortgagor landlord were the plaintiff, and on that basis possession will not be ordered.

NOTES:

1. The existence of the equitable jurisdiction asserted in *Quennell v. Maltby* has been questioned: see Smith [1979] Conv. 266; Pearce [1979] C.L.J. 257.

2. In *Albany Home Loans Ltd v. Massey* [1997] 2 All E.R. 609, noted at [1998] Conv. 391, the Court of Appeal expressly relied on the discretionary equitable jurisdiction asserted in *Quennell v. Maltby* and refused to make a possession order against one of two joint mortgagors in circumstances where it would not benefit the mortgagee because, pending further proceedings, the mortgagee could not obtain an order against the other joint mortgagor.

3. On the leasing powers of the mortgagor, see *supra*, p. 824.

4.4 *Statutory restrictions on the mortgagee's right to possession*
In response to the decision in *Birmingham Citizens Permanent Building Society v. Caunt* [1962] Ch. 883, the right/remedy of the mortgagee to take possession was considered by the Payne Committee on the Enforcement of Judgment Debts. The Committee, which reported in 1969, took the view that (even defaulting) mortgagors required some protection against over-zealous mortgagees; and, although the analogy is not exact, it was argued that the philosophy underlying the protection afforded to tenants under both the general law and the landlord and tenant legislation should be extended to mortgagors, who had been encouraged by successive governments to become owner-occupiers. In particular, the Committee recommended a wider discretion for the courts to protect the mortgagor beyond the protection available under the inherent common law jurisdiction: *Report of the Committee on the Enforcement of Judgment Debts* (1969), Cmnd. 3909, para. 1386.

The recommendations of the Committee were largely implemented by sections 36–39 of the Administration of Justice Act 1970.

Administration of Justice Act 1970, s.36

Additional powers of court in action by mortgagee for possession of dwelling-house

36.—(1) Where the mortgagee under a mortgage of land which consists of or includes a dwelling-house brings an action in which he claims possession of the mortgaged property, not being an action for foreclosure in which a claim for possession of the mortgaged property is also made, the court may exercise any of the powers conferred on it by subsection (2) below if it appears to the court that in the event of its exercising the power the mortgagor is likely to be able within a reasonable period to pay any sums due under the mortgage or to remedy a default consisting of a breach of any other obligation arising under or by virtue of the mortgage.
(2) The court—
(a) may adjourn the proceedings, or
(b) on giving judgment, or making an order, for delivery of possession of the mortgaged property, or at any time before the execution of such judgment or order, may—
  (i) stay or suspend execution of the judgment or order, or
  (ii) postpone the date for delivery of possession,
for such period or periods as the court thinks reasonable.

NOTES:

1. See Haley (1997) 17 *Legal Studies* 483. Smith [1979] Conv. 266.

2. It became apparent that section 36 had failed to achieve the real intention of the Payne Committee and Parliament. The powers of the court conferred by subsection (2) were only available where the condition in subsection (1) was satisfied, namely where it appeared to the court that the mortgagor was likely to be able within a reasonable period to pay *any sums due under the mortgage*. If, as is the normal practice, a mortgage (including an instalment mortgage) makes the entire loan repayable in the event of

default, the section afforded no protection to the mortgagor beyond that already available under the courts' inherent common law jurisdiction: see *Halifax Building Society v. Clark* [1973] Ch. 307. For comment, see (1973) 37 Conv. 133; (1973) 89 L.Q.R. 171; (1973) 36 M.L.R. 550.

3. The Report of the Payne Committee had indicated that the court should have power to postpone the operation of an order for possession when "it appears to the court that the defendant ought to be given the opportunity to pay off *the arrears of instalments or interest* or to have time to make arrangements to redeem the mortgage": para. 1390. This also seems to have been the generally held view expressed during the Parliamentary debates on the Administration of Justice Bill: see H.L. Deb., vol. 306, col. 211, 253.

4. In *First Middlesbrough Trading and Mortgage Co. Ltd v. Cunningham* (1973) 28 P. & C.R. 69 the Court of Appeal adopted a rather more purposive interpretation of section 36: their Lordships doubted whether, in the context of an instalment mortgage, "sums due under the mortgage" referred to the entire loan as opposed to the sums in respect of which the mortgagor was in arrear; but, in any event, they were prepared to find that "a reasonable period" could be construed as the full term of the mortgage. For comment, see (1973) 37 Conv. 213; (1974) 38 Conv. 309; and see also Baker (1973) 89 L.Q.R. 171, 172; Jackson (1973) 36 M.L.R. 550, 553; and see now *Cheltenham and Gloucester Building Society v. Norgan* [1996] 1 W.L.R. 343, *infra*, p. 936.

5. The position in relation to instalment mortgages was clarified by section 8 of the Administration of Justice Act 1973, which provides:

8.—(1) Where by a mortgage of land which consists of or includes a dwelling-house, or by any agreement between the mortgagee under such a mortgage and the mortgagor, the mortgagor is entitled or is to be permitted to pay the principal sum secured by instalments or otherwise to defer payment of it in whole or in part, but provision is also made for earlier payment in the event of any default by the mortgagor or of a demand by the mortgagee or otherwise, then for purposes of section 36 of the Administration of Justice Act 1970 (under which a court has power to delay giving a mortgagee possession of the mortgaged property so as to allow the mortgagor a reasonable time to pay any sums due under the mortgage) a court may treat as due under the mortgage on account of the principal sum secured and of interest on it only such amounts as the mortgagor would have expected to be required to pay if there had been no such provision for earlier payment.

(2) A court shall not exercise by virtue of subsection (1) above the powers conferred by section 36 of the Administration of Justice Act 1970 unless it appears to the court not only that the mortgagor is likely to be able within a reasonable period to pay any amounts regarded (in accordance with subsection (1) above) as due on account of the principal sum secured, together with the interest on those amounts, but also that he is likely to be able by the end of that period to pay any further amounts that he would have expected to be required to pay by then on account of that sum and of interest on it if there had been no such provision as is referred to in subsection (1) above for earlier payment.

See Smith [1979] Conv. 266, 270–281.

6. The effect of section 36 of the 1970 Act, as qualified by section 8 of the 1973 Act, in the common situation where the whole mortgage debt becomes

repayable on default, is summarised in *The Supreme Court Practice 1999*, vol. 1, para. 88/5/13:

> In such a case a court may ... treat the sum due under the mortgage as being only the arrears of instalments or interest. It may exercise its jurisdiction under the section if it appears that the borrower is likely to be able within a reasonable period to bring his payments up to date by paying off all arrears at the date of the order and the payments falling due after the date of the order.

7. Since the conditions for relief under section 36 of the Administration of Justice Act 1970 are rather easier to satisfy in the case of mortgages within section 8(1) of the Administration of Justice Act 1973, the scope of that subsection has been the subject of litigation. The courts will construe the mortgage deed as a whole in order to determine whether "the mortgagor is entitled or is to be permitted to pay the principal sum secured by instalments or otherwise to defer payment of it in whole or in part": see *Centrax Trustees Ltd v. Ross* [1979] 2 All E.R. 952. On that basis, section 8(1) has been held to include traditional mortgages which simply provide for redemption after six months (and which make no provision for the repayment of capital by instalments) but which in their terms indicate that the parties intended an indefinite loan: *ibid.,* noted at [1979] Conv. 371. Section 8(1) has also been held to extend to endowment mortgages, which provide for the payment of instalments of interest only and for the repayment of the principal sum at the end of the term from the proceeds of a separate endowment policy: *Bank of Scotland v. Grimes* [1986] Q.B. 1179. However, section 8(1) has been held *not* to extend to mortgages securing overdraft facilities: *Habib Bank Ltd v. Tailor* [1982] 1 W.L.R. 1218, noted at [1983] Conv. 80. In such cases there is no deferral of repayment of a sum that has become due because the debt becomes due only on demand and there is no right to defer after demand has been made; and endowment mortgages are distinguished on the ground that the *fixed* date for repayment (rarely encountered in overdraft cases) generates the required right to defer. For detailed analysis, see Tromans [1984] Conv. 91.

8. Where a mortgagor has defaulted on repayments and the mortgagee seeks possession of the mortgaged property, the mortgagee is entitled to claim in addition a money judgment for the sums due. However, if the court suspends the possession order pursuant to its jurisdiction under section 36, it should suspend the money judgment on similar terms: see *Cheltenham and Gloucester Building Society v. Grattidge* (1993) 25 H.L.R. 454; *Cheltenham and Gloucester Building Society v. Johnson* (1996) 73 P. & C.R. 293.

9. By virtue of section 39(1) of the Administration of Justice Act 1970 the court may exercise its powers in favour of "any person deriving title under the original mortgagor". This has been held to extend only to assignees of the mortgagor: *Britannia Building Society v. Earl* [1990] 1 W.L.R. 422, 429–430 *per* McCowan L.J. Although the exclusion of tenants (both contractual and statutory) of the mortgagor can be justified in principle, it is arguable that, as a matter of policy, residential tenants should be treated like the spouse or

cohabitant of the mortgagor and should be permitted to invoke section 36: see *infra*, p. 951; and see Bridge [1990] Conv. 450.

4.4.1 *Extent of the jurisdiction under section 36*   The question arises as to whether section 36 constitutes a comprehensive code for the exercise of the mortgagee's right to possession in the context of dwelling-houses. This in fact involves two issues: first, whether the section removes the mortgagee's common law right to take possession by peaceful re-entry so that the right to possession cannot be exercised otherwise than by court proceedings and pursuant to a court order; and, secondly, and irrespective of the answer to the first issue, whether the section applies in all cases where the mortgagee seeks possession by court proceedings, even in the absence of repayment or other default on the part of the mortgagor. It is convenient to consider these two issues in reverse order since that is the order in which they have been litigated.

4.4.1.1 *The application of section 36 in the absence of default*   A literal interpretation of section 36 would appear to restrict the operation of the section to those cases where the mortgagor is in default. However, the Court of Appeal has held that the jurisdiction is exercisable whenever the mortgagee of a dwelling-house applies to the court for a possession order, irrespective of whether the mortgagor is in default.

Western Bank Ltd v. Schindler [1977] Ch. 1

(CA, Buckley, Scarman and Goff L.JJ.)

In 1973 the defendant mortgaged his house to the plaintiff bank to secure the repayment of a loan. The mortgage deed provided for the principal and accrued interest to be payable in 1983. In accordance with the earlier agreement between the parties, and by way of collateral security, the mortgagor also took out an endowment policy in favour of the mortgagees; but the mortgage deed made no reference to that policy. The mortgagor in fact paid three months' interest and three premiums under the endowment policy; but he made no further payments. The mortgagees claimed possession of the mortgaged property. Since there was no express or implied exclusion of the mortgagees' right to possession, the question arose as to the applicability of section 36 of the Administration of Justice Act 1970 where the mortgagor was not in breach of any term in the mortgage deed.

BUCKLEY L.J.:
Goulding J. held that this section applied in the present case, and that he accordingly had a discretion to allow the mortgagees to exercise their common law right to possession or to postpone the exercise of that right. Mr Lightman [counsel for the defendant], on the other hand, contends that, the mortgagor not being in default, the court is by implication positively required by that section to prevent the mortgagees from taking possession, since the only relevant considerations are the existence of some default and its likelihood of being remedied. Alternatively he submits that by inference the section abrogates a mortgagee's right to possession except when some sum is due

under the mortgage or the mortgagor is guilty of some other default under the mortgage.

In the present case, notwithstanding the loan contract, the mortgage and the policy charge must be treated as independent transactions. It is not disputed that the failure of the mortgagor to keep up the original policy, although it was of course a default under the policy charge, was not a default under the mortgage. So, on the evidence before the judge, there was no sum due and no outstanding default under the mortgage.

I have been very much puzzled during the argument about the proper interpretation of section 36. If subsection (1) is read literally, the conditional clause introduced by the words "if it appears to the court" (which I shall refer to as "the conditional clause") appears to restrict the operation of the section to cases in which some sum is due or some default has taken place and remains unremedied when the application comes before the court. This, however, seems to me to lead to a ridiculous result. If a mortgagee applies to the court for a possession order while the mortgagor is in default, the court may keep the matter in abeyance under subsection (2) for a reasonable period to permit the mortgagor to remedy the default: the mortgagor may do so within the time afforded to him by the court: upon the construction of the section now under consideration, if there were no other subsisting default, the mortgagee could thereupon seek an immediate possession order which the court would have no power to refuse or to delay, because no sum would then remain due and there would be no outstanding default. A defaulting mortgagor would therefore be in a better position than one not in default. He could obtain a respite and, having done so, it would be in his interest to remain in default until the last moment of the period of respite. I cannot believe that Parliament can have intended this irrational and unfair result. I must therefore investigate whether the section is capable of some other construction.

Mr Lightman, in the course of his ingenious and helpful argument, has suggested that section 36 by inference abrogates a mortgagee's right to possession when there is no sum due and no subsisting default on the part of the mortgagor under the mortgage. I feel unable to accept this suggestion. Section 36 is an enabling section which empowers the court to inhibit the mortgagee's right to take possession. It confers a discretionary power on the court to achieve this result. It is, in my judgment, impossible to spell out of it a positive abrogation of an important property right, and, moreover, an abrogation of it only in particular circumstances.

I think, however, that the section is capable of interpretation in a way which makes it applicable to a case in which a mortgagee seeks possession when no sum is due and no other default is subsisting under the mortgage. I can see no reason why the legislature should confer the discretionary power on the court when the mortgagor is in default, but should not do so when he is not in default. The manifest unfairness, as I think, of such a position seems to me a strong ground for believing that it must have been Parliament's intention to confer the power, default or no default, notwithstanding the ineptness of the language of the section to achieve this result. The only part of the section which appears to contradict such an intention is the conditional clause. This can only apply when the mortgagor is in arrear with some payment or is otherwise in default. It would be very natural for Parliament to provide that, where the mortgagor is in arrear or otherwise in default, the discretionary power should not be used to prevent the mortgagee from taking immediate possession unless the court were satisfied that there was a genuine likelihood of the mortgagor being able to put himself right within a reasonable time. On this approach, the conditional clause operates as a restriction on the court's free exercise of discretion. This would have been clear, had the conditional clause been framed in some such terms as these: "but, if any sum is due under the mortgage or the mortgagor is in default in respect of any other obligation arising under or by virtue of the mortgage, only if it appears to the court that in the event of its exercising the power the mortgagor is likely to be able within a reasonable period to pay any such sum or to remedy any such default". Although the language of the section is certainly inartistic to achieve this result and interpreting it in this way may involve some violence to the language (not, in my view, very great), nevertheless I think that, when the section is read as a whole in the context of the subject matter and particularly having regard to the arbitrary unfairness of the literal construction, it is possible to spell this meaning out of the words used. Since I do not think that this court should attribute to Parliament so irrational an intention as the literal construction would involve, I feel justified in adopting, and, in my judgment, we should adopt, the more liberal construction. Accordingly, in my judgment, on the true construction of the section, it applies to any case in which a mortgagee seeks possession, whether the mortgagor be in arrear or otherwise in default under the mortgage or not, but, where the mortgagor is in arrear or in default, the discretion is limited by the conditional clause.

. . .

In my judgment, the language of section 36(1) is not incapable of bearing the construction which I favour, and consequently I adopt it as according with what I conceive to have been the true intention of Parliament.

Under section 36(2), the court can hold the matter in abeyance for a "reasonable period". I was at one stage of the argument impressed by the view that the word "reasonable" here related back to the conditional clause in subsection (1), and that this indicated that the discretion was one designed to be exercised only in cases falling within the conditional clause. On consideration, I have reached the conclusion that this is not so. When the mortgagor is in arrear or otherwise in default, a reasonable time for the purpose of subsection (2) must, I think, be measured by what is reasonable for the purposes indicated in the conditional clause in subsection (1). Where the mortgagor is not in arrear or in default, the court will, upon the construction of the section which I favour, be at large in deciding what is reasonable for the purposes of subsection (2). I see nothing unlikely in supposing that Parliament meant this to be so. What would be reasonable must depend upon the circumstances of the case. This may involve, amongst other things, considering why the mortgagee is anxious to obtain possession and what degree of urgency may exist in relation to any particular aspect of the case. It might, perhaps, also involve consideration of whether the mortgagor is likely to be able to pay sums accruing due from time to time under the mortgage punctually as and when they should become due.

. . .

I appreciate that to construe section 36 in this way is in effect to convert the mortgagee's right to possession, which at common law is an absolute right, into a right which is exercisable only with the permission of the court on good cause being shown. I do not, however, regard this as a surprising result of a statutory provision which on any view is aimed at preventing an arbitrary use by the mortgagee of his legal right. It is a construction which, in my opinion, is to be preferred to holding that Parliament has either (1) sub silentio abrogated the mortgagee's right to possession, except when the mortgagor is in arrear or otherwise in default under the mortgage, by a section which in terms only confers a discretionary judicial power to control the exercise of that right, or (2) produced an irrational and unfair position by overlooking or misunderstanding the character of the mortgagee's right to possession at common law and consequently enacting the section in a form which leaves a lacuna which defeats the purpose of the section.

I think, therefore, that the judge was right in holding that the section applied in the present case and that it conferred a discretion upon him. In the exercise of that discretion I think he was entitled to take into account all relevant surrounding circumstances and was not confined to consideration of matters directly arising out of the mortgage. In particular he was, in my opinion, fully entitled to take into account that as a result of the failure of the collateral security provided by the policy charge the debt is now almost certainly inadequately secured. In my judgment, the judge was entitled to make the order which he did upon the grounds which he stated. I would therefore dismiss this appeal.

GOFF L.J.:

I turn to the alternative case for the mortgagor which he based on section 36 of the Administration of Justice Act 1970, and which may be summarised in the following propositions. First, that section applies where there is no money due and unpaid and no default consisting of a breach of any other obligation arising under or by virtue of the mortgage. Secondly, that the failure of the mortgagor to keep up the original policy and the substituted policy, however much it might be a breach of his obligations under the assignment of the policy, was not a breach of any obligation arising under or by virtue of the mortgage, for the mortgagees, for reasons good or bad, kept them separate. Thirdly, it follows on the judge's construction of the mortgage, and on the basis on which this case has proceeded, as no act or event within clause 4(A) has occurred, that this is a case within the first proposition. Fourthly, that in such a case section 36 either abrogates the mortgagee's common law right to take possession unless and until there be default in payment of money or a breach of any other obligation under the mortgage, or the court is bound to exercise its discretion in favour of the mortgagor, I suppose by granting an adjournment sine die.

In my judgment, the second proposition is right, and the third does follow, and the question we have to decide is, therefore, whether the first, and either way of putting the fourth, be right, in which case the appeal must succeed, or whether both or either of the first and fourth propositions are wrong, in which case it fails.

In order to decide these questions, one must in my judgment consider first the purpose and effect of section 36 in the case to which it indubitably applies, namely, where there is default either in payment of money or otherwise. In my judgment, the words in subsection (1), to which Buckley L.J. has referred as the conditional clause:

"if it appears to the court that in the event of its exercising the power the mortgagor is likely to be able within a reasonable period to pay any sums due under the mortgage or to remedy a default consisting of a breach of any other obligation arising under or by virtue of the mortgage"

make it clear that the purpose of the section is to enable the court in any of the ways specified in subsection (2) to grant a limited time, which may of course in a proper case be extended by a further exercise of the statutory powers, within which the mortgagor may put the matter right.

If that were in doubt, and in my view it is not, the legislature has itself removed the doubt by the Administration of Justice Act 1973. This was passed to remedy a defect in the earlier Act, under which in the case of an instalment mortgage with a provision that on default the whole should become due the court could only grant relief on the terms that the mortgagor do pay off the whole principal sum and not merely the instalments in arrear. This remedial Act of 1973 by its very nature emphasises the purpose of the earlier Act, but it goes further, because in section 8(1), it actually describes the purpose of the Act of 1970 in these terms:

"under which a court has power to delay giving a mortgagee possession of the mortgaged property so as to allow the mortgagor a reasonable time to pay any sums due under the mortgage."

This being so, it is argued that the first proposition must be right, both because that is the natural meaning of the words of the section, and because if it be not so a mortgagor who is not in default will be in a worse position than one who is, and it is further argued that the fourth proposition must be right in one or other form, since otherwise the section produces a result which is preposterously absurd. If, so the argument runs, all the court can do is to grant time to enable a mortgagor to pay what is due or to remedy any other default under the mortgage, and when that has been done the mortgagee is left with his absolute proprietary right to take possession, then, save where the money due is the whole amount under the mortgage and the case is not one within section 8 of the Act of 1973 it is idle to grant the mortgagor time to pay the money or remedy the default.

I feel the force of these arguments, but I am not able to accede to them. I am satisfied that section 36 of the Act of 1970 cannot be held, as it were by a side wind, to have wholly abrogated the mortgagee's proprietary right to take possession, even when there is no default. This would not, I think, be applying the principle of liberal construction to avoid absurdity stated in *Luke v. Inland Revenue Commissioners* [1963] A.C. 577, but disregarding the statute or overriding it, which, as Ungoed-Thomas J. pointed out in *In re Maryon-Wilson's Will Trusts* [1968] Ch. 268, 282, and in my judgment rightly pointed out, is what the court is not allowed to do. Nor, in my judgment, by parity of reasoning, can it be said that the court has a discretion but is bound to exercise it against the mortgagee where there is no money due or other default under the mortgage. Apart from the illogicality of saying that the court has a discretion, but is bound to exercise it in a particular way, this would really come back to abrogating the right.

It seems to me that there are only two courses open to the court; the one preferred by Buckley L.J. and Scarman L.J. to construe the clause as conferring a discretion in all cases, reading the conditional clause merely as a qualification on that discretion in the case of unpaid money due or other default; the other to construe the section literally and face whatever anomalies or absurdities that produces. For my part, with all respect, I think the latter is the correct course. It is, in my judgment, inescapable that the result of their construction is that the section operates as a positive enactment disentitling the mortgagee to exercise his proprietary right to take possession save on showing some cause other than the mere existence of his right as legal owner. That is perhaps less startling than saying that the right is wholly abrogated save upon default, but in my view it comes very near to it. Further, I find it very difficult to see how this section can be held to give the court power to adjourn, whether sine die or for a fixed period, where there is no money due which ought to be paid, or other default to be remedied, or by what criterion it could determine what should be a reasonable period. It is one thing to grant an adjournment to enable something specific to be done, such as is contemplated by the conditional clause. It is altogether different to grant an adjournment to see if some act, event or failure may occur which will entitle the mortgagee to exercise a right which at the time of the adjournment he does not possess, since ex hypothesi he is not entitled to exercise his proprietary right save on due cause being shown.

On the other hand, the anomalies and absurdities said to flow from the literal construction may be more apparent than real, because of the equitable liability to account on the footing of wilful default. Where there has never been any default, or where the court has allowed time for it to be remedied, which has been done, the mortgagee will not ordinarily be in a position to exercise any power of sale, and, therefore, will generally not wish to go on and get possession, unless indeed there is some reason apart from default in payment or other obligation, for example if the premises have been left vacant, in which case there is nothing anomalous, unjust or ridiculous in allowing him to do so.

It may be that the legislature overlooked the fact that the mortgagee's right is not dependent on default, or, more probably I think, it was concerned only to give a defaulting mortgagor a chance to make good his default, leaving everything else, that is to say his position on doing so, and the case where there has been no default to the protection of the equitable doctrine of accountability which has sufficed well in the past.

Be that as it may, in my judgment, section 36 does not apply where there is no money due, and no other default, and, therefore, this appeal fails. If that be wrong, however, then in my judgment the construction which Buckley L.J. and Scarman L.J. have adopted must be right, and in that case I respectfully entirely agree both with them and with the judge below that it would not be right, in the circumstances of this case, to exercise the court's discretion under section 36 so as to grant any indulgence to the mortgagor, and I respectfully agree with the order Buckley L.J. has proposed.

NOTES:

1. Scarman L.J. agreed with the reasoning of Buckley L.J. They both declined to interfere with the exercise of the discretion thus conferred on Goulding J. by virtue of section 36. He had made an order for possession (to take effect within one month) on the ground that, given the failure of the collateral security, the mortgage loan was almost certainly inadequately secured.

2. For comment, see (1976) 40 Conv. 310; (1976) 92 L.Q.R. 482; [1979] Conv. 266, 275–278.

3. Harpum (1977) 40 M.L.R. 356 supports the minority view of Goff L.J. that the section was intended to deal only with the mortgagor in default; and he criticises the view of the majority that such an interpretation of the section would produce injustice:

Where the mortgagor is in breach of the mortgage agreement, entry is a prelude to sale by the mortgagee. In view of these drastic consequences it is natural that the court should have a power to control entry. ... If there is no default, entry will be made by the mortgagee to preserve the value of his security and this will often involve an element of urgency. Normally the mortgagor will have gone out of possession and the premises will be falling into disrepair. The mortgagor does not stand to lose his property for ever. Clearly different considerations apply here and there is little justification for a power to postpone entry. ... Abuse is discouraged because at all times the disincentive of strict accountability hangs over the mortgagee.

That the section was intended to deal only with the mortgagor in default seems clear from the terms of the Report of the Payne Committee: see para. 1373; and from the Parliamentary debates on the Administration of Justice Bill: see H.L. Deb., vol. 306, col. 210.

4. As far as mortgages of dwelling-houses are concerned, Clarke [1983] Conv. 293 argued that section 36 should be interpreted as having effectively removed the *right* of the mortgagee to possession of the mortgaged property (although she accepts that that conclusion is based on "the common sense view" of the section rather than its literal interpretation); that possession is available to the mortgagee but only as a remedy to protect or enforce his security, only pursuant to a court order and only on showing good cause; but that the precise implications for the substantive rights of the mortgagor and mortgagee remain uncertain and require careful elaboration and analysis. However, the courts have continued to assert the prima facie right of the mortgagee to possession: see, *e.g. Ladup Ltd v. Williams & Glyn's Bank plc* [1985] 1 W.L.R. 851, 855 *per* Warner J.; *Citybank Trust Ltd v. Ayivor* [1987] 1 W.L.R. 1157, 1161 *per* Mervyn-Davis J.; *Ashley Guarantee plc v. Zacaria* [1993] 1 W.L.R. 62, 69 *per* Nourse L.J.; and see *Cheltenham and Gloucester plc v. Krausz* [1997] 1 W.L.R. 1558, 1564–1567 *per* Phillips L.J., *infra*, p. 944.

4.4.1.2 *Possession by peaceful re-entry*   Prior to the enactment of section 36, and subject to the discretionary equitable jurisdiction asserted in *Quennell v. Maltby* [1979] 1 W.L.R. 318, a mortgagee had the right to possession of the mortgaged property and the right to assert that right to possession by peaceful re-entry. However, since section 36 introduced a regime of protection for the mortgagor of a dwelling-house where the mortgagee seeks possession by court proceedings, it had been suggested that the necessary implication of the section is that it impliedly removed the right of the mortgagee to take possession otherwise than by court proceedings. Although all three members of the Court of Appeal in *Western Bank Ltd v. Schindler* [1977] Ch. 1 assert that the section did *not* abrogate the mortgagee's common law right to possession, the interpretation of the section in the majority judgments of Buckley L.J. and Scarman L.J. restricts the exercise of that right in such a way that, according to Clarke [1983] Conv. 293, the supposed distinction between abrogation and restriction in this context is illusory; see also Bamforth [1996] C.L.P. 207, 237–241. Perhaps surprisingly, the effect of section 36 on the right to take possession by peaceful re-entry was not considered by the courts until 1998.

Ropaigealach v. Barclays Bank plc [1999] 3 W.L.R. 17

(CA, Henry, Chadwick and Clarke L.JJ.)

CHADWICK L.J.:

The statutory purpose
    The genesis of section 36 of the Administration of Justice Act 1970 is not in dispute. Since 1925 a mortgage of freehold land has taken effect as a demise for a term of years absolute, subject to a proviso for redemption: see section 85 of the Law of Property Act 1925. A charge by deed expressed to be by way of legal mortgage takes effect as if a mortgage term of 3000 years had been created in favour of the mortgagee: see section 87(1) of that Act and, where the land is registered land, section 27(1) of the Land Registration Act 1925. The effect, as a matter of legal analysis, is that the mortgagor demises his immediate estate to the mortgagee, who thereupon becomes entitled to possession by virtue of the estate which he has acquired. The position is described in *Halsbury's Laws of England* (4th ed.) vol. 32 (1980), p. 308, para. 672:

> "Where a legal mortgage has been created, whether by demise or legal charge, and no provision is made for retention of possession by the mortgagor, the mortgagee is entitled to immediate possession or receipt of the rents and profits at any time after the execution of the mortgage, and equity does not interfere, notwithstanding that there has been no default on the mortgagor's part."

See also the comparable passage in *Fisher and Lightwood's Law of Mortgages* 10th ed. (1988), p. 331, and the observations of Harman J. in *Four-maids Ltd v. Dudley Marshall (Properties) Ltd* [1957] Ch. 317, 321–2, and of Russell J. in *Birmingham Citizens Permanent Building Society v. Caunt* [1962] Ch. 883, 887.
    It was held, in those cases, that the necessary consequence of the legal foundation upon which a mortgage was based was that the court had no power to refuse, or to suspend, an order for possession sought by a mortgagee who was otherwise entitled to enter by virtue of his estate. Russell J. in *Caunt* expressed the position in these terms, at page 912:

"... where (as here) the legal mortgagee under an instalment mortgage under which by reason of default the whole money has become payable, is entitled to possession, the court has no jurisdiction to decline the order or to adjourn the hearing whether on terms of keeping up payments or paying arrears if the mortgagee cannot be persuaded to agree to this course. To this the sole exception is that the application may be adjourned for a short time to afford to the mortgagor the chance of paying off the mortgage in full or otherwise satisfying him; but this should not be done if there is no reasonable prospect of this occurring."

The decision in *Caunt* put an end to a practice, which had been developed by the Chancery Masters since the introduction, in 1936, of what was then R.S.C., Ord. 55, r. 5A (now Ord. 88, r. 1), under which mortgage possession summonses were adjourned to give the mortgagor an opportunity to pay by instalments. Following the introduction of new Rules of the Supreme Court in 1965, the matter was considered by the Committee on the Enforcement of Judgment Debts under the Chairmanship of Payne J. The Payne Committee recommended at para. 1390 of its Report (1969) (Cmnd. 3909), dated 21 November 1968, that:

"... when possession is sought under a mortgage of a dwelling house having a rateable value which would bring it within the protection of the Rent Acts (whether with or without a concurrent claim for payment) and the defendant is in arrear with any instalments, and it appears to the court that the defendant ought to be given opportunity to pay off the arrears of instalments or interest, or to have time to make arrangements to redeem the mortgage, or otherwise requires the protection of the court, the court should have a discretion to adjourn the application or, if an order or judgment for possession is, or has been, made, and not executed, to stay or suspend the execution of any such order or judgment or postpone the date of possession for such a period or periods as it thinks fit, subject to such conditions (if any) in regard to payment by the mortgagor of arrears as the court thinks fit, and, if such conditions are complied with, the court should have discretion to discharge or rescind any such order or judgment ..."

Section 36 of the Administration of Justice Act 1970 does, of course, go rather further than the Payne Committee had recommended; for it does not restrict the court's powers to adjourn or suspend orders for possession to cases in which the rateable value of the dwelling house would bring it within the protection of the Rent Acts. Be that as it may, it is plain enough that the section was enacted in order to deal with a problem which had arisen following *Caunt* [1962] Ch. 833 and which had been the subject of examination and recommendation by the Payne Committee—see the observation of Scarman L.J. in *Western Bank Ltd v. Schindler* [1977] Ch. 1, 17. There is nothing in the circumstances leading to the enactment of section 36 of the 1970 Act which provides any foundation for a submission that it was intended to deal with a different problem—not then identified—arising from entry without an order of the court.

Nor is there anything in the language of the section itself which lends support to that submission. If the section had been intended to deal with the problems arising from entry without an order of the court, it is (to my mind) inconceivable that the section would have been enacted in the form in which it was ...

The Law Commission Report

The language of the section, as well as the circumstances in which it was enacted, lend strong support to the view expressed in the Law Commission Working Paper No. 99 on Land Mortgages (1986), at p. 103, para. 3.69:

"(a) The court can exercise its discretion [under section 36 of the 1970 Act] only if the mortgagee applies to it for a possession order: technically, therefore, the mortgagee can deprive the mortgagor of protection by electing to seek some other means of enforcement."

There is passage to the same effect in the Report which followed that Working Paper: "Transfer of Land: Land Mortgages" (1991) (Law Com. No. 204) at p.38, para. 6.16:

> "One of the consequences of the relationship created by the mortgage by demise and by the charge by way of legal mortgage is that it is the mortgagee and not the mortgagor who is entitled to possession of the property. Unless the mortgage deed expressly restricts the exercise of the right it is exercisable at any time for any (or no) reason; its exercise is not dependent on any default by the mortgagor, nor on any threat to the security. If the mortgagee prefers to obtain a court order for possession rather than obtain possession extra-judicially the court has power, if the property is a dwelling house, to withhold or delay the order on condition that the mortgagor remedies any default. Otherwise, the court has no power to regulate the exercise of the right: it is a matter in which equity has consistently refused to intervene."

Academic commentary

The view that the protection which section 36 affords to mortgagors of dwelling houses is limited to cases in which the mortgagee seeks an order for possession from the court was criticised in the article "Further Implications of section 36 of the Administration of Justice Act 1970" by Alison Clarke published in *The Conveyancer and Property Lawer* (1993), p.293, to which Mantell L.J. referred when giving leave for this appeal. The article, which may well have provided the inspiration for much of the argument advanced on behalf of Mr Ropaigealach on this appeal, contains a careful and scholarly analysis of the circumstances in which section 36 was enacted. The author recognises the force of the arguments in favour of what may be stigmatised as the literal construction of the section. But she goes on to say this, at pp. 295–6:

> "The courts would therefore be faced with a difficult task in interpreting section 36 as removing the mortgagee's right to take possession peacefully. Arguably, it is a task they should refuse to undertake: reading words into a statute in order to restrict a common law property right is not usually regarded as justifiable, and one would expect the courts to be particularly reluctant to do so where, as here, it is not at all clear either what the words should be or where in the section they should be inserted. In spite of all this, however, it is submitted that the common sense view must prevail. It is anomalous and undesirable to protect mortgagors against eviction by court process yet leave them open to eviction by self-help, particularly if—as apparently would be the case—the mortgagee's right to use self-help continued notwithstanding that he had applied to the court for immediate possession and been refused."

A purposive construction?

In support of the contention that the court should give what he described as a purposive construction to section 36 of the Act of 1970, Mr Scrivener Q.C., counsel for Mr Ropaigealach, relied on two decisions of this Court on the effect of a comparable provision in section 5 of the Increase of Rent and Mortgage Interest (Restrictions) Act 1920: *Remon v. City of London Real Property Co.* [1921] 1 K.B. 49 and *Cruise v. Terrell* [1922] 1 K.B. 664. The Act was enacted shortly after the conclusion of the Great War for the purpose of consolidating and amending the "law with respect to the increase of rent and recovery of possession of premises in certain cases, and the increase of the rate of interest on, and the calling in of securities on such premises...". The Act ... was, of course, an early example of the social housing legislation which was to be developed and re-enacted in subsequent Rent Acts and in the Housing Acts. Section 5 of the Act of 1920 precluded the court from making an order for possession of any dwelling house to which the Act applied unless one or more of a now familiar list of conditions were satisfied:

"(1) No order or judgment for the recovery of possession of any dwelling house to which this Act applies, or for the ejectment of a tenant therefrom, shall be made or given unless ... and in any such case as aforesaid, the court considers it reasonable to make such an order or give such judgment."

It was held by this court, in the two cases to which I have referred, that the effect of the Act of 1920 was to make it unlawful, in circumstances in which a former contractual tenant remained in occupation after the determination of the term, for a landlord to re-enter premises to which the Act applied without first obtaining an order for possession. So, it was argued, the same effect should be given to section 36 of the Administration of Justice Act 1970. That submission overlooks, as it seems to me, the basis upon which this court reached its decision in those two cases.

The question for decision in *Remon* [1921] 1 K.B. 49 was whether the plaintiff, a tenant of rooms to which (once enacted) the Act of 1920 applied and who had been excluded from possession by the landlord's re-entry on the day that the Act came into force following service of a notice to quit, was entitled to an injunction restraining the landlord from interfering with his quiet enjoyment of the premises. It is pertinent to keep in mind that re-entry had been obtained forcibly, by the landlord breaking the locks. It was held that, although the contractual tenancy had come to an end with expiry of the notice to quit, nevertheless, at the time of the re-entry, the plaintiff was to be treated as a tenant who by virtue of the provisions of the Act had retained possession for the purposes of section 15(1); and so was a person entitled to the benefit of the implied covenant for quiet enjoyment under that subsection. Section 15(1) was in these terms (so far as material):

"(1) A tenant who by virtue of the provisions of this Act retains possession of any dwelling house to which this Act applies shall, so long as he retains possession, observe and be entitled to the benefit of all the terms and conditions of the original contract of tenancy so far as the same are consistent with the provisions of this Act..."

. . .

On a proper analysis ... the basis of the decision in *Remon* can be seen to be this: (i) a person holding over after the determination of a contractual tenancy to which the Act applied was protected by section 5 of the Act from eviction by legal process; (ii) it followed that he was a person who, by virtue of the provisions of the Act, retained possession of the dwelling house which had formerly been let to him; (iii) accordingly, he was a person to whom the provisions of section 15 of the Act were plainly intended to apply; (iv) so it was permissible, as a matter of construction, to treat him as a "tenant" for the purposes of section 15; (v) if he were a tenant for those purposes, he had the benefit of the landlord's covenant for quiet enjoyment; and (vi) ejection by forcible re-entry was in breach of the covenant for quiet enjoyment and could be restrained by injunction. The plaintiff was able to bring himself within that analysis because re-entry had not been made before the day on which the Act came into force. The court was able to reach the conclusion that the Act "must have intended and be taken to forbid ejection by the private action of the landlord without the aid of the court" (p. 59) because, giving the word "tenant" a meaning for the purposes of section 15 which was wide enough to include a former contractual tenant holding over against the will of his landlord, "ejection" following forcible re-entry would constitute a breach of the covenant for quiet enjoyment to which, by virtue of that section, the "tenant" was entitled.

The point was before this court again, some eighteen months later, in *Cruise v. Terrell* [1922] 1 K.B. 664. The plaintiffs were "weekenders" to whom a cottage had been let for a fixed term of one year. The contractual term determined on 25 March 1921 and was not renewed. On 7 April, in the absence of the plaintiffs, the defendant sent the local blacksmith to the cottage, who broke into the premises and put a new lock upon the door and locked it. The plaintiffs sued in trespass. The defendant pleaded by way of defence that the tenancy had determined by effluxion of time; in the alternative he counterclaimed for possession of the cottage on one of the statutory grounds. The trial judge awarded damages for trespass, but made an order for possession on the counterclaim. The defendant appealed. After rejecting the contention that the Act of 1920 had no application to a tenancy for a term certain, the court went on to consider whether the effect of the Act was that the defendant's forcible re-entry constituted a trespass. Lord Sterndale M.R. said this, at p. 669:

> "The next point is that assuming the Act does apply and that the plaintiffs are statutory tenants, the Act does not prevent a landlord from exercising a right of re-entry where he is entitled to an immediate order for possession under section 5 of the Act, which order it is contended when obtained relates back to the date of his entry. That point was, however, decided against the appellant in *Remon v. City of London Real Property Co.* It is said that in the judgments in that case the point is dealt with by dicta only. In my opinion they are not dicta, but, even if they are, they are dicta from which we ought not to differ, and by which we are bound."

Warrington L.J. took the same view. ...
Scrutton L.J., the third member of the Court, agreed. He said this, at p. 673:

> "As to the second point it was said that the Act did not destroy the common law right of the landlord to enter. It will not help him to enter, but if he gets in peaceably he is in his right. It is that argument that as a member of the court in *Remon v. City of London Real Property Co.* I listened to from Mr Romer and in my view we decided against it. It is true that in that case the landlord had not obtained an order for possession under section 5 of the Act, as he did here, but in my view the object of the Act was to fetter landlords and to take away their common law rights, and until an order was obtained against him, a tenant stayed on, not as a trespasser, but as a statutory tenant—even against the will of the landlord. If the words of Bankes L.J. and myself in *Remon* which cover this point were obiter, they are now affirmed."

... As I have sought to explain, the true analysis of the decision in *Remon* is not that section 5 of the Act took away the landlord's common law rights; the true analysis is that section 15(1) extended the landlord's obligation to afford quiet enjoyment of the premises to his tenant (an obligation formerly subsisting under the contractual tenancy) to the period of holding over under the new statutory tenancy—so that re-entry, in the circumstances in which it was effected in both *Remon* and *Cruise*, was in breach of that covenant. I do not, myself, think that Scrutton L.J. intended his observations to have any wider application than that.

The view which I have expressed as to the true basis for the decisions in *Remon* and *Cruise* finds support in the decision of Atkinson J. in *Lavender v. Betts* [1942] 2 All E.R. 72. ...

For the reasons which I have set out, I am satisfied that the early decisions on the Increase of Rent and Mortgage Interest (Restrictions) Act 1920 provide no support for Mr Scrivener's contention that section 36 of the Administration of Justice Act 1970 should be given a construction which, on the language used, it cannot bear. *Remon* and *Cruise*, properly understood, provide examples of the court construing statutory provisions to give effect to a clearly identifiable purpose by a legitimate process of interpretation. It was legitimate to consider whether the clear purpose of the Act of 1920 could be served by restricting the meaning of the word "tenant" in section 15(1) to its ordinary sense. To restrict the meaning of that word would, as the court held, be to frustrate the objective which the Act was clearly intended to achieve. So it was necessary to give a wider meaning to that word; but subject to the constraint that that wider meaning must be one which the word was capable of bearing in the context in which it fell to be construed. There is no comparable process of construction by which the words used by the legislature in section 36 of the Act of 1970 can be held to have the effect for which Mr Scrivener contends.

Mr Scrivener sought, also, to rely on *Western Bank Ltd v. Schindler* [1977] Ch. 1. ...

In my view, Mr Scrivener can derive no assistance from *Western Bank Ltd v. Schindler.* It provides clear authority for the proposition that section 36 of the Administration of Justice Act 1970 has not abrogated the mortgagee's common law right to take possession by virtue of his estate. It provides, also, a very good illustration of the principles on which the court acts when faced with the problem that a literal construction of the words used by the legislature would give rise to an obvious lacuna or absurdity. An English judge is not to indulge in judicial legislation. Before he can imply words into an Act, the statutory intention must be plain and the insertion not too big, or too much at variance with the language in fact used by the legislature. The case provides no support for the contention that Parliament must have intended that the mortgagee's right to take possession should be exercisable only with the assistance of the court.

Conclusion

I find it impossible to be satisfied that Parliament must have intended, when enacting section 36 of the Act of 1970, that the mortgagee's common law right to take possession by virtue of his estate should only be exercisable with the assistance of the court. In my view, the only conclusion as to Parliamentary intention that this court can properly reach is that which can be derived from the circumstances in which the section was enacted, the statutory context in which it appears and the language which was used. All point in the same direction. Parliament was concerned with the problem which had arisen following the decision in *Birmingham Citizens Permanent Building Society v. Caunt* [1962] Ch. 883; it intended to restore the position to what it had been thought to be before that decision; and it did not address its mind to the question whether the mortgagor required protection against the mortgagee who took possession without the assistance of the court. It is impossible to be sure what course Parliament would have thought it appropriate to adopt, in 1970, if it had identified and addressed that question. It is impossible to be sure that Parliament did not intend (or would not have intended, if it had addressed its mind to the question) to leave the position as it was in that regard. It is not irrelevant that, at the date at which the Act of 1970 was enacted, the mortgagor who was in occupation had the protection—subsequently replaced in a different and, perhaps, more limited form by section 6 of the Criminal Law Act 1977—afforded by the Statutes of Forcible Entry 1381–1623. It is because it is impossible to be sure that Parliament cannot have intended to leave the position as it was—but must have intended that the mortgagee should only be entitled to exercise his common law right to possession with the assistance of the court—that it cannot be appropriate to embark on an investigation whether the words which have been used are capable of some other construction than that which they naturally bear.

CLARKE L.J.:

I agree, although I must confess that I do so with considerable reluctance. ...

Chadwick L.J. has explained the circumstances in which section 36 came to be enacted, namely as a result of recommendations of the Payne Committee ... which were made in order to deal with the problem which had arisen following the decision of this court in *Birmingham Citizens Permanent Building Society v. Caunt* [1962] Ch. 883. In that case the court was considering the powers of the court where the mortgagee brought an action for possession. Both the Payne Committee and subsequently Parliament took the view that mortgagors should be afforded limited protection in such a case. The nature of that protection was considered by this court in *Cheltenham and Gloucester plc v. Krausz* [1997] 1 W.L.R. 1558. That decision shows that the protection is limited, but it is nevertheless of considerable value to mortgagors who are in default.

It is true to say that neither this court in *Caunt* nor the Payne Committee was considering whether the court should have similar powers in cases in which the mortgagee chooses not to take proceedings for possession but simply takes possession or perhaps sells the property under his power of sale and the purchaser takes possession. In these circumstances I agree that it cannot readily be inferred that Parliament intended to give protection to mortgagors in such a case. It does however strike me as very curious that mortgagors should only have protection in the case where the mortgagee chooses to take legal proceedings and not in the case where he chooses simply to enter the property. As Alison Clarke put it in her illuminating article ... to which Chadwick L.J. has referred, it is anomalous and undesirable to protect mortgagors against eviction by court process yet leave them open to eviction by self-help.

...

As Chadwick L.J. has pointed out, the majority of this court in *Western Bank Ltd v. Schindler* [1977] Ch. 1 rejected the submission that the effect of section 36 was to abrogate the mortgagee's right of possession. However, as appears from the passage from the judgment of Buckley L.J. (at p. 12)..., section 36 is an enabling section which empowers the court to inhibit the mortgagee's right to take possession. He might have added that it also inhibits the right of any person deriving title from the mortgagee to do so. As I see it, the question is whether the section can be construed so as to inhibit the mortgagee's right to take possession by self-help.

It is submitted that it can because of the underlying purpose of the section, as for example stated ... by Griffiths L.J. in *Bank of Scotland v. Grimes* [1985] 1 Q.B. 1179, where he said of section 36 of the Act of 1970 and section 8 of the Administration of Justice Act 1973:

> "It is the intention of both sections to give a measure of relief to those people who find themselves in temporary financial difficulties, unable to meet their commitments under their mortgages and in danger of losing their homes."

It seems to me that if a mortgagor needs that relief he needs it whether the mortgagee chooses to exercise his right of possession by entering into possession with or without an order of the court. Indeed he also needs it if instead of doing either the mortgagee sells the property to a purchaser leaving the purchaser to take possession.

I recognise that Miss Gloster says that responsible mortgagees do not in practice take possession of property in which the mortgagor and his family are living without an order of the court, and I accept that that is so, but in my judgment the problem should be approached by reference to the legal rights of the mortgagee and to the legitimate interests of the mortgagor in the light of the purpose of the Act. In these circumstances, if it were possible to construe section 36 by affording mortgagors protection whether or not the mortgagee chose to obtain possession by self-help or legal action, I for my part would do so. I have however been persuaded that it is not possible.

I agree that the section should be given a purposive construction: see e.g. *Pepper v. Hart* [1993] A.C. 593, 617 *per* Lord Griffiths. But the process remains one of construction and I have reluctantly reached the conclusion that where a section gives the court powers "where the mortgagee ... brings an action in which he claims possession of the mortgaged property" it is not permissible to hold that the effect of the section is to give the court such powers whether or not the mortgagee brings such an action.

[The appellant's] submission amounts to saying that the effect of the section is that a mortgagee is not entitled to take possession of mortgaged property save by order of the court. The problem is that the section does not say so. If Parliament had wished so to provide there is no reason why it should not have done so expressly, as it has in related circumstances. Thus it introduced legislation to protect tenants from eviction by landlords entitled to possession save by order of the court. Section 2 of the Protection from Eviction Act 1977 provides:

"Where any premises are let as a dwelling on a lease which is subject to a right of re-entry or forfeiture it shall not be lawful to enforce that right otherwise than by proceedings in the court while any person is lawfully residing in the premises or any part of them."

Chadwick L.J. has also referred to various provisions of the Rent Acts to which we were referred in argument. Moreover Parliament has considered in what circumstances it should restrict the exercise of a mortgagee's right of possession. It did so in a very limited form in section 126 of the Consumer Credit Act 1974 ... It could have so provided in the case of all mortgages of dwelling-houses, but it did not.

In all the circumstances I respectfully agree with Chadwick L.J., essentially for the reasons which he gives. I accept Miss Gloster's submission that the question what, if any, restrictions to impose upon the exercise of a mortgagee's right of possession is essentially a matter of policy. In order to answer the question it would no doubt be necessary to consider what, if any, such restrictions should be imposed (a) in circumstances in which mortgaged property has been vacated by the mortgagor (which appears to be the case in the vast majority of cases in which mortgagees take possession without an order of the court) and (b) in circumstances in which the mortgagor is residing in the property. In these circumstances, although consideration of the policy behind section 36 supports the appellant's submissions, I do not feel able to accede to them as a matter of construction of the section. I have only added some observations of my own because of my reluctance to reach that conclusion.

HENRY L.J.:

Clarke L.J. has drawn attention to the curious anomaly that mortgagors should have the protection afforded by section 36 of the Administration of Justice Act 1970 in cases in which the mortgagee chooses to take proceedings to enforce his right to possession but should have no such protection where he chooses (and is able) to enter without first obtaining an order from the court. He has pointed out, also, the problem which may exist if the court is asked to exercise the power conferred by section 36 in a case where the mortgagee has already exercised his power of sale, without having taken possession as against the mortgagor. But this anomaly, and this problem, are not identified for the first time in the present case. They have been the subject of academic comment in the past. Perhaps more pertinently, they were considered by the Law Commission in the Working Paper... and the Report... to which Chadwick and Clarke L.JJ. have referred. The Law Commission has made proposals to reform the law in this field. It is for Parliament to decide whether to accept those or other proposals.

NOTE:

1. For comment, see [1999] C.L.J. 281; [1999] Conv. 263.

4.4.2 *Exercise of the discretion under section 36*   Subject to the decision in *Western Bank Ltd v. Schindler*, the jurisdiction under section 36 is dependent upon the ability of the mortgagor "within a reasonable period to pay any sums due under the mortgage or to remedy any default consisting of a breach of any other obligation arising under or by virtue of the mortgage"; but it is not surprising that virtually all the reported cases appear to involve repayment default.

Where a defaulting mortgagor seeks a suspension of a possession order, it appears that there are two options available: either he can seek to persuade the court that he can afford to maintain a repayment schedule in relation to both arrears and continuing instalments; or he can seek to persuade the court that he should be permitted time to sell the mortgaged property and to redeem the mortgage from the proceeds of sale. In either case, whether the condition in section 36(1) is satisfied is a question of fact to be determined on the evidence: *Royal Trust Co. of Canada v. Markham* [1975] 1 W.L.R. 1416, noted at (1976) 40 Conv. 440. If it is clear that there is no prospect of the arrears being repaid within a reasonable period or the property being sold and the mortgage debt being redeemed, the court has no real alternative but to give leave for the possession order to be enforced: *Abbey National Mortgages plc v. Bernard* (1995) 71 P. & C.R. 257.

4.4.2.1 *Repayment schedule*   The cases on repayment default reveal a paradox. Since mortgagees normally prefer to keep mortgages alive, they tend initially to seek to resolve problems of repayment default through negotiation with the mortgagors; and they may renegotiate a series of repayment schedules before finally seeking possession. However, by the time the application is heard by the court, the arrears are likely to be substantial. In such circumstances, it may be unrealistic to conclude that the mortgagor is likely to be able to pay the sums due under the mortgage *within a reasonable period*, unless "reasonable period" is afforded a generous interpretation. Yet, until recently, as a matter of practice two to four years was regarded as the guideline reasonable period: see *The Supreme Court Practice 1995*, vol. 1, para. 88/5/9; and see *Citybank Trust v. Ayivor* [1987] 1 W.L.R. 1157, 1164 *per* Mervyn Davies J.

    The guideline was reconsidered in *Cheltenham and Gloucester Building Society v. Norgan* [1996] 1 W.L.R. 343.

Cheltenham and Gloucester Building Society v. Norgan [1996] 1 W.L.R. 343

(CA, Evans and Waite L.JJ., Sir John May)

In 1986 the defendant borrowed £90,000 from the predecessor of the plaintiff building society in order to finance her husband's business. The loan was secured by a mortgage over the family home, which provided for repayment by monthly instalments over 22 years, although the whole loan became repayable immediately in the event of default. The defendant defaulted on the repayments and by April 1990 the arrears amounted to £7,000; and in November 1990, when the plaintiff obtained a possession order, the arrears amounted to £14,000. Execution of the order was twice suspended on terms as to repayment. In 1991 the plaintiff obtained a warrant for possession, which was twice suspended on terms. Following a brief improvement in the defendant's repayment record, the plaintiff applied again to issue the warrant and the judge refused any further suspension. Arrears amounted to approximately £20,000 while the family home was worth £225,000.

WAITE L.J.:

The issue of principle
    The judge's statement that in the experience of his court "a period of two to four years is the maximum that will ordinarily be allowed" as reasonable for the purposes

of section 36(2) accords with the comment in *The Supreme Court Practice 1995*, vol. 1, para. 88/5/9 ...:

> "The exercise of the discretion under section 36 is by far the commonest matter which arises for decision in disputed mortgage actions. What is a 'reasonable period' for bringing the payments up to date is a question on which there is little guidance. In practice, in any ordinary case a period of at least two years will be allowed to the borrower if it appears that he is likely to be able to clear off the arrears in that time and he may be allowed a much longer time."

The opposing arguments which Mr Croally [counsel for the defendant] and Mr Waters [counsel for the plaintiff] have developed in their helpful written and oral submissions are as follows. Mr Croally contends that there is a primary assumption that a reasonable period is the term of the mortgage, and for that he relies on the dicta already cited from *First Middlesbrough Trading and Mortgage Co. Ltd v. Cunningham* (1974) 28 P. & C.R. 69 and *Western Bank Ltd v. Schindler* [1977] Ch. 1 [see note 2, *infra*]. That assumption is reinforced, he says, in the present case by the fact that there is sufficient equity to protect the mortgagee's eventual entitlement to repayment of the principal debt in full in 2008, that the mortgagor has deposed on affidavit to budgeting proposals under which (with the help she now receives from the Department of Social Security) there is a reasonable prospect of her being able to pay off the arrears in full by the expiry of the mortgage term, and that such a proposal would accord with the policy declared on the face of the C.M.L. statement [see note 3, *infra*]. Mr Waters contends that such an approach takes too narrow a view of the court's discretion. The delaying powers under section 36 represent a substantial interference with the contractual right which the parties have themselves freely negotiated, namely the right of the mortgagee to repayment in full of the whole mortgage debt as soon as a default occurs. In the exercise of its discretion, therefore, the court is bound to be even-handed in its approach to the claims of each side, matching a concern on the one hand that the mortgagor should be allowed a proper opportunity of making good his default with a concern that a mortgagee who has contracted for a steady flow of interest punctually paid by instalments as they fall due should not be compelled to wait for payment through an enforced capitalisation of interest. Given the number of these cases which come before the courts every day, it would lead, so Mr Waters submits, to unnecessary cost and delay if in every case the court was required to undertake the sort of detailed inquiry which would be necessary if one is to weigh to a nicety the effect on the one hand upon the lender of having to submit to a phasing of repayment of arrears over the whole remaining term of the mortgage and the ability on the other hand of the mortgagor to maintain such payments. It would be sufficient for the purposes of a just and fair exercise of the discretion if the courts were to be encouraged to adopt, as the judge did in this case and as many other judges (with encouragement from *The Supreme Court Practice*) regularly do, a period of years (be it two, four or six—Mr Waters leaves us to say which should be chosen) that can, without being applied blindly or rigidly, be adapted by the courts to the demands of each case.

Conclusion

There is no doubt that Mr Waters's argument has strong pragmatic advantages. In the present plight of the housing market possession cases play a major part in the case-load for the county courts. That is particularly true of the district judges, who deal with those cases in such numbers that they develop a "feel" for them and have achieved an excellent disposal record. It is not surprising that they have found it convenient to adopt a relatively short period of years as the rough rule of thumb which aids a just determination of the "reasonable period" for the purposes of section 36 of the Act of 1970 and section 8 of the Act of 1973. Nevertheless, although I would not go quite so far with Mr Croally as to say it should be an "assumption", it does seem to me that the logic and spirit of the legislation require, especially in cases where the parties are proceeding under arrangements such as those reflected in the C.M.L. statement, that the court should take as its starting point the full term of the mortgage and pose at the outset the question: "Would it be possible for the mortgagor to maintain payment-off of the arrears by instalments over that period?"

I accept all the grounds urged on us by Mr Waters for saying that the dicta relied on in *First Middlesbrough Trading and Mortgage Co. Ltd v. Cunningham* (1974) 28 P. & C.R. 69 and *Western Bank Ltd v. Schindler* [1977] Ch. I were directed to situations different from the circumstances of this case and most other cases of it kind, but they nevertheless in my judgment provide confirmation of the view that such is the right approach. I would acknowledge, also, that this approach will be liable to demand a more detailed analysis of present figures and future projections than it may have been customary for the courts to undertake until now. There is likely to be a greater need to require of mortgagors that they should furnish the court with a detailed "budget" of the kind that has been supplied by the mortgagor in her affidavit in the present case. But analysis of such budgets is part of the expertise in which the district judges have already become adept in their family jurisdiction and I would not expect that to present too great a difficulty. There will be instances, too, in which preliminary adjudication will be necessary to determine, when calculating the amount of arrears and assessing the future instalments for their payment-off, which items are to be attributed to the mortgagor's current payment obligations and which to his ultimate liability on capital account. The present case has shown—through the disparity introduced by the disputed items—how problematic that may sometimes prove to be. They are nevertheless disputes that it will be essential to resolve—in this case and others where they arise—before the court can undertake an accurate estimate of the amount which the mortgagor would be required to meet if the arrears were to be made repayable over the full remainder of the mortgage term. There may also be cases, as Mr Waters points out, in which it is less obvious than in this case that the mortgagee is adequately secured—and detailed evidence, if necessary by experts, may be required to see if and when the lender's security will become liable to be put at risk as a result of imposing postponement of payments in arrear. Problems such as these—which I suspect will arise only rarely in practice although they will undeniably be daunting when they do arise—should not however be allowed, in my judgment, to stand in the way of giving effect to the clearly intended scheme of the legislation.

There is another factor which, to my mind, weighs strongly in favour of adopting the full term of the mortgage as the starting point for calculating a "reasonable period" for payment of arrears. It is prompted by experience in this very case. The parties have been before the court with depressing frequency over the years on applications to enforce, or further to suspend, the warrant of possession, while Mrs Norgan and her husband have struggled, sometimes with success and sometimes without, to meet whatever commitment was currently approved by the court. Cheltenham has (in exercise of its power to do so under the terms of the mortgage) added to its security the costs it has incurred in connection with all these attendances. One of the disputed items turns upon the question whether such costs fall to be allocated to capital or to interest account. What is not in dispute, however, is that one day, be it sooner or later, those costs will have to be borne by the mortgagor, and if the day comes when she decides—or is compelled by circumstances—to move to more readily affordable accommodation, her resources for rehousing will be correspondingly reduced. It is an experience which brings home the disadvantages which both lender and borrower are liable to suffer if frequent attendance before the court becomes necessary as a result of multiple applications under section 36 of the Act of 1970—to say nothing of the heavy inroads made upon court hearing time. One advantage of taking the period most favourable to the mortgagor at the outset is that, if his or her hopes of repayment prove to be ill-founded and the new instalments initially ordered as a condition of suspension are not maintained but themselves fall into arrear, the mortgagee can be heard with justice to say that the mortgagor has had his chance, and that the section

36 powers (although of course capable in theory of being exercised again and again) should not be employed repeatedly to compel a lending institution which has already suffered interruption of the regular flow of interest to which it was entitled under the express terms of the mortgage to accept assurances of future payment from a borrower in whom it has lost confidence.

It follows, for all these reasons, that in adopting for this case a period of repayment (four years) unrelated to the remaining term of the mortgage (thirteen years) the judge in my view fell into error. The fault was not his. He applied to a case which he examined with outstanding care and clarity a practice of convenience which has been developed to deal with a widely framed statutory discretion in respect of which guidance from authority has been limited.

In view of the long history of this litigation, and the anxiety it has involved, in particular for Mrs Norgan and her family, it would have been the wish of this court to determine all outstanding issues for ourselves, so that each side might have left this court knowing exactly where they stood. But, as Evans L.J. made clear to the parties at the hearing, there are too many matters unresolved, on evidence which is still not wholly complete, to enable us to do so. I would therefore allow the appeal and remit the case to the county court for (1) a determination of the disputed items and a finding as to what precisely is now, or (as they case may be) will at the expiry of the mortgage term be, due from the mortgagor on capital and interest instalment account respectively—including in the latter account a precise figure for the current interest in arrear; (2) a calculation of (a) the instalments which the mortgagor would be required to pay if the arrears so found were to be made payable by instalments over the whole of the remaining period of the mortgage term and (b) the instalments of interest currently due under the mortgage; (3) a determination of the question whether, in the light of the court's findings as to the current and prospective ability of the mortgagor to discharge the instalments under (2) (a) and (b), there are any unusual circumstances justifying a departure from the remaining term of the mortgage as the period that is prima facie "reasonable" for the purposes of section 36 of the Act of 1970 and section 8 of the Act of 1973; (4) a determination of the question whether, in the light of its conclusions under (1), (2) and (3), this would be a suitable case in which to exercise the court's discretion to suspend the warrant of possession for any and if so what period.

. . .

EVANS L.J.

. . .

In conclusion, a practical summary of our judgments may be helpful in future cases. Drawing on the above and on the judgment of Waite L.J., the following considerations are likely to be relevant when a "reasonable period" has to be established for the purposes of section 36 of the Act of 1970. (a) How much can the borrower reasonably afford to pay, both now and in the future? (b) If the borrower has a temporary difficulty in meeting his obligations, how long is the difficulty likely to last? (c) What was the reason for the arrears which have accumulated? (d) How much remains of the original term? (e) What are relevant contractual terms, and what type of mortgage is it, i.e. when is the principal due to be repaid? (f) Is it a case where the court should exercise its power to disregard accelerated payment provisions (section 8 of the Act of 1973)? (g) Is it reasonable to expect the lender, in the circumstances of the particular case, to recoup the arrears of interest (1) over the whole of the original term, or (2) within a shorter period, or even (3) within a longer period, i.e. by extending the repayment period? Is it reasonable to expect the lender to capitalise the interest or not? (h) Are there any reasons affecting the security which should influence the length of the period for payment? In the light of the answers to the above, the court can proceed to exercise its overall discretion, taking account also of any further factors which may arise in the particular case.

NOTES:

1. For comment, see [1996] Conv. 118; (1996) 112 L.Q.R. 553; (1997) 17 *Legal Studies* 483.

2. In *First Middlesbrough Trading and Mortgage Co. Ltd v. Cunningham* (1974) 28 P. & C.R. 69 Scarman L.J. stated (at 75):

Since the object of the instalment mortgage was, with the consent of the mortgagee, to give the mortgagor the period of the mortgage to repay the capital sum and interest, one begins with a powerful presumption of fact in favour of the period of the mortgage being the "reasonable period".

In *Western Bank Ltd v. Schindler* [1977] Ch. 1 Buckley L.J. stated (at 14):

In a suitable case the specified period might even be the whole remaining prospective life of the mortgage.

3. The Council of Mortgage Lenders publishes a statement (the "C.M.L. statement") of current practice of mortgage lenders when dealing with mortgage arrears and possession cases. The Court of Appeal referred to a section in the February 1995 statement headed "Alleviating arrears problems":

7. Lenders have the following devices which they can use which help some borrowers in arrears difficulties—(a) In the case of a repayment loan the term of the loan can be lengthened, although in most cases this does not make a significant difference to the monthly payments. (b) An endowment mortgage can be changed to a repayment, or interest only, mortgage with a subsequent reduction in monthly outgoings ... (c) Part of the interest can be deferred for a period. This is particularly appropriate where there is a temporary shortfall of income (for example, because of an industrial dispute or a temporary illness), or where there has been a rapid increase in interest rates. Lenders would generally be willing to accept for a reasonable period of time the most the borrower could reasonably afford provided there was the prospect of full repayments being resumed. However, this is not a solution where, because of a permanent reduction in income, a borrower is unable to afford anywhere near the full mortgage repayments and there is no early prospect of a change in the situation. (d) Linked to (c) is the possibility of capitalising interest. This is appropriate where arrears have been built up and when full monthly repayments can be resumed. The arrears can be added to the capital sum and repaid over the life of the loan. ... 8. In addition, lenders try to ensure that the borrower is aware of any income support or other social security benefits that may be available, and, in appropriate cases, many advise the borrower to consider letting the property or taking in a lodger.

4. Any suspension of an order for possession must be for a defined or ascertainable period: *Royal Trust Co. of Canada v. Markham* [1975] 1 W.L.R. 1416; *National Westminster Bank plc v. Skelton (Note)* [1993] 1 W.L.R. 72, 81 *per* Slade L.J. In *Western Bank Ltd v. Schindler* [1977] Ch. 1, 14, Buckley L.J. suggested that an order might be suspended for an indefinite period provided that the parties are given liberty to apply; but, where, as in that case, there has been no default by the mortgagor, postponement for a defined period would be inappropriate.

5. The approach of the Court of Appeal in offering detailed guidelines for the exercise of the jurisdiction under section 36 is in marked contrast to the

earlier approach in *Cheltenham and Gloucester Building Society v. Grant* (1994) 26 H.L.R. 703, noted at [1995] Conv. 51.

6. A mortgagor who is seeking to retain possession of the mortgaged property will be required to provide a detailed budget and financial plan with a schedule for both the payment of continuing instalments and the repayment of arrears: *First National Bank plc v. Syed* [1991] 2 All E.R. 250; *Cheltenham and Gloucester Building Society v. Norgan* [1996] 1 W.L.R. 343. The principal difficulty will normally relate to the repayment of arrears because, after an initial period, social security payments are likely to be available to cover continuing payments of interest (although not payments of capital or endowment policy premiums): see Lundy [1997] Conv. 36. The evidence must establish that the likelihood of the mortgagor's ability to pay is realistic and not merely speculative: *Peckham Mutual Building Society v. Registe* (1980) 42 P. & C.R. 186, 189 *per* Vinelott J.; *Town and Country Building Society v. Julien* (1991) 24 H.L.R. 312, 316–317 *per* Balcombe L.J. Thus the mortgagor cannot rely on the mere hope of a football pools win: *Hastings and Thanet Building Society v. Goddard* [1970] 1 W.L.R. 1544, 1547–1548 *per* Russell L.J. Nor will the court will take into consideration damages that may be awarded to the mortgagor in a counterclaim against the mortgagee or a third party: *Citybank Trust Ltd. v. Ayivor* [1987] 1 W.L.R. 1157; *National Home Loans Corp. plc v. Yaxley* (1997) 73 P. & C.R. D41.

4.4.2.2 *Sale by mortgagor* If the mortgagor is unable to provide a satisfactory repayment schedule, there remains the possibility that he can sell the mortgaged property and redeem the mortgage from the proceeds of sale. The exercise of the jurisdiction under section 36 in these circumstances was considered by the Court of Appeal in *National and Provincial Building Society v. Lloyd* [1996] 1 All E.R. 630 and the current approach is well illustrated by the case of *Bristol and West Building Society v. Ellis* (1996) 73 P. & C.R. 158.

Bristol and West Building Society v. Ellis (1996) 73 P. & C.R. 158

(CA, Hirst and Auld L.JJ.)

In 1987 the respondent and her husband financed the purchase of their matrimonial home with a loan of £40,000 from the appellant building society. The loan, which was subsequently increased to £60,000, was secured by an endowment mortgage over the property. By 1990, when the respondent and her husband separated, there were already substantial arrears. The appellant obtained a possession order which was suspended on terms. The respondent failed to comply with the terms of the order and by 1995 the arrears amounted to £16,000, so that the total debt to the appellant was £76,000. The district judge granted a warrant for possession. The respondent applied for suspension of the execution of the warrant on terms as to repayment of the arrears *and* on the basis that she would sell the property and redeem the mortgage within three to five years (by which time her children would have completed their full-time education). However, the district judge ordered suspension only on terms as to repayment (which terms would mean that it would take the respondent 98 years to repay the arrears). The order was upheld by the county court judge and the appellant appealed to the Court of Appeal.

AULD L.J.:

Mr Michael Duggan, on behalf of Bristol and West, submitted that whether the order upheld by the judge is looked at solely on its terms, so as to envisage a period of 98 years for payment of the arrears, or on its unexpressed basis, that Mrs Ellis would discharge her entire mortgage debt on sale of the house within three to five years, it did not satisfy the requirement of section 36 that the period of repayment should be "reasonable". Mr Duggan submitted that, in making such an order, the district judge had acted outside the bounds of the discretion given to him by the provision and that the judge should have recognised that and should have ordered the issue of the warrant. Mr Duggan's point was that the periods of repayment provided for or contemplated by the order were so long that they were unlawful, not simply discretionary periods with which the judge could decide he need not interfere.

Mr Jan Luba, on behalf of Mrs Ellis, acknowledged that a period extending many decades after the end of the mortgage period could not be a reasonable period for repayment within section 36, but submitted that a period of three to five years until sale of the house was reasonable in the circumstances. The difficulty about that argument is that District Judge Bolton, whatever his expectation, did not express the order so as to suspend it for a period within which Mrs Ellis was required to sell the property. He suspended it only on terms that she pay £10 a month towards the arrears, in addition to payment of an initial sum, for a period over six times the length of the outstanding term of the mortgage. Similarly, Judge McNaught, in his short judgment, while clearly of the view that the order as expressed was for an unreasonably long period, did not vary it to reflect the district judge's apparent expectation. It is difficult to see how, on the face of the order, Bristol and West could rely on that expectation to obtain immediate possession if, after five or more years, Mrs Ellis refused to sell the property while continuing to pay the interest and monthly instalments of £10 in reduction of the arrears. It seems to me that, subject only to the possibility of variation provided by section 36(4), it would be struck with the order in that form until the end of the mortgage period in 16 years time, and with the prospect of substantial arrears of interest still unpaid at that time. The existence of a power of variation in the county courts is no basis for this court, on appeal from it, to uphold an invalid order. I am, therefore, of the view that the order under appeal cannot stand.

Having regard to this court's power in R.S.C. Ord. 59, r. 10(3) to make its own order in the matter, I consider also the issue of reasonableness of the three to five years period apparently underlying the district judge's order.

In the absence of unusual circumstances and where discharge of all arrears by periodic payments is proposed, the outstanding period of the mortgage, whether term or repayment, is the starting point in determining the reasonableness of the period for payment of sums due under a mortgage: see *Cheltenham and Gloucester Building Society v. Norgan* [1996] 1 W.L.R. 343.

However, that convenient starting point is not available to a mortgagor who cannot discharge the arrears by periodic payments and whose only prospect of repaying the entire mortgage loan and accrued and accruing interest is from the sale of the property. In such a case the only general guidance is that the reasonableness of the period is a matter for the court in the circumstances of the case: see *Royal Trust Co. of Canada v. Markham* [1975] 1 W.L.R. 1416 and *National and Provincial Building Society v. Lloyd* [1996] 1 All E.R. 630.

The prospect of settling the mortgage debt, including arrears of principal and/or interest by sale of the property raises a number of questions on the reasonableness of any period which a court may consider allowing for the purpose.

The critical matters are, of course, the adequacy of the property as a security for the debt and the length of the period necessary to achieve a sale. There should be evidence, or at least some informal material (see *Cheltenham and Gloucester Building Society v. Grant* (1994) 26 H.L.R. 703), before the court of the likelihood of a sale the proceeds of which will discharge the debt and of the period within which such a sale is likely to be achieved. If the court is satisfied on both counts and that the necessary period for sale is reasonable, it should, if it decides to suspend the order for possession, identify the period in its order.

The instinct of the courts in determining a reasonable period for this purpose seems to have been to adopt the common law approach before the 1970 Act (see *Birmingham Citizens Permanent Building Society v. Caunt* [1962] Ch. 883) of fixing on a "short" period: see *Markham* and *Target Home Loans Ltd v. Clothier* [1994] 1 All E.R. 439. However, in *Markham* neither the county court judge nor the Court of Appeal considered what, in the circumstances of that case, might have been a reasonable period. The defendants had called no evidence and the judge had not fixed any period in his order. The Court of Appeal contented itself with ruling that he should have fixed a period, but only after hearing evidence on the matter. In *Clothier*, the Court of Appeal, on the strength of evidence before it, but not before the county court judge, made an order for possession, suspending it for three months.

In *Lloyd*, Neill L.J., with whom Bennett J. agreed, after reviewing the above authorities, held that the word "reasonable" in the statute should not necessarily be equated with "short"; what was a reasonable period was "a question for the court in the individual case". He said:

"... if there were, in a hypothetical case, clear evidence that the completion of the sale of a property, perhaps by piecemeal disposal, could take place in six or nine months or even a year, I see no reason why a court could not come to the conclusion in the exercise of its discretion under the two sections that, to use the words of the section 'the mortgagor [was] likely to be able within a reasonable period to pay any sums due under the mortgage'. The question of a 'reasonable period' would be a question for the court in the individual case."

Mr Duggan, on behalf of the building society, sought to extract from that passage a principle that a year is about the maximum period that a court could consider reasonable for this purpose. Whilst that may be a likely maximum in many cases, I do not read Neill L.J.'s words as establishing it as a rule of law or as a matter of general guidance. It all depends on the individual circumstances of each case, though the important factors in most are likely to be the extent to which the mortgage debt and arrears are secured by the value of the property and the effect of time on that security.

Where the property is already on the market and there is some indication of delay on the part of the mortgagor, it may be that a short period of suspension of only a few months would be reasonable (see, *e.g. Clothier*). Where there is likely to be considerable delay in selling the property and/or its value is close to the total of the mortgage debt and arrears so that the mortgagee is at risk as to the adequacy of the security, immediate possession or only a short period of suspension may be reasonable. Where there has already been considerable delay in realising a sale of the property and/ or the likely sale proceeds are unlikely to cover the mortgage debt and arrears or there is simply no sufficient evidence as to sale value, the normal order would be for immediate possession: see, *e.g. Abbey National Mortgages plc v. Rochelle Bernard* (1995) 71 P. & C.R. 257 and *Lloyd*.

Mr Duggan submitted that, here, the material, formal or informal (see *Grant*), before the district judge and judge was insufficient to satisfy them that Mrs Ellis would or could sell the property within three to five years or that its sale proceeds when sold would be sufficient to discharge the mortgage debt and arrears. As to the time of sale, all that the district judge had was her statement in her affidavit that she anticipated selling within three to five years when her children completed their education. As to value, the evidence was not compelling: two estate agents' estimates of between £80,000 and £85,000 as against the redemption figure at the time of just over £77,000 plus costs. As a result of Mrs Ellis's payment of the lump sum ordered by the district judge and subsequent payments, the total figure of indebtedness is now about £70,000, including about £10,000 arrears of interest. Given the inevitable uncertainty as to the movement of property values over the next few years and the reserve with which the courts should approach estate agents' estimates of sale prices (see *Clothier*) no court could be sanguine about the adequacy, now or continuing over that period, of the property as a security for the mortgage debt and arrears. In my view, the evidence was simply insufficient to entitle the district judge to contemplate, behind the order he made, a likelihood that the house would or could be sold at a price sufficient to discharge Mrs Ellis's overall debt to Bristol and West within any reasonable period, and certainly not one of up to three to five years.

It follows that, even if the district judge had made an order, defining a specific period, either three or five years, for the sale of the property, I would not have regarded the evidence before him or the judge as sufficient to enable him to fix on it as a reasonable period for the purpose of section 36 of the 1970 Act. If I am right about that, it is not a case in which this court should be deterred from interfering with the decisions below because of its traditional reluctance to interfere with their exercise of discretion. It is a case in which the court should interfere because the courts below lacked the material to enable them properly to exercise their discretion in the way they did.

I do not consider that the material available below, or to this court, would justify any order other than one of immediate possession. I would, therefore, allow the appeal with an order for the costs of the appeal and before the judge in favour of Bristol and West.

NOTES:

1. For comment on *National and Provincial Building Society v. Lloyd* [1996] 1 All E.R. 630 and *Bristol and West Building Society v. Ellis* (1996) 73 P. & C.R. 158, see [1998] Conv. 125.

2. The mortgagor must establish on the basis of firm evidence that there is a real prospect of a sale within a reasonable period: *National and Provincial Building Society v. Lloyd* [1996] 1 All E.R. 630, 638 *per* Neill L.J.; *Mortgage Service Funding plc v. Steele* (1996) 72 P. & C.R. D40. Subject to the greater flexibility introduced in *National and Provincial Building Society v. Lloyd* as to the timing of such a sale, the standard of proof reflects the approach established in *Royal Trust Co. of Canada v. Markham* [1975] 1 W.L.R. 1416 and in *Target Home Loans Ltd v. Clothier* [1994] 1 All E.R. 439.

The collapse of the property market in the early 1990s and the consequent phenomenon of "negative equity", where the value of the mortgaged property is less than the amount of the outstanding mortgage debt, prompted a series of applications by mortgagors in which, in order to prevent further arrears, they sought an order of the court directing a sale.

Cheltenham and Gloucester plc v. Krausz [1997] 1 W.L.R. 1558

(CA, Butler-Sloss, Millett and Phillips L.JJ.)

The mortgagors had fallen into arrears with their mortgage loan repayments and the mortgagee obtained an order for possession of the mortgaged property. On four occasions warrants for possession were issued and then discharged following agreement between the parties; but on each occasion the mortgagors defaulted on the agreement. When a fifth warrant was issued, the mortgagors negotiated a sale of the property and applied for a suspension of the warrant for possession pending an application for an order for sale pursuant to section 91(2) of the Law of Property Act 1925. The mortgagees resisted the application on the ground that the outstanding mortgage debt significantly exceeded the proposed sale price.

PHILLIPS L.J.:

The law
This appeal requires consideration of the interrelationship of two areas of the law relating to the mortgage of a dwelling house: (1) the circumstances in which the mortgagor is entitled to an order for the sale of the mortgaged property; (2) the circumstances in which the court has jurisdiction to suspend entry into possession of the dwelling house by the mortgagee.

Mortgagor's right of sale
Section 91 of the Law of Property Act 1925 provides:

"(1) Any person entitled to redeem mortgaged property may have a judgment or order for sale instead of for redemption in an action brought by him either for redemption alone, or for sale alone, or for sale or redemption in the alternative. (2) In any action, whether for foreclosure, or for redemption, or for sale, or for the raising and payment in any manner of mortgage money, the court, on the request of the mortgagee, or of any person interested either in the mortgage money or in the right of redemption, and, notwithstanding that—(a) any other person dissents; or (b) the mortgagee or any person so interested does not appear in the action; and without allowing any time for redemption or for payment of any mortgage money, may direct a sale of the mortgaged property, on such terms as it thinks fit, including the deposit in court of a reasonable sum fixed by the court to meet the expenses of sale and to secure performance of the terms."

The origin and history of these provisions are described by Sir Donald Nicholls V.-C. in *Palk v. Mortgage Services Funding Plc* [1993] Ch. 330, 335. Sir Donald Nicholls V.-C. also cited the statement of Lord Jessel M.R. in *Union Bank of London v. Ingram* (1882) 20 Ch.D. 463, 464 about the essentially identical provisions of section 25(2) of the Conveyancing Act 1881:

"The act is a remedial act, one effect of it being to allow a mortgagor whose property is worth more than the mortgage-money, but who cannot raise it, to obtain a sale and get the benefit of the surplus."

Until *Palk's* case it was the practice of the Chancery court only to entertain an application for sale by the mortgagor if the proceeds of sale were expected to be sufficient to discharge the entirety of the mortgage debt. In such circumstances the mortgagor might initiate proceedings by bringing an action for sale under section 91(1), or, if the mortgagee sought to foreclose, the mortgagor could apply for an order for sale in place of foreclosure. The practice thus reflected the heading to section 91: "Sale of mortgaged property in action for redemption or foreclosure".

Palk's case established, for the first time, that the court has power under section 91(2) to make an order for sale on the application of a mortgagor, notwithstanding that the proceeds of sale will be insufficient to discharge the mortgage debt. In *Palk's* case the mortgagees had obtained an order for possession with the intention, not of proceeding to sell the property but of waiting in the hope that the market might improve. The mortgagor was anxious that the property should be sold so that the proceeds would reduce the mortgage debt, on which interest was accruing at an alarming rate. The Court of Appeal held that, as the mortgagees could buy the property themselves if they wished to speculate on an increase in its value, in the interests of fairness the property should be sold.

In *Palk's* case the mortgagor had initially applied for an order for sale to the Eastbourne County Court. It is not clear on what basis that court entertained the claim, for the jurisdiction of the county court to make an order for sale is limited to cases where the value of the property does not exceed £30,000. It also appears from the judgment in the Court of Appeal that the mortgagees obtained an order for possession, which was suspended pending the result of their application. It is not clear which court made the order for possession, or which court suspended that order. What does seem clear is that no challenge was made of the jurisdiction to suspend the possession order.

In *Palk's* case the issue was simply whether or not the property should be sold. No issue arose as to the terms on which it should be sold. As to that matter, section 91(2) empowers the court to direct a sale "on such terms as it thinks fit". In cases before *Palk's* case, where the proceeds of sale were likely to exceed the mortgage debt, the court was prepared to entrust the sale to the mortgagor on the basis that the mortgagor had a keener interest than the mortgagee in obtaining the best price. We have not been referred to any case, however, where there was a contest between the mortgagee and the mortgagor as to who should have conduct of the sale.

Barrett v. Halifax Building Society (1995) 28 H.L.R. 634 marks the next development in this area of the law, and one which demonstrates the importance of the present appeal. In that case the plaintiffs had mortgaged their home and then defaulted on their repayment obligations. The situation was one of negative equity—the mortgage debt substantially exceeded the value of their home. On 6 August 1992 the mortgagees obtained a possession order, with a view to exercising their power of sale. There were numerous suspensions of this order to give the plaintiffs a chance to discharge the instalment arrears. What then occurred was explained by the judge, at p. 636:

> "On 6 March 1995 there was a further suspension of the order for the purpose of leaving [the] mortgagors in possession of the property themselves to find a buyer notwithstanding that there was a deficit over the sum secured so that the property would be on the market, lived in and without it becoming known to the market that it was subject to a forced sale, thereby increasing the realisations available to discharge at least part of the amount due."

The plaintiffs then applied to the Chancery court for an order for sale pursuant to section 91 of the Act of 1925. By the time that their action came on for hearing they had negotiated a sale of the property, subject to contract. They sought an order that they be permitted to proceed with that sale and to remain in possession until completion. The judge summarised the evidence on which they relied, at p. 637:

> "The evidence of the plaintiffs, including the expert evidence of a valuer, is that it is a recognised feature of today's property market that where a mortgagee obtains possession of property and sells in the exercise of its power of sale it is able to obtain a price which is usually not as good as the price which might have been obtained by the mortgagor had the mortgagor remained in possession and the fact of the forced sale not become apparent. It is also the plaintiffs' evidence that if the mortgagee building society were to take over the sale or were now to obtain possession and proceed to sell itself there would be likely to be a delay of some months at least before a fresh purchaser could be found and a sale completed."

The mortgagees resisted the order sought. They did not contend that they would be able to obtain a better price but urged that if the sale went ahead it would break their established policy not to permit borrowers with negative equity themselves to conduct the sale of their property without also at the same time making proposals for the repayment of any resulting deficit. The judge held that this was not a material circumstance which he ought to take into account when exercising his discretion. He held, at p. 640:

"I am left, therefore, with a case [in] which, on the evidence before me, there is no discernible advantage to the building society in refusing to allow this sale to complete, whereas there is an obvious advantage to the mortgagors to complete their proposed sale at what is accepted as the best price that is likely to be obtainable in the current market."

He proceeded to grant the plaintiffs the order that they sought. Just as in *Palk's* case the report does not suggest that in *Barrett's* case any challenge was made by the mortgagees to the order suspending possession pending the plaintiffs' application to the Chancery court.

The consequences of the procedure followed in *Barrett's* case appear to me to be far reaching. In any case in which there is negative equity it will be open to the mortgagor to resist an order for possession on the ground that he wishes to obtain a better price by remaining in possession and selling the property himself. In not every case will the primary motive for such an application be the wish to obtain a better price than that which the mortgagee is likely to obtain on a forced sale. Often the mortgagor will be anxious to postpone for as long as possible the evil day when he has to leave his home. This court has ample experience of hopeless applications for leave to appeal against possession orders designed to achieve just that end. There will be a danger, if the mortgagee does not obtain possession, that the mortgagor will delay the realisation of the property by seeking too high a price, or deliberately procrastinating on completion. At present there is a simple procedure for seeking possession in the county court and the issue tends to be whether there are arrears and whether the mortgagor is likely to be able to discharge these in a reasonable time. If possession is to be suspended whenever this appears reasonable in order to give mortgagors the opportunity to sell the property themselves the courts are going to have to enter into an area of difficult factual inquiry in order to decide in the individual case whether or not this course will be to the common benefit of mortgagor and mortgagee. Furthermore there will be obvious practical difficulties for mortgagees in monitoring the negotiations of mortgagors who are permitted time to market their properties. For these reasons it seems to me that the procedure followed and the decision reached in the *Barrett* case tend fundamentally to undermine the value of the mortgagee's entitlement to possession. Having touched on the implications of the issue raised in this case I turn to consider whether, in law, the county court has jurisdiction to suspend possession in such circumstances.

Suspension of possession

The right of a mortgagee to enter into possession of the mortgaged property was one which the common law protected strictly. The position was accurately stated by Russell J. in *Birmingham Citizens Permanent Building Society v. Caunt* [1962] Ch. 883, 912:

"Accordingly, in my judgment, where (as here) the legal mortgagee under an instalment mortgage under which by reason of default the whole money has become payable, is entitled to possession, the court has no jurisdiction to decline the order or to adjourn the hearing whether on terms of keeping up payments or paying arrears, if the mortgagee cannot be persuaded to agree to this course. To this the *sole exception* is that the application may be adjourned for a short time to afford to the mortgagor a chance of paying off the mortgagee in full or otherwise satisfying him; but this should not be done if there is no reasonable prospect of this occurring.

When I say the sole exception, I do not, of course, intend to exclude adjournments which in the ordinary course of procedure may be desirable in circumstances such as temporary inability of a party to attend, and so forth."

The rigours of the common law in this respect were mitigated by section 36 of the Administration of Justice Act 1970...

The effect of section 36, as amended [by the Administration of Justice Act 1973, s.8], on the power to suspend possession is as follows. (1) The power can be exercised to enable the mortgagor to pay off instalment arrears due under the mortgage agreement from sources other than the sale of the mortgaged property, but (2) if the mortgagor intends to sell the mortgaged property to provide the source of payment, the court must be satisfied that the proceeds will be sufficient to discharge the entirety of the mortgage debt: see *Royal Trust Co. of Canada v. Markham* [1975] 1 W.L.R. 1416; *National and Provincial Building Society v. Lloyd* [1966] 1 All E.R. 630.

Before the decision in *Palk's* case it seemed that section 36 of the Act of 1970 and section 91 of the Act of 1925 were complementary. An application under section 91 would only be contemplated where the proceeds of sale were expected to exceed the mortgage debt. In these circumstances section 36 gave the court the power to suspend possession in order to enable an application for sale under section 91 to be made. It is, however, quite clear that section 36 does not empower the court to suspend possession in order to permit the mortgagor to sell the mortgaged premises where the proceeds of sale will not suffice to discharge the mortgage debt, unless of course other funds will be available to the mortgagor to make up the shortfall. A mortgagor seeking relief in the circumstances of *Palk's* case is thus unable to invoke any statutory power to suspend the mortgagee's right to enter into possession.

For the mortgagors, Mr Smith argued that the provisions of section 36 did not define exclusively the jurisdiction of the court to suspend possession. The section was accurately headed "Additional powers of court in action by mortgagee for possession of dwelling-house". The court enjoyed in addition a power to suspend possession as part of its inherent jurisdiction. He referred us to the general statement or principle, albeit in a criminal context, of Lord Morris of Borth-y-Gest in *Connelly v. Director of Public Prosecutions* [1964] A.C. 1254, 1301:

"There can be no doubt that a court which is endowed with a particular jurisdiction has powers which are necessary to enable it to act effectively within such jurisdiction. I would regard them as powers which are inherent in its jurisdiction. A court must enjoy such powers in order to enforce its rules of practice and to suppress any abuses of its process and to defeat any attempted thwarting of its process."

Mr Smith elaborated his argument as follows. On an application by a mortgagor for sale under section 91 of the Act of 1925 the court has power to order that the mortgagor be entrusted with the sale and that he remain in possession while effecting the sale: see *Barrett's* case (1995) 28 H.L.R. 634. Should the mortgagee attempt to frustrate such an order by entering into possession, the court seized of the section 91 application must have an inherent power to restrain him from doing so. In these circumstances, the county court must also have an inherent power to suspend an order or warrant for possession, at least for such short period as is necessary to enable the mortgagor to make a section 91 application.

In my judgment this argument breaks down at a number of stages. In *Royal Trust Co. of Canada v. Markham* [1975] 1 W.L.R. 1416 Sir John Pennycuick, when delivering the leading judgment of this court, cited with approval the passage from the judgment of Russell J. in *Birmingham Citizens Permanent Building Society v. Caunt* [1962] Ch. 883, 912 which I have myself cited above. He then said, at p. 1420:

"A characteristic instance in which that sole exception is applicable is where the mortgagor has entered or is about to enter into a contract for the sale of the property at a price which will enable the mortgage to be paid off in full. ... So, as the law stood before 1970, the mortgagee had a right, subject only to that one exception mentioned by Russell J., to possession, and it was not in the power of the court to refuse him possession."

Megaw L.J. added, at pp. 1423–1424:

"There was, as I think is clear, no power, before the enactment of section 36 of the Administration of Justice Act 1970, for a court to grant a stay or suspension of execution of an order for possession in a mortgagee's action, such as the present one, based on default in payment or breach of other obligations. Therefore, if there be such power to suspend or stay the execution of the order for possession, it can come only from the provisions of section 36 of the Act of 1970 as amended by section 8 of the Administration of Justice Act 1973."

In my judgment the very specific delimitation of the power given by section 36 makes it clear that the legislature did not intend that the court should have any wider jurisdiction to curtail the mortgagee's right to possession. That right enables the mortgagee to exercise his power of sale in the manner he chooses and in the confidence that he can offer a purchaser vacant possession. Section 36 circumscribes that right where the proceeds of sale are likely to discharge the mortgage debt. It does not do so where the mortgage debt will not be fully discharged, and it is in those circumstances that the mortgagee's rights are of particular importance.

I recognise the principle of the inherent jurisdiction of the court, as explained by Lord Morris in *Connelly v. Director of Public Prosecutions* [1964] A.C. 1254, but I question whether that principle can justify the court in exercising its power to order a sale of mortgaged property under section 91 in circumstances where the mortgagee is seeking to enter into possession in order to sell property in which there is negative equity and where the sole object with which the mortgagor seeks that order is to prevent the mortgagee exercising his right to possession so that the mortgagor can negotiate his own sale while in possession. Even if one assumes that the Chancery court has power to order sale of mortgaged property on terms that displace the mortgagee's right to possession, I do not consider that it follows from this that the county court, as part of its inherent jurisdiction, can properly suspend an order or warrant for possession in order to enable a mortgagor to apply to the High Court for an order under section 91. It seems to me incumbent on the mortgagor to seek from the High Court any relief which that court is empowered to give before the possession warrant takes effect.

In the present case the judge purported in 1995 to suspend a warrant for possession that was properly issued pursuant to an order for possession made in 1991. For the reasons I have given I consider that he had no jurisdiction to make such an order and this appeal should be allowed.

MILLETT L.J.:

I have had the advantage of reading in draft the judgment of Phillips L.J. with which I am in full agreement. *Palk v. Mortgage Services Funding Plc* [1993] Ch. 330 was a case in which the mortgagee had no wish to realise its security in the foreseeable future, whether by sale or foreclosure. It established that in such a case the mortgagor might obtain an order for sale even though the proceeds of sale would be insufficient to discharge the mortgage debt. It does not support the making of such an order where the mortgagee is taking active steps to obtain possession and enforce its security by sale. Still less does it support the giving of the conduct of the sale to the mortgagor in a case where there is negative equity, so that it is the mortgagee who is likely to have the greater incentive to obtain the best price and the quickest sale. Both these steps were taken in *Barrett v. Halifax Building Society* (1995) 28 H.L.R. 634. I have serious doubt whether that case was rightly decided. In fairness to the judge it should be said that it does not appear to have been argued as a matter of principle; the mortgagor's application was resisted on purely pragmatic grounds, and somewhat feeble ones at that. For the reasons given by Phillips L.J. I agree that this appeal should be allowed.

NOTES:

1. For comment, see [1998] Conv. 223; (1998) 18 *Legal Studies* 279.
2. In *Palk v. Mortgage Services Funding plc* [1993] Ch. 330 Sir Michael Kerr stated (at 341–343):

The issue relates solely to the question whether it is an appropriate, or perhaps even a permissible, exercise of the court's discretion to direct a sale against the wishes of the first mortgagee when the circumstances make it clear that this will leave a large part of his debt unsecured and outstanding. But in this connection it is of the greatest significance that the subsection not only places no restriction on the exercise of the court's powers, but that it confers these expressly even when "any other person dissents", or when the mortgagee does not appear at all. The position is therefore that section 91(2) deliberately places no restriction on the power of the court other than the inherent and necessarily implied obligation to exercise the power judicially. Thus, the judicial availability of the power does not depend on whether the mortgagee has taken some step to exercise his rights over the mortgaged property, such as seeking an order for possession, as happened here, although in practice an application for a sale at the request of a mortgagor would no doubt only arise in cases where the mortgagee has taken some such step. Nor does it matter whether the mortgagee's dissent and objection are based on express contractual rights, or on the statutory rights provided by sections 99 to 101 of the Law of Property Act 1925, or on their express incorporation with variations into the mortgage deed, as in the present case.

Are there then any limits to the proper exercise of the court's discretion? The requirement of fairness to both sides goes without saying. But equality in giving effect to their wishes is manifestly impossible, since the plaintiffs request a sale and the company opposes it. The court must decide between them on the basis of what is just in all the circumstances. This will mean giving preference to the commercial interests of one over the other, but there is nothing new in that...

Admittedly, an order for sale against the wishes of the company will deprive it of at least two relevant contractual rights. The first is its negative right not to sell at the present time, given that the decision whether or not to realise his security by sale is undoubtedly a mortgagee's unfettered discretion, both in contract and in tort: see, for example, Lord Templeman in *China and South Sea Bank Ltd v. Tan Soon Gin* [1990] 1 A.C. 536, 545. The second is that a sale will preclude the company from exercising one of its positive rights, to take possession of the property for the purpose of leasing it. However, the court's statutory powers to override these contractual rights cannot be in doubt in the face of section 91(2). They are inherent in it. Any order of sale from which the mortgagee dissents must necessarily deprive him of his contractual right to decide for himself when he wants to sell. And any such order necessarily deprives the mortgagee of the opportunity of exercising any of his alternative rights over the property. Both consequences were inherent in all the cases in which the courts have ordered sales against the wishes of mortgagees.

The only question of principle is therefore whether the court may never exercise its power to order a sale under section 91(2) against a mortgagee's wishes when it is clear that the effect will be not only to deprive him of his security but also to leave a substantial part of the loan outstanding. In this connection two considerations stand out. The first is that the subsection contains no such restriction. The court is given express power to override dissent, and this power is unrestricted. The second is that an order for sale in such circumstances appears never to have been made in the 140-year history of the existence of this power. Counsel for the company concedes the first, but relies on the second for the proposition that it has become a fixed rule of practice that the power will never be exercised unless the terms of the order will have the effect that a sale will only take place if the mortgage debt will be discharged at the same time, without loss to the mortgagee.

I do not accept this proposition. There can be no relevant rule of practice when its existence appears never to have arisen for consideration, let alone been tested, with reference to issues such as those raised by this appeal. I accept, of course, that it must be only in exceptional circumstances that the power will be exercised against the mortgagee's wishes when a substantial part of the mortgage debt will nevertheless remain outstanding. Whenever a mortgagee can demonstrate a real possibility, let alone a probability, that a refusal or postponement of a sale would be financially beneficial, because of the property's likely increase in value or because of the extent of the revenue which it would generate in the interim, then the mortgagor's request for a sale will no doubt be refused out of hand, even though either of these events would also pro tanto inure to his financial benefit. The reason is that when the financial prospects are fairly evenly balanced, let alone when the balance of the argument favours the mortgagee, his wishes should be given preference. An order for sale would deprive him of contractual rights without any fault on his part, and would confer a benefit on the mortgagor to which he is not contractually entitled.

3. *Cheltenham and Gloucester plc v. Krausz* was not cited in *Polonski v. Lloyds Bank Mortgages Ltd* [1998] 1 F.L.R. 896, where Jacob J. applied *Palk v. Mortgage Services Funding plc*. The mortgagor in *Polonski* does not appear to have made the application under section 91(2) in response to proceedings for possession brought by the mortgagee: the mortgage repayments were being met by housing benefit. Rather the mortgagor wished to move to another part of the country in the hope of finding employment and improving her own and her children's circumstances. Jacob J. was of the view that the court was not limited to the consideration of purely financial matters in exercising its discretion under section 91(2); and accordingly he made an order directing a sale of the mortgaged property. For critical comment, see [1998] Conv. 125.

4. For discussion of the jurisdiction of the courts to deny a mortgagee's right to possession in negative equity cases, see Dixon (1998) 18 *Legal Studies* 279.

4.4.2.3 *Default other than non-repayment*   In the case of default other than the non-payment of money due under the mortgage, the breach must be capable of remedy. It has been held that a breach consisting of the unauthorised grant of a tenancy cannot be remedied unless the tenant gives up possession of the property: *Britannia Building Society v. Earl* [1990] 1 W.L.R. 422, 430 *per* McCowan L.J. Moreover, as noted above, a tenant of the mortgagor is not entitled to invoke the protection of section 36: see *supra*, p. 921.

4.4.3 *Section 36 and rights under the Family Law Act 1996*   Potential complications arise where the mortgaged property is co-owned and the co-owners are in dispute. Where the equitable co-owners are also legal co-owners and joint mortgagors, any proceedings for possession will be taken against all the co-owners and each will have the opportunity to rely on section 36. However, the position of an equitable co-owner who is not also a legal owner and mortgagor would seem to be somewhat precarious: the equitable owner has no right to rely on section 36 and his equitable interest is unlikely to be binding on the mortgagee: see *supra*, p. 880.

On the other hand, special provision is made for (former) spouses and cohabitants of mortgagors ("partners"). Where such a partner has matrimonial home rights or other rights of occupation pursuant to the provisions of Part IV of the Family Law Act 1996, any mortgage payments made by the partner are as good as if made by the mortgagor: Family Law Act 1996, ss.30(3), 35(13), 36(13); and the partner can in theory seek to take advantage of section 36 of the Administration of Justice Act 1970. However, where the relationship between the parties breaks down, it would not be uncommon for the mortgagor to stop making repayments but for the partner to know nothing of any default until an order for possession had already been obtained in proceedings against the mortgagor: see *Hastings and Thanet Building Society v. Goddard* [1970] 1 W.L.R. 1544. Even if the partner discovered the default earlier, there would probably be substantial arrears, making it less likely that the partner could satisfy the condition of section 36.

It is now provided that the partner is entitled to be made a party to those possession proceedings if the court is satisfied (i) that the partner is permitted to meet the liabilities of the mortgagor under the mortgage (a reference to sections 30(3), 35(13) and 36(13)); (ii) that the partner has applied to be made a party; (iii) that there is no special reason against the partner being made a party; and (iv) that the partner may be expected to meet the liabilities of the mortgagor so as to affect the outcome of the proceedings or that the expectation of the partner doing so should be considered under section 36 of the 1970 Act: Family Law Act 1996, s.55. Moreover, a spouse who has registered his or her matrimonial home rights is entitled to be served with notice of possession proceedings against the mortgagor: *ibid.* s.56.

However, the fundamental problem remains because there is no requirement on the mortgagee to give the spouse or partner any prior notification of repayment default on the part of the mortgagor: see *Hastings and Thanet Building Society v. Goddard* [1970] 1 W.L.R. 1544, 1548 *per* Russell L.J.; and see (1971) 35 Conv. 48; but the decision in *Cheltenham and Gloucester Building Society v. Norgan* [1996] 1 W.L.R. 343, *supra*, p. 936 may have effected a potential alleviation of the problem.

5. Remedies of equitable mortgagees and chargees

The right to sue on the *personal covenant* is available to equitable mortgagees and chargees.

The remedy of *foreclosure* is available to equitable mortgagees (but not equitable chargees), although the order would direct the mortgagor to convey the property to the mortgagee free of the mortgage.

The statutory power of *sale* under section 101(1) of the Law of Property Act 1925 is only available where the mortgage or charge is made by deed; but even if the equitable mortgage/charge is made by deed, it is not certain that the sale will be effective to convey the legal estate to the purchaser. In *Re*

Hodson and Howes' Contract (1887) 35 Ch D. 668, 673, Cotton L.J. held that such a sale was ineffective to convey the legal estate; but the decision was distinguished in *Re White Rose Cottage* [1965] Ch. 940, 951 *per* Lord Denning M.R., on the ground of the change in wording in the Law of Property Act 1925 from that in section 21(1) of the Conveyancing Act 1881. These limitations may be circumvented by conferring an appropriate power of attorney on the equitable mortgagee/chargee: see the Powers of Attorney Act 1971, ss.4(1), 5(3); or by including in the mortgage deed (i) a declaration that the mortgagor holds the legal estate on trust for the mortgagee/chargee and (ii) a power for the mortgagee/chargee to appoint himself or a nominee as trustee. These same devices are available in the context of registered land, where only a registered chargee has the statutory power of sale. Where the mortgage is not made by deed, any person interested in the mortgage money or in the right of redemption may apply to the court under section 91 of the Law of Property Act 1925, and the court may order a sale: *ibid.* s.91(2); or vest a legal term of years in the applicant so that he can sell as if he were a legal mortgagee: *ibid.* ss.90, 91(7).

The statutory power to appoint a *receiver* under section 101(1) of the Law of Property Act 1925 is similarly only available where the mortgage or charge is made by deed: in all other circumstances it is necessary to apply to the court: Supreme Court Act 1981, s.37(1).

It is arguable that the right/remedy of *possession* should in principle be available as of right to an equitable mortgagee (although not to an equitable chargee) by analogy with the doctrine in *Walsh v. Lonsdale* (1882) 21 Ch D. 9, *ante*, p. 389; and see Wade (1955) 71 L.Q.R. 204. However, the contrary is usually asserted: see *Barclays Bank Ltd v. Bird* [1954] Ch. 274, 280 *per* Harman J.; *Ladup Ltd v. Williams & Glyn's Bank plc* [1985] 1 W.L.R. 851, 855 *per* Warner J.; *Ashley Guarantee plc v. Zacaria* [1993] 1 W.L.R. 62, 69 *per* Nourse L.J. On the other hand, it seems that the equitable mortgagee or chargee may apply to the court for an order for possession: *Barclays Bank Ltd v. Bird, supra*; the jurisdictional basis is not clear but Gray (*Elements of Land Law* (2nd ed., 1993), p. 991) asserts that an application may be made pursuant to section 90(1) of the Law of Property Act 1925.

G. PRIORITY OF MORTGAGES

It is perfectly lawful for a borrower to create two or more mortgages or charges over his property to secure different loans. Provided that the value of the property is at least equal to the combined total of the loans, all the mortgagees should have sufficient security for the repayment of their respective loans. However, circumstances may arise where the value of the property is insufficient to cover all outstanding loans. It may be that the value was never sufficient but the second or subsequent mortgagee, as a result of his own failure or the conduct of the mortgagor or an earlier mortgagee, did not know of the earlier mortgage(s); or, a phenomenon of more recent times, it may be that the value of the property, although originally sufficient to cover all outstanding loans, has fallen so as no longer to be sufficient. In such circumstances, it may be necessary to determine the priority of the mortgages: in particular, if the mortgagor fails to make repayment and the mortgaged property is sold, it will be necessary to determine the order in which the mortgagees are repaid.

The law relating to priorities appears to be complicated; but this is largely because the factual situations include so many variable factors: whether the mortgages relate to a legal estate or an equitable interest; whether the mortgages relate to registered or unregistered land; whether or not the first mortgage is protected by a deposit of title deeds; whether the first mortgage is a legal or equitable mortgage: see Megarry (1940) 7 C.L.J. 243. The date of creation of the mortgages provides yet another variable factor, since a different set of rules applies to mortgages created before 1926; but the following discussion is limited to priorities between post-1925 mortgages. If these variable factors are considered systematically, the position can be stated with reasonable clarity, although, unless the mortgage provides otherwise, the rules may be modified by agreement between the mortgagees: *Cheah Theam Swee v. Equiticorp Finance Group Ltd* [1992] 1 A.C. 472.

1. Mortgages of a legal estate

1.1 *Mortgages of unregistered land*

1.1.1 *First mortgage is protected by a deposit of title deeds*

1.1.1.1 *First mortgage is a legal mortgage*   Prima facie such a mortgage will have priority over any subsequent mortgage (legal or equitable). The rule is based on two pre-1926 principles: first, that the priority of mortgages is determined by the order of their creation; and, secondly, that, where, apart from the order of creation, a legal mortgage and an equitable mortgage had equal claims to priority, the legal mortgage was preferred. Since those principles have not been affected by the 1925 legislation in so far as it relates to mortgages of unregistered land protected by a deposit of the title deeds, it is also assumed that the rule would continue to be displaced in circumstances which would have led to its displacement before 1926; and that a first legal mortgagee would lose prima facie priority over a subsequent mortgagee where the first mortgagee has enabled the mortgagor to obtain a further loan without disclosing the existence of the first mortgage to the subsequent mortgagee.

Thus the prima facie priority of the first legal mortgage has been lost where the first mortgagee has been party to some fraud whereby the subsequent mortgagee has been deceived into believing that there was no earlier mortgage: *Peter v. Russel* (1716) 1 Eq.Ca.Abr. 321. Similarly, where the first mortgagee has enabled the mortgagor to make some misrepresentation to the subsequent mortgagee as to the existence of earlier mortgages (for example by permitting the mortgagor to recover the title deeds), the first mortgagee has been estopped from asserting the prima facie priority of his mortgage: *Perry*

Herrick v. Attwood (1857) 2 De G. & J. 21. Further, the first mortgagee has forfeited priority where he has been grossly negligent in relation to the title deeds: *Walker v. Linom* [1907] 2 Ch. 104, *infra*, p. 956.

1.1.1.2 *First mortgage is an equitable mortgage*   Two preliminary points should be made. First, since 1989 it has no longer been possible to create an equitable mortgage over a legal estate in land simply by the deposit of the title deeds; there must in addition be a valid contract in accordance with the requirements of section 2 of the Law of Property (Miscellaneous Provisions) Act 1989: see *supra*, p. 816. The following discussion must be read against that background.

Secondly, and independently of the above, it has been argued that an equitable mortgage protected by a deposit of title deeds is an estate contract, registrable as a Class C(iv) land charge; and that the normal consequences of non-registration should follow: see Megarry (1940) 7 C.L.J. 243, 250–251; Bailey (1949) 10 C.L.J. 241, 245. However, acceptance of the argument would compromise the perceived scheme of the land charges legislation to exclude all mortgages protected by a deposit of title deeds; and the dictate of practical convenience seems to have been for the mortgagee to rely on possession of the title deeds alone: see Rowley (1962) 26 Conv. 445, 446–449. The precise issue appears not to have been litigated; but it is suggested that on balance the courts would reject the argument and would enforce such mortgages independently of any registration: *ibid.* Alternatively, even if it were argued that the equitable mortgage is registrable but void for non-registration, it might be argued that the mortgagee could rely on its status as an equitable charge, which is not registrable: see Megarry (1940) 7 C.L.J. 243, 252.

On the basis that an equitable mortgage protected by a deposit of title deeds is not registrable, such a mortgage will have priority over a subsequent equitable mortgage, in accordance with the principle that priority is determined by the order of creation. *Taylor v. Russell* [1891] 1 Ch. 8 provides authority that the priority of the earlier mortgage will be subject to displacement in similar circumstances to those discussed above: *ibid.* at 14–20 *per* Kay J.; but, although the point was not argued on appeal, Lord Macnaghten expressed the view that such priority may be displaced by a lesser degree of negligence on the part of the earlier mortgagee: *Taylor v. Russell* [1892] A.C. 244, 262.

However, a subsequent legal mortgage will have priority over the earlier equitable mortgage unless the subsequent mortgagee has acted with gross negligence in his investigation of the mortgagor's title. From the viewpoint of the subsequent legal mortgagee, this rule would appear to be a rather lenient version of the normal bona fide purchaser rule: see *Hewitt v. Loosemore* (1851) 9 Hare 449; *Oliver v. Hinton* [1899] 2 Ch. 264, discussed in *Walker v. Linom* [1907] 2 Ch. 104, *infra*, p. 956.

Walker v. Linom [1907] 2 Ch. 104

(Ch D., Parker J.)

The circumstances under which a mortgagee or purchaser with the legal estate is, by reason of some conduct on his part in relation to the title deeds, postponed to some person having only an equitable interest is discussed fully in the case of *Northern Counties of England Fire Insurance Co. v. Whipp* (1884) 26 Ch.D. 482, in which Fry L.J. delivered the considered judgment of the Court of Appeal. The Lord Justice states the question for decision by referring to the rival contentions of the parties. "It has been contended," he says, "on the part of the plaintiffs that nothing short of fraud will justify the Court in postponing the legal estate. It has been contended by the defendant that gross negligence is enough". He then divides the cases which may assist in answering the question for decision into two categories, namely, (1) those which relate to the conduct of the holder of the legal estate in not getting possession of the deeds, and (2) those which relate to the conduct of such holder in dealing with the deeds after he has got them. In the former category the question may be between the holders of the legal estate and either a prior or a subsequent incumbrancer or purchaser. In the latter case it can only be between the holder of the legal estate and a subsequent incumbrancer or purchaser. The two classes, he says, will not be found to differ in the principles by which they are to be governed, but they do differ much in the kind of fraud which is to be most naturally looked for. In the former case you would naturally look for some such "dolus malus" as indicated by Lord Hardwicke in *Le Neve v. Le Neve* (1747) Amb. 436. In the latter case you look for some actual concurrence in the fraudulent design of another. The learned Lord Justice next discusses at length the judgment of Lord Eldon in *Evans v. Bicknell* (1801) 6 Ves. 74, and comes to the conclusion that the language of Lord Eldon in that case, though loose and difficult to construe, points to fraud as the necessary conclusion before the Court can deprive the holder of the legal estate of the rights derived therefrom. "This fraud," he continues (at p. 490), "no doubt, may be arrived at either by direct evidence or by evidence circumstantial and indirect, and it does not cease to be fraud, because the particular object in contemplation of the parties may have been a fraud in some respects different from the fraud actually accomplished; or because the person intended to have been defrauded may be different from the person actually defrauded; or because the original fraudulent intention had no particular person in view". That fraud, and fraud alone, is the ground for postponing the legal estate is, he says, confirmed by the judgments of Lord Hardwicke in *Le Neve v. Le Neve*, Sir William Grant in *Barnett v. Weston* (1806) 12 Ves. 130, and James L.J. in *Ratcliffe v. Barnard* (1871) L. R. 6 Ch. 652. He then subdivides the cases relating to the conduct of the holder of the legal estate in not getting possession of the deeds into various classes, the first class being where no inquiry has been made for the deeds and the holder of the legal estate has therefore been postponed either to a prior equitable estate, as in *Worthington v. Morgan* (1849) 16 Sim. 547, or, as in *Clarke v. Palmer* (1882) 21 Ch.D. 124, to a subsequent equitable owner who has obtained the deeds. In these cases he says the Courts have considered the conduct of the holder of the legal estate in making no inquiry to be evidence of the fraudulent intent to escape notice of a prior equity, and, in the latter case, that a subsequent mortgagee who has in fact been misled by the mortgagor taking advantage of the conduct of the legal mortgagee could, as against him, take advantage of the fraudulent intent. I need not consider the other classes.

　　The Lord Justice next subdivides and considers the cases relating to the conduct of the holder of the legal estate in dealing with the deeds after he has got them. The case with which he was actually dealing was a case under this category.

　　The conclusion he ultimately arrives at is that in order to postpone a prior legal to a subsequent equitable estate there must be fraud as apart from negligence, and this conclusion is stated in language wide enough to cover cases of postponement based upon the conduct of the holder of the legal estate in not getting possession of the title deeds as well as cases of postponement based upon the conduct of such holder in dealing with the title deeds after he has got them. It would seem at first sight that the Lord Justice uses the word "fraud" throughout this judgment as connoting a dishonest intent, notwithstanding that in the case of fraud to be gathered from conduct in relation to not getting in the title deeds he refers to such cases as *Le Neve v. Le Neve* and *Ratcliffe v. Barnard*.

Now, as I have already said, I cannot under the circumstances of this case find that anyone concerned in the 1896 settlement, with the exception of George Church Walker, acted otherwise than honestly, and, if I treat Fry L.J.'s judgment as meaning that in no case can a prior legal estate be postponed to a subsequent equitable estate without the existence of fraud in its ordinary common law sense as necessarily connoting a dishonest intention, I must hold that the trustees are not postponed. There are, however, subsequent cases which suggest that at any rate in cases of postponement, based on no inquiry having been made for the deeds, fraud is not necessary. It is, for example, clear from the case of *Oliver v. Hinton* [1899] 2 Ch. 264 that a purchaser obtaining the legal estate, but making no inquiry for the title deeds, or making inquiry and failing to take reasonable means to verify the truth of the excuse made for not producing them or handing them over, is, although perfectly honest, guilty of such negligence as to make it inequitable for him to rely on his legal estate so as to deprive a prior incumbrancer of his priority. In this case Lindley M.R. disapproves of the passage in the judgment of James L.J. in *Ratcliffe v. Barnard*, quoted by Fry L.J. in *Northern Counties of England Fire Insurance Co. v. Whipp*, and distinctly says that to deprive a purchaser for value without notice of a prior equitable incumbrance of the benefit of the legal estate it is not essential that he should have been guilty of fraud. And Sir F. H. Jeune, referring also to the judgment of James L.J. in *Ratcliffe v. Barnard*, comes to the conclusion that the word "fraud", as there used, did not mean such conduct as would justify a jury or judge in finding that there had been actual fraud, but such conduct as would justify the Court of Chancery in concluding that there had been fraud in some artificial sense. Similarly in *Berwick & Co. v. Price* [1905] 1 Ch. 632 Joyce J. says (at p. 640): "The omission by a purchaser to investigate the title or to require delivery or production of the title deeds is not to my mind either fraudulent or culpable, nor does it, since the judgment of Lindley M.R. in *Oliver v. Hinton*, seem necessary to characterize it by any such epithet; but the consequence of such omission or wilful ignorance is that it is held to be unjust to prefer the purchaser to the previous mortgagee who has the deeds although such mortgage be equitable and the purchaser have the legal estate".

In both the cases last referred to the question was between a prior equitable and a subsequent legal estate, and I think the later case was actually decided on constructive or imputed notice. But the Master of the Rolls expressly refused to decide *Oliver v. Hinton* on any such ground. The question, however, arises whether the principle laid down in *Oliver v. Hinton* is equally applicable between the holder of the legal estate who has omitted to make inquiry for the title deeds and a subsequent equitable estate the creation of which has been rendered possible by such omission. In my opinion any conduct on the part of the holder of the legal estate in relation to the deeds which would make it inequitable for him to rely on his legal estate against a prior equitable estate of which he had no notice ought also to be sufficient to postpone him to a subsequent equitable estate the creation of which has only been rendered possible by the possession of deeds which but for such conduct would have passed into the possession of the owner of the legal estate. This must, I think, have been the opinion of Fry L.J. in *Northern Counties of England Fire Insurance Co. v. Whipp*; for he explains both *Worthington v. Morgan* and *Clarke v. Palmer* as based upon the same sort of fraud. I do not think, therefore, that there is anything in the authorities to preclude me from holding, and I accordingly hold, that the trustees, although they have the legal estate, are postponed to the defendant.

NOTE:

1. Clearly the issues are different according to whether the priority of the legal mortgage is asserted against an earlier or later equitable mortgage. In the first case the issue is whether priority based on the order of creation is displaced by priority based on the preference afforded to legal mortgages; in the second case the issue is whether both reasons for the priority of the legal mortgage are outweighed by the conduct of the legal mortgagee.

1.1.2 *First mortgage is not protected by a deposit of title deeds*   Such a mortgage is capable of registration under the Land Charges Act 1972. A legal mortgage not protected by a deposit of title deeds is a "puisne mortgage" and registrable as a Class C(i) land charge; and an equitable mortgage not protected by a deposit of title deeds is a "general equitable charge" and registrable as a Class C(iii) land charge. It would therefore seem that the question of priorities should be determined in accordance with the general principles of registration. If the first mortgage is duly protected by registration as a land charge at the time of the creation of the subsequent mortgage, the first mortgage should have priority over the subsequent mortgage (legal or equitable) since, by virtue of section 198(1) of the Law of Property Act 1925, registration is deemed to constitute actual notice; but if the first mortgage is not duly protected at the time of the creation of the subsequent mortgage, according to section 4(5) of the Land Charges Act 1972, the first mortgage will be void as against a subsequent mortgagee (legal or equitable).

However, there is a potential problem where the first mortgage, although not registered at the time of the creation of the subsequent mortgage, is registered subsequently. On the one hand, it has been seen that, according to section 4(5) of the Land Charges Act 1972, the first mortgage would be void as against the subsequent mortgagee. On the other hand, according to section 97 of the Law of Property Act 1925, the priority of mortgages (of the type presently under consideration) is determined by the order in which they are registered: thus the first mortgage would take priority provided only that it is registered before the subsequent mortgage is *registered*. Although section 97 deals in express terms with the priority of mortgages, it is widely assumed that the general principles of registration reflected in section 4(5) will prevail. Megarry (1940) 7 C.L.J. 243, 255–256 asserts that "the subject is not one for dogmatism"; but Megarry and Wade, *The Law of Real Property* (5th ed., 1984), pp. 999–1001, is rather less tentative in according precedence to the Land Charges Act 1972. Significantly, perhaps, the precise point has not arisen for judicial decision. Nor has the so-called *"circulus inextricabilis"* created by the following events: creation of first mortgage (M1), creation of second mortgage (M2), registration of M1, creation of third mortgage (M3). It is argued that, although in accordance with section 198(1) of the Law of Property Act 1925 M1 has priority over M3, in accordance with section 4(5) of the Land Charges Act 1972 M3 has priority over M2 and M2 has priority over M1. For discussion of this and similar conundra, see *Benham v. Keane* (1861) 1 J. & H. 685; *Re Wyatt* [1892] 1 Ch. 188; *Re Weniger's Policy* [1910] 2 Ch. 291; and see Lee (1968) 32 Conv. 325. For a recommended solution, see Law Com. No. 204, *Transfer of Land: Land Mortgages* (1991), para. 3.34.

It should be noted that the Land Charges Act 1972 excludes from the category of general equitable charges equitable mortgages/charges which "arise or affect an interest arising under a trust for sale or a settlement": section 2(4)(iii)(b). For priority between such mortgages, see *infra*.

1.2 *Mortgages of registered land*

1.2.1 *First mortgage is a legal mortgage/charge*   A legal mortgage of registered land necessarily takes the form of a registered charge; but the mortgage is not effective as a *legal* charge until registered. Moreover, subject to any entry to the contrary on the register, a duly registered charge will have priority over any subsequently registered charge, irrespective of the order of creation: Land Registration Act 1925, s.29. It will also have priority over any equitable mortgage/charge created subsequently, and even over an earlier equitable mortgage/charge which had not been protected as a minor interest when the legal charge was registered: *ibid.* ss.20(1), 59(6).

1.2.2 *First mortgage is an equitable mortgage/charge*   A first mortgage/charge which is equitable only (which includes a potential registered charge that has not yet been registered) constitutes a minor interest and is capable of protection by the entry of a notice or caution as appropriate: Land Registration Act 1925, s.106(3). If protected by notice, such a mortgage/charge will take priority over any subsequent mortgage/charge. If protected by caution, the cautioner should have the opportunity to substantiate the mortgage/charge protected; but the entry of a caution *per se* will not afford the mortgage/charge priority over a subsequent registered charge: *Clark v. Chief Land Registrar* [1994] Ch. 370 (except in the unlikely event that the earlier equitable mortgagee/chargee was in actual occupation of the property and could claim to have an overriding interest under section 70(1)(g)). Otherwise, an equitable mortgage/charge will have priority over a subsequent equitable mortgage/charge: *Barclays Bank Ltd v. Taylor* [1974] Ch. 137, discussed at Smith (1977) 93 L.Q.R. 541; and that is so even if the subsequent mortgagee/chargee enters a notice or caution on the register before the earlier mortgagee/chargee: *Mortgage Corp. Ltd v. Nationwide Credit Corp. Ltd* [1994] Ch. 49. It has been stated that the first mortgagee/chargee may forfeit that priority where his conduct justifies the postponement of his equity: *Barclays Bank Ltd v. Taylor* [1974] Ch. 137, 147 *per* Russell L.J.; but it is unclear to what extent the principles relating to fraud, misrepresentation and gross negligence apply in the context of registered land: see *Abigail v. Lapin* [1934] A.C. 491, 500–510 *per* Lord Wright.

2. Mortgages of an equitable interest

Mortgages of equitable interests are necessarily equitable mortgages; but a distinction must be made between different types of equitable interest. On the one hand, it seems that a mortgage of a commercial equitable interest is classified as a general equitable charge in the context of unregistered land, registrable as a Class C(iii) land charge, and as a minor interest in the context of registered land, protectable by notice or caution as appropriate; and that priority is determined in accordance with the principles of registration applicable to mortgages of a legal estate which are not protected by a deposit of the title deeds. On the other hand, it seems that a mortgage of an equitable interest under a trust is not registrable; and that priority between such mortgages is determined by the rule in *Dearle v. Hall* (1823) 3 Russ. 1, as extended by section 137 of the Law of Property Act 1925: see Howell [1993] Conv. 22. Moreover, the rule applies whether title to the mortgaged land is registered or unregistered. In the context of *registered* land, priority used to be determined according to the order of entry in the Index of Minor Interests: Land Registration Act 1925, s.102(2); but the Index was abolished by the Land Registration Act 1986, s.5.

Under the rule in *Dearle v. Hall*, subject to one exception, priority is determined according to the order in which the trustees of the mortgaged land *receive* notice of the mortgages. The crucial time for the operation of the rule is the actual receipt rather than the giving of the notice, although, if two or more notices are received at the same time (for example, by a single postal delivery), priority is determined by the order of creation of the mortgages: *Calisher v. Forbes* (1871) L.R. 1 Ch.App. 109. Moreover, notice should be given to all the relevant trustees to ensure continuing priority: *Re Wasdale* [1899] 1 Ch. 163. The exception is that a subsequent mortgage cannot gain priority over an earlier mortgage where, at the time of the creation of the subsequent mortgage, the mortgagee had actual or constructive knowledge of the earlier mortgage: *Re Holmes* (1885) 29 Ch D. 786. However, the exception does not prevent a subsequent mortgage gaining priority where the mortgagee acquires knowledge of the earlier mortgage after the creation of the subsequent mortgage but before he serves notice on the trustees: *Mutual Life Assurance Society v. Langley* (1886) 32 Ch D. 460.

It has been held that the rule in *Dearle v. Hall* does not apply (in circumstances where it would otherwise apply) to the advantage of a judgment creditor who has been content to give credit without security and who subsequently becomes an equitable mortgagee/chargee without providing further consideration: *United Bank of Kuwait plc v. Sahib* [1997] Ch. 107, 118–120 *per* Chadwick J., citing *Scott v. Lord Hastings* (1858) 4 K. & J. 633, 637–638 *per* Page Wood V.-C.; and see [1995] C.L.J. 249.

3. Tacking

The rules as to priorities outlined above may be modified by the process of "tacking of further advances", whereby a mortgagee who makes a subsequent loan to the mortgagor on the security of the same property may tack (or attach) the subsequent loan to the original mortgage, thereby giving the subsequent loan the same priority as the first over any intervening mortgage: see Rowley (1958) 22 Conv. 44. Thus suppose that A borrows £15,000 from

X and then £10,000 from Y; that each loan is secured by a mortgage over Blackacre; and that the normal rules prioritise the mortgages in the order of creation. If A subsequently borrows another £5,000 from X, in certain circumstances X may tack that loan to his original mortgage and claim priority over Y to the extent of his combined loan total of £20,000.

In the context of unregistered land, X is entitled to tack a further advance in this way, irrespective of whether Y has a legal or equitable mortgage, provided that (i) an arrangement to that effect has been made with Y; or (ii) X had no notice of the intermediate mortgage at the time when he made the further advance; or (iii) the first mortgage imposes an obligation on the mortgagee to make further advances: Law of Property Act 1925, s.94(1). In relation to (ii), X is not deemed to have notice of the intermediate mortgage merely by reason that it is registered as a land charge if the first mortgage was expressly made for the purpose of securing further advances and the intervening mortgage was not registered (presumably by priority notice) at the time when the first mortgage was created or when X last searched the register, whichever is the later: *ibid*. s.94(2).

In the context of registered land, a registered chargee is entitled to tack a further advance, provided that (i) the registered charge is made for securing further advances and the registrar has not given the registered chargee notice of his intention to make an entry on the register which would prejudicially affect the priority of any further advance: Land Registration Act 1925, s.30(1); or (ii) the registered charge imposes an obligation on the chargee to make further advances: *ibid*. s.30(3).

Another version of tacking, the *"tabula in naufragio"* whereby a subsequent mortgagee could acquire an earlier legal mortgage and thereby obtain priority over an intervening mortgage, was abolished in 1925: Law of Property Act 1925, s.94(3).

H. REFORM

It will be apparent from the foregoing discussion that the law relating to land mortgages would benefit significantly from reform. The Law Commission published a Working Paper in 1986, which expressed the provisional view that the law was in need of simplification and modernisation and that in order to achieve this it was necessary to reconsider, first, the structure of the mortgage relationship and, secondly, the rights, duties, protection and remedies of the parties to the relationship, both during the security and on its enforcement: see Law Commission Working Paper No. 99, *Transfer of Land: Land Mortgages* (1986). For discussion of the alternative proposals, see Griffiths [1987] Conv. 191; and for an earlier call for comprehensive reform along similar lines, see Jackson (1978) 94 L.Q.R. 571.

A final Report and draft bill were published in 1991: Law Com. No. 204, *Transfer of Land: Land Mortgages* (1991). Although the Government has decided not to implement the report in its entirety, the Law Commission is to reconsider the report when it has completed its work on land registration: *Hansard* (HL), March 19, 1998, Written Answers 213.

Law Commission Report No. 204, Transfer of Land: Land Mortgages (1991)

Summary of recommendations

The new mortgages

10.2 All existing methods of consensually mortgaging or charging interests in land should be abolished and replaced by new forms of mortgage (the formal land mortgage and the informal land mortgage) the attributes of which would be expressly defined by statute, and which would be the only permissible methods of mortgaging any interest in land, whether legal or equitable.

10.3 In principle, the rights, powers, duties and obligations of mortgagor and mortgagee under a land mortgage should be such as are appropriate for making the mortgaged property security for the performance of the mortgagor's obligations.

Variable and overriding provisions

10.4 The statutory provisions defining the rights, powers, duties and obligations of the parties to a land mortgage should be categorised as either "variable" or "overriding". Variable provisions should be variable or excludable, either directly by an express term of the mortgage or indirectly by necessary implication from any express term. Overriding provisions should apply notwithstanding any provision to the contrary contained in the mortgage or in any other instrument. Any provision of a mortgage or any other instrument should be void to the extent that it (i) purports to impose a liability which has the effect of allowing the mortgagee to escape or mitigate the consequences of an overriding provision, or to be reimbursed the consequences of complying with it or (ii) has the effect of preventing or discouraging the mortgagor or any other person from enforcing or taking advantage of an overriding provision.

Requirement of good faith

10.5 The rights, remedies and powers of a mortgagee under a land mortgage should be expressly stated to be exercisable only in good faith and for the purposes of protecting or enforcing the security. This should apply to all the mortgagee's rights, remedies and powers, whether derived from statute, contract, or elsewhere.

Creation of formal land mortgage

10.6 A formal land mortgage should not be valid unless made by deed, whether the property mortgaged is a legal estate or an equitable interest.... As an additional requirement where the mortgagor's title to all or part of the mortgaged property is registered at H.M. Land Registry, the mortgage should not qualify as a formal land mortgage unless it is substantively registered against that title.

Informal land mortgage

10.7 Informal mortgages should be recognised, to the extent that any purported consensual security over any interest in land that does not constitute a formal land mortgage but would, in the present law, give rise to an equitable mortgage or charge, should take effect as an informal land mortgage, provided the formal requirements for the creation of an informal land mortgage (paragraph 10.9 below) are satisfied.

10.8 A mortgagee under an informal land mortgage should have no right to enforce the security, nor to take any other action in relation to the mortgaged property, but should have a right to have the mortgage perfected by having a formal land mortgage granted to it. In the case of a protected mortgage (paragraph 10.16 below) the mortgagee should not be allowed to have the mortgage perfected without a court order; in all other cases a mortgagee who was able to procure perfection of the mortgage without recourse to the court (for example, by use of a power of attorney) should be entitled to do so.

10.9 An informal land mortgage should not be valid unless it is made by deed or it satisfies requirements equivalent to those set out in section 2 of the Law of Property (Miscellaneous Provisions) Act 1989...

...

Protection and priority

10.11 Where the mortgagor's title to the mortgaged property is registered at H.M. Land Registry, a formal land mortgage of that property should be substantively registrable. Unless and until registered it should take effect as an informal land mortgage. Once registered, it would constitute a registered charge for the purposes of the Land Registration Acts 1925 to 1988. As such, its priority would depend on the date of its registration.

10.12 An informal land mortgage of a legal estate in registered land should be protectable by notice where the informal land mortgage is acknowledged by the registered proprietor. Otherwise, it should be protectable by caution. Protection by notice of deposit and notice of intended deposit should be abolished. The priority of informal land mortgages protected by notice or caution should, for the present, continue to be governed by the rules applicable to the priority of minor interests in the present law.

10.13 Formal and informal land mortgages of commercial equitable interests in registered land should be protectable by entry of notice or caution, but for the present, protection and priority of trust equitable interests should continue to be governed by the rule in *Dearle v. Hall.*

10.14 In unregistered land all formal land mortgages of a legal estate or a commercial equitable interest should be registrable as Class C(i) land charges, and all informal land mortgages of a legal estate or a commercial equitable interest should be registrable as Class C(iii) land charges. Formal and informal mortgages of trust equitable interests should continue to be governed by the rule in *Dearle v. Hall.*

10.15 Section 4(5) of the Land Charges Act 1972 should be amended to remove the possibility of insoluble priority circles arising where there are successive mortgages of the same property.

Protected mortgages

10.16 There should be a class of protected mortgage consisting of all formal and informal land mortgages of any interest in land which includes a dwelling-house except those where either (a) the mortgagor is a body corporate, or (b) enforcement of the mortgage would not affect the occupation of the dwelling-house or (c) the dwelling-house is occupied under a service tenancy.

...

Rights and duties during the security

Documents of title

10.19 It should be a variable provision of a first formal land mortgage that the mortgagee is entitled to possession of the mortgagor's documents of title (including, if title is registered, the mortgagor's land certificate)... The mortgagor should have overriding rights of inspection and production and to take copies.

Insurance

10.20 Variable provisions about insurance should be implied into formal land mortgages. The mortgagor should be under a duty to insure the property.... The mortgagee should have a right to insure for itself if the mortgagor is in default of the obligation to insure, the cost of doing so to be a charge on the mortgaged property.

Repair

10.21 It should be a variable implied term of a formal land mortgage that, except while the mortgagee is in possession, the mortgagor should be under a duty to keep the premises in substantially the same state of repair as they were in at the time the mortgage was created... The mortgagee should have rights to enter and repair on default by the mortgagor.

10.22 It should be an overriding implied term of a formal land mortgage that when the mortgagee is in possession, the mortgagee owes the mortgagor duties of repair corresponding to those the mortgagor has whilst in possession. This should not, however, extend to matters covered by the mortgagor's duty to insure, and the mortgagee's obligation should be set by reference to the state of repair when the mortgagee took possession, not when the mortgage was granted.

Possession

10.23 During the security, the mortgagor should remain entitled to possession. The mortgagee should be entitled to take possession only in specified circumstances for the purposes of protecting or enforcing the security.

Leasing

10.24 It should be an overriding implied term of all formal land mortgages that when in possession the mortgagor is entitled to grant such leases of the property as it thinks fit, without having to obtain the mortgagee's consent. However, no lease granted by the mortgagor will be binding on the mortgagee unless granted with the mortgagee's written consent.

10.25 It should also be an overriding implied term that the mortgagee when in possession, and a receiver appointed by the mortgagee, is entitled to grant leases, but only with the mortgagor's consent, or if required by statute, or if it is reasonably necessary to do so to protect or enforce the security. As an additional requirement in the case of protected mortgages, neither the mortgagee nor a receiver should be entitled to grant a lease of any part of a dwelling-house comprised in the mortgaged property without leave of the court.

Transfer

10.26 There should be no restrictions on the right of a mortgagee to transfer or otherwise deal with the mortgage, if the mortgage is not a protected mortgage. In the case of protected mortgages, if legislation is thought appropriate, it should provide that it is an overriding implied term of a protected mortgage that the mortgagee is not entitled to transfer the mortgage without having first obtained the written consent of the mortgagor, consent not to be unreasonably withheld...

10.27 The mortgagor's interest in the mortgaged property should remain freely alienable, subject to any express restriction contained in the mortgage.

Interest rates

10.28 In all protected mortgages, a provision that purports to increase the rate of interest payable on default should be void. In all other mortgages, such a provision should be challengeable only under the general law relating to penalties or under the new general statutory jurisdiction to set aside or vary mortgage terms.

10.29 In the case of all mortgages, the court should have jurisdiction to vary interest rates under the new general statutory jurisdiction if the mortgage has become challengeable as a result of a variation of or failure to vary the rate of interest payable, even if under the mortgage the mortgagee is fully entitled to vary or not vary interest rates as it chooses.

10.30 In the case of protected mortgages, the court should also be entitled to alter the interest rate payable, if satisfied by the mortgagor that the mortgagee has unreasonably varied or failed to vary the interest rate payable under the mortgage...

Redemption

10.31 The equitable right to redeem the property free from the mortgage after the contractual redemption date by paying and discharging all obligations under it should apply to formal and informal mortgages as it applies to all other mortgages and charges.

10.32 In protected mortgages, any term of the mortgage which postpones the mortgagor's right to redeem should be void, unless the property includes non-residential premises. If it includes non-residential property, or the mortgage is not protected, then a postponement of the right to redeem should be challengeable only under the new general statutory jurisdiction.

10.33 In protected mortgages any term of the mortgage which requires the mortgagor to give notice of intention to redeem, or requires payment of interest in lieu of notice, should be void.

10.34 Mortgagors under a protected mortgage whose repayments are calculated on the basis of the loan remaining outstanding for a specified period should be entitled to the appropriate rebate on earlier repayment.

Consolidation

10.35 In relation to all land mortgages the right to consolidate should be abolished.

Discharge

10.36 A land mortgage should be discharged by the mortgagor discharging all his obligations under it: no document should be necessary in order to complete the discharge...

Enforcement of the security

Sale

10.37 It should be a variable implied term of all formal land mortgages that the mortgagee has power to sell the mortgagor's interest in the mortgaged property, free from the mortgagee's own mortgage and from subsequent mortgages and other interests to which the mortgage has priority, but subject to all prior mortgages and interests taking priority over the mortgage. The power should not be exercisable unless a specified "enforceable event" has occurred and is still operative. This restriction on the exercise of the power of sale should be overriding and should also apply to the statutory power of sale as varied or replaced by any contractual provisions.

10.38 If the mortgage is a protected mortgage, the mortgagee should not be entitled to exercise the power of sale without leave of the court.

10.39 In addition in the case of protected mortgages, before exercising the power of sale the mortgagee should first have served on the mortgagor an enforcement notice in prescribed form specifying the enforceable event on which the mortgagee relies and the action (if any) to be taken by the mortgagor to remedy any default... Once the mortgagor has taken the action required by the notice, or the enforceable event is no longer operative for some other reason, the power of sale should not be exercisable.

10.40 If the mortgagee exercises the power of sale after having been notified that the mortgagor has contracted to sell to someone else, the mortgagee should be liable to indemnify the mortgagor for any sum the mortgagor becomes liable to pay to a third party by reason of being unable to complete his sale contract. This should not apply if the mortgagee contracted to sell before receiving notice of the mortgagor's sale contract, or if it was reasonable for the mortgagee to sell, either because the mortgagor's contract was for sale at a price insufficient to pay off the mortgagee in full, and the mortgagee was able to sell at a higher price than the mortgagor's price, or because the mortgagor's sale was not completed within a reasonable time, or because of some other reason.

10.41 A purchaser from a mortgagee purporting to sell in exercise of the power of sale should get a good title, provided there is a valid formal land mortgage and the purchaser is in good faith, unless the purchaser has notice that the power of sale is not exercisable or that the exercise is improper for some other reason. Notice should include constructive notice.

10.42 A mortgagee under a formal land mortgage should be entitled to exercise the power of sale by selling the property to itself, provided leave of the court is first obtained. The court should not grant leave unless satisfied that sale to the mortgagee is the most advantageous method of realising the security.

10.43 A mortgagee and a receiver appointed under a formal land mortgage should have an overriding duty (owed to the mortgagor, to any guarantors of the mortgagor, and to any subsequent mortgagees) to take reasoanble care to ensure that on a sale the price is the best price that can reasonably be obtained.

10.44 After paying off prior encumbrances, the mortgagee should hold the proceeds of sale on trust to be applied first in payment of the costs of sale, secondly in payment of everything due under the mortgage, and thirdly to be paid to the person next entitled (that is the subsequent encumbrancers or, if none, the mortgagor).

Foreclosure
10.45 The remedy of foreclosure should be abolished.

Possession
10.46 In all formal land mortgages there should be an implied overriding provision that the mortgagee is entitled to take possession of the mortgaged property when it is reasonably necessary to do so to enable the property to be sold pursuant to the mortgagee's power of sale. Once in possession the mortgagee should be under an overriding duty to sell as quickly as is consonant with the duty to take reasonable care to ensure that on sale the price is the best price that can reasonably be obtained.

10.47 In protected mortgages the mortgagee should not be entitled to possession without serving an enforcement notice and obtaining a court order. The court making an order for possession should have discretion to order that interest payable under the mortgage should cease to accrue twelve weeks (or such other period as the court thinks fit) after the execution of the order for possession. Similar provisions should apply if the mortgagor leaves voluntarily in response to a demand for possession from the mortgagee. In both cases the mortgagee should be free to apply to the court for an extension of time at any stage. The Secretary of State should have power by order to vary the period of twelve weeks.

10.48 In formal land mortgages which are not protected, the mortgagee should also have a right to take possession of the property when it is reasonably necessary to do so in order to preserve its value. Once in possession, the mortgagee should be entitled to remain there only for so long as is reasonable, given that the purpose of being there is to preserve the value of the property.

10.49 A mortgagee under a protected mortgage should have no right to take possession of the property for the purpose of preserving its value unless the property includes non-residential property. If non-residential property is included the mortgagee should be entitled to apply to the court for possession for this purpose: the court should be entitled to make an order affecting the non-residential part only on the same grounds as if it were a non-protected mortgage, but should not be entitled to make an order affecting the residential part unless satisfied that it would not otherwise be possible to preserve the value of the property. The court making an order for possession for this purpose should have the same discretion to order that interest should cease to accrue as if possession was for sale, and the same should apply if the mortgagor leaves voluntarily in response to a demand for possession from the mortgagee.

10.50 A mortgagee who is in possession, for whatever purpose, should have a duty to repair (paragraph 10.22 above) and a liability to account. The liability to account should not apply during a period when interest has ceased to accrue.

Appointment of a receiver

10.51 It should be a variable implied term of a formal land mortgage that the mortgagee should have power to appoint a receiver of the income of the property who should be the agent of the mortgagor.

10.52 The power should be exercisable only in circumstances in which the power of sale would be exercisable. In deciding whether to grant leave for the appointment of a receiver under a protected mortgage, the court should consider the effect the appointment would have on the occupation of any dwelling-house on the mortgaged property: if the effect would be to disturb that occupation, leave should be refused unless the court is satisfied that either (i) the object of the appointment is to enable the mortgagee to sell or (ii) the security cannot be protected properly by any other means. All provisions relating to the exercise of the power to appoint should be overriding.

10.53 Provisions defining the powers of a receiver should be variable, but not so as either to exclude or restrict the liability of the receiver to the mortgagor, or to confer on the receiver any powers that a mortgagee could not have.

...

Jurisdiction of the court on enforcement

10.55 In the case of a formal land mortgage which is not protected, if a mortgagee applies to the court for an order to enforce or protect the security, the court should have no specific powers to delay or withhold the remedy requested once the mortgagee has established that the right to take the appropriate action is available and has become exercisable.

10.56 On an application by a mortgagee to protect or enforce a protected mortgage, or for payment of sums due under a protected mortgage, the court should have powers equivalent to those currently applicable to residential mortgages by virtue of Part IV of the Administration of Justice Act 1970 and the Consumer Credit Act 1974. In addition, it should have power to order the mortgagee to accept re-scheduled payments in some circumstances, and it should be allowed to consider whether any of the terms of the mortgage ought to be set aside or varied. It should not have power to refuse or delay an enforcement order on the ground that a tenant of the mortgagor whose tenancy is not binding on the mortgagee has offered to pay all sums due under the mortgage, nor should it have power to order that the mortgagor's interest should be transferred to such a tenant.

Jurisdiction to set aside or vary terms of the mortgage

10.57 There should be a new statutory jurisdiction for the court to set aside or vary terms of a land mortgage. The new jurisdiction should be in addition to the court's general law powers to set aside terms or bargains on grounds such as fraud, mistake, rectification, estoppel, undue influence, or restraint of trade. The equitable jurisdiction to set aside a term of a land mortgage which constitutes a clog or fetter on the equity of redemption should be abolished in so far as it relates to land mortgages, and the extortionate credit bargain provisions of the Consumer Credit Act 1974 should be amended so that they no longer apply to credit bargains secured by a land mortgage.

10.58 Under the new jurisdiction the court should have power to set aside or vary any term of a mortgage with a view to doing justice between the parties if (a) principles of fair dealing were contravened when the mortgage was granted, or (b) the effect of the terms of the mortgage is that the mortgagee now has rights substantially greater than or different from those necessary to make the property adequate security for the liabilities secured by the mortgage, or (c) the mortgage requires payments to be made which are exorbitant, or (d) the mortgage includes a postponement of the right to redeem.

10.59 In deciding whether to exercise its powers on grounds (b) or (d) the court should discount the fact that the terms were freely negotiated between the parties, but in such circumstances should have a discretion to order the mortgagor to compensate the mortgagee. Otherwise, the powers the court should have under the new jurisdiction, and the factors it ought to take into account should be analogous to those now contained in the extortionate credit bargain provisions of the Consumer Credit Act 1974.

Miscellaneous matters

Tacking of further advances

10.60 Section 94 of the Law of Property Act 1925 should be amended to make it clear (a) that registration of a later mortgage under the Companies Act 1989 does not constitute notice of it to an earlier mortgagee seeking to tack advances made after the creation of the later mortgage, and (b) that a mortgagee who is under an obligation to make further advances remains entitled or rely on section 94 despite any default by the mortgagor releasing the mortgagee from the obligation.

10.61 It should be made clear in section 30 of the Land Registration Act 1925 that where it is noted on the register that a charge contains an obligation to make further advances, subsequent charges that are unregistered, as well as those that are registered, will take subject to any such further advances made.

NOTE:

1. For discussion, see [1992] Conv. 69.

INDEX